DICIONÁRIO Escolar
PORTUGUÊS/INGLÊS
INGLÊS/PORTUGUÊS

★ ★ ★ ★ ★

CB047489

Dados Internacionais de Catalogação na Publicação (CIP) de acordo com ISBD

```
C578d    Ciranda Cultural.
             Dicionário escolar Português/ Inglês / Ciranda Cultural. - Jandira, SP :
         Magic Kids, 2023.
             480 p. : 12,00cm x 16,90cm. - (Dicionário).

             ISBN: 978-65-261-0744-7

             1. Dicionários. 2. Língua portuguesa. 3. Inglês. 4. Comunicação. 5.
         Direito da criança e do adolescente. I. Título. II. Série.
                                                              CDD 423.69
2023-1134                                                     CDU 811.134.3`374

                    Elaborado por Lucio Feitosa - CRB-8/8803

                        Índice para catálogo sistemático:
                        1.  Dicionários 423.69
                        2.  Dicionários 811.134.3`374
```

© 2023 Ciranda Cultural Editora e Distribuidora Ltda.
Produção: Ciranda Cultural

1ª Edição em 2023
www.cirandacultural.com.br

Todos os direitos reservados. Nenhuma parte desta publicação pode ser reproduzida, arquivada em sistema de busca ou transmitida por qualquer meio, seja ele eletrônico, fotocópia, gravação ou outros, sem prévia autorização do detentor dos direitos, e não pode circular encadernada ou encapada de maneira distinta daquela em que foi publicada, ou sem que as mesmas condições sejam impostas aos compradores subsequentes.

Crédito das imagens: Shutterstock
Legenda: E = Esquerda, D = Direita, C = Centro, T = Topo, A = Abaixo, F = Fundo.
Capa=Shutterstock; Contracapa=Shutterstock; 8=Jena_Velour; 11=Pixel Embargo; 12/TED e AED=Volodymyr Burdiak; 13/TE=Dusan Milenkovic, TD=Pavel Vakhrushev, AE=Maria Meester, AD= Marafona; 17=Ljupco Smokovski; 19=Miramiska; 20=Robert Kneschke; 21=Warren Goldswain;22=Peter Bernik; 23=pisaphotography 24=Sushaaa; 25=MJTH; 26=GaudiLab; 27=Deborah Kolb; 28=bikeriderlondon; 29=PathDoc; 30=infinity21; 31=Ermolaev Alexander.

DICIONÁRIO Escolar

PORTUGUÊS/INGLÊS
INGLÊS/PORTUGUÊS

Sumário

APRESENTAÇÃO	5
COMO USAR ESTE DICIONÁRIO	6
SINAIS GRÁFICOS	6
ABREVIATURAS	7
A LÍNGUA INGLESA NO MUNDO	7
ALFABETO	8
MOEDA	8
NÚMEROS	9
Cardinais	9
Ordinais	9
HORAS	10
DIAS DA SEMANA E MESES	11
COMO REPRESENTAR DATAS	11
ESTAÇÕES DO ANO	12
TEMPO	13
CORES	13
VERBOS TO BE E TO HAVE	14
Simple present	14
VERBOS IRREGULARES	14
PHRASAL VERBS	16
EXPRESSÕES IDIOMÁTICAS	18
CONHECENDO PESSOAS	20
DIREÇÕES	22
PASSEANDO	24
FAZENDO COMPRAS	25
NO RESTAURANTE	26
INDO A UMA FESTA	27
NO TRABALHO	28
GÍRIAS E EXPRESSÕES	29
NO AEROPORTO	30
VIAJANDO	31

Apresentação

O Dicionário escolar português/inglês – inglês/português foi elaborado para ser o seu companheiro inseparável no dia a dia escolar. Por essa razão, é do tamanho ideal para você carregá-lo para onde for.

Esta obra de referência contém definições claras e precisas de verbetes do português para o inglês e do inglês para o português. Além disso, outras informações importantes são apresentadas, como a maneira correta de utilizar este dicionário e o significado das abreviaturas aqui contidas.

Você vai ter contato com conteúdos importantes, como uma breve história da língua inglesa, uma lista dos países que a utilizam, a pronúncia do alfabeto em inglês, a indicação dos nomes dos números e das formas de dizer os nomes das moedas norte-americanas e canadenses, a maneira correta de representar e dizer as horas, os meses, os dias da semana, as estações e as cores.

O campo linguístico do inglês também é explorado neste dicionário, em que consta a conjugação dos verbos *to be* e *to have*. Além disso, este dicionário conta com uma extensa lista de verbos irregulares. Os *phrasal verbs* e as expressões idiomáticas são também apresentados com exemplos de fácil compreensão.

Para completar esta obra, foram selecionadas frases importantes em inglês relacionadas a situações sociais que podem ser vividas em uma viagem a um país de língua inglesa, por exemplo. Dentre essas situações, destaca-se o que você deve falar quando está em um restaurante, em uma festa, no aeroporto, em um passeio, no trabalho, ou quando está fazendo compras. Essas sessões constituem um importante guia para você se orientar e se comunicar em inglês.

Enfim, os assuntos abordados de modo conciso e eficaz tornam este material um ótimo guia de consulta rápida, auxiliando-o no dia a dia escolar e complementando seus conhecimentos sobre a língua inglesa.

Como usar este dicionário

Para o Dicionário escolar português/inglês – inglês/português ser efetivamente de consulta prática e rápida, é importante entender todos os seus elementos.

Um dicionário de língua se constitui de verbetes, os quais são o conjunto de significados, sinônimos, antônimos, etc. das palavras do idioma em que está escrito. Esses verbetes são organizados em ordem alfabética. Os nomes aparecem no singular e no plural; e os verbos, no infinitivo. Se a palavra a ser consultada é "detected", por exemplo, então você deve procurar o verbete "detect".

Com exceção da página de entrada do conjunto de verbetes, que destaca a letra do alfabeto que os inicia, nas demais páginas constam duas palavras-guia no topo, que indicam o primeiro verbete (à esquerda) e o último (à direita). Este dicionário possui dedeiras nas páginas ímpares, à margem direita, em alturas diferentes, com as letras que correspondem às iniciais das palavras de cada seção.

Agora, entenda as partes que compõem cada verbete:
- Abreviaturas – são as siglas que serão usadas em todo o dicionário. Veja uma lista delas na página seguinte.
- Entrada – em letras maiúsculas, é o vocábulo que inicia o verbete a ser definido.
- Categoria gramatical – é a indicação da classe gramatical (substantivo, adjetivo, por exemplo) à qual pertence a palavra e vem abreviada logo depois da entrada.
- Tradução – vem logo depois da categoria gramatical; é a tradução do vocábulo do inglês para o português.
- Versão – vem logo depois da categoria gramatical; é a versão do vocábulo do português para o inglês.

Sinais gráficos

,	separa as palavras que têm significados semelhantes.
;	separa as palavras que têm significados diferentes.
/	separa as categorias gramaticais.
.	indica a finalização da tradução/versão.

Abreviaturas

abrev.	abreviatura
adj.	adjetivo
adj.2gên.	adjetivo de dois gêneros
adv.	advérbio
art.	artigo
conj.	conjunção
interj.	interjeição
m.q.	mesmo que
num.	numeral
pl.	plural

prep.	preposição
pron.	pronome
s.	substantivo
s.2gên.	substantivo de dois gêneros
s.f.	substantivo feminino
s.f. pl.	substantivo feminino plural
s.m.	substantivo masculino
s.m. pl.	substantivo masculino plural
v.	verbo

A língua inglesa no mundo

A língua inglesa surgiu na Idade Média, no sul da Grã-Bretanha, como desenvolvimento de alguns dialetos falados por povos germanos, principalmente os anglos e os saxões. Gradualmente, o idioma foi evoluindo e sofrendo influência de outras línguas, como o francês, o latim e o grego.

Atualmente, cerca de 400 milhões de pessoas em todo o mundo possuem o inglês como primeira língua, como Estados Unidos, Reino Unido e Canadá. Em mais de 104 países, essa é a segunda língua da população, totalizando aproximadamente 400 milhões de falantes.

Esses números podem tornar-se ainda mais expressivos, na medida em que a língua inglesa tem sido amplamente difundida em todo o mundo por representar uma forma de comunicação Internacional. Desse modo, ter o domínio desse idioma faz-se imprescindível na atualidade.

Belize	Malaui	Austrália	Tuvalu
Botswana	Malta	Ruanda	Uganda
Camarões	Ilhas Marshall	África do Sul	Zâmbia
Canadá	Maurícia	Santa Lúcia	Zimbabwe
Estados Unidos	Micronésia	Samoa	Antígua e Barbuda
Fiji	Namíbia	Seychelles	Bahamas
Gâmbia	Nauru	Serra Leoa	Barbados
Guiana	Nova Zelândia	Singapura	Granada
Índia	Nigéria	Ilhas Salomão	Inglaterra
Quênia	Paquistão	Sudão do Sul	Jamaica
Kiribati	Palau	Tanzânia	São Cristóvão e Nevis
Lesoto	Papua-Nova Guiné	Tonga	São Vicente e Granadinas
Libéria	Filipinas	Trinidad e Tobago	

Alfabeto

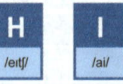

A	/ei/
B	/bi:/
C	/si:/
D	/di:/
E	/i:/
F	/ef/
G	/dʒi:/
H	/eitʃ/
I	/ai/
J	/dʒei/
K	/kei/
L	/el/
M	/em/
N	/en/
O	/oʊ/
P	/pi:/
Q	/kju:/
R	/a:(r)/
S	/es/
T	/ti:/
U	/ju:/
V	/vi:/
W	/dʌbel ju:/
X	/eks/
Y	/wai/
Z	/zi:/

Moeda

Estados Unidos e Canadá

VALOR		NOME
1¢	one cent	a penny
5¢	five cents	a nickel
10¢	ten cents	a dime
25¢	twenty-five cents	a quarter
$1	one dollar	a dollar bill
$5	five dollars	a five-dollar bill
$10	ten dollars	a ten-dollar bill
$20	twenty dollars	a twenty-dollar bill
$50	fifty dollars	a fifty-dollar bill
$100	one hundred dollars	

Números

CARDINAIS

1	one
2	two
3	three
4	four
5	five
6	six
7	seven
8	eight
9	nine
10	ten
11	eleven
12	twelve
13	thirteen
14	fourteen
15	fifteen
16	sixteen
17	seventeen
18	eighteen
19	nineteen
20	twenty
21	twenty-one
22	twenty-two
30	thirty
40	forty
50	fifty
60	sixty
70	seventy
80	eighty
90	ninety
100	one hundred
101	one hundred and one
200	two hundred
1.000	one thousand
10.000	ten thousand
100.000	one hundred thousand
1.000.000	one million

ORDINAIS

1st	first
2nd	second
3rd	third
4th	fourth
5th	fifth
6th	sixth
7th	seventh
8th	eighth
9th	ninth
10th	tenth
11th	eleventh
12th	twelfth
13th	thirteenth
14th	fourteenth
15th	fifteenth
16th	sixteenth
17th	seventeenth
18th	eighteenth
19th	nineteenth
20th	twentieth
21st	twenty-first
22nd	twenty-second
30th	thirtieth
40th	fortieth
50th	fiftieth
60th	sixtieth
70th	seventieth
80th	eightieth
90th	ninetieth
100th	hundredth
101st	thousandth
200th	two hundred
1.000th	one thousand
10.000th	ten-thousandth
100.000th	one hundred thousand
1.000.000th	millionth

Horas

O sistema de contagem de horas nos países de língua inglesa é conhecido como "relógio de 12 horas". A numeração das horas vai de 1 a 12, e os períodos são identificados com as siglas "am" (*ante meridiem:* antes do meio-dia) e "pm" (*post meridiem:* depois do meio-dia). Na linguagem informal, pode-se utilizar *in the morning*, *in the afternoon* ou *in the evening* para distinguir os períodos do dia.

Existe mais de uma maneira de dizer as horas:

(relógio marcando 6h15 ou 18h15)

It's six fifteen am (manhã)/pm (tarde).

It's (a) quarter after/past six am (manhã)/pm (tarde).

(relógio marcando 5h30)

It's five thirty am (manhã)/pm (tarde).

It's half past five am (manhã)/pm (tarde).

It's half five am (manhã)/pm (tarde).

(relógio marcando 8h45)

It's eight forty-five am (manhã)/pm (noite).

It's (a) quarter to/of nine am (manhã)/pm (noite).

(relógio marcando 10h10)

It's ten ten am (manhã)/pm (noite).

It's ten (minutes) after/past ten am (manhã)/pm (noite).

(relógio marcando 5h)

It's five o'clock am (manhã)/pm (noite).

It's five am (manhã)/pm (noite).

(relógio marcando meio-dia ou meia-noite).

It's twelve o'clock pm (meio-dia)/am (meia-noite).

It's midday (meio-dia)/midnight (meia-noite).

> A PREPOSIÇÃO USADA PARA INDICAR O HORÁRIO DE INÍCIO DE ALGUMA ATIVIDADE É "AT": THE PLAY IS AT 8 PM (A PEÇA É ÀS 20H).

Dias da semana e meses

Domingo	Segunda-feira	Terça-feira	Quarta-feira	Quinta-feira	Sexta-feira	Sábado
Sunday	Monday	Tuesday	Wednesday	Thursday	Friday	Saturday

Janeiro	Fevereiro	Março	Abril	Maio	Junho
January	February	March	April	May	June

Julho	Agosto	Setembro	Outubro	Novembro	Dezembro
July	August	September	October	November	December

Como representar datas

No inglês norte-americano, a representação das datas utiliza o padrão mês/dia/ano, enquanto na língua portuguesa se usa o padrão dia/mês/ano. Outra diferença entre esses dois sistemas é que, na língua inglesa, ao escrever-se a data por extenso, o dia transforma-se em numeral ordinal. Assim, se quisermos representar o dia 23 de fevereiro de 2015, as formas escritas serão:

February 23rd, 2015
02/23/15

A PREPOSIÇÃO CORRETA PARA DIAS E DATAS ESPECÍFICAS É "ON":

SHE TRAVELLED ON FEBRUARY 23RD
(ELA VIAJOU EM 23 DE FEVEREIRO).

ON MONDAYS THEY GO TO THE GYM
(ÀS SEGUNDAS-FEIRAS, ELES VÃO À ACADEMIA).

Estações do ano

Hemisfério Norte

Verão
Summer

| Início: 22 e 23 de junho | Fim: 22 e 23 de setembro |

A temperatura aumenta, e os dias são mais longos, podendo ser também chuvosos. É a época das férias de verão.

Curiosidade: *o horário de verão foi uma ideia do norte-americano Benjamin Franklin, em 1784, para economizar os gastos com carvão mineral.*

Outono
Autumn/Fall

| Início: 22 e 23 de setembro | Fim: 21 de dezembro |

As folhas das árvores caem, e os dias são mais curtos e frios, devido à proximidade do inverno.

Curiosidade: *no outono é quando geralmente ocorre a aurora boreal, fenômeno das regiões polares e o qual consiste em efeitos luminosos incríveis vistos no céu.*

Inverno
Winter

| Início: 22 e 23 de dezembro | Fim: 21 de março |

Os dias são bem curtos, com grande queda de temperatura, que pode chegar a níveis inferiores a 0°C e com presença de neve.

Curiosidade: *a temperatura mais baixa já registrada no mundo foi -71,2°C, em 1926, na Rússia.*

Primavera
Spring

| Início: 20 e 21 de março | Fim: 22 e 23 de junho |

Os dias são mais longos; as noites, mais curtas, e há a presença do sol e o aumento de chuvas. Essa é uma época de renovação da flora e da fauna.

Curiosidade: *na primavera, os animais hibernantes, como esquilos e ursos, acordam.*

12

Tempo

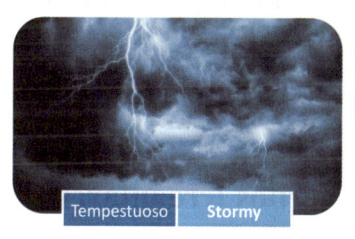

Chuvoso	Rainy
Ensolarado	Sunny
Nublado	Cloudy
Tempestuoso	Stormy

Cores

Vermelho	Red
Cor de Vinho	Burgundy
Marrom	Brown
Laranja	Orange
Amarelo	Yellow
Verde	Green
Azul	Blue
Roxo	Purple
Lilás	Lilac
Cor-de-rosa	Pink
Dourado	Golden
Prateado	Silver
Preto	Black
Cinza	Grey
Branco	White

Verbos to be e to have

SIMPLE PRESENT

Ser/Estar		
To be		
	Afirmativa	Negativa
I	am	am not/ ain't
You	are	are not/ aren't
He/She/It	is	is not/ isn't
We	are	are not/ aren't
You	are	are not/ aren't
They	are	are not/ aren't

Ter		
To have		
	Afirmativa	Negativa
I	have	have not/ haven't
You	have	have not/ haven't
He/She/It	has	has not/ hasn't
We	have	have not/ haven't
You	have	have not/ haven't
They	have	have not/ haven't

Verbos irregulares

INFINITIVE	PAST TENSE	PAST PARTICIPLE
to arise	arose	arisen
to awake	awoke	awoken
to be	was/were	been
to bear	bore	borne/ born
to beat	beat	beaten
to become	became	become
to begin	began	begun
to bet	bet	bet
to bite	bit	bitten
to bleed	bled	bled
to break	broke	broken
to bring	brought	brought
to build	built	built
to burn	burnt/burned	burnt/burned
to buy	bought	bought
to cast	cast	cast
to catch	caught	caught
to choose	chose	chosen
to come	came	come

INFINITIVE	PAST TENSE	PAST PARTICIPLE
to cost	cost	cost
to cut	cut	cut
to deal	dealt	dealt
to dig	dug	dug
to do	did	done
to draw	drew	drawn
to dream	dreamt/ dreamed	dreamt/ dreamed
to drink	drank	drunk
to drive	drove	driven
to eat	ate	eaten
to fall	fell	fallen
to feed	fed	fed
to feel	felt	felt
to fight	fought	fought
to find	found	found
to fly	flew	flown
to forbid	forbade/ forbad	forbidden

INFINITIVE	PAST TENSE	PAST PARTICIPLE
to forget	forgot	forgotten
to forgive	forgave	forgiven
to freeze	froze	frozen
to get	got	got/gotten
to give	gave	given
to go	went	gone
to grow	grew	grown
to hang	hung	hung
to have	had	had
to hear	heard	heard
to hide	hid	hidden
to hit	hit	hit
to hold	held	held
to hurt	hurt	hurt
to keep	kept	kept
to know	knew	known
to lay	laid	laid
to lead	led	led
to learn	learnt/learned	learnt/learned
to leave	left	left
to lend	lent	lent
to let	let	let
to light	lit	lit
to lose	lost	lost
to make	made	made
to mean	meant	meant
to meet	met	met
to fall	fell	fallen
to pay	paid	paid
to partake	partook	partaken
to put	put	put
to quit	quit/quitted	quit/quitted
to read	read	read
to ride	rode	ridden
to ring	rang	rung
to rise	rose	risen
to run	ran	run
to saw	sawed	sawn/sawed
to say	said	said
to see	saw	seen

INFINITIVE	PAST TENSE	PAST PARTICIPLE
to sell	sold	sold
to send	sent	sent
to set	set	set
to sew	sewed	sewn/ sewed
to shake	shook	shaken
to shine	shone	shone
to shoot	shot	shot
to show	showed	shown
to sing	sang	sung
to sink	sank	sunk
to sit	sat	sat
to sleep	slept	slept
to slide	slid	slid
to smell	smelt/smelled	smelt/smelled
to sow	sowed	sown/sowed
to speak	spoke	spoken
to speed	sped/speeded	sped/speeded
to spend	spent	spent
to spoil	spoiled/spoilt	spoiled/spoilt
to spread	spread	spread
to stand	stood	stood
to steal	stole	stolen
to stick	stuck	stuck
to strike	struck	struck
to swear	swore	sworn
to sweep	swept	swept
to swim	swam	swum
to swing	swung	swung
to take	took	taken
to teach	taught	taught
to tell	told	told
to think	thought	thought
to throw	threw	thrown
to understand	understood	understood
to wake	woke	woken
to wear	wore	worn
to wet	wet/wetted	wet/wetted
to win	won	won
to wring	wrung	wrung
to write	wrote	written

Phrasal verbs

Phrasal verbs são combinações de palavras formadas por um verbo e uma preposição ou um verbo e um advérbio. Para entender o significado dos *phrasal verbs*, não é possível fazer uma tradução isolada das palavras. É necessário saber o significado e o uso do conjunto. Estão listados, a seguir, alguns *phrasal verbs*:

Account for: explicar, justificar.

A number of factors account for the fall of profits. (Uma série de fatores justifica/explica a queda dos lucros.)

Ask out: convidar alguém para sair (ir ao cinema, ao teatro, a um jantar, etc.).

He asked me out for dinner. (Ele me convidou para jantar.)

Bring about: causar mudanças em determinada situação, fazer determinada coisa acontecer.

You will have to work harder to bring about changes in the system. (Você terá que trabalhar com mais empenho para que aconteçam mudanças no sistema.)

Bring up: criar uma criança até que ela se torne adulta.

She brought up three kids on her own. (Ela criou três filhos sozinha.)

Call back: retornar uma ligação telefônica.

Please, call me back as soon as possible. (Por favor, retorne minha ligação assim que possível.)

Call off: cancelar determinada coisa que iria acontecer.

She decided to call off the wedding. (Ela decidiu cancelar o casamento.)

Call up: fazer uma ligação telefônica para alguém.

I called him up yesterday. (Eu liguei para ele ontem.)

Catch up: ir rápido até alcançar uma pessoa ou um veículo.

I left before my father, but he soon caught me up. (Eu parti antes do meu pai, mas logo ele me alcançou.)

Cheer up: animar uma pessoa; deixá-la menos triste.

I tried to cheer him up, but he just kept crying. (Eu tentei animá-lo, mas ele continuou chorando.)

Clean up: deixar um lugar completamente limpo.

Go and clean up your room. (Vá e limpe o seu quarto.)

Cross out: riscar determinado item de uma lista escrita.

They crossed my name out the list of the party. (Eles riscaram meu nome da lista da festa.)

Drop in: fazer uma visita a alguém, geralmente sem fazer um convite formal.

I dropped in to see how she was. (Eu fiz uma visita para ver como ela estava.)

Drop out: deixar de frequentar a escola ou a universidade antes do fim do curso.

She dropped out school after the first term. (Ela largou a escola depois do primeiro semestre.)

Figure out: ser capaz de entender ou resolver um problema.

He had to figure out the conection between the two events. (Ele tinha que entender a ligação entre os dois acontecimentos.)

Find out: descobrir um fato ou uma informação.

We have to find out the truth about that case. (Nós temos que descobrir a verdade sobre aquele caso.)

Give up: desistir de algo que se estava tentando fazer.

I gave up the competition. (Eu desisti da competição.)

Keep up: continuar a fazer determinada coisa.

Keep up the good work. (Continue fazendo um bom trabalho.)

Look out: usado para advertir alguém a ser cuidadoso, especialmente se algum acidente estiver prestes a acontecer.

Look out, there's a car coming! (Cuidado, há um carro vindo!)

Pass away: morrer (é uma forma mais branda para o verbo "to die").

My grandfather passed away last year. (Meu avô faleceu ano passado.)

Run out: usar a quantidade toda de determinada coisa até não sobrar mais nada.

Some hospitals are running out their blood suplies. (Alguns hospitais estão com suas reservas de sangue esgotadas.)

Settle down: acalmar-se, acalmar alguém, recuperar o controle.

It was hard to settle down and work after all that. (Foi difícil recuperar o controle e trabalhar depois de tudo aquilo.)

Take over: assumir a atividade que outra pessoa estava fazendo.

Can you take over the cooking while I walk the dog? (Você pode assumir a cozinha enquanto eu passeio com o cachorro?)

Get up: levantar, acordar, sair da cama.

What time do you get up? (Que horas você acorda?)

Expressões idiomáticas

As **expressões idiomáticas**, *idioms*, em inglês, são termos ou frases que apresentam um significado diferente do que teriam as palavras isoladamente. Nesse caso, não basta saber o significado das palavras, é preciso compreender o conjunto que compõe a expressão.

Alguns exemplos de expressões idiomáticas:

Act your age. Não seja infantil.	**Safe and sound.** São e salvo.	**Talk is cheap.** Falar é fácil.
Beyond a shadow of a doubt. Sem sombra de dúvida.	**Hand in hand.** De mãos dadas.	**Piece of cake.** Muito fácil.
Ugly as sin. Extremamente feio.	**Rise and shine!** Acorde e levante-se!	**So far, so good?** Até agora tudo bem?
Are you pulling my leg? Você está brincando comigo?	**I fell flat on my face.** Eu quebrei a cara.	**To be at rock bottom.** Estar no fundo do poço/ Estar por baixo.
By the book. Ao pé da letra.	**Cross my heart!** Juro por Deus!	**It is none of your business.** Não é da sua conta.
Like hell! Uma ova!	**Mum's the word!** Boca de siri!	**To kick the bucket.** Bater as botas, morrer.
Keep your eyes peeled. Fique atento.	**To give a buzz.** Dar uma ligada para alguém.	**It is raining cats and dogs.** Está chovendo muito.
May I have the floor? Posso falar?	**Give it a shot.** Tente.	**To be over the moon.** Estar muito feliz, no mundo da lua de tão contente.
All in good time. Tudo a seu tempo.	**Cross your fingers!** Cruze os dedos! (para dar boa sorte)	**To be on the cres of a wave.** Ser bem-sucedido, estar em uma posição de destaque.

To go from bad to worse.
Ir de mal a pior.

To be in the same boat.
Estar no mesmo barco.
(na mesma situação)

Hold your horses!
Tenha calma!

Help yourself/Be my guest/
Go ahead (informal).
Sirva-se/Pode pegar.

Good thinking.
Bem pensado.

Out of the blue.
Do nada.

Let's keep in touch.
Vamos manter contato.

On second thought.
Pensando bem.

To be a bad egg.
Ser flor que não se cheire.

Look at/on the bright side.
Veja o lado bom das coisas/
Veja o lado positivo.

As good as it gets!
Melhor é impossível!

Snitcher.
Dedo-duro.

I will always be there for you.
Sempre estarei ao seu lado.

Fair play.
Jogo limpo.

Fair game.
Alvo fácil.

Make yourself at home/
comfortable.
Sinta-se em casa/
Fique à vontade.

As lost as a nun
on a honeymoon.
Mais perdido que cego
em tiroteio.

A little birdie told me.
Um passarinho me contou.

Conhecendo pessoas

Hi, what's your name?
Oi, qual é o seu nome?

Hi, how's it going?
Oi, tudo bom?

How old are you?
Quantos anos você tem?

What's your phone number?
Qual é o seu número de telefone?

Excuse me.
Com licença.

See you later!/See you!
Até logo!

Let's keep in touch.
Vamos manter contato.

Have a nice day.
Tenha um bom dia.

How do you spell it?
Como se escreve isso?

Hi, how are you?
Oi, como você está?

I'm fine, and you?
Estou bem, e você?

Nice to meet you.
Prazer em conhecê-la.

Nice to meet you too.
O prazer é meu.

Where are you from?
De onde você é?

Are you from here?
Você é daqui?

What's your address?
Qual é o seu endereço?

What kind of food do you like?
De que tipo de comida você gosta?

Would you like going out with me?
Você gostaria de sair comigo?

Do you have any pets?
Você tem algum animal de estimação?

What's your favorite book?
Qual é o seu livro favorito?

Do you have brothers and sisters?
Você tem irmãos?

What's your job?
No que você trabalha?

Where do you study?
Onde você estuda?

Regards./Give my best.
Mande minhas lembranças.

When's your birthday?
Quando é o seu aniversário?

You're welcome.
De nada.

Thank you.
Obrigada.

Direções

Keep going for about two blocks.

Continue por aproximadamente dois quarteirões.

Turn left/right.

Vire à esquerda/direita.

Across from...

Do outro lado (da rua, da avenida, etc.)...

Go straight...

Vá reto...

It's near to...

É perto do/da...

In front of...

Em frente de...

It's far from here.

É longe daqui.

Excuse me. Where is the...?

Com licença. Onde fica o/a...?

Make a left/right turn.

Faça uma curva à esquerda/direita.

On the corner

Na esquina

How do I get to...?

Como eu chego à/ao...?

Street/Avenue/Road

Rua/Avenida/Estrada

It's in the middle of the block.

É no meio do quarteirão.

You have to go two flights up/down.

Você tem que subir/descer dois lances de escada.

What place is this?

Que lugar é este?

Come along.

Venha comigo.

Is the station far from here?

A estação é longe daqui?

Where is downtown?

Onde é o centro da cidade?

Go up the main street.

Suba a rua principal.

Stay on your left/right side.

Fique à sua esquerda/direita.

You have to use the escalator/elevator.

Você deve usar a escada rolante/o elevador.

I'm lost. Could you repeat, please?

Não entendi. Você pode repetir, por favor?

Keep going for about two blocks.

Continue por aproximadamente dois quarteirões.

Is there a drugstore near here?

Há alguma farmácia aqui perto?

Can you show me where?

Você pode me mostrar onde?

By subway/By bus/By taxi/On foot

De metrô/De ônibus/De táxi/A pé

Passeando

Can you take a picture of us?

Você pode tirar uma foto nossa?

We took a lot of pictures on our trip.

Nós tiramos várias fotos na nossa viagem.

Could I have a ticket to...?

Eu gostaria de uma passagem para...

Excuse me, which way to platform...?

Com licença, para que lado é a plataforma...?

Could you help me, please?

Por favor, você poderia me ajudar?

What time is it?

Que horas são?

Look out for the steps!

Cuidado com o degrau!

Is this the line for...?

Esta é a fila para...?

Is this the end of the line?

Este é o fim da fila?

Where is the nearest taxi rank?

Onde é o ponto de táxi mais próximo?

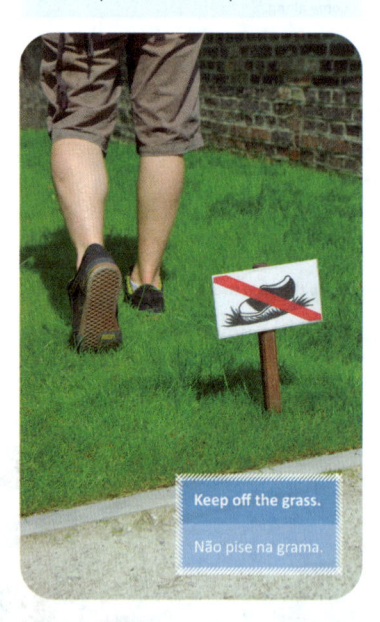

Keep off the grass.

Não pise na grama.

VOCABULÁRIO ÚTIL

Cinema: cinema
Church: igreja
Ferris wheel: roda-gigante
Lookout point: mirante
Museum: museu

Nature reserve: reserva natural
Nightclub: discoteca, boate
Restaurant: restaurante
Roller coaster: montanha-russa
Zoo: zoológico

Fazendo compras

Could I have the receipt please?

Posso ficar com a nota fiscal, por favor?

Here's your receipt.

Aqui está a sua nota fiscal.

Are you being helped?

Você já foi atendido?

No, thanks. I'm just looking.

Não, obrigado. Estou só olhando.

I'd like to try on this shirt, please.

Eu gostaria de experimentar esta camisa, por favor.

Do you take credit card?

Vocês aceitam cartão de crédito?

Everything in the store is on sale today.

Tudo na loja está em liquidação hoje.

The tickets sold out before we could buy any.

Os ingressos esgotaram antes que pudéssemos comprar.

It fits me perfectly.

Serviu perfeitamente.

This shirt is a little loose/tight.

Esta camisa está um pouco larga/apertada.

Do you have a changing room?

Vocês têm provador?

How much does this cost?

Quanto custa isto?

Could I have this gift wrapped, please?

Por favor, poderia embrulhar isto para presente?

No restaurante

I'd like to make a reservation.

Eu gostaria de fazer uma reserva.

Table for two, please!

Mesa para dois, por favor.

Are you ready to order?

Você já está pronto para fazer o pedido?

I have a booking.

Eu tenho uma reserva.

What would you like to eat?

O que você gostaria de comer?

Could you repeat that, please?

Você poderia repetir, por favor?

We need another minute.

Nós precisamos de mais um minuto.

Could you bring...?

Você poderia trazer...?

I'm a vegetarian.

Eu sou vegetariano(a).

I'll have a hot chocolate.

Eu vou querer um chocolate quente.

I didn't order this.

Eu não pedi isto.

Could you bring the check, please?

Você poderia trazer a conta, por favor?

VOCABULÁRIO ÚTIL

Beef: carne vermelha
Beverages: bebidas
Dessert: sobremesa
Dressings: molhos
Menu: cardápio
Poultry: aves
Seafood: frutos do mar
Side dish: acompanhamento

Indo a uma festa

Are you having fun?

Você(s) está(ão) se divertindo?

Let's go for a walk.

Vamos dar uma volta.

Can I get you anything to drink?

Você aceita uma bebida?

I'll take care of it.

Pode deixar comigo.

God bless you!

Saúde! (quando alguém espirra)

Join the fun.

Entre na brincadeira.

Eat something.

Coma alguma coisa.

Are you enjoying the music?

Você está gostando da música?

No, thanks. I've had enough.

Não, obrigado. Estou satisfeito.

How did you like the party?

O que você achou da festa?

Cheers!

Saúde! (brinde)

No trabalho

What do you do for a living?
O que você faz da vida?

What is your job?
Qual é o seu trabalho?

What does your job involve?
Quais são suas atribuições no trabalho?

You got hired by this company.
Você foi contratado por esta empresa.

Today is my day off.
Hoje é meu dia de folga.

My workplace is very cool.
Meu local de trabalho é bem legal.

I'm a hard-working employee.
Eu sou um funcionário esforçado.

How many people work with you?
Quantas pessoas trabalham com você?

Teamwork can make a difference.
O trabalho em equipe pode fazer a diferença.

These are my co-workers.
Estes são meus colegas de trabalho.

Is the company doing well?
A empresa está indo bem?

Today I'll do overtime.
Hoje eu vou fazer hora extra.

Gírias e expressões

Everybody says so!
Todos dizem isso!

Take it easy.
Vá com calma, relaxe.

Never mind.
Tanto faz.

For goodness' sake!
Pelo amor de Deus!

Good Lord!
Meu Deus!

It's awesome!
É impressionante.

What's up, dude?
E aí, cara?

Count me in!
Estou nessa!

You bet!
Pode apostar!

I don't buy that!
Eu não caio nessa!

Never heard of.
Nunca ouvi falar.

All right already!
Pare com isso!

You never know.
Nunca se sabe.

What a let down!
Que decepção!

I did quite well.
Fui muito bem.

Leave it to me.
Deixe comigo.

Once and for all.
De uma vez por todas.

Don't bug me.
Não me chateie/Não me perturbe/Não encha meu saco.

Thank God!
Graças a Deus!

Look here!
Escute aqui!

Look lively!
Vamos logo!

I think so.
Acho que sim.

I don't think so.
Acho que não.

Take your time.
Sem pressa.

So what?
E daí?

It is up to you.
Você que sabe.

29

No aeroporto

May I check your ticket and passport?

Posso verificar seu bilhete e passaporte?

Could you help me with my luggage/baggage, please?

Você poderia me ajudar com a minha bagagem, por favor?

Have you anything to declare?

Você tem algo a declarar?

What is the purpose of your travel/visit?

Qual o motivo da sua viagem/visita?

Where do you come from?

De onde você vem?

Where are you going?

Para onde você está indo?

How long are you staying?

Quanto tempo você vai ficar?

You have excess baggage.

Você tem excesso de bagagem.

Where are the toilets?

Onde ficam os banheiros?

Window seat or aisle seat?

Assento na janela ou no corredor?

What's your flight number?

Qual o número do seu voo?

Your flight has been cancelled.

O seu voo foi cancelado.

I need to change my reservation.

Eu preciso mudar minha reserva.

Viajando

> **I'd like to travel by hitchhiking.**
>
> Eu gostaria de viajar de carona.

Where can I take a taxi/cab?

Onde eu posso pegar um táxi?

Could you save my seat, please?

Você pode guardar meu lugar, por favor?

At what time does the train/bus/plane leave?

A que horas o trem/ônibus/avião parte?

Is this seat free?

Esta poltrona está livre?

Is there another seat available, please?

Há alguma outra poltrona disponível, por favor?

Sit back, relax and enjoy the flight.

Sente-se, relaxe e aproveite o voo.

I'd like a round-trip ticket to...

Eu gostaria de uma passagem de ida e volta para...

Do you know if this train stops in Paris?

Você sabe se este trem para em Paris?

I'd like a standard ticket, please.

Eu gostaria de uma passagem normal, por favor.

PORTUGUÊS/INGLÊS

Aa

A, a *s.m.* the first letter of the Portuguese alphabet / *art.* the / *pron.* her (ela).
À *prep.* at, in, on (lugar).
ABA *s.f.* brim; flap; tab.
ABACATE *s.m.* avocado; avocado pear.
ABACAXI *s.m.* pineapple.
ÁBACO *s.m.* abacus.
ABADE *s.m.* abbot.
ABADESCO *adj.* abbatial; fat.
ABADESSA *s.f.* abbess.
ABADIA *s.f.* abbey.
ABAFADO *adj.* stuffy, suffocating.
ABAFADOR *s.m.* damper.
ABAFAR *v.* to damp; to choke; to suffocate.
ABAFO *s.m.* suffocation, choking; stealing; caress.
ABAIXAMENTO *s.m.* lowering, bringing down.
ABAIXAR *v.* to lower (preço); to reduce (luz, som).
ABAIXO *adv.* down; beneath / *prep.* below; under.
ABAIXO-ASSINADO *s.m.* undersigned.
ABAJUR *s.m.* lampshade; lamp; table lamp.
ABALADO *adj.* shaky; trembled.
ABALAR *v.* to shake; to upset; to weaken.
ABALO *s.m.* shock; quake; shake.
ABANADO *adj.* fanned; waved with a fan.
ABANADOR *s.m.* fanner, winnower / *adj.* fanner, winnower.
ABANAR *v.* to shake; to fan.
ABANCAR *v.* to furnish.
ABANDAR *v.* to gather.
ABANDONADO *adj.* abandoned.
ABANDONAR *v.* to abandon; to leave; to give up.
ABANDONO *s.m.* abandonment.
ABANICAR *v.* to fan.
ABANICO *s.m.* small fan.
ABANO *s.m.* wag.
ABARCA *s.f.* rustic sandal.
ABARCADOR *s.m.* grasper, clasper.
ABARCAR *v.* to cover; to include; to comprehend.
ABARRACAR *v.* to camp.
ABARRANCAR *v.* to form ravines.
ABARROTADO *adj.* crammed; full; overfilled; overloaded.

ABARROTAMENTO *s.m.* overload; overfill; cram.
ABARROTAR *v.* to cram; to full; to filled; to overload.
ABASTADO *adj.* rich; wealthy; well-off; abundant.
ABASTANÇA *s.f.* abundance.
ABASTAR *v.* to provide; to supply.
ABASTARDAR *v.* to corrupt.
ABASTECEDOR *adj.* supplier; provider.
ABASTECER *v.* to supply; to provide; to fuel.
ABASTECIMENTO *s.m.* supplies; provision; fuelling.
ABATE *s.m.* discount; off (valor); slaughter; killing (gado); putting down (árvore).
ABATEDOR *s.m.* knacker.
ABATEDOURO *s.m.* slaughterhouse.
ABATER *v.* to slaughter; to abate; to reduce; to lessen (valor).
ABAULADO *adj.* convex; arched.
ABAULAR-SE *v.* to bulge.
ABDICAÇÃO *s.f.* abdication; renunciation.
ABDICAR *v.* to abdicate; to renounce; to give up.
ABDOME *s.m.* abdomen.
ABDÔMEN *s.m.* m.q. abdome.
ABDOMINAL *adj.* abdominal; sit-ups (exercício).
ABDUÇÃO *s.f.* abduction.
ABDUZIR *v.* to abduct.
ABECEDÁRIO *s.m.* alphabet.
ABEIRAR *v.* to border.
ABELHA *s.f.* bee.
ABELHUDO *adj.* nosy, snoopy.
ABENÇOADO(A) *adj.* blessed
ABENÇOADOR *s.m.* blesser.
ABENÇOAR *v.* to bless.
ABERRAÇÃO *s.f.* aberration.
ABERRANTE *adj.* aberrant.
ABERTA *s.f.* opening, gap.
ABERTO *adj.* opened.
ABERTURA *s.f.* opening; gap.
ABESTALHADO *adj.* stupid; silly.
ABESTALHAR *v.* to become silly, to become imbecile.
ABILOLADO *adj.* crazy; insane.
ABILOLAR *v.* to go insane; to out of mind.
ABISCOITADO *adj.* cookie, biscuit-like.
ABISCOITAR *v.* to gain, to profit by, to arrange, to manage.

ABISMADO *adj.* astonished; shocked.
ABISMAL *adj.* abysmal.
ABISMAR *v.* to stupefy, to shock, to astonish.
ABISMO *s.m.* abyss; abysm; depths.
ABJEÇÃO *s.f.* baseness; degradation; infamy.
ABJETO *adj.* abject.
ABJURAR *v.* to abjure, to renounce.
ABLATIVO *s.m.* ablative.
ABNEGAÇÃO *s.f.* abnegation; renounce; self-denial.
ABNEGADO *adj.* self-sacrificing.
ABNEGAR *v.* to abnegate; to renounce.
ABNEGATIVO *adj.* abnegative.
ABÓBADA *s.f.* vault; dome.
ABOBADADO *adj.* vaulted; dome shaped roof.
ABOBADO *adj.* fool; silly; senseless.
ABÓBORA *s.f.* pumpkin.
ABOBRINHA *s.f.* courgette, zucchini; nonsense talk.
ABOCANHAR *v.* to bite.
ABOLIÇÃO *s.f.* abolition; abolishment.
ABOLICIONISMO *s.m.* abolitionism.
ABOLICIONISTA *s.2gên.* abolitionist / *adj.2gên.* abolitionist.
ABOLIDO *adj.* abolished.
ABOLIMENTO *s.m.* m.q. abolição.
ABOLIR *v.* to abolish; to revoke.
ABOMINAÇÃO *s.f.* abomination; detestation; execration.
ABOMINADO *adj.* abhorred; detested; execrated.
ABOMINADOR *s.m.* abominator; hater.
ABOMINAR *v.* to abhor; to loathe; to hate.
ABOMINÁVEL *adj.* abominable.
ABONAR *v.* to guarantee; to accredit.
ABONO *s.m.* guarantee; bonus; surplus; allowance.
ABORDAGEM *s.f.* approach.
ABORDAR *v.* to approach; to board (navio).
ABORDÁVEL *adj.2gên.* accessible, approachable.
ABORÍGENE *s.2gên.* aborigine / *adj.* aboriginal.
ABORÍGINE *s.2gên.* m.q. aborígene.
ABORRECER *v.* to annoy; to bore; to bother; to irritate.
ABORRECIDO *adj.* bored; annoyed; dull.
ABORRECIMENTO *s.m.* annoyance; boredom.

ABORTADO *adj.* aborted (uma vida); cancelled; interrupted.
ABORTAR *v.* to abort; to miscarry.
ABORTIVO *adj.* abortive.
ABORTO *s.m.* abortion.
ABOTOADURA *s.f.* set of buttons, buttoning.
ABOTOAR *v.* to button up.
ABRACADABRA *s.m.* abracadabra.
ABRAÇADO *adj.* embraced; hugging.
ABRAÇAR *v.* to hug; to embrace.
ABRAÇO *s.m.* hug; embrace.
ABRANDAMENTO *s.m.* mitigation; softening.
ABRANDAR *v.* to reduce; to lower; to mitigate.
ABRANGENTE *adj.* embracing; wide; including.
ABRANGER *v.* to comprehend (assunto); to embrace; to reach (alcançar).
ABRASADO *adj.* burned, burnt; on fire.
ABRASADOR *adj.* burning, scorching.
ABRASAMENTO *s.m.* fervor.
ABRASANTE *adj.* scorching, torrid, burning.
ABRASAR *v.* to burn; to fire.
ABRASIVO *s.m.* abrasive / *adj.* abrasive.
ABREVIAÇÃO *s.f.* abbreviation; reduction.
ABREVIADO *adj.* abbreviated; reduced.
ABREVIAR *v.* to abbreviate; to summarize; to reduce.
ABRIDOR *s.m.* opener.
ABRIGADO *adj.* sheltered; covered; protected.
ABRIGAR *v.* to shelter; to cover; to protect.
ABRIGO *s.m.* shelter, protection; refuge.
ABRIL *s.m.* April.
ABRIR *v.* to open.
ABROLHO *s.m.* reef; thorn.
ABRUPTO *adj.* abrupt.
ABSCEDER *v.* to suppurate, to fester.
ABSCESSO *s.m.* abscess.
ABSOLUTAMENTE *adv.* absolutely; completely; totally.
ABSOLUTO *adj.* absolute.
ABSOLVER *v.* to absolve; to acquit.
ABSOLVIÇÃO *s.f. absolution.*
ABSOLVIDO *adj.* absolved; acquitted.
ABSORÇÃO *s.f.* absorption.
ABSORTO *adj.* absorbed.
ABSORVENTE *adj.* absorbent; absorbing / *s.m.* absorbent; feminine napkin.
ABSORVER *v.* to absorb.

ABSTENÇÃO *s.f.* abstention.
ABSTENCIONISMO *s.m.* abstencionism.
ABSTER *v.* to abstain.
ABSTINÊNCIA *s.f.* abstinence.
ABSTINENTE *adj.* abstinent; abstinentious.
ABSTRAÇÃO *s.f.* abstraction.
ABSTRACIONISMO *s.m.* abstractionism.
ABSTRAIR *v.* to abstract.
ABSTRATO *adj.* abstract.
ABSURDEZA *s.f.* absurdity.
ABSURDO *adj.* absurd / *s.m.* absurdity.
ABULIA *s.f.* abulia.
ABUNDÂNCIA *s.f.* abundance; plentifulness.
ABUNDANTE *adj.* abundant; plentiful.
ABUNDAR *v.* to abound.
ABUSADO(A) *adj.* abused; forced.
ABUSAR *v.* to abuse; to misuse.
ABUSIVO(A) *adj.* abusive.
ABUSO *s.m.* abuse; misuse; overuse.
ABUTRE *s.m.* vulture.
ACABADO(A) *adj.* finished; done, over; accomplished.
ACABAMENTO *s.m.* finish; complement; ending.
ACABAR *v.* to finish; to complete; to complement.
ACABRUNHADO *adj.* depressed; distressed; melancholic.
ACABRUNHAR *v.* to depress; to distress.
ACÁCIA *s.f.* acacia.
ACADEMIA *s.f.* academy, university; gym.
ACADEMICISMO *s.m.* academicism.
ACADÊMICO *s.m.* academic; scholar / *adj.* academic; scholar.
AÇAFRÃO *s.m.* saffron.
AÇAÍ *s.m.* cabbage palm.
ACAJU *s.m.* mahogany.
ACALENTAMENTO *s.m.* soothing.
ACALENTAR *v.* to rock; to cherish; to lull.
ACALENTO *s.m.* lullaby.
ACALMADO *adj.* pacified, calmed, appeased.
ACALMAR *v.* to calm.
ACALORADO *adj.* agitated, excited, inflamed.
ACALORAR *v.* to heat, to warm.
ACAMADO *adj.* bedridden; abed.
ACAMAR *v.* to bed.
ACAMPADO *adj.* encamped.
ACAMPAMENTO *s.m.* camping; camp; encampment.
ACAMPAR *v.* to camp; to encamp.

ACANHADO *adj.* shy; timid.
ACANHAMENTO *s.m.* shyness; timidity.
ACANHAR *v.* to diminish, to shame.
ACANÔNICO *adj.* noncanonical.
AÇÃO *s.f.* action, movement, attitude.
ACAREAÇÃO *s.f.* confrontation.
ACAREAR *v.* to confront; to contract information.
ACARICIAR *v.* to caress; to pet.
ACARINHAR *v.* to caress; to pet; to treat kindness.
ÁCARO *s.m.* acarid; mite.
ACARRETAR *v.* to result in, to bring about; to cart, to cause.
ACASALAMENTO *s.m.* mating.
ACASALAR *v.* to mate, to couple.
ACASO *s.m.* chance; luck; randomly.
ACATADO *adj.* complied; respected.
ACATAMENTO *s.m.* regard, respect.
ACATAR *v.* to obey; to comply; to respect.
ACATÓLICO *s.m.* non-Catholic / *adj.* non--Catholic.
ACAUTELAR *v.* to guard.
ACAVALAR *v.* to superimpose.
ACEBOLADO *adj.* onion-flavored; seasoned with onions.
ACEBOLAR *v.* to season with onions.
ACEDER *v.* to accede, to conform.
ACEFALIA *s.f.* acephalia, acephaly.
ACÉFALO *adj.* acephalous.
ACEITAÇÃO *s.f.* acceptance, acceptation; approval.
ACEITAR *v.* to accept; to consent.
ACEITÁVEL *adj.* acceptable.
ACEITO *adj.* accepted; admitted; received.
ACELERAÇÃO *s.f.* acceleration.
ACELERADO *adj.* accelerated; sped up.
ACELERADOR *s.m.* accelerator, accelerator pedal.
ACELERAR *v.* to accelerate; to speed up.
ACELGA *s.f.* chard.
ACÉM *s.m.* spare rib.
ACENAR *v.* to wave; to beckon; to point.
ACENDEDOR *s.m.* lighter.
ACENDER *v.* to light; to ignite; to turn on.
ACENO *s.m.* wave; sign; gesture.
ACENTO *s.m.* accent; stress; tone, emphasis.
ACENTUAÇÃO *s.f.* accentuation; accent, stress; intonation.
ACENTUADO *adj.* accented; accentuated; marked; emphasized.
ACENTUAR *v.* to accentuate; to accent; to emphasize.
ACEPÇÃO *s.f.* acceptation; meaning; sense.
ACERAR *v.* to steel, to sharpen.
ACERCA *adv.* about; near; concerning; circa (datas).
ACERCAR *v.* to approach, to surround.
ACEROLA *s.f.* acerola.
ACERTADO *adj.* right, correct; fit; proper; adjusted.
ACERTAR *v.* to set right; to adjust, to regulate; to settle (dívida); to hit.
ACERTO *s.m.* hit, judgment.
ACERVO *s.m.* collection.
ACESO *adj.* lighted (fogueira, lareira); turned on (lâmpada).
ACESSAR *v.* to access, to approach, to reach.
ACESSIBILIDADE *s.f.* accessibility.
ACESSÍVEL *adj.* accessible; approachable.
ACESSO *s.m.* access; admission.
ACESSÓRIO *adj.* accessory, addition, complement.
ACETONA *s.f.* acetone.
ACHA *s.f.* log.
ACHADO *adj.* finding, find, discovery.
ACHAQUE *s.m.* ailment; indisposition, illness.
ACHAR *v.* to find (encontrar); to think (opinião).
ACHATADO *adj.* flat, flattened.
ACHATAMENTO *s.m.* flattening.
ACHATAR *v.* to flatten; to squash
ACHEGAR *v.* to arrange; to approximate.
ACHEGO *s.m.* approach, approximation; protection.
ACHINESADO *adj.* Chineselike.
ACIDENTADO *adj.* casualty (ser vivo); rough (terreno).
ACIDENTAL *adj.* accidental, incidental.
ACIDENTAR *v.* to cause.
ACIDENTE *s.m.* accident, incident; misfortune; disaster.
ACIDEZ *s.f.* acidity, sourness.
ACIDIFICAÇÃO *s.f.* acidification.
ACIDIFICAR *v.* to acidify.
ÁCIDO *adj.* acid, sour / *s.m.* acid.
ACIDOSE *s.f.* acisosis.
ACIMA *adv.* above.
ACINTE *s.m.* provocation / *adv.* intentionally.

ACINTOSO *adj.* provocative, spiteful.
ACINZADO *adj.* grayish.
ACINZAR *v.* to make, to paint gray.
ACINZENTADO *adj.* grayish.
ACIONADO *s.m.* defendant / *adj.* to operate, to act; to trigger, to set.
ACIONAR *v.* to sue; to trigger.
ACIONISTA *s.2gên.* shareholder.
ACIRRADO *adj.* incited, irritated, induced, instigated.
ACIRRAR *v.* to incite, to irritate, to induce angrily.
ACLAMAÇÃO *s.f.* acclaim, acclamation.
ACLAMADO *adj.* acclaimed; praised, celebrated.
ACLAMAR *v.* to acclaim, to hail.
ACLAMATIVO *adj.* acclamatory.
ACLARAÇÃO *s.f.* clarification, explanation.
ACLARADO *adj.* cleared; explained.
ACLARAR *v.* to clarify; to explain.
ACLIMAÇÃO *s.f.* acclimation.
ACLIMAR *v.* to aclimate.
ACLIVE *s.m.* acclivity, slope.
ACNE *s.f.* acne; pimples.
AÇO *s.m.* steel.
ACOAR *v.* to bark.
ACOBARDADO *adj.* cowardly.
ACOBARDAMENTO *s.m.* cowardice.
ACOBARDAR *v.* to craven, to discourage.
ACOBERTADO *adj.* protected; concealed; disguised, covered up (notícias, fatos).
ACOBERTAMENTO *s.m.* protection; disguise; cover.
ACOBERTAR *v.* to cover up; to protect; to conceal.
ACOBREAR *v.* to copper.
ACOCHAR *v.* to compress.
ACOCORAR *v.* to hunker.
ACOITAR *v.* to shelter, to protect.
AÇOITAR *v.* to whip; to beat up.
AÇOITE *s.m.* whip, lash.
ACOLÁ *adv.* there.
ACOLCHOADO *adj.* padded, quilted / *s.m.* quilt.
ACOLCHOAR *v.* to quilt, to pad, to stuff.
ACOLHEDOR(A) *adj.* welcoming, hospitable (pessoa); cosy, comfortable (casa, hotel).
ACOLHER *v.* to welcome, to receive.
ACOLHIDA *s.f.* reception, welcome.

ACOMETEDOR *adj.* attacker, aggressor / *s.m.* attacker, aggressor.
ACOMETER *v.* to attack, to assault, hostilized.
ACOMETIDA *s.f.* attack; attempt.
ACOMODAÇÃO *s.f.* accommodation, adaptation.
ACOMODADO *adj.* accommodated, adjusted, adapted.
ACOMODAR *v.* to accommodate, to arrange, to adapt.
ACOMPANHADOR *adj.* companion, companioned; accompanist.
ACOMPANHAMENTO *s.m.* accompaniment.
ACOMPANHANTE *s.2gên.* companion / *adj.2gên.* accompanying.
ACOMPANHAR *v.* to accompany, to escort.
ACONCHEGADO *adj.* near, close; comfortable, cosy.
ACONCHEGANTE *adj.* cosy, comfortable.
ACONCHEGAR *v.* to bring near, closer; to snuggle against.
ACONCHEGO *s.m.* cosiness, snugness, cuddle.
ACONDICIONADO *adj.* conditioned, packed, disposed.
ACONDICIONAMENTO *s.f.* packing (mercadoria); conditioning, arrangement.
ACONDICIONAR *v.* to condition; to pack (mercadoria), to arrange.
ACONSELHADO *adj.* advised, informed, warned.
ACONSELHADOR *s.m.* advisor, counsellor.
ACONSELHAMENTO *s.m.* advise, counselling, consult.
ACONSELHAR *v.* to advise, to counsel, to consult.
ACONSELHÁVEL *adj.* advisable.
ACONTECER *v.* to happen, to occur, to take place.
ACONTECIDO *adj.* happened, done, took place.
ACONTECIMENTO *s.m.* happening, event, occurrence.
ACOPLADO *adj.* coupled, linked.
ACOPLAR *v.* to couple, to link.
ACORDADO *adj.* awake; agreed, dealt, negociated.
ACORDAR *v.* to wake up, to waken, to rouse; to agree, to deal.

ACORDE *s.m.* chord.
ACORDEÃO *s.m.* accordion.
ACORDO *s.m.* agreement, accordance, deal, pact.
ACORRENTADO *adj.* chained.
ACORRENTAR *v.* to fetter, to chain up, to enchain.
ACOSTADO *adj.* parasite.
ACOSTAMENTO *s.m.* coasting, support; bracket; hard shoulders.
ACOSTAR *v.* to lean against; to uphold.
ACOSTUMADO *adj.* accustomed, used to.
ACOSTUMAR *v.* to accustom, to get used to; to habituate, to familiarize.
ACOTOVELAR *v.* to elbow; to jostle.
AÇOUGUE *s.m.* butchery, butcher shop.
AÇOUGUEIRO *adj.* butcher.
ACOVARDADO *adj.* intimidated, threatened.
ACOVARDAR *v.* to craven, to discourage.
ACRACIA *s.f.* anarchy; asthenia, debility.
ÁCRATA *s.2gên.* anarchist.
ACRE *adj.* acre; acrid; sharp; biting.
ACREDITADO *adj.* accredited; believed, trusted, considered.
ACREDITAR *v.* to accredit; to believe, to trust.
ACREDITÁVEL *adj.* credible, convincing.
ACRESCENTAMENTO *s.m.* increase, addition; enlargement; raise (salário).
ACRESCENTAR *v.* to add, to sum; to enlarge, to increase; to raise (salário).
ACRESCER *v.* to increase; to grow; to accrue.
ACRESCIMENTO *s.m.* increase, addition; accrual.
ACRÉSCIMO *s.m.* addition, increase, raise; accrual.
ACRIANÇADO *adj.* childish; childlike.
ACRÍLICO *s.m.* acrylic / *adj.* acrylic.
ACROBACIA *s.f.* acrobatics, loop, aerobatics (acrobacia aérea).
ACROBATA *s.2gên.* acrobat; equilibrist.
ACROBÁTICO *adj.* acrobatic, acrobatical.
ACROFOBIA *s.f.* acrophobia.
ACROFÓBICO *adj.* acrophobic.
ACROMÁTICO *adj.* achromatic, colorless.
ACRÓPOLE *s.f.* acropolis.
ACUADO *adj.* cornered, chased.
ACUAR *v.* to corner, to chase.
AÇÚCAR *s.m.* sugar.
AÇUCARADO *adj.* sugary.
AÇUCARAR *v.* to sugar.

AÇUCAREIRO *s.m.* sugar bowl; sugar basin.
AÇUDE *s.m.* dam, dike, wier.
ACUDIR *v.* to help, to assist; to aid, to run to.
ACUIDADE *s.f.* acuity.
ACULTURAÇÃO *s.f.* acculturation.
ACULTURADO *adj.* acculturative.
ACULTURAR *v.* to acculturate.
ACUMULAÇÃO *s.f.* accumulation, cumulation.
ACUMULAR *v.* to accumulate; to gather, to collect.
ACUMULATIVO *adj.* accumulative.
ACÚMULO *s.m.* accumulation.
ACUPUNTOR *s.m.* acupuncturist / *adj.* acupuncturist.
ACUPUNTURA *s.f.* acupunctur.
ACURADO *adj.* accurate; well-done; precise; exact.
ACUSAÇÃO *s.f.* accusation; indictment; charge.
ACUSADO *adj.* accused; defendant; charged.
ACUSADOR *s.m.* accuser.
ACUSAR *v.* to accuse; to charge; to blame.
ACUSATIVO *s.m.* accusative.
ACÚSTICA *s.f.* acoustics.
ACÚSTICO *adj.* acoustic, acoustical.
ADAGA *s.f.* dagger.
ADÃO *s.m.* Adam.
ADAPTABILIDADE *s.f.* adaptability; adjustment.
ADAPTAÇÃO *s.f.* adaptation.
ADAPTADO *adj.* adapted.
ADAPTADOR *s.m.* adapter.
ADAPTAR *v.* to adapt; to adjust.
ADEGA *s.f.* wine cellar, cellar.
ADEMAIS *adv.* moreover, furthermore, besides.
ADENDO *s.m.* addendum.
ADENOMA *s.m.* adenoma; a benign tumor.
ADENSAR *v.* to densify; to condense.
ADENTADO *adj.* toothed; dentate.
ADENTAR *v.* to indent; to notch; to groove.
ADENTRAR *v.* to enter; to go in, to go inside.
ADENTRO *adv.* in, inside.
ADEPTO *adj.* follower, supporter / *s.m.* adherent.
ADEQUAÇÃO *s.f.* adequacy; adaptation, adjustment.
ADEQUADO *adj.* adequate, appropriate; suitable, proper.

ADEQUAR v. to suit, to adapt; to adjust, to fit.
ADEREÇAMENTO s.m. adornment, decoration.
ADEREÇAR v. to adorn, to decorate; to address.
ADEREÇO s.m. adornment, decoration; address.
ADERÊNCIA s.f. adherence; adhesion; agreement.
ADERENTE adj. adherent; adhesive.
ADERIR v. to adhere.
ADESÃO s.f. adhesion, adherence; agreement.
ADESIVO adj. adhesive, sticky / s.m. sticker, adhesive.
ADESTRADO adj. trained (animais); trained, educated, learned (pessoas).
ADESTRADOR s.m. trainer, instructor, teacher, coach.
ADESTRAMENTO s.m. training, coaching; teaching.
ADESTRAR v. to train, to teach.
ADEUS s.m. goodbye / interj. goodbye!
ADIADO adj. postponed, delayed; procrastinated.
ADIAMENTO s.m. postponement; delay; procastination.
ADIANTADO adj. in advance; advanced; ahead.
ADIANTAMENTO s.m. advance, progress.
ADIANTAR v. to advance; to progress.
ADIANTE adv. forth; in front (of); ahead; forward.
ADIAR v. to postpone, to delay, to procrastinate.
ADIÇÃO s.f. addition.
ADICIONADO adj. added.
ADICIONAL s.2gên. additional; extra, supplement; further.
ADICIONAR v. to add.
ADICTO s.m. addicted, dedicated, devoted / adj. addicted, dedicated, devoted.
ADIETAR v. to keep a diet, to go on a diet.
ADIMPLENTE adj. complying.
ADIMPLIR v. to comply.
ADINHEIRADO adj. wealthy, rich.
ADIPOSE s.f. adipose; fat.
ADIPOSO adj. adipose; fatty.
ADITIVO adj. additive.

ADIVINHAÇÃO s.f. riddle, guessing.
ADIVINHAR v. to guess, to riddle.
ADIVINHO s.m. augur.
ADJACÊNCIA s.f. adjacency; neighborhood.
ADJACENTE adj. adjacente.
ADJETIVAÇÃO s.f. adjective; qualification.
ADJETIVAR v. to adjectivize; to qualify.
ADJETIVO adj. adjective.
ADJUDICAR v. to adjudicate.
ADJUNÇÃO s.f. addition, adjunction.
ADJUNTO s.m. adjunct / adj. joined, added, conected.
ADJUVANTE adj. assistant, assisting; helpful.
ADMINISTRAÇÃO s.f. management; administration; government.
ADMINISTRADOR s.m. manager; administrator / adj. manager; administrator.
ADMINISTRAR v. to manage, to administrate; to conduct.
ADMINISTRATIVO adj. administrative.
ADMIRABILIDADE s.f. admirability; admirableness.
ADMIRAÇÃO s.f. admiration; wonder, amazement.
ADMIRADO adj. admired; surprised; astonished; flabbergasted.
ADMIRADOR s.m. admirer, adorer; fan / adj. admirer, adorer; fan.
ADMIRAR v. to admire; to flabbergast.
ADMIRÁVEL adj.2gên. admirable.
ADMISSÃO s.f. admission; admittance; acceptance.
ADMISSÍVEL adj. admissible; permissible; allowable; acceptable.
ADMITIDO(A) adj. admitted; permited; accepted.
ADMITIR v. to admit; to accept, to allow, to let in; to assume.
ADMOESTAÇÃO s.f. admonition; warning; reprimand.
ADMOESTADOR adj. admonisher; censor; monitory.
ADMOESTAR v. to admonish; to warn; to reprimand; to tell off.
ADNOMINAÇÃO s.f. adnomination.
ADNOMINAL adj. adnominal.
ADOBE s.m. adobe.
ADOÇADO adj. sweetened; sugared.
ADOÇANTE s.m. sweetener.
ADOÇÃO s.f. adoption.

ADOÇAR *v.* to sweeten; to [add] sugar.
ADOCICADO *adj.* sweetish, sweetened; sugary.
ADOCICAR *v. m.q.* adoçar.
ADOECER *v.* to fall ill, to make ill; to sicken.
ADOECIDO *adj.* sick, ill.
ADOENTADO *adj.* sick, unwell.
ADOENTAR *v.* to sicken; to fall ill, to sick.
ADOIDADO *adj.* crazy, mad / *adv.* a lot, so much.
ADOIDAR *v.* to madden; to become crazy.
ADOLESCÊNCIA *s.f.* adolescence.
ADOLESCENTE *adj.* adolescent, teenager / *s.2gên.* adolescent, teenager.
ADOMAR *v.* to tame; to domesticate; to conform.
ADÔNIS *s.m.* Adonis.
ADORAÇÃO *s.f.* adoration; worship; devotion.
ADORADO *adj.* adored; beloved; worshipped.
ADORADOR *adj.* adoring, worshipping / *s.m.* adorer, lover, worshipper.
ADORAR *v.* to adore, to venerate, to worship, to love.
ADORÁVEL *adj.* adorable; lovable; lovely.
ADORMECEDOR *adj.* sleeper; soporific / *s.m.* sleeper; soporific.
ADORMECER *v.* to fall asleep; to sleep.
ADORMECIDO *adj.* asleep; sleeping.
ADORNADO *adj.* adorned.
ADORNAR *v.* to adorn.
ADORNO *s.m.* adornment, ornament.
ADOTADO *adj.* adopted.
ADOTANTE *s.2gên.* adopter.
ADOTAR *v.* to adopt (filhos e cães); to accept, to follow (ideias e estilos).
ADOTÁVEL *adj.2gên.* adoptable.
ADOTIVO *adj.* adoped; adoptive / *s.m.* adoptee.
ADQUIRENTE *s.2gên.* purchaser; buyer / *adj.2gên.* purchaser; buyer.
ADQUIRIÇÃO *s.f.* acquisition; purchase; obtention.
ADQUIRIDO *adj.* acquired; purchased; bought.
ADQUIRIR *v.* to acquire, to obtain, to purchase, to buy.
ADREDE *adv.* purposely, intentionally.
ADRENALINA *s.f.* adrenalin.

ADUANA *s.f.* customs, customhouse.
ADUANAR *v.* to pay customs.
ADUANEIRO *adj.* customs officer.
ADUBAÇÃO *s.f.* fertilization.
ADUBAGEM *s.f.* fertilization, manuring.
ADUBAR *v.* to fertilize, to manure.
ADUBO *s.m.* fertilizer; manure; compost.
ADUÇÃO *s.f.* adduction.
ADULAÇÃO *s.f.* flattery; adulation; coaxing.
ADULADOR *s.m.* flatterer; adulator / *adj.* flatterer; adulator.
ADULAR *v.* to flatter; to adulate.
ADULTERAÇÃO *s.f.* adulteration; falsification; corruption.
ADULTERADO *adj.* corrupted; bogus; falsified.
ADULTERADOR *s.m.* adulterator / *adj.* adulterator.
ADULTERAR *v.* to adulterate; to falsify.
ADULTÉRIO *s.m.* adultery; cheat.
ADÚLTERO *s.m.* adulterer / *adj.* adulterous.
ADULTO *s.m.* adult; grown-up / *adj.* adult; grown-up.
ADUSTO *adj.* adust.
ADUTOR *s.m.* adductor.
ADUZIR *v.* to adduce.
ADVENTÍCIO *adj.* adventitious, accidental / *s.m.* alien, foreign.
ADVENTISMO *s.m.* Adventism.
ADVENTISTA *s.2gên.* Adventist / *adj.2gên.* Adventist.
ADVENTO *s.m.* advent.
ADVERBIAL *adj.* adverbial.
ADVERBIALIZAR *v.* to adverbialize.
ADVÉRBIO *s.m.* adverb.
ADVERSÃO *s.f.* aversion; opposition; objection.
ADVERSAR *v.* to oppose, to resist, to contest.
ADVERSÁRIO *s.m.* adversary, opponent; enemy, antagonist / *adj.* enemy, rival.
ADVERSATIVO *adj.* adversative, oppositive.
ADVERSIDADE *s.f.* adversity; misfortune.
ADVERSO *adj.* adverse; oppositive, contrary.
ADVERTÊNCIA *s.f.* warning, advise.
ADVERTIDO *adj.* warned; advised, noticed.
ADVERTIR *v.* to warn; to advertise.
ADVIR *v.* to come; to occur; to succeed.
ADVOCACIA *s.f.* advocacy; law.
ADVOGADO *s.m.* lawyer; attorney, advocate.

ADVOGAR v. to advocate.
AÉREO adj. aerial; airy.
AEROBARCO s.m. hovercraft.
AERODINÂMICO adj. aerodynamic.
AERÓDROMO s.m. aerodrome; airport.
AERODUTO s.m. vent.
AEROESPACIAL adj.2gên. aerospace.
AEROMOÇO(A) s.m. flight attendant; flight steward.
AEROMODELO s.m. model aircraft.
AERONÁUTICA s.f. aeronautics; aviation.
AERONAVE s.f. aircraft.
AEROPLANO s.m. airplane.
AEROPORTO s.m. airport.
AEROSFERA s.f. aerosphere.
AEROSSOL s.m. aerosol.
AEROVIA s.f. airway.
AEROVIÁRIO adj. air transportation / s.m. airport employer.
AFÃ s.f. eagerness; desire; anxiety.
AFABILIDADE s.f. affability; kindness; friendliness.
AFADIGAR v. to fatigue; to tire.
AFADIGOSO adj. exhausting; fatigue; tiresome.
AFAGADOR s.m. caresser.
AFAGAMENTO s.m. caressing; comforting; fondling.
AFAGANTE adj. m.q. afagador.
AFAGAR v. to caress; to comfort; to pet (animais).
AFAGO s.m. caress; pat; fondling.
AFAMADO adj. famous; notorious; notable.
AFAMAR v. to make famous; to become famous.
AFANAR v. to strive; to work hard; to steal.
AFASIA s.f. aphasia.
AFÁSICO adj. aphasic.
AFASTADO adj. remote; distant; far away from; suspended from (da escola ou do trabalho); aloof.
AFASTADOR s.m. remover; retractor (instrumento cirúrgico).
AFASTAMENTO s.m. removal; distance; suspension.
AFASTAR v. to remove; to suspend, to interrupt.
AFÁVEL adj. affable; friendly; kind.
AFAZER v. to habituate; to adapt; to accustom.

AFAZERES s.m. pl. tasks; duties; business; work.
AFECÇÃO s.f. condition.
AFEIÇÃO s.f. affection.
AFEIÇOADO s.m. affectionate, tender, friend.
AFEIÇOAR v. to shape; to mould; to attach.
AFEITO adj. wont; used to; accustomed to.
AFERENTE adj.2gên. afferent.
AFÉRESE s.f. apheresis.
AFERIÇÃO s.f. checking, calibrating; standardization; admeasurement.
AFERIR v. to assess; to gauge; to check.
AFETAÇÃO s.f. affectation; affection.
AFETADO adj. affected.
AFETAR v. to affect.
AFETIVIDADE s.f. affectivity; affection; kindness.
AFETIVO adj. affective; devoted.
AFETO s.m. affection; tenderness; devotion.
AFETUOSO adj. affectionate.
AFIAÇÃO s.f. sharpening; pointing.
AFIADO adj. sharp.
AFIADOR s.m. sharper.
AFIAR v. to sharpen; to hone.
AFICIONADO s.m. enthusiast / adj. enthusiast.
AFIDALGADO adj. noble; distinguished.
AFIDALGAR v. to raise to nobility.
AFIGURAÇÃO s.f. figuration; representation; imagination.
AFIGURADO adj. figured; represented.
AFIGURAR v. to figure; to represent; to imagine.
AFIGURATIVO adj. figurative.
AFILHADISMO s.m. nepotism; favouritism.
AFILHADO s.m. godson / s.f. goddaughter / s.2gên. godchild.
AFILHAR v. to reproduce; to have children.
AFILIAÇÃO s.f. affiliation.
AFILIAR v. to affiliate; to join.
AFIM adj. related, similar / s.m. relative; kinsman.
AFINAÇÃO s.f. adjustment; improvement; refining (metais); tuning.
AFINADO adj. thinner (líquidos); refined (metais); improved (arte ou método); tuned [in or up], in tune.
AFINAGEM s.f. refining.
AFINAL adv. finally; after all; in conclusion.
AFINAR v. to fine, to refine; to tune.

AFINCADO *adj.* persistent; persevering.
AFINCO *s.m.* hard.
AFINIDADE *s.f.* affinity; connection; kinship.
AFIRMAÇÃO *s.f.* affirmation; statement; assertion.
AFIRMADOR *adj.* affirmer.
AFIRMAR *v.* to affirm; to assert; to say; to claim.
AFIRMATIVO *adj.* affirmative; assertive.
AFIVELAR *v.* to buckle.
AFIXAÇÃO *s.f.* affixation.
AFIXAR *v.* to affix, to fasten; to attach; to stick.
AFIXO *s.m.* affix.
AFLIÇÃO *s.f.* affliction, anguish; distress, agony.
AFLIGIDO *adj.* afflicted.
AFLIGIR *v.* to afflict; to distress.
AFLITIVO *adj.* afflictive.
AFLITO *adj.* distressed, troubled; sorrowful, desolate; afflicted.
AFLORAÇÃO *s.f.* outcrop; appearance; outbreak.
AFLORAMENTO *s.m.* emergence; leveling.
AFLORAR *v.* to crop out; to appear.
AFLUÊNCIA *s.f.* affluence.
AFLUENTE *adj.2gên.* affluent / *s.m.* affluent.
AFLUIR *v.* to flow; to run.
AFLUXO *s.m.* influx; inflow.
AFOBAÇÃO *s.f.* fluster; panic.
AFOBADO *adj.* flustered; panicked.
AFOBAMENTO *s.m. m.q.* afobação.
AFOBAR *v.* to fluster, to hurry.
AFOFAR *v.* to fluff, to soften.
AFOGADIÇO *adj.* suffocating, stifling, sultry.
AFOGADO *s.m.* drowned / *adj.* drowned.
AFOGAR *v.* to drown; to submerge.
AFOGUEADO *adj.* aglow, ablaze.
AFOIÇADO *adj.* scythed.
AFOITAR *v.* to dare bravely.
AFOITEZA *s.f.* audacity; boldness; daring.
AFOITO *adj.* anxious; desperate.
AFONIA *s.f.* aphonia, aphony.
AFÔNICO *adj.* aphonic; voiceless; mute.
AFORA *adv.* outside / *prep.* except, besides.
AFORAR *v.* to except; to exclude.
AFORIA *s.f.* aplasia, defect organ; sterility, agenesis.
AFORISMO *s.m.* aphorism; maxim.
AFORISTA *s.2gên.* aphorist.

AFORÍSTICO *adj.* aphoristic.
AFORTUNADO *adj.* lucky; fortunate; successful.
AFORTUNAR *v.* to succeed; to get rich, to make fortune.
AFRACADO *adj.* weak.
AFRACAR *v.* to weaken; to fade; to attenuate.
AFRANCESADO *adj.* Frenchified.
AFRANCESAR *v.* to Frenchify.
AFRASIA *s.f.* aphasia.
AFREGUESADO *adj.* a loyal client; customer.
AFRESCO *s.m.* cool, fresh; fresco.
ÁFRICA *s.f.* Africa.
AFRICANISMO *s.m.* Africanism.
AFRICANISTA *s.2gên.* Africanist / *adj.2gên.* Africanist.
AFRICANIZAR *v.* to Africanize.
AFRICANO *adj.* African / *s.m.* African.
ÁFRICO *adj.* African / *s.m.* African.
AFRODISIA *s.f.* aphrodisiac.
AFRODISÍACO *s.m.* aphrodisiac / *adj.* aphrodisiac, aphrodisiacal.
AFRONTA *s.f.* affront; insult; outrage; disrespect.
AFRONTADOR *s.m.* offender, insulter.
AFRONTAMENTO *s.m.* confrontation, dyspinea.
AFRONTAR *v.* to affront, to insult; to disrespect, to offend; to confront.
AFRONTOSO *adj.* outrageous; insulting; abusive.
AFROUXAMENTO *s.f.* loose; slackening; relaxation.
AFROUXAR *v.* to loose; to slacken; to relax.
AFTA *s.f.* aphtha; thrush.
AFTOSO *adj.* aphthous.
AFUGENTADO *adj.* driven away, repelled.
AFUGENTADOR *s.m.* chaser; scarier.
AFUGENTAMENTO *s.m.* chasing away; scaring.
AFUGENTAR *v.* to chase; to scare; to drive off.
AFUNDADO *adj.* sunk; submerged.
AFUNDAMENTO *s.m.* sinking.
AFUNDAR *v.* to sink.
AFUNILADO *adj.* tapering; funnel-shaped.
AFUNILAR *v.* to taper.
AGACHADO *v.* crouching.
AGACHAMENTO *s.m.* squatting; crouching.
AGACHAR *v.* to crouch, to squat.

ÁGAPE s.m. agape.
AGAROTADO adj. naughty; childish; childlike.
AGAROTAR v. to childish.
AGARRAÇÃO s.f. gripe; grabbing, holding.
AGARRADIÇO adj. clinging; adherent.
AGARRADO s.m. clinging; stuck.
AGARRADOR s.m. catcher; seizer.
AGARRAMENTO s.m. m.q. agarração.
AGARRAR v. to grab, to hold; to seize; to cling.
AGASALHADO adj. sheltered covered; wrapped.
AGASALHAR v. to cover; to wrap.
AGASALHO s.m. coat, jacket, sweater; warm clothing.
AGASTADO adj. irritated; bored; annoyed.
AGASTAMENTO s.m. irritation; annoyance; anger.
AGASTAR v. to irritate; to annoy; to offense.
AGÊNCIA s.f. agency, office.
AGENCIAÇÃO s.f. agency.
AGENCIADOR s.m. bookingmaker; agent; representative / adj. bookingmaker; agent; representative.
AGENCIAMENTO s.m. m.q. agenciação.
AGENCIAR v. to negotiate; to broker.
AGENDA s.f. agenda; schedule; diary.
AGENDAR v. to schedule.
AGENTE s.2gên. agent, officer; booking maker.
AGIGANTADO adj. aggrandized; enormous, giant.
AGIGANTAMENTO s.m. aggrandizement.
AGIGANTAR v. to aggrandize; to become giant.
ÁGIL adj. agile.
AGILIDADE s.f. agility.
ÁGIO s.m. agio.
AGIOTA s.2gên. moneylender; loan shark; userer / adj.2gên. moneylender; loan shark; userer.
AGIOTAGEM s.f. moneylending.
AGIOTAR v. to lend money.
AGIR v. to act; to move.
AGIRAFADO adj. giraffe-shaped.
AGITAÇÃO s.f. agitation, trouble; excitation.
AGITADIÇO adj. easily agitated.
AGITADO adj. agitated; restless.
AGITADOR s.m. agitator.

AGITANTE adj. agitating.
AGITAR v. to agitate; to shake.
AGITÁVEL adj. agitable.
AGITO s.m. agitation, excitement.
AGLOMERAÇÃO s.f. agglomeration; accumulation; gathering.
AGLOMERADO s.m. agglomerate / adj. agglomerate.
AGLOMERANTE adj. agglomerative.
AGLOMERAR v. to agglomerate.
AGLUTINAÇÃO s.f. agglutination.
AGLUTINADO adj. agglutinated.
AGLUTINAR v. to agglutinate; to unite; to join.
AGLUTINATIVO adj. agglutinative.
AGNOSTICISMO s.m. agnosticism.
AGNÓSTICO s.m. agnostic / adj. agnostic.
AGONIA s.f. agony.
AGONIADO(A) adj. agonizing; anxious, afflicted.
AGONIAR v. to agonize; to afflict.
AGONIZANTE s.2gên. agonizing / adj.2gên. agonizing; dying person.
ÁGONO adj. agonic.
AGORA adv. now.
ÁGORA s.f. agora.
AGORAFOBIA s.f. agoraphobia.
AGOSTINIANO s.m. Augustian / adj. Augustian.
AGOSTO s.m. August.
AGOURAR v. to predict.
AGOURENTO s.m. foreboding / adj. foreboding.
AGOURO s.m. omen; presage.
AGRACIAÇÃO s.f. grace; award; honour.
AGRACIADO adj. honoured; graced.
AGRACIAR v. to grace; to reward.
AGRADAR v. to please, to pleasure; to delight.
AGRADÁVEL adj. pleasant; nice; enjoyable.
AGRADECER v. to thank.
AGRADECIDO adj. thankful; grateful.
AGRADECIMENTO s.m. thanks.
AGRADO s.m. pleasure.
AGRAMATICAL adj.2gên. ungrammatical.
AGRAMATISMO s.m. agrammatism.
AGRÁRIO adj. agrarian.
AGRAVAÇÃO s.f. aggravation.
AGRAVADO s.m. aggravated / adj. aggravated, worse.

AGRAVAMENTO *s.m. m.q.* agravação.
AGRAVANTE *adj.* annoy; exasperate; aggravating (informal).
AGRAVAR *v.* to aggravate; to worsen.
AGRAVO *s.m.* grievance; harm.
AGREDIDO *s.m.* victim; attacked; beaten / *adj.* victim; attacked; beaten.
AGREDIR *v.* to attack; to assault.
AGREGAÇÃO *s.f.* aggregation; aglomeration.
AGREGADO *s.m.* aggregated, attached / *adj.* assembled, aggregated.
AGREGAR *v.* to aggregate; to join; to added.
AGREMIAÇÃO *s.f.* society; association; fellowship; brotherhood.
AGREMIAR *v.* to associate.
AGRESSÃO *s.f.* aggression; attack; assault, battery.
AGRESSIVIDADE *s.f.* aggressiveness.
AGRESSIVO *adj.* aggressive, offensive.
AGRESSOR *s.m.* aggressor / *adj.* aggressive.
AGRESTE *adj.* wild, rural, rustic.
AGRIÃO *s.m.* watercress.
AGRÍCOLA *adj.* agricultural.
AGRICULTAR *v.* to cultivate; to farm.
AGRICULTOR *s.m.* farmer.
AGRICULTURA *s.f.* agriculture.
AGRIDOCE *adj.* bittersweet.
AGRILHOAMENTO *s.m.* shackling; chaining, restrict, control.
AGRILHOAR *v.* to shackle; to chain; to control.
AGRISALHADO *adj.* greyish.
AGRISALHAR *v.* to become grey, greyish.
AGRO *s.m.* camp, bitter taste, heartbreak / *adj.* acid, hard, crust.
AGRONOMÉTRICO *adj.* agronometric.
AGRONOMIA *s.f.* agronomy; agronomics.
AGRONÔMICO *adj.* agronomic, agronomical.
AGRÔNOMO *s.m.* agronomist.
AGROPECUÁRIA *s.f.* agriculture; farming.
AGROTÓXICO *s.m.* pesticide.
AGRUPAÇÃO *s.f.* grouping.
AGRUPAMENTO *s.m. m.q.* agrupação.
AGRUPAR *v.* to group.
ÁGUA *s.f.* water.
AGUAÇA *s.f.* flood.
AGUAÇAL *s.m.* puddle, pond.
AGUACEIRO *s.m.* heavy rain.
AGUADO *adj.* watery.

AGUADOR *s.m.* water can.
AGUAR *v.* to water.
AGUARDAR *v.* to await, to wait for.
AGUARDENTE *s.f.* brandy; rum.
AGUARDENTEIRO *adj.* drunkard.
AGUARDO *s.m.* waiting, expectation.
AGUARRÁS *s.f.* turpentine.
ÁGUA-VIVA *s.f.* medusa; jellyfish.
AGUÇADO *adj.* pointed; sharpened; keen.
AGUÇADOR *s.m.* sharpener.
AGUÇAR *v.* to sharpen.
AGUDEZ *s.f.* acuteness; sharpening; keenness.
AGUDO *adj.* sharp; acute; keen.
AGUENTAR *v.* to hold on, to support; to bear; to endure, to tolerate.
ÁGUIA *s.f.* eagle.
AGULHA *s.f.* needle.
AGULHADA *s.f.* needleful.
AGULHÃO *s.m.* needlefish, swordfish / *adj.* big needle.
AGULHAR *v.* to needle, to provoke.
AGULHEIRO *s.m.* needle-case; switchman, signalman.
AH! *interj.* wow, whew.
AI *interj.* ouch, ow.
AÍ *adv.* there, over there.
AIA *s.f.* chaperon.
AIDS *s.f.* AIDS.
AINDA *adv.* still; yet.
AIPIM *s.m.* cassava.
AIPO *s.m.* celery.
AJARDINAR *v.* to garden; to landscaping.
AJEITADO *adj.* arranged; fixed.
AJEITAR *v.* to arrange; to dispose; to fit.
AJOELHADO *adj.* kneeling; humiliated.
AJOELHAR *v.* to kneel.
AJUDA *s.f.* help; assistance.
AJUDANTE *s.2gên.* helper; assistant.
AJUDAR *v.* to help; to assist.
AJUIZADO *adj.* wise; sensible; reasonable.
AJUIZAR *v.* to judge.
AJUNTA *s.f.* gather; joint, junction.
AJUNTADO *adj.* together; assembled.
AJUNTADOR *s.m.* collector.
AJUNTAMENTO *s.f.* gathering; meeting; union.
AJUNTAR *v.* to gather; to assemble; to collect; to join.
AJURAMENTADO *adj.* sworn.
AJURAMENTAR *v.* to swear; to take an oath.

AJUSTADO *s.m.* adjusted; fit / *adj.* adjusted; fit.
AJUSTADOR *s.m.* adjuster; fitter; setter.
AJUSTAGEM *s.f.* adjustment; regulation (máquinas).
AJUSTAMENTO *s.m.* adjustment; accommodation; setting; settlement (contas, dívidas).
AJUSTAR *v.* to adjust; to regulate; to set; to fit.
AJUSTÁVEL *adj.2gên.* adjustable.
AJUSTE *s.m. m.q.* ajustamento.
ALA *s.f.* row; aisle; wing, side; flank.
ALÁ *s.m.* Allah.
ALABAMA *s.m.* salesman, bagman, traveller.
ALABIRINTADO *adj.* labyrinthine; labyrinth-shaped; confused.
ALADEIRADO *s.m.* hilly, slope / *adj.* hilly, sloping.
ALADO *adj.* winged.
ALADROADO *adj.* thievish; stealing, fraudulent.
ALADROAR *v.* to cheat (em um jogo); to defraud.
ALAGAÇÃO *s.f.* overflow, inundation, flooding.
ALAGADIÇO *adj.* swampy; boggy; marshy.
ALAGADO *adj.* waterlogged; submerged.
ALAGADOR *s.m.* flooder; flooding / *adj.* flooding.
ALAGAMENTO *s.m. m.q.* alagação.
ALAGAR *v.* to overflow; to flood.
ALAGOA *s.f.* pond; lagoon.
ALAGOINHA *s.f.* small pond.
ALAGOSO *adj.* swampish, marshy.
ALAGOSTADO *adj.* lobsterlike; most red.
ALAMAR *s.m.* gold lace.
ALAMARADO *adj.* laced, gold-laced.
ALAMBIQUE *s.m.* alembic; still.
ALAMBIQUEIRO *s.m.* distiller.
ALAMBRA *s.f.* black poplar.
ALAMBRADO *s.m.* wire fence.
ALAMBRAR *v.* to fence in.
ALAMBRE *s.m.* amber.
ALAMBREADO *adj.* amber, yellowish-brown.
ALAMEDA *s.f.* lane, alley, avenue; park.
ALAMIRÉ *s.m.* diapason.
ÁLAMO *s.m.* poplar.
ALANCEADO *adj.* distressed; mortified.
ALANCEADOR *s.m.* lancer / *adj.* lancing.

ALANCEAR *v.* to lance.
ALANHAR *v.* to wound, to cut.
ALAPADO *adj.* hidden; crouched.
ALAPAR *v.* to hide; to cover.
ALAPARDADO *adj.* hidden, crouched.
ALAR *adj.* wing-shaped / *v.* to lift; to go away, to leave.
ALARANJADO *s.m.* orange (cor) / *adj.* orange, orange-colored.
ALARDAR *v.* to boast.
ALARDE *s.m.* vanity; noise.
ALARDEADOR *s.m.* boaster; boastful.
ALARDEAR *v. m.q.* alardar.
ALARDO *s.m.* muster roll.
ALARGADOR *s.m.* counterbore; widener / *adj.* widening.
ALARGAMENTO *s.m.* widening; enlargement; extension.
ALARGAR *v.* to widen; to spread out.
ALARIDO *s.m.* clamour; row.
ALARIFAÇO *adj.* lively.
ALARIFAGEM *s.f.* expertise; skill; great ability.
ALARMANTE *adj.2gên.* alarming; frightening; scaring.
ALARMAR *v.* to alarm.
ALARME *s.m.* alarm; alert; warning.
ALARMISTA *s.2gên.* alarmist / *adj.* alarming.
ALARVADO *adj.* churlish.
ALARVE *s.2gên.* churl, brute.
ALASTRAMENTO *s.m.* spreading, diffusion.
ALASTRANTE *adj.2gên.* spreading, diffusive.
ALASTRAR *v.* to spread, to scatter.
ALATINADO *adj.* Latinized.
ALATINAR *v.* to Latinize.
ALAUDADO *adj.* lute-shaped.
ALAÚDE *s.m.* lute.
ALAVANCA *s.f.* lever; handspike.
ALAVERCAR *v.* to humble; to humiliate.
ALAZÃO *s.m.* sorrel / *adj.* sorrel.
ALAZEIRADO *adj.* hungry, starving.
ALBA *s.f.* alba.
ALBAFAR *s.m.* perfume, incense.
ALBANÊS *s.m.* Albanian / *adj.* Albanian.
ALBARDA *s.f.* pack-saddle.
ALBARDEIRA *s.f.* wild rose.
ALBARDEIRO *s.m.* saddler.
ALBARRADA *s.f.* flowerpot.
ALBATROZ *s.m.* alabatross.
ALBENTE *adj.* whitening.

ALBERCA *s.f.* drain.
ALBERGADO *adj.* sheltered.
ALBERGADOR *s.m.* host / *adj.* sheltering.
ALBERGAMENTO *s.m.* sheltering.
ALBERGAR *v.* to shelter.
ALBERGARIA *s.f.* inn; hostel; shelter.
ALBERGUE *s.m.* hostel; inn.
ALBERGUEIRO *s.m.* hoster, innkeeper.
ALBESCENTE *adj.2gên.* fading, whitening.
ALBICANTE *adj.2gên.* whitish.
ALBICAULE *adj.2gên.* white-stem.
ALBICOLE *adj.* white-necked.
ÁLBIDO *adj.* almost white.
ALBIFICAÇÃO *s.f.* whitening, bleaching.
ALBIFLOR *adj.* whiteblossom.
ALBIGENSE *s.2gên.* Albigense /
adj. Albigensian.
ALBINA *s.f.* yellow alder.
ALBINIA *s.f.* albinism.
ALBINISMO *s.m. m.q.* albinia.
ALBINO *s.m.* albino.
ALBIRROSADO *adj.* pale pink.
ALBIRROSTRO *adj.* white beaked.
ALBITA *s.f.* albite.
ALBOR *s.m.* whiteness, brightness.
ALBORCAR *v.* to exchange.
ALBORQUE *s.m.* exchange.
ALBUGEM *s.f.* leucoma, albugo.
ALBUGINADO *adj.* albugineous.
ALBUGÍNEA *s.f.* albuginea.
ÁLBUM *s.m.* album; book.
ALBUME *s.m.* albumen.
ALBUMINA *s.f.* albumin.
ALBUMINADO *adj.* albuminous, albuminose.
ALBUMINATO *s.m.* albuminate.
ALBUMINOIDE *s.m.* albuminoid /
adj. albuminoidal.
ALBUMINOSO *adj.* albuminous.
ALBURNO *s.m.* alburnum.
ALÇA *s.f.* strap; handle, holder.
ALCAÇARIA *s.f.* street market.
ALCÁCER *s.m.* castle, palace.
ALCACHINADO *adj.* bent; curved.
ALCACHOFRA *s.f.* artichoke.
ALCÁÇOVA *s.f.* castle.
ALCAÇUZ *s.m.* liquorice.
ALÇADA *s.f.* jurisdiction; competence.
ALÇADO *s.m.* elevation, upright projection /
adj. lifted, raised.

ALÇADOR *s.m.* lifter, raiser.
ALÇADURA *s.f.* lifting.
ALÇAGEM *s.f.* hanging up.
ALCAGUETE *s.m.* snitch.
ALCAIOTA *s.f.* gossiper.
ALCALESCÊNCIA *s.f.* alkalescence.
ALCALESCENTE *adj.2gên.* alkalescent.
ÁLCALI *s.m.* alkali.
ALCALIFICANTE *adj.2gên.* alkalifying.
ALCALIFICAR *v.* to alkalify.
ALCALIMETRIA *s.f.* alkalimetry.
ALCALÍMETRO *s.m.* alkalimeter.
ALCALINAR *v.* to alkalise.
ALCALINIZAÇÃO *s.f.* alkalization.
ALCALINIZAR *v. m.q.* alcalinar.
ALCALINO *adj.* alkaline.
ALCALOIDE *s.m.* alkaloid.
ALÇAMENTO *s.m.* raising.
ALCANÇADIÇO *adj.* easily reachable.
ALCANÇADO *adj.* obtained; reached; achieved.
ALCANÇADOR *s.m.* attainer, obtainer /
adj. obtaining, attaining.
ALCANÇAMENTO *s.m.* reaching, obtaining; achieving.
ALCANÇAR *v.* to achieve; to arrive; to reach.
ALCANÇÁVEL *adj.2gên.* reachable; gettable; understandable.
ALCANCE *s.m.* reach; range.
ALCÂNDOR *s.m.* summit; top.
ALCANDORADO *adj.* exalted, sublime.
ALCANDORAR *v.* to sublimate; to be proud of.
ALCANTIL *s.m.* slope, declivity.
ALCANTILADA *s.f.* steep; crags.
ALCANTILADO *adj.* craggy, steep.
ALCANTILAR *v.* to steep; to rise steeply.
ALCANTILOSO *adj.* craggy, cragged.
ALÇAPÃO *s.m.* trapdoor.
ALCAPARRA *s.f.* caper.
ALÇA-PÉ *s.m.* snare; trick, fraud.
ALÇAPREMA *s.f.* crowbar.
ALÇAR *v.* to raise, to lift.
ALCARAVIA *s.f.* caraway seeds.
ALCARAVIZ *s.m.* tuyère.
ALCATEIA *s.f.* pack of wolves; herd; gang.
ALCATIFA *s.f.* carpet; sward.
ALCATIFADO *adj.* covered by carpets; swarded.
ALCATIFAR *v.* to carpet.
ALCATIFEIRO *s.m.* carpetmaker.

ALCATIRA *s.f.* tragacanth.
ALCATRA *s.f.* rump.
ALCATRÃO *s.m.* tar.
ALCATRATE *s.m.* gunwale.
ALCATRAZ *s.m.* frigate bird, pelican.
ALCATREIRO *adj.* big rumped.
ALCATROADO *adj.* tarry.
ALCATROAMENTO *s.m.* tarring.
ALCATROAR *v.* to tar, to asphalt.
ALCATRUZ *s.m.* bucket.
ALCATRUZADO *adj.* bent, arched; clumsy.
ALCAVALA *s.f.* tax; fiscal extorsion.
ALCAVALEIRO *s.m.* taxator, tax colletor.
ALCE *s.m.* moose, elk.
ALCEAMENTO *s.m.* raising, lifting.
ALCEAR *v.* to lift; to raise.
ALCIONÁRIO *s.m.* alcyonarian.
ALCÍONE *s.f.* Alcyon.
ALCOCEIFA *s.f.* brothel; red-light district.
ALCOFA *s.f.* flat-handled-basket / *s.m.* pander.
ALCOFAR *v.* to pander.
ÁLCOOL *s.m.* alcohol; drink.
ALCOOLATO *s.m.* alcoholate.
ALCOÓLATRA *s.2gên.* alcoholic, drunkard / *adj.* alcoholic.
ALCOOLATURA *s.f.* alcoholature, alcoholic.
ALCOÓLICO *s.m.* alcoholic, drunkard / *adj.* alcoholic.
ALCOOLISMO *s.m.* alcoholism.
ALCOOLISTA *s.2gên.* alcoholic, drunkard.
ALCOOLIZAÇÃO *s.f.* alcoholization.
ALCOOLIZADO *adj.* intoxicated, drunk.
ALCOOLIZAR *v.* to intoxicate, to alcoholise.
ALCOOLÔMETRO *s.m.* alcoholometer.
ALCORÃO *s.m.* Koran.
ALCORCA *s.f.* furrow.
ALCORÇA *s.f.* sugar-icing.
ALCORCOVA *s.f.* hump, ditch.
ALCORCOVAR *v.* to ditch; to get humps.
ALCOVA *s.f.* alcove; bedroom.
ALCOVISTA *s.m.* masher.
ALCOVITAGEM *s.f.* panderism; gossip.
ALCOVITAR *v.* to pander; to tell gossip.
ALCOVITEIRA *s.f.* panderess.
ALCOVITEIRICE *s.f.* panderism; gossip.
ALCOVITEIRO *s.m.* procurer; pander, pimp.
ALCUNHA *s.f.* nickname.
ALCUNHAR *v.* to nickname.
ALDAGRANTE *s.m.* vagabond; good-for-nothing.
ALDEÃO *s.m.* countryman, villager / *adj.* rural.
ALDEIA *s.f.* village; hamlet.
ALDEÍDO *s.m.* aldehyde.
ALDEOLA *s.f.* hamlet.
ALDRAVA *s.f.* latch; knocker, door handle.
ALDRAVADO *adj.* patched.
ALDRAVÃO *s.m.* a big latch, door handle.
ALDRAVAR *v.* to latch.
ALDRAVICE *s.f.* roguery, fraud.
ÁLEA *s.f.* alley, walk.
ALEALDAR *v.* to legalise.
ALEATORIEDADE *s.f.* randomization.
ALEATÓRIO *adj.* aleatory; random.
ALECRIM *s.m.* rosemary.
ALECRIM-DO-CAMPO *s.m.* romerillo.
ALECRIM-DO-NORTE *s.m.* bog myrtle.
ALEFRIZ *s.m.* garboard.
ALEGAÇÃO *s.f.* allegation.
ALEGANTE *s.m.* claimant; alleging.
ALEGAR *v.* to allege; to quote; to argue.
ALEGORIA *s.f.* allegory; simile.
ALEGÓRICO *adj.* allegoric, allegorical.
ALEGORISTA *s.2gên.* allegorist / *adj.2gên.* allegorist.
ALEGORIZAR *v.* to allegorise.
ALEGRADO *adj.* gladdened; satisfied; joyful; delighted.
ALEGRADOR *s.m.* delighter / *adj.* delighting.
ALEGRAMENTO *s.m.* joy; cheer; gladness.
ALEGRÃO *s.m.* most happy; innocent.
ALEGRAR *v.* to cheer, to gladden; to rejoice.
ALEGRATIVO *adj.* cheering.
ALEGRE *adj.2gên.* cheerful; glad; happy.
ALEGRETO *s.m.* allegreto / *adj.* allegretto, graceful.
ALEGRIA *s.f. m.q.* alegramento.
ALEGRO *s.m.* allegro / *adv.* alegro.
ALEIA *s.f.* alley; avenue.
ALEIJADO *s.m.* cripple / *adj.* crippled, disabled.
ALEIJAMENTO *s.m.* crippling, maiming.
ALEIJÃO *s.m.* physical deformity; weakness.
ALEIJAR *v.* to maim; to cripple.
ALEITAÇÃO *s.f.* nursing.
ALEITAMENTO *s.m.* breastfeed; suckling, nursing.
ALEITAR *v.* to nurse; to breastfeed.
ALEIVOSIA *s.f.* treachery; calumniousness, meanness.

ALEIVOSO *adj.* calumnious; treacherous.
ALEIXAR *v.* to separate; to remove; to go away.
ALELUIA *s.f.* hallelujah / *interj.* happiness.
ALELUÍTICO *adj.* laudatory.
ALÉM *adv.* over there, there, beyond, further; besides, moreover / *s.m.* post-mortem, afterlife.
ALEMANHA *s.f.* Germany.
ALEMANISMO *s.m.* Germanism.
ALEMANIZAR *v.* to Germanize.
ALEMÃO *s.m.* German / *adj.* German.
ALÉM-MAR *s.m.* overseas / *adj.* overseas / *adv.* overseas.
ALEMOADO *adj.* Germanlike, Germanised.
ALEMOAR *v. m.q.* alemanizar.
ALENTADO *adj.* courageous, brave; diligent, hard-working.
ALENTADOR *adj.* encouraging, heartening.
ALENTAR *v.* to encourage, to animate.
ALENTECER *v.* to slow down.
ALENTO *s.m.* breath; respiration; courage.
ÁLEO *adj.* winged.
ALEQUEADO *adj.* fanlike.
ALERGÊNIO *s.m.* allergen.
ALERGIA *s.f.* allergy, loathing, aversion.
ALÉRGICO *adj.* allergic.
ALERTA *adj.* alert, vigilant / *s.m.* alert, alarm / *interj.* alert.
ALERTADO *adj.* alerted, warned, alar.
ALERTAR *v.* to alert, to give alarm; to be watchful.
ALESADO *adj.* injured.
ALESTAR *v.* to haste.
ALETA *s.f.* a small room.
ALETARGADO *adj.* lethargic.
ALÉTICO *adj.* alexic, alexinic.
ALETOLOGIA *s.f.* alethiology.
ALETRIA *s.f.* vermicelli; angel hair.
ALEUROMANCIA *s.f.* aleuromancy.
ALEUROMÂNTICO *adj.* aleuromantic.
ALEURÔMETRO *s.m.* aleurometer.
ALEVANTADIÇO *adj.* seditious, riotous.
ALEVANTAR *v.* to lift, to raise.
ALEVEDAR *v.* to leaven.
ALEXANDRINO *adj.* Alexandrine.
ALEXANDRITA *s.f.* alexandrite.
ALEXIA *s.f.* alexia.
ALEZIRIADO *adj.* boggy, marshy.
ALFA *s.m.* alpha.

ALFABETAÇÃO *s.f.* literacy; alphabetising.
ALFABETADO *adj.* learned; educated.
ALFABETADOR *s.m.* educator.
ALFABETAR *v.* alphabetise; to educate.
ALFABETÁRIO *adj.* alphabetic, alphabetical.
ALFABÉTICO *adj.* alphabetic.
ALFABETISMO *s.m.* literacy.
ALFABETIZAÇÃO *s.f.* literacy, education.
ALFABETIZADO *s.m.* literate / *adj.* literate.
ALFABETIZAR *v.* to educate; to instruct; to alphabetise.
ALFABETO *s.m.* alphabet, abc.
ALFAÇAL *s.m.* lettuce plantation.
ALFACE *s.f.* lettuce.
ALFAFA *s.f.* alfafa; luzerna.
ALFAFAL *s.m.* alfafa plantation.
ALFAGEME *s.m.* sword cutler.
ALFAIA *s.f.* domestic implement, furniture.
ALFAIAR *v.* to adorn.
ALFAIATAR *v.* to tailor, sew.
ALFAIATARIA *s.f.* tailor's workshop.
ALFAIATE *s.m.* tailor.
ALFÂNDEGA *s.f.* customs.
ALFANDEGAR *v.* to fix, to collect customs.
ALFANDEGÁRIO *adj.* customs.
ALFANDEGUEIRO *s.m.* custom officer.
ALFANJADA *s.f.* stroke.
ALFANJE *s.m.* cutlass, scimitar.
ALFANUMÉRICO *adj.* alphanumeric.
ALFAQUE *s.m.* reef, rock.
ALFAQUI *s.m.* fakir, fakeer.
ALFARRÁBIO *s.m.* old book.
ALFARRABISTA *s.2gên* second-hand bookseller.
ALFARROBA *s.f.* carob, locust bean.
ALFARROBAL *s.m.* carob-trees plantation.
ALFARROBEIRA *s.f.* carob.
ALFAVACA *s.f.* basil.
ALFAZEMA *s.f.* lavender.
ALFEÇA *s.f.* die holder.
ALFEIRE *s.m.* pigsty, pigpen.
ALFEIREIRO *s.m.* shepherd.
ALFEIZAR *s.m.* stretcher.
ALFELOEIRO *s.m.* confectioner.
ALFENA *s.f.* privet.
ALFENINADO *adj.* delicated, fragile.
ALFENINAR *v.* to become fragile, to touchy.
ALFERÇA *s.f.* pick; mattock.
ALFINETADA *s.f.* nip, pin-prick.
ALFINETAR *v.* to pin.

ALFINETE *s.m.* pin.
ALFINETEIRA *s.f.* pincase, pincushion.
ALFOMBRA *s.f.* carpet.
ALFOMBRAR *v.* to carpet.
ALFONSIA *s.f.* mildew.
ALFORJADA *s.f.* a full bag.
ALFORJE *s.m.* a travelling bag.
ALFORRA *s.f.* mildew.
ALFORRAR *v.* to mildew.
ALFORRECA *s.f.* medusa, jellyfish.
ALFORRIA *s.f.* manumission; liberation.
ALFORRIADO *adj.* freed, set free.
ALFORRIAR *v.* to enfranchise.
ALFURJA *s.f.* dunghill.
ALGA *s.f.* seaweed, alga.
ALGÁCEO *adj.* algal.
ALGÁLIA *s.f.* catheter, probe; civet.
ALGALIAR *v.* to catheterise, to proble.
ALGAR *s.m.* cave; den; grotto.
ALGARAVIADA *s.f.* mixpigsty, pigpen.
ALGARISMO *s.m.* digit, number.
ALGAROBEIRA *s.f.* mesquite.
ALGAZARRA *s.f.* clamour, racket, tumult.
ALGAZARRAR *v.* to shout, to clamour.
ÁLGEBRA *s.f.* algebra.
ALGÉBRICO *adj.* algebraic, algebraical.
ALGEBRISTA *s.2gên.* algebraist.
ALGEBRIZAR *v.* to algebraize.
ALGEMA *s.f.* handcuff; oppression, censorship.
ALGEMADO *adj.* handcuffed; arrested.
ALGEMAR *v.* to handcuff, to shackle.
ALGENTE *adj.2gên.* most cold; frozen, glacial.
ALGEROZ *s.m.* gutter.
ALGIA *s.f.* pain.
ALGIBE *s.m.* cistern.
ALGIBEBE *s.m.* hawker; peddler.
ALGIBEIRA *s.f.* pocket, pouch.
ALGIDEZ *s.f.* coldness.
ÁLGIDO *adj.* very cold; chilling.
ALGO *adv.* somewhat / *pron.* something, anything.
ALGODÃO *s.m.* cotton.
ALGODÃO-DOCE *s.m.* cotton candy.
ALGODÃO-PÓLVORA *s.m.* gun cotton.
ALGODOAL *s.m.* cotton field.
ALGODOARIA *s.f.* cotton mill.
ALGODOEIRO *s.m.* cotton plant.
ALGOFILIA *s.f.* algophilia.
ALGÓFILO *s.m.* algophilist.
ALGOFOBIA *s.f.* algophobia.
ALGÓFOBO *s.m.* algophobic / *adj.* algophobic.
ALGOIDE *adj.2gên.* seaweed.
ALGOLOGIA *s.f.* algology.
ALGOLÓGICO *adj.* algologic.
ALGOLOGISTA *s.2gên.* algologist.
ALGOR *s.m.* extremely cold.
ALGORITMO *s.m.* algorithm, algorism.
ALGOZ *s.m.* tormento.
ALGOZAR *v.* to torture.
ALGOZARIA *s.f.* cruelty, barbarity.
ALGRAFIA *s.f.* algraphy.
ALGUAZIL *s.m.* bailiff.
ALGUÉM *pron.* someone; somebody.
ALGUERGUE *s.m.* mosaic.
ALGUM *pron.* some; any.
ALGURES *adv.* somewhere, someplace.
ALHADA *s.f.* garlicky stew.
ALHAL *s.m.* garlic field.
ALHANAR *v.* to be gentile, to polited.
ALHEABILIDADE *s.f.* alienability.
ALHEAÇÃO *s.f.* alienation, distraction.
ALHEADO *adj.* oblivious.
ALHEADOR *adj.* alienating; disturbing.
ALHEAMENTO *s.m.* alienation; distraction.
ALHEAR *v.* to alienate.
ALHEATÓRIO *adj.* aleatory; alienating.
ALHEÁVEL *adj.2gên.* alienable.
ALHEIO *adj.* ignorant / *s.m.* alien, foreigner.
ALHEIRA *s.f.* yellow rocket.
ALHETA *s.f.* trail, track.
ALHO *s.m.* garlic.
ALHURES *adv.* elsewhere.
ALI *adv.* there, that place.
ALIÁCEO *adj.* alliaceous.
ALIADO *adj.* allied / *s.m.* ally.
ALIANÇA *s.f.* alliance, league; ring, pact.
ALIAR *v.* to ally; to join; to make pacts.
ALIÁS *adv.* besides; moreover; by the way.
ALIÁVEL *adj.2gên.* aliable.
ALIAZAR *s.m.* muddy river.
ALIBAMBAR *v.* to fetter.
ÁLIBI *s.m.* alibi.
ALIBILIDADE *s.f.* alibility.
ALICANTINA *s.f.* astuteness, malice, fraud.
ALICANTINADOR *s.m.* cheater, tricker.
ALICATE *s.m.* pliers.
ALICERÇADOR *s.m.* founder, foundation; foundational.
ALICERÇAR *v.* to consolidate, to base.

ALICERCE *s.m.* foundation; base.
ALICIAÇÃO *s.f.* graft, seduction.
ALICIADO *adj.* allured, attracted, seduced.
ALICIADOR *s.m.* seducer / *adj.* seducer.
ALICIAR *v.* to allure, to attract; to seduce.
ALICIENTE *s.m.* that seduces / *adj.* that seduces.
ALICORNE *s.m.* horned screamer.
ALIDADA *s.f.* alidade.
ALIENABILIDADE *s.f.* alienability.
ALIENAÇÃO *s.f.* alienation.
ALIENADO *adj.* alienated / *s.m.* angry, madman.
ALIENADOR *s.m.* alienating, alienator / *adj.* alienating.
ALIENANTE *s.2gên.* alienating.
ALIENAR *v.* to alienate.
ALIENATÓRIO *s.m.* alienee; alienating.
ALIENÁVEL *adj.2gên.* alienable.
ALIENÍGENA *s.2gên.* alien, foreigner / *adj.* alien, foreigner.
ALIENISTA *s.2gên.* alienist / *adj.* alienist.
ALIFÁTICO *adj.* aliphatic.
ALÍFERO *adj.* winged.
ALIFORME *adj.2gên.* aliform.
ALIGÁTOR *s.m.* alligator.
ALIGEIRAR *v.* to speed up; to lighten; to make easier.
ALÍGERO *adj.* winged; quick, swift.
ALIJAÇÃO *s.f.* dumping; throwing overboard, getting rid of.
ALIJAMENTO *s.f.* jettison, dumping; throwing overboard.
ALIJAR *v.* to jettison; to get rid of.
ALIMÁRIA *s.f.* animal; brute.
ALIMENTAÇÃO *s.f.* food, feeding.
ALIMENTADOR *s.m.* feeder, distributor / *adj.* feeding.
ALIMENTAR *v.* to feed.
ALIMENTÍCIO *adj.* alimentary, nourishing; alimony.
ALIMENTO *s.m.* food, feeding.
ALIMENTOSO *adj.* alimentary, nourishing.
ALIMPAMENTO *s.f.* to clean, cleaning, cleanse.
ALINDADO *adj.* adorned, ornamented.
ALINDAMENTO *s.m.* embellishment, ornament.
ALINDAR *v.* to adorn, to make prettier.
ALÍNEA *s.f.* paragraph.

ALINEGRO *adj.* black-winged.
ALINHADO *adj.* aligned, line up.
ALINHADOR *s.m.* aligner / *adj.* aligner.
ALINHAMENTO *s.m.* alignment; carefully arranged.
ALINHAR *v.* to align, to line up.
ALINHAVAR *v.* to tack, to baste; to prepare a project; to delineate.
ALINHAVO *s.m.* basting, tack; sketch; outline.
ALINHO *s.m.* lining up, ranging; ornament, decoration.
ALIPOTENTE *adj.2gên.* strong-winged.
ALÍQUOTA *adj.* aliquot / *s.m.* part.
ALISADO *adj.* smoothed; plain, softer.
ALISAR *v.* to smooth; to equalise; to comb (cabelo).
ALÍSIO *s.m.* trade wind / *adj.* trade.
ALISMA *s.f.* alisma.
ALISTABILIDADE *s.f.* enlistable, listable.
ALISTAMENTO *s.m.* enlistment; recruitment.
ALISTANDO *s.m.* being listed, enlisted; listing person.
ALISTAR *v.* to list, to enlist, to enrol.
ALISTÁVEL *adj.2gên.* enlistable.
ALITERAÇÃO *s.f.* alliteration.
ALITERAR *v.* to alliterate.
ALITÚRGICO *adj.* non-liturgic.
ALIVIAÇÃO *s.f.* relief; comfort; consolation.
ALIVIADO *adj.* relieved.
ALIVIADOR *adj.* balsamic, relief.
ALIVIAR *v.* to alleviate; to mitigate; to calm down.
ALÍVIO *s.m.* relief.
ALIZAR *s.m.* wainscoting; footer; skirting board.
ALIZARINA *s.f.* alizarin, modder.
ALJÔFAR *s.m.* dew, tears.
ALJUBE *s.m.* prison, jail.
ALJUBEIRO *s.m.* gaoler, jailer.
ALJUBETA *s.m.* dim, gown.
ALMA *s.f.* soul.
ALMÁCEGA *s.f.* putty.
ALMAÇO *s.m.* foolscap / *adj.* foolscap.
ALMA-DE-MESTRE *s.m.* thunderbird.
ALMÁDENA *s.f.* minerat.
ALMA GÊMEA *s.f.* soulmate.
ALMAGRAR *v.* to rubricate.
ALMAGRE *s.m.* red ocre; rubric.
ALMAINHA *s.f.* fenced garden.

ALMALHO *s.m.* bullock, a young bull.
ALMANAQUE *s.m.* almanac, calendar.
ALMARGEAL *s.m.* swampy place; meadow.
ALMARGEM *s.m.* pasture.
ALMARGIO *adj.* rubbish.
ALMEIDA *s.f.* counter; helm port.
ALMEIRÃO *s.m.* wild chicory.
ALMEJANTE *adj.2gên.* desirous.
ALMEJAR *v.* to long for, to crave; to desire sorely; to woo.
ALMEJÁVEL *adj.2gên.* sorely desired, wished.
ALMEJO *s.m.* crave, long for.
ALMIRANTA *s.f.* admiral-ship.
ALMIRANTADO *s.m.* admiral, naval staff.
ALMIRANTE *s.m.* flag-officer.
ALMÍSCAR *s.m.* musk.
ALMISCARADO *adj.* musky.
ALMISCARAR *v.* to use musk perfume.
ALMISCAREIRA *s.f.* storks-bill.
ALMISCAREIRO *s.m.* musk deer.
ALMO *adj.* creative fostering; good, benign; adorable, venerable.
ALMOÇADEIRA *s.f.* cup.
ALMOCADÉM *s.m.* commander, leader.
ALMOÇAR *v.* to have lunch.
ALMOÇO *s.m.* lunch.
ALMOCREVE *s.m.* carrier, mule rider.
ALMOEDA *s.f.* auction, public sale.
ALMOEDAR *v.* to auction.
ALMOFAÇA *s.f.* currycomb.
ALMOFAÇAR *v.* to currycomb, to groom.
ALMOFACILHA *s.f.* protective tow around the horse's curb.
ALMOFADA *s.f.* pad, cushion, pillow.
ALMOFADADO *adj.* cushioned; padded.
ALMOFADAR *v.* to cushion.
ALMOFADINHA *s.f.* a small and delicate cushion / *adj.* dandy, fop.
ALMOFADISMO *s.m.* dandyism.
ALMOFARIZ *s.m.* mortar.
ALMOFATE *s.m.* awl, sorte of punch.
ALMOFEIRA *s.f.* olive water.
ALMOFREIXE *s.m.* a large trunck.
ALMOFREZ *s.m.* awl, bodkin.
ALMOLINA *s.f.* blind-man-buff, infant game.
ALMÔNDEGA *s.f.* meatball.
ALMOTOLIA *s.f.* oil can.
ALMOXARIFADO *s.m.* storeroom; warehouse.
ALMOXARIFE *s.m.* storekeeper, warehouse keeper.
ALMUADEM *s.m.* muezzin.
ALNO *s.m.* alder, elder.
ALÓ *adv.* windward.
ALÔ *s.m.* hello (ao telefone) / *interj.* hello!
ALOBRÓGICO *adj.* rough.
ALÓBROGO *s.m.* rustic, rough.
ALOCAÇÃO *s.f.* allocation.
ALOCAR *v.* to allocate, to place in.
ALOCROÍSMO *s.m.* allochroism.
ALOCROMÁTICO *adj.* allochromatic.
ALOCROMIA *s.f.* allochromatism.
ALOCRÔMICO *adj.* allochromatic.
ALÓCTONE *s.2gên.* allochthon / *adj.2gên.* foreign.
ALOCUÇÃO *s.f.* allocution.
ALODIAL *adj.2gên.* allodial.
ALODIALIDADE *s.f.* allodium.
ALÓDIO *s.m.* allod, allodium.
ALOENDRO *s.m.* oleander.
ALOÉ *s.m.* aloe.
ALOÉTICO *adj.* aloetic.
ALOETINA *s.f.* aloin, aloetin.
ALOFTALMIA *s.f.* allophtalmia.
ALOFTÁLMICO *adj.* allophtalmic.
ALOGAMIA *s.f.* allogamy.
ALÓGAMO *adj.* allogamus.
ALÓGENO *adj.* allogeneous.
ALOGIA *s.f.* alogy, nonsense.
ALOGIANO *s.m.* alogian.
ALOGISMO *s.m.* paralogism.
ALOÍNA *s.f.* aloin, barbaloin.
ALOIRADO *adj.* blond, blondie.
ALOIRAR *v.* to make or become blond; to brown.
ALOITE *s.m.* wrestling, battle.
ALOJAÇÃO *s.f.* accommodation; shelter; lodging.
ALOJAMENTO *s.f.* lodge; lodging; accommodation; shelter.
ALOJAR *v.* to house, to dwell; to provide a shelter; to lodge.
ALOMBADO *adj.* cambered; convex; bent; rounding.
ALOMBAMENTO *s.m.* convex; rounding; bending.
ALOMBAR *v.* to bend.
ALOMORFIA *s.f.* allomorphy.
ALOMÓRFICO *adj.* allomorphic.

ALOMORFISMO *s.m.* allomorphism.
ALONGA *s.f.* adapter; border.
ALONGADO *adj.* long, elongated.
ALONGADOR *s.m.* extensor, prolonger / *adj.* prolonging, long; procrastinator.
ALONGAMENTO *s.m.* stretching; elongation; procrastination.
ALONGAR *v.* to stretch; to extend; to length.
ALÔNIMO *s.m.* allonym / *adj.* allonym.
ALOPATA *s.2gên.* allopath.
ALOPATIA *s.f.* allopathy.
ALOPÁTICO *adj.* allopathic.
ALOPECIA *s.f.* alopicia; baldness.
ALOPÉCICO *adj.* m.q. alopático.
ALOPRADO *adj.* mad, nut, agitated.
ALOPRAR *v.* to go crazy; to go out of mind.
ALOQUETE *s.m.* padlock.
ALOR *s.m.* incitement; stimulation; movement.
ALOTADOR *s.m.* stud.
ALOTROPIA *s.f.* allotropy.
ALOTRÓPICO *adj.* allotropic.
ALÓTROPO *s.m.* allotrope.
ALOUCADO *adj.* maddened.
ALOUCAMENTO *s.m.* maddening.
ALOUCAR *v.* to become or go crazy; to behave recklessly.
ALOURADO *adj.* m.q. aloirado.
ALOUSAR *v.* to slate.
ALPACA *s.f.* alpaca, llama.
ALPARCATA *s.f.* sandals, slippers.
ALPARGATA *s.f.* m.q. alparcata.
ALPEDO *adv.* vainly, pointlessly.
ALPENDRE *s.m.* shed, porch.
ALPENSE *adj.2gên.* alpino.
ALPERCHEIRO *s.m.* apricot tree.
ALPES *s.m. pl.* Alps.
ALPESTRE *adj.2gên.* alpine, wild.
ALPINISMO *s.m.* mountaineering; alpinism; climbing.
ALPINISTA *s.2gên.* alpinist, mountaineer.
ALPINO *s.m.* alpino soldier / *adj.* alpine, alpestrine.
ALPISTE *s.m.* birdseed.
ALPONDRAS *s.f. pl.* stepping stones.
ALPORAMA *s.m.* panoramic view.
ALQUEBRADO *adj.* weak, feeble.
ALQUEBRAMENTO *s.m.* weakening, debilitation.
ALQUEBRAR *v.* to weaken, to debilitate

ALQUEIVAR *v.* to lay up.
ALQUEIVE *s.m.* fallow.
ALQUILADOR *s.m.* horse hirer.
ALQUIMIA *s.f.* alchemy.
ALQUÍMICO *adj.* alchemic, alchemical.
ALQUIMISTA *s.m.* alchemist.
ALROTAR *v.* to shout.
ALROTARIA *s.f.* clamour, mockery.
ALSACIANO *s.m.* Alsatian / *adj.* Alsatian.
ALTA *s.f.* raising, rise, increase; boom; discharge (do hospital); high (pressão).
ALTA-COSTURA *s.f.* haute couture.
ALTA-FIDELIDADE *s.f.* high fidelity (hi-fi).
ALTAICO *adj.* altaic, altaian.
ALTAMISA *s.f.* mugwort.
ALTANADICE *s.f.* arrogance, presumption.
ALTANADO *s.m.* arrogant / *adj.* arrogant, frivolous.
ALTANAR *v.* to become arrogant; to behave very proud.
ALTANARIA *s.f.* haughtiness, arrogance.
ALTANEIRO *adj.* soaring; raising very much; haughty, arrogant.
ALTAR *s.m.* altar.
ALTAR-MOR *s.m.* high altar.
ALTAREIRO *s.m.* bigot; devotee.
ALTA-RODA *s.f.* high society.
ALTA-TENSÃO *s.f.* high voltage.
ALTEADOR *s.m.* raiser, lifter / *adj.* raising, lifting.
ALTEAMENTO *s.m.* raising, lifting.
ALTEAR *v.* to raise; to increase; to grow, to enlarge.
ALTERABILIDADE *s.f.* alterability; changeability.
ALTERAÇÃO *s.f.* alteration; modification; change.
ALTERADO *adj.* changed; modified; different, altered.
ALTERADOR *s.m.* changer; cheater / *adj.* changing, alterating.
ALTERAR *v.* to alter; to modify; to change.
ALTERATIVO *adj.* alterative.
ALTERÁVEL *adj.2gên.* changeable; alterable; modifiable.
ALTERCAÇÃO *s.f.* altercation; quarrel.
ALTERCADOR *s.m.* disputer, quarreller / *adj.* quarrelsome.
ALTERCAR *v.* to altercate.
ALTERNAÇÃO *s.f.* alternation, interchange.

ALTERNADO *adj.* alternate, alternating; rotative.
ALTERNADOR *s.m.* alternator, alternating / *adj.* alternative, alternating.
ALTERNÂNCIA *s.f.* alternation, rotation; reversal.
ALTERNANTE *adj.2gên.* alternant.
ALTERNAR *v.* to alternate; to rotate.
ALTERNATIVA *s.f.* alternative; choice / *adj.* alternative; choice.
ALTERNATIVO *adj.* alternative.
ALTERNO *adj.* alternate, periodic.
ALTEROSO *adj.* haughty, grant.
ALTEZA *s.f.* highness, loftiness; elevation, greatness.
ALTICOLÚNIO *adj.* high-columned.
ALTICORNÍGERO *adj.* long-horned.
ALTILOQUÊNCIA *s.f.* high eloquence.
ALTILOQUENTE *adj.2gên.* mouthy, indiscreet in speech; altiloquent.
ALTIMETRIA *s.f.* altimetry.
ALTÍMETRO *s.m.* altimeter.
ALTIPLANO *s.m.* plateau.
ALTIPLANURA *s.f. m.q.* altiplano.
ALTIPOTENTE *adj.2gên.* very powerful.
ALTIRROSTRO *adj.* high-beaked.
ALTÍSSIMO *adj.* very high (coisas), very tall (pessoa).
ALTISSONANTE *adj.2gên.* high-sounding.
ALTÍSSONO *adj. m.q.* altissonante.
ALTISTA *s.2gên.* violist; speculator, manipulator / *adj.* bull; bullish.
ALTITONANTE *adj.2gên.* boisterous.
ALTITUDE *s.f.* altitude; height.
ALTITÚDICO *adj.* altitudinal.
ALTÍVAGO *adj.* high up, flown.
ALTIVAR *v.* to elevate.
ALTIVEZA *s.f.* haughtiness; arrogance; pride.
ALTIVO *adj.* elevated, courageous; haughty, arrogance; pride.
ALTO *adj.* height, high (coisas), tall (pessoas) / *adv.* loud, loudly / *interj.* stop!
ALTO-CÚMULO *s.m.* altocumulus.
ALTO-ESTRATO *s.m.* altostratus.
ALTO-FALANTE *s.m.* speaker, loudspeaker.
ALTO-MAR *s.m.* high seas.
ALTOPLANO *s.m.* plateau.
ALTOR *s.m.* nutritive / *adj.* nutritive.
ALTO-RELEVO *s.m.* high relief, alto-relievo.
ALTRUÍSMO *s.m.* altruism.
ALTRUÍSTA *s.2gên.* altruist / *adj.2gên.* altruistic, altruistical.
ALTRUÍSTICO *adj.* altruistic.
ALTURA *s.f.* height; altitude.
ALUAMENTO *s.m.* lunatic; mad; rut.
ALUAR *v.* to go lunatic, to crazy; rut, period.
ALUCINAÇÃO *s.f.* hallucination; delusion.
ALUCINADO *adj.* hallucinated; deluded; crazy.
ALUCINADOR *adj.* hallucinatory, hallucinating.
ALUCINAMENTO *s.m. m.q.* alucinação.
ALUCINANTE *adj.* hallucinating.
ALUCINAR *v.* to hallucinate; to delude.
ALUCINÓGENO *s.m.* hallucinogen / *adj.* hallucinatory.
ALUCINOSE *s.f.* hallucinosis.
ALUDE *s.m.* avalanche.
ALUDIR *v.* to allude; to mention; to hint; to refer to.
ALUGAÇÃO *s.m.* hiring, renting.
ALUGADO *adj.* rented.
ALUGADOR *s.m.* tenant; hirer, renter.
ALUGAMENTO *s.m.* hiring, renting.
ALUGAR *v.* to rent.
ALUGUEL *s.m.* rent, hire.
ALUIÇÃO *s.f.* shaking; ruin, collapse.
ALUÍDO *adj.* loose; shaky; tumble.
ALUIDOR *adj.* ruinous, destructive / *adj.* ruinous, destructive.
ALUIMENTO *s.m. m.q.* aluição.
ALUIR *v* to shake; to tremble; to collapse.
ÁLULA *s.f.* winglet.
ALUMBRADO *adj.* illuminated, inspiring.
ALUMBRAMENTO *s.m.* illumination; enlightenment; inspiration.
ALUMBRAR *v.* to inspire; to illuminate; to enlighten.
ALUME *s.m.* alum.
ALUMIAÇÃO *s.f.* illumination, enlightenment.
ALUMIADO *adj.* bright; illuminated, luminous.
ALUMIADOR *s.m.* illuminator, inspirer / *adj.* bright, illuminating.
ALUMIAMENTO *s.m.* inspiration, illumination.
ALUMIAR *v.* to illuminate; to enlighten.

ALUMINA *s.f.* alumina.
ALUMÍNICO *adj.* aluminous.
ALUMÍNIO *s.m.* aluminium.
ALUNISSAGEM *s.f.* moonfall.
ALUNO(A) *s.m.* student; pupil.
ALUSÃO *s.f.* allusion; hint, reference.
ALUSIVO *adj.* allusive, hint / *adv.* allusively.
ALUVAI *interj.* stop!
ALUVIAL *adj.2gên.* alluvial.
ALUVIANO *adj.* alluvial.
ALUVIÃO *s.f.* alluvium, alluvion; inundation.
ALVA *s.f.* aurora, dawn; sclera.
ALVACENTO *adj.* whitish; light grey.
ALVAIADAR *v.* to apply white lead to.
ALVAIADE *s.m.* ceruse, snow white.
ALVANEL *s.m.* bricklayer.
ALVAR *adj.2gên.* whitish; stupid, foolish; silly, candid.
ALVARÁ *s.m.* permit, charter; order, patent.
ALVARAZO *s.m.* white leprosy; horse pustules.
ALVEADOR *s.m.* whitewasher, painter.
ALVEAMENTO *s.m.* whitewashing, painting.
ALVEAR *v.* to whitewash, to paint.
ALVEÁRIO *s.m.* beehive; apiary.
ALVEDRIO *s.m.* free will.
ALVEIRO *s.m.* white target / *adj.* white.
ALVEITARIA *s.f.* farriery.
ALVEJANTE *adj.2gên.* whitening, bleaching.
ALVEJAR *v.* to whiten; to become white, to bleach; to hit the target.
ALVENARIA *s.f.* masonry.
ALVENEIRO *s.m. m.q.* alvanel.
ÁLVEO *s.m.* river-bed; furrow, channel.
ALVEOLAR *adj.2gên.* alveolar.
ALVÉOLO *s.m.* alveolus.
ALVERCA *s.f.* marsh; pond; fish-pond.
ALVIÃO *s.m.* hoe; mattock.
ALVINITENTE *adj.2gên.* spotless, white.
ALVIRRUBRO *adj.* white and red.
ALVISSARAR *v.* to tell good news; rumor.
ALVISSAREIRO *adj.* auspicious.
ALVITRADOR *s.m.* proponent, proposer / *adj.* arbitral, arbitrary.
ALVITRAMENTO *s.m.* counselling, advising, consulting.
ALVITRAR *v.* to suggest; to propose; to offer.
ALVITRE *s.m.* reminder, hint; proposal, suggestion.
ALVO *s.m.* white, target / *adj.* white, clean.

ALVOR *s.m.* whiteness, brightness; aurora, dawn.
ALVORADA *s.f.* dawn, morning, twilight; beginning.
ALVORAR *v.* to prance; to hoist.
ALVORECER *v.* to dawn / *s.f.* dawn, aurora.
ALVOREJAR *v.* to whiten, to bleach.
ALVORO *s.m.* dawn.
ALVOROÇADO *adj.* restless, agitated; flustered.
ALVOROÇADOR *adj.* agitating, frightening.
ALVOROÇAMENTO *s.m.* restlessness, alarm, agitation.
ALVOROÇAR *v.* to agitate; to fluster, to frighten.
ALVOROÇO *s.m.* enthusiasm; agitation; alarm, beginning.
ALVOROTO *s.m. m.q.* alvoroço.
ALVURA *s.f.* purity; immaculate; brightness, whiteness.
AMA *s.f.* wet nurse; governess, nursemaid; mistress.
AMÃ *s.f.* Amman.
AMABILIDADE *s.f.* amiability, friendliness; kindness.
AMACACADO *adj.* monkeyish, apish.
AMAÇAROCADO *adj.* entangled.
AMAÇAROCAR *v.* to entangle.
AMACIADO *adj.* soft.
AMACIAMENTO *s.m.* softening.
AMACIAR *v.* to soften, to smooth.
AMADEIRADO *adj.* woody.
AMA DE LEITE *s.f.* wet nurse.
AMADO *s.m.* sweetheart.
AMADOR *s.m.* lover; amateur.
AMADORISMO *s.m.* amateurism.
AMADORISTA *s.2gên.* amateur / *adj.* amateurish.
AMADRINHADO *adj.* gregarious.
AMADURADO *adj.* mature; ripe.
AMADURAMENTO *s.m.* ripening, ripeness.
AMADURAR *v.* to ripen, to be mature.
AMADURECER *v. m.q.* amadurar.
AMADURECIDO *adj. m.q.* amadurado.
AMADURECIMENTO *s.m. m.q.* amaduramento.
ÂMAGO *s.m.* core; heart; essence.
ÂMAGO-FURADO *s.m.* disease in tobbacoes.
AMAGOTADO *adj.* crowds, lots of.

AMAGOTAR v. to heap; to crowd; to accumulate in piles.
AMAINAR v. to strike; to compose; to settle.
AMALDIÇOADO s.m. cursed; accused / adj. cursed; accused.
AMALDIÇOADOR s.m. curser / adj. cursing, damnable.
AMALDIÇOAR v. to curse, to damn.
AMÁLGAMA s.2gên. amalgam; mixture.
AMALGAMAÇÃO s.f. amalgamation; mixture; confusion.
AMALGAMADOR s.m. amalgamator / adj. amalgamative.
AMALGAMAR v. amalgamate; to mix, to blend; to join, to unite.
AMALGÂMICO adj. amalgamative, amalgamate.
AMALHAR v. to drive home; to shelter; to corner.
AMALTAR v. to gang.
AMALUCADO adj. silly.
AMALUCAR v. to go crazy.
AMAMENTAÇÃO s.f. breast-feeding; lactation.
AMAMENTADORA s.f. wet nurse, foster mother / adj. nursing.
AMAMENTAR v. to breastfeed; to feed; to nurse, to suckle.
AMANCEBADO adj. concubinary.
AMANCEBAMENTO s.m. concubinage.
AMANCEBAR-SE v. to live in concubinage.
AMANEIRADO adj. affected; artificial; calculated.
AMANEIRAMENTO s.m. affectation; artificiality.
AMANEIRAR v. to adapt.
AMANHÃ adv. tomorrow / s.m. tomorrow, future.
AMANHAÇÃO s.f. farming, tillage.
AMANHADO adj. farmed; tilled; cultivated.
AMANHADOR s.m. tiller, farmer, cultivator / adj. tilling, farming.
AMANHAR v. to till, to prepare; to farm, to cultivate.
AMANHECENTE adj.2gên. dawning.
AMANHECER v. to dawn / s.m. dawn, dawning, aurora, the beginning.
AMANHECIDO s.m. dawned; old / adj. dawned; old.

AMANHECIMENTO s.m. dawn.
AMANHO s.m. tilling, tillage; arrangement.
AMANINHADOR adj. stagnancy.
AMANINHAR v. to sterilise.
AMANSADOR s.m. tamer.
AMANSAMENTO s.m. taming, domestication.
AMANSAR v. to tame, to domesticate, to break in; to soften, to moderate.
AMANSIA s.f. taming of a bull.
AMANTE s.2gên. lover; concubine / adj.2gên. loving; in love.
AMANTEIGADO adj. buttery.
AMANTEIGAR v. to make butter.
AMANTELAR v. to fortify.
AMANTÉTICO adj. passionate, in love; affectionate, kind.
AMANTILHAR v. to involve, to catch.
AMANTILHO s.m. lift, halyard.
AMANUENSE s.2gên. scribe.
AMAR v. to love.
AMÁRACO s.m. sweet marjoram.
AMARADO adj. full of water; offshore.
AMARAGEM s.f. alighting on water.
AMARANTO s.m. purplewood.
AMARAR v. to alighting on water; to be flooded.
AMARASMEAR v. to become apathic.
AMARELADO adj. yellowish.
AMARELÃO s.m. hookworm, ancylostomiasis.
AMARELAR v. to turn into yellow.
AMARELECER v. m.q. amarelar.
AMARELECIMENTO s.m. turning into yellow.
AMARELENTO adj. yellowing, pale or faded.
AMARELIDÃO s.f. yellow, pale.
AMARELIDEZ s.f. m.q. amarelidão.
AMARELINHA s.f. hopscotch.
AMARELO adj. yellow / s.m. yellow.
AMARESCENTE adj.2gên. bitter, bitterness.
AMARFALHAR v. to crumple, to wrinkle.
AMARFANHAR v. m.q. amarfalhar.
AMARGADO adj. bitter; painful; harsh.
AMARGAR v. to embitter; to bitter, to suffer.
AMARGO adj. bitter, acid / s.m. bitter, acid.
AMARGOR s.m. bitterness.
AMARGOSO adj. a brave man, corageous.
AMARGURA s.f. bitterness.
AMARGURADO adj. distressed; sorrowful, afflicted.
AMARGURAR v. to embitter.

AMARICADO *adj.* effeminate.
AMARILHO *s.m.* bandage.
AMARIOLAR-SE *v.* to hesitate.
AMARO *adj.* bitter.
AMAROTAR-SE *v.* to behave naughty.
AMARRA *s.f.* cable, support, aim.
AMARRAÇÃO *s.f.* fastining, tying.
AMARRADO *s.m.* parcel, bundle / *adj.* fastened, tied.
AMARRADOR *s.m.* master of a float / *adj.* fastening, tying.
AMARRADOURO *s.m.* berth, moorish.
AMARRAR *v.* to fasten, to tie up; to bet money.
AMARRETA *s.f.* m.q. amarra.
AMARRILHO *s.m.* thread.
AMARROADO *adj.* downcast, discouraged.
AMARROAMENTO *s.m.* melancholy.
AMARRONZADO *adj.* brownish; turned brown.
AMARROTADO *adj.* wrinkled, crumple.
AMARROTAR *v.* to crumple, to rumple; to wrinkle, to ruffle.
AMARTELADO *adj.* hammered, squashed, crushed.
AMARTELAR *v.* to hammer.
AMARUJAR *v.* to slightly bitter, to get bored, to upset.
AMARUME *s.m.* bitter taste, bitterness.
AMA-SECA *s.f.* dry nurse, babysitter.
AMÁSIA *s.f.* mistress, concubine.
AMASIAR-SE *v.* to take a mistress.
AMASIO *s.m.* concubinage.
AMÁSIO *s.m.* lover.
AMASSADEIRA *s.f.* knead.
AMASSADELA *s.f.* kneading; crushing.
AMASSADO *adj.* squashed, crushed, flattened; smashed.
AMASSADOR *s.m.* kneading, crushing.
AMASSADURA *s.f.* kneading; bump, blow.
AMASSAMENTO *s.m.* kneading; squash, crush; batch.
AMASSAR *v.* to knead; to squash, to crush.
AMASSARIA *s.f.* bakery.
AMATILHAR *v.* to pack; to join, associate with.
AMATIVIDADE *s.f.* sex appeal.
AMATÓRIO *adj.* loving, amorous.
AMATRONAR *v.* to grow old; to get.
AMAUROSE *s.f.* amaurosis.
AMAURÓTICO *adj.* amaurotic.
AMÁVEL *adj.2gên.* kind, nice; lovable.
AMAVIOS *s.m. pl.* means of seduction; love potion; charms.
AMAVIOSO *adj.* seductive, alluring.
AMAZONA *s.f.* Amazon, warrior.
AMAZONENSE *s.2gên.* Amazonian.
AMAZÔNICO *adj.* Amazonian.
ÂMBAR *s.m.* amber.
AMBÁRICO *adj.* amber.
AMBARINO *adj.* m.q. ambárico.
AMBARIZAR *v.* to amber.
AMBIÇÃO *s.f.* ambition.
AMBICIONAR *v.* to be ambitious, to covet, to strive.
AMBICIONEIRO *adj.* ambitious.
AMBICIOSO *adj.* m.q. ambicioneiro.
AMBIDESTRIA *s.f.* ambidexterity
AMBIDESTRISMO *s.f.* ambidexterity.
AMBIDESTRO *adj.* ambidextrous.
AMBIÊNCIA *s.f.* ambience, environment.
AMBIENTAR *v.* to adapt; to fit in; to acclimatise.
AMBIENTE *s.m.* environment; atmosphere / *adj.2gên.* surround, environmental.
AMBIESQUERDO *adj.* unskillful, very clumsy.
AMBÍGENO *adj.* ambigenus, hybrid.
AMBIGUIDADE *s.f.* ambiguity.
AMBÍGUO *adj.* ambiguous; doubtful.
AMBILÁTERO *adj.* bifacial, two faces.
AMBÍPARO *adj.* ambiparus.
AMBISSÉXUO *adj.* bisexual.
ÂMBITO *s.m.* ambit; scope.
AMBIVALÊNCIA *s.f.* ambivalence.
AMBIVALENTE *adj.2gên.* ambivalent.
AMBÍVIO *s.m.* crossing; crossroads.
AMBLIOPIA *s.f.* amblyopia.
AMBLÓTICO *s.m.* amblotic, abortive / *adj.* amblotic, abortive.
AMBOS *num.* both.
AMBREADA *s.f.* artificial amber, fake.
AMBROSIA *s.f.* ambrosia (mitologia grega); custard (doce).
AMBROSÍACO *adj.* ambrosial.
AMBROSIANO *adj.* ambrosian.
ÂMBULA *s.f.* ampulla.
AMBULACRÁRIO *adj.* ambulacral.
AMBULACRO *s.m.* ambulacrum, ambulacral.
AMBULÂNCIA *s.f.* ambulance.

AMBULANTE *adj.2gên.* moving, walking; ambulant, ambulatory.
AMBULAR *v.* to stroll, to wander.
AMBULATIVO *adj.* ambulatory, ambulant; moving, wandering.
AMBULATÓRIO *s.m.* clinic / *adj.* ambulatory, moving.
AMBUSTÃO *s.f.* cauterization.
AMEAÇA *s.f.* threat.
AMEAÇADO *s.m.* threatened / *adj.* threatened.
AMEAÇADOR s.m threatener / *adj.* threatening, menacing.
AMEAÇANTE *adj.2gên.* threatening, menacing.
AMEAÇAR *v.* to threath, to manace.
AMEADO *adj.* crenellated.
AMEALHADO *adj.* hoarder, saved; economised.
AMEALHADOR *s.m.* hoarder, bargainer.
AMEALHAR *v.* to hoard; to save.
AMEAR *v.* to embattle; to fortify.
AMEBA *s.f.* amoeba, ameba.
AMEBIANO *adj.* amoebic.
AMEBÍASE *s.f.* amoebiasis.
AMÉBICO *adj.* amoebic.
AMEDRONTADO *adj.* frightened; afraid of; scared; fearful.
AMEDRONTADOR *s.m.* scarer, frightener / *adj.* scaring, frighting.
AMEDRONTAMENTO *s.m.* fear, intimidation.
AMEDRONTAR *v.* to frighten; to scare, to intimidate.
AMEIA *s.f.* battlement.
AMEIGADO *adj.* fondled, caressed.
AMEIGADOR *s.m.* fondler, caresser.
AMEIGAR *v.* to fondle, to caress.
AMÊIJOA *s.f.* eatable.
AMEIJOADA *s.f.* cockle stew; pasture ground.
AMEIJOAR *v.* to fold.
AMEIXA *s.f.* plum.
AMEIXAL *s.m.* plum tree orchard.
AMEIXEIRA *s.f.* plum tree.
AMELAÇAR *v.* to color like molasses; to make affected.
AMELOADO *adj.* melonlike.
AMÉM *s.m.* amen / *interj.* amen.
AMÊNCIA *s.f.* amentia.
AMÊNDOA *s.f.* almond.
AMENDOAL *s.m.* almond fields.
AMENDOEIRA *s.f.* almond tree.
AMENDOIM *s.m.* peanut; peanut butter (manteiga de amendoim).
AMENIDADE *s.f.* amenity, serenity.
AMENINADO *adj.* childlike, childish, boyish; weak, feeble.
AMENISTA *s.2gên.* amenable; condescending.
AMENIZADO *adj.* softened, soothed.
AMENIZADOR *s.m.* softener / *adj.* softening.
AMENIZAR *v.* to soften, to ease.
AMENO *adj.* pleasant, bland; kind.
AMENORREIA *s.f.* amenorrhea.
AMENOSO *adj. m.q.* ameno.
AMENTE *adj.2gên.* demented / *s.2gên.* demented, insane, crazy.
AMENTILHO *s.m.* ament.
AMERCEADOR *s.m.* compassionate; merciful.
AMERCEAMENTO *s.m.* compassion; mercifulness.
AMERCEAR *v.* to pardon; to be compassionate, merciful.
AMÉRICA *s.f.* America; profitable business.
AMERICANADA *s.f.* group of americans.
AMERICANISMO *s.m.* americanism.
AMERICANISTA *s.2gên.* Americanist.
AMERICANIZAÇÃO *s.f.* Americanization.
AMERICANIZAR *v.* to Americanize.
AMERICANO *adj.* American.
AMERÍNDIO *adj.* Amerindian / *s.m.* Amerindian.
AMESQUINHADO *adj.* depreciated, humiliated; wretched.
AMESQUINHADOR *s.m.* depreciator, humbler / *adj.* depreciative, humiliating.
AMESQUINHAMENTO *s.m.* demeaning; depreciating; humiliating.
AMESQUINHAR *v.* to depreciate; to wretch; to humiliate.
AMESTRADO *adj.* trained, instructed; domesticated.
AMESTRADOR *s.m.* trainer / *adj.* training.
AMESTRAMENTO *s.m.* training, instructing; domesticating, teaching.
AMESTRAR *v.* to instruct, to train; to domesticate.
AMETISTA *s.f.* amethyst.
AMETÍSTICO *adj.* amethystine.

AMÉTROPE *s.m.* myopic, short-sighted.
AMETROPIA *s.f.* myopia, astigmatism; short-sight.
AMEZINHAR *v.* to treat.
AMIAL *s.m.* alder grove.
AMIANTO *s.m.* asbestos, amianthus.
AMICAL *adj.2gên.* friendly.
AMICÍSSIMO *adj.* very friendly.
AMIDA *s.f.* amide.
AMIDO *s.m.* starch.
AMIDOADO *adj.* starchy.
AMIGAÇÃO *s.f.* making friends, befriending.
AMIGAÇO *s.m.* great friend.
AMIGADO *adj.* being in concubinage.
AMIGAR *v.* to befriend.
AMIGÁVEL *adj.2gên.* friendly.
AMÍGDALA *s.f.* tonsil, amygdala.
AMIGDÁLICO *adj.* tonsilar.
AMIGDALINA *s.f.* amygdalin.
AMIGDALINO *adj.* amygdaline.
AMIGDALITE *s.f.* tonsillitis.
AMIGDALOIDE *adj.2gên.* amygdaloid, amygdaloidal.
AMIGO *s.m.* friend / *adj.* friendly.
AMIGUEIRO *adj.* friendly, attentive.
AMILÁCEO *adj.* amylaceous.
AMÍLASE *s.f.* amylase.
AMIMALHAR *v.* to spoil.
AMINA *s.f.* amine.
AMINGUAR *v.* to lack, to decrease.
AMINOÁCIDO *s.m.* aminoacid.
AMIOSTENIA *s.f.* amyosthenia.
AMIOSTÊNICO *adj.* amyosthenic.
AMIOTROFIA *s.f.* amyotrophy.
AMIR *s.m.* emir, amir.
AMISERAÇÃO *s.f.* compassion.
AMISERAR-SE *v.* to be sorry for; to have compassion.
AMISSÃO *s.f.* loss, miss.
AMISTOSO *adj.* friendly, cordial, play-off.
AMITOSE *s.f.* amistosis.
AMIUDADO *adj.* very often; frequent, repeated.
AMIÚDE *adv.* often; frequently.
AMIZADE *s.f.* friendship.
AMNÉSIA *s.f.* amnesia.
AMNÉSICO *adj.* amnesic.
ÂMNIO *s.m.* amnion.
AMNIÓTICO *adj.* amniotic.
AMO *s.m.* master; owner; boss.

AMOCAMBADO *adj.* hidden refugee, isolated, alone.
AMOCAMBAMENTO *s.m.* hiding; retiring; reclusion.
AMODORRAR *v.* to make drowsy, to get sleepy.
AMOEDAÇÃO *s.f.* coinage, mintage.
AMOEDAR *v.* to coin, to mint.
AMOFINAÇÃO *s.f.* vexation; affliction.
AMOFINADO *adj.* vexed, afflicted.
AMOFINADOR *s.m.* tormentor.
AMOFINAR *v.* to vex, to irritate; to afflict.
AMOITAR-SE *v.* to hide oneself.
AMOJAR *v.* to swell.
AMOLAÇÃO *s.f.* grinding, sharpening, vexation, affliction.
AMOLADEIRA *s.f.* grindstone.
AMOLADO *adj.* sharpened; vexed, annoyed.
AMOLADOR *s.m.* sharpened, grinder / *adj.* annoying, vexatious.
AMOLANTE *s.2gên.* grinder, sharpened / *adj.* tiresome, monotonous.
AMOLAR *v.* to grind, to sharpen; to be boring, tiresome.
AMOLDADO *adj.* moulded.
AMOLDAR *v.* to mould; to shape; to fit.
AMOLDÁVEL *adj.2gên.* mouldable; adjustable.
AMOLECADO *adj.* boyish.
AMOLECAR *v.* to ill-treat, to ridicule, to degrade.
AMOLECEDOR *s.m.* softener / *adj.* softening.
AMOLECER *v.* to soften.
AMOLECIDO *adj.* softened.
AMOLECIMENTO *s.m.* softening, mollification.
AMOLEGAR *v.* to soften, to season.
AMOLENTAMENTO *s.m.* enervation.
AMOLENTAR *v. m.q.* amolecer.
AMOLESTAR *v.* to molest.
AMOLGAÇÃO *s.f.* crushing; beating.
AMOLGAR *v.* to crush, crash; to beat.
AMÔNIA *s.f.* ammonia.
AMONIACADO *adj.* ammoniated.
AMONÍACO *s.m.* ammonia.
AMÔNIO *s.m.* ammonium.
AMONITE *s.f.* ammonite.
AMONÔMETRO *s.m.* ammonia meter.
AMONTADO *adj.* mounted, assembled.

AMONTAR v. to heap; to go up a hill.
AMONTOA s.f. moulding up.
AMONTOAÇÃO s.f. moulding up, earthing up.
AMONTOADO s.m. heap, mass, pile / adj. heaped up, piled up.
AMONTOADOR s.m. heaper.
AMONTOAMENTO s.m. heap, pile.
AMONTOAR v. to heap, to pile up.
AMONTURAR v. to dunghill.
AMOR s.m. love.
AMORA s.f. mulberry, blackberry.
AMORADO adj. mulberry-coloured; in love.
AMORAL adj.2gên. amoral.
AMORALISMO s.m. amoralism.
AMORALISTA s.2gên. amoralist / adj.2gên. amoralistic.
AMORA-PRETA s.f. blackberry.
AMORATIVO v. lovable, worth of love.
AMORÁVEL adj.2gên. loving, affectionate; lovable, lovely.
AMOR-CRESCIDO s.m. sunflower.
AMORDAÇAMENTO s.m. gagging.
AMORDAÇAR v. to gag.
AMOREIRA s.f. mulberry tree.
AMOREIRAL s.m. mulberry tree grove.
AMORFIA s.f. formlessness, shapelessness.
AMORFO adj. amorphous.
AMORICO s.m. flirt.
AMORÍFERO adj. causing or provoking love.
AMORISCADO adj. lovely.
AMORISCAR-SE v. to fall in love, to be in love with.
AMORNADO adj. lukewarm.
AMORNAR v. to warm up.
AMOROSIDADE s.f. lovingness, softness.
AMOROSO s.m. lead / adj. loving, kind.
AMOR-PRÓPRIO s.m. self-love; self-respect.
AMORREADO adj. hilly.
AMORRINHAR-SE v. to be attacked by murrain; to weaken, to enfeeble.
AMORSEGAR v. to bite off, to tear off.
AMORTALHADO adj. shrouded.
AMORTALHAMENTO s.m. shrouding.
AMORTALHAR v. to shroud.
AMORTECEDOR s.m. damper / adj. damping.
AMORTECER v. to weaken; to debilitate, to soften.
AMORTECIDO adj. debilitated, weak.

AMORTECIMENTO s.m. weakening, mitigation.
AMORTIÇAR v. to deaden; to dull, to discourage.
AMORTIZAÇÃO s.f. amortization, paying off.
AMORTIZAR v. to amortize, to pay off.
AMORUDO adj. in love.
AMOSSAR v. to crush, to crumple.
AMOSTRA s.f. sample, specimen, pattern.
AMOSTRADIÇO adj. showy, exhibitive.
AMOSTRAGEM s.f. sampling.
AMOSTRAR v. to show, to demonstrate.
AMOSTRINHA s.f. sample.
AMOTA s.f. embankment; baking.
AMOTAR v. to embank; to land, to ground.
AMOTINAÇÃO s.f. mutiny; insurrection; revolt.
AMOTINADO adj. revolted, mutinying.
AMOTINADOR s.m. rebel, provoker / adj. rebellious, mutinous.
AMOTINAMENTO s.m. m.q. amotinação.
AMOTINAR v. to rebel, to revolt, to mutiny.
AMOTINÁVEL adj.2gên. rebellious.
AMOUCADO adj. rather deaf.
AMOUXAR v. to hoard.
AMOVER v. to remove; to dispossess.
AMOVIBILIDADE s.f. transferability.
AMOVÍVEL adj.2gên. transferable, removable.
AMOXAMAR v. to emaciate.
AMPARADO adj. supported, protected.
AMPARADOR s.m. supporter, protector / adj. supporting, protecting.
AMPARAR v. to support, to protect.
AMPARO s.m. support, protection.
AMPERAGEM s.f. amperage.
AMPERE s.m. ampere.
AMPERÍMETRO s.m. ammeter.
AMPERÔMETRO s.m. m.q. amperímetro.
AMPLEXO s.m. embracement.
AMPLIAÇÃO s.f. enlargement, amplification; zoom in.
AMPLIADO adj. enlarged, amplified.
AMPLIADOR s.m. amplifier, enlarger / adj. amplifying, increasing.
AMPLIAR v. to amplify, to enlarge.
AMPLIATIVO adj. ampliative, enlarging.
AMPLIDÃO s.f. amplitude, ampleness.
AMPLIFICAÇÃO s.f. amplification, enlargement.

AMPLIFICADOR *s.m.* amplifier / *adj.* amplifying.
AMPLIFICAR *v.* to enlarge, to amplify.
AMPLIFICATIVO *adj.* amplifying.
AMPLIFICÁVEL *adj.2gên.* amplifiable.
AMPLITUDE *s.f.* amplitude, largeness.
AMPLO *adj.* ample; wide, vast.
AMPOLA *s.f.* vesicle, blister; ampoule, ampule.
AMPULHETA *s.f.* log glass, sand glass.
AMPUTAÇÃO *s.f.* amputation.
AMPUTADO *adj.* crippled; amputated, mutilated.
AMPUTADOR *s.m.* amputator, mutilator / *adj.* amputative.
AMPUTAR *v.* to amputate; to cut off, to mutilate.
AMUADO *adj.* angry; silent; sad.
AMUAMENTO *s.m.* surliness.
AMUAR *v.* to sulk.
AMULÉTICO *adj.* fetishistic.
AMULETO *s.m.* amulet, talisman.
AMULHERADO *adj.* effeminate.
AMULHERAR-SE *v.* to effeminate.
AMUNHECADO *adj.* weak, debilitated.
AMUNHECAR *v.* to weaken, to grow weak.
AMUNICIAMENTO *s.m.* munitioning.
AMUNICIAR *v.* to munition, to supply ammunition.
AMUO *s.m.* sulkiness.
AMURA *s.f.* main tack.
AMURADA *s.f.* main rail; wall.
AMURADO *adj.* walled in.
AMURALHAR *v.* to wall in.
AMURAR *v. m.q.* amuralhar.
ANABATISMO *s.m.* anabaptism.
ANABATISTA *s.2gên.* anabaptist.
ANABIOSE *s.f.* anabiosis.
ANABÓLICO *adj.* anabolic.
ANABOLISMO *s.m.* anabolism.
ANAÇAR *v.* to mix, to stir up.
ANACARADO *adj.* reddish.
ANACEFALEOSE *s.f.* recapitulation.
ANACOLUTO *s.m.* anacoluthon.
ANACORETA *s.m.* anchorite; unsociable.
ANACORÉTICO *adj.* anchoritic.
ANACRÔNICO *adj.* anachronistic.
ANACRONISMO *s.m.* anachronism.
ANADEL *s.m.* captain, commander.
ANADELARIA *s.f.* captain.

ANAERÓBICO *s.m.* anaerobic.
ANAFA *s.f.* melilot.
ANAFADO *adj.* fat, glossy.
ANAFAR *v.* to comb; to fatten.
ANÁFASE *s.f.* anaphase.
ANÁFEGA *s.f.* jujube fruit.
ANAFILÁCTICO *adj.* anaphylactic.
ANAFILAXIA *s.f.* anaphylaxis.
ANÁFORA *s.f.* anaphora.
ANAFÓRICO *adj.* anaphoric.
ANAFORISMO *s.m.* anachronism.
ANAFRODISIA *s.f.* anaphrodisia.
ANAFRODISÍACO *adj.* anaphrodisiac.
ANAFRODITA *s.2gên.* anaphroditis / *adj.* anaphroditis.
ANAFRODÍTICO *adj.* anaphroditic.
ANAGÊNESE *s.f.* anagenesis.
ANÁGLIFO *s.m.* anaglyph.
ANAGRAMA *s.m.* anagram.
ANAGRAMÁTICO *adj.* anagrammatic.
ANAGRAMATISMO *s.m.* anagrammatism.
ANAGRAMATIZAR *v.* to anagrammatise.
ANÁGUA *s.f.* petticoat, slip.
ANAIS *s.m. pl.* annals; periodical.
ANAL *adj.* anal / *adj.2gên.* yearly, annual.
ANALECTO *s.m.* analecta, collectanea.
ANALECTOR *s.m.* analects, anthology.
ANALÉPTICO *adj.* analeptic.
ANALFABETISMO *s.m.* analphabetism.
ANALFABETO *s.m.* illiterate, unlettered / *adj.* illiterate, unlettered.
ANALGESIA *s.f.* analgesia.
ANALGÉSICO *adj.* analgesic / *s.m.* painkiller; analgesic.
ANALGÉTICO *adj.* analgesic.
ANALGIA *s.f.* analgesia.
ANÁLGICO *adj.* analgestic.
ANALISADOR *s.m.* analyzer, analyst / *adj.* analyzing, critical.
ANALISAR *v.* to analyze.
ANALISÁVEL *adj.2gên.* analyzable.
ANÁLISE *s.f.* analysis.
ANALISTA *s.2gên.* analyst; algebraist.
ANALÍTICO *adj.* analytic.
ANALOGIA *s.f.* analogy.
ANALÓGICO *adj.* analogical.
ANALOGISMO *s.m.* analogism.
ANALOGISTA *s.2gên.* analogistic.
ANALOGÍSTICO *adj.* analogistic.
ANÁLOGO *adj.* analogous, similar.

ANAMNESE *s.f.* anamnesis.
ANAMNÉSIA *s.f. m.q.* anamnese.
ANAMNÉSTICO *adj.* anamnestic.
ANAMNIOTA *s.2gên.* anamniota / *adj.* anamniotic.
ANAMORFOSE *s.f.* anamorphosis.
ANAMORFÓTICO *adj.* anamorphosis, distorted images.
ANANÁS *s.m.* pineapple plant.
ANANICADO *adj.* dwarfish.
ANANICO *adj.* dwarflike; small.
ANANISMO *s.m.* dwarfism.
ANANO *adj. m.q.* ananico.
ANÃO(Ã) *s.m.* dwarf / *adj.* dwarfish, small.
ANAPÉSTICO *adj.* anapaestic.
ANAPESTO *s.m.* anapaest.
ANAPLASTIA *s.f.* plastic surgery, anaplasty.
ANAPLÁSTICO *adj.* anaplastic.
ANAPTIXE *s.f.* anaptyxis.
ANARMÔNICO *adj.* inharmonic.
ANARQUIA *s.f.* anarchy.
ANÁRQUICO *adj.* anarchic.
ANARQUISMO *s.m.* anarchism.
ANARQUISTA *s.2gên.* anarchist / *adj.* anarchistic.
ANARQUIZADOR *adj.* anarchistic.
ANARQUIZAR *v.* to anarchize.
ANARTRIA *s.f.* anarthria.
ANARTRO *adj.* anarthrous.
ANASARCA *s.f.* anasarca.
ANASARCADO *adj.* anasarcous.
ANASTÁTICO *adj.* anastatic.
ANASTIGMÁTICO *adj.* anastigmastic.
ANASTOMOSAR *v.* to anastomose.
ANASTOMOSE *s.f.* anastomosis.
ANASTOMÓTICO *adj.* anastomotic.
ANÁSTROFE *s.f.* anastrophe.
ANATADO *adj.* creamy, creamlike.
ANATAR *v.* to cream; to cover with cream.
ANÁTEMA *s.m.* anathema.
ANATEMATISMO *s.m.* anathematism.
ANATEMATIZAÇÃO *s.f.* anathematization.
ANATEMATIZAR *v.* to anathematise; to curse; to damn.
ANATÍDEOS *s.m. pl.* anathidae.
ANATOCISMO *s.m.* anatocism.
ANATOMIA *s.f.* anatomy.
ANATÔMICO *s.m.* anatomic / *adj.* anatomic.
ANATOMISTA *s.2gên.* anatomist.
ANATOMIZAÇÃO *s.f.* anatomization.

ANATOMIZAR *v.* to dissect, to analyse.
ANATOXINA *s.f.* anatoxin.
ANÁTROPO *adj.* anatropous.
ANAVALHADO *adj.* razor-shaped; sharp, whetted.
ANCA *s.f.* hip, haunch.
ANCADO *adj.* hipshot.
ANCESTRAL *adj.2gên.* ancestral.
ANCESTRALIDADE *s.m.* ancestry.
ANCESTRE *s.m.* ancestor.
ANCHO *adj.* broad, wide.
ANCHOVA *s.f.* anchovy.
ANCHURA *s.f.* width.
ANCIANIA *s.f.* old age; antiquity.
ANCIÃO(Ã) *s.m.* elder, venerable person; ancient.
ANCILA *s.f.* ancilla.
ANCILAR *adj.2gên.* ancillary.
ANCINHAR *v.* to rake.
ANCINHO *s.m.* rake.
ÂNCORA *s.f.* anchor.
ANCORAÇÃO *s.f.* anchoring.
ANCORADOURO *s.m.* anchorage.
ANCORAGEM *s.f.* anchorage.
ANCORAR *v.* to anchor.
ANCORETA *s.f. m.q.* âncora.
ANCUDO *adj.* having large hip, haunches.
ANDA *interj.* come on!
ANDAÇO *s.m.* infection.
ANDADA *s.f.* walk.
ANDADEIRAS *s.f. pl.* leading-strings.
ANDADEIRO *adj.* light-footed; that walks a lot.
ANDADOR *s.m.* errand-boy, messenger; good walker / *adj.* light-footed.
ANDADURA *s.f.* gait.
ANDAIMARIA *s.f.* scaffolding.
ANDAIME *s.m.* scaffol.
ANDAINA *s.f.* row, rank, line.
ANDALUZ *s.m.* Andalusian.
ANDALUZIA *s.f.* Andalusia.
ANDAMENTO *s.m.* process, proceeding; time, measure.
ANDANÇA *s.f.* gait.
ANDANTE *s.m.* andante; passer-by / *adj.2gên.* walking, roving.
ANDANTINO *s.m.* andantino / *adv.* andantino.
ANDAR *v.* to walk; to go / *s.m.* floor, walking.
ANDEJAR *v.* to wander, to walk very much.

ANDESITO s.m. andesite.
ANDINO adj. Andean.
ANDIRÁ s.m. bat.
ANDIROBA s.f. crab-tree.
ÂNDITO s.m. footpath; pavement.
ANDÓ adj. a strange beard.
ANDOR s.m. swallow; steam launch.
ANDORINHA-DO-MAR s.f. royal tern.
ANDORINHA-DO-MATO s.f. smaller swallow-wing.
ANDORINHÃO s.m. swift.
ANDORINHO s.m. a little swallow; stir up.
ANDRAJO s.m. rag, tatter; piece of cloth.
ANDRAJOSO adj. tattered, ragged, a piece of torn cloth.
ANDROCEU s.m. androecium.
ANDROFAGIA s.f. cannibalism.
ANDRÓFAGO s.m. cannibal / adj. androphagous.
ANDROFOBIA s.f. androphobia.
ANDRÓFORO s.m. androphore.
ANDROGÊNESE s.f. androgenesis.
ANDROGINIA s.f. androgyny.
ANDRÓGINO s.m. androgyne / adj. androgynous.
ANDROIDE s.2gên. android / adj.2gên. android.
ANDRÓLATRA s.2gên. worshipper.
ANDROLATRIA s.f. worship a particular man.
ANDROLOGIA s.f. andrology.
ANDROLÓGICO adj. andrologist.
ANDROMANIA s.f. nymphomania.
ANDRÔMEDA s.f. andromeda.
ANDROSTERONA s.m. androsterone.
ANEDIAR v. to make shiny, to polish.
ANEDOTA s.f. joke, anecdote.
ANEDOTÁRIO s.m. collection of anecdotes.
ANEDÓTICO adj. anedoctic.
ANEDOTISTA s.2gên. anecdotist.
ANEDOTIZAR v. to tell anecdotes.
ANEGAR v. to flood, inundate.
ANEGRADO adj. somewhat black; negro.
ANEGRAR v. to blacken, to darken; to become or make black.
ANEGREJAR v. to blacken, to darken.
ANEGRISCADO adj. black, dark.
ANEIRO adj. uncertain, eventual.
ANEJO adj. one year old.
ANEL s.m. ring, circle, link.
ANELAÇÃO s.f. annealing; puffy.

ANELADO adj. ringlike, circular / s.m. annelid.
ANELANTE adj.2gên. puffy.
ANELEIRA s.f. ring box.
ANELÍDEO s.m. annelid.
ANELIFORME adj.2gên. ringlike, ring-shaped.
ANELÍPEDE adj.2gên. having circular paws.
ANÉLITO s.m. breath, respiration.
ANELO s.m. aspiration; anxiety.
ANEMIA s.f. anaemia.
ANEMIAR v. to cause anaemia; to weaken, to feeble, to become anaemic.
ANÊMICO adj. anaemic.
ANEMIZAR v. m.q. anemiar.
ANEMÓFILO adj. anemophilous.
ANEMOGRAFIA s.f. anemography.
ANEMOGRÁFICO adj. anemographic.
ANEMÓGRAFO s.m. anaemograph.
ANEMOLOGIA s.f. anemology.
ANEMOLÓGICO adj. anemological.
ANEMOMETRIA s.f. anemometry.
ANEMOMÉTRICO adj. anemometric.
ANEMÔMETRO s.m. anemometer, wind-gauge.
ANÊMONA s.f. anemone, wind-flower.
ANEMOSCOPIA s.f. anemoscopy.
ANEMOSCÓPIO s.m. anemoscope.
ANENCEFALIA s.f. anencephaly.
ANENCÉFALO s.m. anencephalic monster / adj. anencephalic.
ANEQUIM s.m. porbeagle.
ANEROIDE s.m. aneroid barometer / adj.2gên. aneroid.
ANESTESIA s.f. anaesthesia.
ANESTESIANTE adj. numbing.
ANESTESIAR v. to give anaesthesia.
ANESTÉSICO s.m. anaesthetic / adj. anaesthetic.
ANESTESISTA s.m. anaesthetist.
ANESTÉTICO s.m. m.q. anestésico.
ANETE s.m. anchor ring.
ANETO s.m. drill.
ANEURISMA s.f. aneurism.
ANEURISMAL adj.2gên. aneurismal.
ANEURISMÁTICO adj. aneurismatic.
ANEXAÇÃO s.f. annexation.
ANEXADO adj. attached, annexed.
ANEXADOR s.m. that annexes / adj. attaching, joining.
ANEXAR v. to attach; to annex; to enclose
ANEXIM s.m. saying, proverb.

ANEXIONISTA *s.2gên.* annexationist / *adj.* annexational.
ANEXO *s.m.* annex.
ANFÍBIO *adj.* amphibious / *s.m.* amphibian.
ANFIBIOGRAFIA *s.f.* amphibiography.
ANFIBIOLOGIA *s.f.* amphibiology.
ANFIBÓLIO *s.m.* amphibole.
ANFIBOLOGIA *s.f.* amphibology.
ANFIBOLOIDE *adj.2gên.* amphiboloid.
ANFÍBRACO *s.m.* amphibrachus.
ANFICTIÃO *s.m.* amphictyon.
ANFICTIONIA *s.f.* amphictyony.
ANFICTIÔNICO *adj.* amphictyonic.
ANFIGÊNIO *s.m.* leucite, amphigene.
ANFIGURI *s.m.* amphigory.
ANFIGÚRICO *adj.* amphigoric, meaningless.
ANFIGURISMO *s.m.* amphigoric quality.
ANFIMIXIA *s.f.* amphimixis.
ANFIOXO *s.m.* amphixious.
ANFÍPODE *s.m.* amphipod / *adj.2gên.* amphipod.
ANFISBENA *s.f.* amphisbaena.
ANFÍSCIOS *s.m. pl.* amphiscians.
ANFITEATRAL *adj.* amphitheatric.
ANFITEÁTRICO *adj.* amphitheatrical.
ANFITEATRO *s.m.* amphitheatre.
ANFITRIÃO *s.m.* host.
ANFITRIOA *s.f.* host.
ANFÍTROPO *adj.* amphitropous.
ÂNFORA *s.f.* amphora.
ANFORAL *adj.2gên.* amphoral.
ANFORICIDADE *s.f.* amphoricity.
ANFÓRICO *adj.* amphoric.
ANFÓTERO *adj.* amphoretic.
ANFRACTUOSIDADE *s.f.* anfractuosity.
ANFRACTUOSO *adj.* roundabout; anfractuous.
ANGARIAÇÃO *s.f.* canvass; enlistment, enrolment; attainment.
ANGARIADOR *s.m.* recruiter, engager; canvasser / *adj.* collecting, alluring.
ANGARIAMENTO *s.m.* enlistment; enrolment; canvass.
ANGARIAR *v.* to collect, to recruit.
ANGARILHA *s.f.* wicker.
ANGATECÔ *s.m.* fright, shock.
ANGELICAL *adj.* angelical, pure.
ANGÉLICO *adj. m.q.* angelical.
ANGELITA *s.2gên.* angelist.
ANGELITUDE *s.f.* angelicalness.
ANGELIZAR *v.* to angel.
ANGELOLATRIA *s.f.* angelolatry.
ANGELOLOGIA *s.f.* angelology.
ANGELOLÓGICO *adj.* angelologic.
ANGIALGIA *s.f.* angiagia.
ANGIÁLGICO *adj.* angialgigical.
ANGICAL *s.m.* angico grove.
ANGICO *s.m.* angico.
ANGIITE *s.f.* angiitis.
ANGINA *s.f.* angina.
ANGINOSO *adj.* angious.
ANGIOGRAFIA *s.f.* angiography.
ANGIOGRÁFICO *s.m.* angiographic.
ANGIOLOGIA *s.f.* angiology.
ANGIOMA *s.m.* angioma.
ANGIOSE *s.f.* angiosis.
ANGLICANISMO *s.m.* Anglicanism.
ANGLICANO *s.m.* Anglican / *adj.* Anglican.
ANGLICISMO *s.m.* Anglicism.
ANGLO *s.m.* Angle.
ANGLO-AMERICANO *s.m.* Anglo-American / *adj.* Anglo-American.
ANGLOFOBIA *s.f.* anglophobia.
ANGLÓFOBO *adj.* anglophobic.
ANGULADO *adj.* angled.
ANGULAR *adj.* angular, cornered.
ÂNGULO *s.m.* angle; corner.
ANGÚSTIA *s.f.* anguish; distress.
ANGUSTIADO *adj.* afflicted, distressed.
ANGUSTIAR *v.* to afflict, to distress.
ANHANGUERA *s.m.* evil spirit / *adj.* determined.
ANIL *s.m.* indigo / *adj.2gên.* blue (cor).
ANIMAÇÃO *s.f.* animation; vitality; liveliness.
ANIMADO *adj.* animated, encouraged.
ANIMADOR *s.m.* animator / *adj.* animating.
ANIMAL *s.m.* animal; beast, cruel; awesome / *adj.* animal.
ANIMALISMO *s.m.* animalism.
ANIMALISTA *s.2gên.* animalist.
ANIMAR *v.* to animate; to cheer; liven up.
ÂNIMO *s.m.* courage; will; mind.
ANIMOSIDADE *s.f.* animosity.
ANINAR *v.* to rock to sleep, to sing lullabies.
ANINHAR *v.* to put in a nest, to build a nest.
ANIQUILAÇÃO *s.f.* annihilation.
ANIQUILADOR *s.m.* annihilator / *adj.* annihilating.

ANIQUILAMENTO *s.m.* annihilation.
ANIQUILAR *v.* to annihilate.
ANIVERSARIANTE *adj.* birthday boy, birthday girl.
ANIVERSÁRIO *s.m.* anniversary, birthday.
ANJO *s.m.* angel.
ANO *s.m.* year.
ANO-BASE *s.m.* basis-year.
ANOITECER *v.* to grow dark / *s.m.* nightfall.
ANOJADO *adj.* nauseous; sick.
ANO-LUZ *s.m.* light-years.
ANOMALIA *s.f.* anomaly.
ANOMALÍSTICO *adj.* anomalistic.
ANÔMALO *adj.* anomalous, abnormal.
ANOMIA *s.f.* anomie, anomy.
ANÔNIMO *adj.* anonymous, unnamed / *s.m.* anonym.
ANO-NOVO *s.m.* new year.
ANOREXIA *s.f.* anorexia.
ANORGÂNICO *adj.* inorganic.
ANORMAL *s.2gên.* anormal, abnormal / *adj.2gên.* anormal, abnormal.
ANORMALIDADE *s.f.* abnormality, anomaly.
ANOTAÇÃO *s.f.* annotation; notes.
ANOTADOR *s.m.* noter, marker / *adj.* noting, marking.
ANOTAR *v.* to annotate; to take notes.
ANSEIO *s.m.* longing, anxiety; craving; yearning.
ÂNSIA *s.f.* nausea; anguish, anxiety.
ANSIAR *v.* to crave, to desire; to be anxious.
ANSIEDADE *s.f.* anxiety.
ANSIOSO *adj.* anxious.
ANTAGÔNICO *adj.* antagonistic, opposing.
ANTAGONISMO *s.m.* antagonism.
ANTAGONISTA *s.2gên.* antagonist.
ANTÁRTICO *adj.* Antarctic, southern.
ANTE *prep.* before; in the face of; in the presence / *adv.* before; in the face of; in the presence.
ANTECEDENTE *s.m.* antecedent / *adj.* antecedent, previous.
ANTECEDER *v.* to precede.
ANTECESSOR *s.m.* foregoer, antecessor.
ANTECIPAÇÃO *s.f.* anticipation.
ANTECIPAR *v.* to anticipate.
ANTEFACE *s.m.* veil, mask.
ANTEFERIR *v.* to prefer.
ANTEMÃO *adv.* before, previously.
ANTENA *s.f.* antenna; aerial.
ANTENADO *adj.* tuned.
ANTEONTEM *adv.* the day before yesterday.
ANTEPASSADO *s.m.* forefather, ancestor.
ANTEPASSAR *v.* to precede, to happen before.
ANTEPENÚLTIMO *adj.* last but two.
ANTERIOR *adj.* previous; anterior.
ANTES *adv.* before.
ANTIÁCIDO *s.m.* antiacid.
ANTIAÉREO *adj.* anti-aircraft.
ANTIBIÓTICO *s.m.* antibiotic.
ANTICONCEPCIONAL *s.m.* contraceptive.
ANTICORPO *s.m.* antibody.
ANTÍDOTO *s.m.* antidote.
ANTIGO *adj.* old, antique / *s.m.* ancient, former.
ANTIGUIDADE *s.f.* antiquity.
ANTIQUADO *adj.* old-fashioned; antiquated; outdated.
ANTIQUÁRIO *s.m.* antiquarian (local), antique dealer (pessoa) / *adj.* antiquarian.
ANTROPOFAGIA *s.f.* cannibalism.
ANTROPÓFAGO *s.m.* cannibal / *adj.* androphagous.
ANULAR *v.* to annul; to cancel; to abolish.
ANUNCIANTE *s.2gên.* advertiser (comercial), announcer / *adj.* advertiser (comercial), announcer.
ANUNCIAR *v.* to announce.
ANÚNCIO *s.m.* announcement.
AONDE *adv.* where.
APAGADOR *adj.* eraser.
APAGAR *v.* to extinguish, to put out (fogo); to erase (com borracha); to delete (arquivos eletrônicos); to switch, to turn off (luz).
APAIXONADO *adj.* in love.
APAIXONANTE *adj.* exciting, enthralling.
APAIXONAR *v.* to fall in love; to be in love.
APARAR *v.* to clip, to trim, to prune.
APARECER *v.* to appear; to show up.
APARECIMENTO *s.m.* appearance, emergence.
APARELHAR *v.* to equip, to furnish, to outfit.
APARELHO *s.m.* apparatus; apply; set; equipment.
APARÊNCIA *s.f.* appearance; look; aspect.
APARENTE *adj.* apparent, evident, visible.
APARIÇÃO *s.f.* appearance, apparition; wraith.
APARTAMENTO *s.m.* apartment.

APARTE *s.m.* aside, side-remark.
APATIA *s.f.* apathy.
APÁTICO *adj.* apathetic.
APAVORADO *adj.* terrified, panic-stricken.
APAVORAR *v.* to terrify, to appall.
APAZIGUADOR *s.m.* peacemaker, mollifier / *adj.* peacemaker, mollifier.
APAZIGUAMENTO *s.m.* peacemaking, mollifying.
APAZIGUAR *v.* to pacify, to appease.
APEDREJAMENTO *s.m.* stoning.
APEDREJAR *v.* to stone.
APEGAR-SE *v.* to stick, to adhere.
APEGO *s.m.* fondness, affection.
APELAÇÃO *s.f.* appeal, appellation.
APELAR *v.* to appeal.
APELIDAR *v.* to denominate, to cognominate, to nickname.
APELIDO *s.m.* nickname.
APELO *s.m.* appeal, plea.
APENAS *adv.* only; just.
APÊNDICE *s.m.* appendix.
APENDICITE *s.f.* appendicitis.
APERFEIÇOADO *adj.* improved, ameliorated.
APERFEIÇOAMENTO *adj.* improvement, perfecting.
APERFEIÇOAR *v.* to improve, to perfect.
APERITIVO *s.m.* appetizer, appetiser, starter.
APERREADO *adj.* oppressed, weak, dreary.
APERTADO *adj.* tight, narrow, snug.
APERTAR *v.* to press, to push (botão, interruptor); to shake (mãos); to tighten; to squeeze.
APERTO *s.m.* tightness, squeezed; distress, pinch, scrape, straits.
APESAR *adv.* in spite of, despite; although; even though.
APETECER *v.* to have an appetite for, to desire.
APETECÍVEL *adj.* appetizing, desirable.
APETITE *s.m.* appetite; hunger.
APETITOSO *adj.* appetizing, savory.
ÁPICE *s.m.* apex, summit, top.
APICULTOR *s.m.* apiculturist, beekeeper.
APICULTURA *s.f.* beekeeping.
APIEDAR *v.* to pity, to feel sorry for.
APIMENTADO *adj.* peppered, spicy.
APIMENTAR *v.* to pepper, to spice.
APITAR *v.* to whistle.
APITO *s.m.* whistle.

APLACADO *adj.* placated, appeased, pacified.
APLACADOR *s.m.* placator, soother / *adj.* placator, soother.
APLACAR *v.* to placate, to sooth.
APLAINAR *v.* to plane, to grade.
APLANADO *adj.* level, even, smooth.
APLAUDIDO *adj.* applauded, lauded.
APLAUDIR *v.* to applaud.
APLAUSÍVEL *adj.* praiseworthy.
APLAUSO *s.m.* applause.
APLICAÇÃO *s.f.* application; functionality; investment (dinheiro).
APLICADO *adj.* applied, diligente.
APLICAR *v.* to apply; to invest (dinheiro), to give injection.
APLICATIVO *s.m.* application.
APLICÁVEL *adj.* applicable.
APLIQUE *s.m.* applique.
APODRECER *v.* to rot; to decay.
APODRECIMENTO *s.m.* corruption, rot.
APOIAR *v.* to support, to back.
APOIAR-SE *v.* to rely on, to depend on.
APOIO *s.m.* support; aid.
APÓS *prep.* after, behind / *adv.* after, behind.
APOSENTADO *adj.* retired / *s.m.* retiree, pensioner.
APOSENTADORIA *s.f.* retirement, pension.
APOSENTAR *v.* to retire.
APOSENTO *s.m.* room.
APOSTA *s.f.* bet, betting; gamble (dinheiro).
APOSTAR *v.* to bet; to gamble.
APOSTÓLICO *s.m.* apostolic, apostolical / *adj.* apostolic, apostolical.
APÓSTOLO *s.m.* apostle.
APÓSTROFE *s.f.* apostrophe.
APOTEOSE *s.f.* apotheosis.
APRAZAR *v.* to summon, to convoque.
APRAZIMENTO *s.m.* summoning, convocation.
APRAZÍVEL *adj.* pleasant, delightful.
APRECIAÇÃO *s.f.* appreciation.
APRECIADO *adj.* appreciated.
APRECIAR *v.* to appreciate, to prize, to treasure; to appraise, to value, to estimate.
APRECIÁVEL *adj.* appreciable.
APREÇO *s.m.* valuation, estimation, appraisal.
APREENDER *v.* to apprehend, to arrest.
APREENDIDO *adj.* arresting.
APREENSÃO *s.f.* apprehension, arrest.

APREENSÍVEL *adj.* apprehensible.
APREENSIVO *adj.* apprehensive.
APRENDER *v.* to learn.
APRENDIDO *adj.* learnt.
APRENDIZ *s.m.* apprentice.
APRENDIZADO *s.m.* apprenticed, learning.
APRENDIZAGEM *s.f.* apprenticeship, education.
APRESENTAÇÃO *s.f.* presentation; performance.
APRESENTADO *adj.* presented.
APRESENTADOR *s.m.* presenter.
APRESENTAR *v.* to present, to demonstrate.
APRESENTAR-SE *v.* to present oneself, to report.
APRESENTÁVEL *adj.* presentable.
APRESSADO *adj.* hurried.
APRESSAR *v.* to hurry.
APRESSAR-SE *v.* to bustle, to make haste.
APRESSURADO *adj.* hurried, quick, hasty.
APRIMORADO *adj.* refined, excellent, perfected.
APRIMORAMENTO *s.m.* refinement, elegance.
APRIMORAR *v.* to improve, to perfect.
APRIMORAR-SE *v.* to improve, to perfect oneself.
APRISIONADO *adj.* captive, imprisoned.
APRISIONAMENTO *s.m.* imprisonment.
APRISIONAR *v.* to imprison, to jail.
APROBATIVO *adj.* approbatory, approving.
APROFUNDAMENTO *s.m.* deepening, serious study.
APROFUNDAR *v.* to deepen.
APRONTAR *v.* to prepare, to get ready.
APROPRIAR-SE *v.* to seize upon, to catch hold.
APROPRIAÇÃO *s.f.* appropriation, assumption.
APROPRIADO *adj.* appropriate, suitable.
APROPRIADOR *s.m.* appropriator / *adj.* appropriative.
APROPRIAR *v.* to appropriate, to make suitable.
APROVAÇÃO *s.f.* approval.
APROVADO *adj.* approved, agreed.
APROVAR *v.* to approve.
APROVEITADO *adj.* utilized, useful, profitable.
APROVEITADOR *s.m.* enjoyer, profiteer.

APROVEITAMENTO *s.m.* improvement; enjoyment of, profitting from, use.
APROVEITAR *v.* to take advantage.
APROVEITÁVEL *adj.* profitable, useful, utilizable.
APROXIMAÇÃO *s.f.* approximation, approach.
APROXIMADO *adj.* approximate, close.
APROXIMAR *v.* to bring closer (coisas); to bring together (pessoas); to approach (aproximar-se).
APROXIMATIVO *adj.* approximative, close to.
APRUMO *s.m.* uprightness, haughtiness.
APTIDÃO *s.f.* aptitude.
APTO *adj.* apt.
APUNHALADO *adj.* stabbed with dagger.
APUNHALAR *v.* to stab; to knife.
APURAÇÃO *s.f.* counting, polling; verification.
APURADO *adj.* refined, selected, choice.
APURAR *v.* to choose, to select, to improve.
AQUARELA *s.f.* watercolour.
AQUARELISTA *s.2gên.* watercolourist.
AQUÁRIO *s.m.* aquarium; Aquarius (astrologia).
AQUÁTICO *adj.* aquatic.
AQUECEDOR *s.m.* warmer, heater.
AQUECER *v.* to heat.
AQUECIMENTO *s.m.* heating, warming.
AQUEDUTO *s.m.* aqueduct.
AQUELE(A) *s.f.* that / *adj.* that.
AQUÉM *adv.* beneath, below, less.
AQUI *adv.* here.
AQUIESCÊNCIA *s.f.* acquiescence.
AQUIESCENTE *adj.* acquiescent.
AQUIESCER *v.* to acquiesce, to consent.
AQUIETAÇÃO *s.f.* appeasing, pacifying, quieting.
AQUIETADOR *s.m.* appeaser, pacifier, quieter / *adj.* appeaser, pacifier, quieter.
AQUIETAR *v.* to appease, to pacify, to quiet.
AQUÍFERO *s.m.* aquifer.
AQUILO *pron.* that.
AQUISIÇÃO *s.f.* acquisition, procurement, buy, purchase.
AQUISITIVO *adj.* acquisitive.
AQUOSIDADE *s.f.* acqueousness, wateriness.
AQUOSO *adj.* watery.
AR *s.m.* air.
ÁRABE *adj.* Arabian / *s.m.* Arabian.

ARABESCO *s.m.* arabesque / *adj.* arabesque.
ARÁBIA *s.f.* Arabia.
ARÁBIA SAUDITA *s.f.* Saudi Arabia.
ARÁBICO *s.m.* arab, arabic / *adj.* arab, arabic.
ARAME *s.m.* wire.
ARANHA *s.f.* spider.
ARBITRAGEM *s.m.* arbitration, arbitrage.
ARBITRAL *adj.2gên.* arbitral.
ARBITRAR *v.* to arbitrate.
ARBITRARIEDADE *s.f.* arbitrariness.
ARBITRÁRIO *adj.* arbitrary, despotic.
ARBÍTRIO *s.m.* will, discretion, judgment, freewill (livre-arbítrio).
ÁRBITRO *s.m.* arbitrator.
ARBÓREO *adj.* arboreal.
ARBORESCENTE *adj.2gên.* arborescent.
ARBORESCER *v.* to grow.
ARBUSTO *s.m.* shrub, bush.
ARCA *s.f.* ark, chest, coffer.
ARCADA *s.f.* arcade, vault, arch.
ARCAICO *adj.* archaic.
ARCANJO *s.m.* archangel.
ARCANO *adj.* secret, mystery, arcane.
ARCAR *v.* to afford, to assume; to bend, to arch.
ARCEBISPADO *adj.* archbishopric.
ARCEBISPAL *adj.* archbishopric.
ARCEBISPO *s.m.* archbishop.
ARCO *s.m.* arc, bow.
ARCO-ÍRIS *s.m.* rainbow.
AR-CONDICIONADO *s.m.* air conditioning.
ARDÊNCIA *s.f.* burning; fervency.
ARDENTE *adj.* ardent, burning.
ARDER *v.* to burn.
ARDIDO *adj.* hot.
ARDOR *s.m.* ardor.
ARDÓSIA *s.f.* slate.
ÁRDUO *adj.* arduous, difficult.
ÁREA *s.f.* area.
AREAR *v.* to sand, to scour.
AREIA *s.f.* sand.
AREJADO *adj.* aired, ventilated.
AREJAR *v.* to aerate, to air, to ventilate.
ARENA *s.f.* arena.
ARENOSO *adj.* sandy, gravelly.
ARÉOLA *s.f.* areola, garden bed.
ARESTA *s.f.* edge, corner, brim.
ARESTADO *adj.* edge.
ARFANTE *adj.* panting, gasping.
ARFAR *v.* to gasp, to pant.

ARGAMASSA *s.f.* mortar, building cement.
ARGÉLIA *s.f.* Algeria.
ARGELIANO(A) *s.m.* Algerian / *adj.* Algerian.
ARGENTINA *s.f.* Argentina.
ARGENTINO(A) *s.m.* Argentinian / *adj.* Argentinian.
ARGILA *s.f.* clay.
ARGILOSO *adj.* argillaceous, clayish.
ARGOLA *s.f.* ring, hoop.
ARGONAUTA *s.2gên.* argonaut.
ARGUEIRO *s.m.* trifle.
ARGUIR *v.* to accuse, to condemn; to test orally; to argue.
ARGUMENTAÇÃO *s.f.* argumentation, reasoning.
ARGUMENTADOR *adj.* arguer, disputer.
ARGUMENTAR *v.* to argue, to dispute.
ARGUMENTO *s.m.* argument, argumentation, reason.
ÁRIA *s.f.* aria.
ARIANO *adj.* Aryan.
ARIDEZ *s.f.* aridity, dryness.
ÁRIDO *adj.* arid, dry.
ÁRIES *s.m.* Aries.
ARISCO *adj.* skittish, shy; untamable.
ARISTOCRACIA *s.f.* aristocracy.
ARISTOCRATA *s.2gên.* aristocrat.
ARISTOCRÁTICO *adj.* aristocratic.
ARISTOCRATIZAR *v.* to render aristocratic.
ARITMÉTICA *s.f.* arithmetic.
ARITMÉTICO *adj.* arithmetical.
ARMA *s.f.* weapon, arm, gun.
ARMAÇÃO *s.f.* arming, frame, easel; timberwork, structure; ruse.
ARMADA *s.f.* armada, fleet.
ARMADILHA *s.f.* trap, snare.
ARMADO *adj.* armed, equipped.
ARMADOR *s.m.* ship-owner, trapper.
ARMADURA *s.f.* armour, suit of armour, armament.
ARMAR *v.* to arm; to frame.
ARMARINHO *s.m.* small cupboard, haberdashery.
ARMÁRIO *s.m.* wardrobe, closet.
ARMAZÉM *s.m.* warehouse, repository.
ARMAZENADO *adj.* stored.
ARMAZENADOR *s.m.* storer / *adj.* storer.
ARMAZENAGEM *s.f.* storing, warehousing.
ARMAZENAMENTO *s.m. m.q.* armazenagem.
ARMAZENAR *v.* to store, to warehouse.

AROMA *s.m.* aroma, bouquet.
AROMÁTICO *adj.* aromatic.
AROMATIZAÇÃO *s.f.* aromatization.
AROMATIZANTE *s.m.* aromatizing, flavouring; aromatizer.
AROMATIZAR *v.* to aromatize, to flavour.
ARPÃO *s.m.* harpoon.
ARPEJO *s.m.* arpeggio.
ARPOADOR *s.m.* harpooner.
ARQUEAÇÃO *s.f.* arching, vaulting.
ARQUEADO *adj.* arched, vaulted.
ARQUEAR *v.* to arch, to vault.
ARQUEJANTE *adj.* wheezing, gasping.
ARQUEJAR *v.* to wheeze, to gasp.
ARQUEOLOGIA *s.f.* archeology.
ARQUEÓLOGO *s.m.* archeologist.
ARQUÉTIPO *s.m.* archetypical.
ARQUIBANCADA *s.f.* bleachers.
ARQUIDIOCESANO *adj.* archdiocesan.
ARQUIDIOCESE *s.f.* archdiocese.
ARQUIPÉLAGO *s.m.* archipelago.
ARQUITETAR. *v.* to build, to construct, to project, to plan.
ARQUITETO *s.m.* architect.
ARQUITETÔNICO *adj.* architectural.
ARQUITETURA *s.f.* architecture.
ARQUIVADO *adj.* archived, saved, filed.
ARQUIVAMENTO *s.m.* filing.
ARQUIVAR *v.* to file.
ARQUIVISTA *s.2gên.* archivist, filing clerk.
ARQUIVO *s.m.* file.
ARRAIA *s.f.* ray, skate.
ARRAIAL *s.m.* campground, hamlet, small villag.
ARRAIGADO *adj.* deep-rooted, inveterate, old.
ARRAIGAR *v.* to take root, to settle.
ARRANCADA *s.f.* pull, jerk, jolt; ready start; dash.
ARRANCADO *adj.* jerked, jolted.
ARRANCAR *v.* to pull, to tear, to jerk away.
ARRANCA-RABO *s.m.* scuffle, fight, brawl.
ARRANHA-CÉU *s.m.* skyscraper.
ARRANHADO *adj.* scratched.
ARRANHADURA *s.f.* scratch.
ARRANHAR *v.* to scratch, to graze, to scrabble, to mar (móvel).
ARRANJADO *adj.* lined up, arranged
ARRANJADOR *s.m.* arranger.
ARRANJAR *v.* to arrange.

ARRANJO *s.m.* arrangement, settling.
ARRANQUE *s.m.* start, pull.
ARRASADO *adj.* demolished; knocked down, crushed, depressed.
ARRASADOR *adj.* demolisher; rushing, ruining.
ARRASAR *v.* to demolish, to raze; to crush, to ruin, to humiliate.
ARRASTADIÇO *adj.* easily dragged.
ARRASTADO *adj.* dragged.
ARRASTÃO *s.m.* wrench, dragging, jerk; trawl; draw along.
ARRASTA-PÉ *s.m.* knees-up, shindig.
ARRASTAR *v.* to drag, to pull.
ARREAR *v.* to harness, to furnish, to array.
ARREBANHAR *v.* to herd, to assemble.
ARREBATADO *adj.* vehement, passionate, overhasty.
ARREBATAMENTO *s.m.* ecstasy, vehemence, passion.
ARREBATAR *v.* to snatch, to grab, to enchant.
ARREBENTADO *adj.* ragged.
ARREBENTAR *v.* to break, to burst.
ARREBITADO *adj.* turned up, impudent, insolent, bold.
ARREBITAR *v.* to turn up, to raise, to lift.
ARREBOL *s.m.* afterglow, aurora.
ARRECADAÇÃO *s.f.* collection of taxes, exaction; deposit, gathering.
ARRECADADO *adj.* taxes collected; exact, careful, frugal.
ARRECADADOR *s.m.* collector, tax--collector.
ARRECADAR *v.* to collect; to levy, to secure.
ARREDONDADO *adj.* round, roundish, rotundate.
ARREDONDAMENTO *s.m.* roundness, rounding off.
ARREDONDAR *v.* to roundness, to rounding off.
ARREDOR *adv.* environs, surroundings, outskirts / *s.m.* environs, surroundings, outskirts.
ARREFECEDOR *s.m.* growing indifferent, diminishing / *adj.* growing indifferent, diminishing.
ARREFECER *v.* to cool, to moderate, to subdue.
ARREFECIDO *adj.* cooled, cooled off.

ARREFECIMENTO *s.m.* cooling, refrigeration; moderation, relenting.
ARREGAÇADO *adj.* pinned up, turned up, tucked up.
ARREGAÇAR *v.* to tuck up, to pin up, to turn up.
ARREGANHADO *adj.* showing the teeth.
ARREGANHAR *v.* to snarl, to sneer, to mock; to split, to open.
ARREIO *s.m.* saddlery, harness, gear.
ARRELIA *s.f.* tease, vexation, bad omen.
ARRELIAR *v.* to tease, to annoy, to bother.
ARREMATAÇÃO *s.f.* public sale, auction, end, conclusion, final touch.
ARREMATADO *adj.* outbidden; finished off.
ARREMATADOR *s.m.* outbidder.
ARREMATAR *v.* to finish up, to accomplish.
ARREMATE *s.m.* end, conclusion; knot.
ARREMESSADOR *s.m.* thrower, hurler.
ARREMESSO *s.m.* throw, thrust.
ARREMETER *v.* to assail, to invade, to assault.
ARRENDAMENTO *s.m.* leasehold, renting, lease.
ARRENDAR *v.* to lease, to rent.
ARRENDÁVEL *adj.2gên.* rentable, leasable.
ARREPENDER-SE *v.* to repent, to regret.
ARREPENDIDO *adj.* repentant.
ARREPENDIMENTO *s.m.* regret, repentance.
ARREPIADO *s.m.* bristly, skittish; standing on end (hair), unkempt.
ARREPIANTE *adj.* bristling, frightening, terrifying; bristly, upstanding.
ARREPIAR *v.* to ruffle, to fluff, to frighten.
ARREPIO *s.m.* shiver, fright, goose flesh.
ARRESTADO *s.m.* under embargo, seized for debt.
ARRESTAR *v.* to apprehend, to arrest, to confiscate.
ARREVESAR *v.* to reverse, to complicate.
ARRIAR *v.* to break down, to collapse, to give up; to lower, to strike.
ARRIBA *adv.* upstream, above.
ARRIBAR *v.* to land; to migrate; to depart.
ARRISCADO *adj.* risky.
ARRISCAR *v.* to risk.
ARRITMIA *s.f.* arrhythmia.
ARRÍTMICO *adj.* arrhythmic.
ARROCHAR *v.* to tighten, to compress, to cram.
ARROCHO *s.m.* tightening stick, garrote.
ARROGÂNCIA *s.f.* arrogance.
ARROGANTE *adj.2gên.* arrogant.
ARROIO *s.m.* arroyo, gully.
ARROJADO *adj.* bold, daring, fearless.
ARROJAR *v.* to fling, to repulse.
ARROLHAR *v.* to cork, to intimidate.
ARROMBADO *adj.* forced open, broken up.
ARROMBADOR *s.m.* burglar, housebreaker.
ARROMBAR *v.* to break into, to force open.
ARROTAR *v.* to belch, to burp.
ARROTO *s.m.* belch, burp.
ARROUBAR *v.* to ravish, to enchant.
ARROUBO *s.m.* ravishment, delirium, trance.
ARROXEADO *s.m.* empurpled / *adj.* empurpled.
ARROXEAR *v.* to make purple.
ARROZ *s.m.* rice.
ARROZ-DOCE *s.m.* rice pudding.
ARRUAÇA *s.f.* street riot.
ARRUAÇAR *v.* to riot.
ARRUDA *s.f.* rue (planta).
ARRUELA *s.f.* washer.
ARRUINADO *adj.* ruined, destroyed.
ARRUINAMENTO *s.m.* ruin.
ARRUINAR *v.* to ruin, to destroy.
ARRUMAÇÃO *s.f.* arrangement, disposition; clearing up.
ARRUMADEIRA *s.f.* housemaid.
ARRUMADO *adj.* tidy, neat.
ARRUMAR *v.* to arrange, to dispose; to settle, to tidy up.
ARSENAL *s.m.* arsenal.
ARSÊNICO *s.m.* arsenic / *adj.* arsenic.
ARTE *s.f.* art, skill, craft.
ARTEFATO *s.m.* artifact.
ARTEIRICE *s.f.* craft, artifice, cunning; prank, naughtiness.
ARTEIRO(A) *adj.* crafty; naughty.
ARTÉRIA *s.f.* artery.
ARTERIAL *adj.* arterial.
ARTESANAL *adj.* relating to handicraft.
ARTESANATO *s.m.* workmanship, handicraft.
ARTESÃO *s.m.* artisan, handcrafter.
ARTESIANO *adj.* artesian.
ÁRTICO *s.m.* Arctic / *adj.* Arctic.
ARTICULAÇÃO *s.f.* articulation.

ARTICULADO *adj.* articulated.
ARTICULANTE *s.2gên.* articulate / *adj.2gên.* articulate.
ARTICULAR *v.* to join, to link; to pronounce, to enunciate.
ARTÍCULO *s.m.* article, articulation; joint, knuckle.
ARTÍFICE *s.m.* artifice.
ARTIFICIAL *adj.* artificial.
ARTIFICIALIDADE *s.f.* artificiality.
ARTIFICIALISMO *s.m. m.q.* artificialidade.
ARTIFICIALIZAR *v.* to artificialize.
ARTIFÍCIO *s.m.* artifice.
ARTIGO *s.m.* article.
ARTILHARIA *s.f.* artillery.
ARTILHEIRO *s.m.* artilleryman, gunner.
ARTIMANHA *s.f.* artifice, ruse, trick.
ARTISTA *s.2gên.* artist.
ARTÍSTICO *adj.* artistic.
ARTRITE *s.f.* arthritis.
ARTRÍTICO *adj.* arthritic.
ARTRITISMO *s.m.* arthritism.
ÁRVORE *s.f.* tree.
ÁRVORE-DA-VIDA *s.f.* arborvitae.
ARVOREDO *s.m.* grove.
ARVORETA *s.f.* small tree, sapling.
AS *art. pl.* the.
ÁS *s.m.* ace (baralho).
ASA *s.f.* wing, grip, handle (de um objeto).
ASA-DELTA *s.f.* hang-glider.
ASCENDÊNCIA *s.f.* ascendancy, genealogy.
ASCENDENTE *adj.* ascendant, ancestor; rising, ascending.
ASCENDER *v.* to ascend, to rise, to climb.
ASCENSÃO *s.f.* ascension, rise.
ASCENSOR *s.m.* elevator, lift.
ASCENSORISTA *s.2gên.* elevator operator / *adj.2gên.* elevator operator.
ASCO *s.m.* loathing, repugnance, disgust.
ASFALTADO *adj.* paved, asphalted.
ASFALTAMENTO *s.m.* paving, asphalting.
ASFALTAR *v.* to pave, to asphalt.
ASFALTO *s.m.* asphalt, tarmac.
ASFIXIA *s.f.* asphyxia.
ASFIXIADO *s.m.* asphyxiated / *adj.* asphyxiated.
ASFIXIADOR *s.m.* asphyxiator / *adj.* asphyxiator.
ASFIXIANTE *adj.* stifling, suffocating, asphyxiating.
ASFIXIAR *v.* to asphyxiate, to suffocate.
ÁSIA *s.f.* Asia.
ASIÁTICO(A) *s.m.* Asian / *adj.* Asian.
ASILADO *s.m.* refugee / *adj.* refugee.
ASILAR *v.* to give shelter, to asylum, to refuge.
ASILO *s.m.* asylum, shelter, refuge.
ASMA *s.f.* asthma.
ASMÁTICO *s.m.* asthmatic / *adj.* asthmatic.
ASNEAR *v.* to behave foolishly.
ASNEIRA *s.f.* foolishness, stupidity.
ASNO *s.m.* ass, donkey.
ASPA *s.f.* quotation mark, vane.
ASPARGO *s.m.* asparagus.
ASPECTO *s.m.* aspect, look, appearance.
ASPEREZA *s.f.* roughness, harshness, asperity.
ÁSPERO *adj.* rough, coarse, rude.
ASPIRAÇÃO *s.f.* aspiration, breathing; longing; suction.
ASPIRADOR *s.m.* aspirator, exhaustor; vacuum cleaner.
ASPIRANTE *s.2gên.* aspirer / *adj.2gên.* aspirer.
ASPIRAR *v.* to aspire, to breath; to desire.
ASPIRINA *s.f.* aspirin.
ASQUEROSIDADE *s.f.* loathsomeness, repulsiveness.
ASQUEROSO *adj.* loathsome, repulsive.
ASSADEIRA *s.f.* roasting pan, flat cake tin.
ASSADO *s.m.* roast / *adj.* baked, roasted.
ASSADOR *s.m.* roaster.
ASSADURA *s.f.* roasting, baking; irritation.
ASSALARIADO *adj.* salaried, wage-earner.
ASSALARIAR *v.* to engage, to employ, to bribe.
ASSALTANTE *s.2gên.* assailant, robber.
ASSALTAR *v.* to assault, to rob.
ASSALTO *s.m.* assault, attack, robbery.
ASSANHADIÇO *adj.* irritable.
ASSANHADO *adj.* excited, furious, restless, erotic, flirtatious; unkempt.
ASSANHAMENTO *s.m.* flirtatiousness, lack of composure, restlessness.
ASSANHAR *v.* to provoke anger, to stir up; to dishevel (cabelo).
ASSAR *v.* to roast.
ASSASSINAR *v.* to murder.
ASSASSINATO *s.m.* assassination, murder.
ASSASSINO *s.m.* assassin, murderer / *adj.* assassin, murderer.

ASSEADO *adj.* clean, trim, elegant.
ASSEAR *v.* to clean up, to adorn, to trim.
ASSEDIADOR *s.m.* besieger, bore / *adj.* besieger, bore.
ASSEDIAR *v.* to besiege, to harass.
ASSÉDIO *s.m.* siege, harassment.
ASSEGURAÇÃO *s.f.* assures, ensures.
ASSEGURADO *adj.* insured, secured.
ASSEGURAR *v.* to assure, to ensure, to affirm, to assert.
ASSEIO *s.m.* cleanliness, decency.
ASSELVAJADO *adj.* savage, brutal, uncivilized.
ASSELVAJAR *v.* to make savage, to wild.
ASSEMBLEIA *s.f.* assembly.
ASSEMELHAÇÃO *s.f.* assimilation.
ASSEMELHADO *adj.* similar, alike, resembling.
ASSEMELHAR *v.* to compare, to liken.
ASSENTADA *s.f.* session; sitting.
ASSENTAMENTO *s.m.* settlement, laying, entry.
ASSENTAR *v.* to seat.
ASSENTIMENTO *s.m.* assent, permission.
ASSENTIR *v.* to assent, to consent.
ASSENTO *s.m.* seat, chair.
ASSERTIVO *adj.* assertive.
ASSESSOR *s.m.* advisor, counselor, consultant.
ASSESSORADO *adj.* advisee, assisted.
ASSESSORAMENTO *s.m.* advisement, consideration.
ASSESSORAR *v.* to advise, to assist, to help.
ASSESSORIA *s.f.* advisement, consideration.
ASSEVERAÇÃO *s.f.* averment, affirmation, assertion.
ASSEVERAR *v.* to asseverate, to affirm, to aver, to allege.
ASSEVERATIVO *adj.* asseverative.
ASSEXUADO *s.m.* assexual, non-sexual / *adj.* assexual, non-sexual.
ASSEXUAL *adj.* assexual.
ASSIDUIDADE *s.f.* assiduity, diligence.
ASSÍDUO *adj.* assiduous.
ASSIM *adv.* like this (deste modo); so, therefore (portanto).
ASSIMETRIA *s.f.* asymmetry.
ASSIMÉTRICO *adj.* asymmetrical.
ASSIMILAÇÃO *s.f.* assimilation.
ASSIMILADO *adj.* assimilated.
ASSIMILADOR *s.m.* assimilator / *adj.* assimilator.
ASSIMILAR *v.* to assimilate.
ASSIMILÁVEL *adj.2gên.* assimilable.
ASSINADO *s.m.* signed, subscribed / *adj.* signed, subscribed.
ASSINALADO *adj.* appointed, branded.
ASSINALADOR *s.m.* appointer, brander / *adj.* appointer, brander.
ASSINALAMENTO *s.m.* signalment.
ASSINALAR *v.* to mark, to brand, to designate.
ASSINANTE *s.2gên.* subscriber, signatory.
ASSINAR *v.* to sign, to underwrite; to subscribe (revista).
ASSINATURA *s.f.* signature, subscription.
ASSINERGIA *s.f.* asynergy, asynergia.
ASSINTÁTICO *adj.* asyntactic.
ASSINTOMÁTICO *adj.* asymptomatic.
ASSISTEMÁTICO *adj.* asystematic.
ASSISTÊNCIA *s.f.* assistance, presence, attendance.
ASSISTENCIAL *adj.2gên.* attendance.
ASSISTENTE *adj.2gên.* assistant, helper.
ASSISTIDO *s.m.* helped, attended, aided / *adj.* helped, attended, aided.
ASSISTIR *v.* to attend, to watch.
ASSOALHAR *v.* to lay a wooden floor; to divulge, to brag.
ASSOALHO *s.m.* wooden floor.
ASSOAR *v.* to wipe, to blow.
ASSOBERBADO *adj.* arrogant, proud.
ASSOBERBAR *v.* to disdain, to dominate, to domineer.
ASSOBIADA *s.f.* whistling, hissing.
ASSOBIAR *v.* to whistle, to hiss.
ASSOBIO *s.m.* whistle, hiss.
ASSOCIAÇÃO *s.m.* association, society.
ASSOCIADO *s.m.* associated / *adj.* associated.
ASSOCIAR *v.* to associate, to join, to unite.
ASSOCIÁVEL *adj.2gên.* associable.
ASSOLADOR *s.m.* devastator, destroyer.
ASSOLAMENTO *s.m.* devastation, destruction.
ASSOLAR *v.* to devastate, to destroy.
ASSOMBRAÇÃO *s.f.* spook, apparition, ghost, wraith.
ASSOMBRADO *adj.* haunted, terrified.
ASSOMBRAR *v.* to astonish.
ASSOMBRO *s.m.* astonishment, dread, fright.

ASSOMBROSO *adj.* amazing, terrific, frightening.
ASSOPRAR *v.* to blow; to suggest.
ASSOPRO *s.m.* blowing, blast.
ASSOSSEGAR *v.* to calm, to ease.
ASSOSSEGO *s.m.* tranquility, quiet, peace.
ASSOVIAR *v.* to whistle.
ASSOVIO *s.m.* whistle.
ASSUMIDO *adj.* assumed, convinced.
ASSUMIR *v.* to assume, to take over, to shoulder.
ASSUNTO *s.m.* subject.
ASSUSTADO *adj.* frightened.
ASSUSTADOR *adj.* startling, frightening, alarming.
ASSUSTAR *v.* to frighten.
ASTECA *s.2gên.* Aztec / *adj.* Aztec.
ASTERISCO *s.m.* asterisk.
ASTEROIDE *s.m.* asteroid.
ASTIGMÁTICO *s.m.* astigmatic / *adj.* astigmatic.
ASTIGMATISMO *s.m.* astigmatism.
ASTRAL *s.m.* astral, starry.
ASTROFÍSICA *s.f.* astrophysics.
ASTROFOBIA *s.f.* astrophobia.
ASTROLOGIA *s.f.* astrology.
ASTROLÓGICO *adj.* astrological.
ASTRÓLOGO *s.m.* astrologer / *adj.* astrologer.
ASTROMETRIA *s.f.* astrometry.
ASTRONAUTA *s.2gên.* astronaut.
ASTRONAVE *s.f.* spaceship.
ASTRONOMIA *s.f.* astronomy.
ASTRONÔMICO *adj.* astronomical.
ASTRÔNOMO *s.m.* astronomer.
ASTÚCIA *s.f.* astuteness.
ASTUCIAR *v.* to contrive, to plot.
ASTUCIOSO *adj.* astute.
ASTUTO *adj.* astute.
ATA *s.f.* record, proceedings.
ATACADISTA *s.2gên.* wholesaler, wholesale.
ATACADO *adj.* wholesale (vendas), stricken.
ATACANTE *s.2gên.* aggressor, assailant / *adj.2gên.* aggressor, assailant.
ATACAR *v.* to attack.
ATADO *adj.* tied, hindered, hampered.
ATADURA *s.f.* band, ligature, bandage.
ATALHO *s.m.* bypath, obstacle, obstruction.
ATAPETADO *adj.* carpeted.
ATAPETAR *v.* to carpet.
ATAQUE *s.m.* attack.

ATAR *v.* to tie, to link, to couple.
ATARANTADO *adj.* perplexed, puzzled.
ATARANTAR *v.* to perplex, to puzzle.
ATAREFADO *adj.* very busy, overloaded, overworked.
ATAREFAMENTO *s.m.* bustle.
ATAREFAR *v.* to overload with work.
ATASCADEIRO *s.m.* quagmire, marshy place.
ATASCAR *v.* to bog down, to sink in mud.
ATAÚDE *s.m.* coffin, tombstone.
ATÉ *prep.* until / *adv.* see you later (até logo).
ATEAR *v.* to kindle, to inflame, to foment.
ATEÍSMO *s.m.* atheism.
ATELIÊ *s.m.* atelier, studio.
ATEMORIZADO *adj.* frightened.
ATEMORIZADOR *s.m.* alarming, frightening / *adj.* alarming, frightening.
ATEMORIZANTE *adj.2gên. m.q.* atemorizador.
ATEMORIZAR *v.* to intimidate, to frighten.
ATENAS *s.f.* Athens.
ATENÇÃO *s.f.* attention.
ATENCIOSAMENTE *adv.* respectfully, sincerely.
ATENCIOSO(A) *adj.* attentive.
ATENDENTE *s.2gên.* attendant.
ATENDER *v.* to attend.
ATENDIMENTO *s.m.* attendance, attending, customer service (ao consumidor).
ATENIENSE *s.2gên.* Athenian / *adj.* Athenian.
ATENTADO *s.m.* attack.
ATENTAMENTE *adv.* attentively, closely.
ATENTAR *v.* to attempt, to try, to venture.
ATENTO *adj.* attentive.
ATENUAÇÃO *s.f.* attenuation.
ATENUADO *adj.* attenuated.
ATENUADOR *s.m.* attenuator / *adj.* attenuator.
ATENUANTE *adj.* attenuating, mitigating.
ATENUAR *v.* to attenuate, to weaken.
ATERMIA *s.f.* athermia.
ATÉRMICO *adj.* athermic.
ATERRADOR *adj.* awe-inspiring, appalling.
ATERRAR *v.* to frighten, to fill with earth, to land.
ATERRISSAGEM *s.f.* landing.
ATERRISSAR *v.* to land.
ATERRIZAR *v. m.q.* aterrissar.
ATERRO *s.m.* landfill.
ATERRORIZADO *adj.* terrorized, frightened.

ATERRORIZAR *v.* to terrify, to horrify.
ATESTADO *s.m.* certificate.
ATESTAR *v.* to attest, to certify.
ATEU *s.m.* atheist / *adj.* atheist.
ATIÇADOR *s.m.* instigator, plotter, poker.
ATIÇAMENTO *s.m.* instigation, plotting, stoking (fogo).
ATIÇAR *v.* to stir up, to instigate, to incite.
ATIJOLAR *v.* to brick.
ATINADO *adj.* cautious, prudent, wise.
ATINAR *v.* to guess right, to succeed, to discover.
ATINGIR *v.* to reach.
ATINGÍVEL *adj.* attainable, touchable.
ATÍPICO *adj.* atypical.
ATIRADO *adj.* adventurous, daring.
ATIRADOR *s.m.* rifleman, sharpshooter.
ATIRAR *v.* to shoot, to throw.
ATITUDE *s.f.* attitude.
ATIVAÇÃO *s.f.* activation.
ATIVAR *v.* to enable, to activate.
ATIVIDADE *s.f.* activity.
ATIVISMO *s.m.* activism.
ATIVISTA *s.2gên.* activist / *adj.2gên.* activist.
ATIVO *adj.* active, busy; energetic.
ATLÂNTICO *s.m.* Atlantic / *adj.* Atlantic.
ATLAS *s.m.* atlas.
ATLETA *s.2gên.* athlete / *adj.2gên.* athlete.
ATLÉTICO *adj.* athletic.
ATLETISMO *s.m.* athleticism.
ATMOSFERA *s.f.* atmosphere.
ATMOSFÉRICO *adj.* atmospheric.
ATO *s.m.* act, action, deed.
ATOALHADO *adj.* table-cloth, linen.
ATOALHAR *v.* to cover.
ATOLADO *adj.* bogged down, mired.
ATOLAR *v.* to stick in dirt, to bog down.
ATÔMICO *adj.* atomic.
ATOMIZAÇÃO *s.f.* atomization.
ÁTOMO *s.m.* atom.
ÁTONO *adj.* atonic.
ATOR *s.m.* actor, performer.
ATORDOADO *adj.* stunned, stupefied, dizzy.
ATORDOAR *v.* to stun, to stupefy.
ATORMENTAÇÃO *s.f.* torment, anguish, trouble.
ATORMENTADO *adj.* tormented, anguished.
ATORMENTAR *v.* to torment, to anguish.

ATRACAÇÃO *s.f.* grappling, docking, mooring.
ATRACADOURO *s.m.* wharf, berth.
ATRAÇÃO *s.f.* attraction.
ATRACAR *v.* to moor, to approach.
ATRAENTE *adj.* attractive.
ATRAIÇOADO *adj.* betrayed, perfidious.
ATRAIÇOAR *v.* to betray.
ATRAIR *v.* to attract.
ATRAPALHAÇÃO *s.f.* confusion, disorder.
ATRAPALHADO *adj.* confused, bothered.
ATRAPALHAR *v.* to confuse, to disorder.
ATRÁS *adv.* behind.
ATRASADO *adj.* late.
ATRASAR *v.* to delay, to retard, to defer.
ATRASO *s.m.* delay.
ATRATIVIDADE *s.f.* attractiveness.
ATRATIVO *s.m.* appealing, charming / *adj.* appealing, charming.
ATRAVÉS *adv.* across, through.
ATRAVESSADO *adj.* crossed; pierced, slanting.
ATRAVESSAR *v.* to cross.
ATRELAR *v.* to harness, to link, to yoke, to seduce.
ATREVER-SE *v.* to dare.
ATREVIDO *adj.* daring, bold, impertinent.
ATREVIMENTO *s.m.* daringness, boldness, impudence.
ATRIBUIÇÃO *s.f.* attribution.
ATRIBUIR *v.* to attribute, to assign.
ATRIBUÍVEL *adj.* attributable.
ATRIBULADO *s.m.* troubled, distressed / *adj.* troubled, distressed.
ATRIBULAR *v.* to afflict, to trouble, to distress.
ATRIBUTIVO *adj.* attributive.
ATRIBUTO *s.m.* attribute.
ÁTRIO *s.m.* atrium.
ATRITAR *v.* to rub.
ATRITO *s.m.* rub.
ATRIZ *s.f.* actress.
ATROCIDADE *s.f.* atrocity.
ATROFIA *s.f.* atrophy.
ATROFIADO *adj.* atrophied.
ATROFIAR *v.* to atrophy.
ATROPELADO *s.m.* hit, run over / *adj.* hit, run over.
ATROPELADOR *s.m.* trampler.
ATROPELAMENTO *s.m.* trampling, running over.

ATROPELAR v. to trample, to run over.
ATROPELO s.m. running-over.
ATROZ adj. atrocious, cruel.
ATUAÇÃO s.f. performance, acting.
ATUAL adj. current.
ATUALIDADE s.f. the present.
ATUALIZAÇÃO s.f. update, upgrading.
ATUALIZADO adj. updated.
ATUALIZAR v. to update, to modernize.
ATUALMENTE adv. currently, presently; at present.
ATUANTE adj.2gên. acting, active.
ATUM s.m. tuna.
ATURAR v. to endure, to tolerate.
ATURÁVEL adj.2gên. endurable, tolerable.
ATURDIDO adj. dizzy, stunned, stupefied.
ATURDIMENTO s.m. bewilderment, dizziness.
ATURDIR v. to bewilder, to stun.
AUDÁCIA s.f. audacity.
AUDACIOSO adj. audacious.
AUDIÇÃO s.f. audition, hearing.
AUDIÊNCIA s.f. audience.
ÁUDIO s.m. audio.
AUDIOVISUAL adj. audiovisual.
AUDITIVO s.m. auditory / adj. auditory.
AUDITOR s.m. auditor.
AUDITORIA s.f. audit.
AUDITÓRIO s.m. auditorium.
AUDÍVEL adj. audible.
AUÊ s.m. confusion, disorder.
AUFERIR v. to gain, to make profit, to obtain.
AUFERÍVEL adj. profited.
AUGE s.m. summit, peak, pinnacle.
AULA s.f. class, lesson.
AUMENTADO adj. augmented, increased.
AUMENTAR v. to extend, to increase.
AUMENTÁVEL adj. increasable.
AUMENTO s.m. increase, rise, raise.
AURA s.f. gentle breeze, zephyr; fame.
AURÉOLA s.f. halo, aureole.
AURÍCULA s.f. auricle.
AURICULAR adj. auricular.
AURORA s.f. dawn.
AUSÊNCIA s.f. absence.
AUSENTAR-SE v. to absent oneself.
AUSENTE adj. absent.
AUSPICIAR v. to augur, to predict.
AUSPÍCIO s.m. auspice, augury.
AUSPICIOSO adj. auspicious.

AUSTERIDADE s.f. austerity.
AUSTERO adj. austere, severe.
AUSTRÁLIA s.f. Australia.
AUSTRALIANO(A) s.m. Australian / adj. Australian.
ÁUSTRIA s.f. Austria.
AUSTRÍACO(A) s.m. Austrian / adj. Austrian.
AUTENTICAÇÃO s.f. authentication.
AUTENTICADO adj. authentic, legal.
AUTENTICAR v. to authenticate.
AUTENTICIDADE s.f. authenticity.
AUTÊNTICO adj. authentic.
AUTISMO s.m. autism.
AUTISTA adj. autist.
AUTO s.m. document, writ, deed, act.
AUTOACUSAÇÃO s.f. self-accusation.
AUTOADESIVO s.m. self-adhesive.
AUTOADMIRAÇÃO s.f. self-admiration.
AUTOAFIRMAÇÃO s.f. self-affirmation.
AUTOAGRESSÃO s.f. self-aggression.
AUTOANÁLISE s.f. self-analysis.
AUTOBIOGRAFIA s.f. autobiography.
AUTOCONTROLE s.m. self-control.
AUTOCRACIA s.f. autocracy.
AUTOCRATA s.2gên. autocrat.
AUTOCRÍTICA s.f. self-criticism.
AUTODEFESA s.f. self-defense.
AUTODESTRUIÇÃO s.f. self-destruction.
AUTODIDATA s.2gên. selftaught, self-learner / adj.2gên. selftaught, self-learner.
AUTÓDROMO s.m. autodrome.
AUTOESCOLA s.f. driving school.
AUTOESTRADA s.f. expressway.
AUTOGRAFAR v. to autograph.
AUTOGRAFIA s.f. autography.
AUTÓGRAFO s.m. autograph.
AUTOMAÇÃO s.f. automation.
AUTOMÁTICO adj. automatic.
AUTOMATIZAÇÃO s.m. automatization.
AUTOMATIZAR v. to automatize.
AUTÔMATO s.m. automaton, robot.
AUTOMOBILISMO s.m. automobilism, motoring.
AUTOMOBILISTA s.2gên. automobilist, driver / adj.2gên. automobilist, driver.
AUTOMOBILÍSTICO adj. automobilistic.
AUTOMÓVEL s.m. car.
AUTONOMIA s.m. autonomy.
AUTÔNOMO adj. autonomous.
AUTOPEÇA s.f. car part.

AUTOPROMOÇÃO *s.f.* self-promotion.
AUTÓPSIA *s.f.* autopsy.
AUTOR *s.m.* author.
AUTORIA *s.f.* authorship.
AUTORIDADE *s.f.* authority.
AUTORITÁRIO *adj.* authoritarian, despotic.
AUTORITARISMO *s.m.* authoritarianism.
AUTORIZAÇÃO *s.f.* authorization.
AUTORIZADO *adj.* authorized.
AUTORIZAR *v.* to authorize.
AUTORIZÁVEL *adj.* authorizable.
AUTORRETRATO *s.m.* self-portrait.
AUTOSSUFICIENTE *adj.* self-sufficient.
AUTOSSUSTENTÁVEL *adj.* self-sustainable.
AUTOTROFIA *s.f.* autotrophy.
AUTOTROFISMO *s.m.* autotrophism.
AUTUAÇÃO *s.f.* filing.
AUXILIADOR *s.2gên.* auxiliary, helper / *adj.2gên.* auxiliary, helper.
AUXILIAR *adj.* auxiliary / *s.2gên.* assistant.
AV *abrev.* Ave.
AVACALHAÇÃO *s.f.* demoralization, negligence, sloppiness.
AVACALHAR *v.* to botch; to demoralize, depress.
AVAL *s.m.* surety, guaranty.
AVALANCHE *s.m.* avalanche.
AVALIAÇÃO *s.f.* evaluation, estimation.
AVALIADO *adj.* evaluated, appraised.
AVALIADOR *s.m.* appraiser, evaluator / *adj.* appraiser, evaluator.
AVALIAR *v.* to evaluate, to assess, to estimate, to rate.
AVANÇADO *adj.* advanced, well on, aged.
AVANÇAR *v.* to advance; to proceed.
AVANÇO *s.m.* advance, advancement; headway (progresso).
AVANTAJADO *adj.* superior, strong, stout.
AVANTAJAR *v.* to outreach, to exceed, to surpass.
AVANTE *adv.* to go forward, to go on.
AVARENTO *s.m.* stingy, miser, close-fisted / *adj.* stingy, miser, close-fisted.
AVAREZA *s.f.* avarice, miserliness.
AVASSALADOR *s.m.* conqueror, dominator / *adj.* conqueror, dominator.
AVASSALAR *v.* to vassalize.
AVATAR *s.m.* avatar
AVE *s.f.* bird.

AVEIA *s.f.* oat, oatmeal.
AVELÃ *s.f.* hazelnut.
AVELUDADO *adj.* velvety.
AVELUDAR *v.* to give appearance of velvet.
AVE-MARIA *s.f.* hail-mary.
AVENIDA *s.f.* avenue.
AVENTAL *s.m.* apron.
AVENTURA *s.f.* adventure.
AVENTURADO *adj.* adventurous, brave; blissful (bem-aventurado).
AVENTURAR *v.* to risk, to venture, to chance.
AVENTUREIRO *s.m.* adventurer / *adj.* adventurer.
AVERIGUAÇÃO *s.f.* inquiry, investigation.
AVERIGUAR *v.* to inquire, to investigate.
AVERMELHADO *adj.* reddish, russet.
AVERMELHAR *v.* to redden.
AVERSÃO *s.f.* aversion.
AVESSO *adj.* opposite, contrary, converse / *adv.* inside out (pelo avesso).
AVESTRUZ *s.m.* ostrich.
AVIAÇÃO *s.f.* aviation.
AVIADOR *s.m.* aviator, aeronaut, pilot.
AVIAMENTO *s.m.* accessories, notions; dispatching.
AVIÃO *s.m.* airplane.
AVIDEZ *s.f.* avidity.
ÁVIDO *adj.* avidity.
AVIGORAMENTO *s.m.* invigoration.
AVIGORAR *v.* to invigorate.
AVINDO *adj.* in harmony, in agreement.
AVIR *v.* to adjust, to conciliate.
AVISADO *adj.* advised; discreet, wise, sage.
AVISAR *v.* to warn.
AVISO *s.m.* notice, warning.
AVISTAR *v.* to sight.
AVIVAMENTO *s.m.* enlivenment, revival, invigoration.
AVIVAR *v.* to vivify, to encourage.
AVÓ *s.f.* grandmother.
AVÔ *s.m.* grandfather.
AVOAÇAR *v.* to rouse, to frighten.
AVOADO *adj.* senseless, crackbrained; dizzy, giddy.
AVOAR *v.* to fly.
AVOLUMAR *v.* to increase volume of, to take up space.
AVÓS *s.m. pl.* grandparents.
AVULSO *adj.* separate, detached, sundry.

AVULTAR *v.* to increase, to augment, to enlarge.
AXILA *s.f.* armpit.
AZAFAMAR *v.* to hasten, to hurry.
AZAR *s.m.* bad luck.
AZARADO *adj.* unlucky, luckless.
AZARAR *v.* to cause misfortune, to bring bad luck.
AZEDADO *adj.* sour; angry.
AZEDAR *v.* to acidify, to sour, to ferment.
AZEDO *s.m.* sour, acid, sharp, tart.
AZEDUME *s.m.* sourness, acidity.
AZEITE *s.m.* olive-oil.
AZEITONA *s.f.* olive.
AZIA *s.f.* heartburn.
AZUCRINADO *adj.* bothering, annoying.
AZUCRINANTE *adj.* botherer, annoyer.
AZUCRINAR *v.* to annoy, to bother.
AZUL *s.m.* blue / *adj.* blue.
AZULADO *adj.* blueish, of blue color.
AZULÃO *s.m.* bluebird.
AZULEJADO *adj.* tiled.
AZULEJAR *v.* to tile.
AZULEJO *s.m.* glazed tile.

Bb

B, b *s.m.* the second letter of the Portuguese alphabet.
BABA *s.f.* dribble saliva; slobber.
BABÁ *s.f.* babysitter.
BABACA *adj.* stupid / *s.2gên.* fool, stupid.
BABADO *s.m.* frill, spoony.
BABADOR *s.m.* bib, dickey, pinafore.
BABÃO *s.m.* slobberer.
BABAR *v.* to dribble, to slobber.
BABEL *s.f.* Babel.
BABILÔNIA *s.f.* Babylon, Babel.
BABILÔNICO *s.m.* Babylonian / *adj.* Babylonian, Babilonic.
BABOSA *s.f.* aloe.
BABOSEIRA *s.f.* folly, nonsense.
BABUCHA *s.f.* babouche, baboosh.
BABUGEM *s.f.* drool, saliva, slobber.
BABUÍNO *s.m.* baboon.
BACALHAU *s.m.* cod, codfish, salt cod.
BACALHOADA *s.f.* whipping, beating.
BACAMARTE *s.m.* blunderbuss.
BACANA *adj.2gên.* great, nice, posh.
BACANAL *s.m.* bacchanal, orgy / *adj.* bacchanal.
BACHAREL *s.m.* bachelor.
BACHARELADO *m.q.* bacharel.
BACHARELANDO *s.m.* baccalaureate.
BACIA *s.f.* basin, wash-basin bowl.
BACILO *s.m.* bacillus, bacterium.
BAÇO *adj.* dull / *s.m.* spleen.
BACON *s.m.* bacon.
BACTÉRIA *s.f.* bacterium, bacillus, microbe.
BACTERICIDA *s.m.* bactericide / *adj.2gên.* bactericidal.
BADALAÇÃO *s.f.* flattery.
BADALADO *adj.* popular, well-liked, admired, fashionable, stylish.
BADALAR *v.* to ring, to toll, to blab.
BADERNA *s.f.* commotion, riot.
BADERNAR *v.* to frolic, to laze, to riot.
BADULAQUE *s.m.* trinket.
BAFAFÁ *s.m.* altercation; quarrel.
BAFEJAR *v.* to blow, to fan; to incite, to instigate.
BAFO *s.m.* breath, respiration; exhalation.
BAFÔMETRO *s.m.* breathalyzer.
BAFORADA *s.f.* whiff, puff.
BAGA *s.f.* berry; drop.
BAGACEIRA *s.f.* remainder, residue.
BAGAÇO *s.m.* bagasse.

BAGAGEIRO s.m. porter, luggage van, car rack, roofrack.
BAGAGEM s.f. luggage.
BAGATELA s.f. bagatelle, trifle, trinket.
BAGO s.m. berry; testicle.
BAGRE s.m. catfish; hammerhead (cabeça-de-bagre).
BAGUETE s.f. baguette.
BAGULHO s.m. trash.
BAGUNÇA s.f. mess, shamble.
BAGUNÇADO adj. messy.
BAGUNÇAR v. to mess up.
BAGUNCEIRO s.m. hooligan, rowdy / adj. hooligan, rowdy.
BAIA s.f. pen, stall.
BAÍA s.f. bay, gulf.
BAIANO s.m. Bahian / adj. Bahian.
BAILADO s.m. dance, ballroom.
BAILAR v. to dance.
BAILARINO s.m. dancer.
BAILE s.f. dance, ball.
BAINHA s.f. scabbard, sheath; hem, cuff.
BAIONETA s.f. bayonet, side-arm.
BAIRRISMO s.m. provincialism, localism.
BAIRRISTA s.2gên. provincialist / adj. regional.
BAIRRO s.m. district, neighborhood.
BAITA adj.2gên. enormous.
BAIXA s.f. decrease, reduction, low, lowering depression; loss.
BAIXADA s.f. plain, marshland.
BAIXAR v. to lower, to download, to put down.
BAIXARIA s.f. despicable behavior.
BAIXISTA s.2gên. bassist.
BAIXO adj. low, short / s.m. bassguitar / adv. low.
BAJULAÇÃO s.f. flattery, fawning adulation.
BAJULADOR s.m. toady, flatterer / adj. smarmy.
BAJULAR v. to flatter, to fawn.
BALA s.f. bullet, shot (arma); candy, sweet (doces).
BALAÇO s.m. gunshot.
BALACOBACO s.m. terrific, swell.
BALADA s.f. party.
BALAIO s.m. hamper; buttocks.
BALANÇA s.f. scales, balance, equilibrium.
BALANÇAR v. to balance, to sway.
BALANCEAMENTO s.m. swaying, swinging.
BALANCEAR v. to balance, to sway.

BALANÇO s.m. balance, swinging; vacillation.
BALÃO s.m. balloon.
BALAÚSTRE s.m. banister, baluster.
BALBUCIAR v. to babble, to stammer.
BALBUCIO s.m. stuttering, stammering.
BALBÚRDIA s.f. mess, pandemonium.
BALBURDIAR v. to confuse, to confound.
BALCÃO s.m. balcony.
BALDE s.m. bucket.
BALDEAÇÃO s.f. transshipment, decanting.
BALDEAR v. to transship, to decant, to transfer.
BALDIO s.m. wasteland, fallow land.
BALÉ s.m. ballet.
BALEIA s.f. whale.
BALELA s.f. rumor, unfounded report.
BALISTA s.f. catapult.
BALÍSTICA s.f. ballistics.
BALIZA s.f. landmark, milestone.
BALIZADO adj. signalised, marked.
BALIZAR v. to signalise, to mark.
BALNEÁRIO s.m. bathing resort.
BALOFO adj. puffy, plump, fatty (coloquial).
BALSA s.f. raft.
BALSAMAR v. to aromatize, to scent.
BÁLSAMO s.m. balm, balsam.
BALUARTE s.m. rampart.
BAMBA adj.2gên. expert provoker / s.f. lax, floppy.
BAMBO adj. slack, weak.
BAMBOLÊ s.m. hula hoop.
BAMBOLEAR v. to wobble, to falter.
BAMBU s.m. bamboo.
BAMBUZAL s.m. bamboo grove.
BANAL adj. banal.
BANALIDADE s.f. banality, vulgarity.
BANALIZAR v. to banalize, to vulgarize.
BANANA s.f. banana.
BANANEIRA s.f. banana tree.
BANCA s.f. desk, board.
BANCADA s.f. row of seats, tier; workbench.
BANCAR v. to finance, to pay for, to play.
BANCÁRIO s.m. banking (profissão), bank clerk (atendente).
BANCARROTA s.f. bankruptcy.
BANCO s.m. bench (assento); bank.
BANDA s.f. band, side, flank.
BANDAGEM s.f. dressing, bandaging.
BANDEIRA s.f. flag.

BANDEIRANTE *s.m.* trailbrazer / *s.f.* brownie.
BANDEIRINHA *s.2gên.* pennant.
BANDEJA *s.f.* tray.
BANDIDO *s.m.* bandit, gangster, outlaw.
BANDO *s.m.* band, gang.
BANDOLEIRO *s.m.* outlaw, brigand.
BANGALÔ *s.m.* bungalow.
BANGUELA *s.2gên.* toothless; stutterer / *adj.2gên.* toothless; stutterer.
BANHA *s.f.* fat, lard.
BANHAR *v.* to bath, to wet.
BANHEIRA *s.f.* bathtub.
BANHEIRO *s.m.* bathroom, WC.
BANHO *s.m.* shower (de chuveiro), bath (de banheira).
BANHO-MARIA *s.m.* bain-marie.
BANIDO *s.m.* outcast, exile / *adj.* outcast, exile.
BANIR *v.* to banish.
BANQUEIRO *s.m.* banker.
BANQUETA *s.f.* stool.
BANQUETE *s.m.* banquet, feast.
BAQUE *s.m.* thud, plunk.
BAQUEADO(A) *adj.* under the weather, sick.
BAQUEAR *v.* to tumble, to plop.
BAQUETA *s.f.* drumstick.
BAR *s.m.* bar, pub.
BARALHAR *v.* shuffle; confuse, disorder.
BARALHO *s.m.* pack of cards.
BARÃO *s.m.* baron.
BARATA *s.f.* cockroach.
BARATEAR *v.* to undersell, to undervalue.
BARATO *adj.* cheap.
BARBA *s.f.* beard.
BARBANTE *s.m.* string.
BARBARIDADE *s.f.* barbarity.
BARBARISMO *s.m.* barbarism.
BÁRBARO *adj.* barbarian.
BARBEADOR *s.m.* shaver.
BARBEAR-SE *v.* to shave.
BARBEARIA *s.f.* barbershop.
BARBECUE *s.f.* barbecue sauce (molho).
BARBEIRAGEM *s.f.* bad driving.
BARBEIRO *s.m.* barber.
BARBICHA *s.f.* small beard, goatee.
BARBUDO *adj.* bearded.
BARCA *s.f.* barge.
BARCAÇA *s.f.* barge.
BARCELONA *s.f.* Barcelona.
BARCO *s.m.* boat.
BARGANHA *s.f.* bargain.

BARGANHADO *adj.* swapped; bartered; swindled.
BARGANHAR *v.* to bargain.
BAROMÉTRICO *adj.* barometric.
BARÔMETRO *s.m.* barometer.
BARONESA *s.f.* baroness.
BARQUEIRO *s.m.* boatman.
BARRA *s.f.* bar.
BARRACA *s.f.* tent.
BARRACÃO *s.m.* shed, large tent.
BARRACO *s.m.* hut, shanty.
BARRADO *adj.* barred, mudded.
BARRAGEM *s.f.* dam; din.
BARRANCO *s.m.* ravine.
BARRAR *v.* to bar, to block.
BARREIRA *s.f.* barrier.
BARRICADA *s.f.* barricade.
BARRIGA *s.f.* belly.
BARRIGUDO(A) *adj.* potbellied.
BARRIL *s.m.* barrel.
BARRO *s.m.* mud, clay.
BARROCO *adj.* Barroque.
BARULHEIRA *s.f.* uproar, racket.
BARULHENTO *adj.* noisy.
BARULHO *s.m.* noise.
BASE *s.f.* base.
BÁSICO *adj.* basic.
BASQUETE *s.m.* basketball.
BASQUETEBOL *s.m.* basketball.
BASSÊ *s.m.* dachshund.
BASTA *interj.* enough.
BASTANTE *adj.* enough / *adv.* enough, quite, plenty.
BASTÃO *s.m.* stick.
BASTAR *v.* to be enough.
BASTARDO *adj.* bastard / *s.m.* bastard, illegitimate child.
BASTIDORES *s.m. pl.* backstage.
BATALHA *s.f.* battle.
BATALHADOR(A) *s.m.* fighter, warrior / *adj.* fighter, warrior.
BATALHAR *v.* to battle, to combat.
BATATA *s.f.* potato.
BATE-BOCA *s.m.* squabble, quarrel, argument.
BATEDEIRA *s.f.* beater; mixer.
BATEDOR *s.m.* beater.
BATEDOURO *s.m.* washboard.
BATENTE *s.m.* doorpost.
BATE-PAPO *s.m.* chat.
BATER *v.* to beat, to hit.

BATERIA *s.f.* battery; drums.
BATERISTA *s.2gên.* drummer, drums player.
BATIDA *s.f.* beat.
BATIDO *s.m.* beaten, hit / *adj.* trite, cliché.
BATINA *s.f.* cassock.
BATISMAL *adj.* baptismal.
BATISMO *s.m.* baptism, christening.
BATIZADO(A) *adj.* baptized.
BATIZAR *v.* to baptize, to christen.
BATOM *s.m.* lipstick.
BATUCADA *s.f.* beat, rhythm.
BATUCAR *v.* to drum.
BATUTA *s.f.* baton, wand.
BAÚ *s.m.* trunk.
BAUNILHA *s.f.* vanilla.
BAZAR *s.m.* bazaar, market.
BAZUCA *s.f.* bazooka.
BÊ-Á-BÁ *s.m.* alphabet.
BEATIFICAÇÃO *s.f.* beatification.
BEATIFICAR *v.* beatify.
BEATO *adj.* pious person, devout.
BÊBADO *adj.* drunkard.
BEBÊ *s.2gên.* baby.
BEBEDEIRA *s.f.* drinking bout, binge.
BEBEDOURO *s.m.* drinking fountain.
BEBER *v.* to drink.
BEBERICAR *v.* to sup, to bib.
BEBERRÃO *s.m.* drinker, drunkard.
BEBIDA *s.f.* drink.
BEBÍVEL *adj.* potable.
BECA *s.f.* judge's robe, toga.
BECO *s.m.* alley.
BEDELHAR *v.* to interfere, to meddle.
BEDELHO *s.m.* bolt, latch, lad, urchin.
BEDUÍNO(A) *s.m.* Bedouin / *adj.* Bedouin.
BEGE *adj.2gên.* beige / *s.m.* beige.
BEGÔNIA *s.f.* begonia.
BEHAVIORISMO *s.m.* behaviorism, behaviourism.
BEHAVIORISTA *s.2gên.* behaviorist, behaviourist.
BEICINHO *s.m.* small lip.
BEIÇO *s.m.* lip.
BEIÇUDO(A) *adj.* big lipped.
BEIJA-FLOR *s.m.* hummingbird.
BEIJAR *v.* to kiss.
BEIJO *s.m.* kiss.
BEIJOCA *s.f.* buss, smack.
BEIJOCAR *v.* to buss, to smack.
BEIJOQUEIRO(A) *adj.* kisser.
BEIRA *s.f.* edge.

BEIRADA *s.f.* margin, border.
BEIRAL *s.m.* eave.
BEIRA-MAR *s.f.* seaside.
BEIRAR *v.* to edge.
BEISEBOL *s.m.* baseball.
BELAS-ARTES *s.f. pl.* fine arts.
BELDADE *s.f.* beauty, belle.
BELEZA *s.f.* beauty.
BELGA *adj.* Belgian / *s.2gên.* Belgian.
BÉLGICA *s.f.* Belgium.
BELICHE *s.m.* bunk, bunkbed.
BÉLICO *adj.* bellicose, warlike.
BELIGERÂNCIA *s.f.* belligerence.
BELIGERANTE *adj.* belligerent.
BELISCÃO *s.m.* pinch.
BELISCAR *v.* to nip, to pinch.
BELO(A) *adj.* beautiful.
BEL-PRAZER *s.m.* free will, liking.
BELTRANO *s.m.* so and so, someone.
BEM *adv.* well, good, nice / *s.m.* good, goodness.
BEM-AFORTUNADO *adj.* good-fortuned.
BEM-AMADO *s.m.* well-loved / *adj.* well-loved.
BEM-AVENTURADO *adj.* blessed, lucky.
BEM-AVENTURANÇA *s.f.* bliss, blessedness.
BEM-BOM *s.m.* comfort, ease.
BEM-CASADO *adj.* well married
BEM-CONCEITUADO(A) *adj.* reputable.
BEM-CRIADO *adj.* well-raised.
BEM-DISPOSTO(A) *adj.* fresh.
BEM-EDUCADO *adj.* well-educated, polite.
BEM-ESTAR *s.m.* well-being, comfort.
BEM-HUMORADO(A) *adj.* good-humored, good-humoured.
BEM-ME-QUER *s.m.* daisy.
BEM-NASCIDO *adj.* well-born, noble.
BEM-QUERER *s.m.* love, affection.
BEM-SUCEDIDO *adj.* successful.
BEM-TE-VI *s.m.* tyrant flycatcher.
BEM-VINDO *adj.* welcome.
BÊNÇÃO *s.f.* blessing.
BENDITO *adj.* blessed.
BENDIZER *v.* to praise, to bless, to glorify.
BENEFICÊNCIA *s.f.* beneficence, charity.
BENEFICENTE *adj.* beneficent, charitable.
BENEFICIADO(A) *s.m.* beneficiary / *adj.* beneficiary.
BENEFICIAMENTO *s.m.* benefaction, improvement.

BENEFICIAR *v.* to benefit.
BENEFÍCIO *s.m.* benefit.
BENÉFICO(A) *adj. m.q.* beneficente.
BENEVOLÊNCIA *s.f.* benevolence.
BENEVOLENTE *adj.* benevolent.
BENÉVOLO *adj.* benevolent, kind, charitable.
BENFEITOR *s.m.* benefactor.
BENFEITORIA *s.f.* improvement, melioration.
BENGALA *s.f.* walking stick.
BENIGNIDADE *s.f.* benignity, gentleness.
BENIGNO *adj.* benign.
BENJAMIM *s.m.* youngest son; adapter, adaptor.
BENQUISTO *adj.* beloved, esteemed.
BENS *s.m.* goods.
BENTO *adj.* sacred.
BENZEDEIRO *s.m.* sorcerer, healer.
BENZENO *s.m.* benzene.
BENZER *v.* to bless, to consecrate.
BERÇÁRIO *s.m.* nursery, maternity ward.
BERÇO *s.m.* cradle.
BERGAMOTA *s.f.* bergamot, tangerine, mandarin.
BERIMBAU *s.m.* berimbau.
BERINGELA *s.f.* aubergine.
BERINJELA *s.f. m.q.* beringela.
BERLIM *s.f.* Berlin.
BERMUDAS *s.f. pl.* shorts.
BERRANTE *adj.* bleating, howling, flashy.
BERRAR *v.* to bellow, to cry, to shout.
BERRO *s.m.* bleat, shriek, bray.
BERRUGA *s.f.* wart.
BESOURO *s.m.* beetle.
BESTA *adj.* stupid / *s.2gên.* mare, mule.
BESTEIRA *s.f.* barney, argument; boob.
BETERRABA *s.f.* beetroot.
BETONEIRA *s.f.* cement mixer.
BETUME *s.m.* asphalt.
BEXIGA *s.f.* bladder; balloon.
BEZERRA *s.f.* heifer.
BEZERRO *s.m.* calf.
BIBELÔ *s.m.* bibelot.
BÍBLIA *s.f.* Bible.
BÍBLICO *adj.* biblical.
BIBLIOGRAFIA *s.f.* bibliography.
BIBLIOGRÁFICO(A) *adj.* bibliographic.
BIBLIOTECA *s.f.* library.
BIBLIOTECÁRIO(A) *s.m.* librarian.
BICA *s.f.* tap.

BICAR *v.* to peck.
BICARBONATO *s.m.* bicarbonate.
BICENTENÁRIO *s.m.* bicentenary / *adj.* bicentenary.
BÍCEPS *s.m. pl.* biceps.
BICHA *s.2gên.* queer, faggot.
BICHANO *s.m.* kitten, puss.
BICHARADA *s.f.* animals collectively.
BICHO *s.m.* animal.
BICICLETA *s.f.* bicycle.
BICICLETÁRIO *s.m.* bicycle racks.
BICO *s.m.* beak.
BICUDO *adj.* angry, surly.
BIDÊ *s.m.* bidet.
BIDIMENSIONAL *adj.* two-dimensional, bidimensional.
BIENAL *s.f.* biennial / *adj.* biennial.
BIFÁSICO *adj.* biphasic.
BIFE *s.m.* steak.
BIFURCAÇÃO *s.f.* bifurcation.
BIFURCAR *v.* to bifurcate.
BIGAMIA *s.f.* bigamy.
BÍGAMO *s.m.* bigamist / *adj.* bigamist.
BIGODE *s.m.* moustache.
BIGORNA *s.f.* anvil.
BIJUTERIA *s.f.* costume jewellery.
BILATERAL *adj.* bilateral.
BILE *s.f.* bile.
BILHÃO *s.m.* billion.
BILHAR *s.m.* billiards.
BILHETE *s.m.* ticket (passagem); note (recado).
BILHETERIA *s.f.* box office.
BILÍNGUE *adj.* bilingual.
BILIONÁRIO *s.m.* billionaire / *adj.* billionaire.
BIMESTRAL *adj.2gên.* bimonthly.
BIMESTRE *s.m.* bimester.
BIMOTOR *adj.* bimotor.
BINÁRIO *adj.* binary.
BINGO *s.m.* bingo, game of chance.
BINÓCULO *s.m.* binocular, glass.
BIOCOMBUSTÍVEL *s.m.* biofuel.
BIODIESEL *s.m.* biodiesel.
BIODIVERSIDADE *s.f.* biodiversity.
BIOFÍSICA *s.f.* biophysics.
BIOGRAFIA *s.f.* biography.
BIOLOGIA *s.f.* biology.
BIOMBO *s.m.* screen.
BIÓPSIA *s.f.* biopsy.
BIÓTIPO *s.m.* biotype.
BIPARTIÇÃO *s.f.* bipartition.

BIPE *s.m.* pager.
BÍPEDE *adj.* biped.
BIPOLAR *adj.* bipolar.
BIQUÍNI *s.m.* bikini.
BIRITA *s.f.* tipple.
BIRRA *s.f.* tantrum.
BIRUTA *adj.2gên.* crazy, lunatic / *s.f.* windsock (aeronáutica).
BIS *interj.* encore.
BISAVÓ *s.f.* great-grandmother.
BISAVÔ *s.m.* great-grandfather.
BISAVÓS *s.m. pl.* great-grandparents.
BISBILHOTAR *v.* to snoop.
BISBILHOTEIRO *s.m.* snoop / *adj.* snoop.
BISCATE *s.m.* odd job.
BISCOITO *s.m.* biscuit, cookie, cracker.
BISNAGA *s.f.* tube.
BISNETA *s.f.* great-granddaughter.
BISNETO *s.m.* great-grandson.
BISPO *s.m.* bishop.
BISSEXTO(A) *adj.* leap year, bissextile.
BISSEXUADO *adj.* bisexed.
BISSEXUAL *s.2gên.* bisexual / *adj.2gên.* bisexual.
BISSEXUALIDADE *s.f.* bisexuality.
BISTECA *s.f.* porterhouse.
BISTRÔ *s.m.* bistro.
BISTURI *s.m.* scalpel.
BITOLA *s.f.* gauge.
BITOLADO(A) *adj.* narrow-minded.
BIZARRO *adj.* bizarre.
BLASFEMAR *v.* to curse, to blaspheme.
BLASFÊMIA *s.f.* blasphemy.
BLAZER *s.m.* blazer.
BLECAUTE *s.m.* power cut; black-out.
BLINDADO(A) *adj.* armoured.
BLINDAGEM *s.f.* armour, screening.
BLINDAR *v.* to armour.
BLITZ *s.f.* police road block; blitzkrieg (militar).
BLOCO *s.m.* block.
BLOG *s.m.* blog.
BLOGAR *v.* to blog.
BLOGUEIRO *s.m.* blogger.
BLOQUEADO *adj.* blocked.
BLOQUEADOR *s.m.* blocker.
BLOQUEAR *v.* to blockade.
BLOQUEIO *s.m.* block.
BLUSA *s.f.* shirt.
BOATE *s.f.* club, nightclub.
BOATO *s.m.* rumour.
BOA-VIDA *s.2gên.* idler, lazybones / *adj.2gên.* idler, lazybones.
BOBAGEM *s.f.* silliness, nonsense, trash.
BOBINA *s.f.* reel, bobbin.
BOBO(A) *adj.* silly.
BOCA *s.f.* mouth.
BOCADINHO *s.m.* mite, modicum.
BOCADO *s.m.* mouthful, piece, morsel.
BOCAL *s.m.* mouth, mouthpiece, nozzle.
BOÇAL *adj.* ignorant, rude.
BOCEJAR *v.* to yawn.
BOCEJO *s.m.* yawn.
BOCHECHA *s.f.* cheek.
BOCHECHAR *v.* to rinse the mouth.
BOCHECHUDO *s.m.* round-cheeked.
BODA *s.f.* wedding, marriage.
BODE *s.m.* goat.
BOFETADA *s.f.* slap in the face.
BOFETÃO *s.m.* punch, blow with the fist.
BOI *s.m.* ox.
BOIA *s.f.* buoy.
BOIADA *s.f.* herd of cattle.
BOIAR *v.* to float.
BOICOTADO *adj.* boycotted.
BOICOTAR *v.* to boycott.
BOLA *s.f.* ball.
BOLACHA *s.f.* biscuit, cracker, cookies.
BOLADA *s.f.* kick, stake, jackpot.
BOLERO *s.m.* bolero.
BOLETIM *s.m.* report.
BOLHA *s.f.* blister, bubble.
BOLICHE *s.m.* bowling.
BOLINHO *s.m.* scone.
BOLÍVIA *s.f.* Bolivia.
BOLIVIANO(A) *s.m.* Bolivian / *adj.* Bolivian.
BOLO *s.m.* cake.
BOLOR *s.m.* mould.
BOLOTA *s.f.* acorn.
BOLSA *s.f.* bag.
BOLSO *s.m.* pocket.
BOM(A) *adj.* good, nice.
BOMBA *s.f.* bomb.
BOMBADO(A) *s.m.* muscleman.
BOMBARDEADO *adj.* bombed.
BOMBARDEAR *v.* to bomb.
BOMBARDEIO *s.m.* bombardment.
BOMBEAR *v.* to pump.
BOMBEIRO *s.m.* fireman.
BOMBOM *s.m.* chocolate.
BONDADE *s.m.* goodness.
BONDE *s.m.* tram.

BONDOSO(A) *adj.* kindhearted.
BONÉ *s.m.* cap.
BONECA *s.f.* doll.
BONECO *s.m.* dummy, puppet.
BONITO(A) *adj.* pretty.
BÔNUS *s.m.* bonus.
BOQUIABERTO *adj.* dumbfounded.
BORBOLETA *s.f.* butterfly.
BORBULHA *s.f.* bubble, bleb; acne, pimple.
BORBULHAR *v.* to bubble.
BORBULHENTO *adj.* pimpled, gushing.
BORDA *s.f.* border, fringe, brim.
BORDADA *s.f.* tack, board, border.
BORDADEIRA *s.f.* embroideress.
BORDADO *s.m.* embroidery / *adj.* embroidered.
BORDÃO *s.m.* staff.
BORDAR *v.* to embroider.
BORDEL *s.m.* brothel.
BORDO *s.m.* maple (árvore); log (navegação).
BORDOADA *s.f.* strike, blow, knock.
BOROCOXÔ *adj.* listless, inert.
BORRA *s.f.* dregs, lees.
BORRACHA *s.f.* rubber, eraser.
BORRACHUDO *adj.* bulgy; rubbery.
BORRÃO *s.m.* blot, stain, sketch.
BORRAR *v.* to blot.
BORRIFAR *v.* to sprinkle.
BORRIFO *s.m.* sprinkling, drizzle.
BOSQUE *s.m.* forest, woods.
BOSSA *s.f.* bump, hump.
BOTA *s.f.* boot.
BOTÂNICA *s.f.* botany.
BOTÂNICO *s.m.* botanist.
BOTÃO *s.m.* button.
BOTAR *v.* to last, to cast, to set.
BOTE *s.m.* boat.
BOTEQUIM *s.m.* bar, tavern.
BOVINO *s.m.* bovine / *adj.* bovine.
BOXE *s.m.* boxing.
BOXEADOR *s.m.* boxer.
BOXEAR *v.* to box.
BRAÇADA *s.f.* armful.
BRAÇADEIRA *s.f.* armband.
BRACELETE *s.m.* bracelet.
BRAÇO *s.m.* arm.
BRAÇUDO *s.m.* brawny / *adj.* brawny.
BRADAR *v.* to shout.
BRAGUILHA *s.f.* fly (calça).
BRAILE *s.m.* Braille.
BRANCO(A) *adj.* white / *s.m.* white.

BRANQUEAR *v.* to whiten.
BRASA *s.f.* hot coal.
BRASEIRO *s.m.* brazier.
BRASIL *s.m.* Brazil.
BRASILEIRISMO *s.m.* Brazilianism.
BRASILEIRO(A) *adj.* Brazilian / *s.m.* Brazilian.
BRAVATA *s.f.* bravado.
BRAVATEAR *v.* to defy, to provoke, to challenge.
BRAVATEIRO *s.m.* swaggerer, boaster, braggart / *adj.* swaggerer, boaster, braggart.
BRAVEJAR *v.* to rage, to fume.
BRAVEZA *s.f.* ferocity, savagery.
BRAVO(A) *adj.* angry / *interj.* bravo.
BRAVURA *s.f.* bravery, courage.
BRECAR *v.* to stop, to brake.
BRECHA *s.f.* breach, gap.
BRECHÓ *s.m.* garage sale.
BREGA *adj.* corny, tacky, excessive.
BREJO *s.m.* marsh.
BREQUE *s.m.* brake.
BREVE *adj.* short.
BREVIDADE *s.f.* brevity; crumpet.
BRIGA *s.f.* fight.
BRIGADA *s.f.* brigade.
BRIGADEIRO *s.m.* brigadier; brigadeiro.
BRIGAR *v.* to fight.
BRIGUENTO *adj.* belligerent.
BRILHANTE *adj.* bright / *s.m.* diamond.
BRILHANTINA *s.f.* brilliantine.
BRILHANTISMO *s.m.* brilliancy, splendour.
BRILHAR *v.* to shine.
BRILHO *s.m.* brightness, shine.
BRIM *s.m.* denim.
BRINCADEIRA *s.f.* fun.
BRINCALHÃO(ONA) *adj.* playful / *s.m.* joker.
BRINCAR *v.* to play, to have fun.
BRINCO *s.m.* earring.
BRINDAR *v.* to toast.
BRINDE *s.m.* toast.
BRINQUEDO *s.m.* toy.
BRIO *s.m.* self-respect.
BRIOCHE *s.m.* brioche.
BRISA *s.f.* breeze.
BRITADEIRA *s.f.* jackhammer.
BRITÂNICO *adj.* British / *s.m.* British.
BRITAR *v.* to crush, to grind.
BROA *s.f.* corn mush, corn bread (pão de milho).
BROCA *s.f.* bit, auger, chisel.
BROCAR *v.* to drill, to bore, to perforate.

BROCHA *s.f.* tack, peg; impotent.
BROCHAR *v.* to lose an erection.
BROCHE *s.m.* brooch.
BROCHURA *s.f.* paper-back, brochure.
BRÓCOLIS *s.m.* broccoli.
BRONCA *s.f.* telling off.
BRONCO(A) *adj.* coarse / *s.m.* idiot, dunce.
BRONQUICE *s.f.* stupidity, foolishness.
BRÔNQUIO *s.m.* bronchus.
BRONQUITE *s.f.* bronchitis.
BRONTOSSAURO *s.m.* brontosaurus.
BRONZE *s.m.* bronze.
BRONZEADO(A) *adj.* tanned, suntan.
BRONZEADOR *s.m.* tanning lotion, suntan lotion.
BRONZEAMENTO *s.f.* tanning.
BRONZEAR *v.* to tan.
BROTAMENTO *s.m.* budding, sprouting.
BROTAR *v.* to produce, to sprout, to bud.
BROTINHO *s.m.* small pizza; flapper.
BROTO *s.m.* youngster, bud, sprout.
BROTOEJA *s.f.* rash.
BRUACA *s.f.* travel bag; hag, ugly woman; prostitute.
BRUÇOS *s.m. pl.* face-down, breaststroke (nado de bruços).
BRUMA *s.f.* fog, haze, mystery.
BRUNIDO *s.m.* burnished, polished / *adj.* burnished, polished.
BRUNIR *v.* to burnish, to polish.
BRUSCO *adj.* rough, harsh, brusque.
BRUSQUIDÃO *s.f.* roughness, harshness, brusqueness.
BRUTAL *adj.* brutal.
BRUTALIDADE *s.f.* brutality.
BRUTALIZAR *v.* to brutalize.
BRUTAMONTES *s.m.* brute, yahoo, boor.
BRUTO(A) *adj.* rude, rough, coarse.
BRUXA *s.f.* witch.
BRUXELAS *s.f.* Brussels.
BRUXO *s.m.* wizard.
BUCHO *s.m.* stomach, paunch.
BUÇO *s.m.* down.
BUCÓLICO *adj.* bucolic.
BUDISMO *s.m.* Buddhism.
BUDISTA *s.2gên.* Buddhist / *adj.2gên.* Buddhist.
BUEIRO *s.m.* manhole.
BÚFALO *s.m.* buffalo.
BUFAR *v.* to puff.
BUFÊ *s.m.* sideboard.
BUFFER *s.m.* buffer.
BUGIGANGA *s.f.* trinket.
BUJÃO *s.m.* gas cylinder.
BULA *s.f.* bulla, package insert.
BULBO *s.m.* bulb.
BULDOGUE *s.m.* bull dog.
BULE *s.m.* teapot.
BULGÁRIA *s.f.* Bulgaria.
BÚLGARO *adj.* Bulgarian / *s.m.* Bulgarian.
BULIMIA *s.f.* bulimia.
BULÍMICO *s.m.* bulimic / *adj.* bulimic.
BULIR *v.* to agitate, to move, to stir.
BUMBUM *s.m.* buttocks, behind, buns.
BUMERANGUE *s.m.* boomerang.
BUNDA *s.f.* backside (coloquial).
BUQUÊ *s.m.* bouquet, bunch.
BURACO *s.m.* hole.
BURBUREJAR *v.* to bubble, to gurgle.
BURBURINHO *s.m.* murmuring, rustling.
BURGUÊS(ESA) *adj.* bourgeois / *s.m.* bourgeois.
BURGUESIA *s.f.* bourgeoisie.
BURLA *s.f.* jest, trick, prank.
BURLÃO *s.m.* joker, jester.
BURLAR *v.* to jest, to joke, to tease.
BURLESCO *s.m.* burlesque, mocking, teasing / *adj.* burlesque, mocking, teasing.
BUROCRACIA *s.f.* bureaucracy.
BUROCRATA *s.m.* bureaucrat.
BUROCRÁTICO(A) *adj.* bureaucratic.
BUROCRATIZAÇÃO *s.f.* bureaucratization.
BUROCRATIZAR *v.* to bureaucratize.
BURRADA *s.f.* drove of donkeys; foolish act, nonsense, blunder.
BURRICE *s.f.* stupidity, dullness.
BURRO(A) *adj.* stupid, dumb / *s.m.* donkey.
BUSCA *s.f.* search.
BUSCADOR *s.m.* seeker, investigator.
BUSCAR *v.* to fetch, to seek.
BÚSSOLA *s.f.* compass.
BUSTO *s.m.* bust.
BUTIQUE *s.m.* boutique.
BUZINA *s.f.* horn, honk.
BUZINAR *v.* to honk.
BÚZIO *s.m.* seashell, trumpet.

Cc

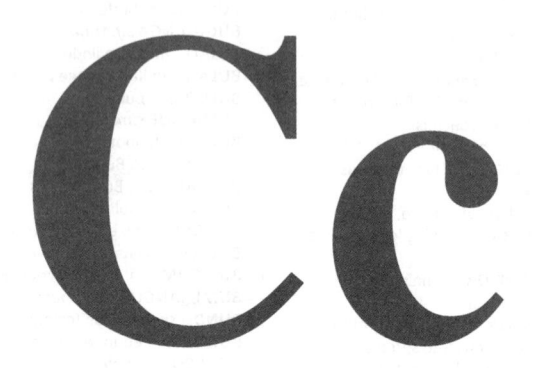

C, c *s.m.* the third letter of the Portuguese alphabet.
CÁ *adv.* here, in this place.
CAATINGA *s.f.* scrubland.
CABAÇA *s.f.* calabash.
CABAÇO *s.m.* bottle; gourd.
CABAL *adj.2gên.* full, complete, as a whole.
CABALA *s.f.* kabbalah.
CABALAR *v.* to cabal, to plot, to intrigue.
CABANA *s.f.* cottage, shack, hut.
CABARÉ *s.m.* cabaret, honky-tonk.
CABEÇA *s.f.* head; the leader, responsible.
CABEÇADA *s.f.* butt; header.
CABEÇA-DE-VENTO *s.2gên.* scatterbrain.
CABEÇA-DURA *s.2gên.* stupid, stubborn, blockhead.
CABEÇAL *s.m.* headband, headboard; head; pillow, cushion.
CABEÇALHO *s.m.* header, heading, pillow, title page.
CABEÇÃO *s.m.* big head, blackcap, headstall.
CABECEAR *v.* to beckon, to nod.
CABECEIRA *s.f.* headband, headboard, head, pillow, cushion.
CABEÇOTE *s.m.* head.
CABEÇUDO(A) *adj.* bigheaded.
CABELEIRA *s.f.* hair; wig; mane / *s.m.* hariness.
CABELEIREIRO(A) *s.m.* hairdresser; stylist; coiffeur.
CABELO *s.m.* hair.
CABELUDO *adj.* hairy.
CABER *v.* to fit.
CABIDE *s.m.* hanger, rack, hook.
CABIDO *adj.* proper, appropriate; fit, suitable.
CABIMENTO *s.m.* suitability, relevancy, pertinence.
CABINA *s.f.* cabin, box, booth.
CABINE *s.f.* cabin, cockpit.
CABISBAIXO(A) *adj.* downcast, depressed.
CABÍVEL *adj.2gên.* reasonable, wise, plausible, appropriate.
CABO *s.m.* doorhandle, holder; cable; commander; cape.
CABOCLO *s.m.* mixed-race Brazilian, ranger, farm hand.
CABO DE GUERRA *s.m.* tug of war.

CABOTAGEM *s.f.* cabotage.
CABRA *s.f.* goat.
CABRA-CEGA *s.f.* blindman's bluff.
CABRA DA PESTE *s.2gên.* corageous, brave.
CABRA-MACHO *s.m.* bully, tough / *adj.* ruffian.
CABREIRO(A) *adj.* suspicious.
CABRESTO *s.m.* halter, frenum.
CABRITO *s.m.* young goat, kid.
CÁBULA *s.f.* lazy student, truant.
CABULAR *v.* to truancy, to skip classes.
CABULOSO *adj.* unlucky, tiresome, preachy, confused.
CACA *s.f.* feces, excrement.
CAÇA *s.f.* hunting.
CAÇADA *s.f.* hunting party, hunt, chase.
CAÇADO *adj.* hunted, chased; pusued.
CAÇADOR *s.m.* hunter, huntsman; sniper.
CAÇADORA *s.f.* huntress, sportswoman.
CAÇA-DOTES *s.m.* fortune hunter.
CAÇAMBA *s.f.* bucket; dump-cart.
CAÇA-NÍQUEIS *s.m.* shot machine / *adj.* shot machine.
CAÇÃO *s.m.* dogfish, shark.
CAÇAR *v.* to hunt.
CACAREJAR *v.* to cluck.
CACAREJO *s.m.* clucking, cluck, cackling, cackle.
CAÇAROLA *s.f.* saucepan, casserole, skillet.
CAÇA-SUBMARINOS *s.m.* submarine chaser.
CACATUA *s.f.* cockatoo.
CACAU *s.m.* cocoa, cacao.
CACETADA *s.f.* blow, beating, thrashing.
CACETE *s.m.* club; mace; rod; dick.
CACHAÇA *s.f.* white rum, sugar cane liquor.
CACHACEIRO(A) *s.m.* drunkard / *adj.* drunkard.
CACHÊ *s.m.* pay, fee.
CACHEADO *adj.* curly.
CACHEAR *v.* to curl.
CACHECOL *s.m.* scarf.
CACHIMBAR *v.* to smoke a pipe, to trick.
CACHIMBO *s.m.* pipe.
CACHO *s.m.* bunch; curl (cabelo).
CACHOEIRA *s.f.* overfall, waterfall.
CACHORRA *s.f.* bitch, female dog.
CACHORRADA *s.f.* pack of dogs.
CACHORRINHO *s.m.* puppy, young dog
CACHORRO *s.m.* dog.
CACHORRO-QUENTE *s.m.* hot dog.

CACIQUE *s.m.* chief.
CACO *s.m.* fragment.
CAÇOADA *s.f.* making jokes of, mocking.
CAÇOANTE *s.2gên.* mocker, teaser / *adj.* mocking, teasing.
CAÇOAR *v.* to mock, to tease.
CACOETE *s.m.* twitch.
CACOFONIA *s.f.* cacophony.
CACOFONIAR *v.* to make cacophony.
CACOFÔNICO *adj.* cacophonous.
CACOGRAFIA *s.f.* cacography.
CACOGRÁFICO *adj.* cacographycal.
CACTO *s.m.* cactus.
CAÇULA *s.m.* youngest / *adj.* youngest.
CACUNDA *s.f.* back, shoulders, humpback, hump / *s.2gên.* humpback.
CADA *pron.* each, every / *adv.* such, what.
CADARÇO *s.m.* shoelace, shoestring, floss silk.
CADASTRADO *adj.* registered.
CADASTRAL *adj.2gên.* cadastral.
CADASTRAR *v.* to register, to access, to book in, to record.
CADASTRO *s.m.* register, records, official registration.
CADÁVER *s.m.* cadaver, corpse, dead body.
CADÊ *adv.* where is? (coloquial).
CADEADO *s.m.* padlock, lock.
CADEIA *s.f.* chain (de lojas), range (de montanhas), prison, jail, penitentiary.
CADEIÃO *s.m.* carriages.
CADEIRA *s.f.* chair, seat, professorship.
CADEIRAS *s.f. pl.* hips.
CADELA *s.f.* bitch; female dog; slut, prostitute.
CADÊNCIA *s.f.* cadence, cadency.
CADENCIAR *v.* to rhythm, to accent.
CADENCIOSO *adj.* cadence, regular, rhythmic.
CADENTE *adj.2gên.* cadenced, rhythmic; shooting star.
CADERNETA *s.f.* notebook, school register.
CADERNO *s.m.* notebook, book, copybook.
CADETE *s.m.* cadet.
CADUCANTE *adj.2gên.* growing older, decaying, expiring.
CADUCAR *v.* to lapse, to expire, to grow older, to become feeble.
CADUCO *adj.* expired, lapsed, invalid.
CADUQUICE *s.f.* senility, lapse, old aged.
CÃES *s.m. pl.* dogs.

CAFAJESTADA *s.f.* rascality, roguishness, dishonesty.
CAFAJESTE *adj.* boor, roguish, vulgar / *s.2gên.* rogue.
CAFÉ *s.m.* coffee.
CAFÉ COM LEITE *s.m.* white coffee.
CAFÉ DA MANHÃ *s.m.* breakfast.
CAFEÍNA *s.f.* caffeine.
CAFETÃ *s.m.* caftan, kaftan.
CAFETÃO *s.m.* pimp, protector.
CAFETEIRA *s.f.* coffee pot.
CAFEZAL *s.m.* coffee field.
CAFUNÉ *s.m.* caress, affection.
CAFUNGAR *v.* to inhale, to smell.
CÁGADO *s.m.* tortoise, turtle.
CAGANEIRA *s.f.* diarrhea.
CAGAR *v.* to shit, to defecate.
CÃIBRA *s.f.* cramp.
CAÍDA *s.f.* decline, decay, slope, downhill.
CAÍDO *adj.* dejected, fallen, decayed.
CÂIMBRA *s.f. m.q.* cãibra.
CAIMENTO *s.m.* hang, fall, decadence, decay.
CAIPIRA *s.2gên.* peasant, yokel, redneck.
CAIPIRINHA *s.f.* caipirinha; cocktail.
CAIR *v.* to fall, to fall down, to drop, to succumb.
CAIS *s.m.* wharf, quay, dock, pier.
CAIXA *s.f.* box, kit, case, chase, set.
CAIXA-ALTA *s.f.* uppercase.
CAIXA-BAIXA *s.f.* lowercase.
CAIXA-FORTE *s.f.* strongbox.
CAIXÃO *s.m.* coffin.
CAIXA-PRETA *s.f.* black box.
CAIXEIRO *s.m.* cashier.
CAIXOTE *s.m.* packing case, packing box.
CAJADO *s.m.* staff, stick, cane.
CAJU *s.m.* cashew, cashew nut.
CAL *s.f.* lime.
CALA *s.f.* silence, stillness.
CALA-BOCA *s.m.* shut up.
CALABOUÇO *s.m.* dungeon.
CALADÃO *adj.* introverted.
CALADO(A) *adj.* quiet, silent, introverted.
CALAFRIO *s.m.* shiver, chill.
CALAMIDADE *s.f.* calamity; catastrophe, disaster.
CALAMITOSO *adj.* calamitous, catastrophic, disastrous.
CALAR *v.* to keep silent, to get to be quiet.

CALÇA *s.f.* pants, trousers, denim trousers (jeans), racksuit trousers (moletom).
CALÇADA *s.f.* pavement, sidewalk.
CALÇADÃO *s.m.* pedestrian street.
CALÇADO *adj.* paved / *s.m.* footwear.
CALÇAMENTO *s.m.* paving, pavement.
CALCANHAR *s.m.* heel.
CALÇÃO *s.m.* shorts.
CALCAR *v.* to trample, to tread on.
CALÇAR *v.* to put on.
CALÇAS *s.f. pl.* pants, trousers.
CALCINHA *s.f.* panties.
CÁLCIO *s.m.* calcium.
CALÇOLA *s.f.* knicker.
CALCULAR *v.* to calculate, to compute.
CALCULÁVEL *adj.2gên.* computable, countable.
CALCULISTA *s.2gên.* calculating, computer / *adj.* calculating.
CÁLCULO *s.m.* calculation, computation.
CALDA *s.f.* syrup, sauce.
CALDEIRA *s.f.* boiler, kettle.
CALDEIRÃO *s.m.* cauldron.
CALDO *s.m.* broth, soup, sauce.
CALEFAÇÃO *s.f.* calefaction, heating, warming.
CALEIDOSCÓPIO *s.m.* kaleidoscope.
CALEJADO *adj.* callous, horny; experienced, practical.
CALEJAR *v.* to make callous, to harden.
CALENDÁRIO *s.m.* calendar, diary, almanac, chronological list.
CALHA *s.f.* gutter, channel.
CALHAMAÇO *s.m.* voluminous book.
CALHAMBEQUE *s.m.* jalopy, anything old.
CALHAR *v.* to suit, to be just right, to wear well.
CALHORDA *s.2gên.* hoodlum, despicable / *adj.2gên.* hoodlum, despicable.
CALIBRADO *adj.* calibrated.
CALIBRAGEM *s.f.* calibration.
CALIBRAR *v.* to gauge, to standardise.
CÁLICE *s.m.* wine glass, cup, calix.
CÁLIDO *adj.* hot, heated, ardent, burning.
CALIFORNIANO(A) *s.m.* Californian / *adj.* Californian.
CALIGRAFIA *s.f.* calligraphy, handwriting.
CALMA *s.f.* calmness, serenity, tranquility.
CALMANTE *s.m.* sedative, tranquilliser / *adj.2gên.* soothing, sedative.

CALMAR *v.* to calm down, to quiet, to still.
CALMARIA *s.f.* calm, quiet.
CALMO(A) *adj.* calm, quiet, peaceful.
CALO *s.m.* corn, callus.
CALOMBO *s.m.* swelling, knob, pustule.
CALOR *s.m.* heat, warmth.
CALORÃO *s.m.* heat wave, stuffy, airless.
CALORENTO *adj.* hot, warm.
CALORIA *s.f.* calorie.
CALÓRICO *s.m.* caloric / *adj.* caloric.
CALOROSO *adj.* hot, warm, hearty, cordial, friendly.
CALOSIDADE *s.f.* callosity, callousness, hardened skin.
CALOTA *s.f.* cap, hubcap.
CALOTE *s.m.* default, cheat, unpaid loans.
CALOTEAR *v.* to bilk, to cheat.
CALOTEIRO *s.m.* swindler, cheater.
CALOURO(A) *s.m.* fresher, freshman, newbie, beginner.
CALÚNIA *s.f.* slander, calumny, defamatory.
CALUNIADO *s.m.* slandered / *adj.* slandered.
CALUNIADOR *s.m.* calumniator, slanderer / *adj.* defamatory, slanderous.
CALUNIAR *v.* to calumniate, to slander, to defame.
CALVA *s.f.* baldness, bald.
CALVÁRIO *s.m.* calvary.
CALVÍCE *s.f.* baldness.
CALVO *s.m.* bald-headed, hairless / *adj.* bald--headed, hairless
CAMA *s.f.* bed.
CAMACHO *s.m.* cripple / *adj.* crippled.
CAMADA *s.f.* layer.
CAMAFEU *s.m.* cameo.
CAMALEÃO *s.m.* chameleon.
CÂMARA *s.f.* chamber, room.
CAMARADA *s.2gên.* comrade, pal, buddy / *adj.* pally.
CAMARADAGEM *s.f.* camaraderie, fellowship, comradeship.
CAMARÃO *s.m.* shrimp, prawn.
CAMAREIRO *s.m.* cleaner, room servant, housekeeping, steward.
CAMARIM *s.m.* dressing room, backstage.
CAMAROTE *s.m.* teatro cabin, box.
CAMBALEANTE *adj.2gên.* reeling, staggering, dizzy.
CAMBALEAR *v.* to stagger, to reel, to wobble.
CAMBALHOTA *s.f.* somersault, tumble.
CAMBIAR *v.* to change, to exchange, to convert, to gear.
CAMBIÁVEL *adj.2gên.* exchangeable.
CÂMBIO *s.m.* exchange, banknotes, bills, valuta.
CAMBISTA *s.2gên.* moneychanger, exchange dealer; broker, ticket jobber.
CAMBITO *s.m.* gammon, ham.
CAMBRAIA *s.f.* cambric.
CAMBURÃO *s.m.* Black Maria.
CAMELO *s.m.* camel.
CAMELÔ *s.m.* street peddler, hawker, packman.
CÂMERA *s.f.* chamber, room, camera.
CAMINHADA *s.f.* walk, walking, stroll, hike.
CAMINHANTE *s.2gên.* walking / *adj.2gên.* walking.
CAMINHÃO *s.m.* gum benzoin, lorry, truck.
CAMINHAR *v.* to walk.
CAMINHO *s.m.* way, path, road, route.
CAMINHONEIRO *s.m.* truck driver, carman.
CAMINHONETE *s.f.* station wagon, truck.
CAMISA *s.f.* shirt, jacket.
CAMISA DE FORÇA *s.f.* straight jackets, straitjacket.
CAMISÃO *s.m.* long shirt.
CAMISEIRO *s.m.* shirtmaker.
CAMISETA *s.f.* T-shirt, undershirt.
CAMISINHA *s.f.* condom.
CAMISOLA *s.f.* nightshirt, nightdress, nighty, jersey.
CAMPAINHA *s.f.* bell, small bell, handbell.
CAMPANHA *s.f.* campaign.
CAMPEÃO(Ã) *s.m.* champion.
CAMPEONATO *s.m.* championship.
CAMPESINO *adj.* rural, rustic.
CAMPESTRE *adj. m.q.* campesino.
CAMPINA *s.f.* meadow, plain.
CAMPINO *s.m.* farmer, rural worker / *adj.* rural.
CAMPISTA *s.m.* camper.
CAMPO *s.m.* countryside, country, field.
CAMPONÊS *s.m.* peasant, farmer, countryman.
CAMPONESA *s.f.* countrywoman, peasant.
CAMPUS *s.m.* campus.
CAMUFLADO *adj.* camouflaged.
CAMUFLAGEM *s.f.* camouflage, disguise.

CAMUFLAR *v.* to camouflage, to disguise, to mask; to fake.
CAMUNDONGO *s.m.* mouse.
CAMURÇA *s.f.* suede, chamois leather / *adj.* chamois-coloured.
CANA *s.f.* cane, sugar cane.
CANADÁ *s.f.* Canada.
CANA-DE-AÇÚCAR *s.m.* sugar cane.
CANAL *s.m.* channel, waterway, canal.
CANALHA *s.f.* rabble, mob / *adj.2gên.* infamous.
CANALHICE *s.f.* roguishness, rascality.
CANALIZAÇÃO *s.f.* plumbing, canalization, drain.
CANALIZADO *adj.* pipy, canalized.
CANALIZAR *v.* to canalize, to pipe.
CANAPÉ *s.m.* sofa, couch, appetiser.
CANÁRIO *s.m.* canary, canary bird.
CANAVIAL *s.m.* sugar cane field, reed plot.
CANÇÃO *s.f.* song, folksong, ballad.
CANCELA *s.f.* farm gate, gate, barrier.
CANCELADO *adj.* cancelled, invalid.
CANCELAMENTO *s.m.* cancellation, invalidation.
CANCELAR *v.* to cancel, to invalidate, to delete.
CÂNCER *s.m.* cancer; cancer (astrologia).
CANCERÍGENO *adj.* carcinogen.
CANDELABRO *s.m.* candelabrum, candlestick.
CANDIDATAR-SE *v.* to candidate.
CANDIDATO *s.m.* candidate, applicant.
CANDIDATURA *s.f.* candidature, candidacy.
CANDOR *s.m.* whiteness, pureness, innocence.
CANDOROSO *adj.* white, snow-white, pure.
CANECA *s.f.* mug, cup.
CANECADA *s.f.* mugful.
CANECO *s.m.* cup, tankard.
CANELA *s.f.* cinnamon (especiaria); shin (perna).
CANETA *s.f.* pen.
CANGA *s.f.* beach towels.
CANGACEIRO *s.m.* outlaw, highway robber, bandit.
CANGOTE *s.m.* scruff.
CANGURU *s.m.* kangaroo.
CANHÃO *s.m.* cannon, gun.
CANHOTA *s.f.* left hand.
CANHOTO *adj.* left-handed, awkward, clumsy.
CANIBAL *s.2gên.* cannibal, man-eater / *adj.2gên.* cannibal, man-eater.
CANIBALESCO *adj.* cannibalistic, cruel, ferocious.
CANIBALISMO *s.m.* cannibalism, man-eating, anthropophagy.
CANIL *s.m.* kennel, dog shelter.
CANINO *s.m.* canine tooth / *adj.* canine, doglike.
CANIVETE *s.m.* penknife, pocketknife.
CANJA *s.f.* chicken soup, broth.
CANJICA *s.f.* maize porridge.
CANO *s.m.* pipe, tube, connection, bar.
CANOA *s.f.* canoe, boat.
CANÔNICO *adj.2gên.* canonic, canonical.
CANONIZAÇÃO *s.f.* canonisation, sanctification.
CANONIZADOR *s.m.* canonizer, adulator / *adj.* canonising.
CANONIZAR *v.* to canonize, to flatter, to adulate.
CANSAÇO *s.m.* tiredness, fatigue.
CANSADO *adj.* tired, fatigued, weary.
CANSAR *v.* to tire, to fatigue.
CANSATIVO *adj.* tiring, tiresome, fatiguing, stressful.
CANSEIRA *s.f.* tiredness, fatigue, exhaustion.
CANTADA *s.f.* flirting.
CANTAR *v.* to sing, to tune; to flirt.
CANTAROLAR *v.* to sing, to hum.
CANTEIRO *s.m.* stone-mason (obras); flower bed (flores).
CÂNTICO *s.m.* canticle, chant.
CANTIGA *s.f.* song, ditty, ballad.
CANTINA *s.f.* canteen, messroom, mess.
CANTO *s.m.* corner, angle, folk song, song.
CANTOR *s.m.* singer, vocalist.
CANTORIA *s.f.* singing.
CANUDO *s.m.* straw, pipe, tube.
CÃO *s.m.* dog, canine, canis.
CAOLHO *s.m.* one-eyed, cross-eyed / *adj.* one-eyed, cross-eyed.
CAOS *s.m.* chaos.
CAÓTICO *adj.* chaotic, confused.
CAPA *s.f.* cover, cape, cloak.
CAPACETE *s.m.* helmet.

CAPACIDADE *s.f.* capacity, capability, ability, skill.
CAPACITAÇÃO *s.f.* capacity, function.
CAPACITAR *v.* to capacitate, to enable.
CAPAR *v.* to castrate.
CAPATAZ *s.m.* foreman, overseer.
CAPAZ *adj.2gên.* able, capable, skilful.
CAPCIOSO *adj.* catchy, captious, tricky.
CAPELA *s.f.* chapel, little church, sanctuary.
CAPELÃO *s.m.* chaplain, father.
CAPENGA *s.2gên.* cripple, handicapped / *adj.2gên.* lame, crippled.
CAPENGAR *v.* to limp, to hobble.
CAPILAR *adj.2gên.* capillary.
CAPIM *s.m.* grass.
CAPINAR *v.* to weed, to clear off.
CAPITAÇÃO *s.f.* capitation, head tax, poll.
CAPITAL *s.f.* capital, funds, resources / *adj.* capital, essential.
CAPITALISMO *s.m.* capitalism.
CAPITALISTA *s.2gên.* capitalist.
CAPITALIZAÇÃO *s.f.* capitalization.
CAPITALIZAR *v.* to capitalize.
CAPITANIA *s.f.* captaincy, captainship.
CAPITÃO *s.m.* captain, commander.
CAPITULAR *v.* to capitular.
CAPÍTULO *s.m.* chapter, capitulum.
CAPÔ *s.m.* bonnet, hood.
CAPOEIRA *s.f.* hencoop, hutch; capoeira.
CAPOTA *s.f.* hood, bonnet.
CAPOTAR *v.* to overturn, to capsize.
CAPOTE *s.m.* cloack, overcoat, overturn.
CAPRICHAR *v.* to do carefully, to caprice.
CAPRICHO *s.m.* whim, caprice.
CAPRICÓRNIO *s.m.* Capricorn (astrologia).
CÁPSULA *s.f.* capsule.
CAPSULAR *v.* to capsulate / *adj.* capsular.
CAPTAÇÃO *s.f.* collection, stock, storage.
CAPTADO *adj.* perceived.
CAPTAR *v.* to capture, to collect, to pick up.
CAPTURA *s.f.* capture, taking, arrest.
CAPUZ *s.m.* hood, cap, bonnet.
CÁQUI *adj.* khaki.
CAQUI *s.m.* persimmon.
CARA *s.f.* face, guy.
CARACA *interj.* wow, gosh!
CARACOL *s.m.* snail.
CARACOLADO *adj.* spiral-shaped, curl, curly.
CARACTERE *s.m.* character.
CARACTERES *s.m. pl.* characters, signs, letters.
CARACTERÍSTICA *s.f.* characteristic, attribute, personality.
CARACTERÍSTICO *adj.* characteristic, typical, distinctive.
CARACTERIZAÇÃO *s.f.* characterization.
CARACTERIZAR *v.* to characterize, to feature.
CARA DE PAU *adj.* brazen.
CARADURA *s.2gên.* shameless / *adj.2gên.* shameless.
CARAMBA *interj.* whew!
CARAMBOLA *s.f.* carom, carombole.
CARAMELO *s.m.* caramel, blackjack.
CARA-METADE *s.f.* better half, beloved one.
CARAMUJO *s.m.* conch, snail.
CARANGUEJO *s.m.* crab.
CARAPUÇA *s.f.* cap, skullcap, carapace.
CARATÊ *s.m.* karate.
CARÁTER *s.m.* character.
CARAVANA *s.f.* caravan.
CARAVELA *s.f.* caravel, carvel.
CARBONIZADO *adj.* carbonized, burnt.
CARBONIZADOR *s.m.* carbonizer, carbon agent.
CARBONIZAR *v.* to carbonize, to burn.
CARBONO *s.m.* carbon.
CARBURADOR *s.m.* carburettor.
CARCAÇA *s.f.* carcass.
CARCERAGEM *s.f.* incarceration, prison, jail.
CÁRCERE *s.m.* prison, jail.
CARCEREIRO *s.m.* jailer, gaoler.
CARDÁPIO *s.m.* menu, carte (vinho).
CARDEAL *s.m.* Cardinal, redbird.
CARDÍACO *s.m.* cardiac / *adj.* cardiac.
CARDIOLOGIA *s.f.* cardiology.
CARDIOLOGISTA *s.2gên.* cardiologist.
CARDIOVASCULAR *adj.* cardiovascular.
CARDUME *s.m.* shoal.
CAREAÇÃO *s.f.* confrontation, being confronted.
CARECA *adj.* bald, hairless / *s.f.* baldness, alopecia.
CARECER *v.* to need, to lack.
CARÊNCIA *s.f.* lack, shortage, deficiency.
CARENTE *adj.2gên.* lacking.
CARETA *adj.* straight / *s.f.* grimace
CARGA *s.f.* load, burden, cargo.

CARGO *s.m.* load, burden, charge, duty, job position, employment.
CARGUEIRO *s.m.* cargo boat; ship, freighter / *adj.* carrying, freighting.
CARICATO *s.m.* satirical actor, parodist / *adj.* ridiculous, funny, comical.
CARICATURA *s.f.* caricature, cartoon.
CARICATURAR *v.* to caricature.
CARICATURESCO *adj.* caricatural, ridiculous.
CARICATURISTA *s.2gên.* caricaturist, cartoonist.
CARÍCIA *s.f.* caress.
CARICIAR *v.* to caress; to cuddle.
CARIDADE *s.f.* charity.
CARIDOSO(A) *adj.* charitable, gentle, kind.
CÁRIE *s.f.* dental caries, tooth decay.
CARIMBADO *adj.* marked, stamped, sealed.
CARIMBAR *v.* to stamp, to postmark.
CARIMBO *s.m.* stamp, seal, postmark.
CARINHO *s.m.* affection, caress, kindness.
CARINHOSO(A) *adj.* affectionate, loving, fond.
CARISMA *s.f.* charism.
CARISMÁTICO(A) *adj.* charismatic.
CARMA *s.m.* karma.
CARMIM *s.m.* carmine.
CARNAL *adj.2gên.* fleshly, carnal.
CARNAVAL *s.m.* carnival, happiness, party, mess.
CARNAVALESCO *adj.* reveller, funny.
CARNE *s.f.* meat, flesh.
CARNÊ *s.m.* card, notebook, adressbook.
CARNEIRO *s.m.* sheep, mutton, grave, tomb.
CARNIÇA *s.f.* carrion, carcass, rotten flesh.
CARNICEIRO *s.m.* butcher; slaughterer / *adj.* carnivorous.
CARNIFICINA *s.f.* carnage, bloodshed, massacre, slaughter.
CARNÍVORO *s.m.* carnivore, flesh-eater / *adj.* carnivorous.
CARNUDO *adj.* plump, fleshy, beefy; succulent.
CARO *adj.* expensive, dear.
CAROÇO *s.m.* lump, stone, seed.
CAROÇUDO *adj.* fruit that contains lump; stone.
CARONA *s.f.* ride, lift.
CARPA *s.f.* carp, weeding, hoeing.
CARPETE *s.m.* carpet.

CARPINTARIA *s.f.* carpentry, woodwork.
CARPINTEIRO *s.m.* carpenter.
CARPIR *v.* to gather, to pick, to weed.
CARRANCA *s.f.* frown, surly, grumpy.
CARRANCUDO *adj.* scowling, frowning, surly.
CARRÃO *s.m.* big car.
CARRAPATO *s.m.* tick, louse.
CARRAPICHO *s.m.* burr.
CARRASCO *s.m.* executioner, torturer, hangman.
CARREGADO *adj.* loaded, charged; cloudy.
CARREGADOR *s.m.* loader, carrier, charger.
CARREGAMENTO *s.m.* loading, cargo, shipment.
CARREGAR *v.* to load, to charge, to bear.
CARREIRA *s.f.* career, occupation, running; route, row.
CARRETA *s.f.* cart, lorry; truck.
CARRETEL *s.m.* reel, spool.
CARRO *s.m.* car, cart.
CARROÇA *s.f.* waggon, cart.
CARRO-CHEFE *s.m.* flagship.
CARROSSEL *s.m.* carousel, merry-go-round.
CARRUAGEM *s.f.* carriage, coach.
CARTA *s.f.* card, letter, chart, map, epistle.
CARTADA *s.f.* trump card, try, effort.
CARTÃO *s.m.* card, cardboard.
CARTAZ *s.m.* poster, billboard, sticker.
CARTEIRA *s.f.* wallet, purse.
CARTEIRO *s.m.* postman.
CARTEL *s.m.* cartel, provocation.
CARTELA *s.f.* cartouche, memorial panel.
CARTILAGEM *s.f.* cartilage, gristle.
CARTILHA *s.f.* hornbook, primer, spelling book.
CARTOLA *s.f.* top hat, topper.
CARTOLINA *s.f.* bristol board, cardboard, board paper.
CARTOMANTE *s.2gên.* fortuneteller.
CARTONADO *adj.* paperback.
CARTONAGEM *s.f.* bookbinding.
CARTONAR *v.* to board.
CARTONISTA *s.2gên.* pattern maker.
CARTÓRIO *s.m.* notary's office, registry.
CARTUCHO *s.m.* cartridge, cartouche, shell.
CARVALHO *s.m.* oak, oak tree.
CARVÃO *s.m.* coal, charcoal, cinder.
CASA *s.f.* house, building, habitation, office.
CASACA *s.f.* dress coat.

CASACO *s.m.* coat, jacket.
CASAL *s.m.* couple.
CASALAR *v.* to couple, to make pair, to mate, to reproduce.
CASAMENTEIRO *s.m.* matchmaker / *adj.* match-making.
CASAMENTO *s.m.* marriage, wedding, matrimony.
CASAR *v.* to marry, to get married.
CASARÃO *s.m.* mansion.
CASCA *s.f.* skin, bark, shell, peel.
CASCA-GROSSA *s.2gên.* bounder, rude.
CASCALHO *s.m.* gravel, rubble; money.
CASCÃO *s.m.* crusty, hard bark.
CASCAR *v.* to strip, to peel.
CASCATA *s.f.* waterfall, cascade.
CASCO *s.m.* hull, hoof, skull, scalp, shell.
CASEIRA *s.f.* farmer's wife, peasant woman, housekeeper.
CASEIRO *s.m.* tenant, housekeeper, caretaker / *adj.* domestic, homemade.
CASIMIRA *s.f.* cashmere.
CASINHA *s.f.* cottage.
CASMURRO *s.m.* stubborn / *adj.* grumpy, pigheaded, sullen.
CASO *s.m.* case, event, chance, accident, situation, matter.
CASÓRIO *s.m.* marriage, wedding.
CASPA *s.f.* dandruff, scurf.
CASSAÇÃO *s.f.* repealing, annul.
CASSAR *v.* to cancel, to revoke, to annul.
CASSETE *s.m.* cassette.
CASSINO *s.m.* casino.
CASTA *s.f.* caste, specie, breed, class, sort, kind.
CASTANHA *s.f.* chestnut, nut.
CASTANHO *s.m.* brown, nut-brown.
CASTELÃO *s.m.* castellan.
CASTELHANO *s.m.* Castilian / *adj.* Castilian.
CASTELO *s.m.* castle.
CASTIÇAL *s.m.* candlestick, candle-holder.
CASTIDADE *s.f.* chastity, purity, sexual abstinence.
CASTIFICAR *v.* to purify.
CASTIGADO *adj.* punished, beaten, chastised.
CASTIGAR *v.* to punish, to castigate.
CASTIGO *s.m.* punishment, penalty, reprimand.

CASTO *adj.* chaste, pure, clean, virgin, honest.
CASTOR *s.m.* beaver.
CASTRAÇÃO *s.f.* castrating, castration.
CASTRADO *s.m.* eunuch, castrated, gelded / *adj.* eunuch, castrated, gelded.
CASTRAR *v.* to castrate, to spay.
CASUAL *adj.2gên.* casual, occasional, accidental.
CASUALIDADE *s.f.* casualty, fortuity, accident.
CASULO *s.m.* boll, cocoon.
CATACUMBA *s.f.* catacomb.
CATALISAR *v.* to catalyze, to promote, to inspire.
CATALISADOR *s.m.* catalyst.
CATALOGAÇÃO *s.f.* cataloging, tabulation.
CATALOGADO *adj.* catalogued.
CATALOGAR *v.* to catalogue.
CATÁLOGO *s.m.* catalogue, list, roll.
CATAPORA *s.f.* chicken pox, varicella.
CATAPULTA *s.f.* catapult.
CATAR *v.* to pick up, to seek, to collect.
CATARATA *s.f.* waterfall, cataract.
CATARRO *s.m.* catarrh.
CATARSE *s.f.* catharsis, purgation.
CATÁSTROFE *s.f.* catastrophe, disaster.
CATASTRÓFICO *adj.* catastrophic.
CATA-VENTO *s.m.* weather vane, windmill.
CATECISMO *s.m.* catechism.
CATEDRAL *s.m.* cathedral.
CATEGORIA *s.f.* category, class.
CATEGÓRICO *adj.* categorical.
CATEGORIZAR *v.* to class, to classify, to categorize.
CATEQUESE *s.m.* catechism.
CATEQUISMO *s.m. m.q.* catecismo.
CATEQUIZAR *v.* to catechize.
CATETER *s.m.* catheter.
CATINGA *s.f.* caatinga.
CATIVANTE *adj.2gên.* catchy, captivating.
CATIVAR *v.* to captivate, to catch.
CATIVEIRO *s.m.* captivity, bondage, prison.
CATIVO *s.m.* captive, prisoner / *adj.* captive, prisoner.
CATOLICISMO *s.m.* Catholicism.
CATÓLICO *s.m.* Catholic / *adj.* Catholic.
CATOLIZAR *v.* to Catholicize.
CATORZE *s.m.* fourteen.
CATRACA *s.f.* turnstile, baffle gate.

CAUDA *s.f.* tail.
CAULE *s.m.* stalk.
CAUSA *s.f.* cause, motive, reason, origin.
CAUSAR *v.* to cause, to be the cause of, to be the reason of.
CÁUSTICO *s.m.* caustic / *adj.* caustic.
CAUTELA *s.f.* caution, precaution, care, warning.
CAUTELAR *v.* to caution, to warn, to forewarn.
CAUTELOSO *adj.* cautious, prudent, careful, watchful, vigilant.
CAUTERIZAÇÃO *s.f.* cautery, cauterization.
CAUTERIZAR *v.* to cauterize.
CAVAÇÃO *s.f.* digging, hole, pit.
CAVADEIRA *s.f.* hoe.
CAVADO *adj.* hollow, pit, excavated; low-cut.
CAVALEIRO *s.m.* horseman, rider, trooper / *adj.* horseman, rider, trooper.
CAVALGAR *v.* to ride, to jockey.
CAVALHEIRO *s.m.* gentleman / *adj.* gentleman.
CAVALO *s.m.* horse.
CAVAR *v.* to dig.
CAVEIRA *s.f.* skull, death.
CAVERNA *s.f.* cavern, cave.
CAVERNOSO *adj.* cavernous.
CAVIDADE *s.f.* cavity, hole, cave.
CAXUMBA *s.f.* mumps, parotitis.
CEAR *v.* to sup.
CEBOLA *s.f.* onion.
CEBOLINHA *s.f.* welsh onion.
CÊ-DÊ-EFE *s.2gên.* nerd, swot / *adj.2gên.* nerd, swot.
CEDER *v.* to give up, to assign, to transfer.
CEDIDO *adj.* granted, transferred.
CEDILHA *s.f.* cedilla.
CEDO *adv.* early, soon, quickly.
CEDRO *s.f.* cedar, cedar tree.
CÉDULA *s.f.* banknote, note, voting paper.
CEFALEIA *s.f.* headache.
CEFÁLICO *adj.* cephalic.
CEGAMENTO *s.m.* blindness, ignorance, fanaticism.
CEGANTE *adj.2gên.* blinding, dazzling, obfuscating.
CEGAR *v.* to blind.
CEGO(A) *s.m.* blind / *adj.* blind.
CEGONHA *s.f.* stork.
CEGUEIRA *s.f.* blindness.

CEIA *s.f.* supper.
CEIFA *s.f.* harvest, harvesting; destruction, massacre.
CEIFADOR *s.m.* reaper, harvest-man, murderer / *adj.* reaping, harvesting.
CEIFAR *v.* to reap, to harvest, to destruct.
CELA *s.f.* cell, small dormitory, prison cell, ward.
CELEBRAÇÃO *s.f.* celebration.
CELEBRADO *adj.* celebrated, renowned, glorified.
CELEBRANTE *s.m.* celebrant / *adj.2gên.* celebrant.
CELEBRAR *v.* to celebrate.
CÉLEBRE *adj.* famous, renowned, eminent.
CELEBRIDADE *s.f.* celebrity, famous.
CELEIRO *s.m.* barn, cellar, granary.
CELESTE *adj.2gên.* celestial, heavenly.
CELIBATÁRIO *s.m.* celibate, bachelor / *adj.* celibate, unmarried.
CELIBATO *s.m.* celibacy, bachelorhood.
CELOFANE *s.m.* cellophane.
CELTA *s.2gên.* Celtic, celt / *adj.2gên.* Celtic, celt.
CÉLULA *s.f.* cell.
CELULAR *adj.* cellular.
CELULITE *s.f.* cellulitis.
CEM *num.* one hundred, a hundred.
CEMITÉRIO *s.m.* cemetery, necropolis.
CENA *s.f.* scene, stage, drama.
CENÁRIO *s.m.* scenery, stage setting, set.
CENARISTA *s.2gên.* screenwriter, scenarist.
CÊNICO *adj.* scenic, theatrical.
CENOGRAFIA *s.f.* scenography.
CENOURA *s.f.* carrot.
CENSO *s.m.* census.
CENSOR *s.m.* censor.
CENSURA *s.f.* censorship, censure.
CENSURADO *adj.* censured, reproved, condemned.
CENSURAR *v.* to censor, to control.
CENTAURO *s.m.* centaur, centaurus.
CENTAVO *s.m.* cent, penny.
CENTEIO *s.m.* rye.
CENTELHA *s.f.* spark, sparkle.
CENTENA *num.* one hundred.
CENTENÁRIO *s.m.* centenary / *adj.* centenary.
CENTESIMAL *adj.2gên.* centesimal.

CENTÉSIMO *num.* hundredth / *s.m.* hundredth.
CENTÍGRADO *adj.* centigrade.
CENTÍMETRO *s.m.* centimetre.
CENTO *num.* one hundred / *s.m.* one hundred.
CENTOPEIA *s.f.* centipede.
CENTRAL *s.f.* central, headquarter / *adj.2gên.* central.
CENTRALISTA *s.2gên.* centralist, centralistic / *adj.2gên.* centralist, centralistic.
CENTRALIZAÇÃO *s.f.* centralization.
CENTRALIZAR *v.* to centralize.
CENTRAR *v.* to centre.
CENTRÍFUGA *s.f.* centrifuge machine.
CENTRIFUGAR *v.* to centrifuge.
CENTRO *s.m.* centre, downtown (da cidade).
CENTROAVANTE *s.m.* centre-foward.
CENTRO-OESTE *s.m.* Middle west, Midwest.
CERA *s.f.* wax, beeswax.
CERÂMICA *s.f.* ceramics, pottery.
CERÂMICO *adj.* ceramic.
CERCA *s.f.* fence, wall / *adv.* circa, about, around.
CERCADO *s.m.* fence, protected, enclosure / *adj.* cornered, surrounded, walled.
CERCAR *v.* to corner, to surround, to enclose.
CERCO *s.m.* siege, restriction, encirclement.
CEREAL *s.m.* cereal, corn meal.
CEREBRAL *adj.2gên.* cerebral.
CÉREBRO *s.m.* brain.
CEREJA *s.f.* cherry.
CEREJEIRA *s.f.* cherry tree.
CERIMÔNIA *s.f.* ceremony, rite.
CERIMONIAL *s.m.* ceremonial, ritual.
CERIMONIOSO *adj.* ceremonial, formal solemn.
CEROULAS *s.f. pl.* underpants, drawers.
CERRAÇÃO *s.f.* fog, haziness, mistiness.
CERRADO *s.m.* hedge; bushy (vegetação) / *adj.* closed; bushy (vegetação).
CERRAR *v.* to close, to shut, to join.
CERTA *s.f.* certainty, sureness, surely.
CERTAR *v.* to fight, to argue, to discuss.
CERTEIRO *adj.* accurate, right, correct.
CERTEZA *s.f.* certainty, certain, to be sure.
CERTIDÃO *s.f.* certificate, testimonial.
CERTIFICAÇÃO *s.f.* certification.
CERTIFICADO *s.m.* certification, testimonial / *adj.* certified, attested.
CERTIFICAR *v.* to certify, to certificate, to attest, to confirm.
CERTO *s.m.* certain, correct / *adj.* certain, right, exact.
CERVEJA *s.f.* beer.
CERVEJARIA *s.f.* brewery, pub, bar, beershop.
CERVICAL *adj.2gên.* cervical.
CERVO *s.m.* deer.
CESARIANA *s.f.* Caesarian surgery / *adj.* Caesarian surgery.
CESSAÇÃO *s.f.* cessation, ceasing, suspension.
CESSANTE *adj.2gên.* interruption.
CESSÃO *s.f.* giving up, surrender.
CESSAR *v.* to give up, to cease, to leave.
CESTA *s.f.* basket.
CESTEIRO *s.m.* basketmaker.
CESTO *s.m.* basket, bin.
CETICISMO *s.m.* scepticism, skepticism.
CÉTICO *s.m.* sceptic, skeptical / *adj.* sceptic, skeptical.
CETIM *s.m.* satin.
CETRO *s.m.* sceptre.
CÉU *s.m.* sky, sphere, heaven, paradise.
CEVADA *s.f.* barley, corn.
CHÁ *s.m.* tea.
CHÁCARA *s.f.* small farm, country house.
CHACINA *s.f.* slaughter, massacre.
CHACINAR *v.* to slaughter, to mince, to massacre.
CHACOALHADO *adj.* shaken violently, agitated.
CHACOALHAR *v.* to shake violently, to agitate.
CHACOTA *s.f.* mockery, joke.
CHAFARIZ *s.m.* fountain.
CHAGA *s.f.* wound, sore, ulcer.
CHALÉ *s.m.* chalet, cabin, cottage.
CHALEIRA *s.f.* kettle.
CHAMA *s.f.* flame, blaze.
CHAMADA *s.f.* call, calling, notification.
CHAMADO *s.m.* call, calling, convocation / *adj.* called, summoned.
CHÁ-MATE *s.m.* maté tea, yerba maté.
CHAMAR *v.* to call, to invoke, to convoke.
CHAMARIZ *s.f.* advertisement, attraction, decoy.
CHAMATIVO *adj.* calling.
CHAMEGO *s.m.* cuddle, care, affection.
CHAMINÉ *s.f.* chimney, lamp-chimney.

CHAMPANHE *s.m.* sparkling wine, champagne.
CHAMUSCADO *adj.* singed, slightly burned, toasted.
CHAMUSCAR *v.* to singe, to burn slightly, to toast.
CHANCE *s.f.* chance, opportunity.
CHANCELA *s.f.* seal, official stamp; seal, signing.
CHANCELAR *v.* to seal, to stamp, to approve, to confirm.
CHANCELER *s.m.* chancellor.
CHANTAGEAR *v.* to blackmail, to extort, to chantage.
CHANTAGEM *s.f.* blackmail, extortion, chantage.
CHANTAGISTA *s.2gên.* blackmailer / *adj.* blackmailer.
CHÃO *s.m.* ground, floor, pavement.
CHAPA *s.f.* plate, sheet, slab / *s.2gên.* friend, buddy.
CHAPADA *s.f.* plateau, plain, flatted, high.
CHAPADO *adj.* flatted, plain, stoned, high, drunk.
CHAPAR *v.* to plate, to get flattered.
CHAPELADA *s.f.* capful, hatful.
CHAPELARIA *s.f.* hat maker, hat shop, millinery.
CHAPELEIRO *s.m.* hatter, hat maker.
CHAPÉU *s.m.* hat.
CHARADA *s.f.* charade, riddle.
CHARLA *s.f.* chat, talk.
CHARLAR *v.* to chatter, to talk, to gossip.
CHARLATÃO *s.m.* charlatan, quack, impostor.
CHARME *s.m.* charm.
CHARMOSO *adj.* charming, good-looking, charmer.
CHARUTO *s.m.* cigar.
CHATEAÇÃO *s.f.* nuisance, annoyance, bother.
CHATEAR *v.* to annoy, to importune, to upset.
CHATICE *s.f.* nuisance.
CHATO(A) *adj.* flat (plano); boring (entediante).
CHAUVINISMO *s.m.* chauvinism.
CHAUVINISTA *adj.2gên.* chauvinist, chauvinistic / *s.2gên.* chauvinist, chauvinistic.
CHAVE *s.f.* key, wrench, clave.
CHAVEIRO *s.m.* key ring; chain, doorman, key maker.
CHECAR *v.* to check, to examine, to verify.
CHECK-UP *s.m.* check-up.
CHEFÃO *s.m.* warlord, big boss.
CHEFE *s.2gên.* boss, leader, head, principal, chef.
CHEFIA *s.f.* leadership, leading, supervision.
CHEFIAR *v.* to head, to lead, to instruct.
CHEGADA *s.f.* arrival, coming.
CHEGADO *adj.* close, intimate, familiar, arrived.
CHEGAR *v.* to arrive, to reach, to come, to approach.
CHEIA *s.f.* inundation, flood, overflowing.
CHEIO *adj.* full, filled up, replete.
CHEIRADOR *s.m.* sniffer.
CHEIRAR *v.* to smell, to breath, to inhale.
CHEIRO *s.f.* smell, odour, scent.
CHEIROSO(A) *adj.* smelly, fragrant, odoriferous.
CHEQUE *s.m.* cheque, bank cheque.
CHIADEIRA *s.f.* squeaking, noise, fizzle.
CHIADO *s.m.* squeak, wheeze, wheezing.
CHIAR *v.* to squeak, to hiss.
CHIBATA *s.f.* cane, switch, whip
CHIBATADA *s.f.* whipping, whiplash.
CHIBATAR *v.* to cane, to swish, to beat
CHICLETE *s.m.* chewing; bubble gum.
CHICÓRIA *s.f.* chicory, endive.
CHICOTADA *s.f.* flogging, whipping.
CHICOTAR *v.* to whip, to spank, to scourge.
CHICOTE *s.m.* whip, horsewhip.
CHIFRADA *s.f.* horns blow; hit, butt.
CHIFRAR *v.* to horn, to attack.
CHIFRE *s.m.* horn.
CHIFRUDO *s.m.* cuckold / *adj.* cuckold.
CHILE *s.m.* Chile.
CHILENO(A) *s.m.* Chilean / *adj.* Chilean.
CHIMPANZÉ *s.m.* chimpanzee.
CHINA *s.f.* China.
CHINELO *s.m.* slipper, sandals.
CHINÊS *s.m.* Chinese / *adj.* Chinese.
CHIQUE *adj.* elegant, chic, stylish.
CHIQUEIRO *s.m.* pigsty, pigpen.
CHISPA *s.f.* spark, sparkle.
CHITA *s.f.* cheetah.
CHOCADEIRA *s.f.* brooder, hatcher, incubator.
CHOCADO *adj.* shocked, surprised, amazed.

CHOCALHO *s.m.* cattle bell, rattle, clapper, gossip.
CHOCANTE *adj.2gên.* shocking, frightful, scandalous.
CHOCAR *v.* to hatch (ovo); to crash (colidir).
CHOCOLATE *s.m.* chocolate.
CHOCÓLATRA *s.2gên.* chocoholic.
CHOFER *s.m.* chauffeur, driver, motorist.
CHOPE *s.m.* draught beer.
CHOQUE *s.m.* collision, crash, impact, shock.
CHORADEIRA *s.f.* weeping, whining, crying, lamentation.
CHORAMINGAR *v.* to whimper, to whine.
CHORÃO *s.m.* crybaby, whiner / *adj.* whining, crying.
CHORAR *v.* to cry, to weep, to regret, to lament.
CHORO *s.m.* cry, crying, weeping, moan.
CHORUMELA *s.f.* trifle, nothingness, useless.
CHOURIÇO *s.m.* sausage, smoked sausage, blood pudding.
CHOVER *v.* to rain.
CHUCHU *s.m.* chayote.
CHULÉ *s.m.* foot odour, bad foot smel.
CHULO *adj.* ponce, crude, vulgar.
CHUMAÇO *s.m.* wad, pad.
CHUMBADO *adj.* leaded.
CHUMBAR *v.* to fasten, to plumb; to solder.
CHUMBINHO *s.m.* shot.
CHUMBO *s.m.* lead, bullets, shoot.
CHUPADO *adj.* skinny, sucked.
CHUPAR *v.* to suck, to absorb, to soak, to gain.
CHUPETA *s.f.* dummy, pacifier, nursing nipple.
CHURRASCARIA *s.f.* steak house, barbecue house.
CHURRASCO *s.m.* barbecue.
CHURRASQUEIRO *s.m.* barbecue chef.
CHUTAR *v.* to kick.
CHUTE *s.m.* kick, shot.
CHUTEIRA *s.f.* football boot, shoes.
CHUVA *s.f.* rain, water, rainfall.
CHUVÃO *s.m.* heavy rain.
CHUVEIRO *s.m.* shower.
CHUVISCAR *v.* to drizzle, to mizzle.
CHUVISCO *s.m.* drizzling rain, drizzle.
CHUVOSO *adj.* rainy.
CIA *abrev.* cia (companhia).
CIBERCAFÉ *s.m.* cybercafe.
CIBERESPAÇO *s.m.* cyberspace.
CIBERNÉTICA *s.f.* cybernetics.
CICATRIZ *s.f.* scar, cicatrix.
CICATRIZAÇÃO *s.f.* cicatrization, healing.
CICATRIZADO *adj.* healed.
CICATRIZAR *v.* to heal, to scar.
CICERONE *s.2gên.* tourist guide.
CÍCLICO *adj.* cyclic.
CICLISMO *s.m.* cyclism.
CICLISTA *s.2gên.* cyclist, rider.
CICLONE *s.m.* hurricane, twister, cyclone.
CICLOPE *s.m.* Cyclops.
CIDADANIA *s.f.* citizenship.
CIDADÃO *s.m.* citizen.
CIDADE *s.f.* town, city.
CIDADELA *s.f.* stronghold, tower.
CIDREIRA *s.f.* citron, cedrat.
CIÊNCIA *v.* science, knowledge, wisdom.
CIENTE *adj.2gên.* aware, conscious.
CIENTÍFICO *adj.* scientific.
CIENTISTA *s.2gên.* scientist.
CIFRA *s.f.* cypher, figure, code.
CIFRÃO *s.m.* currency symbol.
CIFRAR *v.* to cypher, to write in codes.
CIGANO *s.m.* gypsy.
CIGARRA *s.f.* cicada, cricket.
CIGARRILHA *s.f.* cheroot, cigarillo.
CIGARRO *s.m.* cigarette.
CILADA *s.f.* trap, trick, ambush, pothole, intrigue.
CILINDRADA *s.f.* piston displacement.
CILINDRAR *v.* to cylinder.
CILINDRO *s.m.* cylinder, roll.
CÍLIO *s.m.* eyelash, cilium.
CIMA *s.f.* top, summit.
CIMENTAR *v.* to cement.
CIMENTO *s.m.* cement, concrete, basis.
CINCO *s.m.* five.
CINEASTA *s.2gên.* film maker.
CINECLUBE *s.m.* cinema club.
CINEGRAFISTA *s.2gên.* cameraman, camerawoman.
CINEMA *s.m.* movies, cinema, movie theatre.
CINEMATECA *s.f.* cinematheque.
CINEMATOGRAFIA *s.f.* cinematography.
CINESTESIA *s.f.* kinaesthetic.
CINÉTICO *adj.* kinetic.
CINGIR *v.* to belt, to encircle, to unite.
CÍNICO(A) *s.m.* cynic / *adj.* cynical.
CINISMO *s.m.* cynicism.

CINQUENTA *s.m.* fifty.
CINQUENTENÁRIO *s.m.* fiftieth.
CINTA *s.f.* strap, girdle, belt.
CINTA-LIGA *s.f.* garter belt.
CINTAR *v.* to girdle, to belt.
CINTILAÇÃO *s.f.* scintillation, twinkle, spark.
CINTILANTE *adj.2gên.* scintillant, sparkling, twink.
CINTILAR *v.* to sparkle, to scintillate, to twinkle.
CINTO *s.m.* belt, girdle, sash.
CINTURA *s.f.* waist.
CINTURÃO *s.m.* belt; girdle.
CINZA *s.m.* ash, cinder / *adj.* grey.
CINZEIRO *s.m.* ashtray.
CINZENTO *s.m.* grey, grizzly, ashy / *adj.* grey, grizzly, ashy.
CIO *s.m.* rut, heat.
CIPÓ *s.m.* liana.
CIRCO *s.m.* circus, amphitheatre.
CIRCUITAR *v.* to circuit.
CIRCUITO *s.m.* circuit, cycle, circle.
CIRCULAÇÃO *s.f.* circulation, rotation, circle, cycle.
CIRCULADOR *s.m.* circulator / *adj.* circulating.
CIRCULAR *v.* to circulate, to circle / *s.f.* circular / *adj.* circular, rotate.
CÍRCULO *s.m.* circle, ring, circumference.
CIRCUNAVEGAÇÃO *s.f.* circumnavigation.
CIRCUNAVEGAR *v.* to circumnavigate.
CIRCUNCIDAR *v.* to circumcise.
CIRCUNCISÃO *s.f.* circumcision.
CIRCUNDAR *v.* to circle, to surround, to circuit.
CIRCUNFERÊNCIA *s.f.* circumference, circle, round.
CIRCUNFLEXO *adj.* circumflex, caret.
CIRCUNSTÂNCIA *s.f.* circumstance, condition, fact.
CIRCUNSTANCIAL *adj.2gên.* circumstantial.
CÍRIO *s.m.* taper.
CIRROSE *s.f.* cirrhosis.
CIRROSO *adj.* cirrhotic, scirrhous.
CIRURGIA *s.f.* surgery.
CIRURGIÃO(Ã) *s.m.* surgeon.
CIRÚRGICO *adj.* surgical.
CISCAR *v.* to clean up trash, to sweep.
CISCO *s.m.* speck, dust, rubbish.
CISMA *s.m.* schism, worry, suspicious.
CISMADO(A) *adj.* suspicious, distrustful, worried, cautious.

CISMAR *v.* to brood, to dislike, to worry, to suspect.
CISNE *s.m.* swan.
CITAÇÃO *s.f.* quotation.
CITADO *adj.* summoned.
CITAR *v.* to quote.
CITOPLASMA *s.m.* cytoplasm.
CÍTRICO *adj.* citrus.
CIUMAR *v.* to be jealousy.
CIÚME *s.m.* jealousy.
CIUMEIRA *s.f.* extremely jealousy.
CÍVICO *adj.* civic, civil.
CIVIL *adj.* civil / *s.2gên.* civilian.
CIVILIDADE *s.f.* civility, urbanity.
CIVILIZAÇÃO *s.f.* civilization.
CIVILIZADO *adj.* civil, civilized.
CLÃ *s.m.* clan.
CLAMANTE *adj.2gên.* clamant, crying out.
CLAMAR *v.* to cry, to shout.
CLAMOR *s.m.* clamour.
CLANDESTINIDADE *s.f.* underground, clandestinity.
CLANDESTINO *s.m.* underground / *adj.* clandestine.
CLARA *s.f.* egg white.
CLARABOIA *s.f.* skylight, light.
CLAREAR *v.* to clarify, to enlighten, to have an idea.
CLAREZA *s.f.* clarity, clearness.
CLARO *adj.* clear, light.
CLASSE *s.f.* class, category, group.
CLASSICISMO *s.m.* classicism.
CLÁSSICO *adj.* classical.
CLASSIFICAÇÃO *s.f.* classification.
CLASSIFICADO *s.m.* advertisement / *adj.* classified, ranked.
CLASSIFICAR *v.* to classify.
CLAUSTROFOBIA *s.f.* claustofobia.
CLAUSTROFÓBICO *s.m.* claustrofobic.
CLÁUSULA *s.f.* clause, condition.
CLAUSURA *s.f.* clausure, enclosure.
CLAUSURADO *adj.* secluded.
CLAVÍCULA *s.f.* clavicle, collarbone.
CLEMÊNCIA *s.f.* mercy, lenity.
CLEMENTE *adj.2gên.* clement.
CLEPTOMANIA *s.f.* kleptomania.
CLEPTOMANÍACO *adj.* kleptomaniaco.
CLERO *s.m.* clergy, priesthood.
CLICAR *v.* to click.
CLICHÊ *s.m.* cliché, stereotype.

CLIENTE *s.2gên.* client, consumer, customer.
CLIENTELA *s.f.* clientage, clients, consumers.
CLIMA *s.m.* climate, clime.
CLIMÁTICO *adj.* climatic.
CLIMATIZAÇÃO *s.f.* climatization, acclimatization.
CLIMATIZAR *v.* to acclimate.
CLIMATOLOGIA *s.f.* climatology.
CLÍMAX *s.m.* climax.
CLÍNICA *s.f.* clinic, medical clinic.
CLINICAR *v.* to practise medicine.
CLÍNICO *s.m.* doctor / *adj.* clinical.
CLIPE *s.m.* clip.
CLIQUE *s.m.* click.
CLITÓRIS *s.m.* clitoris.
CLONE *s.m.* clone.
CLORO *s.m.* chlorine.
CLOROFILA *s.f.* chlorophyll.
CLUBE *s.m.* club, association, society.
COABITAR *v.* to cohabit.
COADJUVANTE *adj.2gên.* supporting, cooperator, background.
COADJUVAR *v.* to help, to aid, to assist.
COADO *adj.* strained, filtered.
COADOR *s.m.* strainer, filter, percolator.
COAGIDO *adj.* coerced, forced.
COAGIR *v.* to coerce.
COAGULADO *adj.* coagulated, clotted, curdy.
COAGULAR *v.* to coagulate.
COÁGULO *s.m.* coagulant; clot.
COALHADA *s.f.* curdle milk, clabber.
COALHADO *adj.* curdled, curdy, sour.
COALHAR *v.* to curdle.
COAR *v.* strain, to filter.
COAUTOR *s.m.* co-author, collaborator.
COAUTORIA *s.f.* co-authorship.
COBAIA *s.f.* guinea pig.
COBERTA *s.f.* cover, bedspread, blanket.
COBERTO *adj.* covered, coverture, shelter.
COBERTOR *s.m.* blanket, coverlet.
COBERTURA *s.f.* covering.
COBIÇA *s.f.* greed, envy.
COBIÇAR *v.* to covet, to lust.
COBRA *s.f.* snake, serpent; treacherous friend.
COBRADOR *s.m.* bill collector, collector, receiver.
COBRANÇA *s.f.* collection.
COBRAR *v.* to receive, to take back.
COBRE *s.m.* copper.

COBRIR *v.* to cover, to hood, to give shelter.
COCA *s.f.* coca.
COCADA *s.f.* coconut sweet.
COCAÍNA *s.f.* cocaine, dope.
COÇAR *v.* to scratch.
CÓCCIX *s.m.* coccyx.
CÓCEGAS *s.f. pl.* tickle, tickling, itching.
COCEIRA *s.f.* itching, itch.
COCHICHADA *s.f.* whisper, mutter.
COCHICHAR *v.* to whisper, to mutter.
COCHICHO *s.m.* whispering, whisper, muttering.
COCHILADA *s.f.* nap.
COCHILAR *v.* to nap, to drop off.
COCHILO *s.m.* napping, error, mistake.
COCO *s.m.* coconut.
COCÔ *s.m.* excrement, feces, poop.
CÓCORAS *s.f. pl.* squatting.
CODIFICADO *adj.* encoded, ciphered, concealed.
CODIFICAR *v.* to code, to encode, to codify.
CÓDIGO *s.m.* code.
CODORNA *s.f.* quail.
COEDUCAR *v.* to co-educate.
COEFICIENTE *s.m.* coefficient.
COELHO *s.m.* rabbit, jack rabbit.
COENTRO *s.m.* coriander.
COERÇÃO *s.f.* coercion, coacction.
COERÊNCIA *s.f.* coherence, consistency.
COERENTE *adj.2gên.* coherent.
COESÃO *s.f.* cohesion.
COESIVO *adj.* cohesive.
COESO *adj.* coherent, united, joint.
COEXISTÊNCIA *s.f.* coexistence.
COEXISTENTE *adj.2gên.* coexistent.
COEXISTIR *v.* to coexist.
COFRE *s.m.* safe, strongbox.
COGITAÇÃO *s.f.* cogitation, thought.
COGITAR *v.* to cogitate, to contemplate.
COGNATO *s.m.* cognate, related / *adj.* cognate, related.
COGNIÇÃO *s.f.* cognition.
COGNITIVO *adj.* cognitive.
COGNOME *s.m.* cognomen, surname, nickname.
COGNOMINAR *v.* to cognominate, to name, to surname.
COGUMELO *s.m.* mushroom.
COIBIÇÃO *s.f.* restraint, restraining.
COIBIR *v.* to restrain.

COIBITIVO *adj.* cohibitive.
COICE *s.m.* kick, recoil.
COINCIDÊNCIA *s.f.* coincidence.
COINCIDENTE *adj.2gên.* coincident.
COINCIDIR *v.* to coincide.
COIOTE *s.m.* coyote.
COISA *s.f.* thing.
COITADO *s.m.* poor, miserable / *adj.* poor, miserable.
COLA *s.f.* glue.
COLABORADOR *s.m.* collaborator, employer, worker.
COLABORAR *v.* to collaborate.
COLADO *adj.* glued, adhered, pasted.
COLANTE *adj.* skintight.
COLAPSO *s.m.* collapse.
COLAR *v.* to stick / *s.m.* necklace.
COLCHA *s.f.* bedspread.
COLCHÃO *s.m.* mattress.
COLCHETE *s.m.* hook, clasp.
COLEÇÃO *s.f.* collection.
COLÉGIO *s.m.* school.
COLEIRA *s.f.* collar.
COLHEITA *s.f.* crop.
COLHER *s.f.* spoon.
COLHER *v.* to gather.
COLHIDO *adj.* picked.
COLINA *s.f.* hill.
COLISÃO *s.f.* collision.
COLLANT *s.m.* pantyhose.
COLMEIA *s.f.* beehive.
COLOCAÇÃO *s.f.* collocation, emplacement, setting.
COLOCADO *adj.* collocated, set.
COLOCAR *v.* to put, to place.
COLÔNIA *s.f.* colony, community.
COLORIDO *s.m.* colour / *adj.* colourful.
COLORIR *v.* to colour.
COLUNA *s.f.* column.
COM *prep.* with.
COMA *s.m.* coma.
COMADRE *s.f.* godmother, midwife.
COMANDANTE *s.m.* commander / *adj.* commander.
COMANDAR *v.* to command, to order.
COMANDO *s.m.* command, order.
COMARCA *s.f.* county.
COMBATE *s.m.* combat, fight.
COMBATENTE *s.2gên.* combatant / *adj.* combatant.

COMBATER *v.* to flight, to combat.
COMBATIVIDADE *s.f.* combativeness.
COMBATIVO *adj.* combative.
COMBINAÇÃO *s.f.* combination.
COMBINADO *adj.* agreement, agreed.
COMBINAR *v.* to combine, to match.
COMBINÁVEL *adj.2gên.* combinable.
COMBOIAR *v.* to convoy, to escort.
COMBOIO *s.m.* convoy, transport.
COMBUSTÃO *s.f.* combustion.
COMBUSTÍVEL *s.m.* fuel.
COMEÇAR *v.* to begin, to start.
COMEÇO *s.m.* beginning, start.
COMÉDIA *s.f.* comedy.
COMEDIANTE *s.2gên.* comedian / *adj.2gên.* comedian.
COMEDIDO(A) *adj.* moderate, unpretentious, cautious.
COMEMORAÇÃO *s.f.* commemoration.
COMEMORAR *v.* to commemorate, to celebrate.
COMEMORATIVO *adj.* commemorative.
COMENTAR *v.* to comment.
COMENTÁRIO *s.m.* comment, remark.
COMENTARISTA *s.2gên.* commentator / *adj.2gên.* commentator.
COMER *v.* to eat.
COMERCIAL *adj.* commercial.
COMERCIANTE *s.2gên.* merchant, trader / *adj.2gên.* merchant, trader.
COMÉRCIO *s.m.* commerce.
COMESTÍVEL *s.m.* comestible.
COMETER *v.* to commit, to perpetrate.
COMICHÃO *s.m.* itching, ardent desire.
COMICIDADE *s.f.* comicality.
COMÍCIO *s.m.* meeting, rally, demonstration.
CÔMICO *adj.* comical, humorous, comic.
COMIDA *s.f.* food.
COMIGO *pron.* with me.
COMILANÇA *s.f.* binge.
COMILÃO *s.m.* glutton, overeater / *adj.* glutton, overeater.
COMINAÇÃO *s.f.* commination; threat, menace.
COMINAR *v.* to comminate; to threaten, to menace.
COMISSÃO *s.f.* commission; committe.
COMISSÁRIO *s.m.* commissioner, officer.
COMITÊ *s.m.* committee.

COMO *adv.* how / *conj.* as / *prep.* like.
COMOÇÃO *s.f.* commotion, disturbance, riot.
CÔMODA *s.f.* commode.
COMODIDADE *s.f.* coziness, convenience, comfort.
COMODISMO *s.m.* selfishness, self-indulgence.
CÔMODO(A) *adj.* confortable, easy.
COMODORO *s.m.* commodore.
COMOVENTE *adj.* moving, touching.
COMOVER *v.* to move, to touch.
COMOVIDO(A) *adj.* moved, touched, upset.
COMPACTADOR *s.m.* compactor.
COMPACTAR *v.* to compact.
COMPACTO *s.m.* compact, crowded, dense / *adj.* compact, crowded, dense.
COMPADECER-SE *v.* to pity, to sympathize.
COMPADECIMENTO *s.m.* compassion, sympathy.
COMPADRE *s.m.* godfather, pal.
COMPAIXÃO *s.f.* compassion.
COMPANHEIRISMO *s.m.* companionship.
COMPANHEIRO(A) *s.m.* companion.
COMPANHIA *s.f.* company.
COMPARAÇÃO *s.f.* comparison.
COMPARADO *adj.* compared.
COMPARAR *v.* to compare.
COMPARECER *v.* to attend, to show up, to report.
COMPARECIMENTO *s.m.* attendance; appearance.
COMPARSA *s.2gên.* accomplice, crony (amigo).
COMPARTILHAMENTO *s.m.* share, sharing.
COMPARTILHAR *v.* to share, to partake.
COMPARTIMENTO *s.m.* partitioning, compartmentalizing.
COMPASSO *s.m.* compass, measure, beat.
COMPATIBILIDADE *s.f.* compatibility.
COMPATÍVEL *adj.* compatible.
COMPATRIOTA *s.2gên.* compatriot / *adj.2gên.* compatriot.
COMPENSADO *s.m.* compensated; hardboard; cleared.
COMPENSAR *v.* to compensate, to pay.
COMPETÊNCIA *s.f.* competence, ability.
COMPETENTE *adj.2gên.* competent, capable.
COMPETIÇÃO *s.f.* competition.
COMPETIDOR(A) *s.m.* competitor.
COMPETIR *v.* to compete.
COMPETITIVO(A) *adj.* competitive.
COMPLEMENTAR *v.* to complement / *adj.2gên.* complementary.
COMPLEMENTO *s.m.* complement.
COMPLETAMENTE *adv.* completely, entirely, absolutely.
COMPLETAR *v.* to complete, to conclude.
COMPLETO(A) *adj.* complete, entire.
COMPLEXIDADE *s.f.* complexity.
COMPLEXO(A) *s.m.* complex / *adj.* complex.
COMPLICAÇÃO *s.f.* complication, trouble.
COMPLICADO(A) *adj.* complicated, complex.
COMPLICAR *v.* to complicate.
COMPLÔ *s.m.* conspiracy.
COMPONENTE *s.m.* component.
COMPOR *v.* to compose, to arrange.
COMPORTAMENTO *s.m.* behaviour.
COMPORTAR *v.* to put up, to admit, to bear.
COMPOSIÇÃO *s.f.* composition.
COMPOSITOR(A) *s.m.* composer / *adj.* composer.
COMPOSTO *s.m.* composed / *adj.* composed.
COMPOTA *s.f.* compote.
COMPRA *s.f.* purchase, buy.
COMPRADOR(A) *s.m.* buyer, purchaser.
COMPRAR *v.* to buy.
COMPREENDER *v.* to understand, to realize.
COMPREENSÃO *s.f.* understanding.
COMPREENSÍVEL *adj.2gên.* comprehensible.
COMPREENSIVO(A) *adj.* comprehensive.
COMPRESSA *s.f.* compress.
COMPRESSÃO *s.f.* compression.
COMPRIDO(A) *adj.* lengthy, long.
COMPRIMENTO *s.m.* length.
COMPRIMIR *v.* to compress, to squeeze.
COMPROMETER *v.* to commit, to promise, to oblige.
COMPROMISSO *s.m.* commitment, engagement.
COMPROVANTE *s.m.* receipt, voucher.
COMPROVAR *v.* to confirm, to prove, to vouch.
COMPULSIVO(A) *adj.* compulsive.
COMPULSÓRIO(A) *adj.* compulsory.
COMPUTAÇÃO *s.f.* computation.
COMPUTADOR *s.m.* computer.
COMPUTAR *v.* to compute.
COMUM *adj.* common.
COMUNGAR *v.* to commune.

COMUNHÃO *s.f.* communion.
COMUNICAÇÃO *s.f.* communication.
COMUNICADO *s.m.* communication, official report.
COMUNICAR *v.* to report.
COMUNIDADE *s.f.* community.
COMUNISMO *s.m.* communism.
COMUNISTA *s.2gên.* communist / *adj.2gên.* communist.
CONCEBER *v.* to conceive, to think.
CONCEBIDO(A) *adj.* planned, schemed, designed.
CONCEDER *v.* to concede, to grant.
CONCEDIDO(A) *adj.* granted, conceded.
CONCEITO *s.m.* concept.
CONCEITUAÇÃO *s.f.* conceptualization.
CONCENTRAÇÃO *s.f.* concentration.
CONCENTRADO(A) *adj.* concentrated.
CONCENTRAR *v.* to concentrate.
CONCEPÇÃO *s.f.* conception.
CONCERTO *s.m.* concert.
CONCESSÃO *s.f.* concession.
CONCHA *s.f.* shell, ladle, scoop.
CONCILIAÇÃO *s.f.* conciliation.
CONCILIAR *v.* to conciliate, to reconcile.
CONCLUIR *v.* to conclude.
CONCLUSÃO *s.f.* conclusion.
CONCORDÂNCIA *s.f.* concordance, agreement.
CONCORDAR *v.* to agree, to consent.
CONCORRÊNCIA *s.f.* competition, rivalry.
CONCORRENTE *s.2gên.* concurrent, rival / *adj.2gên.* concurrent, rival.
CONCORRER *v.* to compete, to rival.
CONCRETIZAR *v.* to accomplish, to achieve, to fulfill.
CONCRETO *s.m.* concrete / *adj.* concrete.
CONCURSO *s.m.* concourse; competition; concurrence.
CONDE *s.m.* count.
CONDENAÇÃO *s.f.* condemnation, conviction.
CONDENADO(A) *adj.* condemned.
CONDENAR *v.* to condemn, to convict, to sentence.
CONDENSAR *v.* to condense.
CONDESSA *s.f.* countess.
CONDIÇÃO *s.f.* condition.
CONDICIONAMENTO *s.m.* conditioning.
CONDICIONAR *v.* to condition, to prepare; to stipulate.
CONDIMENTO *s.m.* condiment, seasoning.
CONDOMÍNIO *s.m.* joint ownership, condominium.
CONDUÇÃO *s.f.* conduction.
CONDUTOR *s.m.* conduction.
CONDUZIR *v.* to conduct, to lead.
CONECTADO *adj.* connected.
CONECTAR *v.* to connect.
CONEXÃO *s.f.* connection.
CONFECÇÃO *s.f.* confection.
CONFECCIONAR *v.* to make, to fabricate, to manufacture.
CONFEITARIA *s.f.* confectionery.
CONFERÊNCIA *s.f.* conference, lecture.
CONFERIR *v.* to check.
CONFESSAR *v.* to confess, to reveal.
CONFIANÇA *s.f.* confidence.
CONFIAR *v.* to trust.
CONFIÁVEL *adj.2gên.* trustworthy, reliable.
CONFIDÊNCIA *s.f.* confidence, trust.
CONFIDENCIAL *adj.2gên.* confidential, classified, private / *s.f.* confidentiality.
CONFIDENTE *s.m.* confidante.
CONFIRMAÇÃO *s.f.* confidante.
CONFIRMADO *adj.* confirmed.
CONFIRMAR *v.* to confirm, to affirm.
CONFISSÃO *s.f.* confession.
CONFORMAR *v.* to conform, to shape.
CONFORME *adv.* conformably, accordingly, correspondingly.
CONFORMIDADE *s.f.* conformity.
CONFORTAR *v.* to comfort, to console.
CONFORTÁVEL *adj.* comfortable.
CONFORTO *s.m.* comfort.
CONFRONTAR *v.* to confront.
CONFRONTO *s.m.* confrontation.
CONFUSÃO *s.f.* confusion, tumult; disorder.
CONFUSO(A) *adj.* confused.
CONGELADO *adj.* frozen.
CONGELADOR *s.m.* freezer.
CONGELAMENTO *s.m.* freeze, freezing.
CONGELAR *v.* to freeze, to ice.
CONGESTIONADO *adj.* congested.
CONGESTIONAMENTO *s.m.* congestion.
CONGESTIONAR *v.* to congest.
CONGRESSISTA *s.2gên.* congressman / *adj.2gên.* congressman.
CONGRESSO *s.m.* congress.

CONHAQUE *s.m.* cognac.
CONHECEDOR *s.m.* connoisseur, expert, specialist.
CONHECER *v.* to know, to meet.
CONHECIDO *s.m.* acquaintance / *adj.* known, notorious.
CONHECIMENTO *s.m.* knowledge, understanding.
CONJUGADO *adj.* conjoined, combined.
CONJUGAR *v.* to conjugate.
CÔNJUGE *s.m.* spouse, mate, partner.
CONJUNÇÃO *s.f.* conjunction.
CONOSCO *pron.* with us.
CONQUISTA *s.f.* conquest.
CONQUISTAR *v.* to conquer, to vanquish, to defeat.
CONSCIÊNCIA *s.f.* conscience.
CONSCIENTE *adj.* conscious, aware, knowing, conscientious.
CONSEGUIR *v.* to obtain, to achieve.
CONSELHO *s.m.* advice, opinion, council, board.
CONSENTIMENTO *s.m.* consent, approval, permission.
CONSENTIR *v.* to consent, to approve, to permit.
CONSEQUÊNCIA *s.f.* consequence.
CONSEQUENTE *adj.* consequent, consequential.
CONSERTAR *v.* to repair, to fix.
CONSERTO *s.m.* repair, restoration, fix
CONSERVA *s.f.* conserve.
CONSERVAÇÃO *s.f.* conservation.
CONSERVADOR(A) *s.m.* conserver, conservative / *adj.* conserver, conservative.
CONSERVADORISMO *s.m.* conservatism.
CONSERVANTE *s.m.* conserving, preserving.
CONSERVAR *v.* to conserve, to preserve.
CONSERVATÓRIO *s.m.* conservatory.
CONSIDERAÇÃO *s.f.* consideration, thought.
CONSIDERADO *adj.* considerate, considerable, deliberate.
CONSIDERAR *v.* to consider.
CONSIDERÁVEL *adj.* considerable.
CONSIGO *pron.* with him, with himself.
CONSISTENTE *adj.2gên.* consistent, solid.
CONSISTIR *v.* to consist.
CONSOANTE *s.f.* consonant; rhyme.
CONSOLAÇÃO *s.f.* consolation.
CONSOLAR *v.* to console, to comfort.
CONSOLIDADO *s.m.* consolidated / *adj.* consolidated.
CONSOLIDAR *v.* to consolidate.
CONSOLO *s.m.* console, consolation, comfort.
CONSÓRCIO *s.m.* consortium, partnership, marriage.
CONSPIRAÇÃO *s.f.* conspiracy.
CONSPIRAR *v.* to conspire.
CONSTANTE *adj.* constant.
CONSTAR *v.* to consist of.
CONSTATAR *v.* to verify, to certify.
CONSTERNADO(A) *adj.* consternated, depressed.
CONSTIPAÇÃO *s.f.* constipation.
CONSTIPAR *v.* to constipate.
CONSTITUIÇÃO *s.f.* constitution.
CONSTITUINTE *adj.2gên.* constituting.
CONSTITUIR *v.* to constitute, to form.
CONSTRANGER *v.* to constrain, to oblige, to impel.
CONSTRANGIMENTO *s.m.* constraint, compulsion, embarrassment.
CONSTRUÇÃO *s.f.* building.
CONSTRUÍDO *adj.* built, constructed.
CONSTRUIR *v.* to construct.
CONSTRUTIVO(A) *adj.* constructive.
CONSTRUTOR(A) *s.m.* constructor.
CÔNSUL *s.m.* consul.
CONSULADO *s.m.* consulate.
CONSULTA *s.f.* consulting, consultancy.
CONSULTAR *v.* to consult, to look up.
CONSULTOR *s.m.* consultant, examiner / *adj.* consultant, advisor.
CONSULTORIA *s.f.* consultancy.
CONSULTÓRIO *s.m.* office; clinic.
CONSUMIDO *adj.* consumed, used up, worried.
CONSUMIDOR *s.m.* consumer, consuming / *adj.* consumer, consuming.
CONSUMIR *v.* to consume.
CONSUMO *s.m.* consumption.
CONTA *s.f.* account, count, bill.
CONTABILIDADE *s.f.* accounting.
CONTABILIZAR *v.* to do accounting.
CONTADOR(A) *s.m.* accountant, auditor.
CONTAGIANTE *adj.2gên.* contagious.
CONTAGIAR *v.* to infect, to transmit.
CONTÁGIO *s.m.* contagion, infection.

CONTAGIOSO(A) *adj.* contagious.
CONTAMINADO(A) *adj.* contaminated, infected.
CONTAMINAR *v.* to contaminate, to infect.
CONTAR *v.* to count.
CONTATO *s.m.* contact.
CONTEMPLAR *v.* contemplate.
CONTEMPLATIVO(A) *adj.* contemplative.
CONTEMPORANEIDADE *s.f.* contemporaneity.
CONTEMPORÂNEO(A) *adj.* contemporaneous, contemporary.
CONTENTAMENTO *s.m.* contentment, satisfaction, enjoyment.
CONTENTAR *v.* to content, to satisfy, to suffice.
CONTENTE *adj.* contented, satisfied, joyful, happy.
CONTER *v.* to contain, to comprise.
CONTERRÂNEO(A) *s.m.* fellow countryman / *adj.* fellow countryman.
CONTESTAÇÃO *s.f.* dispute, contestation.
CONTESTADO *s.m.* refuted, contradicted / *adj.* refuted, contradicted.
CONTESTAR *v.* to contest, to refute.
CONTEÚDO *s.m.* content.
CONTEXTO *s.m.* context.
CONTEXTUALIZAR *v.* to contextualize.
CONTIDO(A) *adj.* restrained.
CONTIGO *pron.* with you.
CONTÍGUO *adj.* contiguous.
CONTINENTAL *adj.* continental.
CONTINENTE *s.m.* continent.
CONTINUAÇÃO *s.f.* continuation.
CONTINUAR *v.* to continue.
CONTINUIDADE *s.f.* continuity.
CONTO *s.m.* narrative.
CONTORCER *v.* to contort.
CONTORNAR *v.* to bypass, to circumvent; to contour.
CONTORNO *s.m.* outline, profile.
CONTRA *prep.* against / *s.m.* opposed, contra / *adv.* counter.
CONTRA-ATAQUE *s.m.* counter-attack.
CONTRABANDEAR *v.* to smuggle, to contraband.
CONTRABANDO *s.m.* smuggling, contraband.
CONTRAÇÃO *s.f.* contraction.
CONTRACAPA *s.f.* back cover, inside cover.
CONTRACEPTIVO *s.m.* contraceptive.
CONTRADIÇÃO *s.f.* contradiction.
CONTRADITÓRIO(A) *adj.* contradictory.
CONTRAGOSTO *s.m.* dislike, aversion.
CONTRAÍDO *adj.* contracted.
CONTRAIR *v.* to contract.
CONTRAMÃO *s.f.* wrong way, contraflow.
CONTRARIAR *v.* to oppose; to counter.
CONTRÁRIO(A) *adj.* contrary.
CONTRASTADO *adj.* contrasted.
CONTRASTAR *v.* to contrast.
CONTRASTE *s.m.* contrast.
CONTRATADO *adj.* contracted.
CONTRATAR *v.* to contract.
CONTRATEMPO *s.m.* setback, mischance.
CONTRATO *s.m.* contract, agreement.
CONTRIBUIÇÃO *s.f.* contribution.
CONTRIBUINTE *s.2gên.* contributor / *adj.2gên.* contributor.
CONTRIBUIR *v.* to contribute.
CONTROLADO(A) *adj.* controlled.
CONTROLADOR(A) *s.m.* controller / *adj.* controller.
CONTROLAR *v.* to control.
CONTROLE *s.m.* control.
CONTROVÉRSIA *s.f.* controversy.
CONTROVERSO *adj.* controversial, contentious, polemic.
CONTUDO *conj.* however, yet, nevertheless.
CONTUNDIDO(A) *adj.* bruised.
CONTUNDIR *v.* to bruise.
CONTUSÃO *s.f.* contusion, bruise.
CONVENÇÃO *s.f.* convention.
CONVENCER *v.* to convince.
CONVENCIDO(A) *adj.* conceited, cocky.
CONVENCIONAL *adj.* conventional.
CONVENIÊNCIA *s.f.* convenience.
CONVENIENTE *s.2gên.* convenient / *adj.2gên.* convenient.
CONVÊNIO *s.m.* covenant, accord, convention.
CONVENTO *s.m.* convent.
CONVERSA *s.f.* chat, conversation, talk.
CONVERSADO *adj.* conversed, talked about.
CONVERSÃO *s.f.* conversion.
CONVERSAR *v.* to talk, to converse.
CONVERTER *v.* to convert.
CONVERTIDO *s.m.* converted.
CONVÉS *s.m.* deck.

CONVICÇÃO *s.f.* conviction.
CONVIDADO(A) *s.m.* guest; invited.
CONVIDAR *v.* to invite.
CONVINCENTE *adj.2gên.* convincing.
CONVITE *s.m.* invitation.
CONVIVÊNCIA *s.f.* companionship, familiarity.
CONVIVER *v.* to cohabit, to live together.
CONVOCADO *s.m.* drafted, summoned / *adj.* drafted, summoned.
CONVOCAR *v.* to summon, to convoke.
CONVOSCO *pron.* with you.
CONVULSÃO *s.f.* convulsion.
CONVULSIONAR *v.* to convulse.
COOPER *s.m.* jogging.
COOPERAÇÃO *s.f.* cooperation.
COOPERAR *v.* cooperate.
COORDENADA *s.f.* coordinate.
COORDENADO(A) *adj.* coordinated.
COORDENADOR *s.m.* coordinator; coordinating.
COPA *s.f.* cup (esporte), kitchenette (casa).
COPEIRA *s.f.* kitchen maid.
CÓPIA *s.f.* copy.
COPIADO *adj.* copied, duplicated; imitated.
COPIAR *v.* to copy.
COQUE *s.m.* bun; coke.
COQUEIRO *s.m.* coconut palm.
COQUETEL *s.m.* cocktail.
COR *s.f.* colour, color.
CORAÇÃO *s.m.* heart.
CORADO *adj.* ruddy, rosy.
CORAGEM *s.f.* courage.
CORAJOSO(A) *adj.* courageous.
CORAL *s.m.* coral; choral (música)
CORAR *v.* to colour, to dye.
CORDA *s.f.* rope.
CORDÃO *s.m.* string, twine.
CORDEIRO *s.m.* lamb.
COR-DE-ROSA *s.m.* pink / *adj.2gên.* pink.
CORDEL *s.m.* string.
COREANO(A) *s.m.* Korean / *adj.* Korean.
COREIA *s.f.* Korea.
CORO *s.m.* choir, chorus.
COROA *s.f.* crown.
COROAÇÃO *s.f.* coronation, crowning.
COROADO *adj.* crowned.
COROAR *v.* to crown.
CORONEL *s.m.* colonel.
CORPO *s.m.* body.
CORPULENTO *s.m.* corpulent, stout, fat / *adj.* corpulent, stout, fat.
CORREÇÃO *s.f.* correction.
CORREDOR *s.m.* corridor, gangway, runner, racer.
CORREIO *s.m.* post, mail.
CORRENTE *s.f.* chain; draught, draft / *adj.* current.
CORRENTEZA *s.f.* current, stream, watercourse.
CORRER *v.* to run.
CORRESPONDÊNCIA *s.f.* correspondence.
CORRESPONDER *v.* to correspond.
CORRESPONDIDO(A) *adj.* unrequited.
CORRETO(A) *adj.* correct.
CORRETOR(A) *s.m.* broker (da Bolsa); underwriter (de seguros); realtor (de imóveis).
CORRIDA *s.f.* race, run.
CORRIDO(A) *adj.* rushed.
CORRIGIR *v.* to correct.
CORRIMENTO *s.m.* discharge.
CORRIQUEIRO(A) *adj.* everyday.
CORROMPER *v.* to corrupt.
CORROSIVO(A) *adj.* corrosive.
CORRUPÇÃO *s.f.* corruption.
CORRUPTO(A) *adj.* corrupt.
CORTADA *s.f.* cut; undercut (golfe).
CORTANTE *s.m.* sharp / *adj.2gên.* sharp.
CORTAR *v.* to cut, to chop, to clip.
CORTE *s.m.* cut.
CORTE *s.f.* court.
CORTEJADOR *s.m.* flatterer; overcourteous.
CORTEJAR *v.* to court.
CORTEJO *s.m.* procession, cortège.
CORTESIA *s.f.* courtesy.
CORTIÇA *s.f.* cork.
CORTIÇO *s.m.* slum, tenement; hive, beehive.
CORTINA *s.f.* curtain, drape.
CORTINADO *adj.* tieback.
CORUJA *s.f.* owl.
CORVO *s.m.* crow, raven.
COSMÉTICO *s.m.* cosmetic / *adj.* cosmetic.
COSTA *s.f.* coast (litoral).
COSTAS *s.f. pl.* back, dorsal area.
COSTELA *s.f.* rib.
COSTELETA *s.f.* chop, cutlet; sideburns.
COSTUMAR *v.* to be accustomed, to used.
COSTUME *s.m.* custom, habit.
COSTUMEIRO *adj.* customary, usual.

COSTURA *s.f.* sewing.
COSTURADO *adj.* seamed.
COSTURAR *v.* to sew, to tailor.
COTA *s.f.* quota.
COTAÇÃO *s.f.* quotation.
COTADO *adj.* well priced.
COTAR *v.* to quote.
COTEJAR *v.* to compare.
COTIDIANO *adj.* everyday.
COTONETE *s.m.* swab.
COTOVELADA *s.f.* nudge.
COTOVELAR *v.* to elbow.
COTOVELO *s.m.* elbow.
COURO *s.m.* leather.
COUVE *s.f.* kale, cole.
COUVE-FLOR *s.f.* cauliflower.
COUVERT *s.m.* cover charge.
COVA *s.f.* cavity, hole; grave.
COVARDE *s.2gên.* coward / *adj.2gên.* coward.
COVARDIA *s.f.* cowardice, cowardliness.
COVIL *s.m.* lair.
COXA *s.f.* thigh.
COXO(A) *adj.* lame, limping, halting.
COZER *v.* to cook.
COZIDO(A) *adj.* cooked.
COZINHA *s.f.* kitchen.
COZINHAR *v.* to cook.
COZINHEIRO *s.m.* cook.
CRACHÁ *s.m.* badge, tag; name tag.
CRÂNIO *s.m.* cranium, skull, braincase.
CRAQUE *s.2gên.* expert.
CRATERA *s.f.* crater.
CRAVO *s.m.* clove (especiaria), carnation (flor), comedo, blackhead (acne).
CRECHE *s.f.* daycare, nursery.
CREDENCIAL *s.f.* credential.
CREDITAR *v.* to deposit.
CRÉDITO *s.m.* credit.
CREME *s.m.* cream.
CRENÇA *s.f.* belief, faith.
CRENTE *s.2gên.* believer, believing / *adj.2gên.* believer, believing.
CREPÚSCULO *s.m.* dusk, dawn, twilight.
CRER *v.* to believe.
CRESCENTE *adj.* growing.
CRESCER *v.* to grow, to expand, to enlarge.
CRESCIDO *adj.* grown.
CRESCIMENTO *s.m.* growth, increase.
CRESPO *adj.* wrinkles; crisped, curly, curled, frizzled.

CRETINO(A) *s.m.* cretin / *adj.* cretin.
CRIA *s.f.* breed, brood, litter, offspring.
CRIAÇÃO *s.f.* creation.
CRIADO *s.m.* raised, created.
CRIADOR(A) *s.m.* creator; creative.
CRIANÇA *s.f.* child, kid.
CRIAR *v.* to rise, to create.
CRIATURA *s.f.* creature.
CRIME *s.m.* crime, offense.
CRIOULO(A) *s.m.* creole / *adj.* creole.
CRISE *s.f.* crisis.
CRISTAL *s.m.* crystal.
CRISTALIZADO *adj.* crystallized.
CRISTÃO(Ã) *s.m.* Christian / *adj.* Christian.
CRISTIANISMO *s.m.* Christianity.
CRISTO *s.m.* Christ.
CRITÉRIO *s.m.* criterion.
CRITERIOSO(A) *adj.* judicious, discerning, selective.
CRÍTICA *s.f.* critique, criticism.
CRITICAR *v.* to criticize, to judge.
CRÍTICO(A) *adj.* critic.
CROCANTE *adj.* crunchy.
CRÔNICA *s.f.* chronicle.
CRONOLOGIA *s.f.* chronology.
CRONOLÓGICO *adj.* chronologic, chronological.
CROQUETE *s.m.* croquette.
CRU(A) *adj.* raw.
CRUCIAL *s.m.* crucial / *adj.2gên.* crucial.
CRUCIFICADO *s.m.* crucified / *adj.* crucified.
CRUCIFICAR *v.* to crucify.
CRUCIFIXO *s.m.* crucifix.
CRUEL *adj.* cruel.
CRUELDADE *s.f.* cruelty.
CRUZ *s.f.* cross.
CRUZADO *adj.* crusader, cross (boxe).
CRUZAMENTO *s.m.* crossing.
CRUZAR *v.* to cross.
CRUZEIRO *s.m.* cruise.
CU *s.m.* asshole, arse.
CUBA *s.f.* Cuba.
CUBANO(A) *s.m.* Cuban / *adj.2gên.* Cuban.
CUCO *s.m.* cuckoo.
CUECA *s.f.* underpants.
CUIDADO *s.m.* care, precaution.
CUIDAR *v.* to take care.
CUJO(A) *pron.* whose, which.
CULINÁRIA *s.f.* culinary, cookery.

CULPA *s.f.* fault, guilt, blame; offense.
CULPAR *v.* to blame, to accuse, to incriminate.
CULTIVAR *v.* to cultivate.
CULTIVO *s.m.* cultivation.
CULTO *s.m.* cult.
CULTURA *s.f.* culture.
CULTURAL *adj.* cultural.
CÚMPLICE *s.2gên.* accomplice / *adj.2gên.* accomplice.
CUMPRIMENTAR *v.* to greet, to salute; to compliment.
CUMPRIMENTO *s.m.* greeting, congratulation.
CUMPRIR *v.* to comply, to abide.
CÚMULO *s.m.* cumulus, pile; paroxysm, spasm.
CUNHADA *s.f.* sister-in-law.
CUNHADO *s.m.* brother-in-law.
CUPIM *s.m.* termite.
CURA *s.f.* cure.
CURADO *adj.* cured.
CURADOR *s.m.* guardian, curator.
CURANDEIRO *s.m.* healer, witch doctor / *adj.* healer, witch doctor.
CURAR *v.* to cure.
CURATIVO *s.m.* dressing, treatment / *adj.* dressing, treatment.
CURIOSIDADE *s.f.* curiosity.
CURIOSO(A) *adj.* curious, inquisitive, interesting.
CURRAL *s.m.* pen; pinfold, corral.
CURRÍCULO *s.m.* curriculum vitae, résumé.
CURSAR *v.* to attend.
CURSO *s.m.* course.
CURSOR *s.m.* cursor.
CURTIÇÃO *s.f.* fun.
CURTIDO *adj.* tanned, hardened.
CURTIR *v.* to enjoy.
CURTO(A) *adj.* short.
CURVA *s.f.* curve, bend.
CUSCUZ *s.m.* couscous.
CUSPE *s.m.* spit.
CUSPIR *v.* to spit.
CUSTAR *v.* to cost.
CUSTO *s.m.* cost, expense, price.
CUTÍCULA *s.f.* cuticle.
CUTUCADA *s.f.* poke, nudge.
CUTUCÃO *s.m.* jab, vigorous nudge.
CUTUCAR *v.* to prod.

Dd

D, d *s.m.* the fourth letter of the Portuguese alphabet.
DÁBLIU *s.m.* letter w.
DADÁ *s.m.* Dada.
DADAÍSMO *s.m.* Dadaism.
DADAÍSTA *adj.2gên.* Dadaist / *s.2gên.* Dadaist.
DÁDIVA *s.f.* donation, gift, present.
DADIVAR *v.* to gift, to present.
DADO *s.m.* dice, data.
DAÍ *prep.* then, therefore, that for.
DALI *prep.* from there.
DÁLIA *s.f.* dahlia.
DÁLMATA *adj.2gên.* Dalmatian / *s.2gên.* Dalmatian.
DÁLTON *s.m.* dalton.
DALTÔNICO(A) *adj.* daltonian, color blind / *s.m.* daltonian, color blind.
DALTONISMO *s.m.* daltonism, color blindness.
DAMA *s.f.* lady, maid, dame.
DAMAS *s.f. pl.* checkers, draughts.
DAMASCO *s.m.* apricot, damask.
DAMASQUEIRO *s.m.* apricot tree.

DANADO(A) *adj.* damned; naughty; damaged.
DANAR *v.* to harm, to hurt.
DANÇA *s.f.* dance.
DANÇANTE *adj.2gên.* dancing / *s.2gên.* dancing.
DANÇAR *v.* to dance.
DANÇARINO(A) *s.m.* dancer.
DANÊS *adj.* Danish, Dane / *s.m.* Danish, Dane.
DANIFICAÇÃO *s.f.* damaging, damnification.
DANIFICADO(A) *adj.* damaged.
DANIFICAR *v.* to damage.
DANINHO(A) *adj.* damaging, detrimental.
DANO *s.m.* damage, injury.
DANTESCO(A) *adj.* Dantesque, awful, horrible.
DAQUELE *prep.* from that, of that.
DAQUI *prep.* from here.
DAR *v.* to give.
DARDO *s.m.* dart, spear, sarcarsm, irony.
DARWINISMO *s.m.* Darwinism.

DARWINISTA *adj.2gên.* Darwinist / *s.2gên.* Darwinist.
DATA *s.f.* date, period.
DATAR *v.* to date.
DATILOGRAFAR *v.* to type.
DATILOGRAFIA *s.f.* typewriting.
DATILÓGRAFO *s.m.* typist.
DATILOSCOPIA *s.f.* dactyloscopy.
DATIVO *adj.* dative / *s.m.* dative.
DE *prep.* of, from.
DEAMBULAÇÃO *s.f.* walk, stroll.
DEAMBULAR *v.* to walk around, to stroll.
DEBAIXO *adv.* below, under.
DEBALDE *adv.* in vain.
DEBANDADA *s.f.* flight, escape.
DEBANDAR *v.* to put to flight, to scatter.
DEBATE *s.m.* discussion, debate.
DEBATER *v.* to debate.
DEBELAR *v.* to subdue, to overcome.
DÉBIL *adj.2gên.* weak.
DEBILIDADE *s.f.* weakness.
DEBILITAÇÃO *s.f.* debilitation.
DEBILITAR *v.* to debilitate.
DEBITAR *v.* to debit, to bill, to charge.
DÉBITO *s.m.* debit.
DEBOCHADO(A) *adj.* lewd; scornful; mocking.
DEBOCHAR *v.* to mock.
DEBOCHE *s.m.* debauch, mockery, jeer.
DEBRUÇAR *v.* to bend over.
DEBULHAR *v.* to thresh.
DEBUTANTE *adj.2gên.* debutante / *s.2gên.* debutante.
DEBUTAR *v.* to make a debut, to debut.
DÉCADA *s.f.* decade.
DECADÊNCIA *s.f.* decadence, decline, decay.
DECADENTE *adj.2gên.* decadent, declining, decaying.
DECÁGONO *s.m.* decagon.
DECAÍDA *s.f.* decay, decline, fall.
DECAIR *v.* to decay, to decline.
DECÁLOGO *s.m.* Decalogue.
DECALQUE *s.m.* decalcomania, copying, tracing.
DECANTAÇÃO *s.f.* decantation.
DECANTAR *v.* to decant.
DECAPITAÇÃO *s.f.* decapitation.
DECAPITAR *v.* to behead.
DECASSÍLABO(A) *adj.* decasyllable, decasyllabic / *s.m.* decasyllable, decasyllabic.
DECATLO *s.m.* decathlon.
DECÊNCIA *s.f.* decency.
DECÊNIO *s.m.* decennium.
DECENTE *adj.2gên.* decent, honest.
DECEPAMENTO *s.m.* amputation.
DECEPAR *v.* to cut off, to ampute.
DECEPÇÃO *s.f.* disappointment.
DECEPCIONADO(A) *adj.* disappointed.
DECEPCIONANTE *adj.2gên.* disappointing.
DECERTO *adv.* certainly, surely.
DECIBEL *s.m.* decibel.
DECIDIDO(A) *adj.* decided, determined.
DECIDIR *v.* to decide.
DECIFRAR *v.* to decipher, to decode.
DECIMAL *adj.2gên.* decimal.
DÉCIMO *num.* tenth.
DECISÃO *s.f.* decision.
DECISIVO(A) *adj.* decisive.
DECLAMAÇÃO *s.f.* declamation, recitation.
DECLAMAR *v.* to recite, to declaim.
DECLARAÇÃO *s.f.* declaration.
DECLARAR *v.* to declare.
DECLARATIVO(A) *adj.* declarative.
DECLINAÇÃO *s.f.* declension.
DECLINAR *v.* to decline, to reject, to refuse.
DECLÍNIO *s.m.* decline, declination.
DECLIVE *s.m.* slope, declivity.
DECODIFICAÇÃO *s.f.* decoding.
DECODIFICAR *v.* to decode, to decipher.
DECOLAGEM *s.f.* take-off.
DECOLAR *v.* to take off.
DECOMPOR *v.* to analyse, to decompose.
DECOMPOSIÇÃO *s.f.* analysis, decomposition.
DECOMPOSTO(A) *adj.* decomposed.
DECORAÇÃO *s.f.* decoration, adornment.
DECORADOR *adj.* decorator / *s.m.* decorator.
DECORAR *v.* to decorate, to adorn, to remember, to retain.
DECORATIVO(A) *adj.* decorative.
DECORO *s.m.* decorum, decency.
DECORRÊNCIA *s.f.* consequence.
DECORRENTE *adj.2gên.* deriving.
DECORRER *v.* to pass.
DECOTADO(A) *adj.* low-necked.
DECOTAR *v.* to make low-necked; to trim.
DECOTE *s.m.* low neck, neckline.

DECRÉPITO(A) *adj.* decrepit.
DECRESCENTE *adj.2gên.* decreasing, decrescent.
DECRESCER *v.* to decrease, to diminish.
DECRESCIMENTO *s.m.* decrease.
DECRETAR *v.* to decree, to proclaim.
DECRETO *s.m.* decree, order.
DECÚBITO *s.m.* decubitus, decumbency.
DEDAL *s.m.* thimble.
DEDÃO *s.m.* thumb (da mão), big toe (do pé).
DEDETIZAÇÃO *s.f.* spraying of pesticide.
DEDETIZAR *v.* to spray pesticide.
DEDICAÇÃO *s.f.* dedication.
DEDICADO *adj.* dedicated.
DEDICAR *v.* to dedicate.
DEDICATÓRIA *s.f.* dedication.
DEDILHAR *v.* to finger, to play with the fingers.
DEDO *s.m.* finger (da mão), toe (do pé).
DEDO-DURO *adj.2gên.* informer, whistleblower / *s.m.* informer, whistleblower.
DEDUÇÃO *s.f.* deduction.
DEDURAR *v.* to acuse, to rat.
DEDUZIR *v.* to deduct, to deduce, to reduce.
DEFASAGEM *s.f.* discrepancy.
DEFASAR *v.* to dephase.
DEFECAR *v.* to defecate.
DEFECTIVO(A) *adj.* defective.
DEFEITO *s.m.* defect, fault.
DEFEITUOSO(A) *adj.* defective, faulty.
DEFENDER *v.* to defend, to protect.
DEFENSIVA *s.f.* defensive.
DEFENSOR *s.m.* defender, protector.
DEFERÊNCIA *s.f.* deference.
DEFERIDO(A) *adj.* granted, conferred.
DEFERIR *v.* to grant, to concede.
DEFESA *s.f.* defence.
DEFICIÊNCIA *s.f.* deficiency.
DEFICIENTE *adj.2gên.* deficient.
DÉFICIT *s.m.* deficit.
DEFINHADO(A) *adj.* thin, weak.
DEFINHAR *v.* to make thin; to debilitate.
DEFINIÇÃO *s.f.* definition.
DEFINIDO(A) *adj.* defined.
DEFINIR *v.* to define.
DEFINITIVAMENTE *adv.* definitively.
DEFINITIVO(A) *adj.* definitive.
DEFLACIONAR *v.* to deflate.
DEFLAGRAR *v.* to burn, to deflagrate.

DEFLEXÃO *s.f.* deflection
DEFLORAR *v.* to deflower.
DEFLUIR *v.* to flow down.
DEFORMAÇÃO *s.f.* deformation.
DEFORMADO(A) *adj.* deformed.
DEFORMAR *v.* to deform.
DEFORMIDADE *s.f.* deformity.
DEFRAUDAÇÃO *s.f.* defraudation.
DEFRAUDAR *v.* to defraud.
DEFRONTE *adv.* opposite to, in front of.
DEFUMADO(A) *adj.* smoked.
DEFUMAR *v.* to smoke-dry, to cure with smoke.
DEFUNTO(A) *adj.* dead; corpse / *s.m.* dead; corpse.
DEGELAR *v.* to defrost, to thaw.
DEGELO *s.m.* thawing, thaw.
DEGENERAÇÃO *s.f.* degeneration.
DEGENERADO(A) *adj.* degenerate, degraded.
DEGENERAR *v.* to degenerate.
DEGENERATIVO(A) *adj.* degenerative.
DEGLUTIÇÃO *s.f.* swallowing.
DEGLUTIR *v.* to swallow.
DEGOLAR *v.* to decapitate.
DEGRADAÇÃO *s.f.* degradation.
DEGRADADO(A) *adj.* degraded.
DEGRADANTE *adj.2gên.* degrading.
DEGRADAR *v.* to degrade.
DEGRAU *s.m.* step.
DEGREDAR *v.* to exile, to banish.
DEGREDO *s.m.* exile, banishment.
DEGRINGOLAR *v.* to roll down, to fall; to come down.
DEGUSTAÇÃO *s.f.* tasting.
DEGUSTAR *v.* to taste.
DEITADO(A) *adj.* lying, stretched out.
DEITAR *v.* to lay down.
DEIXA *s.f.* cue, hint.
DEIXAR *v.* to leave, to quit.
DEJETAR *v.* to defecate.
DEJETO *s.m.* defecation, evacuation.
DELAÇÃO *s.f.* accusation, delation.
DELATAR *v.* to delate, to denounce.
DELEGAÇÃO *s.f.* delegation.
DELEGACIA *s.f.* police station.
DELEGADO(A) *s.m.* delegate, police chief.
DELEGAR *v.* to delegate.
DELEITAR *v.* to delight.
DELEITE *s.m.* delight.
DELGADO(A) *adj.* thin, slender.

DELIBERAR *v.* to deliberate.
DELICADEZA *s.f.* delicacy, courtesy.
DELICADO(A) *adj.* delicate.
DELÍCIA *s.f.* pleasure, delight, delicacy.
DELICIAR *v.* to delight.
DELICIOSO(A) *adj.* delicious.
DELIMITAR *v.* to delimit, to bound, to demarcate.
DELINEAMENTO *s.m.* delineation.
DELINEAR *v.* to outline.
DELINQUÊNCIA *s.f.* delinquency.
DELINQUIR *v.* to commit an offense.
DELIRADO(A) *adj.* delirious, mad, frantic.
DELIRANTE *adj.2gên.* delirious, insane.
DELIRAR *v.* to be delirious.
DELÍRIO *s.m.* delirium, insanity.
DELITO *s.m.* crime.
DELONGA *s.f.* delay.
DELTA *s.m.* delta.
DEMAGOGIA *s.f.* demagogy.
DEMAGOGO(A) *s.m.* demagogue.
DEMAIS *adv.* too much, extrordinary, excessive.
DEMANDA *s.f.* lawsuit.
DEMANDAR *v.* to demand, to require.
DEMANDISTA *s.2gên.* plaintiff, demandant.
DEMÃO *s.f.* layer, coat.
DEMARCAR *v.* to demarcate.
DEMASIA *s.f.* excess.
DEMÊNCIA *s.f.* dementia.
DEMENTE *adj.2gên.* insane, mad, lunatic / *s.2gên.* insane, mad, lunatic.
DEMISSÃO *s.f.* dismissal.
DEMITIDO(A) *adj.* dismissed, fired.
DEMITIR *v.* to dismiss.
DEMO *s.m.* demon, devil; demo, demonstration.
DEMOCRACIA *s.f.* democracy.
DEMOCRATA *adj.2gên.* democrata / *s.2gên.* democrat.
DEMOLIÇÃO *s.f.* demolition.
DEMOLIR *v.* to demolish.
DEMONÍACO(A) *adj.* demonic, demoniac.
DEMÔNIO *s.m.* devil, demon.
DEMONISMO *s.m.* demonism.
DEMONSTRAÇÃO *s.f.* proof, demonstration.
DEMONSTRAR *v.* to demonstrate, to show, to prove.
DEMORA *s.f.* delay, lateness.
DEMORAR *v.* to delay, to detain, to retard.

DENDROLOGIA *s.f.* dendrology.
DENEGRIR *v.* to blacken, to defame.
DENGOSO(A) *adj.* whining, affected, finical.
DENGUE *s.f.* dengue.
DENOMINAÇÃO *s.f.* denomination.
DENOMINADOR *adj.* denominator; denominative / *s.m.* denominator; denominative.
DENOMINAR *v.* to denominate, to name, to designate.
DENOTAÇÃO *s.f.* denotation.
DENOTAR *v.* to show, to indicate.
DENSIDADE *s.f.* density.
DENSO(A) *adj.* dense.
DENTADA *s.f.* bite.
DENTADURA *s.f.* denture, false teeth.
DENTAR *v.* to bite, to snap.
DENTE *s.m.* tooth.
DENTEAR *v.* to indent, to notch.
DENTIÇÃO *s.f.* dentition, teething.
DENTIFRÍCIO(A) *adj.* dentifrice / *s.m.* dentifrice.
DENTISTA *s.2gên.* dentist.
DENTRE *prep.* among.
DENTRO *adv.* in, inside.
DENTUÇO(A) *adj.* buck teeth / *s.m.* buck teeth.
DENÚNCIA *s.f.* denunciation.
DENUNCIAR *v.* to denounce, to accuse.
DEPARAR *v.* to come across.
DEPARTAMENTO *s.m.* department.
DEPENADOR *adj.* plucker / *s.m.* plucker.
DEPENAR *v.* to pluck.
DEPENDÊNCIA *s.f.* dependence, dependency.
DEPENDENTE *adj.2gên.* dependent / *s.2gên.* dependent.
DEPENDER *v.* to depend on.
DEPENDURAR *v.* to hang, to suspend.
DEPILAR *v.* to wax, to pluck.
DEPILATÓRIO(A) *adj.* depilatory / *s.m.* depilatory.
DEPLORAR *v.* to deplore, to bemoan, to lament.
DEPLORÁVEL *adj.2gên.* deplorable, lamentable.
DEPOENTE *adj.2gên.* deponent, affiant / *s.2gên.* deponent, affiant.
DEPOIMENTO *s.m.* testimony, state.
DEPOIS *adv.* after, afterwards, later on, then.

DEPOR *v.* to testify.
DEPORTAR *v.* to deport, to exile.
DEPOSITANTE *adj.2gên.* depositing / *s.2gên.* depositor.
DEPOSITAR *v.* to deposit.
DEPOSITÁRIO *s.m.* depositary.
DEPÓSITO *s.m.* deposit.
DEPRAVADO(A) *adj.* depraved / *s.m.* depraved.
DEPRAVAR *v.* to deprave, to corrupt.
DEPRECIAÇÃO *s.f.* depreciation.
DEPRECIAR *v.* to depreciate, to devalue.
DEPREDAR *v.* to depredate, to despoil, to plunder.
DEPREENDER *v.* to infer, to deduce.
DEPRESSA *adv.* fast, quickly.
DEPRESSÃO *s.f.* depression.
DEPRESSIVO(A) *adj.* depressive; depressing.
DEPRIMENTE *adj.2gên.* depressing.
DEPRIMIDO(A) *adj.* depressed.
DEPRIMIR *v.* to depress.
DEPURADOR *adj.* purifier, depurator / *s.m.* purifier, depurator.
DEPURAR *v.* to purify, to depurate, to cleanse.
DEPUTADO(A) *s.m.* deputy, representative.
DEPUTAR *v.* to depute, to delegate.
DERIVA *s.f.* drift, leeway.
DERIVAÇÃO *s.f.* derivation.
DERIVADO(A) *adj.* derivative / *s.m.* derivative.
DERIVAR *v.* to derive.
DERMATITE *s.f.* dermatitis.
DERMATOLOGIA *s.f.* dermatology.
DERME *s.f.* dermis.
DERRABAR *v.* to bobtail, to dock.
DERRADEIRO(A) *adj.* last; conclusive, ultimate.
DERRAMA *s.f.* looping, pruning.
DERRAMAR *v.* to spill.
DERRAME *s.m.* shedding; stroke.
DERRAPAR *v.* to skid.
DERREAMENTO *s.m.* exhaustion, prostration.
DERREAR *v.* to bend down, to stoop; to wear out.
DERREDOR *adv.* around, about.
DERRETER *v.* to melt.
DERRETIDO(A) *adj.* melted.
DERRIBAR *v.* to throw down, to knock down; to pull down.

DERROTA *s.f.* defeat.
DERROTAR *v.* to defeat.
DERROTISMO *s.m.* defeatism.
DERRUBADA *s.f.* falling of trees.
DERRUBAR *v.* to knock down.
DERRUIR *v.* to collapse; to founder; to destroy.
DESABAFAR *v.* to confide, to give vent to, to uncover.
DESABAFO *s.m.* ease, alleviation, relief.
DESABALADO(A) *adj.* precipitate, overhasty; excessive.
DESABAMENTO *s.m.* collapse.
DESABAR *v.* to collapse.
DESABILITAR *v.* to incapacitate, to disable.
DESABITUAR *v.* to disaccustom, to break a habit.
DESABONADO(A) *adj.* discredited, disreputed.
DESABOTOAR *v.* to unbotton.
DESABRIGADO *adj.* unsheltered, unprotected.
DESABROCHAR *v.* to blossom, to bloom.
DESACATAR *v.* to disrespect, to affront, to insult.
DESACONSELHAR *v.* to dissuade, to advise against.
DESACORDADO(A) *adj.* unconscious, senseless.
DESACORDO *s.m.* disagreement.
DESACOSTUMAR *v.* to disaccustom.
DESACREDITAR *v.* to discredit.
DESAFETO *s.m.* disaffection.
DESAFIAR *v.* to challenge, to defy.
DESAFINAÇÃO *s.f.* disharmony, dissonance.
DESAFINAR *v.* to untune.
DESAFIO *s.m.* challenge, defiance, competition.
DESAFOGAR *v.* to ease, to relieve.
DESAFOGO *s.m.* relief.
DESAFORADO(A) *adj.* insolent, impertinent; rude.
DESAFORAR *v.* to make insolent.
DESAFORO *s.m.* insolence.
DESAFORTUNADO(A) *adj.* unfortunate.
DESAFRONTAR *v.* to revenge, to vindicate; to requite.
DESAGASALHAR *v.* to unshelter; to uncover.
DESAGRADAR *v.* to displease.
DESAGRADÁVEL *adj.2gên.* unpleasant.

DESAGRAVAR *v.* to redress, to make amends; to avenge, to revenge.
DESAGRAVO *s.m.* amends, reparation, revenge, retaliation.
DESAGREGAÇÃO *s.f.* disaggregation, dissolution.
DESAGREGAR *v.* to disaggregate, to dissolve.
DESAGUAR *v.* to drain, to dry.
DESAJEITADO(A) *adj.* clumsy, unskillful.
DESAJEITAR *v.* to disarrange, to deform.
DESAJUIZADO(A) *adj.* witless, unwise.
DESAJUIZAR *v.* to become irresponsible.
DESAJUNTAR *v.* to disjoin, to disunite.
DESAJUSTAR *v.* to disarrange.
DESALENTO *s.m.* discouragement.
DESALINHADO(A) *adj.* out of line; sloppy.
DESALINHAR *v.* to put out of line; to dishevel.
DESALINHO *s.m.* disorder, disarray.
DESALMADO(A) *adj.* soulless, inhuman.
DESALOJAR *v.* to dislodge, to drive out.
DESALUMIADO(A) *adj.* dark, gloomy.
DESAMARRAR *v.* to untie.
DESAMASSAR *v.* to smooth, to straighten out.
DESAMBIÇÃO *s.f.* unambitiousness; modesty, unselfishness.
DESAMBIENTAR *v.* to displace.
DESAMOR *s.m.* lovelessness, disaffection.
DESAMPARAR *v.* to abandon, to forsake.
DESANDAR *v.* to turn or draw back.
DESANIMADO(A) *adj.* discouraged, dispirited.
DESANIMAR *v.* to dishearten, to discourage.
DESANUVIAR *v.* to uncloud, to clear up.
DESAPAIXONAR *v.* to free from passion, to calm.
DESAPARECER *v.* to disappear.
DESAPARECIMENTO *s.m.* disappearance.
DESAPEGO *s.m.* indifference.
DESAPERCEBIDO(A) *adj.* unprepared, destitute.
DESAPERTAR *v.* to loosen; to unfasten.
DESAPONTAR *v.* to disappoint.
DESAPROPRIAR *v.* to dispossess, to deprive.
DESAPROVAR *v.* to disapprove.
DESARMAR *v.* to disarm.
DESARMONIA *s.f.* disharmony, discord.
DESARMONIZAR *v.* to disharmonize.

DESARRAIGAR *v.* to uproot.
DESARRANJAR *v.* to disarrange.
DESARRUMADO(A) *adj.* untidy.
DESARRUMAR *v.* to mess up.
DESASSOMBRAR *v.* to expose to the sun, to brighten; to embolden.
DESASSOMBRO *s.m.* frankness, firmness; boldness.
DESASSOSSEGAR *v.* to bother, to disquiet, to disturb.
DESASSOSSEGO *s.m.* unquietness, uneasiness.
DESASTRADO(A) *adj.* clumsy.
DESASTRE *s.m.* disaster.
DESATAR *v.* to undo, to untie.
DESATENÇÃO *s.f.* carelessness, inattention, absence of mind.
DESATENTO(A) *adj.* distracted, inadvertent.
DESATINAR *v.* to madden.
DESATINO *s.m.* madness, nonsense.
DESATIVAR *v.* to shut down.
DESATUALIZADO(A) *adj.* outdated.
DESAVENÇA *s.f.* quarrel.
DESAVISADO(A) *adj.* not informed, imprudent / *s.m.* not informed, imprudent.
DESBANCAR *v.* to surpass, to excel; to take away the benches.
DESBARATAR *v.* to waste, to squander.
DESBLOQUEAR *v.* to unblock.
DESBOCADO(A) *adj.* foul-mouthed.
DESBOTAR *v.* to discolour, to fade.
DESBRAVAR *v.* to break, to cultivate.
DESCABELAR *v.* to disarrange someone's hair.
DESCABIDO(A) *adj.* improper, not suitable.
DESCALÇAR *v.* to take off.
DESCALÇO(A) *adj.* barefoot.
DESCAMAÇÃO *s.f.* scaling.
DESCAMAR *v.* to scale.
DESCAMBAR *v.* to slide; to talk imprudently.
DESCAMPADO(A) *adj.* open field, desert / *s.m.* open field, desert.
DESCANSAR *v.* to rest.
DESCARADO(A) *adj.* shameless.
DESCARGA *s.f.* unloading.
DESCARREGAR *v.* to unload.
DESCARTAR *v.* to discard, to get rid of.
DESCARTÁVEL *adj.2gên.* disposable, expendable.
DESCASAR *v.* to divorce; to separate.
DESCASCAR *v.* to peel.

DESCASO *s.m.* negligence, inattention.
DESCENDÊNCIA *s.f.* descent, ancestry.
DESCENDENTE *adj.2gên.* descendent / *s.2gên.* descendant.
DESCENDER *v.* to descend, to come from.
DESCENTRALIZAR *v.* to decentralize.
DESCER *v.* to go down, to come down, to descend.
DESCEREBRAR *v.* to turn insane; to decerebrate.
DESCIDA *s.f.* descent; slope, hillside.
DESCLASSIFICAR *v.* to disqualify.
DESCOBRIR *v.* to discover, to find, to reveal.
DESCOLAR *v.* to unglue, to unpaste.
DESCOLORIR *v.* to discolour.
DESCOMPOR *v.* to disarrange, to discompose.
DESCOMPOSTURA *s.f.* disorder, discomposure.
DESCOMUNAL *adj.2gên.* uncommon, rare.
DESCONCERTAR *v.* to disconcert; to confuse.
DESCONFIANÇA *s.f.* suspicion.
DESCONFIAR *v.* to be suspicious, to suspect.
DESCONFORTO *s.m.* discomfort.
DESCONGELAR *v.* to thaw, to defrost.
DESCONGESTIONAR *v.* to decongest.
DESCONHECER *v.* to ignore.
DESCONHECIDO(A) *adj.* unknown.
DESCONSERTAR *v.* to disarrange.
DESCONSIDERAR *v.* to disregard.
DESCONTAR *v.* to deduct, to discount.
DESCONTENTAR *v.* to discontent, to displease.
DESCONTENTE *adj.2gên.* discontent.
DESCONTO *s.m.* discount.
DESCONTRAIR *v.* to relax; to become spontaneous.
DESCONTROLAR *v.* to lose control.
DESCONVERSAR *v.* to dissimulate; to break off a conversation.
DESCORADO(A) *adj.* discoloured, colourless.
DESCORAR *v.* to discolour.
DESCORTESIA *s.f.* discourtesy, unkindness.
DESCRENÇA *s.f.* disbelief, incredulity.
DESCRENTE *adj.2gên.* incredulous, unbelieving / *s.2gên.* unbeliever.
DESCREVER *v.* to describe.
DESCRIÇÃO *s.f.* description.
DESCRIMINAR *v.* to decriminalize; to absolve.

DESCRITIVO(A) *adj.* descriptive.
DESCUIDAR *v.* to neglect.
DESCUIDO *s.m.* carelessness, negligence.
DESCULPA *s.f.* excuse, apology.
DESCULPAR *v.* to apologize, to excuse.
DESCUMPRIR *v.* to disobey.
DESDE *prep.* from, since.
DESDÉM *s.m.* disdain.
DESDENHAR *v.* to disdain, to scorn.
DESDIZER *v.* to unsay; to deny.
DESDOBRAR *v.* to unfold.
DESEJAR *v.* to want, to wish.
DESEJO *s.m.* wish, desire.
DESEMBAÇAR *v.* to clean, to wipe steam.
DESEMBALAR *v.* to unpack, to uncase.
DESEMBARCAR *v.* to land.
DESEMBARGADOR *adj.* chief judge / *s.m.* chief judge.
DESEMBARQUE *s.m.* disembarkation, debarkation.
DESEMBESTADO(A) *adj.* unrestraint, unruled.
DESEMBOLSAR *v.* to disburse, to spend, to expend.
DESEMBRULHAR *v.* to unwrap, to unpack.
DESEMPENHAR *v.* to carry out, to perform.
DESEMPREGADO(A) *adj.* unemployed / *s.m.* unemployed.
DESEMPREGO *s.m.* unemployment.
DESENCADEAR *v.* to unleash, to unchain.
DESENCAMINHAR *v.* to misguide, to mislead.
DESENCANTAR *v.* to disenchant.
DESENCARNAR *v.* to leave the body.
DESENCARREGAR *v.* to discharge.
DESENCHARCAR *v.* to drain, to dry out.
DESENCORAJAR *v.* to discourage.
DESENCOSTAR *v.* to straighten.
DESENFREAR *v.* to unbridle, to set loose.
DESENGAJAR *v.* to disengage.
DESENGONÇADO(A) *adj.* unhinged; clumsy, awkward.
DESENHAR *v.* to draw.
DESENHO *s.m.* drawing.
DESENLACE *s.m.* unfolding, conclusion, outcome.
DESENROLAR *v.* to unroll, to unwind.
DESENTENDIMENTO *s.m.* misunderstanding.
DESENTUPIR *v.* to unblock.

DESENVOLTURA *s.f.* nimbleness, agility.
DESENVOLVER *v.* to develop.
DESENVOLVIDO(A) *adj.* developed.
DESEQUILIBRADO(A) *adj.* unbalanced.
DESEQUILIBRAR *v.* to throw out of balance, to unbalance.
DESEQUILÍBRIO *s.m.* unbalance; instability.
DESERÇÃO *s.f.* desertion.
DESERDADO(A) *adj.* disinherited.
DESERDAR *v.* to disinherit.
DESERTAR *v.* to desert.
DESERTO(A) *adj.* desert, uninhabited / *s.m.* desert.
DESERTOR *adj.* deserter / *s.m.* deserter.
DESESPERADO(A) *adj.* desperate.
DESESPERAR *v.* to despair.
DESESPERO *s.m.* despair.
DESFALCAR *v.* to embezzle.
DESFALECER *v.* to faint.
DESFALECIDO(A) *adj.* faint.
DESFALQUE *s.m.* peculation, embezzlement.
DESFAVORÁVEL *adj.2gên.* unfavourable.
DESFAZER *v.* to undo, to unmake.
DESFECHO *s.m.* outcome, conclusion.
DESFEITA *s.f.* insult.
DESFEITO(A) *adj.* undone.
DESFERIR *v.* to brandish; to fling.
DESFIADO(A) *adj.* unweaving; untwisted.
DESFIAR *v.* to unravel, to unknit.
DESFIGURADO(A) *adj.* disfigured.
DESFIGURAR *v.* to disfigure, to deform.
DESFILADEIRO *s.m.* ravine.
DESFILAR *v.* to parade.
DESFILE *s.m.* parade.
DESFLORESTAR *v.* to deforest.
DESFOLHAR *v.* to defoliate.
DESFORRA *s.f.* revenge, retaliation.
DESFORRAR *v.* to unline.
DESFRUTAR *v.* to enjoy; to mock.
DESGARRADO(A) *adj.* lost, stray.
DESGASTAR *v.* to wear down.
DESGASTE *s.m.* wearing, wastage; abrasion.
DESGRAÇA *s.f.* misfortune.
DESGRAÇADO(A) *adj.* rascal, scoundrel; unlucky, miserable / *s.m.* rascal, scoundrel; unlucky, miserable.
DESGRAÇAR *v.* to disgrace.
DESGRENHAR *v.* to dishevel, to rumple.
DESGRUDAR *v.* to unstick.
DESIDRATAÇÃO *s.f.* dehydration.
DESIDRATAR *v.* to dehydrate.
DESIGNAR *v.* to designate, to appoint.
DESÍGNIO *s.m.* intention, purpose, aim.
DESIGUAL *adj.2gên.* unequal.
DESIGUALDADE *s.f.* inequality, unlikeness.
DESILUDIR *v.* to disillusion.
DESIMPEDIR *v.* to disengage, to clear.
DESINÊNCIA *s.f.* extremity, termination; ending, inflection.
DESINFETANTE *adj.2gên.* disinfectant / *s.m.* disinfectant.
DESINFETAR *v.* to disinfect.
DESINTEGRAR *v.* to disintegrate.
DESINTERESSADO(A) *adj.* uninterested, disinterested.
DESINTERESSAR *v.* to disinterest.
DESINTERESSE *s.m.* disinterest.
DESINTOXICAR *v.* to disintoxicate, to detoxify.
DESISTÊNCIA *s.f.* desistance; giving up.
DESISTIR *v.* to give up, to quit.
DESJEJUM *s.m.* breakfast.
DESLACRAR *v.* to break the seal.
DESLAVADO(A) *adj.* discoloured, faded; shameless, impudent.
DESLEAL *adj.2gên.* disloyal.
DESLEALDADE *s.f.* disloyalty.
DESLEIXADO(A) *adj.* neglectful, messy, untidy.
DESLIGADO(A) *adj.* off, turned off; disconnected.
DESLIGAR *v.* to disconnect.
DESLIZAR *v.* to slide, to slip.
DESLOCADO(A) *adj.* dislocated; out of place.
DESLOCAMENTO *s.m.* displacement.
DESLOCAR *v.* to dislocate.
DESLUMBRANTE *adj.2gên.* dazzling.
DESLUMBRAR *v.* to dazzle.
DESMAIAR *v.* to faint.
DESMAIO *s.m.* faint.
DESMAMAR *v.* to wean.
DESMANCHA-PRAZERES *s.2gên.* killjoy, spoilsport.
DESMANCHAR *v.* to undo.
DESMANCHE *s.m.* chop shop.
DESMANDAR *v.* to repeal an order.
DESMANDO *s.m.* disobedience, insubordination.
DESMANTELAR *v.* to dismantle.

DESMARCAR *v.* to take away the marks; to cancel.
DESMASCARAR *v.* to unmask; to expose.
DESMEMBRAR *v.* to dismember.
DESMEMORIADO(A) *adj.* forgetful, oblivious / *s.m.* forgetful, oblivious.
DESMENTIR *v.* to deny.
DESMONTAR *v.* to dismount, to disassemble.
DESMORALIZADO(A) *adj.* demoralized.
DESMORALIZAR *v.* to demoralize.
DESMORONAR *v.* to collapse.
DESMOTIVAR *v.* to demotivate.
DESNACIONALIZAR *v.* to denationalize.
DESNATADO(A) *adj.* skimmed.
DESNATAR *v.* to skim.
DESNATURADO(A) *adj.* unnatural, cruel.
DESNECESSÁRIO(A) *adj.* unnecessary.
DESNÍVEL *s.m.* unevenness.
DESNIVELAR *v.* to make uneven, to unlevel.
DESNORTEADO(A) *adj.* bewildered, confused.
DESNORTEAR *v.* to bewilder, to confuse.
DESNUDAR *v.* to undress.
DESNUTRIÇÃO *s.* malnutrition.
DESNUTRIR *v.* to nourish poorly, to unfeed.
DESOBEDECER *v.* to disobey.
DESOBEDIENTE *adj.2gên.* disobedient.
DESOBSTRUIR *v.* to clear.
DESOCUPADO(A) *adj.* vacant, unoccupied.
DESOCUPAR *v.* to vacate.
DESODORANTE *adj.2gên.* deodorant / *s.m.* deodorant.
DESODORIZAR *v.* to deodorize.
DESOLAÇÃO *s.f.* desolation; sadness.
DESOLAR *v.* to desolate.
DESONERAR *v.* to exempt, to release; to liquidize; to degenerate.
DESONESTIDADE *s.f.* dishonesty.
DESONESTO(A) *adj.* dishonest.
DESONRA *s.f.* dishonour.
DESONRAR *v.* to dishonour.
DESONROSO(A) *adj.* dishonourable, unworthy.
DESORDEIRO(A) *adj.* turbulent, riotous / *s.m.* ruffian, rioter.
DESORDEM *s.f.* disorder.
DESORDENAR *v.* to disorder, to disarrange.
DESORGANIZAÇÃO *s.f.* disorganization.
DESORGANIZAR *v.* to disorganize.

DESORIENTADOR *adj.* perplexing, bewildering / *s.m.* disorientator.
DESORIENTAR *v.* to disorient.
DESOVAR *v.* to spawn, to spat.
DESOXIDAR *v.* to deoxidize.
DESOXIGENAR *v.* to deoxygenate.
DESPACHAR *v.* to dispatch, to send.
DESPEDAÇAR *v.* to tear into pieces.
DESPEDIDA *s.f.* farewell.
DESPEDIR *v.* to dismiss.
DESPEGAR *v.* to unglue, to detach, to unstick; to withdraw.
DESPEITADO(A) *adj.* envious.
DESPEITAR *v.* to despise.
DESPEITO *s.m.* spite.
DESPEJAR *v.* to pour; to evict.
DESPEJO *s.m.* eviction.
DESPENCAR *v.* to fall.
DESPENSA *s.f.* larder, store-room.
DESPERDIÇAR *v.* to waste (dinheiro); to squander.
DESPERDÍCIO *s.m.* waste.
DESPERTADOR *adj.* awakening, rousing / *s.m.* alarm clock.
DESPERTAR *v.* to awake / *s.m.* awakening.
DESPERTO(A) *adj.* awake.
DESPESA *s.f.* expense.
DESPIDO(A) *adj.* naked.
DESPIR *v.* to take off, to undress.
DESPISTAR *v.* to foil, to mislead.
DESPOJAR *v.* to loot.
DESPOJO *s.m.* booty; plunder, robbing.
DESPONTAR *v.* to blunt; to rise.
DÉSPOTA *adj.2gên.* despot, tyrant / *s.2gên.* despot, tyrant.
DESPREZAR *v.* to despise, to scorn.
DESPREZO *s.m.* scorn, disdain.
DESPROPORÇÃO *s.f.* disproportion.
DESQUALIFICAR *v.* to disqualify.
DESRESPEITAR *v.* to disrespect.
DESRESPEITO *s.m.* disrespect.
DESTACAR *v.* to point, to detach.
DESTAMPADO(A) *adj.* bare, uncovered.
DESTAMPAR *v.* to take off the lid, to open.
DESTAQUE *s.m.* prominence, eminence; highlight.
DESTE *prep.* of this, from this.
DESTEMIDO(A) *adj.* fearless, daring, bold.
DESTEMOR *s.m.* fearlessness, boldness.
DESTILAR *v.* to distill.

DESTINAR *v.* to destine.
DESTINATÁRIO(A) *s.m.* addressee.
DESTINO *s.m.* destiny.
DESTITUIR *v.* to deprive.
DESTOAR *v.* to be out of tune; to differ, to diverge.
DESTRAMBELHADO(A) *adj.* giddy, foolish / *s.m.* disorganized.
DESTRATAR *v.* to affront, to insult, to outrage.
DESTREZA *s.f.* skill.
DESTRO(A) *adj.* dexterous.
DESTROÇO *s.m.* destruction.
DESTRONADO(A) *adj.* dethroned.
DESTRONCAR *v.* to truncate, to lop; to sprain, to dislocate.
DESTRUIÇÃO *s.f.* destruction.
DESTRUIR *v.* to destroy.
DESUMANO(A) *adj.* inhuman.
DESVAIRADO(A) *adj.* crazy.
DESVALORIZAÇÃO *s.f.* devaluation.
DESVALORIZAR *v.* to devalue.
DESVANECER *v.* to dispel.
DESVANECIDO(A) *adj.* dispelled.
DESVANTAGEM *s.f.* disadvantage.
DESVARIO *s.m.* madness.
DESVENDAR *v.* to unmask, to reveal.
DESVENTURA *s.f.* misfortune.
DESVIAR *v.* to divert.
DESVINCULAR *v.* to detach.
DESVIO *s.m.* diversion, detour.
DESVIRTUAR *v.* to misinterpret.
DETALHAR *v.* to detail, to specify.
DETALHE *s.m.* detail.
DETECTAR *v.* to detect.
DETENÇÃO *s.f.* detention.
DETENTO(A) *s.m.* prisoner.
DETENTOR *adj.* detainer / *s.m.* detainer.
DETER *v.* to stop, to arrest.
DETERGENTE *adj.2gên.* detergent / *s.m.* detergent.
DETERIORAÇÃO *s.f.* deterioration.
DETERIORAR *v.* to deteriorate.
DETERMINAÇÃO *s.f.* determination.
DETERMINAR *v.* to determine.
DETESTAR *v.* to detest.
DETETIVE *s.2gên.* detective.
DETIDO(A) *adj.* detained / *s.m.* detained.
DETONAÇÃO *s.f.* detonation.
DETONANTE *adj.2gên.* detonating.

DETONAR *v.* to detonate.
DETRÁS *adv.* behind.
DETRIMENTO *s.m.* detriment.
DETRITO *s.m.* debris.
DETURPAR *v.* to corrupt, to distort.
DEUS *s.m.* God.
DEUSA *s.f.* goddess, divinity.
DEUTERONÔMIO *s.m.* Deuteronomy.
DEVAGAR *adv.* slowly.
DEVANEAR *v.* to daydream.
DEVANEIO *s.m.* daydream.
DEVASSA *s.f.* judicial inquiry.
DEVASSO(A) *adj.* debauched.
DEVASTAÇÃO *s.f.* devastation.
DEVASTAR *v.* to devastate.
DEVER *v.* to owe / *s.m.* duty, task.
DEVERAS *adv.* really.
DEVIDO(A) *adj.* proper / *s.m.* due, debt.
DEVOÇÃO *s.f.* devotion.
DEVOLUÇÃO *s.f.* devolution.
DEVOLVER *v.* to give back.
DEVORAR *v.* to devour.
DEVOTAR *v.* to devote.
DEVOTO(A) *adj.* devout.
DEZ *num.* ten.
DEZEMBRO *s.m.* December.
DEZENA *s.f.* ten, set of ten.
DEZENOVE *num.* nineteen.
DEZESSEIS *num.* sixteen.
DEZESSETE *num.* seventeen.
DEZOITO *num.* eighteen.
DIA *s.m.* day.
DIABETES *s.2gên.* diabetes.
DIABO *s.m.* devil.
DIADEMA *s.m.* diadem, crown.
DIAFRAGMA *s.m.* diaphragm.
DIAGNÓSTICO *s.m.* diagnosis.
DIAGONAL *adj.2gên.* diagonal.
DIAGRAMA *s.m.* diagram.
DIAGRAMAR *v.* to diagram.
DIALÉTICA *s.f.* dialectics.
DIALETO *s.m.* dialect.
DIALOGAR *v.* to talk, to dialogue.
DIÁLOGO *s.m.* dialogue.
DIAMANTE *s.m.* diamond.
DIÂMETRO *s.m.* diameter.
DIANTE *adv.* in front.
DIANTEIRO(A) *adj.* front, foremost, fore / *s.f.* lead.
DIAPASÃO *s.m.* diapason, tuning fork.

DIÁRIO(A) *adj.* diary / *s.m.* diary / *s.f.* daily rate.
DIARISTA *s.2gên.* day-worker; journalist; diarist.
DIARREIA *s.f.* diarrhoea.
DIATERMIA *s.f.* diathermy.
DIATÉRMICO(A) *adj.* diathermic.
DICA *s.f.* hint, clue.
DICÇÃO *s.f.* diction.
DICIONÁRIO *s.m.* dictionary.
DICIONARISTA *s.2gên.* lexicographer.
DICIONARIZAR *v.* to include in a dictionary, to compile a dictionary.
DICOTILEDÔNEA *s.f.* dicotyledons.
DIDÁTICO(A) *adj.* didactic, educational / *s.f.* didactics.
DIEDRO *adj.* dihedral / *s.m.* dihedron.
DIESEL *s.m.* diesel.
DIETA *s.f.* diet.
DIETÉTICO(A) *adj.* dietary / *s.f.* dietetics.
DIFAMAR *v.* to slander.
DIFERENÇA *s.f.* difference.
DIFERENCIAL *adj.2gên.* differential.
DIFERENCIAR *v.* to differentiate, to distinguish.
DIFERENTE *adj.2gên.* different.
DIFÍCIL *adj.2gên.* difficult.
DIFICULDADE *s.f.* difficulty.
DIFICULTAR *v.* to make difficult.
DIFUNDIR *v.* to diffuse; to spread, to scatter; to propagate.
DIFUSÃO *s.f.* diffusion.
DIFUSO(A) *adj.* diffuse.
DIGERIR *v.* to digest.
DIGESTÃO *s.f.* digestion.
DIGESTIVO(A) *adj.* digestive.
DIGITAÇÃO *s.f.* digitation, typing.
DIGITADOR *s.m.* typist.
DIGITAL *adj.2gên.* digital.
DIGITAR *v.* to type, to key in.
DÍGITO *s.m.* digit.
DIGLADIAR *v.* to digladiate, to quarrel.
DIGNAR *v.* to deign, to vouchsafe.
DIGNIDADE *s.f.* dignity.
DIGNIFICAR *v.* to dignify.
DIGNO(A) *adj.* worthy.
DIGRESSÃO *s.f.* digression.
DILACERAR *v.* to dilacerate, to tear.
DILATAR *v.* to dilate, to delay.
DILEMA *s.m.* dilemma.
DILUIR *v.* to dilute.
DILÚVIO *s.m.* flood.
DIMENSÃO *s.f.* dimension.
DIMINUIÇÃO *s.f.* reduction.
DIMINUIR *v.* to reduce.
DIMINUTIVO(A) *adj.* diminutive.
DIMINUTO(A) *adj.* minute.
DINAMARCA *s.f.* Denmark.
DINÂMICO(A) *adj.* dynamic.
DINAMISMO *s.m.* dynamism.
DINAMITE *s.f.* dynamite.
DÍNAMO *s.m.* dynamo, generator.
DINASTIA *s.f.* dynasty.
DINHEIRO *s.m.* money.
DINOSSAURO *s.m.* dinosaur.
DIOCESE *s.f.* diocese.
DIÓXIDO *s.m.* dioxide.
DIPLOMA *s.m.* diploma.
DIPLOMACIA *s.f.* diplomacy.
DIPLOMADO(A) *adj.* certificated, graduate / *s.m.* certificated, graduate.
DIPLOMAR *v.* to graduate.
DIPLOMATA *s.2gên.* diplomat.
DIPLOMÁTICO(A) *adj.* diplomatic.
DIPLOPIA *s.f.* diplopia.
DIQUE *s.m.* dyke.
DIREÇÃO *s.f.* direction.
DIRECIONAR *v.* to direct, to orientate.
DIREITO(A) *adj.* honest, just / *s.m.* right; law / *s.f.* right.
DIRETO(A) *adj.* direct, straight.
DIRETOR *s.m.* director.
DIRETORIA *s.f.* direction, administration; board of directors.
DIRETÓRIO *s.m.* directory.
DIRETRIZ *adj.2gên.* guideline.
DIRIGENTE *adj.2gên.* director / *s.2gên.* director.
DIRIGIDO(A) *adj.* directed, managed.
DIRIGIR *v.* to direct (filme, peça de teatro); to drive (carro).
DIRIGÍVEL *adj.2gên.* steerable.
DIRIMIR *v.* to nullify, to cancel.
DISCAGEM *s.f.* dialing.
DISCAR *v.* to dial.
DISCENTE *adj.2gên.* learning.
DISCERNENTE *adj.2gên.* discerning, distinguishing.
DISCERNIR *v.* to discern.

DISCIPLINA *s.f.* discipline; subject (matéria).
DISCO *s.m.* disc.
DISCORDAR *v.* to disagree.
DISCÓRDIA *s.f.* discord.
DISCORRER *v.* to discourse, to converse; to reason; to narrate.
DISCREPÂNCIA *s.f.* discrepancy.
DISCRETO(A) *adj.* discreet.
DISCRIÇÃO *s.f.* discretion.
DISCRIMINAÇÃO *s.f.* discrimination.
DISCRIMINAR *v.* to discriminate, to segregate.
DISCRIMINATÓRIO(A) *adj.* discriminatory.
DISCURSADOR *adj.* discoursing / *s.m.* speaker, orator, discourser.
DISCURSAR *v.* to discourse.
DISCURSIVO(A) *adj.* discursive.
DISCURSO *s.m.* speech.
DISCUSSÃO *s.f.* discussion, debate.
DISCUTIR *v.* to discuss, to argue.
DISFARÇAR *v.* to disguise.
DISFARCE *s.m.* disguise.
DISFORME *adj.2gên.* deformed, disfigured.
DISFUNÇÃO *s.f.* dysfunction.
DISLEXIA *s.f.* dyslexia.
DISPARAR *v.* to fire, to shoot.
DISPARIDADE *s.f.* disparity.
DISPENSA *s.f.* dispensation, discharge.
DISPENSAR *v.* to excuse.
DISPENSÁRIO *s.m.* dispensary.
DISPENSÁVEL *adj.2gên.* expendable.
DISPEPSIA *s.f.* dyspepsia.
DISPERSÃO *s.f.* dispersion.
DISPERSAR *v.* to disperse.
DISPERSO(A) *adj.* dispersed.
DISPLICÊNCIA *s.f.* negligence.
DISPONÍVEL *adj.2gên.* available.
DISPOR *v.* to arrange.
DISPOSIÇÃO *s.f.* arrangement.
DISPOSITIVO(A) *adj.* dispositive, disposing / *s.m.* gadget, device.
DISPOSTO(A) *adj.* disposed, ordered; ready, willing.
DISPUTA *s.f.* dispute.
DISPUTAR *v.* to dispute.
DISSECAR *v.* to dissect.
DISSEMINAÇÃO *s.f.* dissemination.
DISSEMINAR *v.* to disseminate.
DISSENSÃO *s.f.* dissension.

DISSENTIR *v.* to dissent.
DISSERTAÇÃO *s.f.* dissertation.
DISSERTAR *v.* to lecture.
DISSIMULAR *v.* to disguise, to dissimulate.
DISSIPAR *v.* to dissipate, to disperse.
DISSOLVER *v.* to dissolve.
DISSUADIR *v.* to dissuade.
DISTÂNCIA *s.f.* distance.
DISTANCIAR *v.* to distance, to separate.
DISTANTE *adj.2gên.* distant.
DISTENDER *v.* to stretch.
DISTINÇÃO *s.f.* distinction.
DISTINGUIR *v.* to distinguish.
DISTINTO(A) *adj.* distinct, different.
DISTORÇÃO *s.f.* distortion.
DISTORCER *v.* to distort.
DISTRAÇÃO *s.f.* distraction.
DISTRAÍDO(A) *adj.* forgetful, absent--minded.
DISTRAIR *v.* to distract, to amuse.
DISTRIBUIÇÃO *s.f.* distribution.
DISTRIBUIDOR *s.m.* distributor.
DISTRIBUIR *v.* to distribute.
DISTRIBUTIVO(A) *adj.* distributive.
DISTRITO *s.m.* district.
DISTÚRBIO *s.m.* disturbance.
DITADO *s.m.* saying, proverb.
DITADOR *s.m.* dictator.
DITADURA *s.f.* dictatorship.
DITAR *v.* to dictate.
DITO *adj.* aforementioned, said / *s.m.* aforementioned, said.
DITONGO *s.m.* diphthong.
DIURÉTICO(A) *adj.* diuretic / *s.m.* diuretic.
DIURNO(A) *adj.* diurnal.
DIVA *s.f.* diva.
DIVÃ *s.m.* divan.
DIVAGAR *v.* to divagate, to wander.
DIVERGÊNCIA *s.f.* divergence.
DIVERSÃO *s.f.* amusement.
DIVERSIDADE *s.f.* diversity.
DIVERSO(A) *adj.* diverse, different.
DIVERTIDO(A) *adj.* amusing.
DIVERTIMENTO *s.m.* amusement.
DIVERTIR *v.* to amuse.
DÍVIDA *s.f.* debt.
DIVIDENDO *s.m.* dividend.
DIVIDIR *v.* to divide, to share.
DIVINDADE *s.f.* divinity.
DIVINO(A) *adj.* divine.

DIVISA *s.f.* device, motto; emblem, badge; boundary, frontier.
DIVISÃO *s.f.* division.
DIVORCIAR *v.* to divorce.
DIVÓRCIO *s.m.* divorce.
DIVULGAÇÃO *s.f.* publicizing.
DIVULGAR *v.* to spread.
DIZER *v.* to say, to tell.
DÍZIMA *s.f.* tithe.
DÓ *s.m.* pity; C (nota musical).
DOAÇÃO *s.f.* donation, gift.
DOADOR *adj.* donor / *s.m.* donor.
DOAR *v.* to donate.
DOBRA *s.f.* fold.
DOBRADEIRA *s.f.* folding stick.
DOBRADIÇA *s.f.* hinge.
DOBRADO(A) *adj.* folded.
DOBRADURA *s.f.* fold, folding.
DOBRAR *v.* to double; to fold up.
DOBRO *num.* double / *s.m.* double.
DOCA *s.f.* dock, basin.
DOCE *adj.2gên.* sweet / *s.m.* sweet.
DOCENTE *adj.2gên.* teacher, professor.
DÓCIL *adj.2gên.* docile.
DOCUMENTAÇÃO *s.f.* documentation.
DOCUMENTAR *v.* to document.
DOCUMENTÁRIO *adj.* documentary / *s.m.* documentary.
DOCUMENTO *s.m.* document.
DOÇURA *s.f.* sweetness.
DODÓI *s.m.* wound.
DOENÇA *s.f.* illness, sickness.
DOENTE *adj.2gên.* sick, ill.
DOER *v.* to hurt, to ache.
DOGMA *s.m.* dogma.
DOGMÁTICO(A) *adj.* dogmatic.
DOGMATISMO *s.m.* dogmatism.
DOIDO(A) *adj.* mad, crazy / *s.m.* fool.
DOÍDO(A) *adj.* painful.
DOIS *num.* two.
DÓLAR *s.m.* dollar.
DOLÊNCIA *s.f.* melancholy, dejection, sorrow.
DOLO *s.m.* fraud.
DOLORIDO(A) *adj.* sore.
DOLOROSO(A) *adj.* painful.
DOLOSO(A) *adj.* premeditated.
DOM *s.m.* gift, talent.
DOMAR *v.* to tame.
DOMESTICAR *v.* to domesticate.

DOMÉSTICO(A) *adj.* domestic / *s.f.* maid.
DOMICÍLIO *s.m.* home, residence.
DOMINAÇÃO *s.f.* domination.
DOMINANTE *adj.2gên.* dominant.
DOMINAR *v.* to dominate.
DOMINGO *s.m.* Sunday.
DOMÍNIO *s.m.* dominion.
DONATÁRIO(A) *s.m.* donee; proprietary.
DONATIVO *s.m.* donation.
DONO(A) *s.m.* owner / *s.f.* lady.
DONZELA *s.m.* maiden.
DOPAR *v.* to dope, to drug.
DOR *s.f.* ache, pain.
DORMÊNCIA *s.f.* dormancy.
DORMIR *v.* to sleep.
DORMITÓRIO *s.m.* dormitory.
DORSAL *adj.2gên.* dorsal.
DORSO *s.m.* back.
DOSAGEM *s.f.* dose.
DOSAR *v.* to dose.
DOSE *s.f.* dose.
DOSSIÊ *s.m.* dossier.
DOTAÇÃO *s.f.* endowment.
DOTAR *v.* to endow.
DOTE *s.m.* dowry.
DOURADO(A) *adj.* golden.
DOURAR *v.* to gild.
DOUTO(A) *adj.* learned, erudite / *s.m.* learned, erudite.
DOUTOR *s.m.* doctor.
DOUTORADO *s.m.* doctorate.
DOUTORANDO(A) *s.m.* candidate for a doctorate.
DOUTORAR *v.* to doctorate.
DOUTRINA *s.f.* doctrine.
DOZE *num.* twelve.
DRAGA *s.f.* dredger.
DRAGÃO *s.m.* dragon.
DRÁGEA *s.f.* tablet.
DRAMA *s.m.* drama.
DRAMALHÃO *s.m.* melodrama.
DRAMÁTICO(A) *adj.* dramatic.
DRAMATIZAR *v.* to dramatize.
DRAMATURGIA *s.f.* dramaturgy.
DRAMATURGO *s.m.* playwright.
DRÁSTICO(A) *adj.* drastic.
DRENAR *v.* to drain.
DRENO *s.m.* drain.
DRIBLAR *v.* to dribble.
DRINQUE *s.m.* drink.

DROGA *s.f.* drug.
DROGARIA *s.f.* drugstore.
DROGUISTA *s.2gên.* druggist.
DROMEDÁRIO *s.m.* dromedary.
DUAL *adj.2gên.* dual / *s.m.* dual.
DUALISMO *s.m.* dualism.
DUALISTA *adj.2gên.* dualist.
DUBLAGEM *s.f.* dubbing.
DUBLAR *v.* to dub.
DUCADO *s.m.* dukedom.
DUCHA *s.f.* shower.
DÚCTIL *adj.2gên.* ductile.
DUCTILIDADE *s.f.* ductility.
DUELAR *adj.2gên.* dueling / *v.* to duel.
DUELISTA *s.2gên.* dueler, duelist.
DUELO *s.m.* duel.
DUENDE *s.m.* elf, goblin.
DUO *s.m.* duo, duet.
DUODENO *s.m.* duodenum.
DUPLA *s.f.* duo.
DUPLICAR *v.* to duplicate.
DUQUE *s.m.* duke.
DURAÇÃO *s.f.* duration, length.
DURANTE *prep.* during, while.
DURAR *v.* to last, to endure.
DUREZA *s.f.* hardness.
DURO(A) *adj.* hard.
DÚVIDA *s.f.* doubt.
DUVIDAR *v.* to doubt.
DUVIDOSO(A) *adj.* doubtful.
DUZENTOS *num.* two hundred.
DÚZIA *s.f.* dozen.

E e

E, e *s.m.* the fifth letter of the Portuguese alphabet / *conj.* and.
ÉBANO *s.m.* ebony.
EBRIÁTICO *adj.* intoxicating, inebriating.
EBRIEDADE *s.f.* drunkness, inebriation.
ÉBRIO *s.m.* drunkard, toper / *adj.* drunk, intoxicated, inebriated.
EBULIÇÃO *s.f.* boiling, ebullition; agitation, living.
EBULIR *v.* to boil.
ECHARPE *s.f.* scarf.
ECLAMPSIA *s.f.* eclampsia.
ECLESIAL *adj.2gên.* ecclesial,
ECLESIASTES *s.m.* Ecclesiastes.
ECLESIÁSTICO *adj.* ecclesiastic, clericalist.
ECLÉTICO *adj.* eclectic.
ECLIPSAR *v.* to eclipse, to outshine.
ECLIPSE *s.m.* eclipse.
ECLÍPTICA *s.f.* ecliptic.
ECLÍPTICO *adj.* ecliptic.
ECLODIR *v.* to arise, to emerge, to appear.
ECLUSA *s.f.* sluice, lockage.
ECLOSÃO *s.f.* outbreak, appearance.
ECO *s.m.* echo.
ECOAR *v.* to echo.
ECOLOGIA *s.f.* ecology.
ECOLÓGICO *adj.* ecologic.
ECÔMETRO *s.m.* echometre.
ECONOMIA *s.f.* economy.
ECONÔMICO *adj.* economical.
ECONOMISTA *s.2gên.* economist.
ECONOMIZAR *v.* to economize, to save.
ECOSSISTEMA *s.m.* ecosystem.
ECTOPLASMA *s.m.* ectoplasm.
ECUMÊNICO *adj.* ecumenical.
EDEMA *s.m.* oedema.
ÉDEN *s.m.* Eden, heaven.
EDÊNICO *adj.* Edenic, paradisiacal.
EDIÇÃO *s.m.* publication, edition.
EDÍCULA *s.f.* a small house, little house.
EDIFICAÇÃO *s.f.* edification, construction, building.
EDIFICADOR *s.m.* builder, constructor / *adj.* constructive, edifying.
EDIFICANTE *adj.2gên.* edifying, building, uplifting.
EDIFICAR *v.* to edify, to construct, to build.
EDIFÍCIO *s.m.* building.

EDITAÇÃO *s.f.* edictal, edition, publication.
EDITAL *s.m.* edictal.
EDITAR *v.* to publish, to edit.
EDITO *s.m.* edict.
ÉDITO *s.m.* edict, command.
EDITOR *s.m.* publisher, editor.
EDITORA *s.f.* publishing house.
EDITORAÇÃO *s.f.* publication, publishing.
EDITORAR *v.* to publish, to edit.
EDITORIAL *s.m.* editorial.
EDREDOM *s.m.* comforter, continental quilt.
EDUCABILIDADE *s.f.* educability.
EDUCAÇÃO *s.f.* education.
EDUCACIONAL *adj.2gên.* educational, pedagogical.
EDUCADO *adj.* educated, trained; polite, gracious.
EDUCADOR *s.m.* educator, teacher, coach, instructor / *adj.* educating, educative.
EDUCANDÁRIO *s.m.* school, educational place.
EDUCANDO *s.m.* pupil, student.
EDUCAR *v.* to educate, to bring up.
EDUCATIVO *adj.* educative, educational.
EDUCÁVEL *adj.2gên.* teachable.
EDULCORANTE *adj.2gên.* edulcorant.
EFEITO *s.m.* effect.
EFEITUAR *v.* to execute.
EFEMERIDADE *s.f.* ephemerality, frailty.
EFÊMERO *adj.* ephemeral, transitory.
EFERVESCÊNCIA *s.f.* effervescence; commotion, agitation.
EFERVESCENTE *adj.2gên.* fizzy, effervescent.
EFERVESCER *v.* to effervesce.
EFÉSIO *adj.* ephesian.
EFETIVAÇÃO *s.f.* effectuation.
EFETIVAR *v.* to carry out, to execute.
EFETIVIDADE *s.f.* effectiveness, action, activity.
EFETIVO *adj.* effective.
EFETUAÇÃO *s.f.* effectuation, performance, execution.
EFETUAR *v.* to carry out, to accomplish.
EFICÁCIA *s.f.* effectiveness, efficiency.
EFICAZ *adj.2gên.* efficient.
EFICIÊNCIA *s.f.* efficiency.
EFICIENTE *adj.2gên.* efficient.
EFLORESCÊNCIA *s.f.* efflorescence.
EFLORESCENTE *adj.2gên.* efflorescent.

EFLORESCER *v.* to effloresce; to blossom, to bloom.
EFLUÊNCIA *s.f.* effluence, effusion.
EFLUIR *v.* to irradiate.
EFLUENTE *adj.2gên.* effluent.
EFÚGIO *s.m.* subterfuge, evasion.
EFUSÃO *s.f.* effusion.
EFUSIVO *adj.* effusive, effluent.
EFUSO *adj.* effuse.
ÉGIDE *s.f.* aegis; shelter, protection.
EGÍPCIO *adj.* Egyptian.
EGITO *s.m.* Egypt.
ÉGLOGA *s.f.* eclogue.
EGO *s.m.* ego.
EGOCÊNTRICO *adj.* egocentric, self-centered.
EGOCENTRISMO *s.m.* egocentricity.
EGOÍSMO *s.m.* selfishness, egoism.
EGOÍSTA *adj.2gên.* selfish.
EGÓLATRA *s.2gên.* egomaniac, self-worshipper.
EGOLATRIA *s.f.* egomania.
EGOTISMO *s.m.* egotism.
EGOTISTA *s.2gên.* egoist.
EGRESSÃO *s.f.* egress, going out.
EGRESSO *s.m.* egress / *adj.* egressed.
ÉGUA *s.f.* mare.
EIRA *s.f.* threshing floor, barn floor.
EIS *adv.* here it is.
EIXO *s.m.* axis, spindle; pivot.
EJACULAÇÃO *s.f.* ejaculation, emission.
EJACULADOR *adj.* ejaculatory, ejaculating.
EJACULAR *v.* to ejaculate, to eject, to discharge.
EJACULATÓRIO *adj.* ejaculatory.
EJEÇÃO *s.f.* ejection, expulsion.
EJETAR *v.* to eject, to expel.
EJETOR *s.m.* ejector.
ELA *pron.* she.
ELABORAÇÃO *s.f.* elaboration; preparation, formulation.
ELABORAR *v.* to prepare, to elaborate; to formulate.
ELASTICIDADE *s.f.* elasticity.
ELÁSTICO *adj.* elastic.
ELE *pron.* he.
ELEFANTE *s.m.* elephant.
ELEFANTÍASE *s.f.* elephantiasis.
ELEGÂNCIA *s.f.* elegance.
ELEGANTE *adj.2gên.* elegant.

ELEGER v. to elect.
ELEGIA s.f. elegy.
ELEGÍACO adj. elegiac.
ELEGIBILIDADE s.f. eligibility.
ELEGIDO adj. elected, selected, chosen.
ELEGÍVEL adj.2gên. eligible.
ELEIÇÃO s.f. election; choice, preference, option.
ELEITO adj. elected; chosen, opted / s.m. elect, selected.
ELEITOR(A) s.m. voter, elector.
ELEITORADO s.m. electorate; right to elect.
ELEITORAL adj.2gên. electoral, elective.
ELEMENTAR adj.2gên. elementary.
ELEMENTO s.m. element.
ELENCO s.m. list, cast.
ELETIVO adj. selectivity; selecting, choosing.
ELETRACÚSTICO adj. electroacoustic.
ELETRICIDADE s.f. electricity.
ELETRICISTA s.2gên. electrician.
ELÉTRICO adj. electrical / s.m. electric.
ELETRIFICAÇÃO s.f. electrification, electrifying.
ELETRIFICAR v. to electrify.
ELETRIZAÇÃO s.f. electrization.
ELETRIZANTE adj.2gên. thrilling, exciting, stirring.
ELETRIZAR v. to electrify.
ELETROCARDIOGRAFIA s.f. electrocardiography.
ELETROCARDIÓGRAFO s.m. electrocardiograph.
ELETROCARDIOGRAMA s.m. electrocardiogram.
ELETROCHOQUE s.m. electroshock.
ELETROCINÉTICO adj. electrokinetic.
ELETROCUTAR v. to electrocute.
ELETRODINÂMICA s.f. electrodynamics.
ELETRODO s.m. eletrode.
ELETRODOMÉSTICO s.m. domestic appliance.
ELETROÍMÃ s.m. electromagnet, magnet.
ELETRÓLISE s.f. electrolysis.
ELETRÓLITO s.m. electrolyte.
ELETROMAGNÉTICO adj. electromagnetic.
ELETROMAGNETISMO s.m. electromagnetism.
ELÉTRON s.m. electron.
ELETRÔNICA s.f. electronics.
ELETRÔNICO adj. electronic.
ELETROQUÍMICA s.f. electrochemistry.
ELETROSCÓPIO s.m. electroscope.
ELETROSTÁTICA s.f. electrostatics.
ELEVAÇÃO s.f. elevation, raising; lift up, rising, ascension.
ELEVADO s.m. elevated / adj. high, raised, lifted up.
ELEVADOR s.m. elevator, lift / adj. elevating, lifting.
ELEVAR v. to lift up, to raise; to exalt, to ennoble.
ELEVATÓRIO adj. lifting, elevatory.
ELFO s.m. elf, sprite.
ELIDIR v. to elide.
ELIMINAÇÃO s.f. elimination; removal, deletion.
ELIMINAR v. to eliminate; to remove, to banish; to delete.
ELIMINATÓRIA s.f. heat, runoff.
ELIMINATÓRIO adj. eliminatory, eliminating.
ELIMINÁVEL adj.2gên. eliminable, clearable.
ELIPSE s.f. ellipse, ellipsis.
ELÍPTICO adj. elliptical, elliptic.
ELISÃO s.f. elision; suppression, elimination.
ELITE s.f. elite.
ELITISMO s.m. elitism.
ELITISTA adj.2gên. elitist.
ELMO s.m. helmet, helm.
ELO s.m. link, bond; connection, connecting.
ELOCUÇÃO s.f. elocution, utterance, diction.
ELOGIAR v. to eulogise, to praise; to exalt, to compliment.
ELOGIÁVEL adj.2gên. praiseworthy.
ELOGIO s.m. praise, compliment; eulogy, commendation.
ELOGIOSO adj. eulogistic.
ELOQUÊNCIA s.f. eloquence; oratory.
ELOQUENTE adj.2gên. eloquent, fluent; expressive, talkative.
ELUCIDAÇÃO s.f. elucidation, explanation.
ELUCIDAR v. to elucidate, to clarify; to clear, to explain.
ELUCIDÁRIO s.m. glossary, vocabulary, commentary.
ELUCIDATIVO adj. elucidatory, explanatory; elucidating.

EM *prep.* in, into; on, at; upon.
EMA *s.f.* emu, Brazilian ostrich.
EMAGRECER *v.* to get thin, to loose weight; to attenuate.
EMAGRECIMENTO *s.m.* emaciation, thinning; attenuation, reduction.
EMANAÇÃO *s.f.* emanation.
EMANANTE *adj.2gên.* emanative, emanating.
EMANAR *v.* to emanate.
EMANCIPAÇÃO *s.f.* emancipation; freeing, liberation.
EMANCIPADO *adj.* emancipated.
EMANCIPAR *v.* to emancipate; to set free, to free.
EMARANHADO *adj.* angled, confusion, intricacy.
EMARANHAR *v.* to entangle, to tangle; to puzzle.
EMBAÇADO *adj.* blurry, lustreless.
EMBAÇAR *v.* to tarnish; to dim, to confuse.
EMBAINHAR *v.* to sheath.
EMBAIXADA *s.f.* embassy.
EMBAIXADOR *s.m.* ambassador.
EMBAIXATRIZ *s.m.* ambassadress.
EMBAIXO *adv.* below, under; beneath, underneath.
EMBALADO(A) *adj.* wrapped, packed.
EMBALADOR *s.m.* packager, rocker / *adj.* packing, rocking.
EMBALAGEM *s.f.* package, packaging.
EMBALAR *v.* to pack up, to wrap; to rock (criança).
EMBALO *s.m.* lulling, rocking.
EMBALSAMENTO *s.m.* embalming.
EMBALSAMAR *v.* to embalm.
EMBANANAR *v.* to become confused; to make confused.
EMBANDEIRAR *v.* to adorn with flags; to flatter; to dress one up.
EMBARAÇADO *adj.* embarrassed, concerned.
EMBARAÇADOR *s.m.* embarrassing; difficult, worrying.
EMBARAÇAR *v.* to hinder, to embarrass, to detain.
EMBARAÇO *s.m.* impediment, embarrassment.
EMBARAÇOSO *adj.* embarrassing, perplexing.
EMBARALHAR *v.* to shuffle, to mix.
EMBARCAÇÃO *s.f.* vessel, ship.
EMBARCAR *v.* to embark, to go onboard, to board.
EMBARGADO *adj.* embargoed; under a embargo.
EMBARGADOR *s.m.* confiscator / *adj.* confiscating, hindering, embarrassing.
EMBARGAR *v.* to embargo, to confiscate.
EMBARGO *s.m.* embargo, seizure, arrest; impediment.
EMBARQUE *s.m.* embarkation, boarding.
EMBASAMENTO *s.m.* basement, foundation; base.
EMBASAR *v.* to base on, to found upon.
EMBASBACAR *v.* to intoxicate.
EMBATE *s.m.* collision, clash, shock; resistance, opposition.
EMBEBEDAR *v.* to intoxicate; to drink alcohol.
EMBEBER *v.* to soak, to absorb.
EMBELEZADOR *adj.* beautifying.
EMBELEZAMENTO *s.m.* embellishment, beautification.
EMBELEZAR *v.* to beautify, to decorate, to adorn.
EMBEVECER *v.* to delight.
EMBEVECIDO *adj.* delighted.
EMBICAR *v.* to shape like a beak; to be confused, to be embarrassed; to stop, to halt.
EMBIRRAR *v.* to be obstinate; to be stubborn, to dislike.
EMBLEMA *s.m.* emblem, ensign; badge, symbol, allegory.
EMBLEMÁTICO *adj.* emblematic; significative, symbolic.
ÊMBOLO *s.m.* piston, forcer; embolus.
EMBOLORAR *v.* to make or become mouldy, musty.
EMBOLSAR *v.* to pocket; to steal.
EMBORA *conj.* although, while / *adv.* though, away.
EMBOSCADA *s.f.* ambush, ambuscade.
EMBOSCAR *v.* to ambush.
EMBRANDECER *v.* to soften.
EMBRANQUECER *v.* to whiten, to make white; to grow older.
EMBREAGEM *s.f.* clutch, gearing.

EMBRIAGAR *v.* to make drunk; to intoxicate; to inebriate.
EMBRIAGUEZ *s.f.* intoxication, inebriation; inebriety; enthusiasm.
EMBRIÃO *s.m.* embryo, germ.
EMBRIOLOGIA *s.f.* embryology.
EMBROMAR *v.* to swindle; to cheat, to defraud; to make false promises.
EMBRULHAR *v.* to wrap up, to pack up.
EMBRULHO *s.m.* package, packet, parcel.
EMBRUTECER *v.* to make brutal.
EMBRUTECIMENTO *s.m.* brutalization.
EMBUCHAR *v.* to overeat, to be full; to keep in silence; to become pregnant.
EMBURRAR *v.* to become brutish; to sulk, to pout; to become sullen.
EMBUSTE *s.m.* hoax, swindle, quiz.
EMBUTIR *v.* to inlay, to encrust, to imbed.
EMENDA *s.f.* correction, amendment; rectification, converting.
EMENDAR *v.* to correct, to amend; to emend, to right, to rectify.
EMERGÊNCIA *s.f.* emergency.
EMERGENTE *adj.2gên.* emergent, emerging; forthcoming, resultant.
EMERGIR *v.* to emerge; to rise, to appear.
EMÉRITO *adj.* emeritus, honourably, eminent.
EMERSO *adj.* emersed, emerged.
EMIGRAÇÃO *s.f.* emigration.
EMIGRANTE *adj.2gên.* emigrant.
EMIGRAR *v.* to emigrate.
EMINÊNCIA *s.f.* eminence; altitude, height.
EMINENTE *adj.2gên.* eminent, prominent; great, notable.
EMIR *s.m.* emir, amir.
EMIRADO *s.m.* emirate.
EMISSÃO *s.f.* emission, transmission.
EMISSÁRIO *s.m.* emissary, envoy; messenger, agent.
EMISSORA *s.f.* broadcast station.
EMITIR *v.* to emit, to issue.
EMOÇÃO *s.f.* emotion, thrill, commotion.
EMOCIONADO *adj.* thrilled, affected.
EMOCIONAL *adj.2gên.* emotional.
EMOCIONANTE *adj.2gên.* exciting, thrilling; emotive.
EMOCIONAR *v.* to thrill, to stir emotions, to impress.
EMOLDURAR *v.* to frame, to profile.
EMOLIENTE *s.2gên.* emollient / *adj.2gên.* emollient, mollifier, mitigatory.
EMOTIVO *adj.* emotional, emotive.
EMPACAR *v.* to balk.
EMPACOTAR *v.* to pack up, to wrap; to incase, to put in a box.
EMPADA *s.f.* pie, patty.
EMPALHAR *v.* to pack or wrap in straws; to stuff with straws.
EMPALIDECER *v.* to pale, to blanch; to fade.
EMPANAR *v.* to cover, to wrap.
EMPANTURRAR *v.* to stuff, to fill; to overeat, to eat a lot.
EMPAREDAR *v.* to wall.
EMPARELHAR *v.* to pair, to link, to match.
EMPATADO *adj.* drawn.
EMPATAR *v.* to be or end drawn; to hinder, to tie up.
EMPATE *s.m.* tie.
EMPECILHO *s.m.* obstacle, embarrassment; difficulty, obstruction.
EMPENHAR *v.* to engage, to commit; to hock, to pledge; to pawn.
EMPENHO *s.m.* effort, interest; endeavour, engage.
EMPERRADO *adj.* stuck, jammed.
EMPERRAR *v.* to get stuck or blocked; to stiffen.
EMPILHAR *v.* to pile up, to heap.
EMPINADO *adj.* straight, upright; craggy, rearing, prancing.
EMPINAR *v.* to raise or lift up; to put straight.
EMPIPOCAR *v.* to pustulate.
EMPÍRICO *adj.* empiric, empiricist.
EMPIRISMO *s.m.* empiricism.
EMPLASTRO *s.m.* plaster.
EMPOBRECER *v.* to impoverish, to pauperise.
EMPOEIRADO *adj.* dusty.
EMPOLEIRAR *v.* to perch, to sit on a branch.
EMPOLGANTE *adj.2gên.* exciting, breathtaking, gripping.
EMPOLGAR *v.* to stimulate, to thrill; to excite.
EMPORCALHAR *v.* to dirt, to mess up.
EMPÓRIO *s.m.* emporium, grocery store.
EMPOSSAR *v.* to induct, to enthrone.

EMPREENDEDOR(A) *s.m.* enterprising, adventurous / *adj.* enterprising, courageous.
EMPREENDER *v.* to undertake, to engage.
EMPREENDIMENTO *s.m.* undertaking, enterprise.
EMPREGADA *s.f.* maid, domestic servant.
EMPREGADO(A) *s.m.* employee / *adj.* employed.
EMPREGADOR(A) *s.m.* employer; owner, boss, master.
EMPREGAR *v.* to employ, to use; to give a function to, to make use of.
EMPREGO *s.m.* job, work, employment; use, utility, application.
EMPREITADA *s.f.* job contract, agreement.
EMPREITEIRO *s.m.* contractor, undertaker.
EMPRENHAR *v.* to impregnate; to get one pregnant.
EMPRESA *s.f.* firm, company, enterprise.
EMPRESARIAL *adj.2gên.* business.
EMPRESÁRIO *s.m.* businessman, manager, executive officer.
EMPRESTADO *adj.* lent, borrowed; loaned.
EMPRESTAR *v.* to lend, to borrow; to loan.
EMPRÉSTIMO *s.m.* lending, borrowing; loan.
EMPUNHAR *v.* to handle, to hold up, to carry.
EMPURRÃO *s.m.* push, shove, poke violently.
EMPURRAR *v.* to push, to thrust.
EMPUXO *s.m.* pushing.
EMUDECER *v.* to make silence, to be quite, to dumbfound.
EMULAÇÃO *s.f.* emulation.
EMULAR *v.* to emulate; to fight or compete with.
ENALTECER *v.* to praise, to extol; to magnify, to aggrandise, to ennoble.
ENAMORAR *v.* to enamour, to fascinate, to fall in love.
ENCABEÇAR *v.* to head, to lead, to direct; to be convinced.
ENCABULADO *adj.* timid, shy; bullheaded, vexed.
ENCABULAR *v.* to be ashamed, to worry.
ENCADEADO *adj.* linked, connected, joined.
ENCADEAR *v.* to link, to connect, to enchain, to unite.
ENCADERNAÇÃO *s.f.* binding, bookbinding.
ENCADERNAR *v.* to bind, to tie, to fasten.
ENCAFIFAR *v.* to puzzle, to worry, to brood.
ENCAIXAR *v.* to fit in, to box, to pack.
ENCAIXE *s.m.* setting in, fitting in; encasement.
ENCAIXOTAR *v.* to incase, to box, to pack.
ENCALÇAR *v.* to follow closely, to pursue; to walk on one's shoes.
ENCALHADO *adj.* stranded, aground.
ENCALHAR *v.* to strand, to run aground; to get stuck, to be stagnated.
ENCALHE *s.m.* stranding, grounding; obstacle, obstruction.
ENCALVECER *v.* to be bald, to get bald.
ENCAMAR *v.* to get sick, to be abed.
ENCAMINHAMENTO *s.m.* direction, guiding, leading.
ENCAMINHAR *v.* to direct, to conduct, to lead.
ENCANADOR *s.m.* plumber.
ENCANAMENTO *s.m.* plumbing, piping; drainage system.
ENCANAR *v.* to channel; to canalise; to imprison.
ENCANDEAR *v.* to dazzle; to hallucinate, to fascinate.
ENCANTADO *adj.* delighted, overjoyed.
ENCANTADOR *s.m.* enchanter, magician, sorcerer / *adj.* charming, delightful.
ENCANTAR *v.* to bewitch, to charm.
ENCANTO *s.m.* delight, charm.
ENCAPAR *v.* to cover, to put a cover on.
ENCARACOLAR *v.* to spiral, to twist and turn; to curl.
ENCARAR *v.* to face, to stare at.
ENCARDIDO *adj.* soiled, greasy, dirty; scowling, threatening.
ENCARECER *v.* to raise the prices; to exalt someone, to estimate.
ENCARGO *s.m.* responsibility, incumbency, obligation; tax.
ENCARNAÇÃO *s.f.* incarnation, personification.
ENCARNAR *v.* to incarnate.
ENCARREGADO *s.m.* manager, boss, one who's in charge / *adj.* charged, in charge.
ENCARREGAR *v.* to charge, to commit, to be responsible for.
ENCARTE *s.m.* registration of a document.
ENCASQUETADO *adj.* obstinate, obsessed.

ENCASQUETAR *v.* to insist, to make believe.
ENCASTELAR *v.* to place in a castle; to be fortified.
ENCAVALAR *v.* to superpose.
ENCÉFALO *s.m.* encephalon, brain.
ENCENAÇÃO *s.f.* staging; simulation.
ENCENAR *v.* to stage; to mount.
ENCERADEIRA *s.f.* floor polisher machine.
ENCERADO *s.m.* tarpaulin, wax cloth, oilcloth / *adj.* polished, waxed.
ENCERAR *v.* to wax, to polish.
ENCERRAMENTO *s.m.* closing, termination; finishing, conclusion.
ENCERRAR *v.* to close, to shut, to finish; to contain, to enclose.
ENCERRO *s.m.* end, finish, close.
ENCESTAR *v.* to throw-in; to put in a basket.
ENCETAR *v.* to begin, to start.
ENCHARCADO *adj.* swampy, marshy; flooded, wet.
ENCHARCAR *v.* to soak, to wet; to give form of a puddle.
ENCHENTE *s.f.* flood, inundation, overflow.
ENCHER *v.* to fill up, to stuff; to charge, to load, to get full.
ENCHIMENTO *s.m.* filling up, stuffing, inflation.
ENCHOVA *s.f.* anchovy.
ENCICLOPÉDIA *s.f.* encyclopaedia, thesaurus.
ENCICLOPÉDICO *adj.* encyclopaedic.
ENCICLOPEDISTA *s.2gên.* encyclopaedist.
ENCIUMAR *v.* to make jealous.
ENCLAUSURAR *v.* to confine in an enclosure.
ENCOBERTO *adj.* hidden, secret; disguised, dissimulated.
ENCOBRIR *v.* to cover, to occult, to keep secret.
ENCOLHER *v.* to contract, to shrink.
ENCOLHIDO *s.m.* shy, timid / *adj.* shrunken, contracted.
ENCOMENDA *s.f.* order (produtos), task, incumbency.
ENCOMENDAR *v.* to order, to ask for.
ENCONTRADO *adj.* united, joint; found, close.
ENCONTRAR *v.* to find (objetos); to meet (pessoas).
ENCONTRO *s.m.* meeting, encounter; finding, shock.
ENCORAJAR *v.* to encourage.
ENCORDOAMENTO *s.m.* stringing.
ENCORPAR *v.* to thicken.
ENCOSTA *s.f.* slope, hill, acclivity.
ENCOSTAR *v.* to lean, to backboard.
ENCOSTO *s.m.* back of seat; support.
ENCRAVADO *adj.* nailed, stuck.
ENCRAVAR *v.* to nail, to deceit, to trick.
ENCRENCA *s.f.* trouble, difficulty.
ENCRENCAR *v.* to complicate, to be in trouble.
ENCRENQUEIRO *s.m.* troublemaker / *adj.* bothersome, quarrelsome.
ENCRUZILHADA *s.f.* crossroad, crossing, intersection.
ENCUCAR *v.* to confound, to disturb, to worry, to get crazy.
ENCURRALAR *v.* to corral, to corner, to surround.
ENCURTAMENTO *s.m.* shortening, diminution, curtailment.
ENCURTAR *v.* to shorten, to reduce.
ENDEMIA *s.f.* endemic disease.
ENDEREÇAR *v.* to address, to give directions.
ENDEREÇO *s.m.* address.
ENDEUSADO *adj.* deified.
ENDEUSAMENTO *s.m.* deification.
ENDEUSAR *v.* to deify.
ENDIABRADO *adj.* demoniac, devilish.
ENDINHEIRADO *adj.* moneyed, wealthy.
ENDIREITADO *adj.* straightened.
ENDIREITAR *v.* to straighten, to make right.
ENDÍVIA *s.f.* endive, chicory.
ENDIVIDADO *adj.* indebted, overdrawn.
ENDIVIDAMENTO *s.m.* indebtedness.
ENDIVIDAR *v.* to debt.
ENDÓCRINO *s.m.* endocrinous.
ENDOCRINOLOGIA *s.f.* endocrinology.
ENDOCRINOLOGISTA *s.2gên.* endocrinologist.
ENDOGAMIA *s.f.* endogamy.
ENDOIDANTE *adj.2gên.* maddening.
ENDOIDAR *v.* to become crazy, to be angry.
ENDOIDECER *v.* to go insane, to go mad.
ENDOMÉTRIO *s.m.* endometrium.

ENDOMETRIOSE *s.f.* endometriosis.
ENDORFINA *s.f.* endorphin.
ENDOSCOPIA *s.f.* endoscopy.
ENDOSSAR *v.* to endorse.
ENDURECER *v.* to harden.
ENEGRECER *v.* to blacken, to darken.
ENERGÉTICO *s.m.* energetic, energy-giving.
ENERGIA *s.f.* energy, power, strength.
ENÉRGICO *adj.* energetic, powerful, strong.
ENERGÚMENO *adj.* energumen.
ENERGIZAR *v.* to energize.
ENERVAR *v.* to weaken, to debilitate.
ENÉSIMO *num.* nth, umpteenth.
ENEVOADO *adj.* foggy.
ENEVOAR *v.* to fog, to haze, to cover with mist.
ENFADAR *v.* to bore, to miff.
ENFADO *s.m.* boredom, vexation, tedium.
ENFADONHO *adj.* tiresome, boring, tedious.
ENFAIXAR *v.* to swathe, to bandage.
ENFARINHAR *v.* to pour flour, to add flour.
ENFARTAR *v.* to have a heart attack.
ÊNFASE *s.f.* emphasis.
ENFATIZAR *v.* to emphasise.
ENFEAR *v.* to uglify.
ENFEITADO *adj.* adorned, ornate.
ENFEITAR *v.* to decorate, to adorn.
ENFEITE *s.m.* ornament, decoration.
ENFEITIÇAR *v.* to bewitch, to charm, to fascinate.
ENFERMAGEM *s.f.* nursing.
ENFERMARIA *s.f.* infirmary, hospital ward.
ENFERMEIRO(A) *s.m.* nurse.
ENFERMIDADE *s.f.* illness, sickness.
ENFERMO(A) *s.m.* patient, suffer / *adj.* sick, weak, feeble.
ENFERRUJADO *adj.* rusty.
ENFERRUJAR *v.* to rust.
ENFEZAR *v.* to stunt; to annoy, to irritate.
ENFIADA *s.f.* threaded.
ENFIAR *v.* to put on, to thread.
ENFILEIRADO *adj.* queued, in a line.
ENFILEIRAR *v.* to queue, to make line, to align.
ENFIM *adv.* finally, at last; after all.
ENFOQUE *s.m.* approach, focus, outlook.
ENFORCAR *v.* to hang.
ENFRAQUECER *v.* to weaken, to debilitate.

ENFREAR *v.* to break, to slow down, to reduce.
ENFRENTAR *v.* to face, to confront.
ENFUMAÇAR *v.* to smoke; to fill with smoke.
ENFURECER *v.* to infuriate, to enrage.
ENFURECIDO(A) *adj.* furious, angry, wild.
ENGAIOLADO *adj.* caged (animal); imprisoned (pessoa).
ENGAIOLAR *v.* to encage, to arrest, to isolate.
ENGAJADO *adj.* engaged.
ENGAJAMENTO *s.m.* engagement.
ENGAJAR *v.* to engage, to take on.
ENGALFINHAR *v.* to wrestle, to tangle.
ENGANAÇÃO *s.f.* deception, illusion.
ENGANADO *adj.* cheated, deceived; mistaken, wrong.
ENGANAR *v.* to deceive, to cheat.
ENGANO *s.m.* mistake, error.
ENGANOSO *adj.* deceiving, deceitful, illusory, fallacious.
ENGARRAFAMENTO *s.m.* bottling; obstruction, obstacle.
ENGARRAFAR *v.* to bottle.
ENGASGAR *v.* to choke, to suffocate.
ENGASGO *s.m.* choking, obstacle.
ENGATAR *v.* to clamp, to engage, to gear.
ENGATE *s.m.* clamp, gear, hook.
ENGATINHAR *v.* to crawl; to begin, to be beginner.
ENGAVETAR *v.* to store in a drawer; to pile.
ENGENDRAR *v.* to engender, to engineer, to create.
ENGENHAR *v.* to engineer, to scheme, to invent.
ENGENHARIA *s.f.* engineering.
ENGENHEIRO(A) *s.m.* engineer.
ENGENHO *s.m.* inventive power; talent, ingenuity.
ENGENHOCA *s.f.* gadget, contraption.
ENGENHOSO(A) *adj.* talent, smart, clever.
ENGESSAR *v.* to plaster, to apply plaster to.
ENGLOBAR *v.* to unite, to join, to conglomerate.
ENGODO *s.m.* allurement, bait, decoy.
ENGOLFAR *v.* to engulf.
ENGOLIR *v.* to swallow, to engulf, to absorb.
ENGOMAR *v.* to iron, to size, to starch.

ENGORDAR *v.* to fatten, to get fatter.
ENGRAÇADO *adj.* funny, comic, amusing.
ENGRADADO *s.m.* crate; packing box.
ENGRANDECER *v.* to enlarge, to increase; to magnify.
ENGRAVATAR *v.* to wear a tie.
ENGRAVIDAR *v.* to become pregnant.
ENGRAXAR *v.* to shine shoes; to smear grease.
ENGRENAGEM *s.f.* gear, gearing.
ENGRENAR *v.* to gear, to put in gear.
ENGROSSAR *v.* to enlarge, to swell, to increase.
ENGUIA *s.f.* eel.
ENGUIÇAR *v.* to stunt, to bring bad luck.
ENIGMA *s.m.* enigma, puzzle, mystery, riddle.
ENIGMÁTICO *adj.* enigmatic.
ENJAULAR *v.* to encage, to jail.
ENJOADO *adj.* sick, bored.
ENJOAR *v.* to sicken, to nauseate.
ENJOATIVO *adj.* nauseating, repugnant.
ENJOO *s.m.* sickness, nausea.
ENLAÇADO *adj.* fastened, laced; tied.
ENLAÇAR *v.* to tie, to fasten; to link, to join.
ENLACE *s.m.* union, wedding.
ENLAMEADO *adj.* muddied, muddy.
ENLAMEAR *v.* to dirty, to puddle.
ENLATAR *v.* to can, to tin.
ENLOUQUECER *v.* to drive mad, to madden.
ENOJADO *adj.* annoyed, nauseated.
ENOJAR *v.* to disgust, to nauseate.
ENORME *adj.2gên.* enormous, huge.
ENORMIDADE *s.f.* enormity, enormousness.
ENOVELAR *v.* to clew, to coil.
ENQUADRAR *v.* to frame; to square, to conform.
ENQUANTO *conj.* while, whilst, as long as.
ENQUETE *s.f.* survey, search.
ENRAIVECIDO *adj.* angry, furious, enraged.
ENRAIZADO *adj.* rooted, fixed.
ENRAIZAR *v.* to root, to establish, to fix.
ENRASCADA *s.f.* difficulty, dangerous situation.
ENREDO *s.m.* plot, intrigue.
ENRIJECER *v.* to stiffen, to harden, to make rigid.
ENRIQUECER *v.* to enrich, to obtain wealth.

ENRIQUECIMENTO *s.m.* enrichment.
ENROLAR *v.* to roll up.
ENROSCADO *adj.* spiralled, tolled; tangled, twisted.
ENROSCAR *v.* to twist, to twine.
ENRUGAR *v.* to wrinkle, to crease.
ENRUSTIDO *adj.* closeted.
ENSABOADO *adj.* soapy, lathery.
ENSABOAR *v.* to soap, to lather.
ENSAIAR *v.* to test, to rehearse.
ENSAIO *s.m.* test, rehearsal; essay.
ENSANDECER *v.* to make or become mad; to go crazy.
ENSANGUENTAR *v.* to bloody, to stain with blood.
ENSEADA *s.f.* cove, inlet, bay.
ENSEJO *s.m.* chance, occasion.
ENSINAMENTO *s.m.* teaching, education, doctrine.
ENSINAR *v.* to teach, to coach, to educate; to instruct.
ENSINO *s.m.* teaching, training.
ENSOLARADO *adj.* sunny.
ENSOPADO *s.m.* stew / *adj.* wet, dripping wet.
ENSOPAR *v.* to sop in, to soak; to cook a stew.
ENSURDECEDOR *adj.* deafening.
ENSURDECER *v.* to deafen.
ENTALADO *adj.* pressed, stuck.
ENTALAR *v.* to splint, to pinch.
ENTALHAR *v.* to carve, to engrave, to sculpture, to groove.
ENTALHE *s.m.* notch, cut.
ENTALHO *s.m.* intaglio.
ENTANTO *adv.* in the interim / *conj.* nevertheless.
ENTÃO *adv.* then.
ENTARDECER *s.m.* sunset.
ENTE *s.m.* being, a person, living creature.
ENTEADO *s.m.* stepchild, stepson, stepdaughter.
ENTEDIADO(A) *adj.* peevish, bored.
ENTEDIAR *v.* to bore.
ENTENDER *v.* to understand.
ENTENDIDO *adj.* expert; understood.
ENTENDIMENTO *s.m.* understanding.
ENTERNECER *v.* to touch; to warm.
ENTERRAR *v.* to bury.
ENTERRO *s.m.* burial, funeral.
ENTIDADE *s.f.* entity.

ENTOAR *v.* to intone, to modulate.
ENTONAÇÃO *s.f.* intonation.
ENTORPECENTE *adj.2gên.* narcotic.
ENTORPECER *v.* to benub, to drug.
ENTORTAR *v.* to bend, to bow.
ENTRADA *s.f.* entrance, entry.
ENTRANÇAR *v.* to mat, to twist.
ENTRÂNCIA *s.f.* instance.
ENTRANHA *s.f.* viscera, bowels, entrails; tripe.
ENTRANHAR *v.* to pierce.
ENTRANTE *adj.2gên.* beginning, entering.
ENTRAR *v.* to go in, to enter.
ENTRAVAR *v.* to hinder, to encumber.
ENTRAVE *s.m.* hindrance, impediment.
ENTRE *prep.* between.
ENTREABERTO *adj.* half-open, ajar.
ENTREABRIR *v.* to set ajar.
ENTREGA *s.f.* delivery.
ENTREGADOR(A) *s.m.* deliverer.
ENTREGAR *v.* to hand over, to deliver.
ENTREGUE *adj.2gên.* delivered.
ENTRELAÇADO *adj.* interlaced.
ENTRELAÇAR *v.* to interlace.
ENTRELINHA *s.m.* interlineation; lead; comment.
ENTREMEIO *s.m.* interval.
ENTREOLHAR *v.* to look at one another.
ENTREOUVIR *v.* to heard indistinctly, to overhear.
ENTREPOSTO *s.m.* depository; warehouse.
ENTRETANTO *conj.* however / *adv.* meantime.
ENTRETENIMENTO *s.m.* entertainment.
ENTRETER *v.* to entertain.
ENTRETIDO *adj.* busy; amused, entertained.
ENTREVER *v.* to see indistinctly.
ENTREVISTA *s.f.* interview.
ENTREVISTADOR(A) *s.m.* interviewer.
ENTREVISTAR *v.* to interview.
ENTRISTECER *v.* to sadden.
ENTRONIZAR *v.* to enthrone.
ENTROSADO *adj.* integrated.
ENTROSAMENTO *s.m.* adjustment.
ENTROSAR *v.* to gear, to mesh.
ENTUBAR *v.* to channel.
ENTULHAR *v.* to clutter up.
ENTULHO *s.m.* rubble, rubbish.
ENTUPIDO *adj.* blocked.
ENTUPIR *v.* to block.

ENTURVAR *v.* to make turbid.
ENTUSIASMADO *adj.* ravished, excited; enthusiastic.
ENTUSIASMAR *v.* to excite, to animate.
ENTUSIASMO *s.m.* enthusiasm.
ENUMERAÇÃO *s.f.* enumeration.
ENUMERAR *v.* to enumerate.
ENUNCIAÇÃO *s.f.* enunciation.
ENUNCIADO *s.m.* enunciation.
ENUNCIAR *v.* to enunciate.
ENVAIDECER *v.* to make proud.
ENVELHECER *v.* to age, to get old.
ENVELHECIMENTO *s.m.* aging.
ENVELOPAR *v.* to wrap.
ENVELOPE *s.m.* envelope, mailer.
ENVENENADO *adj.* poisoned.
ENVENENAMENTO *s.m.* poisoning.
ENVENENAR *v.* to poison.
ENVERGADURA *s.f.* span; wingspan.
ENVERGAR *v.* to bend.
ENVERGONHADO *adj.* ashamed, embarrassed.
ENVERGONHAR *v.* to shame.
ENVERNIZADO *adj.* varnished.
ENVERNIZAR *v.* to varnish.
ENVESGAR *v.* to squint.
ENVIADO *adj.* sent.
ENVIAR *v.* to send.
ENVIDRAÇADO *adj.* glazed.
ENVIDRAÇAR *v.* to glaze.
ENVIO *s.m.* sending, dispatch.
ENVIUVAR *v.* to widow.
ENVOLTO *adj.* wrapped.
ENVOLTÓRIO *s.m.* wrapper.
ENVOLVENTE *adj.2gên.* involving.
ENVOLVER *v.* to involve, to wrap.
ENVOLVIMENTO *s.m.* involvement; implication.
ENXADA *s.f.* hoe.
ENXADRISTA *s.m.* chess player.
ENXAGUAR *v.* to rinse.
ENXÁGUE *s.m.* rinsing.
ENXAME *s.m.* swarm.
ENXAMEAR *v.* to swarm, to teem.
ENXAQUECA *s.f.* migraine.
ENXERGAR *v.* to see.
ENXERIDO *adj.* intrusive, nosy / *s.m.* meddler, busybody, intruder; snooper, eavesdropper.
ENXERTO *s.m.* graft; scion (planta).

ENXOFRE *s.m.* sulphur.
ENXOTAR *v.* to throw out.
ENXOVAL *s.m.* trousseau (de noiva), layette (de bebê).
ENXUGAR *v.* to dry.
ENXURRADA *s.f.* torrent.
ENXUTO *adj.* dry.
ÉPICO *adj.* epic.
EPIDEMIA *s.f.* epidemic.
EPIDÊMICO *adj.* epidemic.
EPIDERME *s.f.* epidermis.
EPIFANIA *s.f.* epiphany.
EPIGLOTE *s.f.* epiglottis.
EPÍGRAFE *s.f. s.f.* epigraph.
EPILEPSIA *s.f.* epilepsy.
EPILÉPTICO *adj.* epileptic.
EPÍLOGO *s.m.* epilogue.
EPISÓDIO *s.m.* episode.
EPÍSTOLA *s.f.* epistle.
EPISTOLAR *adj.2gên.* epistolary.
EPITÁFIO *s.m.* epitaph.
EPÍTETO *s.m.* epithet.
ÉPOCA *s.f.* period, time.
EQUAÇÃO *s.f.* equation.
EQUADOR *s.m.* Ecuador (país); equator (linha).
EQUALIZAÇÃO *s.f.* equalization.
EQUALIZADOR *adj.* equalizer.
EQUALIZAR *v.* to equalize.
EQUATORIAL *adj.2gên.* equatorial.
EQUATORIANO *adj.* Ecuadorian.
EQUESTRE *adj.2gên.* equestrian.
EQUIDADE *s.f.* equity.
EQUÍDEOS *adj.* horses.
EQUIDISTÂNCIA *s.f.* equidistance.
EQUIDISTANTE *adj.2gên.* equidistant.
EQUILIBRADO *adj.* balanced; level.
EQUILIBRAR *v.* to balance.
EQUILÍBRIO *s.m.* balance.
EQUILIBRISTA *adj.2gên.* acrobat.
EQUINO *adj.* equine.
EQUINÓCIO *s.m.* equinox.
EQUIPAMENTO *s.m.* equipment.
EQUIPAR *v.* to equip.
EQUIPARAÇÃO *s.f.* equalizatiom.
EQUIPARAR *v.* to equate.
EQUIPARÁVEL *adj.2gên.* comparable.
EQUIPE *s.f.* team.
EQUITAÇÃO *s.f.* equitation.
EQUITATIVO *adj.* equitable.

EQUIVALÊNCIA *s.f.* equivalence.
EQUIVALENTE *adj.2gên.* equivalent.
EQUIVOCAR *v.* to mistake.
EQUÍVOCO *s.m.* mistake.
ERA *s.f.* era, age.
ERÁRIO *s.m.* exchequer.
EREÇÃO *s.f.* erection.
EREMITA *s.2gên.* hermit.
ERETO *adj.* erect.
ERGUER *v.* to raise; to elevate, to rear; to build, to erect.
ERGUIDO *adj.* bristly.
ERIÇAR *v.* to bristle.
ERIGIR *v.* to build.
ERMITÃO *s.m.* hermit.
ERMO *adj.* desert, solitary place.
ERODIR *v.* to erode.
ERÓGENO *adj.* erogenous.
EROSÃO *s.f.* erosion.
EROSIVO *adj.* erosive.
ERÓTICO *adj.* erotic.
EROTISMO *s.m.* erotism.
EROTIZAR *v.* to eroticize.
ERRADICAÇÃO *s.f.* eradication.
ERRADICAR *v.* to eradicate.
ERRADO *adj.* wrong, mistaken.
ERRANTE *adj.2gên.* erring.
ERRAR *v.* to miss, to err.
ERRATA *s.f.* erratum.
ERRÁTICO *adj.* erratic.
ERRO *s.m.* mistake, error.
ERRÔNEO *adj.* erroneous.
ERUDIÇÃO *s.f.* erudition.
ERUDITO *adj.* erudite.
ERUPÇÃO *s.f.* eruption.
ERUPTIVO *adj.* eruptive.
ERVA *s.f.* herb.
ERVA-CIDREIRA *s.f.* lemon balm.
ERVILHA *s.f.* pea.
ESBAFORIDO *adj.* hasty, panting, gasping.
ESBANJAR *v.* to squander.
ESBARRÃO *s.m.* collision.
ESBARRAR *v.* to collide.
ESBARRO *s.m.* jostle.
ESBELTO *adj.* slim, slender.
ESBOÇAR *v.* to sketch, to outline.
ESBOÇO *s.m.* sketch, outline.
ESBOFETEAR *v.* to slap.
ESBORRACHADO *adj.* burst, crush, squash.

ESBORRACHAR v. to burst, to crush, to squash.
ESBRANQUIÇADO adj. whitish.
ESBRAVEJAR v. to roar.
ESBUGALHADO adj. pop-eyed.
ESBUGALHAR v. to pop out.
ESBURACADO adj. perfurated, pitted, bumpy, holey.
ESBURACAR v. to bore, to perforate.
ESCABECHE s.m. marinade.
ESCADA s.f. staircase, stairs.
ESCADARIA s.f. stairwell, stairway.
ESCAFANDRO s.m. standard diving dress, hard-hat equipment.
ESCAFEDER v. to disappear.
ESCALA s.f. scale.
ESCALADA s.f. scaling.
ESCALADOR s.m. scaler.
ESCALÃO s.m echelon; step.
ESCALAR v. to climb.
ESCALDADO adj. scalded, burned.
ESCALDAR v. to scald, to burn; to rebuke, to reprimed.
ESCALENO adj. scalene.
ESCALOPE s.m. escalope, scallop.
ESCAMA s.f. scale.
ESCAMAÇÃO s.f. scaling.
ESCAMOSO ad. scaly.
ESCAMOTEAR v. to pilfer, to filch.
ESCAMPADO s.m. open field / adj. unsheltered, desert.
ESCANCARADO adj. wide-open.
ESCANCARAR v. to set wide open.
ESCANDALIZADO adj. shocked.
ESCANDALIZAR v. to shock, to scandalize.
ESCÂNDALO s.m. scandal, outrage.
ESCANDALOSO adj. scandalous.
ESCANDINAVO adj. Scandinavian.
ESCANTEIO s.m. corner.
ESCAPADA s.f. escapade.
ESCAPAMENTO s.m. exhaust, escape.
ESCAPAR v. to escape, to run away.
ESCAPATÓRIA s.f. loophole.
ESCAPE s.m. escape.
ESCAPISMO s.m. escapism.
ESCÁPULA s.f. hook, spike.
ESCAPULÁRIO s.m. scapular.
ESCAPULIDA s.f. flight.
ESCAPULIR v. to escape, to run away.
ESCARAVELHO s.m. beetle, scarab.

ESCARCÉU s.m. billow; ado, uproar; exaggeration.
ESCARLATE adj.2gên. scarlet.
ESCARLATINA s.f. scarlatina.
ESCARNECER v. to mock.
ESCÁRNIO s.m. mocking, derision, scoff, scorn.
ESCAROLA s.f. endive.
ESCARPA s.f. slope.
ESCARPADO adj. sloped.
ESCARPAR v. to slope.
ESCARRAR v. to expectorate, to spit.
ESCARRO s.m. spittle, spawl, mucus.
ESCASSEAR v. to become scarce.
ESCASSEZ s.f. scarcity.
ESCASSO adj. scarce.
ESCATOLOGIA s.f. scatology, eschatology.
ESCATOLÓGICO adj. scatological; eschatological.
ESCAVAÇÃO s.f. digging, excavation.
ESCAVADO adj. dug.
ESCAVADOR s.m. digger.
ESCAVADORA s.f. digging machine, digger, bulldozer.
ESCAVAR v. to dig.
ESCLARECEDOR adj. elucidator, clarifier; clarifying, enlightening.
ESCLARECER v. to explain, to brighten.
ESCLARECIMENTO s.m. clarification, enlightenment.
ESCLEROSAR v. to indurate, to become sclerotic.
ESCLEROSE s.f. sclerosis.
ESCOADOURO s.m. drain.
ESCOAMENTO s.m. drainage, flowage; discharge, outflow.
ESCOAR v. to flow off, to drain, to decant.
ESCOCÊS adj. Scotsman.
ESCOCESA adj. Scotswoman.
ESCÓCIA s.f. Scotland.
ESCOLA s.f. school.
ESCOLAR adj.2gên. school.
ESCOLARIDADE s.f. schooling.
ESCOLARIZAÇÃO s.f. schooling, education.
ESCOLARIZADO(A) s.m. educated.
ESCOLARIZAR v. to educate, to school.
ESCOLÁSTICA s.f. scholasticism.
ESCOLHA s.f. choice.
ESCOLHER v. to choose.
ESCOLHIDO adj. chosen / s.m. the chosen one. 133

ESCOLIOSE *s.f.* scoliosis.
ESCOLTA *s.f.* escort.
ESCOLTAR *v.* to escort.
ESCOMBROS *s.m. pl.* debris; wreckage.
ESCONDE-ESCONDE *s.m.* hide and seek.
ESCONDER *v.* to hide.
ESCONDERIJO *s.m.* hiding place.
ESCONDIDO *adj.* hidden.
ESCONJURAR *v.* to exorcise.
ESCONJURO *s.m.* exorcism.
ESCOPETA *s.f.* shotgun.
ESCOPO *s.m.* scope.
ESCORA *s.f.* prop, brace.
ESCORAMENTO *s.m.* propping.
ESCORAR *v.* to prop, to brace, to support, to uphold, to sustain.
ESCORBUTO *s.m.* scurvy.
ESCÓRIA *s.f.* slag.
ESCORIAÇÃO *s.f.* excoriation.
ESCORIAR *v.* to excoriate.
ESCORPIANO *adj.* Scorpios.
ESCORPIÃO *s.m.* Scorpio (astrologia); scorpion.
ESCORRAÇADO *adj.* expulsed, rejected.
ESCORRAÇAR *v.* to put to flight, to expule, to reject, to refuse.
ESCORREDOR *s.m.* drainer.
ESCORREGADELA *s.f.* slipping.
ESCORREGADIO *adj.* slippery.
ESCORREGADOR *s.m.* slipping, sliding, child's slide.
ESCORREGÃO *s.m.* slipping, sliding.
ESCORREGAR *v.* to slide, to slip, to skid, to glide.
ESCORRER *v.* to drain.
ESCORRIDO *adj.* drained.
ESCOTEIRO *s.m.* scout.
ESCOTILHA *s.f.* hatch.
ESCOTISMO *s.m.* scouting.
ESCOVA *s.f.* brush.
ESCOVAÇÃO *s.f.* brushing.
ESCOVADELA *s.f.* brushing.
ESCOVADO *adj.* brushed.
ESCOVADOR *s.m.* brusher.
ESCOVÃO *s.m.* brush, big brush.
ESCOVAR *v.* to brush.
ESCRAVATURA *s.f.* slavery.
ESCRAVIDÃO *s.f.* slavery.
ESCRAVISTA *adj.2gên.* proslavery.
ESCRAVIZAÇÃO *s.f.* enslavement.

ESCRAVIZAR *v.* enslave.
ESCRAVO *adj.* captive / *s.m.* slave.
ESCREVENTE *s.2gên.* clerk, copyist, scribe, notary.
ESCREVER *v.* to write.
ESCRIBA *s.m.* scribe.
ESCRITA *s.f.* writing.
ESCRITOR *s.m.* writer.
ESCRITÓRIO *s.m.* office.
ESCRITURA *s.f.* deed.
ESCRITURAÇÃO *s.f.* book-keeping.
ESCRITURAR *v.* to enter into a book.
ESCRITURÁRIO *s.m.* book-keeper.
ESCRIVANINHA *s.f.* desk, workstation, bureau, carrel.
ESCRIVÃO *s.m.* scrivener.
ESCROTO *s.m.* scrotum.
ESCRÚPULO *s.m.* scruple.
ESCRUPULOSO *adj.* scrupulous.
ESCUDEIRO *s.m.* shield-bearer, page, henchman.
ESCUDO *s.m.* shield.
ESCULACHADO *adj.* demoralized, ridiculed; careless, messy.
ESCULACHAR *v.* to blow; to shatter, to ridicule.
ESCULHAMBADO *adj.* sloopy person; mesy, disorderly.
ESCULHAMBAR *v.* to decompose, to ridicule, to deride.
ESCULPIDO *adj.* sculptured.
ESCULPIR *v.* to sculpture, to carve out.
ESCULTOR *s.m.* sculptor, carver.
ESCULTÓRICO *adj.* sculptural.
ESCULTURA *s.f.* sculpture.
ESCUMADEIRA *s.f.* skimmer.
ESCUNA *s.f.* schooner.
ESCURECER *v.* to darken.
ESCURECIMENTO *s.m.* darkening.
ESCURIDÃO *s.f.* darkness.
ESCURO *adj.* dark / *s.m.* darkness.
ESCUSAR *v.* to excuse.
ESCUSO *adj.* shady, obscure.
ESCUTAR *v.* to listen, to hear.
ESDRÚXULO *adj.* proparoxytone; dactylic; odd.
ESFAQUEAR *v.* to stab.
ESFARELADO *adj.* crumbled.
ESFARELAR *v.* to crumble.
ESFARRAPADO *adj.* torn; ragged; mean.

ESFARRAPAR *v.* to tear.
ESFERA *s.f.* sphere.
ESFÉRICO *adj.* spherical.
ESFEROGRÁFICA *s.f.* biro, rollerball, ballpoint pen.
ESFÍNCTER *s.m.* sphincter.
ESFINGE *s.f.* sphinx.
ESFOLADO *adj.* peeled.
ESFOLAMENTO *s.m.* flaying.
ESFOLAR *v.* to flay.
ESFOLIAÇÃO *s.f.* exfoliation.
ESFOLIADO *adj.* exfoliated.
ESFOLIAR *v.* to exfoliate.
ESFOMEADO *adj.* hungry, famished, ravenous.
ESFORÇADO *adj.* diligent, courageous; industrious.
ESFORÇAR *v.* to struggle, to strain, to strengthen, to try hard.
ESFORÇO *s.m.* effort.
ESFREGÃO *s.m.* rubbing cloth, rubber, scrubber; mop; scrubbing brush.
ESFREGAR *v.* to rub, to scrub.
ESFRIAMENTO *s.m.* cooling.
ESFRIAR *v.* to cool, to chill.
ESFUMAÇADO *adj.* smoky.
ESFUMADO *adj.* charcoal drawing.
ESFUMAR *v.* to smoke.
ESGANADO *adj.* greedy; gluttonous.
ESGANAR *v.* to strangle, to suffocate.
ESGANIÇAR *v.* to scream, to shout.
ESGARÇAR *v.* to rend, to rip.
ESGOELAR *v.* to cry, to bawl, to yell; to strangle.
ESGOTADO *adj.* exhausted, drained.
ESGOTAR *v.* to drain, to exhaust.
ESGOTO *s.m.* drain, sewage.
ESGRIMA *s.f.* fencing.
ESGRIMIR *v.* to brandish, to fence.
ESGRIMISTA *s.2gên.* fencer.
ESGUEIRAR *v.* to creep into, to edge, to slink.
ESGUELHA *s.f.* obliquity, bias, slant.
ESGUICHAR *v.* to spurt.
ESGUICHO *s.m.* spout, jet, gush, squish.
ESGUIO *adj.* lanky; slender.
ESLAVO *adj.* Slav, Slavonian.
ESMAGADOR *adj.* overwhelming.
ESMAGADURA *s.f.* compressing, squeezing.
ESMAGAR *v.* to crush, to squeeze.

ESMALTAR *v.* to enamel.
ESMALTE *s.m.* enamel, nail polish.
ESMERALDA *s.f.* emerald.
ESMERO *s.m.* care, diligence, carefulness; perfection, accuracy.
ESMIGALHAR *v.* to crumble, to crunch.
ESMIUÇADO *adj.* detailed, precise.
ESMO *s.m.* conjecture, guess; estimate, estimation.
ESMOLA *s.f.* alms.
ESMORECER *v.* to dismay, to discourage.
ESNOBAR *v.* to snob.
ESNOBE *adj.2gên.* snob, snobby.
ESÔFAGO *s.m.* esophagus, gullet.
ESOTÉRICO *adj.* esoteric.
ESOTERISMO *s.m.* esoterism.
ESPAÇADO *adj.* spaced.
ESPACIAL *adj.2gên.* spatial, spacial.
ESPAÇO *s.m.* space.
ESPAÇONAVE *s.f.* spacecraft, spaceship.
ESPAÇOSO *adj.* spacious, wide.
ESPADA *s.f.* sword.
ESPADACHIM *s.m.* swordsman.
ESPÁDUA *s.f.* shoulder blade.
ESPAGUETE *s.m.* spaghetti.
ESPAIRECER *v.* to amuse, to recreate, to distract.
ESPALHADO *adj.* scattered.
ESPALHAFATO *s.m.* fuss; uproar; glitz; swash.
ESPALHAFATOSO *adj.* fussy; blatant; ostentatious, flauting; garish.
ESPALHAR *v.* to spread.
ESPALMADO *adj.* flattened, palmated.
ESPALMAR *v.* to flatten, to spread; to palm.
ESPANCAR *v.* to thresh.
ESPANHA *s.f.* Spain.
ESPANHOL *adj.* Spanish; Spaniard.
ESPANTADIÇO *adj.* skittish.
ESPANTADO *adj.* scared.
ESPANTALHO *s.m.* scarecrow.
ESPANTAR *v.* to frighten.
ESPANTO *s.m.* fright.
ESPANTOSO *adj.* frightening.
ESPARADRAPO *s.m.* adhesive plaster, sticking plaster.
ESPARRAMADO *adj.* dispersed.
ESPARRAMAR *v.* to disperse; to awash; to sprawl.
ESPARSO *adj.* sparse.

ESPARTANO adj. Spartan.
ESPARTILHO s.m. corset.
ESPASMO s.m. spasm.
ESPATIFADO adj. shattered.
ESPATIFAR v. to shatter, to smash.
ESPÁTULA s.f. spatula.
ESPECIAL adj.2gên. special.
ESPECIALIDADE s.f. speciality.
ESPECIALISTA adj.2gên. specialist; sharp; expert.
ESPECIALIZAÇÃO s.f. specialization; major; minor.
ESPECIALIZADO adj. specialized.
ESPECIALIZAR v. to speacialize; to major.
ESPECIARIA s.f. spice, flavoring.
ESPÉCIE s.f. species, sort, kind.
ESPECIFICAÇÃO s.f. specification.
ESPECIFICAMENTE adv. specifically.
ESPECIFICAR v. to specify.
ESPECÍFICO adj. specific.
ESPECTADOR(A) s.m. spectator.
ESPECTRO s.m. spectrum.
ESPECULAÇÃO s.f. speculation.
ESPECULAR v. to speculate.
ESPECULATIVO adj. speculative.
ESPELHADO adj. mirrored.
ESPELHAR v. to mirror.
ESPELHARIA s.f. mirror factory; mirror shop.
ESPELHO s.m. mirror.
ESPERA s.f. hope, expectation.
ESPERANÇA s.f. hope.
ESPERANÇOSO adj. hopeful.
ESPERANTO s.m. Esperanto.
ESPERAR v. to wait for; to hope for.
ESPERMA s.m. sperm, semen.
ESPERMATOZOIDE s.m. spermatozoon.
ESPERMICIDA s.m. spermicide.
ESPERNEAR v. to kick about; to complain.
ESPERTALHÃO s.m. sly, tricky-guy; hotshot.
ESPERTEZA s.f. cleverness.
ESPERTO adj. clever.
ESPESSAR v. to thicken.
ESPESSO adj. thick.
ESPESSURA s.f. thickness.
ESPETACULAR adj.2gên. spectacular.
ESPETÁCULO s.m. show.
ESPETAR v. to broach, to pierce, to prick.
ESPETO s.m. spit.
ESPEVITADO adj. snuffed; brisk, lively.
ESPIÃO s.m. spy.

ESPIAR v. to spy.
ESPIGA s.f. ear of corn, spike.
ESPINAFRE s.m. spinach.
ESPINGARDA s.f. rifle.
ESPINHA s.f. spine.
ESPINHEIRO s.m. thornbush.
ESPINHO s.m. thorn.
ESPINHOSO adj. thorny.
ESPIONAGEM s.f. spying, espionage.
ESPIONAR v. to spy.
ESPIRAL adj.2gên. spiral, swirling.
ESPIRALAR v. to spiral.
ESPIRAR v. to breathe.
ESPÍRITA s.2gên. spiritualist.
ESPIRITISMO s.m. spiritualism.
ESPÍRITO s.m. spirit, soul.
ESPIRITUAL adj.2gên. spiritual.
ESPIRITUALIDADE s.f. spirituality.
ESPIRRAR v. to sneeze.
ESPIRRO s.m. sneeze.
ESPLANADA s.f. esplanade.
ESPLÊNDIDO adj. splendid.
ESPLENDOR s.m. splendor.
ESPOLETA s.f. fuse; detonator.
ESPÓLIO s.m. estate, assets.
ESPONJA s.f. sponge.
ESPONJOSO adj. spongy.
ESPONSAIS s.m. espousals.
ESPONTANEIDADE s.f. spontaneity.
ESPONTÂNEO adj. spontaneous.
ESPORA s.f. spur.
ESPORÁDICO adj. sporadic.
ESPORRO s.m. reprimand; come, cum; ranting.
ESPORTE s.m. sport.
ESPORTISTA s.2gên. sportsman.
ESPORTIVA s.f. fair-mindedness, sportsmanship; soccer lottery.
ESPORTIVO adj. sportive.
ESPOSA s.f. wife.
ESPOSAR v. to marry.
ESPOSO s.m. husband.
ESPREGUIÇADEIRA s.f. chaise longue, deck chair, reclining chair.
ESPREGUIÇAR-SE v. to stretch oneself.
ESPREITA s.f. peep, pry; lookout, ambush.
ESPREITAR v. to peep, to pry, to watch, to spy.
ESPREMEDOR s.m. squeezer.

ESPREMER *v.* to squeeze.
ESPREMIDO *adj.* squeezed.
ESPUMA *s.f.* foam; froth; lather.
ESPUMADEIRA *s.f.* skimmer.
ESPUMANTE *s.m.* sparkling wine / *adj.2gên.* foaming, frothy, foamy, bubbly, fizzy.
ESPUMAR *v.* to skim, to foam, to froth, to bubble.
ESQUADRA *s.f.* fleet.
ESQUADRÃO *s.m.* squadron.
ESQUADRIA *s.f.* sash.
ESQUADRILHA *s.f.* squadrom.
ESQUADRO *s.m.* square; set-square.
ESQUARTEJADO *adj.* quartered.
ESQUARTEJAMENTO *s.m.* quartering.
ESQUARTEJAR *v.* to quarter.
ESQUECER *v.* to forget.
ESQUECIDO *adj.* forgotten, forgetful.
ESQUECIMENTO *s.m.* forgetfulness, oblivion.
ESQUELÉTICO *adj.* skeleton, rawboned.
ESQUELETO *s.m.* skeleton.
ESQUEMA *s.m.* outline, scheme.
ESQUEMATIZAR *v.* to schematize.
ESQUENTADO *adj.* heated, warmed; hot.
ESQUENTAR *v.* to heat, to warm.
ESQUERDISTA *adj.2gên.* leftist.
ESQUERDO *adj.* left.
ESQUI *s.m.* ski.
ESQUIAR *v.* to ski.
ESQUIFE *s.m.* coffin, casket, bier.
ESQUILO *s.m.* squirrel.
ESQUIMÓ *adj.2gên.* eskimo.
ESQUINA *s.f.* corner.
ESQUISITICE *s.f.* eccentricity, oddity.
ESQUISITO *adj.* strange, weird.
ESQUIVAR *v.* to shun, to avoid, to dodge, to duck.
ESQUIVO *adj.* slinky, rare, difficult to get at.
ESQUIZOFRENIA *s.f.* schizophrenia.
ESQUIZOFRÊNICO *adj.* schizophrenic.
ESSE(A) *pron.* this (*pl.* these).
ESSÊNCIA *s.f.* essence.
ESSENCIAL *adj.2gên.* essential.
ESTABANADO *adj.* clumsy, awkward.

ESTABELECER *v.* to establish, to set, to settle.
ESTABELECIMENTO *s.m.* establishment.
ESTABILIDADE *s.f.* stability.
ESTABILIZAÇÃO *s.f.* stabilization.
ESTABILIZAR *v.* to stabilize, to settle.
ESTÁBULO *s.m.* barn.
ESTACA *s.f.* stake.
ESTAÇÃO *s.f.* station.
ESTACIONAMENTO *s.m.* parking lot.
ESTACIONAR *v.* to park.
ESTADIA *s.f.* stay, sojourn.
ESTÁDIO *s.m.* stadium.
ESTADISTA *s.2gên.* statesman; stateswoman.
ESTADO *s.m.* state.
ESTADO CIVIL *s.m.* marital status.
ESTADO-MAIOR *s.m.* general staff; captain--general.
ESTADUAL *adj.2gên.* state.
ESTADUNIDENSE *adj.2gên.* American.
ESTAFA *s.f.* exhaustion.
ESTAGIAR *v.* to apprentice, to intern.
ESTAGIÁRIO *s.m.* trainee, intern.
ESTÁGIO *s.m.* stage, internship.
ESTAGNAÇÃO *s.f.* stagnation.
ESTAGNADO *adj.* stagnant.
ESTAGNAR *v.* to stagnate.
ESTALACTITE *s.f.* stalactite.
ESTALAGEM *s.f.* inn, lodge, hostel, auberge.
ESTALAGMITE *s.f.* stalagmite.
ESTALAR *v.* to crack.
ESTALEIRO *s.m.* shipyard.
ESTALIDO *s.m.* clapping, cracking, smacking, snapping.
ESTALO *s.m.* crack, crackling, burst; illumination.
ESTAME *s.m.* stamen.
ESTAMPA *s.f.* impression; printed image; pattern, stencil.
ESTAMPADO *adj.* printed, impressed, stamped.
ESTAMPAR *v.* to print, to stamp.
ESTAMPARIA *s.f.* printworks, printery.
ESTAMPIDO *s.m.* clap, crack, report (arma); explosion, detonation.
ESTANCAR *v.* to stanch.
ESTÂNCIA *s.f.* ranch, farm.
ESTANDARTE *s.m.* flag, standard, banner, guidon.
ESTANDE *s.m.* box, booth.

ESTANHO *s.m.* tin.
ESTANQUE *adj.2gên.* stanch, standing, stagnant.
ESTANTE *s.f.* bookcase.
ESTAR *v.* to be.
ESTARDALHAÇO *s.m.* bustle.
ESTARRECER *v.* to terrify.
ESTATAL *adj.2gên.* state.
ESTATELAR *v.* to plop, to crash (carros).
ESTÁTICA *s.f.* statics.
ESTÁTICO *adj.* static.
ESTATÍSTICA *s.f.* statistics.
ESTATÍSTICO *s.m.* statistician / *adj.* statistical, statistician.
ESTATIZAÇÃO *s.f.* nationalization.
ESTATIZAR *v.* to nationalize.
ESTÁTUA *s.f.* statue.
ESTATURA *s.f.* stature.
ESTATUTO *s.m.* statute.
ESTÁVEL *adj.2gên.* stable, firm, steady.
ESTE(A) *pron.* this (*pl.* these).
ESTEIRA *s.f.* wake; treadmill; carousel, conveyor belt.
ESTELAR *adj.2gên.* stellar.
ESTELIONATO *s.m.* embezzlement.
ESTENDER *v.* to extend.
ESTEPE *s.f.* steppe (formação vegetal); spare (pneu reserva).
ESTERCO *s.m.* dung, manure; excrement, garbage.
ESTÉREO *s.m.* stereo, stereophonic.
ESTEREOTIPADO *adj.* stereotyped.
ESTEREÓTIPO *s.m.* stereotype.
ESTÉRIL *adj.2gên.* sterile, barren.
ESTERILIZADOR *adj.* sterilizer, sterilizing.
ESTERILIZAR *v.* to sterilize.
ESTERNO *s.m.* sternum, breastbone.
ESTÉTICA *s.f.* esthetics.
ESTETICISTA *adj.2gên.* estheticist.
ESTIAGEM *s.f.* dry weather.
ESTIAR *v.* to stop raining, to dry up.
ESTICAR *v.* to stretch out, to lengthen, to dilate.
ESTIGMA *s.m.* stigma.
ESTIGMATIZADO *adj.* stigmatized.
ESTILETE *s.m.* probe, stiletto.
ESTILHAÇAR *v.* to shatter, to splinter.
ESTILHAÇO *s.m.* chip, fragment, scrap.
ESTILINGUE *s.m.* slingshot, sling.

ESTILISTA *adj.2gên.* stylist, fashion designer.
ESTILÍSTICA *s.f.* stylistics.
ESTILIZAR *v.* to stylize.
ESTILO *s.m.* style.
ESTIMA *s.f.* esteem.
ESTIMAÇÃO *s.f.* affection, esteem.
ESTIMADO *adj.* esteemed, appreciated.
ESTIMAR *v.* to esteem, to appreciate, to apraise.
ESTIMATIVA *s.f.* estimation; guess; figure.
ESTIMATIVO *adj.* estimative, esteeming.
ESTIMÁVEL *adj.2gên.* estimable, respectable.
ESTIMULAÇÃO *s.f.* stimulation, excitement, incitement.
ESTIMULANTE *adj.2gên.* stimulant, stimulating.
ESTIMULAR *v.* to stimulate.
ESTÍMULO *s.m.* stimulus, incentive.
ESTIPULAR *v.* to stipulate, to specify.
ESTIRAR *v.* to stretch, to lengthen, to distend.
ESTIRPE *s.f.* stock, race, lineage, family tree.
ESTIVADOR *s.m.* longshoreman, stevedore.
ESTOCAGEM *s.f.* stowage.
ESTOCAR *v.* to stock.
ESTOFAMENTO *s.m.* upholstering, upholstery.
ESTOFAR *v.* upholster, stuff, quilt.
ESTOFO *s.m.* stuff, material, padding, wadding.
ESTOJO *s.m.* case, box.
ESTOLA *s.f.* stole.
ESTOMACAL *adj.2gên.* stomachic; stomachal.
ESTÔMAGO *s.m.* stomach.
ESTOQUE *s.m.* stock, stash.
ESTOQUISTA *adj.2gên.* stockist.
ESTÓRIA *s.f.* story.
ESTORRICAR *v.* to dry, to toast, to parch.
ESTORVAR *v.* to hinfer, to obstruct, to impede.
ESTOURAR *v.* to burst, to split, to shatter.
ESTOURO *s.m.* explosion, burst.
ESTRÁBICO *adj.* cross-eyed; lazy eye.
ESTRABISMO *s.m.* strabismus.
ESTRAÇALHAR *v.* to tear, to shred, to shatter.
ESTRADA *s.f.* road, railroad, railway.

ESTRADO *s.m.* bed frame.
ESTRAGADO *adj.* spoiled, rotten.
ESTRAGÃO *s.m.* tarragon.
ESTRAGAR *v.* to spoil, to ruin.
ESTRAGO *s.m.* damage, harm, injury.
ESTRALAR *v.* to crackle, to crack, to burst.
ESTRAMBÓLICO *adj.* extravagant, capricious.
ESTRAMÔNIO *s.m.* stramonium.
ESTRANGEIRISMO *s.m.* loan word, borrowing.
ESTRANGEIRO *adj.* foreign / *s.m.* foreigner.
ESTRANGULAÇÃO *s.f.* strangulation.
ESTRANGULADOR *s.m.* strangler.
ESTRANGULAMENTO *s.m.* strangling.
ESTRANGULAR *v.* to strangler.
ESTRANHAR *v.* to wonder, to admire, to be astonished, to marvel.
ESTRANHEZA *s.f.* strangeness, oddity, astonishment, surprise.
ESTRANHO *adj.* strange / *s.m.* stranger.
ESTRATAGEMA *s.m.* stratagem, ruse, trick.
ESTRATÉGIA *s.f.* strategy.
ESTRATÉGICO *adj.* strategic.
ESTRATEGISTA *s.2gên.* strategist.
ESTRATIFICAR *v.* to stratify.
ESTRATO *s.m.* stratum, bed, layer.
ESTRATO-CÚMULO *s.m.* strato-cumulus.
ESTRATOSFERA *s.f.* stratosphere.
ESTRATOSFÉRICO *adj.* stratospheric.
ESTREANTE *adj.2gên.* debutant, begginer, novice.
ESTREAR *v.* to inaugurate, to begin.
ESTREBUCHAR *v.* to flounder, to struggle helplessly.
ESTREIA *s.f.* premiere, opening.
ESTREITAR *v.* to narrow, to tighten.
ESTREITEZA *s.f.* narrowness, tightness, intimacy.
ESTREITO *adj.* narrow.
ESTRELA *s.f.* star.
ESTRELA-D'ALVA *s.f.* Morning Star.
ESTRELA DE DAVI *s.f.* Star of David.
ESTRELADO *adj.* starry.
ESTRELA-DO-MAR *s.f.* starfish.
ESTRELAR *v.* to star, to shine, to scintillate.
ESTRELATO *s.m.* stardom.
ESTREMECEDOR *adj.* trembling.
ESTREMECER *v.* to tremble, to shake, to frighten.

ESTRESSADO *adj.* stressed.
ESTRESSANTE *adj.2gên.* stressful.
ESTRESSAR *v.* to stress.
ESTRESSE *s.m.* stress.
ESTRIA *s.f.* stria, stretch mark; groove, channel, bloodsucker.
ESTRIADO *adj.* striated, grooved.
ESTRIBEIRA *s.f.* step, foot-board, stirrup.
ESTRIBEIRO *s.m.* stableman, equerry.
ESTRIBILHO *s.m.* refrain, chorus.
ESTRIBO *s.m.* stirrup, step, foot-board.
ESTRICNINA *s.f.* strychnine.
ESTRIDÊNCIA *s.f.* stridency.
ESTRIDENTE *adj.2gên.* shrill, strident, jangling; yelling.
ESTRIPADOR *adj.* ripper.
ESTRIPAR *v.* to disembowel, to extirpate.
ESTRIPULIA *s.f.* naughtiness, prank, tumult.
ESTRITO *adj.* strict, rigorous, severe.
ESTROFE *s.f.* strophe, stanza.
ESTRÓFICO *adj.* strophic.
ESTROGÊNIO *s.m.* estrogen.
ESTRÔNCIO *s.m.* strontium.
ESTRONDAR *v.* to roar, to thunder.
ESTRONDO *s.m.* noise, racket, rumble, thundering.
ESTRONDOSO *adj.* noisy, loud, tumultuous.
ESTROPIADO *adj.* maimed, mangled, mutilated.
ESTROPIAR *v.* to maim, to mutilate, to cripple.
ESTROPÍCIO *s.m. m.q.* estrupício.
ESTRUME *s.m.* manure, dung, fertilizer.
ESTRUPÍCIO *s.m.* blunder; mutinity, riot, revolt; damage, evil deed.
ESTRUTURA *s.f.* structure; frame, framework.
ESTRUTURAL *adj.2gên.* structural.
ESTRUTURALISMO *s.m.* structuralism.
ESTRUTURALISTA *adj.2gên.* structuralist.
ESTRUTURAR *v.* to structure.
ESTUÁRIO *s.m.* estuary.
ESTUDADO *adj.* studied; examined; affected.
ESTUDANTE *adj.2gên.* student.
ESTUDAR *v.* to study.
ESTÚDIO *s.m.* studio.
ESTUDIOSO *adj.* studious.
ESTUDO *s.m.* study.
ESTUFA *s.f.* stove, greenhouse.

ESTUFAR v. to stew, to heat.
ESTULTO adj. foolish, silly, stupid.
ESTUPEFAÇÃO s.f. stupefaction.
ESTUPEFACIENTE adj.2gên. stupefying.
ESTUPEFATO adj. stupefied; astonished; glazed.
ESTUPEFAZER v. to stupefy, to amaze, to astonish.
ESTUPENDO adj. stupendous.
ESTUPIDEZ s.f. stupidity, foolishness.
ESTÚPIDO adj. stupid, obtuse / s.m. brute, dunce.
ESTUPOR s.m. stupor.
ESTUPRADOR s.m. rapist, raping.
ESTUPRAR v. to rape.
ESTUPRO s.m. rape.
ESTUQUE s.m. stucco.
ESVAECER v. to evanescence, to dissolve, to vanish.
ESVAECIMENTO s.m. disappearance, vanishing.
ESVAIR v. to dissipate, to evaporate.
ESVAZIAMENTO s.m. emptying, deflating.
ESVAZIAR v. to empty.
ESVERDEADO adj. green, greenish.
ESVOAÇANTE adj.2gên. fluttering.
ESVOAÇAR v. to flutter.
ETANO s.m. ethane.
ETANOL s.m. ethanol.
ETAPA s.f. stage.
ÉTER s.m. ether.
ETERIZAÇÃO s.f. etherization.
ETERNAMENTE adv. eternally.
ETERNIDADE s.f. eternity.
ETERNIZAR v. to eternalize, to immortalize.
ETERNO adj. eternal.
ÉTICA s.f. ethics.
ÉTICO adj. ethical.
ETILENO s.m. ethylene.
ETÍLICO adj. ethylic.
ETIMOLOGIA s.f. etymology.
ETIMOLÓGICO adj. etymological.
ETIMOLOGISTA s.2gên. etymologist.
ETÍOPE s.2gên. Ethiopian.
ETIÓPIA s.f. Ethiopia.
ETIQUETA s.f. etiquette, label, tag.
ETIQUETAGEM s.f. labeling.
ETIQUETAR v. to label.
ETNIA s.f. ethinic group.
ÉTNICO adj. ethnic.

EU pron. I.
EUCALIPTO s.m. eucalyptus.
EUCARISTIA s.f. Eucharist.
EUFEMISMO s.m. euphemism.
EUFONIA s.f. euphony.
EUFORIA s.f. euphoria.
EUFÓRICO adj. euphoric.
EUGENIA s.f. eugenics.
EUGÊNICO adj. eugenic.
EUNUCO s.m. eunuch.
EURECA interj. eureka!
EURO s.m. Euro.
EURO-ASIÁTICO adj. Euro-Asian.
EUROPA s.f. Europe.
EUROPEIA s.f. European woman / adj. European.
EUROPEÍSMO s.m. Europeanism.
EUROPEÍSTA adj. Europeanist.
EUROPEIZAÇÃO s.f. Europeanization.
EUROPEIZAR v. to Europeanize.
EUROPEU s.m. European man / adj. European.
EUTANÁSIA s.f. euthanasia.
EVACUAÇÃO s.f. evacuation.
EVACUAR v. to evacuate, to empty.
EVADIR v. to evade, to avoid, to elude.
EVANESCÊNCIA s.f. evanescence.
EVANESCENTE adj.2gên. evanescent.
EVANGELHO s.m. Gospel.
EVANGÉLICO adj. evangelic.
EVANGELISMO s.m. evangelism.
EVANGELISTA adj.2gên. evangelist.
EVANGELIZAÇÃO s.f. evangelization.
EVANGELIZADOR s.m. evangelist, preacher.
EVANGELIZAR v. to evangelize.
EVAPORAÇÃO s.f. evaporation.
EVAPORAR v. to evaporate.
EVAPORIZAR v. m.q. evaporar.
EVASÃO s.f. escape.
EVASIVA s.f. evasion, subterfuge, pretext.
EVASIVO adj. evasive.
EVENTO s.m. event.
EVENTUAL adj.2gên. fortuitous, occasional.
EVENTUALIDADE s.f. eventuallity.
EVIDÊNCIA s.f. evidence.
EVIDENCIAR v. to evidence, to make clear.
EVIDENTE adj.2gên. evident.
EVIDENTEMENTE adv. evidently, clearly, obviously.
EVITAR v. to avoid, to prevent.

EVOCAÇÃO *s.f.* evocation.
EVOCADOR *adj.* remindful.
EVOCAR *v.* to evoke, to call, to remind.
EVOCATIVO *adj.* evocative.
EVOLUÇÃO *s.f.* development, evolution.
EVOLUCIONAR *v.* to evolve, to develop, to progress.
EVOLUCIONISMO *s.m.* evolutionism.
EVOLUCIONISTA *adj.2gên.* evolutionist.
EVOLUIR *v.* to develop, to evolve.
EVOLUTIVO *adj.* evolutionary.
EVOLVER *v.* to evolve.
EXACERBAÇÃO *s.f.* exacerbation.
EXACERBAR *v.* to exacerbate, to aggravate.
EXAGERAÇÃO *s.f.* exaggeration.
EXAGERADO *adj.* exaggerated.
EXAGERAR *v.* to exaggerate.
EXAGERO *s.m.* exaggeration, overstatement.
EXALAÇÃO *s.f.* exhalation.
EXALAR *v.* to exhale.
EXALTAÇÃO *s.f.* exaltation, enthusiasm.
EXALTADO *adj.* exalted, exaggerated.
EXALTAR *v.* to exalt, to glorify, to praise.
EXAME *s.m.* exam, examination.
EXAMINADOR *s.m.* examiner, examining.
EXAMINAR *v.* to examine.
EXASPERAÇÃO *s.f.* exasperation.
EXASPERAR *v.* to exasperate, to provoke, to irritate.
EXATIDÃO *s.f.* exactness, accuracy.
EXATO *adj.* right, correct, accurate, precise.
EXAURIR *v.* to exhaust, to drain, to dry up.
EXAUSTÃO *s.f.* exhaustion.
EXAUSTIVO *adj.* exhaustive.
EXAUSTO *adj.* exhausted, drained, emptied.
EXAUSTOR *s.m.* exhaust, suction, ventilation.
EXCEÇÃO *s.f.* exception.
EXCEDENTE *s.m.* excess, remainder.
EXCEDER *v.* to exceed, to excel; to transcend.
EXCELÊNCIA *pron.* excellence / *s.f.* excellence.
EXCELENTE *adj.2gên.* excellent.
EXCELENTÍSSIMO *s.m.* most excellent.
EXCELSO *adj.* excellent, lofty, eminent.
EXCENTRICIDADE *s.f.* eccentricity.
EXCÊNTRICO *adj.* eccentric.
EXCEPCIONAL *adj.2gên.* exceptional.

EXCEPCIONALIDADE *s.f.* exceptionality.
EXCEPCIONALMENTE *adv.* exceptionally.
EXCESSIVO *adj.* excessive.
EXCESSO *s.m.* excess.
EXCETO *prep.* except.
EXCETUAR *v.* to except, to exclude, to exempt, to object.
EXCIPIENTE *s.m.* excipient.
EXCITABILIDADE *s.f.* excitability.
EXCITAÇÃO *s.f.* excitement.
EXCITADO *adj.* excited.
EXCITAMENTO *s.m.* excitation.
EXCITANTE *adj.2gên.* exciting.
EXCITAR *v.* to excite.
EXCLAMAÇÃO *s.f.* exclamation.
EXCLAMAR *v.* to exclaim.
EXCLAMATIVO *adj.* exclamatory.
EXCLUDENTE *adj.2gên.* excluding, excluder.
EXCLUIR *v.* to exclude.
EXCLUSÃO *s.f.* exclusion.
EXCLUSIVIDADE *s.f.* exclusivity.
EXCLUSIVISMO *s.m.* exclusivism.
EXCLUSIVISTA *adj.2gên.* exclusivist.
EXCLUSIVO *adj.* exclusive.
EXCOMUNGADO *adj.* excommunicated.
EXCOMUNGAR *v.* to excommunicate.
EXCOMUNHÃO *s.f.* excommunication.
EXCREÇÃO *s.f.* excretion.
EXCREMENTO *s.m.* excrement.
EXCRESCÊNCIA *s.f.* excrescence, wart, tubercule.
EXCRETAR *v.* to excrete, to expel, to secrete.
EXCRETOR *adj.* excretory.
EXCRETÓRIO *adj. m.q.* excretor.
EXCURSÃO *s.f.* outing, excursion.
EXCURSIONAR *v.* to go on an excursion.
EXECRAÇÃO *s.f.* execration.
EXECRAR *v.* to execrate.
EXECRÁVEL *adj.* execrable, hateful.
EXECUÇÃO *s.f.* execution; accomplishment.
EXECUTAR *v.* to execute, to perform.
EXECUTÁVEL *adj.2gên.* executable.
EXECUTIVA *s.f.* executive commission.
EXECUTIVO(A) *s.m.* executive / *adj.* executive.
EXECUTOR *s.m.* executor, doer.
EXEGESE *s.f.* exegesis.
EXEGETA *s.m.* exegete.

EXEMPLAR *adj.2gên.* exemplary / *s.m.* example.
EXEMPLIFICAÇÃO *s.f.* exemplification.
EXEMPLIFICAR *v.* to exemplify.
EXEMPLO *s.m.* example, model.
EXERCER *v.* to exercise.
EXERCÍCIO *s.m.* exercise.
EXERCITAÇÃO *s.f.* exercitation, practise, use.
EXERCITANTE *adj.2gên.* exercising.
EXERCITAR *v.* to exercise, to practise.
EXÉRCITO *s.m.* army.
EXIBIÇÃO *s.f.* exhibition.
EXIBICIONISMO *s.m.* exhibitionism, flashing; ballyhoo.
EXIBICIONISTA *s.2gên.* exhibitionist, showoff / *adj.2gên.* flamboyant.
EXIBIDO *adj.* exhibitionist.
EXIBIR *v.* to show.
EXIGÊNCIA *s.f.* demand to urge.
EXIGENTE *adj.2gên.* demanding, choosy, exigent.
EXIGIR *v.* to demand.
EXÍGUO *adj.* exiguous, lean, scanty.
EXILADO *adj.* exile, deportee, exiled, banished.
EXILAR *v.* to exile, to banish.
EXÍLIO *s.m.* exile.
EXÍMIO *adj.* eximious, eminent, distinguished, excellent.
EXIMIR *v.* to exempt, to exonerate, to clear.
EXISTÊNCIA *s.f.* existence.
EXISTENCIAL *adj.2gên.* existencial.
EXISTENCIALISMO *s.m.* existentialism.
EXISTENCIALISTA *adj.2gên.* existentialist.
EXISTIR *v.* to exist.
ÊXITO *s.m.* effect, outcome, success.
ÊXODO *s.m.* exodus, migration.
EXOESQUELETO *s.m.* exoeskeleton.
EXOGAMIA *s.f.* exogamy.
EXÓGENO *adj.* exogenous.
EXONERAÇÃO *s.f.* exoneration.
EXONERAR *v.* to exonerate.
EXORBITÂNCIA *s.f.* exorbitance.
EXORBITANTE *adj.2gên.* exorbitant.
EXORBITAR *v.* to exceed, to go too far.
EXORCISMO *s.m.* exorcism.
EXORCISTA *s.m.* exorcist.
EXORCIZAR *v.* to exorcize.
EXÓRDIO *s.m.* preface, introduction, prologue.

EXORTAÇÃO *s.f.* exhortation.
EXORTAR *v.* to exhort.
EXÓTICO *adj.* exotic.
EXOTISMO *s.m.* exoticism.
EXPANDIR *v.* to expand.
EXPANSÃO *s.f.* expansion.
EXPANSIONISMO *s.m.* expansionism.
EXPANSIVO *adj.* expansive, enthusiastic.
EXPATRIAÇÃO *s.f.* expatriation.
EXPATRIADO *adj.* expatriate, expatriated.
EXPATRIAR *v.* to expatriate.
EXPECTAÇÃO *s.f.* expectation.
EXPECTANTE *adj.2gên.* expectant, expecting.
EXPECTATIVA *s.f.* expectation.
EXPECTORAÇÃO *s.f.* expectoration.
EXPECTORANTE *adj.2gên.* expectorant, expectorating.
EXPECTORAR *v.* to expectorate, to spit.
EXPEDIÇÃO *s.f.* expedition.
EXPEDICIONÁRIO *s.m.* expeditionary.
EXPEDIENTE *adj.2gên.* business hours, expedient.
EXPEDIR *v.* to dispatch.
EXPEDITO *adj.* expeditious, swift, quick.
EXPELIR *v.* to expel, to pass, to exhale.
EXPERIÊNCIA *s.f.* experience.
EXPERIENTE *adj.2gên.* expert, experienced, skilled.
EXPERIMENTAÇÃO *s.f.* experimentation.
EXPERIMENTADO *adj.* experienced, able, skilled.
EXPERIMENTAL *adj.2gên.* experimental; tentative.
EXPERIMENTAR *v.* to experiment, to taste, to try, to prove, to attempt.
EXPERIMENTO *s.m.* experiment, trial, proof.
EXPERTO *adj.* skilful, experienced.
EXPIAÇÃO *s.f.* expiation.
EXPIAR *v.* to expiate.
EXPIATÓRIO *s.m.* expiatory.
EXPIRAÇÃO *s.f.* expiration, exhalation.
EXPIRAR *v.* to expire, to die, to breathe out.
EXPLANAÇÃO *s.f.* explanation.
EXPLANAR *v.* to explain, to explicate.
EXPLICAÇÃO *s.f.* explanation.
EXPLICAR *v.* to explain.
EXPLICATIVO *adj.* explicative, explanatory.
EXPLICITAR *v.* to make explicit.
EXPLÍCITO *adj.* explicit.
EXPLODIR *v.* to explode, to burst.
EXPLORAÇÃO *s.f.* exploration.
EXPLORADOR(A) *s.m.* explorer.

EXPLORAR *v.* to explore.
EXPLORATÓRIO *adj.* exploratory.
EXPLOSÃO *s.f.* explosion.
EXPLOSIVO *adj.* explosive.
EXPONENCIAL *adj.2gên.* exponential.
EXPOENTE *s.2gên.* exponent.
EXPOR *v.* to expose, to show, to display.
EXPORTAÇÃO *s.f.* export.
EXPORTADOR *adj.* exporter.
EXPORTADORA *s.f.* exporting company.
EXPORTAR *v.* to export.
EXPOSIÇÃO *s.f.* display.
EXPOSITOR *s.m.* exhibitor, expositor.
EXPOSTO *adj.* exposed.
EXPRESSÃO *s.f.* expression.
EXPRESSAR *v.* to express, to depict, to show.
EXPRESSIONISMO *s.m.* expressionism.
EXPRESSIONISTA *adj.2gên.* expressionist.
EXPRESSIVIDADE *s.f.* expressiveness.
EXPRESSO *adj.* expressive, meaningful / *s.m.* express train, express, clear.
EXPRIMIR *v.* to express, to declare, to speak, to say.
EXPROPRIAÇÃO *s.f.* expropriation.
EXPROPRIAR *v.* to expropriate.
EXPULSÃO *s.f.* expulsion, banishment.
EXPULSAR *v.* to expel, to banish.
EXPULSO *adj.* expelled.
EXPURGAR *v.* to expurgate, to purge, to clear.
ÊXTASE *s.m.* ecstasy.
EXTASIADO *adj.* ecstatic, enraptured.
EXTASIAR *v.* to ravish, to transport.
EXTENSÃO *s.f.* extension.
EXTENSÍVEL *adj.2gên.* extensible.
EXTENSIVO *adj.* extensive, extending.
EXTENSO *adj.* extensive, ample, large, broad.
EXTENUAÇÃO *s.f.* extenuation.
EXTENUAR *v.* to extenuate, to weaken.
EXTERIOR *adj.2gên.* outside / *s.m.* exterior, outside.
EXTERIORIZAÇÃO *s.f.* exteriorization.
EXTERIORIZAR *v.* to utter, to express, to externalize.
EXTERMINAÇÃO *s.f.* extermination.
EXTERMINAR *v.* to exterminate
EXTERMÍNIO *s.m.* extermination, extinction, massacre.
EXTERNATO *s.m.* day-school.
EXTERNO *adj.* external.
EXTINÇÃO *s.f.* extinction.
EXTINGUIR *v.* to extinguish; to douse, to starve (chamas).
EXTINTO *adj.* extinct.
EXTINTOR *adj.* extinguisher.
EXTIRPAR *v.* to extirpate, to destroy.
EXTORQUIR *v.* to extort, to rob, to steal.
EXTORSÃO *s.f.* extortion.
EXTRA *adj.2gên.* extra, additional, supplementary.
EXTRAÇÃO *s.f.* extraction.
EXTRACONJUGAL *adj.2gên.* extramarital.
EXTRADIÇÃO *s.f.* extradition.
EXTRADITAR *v.* to extradite.
EXTRAESCOLAR *adj.2gên.* extracurricular.
EXTRAIR *v.* to extract, to draw out, to withdraw.
EXTRAORDINÁRIO *adj.* extraordinary, outstanding.
EXTRAPOLAR *v.* to extrapolate, to infer.
EXTRATERRESTRE *s.2gên.* extraterrestrial.
EXTRATO *s.m.* extract.
EXTRAVAGÂNCIA *s.f.* extravagance.
EXTRAVAGANTE *adj.2gên.* extravagant.
EXTRAVASAR *v.* to extravasate, to pour out.
EXTRAVIADO *adj.* astray, corrupt, perverted.
EXTRAVIAR *v.* to embezzle, to lead astray, to misdirect.
EXTRAVIO *s.m.* misleading, loss, embezzlement.
EXTREMAR *v.* to exalt, to elevate.
EXTREMIDADE *s.f.* extremity.
EXTREMISMO *s.m.* extremism.
EXTREMISTA *adj.2gên.* extremist.
EXTREMO *adj.* extreme, utmost, the end.
EXTROVERSÃO *s.f.* extroversion.
EXTROVERTIDO *adj.* extroverted, extrovert, outgoing.
EXUBERÂNCIA *s.f.* exuberance.
EXUBERANTE *adj.2gên.* exuberant, exuberating.
EXUBERAR *v.* to exuberate.
EXULTAÇÃO *s.f.* exultating, gaiety; exultancy.
EXULTANTE *adj.2gên.* exulting, exultant.
EXULTAR *v.* to exult, to jubilate.
EXUMAÇÃO *s.f.* exhumation.
EXUMAR *v.* to exhume.

Ff

F, f *s.m.* the sixth letter of the Portuguese alphabet.
FÃ *s.m.* fan.
FÁ *s.m.* F (nota musical).
FÁBRICA *s.f.* factory.
FABRICAÇÃO *s.f.* manufacture.
FABRICAR *v.* to manufacture; to make.
FÁBULA *s.f.* fable.
FABULOSO *adj.* fabulous.
FACA *s.f.* knife.
FAÇANHA *s.f.* exploit.
FACÃO *s.m.* carving knife.
FACÇÃO *s.f.* faction.
FACE *s.f.* face.
FACETA *s.f.* facet.
FACHADA *s.f.* façade, front.
FACHO *s.m.* torch; lantern, signal light.
FÁCIL *adj.2gên.* easy.
FACILIDADE *s.f.* facility.
FACILITAR *v.* to facilitate.
FAC-SÍMILE *s.m.* facsimile, exact copy.
FACULDADE *s.f.* faculty; university.
FACULTATIVO *adj.* optional.
FADA *s.f.* fairy.
FADADO *adj.* predestined.
FADIGA *s.f.* fatigue, tiredness.
FADO *s.m.* fate, destiny; Portuguese folk song, dance and music.
FAGULHA *s.f.* spark.
FAISÃO *s.m.* pheasant.
FAÍSCA *s.f.* spark, flash.
FAISCAR *v.* to spark.
FAIXA *s.f.* belt, band, strip.
FAJUTO *adj.* of poor quality, fake.
FALÁCIA *s.f.* fallacy, fraud.
FALANGE *s.f.* phalanx, body of soldiers.
FALANTE *adj.2gên.* talkative.
FALAR *v.* to speak, to talk.
FALATÓRIO *s.m.* talking, chit-chat.
FALCÃO *s.m.* falcon, hawk.
FALCATRUA *s.f.* imposture, fraud.
FALECER *v.* to die, to pass away.
FALECIDO *s.m.* dead, deceased / *adj.* dead, deceased.
FALECIMENTO *s.m.* death, demise.
FALÊNCIA *s.f.* bankruptcy.
FALÉSIA *s.f.* sea cliff.
FALHA *s.f.* fault, error, mistake.

FALHAR *v.* to fail.
FALIDO(A) *adj.* bankrupt, ruined.
FALIR *v.* to fail, to go bankrupt.
FALSÁRIO(A) *s.m.* forger.
FALSETE *s.m.* falsetto (música).
FALSIDADE *s.f.* falsehood.
FALSIFICAR *v.* to forge.
FALSO(A) *adj.* false, untrue.
FALTA *s.f.* lack; absence.
FALTAR *v.* to be lacking, to be absent, to miss.
FAMA *s.f.* fame.
FAMIGERADO *s.m.* famous, renowned.
FAMÍLIA *s.f.* family.
FAMILIAR *adj.2gên.* family, familiar.
FAMINTO(A) *adj.* hungry, starving.
FAMOSO(A) *adj.* famous, renowned.
FANÁTICO(A) *adj.* fanatical / *s.m.* fanatic.
FANFARRA *s.f.* flourish of trumpets, fanfare.
FANTASIA *s.f.* fantasy.
FANTASIAR *v.* to imagine.
FANTASMA *s.m.* ghost.
FANTÁSTICO(A) *adj.* fantastic.
FANTOCHE *s.m.* puppet.
FARAÓ *s.m.* pharaoh.
FARDA *s.f.* uniform.
FARELO *s.m.* bran, chaff.
FARINGE *s.f.* pharynx.
FARINHA *s.f.* flour.
FARMACÊUTICO(A) *adj.* pharmaceutical / *s.m.* pharmacist.
FARMÁCIA *s.f.* pharmacy, drugstore.
FARO *s.m.* sense of smell.
FAROL *s.m.* lighthouse.
FARRA *s.f.* binge.
FARRAPO *s.m.* rag.
FARSA *s.f.* farce.
FARTAR *v.* to satiate, sate.
FARTO(A) *adj.* full.
FARTURA *s.f.* abundance, wealth.
FASCINANTE *adj.2gên.* fascinating.
FASCINAR *v.* to fascinate.
FASCISMO *s.m.* fascismo.
FASE *s.f.* phase, stage.
FATAL *adj.2gên.* fatal.
FATIA *s.f.* slice, piece.
FATIGANTE *adj.2gên.* tiresome.
FATIGAR *v.* to tire.
FATO *s.m.* fact.

FATOR *s.m.* factor, agent.
FATURA *s.f.* invoice.
FAVA *s.f.* broad bean.
FAVELA *s.f.* slum.
FAVOR *s.m.* favour.
FAXINA *s.f.* brushwood.
FAZENDA *s.f.* farm.
FAZER *v.* to make, to do.
FÉ *s.f.* faith, creed.
FEBRE *s.f.* fever, temperature.
FECHADO(A) *adj.* shut, closed.
FECHADURA *s.f.* lock.
FECHAR *v.* to close, to shut.
FECHO *s.m.* fastening, zipper.
FÉCULA *s.f.* starch.
FECUNDAR *v.* to fertilize.
FEDER *v.* to stink.
FEDERAÇÃO *s.f.* federation.
FEDERAL *adj.2gên.* federal.
FEIÇÃO *s.f.* form.
FEIJÃO *s.m.* bean.
FEIO(A) *adj.* ugly.
FEIRA *s.f.* fair.
FEITICEIRO(A) *s.m.* witch.
FEITIÇO *s.m.* charm, spell.
FEITIO *s.m.* shape; make, fabric.
FEITO *s.m.* fact, action / *adj.* made, done.
FEIURA *s.f.* ugliness.
FEIXE *s.m.* bundle.
FEL *s.m.* bile, gall.
FELICIDADE *s.f.* happiness.
FELINO *s.m.* feline.
FELIZ *adj.2gên.* happy.
FELPUDO(A) *adj.* fuzzy, fluffy.
FELTRO *s.m.* felt.
FÊMEA *s.f.* female.
FEMININO(A) *adj.* feminine.
FEMINISTA *adj.2gên.* feminist / *s.2gên.* feminist.
FENDA *s.f.* slit; crack.
FENDER *v.* to split.
FENO *s.m.* hay.
FENOMENAL *adj.2gên.* phenomenal.
FERA *s.f.* wild animal.
FÉRETRO *s.m.* coffin.
FERIADO *s.m.* holiday.
FÉRIAS *s.f. pl.* holiday, vacation.
FERIDA *s.f.* wound.
FERIDO(A) *adj.* injured, wounded, hurt.
FERIMENTO *s.m.* injury, wound.

FERIR v. to injure, to wound.
FERMENTAR v. to ferment.
FERMENTO s.m. yeast.
FEROZ adj.2gên. fierce.
FERRADURA s.f. horseshoe.
FERRAGEM s.f. hardware, metalwork.
FERRAMENTA s.f. tool.
FERRÃO s.m. goad, prick, spike.
FERREIRO s.m. blacksmith, forger.
FERRO s.m. iron.
FERROVIA s.f. railroad, railway.
FERRUGEM s.f. rust.
FÉRTIL adj.2gên. fertile.
FERVENTE adj.2gên. boiling.
FERVER v. to boil.
FERVILHAR v. to simmer.
FERVOR s.m. fervour.
FERVOROSO adj. fervent.
FESTA s.f. party.
FESTEJAR v. to celebrate.
FESTIM s.m. feast.
FESTIVAL s.m. festival.
FESTIVIDADE s.f. festivity.
FESTIVO(A) adj. festive.
FETICHE s.m. fetish.
FÉTIDO(A) adj. stinking, rank.
FETO s.m. foetus.
FEUDO s.m. feud, fief.
FEVEREIRO s.m. February.
FEZES s.f. pl. faeces, excrements.
FIADA s.f. row, line.
FIADOR(A) s.f. backer, warrantor.
FIANÇA s.f. guarantee.
FIAR v. to spin; to rely, to trust.
FIASCO s.m. fiasco, failure.
FIBRA s.f. fibre.
FICAR v. to stay, to remain.
FICÇÃO s.f. fiction.
FICHA s.f. ticket.
FICHÁRIO s.m. card index, file.
FICTÍCIO(A) adj. fictitious.
FIDALGO s.m. nobleman.
FIDEDIGNO adj. trustworthy; authentical.
FIDELIDADE s.f. fidelity, loyalty.
FIEL adj.2gên. faithful.
FIGA s.f. talisman.
FÍGADO s.m. liver.
FIGO s.m. fig.
FIGURA s.f. figure.
FIGURANTE s.2gên. extra.
FIGURAR v. to appear.
FIGURINO s.m. model.
FILA s.f. row, line, queue.
FILAMENTO s.m. filament.
FILATELIA s.f. philately.
FILÉ s.m. steak.
FILEIRA s.f. file, row, wing.
FILHA s.f. daughter.
FILHO s.m. son.
FILHOTE s.m. puppy (de cachorro); cub (de leão).
FILIAL s.f. branch.
FILIPINAS s.f. pl. Philippines.
FILMADORA s.f. camcorder.
FILMAR v. to film, to shoot.
FILME s.m. film.
FILOLOGIA s.f. philology.
FILOSOFIA s.f. philosophy.
FILTRAR v. to filter.
FILTRO s.m. filter.
FIM s.m. end, termination.
FINAL adj.2gên. final / s.m. end.
FINANÇAS s.f. pl. finance.
FINCAR v. to thrust in, to drive in.
FINEZA s.f. finesse.
FINGIMENTO s.m. pretense, dissimulation.
FINGIR v. to pretend.
FINITO(A) adj. finite / s.m. finite.
FINLÂNDIA s.f. Finland.
FINO(A) adj. fine; thin, slim.
FIO s.m. thread, twine.
FIRMA s.f. company.
FIRMAR v. to secure, to firm.
FIRME adj.2gên. firm.
FISCAL s.m. custom officer, fiscal.
FÍSICA s.f. physics.
FÍSICO(A) adj. physical.
FISIONOMIA s.f. expression, look.
FISIOTERAPIA s.f. physiotherapy.
FISSURA s.f. crack, split.
FITA s.f. strip, band, ribbon.
FITAR v. to stare.
FIVELA s.f. buckle.
FIXAR v. to fix.
FIXO(A) adj. fixed, stable.
FLÁCIDO adj. flaccid, flabby.
FLAGELO s.m. scourge, whip.
FLAGRANTE s.m. flagrant.
FLAGRAR v. to catch.
FLÂMULA s.f. pennant.

FLANELA *s.f.* flannel.
FLAUTA *s.f.* flute.
FLECHA *s.f.* arrow.
FLEXÍVEL *adj.2gên.* flexible.
FLIPERAMA *s.m.* pinball machine.
FLOCO *s.m.* flake.
FLOR *s.f.* flower.
FLORESCENTE *adj.2gên.* flourishing.
FLORESCER *v.* to flower, to bloom, to blossom.
FLORESTA *s.f.* forest.
FLORIDO(A) *adj.* flowery.
FLUÊNCIA *s.f.* fluency.
FLUIDO *adj.* fluid / *s.m.* fluid, liquid.
FLUIR *v.* to flow.
FLÚOR *s.m.* fluorine.
FLUTUAR *v.* to float.
FLUVIAL *adj.2gên.* river, fluvial.
FLUXO *s.m.* flow.
FOBIA *s.f.* phobia.
FOCA *s.f.* seal.
FOCALIZAR *v.* to focus.
FOCINHO *s.m.* snout.
FOCO *s.m.* focus.
FOFO(A) *adj.* soft; cute (pessoa).
FOFOCA *s.f.* gossip.
FOGÃO *s.m.* stove.
FOGO *s.m.* fire.
FOGOSO(A) *adj.* fiery.
FOGUETE *s.m.* rocket.
FOLCLORE *s.m.* folklore.
FÔLEGO *s.m.* breath.
FOLGA *s.f.* rest, break.
FOLHA *s.f.* leaf; page (livro), sheet (papel).
FOLHAGEM *s.f.* foliage.
FOLIA *s.f.* revelry.
FOLÍCULO *s.m.* follicle; crypt.
FOME *s.f.* hunger.
FONEMA *s.m.* phoneme.
FONOAUDIOLOGIA *s.f.* speech therapy.
FONTE *s.f.* fountain; origin.
FORA *adv.* out, outside.
FORAGIDO(A) *adj.* fugitive / *s.m.* fugitive, outlaw.
FORASTEIRO(A) *s.m.* outsider, foreigner, outlander.
FORCA *s.f.* gallows.
FORÇA *s.f.* power, force, strength.
FORÇAR *v.* to force.
FORJAR *v.* to forge.

FORMA *s.f.* form, shape; mold, cake pan.
FORMAÇÃO *s.f.* formation.
FORMAL *adj.2gên.* formal.
FORMAR *v.* to form.
FORMATAR *v.* to format.
FORMATURA *s.f.* formation; graduation.
FORMIDÁVEL *adj.2gên.* formidable, splendid.
FORMIGA *s.f.* ant.
FORMOSO(A) *adj.* beautiful, charming.
FÓRMULA *s.f.* formula.
FORMULAR *v.* to formulate.
FORMULÁRIO *s.m.* form.
FORNECEDOR(A) *s.m.* supplier.
FORNECER *v.* to supply, to provide.
FORNO *s.m.* oven.
FORRAR *v.* to cover.
FORTALECER *v.* to strengthen.
FORTALEZA *s.f.* fortress, fort.
FORTE *adj.2gên.* strong.
FORTUITO(A) *adj.* accidental, casual.
FORTUNA *s.f.* fortune.
FOSCO(A) *adj.* dull, dim, opaque.
FÓSFORO *s.m.* match.
FÓSSIL *s.m.* fossil.
FOTO *s.f.* photo.
FOTOGRAFAR *v.* to photograph.
FOTOGRAFIA *s.f.* photography.
FOTÓGRAFO(A) *s.m.* photographer.
FOZ *s.f.* mouth of a river.
FRAÇÃO *s.f.* fraction.
FRACASSAR *v.* to fail.
FRACO(A) *adj.* weak.
FRAGATA *s.f.* frigate.
FRÁGIL *adj.2gên.* fragile.
FRAGMENTO *s.m.* fragment.
FRAGRÂNCIA *s.f.* fragrance.
FRALDA *s.f.* diaper, nappy.
FRAMBOESA *s.f.* raspberry.
FRANÇA *s.f.* France.
FRANCAMENTE *adv.* frankly.
FRANGO *s.m.* chicken.
FRANJA *s.f.* fringe (enfeite), bangs (cabelo).
FRANQUEZA *s.f.* frankness.
FRANQUIA *s.f.* postage; franchise.
FRANZIR *v.* to pleat.
FRAQUEZA *s.f.* weakness.
FRASCO *s.m.* bottle, flask.
FRASE *s.f.* sentence, phrase.
FRATURA *s.f.* fracture.

FRAUDE *s.f.* fraud.
FREAR *v.* to curb, to brake.
FREIRA *s.f.* nun, sister.
FRENTE *s.f.* front.
FREQUÊNCIA *s.f.* frequency.
FREQUENTAR *v.* to frequent, to attend.
FREQUENTE *adj.2gên.* frequent, often.
FRESCO(A) *adj.* fresh, new.
FRESCURA *s.f.* freshness; fussy.
FRETAR *v.* to charter.
FRETE *s.m.* freight.
FRIEZA *s.f.* coldness.
FRIGIDEIRA *s.f.* frying pan.
FRÍGIDO(A) *adj.* frigid.
FRIGIR *v.* to fry.
FRIGORÍFICO *s.m.* refrigerator.
FRIO(A) *adj.* cold / *s.m.* coldness.
FRISAR *v.* to curl, to frizzle, emphasize.
FRITAR *v.* to fry.
FRITAS *s.f. pl.* chips, French fries.
FRITO(A) *adj.* fried.
FRONHA *s.f.* pillowcase.
FRONTE *s.f.* forehead.
FRONTEIRA *s.f.* border, frontier.
FROTA *s.f.* fleet.
FROUXO(A) *adj.* loose.
FRUSTRAR *v.* to frustrate.
FRUTA *s.f.* fruit.
FUBÁ *s.m.* corn meal.
FUGA *s.f.* flight, escape.
FUGAZ *adj.* fleeting.
FUGIR *v.* to flee, to run away, to escape.
FUGITIVO(A) *adj.* fugitive / *s.m.* fugitive, evader.
FULMINANTE *adj.2gên.* devastating, withering.

FUMAÇA *s.f.* smoke.
FUMANTE *s.m.* smoker.
FUMAR *v.* to smoke.
FUMO *s.m.* smoke.
FUNÇÃO *s.f.* function.
FUNCIONAR *v.* to work, to function.
FUNCIONÁRIO(A) *s.m.* employee, clerk; official.
FUNDAÇÃO *s.f.* foundation.
FUNDAMENTAL *adj.2gên.* fundamental.
FUNDAMENTO *s.m.* foundation.
FUNDAR *v.* to found; to establish.
FUNDIÇÃO *s.f.* fusion, melting.
FUNDIR *v.* to fuse, to melt.
FUNDO(A) *adj.* deep / *s.m.* bottom.
FÚNEBRE *adj.2gên.* funereal.
FUNERAL *s.m.* funeral.
FUNESTO(A) *adj.* fatal, funest.
FUNGO *s.m.* fungus.
FUNIL *s.m.* funnel.
FURACÃO *s.m.* hurricane.
FURADO(A) *adj.* perforated, pierced.
FURAR *v.* to bore, to perforate, to pierce, to drill.
FURGÃO *s.m.* van.
FÚRIA *s.f.* fury.
FURO *s.m.* hole.
FURTAR *v.* to steal.
FUSÃO *s.f.* fusion, merger.
FUSÍVEL *s.m.* fuse.
FUSO *s.m.* spindle, spool.
FUTEBOL *s.m.* football; soccer.
FÚTIL *adj.2gên.* futile.
FUTILIDADE *s.f.* shallowness, futility.
FUTURO *s.m.* future / *adj.* future.
FUZIL *s.m.* rifle, gun.

G g

G, g *s.m.* the seventh letter of the Portuguese alphabet.
GABAÇÃO *s.f.* praising.
GABADOR *s.m.* praiser.
GABÃO *s.m.* Gabon.
GABAR *v.* to praise.
GABAR-SE *v.* to boast.
GABARITADO *adj.* qualified.
GABARITO *s.m.* templet, template, pattern; answer key.
GABINETE *s.m.* office, cabinet.
GABO *s.m. m.q.* gabação.
GADANHA *s.f.* scythe.
GADO *s.m.* live stock, cattle, herd, stock.
GAÉLICO *adj.* Gaelic.
GAFANHOTO *s.m.* grasshopper.
GAFE *s.f.* gaffe, blunder.
GAFIEIRA *s.f.* gaff, honky-tonk.
GAGÁ *adj.2gên.* gaga, senile / *s.2gên.* gaga, senile.
GAGO *adj.* stutterer, falterer, stammerer / *s.m.* stutterer, falterer, stammerer.
GAGUEIRA *s.f.* stutter, stammer.
GAGUEJAMENTO *s.m.* stutter, stammer, faltering.
GAGUEJAR *v.* to stutter, to stammer.
GAGUEZ *s.f.* stammer, stutter.
GAGUICE *s.f.* stammer, stutter.
GAIATO(A) *adj.* joyous, mischievous, naughty.
GAIO *s.m.* European jay.
GAIOLA *s.f.* cage, bird-cage, mew, hutch.
GAITA *s.f.* flute, reed, mouth-organ, harmonica.
GAITA DE FOLES *s.f.* bagpipe.
GAITEAR *v.* to flute.
GAITEIRO *s.m.* bagpipe, mouth-organ player.
GAIVÃO *s.m.* swift, martlet.
GAIVOTA *s.f.* seagull.
GAJO *s.m.* guy, chap.
GALA *s.f.* gala, pomp.
GALÃ *s.m.* coquet, leading man.
GALÁCTICO *adj.* galactic.
GALACTÔMETRO *s.m.* lactometer.
GALACTOSE *s.f.* galactose, lactose.
GALADO *adj.* fecundated, fertilized; fecundated hen.

GALAICO *adj.* Galician.
GALAICO-PORTUGUÊS *adj.* Galician-portuguese.
GALANTARIA *s.f.* gallantry, courteous behavior, genteelness.
GALANTE *adj.2gên.* graceful / *s.2gên.* gallant, gentleman.
GALANTEADOR *adj.* gallant, court, woo.
GALANTEAR *v.* to gallant, to court, to woo.
GALANTEIO *s.m.* gallantry, court, courtesy, politeness, courtship, wooing.
GALÃO *s.m.* stripe (uniforme); galloon, tun (medida).
GALAR *v.* to fecundate.
GALARDÃO *s.m.* premium, reward, recompense, award, accolade.
GALARDOAR *v.* to recompense, to reward.
GÁLATA *s.2gên.* Galatian / *adj.2gên.* Galatian.
GALÁXIA *s.f.* galaxy.
GÁLBANO *s.m.* galbanum.
GALÉ *s.f.* galley.
GALEÃO *adj.* galleon, carrack.
GALEGADA *s.f.* Galicians.
GALEGO(A) *s.2gên.* Galician / *adj.* Galician.
GALENO *s.m.* physician.
GALEOTE *adj.* galliot.
GALERA *s.f.* galley; gang.
GALERIA *s.f.* gallery.
GALERIA DE ARTE *s.f.* art gallery.
GALERIA SUBTERRÂNEA *s.f.* sap, heading, undercroft.
GALES *s.m.* Wales.
GALÊS *adj.* Welshman.
GALETO *s.m.* cockerel.
GALGAR *v.* to jump over, to leap over, to spring, to overstep.
GALGAZ *adj.2gên.* slender, long and thin, slim.
GALGO *s.m.* greyhound.
GALHADA *s.f.* antler.
GALHARDEAR *v.* to show off, to make a display.
GALHARDETE *s.m.* pennant.
GALHARDIA *s.f.* gallantry, chivalry, bravery.
GALHARDO *adj.* elegant, refined, chivalrous, merry, graceful.
GALHETEIRO *s.m.* caster, cruet.
GALHO *s.m.* branch, limb.
GALHOFA *s.f.* jest, joke, mockery.

GALHOFAR *v.* to joke, to jest; to romp.
GALHOFEIRO *adj.* sportful, sportive, lively.
GALHUDO *adj.* branchy; antlered, cuckolded.
GÁLIA *s.f.* Gaul.
GALICISMO *s.m.* Gallicism.
GALICISTA *adj.2gên.* Gallicizer.
GÁLICO *adj.* Gallic.
GALILEU *s.m.* galilean / *adj.* galilean.
GALINÁCEO *adj.* gallinaceous.
GALINHA *s.f.* hen, chicken.
GALINHA-CHOCA *s.f.* broody hen.
GALINHA-D'ANGOLA *s.f.* Helmeted Guinea fowl, Guinea hen.
GALINHAGEM *s.f.* faint-heartedness, weakness, cowardice; promiscuity.
GALINHEIRO *s.m.* poulterer, poultry-dealer, hennery.
GALINHOLA *s.f.* woodcock.
GÁLIO *s.m.* gallium.
GALO *s.m.* cock, rooster.
GALOCHA *s.f.* wellington (bota), galosh.
GALO DE BRIGA *s.m.* game cock, fighting cock.
GALO GARNISÉ *s.m.* cockalorum.
GALOPADA *s.f.* gallop, gallopade.
GALOPADOR *s.m.* galloper.
GALOPANTE *adj.2gên.* galloping.
GALOPAR *v.* to gallop.
GALOPE *s.m.* gallop.
GALPÃO *s.m.* shed.
GALRAR *v.* to prattle, to chatter, to babble; to boast, to brag.
GALVÂNICO *adj.* galvanic.
GALVANISMO *s.m.* galvanism.
GALVANIZAÇÃO *s.f.* galvanization.
GALVANIZAR *v.* to galvanize.
GALVANÔMETRO *s.m.* galvanometer.
GALVANOTIPIA *s.f.* galvanotype, electrotype.
GAMA *s.f.* gamma, scale.
GAMAÇÃO *s.f.* passion, desire.
GAMADO *adj.* hooked.
GAMÃO *s.m.* backgammon, gammon.
GAMAR *v.* to be in love with, to be fascinated.
GAMARRA *s.f.* martingale, harness strap.

GAMBÁ *s.m.* opossum.
GAMBETA *s.f.* doubling, dodging, craftiness.
GÂMBIA *s.f.* leg; Gambia.
GAMBIANO *adj.* Gambian.
GAMBIARRA *s.f.* stage lights, footlights.
GAMELA *s.f.* wooden trough, kneading trough.
GAMETA *s.m.* gamete.
GAMETÓFITO *s.m.* gametophyte.
GAMO *s.m.* buck.
GANA *s.f.* craving, wish, hunger, hate; Ghana.
GANÂNCIA *s.f.* greed.
GANANCIAR *v.* to win, to obtain, to get greedily.
GANANCIOSO *adj.* greedy, rapacious; acquisitive, grasping.
GANCHO *s.m.* hook.
GANDAIA *s.f.* vagrancy, idleness, idling, dissolute life.
GANDAIAR *v.* to loiter, to idle about, to hang about.
GANDAIEIRO *s.m.* vagrant, loafer.
GANDULA *s.2gên.* ball boy, ball girl.
GANENSE *adj.2gên.* Ghanaian, Ghanian.
GÂNGLIO *s.m.* ganglion.
GANGLIOMA *s.m.* ganglioma.
GANGLIONAR *v.* to gangliar, to ganglionated.
GANGORRA *s.f.* seesaw.
GANGRENA *s.f.* gangrene.
GANGRENADO *adj.* gangrenous.
GANGRENAR *v.* to gangrene.
GÂNGSTER *s.m.* gangster, gangsta.
GANGUE *s.f.* gang.
GANHADOR(A) *s.2gên.* winner / *adj.* winning.
GANHA-PÃO *s.m.* livelihood, breadwinner, means of living.
GANHAR *v.* to win; to earn.
GANHO *s.m.* profit, gain, lucre, earnings.
GANIDO *s.m.* yelping, yelp, bark, yap, yip.
GANIR *v.* to yelp.
GANSO(A) *s.m.* gander, goose.
GARAGEM *s.f.* garage.
GARAGISTA *s.2gên.* owner of a garage.
GARANHÃO *s.m.* stallion.
GARANTIA *s.f.* warranty, guarantee.
GARANTIR *v.* to guarantee.
GARAPA *s.f.* juice of sugar-cane.
GARATUJA *s.f.* scrawl, scribble, doodle.
GARATUJAR *v.* to scribble, to scrabble, to doodle.

GARAVATO *s.m.* hook.
GARBO *s.m.* elegance, garb.
GARBOSO *adj.* elegant, graceful.
GARÇA *s.f.* heron.
GARÇOM *s.m.* waiter.
GARÇONETE *s.f.* waitress.
GARDÊNIA *s.f.* gardenia.
GARFADA *s.f.* clawing, scratching.
GARFAR *v.* to fork, to graft.
GARFO *s.m.* fork.
GARGALHADA *s.f.* laughter.
GARGALHAR *v.* to guffaw, to hoot, to laugh loudly.
GARGALHO *s.m.* tough sputum.
GARGALO *s.m.* bottleneck.
GARGANTA *s.f.* throat.
GARGANTEAR *v.* to quaver, to warble, to vibrate; to brag, to boast.
GARGANTILHA *s.f.* neckband, necklace.
GARGAREJAR *v.* to gargle.
GARGAREJO *s.m.* gargling, gargle.
GÁRGULA *s.f.* gargoyle.
GARI *s.2gên.* roadsweeper.
GARIMPAGEM *s.f.* gold digging.
GARIMPAR *v.* to prospect.
GARIMPEIRO *s.m.* prospector.
GARIMPO *s.m.* prospecting.
GAROA *s.f.* drizzle.
GAROAR *v.* to drizzle, to mizzle, to dribble.
GAROENTO *adj.* drizzling, misty.
GAROTA *s.f.* girl.
GAROTADA *s.f.* the kids.
GAROTICE *s.f.* pranks.
GAROTO *s.m.* boy.
GAROUPA *s.f.* grouper.
GARRA *s.f.* claw.
GARRAFA *s.f.* bottle.
GARRAFADA *s.f.* bottleful.
GARRAFAL *adj.2gên.* bottle-shaped.
GARRAFÃO *s.m.* carboy, demijohn.
GARRAFA TÉRMICA *s.f.* thermos bottle, vacuum bottle, thermos.
GARRANCHO *s.m.* scribble.
GARRIDO *adj.* dandyish, foppish, smug.
GARROTE *s.m.* garrote, iron collar.
GARUPA *s.f.* hindquarters.
GÁS *s.m.* gas.
GASEAR *v.* to gasify.
GASEIFICAÇÃO *s.f.* gasification.
GASEIFICAR *v.* to gasify.

GASEIFORME *adj.2gên.* gasiform.
GASODUTO *s.m.* gas pipeline.
GASOGÊNIO *s.m.* gazogene.
GASÓLEO *s.m.* diesel oil.
GASOLINA *s.f.* petrol, gas.
GASÔMETRO *s.m.* gasometer.
GASOSO(A) *adj.* sparkling.
GASPACHO *s.m.* gazpacho.
GASTADOR *adj.* squanderer, prodigal, wastrel, waster.
GASTAR *v.* to spend; to waste.
GASTO *s.m.* expense, expenditure; spent, worn out / *adj.* old.
GASTRENTERITE *s.f.* gastroenteritis.
GASTRENTEROLOGIA *s.f.* gastroenterology.
GÁSTRICO(A) *adj.* gastric.
GASTRINTESTINAL *adj.2gên.* gastrointestinal.
GASTRITE *s.f.* gastritis.
GASTRODUODENAL *adj.2gên.* gastroduodenal.
GASTRONOMIA *s.f.* gastronomy.
GASTRONÔMICO *adj.* gastronomic, gastronomical.
GASTRÔNOMO *s.m.* gastronome, gastronomist.
GATA *s.f.* babe, foxy, cat.
GATÃO *s.m.* hunk, stud.
GATARIA *s.f.* a lot of cats.
GATEADO *adj.* stealed, clamped.
GATEADOR *adj.* sly hunter, scoundrel / *s.m.* sly hunter, scoundrel.
GATEAR *v.* to steal.
GATEIRA *s.f.* cat flap.
GATICÍDIO *s.m.* cat killing.
GATILHO *s.m.* trigger.
GATINHAR *v.* to crawl.
GATO *s.m.* cat.
GATUNAGEM *s.f.* robbery.
GATUNAR *v.* to steal.
GATUNO *adj.* thief, stealer / *s.m.* thief, stealer.
GAÚCHO *s.m.* gaucho.
GAULÊS *adj.* Gaul, Gaulish.
GÁVEA *s.f.* topsail.
GAVETA *s.f.* drawer.
GAVIÃO *s.m.* hawk.
GAVINHA *s.f.* tendril.
GAY *adj.2gên.* gay, homosexual / *s.2gên.* gay, homosexual.
GAZE *s.f.* gauze, bandage.
GAZELA *s.f.* gazelle.
GAZETA *s.f.* newspaper.
GAZETEIRO *s.m.* truant.
GAZUA *s.f.* picklock.
GEADA *s.f.* frost.
GEADO *adj.* frosted.
GEAR *v.* to frost.
GÊISER *s.m.* geyser.
GEL *s.m.* gel.
GELADEIRA *s.f.* refrigerator, fridge.
GELADO(A) *adj.* frozen.
GELAR *v.* to freeze.
GELATINA *s.f.* gelatine, jelly.
GELATINOSO *adj.* gelatinous, jellying.
GELEIA *s.f.* jelly, jam.
GELEIRA *s.f.* glacier.
GÉLIDO *adj.* gelid, icy.
GELO *s.m.* ice.
GELOSIA *s.f.* latticework, trellis.
GEMA *s.f.* yolk.
GEMAÇÃO *s.f.* gemmation.
GEMADA *s.f.* egg flip.
GÊMEO(A) *adj.* twin / *s.m.* twin.
GÊMEOS *s.m. pl.* Gemini (astrologia).
GEMER *v.* to groan, to moan.
GEMICAR *v.* to wail, to groan.
GEMIDO *s.m.* groan.
GEMINAÇÃO *s.f.* gemination.
GEMINADO *adj.* geminate.
GEMINAR *v.* to geminate.
GEMINIANO *adj.* Geminian.
GEMÍPARO *s.m.* gemmiparous.
GEMOLOGIA *s.f.* gemology.
GEMOLÓGICO *adj.* gemological.
GEMÓLOGO *adj.* gemologist / *s.m.* gemologist.
GENCIANA *s.f.* gentian.
GENE *s.m.* gene.
GENEALOGIA *s.f.* genealogy.
GENEALÓGICO *adj.* genealogical.
GENEBRA *s.f.* Geneva.
GENEBRÊS *adj.* Genevan.
GENERAL *s.m.* general.
GENERALIZAÇÃO *s.f.* generalization.
GENERALIZAR *v.* to generalize.
GENERATIVO *adj.* generative.
GENERATRIZ *s.f.* generatrix.
GENÉRICO *adj.* generical.
GÊNERO *s.m.* genre; type, kind.

GENEROSIDADE *s.f.* generosity.
GENEROSO(A) *adj.* generous.
GÊNESE *s.f.* genesis.
GENÉTICA *s.f.* genetics.
GENETICISTA *s.2gên.* geneticist.
GENÉTICO *adj.* genetical, genetic.
GENGIBRE *s.m.* ginger.
GENGIVA *s.f.* gum.
GENGIVITE *s.f.* gingivitis.
GENIAL *adj.2gên.* brilliant.
GENIALIDADE *s.f.* geniality.
GÊNIO *s.m.* genius.
GENIOSO *adj.* ill-tempered.
GENITAL *adj.2gên.* genital.
GENITÁLIA *s.f.* genitals, genitalia.
GENITIVO *s.m.* genitive / *adj.* genitive.
GENITOR *s.m.* genitor, father.
GENOCÍDIO *s.m.* genocide.
GENOMA *s.m.* genome.
GENÓTIPO *s.m.* genotype.
GENOVÊS *adj.* Genoese.
GENRO *s.m.* son-in-law.
GENTALHA *s.f.* rabble.
GENTE *s.f.* people.
GENTIL *adj.2gên.* kind.
GENTILEZA *s.f.* politeness.
GENTÍLICO *adj.* gentilic.
GENTINHA *s.f.* rabble.
GENTIO *adj.* pagan, heathen; gentile.
GENUÍNO *adj.* genuine.
GEOBIOLOGIA *s.f.* geobiology.
GEOBOTÂNICA *s.f.* geobotany.
GEOCÊNTRICO *adj.* geocentric.
GEODESIA *s.f.* geodesy.
GEODINÂMICA *s.f.* geodynamics.
GEODO *s.m.* geode.
GEOFAGIA *s.f.* geophagy.
GEOFÍSICA *s.f.* geophysics.
GEOGRAFIA *s.f.* geography.
GEOGRÁFICO *adj.* geographical, geographic.
GEÓGRAFO *s.m.* geographer.
GEOLOGIA *s.f.* geology.
GEÓLOGO *s.f.* geologist.
GEOMAGNETISMO *s.m.* geomagnetism.
GEÔMETRA *s.2gên.* geometer, geometrician.
GEOMETRIA *s.f.* geometry.
GEOMÉTRICO *adj.* geométrico.
GEOPOLÍTICA *s.f.* geopolitics.
GEOQUÍMICA *s.f.* geochemistry.
GEORGIANO *adj.* Georgian.
GEOSTÁTICA *s.f.* geostatics.
GEOTECTÔNICA *s.f.* geotectonic.
GEOTERMIA *s.f.* geothermy.
GEOTÉRMICO *adj.* geothermic.
GEOTERMÔMETRO *s.m.* geothermometer.
GEOTRÓPICO *adj.* geotropic.
GEOTROPISMO *s.m.* geotropism.
GERAÇÃO *s.f.* generation.
GERACIONAL *adj.2gên.* generational.
GERADOR *adj.* generator.
GERAL *adj.2gên.* general.
GERALMENTE *adv.* generally.
GERÂNIO *s.m.* geranium.
GERAR *v.* to produce, to generate.
GERATIVO *adj.* generative.
GERATRIZ *adj.* generating / *s.f.* generating.
GERÊNCIA *s.f.* management.
GERENCIAR *v.* to manage.
GERENTE *s.m.* manager.
GERGELIM *s.m.* sesame.
GERIATRIA *s.f.* geriatrics.
GERIÁTRICO(A) *adj.* geriatric.
GERINGONÇA *s.f.* botch, shoddy.
GERIR *v.* to manage.
GERMÂNICO *adj.* Germanic.
GERMANISMO *s.m.* Germanism.
GERMANISTA *s.2gên.* Germanism.
GERMANIZAR *v.* to Germanize.
GERMANO *adj.* German.
GERME *s.m.* germ.
GERMICIDA *s.m.* germicide.
GERMINAÇÃO *s.f.* germination.
GERMINADOR *s.m.* germinator.
GERMINADOURO *s.m.* germinator room.
GERMINAL *adj.2gên.* germinal.
GERMINAR *v.* to germinate.
GERMINATIVO *adj.* germinative.
GERONTOLOGIA *s.f.* gerontology.
GERONTOLOGISTA *s.2gên.* gerontologist.
GERÚNDIO *s.m.* gerund.
GESSAGEM *s.f.* plastering.
GESSAR *v.* to plaster.
GESSO *s.m.* plaster.
GESTAÇÃO *s.f.* pregnancy.
GESTANTE *s.f.* pregnant woman / *adj.2gên.* pregnant.
GESTÃO *s.f.* management.

GESTICULAR v. to make gestures, to gesticulate.
GESTO s.m. gesture.
GESTOR s.m. manager.
GESTUAL adj.2gên. gestural.
GIBA s.f. hunchback.
GIBÃO s.m. doublet; gibbon.
GIBI s.m. comic book.
GIBRALTARINO adj. Gibraltarian / s.m. Gibraltarian.
GIGABYTE s.m. gigabyte.
GIGANTE adj.2gên. gigantic, giant / s.m. giant.
GIGANTISMO s.m. giantism, gigantism.
GIGOLÔ s.m. gigolo.
GIM s.m. gin.
GIMNOSPERMA s.f. gymnosperm.
GINASIAL adj.2gên. secondary school.
GINÁSIO s.m. gymnasium.
GINASTA s.2gên. gymnast.
GINÁSTICA s.f. gymnastics.
GINCANA s.f. scavenger hunt.
GINECEU s.m. gynaeceum.
GINECOLOGIA s.f. gynecology.
GINECOLOGISTA s.2gên. gynecologist.
GINETA adj.2gên genet / s.f. genet.
GINGA s.f. shimmy.
GINGAR v. to waddle.
GIRAFA s.f. giraffe.
GIRAR v. to turn.
GIRASSOL s.m. sunflower.
GIRATÓRIO(A) adj. revolving.
GÍRIA s.f. slang.
GIRINO s.m. tadpole, polliwog.
GIRO s.m. rotation, turn.
GIZ s.m. chalk.
GLAÇAR v. to glaze.
GLACÊ s.m. glacé.
GLACIAÇÃO s.f. glaciation.
GLACIAL adj.2gên. icy.
GLACIÁRIO adj. glacial.
GLADIADOR s.m. gladiator.
GLAMOROSO(A) adj. glamorous.
GLANDE s.f. glands.
GLÂNDULA s.f. gland.
GLAUCOMA s.m. glaucoma.
GLEBA s.f. glebe.
GLICEMIA s.f. glycemia.
GLICERINA s.f. glycerine.
GLICÓLISE s.f. glycolysis.
GLICOSE s.f. glucose.
GLÍPTICA s.f. glyptics.
GLOBAL adj.2gên. global.
GLOBALIZAÇÃO s.f. globalization.
GLOBALIZAR v. to globalize.
GLOBO s.m. globe.
GLOBULINA s.f. globulin.
GLÓBULO s.m. globule.
GLÓRIA s.f. glory.
GLORIFICAÇÃO s.f. glorification.
GLORIFICAR v. to glorify.
GLORIOSO adj. glorious.
GLOSAR v. to comment, to gloss.
GLOSSÁRIO s.m. glossary.
GLOTE s.f. glottis.
GLUTÃO adj. glutton / s.m. glutton.
GLÚTEN s.m. gluten.
GLÚTEO s.m. gluteal.
GNOMO s.m. gnome.
GNOSE s.f. gnosis.
GNU s.m. gnu.
GODÊ s.m. godet.
GODO s.m. Goth.
GOELA s.f. throat, gullet.
GOFRAGEM s.f. stamped nervures.
GOIABEIRA s.f. guava tree.
GOIABA s.f. guava.
GOIABADA s.f. guava jam.
GOL s.m. goal.
GOLA s.f. collar.
GOLE s.m. gulp.
GOLEIRO s.m. goalkeeper.
GOLFADA s.f. gush, spew.
GOLFAR v. to gush.
GOLFE s.m. golf.
GOLFINHO s.m. dolphin.
GOLFISTA s.2gên. golfer.
GOLFO s.m. gulf.
GOLPE s.m. blow.
GOLPEAR v. to strike, to beat.
GOMA s.f. gum.
GOMA-ARÁBICA s.f. gum arabic.
GOMA-ELÁSTICA s.f. india rubber.
GOMO s.m. bud, shoot, gemma.
GOMOSO adj. gummy, gummous.
GÔNADA s.f. gonad.
GÔNDOLA s.f. gondola.
GONDOLEIRO s.m. gondolier.
GONGO s.m. gong.

GONORREIA *s.f.* gonorrhoea.
GONZO *s.m.* hinge.
GORAR *v.* to frustrate.
GORDO(A) *adj.* fat.
GORDURA *s.f.* fat; grease.
GORDUROSO *adj.* greasy.
GORILA *s.m.* gorilla.
GORJEAR *v.* to warble.
GORJEIO *s.m.* warble.
GORJETA *s.f.* tip.
GOROROBA *s.f.* slop.
GORRO *s.m.* cap.
GOSMA *s.f.* spittle.
GOSMENTO *adj.* slimy, phlegmy.
GOSTAR *v.* to like.
GOSTO *s.m.* taste.
GOSTOSO *adj.* tasty.
GOSTOSURA *s.f.* delight, tastiness.
GOTA *s.f.* drop.
GOTEIRA *s.f.* gutter; leak.
GOTEJAMENTO *s.m.* dropping.
GOTEJAR *v.* to drip.
GÓTICO *s.m.* Gothic.
GOVERNADOR(A) *s.2gên.* governor.
GOVERNAMENTAL *adj.2gên.* government.
GOVERNANTA *s.f.* governess.
GOVERNAR *v.* to govern.
GOVERNO *s.m.* government.
GOZAÇÃO *s.f.* mockery.
GOZADO(A) *adj.* funny.
GOZADOR *adj.* enjoyer, idler / *s.m.* enjoyer, idler.
GOZAR *v.* to enjoy.
GRAAL *s.m.* grail.
GRÃ-BRETANHA *s.f.* Great Britain.
GRAÇA *s.f.* grace.
GRACEJAR *v.* to joke.
GRACEJO *s.m.* joke.
GRACIOSO(A) *adj.* charming.
GRADAÇÃO *s.f.* gradation.
GRADATIVO(A) *adj.* gradual.
GRADE *s.f.* grating.
GRADEAR *v.* to fence in.
GRADIENTE *s.m.* gradient.
GRADO *s.m.* will, wish.
GRADUAÇÃO *s.f.* graduation.
GRADUAL *adj.2gên.* gradual.
GRADUAR *v.* to graduate.
GRADUÁVEL *adj.2gen.* adjustable.
GRÃ-DUQUE *s.m.* grand-duke.

GRAFAR *v.* to spell.
GRAFEMA *s.m.* grapheme.
GRAFIA *s.f.* writing.
GRÁFICA *s.f.* graphics, printing company.
GRÁFICO *adj.* graphic.
GRÃ-FINO *adj.* upper-class man / *s.m.* upper-class man.
GRAFISMO *s.m.* graphism.
GRAFITE *s.f.* graphite, graffiti.
GRALHA *s.f.* carrion crow.
GRAMA *s.f.* gramme, gram (medida); grass (planta).
GRAMADO *s.m.* lawn.
GRAMAR *v.* to plant grass.
GRAMÁTICA *s.f.* grammar.
GRAMATICAL *adj.2gên.* grammatical.
GRAMÁTICO *adj.* grammarian.
GRAMÍNEAS *s.f. pl.* gramineous plant.
GRAMOFONE *s.m.* gramophone.
GRAMPEADOR *s.m.* stapler.
GRAMPEAR *v.* to staple.
GRAMPO *s.m.* hairpin.
GRANA *s.f.* money, buck.
GRANADA *s.f.* shell.
GRANADINA *s.f.* grenadine.
GRANDE *adj.2gên.* big, large.
GRANDEZA *s.f.* largeness; grandeur.
GRANDIOSO(A) *adj.* magnificent.
GRANDIOSIDADE *s.f.* grandiosity.
GRANEL *s.m.* in bulk.
GRANITO *s.m.* granite.
GRANÍVORO *adj.* granivorous.
GRANIZADA *s.f.* hailstorm.
GRANIZO *s.m.* hailstone.
GRANJA *s.f.* farm, ranch.
GRANJEAR *v.* to acquire, to obtain.
GRANULAÇÃO *s.f.* granulation.
GRANULADO(A) *adj.* grainy.
GRANULAR *adj.2gên.* granulate.
GRÂNULO *s.m.* granule.
GRÃO *s.m.* grain.
GRÃO-DE-BICO *s.m.* chick pea.
GRASNAR *v.* to caw, to croak, to clang.
GRATIDÃO *s.f.* gratitude.
GRATIFICAÇÃO *s.f.* gratification, reward, tip.
GRATIFICANTE *adj.2gên.* rewarding.
GRATIFICAR *v.* to tip, to reward.
GRATINADO *adj.* graitin,
GRÁTIS *adj.2gên.* free.
GRATO(A) *adj.* grateful.

GRATUITO(A) *adj.* free.
GRAU *s.m.* degree.
GRAÚDO(A) *adj.* grown, developed.
GRAVAÇÃO *s.f.* recording.
GRAVADOR *s.m.* tape recorder; engraver.
GRAVAR *v.* to record; to engrave.
GRAVATA *s.f.* tie.
GRAVATARIA *s.f.* necktie workshop.
GRAVATEIRO *s.m.* necktie manufacturer.
GRAVE *adj.2gên.* serious.
GRAVETO *s.m.* kindling wood.
GRÁVIDA *adj.* pregnant.
GRAVIDADE *s.f.* gravity.
GRAVIDEZ *s.f.* pregnancy.
GRAVITAÇÃO *s.f.* gravitation.
GRAVITACIONAL *adj.2gên.* gravitational.
GRAVITAR *v.* to gravitate.
GRAVURA *s.f.* engraving.
GRAXA *s.f.* polish.
GRAXENTO *adj.* oily, greasy.
GRÉCIA *s.f.* Greece.
GREGÁRIO *adj.* gregarious.
GREGO(A) *s.m.* Greek.
GREGORIANO *adj.* Gregorian.
GRELHA *s.f.* grill.
GRELHADO *adj.* grilled.
GRELHAR *v.* to broil, to grill.
GRÊMIO *s.m.* guild.
GRENHA *s.f.* mane, shag.
GRÉS *s.m.* sandstone.
GRETA *s.f.* crack, fissure.
GREVE *s.f.* strike.
GRIFAR *v.* to underline (palavras).
GRIFO *s.m.* griffin, griffon; italic type, italics.
GRILAR *v.* to worry.
GRILHÃO *s.m.* fetters, shackles.
GRILO *s.m.* cricket.
GRINALDA *s.f.* garland.
GRINGO *s.m.* gringo.
GRIPADO(A) *adj.* get a cold.
GRIPE *s.f.* flu (influenza).
GRISALHO(A) *adj.* grey.
GRITANTE *adj.2gên.* glaring, gross.
GRITAR *v.* to shout.
GRITO *s.m.* scream.
GROENLANDÊS *adj.* greenlander.
GROENLÂNDIA *s.f.* Greenland.
GROGUE *adj.2gên.* grog; staggering.
GROSELHA *s.f.* gooseberry.
GROSSEIRO(A) *adj.* rude.
GROSSERIA *s.f.* coarseness, roughness.
GROSSO(A) *adj.* thick.
GROSSURA *s.f.* thickness, stoutness.
GROTESCO(A) *adj.* grotesque.
GRUA *s.f.* water crane; derrick.
GRUDADO *adj.* glued, stuck.
GRUDAR *v.* to glue.
GRUDE *s.m.* glue, paste.
GRUDENTO *adj.* sticky.
GRUMETE *s.m.* cabin-boy.
GRUMO *s.m.* lump, clot.
GRUMOSO *adj.* lumpy, clotted.
GRUNHIDO *s.m.* grunt.
GRUNHIR *v.* to grunt.
GRUPAMENTO *s.m.* grouping.
GRUPO *s.m.* group.
GRUTA *s.f.* grotto, cave.
GUACHE *s.m.* gouache.
GUAPO *adj.* courageous; beautiful; slim.
GUARÁ *s.m.* maned wolf or dog.
GUARDA *s.2gên.* guard.
GUARDA-CHUVA *s.m.* umbrella.
GUARDA-CIVIL *s.m.* civil guard.
GUARDA-COSTAS *s.m.* bodyguard.
GUARDA-FLORESTAL *s.m.* forest ranger.
GUARDA-JOIAS *s.m.* jewelry box.
GUARDANAPO *s.m.* napkin.
GUARDA-NOTURNO *s.m.* night watchman.
GUARDAR *v.* to guard; to keep.
GUARDA-ROUPA *s.m.* wardrobe.
GUARDA-SOL *s.m.* sunshade.
GUARDIÃO(Ã) *s.2gên.* guardian.
GUARIDA *s.f.* shelder, protection.
GUARITA *s.f.* sentry-box, watchtower.
GUARNECER *v.* to trim, to garnish.
GUARNECIDO *adj.* garnished, ribboned; furnished, equipped.
GUARNIÇÃO *s.f.* garrison (militar); garnish (culinária).
GUEIXA *s.f.* geisha.
GUELRA *s.f.* gills, branchiae.
GUERRA *s.f.* war.
GUERREAR *v.* to war, to combat.
GUERREIRO *adj.* warrior.
GUERRILHA *s.f.* guerrilla.
GUERRILHEIRO *s.m.* guerrilla.
GUETO *s.m.* ghetto.
GUIA *s.2gên.* guide, leader.
GUIADO *adj.* guided.
GUIANA *s.f.* Guyana.

GUIANENSE *adj.2gên.* Guyanese / *s.2gên.* Guyanese.
GUIAR *v.* to guide, to lead.
GUICHÊ *s.m.* ticket window.
GUIDOM *s.m.* handlebars.
GUILHOTINA *s.f.* guillotine.
GUILHOTINAR *v.* to guillotine, to behead.
GUINADA *s.f.* swerve.
GUINCHAR *v.* to squeal (gritar); to winch (veículo).
GUINCHO *s.m.* squeal (grito); tow truck (veículo).
GUINDASTE *s.m.* hoist, crane.
GUINÉ-BISSAU *s.f.* Guinea-Bissau.
GUIRLANDA *s.f.* garland.
GUISA *s.f.* mode.
GUISADO *adj.* stew, ragout.
GUISAR *v.* to stew; to outline.
GUITARRA *s.f.* electric guitar.
GUITARRISTA *s.2gên.* guitar player.
GUIZO *s.m.* bell.
GULA *s.f.* gluttony, greed.
GULODICE *s.f.* delicacy, tidbit.
GULOSEIMA *s.f.* delicacy, dainties.
GULOSO(A) *adj.* greedy / *s.m.* glutton.
GUME *s.m.* knife-edge.
GURI *s.m.* kid.
GURU *s.m.* guru.
GUSTAÇÃO *s.f.* gustation, taste.
GUSTATIVO *adj.* gustatory.
GUTURAL *adj.2gên.* guttural.

H h

H, h *s.m.* the eighth letter of the Portuguese alphabet.
HÁBIL *adj.2gên.* skilful, clever.
HABILIDADE *s.f.* skill, hability.
HABILIDOSO *adj.* skilful, skilled; handy; clever.
HABILITAÇÃO *s.f.* competence, qualification.
HABILITADO(A) *adj.* qualified.
HABILITANTE *s.2gên.* habilitator, litigator / *adj.2gên.* plaintiff.
HABILITAR *v.* to enable, to qualify.
HABILMENTE *adv.* skilfully, ably, cleverly, subtly.
HABITAÇÃO *s.f.* habitation, residence.
HABITACIONAL *adj.2gên.* housing, dwelling.
HABITANTE *s.2gên.* inhabitant.
HABITAR *v.* to live.
HABITAT *s.m.* habitat.
HABITÁVEL *adj.2gên.* habitable, tenantable.
HÁBITO *s.m.* habit, use.
HABITUAL *adj.2gên.* usual.
HABITUAR *v.* to habituate, to familiarize.
HADOQUE *s.m.* haddock.
HAICAI *s.m.* haiku.
HAITI *s.m.* Haiti.
HAITIANO(A) *s.m.* Haitian / *adj.* Haitian.
HÁLITO *s.m.* breath.
HALITOSE *s.f.* halitosis, bad breath.
HALO *s.m.* halo, corona; areola; aureole, nimbus.
HALOGENAÇÃO *s.f.* halogenation.
HALOGÊNIO *s.m.* halogen.
HALTER *s.m. m.q.* haltere.
HALTERE *s.m.* haltere.
HAMBÚRGUER *s.m.* hamburger.
HANDEBOL *s.m.* handball.
HANGAR *s.m.* hangar.
HANSENÍASE *s.f.* Hansen's disease, leprosy.
HARAS *s.m.* stud, stud farm.
HARÉM *s.m.* harem, seraglio.
HARMONIA *s.f.* harmony.
HARMÔNICA *s.f.* glass harmonica; concertina; harmonica, mouth organ.
HARMÔNICO(A) *adj.* harmonic, tuneful; concordant, consonant.

HARMONIOSO(A) *adj.* harmonious.
HARMONIZAR *v.* to harmonize.
HARPA *s.f.* harp.
HARPISTA *s.2gên.* harpist, harper.
HASTE *s.f.* flagpole.
HAVAÍ *s.m.* Hawaii.
HAVAIANO(A) *s.m.* Hawaiian / *adj.* Hawaiian.
HAVANA *s.m.* Havana.
HAVER *v.* to have; there is, there are (existir).
HEBRAICO(A) *s.m.* Hebrew, the Hebrew language / *adj.* Hebraic.
HEBREIA *s.f.* Hebrew.
HEBREU *s.m.* Hebrew.
HECTARE *s.m.* hectare.
HEDIONDO(A) *adj.* hideous, dreadful.
HEIN *interj.* what?; huh?.
HÉLICE *s.f.* propeller.
HELICÓPTERO *s.m.* helicopter.
HÉLIO *s.m.* helium.
HELIPORTO *s.m.* heliport.
HEMATOMA *s.m.* bruise.
HEMISFÉRICO(A) *adj.* hemispherical.
HEMISFÉRIO *s.m.* hemisphere.
HEMOCULTURA *s.f.* blood culture.
HEMODIÁLISE *s.f.* hemodialysis.
HEMORRAGIA *s.f.* hemorrhage.
HEMORRÁGICO(A) *adj.* hemorrhagic.
HEMORROIDAS *s.f. pl.* hemorrhoids.
HENA *s.f.* henna.
HEPÁTICO(A) *adj.* hepatic, hepatical.
HEPATITE *s.f.* hepatitis.
HERA *s.f.* ivy, English ivy.
HERANÇA *s.f.* inheritance.
HERBÁCEO(A) *adj.* herbaceous.
HERBÍVORO(A) *s.m.* herbivore / *adj.* herbivorous, graminivorous.
HERDAR *v.* to inherit.
HERDEIRO(A) *s.m.* heir.
HEREDITÁRIO(A) *adj.* hereditary; heritable, descendible, hereditable.
HEREGE *s.2gên.* heretic; dissenter, misbeliever / *adj.2gên.* heretic, heretical.
HERESIA *s.f.* heresy.
HERMAFRODITA *s.2gên.* hermaphrodite / *adj.2gên.* hermaphroditic.
HERÓI *s.m.* hero.
HEROICO(A) *adj.* heroic, heroical, noble bold, daring; valorous, courageous.
HEROÍNA *s.f.* heroine.
HERPES *s.m.* herpes.

HESITAÇÃO *s.f.* hesitation.
HESITANTE *adj.2gên.* hesitant.
HESITAR *v.* to hesitate.
HETEROGÊNESE *s.f.* heterogenesis.
HETEROSSEXUAL *s.2gên.* heterosexual / *adj.2gên.* heterosexual.
HETEROSSEXUALIDADE *s.m.* heterosexuality.
HEXACAMPEÃO(Ã) *s.m.* six times champion.
HEXAGONAL *adj.2gên.* hexagonal.
HEXÁGONO *s.m.* hexagon.
HIATO *s.m.* hiatus, interruption; opening, gap.
HIBERNAÇÃO *s.f.* hibernation.
HIBERNAR *v.* to hibernate.
HIBISCO *s.m.* hibiscus.
HÍBRIDO(A) *adj.* hybrid / *s.m.* hybrid.
HIDRA *s.f.* hydra.
HIDRANTE *s.m.* hydrant, fire hydrant.
HIDRATAÇÃO *s.f.* hydration.
HIDRATANTE *s.m.* moisturizer.
HIDRATAR *v.* to hydrate.
HIDRÁULICO(A) *adj.* hydraulic.
HIDRELÉTRICO(A) *adj.* hydroelectric.
HIDRODINÂMICA *s.f.* hydrodynamics.
HIDROFOBIA *s.f.* hydrophobia, rabies.
HIDROFONE *s.m.* hydrophone.
HIDRÓFORO(A) *adj.* hydrophorous, hydrophore.
HIDROGENAÇÃO *s.f.* hydrogenation.
HIDROGENAR *v.* to hydrogenate, to hydrogenize.
HIDROGÊNIO *s.m.* hydrogen.
HIDROGINÁSTICA *s.f.* water aerobics.
HIDRÓLISE *s.f.* hydrolysis.
HIENA *s.f.* hyena.
HIERARCA *s.m.* hierarch.
HIERARQUIA *s.f.* hierarchy.
HIERÁRQUICO(A) *adj.* hierarchic.
HIERARQUIZAR *v.* to hierarchize.
HIERÓGLIFO *s.m.* hieroglyph.
HÍFEN *s.m.* hyphen.
HIGIENE *s.f.* hygiene.
HIGIENIZAR *v.* to make hygienic.
HIGRÔMETRO *s.m.* hygrometer.
HILÁRIO(A) *adj.* hilarious.
HÍMEN *s.m.* hymen.
HINÁRIO *s.m.* hymnbook, hymnary.
HÍNDI *s.m.* Hindi.
HINDU *adj.2gên.* Hindu, Hindoo.
HINDUÍSMO *s.m.* hinduism.

HINDUÍSTA *adj.2gên.* Hindu.
HINO *s.m.* hymn, anthem.
HIPERMERCADO *s.m.* hypermarket.
HIPERMETROPIA *s.f.* hypermetropia, hyperopia, far-sightedness.
HIPERSENSIBILIDADE *s.f.* hypersensitivity, hypersensitiveness.
HIPERTENSÃO *s.f.* hypertension.
HIPERTENSO(A) *s.m.* hypertensive / *adj.* hypertensive.
HIPERTERMIA *s.f.* hyperthermia.
HIPERTROFIA *s.f.* hypertrophy.
HIPERVENTILAR *v.* to hyperventilate.
HÍPICO(A) *adj.* riding club.
HIPISMO *s.m.* horsemanship, equestrianism.
HIPNOSE *s.f.* hypnosis.
HIPNOTISMO *s.m.* hypnotism.
HIPOCONDRÍACO(A) *s.m.* hypochondriac / *adj.* hyponchondriac.
HIPOCRISIA *s.f.* hypocrisy.
HIPÓCRITA *s.2gên.* hypocrite; pretender, dissimulator / *adj.2gên.* hypocritic, hypocritical; pharisaic, pharisaical.
HIPÓDROMO *s.m.* race-course.
HIPOPÓTAMO *s.m.* hippopotamus.
HIPOTECA *s.f.* mortgage.
HIPOTECAR *v.* to mortgage; to bond, to pledge.
HIPOTENSÃO *s.f.* hypotension.
HIPOTERMIA *s.f.* hypothermia.
HIPÓTESE *s.f.* hypothesis.
HIPOTROFIA *s.f.* atrophy, undergrowth.
HISPÂNICO(A) *adj.* Hispanic.
HISTERIA *s.m.* hysteria.
HISTÓRIA *s.f.* history, story, tale.
HISTORIADOR *s.m.* historian, historiographer, chronicler.
HISTÓRICO *s.m.* description, detailed report / *adj.* true, veracious; traditional.
HOJE *adv.* today.
HOLANDA *s.f.* Holland, Netherlands.
HOLANDÊS *s.m.* Dutchman, Netherlander; Dutch / *adj.* Dutch, Netherlandish.
HOLOCAUSTO *s.m.* holocaust.
HOLOFOTE *s.m.* searchlight.
HOMEM *s.m.* man.
HOMENAGEAR *v.* to pay tribute.
HOMENAGEM *s.f.* tribute.
HOMEOPÁTICO *adj.* homeopathic.
HOMÉRICO *adj.* Homeric.

HOMICIDA *adj.2gên.* homicidal / *s.2gên.* murderer.
HOMICÍDIO *s.m.* murder.
HOMOFONIA *s.f.* homophony.
HOMOLOGAR *v.* to ratify.
HOMONÍMIA *s.f.* homonymy.
HOMOSSEXUAL *adj.2gên.* homosexual / *s.2gên.* homosexual.
HOMOZIGOTO *s.m.* homozygote.
HONDURAS *s.f. pl.* Honduras.
HONDURENHO(A) *s.m.* Honduran / *adj.* Honduran.
HONESTIDADE *s.f.* honesty.
HONESTO(A) *adj.* honest.
HONORÁRIO *s.m.* fee, pay / *adj.* honorary.
HONRA *s.f.* honour, honor.
HONRADO(A) *adj.* honest.
HONRAR *v.* to honour.
HONROSO(A) *adj.* honourable.
HÓQUEI *s.m.* hockey.
HORA *s.f.* time, hour.
HORÁRIO DE VERÃO *s.m.* daylight saving.
HORÁRIO NOBRE *s.m.* prime time.
HORDA *s.f.* horde; troop, gang.
HORISTA *s.2gên.* hourly worker.
HORIZONTAL *s.f.* horizontal / *adj.2gên.* horizontal.
HORIZONTE *s.m.* horizon.
HORMONAL *adj.2gên.* hormonal.
HORMÔNIO *s.m.* hormone.
HORÓSCOPO *s.m.* horoscope.
HORRENDO(A) *adj.* horrendous.
HORRIPILANTE *adj.2gên.* horrifying.
HORRÍVEL *adj.2gên.* awful, horrible.
HORROR *s.m.* horror.
HORRORIZAR *v.* to horrify, to frighten.
HORTA *s.f.* vegetable garden.
HORTALIÇA *s.f.* vegetable.
HORTELÃ *s.m.* mint, peppermint.
HORTÊNSIA *s.f.* hydrangea.
HORTICULTOR(A) *s.m.* horticulturist.
HORTO *s.m.* plant nursery.
HOSPEDAGEM *s.f.* accomodation, lodging.
HOSPEDAR *v.* to put up, to lodge.
HOSPEDARIA *s.f.* inn, lodging-house; hotel, hostelry.
HÓSPEDE *s.2gên.* guest.
HOSPEDEIRO(A) *s.m.* host, landlord, innkeeper.
HOSPÍCIO *s.m.* madhouse, asylum.
HOSPITAL *s.m.* hospital.

HOSPITALAR *adj.2gên.* pertaining to a hospital, nosocomial.
HOSPITALEIRO *adj.* hospitable.
HOSPITALIDADE *s.f.* hospitality.
HÓSTIA *s.f.* host.
HOSTIL *adj.2gên.* hostile, inimical; adverse; aggressive.
HOSTILIDADE *s.f.* hostility.
HOSTILIZAR *v.* to hostilize; to oppose; to hurt, to wound.
HOTEL *s.m.* hotel.
HOTELEIRO(A) *s.m.* hotelkeeper, owner of a hotel.
HULHA *s.f.* coal, black coal, stone coal, mineral coal.
HUMANAMENTE *adv.* humanly, kindly, gently.
HUMANIDADE *s.f.* humanity; human nature; kindness, humaneness.
HUMANISTA *s.2gên.* humanist.
HUMANITÁRIO(A) *adj.* humane / *s.m.* humanitarian.
HUMANIZAÇÃO *s.f.* humanization.
HUMANO(A) *adj.* human, humane / *s.m.* human.
HUMILDADE *s.f.* humility.
HUMILDE *adj.2gên.* humble.
HUMILHAÇÃO *s.f.* humiliation; mortification.
HUMILHAR *v.* to humiliate.
HUMOR *s.m.* mood, humour.
HUMORADO *adj.* humoured, humorous, tempered; funny, witty.
HUMOR NEGRO *s.m.* black humour, morbid humour.
HÚNGARO(A) *s.m.* Hungarian / *adj.* Hungarian.
HUNGRIA *s.f.* Hungary.

I, i

I, i *s.m.* the ninth letter of the Portuguese alphabet.
IÁ *interj.* gee-ho!
IÂMBICO *adj.* iambic.
IAMBO *s.m.* iamb.
IANQUE *s.2gên.* yankee / *adj.* yankee.
IATE *s.m.* yacht.
IATISMO *s.m.* yachting.
IBÉRICO(A) *s.m.* Iberian / *adj.* Iberian.
IBERO *s.m.* Iberian / *adj.* Iberian.
IBERO-AMERICANO *s.m.* Ibero-American / *adj.* Ibero-American.
ÍBIS *s.2gên.* ibis.
IÇADO *adj.* atrip; hoisted.
IÇAR *v.* to hoist, to boost.
ÍCARO *s.m.* Icarus.
ICEBERG *s.m.* iceberg.
ICNOGRAFIA *s.f.* ichnography.
ICNOGRÁFICO *adj.* ichnographic.
ÍCONE *s.m.* icon.
ICÔNICO *adj.* iconic.
ICONOCLASTA *s.2gên.* iconoclast.
ICONOLATRIA *s.f.* iconolatry.
ICONOLOGIA *s.f.* iconology.
ICONOLÓGICO *adj.* iconological.
ICONOLOGISTA *s.2gên.* iconologist.
ICTIOLOGIA *s.f.* ichthyology.
ID *s.m.* id.
IDA *s.f.* departure, leaving, going.
IDADE *s.f.* age, time, lifetime.
IDADE DA PEDRA *s.f.* Stone Age.
IDADE DA RAZÃO *s.f.* adulthood.
IDADE DO OURO *s.f.* Gold Age.
IDADE MÉDIA *s.f.* Middle Age, Dark Age.
IDEAÇÃO *s.f.* ideation, notion, conception.
IDEAL *s.m.* ideal, model, paradigm / *adj.2gên.* ideal, idealistic.
IDEALIDADE *s.f.* ideality.
IDEALISMO *s.m.* idealism.
IDEALISTA *s.2gên.* idealist; dreamer / *adj.2gên.* idealist; dreamer.
IDEALÍSTICO *adj.* idealistic, platonic.
IDEALIZAÇÃO *s.f.* idealisation.
IDEALIZADOR(A) *s.m.* idealiser, organiser, creator.
IDEALIZAR *v.* to idealize, to imagine, to dream.
IDEÁRIO *s.m.* ideas, a set of ideas.
IDEIA *s.f.* idea, thought; notion, concept.
IDEM *pron.* idem, ditto.

IDÊNTICO *adj.* identical; similar, equal.
IDENTIDADE *s.f.* identity, sameness.
IDENTIFICAÇÃO *s.f.* identification.
IDENTIFICAR *v.* to identify.
IDENTIFICÁVEL *adj.2gên.* recognisable, identifiable.
IDEOGRAFISMO *s.m.* ideographics.
IDEÓGRAFO *s.m.* ideographer.
IDEOGRAMA *s.m.* ideogram, ideography.
IDEOLOGIA *s.f.* ideology.
IDEOLÓGICO *adj.* ideologic, ideological.
IDEÓLOGO(A) *adj.* ideologist.
IDÍLICO *adj.* idyllic, pleasing.
IDÍLIO *s.m.* idyll.
IDILISTA *s.2gên.* dreamer, utopian.
IDIOCROMÁTICO *adj.* idiochromatic.
IDIÓLATRA *s.2gên.* self-worshipper.
IDIOLATRIA *s.f.* idiolatry; self-worship.
IDIOMA *s.f.* idiom, language.
IDIOMÁTICO *adj.* idiomatic.
IDIOMOGRAFIA *s.f.* idiomography.
IDIOMOGRÁFICO *adj.* idiomographic.
IDIOMÓRFICO *adj.* idiomorphic.
IDIOPATIA *s.f.* idiopathic.
IDIOPÁTICO *adj.* idiopathic.
IDIOPLASMA *s.f.* idioplasm.
IDIOSSINCRASIA *s.f.* idiosyncrasy.
IDIOSSINCRÁTICO *adj.* idiosyncratic.
IDIOTA *adj.2gên.* idiotic, stupid; silly, moron / *s.2gên.* idiot.
IDIOTAR *v.* to become idiot.
IDIOTIA *s.f.* idiocy, imbecility.
IDIOTICE *s.f.* stupidity, silliness.
IDIOTISMO *s.m.* idiocy, foolishness.
IDIOTIZAR *v. m.q.* idiotar.
IDO *adj.* departed, past, gone.
IDÓLATRA *s.2gên.* idolater, heathen / *adj.2gên.* idolatrous, pagan.
IDOLATRAR *v.* to idolise, to deify.
IDOLATRIA *s.f.* idolatry, paganism.
IDOLÁTRICO *adj.* idolatrous.
ÍDOLO(A) *s.m.* idol; icon, effigy.
IDONEIDADE *s.f.* suitability, capacity.
IDÔNEO(A) *adj.* competent, qualified, suitable.
IDOSO(A) *adj.* old, elderly, aged / *s.m.* elder.
IENE *s.m.* yen.
IGLU *s.m.* igloo.
IGNESCÊNCIA *s.f.* ignition, burning.
IGNESCENTE *adj.2gên.* ignescent, inflammatory.
IGNIÇÃO *s.f.* ignition, combustion.

IGNORADO *adj.* unknown, unrecognised.
IGNORÂNCIA *s.f.* ignorance, illiteracy.
IGNORANTÃO *s.m.* blockhead, ignoramus / *adj.* stupid, moron, impolite.
IGNORANTE *s.2gên.* ignorant, heathen / *adj.2gên.* ignorant, unlettered.
IGNORANTISMO *s.m.* obscurantism.
IGNORANTISTA *s.2gên.* obscurantist.
IGNORAR *v.* to ignore, to bypass, to disregard.
IGNOTO *adj.* unknown, incognito, obscure.
IGREJA *s.f.* church; sanctuary.
IGREJINHA *s.f.* little church; chapel.
IGUAL *s.2gên.* the same, equal, fellow / *adj.2gên.* equal, like, uniform.
IGUALAÇÃO *s.f.* equalisation, equation, standardisation.
IGUALADOR *s.m.* equaliser.
IGUALAMENTO *s.m.* equalising, levelling off.
IGUALAR *v.* to equal, to level, to become equal.
IGUALÁVEL *adj.2gên.* equaled.
IGUALDADE *s.f.* equality, equity; levelness.
IGUALITÁRIO *s.m.* egalitarian, leveller / *adj.* egalitarian.
IGUALITARISMO *s.m.* egalitarianism.
IGUALMENTE *adv.* equally; also, too.
IGUANA *s.f.* iguana.
IGUANODONTE *s.m.* iguanodon.
IGUARIA *s.f.* delicacy; dish, food.
IH! *interj.* oh!
IÍDICHE *s.m.* Yiddish.
ILAÇÃO *s.f.* illation, deduction; conclusion.
ILACERÁVEL *adj.2gên.* unlacerable.
ILACRIMÁVEL *adj.2gên.* inexorable, cruel.
ILAPSO *s.m.* elapse; inspiration, divine influx.
ILEGAL *adj.* illegal, unlawful.
ILEGALIDADE *s.f.* illegality, falseness.
ILEGIBILIDADE *s.f.* illegibility.
ILEGITIMIDADE *s.f.* illegitimacy, bastardy.
ILEGITIMAR *v.* to illegitimate.
ILEGÍTIMO *adj.* illegitimate, unlawful.
ILEGÍVEL *adj.2gên.* illegible, unreadable.
ÍLEO *s.m.* ileum.
ILESO *adj.* unharmed, unhurt; uninjured.
ILETRADO *s.m.* illiterate, untaught / *adj.* illiterate, unlearned.
ILHA *s.f.* island.
ILHAR *v.* to separate, to isolate.
ILHÉU *s.m.* islander.
ILHOTA *s.f.* islet, cay.

ILÍACO s.m. ilium, thighbone / adj. Iliac.
ILÍADA s.f. Iliad.
ILIBAÇÃO s.f. exoneration, exculpation.
ILIBADO adj. cleared, purified; stainless, pure.
ILIBAR v. to purify, to clean.
ILIBERAL adj.2gên. illiberal, intolerant.
ILIBERALIDADE s.f. parsimony, meanness.
ILIBERALISMO s.m. illiberalism.
ILIÇADOR s.m. impostor, swindler.
ILIÇÃO s.f. fraud, swindle, deceit.
ILIÇAR v. to cheat, to deceive.
ILÍCIO s.m. false, fraud; liar.
ILÍCITO adj. illicit, illegal; false, fraud.
ILÍDIMO adj. unlawful, unauthorised.
ILIDIR v. to destroy, to prove false.
ILIDÍVEL adj.2gên. refutable, repealable.
ILIMITADO adj. unlimited.
ILIMITÁVEL adj.2gên. illimitable, immeasurable.
ÍLION s.m. Ilium; hipbone.
ILÍQUIDO adj. non-liquid matter; gross, total.
ILITERATO s.m. illiterate, unlettered.
ILOCÁVEL adj.2gên. unplaced; not leasable, not rentable.
ILÓGICO adj. illogical, irrational; absurd, incoherent.
ILOGISMO s.m. illogicality.
ILUDENTE adj.2gên. misleading, illusive, illusory.
ILUDIR v. to delude, to deceive, to elude.
ILUDÍVEL adj.2gên. able to elude.
ILUMINAÇÃO s.f. illumination, enlightenment.
ILUMINADO s.m. illuminate, prophet / adj. illuminated, lighted.
ILUMINADOR s.m. illuminator / adj. illuminating, illuminative.
ILUMINANTE adj.2gên. illuminant.
ILUMINAR v. to illuminate, to enlighten.
ILUMINATIVO adj. illuminative, enlightening.
ILUMINISMO s.m. Illuminism, Illuminati.
ILUMINISTA s.2gên. illuminist.
ILUMINURA s.f. illumination.
ILUSÃO s.f. illusion; delusion.
ILUSIONISMO s.m. illusionism.
ILUSIONISTA s.2gên. illusionist.
ILUSIVO adj. illusive, delusive.
ILUSO adj. tricked, deceived.
ILUSOR s.m. mocker, cheater, deluder.
ILUSÓRIO(A) adj. illusory, illusive; delusory.
ILUSTRAÇÃO s.f. illustration.
ILUSTRADO(A) adj. illustrated.
ILUSTRADOR(A) s.m. illustrator.
ILUSTRAR v. to illustrate; to explain.
ILUSTRATIVO adj. illustrative, elucidative.
ILUSTRE adj.2gên. illustrious, eminent; noble, honourable.
ILUSTRÍSSIMO(A) s.m. illustrious; distinguished.
ÍMÃ s.m. magnet.
IMACULIDADE s.f. pure.
IMACULADO(A) adj. immaculate; spotless, stainless, clean.
IMACULÁVEL adj.2gên. impeccable, pure, perfect.
IMAGEM s.f. image; picture, representation.
IMAGINAÇÃO s.f. imagination; idea, vision, conceit.
IMAGINADOR s.m. imaginer / adj. imagining.
IMAGINANTE adj.2gên. imaging, imaginer, conceiving.
IMAGINAR v. to imagine, to think, to guess, to suppose.
IMAGINÁRIO s.m. imaginary; notional, fictional / adj. imaginary; notional, fictional.
IMAGINATIVO s.m. imaginer / adj. imaginative.
IMAGINÁVEL adj.2gên. imaginable.
IMAGINOSO adj. imaginative, imaginer.
IMAGO s.f. imago.
IMALEABILIDADE s.f. imalleability.
IMALEÁVEL adj.2gên. non-malleable, incapable.
IMAME s.m. imam, imaum.
IMANAR v. to magnetize; to attract.
IMANE adj.2gên. huge, enormous; cruel, atrocious.
IMANÊNCIA s.f. immanence, immanency.
IMANENTE adj.2gên. immanent.
IMANENTISMO s.m. immanentism.
IMANIDADE s.f. hugeness, enormousness.
IMANIZAÇÃO s.f. magnetisation.
IMANIZAR v. to magnetise.
IMANTAÇÃO s.f. magnetisation.
IMANTAR v. to magnetise.
IMATERIAL s.m. immaterial / adj.2gên. immaterial.
IMATERIALIDADE s.f. immateriality.
IMATERIALISMO s.m. immaterialism.
IMATERIALISTA s.2gên. immaterialist.
IMATERIALIZAR v. to immaterialise.
IMATURIDADE s.f. immaturity.
IMATURO(A) adj. immature.

IMBATÍVEL *adj.2gên.* unbeatable, insuperable.
IMBECIALIDADE *s.f.* imbecility, stupidity, silliness.
IMBECIALIZAR *v.* to become imbecile, to be silly.
IMBECIL *adj.2gên.* stupid, dumb / *s.2gên.* idiot, imbecile.
IMBELE *adj.2gên.* not for war; weak, coward.
IMBERBE *adj.2gên.* young, youth.
IMBICAR *v.* to land, to put into port.
IMBRICAÇÃO *s.f.* imbrication.
IMBRICADO *adj.* imbricated.
IMBRICAR *v.* to imbricate.
IMBUIR *v.* to imbue, to pervade, to leaven.
IMEDIAÇÃO *s.f.* immediacy, outskirts.
IMEDIATAR *v.* to immediate.
IMEDIATISMO *s.m.* immediacy.
IMEDIATO *s.2gên.* chief officer / *adj.* immediate, close, near.
IMEDICÁVEL *adj.2gên.* incurable, impossible to heal.
IMEMORADO *adj.* forgotten, not reported.
IMEMORÁVEL *adj.2gên.* immemorial.
IMENSIDÃO *s.f.* wilderness, vastness; ocean.
IMENSIDADE *s.f.* immensity, hugeness.
IMENSO *adj.* immense, unlimited.
IMENSURABILIDADE *s.f.* immeasurability.
IMENSURÁVEL *adj.2gên.* immeasurable.
IMERECIDO *adj.* undeserved, unmerited.
IMERGENTE *adj.2gên.* immersing.
IMERGIR *v.* to immerse.
IMÉRITO *adj.* unmerited, virtueless, worthless.
IMERSÃO *s.f.* immersion, submersion.
IMERSÍVEL *adj.2gên.* immersible, submersible.
IMERSIVO *adj.* immersive.
IMERSO *adj.* immersed, submerged.
IMIGRAÇÃO *s.f.* immigration.
IMIGRADO *adj.* immigrated.
IMIGRANTE *s.2gên.* immigrant, incomer / *adj.2gên.* immigrant.
IMIGRAR *v.* to immigrate.
IMIGRATÓRIO *adj.* migratory.
IMINÊNCIA *s.f.* imminence.
IMINENTE *adj.2gên.* imminent.
IMISÇÃO *s.f.* intervention, intromission.
IMISCIABILIDADE *s.f.* immiscibility.
IMISCÍVEL *adj.2gên.* immiscible.
IMISCUIR-SE *v.* to interfere, to invade.
IMISSÃO *s.f.* immixture.

IMITAÇÃO *s.f.* imitation, mimesis; falsification, copy.
IMITADO(A) *adj.* imitated, copied, false, fake.
IMITADOR(A) *s.m.* imitator, copier, mimic / *adj.* imitating.
IMITANTE *adj.2gên.* imitational, artificial.
IMITAR *v.* to imitate, to fake, to copy, to falsify.
IMITATIVO *adj.* imitative, mimetic, mimic.
IMITÁVEL *adj.2gên.* imitable.
IMITIR *v.* to invest; to enthrone; to let in.
IMOBILIÁRIO *adj.* real estate.
IMOBILIDADE *s.f.* immobility.
IMOBILISMO *s.m.* immobilism.
IMOBILISTA *s.2gên.* immobilist / *adj.2gên.* anti-progressionist.
IMOBILIZAÇÃO *s.f.* immobilisation, standstill.
IMOBILIZADOR(A) *s.m.* immobiliser, immobilising.
IMOBILIZAR *v.* to immobilise, to fix, to standstill.
IMODERAÇÃO *s.f.* immoderation, insobriety.
IMODERADO *adj.* immoderate; exaggerated.
IMODÉSTIA *s.f.* immodesty; arrogance.
IMODESTO(A) *adj.* immodest, arrogant.
IMODIFICÁVEL *adj.2gên.* unmodifiable, unalterable.
IMOLAÇÃO *s.f.* immolation, sacrifice.
IMOLADO *adj.* immolated, sacrificed.
IMOLADOR(A) *s.m.* immolator / *adj.* immolating.
IMOLANDO *adj.* immolating, sacrificing.
IMOLANTE *adj.2gên.* immolating, sacrificial.
IMOLAR *v.* to immolate, to sacrificed.
IMORAL *adj.2gên.* immoral, impure.
IMORALIDADE *s.f.* immorality.
IMORALISMO *s.m.* immoralism.
IMORIGERADO *adj.* libertine, dissolute.
IMORTAL *s.m.* immortal, deathless, eternal / *adj.2gên.* immortal, deathless, eternal.
IMORTALIDADE *s.f.* immortality, eternity.
IMORTALIZAÇÃO *s.f.* immortalisation.
IMORTALIZADOR(A) *s.m.* that immortalises / *adj.* immortalising.
IMORTALIZAR *v.* to immortalise, to eternalise.
IMOTO *adj.* immotile, immovable, stationary.
IMÓVEL *s.m.* property / *adj.2gên.* immovable, immobile fixed.

IMPACIÊNCIA s.f. impatience, eagerness; anxiety.
IMPACIENTAR v. to importune, to fidget, to annoy.
IMPACIENTE adj.2gên. impatient, eager.
IMPACTO s.m. impact, impulse; hit, bump.
IMPAGÁVEL adj.2gên. priceless, not payable, precious.
IMPALPABILIDADE s.f. impalpability.
IMPALPÁVEL adj.2gên. impalpable, intangible.
IMPALUDAR v. to infect with Malaria.
IMPALUDISMO s.m. impaludism, paludism.
IMPAR v. to breathe difficultly; to be full, to overeat.
ÍMPAR adj.2gên. odd, uneven; unique, unpaired.
IMPARCIAL adj.2gên. impartial, neutral.
IMPARCIALIDADE s.f. impartiality, neutrality.
IMPARCIALIZAR v. to be impartial, to behave neutral.
IMPARIDADE s.f. impairment, oddness.
IMPARISSILÁBICO adj. imparisyllabic.
IMPARISSÍLABO adj. m.q. imparissilábico.
IMPARTÍVEL adj.2gên. indivisible.
IMPASSE s.m. impasse; dilemma, plight.
IMPASSIBILIDADE s.f. impassibility; stolidity.
IMPASSIBILIZAR v. to face dilemma, to impasse, to obstacle.
IMPASSÍVEL adj.2gên. impassible, impassive, stolid.
IMPATRIÓTICO s.m. unpatriotic / adj. unpatriotic.
IMPAVIDEZ s.f. fearlessness, courage, bravery.
IMPÁVIDO adj. fearless, courageous, undaunted.
IMPEACHMENT s.m. impeachment.
IMPECABILIDADE s.f. impeccability.
IMPECÁVEL adj.2gên. impeccable, flawless.
IMPEDÂNCIA s.f. impedance.
IMPEDIÇÃO s.f. hindering, impediment.
IMPEDIDO adj. hindered, obstructed, blocked; offside.
IMPEDIDOR s.m. hinderer, obstructor / adj. impeding, hindering, detainee.
IMPEDIENTE adj.2gên. hindering, impeding.
IMPEDIMENTO s.m. impediment, hindrance, prevention; offside.
IMPEDIR v. to prevent, to block, to impede; to hinder, to stop.
IMPEDITIVO adj. deterrent, preventive.
IMPELENTE adj.2gên. impellent, impelling.
IMPELIR v. to impel; to push, to urge.
IMPENETRABILIDADE s.f. impenetrability.
IMPENETRADO adj. not penetrated yet.
IMPENETRÁVEL adj.2gên. impenetrable.
IMPENHORÁVEL adj.2gên. non-extendible.
IMPENITÊNCIA s.f. impenitence, impenitency.
IMPENITENTE adj.2gên. impenitent, unrepentant.
IMPENSADO adj. thoughtless, unintended, unpremeditated.
IMPENSÁVEL adj.2gên. unthinkable, unimaginable.
IMPERADOR s.m. emperor; Caesar, kaiser.
IMPERANTE adj.2gên. prevalent, regnant; commanding.
IMPERAR v. to reign, to govern; to rule, to command.
IMPERATIVO s.m. imperative, order; imperative / adj. imperative.
IMPERATÓRIO adj. imperatorial, imperative.
IMPERATRIZ s.f. empress.
IMPERCEBÍVEL adj.2gên. imperceptible, invisible.
IMPERCEPTIBILIDADE s.f. imperceptibility.
IMPERCEPTÍVEL adj.2gên. imperceptible, invisible.
IMPERDÍVEL adj.2gên. unmissable.
IMPERDOÁVEL adj.2gên. inexcusable, unforgivable.
IMPERECEDOURO adj. imperishable, eternal, immortal.
IMPERECÍVEL adj.2gên. undying, unfading, everlasting.
IMPERFECTIBILIDADE s.f. imperfectibility.
IMPERFECTÍVEL adj.2gên. non-perfectible.
IMPERFEIÇÃO s.f. imperfection.
IMPERFEIÇOAR v. to imperfect, to impair.
IMPERFEITO s.m. imperfect tense / adj. imperfect, incorrect.
IMPERFURAÇÃO s.f. imperforation; occlusion.
IMPERFURADO adj. imperforate.
IMPERFURÁVEL adj.2gên. imperforable.
IMPERIAL adj.2gên. imperial.
IMPERIALISMO s.m. imperialism.
IMPERIALISTA s.2gên. imperialist / adj.2gên. imperialistic.

IMPERÍCIA *s.f.* malpractice, inadequacy, incapacity.
IMPÉRIO *s.m.* empire, governance; realm, domain.
IMPERIOSIDADE *s.f.* imperiousness.
IMPERIOSO *adj.* imperious, imperative; masterful.
IMPERITO *adj.* inexpert, ignorant.
IMPERMANÊNCIA *s.f.* impermanence, instability.
IMPERMANENTE *adj.2gên.* impermanent, unstable.
IMPERMEABILIDADE *s.f.* impermeability.
IMPERMEABILIZAÇÃO *s.f.* waterproofing.
IMPERMEABILIZADOR *s.m.* waterproofer.
IMPERMEABILIZANTE *s.f.* waterproofing.
IMPERMEÁVEL *s.m.* raincoat / *adj.2gên.* impermeable, impenetrable.
IMPERMISTO *adj.* pure, unmixed.
IMPERMUTABILIDADE *s.f.* impermutability.
IMPERMUTÁVEL *adj.2gên.* impermutable.
IMPERSCRUTÁVEL *adj.2gên.* impenetrable; unfathomable.
IMPERSISTENTE *adj.2gên.* inconstant, changeable.
IMPERSONALIDADE *s.f.* impersonality; absence of personality.
IMPERTÉRRITO *adj.* undeterred, fearless, intrepid.
IMPERTINÊNCIA *s.f.* impertinence, impertinency; insolence, petulance.
IMPERTINENTE *s.m.* impertinent, irrelevant, peevish / *adj.2gên.* impertinent, irrelevant, peevish.
IMPERTURBABILIDADE *s.f.* calmness, serenity.
IMPERTURBADO *adj.* unperturbed, undisturbed; calm.
IMPERTURBÁVEL *adj.2gên.* imperturbable; calm, cool.
IMPÉRVIO *adj.* impervious; impassable.
IMPESSOAL *adj.2gên.* impersonal, objective.
IMPESSOALIDADE *s.f.* impersonality.
IMPETAR *v.* to throw, to hurl.
IMPETICAR *v.* to involve, to implicate.
IMPETIGEM *s.f.* impetigo.
IMPETIGINOSO *adj.* impetiginosus.
IMPETIGO *s.m.* impetigo.
ÍMPETO *s.m.* impetus, momentum, impulse.
IMPETRA *s.f.* impetration, procurement, petition.
IMPETRABILIDADE *s.f.* impetrability.
IMPETRAÇÃO *s.f.* impetration, petition.
IMPETRANTE *s.2gên.* supplicant, petitioner / *adj.2gên.* supplicant, supplicatory.
IMPETRAR *v.* to impetrate.
IMPETRATIVO *adj.* impetrative, impetratory.
IMPETRÁVEL *adj.2gên.* impetrative, persuasive.
IMPETUOSIDADE *s.f.* impetuosity; fury, anger.
IMPETUOSO *adj.* impetuous, furious, angry.
IMPIEDADE *s.f.* impiety, profanity.
IMPIEDOSO *adj.* cruel, impious; ruthless, merciless.
IMPINGEM *s.f.* tetter, ringworm.
IMPINGIDELA *s.f.* impingiment, deception; mean action.
IMPINGIR *v.* to impinge, to strike.
ÍMPIO *s.m.* impious man, heretic / *adj.* impious, profane, wicked.
IMPLACABILIDADE *s.f.* implacability, insensibility.
IMPLACÁVEL *adj.2gên.* implacable, inexorable, merciless.
IMPLACIDEZ *s.f.* unrest, lack of placidness, commotion.
IMPLANTAÇÃO *s.f.* implantation.
IMPLANTADOR *s.m.* implanter, planter.
IMPLANTAR *v.* to plant, to implant; to introduce, to insert.
IMPLANTE *s.m.* implantation.
IMPLANTOLOGIA *s.f.* implantology.
IMPLAUSÍVEL *adj.2gên.* implausible, reasonable.
IMPLEMENTO *s.m.* implement, accessory.
IMPLEXO *adj.* implex, intricate.
IMPLICAÇÃO *s.f.* implication, involvement.
IMPLICADO *adj.* entangled, involved, implied.
IMPLICÂNCIA *s.f.* implication, involvement.
IMPLICANTE *s.2gên.* implicate / *adj.2gên.* captious, quarrelsome, implicant.
IMPLICAR *v.* to implicate, to involve; to imply, to include.
IMPLICATIVO *adj.* implicative.
IMPLÍCITO *adj.* implicit, implicate.
IMPLORAÇÃO *s.f.* imploring, supplication.
IMPLORADOR *s.m.* implorer / *adj.* imploring.
IMPLORANTE *s.2gên.* implorer / *adj.2gên.* imploring.
IMPLORAR *v.* to beg, to implore; to supplicate.

IMPLORATIVO *adj.* imploring, supplicatory.
IMPLORÁVEL *adj.2gên.* implorable.
IMPLUME *adj.2gên.* featherless, plumeless.
IMPLÚVIO *s.m.* impluvium; cistern, tank.
IMPOLIDEZ *s.f.* impoliteness; rudeness.
IMPOLIDO *adj.* impolite, rude; disrespectful.
IMPOLÍTICA *s.f.* rudeness, incivility; discourtesy.
IMPOLÍTICO *adj.* impolitic, injudicious.
IMPOLUÍVEL *adj.2gên.* impolluted; immaculate.
IMPOLUTO *adj.* intact, unspotted.
IMPONDERABILIDADE *s.f.* imponderable.
IMPONDERADO *adj.* ill-considered, unweighed.
IMPONDERÁVEL *s.m.* indefinable, unpredictable / *adj.2gên.* disregarded.
IMPONÊNCIA *s.f.* loftiness, grandiosity; pomposity, pride.
IMPONENTE *adj.2gên.* imposing; proud, arrogant, superb.
IMPONTUAL *adj.2gên.* unpunctual; inexact.
IMPONTUALIDADE *s.f.* lateness; impunctuality.
IMPOPULAR *adj.2gên.* unpopular.
IMPOPULARIDADE *s.f.* unpopularity.
IMPOR *v.* to impose, to lay on, to put on.
IMPORTAÇÃO *s.f.* importation.
IMPORTADOR(A) *s.m.* importer / *adj.* importing.
IMPORTÂNCIA *s.f.* importance, consideration.
IMPORTANTE *s.m.* important, essential / *adj.2gên.* important, relevant.
IMPORTAR *v.* to import, to matter; to be important.
IMPORTÁVEL *adj.2gên.* importable.
IMPORTE *s.m.* cost, sum; price, total.
IMPORTUNAÇÃO *s.f.* harassment, importunity; molestation.
IMPORTUNADOR *s.m.* importuner, teaser / *adj.* importunate, vexatious.
IMPORTUNAR *v.* to importune, to tease, to incommode.
IMPORTUNIDADE *s.f.* importunity, bother; annoyance, molestation.
IMPORTUNO *s.m.* annoyer, molester / *adj.* importunate, troublesome.
IMPOSIÇÃO *s.f.* imposition, obligation.
IMPOSITIVO *adj.* authoritative, imposing.
IMPOSSIBILIDADE *s.f.* impossibility.
IMPOSSIBILITAR *v.* to make impossible; to disable.
IMPOSSÍVEL *s.m.* impossible, intolerable / *adj.2gên.* impossible, intolerable.
IMPOSTA *s.f.* imposed, due to, forced.
IMPOSTO *s.m.* imposition; tax, tribute, duty.
IMPOSTOR *s.m.* impostor, charlatan / *adj.* fake, false, fraud.
IMPOSTORIA *s.f.* imposture, deception; vanity, pride.
IMPOSTURA *s.f.* imposture, imposition; fraud, calumny.
IMPOSTURAR *v.* to make imposture; to deceive.
IMPOTABILIDADE *s.f.* non-drinkable; impotability.
IMPOTÁVEL *adj.2gên.* non-drinkable; impotable.
IMPOTÊNCIA *s.f.* impotence, impotency; feebleness, weakness.
IMPOTENTE *s.m.* impotent, feeble / *adj.2gên.* feeble, weak, unable.
IMPRATICABILIDADE *s.f.* impracticability.
IMPRATICÁVEL *adj.2gên.* impractical, impracticable.
IMPRECAÇÃO *s.f.* imprecation; oath, conjuration.
IMPRECAR *v.* to swear, to curse; to profane, to desecrate.
IMPRECATADO *adj.* cursed, profaned; desecrated.
IMPRECATIVO *adj.* imprecatory; that swears or curses.
IMPRECATÓRIO *adj.* maledictory, imprecatory.
IMPRECAUÇÃO *s.f.* oversight; hindsight.
IMPRECISÃO *s.f.* imprecision, inexactness; haziness.
IMPRECISO *adj.* inaccurate, imprecise; incorrect, vague.
IMPREENCHÍVEL *adj.2gên.* unfillable.
IMPREGNAÇÃO *s.f.* impregnation, permeation, saturation.
IMPREGNADO *adj.* impregnated, saturated, penetrated.
IMPREGNAR *v.* to impregnate, to pervade, to penetrate.
IMPREMEDITAÇÃO *s.f.* unpremeditation, forethought.
IMPREMEDITADO *adj.* unpremeditated, spontaneous.
IMPRENSA *s.f.* press, printing.

IMPRENSADO *adj.* pressed, printed.
IMPRENSADOR *s.m.* pressman; calender.
IMPRENSAR *v.* to press, to compress; to print, to stamp.
IMPRESCIÊNCIA *s.f.* imprescience; lack of foreknowledge.
IMPRESCINDÍVEL *adj.2gên.* vital, essential, necessary.
IMPRESCRITIBILIDADE *s.f.* imprescriptibility.
IMPRESCRITÍVEL *adj.2gên.* imprescriptibile.
IMPRESSÃO *s.f.* impression, impress; print, printing.
IMPRESSIONABILIDADE *s.f.* impressionability, sensibility.
IMPRESSIONADO(A) *adj.* impressed; touched, shocked.
IMPRESSIONANTE *adj.2gên.* impressing, moving, touching.
IMPRESSIONAR *v.* to impress, to mark, to stamp in.
IMPRESSIONÁVEL *adj.2gên.* impressionable; sensitive.
IMPRESSIONISMO *s.m.* impressionism.
IMPRESSIONISTA *s.2gên.* impressionist / *adj.2gên.* impressionistic.
IMPRESSIVO *adj.* impressive, susceptible.
IMPRESSO *s.m.* print, copy, printed matter / *adj.* printed.
IMPRESSOR *s.m.* printer, presser; pressman, press worker.
IMPRESTÁVEL *adj.2gên.* worthless, useless, unfit.
IMPRETERÍVEL *adj.2gên.* necessary, forcible; non-extendable, urgent.
IMPREVIDÊNCIA *s.f.* improvidence, imprudence, hindsight.
IMPREVIDENTE *adj.2gên.* improvident, wasteful, casual, unwary.
IMPREVISÃO *s.f.* negligence, improvidence.
IMPREVISÍVEL *adj.2gên.* unpredictable, unforeseeable.
IMPREVISTO *s.m.* unforeseen, unexpected; surprising / *adj.* unforeseen, unexpected; surprising.
IMPRIMIR *v.* to print, to imprint; to press, to stamp in.
IMPROBABILIDADE *s.f.* improbability.
IMPROBIDADE *s.f.* dishonesty, improbity.
ÍMPROBO *adj.* unrighteous, unfair; infamous.
IMPROCEDÊNCIA *s.f.* absurd, improbability; incoherent.

IMPROCEDENTE *adj.2gên.* unfounded, groundless; illogical, unfair.
IMPRODUTÍVEL *adj.2gên.* unable to produce.
IMPRODUTIVIDADE *s.f.* unproductiveness; fruitlessness.
IMPRODUTIVO *adj.* unproductive, useless.
IMPROFERÍVEL *adj.2gên.* unutterable.
IMPROFICIÊNCIA *s.f.* improficiency, improficience.
IMPROFICIENTE *adj.2gên.* improficient, incompetent.
IMPROFÍCUO *adj.* unprofitable; useless, vain.
IMPROGRESSIVO *adj.* improgressive.
IMPROLÍFERO *adj.* unprolific, infertile.
IMPROPERAR *v.* to reprimand, to insult, to accuse.
IMPROPÉRIO *s.m.* affront, insult, outrage.
IMPROPRIAR *v.* to make improper.
IMPROPRIEDADE *s.f.* impropriety, inadequacy.
IMPRÓPRIO *adj.* improper, inappropriate, unfit.
IMPRORROGABILIDADE *s.f.* not prorogable; unextendability.
IMPRORROGÁVEL *adj.2gên.* undelayable, non-postponable.
IMPRÓSPERO *adj.* improsperous, non--successful.
IMPROVAR *v.* to disapprove, to censure, to interpose.
IMPROVÁVEL *adj.2gên.* improbable, unlikely.
IMPROVIDÊNCIA *s.f.* improvidence; imprudence.
IMPROVIDENTE *adj.2gên.* improvident, imprudent, careless.
IMPRÓVIDO *adj. m.q.* improvidente.
IMPROVISAÇÃO *s.f.* improvisation; impromptu.
IMPROVISADO *adj.* improvised, makeshift; impromptu.
IMPROVISADOR *s.m.* improviser; improvisator.
IMPROVISAR *v.* to improvise.
IMPROVISO *s.m.* improvisation / *adj.* improvised, unexpected.
IMPRUDÊNCIA *s.f.* imprudence, indiscretion, rashness.
IMPRUDENTE *s.2gên.* imprudent / *adj.2gên.* imprudent, precipitate.
IMPUBERDADE *s.f.* impuberty.

IMPÚBERE *s.2gên.* impubic, impuberal, impubescent.
IMPUBESCÊNCIA *s.f.* immatureness.
IMPUBESCENTE *s.2gên.* underage, child / *adj.2gên.* underage, child.
IMPUBLICÁVEL *adj.2gên.* unprintable; unpostable.
IMPUDÊNCIA *s.f.* impudence, impertinence.
IMPUDENTE *adj.2gên.* impudent, shameless; impertinent.
IMPUDOR(A) *s.m.* impudence, insolence, immodesty.
IMPUGNABILIDADE *s.f.* refutability.
IMPUGNAÇÃO *s.f.* accusation, impugnment; opposition.
IMPUGNADOR(A) *s.m.* opposer, contester; impugner.
IMPUGNAR *v.* to impugn, to contest; to oppose.
IMPUGNÁVEL *adj.2gên.* impugnable.
IMPULSÃO *s.f.* impulsion, impulse, propulsion; stimulation.
IMPULSAR *v.* to push, to force; to impel; to stimulate.
IMPULSIONAR *v.* to stimulate, to animate; to push, to proper.
IMPULSIVIDADE *s.f.* impulsiveness, impulsivity.
IMPULSIVO(A) *adj.* impulsive; irritable, warm-blooded.
IMPULSO *s.m.* impulse, push; impulsion, propulsion.
IMPULSOR *s.m.* impeller, propulsor, propellant / *adj.* impelling, impulsive.
IMPUNE *adj.2gên.* unpunished; scot-free.
IMPUNIDADE *s.f.* impunity.
IMPUNIDO *adj. m.q.* impune.
IMPUNÍVEL *adj.2gên.* unpunishable.
IMPUREZA *s.f.* impurity, dirt, filth.
IMPURIDADE *s.f.* impureness, uncleanness.
IMPURIFICAR *v.* to become impure.
IMPURO *adj.* impure, unclean; obscene, profane.
IMPUTABILIDADE *s.f.* imputability, liability.
IMPUTAÇÃO *s.f.* imputation, attribution; accusation.
IMPUTADOR *s.m.* accuser, reproacher / *adj.* imputative.
IMPUTAR *v.* to impute, to attribute; to accuse, to consider.

IMPUTÁVEL *adj.2gên.* chargeable, imputable.
IMPUTRESCÍVEL *adj.2gên.* incorruptible.
IMUDÁVEL *adj.2gên.* unchangeable, unalterable, invariable.
IMUNDÍCIA *s.f.* filthiness, foulness.
IMUNDÍCIE *s.f. m.q.* imundícia.
IMUNDO *adj.* filthy, dirty; impure, indecent.
IMUNE *adj.2gên.* immune, exempt; proof, protected (doença).
IMUNIDADE *s.f.* immunity, exemption; protection.
IMUNIZAÇÃO *s.f.* immunisation.
IMUNIZADO *adj.* immune, immunised.
IMUNIZADOR(A) *s.m.* immuniser / *adj.* immunising.
IMUNIZAR *v.* to immunise, to protect from.
IMUTABILIDADE *s.f.* immutability, immovability.
IMUTAÇÃO *s.f.* immutation.
IMUTAR *v.* to immutate, to be fixed.
IMUTÁVEL *adj.2gên.* immutable, changeless, immovable.
INABALÁVEL *adj.2gên.* unshakable, unswerving, constant.
INABDICÁVEL *adj.2gên.* inabidicable, unwaivable; unabandonable.
INÁBIL *adj.2gên.* unskilful, unfit; incapable, awkward.
INABILIDADE *s.f.* inability, incapability, disablement.
INABILITAÇÃO *s.f.* disqualification, disablement.
INABILITADO *adj.* disqualified, unqualified.
INABILITAR *v.* to incapacitate, to disable.
INABITADO *adj.* uninhabited, deserted; unoccupied.
INABITÁVEL *adj.2gên.* uninhabitable.
INABORDÁVEL *adj.2gên.* unapproachable, inaccessible.
INACABADO *adj.* unfinished, uncompleted; undone.
INACABÁVEL *adj.2gên.* endless, interminable.
INAÇÃO *s.f.* inaction, inactivity, idleness.
INACEITÁVEL *adj.2gên.* unacceptable, inadmissible.
INACESSIBILIDADE *s.f.* inaccessibility.
INACESSÍVEL *adj.2gên.* inaccessible, unapproachable.
INACESSO *adj.* inaccessible.
INÁCIA *s.f.* routine.
INACLIMÁVEL *adj.2gên.* non-acclimatised.

INACREDITÁVEL *adj.2gên.* incredible, unbelievable.
INACUSÁVEL *adj.2gên.* unindictable, unaccusable.
INADAPTAÇÃO *s.f.* inadaptation; inadequacy, unsuitability.
INADAPTADO *adj.* unadapted, unsuitable.
INADAPTÁVEL *adj.2gên.* unadaptable, unsuitable.
INADEQUABILIDADE *s.f.* inadequacy, unsuitability.
INADEQUADO *adj.* inappropriate, inadequate; improper.
INADERENTE *adj.2gên.* inadherent, inadhesive.
INADESTRADO *adj.* unskilful, untrained.
INADESTRAR *v.* to untrain, to unteach.
INADIÁVEL *adj.2gên.* undelayable, urgent.
INADIMPLÊNCIA *s.f.* default.
INADIMPLIR *v.* to breach an agreement; to not pay the bills.
INADMISSÃO *s.f.* inadmition, exclusion.
INADMISSIBILIDADE *s.f.* inadmissibility.
INADMISSÍVEL *adj.2gên.* inadmissible.
INADVERTÊNCIA *s.f.* inadvertence, inadvertency.
INADVERTIDO *adj.* inadvertent, unintentional.
INAFIANÇÁVEL *adj.2gên.* non-bailable.
INAJÁ *s.2gên.* inaja palm.
INALAÇÃO *s.f.* inhalation, inspiration.
INALADO *adj.* inhaled, imbibed.
INALADOR *s.m.* inhaler, inspiring / *adj.* inhaling, inhalant.
INALANTE *adj.2gên.* inhalant.
INALAR *v.* to inhale, to breathe, to imbibe.
INALCANÇADO *adj.* unreached, unapproached.
INALCANÇÁVEL *adj.2gên.* unachievable, unapproachable.
INALIÁVEL *adj.2gên.* unalliable, unaloyable.
INALIENABILIDADE *s.f.* inalienability.
INALIENAÇÃO *s.f.* inalienation, unmadness.
INALIENADO *adj.* non-alienated.
INALIENAR *v.* to prevent to be alienated.
INALIENÁVEL *adj.2gên.* inalienable.
INALTERABILIDADE *s.f.* unalterability, immutability.
INALTERADO *adj.* unaltered, unchanged.
INALTERÁVEL *adj.2gên.* unalterable, unchangeable.
INAMÁVEL *adj.2gên.* unlovable, unfriendly.

INAMBULAÇÃO *s.f.* unambulation.
INAMISSIBILIDADE *s.f.* inamissibleness.
INAMISSÍVEL *adj.2gên.* inamissible.
INAMISTOSO *adj.* unfriendly; adverse, hostile.
INANE *adj.2gên.* inane; empty, futile.
INANIÇÃO *s.f.* inanition, starvation, weakness.
INANIDADE *s.f.* inanity, emptiness.
INANIMADO(A) *adj.* inanimate, lifeless.
INÂNIME *adj.2gên.* inanimate, lifeless, spiritless.
INAPAGÁVEL *adj.2gên.* ineffaceable.
INAPELABILIDADE *s.f.* inapellability, irrepealability.
INAPELÁVEL *adj.2gên.* inappellable.
INAPENDICULADO *adj.* inappendiculate.
INAPERTO *adj.* inapertous.
INAPETÊNCIA *s.f.* inappetence.
INAPETENTE *adj.2gên.* inappetent.
INAPLICABILIDADE *s.f.* inapplicability, irrelevance.
INAPLICADO *adj.* non-applied, inattentive, negligent.
INAPLICÁVEL *adj.2gên.* inapplicable, irrelevant.
INAPRECIÁVEL *adj.2gên.* inappreciable, inestimable.
INAPRESENTÁVEL *adj.2gên.* unpresentable.
INAPROPRIADO *adj.* improper, inadequate.
INAPROVEITADO *adj.* unused, waste.
INAPROVEITÁVEL *adj.2gên.* inefficient, useless, unserviceable.
INAPTIDÃO *s.f.* disability, inability.
INAPTO *adj.* inapt, unfit, unable, incapable.
INARMONIA *s.f.* dissonance, discord.
INARMÔNICO *adj.* unmusical, dissonant, discordant.
INARMONIOSO *adj.* inharmonic; conflicting, disagreeing.
INARRÁVEL *adj.2gên.* untellable, unspeakable.
INARRECADÁVEL *adj.2gên.* uncollectable, unreapable.
INARTICULADO *adj.* inarticulated.
INARTICULÁVEL *adj.2gên.* inarticulable.
INARTÍSTICO *adj.* inartistic, unskilful.
INASCÍVEL *adj.2gên.* innascible; unborn.
INASSIDUIDADE *s.f.* unassiduity, unassiduousness.
INASSIMILÁVEL *adj.2gên.* unassimilable.

INASSINÁVEL *adj.2gên.* unassignable, unsignable.
INATACABILIDADE *s.f.* inimpeachableness.
INATACÁVEL *adj.2gên.* unassailable, incontestable.
INATINGIDO *adj.* unattained, unachieved.
INATINGÍVEL *adj.2gên.* unachievable, unbearable, unattainable.
INATIVIDADE *s.f.* inactivity, inaction; idleness.
INATIVO *adj.* inactive, idle; indolent, stagnant.
INATO *adj.* innate, inborn, congenital.
INATURAL *adj.2gên.* unnatural, artificial.
INATURALIDADE *s.f.* unnaturalness.
INATURÁVEL *adj.2gên.* intolerable, unbearable, unendurable.
INAUDITO *adj.* unheard of, unprecedented.
INAUDÍVEL *adj.2gên.* inaudible.
INAUFERÍVEL *adj.2gên.* intrinsic, inherent.
INAUGURAÇÃO *s.f.* inauguration; opening, initiation.
INAUGURADO *adj.* opened, inaugurated.
INAUGURADOR(A) *s.m.* inaugurator; opener.
INAUGURAL *adj.2gên.* inaugural, opening.
INAUGURAR *v.* to inaugurate, to open, to begin.
INAUGURATIVO(A) *adj.* inauguratory, opening.
INAUSPICIOSO *adj.* inauspicious; unlikely, unlucky.
INAUTENTICIDADE *s.f.* inauthenticity.
INAUTÊNTICO *adj.* inauthentic, fake, untrue.
INAVALIÁVEL *adj.2gên.* invaluable.
INAVEGABILIDADE *s.f.* unseaworthiness.
INAVEGÁVEL *adj.2gên.* unnavigable.
INCA *s.2gên.* Inca, indian nation / *adj.2gên.* Incan.
INCABÍVEL *adj.2gên.* non-applicable, unfit, irrelevant.
INCAICO *adj.* Incan.
INCALCINÁVEL *adj.2gên.* that cannot burnout.
INCALCULÁVEL *adj.2gên.* incalculable, invaluable, inestimable.
INCANDESCÊNCIA *s.f.* incandescence, candescence; glow.
INCANDESCENTE *adj.2gên.* incandescent; glowing.
INCANDESCER *v.* to incandescence, to glow.
INCANSÁVEL *adj.2gên.* tireless, indefatigable.
INCAPACIDADE *s.f.* incapacity, inability, disability.

INCAPACITADO *adj.* disabled, unable, disqualified.
INCAPACITAR *v.* to disable, to incapacitate, to unable.
INCAPACITÁVEL *adj.2gên.* uncapacitate; unconvincible.
INCAPAZ *adj.2gên.* unable, incapable, disabled.
INÇAR *v.* to crowd, to infect, to proliferate.
INCARACTERÍSTICO *adj.* uncharacteristic.
INCENDER *v.* to light, to kindle.
INCENDIADO *adj.* afire, flared up.
INCENDIAR *v.* to set fire to, to fire; to burn, to inflame.
INCENDIÁRIO *s.m.* incendiary, inflammatory / *adj.* incendiary, inflammatory.
INCÊNDIO *s.m.* fire, burning; calamity, disaster.
INCENSAÇÃO *s.f.* incensation.
INCENSAR *v.* to incense; to provoke, to irritate.
INCENSÁRIO *s.m.* censer, incense burner.
INCENSO *s.m.* incense.
INCENSURÁVEL *adj.2gên.* irreproachable, uncensurable.
INCENTIVAR *v.* to encourage, to stimulate, to incite.
INCENTIVO *s.m.* incentive, fuel, impulse, stimulus.
INCENTOR(A) *s.m.* stimulator.
INCERIMONIOSO *adj.* unceremonious, informal.
INCERTA *s.f.* surprising visit of an officer.
INCERTEZA *s.f.* uncertainty, doubt; suspense.
INCERTO *adj.* uncertain, unsure, insecure.
INCESSANTE *adj.2gên.* incessant, unceasing, constant.
INCESSÍVEL *adj.2gên.* untransferable, inalienable.
INCESTAR *v.* to commit incest.
INCESTO *s.m.* incest.
INCESTUOSO *adj.* incestuous.
INCHAÇÃO *s.f.* swelling, swell.
INCHAÇO *s.m.* swelling, bump, lump.
INCHADO *adj.* swollen, bloated.
INCHAR *v.* to swell, to bloat, to bulge.
INCICATRIZÁVEL *adj.2gên.* unhealable.
INCIDÊNCIA *s.f.* incidence.
INCIDENTADO *adj.* incidental; accidental.
INCIDENTAL *adj.2gên.* incidental; accidental.
INCIDIR *v.* to happen, to occur; to cut, to incise.

INCINERAÇÃO *s.f.* incineration, cremation.
INCINERADO *adj.* burnt, cremated, incinerated.
INCINERADOR *s.m.* incinerator, crematory, destructor.
INCINERAR *v.* to incinerate, to burn, to cremate.
INCIPIENTE *adj.2gên.* incipient, initial, beginning.
INCIRCUNCIDADO *s.m.* uncircumcised / *adj.* uncircumcised, impure.
INCIRCUNCISO *s.m. m.q.* incircuncidado.
INCIRCUNSCRITO *adj.* uncircumscribed; unlimited, boundless.
INCISÃO *s.f.* incision; cutting, slit.
INCISAR *v.* to incise; to cut into.
INCISIVO *s.m.* incisor / *adj.* incisive, sharp, cutting.
INCISO *s.m.* item; proposition, sentence.
INCISOR *s.m.* incisor, foretooth / *adj.* incisive, cutting.
INCISÓRIO *adj.* incisorial, cutting, incisive.
INCISURA *s.f.* incision, cut; notch, kerb.
INCITABILIDADE *s.f.* excitability, irritability.
INCITAÇÃO *s.f.* incitement, instigation, stimulation.
INCITADOR *s.m.* inciter, instigator; provoker / *adj.* inciting, stimulating.
INCITAMENTO *s.m.* incitement, inducement; provocation.
INCITANTE *adj.2gên.* inciting, inflammatory.
INCITAR *v.* to incite, to urge; to stimulate.
INCITATIVO *adj.* incitive, stimulative, hortative
INCITÁVEL *adj.2gên.* incitable.
INCIVIL *adj.2gên.* uncivil; rude.
INCIVILIDADE *s.f.* incivility; disrespect, rudeness.
INCIVILIZADO *adj.* uncivilised, uncultured; rude, savage.
INCIVILIZÁVEL *adj.2gên.* uneducatable.
INCLASSIFICÁVEL *adj.2gên.* unclassifiable, nondescript.
INCLEMÊNCIA *s.f.* inclemency, mercilessness, rigorous.
INCLEMENTE *adj.2gên.* inclement, merciless; cruel, severe.
INCLINAÇÃO *s.f.* inclination, incline; bending.
INCLINADO *adj.* inclined, bowed, bent.
INCLINADOR *s.m.* incliner.
INCLINAR *v.* to incline, to recline, to bow, to bend.
INCLINÁVEL *adj.2gên.* inclinable, bendable.
ÍNCLITO *adj.* famous, eminent, prominent.
INCLUÍDO *adj.* included, involved, implicate.
INCLUIR *v.* to include, to involve, to enclose.
INCLUSÃO *s.f.* inclusion.
INCLUSIVO *adj.* inclusive, including.
INCLUSO *adj.* included, enclosed.
INCOAGULÁVEL *adj.2gên.* incoagulable.
INCOATIVO *s.m.* uncoercive / *adj.* inchoative.
INCOBRÁVEL *adj.2gên.* uncollectible, uncoverable.
INCOERCIBILIDADE *s.f.* incoercibility.
INCOERCÍVEL *adj.2gên.* incoercible.
INCOERÊNCIA *s.f.* incoherence, contradiction.
INCOERENTE *adj.2gên.* incoherent, unconnected.
INCOESÃO *s.f.* incohesion, incoherent.
INCOGITADO *adj.* unthought, unconsidereted.
INCOGITÁVEL *adj.2gên.* incogitable, unthinkable.
INCÓGNITA *s.f.* unknown quantity.
INCÓGNITO *s.m.* incognito, unrecognisable.
INCOGNOSCIBILIDADE *s.f.* incognoscibility.
INCOGNOSCÍVEL *s.2gên.* incognoscible; unknowable / *adj.2gên.* incognoscible; unknowable.
ÍNCOLA *s.2gên.* inhabitant, resident, dweller.
INCOLOR *adj.2gên.* uncoloured, colourless; blank.
INCÓLUME *adj.2gên.* unscathed, unharmed, unhurt.
INCOLUMIDADE *s.f.* safety, well-being.
INCOMBUSTIBILIDADE *s.f.* incombustibility.
INCOMBUSTÍVEL *adj.2gên.* incombustible; fireproof.
INCOMBUSTO *adj.* unburnt.
INCOMENSURABILIDADE *s.f.* incommensurability.
INCOMENSURÁVEL *adj.2gên.* incommensurable.
INCOMÍVEL *adj.2gên.* uneatable.
INCOMODADO *adj.* incommodated, inconvenienced; troubled.
INCOMODADOR *s.m.* troublemaker / *adj.* troubling, importunate.
INCOMODANTE *adj.2gên.* importunate, bothersome.
INCOMODAR *v.* to bother, to annoy.
INCOMODATIVO *adj.* troublesome, bothersome.

INCOMODIDADE *s.f.* unconvenience, discomfort.
INCÔMODO *s.m.* discomfort, annoyance / *adj.* worrisome, uncomfortable.
INCOMPARABILIDADE *s.f.* incomparability, match.
INCOMPARÁVEL *adj.2gên.* unmatched, imcomparable.
INCOMPASSÍVEL *adj.2gên.* incompassionate, merciless.
INCOMPATIBILIDADE *s.f.* incompatibility, inconsistency.
INCOMPATIBILIZAR *v.* to unmatch, to unfit.
INCOMPATÍVEL *adj.2gên.* incompatible, inconsistent.
INCOMPENSADO *adj.* unrewarded.
INCOMPENSÁVEL *adj.2gên.* irreparable, irrecoverable.
INCOMPETÊNCIA *s.f.* incompetence, incapacity.
INCOMPETENTE *s.2gên.* incompetent, unfit, unable / *adj.2gên.* incompetent, unfit, unable.
INCOMPLACÊNCIA *s.f.* incompliance.
INCOMPLACENTE *adj.2gên.* incompliant.
INCOMPLETO *adj.* incomplete, fragment; piece.
INCOMPLEXIDADE *s.f.* incomplexity.
INCOMPLEXO *adj.* incomplex, simple.
INCOMPORTÁVEL *adj.2gên.* incomportable, unaffordable; unbearable, intolerable.
INCOMPREENDIDO *adj.* misunderstood.
INCOMPREENSÃO *s.f.* incomprehension, unwisdom.
INCOMPREENSIBILIDADE *s.f.* incomprehensibility.
INCOMPREENSÍVEL *adj.2gên.* incomprehensible, impenetrable.
INCOMPREENSIVO *adj.* uncomprehending.
INCOMPRESSIBILIDADE *s.f.* incompressibility.
INCOMPRESSÍVEL *adj.2gên.* incompressible.
INCOMPRIMIDO *adj.* non-compressed.
INCOMPTO *adj.* rough, simple; non--complex.
INCOMPUTÁVEL *adj.2gên.* incomputable.
INCOMUM *adj.2gên.* uncommon, unusual; strange, weird.
INCOMUNICABILIDADE *s.f.* incommunicability.
INCOMUNICÁVEL *adj.2gên.* incommunicable.
INCOMUTABILIDADE *s.f.* incommutability.
INCOMUTÁVEL *adj.2gên.* unchangeable.
INCONCEBÍVEL *adj.2gên.* unthinkable, unimaginable.
INCONCEPTO *adj.* inconceptus, inconceivable.
INCONCESSÍVEL *adj.2gên.* unconcessible, unpermissible.
INCONCESSO *adj.* illicit, forbidden.
INCONCILIABILIDADE *s.f.* irreconcilability.
INCONCILIAÇÃO *s.f.* irreconciliation.
INCONCILIÁVEL *adj.2gên.* irreconcilable, incompatible.
INCONCLUDENTE *adj.2gên.* undetermined, inconclusive.
INCONCLUSIVO *adj.* inconclusive.
INCONCLUSO *adj.* incomplete, unfinished.
INCONCORDÁVEL *adj.2gên.* unagreeable, incompatible.
INCONCUSSO *adj.* indisputable; undeniable; austere.
INCONDICIONADO *s.m.* absoluteness, infinite / *adj.* unconditioned, absolute.
INCONDICIONAL *adj.2gên.* unconditional, absolute; categorical.
INCONDICIONALIDADE *s.f.* absoluteness, unconditionality.
INCONDICIONALISMO *s.m.* absolutism, despotism.
INCÔNDITO *adj.* mess; disorderly, disarranged.
INCONEXÃO *s.f.* disconnection.
INCONEXO *adj.* unconnected, irrelational.
INCONFESSADO *adj.* unconfessed, unconfessant.
INCONFESSÁVEL *adj.2gên.* unconfessable.
INCONFESSO *adj.* unconfessed.
INCONFIDÊNCIA *s.f.* disloyalty, infidelity, distrust.
INCONFIDENTE *adj.2gên.* disloyal, false; conspirator.
INCONFORMADO *adj.* nonconformist; irresigned.
INCONFORTÁVEL *adj.2gên.* uncomfortable, uneasy.
INCONFUNDÍVEL *adj.2gên.* unmistakable, distinct.
INCONGELADO *adj.* unfrozen.
INCONGELÁVEL *adj.2gên.* unfreezable.

INCONGRUÊNCIA *s.f.* incongruity, inconsequence.
INCONGRUENTE *adj.2gên.* incongruous, absurd; inconsequent.
INCONGRUIDADE *s.f.* incongruity.
INCÔNGRUO *adj. m.q.* incongruente.
INCONIVENTE *adj.2gên.* non-accessary.
INCONJUGÁVEL *adj.2gên.* unconjugable.
INCONQUISTABILIDADE *s.f.* quality of unconquerable.
INCONQUISTADO *adj.* unconquered.
INCONQUISTÁVEL *adj.2gên.* unconquerable, invincible.
INCONSCIÊNCIA *s.f.* unconsciousness; comma.
INCONSCIENCIOSO *adj.* unconscientious; unscrupulous.
INCONSCIENTE *adj.2gên.* unconscious, senseless; comma.
INCÔNSCIO *adj.* unconscious, insensible.
INCONSEQUÊNCIA *s.f.* inconsequence.
INCONSEQUENTE *adj.2gên.* inconsequent, inconsistent.
INCONSIDERAÇÃO *s.f.* inconsideration, regardlessness.
INCONSIDERADO(A) *adj.* inconsiderate, indiscreet.
INCONSIDERÁVEL *adj.2gên.* inconsiderable, unimportant; trivial.
INCONSISTÊNCIA *s.f.* inconsistency, contradiction.
INCONSISTENTE *adj.2gên.* inconsistent, discrepant.
INCONSOLADO *adj.* uncomforted; unconsoled.
INCONSOLÁVEL *adj.2gên.* unconsolable.
INCONSONÂNCIA *s.f.* inconsonance, discordance.
INCONSONANTE *adj.2gên.* inconsonant.
INCONSTÂNCIA *s.f.* inconstancy; fickleness.
INCONSTANTE *adj.2gên.* inconstant; fickle, unstable.
INCONSTITUCIONAL *adj.2gên.* unconstitutional.
INCONSTITUCIONALIDADE *s.f.* unconstitutionality.
INCONSULTO *adj.* unconsulted, disregarded.
INCONSUMÍVEL *adj.2gên.* inconsumable.
INCONSUNTO(A) *adj.* unbroken, intact.
INCONTAMINADO *adj.* uncontaminated, undefiled; unpolluted, pure.

INCONTÁVEL *adj.2gên.* uncountable; untold.
INCONTENTÁVEL *adj.2gên.* incontentable; unsatisfiable.
INCONTESTABILIDADE *s.f.* incontestability, indisputability.
INCONTESTADO(A) *adj.* uncontested, undisputed.
INCONTESTÁVEL *adj.2gên.* incontestable, undeniable.
INCONTESTE *adj.2gên.* uncontested, undisputed.
INCONTIDO *adj.* unrestricted, uncurbed; uncontainable.
INCONTINÊNCIA *s.f.* incontinence.
INCONTINENTE *adj.2gên.* incontinent, unrestrained.
INCONTINGÊNCIA *s.f.* certainty, assurance.
INCONTINGENTE *adj.2gên.* certain, sure.
INCONTINUIDADE *s.f.* uncontinuity, non-permanence.
INCONTÍNUO *adj.* ceased, stopped; stuck.
INCONTRASTÁVEL *adj.2gên.* contrastable, irresistible.
INCONTRITO *adj.* unrepentant, uncontrite.
INCONTROLÁVEL *adj.2gên.* uncontrollable; ungovernable.
INCONTROVERSO *adj.* incontrovertible, undisputed.
INCONTROVERTIDO *adj. m.q.* incontroverso.
INCONTROVERTÍVEL *adj.2gên.* incontrovertible, undisputable.
INCONVENCÍVEL *adj.2gên.* unconverted, unconvincible.
INCONVENIÊNCIA *s.f.* inconvenience, impropriety.
INCONVENIENTE *s.m.* inconvenience, trouble / *adj.2gên.* inconvenient, improper.
INCONVERSÍVEL *adj.2gên.* inconvertible.
INCONVERTÍVEL *adj.2gên.* immutable, unchangeable.
INCONVICTO *adj.* unconvinced.
INCOORDENAÇÃO *s.f.* incoordination.
INCORPORAÇÃO *s.f.* incorporation; annexation.
INCORPORADO(A) *adj.* incorporated; annexed.
INCORPORADOR(A) *s.m.* incorporator; developer.
INCORPORAR *v.* to incorporate; to join, to unite.
INCORPÓREO *adj.* incorporeal, immaterial; spiritual.

INCORREÇÃO *s.f.* inaccuracy; error, mistake.
INCORRER *v.* to incur, to occur; to pass through.
INCORRETO *adj.* incorrect; wrong, improper.
INCORRIGIBILIDADE *s.f.* incorrigibility.
INCORRIGÍVEL *adj.2gên.* incorrigible; hopeless.
INCORRUPTIBILIDADE *s.f.* incorruptibility; integrity, honesty.
INCORRUPTÍVEL *adj.2gên.* incorruptible; unbribable.
INCORRUPTIVO *adj.* incorruptive.
INCORRUPTO *adj.* incorrupt; clean-fingered.
INCREDIBILIDADE *s.f.* incredibility.
INCREDULIDADE *s.f.* incredulity.
INCRÉDULO(A) *s.m.* unbeliever, disbeliever / *adj.* incredulous, sceptical.
INCREMENTADO(A) *adj.* incremented, developed.
INCREMENTAR *v.* to increment; to increase, to develop.
INCREMENTO *s.m.* increment; development, increase.
INCRIMINAÇÃO *s.f.* crimination; accusation.
INCRIMINADO *adj.* incriminated, accused.
INCRIMINAR *v.* to incriminate, to accuse.
INCRITICÁVEL *adj.2gên.* uncriticisable; unexceptionable.
INCRÍVEL *adj.2gên.* incredible, unbelievable.
INCRUSTAÇÃO *s.f.* incrustation, inlay.
INCRUSTANTE *adj.2gên.* incrusting; fouling.
INCRUSTAR *v.* to encrust, to incrust; to inlay.
INCUBAÇÃO *s.f.* incubation.
INCUBADOR *adj.* incubative, incubator.
INCUBADORA *s.f.* incubator, hatchery; broody hen.
INCUBAR *v.* to incubate; to hatch.
INCULCAR *v.* to inculcate; to engrain, to implant.
INCULPAÇÃO *s.f.* inculpation, imputation; charge, accusation.
INCULPAR *v.* to inculpate, to accuse; to incriminate.
INCULTIVÁVEL *adj.2gên.* uncultivable, unproductive.
INCULTO *adj.* unlearned, uncultivated; uncultured.
INCULTURA *s.f.* wildness; lack of culture.
INCUMBÊNCIA *s.f.* incumbency, obligation; commission, task.
INCUMBIDO(A) *adj.* charged; entrusted.
INCUMBIR *v.* to charge, to engage in; to entrust, to task.
INCURABILIDADE *s.f.* incurability.
INCURÁVEL *adj.2gên.* incurable; hopeless, incorrigible.
INCURIOSIDADE *s.f.* incuriosity.
INCURIOSO *adj.* incurious; careless, negligent.
INDAGAÇÃO *s.f.* investigation, inquiry, quest.
INDAGADOR *s.m.* inquirer, querist.
INDAGAR *v.* to ask, to inquire.
INDECÊNCIA *s.f.* indecency.
INDECENTE *adj.2gên.* indecent, obscene.
INDECIDIDO *adj.* undecided.
INDECIFRÁVEL *adj.2gên.* indecipherable.
INDECISÃO *s.f.* indecision.
INDECISO *adj.* indecisive, vacillating.
INDECLARÁVEL *adj.2gên.* undeclarable.
INDECLINABILIDADE *s.f.* indeclinability.
INDECLINÁVEL *adj.2gên.* indeclinable.
INDECORO *s.m.* indecorum, indecency.
INDECOROSO *adj.* indecorous, unclean, shocking.
INDEFECTÍVEL *adj.2gên.* indefectible.
INDEFENSÁVEL *adj.2gên.* indefensible, unsustainable.
INDEFERIDO *adj.* rejected, refused.
INDEFERIMENTO *s.m.* rejection; dismissal.
INDEFERIR *v.* to reject, to refuse; to dismiss.
INDEFESO *adj.* undefended, resistless.
INDEFICIENTE *adj.2gên.* indeficient; unfaulty.
INDEFINIDO *adj.* indefinite; vague, neutral.
INDEFINÍVEL *adj.2gên.* indefinable; vague.
INDELIBERAÇÃO *s.f.* indeliberation.
INDELIBERADO *adj.* undeliberate; unadvised.
INDELICADEZA *s.f.* indelicacy; incivility.
INDELICADO *adj.* indelicate, impolite; rude.
INDELINEÁVEL *adj.2gên.* undelineative, untraceable.
INDEMONSTRÁVEL *adj.2gên.* indemonstrable.
INDENIZAÇÃO *s.f.* indemnification, indemnity.
INDENIZADO *adj.* indemnified.
INDENIZADOR *s.m.* indemnitor; indemnifier.
INDENIZAR *v.* to indemnify; to compensate.

INDEPENDÊNCIA *s.f.* independence; freedom, autonomy.
INDEPENDENTE *adj.2gên.* independent; free, autonomous.
INDESATÁVEL *adj.2gên.* indissoluble, untied.
INDESCONFIÁVEL *adj.2gên.* unsuspecting, reliable.
INDESCRITÍVEL *adj.2gên.* indescribable, unspeakable.
INDESCULPÁVEL *adj.2gên.* inexcusable, unjustifiable.
INDESEJADO(A) *adj.* unwanted, undesired.
INDESEJÁVEL *adj.2gên.* undesirable.
INDESTRUTÍVEL *adj.2gên.* indestructible.
INDETERMINAÇÃO *s.f.* indetermination; indeterminacy.
INDETERMINADO *s.f.* undetermined, indeterminate.
INDETERMINAR *v.* to indetermine, to undefine.
INDETERMINISMO *s.m.* indeterminism.
INDEVIDO *adj.* undue; improper, unjustified.
INDEVOÇÃO *s.f.* undevotion; religiousless.
INDEVOTO *adj.* undevout; irreligious.
ÍNDEX *s.m.* index; index-finger, forefinger.
INDIANISMO *s.m.* Indianism.
INDIANISTA *s.2gên.* Indianist / *adj.2gên.* Indianist.
INDIANO(A) *s.m.* Indian / *adj.* Indian.
INDICAÇÃO *s.f.* indication.
INDICADO *adj.* indicated.
INDICADOR *s.m.* indicator, pointer.
INDICAR *v.* to indicate, to show; to guide, to direct.
INDICATIVO *s.m.* indicative mode / *adj.* indicatory, denotative.
ÍNDICE *s.m.* index, table of contents; catalogue.
INDICIADO(A) *s.m.* indicted, accused / *adj.* indicted, accused.
INDICIAR *v.* to indict, to accuse.
INDÍCIO *s.m.* evidence, trace, clue.
INDIFERENÇA *s.f.* indifference, apathy.
INDIFERENTE *s.2gên.* indifferent / *adj.2gên.* indifferent.
INDÍGENA *s.2gên.* native, aboriginal, indigene / *adj.2gên.* indian, indigenous.
INDIGÊNCIA *s.f.* indigence, poverty, pauper.
INDIGENTE *adj.2gên.* indigent, poor.

INDIGESTÃO *s.f.* indigestion.
INDIGESTO *adj.* indigestible.
INDIGNAÇÃO *s.f.* indignation, abhorrence.
INDIGNADO(A) *adj.* indignant; angry.
INDIGNIDADE *s.f.* indignity; offence.
INDIGNO *adj.* unworthy, undignified.
ÍNDIO *s.m.* Indian / *adj.* Indian.
INDIRETA *s.f.* indirect; allusion, hint.
INDIRETO *adj.* indirect, collateral.
INDISCIPLINA *s.f.* indiscipline.
INDISCIPLINADO *adj.* undisciplined, unruly.
INDISCIPLINAR *v.* to demoralise.
INDISCRETO *s.m.* indiscreet / *adj.* indiscreet, chattering.
INDISCRIÇÃO *s.f.* indiscretion, imprudence.
INDISCRIMINADO *adj.* indiscriminate.
INDISCUTÍVEL *adj.2gên.* unquestionable, unarguable.
INDISPENSÁVEL *adj.2gên.* indispensable, necessary.
INDISPONIBILIDADE *s.f.* unavailability.
INDISPONÍVEL *adj.2gên.* unavailable.
INDISPOR *v.* to indispose; to irritate, to annoy.
INDISPOSIÇÃO *s.f.* indisposition; illness.
INDISPOSTO *adj.* indisposed.
INDISTINÇÃO *s.f.* indistinctness.
INDISTINTO *adj.* indistinct.
INDIVIDUAL *adj.2gên.* individual, peculiar; singular.
INDIVIDUALIDADE *s.f.* individuality; personality.
INDIVIDUALISMO *s.m.* individualism.
INDIVIDUALISTA *s.2gên.* individualist / *adj.2gên.* individualistic.
INDIVIDUALIZAR *v.* to individualise; to distinguish.
INDIVÍDUO *s.m.* individual; person, being.
INDIVISÃO *s.f.* indivision; unity, atom.
INDIVISÍVEL *s.m.* indivisible, impartible / *adj.2gên.* indivisible, impartible.
INDIZÍVEL *adj.2gên.* unspeakable, unutterable.
INDÓCIL *adj.2gên.* indocile, ungovernable.
ÍNDOLE *s.f.* natural, character.
INDOLÊNCIA *s.f.* indolence, laziness.
INDOLENTE *adj.2gên.* indolent; apathetic.
INDOLOR *adj.2gên.* painless.
INDOMADO *adj.* untamed, wild.

INDOMÁVEL *adj.2gên.* uncontrollable; tameless.
INDOMESTICÁVEL *adj.2gên.* undomesticated; savage, wild.
INDUBITÁVEL *adj.2gên.* indubitable, undoubted.
INDUÇÃO *s.f.* induction, influence.
INDULGÊNCIA *s.f.* indulgence, lenience.
INDULGENTE *adj.2gên.* indulgent, clement; lenient.
INDULTO *s.m.* indult; permission, grant.
INDÚSTRIA *s.f.* industry.
INDUSTRIAL *s.2gên.* industrial / *adj.2gên.* industrial.
INDUSTRIALISMO *s.m.* industrialism.
INDUSTRIALISTA *s.2gên.* industrialist; industrial / *adj.2gên.* industrialist; industrial.
INDUSTRIALIZAÇÃO *s.f.* industrialisation.
INDUSTRIALIZAR *v.* to industrialise.
INDUTIVO *adj.* inductive; inducing.
INDUTOR *s.m.* inductor / *adj.* inductive.
INDUZIDO *adj.* induced.
INDUZIR *v.* to induce, to incite.
INEBRIANTE *adj.2gên.* intoxicant, inebriant.
INEBRIAR *v.* to inebriate; to intoxicate.
INÉDITO *adj.* unpublished, inedited; original.
INEFÁVEL *adj.2gên.* ineffable, unspeakable.
INEFICÁCIA *s.f.* ineffectiveness; uselessness.
INEFICAZ *adj.2gên.* ineffective, ineffectual.
INEFICIÊNCIA *s.f.* inefficiency; incompetence.
INEFICIENTE *adj.2gên.* inefficient; weak, feeble.
INEGÁVEL *adj.2gên.* undeniable; evident.
INEGOCIÁVEL *adj.2gên.* undeniable.
INELEGÂNCIA *s.f.* inelegance; inelegancy.
INELEGANTE *adj.2gên.* Inelegant; unrefined, ungraceful.
INELEGIBILIDADE *s.f.* ineligibility.
INELEGÍVEL *adj.2gên.* ineligible.
INÉPCIA *s.f.* ineptitude, ineptness.
INEPTO *adj.* inept; unfit.
INEQUÍVOCO *adj.* unequivocal, unmistakable.
INÉRCIA *s.f.* inertia; unmovable, static.
INERÊNCIA *s.f.* inherence; inhesion.
INERENTE *adj.2gên.* inherent, native, intrinsic.
INERTE *adj.2gên.* inert, inactive; stagnant, lifeless.
INERVAÇÃO *s.f.* innervation.
INERVAR *v.* to innervate, to unnerve.

INESCRUPULOSO *adj.* unscrupulous; unprincipled.
INESCUSÁVEL *adj.2gên.* inexcusable.
INESGOTÁVEL *adj.2gên.* inexhaustible; abundant, endless.
INESPECÍFICO *adj.* nonspecific, unspecific.
INESPERADO *adj.* unexpected, accidental; unhoped.
INESQUECÍVEL *adj.2gên.* unforgettable.
INESTIMÁVEL *adj.2gên.* inestimable, priceless, precious.
INEVITÁVEL *adj.2gên.* inevitable, necessary; unavoidable.
INEXATIDÃO *s.f.* inexactness; inaccuracy, untruth.
INEXATO *adj.* inexact; inaccurate, untrue.
INEXAURÍVEL *adj.2gên.* inexhaustible; inexhaustive.
INEXCEDÍVEL *adj.2gên.* unexcelled.
INEXCITÁVEL *adj.2gên.* unexcitable.
INEXISTÊNCIA *s.f.* inexistence; absence.
INEXISTENTE *adj.2gên.* inexistent, absent.
INEXISTIR *v.* to inexist; to unlive.
INEXPERIÊNCIA *s.f.* inexperience; rawness, greenness.
INEXPERIENTE *adj.2gên.* inexperienced.
INEXPLICÁVEL *adj.2gên.* inexplicable; uncountable.
INEXPLORADO *adj.* unexplored, unexploited.
INEXPRESSIVO *adj.* expressionless, inexpressive; blank.
INEXTINGUÍVEL *adj.2gên.* inextinguishable, indestructible.
INFALÍVEL *adj.2gên.* infallible; foolproof.
INFALSIFICÁVEL *adj.2gên.* unfalsifiable, unadulterable.
INFAMAÇÃO *s.f.* defamation; calumny, infamy.
INFAME *adj.2gên.* infamous; scandalous.
INFÂMIA *s.f.* infamy.
INFÂNCIA *s.f.* childhood, infancy.
INFANTARIA *s.f.* infantry.
INFANTIL *adj.2gên.* infant; childlike, puerile.
INFANTILISMO *s.m.* infantilism.
INFANTILIZAR *v.* to infantilise.
INFARTO *s.m.* heart attack; infarct.
INFECÇÃO *s.f.* infection.
INFECCIOSO *adj.* infectious, infective.
INFELICIDADE *s.f.* unhappiness.
INFELIZ *adj.2gên.* unhappy.

INFERIOR *s.2gên.* inferior; less / *adj.2gên.* inferior; less.
INFERIORIDADE *s.f.* inferiority, poorness.
INFERNAL *adj.2gên.* terrible; diabolic, diabolical; infernal.
INFERNO *s.f.* hell.
INFÉRTIL *adj.2gên.* infertile.
INFERTILIDADE *s.f.* infertility; unfruitfulness.
INFESTADO *adj.* infested.
INFESTAR *v.* to infest; to attack.
INFIDELIDADE *s.f.* infidelity, disloyalty.
INFIEL *s.2gên.* infidel, unbeliever / *adj.2gên.* unfaithful, dishonest.
INFILTRAÇÃO *s.f.* infiltration.
INFILTRAR *v.* to infiltrate, to filter.
INFINIDADE *s.f.* infinity, infinitude.
INFINITIVO *s.m.* infinitive mood / *adj.* infinitive.
INFINITO *s.m.* infinite, infinitive / *adj.* infinite, infinitive.
INFLAÇÃO *s.f.* inflation.
INFLADO *adj.* inflated, swollen.
INFLAMAÇÃO *s.f.* inflammation.
INFLAMADO *adj.* ablaze, aglow; exalted, sore.
INFLAMAR *v.* to inflame, to set on fire.
INFLAMÁVEL *adj.2gên.* flammable; inflammable.
INFLAR *v.* to inflate; to blow up.
INFLEXIBILIDADE *s.f.* inflexibility, rigidity.
INFLEXÍVEL *adj.2gên.* inflexible.
INFLIÇÃO *s.f.* infliction.
INFLIGIR *v.* to inflict; to penalise.
INFLUÊNCIA *s.f.* influence, importance.
INFLUENCIAR *v.* to influence.
INFLUENTE *adj.2gên.* influential, important.
INFLUENZA *s.f.* flu, grippe.
INFLUIR *v.* to flow.
INFORMAÇÃO *s.f.* information.
INFORMADO *adj.* informed, aware; noticed.
INFORMANTE *adj.2gên.* informant; informer, insider.
INFORMAR *v.* to inform; to tell, to notify.
INFORMATIVO *adj.* informative.
INFORTUNA *s.f.* misfortune, misery, unhappiness.
INFORTUNADO(A) *adj.* unhappy, miserable, wretched.

INFRAÇÃO *s.f.* infraction; violation, infringement.
INFRAESTRUTURA *s.f.* infrastructure; substructure.
INFRATOR *s.m.* infractor, infringer; violator.
INFRAVERMELHO *s.m.* infra-red / *adj.* infra-red.
INFRINGIR *v.* break; invade, infringe.
INFUNDADO *adj.* unfounded, baseless.
INFUSÃO *s.f.* infusion.
INGENUIDADE *s.f.* simplicity, ingenuity; naivety.
INGÊNUO *adj.* naive, silly, fool.
INGERIR *v.* to swallow, to ingest.
INGESTÃO *s.f.* ingestion, swallowing; intake.
INGLÓRIO *adj.* inglorious; obscure.
INGOVERNÁVEL *adj.2gên.* ungovernable; unmanageable.
INGRATIDÃO *s.f.* ingratitude.
INGRATO *s.m.* ungrateful; unthankful / *adj.* ungrateful; unthankful.
INGREDIENTE *s.m.* ingredient, material; component.
INGRESSAR *v.* to enter, to join.
INGRESSO *s.m.* entrance, admission; ticket.
INIBIÇÃO *s.f.* inhibition; embargo.
INIBIR *v.* to inhibit.
INICIAÇÃO *s.f.* initiation; beginning, start.
INICIADO *s.m.* supporter, follower / *adj.* initiate, adept.
INICIAR *v.* to start, to begin; to initiate.
INICIATIVA *s.f.* initiative; enterprise.
INÍCIO *s.m.* beginning, start; opening.
INIGUALÁVEL *adj.2gên.* unequaled, surpassing.
INIMAGINÁVEL *adj.2gên.* unthinkable; unimaginable.
INIMIGO(A) *s.m.* enemy, adversary / *adj.* inimical, averse.
INIMIZADE *s.f.* enmity, hostility.
INJEÇÃO *s.f.* injection; shot.
INJETAR *v.* to inject; to insert.
INJÚRIA *s.f.* injury; offence, insult.
INJURIAR *v.* to injure; to provoke, to insult.
INJUSTIÇA *s.f.* injustice; inequity.
INJUSTIFICÁVEL *adj.2gên.* unjustifiable.
INJUSTO *adj.* unfair, unjust.
INOBEDIÊNCIA *s.f.* disobedience.
INOCÊNCIA *s.f.* innocence.

INOCENTE *s.2gên.* child / *adj.2gên.* innocent.
INOCULAR *v.* to inoculate; to transfuse.
INOFENSIVO *adj.* inoffensive, harmless.
INOMINÁVEL *adj.2gên.* unnamable; nameless.
INOPERANTE *adj.2gên.* inoperative; inert.
INÓPIA *s.f.* poverty, penury; poorness.
INOPORTUNO *adj.* inopportune.
INORGÂNICO *adj.* inorganic.
INÓSPITO *adj.* inhospitable.
INOVAÇÃO *s.f.* innovation.
INOVADOR(A) *s.m.* innovator / *adj.* innovatory.
INOVAR *v.* to innovate.
INQUÉRITO *s.m.* inquiry, question; inquest.
INQUESTIONÁVEL *adj.2gên.* unquestionable.
INQUIETAÇÃO *s.f.* inquietude, unrest.
INQUIETANTE *adj.2gên.* disquieting, anxious.
INQUIETAR *v.* to disquiet, to disturb.
INQUIETUDE *s.f.* disquietude.
INQUILINO(A) *s.m.* tenant; renter, occupant.
INQUIRIMENTO *s.m.* inquest, inquiry.
INQUIRIR *v.* to inquire; to query.
INQUISIÇÃO *s.f.* inquisition.
INQUISIDOR *s.m.* inquisitor.
INQUISITIVO *adj.* inquisitive.
INSACIADO *adj.* insatiate.
INSACIÁVEL *adj.2gên.* insatiable; greedy.
INSALUBRE *adj.2gên.* insalubrious; unhealthy.
INSALUBRIDADE *s.f.* insalubrity.
INSÂNIA *s.f.* insanity; madness, lunacy.
INSANIDADE *s.f.* insanity.
INSANO(A) *adj.* insane, deranged; crazy.
INSATISFAÇÃO *s.f.* dissatisfaction.
INSATISFEITO(A) *adj.* dissatisfied; unsatisfied.
INSCREVER *v.* to inscribe, to register; to enlist.
INSCRIÇÃO *s.f.* inscription, registration.
INSCRITO(A) *adj.* inscribed; registered.
INSECÁVEL *adj.2gên.* undryable.
INSEGURANÇA *s.f.* insecurity; unsafeness.
INSEGURO(A) *adj.* unsafe, insecure; unsure.
INSEMINAÇÃO *s.f.* insemination.
INSENSATEZ *s.f.* insanity, madness; stupidity.

INSENSATO(A) *adj.* insensate; unwise, foolish.
INSENSIBILIDADE *s.f.* insensibility; callousness.
INSENSIBILIZAR *v.* to insensibilise; to deaden.
INSENSÍVEL *adj.2gên.* insensible; insensitive.
INSERIR *v.* to insert, to put in.
INSETICIDA *s.m.* insecticide / *adj.2gên.* insecticidal.
INSETO *s.m.* insect.
INSIGNIFICANTE *s.2gên.* insignificant / *adj.2gên.* insignificant, unimportant.
INSIGNIFICATIVO(A) *adj.* insignificant; meaningless.
INSINUAÇÃO *s.f.* insinuation; hint, suggestion.
INSINUANTE *adj.2gên.* insinuating, insinuative.
INSINUAR *v.* to insinuate; to suggest.
INSISTÊNCIA *s.f.* insistence; persistence.
INSISTIR *v.* to insist; to persist.
INSOLAÇÃO *s.f.* insolation.
INSOLÊNCIA *s.f.* insolence, impertinence.
INSOLENTE *adj.2gên.* insolent, impertinent; arrogant.
INSONE *adj.2gên.* wakeful.
INSÔNIA *s.f.* insomnia; sleepless.
INSPEÇÃO *s.f.* inspection.
INSPECIONAR *v.* to inspect; to examine.
INSPETOR(A) *s.m.* inspector; supervisor.
INSPIRAÇÃO *s.f.* inspiration.
INSPIRAR *v.* to inspire; to breath.
INSTABILIDADE *s.f.* instability, inconstancy.
INSTALAÇÃO *s.f.* installation; accomodation.
INSTALAR *v.* to instal; to set up.
INSTÂNCIA *s.f.* instance;
INSTANTANEIDADE *s.f.* instantaneity.
INSTANTÂNEO *adj.* instantaneous, immediate; momentary.
INSTANTE *s.m.* instant, moment / *adj.2gên.* instant, urgent.
INSTAURAÇÃO *s.f.* instauration; establishment.
INSTAURADOR(A) *s.m.* establisher, restorer; renewer.
INSTAURAR *v.* to begin, to initiate; to establish.
INSTÁVEL *adj.2gên.* unstable; changeable.
INSTIGAÇÃO *s.f.* instigation; inducement.
INSTIGADO *adj.* instigated.

INSTIGAR v. to instigate, to incite; to set on.
INSTINTO s.m. instinct, intuition.
INSTINTIVO(A) adj. instinctive; intuitive.
INSTITUIÇÃO s.f. institution; foundation.
INSTITUIR v. to institute, to found.
INSTITUTO s.m. institute, institution.
INSTRUÇÃO s.f. education; instruction.
INSTRUÍDO(A) adj. trained; learned, informed.
INSTRUIR v. to instruct; to train, to educate.
INSTRUMENTAL s.m. instrumental / adj.2gên. instrumental.
INSTRUMENTO s.m. instrument; tool, apparatus.
INSTRUTIVO adj. instructive, didactic.
INSTRUTOR s.m. instructor; trainer, coach.
INSUBMISSÃO s.f. disobedience.
INSUBMISSO(A) adj. ungovernable; unruly, refractory.
INSUBORDINAÇÃO s.f. insubordination; rebellion.
INSUBORDINAR v. to revolt; to rebel.
INSUBORNÁVEL adj.2gên. unbriable; clean-fingered.
INSUBSTITUÍVEL adj.2gên. irreplaceable.
INSUFICIÊNCIA s.f. insufficiency; failure, deffect.
INSUFICIENTE adj.2gên. inadequate, insufficient.
INSUFLAR v. to insufflate.
INSULINA s.f. insulin.
INSULTADO(A) adj. insulted, offended.
INSULTANTE adj.2gên. abusive, offending, insulting.
INSULTAR v. to insult, to offend; to affront.
INSULTO s.m. insult; offence, abuse.
INSUPERÁVEL adj.2gên. insuperable, surpassing.
INSUPORTÁVEL adj.2gên. unbearable, intolerable; unendurable.
INSURGENTE s.2gên. insurgent; rebel / adj.2gên. insurgent; rebel.
INSURGIR v. to revolt, to rebel; to rise against.
INSURREIÇÃO s.f. insurrection, uprising; rebellion.
INSUSTENTÁVEL adj.2gên. untenable, unbearable; unsupportable.
INTACTO adj. intact; untouched, entire.
ÍNTEGRA s.f. totality, completeness; entireness.
INTEGRAÇÃO s.f. integration.

INTEGRAL adj.2gên. whole, integral.
INTEGRANTE adj.2gên. integrant; integral.
INTEGRIDADE s.f. integrity; entirety; honesty.
ÍNTEGRO adj. integrate, incorruptible; straightforward.
INTEIRADO adj. aware; informed, initiate.
INTEIRAR v. to entire, to complete.
INTEIRO adj. all, entire, full; total.
INTELECTO s.m. intellect; mind, brain.
INTELECTUAL s.2gên. intellectual, scholar / adj.2gên. intellectual, intelligent.
INTELECTUALISMO s.m. intellectualism.
INTELIGÊNCIA s.f. intelligence.
INTELIGENTE adj.2gên. intelligent, smart; clever.
INTELIGÍVEL adj.2gên. intelligible, clear.
INTENÇÃO s.f. intent, intent; aim, purpose.
INTENCIONAL adj.2gên. intentional, calculated; intended.
INTENSIDADE s.f. intensity, magnitude.
INTENSIFICAÇÃO s.f. intensification; escalation.
INTENSIFICAR v. to intensify, to exalt.
INTENSIVO adj. intensive.
INTENSO adj. intense, profound.
INTERAÇÃO s.f. interaction.
INTERCALADO adj. intercalary.
INTERCALAR v. to intercalate; to insert, to put in.
INTERCÂMBIO s.m. exchange, interchange; trade.
INTERCAMBIAR v. to exchange, to trade.
INTERCEPTAR v. to intercept; to interrupt.
INTERDIÇÃO s.f. prohibition, interdict.
INTERDITAR v. to interdict, to stop; to prohibit.
INTERESSADO adj. interested; concerned.
INTERESSANTE adj.2gên. interesting; concerning.
INTERESSAR v. to interest, to concern.
INTERESSE s.m. interest; concern.
INTERFERÊNCIA s.f. interference.
INTERFERENTE adj.2gên. interfering, interferential.
INTERFERIR v. to interfere.
INTERINO adj. interim; acting, provisional.
INTERIOR adj. inner, internal, inside / s.m. inland, interior; countryside.
INTERJEIÇÃO s.f. interjection.
INTERLOCUÇÃO s.f. interlocution.
INTERLOCUTOR(A) s.m. interlocutor.
INTERMEDIAR v. to intermediate.

INTERMEDIÁRIO *s.m.* intermediate, intermediary; middle / *adj.* intermediate, intermediary; middle.
INTERMÉDIO *s.m.* medium, intervention / *adj.* middle, intermediate.
INTERMINÁVEL *adj.2gên.* endless, unending; interminable.
INTERMITÊNCIA *s.f.* intermittence; interval.
INTERMITENTE *adj.2gên.* intermittent; periodical.
INTERNAÇÃO *s.f.* internment, confinement; admission.
INTERNACIONAL *adj.2gên.* international.
INTERNAR *v.* to intern.
INTERNO *s.m.* student / *adj.* internal; inner, inside.
INTERPRETAÇÃO *s.f.* interpretation, understanding.
INTERPRETAR *v.* to interpret.
INTÉRPRETE *s.2gên.* interpreter.
INTERROGAR *v.* to interrogate; to quest, to ask.
INTERROMPER *v.* to interrupt.
INTERRUPÇÃO *s.f.* interruption.
INTERVALO *s.m.* interval, break; gap, distance.
INTERVENÇÃO *s.f.* intervention, interference.
INTESTINO *s.m.* intestine.
INTIMAÇÃO *s.f.* intimation, demand; ultimatum.
INTIMAR *v.* to summon; to cite, to evoke.
INTIMIDAÇÃO *s.f.* intimidation.
INTIMIDADE *s.f.* intimacy.
INTIMIDAR *v.* to intimidate.
ÍNTIMO *adj.* intimate, familiar; confidential, secret.
INTITULAÇÃO *s.f.* naming; entitling.
INTITULAR *v.* to entitle; to address.
INTOCÁVEL *adj.2gên.* untouchable.
INTOLERÂNCIA *s.f.* intolerance, impatience.
INTOLERANTE *adj.2gên.* intolerant, impatient.
INTONAÇÃO *s.f.* intonation.
INTOXICAR *v.* to intoxicate, to poison.
INTRIGA *s.f.* intrigue.
INTUIÇÃO *s.f.* intuition.
INÚTIL *adj.2gên.* useless, futile, vain / *s.2gên.* worthless person.
INVADIR *v.* to invade.
INVEJA *s.f.* envy.
INVEJOSO *adj.* envious.
INVENÇÃO *s.f.* invention.
INVENTAR *v.* to invent.
INVENTOR *s.m.* inventor; author; discoverer, finder.
INVERNO *s.m.* winter.
IR *v.* to go.
IRA *s.f.* anger, rage.
IRMÃ *s.f.* sister.
IRMÃO *s.m.* brother.
IRONIA *s.f.* irony.
IRÔNICO *adj.* ironic.
IRRITADO *adj.* angry, peeved.
IRRITAR *v.* to irritate.
ITINERÁRIO *s.m.* itinerary.

J, j *s.m.* the tenth letter of the Portuguese alphabet.
JÁ *adv.* already / *conj.* now.
JABÁ *s.m.* dried meat.
JABACULÊ *s.m.* money; tip.
JACA *s.f.* jack fruit.
JACARANDÁ *s.m.* rosewood.
JACARÉ *s.m.* alligator.
JACENTE *adj.2gên.* recumbent.
JACTAÇÃO *s.f.* jactitation.
JACTÂNCIA *s.f.* vanity.
JACULAR *v.* to jaculate, to throw.
JADE *s.m.* jade.
JAGUAR *s.m.* jaguar.
JAGUNÇO *s.m.* gunman.
JALECO *s.m.* short coat.
JALOFO *adj.* rude, barbariac.
JAMAICA *s.f.* Jamaica.
JAMAICANO *s.m.* Jamaican / *adj.* Jamaican.
JAMAIS *adv.* never.
JAMANTA *s.f.* devilfish; unkempt person.
JAMELÃO *s.m.* jambolan.
JANEIRO *s.m.* January
JANELA *s.f.* window.
JANGADA *s.f.* raft, float.
JANGADEIRO *s.m.* raftsman.
JANOTA *adj.2gên.* coxcomb, dude.
JANSENISTA *s.2gên.* Jansenist.
JANTA *s.f.* dinner.
JANTAR *s.m.* dinner / *v.* to dine.
JAPÃO *s.m.* Japan.
JAPECANGA *s.f.* sarsaparilla.
JAPONA *s.f.* jacket.
JAPONÊS *s.m.* Japanese / *adj.* Japanese.
JAQUETA *s.f.* jacket.
JARDA *s.f.* yard.
JARDIM *s.m.* garden.
JARDIM BOTÂNICO *s.m.* botanical garden.
JARDIM DE INFÂNCIA *s.m.* kindergarten.
JARDINAGEM *s.f.* gardening.
JARDINAR *v.* to garden, to cultivate.
JARDINEIRA *s.f.* jardiniere, ornamental plant pot.
JARDINEIRO(A) *s.m.* gardener.
JARGÃO *s.m.* slang.
JARRA *s.f.* vase, flowerpot.
JARRO *s.m.* jug.
JASMIM *s.m.* jasmine, jasmin.

JATO s.m. jet.
JAULA s.f. cage.
JAVALI s.m. boar, wild pig.
JAVANÊS s.m. Javanese.
JAZER v. to rest.
JAZIDA s.f. resting-place.
JAZIGO s.m. grave.
JAZZ s.m. jazz.
JAZZISTA s.2gên. jazzman.
JECA s.2gên. rube, rustic fellow, countryman / adj.2gên. clumsy, rustic.
JEGUE s.m. donkey.
JEITO s.m. way; aptitude, talent.
JEITOSO adj. skillful, handy.
JEJUAR v. to fast.
JEJUM s.m. fast, fasting.
JEJUNO s.m. jejunum.
JEOVÁ s.m. Jehovah.
JERIMUM s.m. pumpkin.
JERRA s.f. picnic.
JERUSALÉM s.f. Jerusalem.
JESUÍTA s.m. Jesuit.
JESUÍTICO adj. Jesuitic, Jesuitical.
JIBOIA s.f. boa constrictor.
JIBOIAR v. to digest while at rest.
JINGOÍSMO s.m. jingoism.
JINGOÍSTA s.2gên. jingoist.
JIPE s.m. jeep.
JOALHEIRO s.m. jeweller.
JOALHERIA s.f. jewellery.
JOANETE s.m. bunion.
JOANINHA s.f. ladybug.
JOCOSO adj. jocose.
JOELHEIRA s.f. kneepad.
JOELHO s.m. knee.
JOGADA s.f. move, throw, hit.
JOGADO adj. prostrate, abandoned; played.
JOGADOR(A) s.m. player.
JOGAR v. to play; to throw.
JOGO s.m. play, game.
JOGRAL s.m. jester; troubadour.
JOGUETE s.m. toy, plaything.
JOIA s.f. jewel.
JOIO s.m. darnel.
JÓQUEI s.m. jockey.
JORDÂNIA s.f. Jordan.
JORNADA s.f. journey; trip.
JORNAL s.m. newspaper.
JORNALEIRO s.m. newsboy, day labourer.
JORNALISMO s.m. journalism.

JORNALISTA s.2gên. journalist.
JORNALÍSTICO adj. journalistic.
JORRAR v. to spout out, to gush.
JOVEM adj.2gên. young / s.2gên. young person.
JOVIAL adj.2gên. jovial, merry, jolly.
JOVIALIDADE s.f. joviality.
JUBA s.f. mane.
JUBILAÇÃO s.f. jubilation, exultation; retirement.
JUBILADO adj. retired.
JUBILAR v. to jubilate, to exult.
JUBILEU s.m. jubilee.
JÚBILO s.m. jubilation, satisfaction.
JUCUNDO adj. jocund, cheerful.
JUDAICO adj. Judaic.
JUDAÍSMO s.m. Judaism.
JUDEU s.m. Jew / adj. Jew.
JUDIAR v. to torment, to mistreat.
JUDICIAL adj.2gên. judicial.
JUDICIÁRIO adj. judiciary, judicial.
JUDÔ s.m. judo.
JUDOCA s.2gên. judoka.
JUDOÍSTA s.2gên. judoist.
JUGA s.f. peak, top.
JUGULAR s.f. jugular.
JUIZ(ÍZA) s.m. judge; referee, umpire.
JUIZADO s.m. court.
JUÍZO s.m. judgment; wits, sense.
JULGADO adj. judged, sentenced.
JULGAMENTO s.m. judgement, trial.
JULGAR v. to judge; to think.
JULHO s.m. July.
JUMENTO s.m. donkey.
JUNÇA s.f. sedge.
JUNÇÃO s.f. junction; union.
JUNCAR v. to bestrew, to cover.
JUNCO s.m. bulrush, cattail.
JUNHO s.m. June.
JÚNIOR adj. junior, younger.
JUNQUILHO s.m. jonquil.
JUNTA s.f. joint; committee.
JUNTAMENTE adv. along, togheter.
JUNTAR v. to join, to connect.
JUNTIVO s.m. juncture.
JUNTO adj. near, joined / adv. togheter, near.
JUNTURA s.f. junction; joint.
JÚPITER s.m. Jupiter.
JURA s.f. oath, vow.

JURADO *s.m.* jury, juryman.
JURAMENTADO *adj.* sword in, authenticated.
JURAMENTAR *v.* to pledge.
JURAMENTO *s.m.* oath, vow.
JURAR *v.* to swear, to promise.
JURÁSSICO *adj.* Jurassic.
JURATÓRIO *adj.* juratory.
JÚRI *s.m.* jury.
JURÍDICO *adj.* juridical, legal.
JURISDIÇÃO *s.f.* jurisdiction; authority, power; district.
JURISPRUDÊNCIA *s.f.* jurisprudence.
JURISPRUDENTE *s.2gên.* jurisprudent.
JURISTA *s.2gên.* jurist, lawyer.
JURO *s.m.* interest; compensation, reward.
JUS *s.m.* right.
JUSTA *s.f.* joust, tourney.
JUSTAPOR *v.* to overlap, to juxtapose.
JUSTAPOSIÇÃO *s.f.* juxtaposition, contiguity.
JUSTIÇA *s.f.* justice.
JUSTIÇAR *v.* to execute.
JUSTICEIRO *adj.* righteous.
JUSTIFICAÇÃO *s.f.* justification, excuse.
JUSTIFICAR *v.* to justify.
JUSTIFICÁVEL *adj.2gên.* justifiable.
JUSTILHO *s.m.* jerkin.
JUSTO *s.m.* fair person / *adj.* fair, just, right.
JUVENIL *adj.2gên.* juvenile, young.
JUVENTUDE *s.f.* youth, young people.

K

K, k *s.m.* the eleventh letter of the Portuguese alphabet.
KABUQUI *s.m.* kabuki.
KAFKIANO *adj.* Kafkaesque.
KAISER *s.m.* kaiser, emperor.
KAMIKAZE *s.m.* kamikaze.
KANTISMO *s.m.* Kantianism, Kantism.
KANTISTA *s.2gên.* Kantian, Kantist / *adj.2gên.* Kantian.
KARAOKE *s.m.* karaoke.
KARDECISMO *s.m.* Kardecism.
KARDECISTA *adj.2gên.* Kardecist / *s.2gên.* Kardecist.
KART *s.m.* kart, go-kart.
KARTISMO *s.m.* karting.
KARTISTA *s.2gên.* karter.
KARTÓDROMO *s.m.* kart track.
KC *abrev.* kilocycle.
KEPLERIANO *adj.* Keplerian.
KETCHUP *s.m.* ketchup, catsup.
KG *abrev.* kilogram.
KHZ *abrev.* kilohertz.
KIBUTZ *s.m.* kibbutz.
KICK BOXING *s.m.* kick boxing.
KILT *s.m.* kilt.
KIMBERLITO *s.m.* kimberlite.
KIRSCH *s.m.* kirsch.
KIT *s.m.* kit.
KITCHENETTE *s.f.* kitchenette, studio flat, studio apartment.
KITSCH *adj.2gên.* kitsch.
KIWI *s.m.* kiwi.
KL *abrev.* kiloliter.
KM *abrev.* kilometer.
KM^2 *abrev.* square kilometer.
KM^3 *abrev.* cubic kilometer.
KR *abrev.* krypton.
KÜMMEL *s.m.* kümmel.
KUWAITIANO *adj.* Kuwaiti / *s.m.* Kuwaiti.
KV *abrev.* kilovolt.
KW *abrev.* kilowatt.
KWH *abrev.* kilowatt-hour.
KYRIE *s.m.* kyrie.

Ll

L, l *s.m.* the twelfth letter of the Portuguese alphabet.
LÁ *adv.* there, over there.
LÃ *s.f.* wool.
LABAREDA *s.f.* blaze.
LÁBARO *s.m.* standard, flag.
LÁBIA *s.f.* patter, pitch.
LABIAL *adj.2gên.* labial.
LÁBIO *s m.* lip.
LABIRINTITE *s.f.* labyrinthitis.
LABIRINTO *s.m.* labyrinth, maze.
LABORATÓRIO *s.m.* laboratory, lab.
LABORIOSO(A) *adj.* laborious, difficult.
LABUTA *s.f.* drudgery.
LACA *s.f.* lac; shellac.
LAÇADA *s.f.* bowknot.
LAÇADO(A) *adj.* laced, tied.
LACAIO *s.m.* lackey.
LAÇAR *v.* to bind, to lace.
LACERAÇÃO *s.f.* laceration.
LACERANTE *adj.2gên.* dilacerating.
LAÇO *s.m.* bowknot.
LACÔNICO(A) *adj.* laconic, concise.
LACRADO(A) *adj.* sealed.
LACRAIA *s.f.* centipede.
LACRAR *v.* to seal; to plumb.
LACRE *s.m.* seal, sealing wax.
LACRIMAL *adj.2gên.* lacrimal.
LACRIMEJAR *v.* to shed tears.
LACRIMOGÊNEO(A) *adj.* lacrimating.
LACRIMOSO(A) *adj.* tearful.
LACTANTE *adj.2gên.* nursing.
LÁCTEO(A) *adj.* milky.
LACTOBACILO *s.m.* lactobacillus.
LACTOSE *s.f.* lactose.
LACUNA *s.f.* gap.
LACUSTRE *adj.2gên.* lacustrine.
LADAINHA *s.f.* litany.
LADEAR *v.* to hedge; to skirt.
LADEIRA *s.f.* slope.
LADINO(A) *adj.* foxy, astute.
LADO *s.m.* side.
LADRÃO(DRA) *s.m.* thief, robber.
LADRAR *v.* to bark.
LADRILHAR *v.* to tile.
LADRILHEIRO(A) *s.m.* tilemaker.
LADRILHO *s.m.* tile.
LAGARTA *s.f.* caterpillar.

LAGARTIXA *s.f.* gecko.
LAGARTO *s.m.* lizard.
LAGO *s.m.* lake.
LAGOA *s.f.* pond.
LAGOSTA *s.f.* lobster.
LAGOSTIM *s.m.* crayfish.
LÁGRIMA *s.f.* tear.
LAGUNA *s.f.* lagoon.
LAIA *s.f.* kind, sort.
LAICO(A) *adj.* lay.
LAJE *s.f.* flagstone.
LAJEADO *s.m.* slab covering.
LAJEAR *v.* to pave.
LAMA *s.f.* mud.
LAMAÇAL *s.m.* marsh.
LAMACENTO(A) *adj.* muddy.
LAMBADA *s.f.* lambada; stroke.
LAMBER *v.* to lick.
LAMBIDA *s.f.* lick.
LAMBISGOIA *s.2gên.* meddler.
LAMBRETA *s.f.* scooter.
LAMBUJA *s.f.* advantage.
LAMBUZADO(A) *adj.* smeared.
LAMBUZAR *v.* to slather, to smear.
LAMENTAR *v.* to lament, to regret.
LAMENTÁVEL *adj.2gên.* tragic; regrettable.
LAMENTO *s.m.* lamentation.
LAMENTOSO(A) *adj.* lamentable, sad.
LÂMINA *s.f.* sheet; blade.
LAMINADO(A) *adj.* laminated / *s.m.* laminate.
LAMINAR *v.* to laminate.
LÂMPADA *s.f.* lamp.
LAMPARINA *s.f.* oil lamp.
LAMPEJANTE *adj.2gên.* sparkling.
LAMPEJAR *v.* to sparkle.
LAMPEJO *s.m.* sparkle, glitter.
LAMPIÃO *s.m.* gas lamp.
LAMPREIA *s.f.* lamprey.
LAMÚRIA *s.f.* complaint; whimpering.
LANÇA *s.f.* spear.
LANÇA-CHAMAS *s.m.* flamethrower.
LANÇADEIRA *s.f.* sewing shuttle.
LANÇADOR(A) *s.m.* thrower.
LANÇAMENTO *s.m.* throwing, launching.
LANÇAR *v.* to throw; to release.
LANCE *s.m.* bid; stile; throwing.
LANCHA *s.f.* launch, motor-boat.
LANCHAR *v.* to snack.
LANCHE *s.m.* snack.
LANCHEIRA *s.f.* lunchbox.
LANCHONETE *s.f.* diner, cafeteria, café.
LANCINANTE *adj.2gên.* lancinating.
LANCINAR *v.* to pierce.
LANGUIDEZ *s.f.* languidness.
LÂNGUIDO(A) *adj.* languid.
LANOLINA *s.f.* lanolin.
LANTEJOULA *s.f.* sequin.
LANTERNA *s.f.* lantern, flashlight.
LANTERNINHA *s.2gên.* usher / *s.f.* small lantern.
LAPA *s.f.* limpet; slap; shelter.
LAPADA *s.f.* beating, lashing.
LAPÃO *s.m.* boor, churl.
LAPELA *s.f.* lapel, buttonhole.
LAPIDAÇÃO *s.f.* lapidation.
LAPIDADOR *s.m.* lapidary.
LAPIDAR *v.* to polish; to educate.
LÁPIDE *s.f.* gravestone.
LÁPIS *s.m.* pencil.
LAPISEIRA *s.f.* mechanical pencil.
LAPSO *s.m.* lapse.
LAQUÊ *s.m.* hairspray.
LAQUEADO(A) *adj.* lacquered.
LAQUEADURA *s.f.* tubal ligation.
LAR *s.m.* home.
LARANJA *s.f.* orange / *adj.2gên.* orange.
LARANJADA *s.f.* orangeade.
LARANJAL *s.m.* orangery.
LARANJEIRA *s.f.* orange tree.
LARÁPIO(A) *adj. s.m.* filcher.
LAREIRA *s.f.* fireplace.
LARGADA *s.f.* start.
LARGADO(A) *adj.* abandoned; careless.
LARGAR *v.* to release.
LARGO(A) *adj.* wide.
LARGURA *s.f.* width.
LARINGE *s.f.* larynx.
LARINGITE *s.f.* laryngitis.
LARVA *s.f.* grub.
LASANHA *s.f.* lasagna.
LASCA *s.f.* splinter.
LASCADO(A) *adj.* cracked, fudged.
LASCAR *v.* to splinter, to crack.
LASCIVO(A) *adj.* lascivious.
LÁSTIMA *s.f.* pity.
LASTIMAR *v.* to lament.
LASTIMÁVEL *adj.2gên.* regrettable.
LASTRAR *v.* to ballast.
LASTRO *s.m.* ballast.
LATA *s.f.* can.

LATÃO *s.m.* brass.
LATARIA *s.f.* bodywork.
LATEJANTE *adj.2gên.* pulsing.
LATEJAR *v.* to pulse.
LATÊNCIA *s.f.* latency.
LATENTE *adj.2gên.* latent.
LATERAL *s.f.* sideline / *adj.2gên.* lateral.
LÁTEX *s.m.* latex.
LATICÍNIO *s.m.* dairy.
LÁTICO(A) *adj.* lactic.
LATIDO *s.m.* barking.
LATIFUNDIÁRIO(A) *s.m.* landowner.
LATIFÚNDIO *s.m.* estate.
LATIM *s.m.* Latin.
LATINO(A) *adj.* Latin.
LATINO-AMERICANO(A) *adj.* Latin American.
LATIR *v.* to bark.
LATITUDE *s.f.* latitude.
LATITUDINAL *adj.2gên.* latitudinal.
LATRINA *s.f.* latrine.
LATROCÍNIO *s.f.* armed robbery.
LAUDA *s.f.* laud; page.
LAUDO *s.m.* appraisal; report.
LÁUREA *s.f.* laurel.
LAUREAR *v.* to praise; to reward.
LAVA *s.f.* lava.
LAVABO *s.m.* washbasin.
LAVADA *s.f.* blowout; whitewash.
LAVADEIRA *s.f.* laundry worker.
LAVADORA *s.f.* washing machine.
LAVAGEM *s.f.* wash, laundry.
LAVA-LOUÇAS *s.m.* dishwasher.
LAVANDA *s.f.* lavender.
LAVANDERIA *s.f.* laundry; laundry room.
LAVAR *v.* to wash.
LAVA-RÁPIDO *s.m.* car wash.
LAVATÓRIO *s.m.* lavatory; washstand.
LAVÁVEL *adj.2gên.* washable.
LAVOURA *s.f.* farming; tillage.
LAVRADOR(A) *s.m.* tiller, farmer.
LAVRAR *v.* to till, to cultivate.
LAXANTE *adj.2gên.* laxative / *s.m.* laxative.
LAZARENTO *s.m.* lazar, leprous.
LAZER *s.m.* leisure.
LEAL *adj.2gên.* loyal.
LEALDADE *s.f.* loyalty.
LEÃO *s.m.* lion; Leo.
LEÃO-MARINHO *s.m.* sea lion.
LEBRÃO *s.m.* male hare.
LEBRE *s.f.* hare.

LECIONAR *v.* to teach, to lecture.
LEDO(A) *adj.* joyful, merry.
LEGADO *s.m.* legacy.
LEGAL *adj.2gên.* nice, cool.
LEGALIDADE *s.f.* legality.
LEGALIZAÇÃO *s.f.* legalization.
LEGALIZAR *v.* to legalize.
LEGENDA *s.f.* subtitle; legend.
LEGENDAGEM *s.f.* subtitling.
LEGENDAR *v.* to subtitle.
LEGENDÁRIO(A) *adj.* legendary.
LEGIÃO *s.f.* legion.
LEGIONÁRIO(A) *adj.* legionary.
LEGISLAÇÃO *s.f.* legislation.
LEGISLADOR(A) *adj.* legislating / *s.m.* legislator.
LEGISLATIVO(A) *adj.* legislative.
LEGISLATURA *s.f.* legislature.
LEGISTA *s.2gên.* jurist; coroner.
LEGITIMAR *v.* to legitimate.
LEGÍTIMO(A) *adj.* legitimate.
LEGÍVEL *adj.2gên.* legible, readable.
LÉGUA *s.f.* league.
LEGUME *s.m.* vegetable.
LEGUMINOSA *s.f.* leguminous plant.
LEI *s.f.* law.
LEIAUTE *s.m.* layout.
LEIGO(A) *adj.* lay.
LEILÃO *s.m.* auction.
LEILOAR *v.* to auction.
LEILOEIRO(A) *s.m.* auctioneer.
LEITÃO *s.m.* piggy
LEITE *s.m.* milk.
LEITEIRA *s.f.* milk can.
LEITEIRO(A) *s.m.* milkman.
LEITO *s.m.* bed, berth.
LEITOR(A) *s.m.* reader.
LEITORADO *s.m.* readership.
LEITOSO(A) *adj.* milky.
LEITURA *s.f.* reading.
LELÉ *adj.2gên.* loony, cuckoo.
LEMA *s.m.* motto.
LEMBRANÇA *s.f.* souvenir, gift.
LEMBRAR *v.* to remember; to remind.
LEMBRETE *s.m.* reminder, note.
LEME *s.m.* rudder, helm.
LÊMURE *s.m.* lemur.
LENÇO *s.m.* handkerchief.
LENÇOL *s.m.* sheet.
LENDA *s.f.* legend.

LENDÁRIO(A) *adj.* legendary.
LÊNDEA *s.f.* nit.
LENHA *s.f.* firewood.
LENHADOR(A) *s.m.* woodcutter.
LENTE *s.f.* lens.
LENTIDÃO *s.f.* slowness.
LENTILHA *s.f.* lentil.
LENTO *adj.* slow.
LEOPARDO *s.m.* leopard.
LEPORINO(A) *adj.* leporine.
LEPRA *s.f.* leprosy.
LEPROSO(A) *adj.* leprous.
LEPTOSPIROSE *s.f.* leptospirosis.
LEQUE *s.m.* fan.
LER *v.* to read.
LERDEZA *s.f.* sluggishness.
LERDO(A) *adj.* slow, dull.
LERO-LERO *s.m.* twaddle.
LESADO(A) *adj.* damaged.
LESÃO *s.f.* lesion, wound.
LESAR *v.* to injure.
LÉSBICA *s.f.* lesbian.
LESEIRA *s.f.* laziness.
LESIONAR *v.* to injure, to wound.
LESMA *s.f.* slug.
LESTE *s.m.* east.
LETAL *adj.2gên.* lethal.
LETARGIA *s.f.* lethargy.
LETÁRGICO(A) *adj.* lethargic.
LETRA *s.f.* letter.
LETRADO(A) *adj.* literate.
LETREIRO *s.m.* placard, sign.
LETRISTA *s.2gên.* lyricist; sign painter.
LÉU *s.m.* leisure, idleness.
LEUCEMIA *s.f.* leukemia.
LEUCÓCITO *s.m.* leukocyte.
LEVA *s.f.* batch; group.
LEVADA *s.f.* leat, sluice; slope.
LEVADIÇO(A) *adj.* moveable, raiseable.
LEVADO(A) *adj.* mischievous, naughty.
LEVANTAMENTO *s.m.* lifting; survey.
LEVANTAR *v.* to raise, to lift.
LEVAR *v.* to take.
LEVE *adj.2gên.* light.
LÊVEDO *s.m.* yeast.
LEVEDURA *s.f.* leaven, yeast.
LEVEZA *s.f.* lightness, delicacy.
LEVIANO(A) *adj.* frivolous.
LEVITAÇÃO *s.f.* levitation.
LEVITAR *v.* to levitate.

LÉXICO *s.m.* lexicon.
LEXICOGRAFIA *s.f.* lexicography.
LEXICÓLOGO(A) *s.m.* lexicologist.
LHAMA *s.f.* llama.
LHE *pron.* her; him; it.
LIBÉLULA *s.f.* dragonfly.
LIBERAÇÃO *s.f.* liberation; release.
LIBERADO(A) *adj.* released.
LIBERAL *adj.2gên.* liberal.
LIBERAR *v.* to discharge; to release.
LIBERDADE *s.f.* freedom, liberty.
LÍBERO *s.m.* libero.
LIBERTAÇÃO *s.f.* liberation, release.
LIBERTADOR(A) *adj.* liberating / *s.m.* liberator.
LIBERTAR *v.* to liberate.
LIBERTÁRIO(A) *adj.* libertarian.
LIBERTINAGEM *s.f.* lewdness.
LIBERTINO(A) *adj.* libertine.
LIBERTO(A) *adj.* freed, unstuck.
LIBIDINAGEM *s.f.* lustfulness.
LIBIDO *s.f.* libido.
LIBRA *s.f.* Libra; pound.
LIBRETO *s.m.* libretto, book.
LIÇÃO *s.f.* lesson; homework.
LICENÇA *s.f.* license.
LICENCIADO(A) *adj.* licensed, licenciated.
LICENCIAMENTO *s.m.* licensing, permission.
LICENCIAR *v.* to license, to permit.
LICENCIATURA *s.f.* bachelor's degree.
LICEU *s.m.* lyceum.
LICHIA *s.f.* litchi.
LICITAÇÃO *s.f.* bid; licitation.
LICITAR *v.* to bid.
LÍCITO(A) *adj.* licit; lawful.
LICOR *s.m.* liqueur.
LIDA *s.f.* drudgery.
LIDAR *v.* to deal.
LÍDER *s.2gên.* leader.
LIDERANÇA *s.f.* leadership.
LIDERAR *v.* to lead.
LIGA *s.f.* league.
LIGAÇÃO *s.f.* connection, relation.
LIGADO(A) *adj.* connected; on.
LIGADURA *s.f.* ligature; bandage.
LIGAMENTO *s.m.* ligament.
LIGAR *v.* to bind, to join, to connect.
LIGEIRO(A) *adj.* quick, fast.
LILÁS *adj.2gên.* lilac / *s.m.* lilac.

LIMA *s.f.* sweet lime; file.
LIMAGEM *s.f.* filing.
LIMALHA *s.f.* filings, file dust.
LIMÃO *s.m.* lemon.
LIMAR *v.* to file.
LIMBO *s.m.* limb; edge.
LIMEIRA *s.f.* sweet lime tree.
LIMIAR *s.m.* threshold.
LIMINAR *adj.2gên.* preliminary.
LIMITAÇÃO *s.f.* limitation.
LIMITADO(A) *adj.* limited.
LIMITANTE *adj.2gên.* limiting.
LIMITAR *v.* to limit; to restrict.
LIMITE *s.m.* limit.
LIMÍTROFE *adj.2gên.* bordering.
LIMOEIRO *s.m.* lime tree.
LIMONADA *s.f.* lemonade.
LIMPA *s.f.* cleaning.
LIMPADOR(A) *s.m.* cleaner.
LIMPAR *v.* to clean, to cleanse.
LIMPA-VIDROS *s.m.* glass cleaner.
LIMPEZA *s.f.* cleansing, cleaning.
LÍMPIDO(A) *adj.* limpid, clear.
LIMPO(A) *adj.* clean.
LIMUSINE *s.f.* limousine, limo.
LINCE *s.m.* lynx; bobcat.
LINCHAMENTO *s.m.* lynching.
LINCHAR *v.* to lynch.
LINDO(A) *adj.* beautiful; handsome.
LINEAR *adj.2gên.* linear.
LINEARIDADE *s.f.* linearity.
LINFA *s.f.* lymph.
LINFÁTICO(A) *adj.* lymphatic.
LINFOMA *s.m.* lymphoma.
LÍNGUA *s.f.* tongue; language.
LINGUADO *s.m.* flatfish, flounder.
LINGUAGEM *s.f.* language.
LINGUAJAR *s.m.* talk; dialect.
LINGUARUDO(A) *adj.* slanderous / *s.m.* chatterbox.
LINGUIÇA *s.f.* sausage.
LINGUISTA *s.2gên.* linguist.
LINGUÍSTICA *s.f.* linguistics.
LINGUÍSTICO(A) *adj.* linguistic.
LINHA *s.f.* line; thread.
LINHAÇA *s.f.* linseed.
LINHA-DURA *s.2gên.* hard liner / *adj.2gên.* severe.
LINHAGEM *s.f.* lineage.
LINHO *s.m.* linen, flax.

LINÓLEO *s.m.* linoleum.
LIPÍDIO *s.m.* lipid.
LIPOASPIRAÇÃO *s.f.* liposuction.
LIQUEFAÇÃO *s.f.* liquefaction.
LÍQUEN *s.m.* lichen.
LIQUIDAÇÃO *s.f.* sale; liquidation.
LIQUIDAR *v.* to liquidate.
LIQUIDEZ *s.f.* liquidity.
LIQUIDIFICADOR *s.m.* blender.
LÍQUIDO *adj.* liquid / *s.m.* liquid.
LIRA *s.f.* lyre.
LÍRICA *s.f.* lyric poem.
LÍRICO(A) *adj.* lyrical.
LÍRIO *s.m.* lily.
LIRISMO *s.m.* lyricism.
LISO(A) *adj.* smooth.
LISONJEADO(A) *adj.* flattered.
LISONJEAR *v.* to flatter.
LISTA *s.f.* list, roll.
LISTADO(A) *adj.* listed.
LISTAGEM *s.f.* listing.
LISTRA *s.f.* stripe.
LISTRADO(A) *adj.* striped.
LISTRAR *v.* to stripe.
LITERAL *adj.2gên.* literal.
LITERÁRIO(A) *adj.* literary.
LITERATURA *s.f.* literature.
LITIGANTE *adj.2gên.* litigant.
LITIGAR *v.* to litigate.
LITÍGIO *s.m.* lawsuit; dispute.
LITIGIOSO(A) *adj.* litigious, contentious.
LÍTIO *s.m.* lithium.
LITORAL *s.m.* coastline / *adj.2gên.* coastal.
LITORÂNEO(A) *adj.* coastal.
LITOSFERA *s.f.* lithosphere.
LITRO *s.m.* liter.
LITURGIA *s.f.* liturgy.
LITÚRGICO(A) *adj.* liturgical.
LÍVIDO(A) *adj.* livid; black and blue.
LIVRAMENTO *s.m.* liberation.
LIVRAR *v.* to liberate.
LIVRARIA *s.f.* bookshop, bookstore.
LIVRE *adj.2gên.* free.
LIVRE-ARBÍTRIO *s.m.* free will.
LIVREIRO(A) *s.m.* bookseller.
LIVRO *s.m.* book.
LIXA *s.f.* sandpaper.
LIXÃO *s.m.* landfill.
LIXAR *v.* to file, to strip.
LIXEIRA *s.f.* trashcan, dustbin.

LIXEIRO(A) *s.m.* garbage collector.
LIXO *s.m.* garbage, trash.
LOBISOMEM *s.m.* werewolf.
LOBO *s.m.* wolf.
LOBOTOMIA *s.f.* lobotomy.
LÓBULO *s.m.* lobule, lobe; earlobe.
LOCAÇÃO *s.f.* renting, leasing.
LOCADOR(A) *s.m.* landlord.
LOCADORA *s.f.* rental shop.
LOCAL *s.m.* place, site / *adj.2gên.* local.
LOCALIDADE *s.f.* locality.
LOCALIZAÇÃO *s.f.* location; localization.
LOCALIZAR *v.* to spot; to locate.
LOÇÃO *s.f.* lotion.
LOCAR *v.* to rent, to lease.
LOCATÁRIO(A) *s.m.* renter.
LOCOMOÇÃO *s.f.* locomotion.
LOCOMOTIVA *s.f.* locomotive.
LOCOMOTOR(A) *adj.* locomotor.
LOCOMOVER *v.* to locomote, to move about.
LOCUÇÃO *s.f.* locution.
LOCUTOR(A) *s.m.* announcer, speaker.
LODO *s.m.* slurry, mud.
LOGARITMO *s.m.* logarithm.
LÓGICA *s.f.* logic.
LÓGICO(A) *adj.* logical, rational.
LOGÍSTICA *s.f.* logistics.
LOGÍSTICO(A) *adj.* logistic, logistical.
LOGO *adv.* at once, soon / *conj.* therefore.
LOGOTIPO *s.m.* logotype.
LOGRADOURO *s.m.* public area.
LOGRAR *v.* to get; to cheat.
LOGRO *s.m.* trap, spoof.
LOIRO(A) *adj.* blond, blonde.
LOJA *s.f.* shop, store.
LOJISTA *s.2gên.* shopkeeper.
LOMBA *s.f.* ridge.
LOMBADA *s.f.* speed bump.
LOMBAR *adj.* lumbar.
LOMBINHO *s.m.* tenderloin.
LOMBO *s.m.* loin.
LOMBRIGA *s.f.* roundworm.
LONA *s.f.* canvas; duffel.
LONGA-METRAGEM *s.m.* feature, full--length film.
LONGE *adv.* far / *adj.2gên.* distant.
LONGEVIDADE *s.f.* longevity.
LONGEVO(A) *adj.* longevous.
LONGÍNQUO(A) *adj.* distant, far-away.

LONGITUDE *s.f.* longitude.
LONGITUDINAL *adj.2gên.* longitudinal.
LONGO(A) *adj.* long.
LONJURA *s.f.* great distance.
LONTRA *s.f.* otter.
LORDE *s.m.* lord.
LORDOSE *s.f.* lordosis, swayback.
LOROTA *s.f.* fib, lie; nonsense.
LOSANGO *s.m.* lozenge.
LOTAÇÃO *s.f.* capacity.
LOTAR *v.* to allot, to pack.
LOTE *s.m.* lot; batch.
LOTEAMENTO *s.m.* lot, parcel.
LOTEAR *v.* to lot, to divide.
LOTERIA *s.f.* lottery.
LOTÉRICA *s.f.* betting shop.
LOUÇA *s.f.* dishware.
LOUCO(A) *adj.* crazy, mad / *s.m.* mad person.
LOUCURA *s.f.* madness, insanity.
LOURO(A) *adj.* blond, blonde / *s.m.* bay leaf; parrot.
LOUSA *s.f.* blackboard.
LOUVA-A-DEUS *s.m.* praying mantis.
LOUVADO(A) *adj.* praised / *s.m.* umpire.
LOUVAR *v.* to praise.
LOUVÁVEL *adj.2gên.* praiseworthy.
LOUVOR *s.m.* praise, laud.
LUA *s.f.* moon.
LUAR *s.m.* moonlight.
LUARENTO(A) *adj.* moonlit.
LUAU *s.m.* luau.
LUBRIFICAÇÃO *s.f.* lubrication.
LUBRIFICANTE *s.m.* lubricant / *adj.2gên.* lubricant.
LUBRIFICAR *v.* to lubricate.
LUCIDEZ *s.f.* lucidity.
LÚCIDO(A) *adj.* lucid.
LÚCIFER *s.m.* Lucifer.
LÚCIO *s.m.* pike, pickerel.
LUCRAR *v.* to profit, to gain.
LUCRATIVO(A) *adj.* profitable.
LUCRO *s.m.* profit, gain.
LUDIBRIAR *v.* to cheat, to entrap.
LÚDICO(A) *adj.* ludic, playful.
LUDO *s.m.* ludo.
LUGAR *s.m.* place.
LUGAR-COMUM *s.m.* commonplace, cliché.
LUGAREJO *s.m.* hamlet, village.
LÚGUBRE *adj.2gên.* lugubrious, grim.
LULA *s.f.* squid.

LÚMEN *s.m.* lumen.
LUMINÁRIA *s.f.* lantern.
LUMINESCÊNCIA *s.f.* luminescence.
LUMINOSIDADE *s.f.* luminosity.
LUMINOSO(A) *adj.* luminous.
LUNAR *adj.2gên.* lunar.
LUNÁTICO(A) *adj.* lunatic, crazy.
LUNETA *s.f.* field glass.
LUPA *s.f.* magnifying glass.
LÚPUS *s.m.* lupus.
LUSITANO(A) *adj.* Portuguese.
LUSTRA-MÓVEIS *s.m.* furniture polish.
LUSTRAR *v.* to polish.
LUSTRE *s.m.* chandelier; lustre.
LUSTROSO(A) *adj.* lustrous, glossy.

LUTA *s.f.* fight.
LUTADOR(A) *adj.* fighter; wrestler.
LUTAR *v.* to fight.
LUTO *s.m.* mourning, grieve.
LUVA *s.f.* glove.
LUXAÇÃO *s.f.* luxation, strain.
LUXAR *v.* to sprain, to wrench.
LUXO *s.m.* luxury.
LUXUOSO(A) *adj.* luxurious.
LUXÚRIA *s.f.* lust.
LUZ *s.f.* light.
LUZEIRO *s.m.* lighthouse.
LUZENTE *adj.2gên.* luminous
LUZIMENTO *s.m.* splendour.
LUZIR *v.* to shine, to glitter.

M m

M, m *s.m.* the thirteenth letter of the Portuguese alphabet.
MACA *s.f.* stretcher, litter, hammock.
MAÇÃ *s.f.* apple.
MACABRO *adj.* macabre; gruesome.
MACACADA *s.f.* gang; friends.
MACACÃO *s.m.* big ape; overalls, dungaree.
MACACO *s.m.* monkey; ape.
MAÇANETA *s.f.* knob, handle; doorknob, door handle.
MAÇANTE *s.2gên.* preachy / *adj.2gên.* tiresome, boring, monotonous.
MACAQUEAR *v.* to ape, to imitate; to mock, to mimic.
MACAQUICE *s.f.* apery, monkeyshine.
MAÇARICO *s.m.* blowtorch, blowpipe; burner.
MACARRÃO *s.m.* pasta, spaghetti; noodle, macaroni.
MACARRONADA *s.f.* pasta.
MACARRÔNICO *adj.* macaronic; burlesque.
MACETE *s.m.* trick, artifice.
MACHADO *s.m.* axe; hatchet.
MACHÃO *adj.* macho man; robust, rude.

MACHISMO *s.m.* machism; chauvinism, manliness.
MACHISTA *adj.2gên.* macho; sexist, chauvinist.
MACHO *s.m.* male, masculine / *adj.* male; brave, courageous.
MACHUCADO *adj.* hurt, injured; bruised, wounded.
MACHUCAR *v.* to injure; to wound, to hurt.
MACIÇO *adj.* massive, solid; compact, massy.
MACIEIRA *s.f.* apple tree.
MACIEZ *s.f.* softness, smoothness; gentleness.
MACIO(A) *adj.* soft, smooth, tender.
MACIOTA *s.f.* easygoingness; slowly.
MAÇO *s.m.* mallet; bunch, pack, pile.
MAÇOM *s.m.* Mason, Freemason.
MAÇONARIA *s.f.* masonry.
MAÇONICO *adj.* Masonic.
MÁ-CRIAÇÃO *s.f.* discourtesy; bad manners.
MACROECONOMIA *s.f.* macroeconomics.
MÁCULA *s.f.* macula, spot, stain; dishonour, disgrace.

MACULADO *adj.* spotted, stained, impure.
MACULAR *v.* to maculate, to stain; to pollute, to blemish.
MADAMA *s.f.* madam, mistress; prostitute.
MADEIRA *s.f.* wood; timber.
MADEIRAMENTO *s.m.* heap of wood; framework.
MADEIRAR *v.* to set up a frame.
MADEIXA *s.f.* skein; strand, lock of hair.
MADRASTA *s.f.* stepmother.
MADRE *s.f.* mother; nun.
MADRIGAL *s.m.* madrigal.
MADRINHA *s.f.* godmother; made of honour; sponsor, protector.
MADRUGADA *s.f.* dawning, daybreak.
MADRUGAR *v.* to get up early.
MADURAÇÃO *s.f.* ripening, maturation.
MADURAR *v.* to mature, to ripen.
MADUREZA *s.f.* maturity, ripeness; prudence.
MADURO(A) *adj.* mature, ripe.
MÃE *s.f.* mother; mum, mommy.
MAESTRIA *s.f.* mastery; control, knowledge.
MAESTRO *s.m.* maestro, composer; leader.
MÁ-FÉ *s.f.* bad-faith; fraud, hoax.
MÁFIA *s.f.* mafia; mob.
MAFIOSO(A) *adj.* mafioso; criminal.
MÁ-FORMAÇÃO *s.f.* malformation.
MAGAZINE *s.f.* store; periodical.
MAGIA *s.f.* magic, spell; sorcery, witchery.
MÁGICA *s.f.* magic, sorcery; witch, magician.
MÁGICO *s.m.* magician, illusionist / *adj.* magical, magic; mystical.
MAGÍSTER *s.m.* master.
MAGISTÉRIO *s.m.* mastership, professorship.
MAGISTRAL *adj.2gên.* masterly; perfect, complete, excellent.
MAGISTRATURA *s.f.* magistrature, magistracy; judiciary.
MAGNÂNIMO *adj.* magnanimous; noble, generous.
MAGNATA *s.2gên.* magnate; tycoon.
MAGNÉTICO *adj.* magnetic; attractive.
MAGNETISMO *s.m.* magnetism.
MAGNETIZAÇÃO *s.f.* magnetisation; attraction.
MAGNETIZAR *v.* to magnetise; to attract.
MAGNIFICAR *v.* to magnify.
MAGNÍFICO *adj.* magnificent, glorious, splendid.
MAGNITUDE *s.f.* magnitude; scale, dimension.
MAGO *s.m.* magician, wizard.
MÁGOA *s.f.* sorrow, grief; heartache, hurt.
MAGOADO(A) *adj.* hurt, sad; unhappy.
MAGOAR *v.* to hurt, to wound; to sadden.
MAGRELO(A) *adj.* skinny, lean, scraggy.
MAGREZA *s.f.* slimness, leanness, thinness.
MAGRO(A) *adj.* thin, skinny.
MAIO *s.m.* May.
MAIÔ *s.m.* swimming suit; bathing suit.
MAIONESE *s.f.* mayonnaise.
MAIOR *adj.2gên.* bigger, larger, longer.
MAIORAL *s.2gên.* foreman, chief, boss.
MAIORIA *s.f.* majority.
MAIORIDADE *s.f.* full age, adulthood; emancipation.
MAIS *adv.* more, also / *prep.* plus.
MAISQUERER *v.* to prefer, to love more.
MAIS-VALIA *s.f.* added value, capital gain.
MAIÚSCULA *s.f.* capital letter.
MAIUSCULIZAR *v.* to captalise.
MAIÚSCULO *adj.* capital.
MAJESTADE *s.f.* majesty; grandiosity, royalty.
MAJESTOSO *adj.* majestic; kingly, imperial.
MAJOR *s.2gên.* major.
MAJORITÁRIO *adj.* majority.
MAL *adv.* badly, hardly / *s.m.* evil, illness.
MALA *s.f.* suitcase, handbag / *adj.2gên.* tiresome, boring.
MALABARISMO *s.m.* juggling; juggle, jugglery.
MALABARISTA *s.2gên.* juggler, conjurer, trickster.
MAL-ACABADO(A) *adj.* badly-finished, maladjusted; tired, old.
MAL-AGRADECIDO(A) *adj.* ungrateful, ingrate; thankless.
MAL-AMADO(A) *s.m.* unloved / *adj.* unloved.
MALANDRAGEM *s.f.* roguery, trickery; vagabondage.
MALANDRICE *s.f.* rascality, roguery.
MALANDRO *s.m.* rascal, vagabond, scoundrel / *adj.* roguish, scoundrelly.

MAL-ASSOMBRADO(A) *s.m.* ghost, spectre / *adj.* haunted, spooky.
MAL-AVENTURADO(A) *adj.* ill-fated; evil blessed, unfortunate.
MALCHEIROSO *adj.* smelly, stink; fetid.
MALCRIAÇÃO *s.f. m.q.* má-criação.
MALCRIADO *adj.* naughty; insolent, uncivil.
MALDADE *s.f.* badness, wickedness; evil.
MALDIÇÃO *s.f.* curse, damn; malediction.
MALDITO *s.m.* devil, accursed / *adj.* cursed, unblessed.
MALDIZENTE *s.2gên.* defamer, backbiter / *adj.2gên.* defamatory, calumnious.
MALDIZER *v.* to slander, to defame, to backbite / *s.m.* backbiting.
MALDOSO *adj.* wicked, bad; spiteful.
MALEABILIDADE *s.f.* malleability.
MALEÁVEL *adj.2gên.* malleable; tractable.
MAL-EDUCADO(A) *adj.* bad mannered, discourteous; impolite.
MALEFICÊNCIA *s.f.* maleficence; malignancy.
MALEFÍCIO *s.m.* malefaction, witchcraft; harm.
MALÉFICO *adj.* maleficent, malefic; malign.
MAL-EMPREGADO *adj.* misused.
MAL-ENCARADO(A) *adj.* ugly; evil-looking.
MAL-ENTENDIDO(A) *s.m.* misunderstanding, disagreement / *adj.* misunderstood.
MAL-ESTAR *s.m.* malaise; illness, indisposition.
MALETA *s.f.* suitcase, bag; handbag.
MALEVOLÊNCIA *s.f.* malevolence; malignancy.
MALEVOLENTE *adj.2gên.* malevolent, unkind.
MALÉVOLO(A) *adj.* malignant, mean; malevolent.
MALFEITO *adj.* deformed; badly-done.
MALFEITOR(A) *s.m.* wrongdoer, malefactor.
MALFEITORIA *s.f.* malefaction, delict; misdeed, wrongdoing.
MALFORMAÇÃO *s.f. m.q.* má-formação.
MALFORMADO *adj.* malformed.
MALHA *s.f.* mesh, jersey; sweater.
MALHADO *adj.* brindled, tabby, piebald; worked out.
MALHAR *v.* to strike, to beat up; to work out.
MAL-HUMORADO(A) *adj.* bad-tempered, grumpy, moody.
MALÍCIA *s.f.* malice, guile.

MALICIOSO(A) *adj.* malicious; mischievous.
MALIGNO *adj.* malignant, malign.
MÁ-LÍNGUA *s.2gên.* whisperer, taleteller / *adj.2gên.* slander, long-tongued.
MAL-INTENCIONADO(A) *adj.* perfidious, malicious, evil-minded.
MALOTE *s.m.* pouch, express mail.
MALQUISTO *adj.* dislike, detested, hated.
MALTRATADO *adj.* mistreated, insulted; abused.
MALTRATAR *v.* to mistreat, to abuse; to maltreat.
MALUCO(A) *adj.* crazy, mad, nutty / *s.m.* nut, fool; madman.
MALUQUICE *s.f.* madness; craziness.
MALVADEZ *s.f.* perversity; meanness.
MALVADO(A) *adj.* perverse, wicked; bad, mean.
MALVISTO *adj.* disliked, suspected.
MAMA *s.f.* breast, teat; mommy.
MAMADA *s.f.* feeding, suckling.
MAMADEIRA *s.f.* nursing bottle; babies bottle.
MAMÃE *s.f.* mother, mom; mum, mummy.
MAMÃO *s.m.* papaya.
MAMAR *v.* to suck, to take the breast.
MAMÍFERO *s.m.* mammal.
MAMILO *s.m.* nipple.
MAMUTE *s.m.* mammoth.
MANA *s.f.* sis.
MANADA *s.f.* herd (gado).
MANANCIAL *s.m.* spring, source, wellspring.
MANCADA *s.f.* mistake; slip-up.
MANCAR *v.* to limp; to hobble.
MANCEBO *s.m.* boy, youth.
MANCHA *s.f.* stain, spot; blur.
MANCHADO *adj.* stained, spotted.
MANCHAR *v.* to spot, to stain.
MANCHETE *s.f.* headline.
MANCO *adj.* lame, cripple / *s.m.* hobbler, limper.
MANDAMENTO *s.m.* commandment; command, order.
MANDANTE *s.2gên.* leader, boss / *adj.2gên.* ordering, commanding.
MANDAR *v.* to order; to govern, to rule.
MANDÍBULA *s.f.* jaw; mandible.
MANDIBULAR *adj.2gên.* mandibular.
MANDINGA *s.f.* sorcery, witchcraft.

MANDIOCA *s.f.* cassava, manioc.
MANDO *s.m.* order, command.
MANEIRA *s.f.* way, manner, form.
MANEIRAR *v.* to go easy on; to take easy.
MANEIRO *adj.* easy, light; portable, manageable.
MANEJAR *v.* to handle, to manage; to carry, to deal with.
MANEJO *s.m.* management, attendance; handling.
MANEQUIM *s.m.* mannequin; manikin; dummy.
MANGA *s.f.* mango; sleeve, arm (roupa).
MANGAÇÃO *s.f.* mockery, kidding; joke.
MANGUEIRA *s.f.* mangoes tree; hose, garden hose.
MANHA *s.f.* whining, artfulness; slyness, trick.
MANHÃ *s.f.* morning.
MANHOSO(A) *adj.* sly, tricky; foxy, cunning.
MANIA *s.f.* mania, obsession; craze, trade.
MANÍACO(A) *adj.* manic, maniac; crazy.
MANICÔMIO *s.m.* asylum, madhouse.
MANIFESTAÇÃO *s.f.* demonstration, expression; riot, parade.
MANIFESTANTE *s.2gên.* protestor, rioter / *adj.2gên.* manifesting, demonstrating.
MANIFESTAR *v.* to manifest, to express; to show.
MANIFESTO *s.m.* manifest; plan, circular / *adj.* visible, palpable.
MANILHA *s.f.* bracelet, armlet; shackle.
MANIPULAÇÃO *s.f.* manipulation, handling.
MANIPULADO *adj.* manipulated, handle; prepared.
MANIPULADOR *s.m.* manipulator, operator / *adj.* manipulator.
MANIPULAR *v.* to manipulate, to operate, to handle.
MANIPULÁVEL *adj.2gên.* manipulable.
MANIQUEÍSMO *s.m.* Manichaeism.
MANIQUEÍSTA *s.2gên.* Manichaean / *adj.2gên.* Manichaeaist.
MANIVELA *s.f.* crank, handle.
MANJADO *adj.* very known; cliché.
MANO *s.m.* bro; brother.
MANOBRA *s.f.* shunt, maneuver; handling, manipulation.
MANOBRAR *v.* to maneuver, to handle; to manipulate.
MANOBRISTA *s.2gên.* parking valet; valet.

MANSÃO *s.f.* mansion, manor house.
MANSO *adj.* tame, meek, gentle, domesticated.
MANTA *s.f.* blanket, cover; wrap.
MANTEIGA *s.f.* butter.
MANTER *v.* to maintain, to preserve; to hold, to sustain; to keep.
MANTIMENTO *s.m.* provision, supply; grocery, food.
MANTO *s.m.* mantle, cape.
MANTRA *s.m.* mantra.
MANUAL *s.m.* handbook, manual, guide / *adj.2gên.* manual.
MANUFATURA *s.f.* manufacture, preparation, production.
MANUFATURAÇÃO *s.f.* manufacturing.
MANUSCRITO *s.m.* manuscript, handwriting / *adj.* manuscript, handwritten.
MANUSEAR *v.* to handle, to manipulate.
MANUSEIO *s.m.* handing, manipulation.
MANUTENÇÃO *s.f.* maintenance, keeping; conservation, preservation.
MÃO *s.f.* hand; paw; traffic flow (trânsito).
MÃO-ABERTA *s.2gên.* prodigal, liberal, generous.
MÃO-CHEIA *s.f.* handful; portion, measure.
MÃO DE FERRO *s.f.* iron hand, tyranny, oppressor.
MÃO DE OBRA *s.f.* labour; manpower, workmanship.
MÃO DE VACA *s.2gên.* penny-pincher / *adj.2gên.* mingy, iron fisted.
MÃO-FRANCESA *s.f.* strut, brace.
MÃOZINHA *s.f.* small hand; helping hand, little help.
MAPA *s.m.* map, chart, graph.
MAPA-MÚNDI *s.m.* map of the world; world map.
MAPEAMENTO *s.m.* mapping.
MAPEAR *v.* to map; to chart.
MAQUETE *s.f.* maquette; model, mockup.
MAQUETISTA *s.2gên.* modeler.
MAQUIAGEM *s.f.* makeup, cosmetics.
MAQUIAR *v.* to make up; to hide, to mask.
MÁQUINA *s.f.* machine; engine.
MAQUINAÇÃO *s.f.* machination; intrigue, scheming.
MAQUINAR *v.* to machinate, to scheme; to plot.

MAQUINISTA *s.2gên.* machinist; train engineer.
MAR *s.m.* sea; beach.
MARACUJÁ *s.m.* passion fruit.
MARAJÁ *s.m.* maharajah; boss, leader.
MARASMO *s.m.* marasmus.
MARATONA *s.f.* marathon; marathon race.
MARATONISTA *s.2gên.* marathon runner.
MARAVILHA *s.f.* wonder, marvel.
MARAVILHAR *v.* to amaze, to marvel; to surprise.
MARAVILHOSO(A) *adj.* wonderful, amazing; admirable.
MARCA *s.f.* mark, tag; brand.
MARCAÇÃO *s.f.* marking, limit; branding with an iron.
MARCADO *adj.* marked, tagged; reserved.
MARCADOR(A) *s.m.* marker, scorer.
MARCANTE *adj.2gên.* marking, remarkable; outstanding.
MARCAPASSO *s.m.* pacemaker.
MARCAR *v.* to mark, to score; to tag.
MARCENARIA *s.f.* joinery; woodwork shop.
MARCENEIRO(A) *s.m.* joiner, cabinet-maker; woodworker.
MARCHA *s.f.* march, walking; process; gear (carro).
MARCHAR *v.* to march, to walk.
MARCIAL *adj.2gên.* martial; warlike, military.
MARCIANO(A) *s.m.* Martian / *adj.* Martian.
MARCO *s.m.* mark; sign.
MARÇO *s.m.* March.
MARÉ *s.f.* tide, water.
MAREADO *adj.* seasick.
MARÉ-ALTA *s.f.* high tide.
MAREAR *v.* to steer, to navigate.
MARÉ-BAIXA *s.f.* low tide.
MARECHAL *s.m.* marshal; commander.
MARÉ-CHEIA *s.f. m.q.* maré-alta.
MAREMOTO *s.m.* seaquake.
MARESIA *s.f.* whitecaps; salty air.
MARFIM *s.m.* ivory.
MARGARIDA *s.f.* daisy.
MARGARINA *s.f.* margarine.
MARGEAR *v.* to border, to skirt; to lay on.
MARGEM *s.f.* border, shore; margin, bank.
MARGINAL *adj.2gên.* marginal, outside; outcast.
MARGINALIDADE *s.f.* marginality.
MARGINALIZAÇÃO *s.f.* marginalisation.

MARGINALIZADO *adj.* marginalised; excluded.
MARGINALIZAR *v.* to marginalise; to exclude.
MARICAS *s.m.* sissy, molly.
MARIDO *s.m.* husband.
MARINHA *s.f.* navy.
MARINHEIRO *s.m.* seaman, sailor; mariner.
MARINHO *adj.* marine.
MARIOLA *s.f.* scamp; sirrah.
MARIONETE *s.f.* puppet, marionette.
MARIPOSA *s.f.* moth.
MARISCO *s.m.* shellfish; seafood.
MARITAL *adj.2gên.* marital; husbandly.
MARÍTIMO *s.m.* seaman, marine / *adj.* maritime, marine, naval.
MARMANJO *s.m.* grown man; adult / *adj.* grown man; adult.
MARMELADA *s.f.* marmalade.
MARMELO *s.m.* quince.
MARMITA *s.f.* lunch box, pan; mess kit.
MÁRMORE *s.m.* marble.
MARMORÍSTA *s.2gên.* marble worker.
MARMOTA *s.f.* marmot.
MAROTAGEM *s.f.* gang of rascals.
MAROTO *s.m.* rascal, scoundrel / *adj.* roguish.
MARQUÊS *s.m.* marquis, marquess.
MARQUESADO *adj.* marquisate.
MARQUISE *s.f.* marquise.
MARRA *s.f.* weeding tool; persistence, insistence.
MARROCOS *s.m.* Morocco.
MARRECO *s.m.* drake.
MARRETA *s.f.* sledgehammer; mallet.
MARRETEIRO *s.m.* hammer maker; hammer worker.
MARROM *s.m.* brown / *adj.2gên.* brown.
MARSUPIAL *s.m.* marsupial / *adj.2gên.* marsupial.
MARTE *s.m.* Mars.
MARTELAR *v.* to hammer.
MARTELO *s.m.* hammer, striker.
MÁRTIR *s.2gên.* martyr.
MARTÍRIO *s.m.* martyrdom; passion.
MARTIRIZADOR *s.m.* martyrisor.
MARTIRIZANTE *adj.2gên.* martyrising.
MARTIRIZAR *v.* to martyr.
MARUJADA *s.f.* gang of sailors.
MARUJO *s.m.* sailor, seaman.
MARXISMO *s.m.* Marxism.

MARXISTA *s.2gên.* Marxist / *adj.* Marxist.
MAS *conj.* but, however.
MASCADOR *s.m.* chewer / *adj.* chewing.
MASCAR *v.* to chew; to bite.
MÁSCARA *s.f.* mask.
MASCARADA *s.f.* masquerade; masque.
MASCARADO *adj.* masked, disguised.
MASCARAR *v.* to mask, to disguised.
MASCATE *s.m.* peddler; hawk.
MASCATEAR *v.* to vend, to huckster.
MASCOTE *s.f.* mascot.
MASCULINIDADE *s.f.* masculinity; manhood, manliness.
MASCULINIZAR *v.* to masculinise.
MASCULINO *adj.* masculine; manly, virile.
MÁSCULO *adj.* manlike, manful.
MASMORRA *s.f.* dungeon, donjon.
MASOQUISMO *s.m.* masochism.
MASOQUISTA *s.2gên.* masochist / *adj.2gên.* masochist.
MASSA *s.f.* mass; dough; pasta.
MASSACRANTE *adj.2gên.* crushing; boring, dull.
MASSACRAR *v.* to massacre, to slaughter.
MASSACRE *s.m.* massacre, carnage.
MASSAGEADOR(A) *s.m.* massager / *adj.* massager.
MASSAGEAR *v.* to massage; to rub.
MASSAGEM *s.f.* massage; rubbing.
MASSAGISTA *s.2gên.* masseuse; rubber.
MASSIFICAÇÃO *s.f.* massification.
MASSIFICADO(A) *adj.* massified;
MASSUDO(A) *adj.* massive, compact, bulky.
MASTECTOMIA *s.f.* mastectomy.
MASTIGAÇÃO *s.f.* mastication; chewing.
MASTIGADO *adj.* masticated, chewed.
MASTIGADOR(A) *s.m.* masticator, chewer.
MASTIGADOURO *s.m.* masticatory.
MASTIGAR *v.* to masticate; to chew.
MASTITE *s.f.* mastitis.
MASTRO *s.m.* mast, pole.
MASTURBAÇÃO *s.f.* masturbation.
MASTURBAR *v.* to masturbate.
MASTURBATÓRIO *adj.* masturbatory.
MATA *s.f.* forest, wood, jungle.
MATA-BORRÃO *s.m.* blotter; blotting paper.
MATADOR *adj.* killer, assassin, murder / *s.m.* killer, assassin, murder.
MATADOURO *s.m.* slaughterhouse.
MATAGAL *s.m.* underwood, thicket; brushwood.
MATANÇA *s.f.* killing, massacre, butchery.
MATAR *v.* to kill, to slaughter; to assassinate.
MATA-RATOS *s.m.* rat poison; arsenic.
MATAR-SE *v.* to suicide.
MATE *s.m.* checkmate; mate tea.
MATEMÁTICA *s.f.* Mathematics.
MATEMÁTICO *s.m.* mathematician / *adj.* mathematical.
MATÉRIA *s.f.* matter, substance; subject, topic.
MATERIAL *adj.2gên.* material.
MATERIALIDADE *s.f.* materiality.
MATERIALISMO *s.m.* materialism.
MATERIALISTA *s.2gên.* materialist.
MATERIALIZAÇÃO *s.f.* materialisation.
MATERIALIZAR *v.* to materialise, to objectify.
MATÉRIA-PRIMA *s.f.* raw material.
MATERNAL *adj.2gên.* maternal; motherly.
MATERNIDADE *s.f.* maternity; motherhood.
MATERNO *adj.* maternal, motherly.
MATILHA *s.f.* pack of hounds; gang of rascals.
MATINA *s.f.* dawn, daybreak; morning.
MATINAL *adj.2gên.* matutinal, morning.
MATINAR *v.* to get up early.
MATINÊ *s.f.* matinee.
MATIZ *s.m.* tint, shade; nuance.
MATIZAÇÃO *s.f.* tinting, shading.
MATIZAR *v.* to shade, to tint.
MATO *s.m.* bush, thicket; wood.
MATOSO *adj.* brushy, jungly.
MATRACA *s.f.* eloquent, talkative; noisemaker.
MATRIARCA *s.f.* matriarch.
MATRIARCADO *s.m.* matriarchy.
MATRIARCAL *adj.2gên.* matriarchal.
MATRICIDA *s.2gên.* matricidal.
MATRICÍDIO *s.m.* matricide.
MATRÍCULA *s.f.* registration, enrolment; matriculation.
MATRICULAR *v.* to matriculate; to register.
MATRIMONIAL *adj.2gên.* spousal, matrimonial.
MATRIMÔNIO *s.m.* marriage, matrimony, wedding.
MATRIZ *s.f.* matrix; womb.
MATRONA *s.f.* matron; motherly woman.

MATURAÇÃO s.f. maturation (humano); ripeness (fruta).
MATURAR v. to mature; to ripe.
MATURIDADE s.f. maturity, adulthood; ripeness.
MATUTAÇÃO s.f. meditation, thought.
MATUTAR v. to think, to meditate.
MATUTINO adj. morning.
MATUTO s.m. rural, simple; hick / adj. rural, simple; hick.
MAU adj. bad; mean.
MAU-CARÁTER s.2gên. knave, villain; bad character / adj.2gên. knave, villain; bad character.
MAU-OLHADO s.m. evil-eyed.
MAUSOLÉU s.m. mausoleum.
MAUS-TRATOS s.m. pl. mistreatment.
MAXILA s.f. jaw.
MAXILAR s.m. jaw / adj.2gên. maxillary.
MÁXIMA s.f. maxim, proverb; precept.
MAXIMIZAR v. to maximise.
MÁXIMO adj. greatest, highest, best / s.m. maximum.
ME pron. me, myself.
MEADO adj. mid, middle; halve / s.m. mid, middle; halve.
MEAR v. to halve.
MECÂNICA s.f. mechanics.
MECANICISMO s.m. mechanism.
MECÂNICO s.m. mechanic / adj. mechanical.
MECANISMO s.m. mechanism; gear.
MECANISTA adj.2gên. mechanist.
MECANIZAR v. to mechanise.
MECENATO s.m. patronage.
MECHA s.f. wick, fuse.
MEDALHA s.f. medal.
MEDALHÃO s.m. medallion, locket.
MEDALHISTA s.2gên. medalist.
MÉDIA s.f. average, mean; medium.
MEDIAÇÃO s.f. mediation.
MEDIADOR(A) s.m. mediator; peacekeeper / adj. mediator; peacekeeper.
MEDIANO adj. median; average.
MEDIANTE adj.2gên. intermediary / prep. means of, by.
MEDIAR v. to mediate; to interfere.
MEDICAÇÃO s.f. medication.
MEDICAMENTO s.m. medicine, remedy; medicament.
MEDIÇÃO s.f. measurement; metering.

MEDICAR v. to medicate; to remedy.
MEDICÁVEL adj.2gên. medicable, curable.
MEDICINA s.f. medicine.
MEDICINAL adj.2gên. medicinal, healing.
MÉDICO(A) s.m. doctor, medic / adj. medical.
MEDIDA s.f. measurement; measure.
MEDIDOR s.m. measurer, meter / adj. measuring.
MEDIEVAL adj.2gên. medieval; mediaeval.
MEDIEVALISMO s.m. medievalism.
MEDIEVALISTA s.2gên. medievalist.
MÉDIO adj. medium; mean, halfback.
MEDÍOCRE s.2gên. mediocre / adj.2gên. mediocre, poor, so-so.
MEDIOCRIDADE s.f. mediocrity; meanness.
MEDIR v. to measure, to gauge.
MEDITAÇÃO s.f. meditation; wondering.
MEDITADOR(A) s.m. meditator.
MEDITAR v. to meditate; to muse.
MEDITATIVO(A) adj. meditative; musing.
MEDITERRÂNEO s.m. Mediterranean / adj. Mediterranean.
MÉDIUM s.2gên. medium.
MEDO s.m. fear; afraid (com medo de).
MEDONHO adj. scary, frightful; hideous.
MEDRAR v. to prosper, to grow, to develop.
MEDROSO adj. fearful, fearsome; timid, shy.
MEDULA s.f. medulla; marrow.
MEDULAR adj.2gên. medullary; essential.
MEDUSA s.f. Medusa, jellyfish.
MEGAFONE s.m. megaphone; loudspeaker.
MEGALOMANIA s.f. megalomania.
MEGALOMANÍACO(A) adj. megalomaniac.
MEGALÓPOLE s.f. megalopolis.
MEGERA s.f. shrew, vixen.
MEIA s.f. sock, stocking.
MEIA-CALÇA s.f. pantyhose, collant, tights.
MEIA-IDADE s.f. middle age; midlife.
MEIA-LUA s.f. half moon.
MEIA-NOITE s.f. midnight.
MEIA-TIGELA s.f. valueless, second-rate.
MEIA-VIDA s.f. half-life; used.
MEIA-VOLTA s.f. U-turn / interj. about-face!
MEIGO adj. mild, gentle; sweet.
MEIGUICE s.f. tenderness, kindness.
MEIO s.m. means, middle / adj. half.
MEIO-CAMPISTA s.2gên. midfielder.
MEIO-DIA s.m. midday, noon.
MEIO-FIO s.m. kerb, curb.

MEIO-IRMÃO *s.m.* half-brother; stepbrother.
MEIO-TERMO *s.m.* mid-term; mean, medium.
MEIO-TOM *s.m.* halftone, undertone.
MEL *s.f.* honey.
MELAÇO *s.m.* molasses, treacle.
MELADO *s.m.* molasses / *adj.* honeyed, luscious.
MELANCIA *s.f.* watermelon.
MELANCIEIRA *s.f.* watermelon plant.
MELANCOLIA *s.f.* melancholy; sadness.
MELANCÓLICO *adj.* melancholic; gloomy, sad, blue.
MELANINA *s.f.* melanin; skin pigment.
MELÃO *s.m.* melon.
MELAR *v.* to sweeten; to cover with honey.
MELECA *s.f.* goo; booger.
MELHOR *adj.* better; the best.
MELHORA *s.f.* improvement; reformation.
MELHORAMENTO *s.m.* improvement, upgrading.
MELHORAR *v.* to improve, to better; to upgrade.
MELHORIA *s.f.* m.q. melhora.
MELIANTE *s.2gên.* miscreant.
MELÍFLUO *adj.* mellifluous.
MELINDRAR *v.* to offend, to shock; to scandalise.
MELINDRE *s.m.* politeness; modesty, scruple.
MELINDROSO *adj.* polite; scrupulous, modest.
MELODIA *s.f.* melody.
MELODIAR *v.* to melodise; to harmonise.
MELÓDICO *adj.* melodic, melodious.
MELODIOSO(A) *adj.* melodious; harmonious, musical.
MELODRAMA *s.m.* melodrama.
MELODRAMÁTICO(A) *adj.* melodramatic.
MELOSO(A) *adj.* sweet, treacly.
MEMBRANA *s.f.* membrane.
MEMBRANOSO(A) *adj.* membranous.
MEMBRO *s.m.* member.
MEMORANDO *s.m.* memo, memorandum.
MEMORAR *v.* to memorise, to remind.
MEMORÁVEL *adj.2gên.* memorable; remarkable.
MEMÓRIA *s.f.* memory, record (pessoa); storage (máquina).
MEMORIAL *s.m.* memorial / *adj.2gên.* memorial.

MEMORIZAÇÃO *s.f.* memorisation.
MEMORIZAR *v.* to memorise.
MENÇÃO *s.f.* mention, reference.
MENCIONAR *v.* to mention, to cite.
MENDICÂNCIA *s.f.* mendacity; beggary.
MENDIGAR *v.* to beg; to mump.
MENDIGO *s.m.* beggar, tramp.
MENINA *s.f.* girl.
MENINGE *s.f.* meninges.
MENINGITE *s.f.* meningitis.
MENINO *s.m.* boy.
MENOPAUSA *s.f.* menopause.
MENOR *s.2gên.* underage, child, minor / *adj.* smaller; less, minor.
MENORIDADE *s.f.* minority.
MENOS *adv.* less / *prep.* except.
MENOSPREZAR *v.* to despise, to underestimate.
MENOSPREZÍVEL *adj.2gên.* disdainful.
MENOSPREZO *s.m.* contempt; underestimation.
MENSAGEIRO(A) *s.m.* messenger.
MENSAGEM *s.f.* message.
MENSAL *adj.2gên.* monthly.
MENSALIDADE *s.f.* monthly payment.
MENSALISTA *s.2gên.* salaried.
MENSTRUAÇÃO *s.f.* menstruation, period; menses.
MENSTRUAL *adj.2gên.* menstrual.
MENSTRUAR *v.* to menstruate.
MENSURABILIDADE *s.f.* measurability.
MENSURAR *v.* to measure; to quantify.
MENSURÁVEL *adj.2gên.* measurable; quantifiable.
MENTA *s.f.* mint.
MENTAL *adj.2gên.* mental.
MENTALIDADE *s.f.* mentality.
MENTALIZAR *v.* to conceptualise, to imagine.
MENTE *s.f.* mind.
MENTECAPTO *s.m.* madman, fool / *adj.* madman, fool.
MENTIR *v.* to lie.
MENTIRA *s.f.* lie; untruth.
MENTIROSO(A) *adj.* lying, untrue / *s.m.* liar.
MENTOL *s.m.* menthol.
MENTOLADO *adj.* mentholated.
MENTOR *s.m.* mentor, oracle; guide, leader.
MENU *s.m.* menu.

MERCADINHO s.m. grocery store; small market.
MERCADO s.m. market, marketplace.
MERCADOLOGIA s.f. marketing.
MERCADOR s.m. merchant; seller, trader.
MERCADORIA s.f. merchandise; goods, commodities.
MERCANTE adj.2gên. trade, mercantile.
MERCANTIL adj.2gên. m.q. mercante.
MERCANTILISMO s.m. mercantilism.
MERCANTILIZAR v. to buy, to sell.
MERCÊ s.f. grace, mercy, boon.
MERCEARIA s.f. grocery store.
MERCENÁRIO(A) adj. mercenary / s.m. mercenary.
MERCÚRIO s.m. Mercury (planeta); mercury (química).
MERECEDOR(A) s.m. deserver / adj. worthy, dignified.
MERECER v. to deserve; to merit.
MERECIDO adj. deserved; merited, dignified.
MERENDA s.f. light meal, snack.
MERENDAR v. to eat light meal; to snack.
MERENDEIRA s.f. lunch box; woman cooker.
MERENGUE s.m. meringue.
MERETRIZ s.f. prostitute.
MERGULHADOR adj. diver / s.m. diver.
MERGULHAR v. to dive; to submerge.
MERGULHO s.m. dive, plunge.
MERIDIANO s.m. meridian / adj. meridian.
MERIDIONAL adj.2gên. southern; south, meridional.
MERITÍSSIMO(A) s.m. Your Honour; judge.
MÉRITO s.m. merit.
MERO adj. mere, simple.
MÊS s.m. month.
MESA s.f. table.
MESADA s.f. allowance.
MESA DE CABECEIRA s.f. beside table, night table.
MESA-REDONDA s.f. roundtable (discussão).
MESÁRIO(A) s.m. board member.
MESCLA s.f. miscellany, mixture.
MESCLADO adj. mixed, mixing.
MESCLAR v. to mix.
MESMICE s.f. sameness.
MESMO adj. same, equal, identical / adv. even, yet; exactly.

MESQUINHEZ s.f. avarice, meanness; stinginess.
MESQUINHO(A) adj. stingy, mean, misery.
MESQUITA s.f. mosque.
MESSIÂNICO(A) adj. messianic.
MESSIANISMO s.m. messianism.
MESSIAS s.m. messiah.
MESTIÇAGEM s.f. miscegenation.
MESTIÇO(A) s.m. crossbreed, half-breed / adj. mongrel, hybrid.
MESTRADO s.m. Mastership, Master's degree.
MESTRE s.m. Master.
MESTRE DE CERIMÔNIAS s.m. Master of ceremonies, Mc.
MESURA s.f. curtsy; reverence.
META s.f. goal, target; aim, purpose.
METABÓLICO adj. metabolic.
METABOLISMO s.m. metabolism.
METABOLIZAR v. to metabolise.
METADE s.f. half.
METAFÍSICA s.f. metaphysics.
METÁFORA s.f. metaphor; allegory.
METAFÓRICO adj. metaphoric; allegoric.
METAL s.m. metal.
METÁLICO adj. metallic.
METALINGUAGEM s.f. metalanguage.
METALINGUÍSTICO(A) adj. metalinguistic.
METALIZAR v. to metallise.
METALURGIA s.f. metallurgy.
METALÚRGICA s.f. metallurgy workshop; metallurgical.
METAMÓRFICO adj. metamorphic.
METAMORFISMO s.m. metamorphism.
METAMORFOSE s.f. metamorphosis.
METANO s.m. methane.
METANOL s.m. methanol.
METÁSTASE s.f. metastasis.
METATARSO s.m. metatarsus.
METEÓRICO adj. meteoric.
METEORITO s.m. meteorite.
METEORO s.m. meteor.
METEOROLOGIA s.f. meteorology.
METEOROLOGISTA s.2gên. meteorologist; weather(wo)man.
METER v. to put, to place; to deposit, to insert.
METICULOSIDADE s.f. meticulousness.
METICULOSO adj. meticulous; careful, rigorous.

METIDO *adj.* audacious, meddlesome, cheeky.
METÓDICO(A) *adj.* methodic; systematic.
METODISMO *s.m.* methodism.
MÉTODO *s.m.* method.
METODOLOGIA *s.f.* methodology.
METODOLÓGICO *adj.* methodological.
METONÍMIA *s.f.* metonymy.
METRAGEM *s.f.* metreage; measure in meters.
METRALHADORA *s.f.* machine-gun.
METRALHAR *v.* to strafe; to machine-gun.
MÉTRICA *s.f.* metrics, meter; prosody (poema).
MÉTRICO *adj.* metric.
METRIFICAÇÃO *s.f.* metrification.
METRIFICAR *v.* to measure.
METRO *s.m.* meter.
METRÔ *s.m.* subway, tube.
METRÔNOMO *s.m.* metronome.
METRÓPOLE *s.f.* metropolis, metropole.
METROPOLITANO(A) *adj.* metropolitan.
METROSSEXUAL *s.m.* metrosexual.
MEU *pron.* my, mine.
MEXEDOR *s.m.* provoker, stirrer / *adj.* provoker, stirrer.
MEXER *v.* to move, to stir; to provoke.
MEXERICA *s.f.* tangerine.
MEXIDA *s.f.* movement, stirring; disturbance.
MEXIDO *adj.* moved, touched; stirred.
MEXILHÃO *s.m.* mussel.
MI *s.m.* E (nota musical).
MIADO *s.m.* meow, mewing.
MIALGIA *s.f.* myalgia.
MIAR *v.* to meow.
MIAU *s.m.* meow.
MICCÇÃO *s.f.* urination.
MICCIONAL *adj.2gên.* micturition.
MICO *s.m.* small monkey; make a fool of.
MICOSE *s.f.* ringworm.
MICRO *s.m.* microcomputer.
MICROBICIDA *adj.2gên.* microbicidal / *s.m.* microbicidal.
MICRÓBIO *s.m.* microbe.
MICROBIOLOGIA *s.f.* microbiology.
MICROCIRURGIA *s.f.* microsurgery.
MICROFONE *s.m.* microphone.
MICROPROCESSADOR *s.m.* microprocessor.

MICRORGANISMO *s.m.* microorganism.
MICROSCÓPICO *adj.* microscopic.
MICROSCÓPIO *s.m.* microscope.
MICTÓRIO *s.m.* urinal.
MIGALHA *s.f.* crumb, bit; tiny portion.
MIGRAÇÃO *s.f.* migration.
MIGRAR *v.* to migrate.
MIGRATÓRIO *adj.* migratory.
MIL *num.* one thousand.
MILAGRE *s.m.* miracle.
MILAGREIRO *adj.* miracle worker.
MILAGROSO(A) *adj.* miraculous.
MILANESA *s.f.* breaded.
MILENAR *adj.2gên.* millenary.
MILÊNIO *s.m.* millennium.
MILÉSIMO *s.m.* millesimal, thousandth / *adj.* millesimal, thousandth.
MILHA *s.f.* mile.
MILHÃO *num.* one million.
MILHAR *s.m.* a thousand / *v.* to give corn to.
MILHARAL *s.m.* cornfield.
MILHO *s.m.* corn.
MILÍCIA *s.f.* militia.
MILICIANO(A) *adj.* militia(wo)man.
MILIGRAMA *s.m.* milligram.
MILILITRO *s.m.* millilitre.
MILIMETRAR *v.* to measure in millimetres.
MILIMÉTRICO *adj.* millimetric.
MILÍMETRO *s.m.* millimetre.
MILIONÁRIO *s.m.* millionaire.
MILIONÉSIMO *adj.* millionth.
MILITÂNCIA *s.f.* militancy.
MILITANTE *adj.* militant.
MILITAR *adj.2gên.* military, warlike / *s.m.* soldier, serviceman.
MILITARISMO *s.m.* militarism.
MILITARIZAÇÃO *s.f.* militarisation.
MILITARIZAR *v.* to militarise.
MIM *pron.* me.
MIMADO(A) *adj.* spoilt.
MIMAR *v.* to spoil; to cuddle, to mimic.
MIMESE *s.f.* mimesis.
MIMETISMO *s.m.* mimicry, mimesis.
MIMETIZAR *v.* to mimic.
MÍMICA *s.f.* mime, mimic.
MIMO *s.m.* tenderness, caress; mime, fool.
MIMOSO *adj.* darling, beloved.
MINA *s.f.* mine, quarry.
MINAR *v.* to mine, to undermine.
MINDINHO *s.m.* little finger.

MINEIRO *adj.* miner.
MINERAÇÃO *s.f.* mining.
MINERAL *adj.2gên.* mineral.
MINERALOGIA *s.f.* mineralogy.
MINERALOGISTA *s.2gên.* mineralogist.
MINERAR *v.* to mine, to exploit a mine.
MINÉRIO *s.m.* ore, mineral.
MINGAU *s.m.* porridge; manioc pap.
MÍNGUA *s.f.* shortage, misery; lack of.
MINGUADO *adj.* lacking of; abated, thin.
MINGUAR *v.* to lack, to wane.
MINHA *pron.* my, mine.
MINHOCA *s.f.* earthworm; worm, lobworm.
MINIATURA *s.f.* miniature.
MÍNIMA *s.f.* minimum; minim.
MINIMALISMO *s.m.* minimalism.
MINIMALISTA *s.2gên.* minimalist / *adj.* minimalist.
MINIMIZAR *v.* to minimalise.
MÍNIMO *adj.* minimum, minimal.
MINISSAIA *s.f.* miniskirt.
MINISTERIAL *adj.2gên.* ministerial; cabinet, office.
MINISTÉRIO *s.m.* ministry; department.
MINISTRAR *v.* to minister; to administer, to provide.
MINISTRO *s.m.* minister; officer.
MINORAÇÃO *s.f.* decrease; lessening, softening.
MINORAR *v.* to lessen, to soften; to decrease.
MINORIA *s.f.* minority.
MINORITÁRIO *adj.* minority.
MINÚCIA *s.f.* minutia, detail.
MINUCIAR *v.* to particularise, to detail.
MINUCIOSO *adj.* detailed, precise, meticulous.
MINUETO *s.m.* minuet.
MINÚSCULA *s.f.* lower case letter.
MINÚSCULO *adj.* tiny, miniscule.
MINUTA *s.f.* minutes; protocol.
MINUTO *s.m.* minute.
MIOCÁRDIO *s.m.* myocardium.
MIOCARDITE *s.f.* myocarditis.
MIOLO *s.m.* grain, kernel; brain.
MIOMA *s.m.* myoma.
MIOPATIA *s.f.* myopathy.
MÍOPE *s.2gên.* myope / *adj.2gên.* myopic; nearsighted, short-sighted.
MIOPIA *s.f.* myopia.
MIRA *s.f.* sight, mark; aim, target.

MIRABOLANTE *adj.2gên.* fanciful, delirium, gaudy.
MIRACULOSO(A) *adj.* miraculous.
MIRADA *s.f.* glance, look, squint.
MIRAGEM *s.f.* mirage.
MIRANTE *s.m.* gazebo, observatory.
MIRAR *v.* to stare, to look at; to examine.
MIRÍADE *s.f.* myriad.
MIRIM *adj.2gên.* young (pessoa), small (objeto).
MIRRA *s.f.* myrrh, cicely.
MIRRADO *adj.* withered, wizen.
MIRRAR *v.* to wither; to blight.
MISANTROPIA *s.f.* misanthropy.
MISANTROPO *s.m.* misanthrope, misanthropist / *adj.* unsocial.
MISCELÂNEA *s.f.* miscellanea, medley.
MISCIGENAÇÃO *s.f.* miscegenation.
MISCIGENADO *adj.* mestizo, mixed; half-caste.
MISCÍVEL *adj.2gên.* miscible.
MISERAR *v.* to disgrace, to be unhappy.
MISERÁVEL *adj.2gên.* miserable; wretched.
MISÉRIA *s.f.* misery; unhappiness.
MISERICÓRDIA *s.f.* mercy, mercifulness.
MISERICORDIOSO(A) *adj.* merciful, compassionate.
MÍSERO *adj.* wretched, miserable.
MISOGINIA *s.f.* misogyny.
MISÓGINO *s.m.* misogynist, woman hater / *adj.* woman-hating.
MISSA *s.f.* mass.
MISSÃO *s.f.* mission, legacy.
MÍSSIL *s.m.* missile.
MISSIONÁRIO *s.m.* missionary / *adj.* missionary.
MISSIONEIRO *s.m. m.q.* missionário.
MISSIVA *s.f.* missive, letter; epistle.
MISTER *s.m.* occupation, profession; service, work.
MISTÉRIO *s.m.* mystery.
MISTERIOSO(A) *adj.* mysterious.
MÍSTICA *s.f.* mystic, mystique.
MISTICISMO *s.m.* mysticism.
MÍSTICO *adj.* mystical.
MISTIFICAÇÃO *s.f.* mystification.
MISTIFICAR *v.* to mystify.
MISTO *adj.* mixed, miscellaneous.
MISTURA *s.f.* mix, blend; mixture, cross, fusion.
MISTURAR *v.* to mix, to fuse, to cross.

MÍTICO *adj.* mythical.
MITIFICAÇÃO *s.f.* mythification.
MITIFICAR *v.* to mythicise.
MITIGAÇÃO *s.f.* mitigation.
MITIGAR *v.* to mitigate; to assuage, to quench.
MITO *s.m.* myth.
MITOLOGIA *s.f.* mythology.
MITOLÓGICO *adj.* mythological; fabled.
MIÚDO *s.m.* kid, child; small quantity.
MIXAGEM *s.f.* mixing, mix (música).
MIXARIA *s.f.* bauble, trifle.
MNEMÔNICO *adj.* mnemonic.
MÓBIL *adj.2gên.* mobile, moveable.
MOBÍLIA *s.f.* furniture.
MOBILIAR *v.* to furnish.
MOBILIÁRIA *s.f.* furniture factory.
MOBILIÁRIO *adj.* furniture.
MOBILIDADE *s.f.* mobility.
MOBILIZAR *v.* to mobilise.
MOÇA *s.f.* girl, maiden; miss, young woman.
MOÇÃO *s.f.* motion, movement.
MOCHILA *s.f.* backpack, schoolbag.
MOCIDADE *s.f.* youth, young age.
MOÇO *s.m.* young man.
MODA *s.f.* fashion; mode.
MODAL *adj.2gên.* modal.
MODALIDADE *s.f.* modality.
MODELAGEM *s.f.* modeling, moulding; shaping.
MODELAR *v.* to model, to mould / *adj.2gên.* model, exemplary.
MODELO *s.2gên.* model; sample, form.
MODERAÇÃO *s.f.* moderation.
MODERADOR *s.m.* moderator, mediator / *adj.* moderating.
MODERAR *v.* to moderate; to control.
MODERNIDADE *s.f.* modernity.
MODERNISMO *s.m.* modernism.
MODERNISTA *s.2gên.* modernist / *adj.2gên.* modernist.
MODERNIZAR *v.* to modernise.
MODERNO *adj.* modern.
MODÉSTIA *s.f.* modesty.
MODESTO *adj.* modest, humble.
MODIFICAÇÃO *s.f.* modification; alteration.
MODIFICAR *v.* to modify; to change, to alter.
MODIFICÁVEL *adj.2gên.* modifiable, changeable.
MODISMO *s.m.* mania, trend.

MODISTA *s.2gên.* modiste, fashion designer; dressmaker.
MODO *s.m.* way, manner; mode, means.
MODULAÇÃO *s.f.* modulation; change.
MODULADOR *s.m.* modulator / *adj.* modulated.
MODULAR *v.* to modulate.
MÓDULO *s.m.* module, modulus.
MOEDA *s.f.* coin; currency (monetário).
MOEDOR *s.m.* grinder, miller; pounder.
MOEDURA *s.f.* grinding; milling.
MOELA *s.f.* gizzard.
MOER *v.* to grind, to crush; to triturate.
MOFA *s.f.* mockery, scorn.
MOFADO *adj.* mouldy, musty.
MOFAR *v.* to mock, to scorn; to mould, to get musty.
MOFINO *adj.* unhappy, miserable.
MOFO *s.m.* mould, mildew.
MOÍDO *adj.* ground, milled; crushed, beat.
MOINHO *s.m.* mill; flour mill.
MOITA *s.f.* shrub, bush.
MOLA *s.f.* spring; motive, incentive.
MOLAR *adj.2gên.* molar.
MOLDADO *adj.* moulded.
MOLDAR *v.* to shape; to mould.
MOLDE *s.m.* mould, patter; norm.
MOLDURA *s.f.* frame; moulding.
MOLE *adj.2gên.* soft, limp; floppy.
MOLECADA *s.f.* gang of boys.
MOLECAGEM *s.f.* boyish tricks; childlike behaviour.
MOLÉCULA *s.f.* molecule.
MOLECULAR *adj.2gên.* molecular.
MOLEIRO *s.m.* miller, mill worker.
MOLENGA *adj.2gên.* lazy, lazybones.
MOLENGAR *v.* to behave lazily.
MOLEQUE *s.m.* brat, kid, boy / *adj.* funny, mocking.
MOLESTAR *v.* to harass, to molest; to annoy, to vex.
MOLÉSTIA *s.f.* disease, sickness.
MOLESTO *adj.* onerous, vexatious.
MOLEZA *s.f.* softness, weakness.
MOLHADELA *s.f.* wetting.
MOLHADO(A) *adj.* wet, soaked; watery.
MOLHAMENTO *s.m.* wetness.
MOLHAR *v.* to wet, to dampen; to soak, to water.
MOLHE *s.m.* mole, pier.

MOLHO s.m. sauce, dressing; bunch (chaves).
MOLUSCO s.m. mollusk.
MOMENTÂNEO adj. momentary, transitory; instantaneous.
MOMENTO s.m. moment, instant; time.
MONARCA s.m. monarch.
MONARQUIA s.f. monarchy.
MONÁRQUICO adj. monarchic.
MONARQUISMO s.m. monarchism.
MONASTÉRIO s.m. monastery.
MONÁSTICO adj. monastic, monkish.
MONÇÃO s.f. monsoon.
MONETÁRIO adj. monetary.
MONGE s.m. monk; friar.
MONITOR s.m. monitor; supervisor.
MONITORAMENTO s.m. monitoring.
MONITORAR v. to monitor; to watch over.
MONITORIA s.f. monitoring.
MONJA s.f. nun.
MONOCICLO s.m. unicycle.
MONOCROMÁTICO adj. monochromatic.
MONOCROMO s.m. monochrome.
MONÓCULO s.m. monocle, eyeglass / adj. monocular.
MONOGAMIA s.f. monogamy.
MONOGÂMICO adj. monogamous.
MONÓGAMO s.m. monogamist.
MONOGRAFIA s.f. monograph.
MONOGRÁFICO adj. monographic.
MONOGRAMA s.m. monogram.
MONÓLOGO s.m. monologue.
MONOLOGUISTA s.2gên. monologist.
MONOPÓLIO s.m. monopoly.
MONOPOLISTA s.2gên. monopolist.
MONOPOLIZAÇÃO s.f. monopolisation.
MONOPOLIZADOR s.m. monopoliser / adj. monopolistic.
MONOPOLIZAR v. to monopolise.
MONOSSILÁBICO adj. monosyllabic.
MONOSSÍLABO s.m. monosyllable.
MONOTEÍSMO s.m. monotheism.
MONOTEÍSTA s.2gên. monotheistic.
MONOTONIA s.f. monotony.
MONÓTONO adj. monotone, monotonous.
MONÓXIDO s.m. monoxide.
MONSTRENGO s.m. monster, scarecrow.
MONSTRO s.m. monster.
MONSTRUOSIDADE s.f. monstrosity; abnormity.
MONSTRUOSO adj. monstrous, abnormal; ugly.

MONTADO adj. mounted, built; assembled, sitting.
MONTAGEM s.f. montage, mounting; building.
MONTANHA s.f. mountain.
MONTANHA-RUSSA s.f. roller coaster.
MONTANHOSO adj. mountainous; hilly, rangy.
MONTANTE s.m. amount, sum.
MONTÃO s.m. heap, pile; a lot of.
MONTAR v. to mount, to ride (cavalo); to set, to assemble.
MONTARIA s.f. riding, mount (cavalo).
MONTE s.m. heap, pile; accumulation, portion.
MONTURO s.m. dunghill, scrap heap.
MONUMENTAL adj.2gên. monumental.
MONUMENTO s.m. monument.
MORA s.f. delay, respite.
MORADA s.f. residence, home; dwelling-place.
MORADIA s.f. dwelling house, home; habitation.
MORADOR(A) adj. dweller, resident; inhabitant.
MORAL adj.2gên. moral, ethic / s.f. moral, morality.
MORALIDADE s.f. morality; morals.
MORALISMO s.m. moralism.
MORALISTA adj.2gên. moralist / s.2gên. moralist.
MORALIZAÇÃO s.f. moralisation.
MORALIZAR v. to moralise, to censure.
MORANGO s.m. strawberry.
MORANGUEIRO s.m. strawberry vendor.
MORAR v. to live, to inhabit.
MORATÓRIA s.f. moratorium.
MORATÓRIO adj. moratory.
MORBIDEZ s.f. morbidity, morbidness.
MÓRBIDO adj. morbid, unhealthy.
MORCEGO s.m. bat.
MORDAÇA s.f. muzzle, gag.
MORDACIDADE s.f. mordacity; sarcasm, causticity.
MORDAZ adj.2gên. mordent, sarcastic, caustic.
MORDEDOR s.m. biter, nipper; teething ring.
MORDER v. to bite, to torment; to hurt.
MORDICAR v. to nibble, to bite, to sting.
MORDIDA s.f. bite; snap.

MORDOMIA *s.f.* stewardship; comfort, well-being.
MORDOMO *s.m.* butler; steward.
MORENO(A) *adj.* brunette; tanned.
MORFEMA *s.f.* morpheme.
MORFINA *s.f.* morphine.
MORFOLOGIA *s.f.* morphology.
MORFOLÓGICO *adj.* morphologic.
MORFOSSINTAXE *s.f.* morphossyntax.
MORIBUNDO *adj.* moribund, dying / *s.m.* moribund.
MORMAÇO *s.m.* sultriness; haze.
MÓRMON *s.2gên.* Mormon / *adj.2gên.* Mormon.
MORMONISMO *s.m.* Mormonism.
MORNO(A) *adj.* warm, tepid.
MOROSIDADE *s.f.* slowness, laxness.
MOROSO *adj.* slow, lax.
MORRER *v.* to die; to decease, to expire.
MORRO *s.m.* hill, mount.
MORTADELA *s.f.* bologna.
MORTAL *s.m.* mortal; deathly / *adj.2gên.* mortal; deathly.
MORTALHA *s.f.* shroud.
MORTALIDADE *s.f.* mortality.
MORTANDADE *s.f.* slaughter, carnage; massacre.
MORTE *s.f.* death.
MORTEIRO *s.m.* mortar, howitzer.
MORTICÍNIO *s.m.* slaughter, carnage.
MORTÍFERO *adj.* lethal, deadly.
MORTIFICAÇÃO *s.f.* mortification.
MORTIFICADO *adj.* mortified.
MORTIFICANTE *adj.2gên.* mortifying; grievous.
MORTIFICAR *v.* to mortify, to humiliate; to torment.
MORTO *adj.* dead, deceased.
MORTUÁRIO *adj.* mortuary.
MORTUÓRIO *s.m.* funeral, obsequies.
MOSAICO *s.m.* mosaic.
MOSCA *s.f.* fly.
MOSQUITO *s.m.* mosquito.
MOSTARDA *s.f.* mustard.
MOSTEIRO *s.m.* convent, monastery.
MOSTRA *s.f.* display, demonstration.
MOSTRADOR *adj.* demonstration / *s.m.* demonstrator.
MOSTRAR *v.* show, display, exhibit.
MOSTRUÁRIO *s.m.* showcase.
MOTEJAR *v.* to mock, to make jokes.

MOTEJO *s.m.* mockery, joke; taunt.
MOTEL *s.m.* motel, hotel.
MOTILIDADE *s.f.* motility.
MOTIM *s.m.* mutiny, revolt; rebellion, insurrection.
MOTIVAÇÃO *s.f.* motivation; provocation.
MOTIVADO *adj.* motivated, provoked.
MOTIVAR *v.* to motivate; to provoke, to stimulate.
MOTIVO *s.m.* motive, reason, purpose.
MOTO *s.f.* motorcycle; / *s.m.* motto.
MOTOCICLETA *s.f.* motorcycle.
MOTOCICLISMO *s.m.* motorcycling.
MOTOCICLISTA *s.2gên.* motorcyclist, biker.
MOTOR *s.m.* motor, engine.
MOTORISTA *s.2gên.* motorist; driver.
MOTORIZADO *adj.* motorised, motor vehicle.
MOTORIZAR *v.* to motorise.
MOTRICIDADE *s.f.* motility.
MOTRIZ *s.f.* motive, driving; motor, moving.
MOURO *s.m.* Moor / *adj.* Moorish.
MOVEDIÇO *adj.* moveable, unstable, fickle.
MÓVEL *adj.2gên.* mobile, movable / *s.m.* furniture.
MOVER *v.* to move; to persuade.
MOVIDO *adj.* moved, taken.
MOVIMENTAÇÃO *s.f.* movement, moving.
MOVIMENTAR *v.* to move; to stir, to animate.
MOVIMENTO *s.m.* movement.
MUAMBA *s.f.* knapsack, theft; thievery.
MUAMBEIRO(A) *adj.* smuggler.
MUCO *s.m.* mucus.
MUCOSA *s.f.* mucus, membrane.
MUCOSIDADE *s.f.* mucosity.
MUCOSO *adj.* mucous, viscous.
MUÇULMANO *s.m.* Muslim / *adj.* Muslim.
MUDA *s.f.* change of clothes; shift, change; mute woman.
MUDADO *adj.* changed, moved.
MUDANÇA *s.f.* change; move, relocation; shift.
MUDAR *v.* to change, to alter; to modify.
MUDÁVEL *adj.2gên.* changeable.
MUDEZ *s.f.* dumbness, mutism, silence.
MUDO *adj.* mute, dumb; voiceless.
MUGIDO *s.m.* moo, mooing.
MUGIR *v.* to moo.
MUITO *adv.* very, much, a lot of / *pron.* much, many.
MULA *s.f.* mule.

MULATO *s.m.* mulatto.
MULETA *s.f.* crutch; support.
MULHER *s.f.* woman.
MULHERENGO *adj.* womaniser; stud, unmanly / *s.m.* womaniser; stud, unmanly.
MULTA *s.f.* fine, penalty; ticket.
MULTAR *v.* to fine, to penalise; to give a ticket.
MULTICELULAR *adj.2gên.* multicellular.
MULTICOLOR *adj.2gên.* multicolour.
MULTIDÃO *s.f.* crowd, mob; multitude.
MULTIDISCIPLINAR *adj.2gên.* multidisciplinary; cross-functional.
MULTINACIONAL *adj.2gên.* multinational.
MULTIPLICAÇÃO *s.f.* multiplication.
MULTIPLICAR *v.* to multiply; to proliferate.
MÚLTIPLO *adj.* multiple.
MÚMIA *s.f.* mummy.
MUMIFICAÇÃO *s.f.* mummification.
MUMIFICAR *v.* to mummify.
MUNDANISMO *s.m.* worldliness.
MUNDANO(A) *adj.* mundane, worldly; earthly.
MUNDÃO *s.m.* a lot of people; very distant.
MUNDIAL *adj.2gên.* worldwide; global.
MUNDO *s.m.* world.
MUNHECA *s.f.* wrist; hand.
MUNIÇÃO *s.f.* ammunition, fortification; bullets.
MUNICIPAL *adj.2gên.* municipal.
MUNICIPALIZAR *v.* to municipalise.
MUNICÍPIO *s.m.* municipality, town.
MUNIR *v.* to supply, to reload; to furnish.
MURAL *s.m.* wall, mural; board.
MURALHA *s.f.* wall; battlement.
MURAR *v.* to wall, to fence; to fortify.
MURCHAMENTO *s.m.* flatting.
MURCHAR *v.* to flat, to wither; to fade.
MURCHO(A) *adj.* wilted, withered, languid.
MURMURANTE *adj.2gên.* murmuring, muttering; whispering.
MURMURAR *v.* to murmur, to mutter; to whisper.
MURMÚRIO *s.m.* mutter, murmur; whisper, chatter.
MURO *s.m.* wall.
MURRO *s.m.* punch, jab; slug, blow.
MUSA *s.f.* muse.
MUSCULAÇÃO *s.f.* bodybuilding; weightlifting.
MUSCULAR *adj.2gên.* muscular, musclebound.
MUSCULATURA *s.f.* musculature.
MÚSCULO *s.m.* muscle; meat, beef.
MUSCULOSO(A) *adj.* beefy, brawny; muscled, strong.
MUSEOLOGIA *s.f.* museology.
MUSEOLOGISTA *s.2gên.* museologist.
MUSEU *s.m.* museum.
MUSGO *s.m.* moss.
MUSGOSO *adj.* mossy.
MÚSICA *s.f.* music; song.
MUSICAL *adj.2gên.* musical.
MUSICALIDADE *s.f.* musicality.
MUSICAR *v.* to musicalise.
MUSICISTA *s.2gên.* musician.
MÚSICO *s.m.* musician; player, performer / *adj.* musical.
MUSSE *s.m.* mousse.
MUTAÇÃO *s.f.* mutation; change, metamorphosis.
MUTANTE *s.2gên.* mutant / *adj.2gên.* mutant.
MUTÁVEL *adj.2gên.* mutable; changeable.
MUTILAÇÃO *s.f.* mutilation; deformation.
MUTILADO *adj.* mutilated, deformed / *s.m.* amputee.
MUTILAR *v.* to mutilate, to deform.
MUTIRÃO *s.m.* collective effort.
MUTISMO *s.m.* mutism; speechless.
MÚTUA *s.f.* mutual change; reciprocal trade.
MUTUALISMO *s.m.* mutualism.
MUTUANTE *adj.2gên.* mutual; equivalent.
MUTUAR *v.* to mutualise; to lend, to borrow.
MUTUÁRIO *s.m.* borrower, mortgagee.
MÚTUO *adj.* equivalent, reciprocal; mutual.

Nn

N, n *s.m.* the fourteenth letter of the Portuguese alphabet.
NABO *s.m.* turnip.
NAÇÃO *s.f.* nation, land, country.
NÁCAR *s.m.* nacre.
NACIONAL *adj.2gên.* national.
NACIONALIDADE *s.f.* nationality.
NACIONALISMO *s.m.* nationalism.
NACIONALISTA *adj.2gên.* nationalist.
NACIONALIZAÇÃO *s.f.* nationalization.
NACIONALIZAR *v.* to nationalize.
NACO *s.m.* piece, portion.
NADA *pron.* nothing.
NADADEIRA *s.f.* flipper, paddle, fin.
NADADOR(A) *s.m.* swimmer / *adj.* swimmer.
NADAR *v.* to swim, to bathe.
NÁDEGA *s.f.* buttock, rump.
NADO *s.m.* swim, swimming.
NAFTA *s.f.* naphta, kerosene.
NAFTALINA *s.f.* naphthalene.
NÁILON *s.m.* nylon.
NAIPE *s.m.* suit.
NAMIBIANO(A) *adj.* Namibian.
NAMORADA *s.f.* girlfriend.
NAMORADO *s.m.* boyfriend.
NAMORAR *v.* to date.
NAMORO *s.m.* relationship; love affair; love making.
NANAR *v.* to sleep, to slumber.
NANICO *adj.* dwarfish, undersized, tiny.
NANISMO *s.m.* dwarfism.
NANOCEFALIA *s.f.* microcephaly.
NANQUIM *s.m.* nankeen, nankin.
NÃO *adv.* no, not.
NAPOLEÔNICO *adj.* Napoleonic.
NAPOLITANO(A) *adj.* Neapolitan.
NAQUILO *prep.* in that, at that, on that.
NARCISISMO *s.m.* narcissism.
NARCISISTA *adj.2gên.* narcissist.
NARCISO *s.m.* Narcissus.
NARCOLEPSIA *s.f.* narcolepsy.
NARCOLÉPTICO *adj.* narcoleptic.
NARCÓTICO *adj.* narcotic / *s.m.* narcotic, opiate, drug.
NARCOTINA *s.f.* narcotine.
NARCOTISMO *s.m.* narcotism.
NARCOTRAFICANTE *adj.2gên.* drug dealer.
NARCOTRÁFICO *s.m.* drug trafficking
NARÍCULA *s.f.* nostril.
NARIGÃO *s.m.* big nose, schnozzle.

NARIGUDO *adj.* conky, long-nosed, big-nosed / *s.m.* conky, long-nosed, big-nosed.
NARINA *s.f.* nostril.
NARIZ *s.m.* nose.
NARRAÇÃO *s.f.* narration.
NARRADOR *adj.* narrator, teller / *s.m.* narrator, teller.
NARRAR *v.* to narrate, to tell, to relate.
NARRATIVO(A) *adj.* narrative, descriptive / *s.f.* account; narration, narrative; story, tale.
NASA *s.f.* NASA.
NASAL *adj.2gên.* nasal.
NASALAÇÃO *s.f.* nasalization.
NASALAR *v.* to nasalize.
NASALIDADE *s.f.* nasality.
NASCENÇA *s.f.* nascency, birth.
NASCENTE *adj.2gên.* nascent / *s.f.* fountain; source; origin; head, wellhead wellspring.
NASCER *v.* to be born.
NASCER DO SOL *s.m.* sunrise.
NASCIMENTO *s.m.* birth.
NASOFARÍNGEO *adj.2gên.* nasopharyngeal.
NATA *s.f.* cream, butterfat.
NATAÇÃO *s.f.* swimming, swim.
NATAL *adj.2gên.* native (lugar).
NATAL *s.m.* Christmas, Xmas, Noel.
NATALIDADE *s.f.* natality, birth-rate.
NATIMORTO *adj.* stillborn, dead at birth / *s.m.* stillborn, dead at birth.
NATIVIDADE *s.f.* nativity, birth.
NATIVO(A) *adj.2gên.* native / *s.m.* native, aboriginal.
NATO *adj.* born, native.
NATURA *s.f.* nature.
NATURAL *adj.2gên.* natural.
NATURALIDADE *s.f.* birthplace.
NATURALISMO *s.m.* naturalism.
NATURALISTA *adj.2gên.* naturalist.
NATURALIZAÇÃO *s.f.* naturalization.
NATURALIZADO *adj.* naturalized, acclimatized.
NATURALIZAR *v.* to naturalize, to domesticate, to nationalize.
NATUREZA *s.f.* nature.
NATUREZA-MORTA *s.f.* still life.
NATURISMO *s.m.* naturism, nudism.
NATURISTA *adj.2gên.* naturist, nudist.
NAU *s.f.* vessel, ship.
NAUFRAGADO *adj.* wrecked, castaway, shipwrecked person.
NAUFRAGAR *v.* to wreck, to shipwreck.
NAUFRÁGIO *s.m.* shipwreck, wreck.

NÁUFRAGO *adj.* castaway / *s.m.* castaway.
NÁUSEA *s.f.* nausea, queasiness, qualm.
NAUSEABUNDO *adj.* nauseating, repulsive, putrid, foul.
NAUSEADO *adj.* nauseous, queasy, sickened, disgusted.
NAUSEAR *v.* to nauseate.
NAUTA *s.m.* navigator.
NÁUTICA *s.f.* navigation, seamanship.
NÁUTICO *adj.* marine, maritime, nautical.
NAVAL *adj.2gên.* naval, marine, maritime.
NAVALHA *s.f.* razor, knife, claw.
NAVALHAR *v.* to razor.
NAVE *s.f.* ship, aircraft, nave, vessel.
NAVEGABILIDADE *s.f.* navigability.
NAVEGAÇÃO *s.f.* navigation, sailing, navigate.
NAVEGADOR *adj.* navigator, seaman, pilot.
NAVEGANTE *adj.2gên.* navigating, navigator, sailor / *s.2gên.* sailor, seafarer, officer.
NAVEGAR *v.* to sail, to navigate.
NAVEGÁVEL *adj.2gên.* navigable, seaworthy, passable.
NAVIO *s.m.* ship.
NAVIO CARGUEIRO *s.m.* cargo ship.
NAZARENO *adj.* Nazarene.
NAZISMO *s.m.* Nazism.
NAZISTA *adj.2gên.* Nazi.
NEBLINA *s.f.* mist.
NEBLINAR *v.* to drizzle, to be foggy.
NEBULOSA *s.f.* nebula.
NEBULOSIDADE *s.f.* haziness, nebulosity, cloudiness.
NEBULOSO *adj.* foggy, hazy, misty; nebulous, unclear.
NÉCESSAIRE *s.m.* toiletries bag, cosmetic bag.
NECESSARIAMENTE *adv.* necessarily, unavoidably.
NECESSÁRIO *adj.* necessary, required.
NECESSIDADE *s.f.* requirement, necessity; must, need; necessary; poverty.
NECESSITADO *adj.* needy, pauper, beggar / *s.m.* pauper, beggar.
NECESSITAR *v.* to require, to need.
NECROFAGIA *s.f.* necrophagia.
NECRÓFAGO *adj.* necrophagous / *s.m.* necrophagous.
NECROFILIA *s.f.* necrophilia.
NECRÓFILO *adj.* necrophile.
NECRÓPOLE *s.f.* necropolis, cemetery.
NECROPSIA *s.f.* necropsy, autopsy.

NECROSAR v. to mortify.
NECROSCOPIA s.f. necroscopy.
NECROSE s.f. necrosis, canker.
NECROTÉRIO s.m. morgue, mortuary.
NÉCTAR s.m. nectar.
NECTARINA s.f. nectarine.
NEFASTO adj. nefário, malign, fatal.
NEFELIBATA adj.2gên. dreamer, fantasizer.
NEFROLOGIA s.f. nephrology.
NEFROLOGISTA adj.2gên. nephrologist / s.2gên. nephrologist.
NEGAÇÃO s.f. denial, negation.
NEGAR v. to deny, to refuse, to negate.
NEGATIVAMENTE adv. negatively.
NEGATIVIDADE s.f. negativity.
NEGATIVISMO s.m. negativism.
NEGATIVO(A) adj. negative, pessimistic / s.f. negative, no.
NEGÁVEL adj.2gên. deniable.
NEGLIGÊNCIA s.f. negligence.
NEGLIGENCIAR v. to neglect.
NEGLIGENTE adj.2gên. negligent.
NEGOCIAÇÃO s.f. negotiation, deal.
NEGOCIADOR(A) adj. negotiant, negotiator.
NEGOCIANTE s.2gên. negotianting; merchandiser; businessman; seller; trader; marketer.
NEGOCIAR v. to negotiate.
NEGOCIÁVEL adj.2gên. negotiable.
NEGÓCIO s.m. business.
NEGRITO adj. bold, boldface / s.m. bold, boldface.
NEGRO(A) adj. black.
NEM conj. neither.
NEM SEQUER adv. not even, neither.
NENÊ s.2gên. baby.
NENÉM s.2gên. baby, infant.
NENHUM pron. any, no, none, neither.
NENHUMAMENTE adv. by no means, under no condition, in no way.
NENÚFAR s.m. nenuphar, waterlily.
NEOLOGISMO s.m. neologism.
NÉON s.m. neon.
NEONAZISMO s.m. neonazism.
NEOPLATÔNICO adj. Neo-Platonic.
NEOPLATONISMO s.m. Neo-Platonism.
NEOZELÂNDES adj.2gên. New Zealander.
NEPALÊS(ESA) adj. Nepalese.
NEPOTISMO s.m. nepotism.
NEPOTISTA adj.2gên. nepotist.
NERVO s.m. nerv.

NERVOSISMO s.m. nervousness, jitters.
NERVOSO adj. nervous.
NETA s.f. granddaughter.
NETO s.m grandson.
NETUNO s.m. Neptune.
NEUROLOGIA s.f. neurology.
NEURÔNIO s.m. neuron.
NEUROSE s.f. neurosis.
NEURÓTICO adj. neurotic.
NEUTRALIDADE s.f. neutrality.
NEUTRALIZAR v. to neutralize.
NEUTRO adj. neuter; neutral; non--belligerent.
NÊUTRON s.m. neutron.
NEVAR v. to snow.
NEVASCA s.f. snowstorm, blizzard.
NEVE s.f. snow.
NÉVOA s.f. mist, fog; haze.
NEVOEIRO s.m. mist, fog; haze.
NEXO s.m. nexus, joint.
NHOQUE s.m. gnocchi.
NICHO s.m. niche; break; corner; housing.
NICOTINA s.f. nicotine.
NIGERIANO adj. Nigerian.
NIILISMO s.m. nihilism.
NIILISTA adj.2gên. nihilist.
NIMBO s.m. nimbus, aureole, halo.
NINAR v. to cradle, to lull.
NINFA s.f. nymph.
NINFOMANIA s.f. nymphomania.
NINFOMANÍACO(A) s.2gên. nymphomaniac.
NINGUÉM pron. nobody.
NINHO s.m. nest.
NINJA s.2gên. ninja.
NIPÔNICO adj. Japanese / s.m. Japanese.
NÍQUEL s.m. nickel.
NIRVANA s.m. nirvana.
NITIDAMENTE adv. neatly; risply.
NITIDEZ s.f. clearness, distinctness.
NÍTIDO adj. clear, sharp, brilliant.
NITRATO s.m. nitrate.
NÍTRICO adj. nitric.
NITRITO s.m. nitrite.
NITRO s.m. niter.
NITROGÊNIO s.m. nitrogen.
NITROGLICERINA s.f. nitro-glycerine.
NÍVEL s.m. level.
NIVELADOR(A) adj. grader, leveler; leveller / s.m. grader, screed, bulldozer.
NIVELAR v. to grade, to level, to even, to plane; to flat.

NO(A) prep. at, on, to.
NÓ s.m. knot, node.
NOBRE adj.2gên. noble, exalted.
NOBREZA s.f. nobility.
NOÇÃO s.f. notion, idea, sense.
NOCAUTE s.m. knockout.
NOCAUTEAR v. to plunk down.
NOCIVO adj. noxious, pernicious; bad, evil.
NOCTÂMBULO(A) adj. sleep-walker, night-hawk.
NÓDOA s.f. spot, blot, blur, fleck, speck.
NÓDULO s.m. nodule.
NOGUEIRA s.f. walnut tree, walnut wood.
NOITADA s.f. sleeplessness.
NOITE s.f. night; evening.
NOIVADO s.m. engagement.
NOIVAR v. to engage.
NOIVO(A) s.m. groom, fiancé. / s.f. bride, fiancée.
NOJENTO(A) adj. disgusting, filthy.
NOJO s.m. nausea, disgust.
NÔMADE adj.2gên. nomad.
NOME s.m. name.
NOMEAÇÃO s.f. nomination.
NOMEADO(A) adj. named, called.
NOMEAR v. to name, to call.
NOMENCLATURA s.f. nomenclature, terminology.
NOMINAL adj.2gên. nominal.
NORA s.f. daughter-in-law.
NORDESTE s.m. northeast.
NÓRDICO adj. Nordic, Norse.
NORMA s.f. norm, rule; standard.
NORMAL adj.2gên. normal, regular, natural.
NORMALIDADE s.f. normality.
NORMALIZAR v. to normalize.
NORMATIVO adj. normative, standard.
NOROESTE s.m. northwest.
NORTE s.m. north.
NORTE-AMERICANO adj. North American.
NORTEAR v. to lead, to guide.
NORTISTA adj.2gên. northerner, northern.
NOS pron. us.
NÓS pron. we.
NOSSO pron. our.
NOSTALGIA s.f. nostalgia.
NOSTÁLGICO adj. nostalgic.
NOTA s.f. note, reminder.
NOTAÇÃO s.f. notation.
NOTAR v. to notice, to tell.
NOTÁRIO s.m. notary.
NOTÁVEL adj.2gên. notable, remarkable.
NOTÍCIA s.f. information, news.
NOTICIAR v. to inform, to report.
NOTICIÁRIO s.m. news, newscast.
NOTIFICAÇÃO s.f. notification; notice.
NOTIFICAR v. to notify.
NOTORIEDADE s.f. notoriety.
NOTÓRIO adj. notorius, noted.
NOTURNO adj. nocturne.
NOVAMENTE adv. again.
NOVATO(A) s.m. beginner, newcommer; tyro; novice, colt; freshman.
NOVE num. nine.
NOVECENTOS num. nine hundred.
NOVELA s.f. soap opera.
NOVELO s.m. hank; ball; clew.
NOVEMBRO s.m. November.
NOVENA s.f. novena.
NOVENTA num. ninety.
NOVIÇO adj. novice, apprentice.
NOVIDADE s.f. news; fad; innovation.
NOVILHO s.m. steer; bullock.
NOVO(A) adj. new; young.
NOZ s.f. walnut.
NOZ-MOSCADA s.f. nutmeg.
NU(A) adj. naked / s.m. nude.
NUANCE s.f. nuance; shading.
NUBLADO adj. cloudy.
NUCA s.f. nape; scruff; cervix.
NUCLEAR adj.2gên. nucleate, nuclear.
NÚCLEO s.m. nucleous; core.
NUDEZ s.f. nudity, bareness, nakedness.
NUDISMO s.m. nudism.
NULO adj. null, void, invalid.
NUMERAÇÃO s.f. numeration, enumeration, numbering.
NUMERAL adj.2gên. numeral.
NUMERAR v. to number, to enumerate.
NUMÉRICO adj. numeric.
NÚMERO s.m. number.
NUMEROLOGIA s.f. numerology.
NUMEROLOGISTA s.2gên. numerologist.
NUMEROSO adj. numerous, copious.
NUNCA adv. never.
NÚPCIAS s.f. nuptials.
NUTRIÇÃO s.f. nutrition.
NUTRICIONISTA adj.2gên. nutritionist.
NUTRIDO(A) adj. nourished.
NUTRIENTE adj.2gên. nutrient.
NUTRIR v. to nourish, to maintain, to feed.
NUTRITIVO adj. nutritive.
NUVEM s.f. cloud.

Oo

O, o *s.m.* the fifteenth letter of the Portuguese alphabet.
Ó *interj.* oh.
OÁSIS *s.m.* oasis.
OBA *interj.* whoopee.
OBCECADO(A) *adj.* obsessed.
OBCECAR *v.* to obsess.
OBEDECER *v.* to obey.
OBEDIÊNCIA *s.f.* obedience.
OBEDIENTE *adj.2gên.* obedient.
OBELISCO *s.m.* obelisk.
OBESIDADE *s.f.* obesity.
OBESO(A) *adj.* obese.
ÓBITO *s.m.* death.
OBITUÁRIO *s.m.* obituary.
OBJEÇÃO *s.f.* objection, opposition.
OBJETAR *v.* to object.
OBJETIVO(A) *adj.* objective / *s.m.* objective, aim.
OBJETO *s.m.* object.
OBLAÇÃO *s.m.* oblation.
OBLÍQUO(A) *adj.* oblique.
OBLITERAÇÃO *s.f.* obliteration.
OBLITERAR *v.* to obliterate.
OBNUBILAR *v.* to obnubilate.
OBOÉ *s.m.* oboe.
OBRA *s.f.* work.
OBRA-PRIMA *s.f.* masterpiece.
OBREIRO *s.m.* worker.
OBRIGAÇÃO *s.f.* obligation, duty.
OBRIGADO(A) *adj.* required / *interj.* thanks, thank you.
OBRIGAR *v.* to compel; to force.
OBRIGATÓRIO(A) *adj.* compulsory, obligatory.
OBSCENIDADE *s.f.* obscenity.
OBSCENO(A) *adj.* obscene.
OBSCURECER *v.* to obfuscate, to obscure.
OBSCURIDADE *s.f.* obscurity.
OBSCURO(A) *adj.* obscure; dark.
OBSÉQUIO *s.m.* favour.
OBSERVAÇÃO *s.f.* observation.
OBSERVADOR(A) *adj.* observant / *s.m.* observer.
OBSERVAR *v.* to observe, to look.
OBSERVATÓRIO *s.m.* observatory.
OBSESSÃO *s.f.* obsession.
OBSESSIVO(A) *adj.* obsessive.

OBSESSO(A) *adj.* obsessive, tormented.
OBSOLETO(A) *adj.* obsolete.
OBSTÁCULO *s.m.* obstacle.
OBSTETRA *s.2gên.* obstetrician.
OBSTETRÍCIA *s.f.* obstetrics.
OBSTINAÇÃO *s.f.* obstinacy.
OBSTINADO(A) *adj.* stubborn, obstinate.
OBSTRUÇÃO *s.f.* obstruction; obstacle.
OBSTRUIR *v.* to obstruct.
OBTENÇÃO *s.f.* obtainment.
OBTER *v.* to obtain.
OBTURAÇÃO *s.f.* filling.
OBTURAR *v.* to fill.
OBVIEDADE *s.f.* obviousness.
ÓBVIO(A) *adj.* obvious.
OCASIÃO *s.f.* opportunity, occasion.
OCASIONAL *adj.2gên.* occasional.
OCASIONAR *v.* to occasion; to bring about.
OCASO *s.m.* sunset, occident.
OCEÂNICO(A) *adj.* oceanic.
OCEANO *s.m.* ocean.
OCEANOGRAFIA *s.f.* oceanography.
OCIDENTAL *adj.2gên.* western, west.
OCIDENTE *s.m.* west.
ÓCIO *s.m.* leisure; laziness.
OCIOSO(A) *adj.* idler.
OCLUIR *v.* to close.
OCLUSÃO *s.f.* closure.
OCLUSIVO(A) *adj.* occlusive.
OCO(A) *adj.* hollow.
OCORRÊNCIA *s.f.* event, happening, incident.
OCORRER *v.* to occur, to happen.
OCRE *s.m.* ochre.
OCTAEDRO *s.m.* octahedron.
OCTOGONAL *adj.2gên.* octagonal.
OCTÓGONO *s.m.* octagon.
ÓCTUPLO *num.* octuplet.
OCULAR *adj.2gên.* ocular.
OCULISTA *s.2gên.* oculist; optician.
ÓCULOS *s.m.* glasses.
OCULTAR *v.* to conceal, to hide.
OCULTISMO *s.m.* occultism.
OCULTO(A) *adj.* occult; hidden.
OCUPAÇÃO *s.f.* occupation.
OCUPACIONAL *adj.2gên.* occupational.
OCUPADO(A) *adj.* busy.
OCUPAR *v.* to occupy; to get busy.
ODALISCA *s.f.* odalisque.
ODE *s.f.* ode.

ODIADO(A) *adj.* hated.
ODIAR *v.* to hate.
ÓDIO *s.m.* hate.
ODISSEIA *s.f.* odyssey.
ODONTOLOGIA *s.f.* odontology.
ODONTOLÓGICO(A) *adj.* odontological.
ODOR *s.m.* smell.
ODORÍFERO(A) *adj.* odoriferous; fragrant.
OESTE *s.m.* west.
OFEGANTE *adj.2gên.* puffed, breathless.
OFEGAR *v.* to pant, to wheeze.
OFENDER *v.* to offend.
OFENDIDO(A) *adj.* offended.
OFENSA *s.f.* offense.
OFENSIVA *s.f.* offensive.
OFENSIVO(A) *adj.* offensive.
OFENSOR *s.m.* offender.
OFERECER *v.* to offer.
OFERENDA *s.f.* offering.
OFERTA *s.f.* offer.
OFICIAL *adj.2gên.* official / *s.2gên.* officer.
OFICIALIZAR *v.* to officialize.
OFICINA *s.f.* workshop.
OFÍCIO *s.m.* occupation.
OFTALMIA *s.f.* ophthalmia.
OFTÁLMICO(A) *adj.* ophthalmic.
OFTALMOLOGIA *s.f.* ophthalmology.
OFTALMOLOGISTA *s.2gên.* ophthalmologist.
OFTALMOSCÓPIO *s.m.* ophthalmoscope.
OFUSCAR *v.* to overshadow.
OGRO *s.m.* ogre.
OI *interj.* hi, hello.
OITAVA *s.f.* octave.
OITAVO *num.* eighth.
OITENTA *num.* eighty.
OITO *num.* eight.
OITOCENTOS *num.* eight hundred.
OLÁ *interj.* hi, hello.
ÓLEO *s.m.* oil.
OLEODUTO *s.m.* pipeline.
OLEOSIDADE *s.f.* oiliness.
OLEOSO(A) *adj.* oily; greasy.
OLFATO *s.m.* smell.
OLHADA *s.f.* glance.
OLHAR *v.* to see, to look.
OLHO *s.m.* eye.
OLIGARQUIA *s.f.* oligarchy.
OLIGÁRQUICO(A) *adj.* oligarchic.
OLIMPÍADA *s.f.* Olympiad.

OLÍMPICO(A) *adj.* Olympic.
OLIVA *s.f.* olive.
OLIVEIRA *s.f.* olive tree.
OLVIDAR *v.* to forget.
OMBREIRA *s.f.* shoulder piece; jamb.
OMBRO *s.m.* shoulder.
ÔMEGA *s.m.* omega.
OMELETE *s.2gên.* omelet.
OMISSÃO *s.f.* omission.
OMITIDO(A) *adj.* omitted.
OMITIR *v.* to omit.
OMÓFAGO *adj.* omophagous.
ONÇA *s.f.* jaguar; ounce.
ONCOLOGIA *s.f.* oncology.
ONCOLOGISTA *s.2gên.* oncologist.
ONDA *s.f.* wave.
ONDE *adv.* where.
ONDULAÇÃO *s.f.* curl.
ONDULADO(A) *adj.* curly; wavy.
ONDULAR *v.* to wave.
ONERAR *v.* to burden, to tax.
ÔNIBUS *s.m.* bus.
ONIPOTÊNCIA *s.f.* omnipotence.
ONIPOTENTE *adj.2gên.* omnipotent.
ONIPRESENÇA *s.f.* omnipresence.
ONIPRESENTE *adj.2gên.* omnipresent.
ONISCIÊNCIA *s.f.* omniscience.
ONISCIENTE *adj.2gên.* omniscient.
ONÍVORO(A) *adj.* omnivorous.
ONOMÁSTICA *s.f.* onomastics.
ONOMÁSTICO(A) *adj.* onomastic.
ONOMATOPEIA *s.f.* onomatopoeia.
ONTEM *adv.* yesterday.
ONTOGENIA *s.f.* ontogenesis.
ONTOLOGIA *s.f.* ontology.
ONTOLOGISTA *s.2gên.* ontologist.
ÔNUS *s.m.* onus.
ONZE *num.* eleven.
OPA *interj.* whoops
OPACIDADE *s.f.* opacity.
OPACO(A) *adj.* opaque.
OPALA *s.f.* opal.
OPÇÃO *s.f.* option, choice.
OPCIONAL *adj.2gên.* optional.
ÓPERA *s.f.* opera.
OPERAÇÃO *s.f.* operation.
OPERACIONAL *adj.2gên.* operational.
OPERADOR(A) *s.m.* operator.
OPERANTE *adj.2gên.* operative, operating.
OPERAR *v.* to operate.
OPERÁRIO(A) *s.m.* worker.
OPERATIVO(A) *adj.* operative.
OPERATÓRIO(A) *adj.* operative; surgical.
OPERETA *s.f.* operetta.
OPINAR *v.* to opine.
OPINIÃO *s.f.* opinion.
ÓPIO *s.m.* opium.
OPONENTE *s.2gên.* opponent.
OPOR *v.* to oppose.
OPORTUNIDADE *s.f.* opportunity.
OPORTUNISMO *s.m.* opportunism.
OPORTUNISTA *s.2gên.* opportunist / *adj.2gên.* opportunistic.
OPORTUNO(A) *adj.* opportune.
OPOSIÇÃO *s.f.* opposition.
OPOSTO(A) *adj.* opposite.
OPRESSÃO *s.f.* oppression.
OPRESSIVIDADE *s.f.* oppressiveness.
OPRESSIVO(A) *adj.* oppressive.
OPRESSOR(A) *s.m.* oppressor.
OPRIMIR *v.* to oppress; to overbear.
OPRÓBRIO *s.m.* opprobrium.
OPTAR *v.* to choose, to decide for.
OPTATIVO(A) *adj.* optative.
ÓPTICO(A) *adj.* optic, optical.
OPULÊNCIA *s.f.* opulence.
ORA *interj.* well.
ORAÇÃO *s.f.* prayer.
ORÁCULO *s.m.* oracle.
ORADOR(A) *s.m.* orator.
ORAL *adj.2gên.* oral.
ORALIDADE *s.f.* orality.
ORANGOTANGO *s.m.* orangutan.
ORAR *v.* to pray.
ÓRBITA *s.f.* orbit.
ORCA *s.f.* orca.
ORÇAMENTO *s.m.* budget.
ORÇAR *v.* to calculate.
ORDEM *s.f.* order.
ORDENADO *s.m.* wage.
ORDENAR *v.* to command.
ORDENHAR *v.* to milk.
ORDINAL *adj.2gên.* ordinal.
ORDINÁRIO(A) *adj.* ordinary.
ORELHA *s.f.* ear.
ORFANATO *s.m.* orphanage.
ÓRFÃO(Ã) *s.m.* orphan / *adj.* orphan.
ORGÂNICO *adj.* organic(al).
ORGANISMO *s.m.* organism.
ORGANIZAÇÃO *s.f.* organization.

ORGANIZACIONAL *adj.2gên.* organizacional.
ORGANIZADO(A) *adj.* organized.
ORGANIZAR *v.* to organize.
ORGANOGRAMA *s.m.* organogram.
ÓRGÃO *s.m.* organ.
ORGASMO *s.m.* orgasm.
ORGIA *s.f.* orgy.
ORGULHO *s.m.* pride.
ORGULHOSO(A) *adj.* proud.
ORIENTAÇÃO *s.f.* orientation; guidance.
ORIENTAL *adj.2gên.* east, oriental.
ORIENTAR *v.* to guide.
ORIENTE *s.m.* Orient, east.
ORIFÍCIO *s.m.* orifice.
ORIGAMI *s.m.* origami.
ORIGEM *s.f.* origin.
ORIGINAL *adj.2gên.* original.
ORIGINALIDADE *s.f.* originality.
ORIGINAR *v.* to originate.
ORLA *s.f.* edge.
ORNAMENTAR *v.* to ornament, to decorate.
ORNAMENTO *s.m.* ornament.
ORNITORRINCO *s.m.* platypus.
ORQUESTRA *s.f.* orchestra.
ORQUESTRAR *v.* to orchestrate.
ORQUÍDEA *s.f.* orchid.
ORTODOXO(A) *adj.* orthodox.
ORTOGRAFIA *s.f.* spelling.
ORTOPEDIA *s.f.* orthopaedics.
ORTOPÉDICO(A) *adj.* orthopaedic.
ORTOPEDISTA *s.2gên.* orthopaedist.
ORVALHO *s.m.* dew.
OSCILAÇÃO *s.f.* oscillation.
OSCILAR *v.* to oscillate.
OSMOSE *s.f.* osmosis.
ÓSSEO(A) *adj.* osseus.
OSSIFICAÇÃO *s.f.* ossification.
OSSIFICAR *v.* to ossify.
OSSO *s.m.* bone.
OSTENSIVO(A) *adj.* ostensible.
OSTENTAÇÃO *s.f.* ostentation.
OSTENTAR *v.* to flaunt.
OSTRA *s.f.* oyster.
OSTRACISMO *s.m.* ostracism.
OTÁRIO(A) *s.m.* fool.
OTIMISMO *s.m.* optimism.
OTIMISTA *s.2gên.* optimist / *adj.2gên.* optimistic.
OTIMIZAR *v.* to optimize.
ÓTIMO(A) *adj.* excellent.
OU *conj.* or, either.
OURIÇO *s.m.* hedgehog.
OURO *s.m.* gold.
OUSADIA *s.f.* daring.
OUSADO(A) *adj.* daring.
OUSAR *v.* to dare.
OUTONO *s.m.* autumn, fall.
OUTRO(A) *adj.* another, other.
OUTUBRO *s.m.* October.
OUVIDO *s.m.* ear.
OUVINTE *s.2gên.* listener.
OUVIR *v.* to listen, to hear.
OVAÇÃO *s.f.* ovation.
OVACIONAR *v.* to acclaim.
OVAL *s.f.* oval / *adj.2gên.* oval.
OVÁRIO *s.m.* ovary.
OVELHA *s.f.* sheep.
OVERDOSE *s.f.* overdose.
OVÍPARO *adj.* oviparous.
OVO *s.m.* egg.
OVULAÇÃO *s.f.* ovulation.
ÓVULO *s.m.* ovum.
OXALÁ *interj.* let`s hope.
OXICOCO *s.m.* cranberry.
OXIDAÇÃO *s.f.* oxidation.
OXIDAR *v.* to oxidize.
ÓXIDO *s.m.* oxide.
OXIGENAÇÃO *s.f.* oxygenation.
OXIGENAR *v.* to oxygenate.
OXIGÊNIO *s.m.* oxygen.
OZÔNIO *s.m.* ozone.

Pp

P, p *s.m.* the sixteenth letter of the portuguese alphabet.
PÁ *s.f.* shovel, blade, dustpan.
PACATO(A) *adj.* peaceful, pacific, quiet.
PACIÊNCIA *s.f.* patience.
PACIENTE *s.2gên.* patient / *adj.2gên.* patient, persistent.
PACÍFICO(A) *adj.* pacific / *s.m.* Pacific Ocean.
PACOTE *s.m.* packet; parcel; package.
PACTO *s.m.* pact, agreement.
PADARIA *s.f.* bakery.
PADECER *v.* to suffer.
PADEIRO *s.m.* baker.
PADRÃO *s.m.* standard.
PADRASTO *s.m.* stepfather.
PADRE *s.m.* priest.
PADRINHO *s.m.* godfather; best man.
PADROEIRO(A) *s.2gên.* patron.
PADRONIZAÇÃO *s.f.* standardization.
PADRONIZAR *v.* to standardize.
PAETÊ *s.m.* spangle.
PAGAMENTO *s.m.* payment.
PAGAR *v.* to pay.
PÁGINA *s.f.* page.
PAI *s.m.* father.
PAINEL *s.m.* panel; picture.
PAÍS *s.m.* country; native land.
PAISAGEM *s.f.* scenery, landscape.
PAISAGISTA *s.2gên.* landscape painter, landscape gardener.
PAIXÃO *s.f.* passion.
PAIXONITE *s.f.* crush, infatuation.
PAJÉ *s.m.* shaman, witch-doctor.
PAJEM *s.m.* page, attendant.
PALACETE *s.m.* a small palace, stately house.
PALÁCIO *s.m.* palace.
PALADAR *s.m.* taste, palate.
PALANQUE *s.m.* stand, scaffold.
PALATO *s.m.* palate.
PALAVRA *s.f.* word; speech.
PALAVRÃO *s.m.* insulting word, curse word.
PALCO *s.m.* stage.
PALERMA *adj.2gên.* idiot, fool.
PALESTINA *s.f.* Palestine.
PALESTINO(A) *s.m.* Palestinian / *adj.* Palestinian.

PALESTRA s.f. conversation, talk.
PALESTRAR v. to converse, to talk.
PALETA s.f. palette, killjoy.
PALETÓ s.m. jacket, blazer.
PALHA s.f. straw.
PALHAÇADA s.f. buffoonery, clowning.
PALHAÇO s.m. buffoon, clown.
PALHETA s.f. musical reed, straw hat.
PÁLIDO(A) adj. pale.
PALITO s.m. match, toothpick.
PALMA s.f. palm, palm leaf.
PALMADA s.f. slap.
PALMEIRA s.f. palm tree.
PALMILHA s.f. insole.
PALMITO s.m. palm cabbage.
PÁLPEBRA s.f. eyelid.
PALPITAR v. to palpitate.
PALPITE s.m. suggestion, tip.
PANAMÁ s.m. Panama.
PANCADA s.f. blow, knock.
PANCADARIA s.f. scuffle, fray.
PANDA s.m. panda.
PANDEMIA s.f. pandemic.
PANDEIRO s.m. tambourine.
PANELA s.f. pot, pan, pressure cooker.
PANFLETO s.m. pamphlet.
PÂNICO s.m. panic.
PANO s.m. cloth.
PANQUECA s.f. pancake.
PANTANAL s.m. swampland.
PÂNTANO s.m. swamp, marsh.
PANTERA s.f. panther.
PÃO s.m. bread.
PAPA s.m. pope.
PAPAGAIO s.m. parrot; kite.
PAPAI s.m. daddy.
PAPEL s.m. paper; role; wrapping paper.
PAPELADA s.f. heap of papers, documents.
PAPO s.m. crop, pouch, craw, goitre.
PAQUERAR v. to flirt.
PAQUISTANÊS(ESA) s.m. Pakistani / adj. Pakistani.
PAQUISTÃO s.m. Pakistan.
PAR s.m. pair, couple.
PARA prep. to, for.
PARABENIZAR v. to congratulate.
PARABÉNS s.m. congratulations.
PARA-BRISA s.m. windshield.
PARA-CHOQUE s.m. bumper.
PARADA s.f. parade; stop; halt.

PARADO adj. still, quiet.
PARAFUSO s.m. screw.
PARÁGRAFO s.m. paragraph.
PARAGUAI s.m. Paraguay.
PARAGUAIO(A) s.m. Paraguayan / adj. Paraguayan.
PARAÍSO s.m. paradise.
PARA-LAMA s.m. mudguard.
PARAPEITO s.m. parapet.
PARAPENTE s.m. parasail, parasailing.
PARAQUEDAS s.m. parachute.
PARAR v. to stop.
PARA-RAIOS s.m. pl. lightning-rod.
PARASITA s.m. parasite.
PARCEIRO s.m. partner.
PARCELA s.f. parcel, portion.
PARCERIA s.f. partnership.
PARCIAL adj.2gên. partial.
PARDO s.m. mulatto, dark, dusky.
PARECER v. to appear, to seem / s.m. opinion.
PARECIDO s.m. similar, resembling.
PAREDE s.f. wall.
PARENTE s.m. relative, kinsman.
PARÊNTESES s.m. parenthesis.
PÁREO s.m. heat.
PARIS s.f. Paris.
PARLAMENTAR s.2gên. parliamentarian, parliamentary.
PARÓQUIA s.f. parish, city district.
PARQUE s.m. park.
PARTE s.f. part.
PARTICIPAR v. to participate.
PARTICULAR adj.2gên. private.
PARTIDA s.f. departure; match; game.
PARTIDO s.m. party, political organization.
PARTILHAR v. to divide, to partition.
PARTIR v. to leave; to split.
PARTO s.m. childbirth, delivery.
PÁSCOA s.f. Easter.
PASMO s.m. amazement, astonishment.
PASSADO s.m. past / adj. last, past.
PASSAGEIRO s.m. passenger, traveller.
PASSAGEM s.f. passage.
PASSAPORTE s.m. passport.
PASSAR v. to pass.
PASSARELA s.f. footbridge, catwalk.
PÁSSARO s.m. bird.
PASSATEMPO s.m. pastime, hobby.
PASSE s.m. pass, permission.

PASSEAR *v.* to stroll; to hang out; to ramble.
PASSEATA *s.f.* protest march.
PASSIVO *adj.* passive.
PASSO *s.m.* pace, step, walk, gait.
PASTA *s.f.* past.
PASTEL *s.m.* fried pie, pastel, pastel crayon.
PASTELARIA *s.f.* pastry shop.
PASTILHA *s.f.* pastille, lozenge.
PASTOR *s.m.* pastor, minister.
PATA *s.f.* paw, pad, female duck.
PATETA *s.2gên.* simpleton, fool / *adj.2gên.* goofy.
PATÉTICO *s.m.* pathetic.
PATIM *s.m.* skate, runner.
PATINAR *v.* to skate, to roller-skate.
PÁTIO *s.m.* patio, yard.
PATO *s.m.* duck.
PATRÃO *s.m.* boss.
PÁTRIA *s.f.* native country, motherland, fatherland.
PATRIMÔNIO *s.m.* birthright, heritage, inheritance, patrimony.
PATRIOTA *s.2gên.* patriot.
PATROCINAR *v.* to sponsor.
PATRULHA *s.f.* patrol, patrollilng.
PAUSA *s.f.* pause.
PAUTA *s.f.* staff, list, roll, guidelines.
PAVÃO *s.m.* peacock.
PAVILHÃO *s.m.* pavilion, canopy, banner.
PAVIMENTO *s.m.* pavement, floor, story.
PAVOR *s.m.* fear, dread, terror.
PAZ *s.f.* peace.
PÉ *s.m.* foot.
PEÃO *s.m.* peon, drudge; pawn.
PEÇA *s.f.* piece; play.
PECADO *s.m.* sin.
PECAR *v.* to sin, to commit a sin.
PECHINCHA *s.f.* bargain.
PEDAÇO *s.m.* piece, bit, fragment.
PEDÁGIO *s.m.* toll.
PEDAL *s.m.* pedal.
PEDESTRE *s.2gên.* pedestrian.
PEDIDO *s.m.* order; request.
PEDIR *v.* to ask for, to beg.
PEDÓFILO *s.m.* pedophile.
PEDRA *s.f.* stone.
PEGADA *s.f.* act of catching; footprint.
PEGAJOSO(A) *adj.* sticky.
PEGAR *v.* to catch, to get.
PEITO *s.m.* chest, breast.

PEIXE *s.m.* fish.
PEIXES *s.m.* Pisces.
PELADA *s.f.* football game.
PELADO *adj.* naked, bare.
PELE *s.f.* skin; fur.
PELÍCULA *s.f.* film.
PELO *prep.* for the.
PELO *s.m.* fur, hair.
PELÚCIA *s.m.* plush.
PELUDO *adj.* hairy; furry.
PENA *s.f.* feather. pity.
PÊNALTI *s.m.* penalty.
PENDURAR *v.* to hang.
PENEIRA *s.f.* sieve.
PENETRAR *v.* to penetrate, to invade.
PENHASCO *s.m.* cliff.
PENICILINA *s.f.* penicillin.
PENÍNSULA *s.f.* peninsula.
PÊNIS *s.m.* penis.
PENITÊNCIA *s.f.* contrition, penance.
PENSAMENTO *s.m.* thought.
PENSÃO *s.f.* pension, allowance.
PENSAR *v.* to think.
PENSIONISTA *s.2gên.* boarder.
PENTE *s.m.* comb.
PENÚLTIMO *adj.* last but one.
PEPINO *s.m.* cucumber.
PEQUENO(A) *adj.* little, small.
PEQUIM *s.m.* Beijing.
PERA *s.f.* pear.
PERAMBULAR *v.* to perambulate, to wander.
PERANTE *prep.* in the presence; before.
PERCEBER *v.* to perceive, to notice.
PERCENTAGEM *s.f.* percentage.
PERCEPÇÃO *s.f.* perception.
PERCEVEJO *s.m.* bedbug.
PERCORRER *v.* to go through.
PERCURSO *s.m.* route, passage, course.
PERDA *s.f.* loss.
PERDÃO *s.f.* pardon, forgiveness; sorry.
PERDER *v.* to lose.
PERDOAR *v.* to forgive.
PERECÍVEL *adj.2gên.* perishable.
PEREGRINAÇÃO *s.f.* pilgrimage.
PEREGRINO *s.m.* pilgrim, traveler.
PERFEIÇÃO *s.f.* perfection.
PERFEITO *adj.* perfect.
PERFIL *s.m.* profile.

PERFUME *s.m.* perfume, fragrance.
PERFURAR *v.* to perforate.
PERGUNTA *s.f.* question.
PERÍCIA *s.f.* skill, expertise.
PERIFERIA *s.f.* periphery, outskirts.
PERIGO *s.m.* danger.
PERIGOSO *adj.* dangerous.
PERÍODO *s.m.* period.
PERIQUITO *s.m.* parakeet.
PERITO *adj.* expert, specialist.
PERMANECER *v.* to remain.
PERMISSÃO *s.f.* permission.
PERMITIR *v.* to allow, to permit.
PERNA *s.f.* leg.
PERNILONGO *s.m.* mosquito, insect.
PÉROLA *s.f.* pearl.
PERSEGUIÇÃO *s.f.* persecution.
PERSEGUIR *v.* to pursue; to persecute.
PERSIANA *s.f.* blind, venetian blinds.
PERSISTIR *v.* to persist.
PERSONAGEM *s.f.* personage, character.
PERSONALIDADE *s.f.* personality.
PERSPECTIVA *s.f.* perspective.
PERSPICÁCIA *s.f.* perspicacity, perspicaciousness, insight.
PERSUADIR *v.* to persuade.
PERTENCER *v.* to belong.
PERTINÊNCIA *s.f.* pertinence.
PERTO *adv.* near, close / *adj.* near, close.
PERTURBAR *v.* to perturb.
PERU *s.m.* turkey; Peru (país).
PERUCA *s.f.* wig.
PESADELO *s.m.* nightmare.
PESADO *adj.* heavy.
PÊSAMES *s.m.* condolences.
PESAR *s.m.* sadness; weigh.
PESCA *s.f.* fishing.
PESCAR *v.* to fish.
PESCOÇO *s.m.* neck.
PESO *s.m.* weight.
PESQUISA *s.f.* research; investigation.
PÊSSEGO *s.m.* peach.
PESSIMISTA *s.2gên.* pessimist.
PÉSSIMO(A) *adj.* terrible.
PESSOA *s.f.* person (pl. people).
PESTANA *s.f.* eyelash
PESTE *s.f.* pest.
PÉTALA *s.f.* petal.
PETIÇÃO *s.f.* petition.
PETISCO *s.m.* tidbit, morsel.

PETRÓLEO *s.m.* oil, petroleum.
PIA *s.f.* sink.
PIADA *s.f.* joke.
PIANISTA *s.2gên.* pianist.
PIANO *s.m.* piano.
PICADA *s.f.* prick, to bite.
PICANTE *adj.2gên.* spicy, picante.
PICAR *v.* to prick; bite.
PICO *s.m.* peak, apex.
PICOLÉ *s.m.* popsicle, ice pop.
PICOTAR *v.* to perforate.
PIEDADE *s.f.* piety, mercy.
PIFAR *v.* to break down.
PIJAMA *s.m.* pijamas.
PILAR *s.m.* pillar; grind.
PILHA *s.f.* pile; battery.
PILOTAR *v.* to pilot.
PILOTO *s.m.* pilot.
PÍLULA *s.f.* pill.
PIMENTA *s.f.* pepper.
PIMENTÃO *s.m.* bell pepper.
PINÇA *s.f.* tweezers, nippers, tongs.
PINCEL *s.m.* brush.
PINGAR *v.* to drip; to drizzle.
PINGO *s.m.* drop; little bite.
PINGUE-PONGUE *s.m.* ping pong, table tennis.
PINGUIM *s.m.* penguin.
PINO *s.m.* plug, pin, peg.
PINTA *s.f.* mole, spot; appearance.
PINTAR *v.* to paint.
PINTO *s.m.* chick; prick.
PINTOR(A) *s.m.* painter.
PINTURA *s.f.* painting.
PIOLHO *s.m.* louse.
PIONEIRO(A) *s.m.* pioneer.
PIOR *adj.2gên.* worse / *adv.* worse.
PIPOCA *s.f.* popcorn.
PIPOCAR *v.* to pop, to burst.
PIQUENIQUE *s.m.* picnic.
PIRATA *s.m.* pirate.
PIRULITO *s.m.* lollipop.
PISCA-PISCA *s.m.* blinker.
PISCINA *s.f.* swimming pool.
PISO *s.m.* floor.
PISTA *s.f.* lane, trail; trace, clue.
PISTOLA *s.f.* pistol.
PLACA *s.f.* sign, plate, plaque, tag.
PLACAR *v.* to score; to plaque; to placate.

PLANALTO *s.m.* plateau.
PLANEJAMENTO *s.m.* planning.
PLANEJAR *v.* to plan.
PLANETA *s.m.* planet.
PLANÍCIE *s.f.* plain.
PLANILHA *s.f.* spreadsheet.
PLANO *s.m.* plan.
PLANTA *s.f.* plant.
PLANTAR *v.* to plant.
PLÁSTICO *s.m.* plastic.
PLATEIA *s.f.* stalls; audience.
POBRE *adj.2gên.* poor.
PODER *s.m.* power / *v.* to can.
PODRE *adj.2gên.* rotten, putrid.
POLÍCIA *s.f.* police.
POLPA *s.f.* pulp.
POLUIÇÃO *s.f.* pollution.
POLVO *s.m.* octopus.
POMADA *s.f.* pomade, ointment.
POMBA *s.f.* dove, pigeon.
PONTE *s.f.* bridge.
PONTO *s.m.* point, dot.
PÔR *v.* to put, to place / *s.m.* sunset (pôr do sol).
PORCO *s.m.* pig / *adj.* filthy.
PORÉM *conj.* however.
PORQUE *conj.* because.
PORTA *s.f.* door.
PORTANTO *conj.* so, therefore.
POSIÇÃO *s.f.* position.
POSITIVO *adj.* positive.
POSSIBILIDADE *s.f.* possibility.
POTÊNCIA *s.f.* power.
POUCO *adj.* few, not many, not much, little.
POVO *s.m.* people.

PRAÇA *s.f.* square.
PRAIA *s.f.* beach.
PRATA *s.f.* silver.
PRECE *s.f.* prayer.
PREÇO *s.m.* price.
PREENCHER *v.* to fill, to complete.
PREFEITO *s.m.* mayor.
PREGUIÇA *s.f.* laziness.
PREOCUPAÇÃO *s.f.* preoccupation, worry.
PRESENÇA *s.f.* presence.
PRESIDÊNCIA *s.f.* presidency.
PRESSÃO *s.f.* pressure.
PRESUNTO *s.m.* ham.
PREZADO(A) *adj.* dear.
PRIMAVERA *s.f.* spring.
PRIMEIRO(A) *adj.* first.
PRIMITIVO(A) *adj.* primitive.
PRIMO(A) *s.m.* cousin.
PRINCESA *s.f.* princess.
PRÍNCIPE *s.m.* prince.
PRIVILÉGIO *s.m.* privilege.
PROBLEMA *s.m.* problem.
PROMESSA *s.f.* promise.
PROMETER *v.* to promise.
PROMOÇÃO *s.f.* promotion.
PRONÚNCIA *s.f.* pronunciation.
PRÓPRIO(A) *adj.* own, proper.
PROTEÍNA *s.f.* protein.
PROVA *s.f.* test, proof, evidence.
PRÓXIMO(A) *adj.* near, next.
PULSEIRA *s.f.* bracelet.
PULSO *s.m.* wrist, pulse.
PUNHO *s.m.* fist.
PUREZA *s.f.* purity, pureness.
PÚRPURA *s.f.* purple.

Q q

Q, q *s.m.* the seventeenth letter of the Portuguese alphabet.
QUADRA *s.f.* block; court; season; quatrain.
QUADRADO *adj.* square, quadrate; four square; pane / *s.m.* square, quadrate; four square; pane.
QUADRAGENÁRIO *s.m.* quadragenarian.
QUADRAGÉSIMO *num.* fortieth.
QUADRANGULADO *adj.* quadrangular.
QUADRANGULAR *adj. m.q.* quadrangulado.
QUADRANTE *s.m.* quadrant, four square.
QUADRAR *v.* to square, to quadrate, to make square; to agree with.
QUADRÍCEPS *s.m.* quadriceps.
QUADRICULAR *v.* to chequer, to checker, to cross line / *adj.2gên.* ruled in squares, square-lined.
QUADRÍCULO *s.m.* small square.
QUADRIÊNIO *s.m.* quadriennium, quadrennium.
QUADRIGÊMEO *adj.* quadrigeminal, quadrigeminous / *s.m.* quadruplet.
QUADRIL *s.m.* hip.
QUADRILÁTERO *s.m.* quadrangle / *adj.* quadrilateral.
QUADRILHA *s.f.* quadrille, square dance; gang, band; squadron.
QUADRINHOS *s.m. pl.* comic book.
QUADRO *s.m.* painting, picture; chart; table, schedule.
QUADRO-NEGRO *s.m.* blackboard, whiteboard, chalkboard.
QUADRÚPEDE *adj.2gên.* beast, quadruped / *s.2gên.* beast, quadruped.
QUADRUPLICAR *v.* to quadruple, to quadruplicate.
QUÁDRUPLO *num.* quadruple / *s.m.* quadruple.
QUAL *pron.* what, which.
QUALIDADE *s.f.* quality.
QUALIFICAÇÃO *s.f.* qualification.
QUALIFICADO *adj.* qualified, able, competent.
QUALIFICAR *v.* to qualify, to modify, to estimate, to appreciate; to mutate.
QUALITATIVO *adj.* qualitative.

QUALQUER *pron.* any.
QUANDO *adv.* when / *conj.* when.
QUANTIA *s.f.* quantity, amount, sum.
QUANTIDADE *s.f.* quantity; deal; amount; number.
QUANTIFICAR *v.* to quantify.
QUANTITATIVO *adj.* quantitative, measurable.
QUANTO *pron.* how much; how many / *conj.* as.
QUÃO *adv.* how, as.
QUARENTA *num.* forty.
QUARENTÃO *adj.* quadragenarian; forties / *s.m.* quadragenarian; forties.
QUARENTENA *s.f.* quarantine, confinement; sexual abstention.
QUARESMA *s.f.* Lent, Quadragesima.
QUARTA *s.f.* quarter.
QUARTA-FEIRA *s.f.* Wednesday.
QUARTEIRÃO *s.m.* block.
QUARTEL *s.m.* barracks, quarters.
QUARTETO *s.m.* quartet.
QUARTO *s.m.* bedroom, room; quarter / *num.* fourth.
QUARTZO *s.m.* quartz.
QUASE *adv.* almost.
QUASÍMODO *s.m.* Quasimodo.
QUATERNÁRIO *adj.* quaternary, quadruple.
QUATI *s.m.* coati.
QUATORZE *num.* fourteen.
QUATRO *num.* four.
QUATROCENTOS *num.* four hundred.
QUE *pron.* what, that, which.
QUEBRA *s.f.* breakage, abatement, rebate; breaking, fracture; smash.
QUEBRA-CABEÇA *s.m.* puzzle.
QUEBRADA *s.f.* slope, incline, hillside; ravine; bend of a road; remote place.
QUEBRADEIRA *s.f.* puzzle, problem; weariness; lack of money.
QUEBRADIÇO *adj.* fragile, frail.
QUEBRADO *adj.* broken; broke, bankrupt.
QUEBRA-GALHO *s.m.* stopgap.
QUEBRA-MAR *s.m.* breakwater.
QUEBRA-MOLAS *s.m.* road humps.
QUEBRA-NOZES *s.m.* pl. nutcracker.
QUEBRANTADO *adj.* debilitated, enfeebled, weakened; damaged, harmed.
QUEBRANTAR *v.* to debilitate, to weaken, to enfeeble; to break, to shatter, to crack.
QUEBRANTO *s.m.* prostration, weakness, bewitching; enfeeblement.
QUEBRA-QUEBRA *s.m.* shower of blows, brawl, fracas.
QUEBRAR *v.* to break.
QUEDA *s.f.* fall, drop.
QUEDA-D'ÁGUA *s.f.* waterfall.
QUEIJEIRA *s.f.* cheese making, dairy, female cheese maker, cheese-mould.
QUEIJO *s.m.* cheese.
QUEIMA *s.f.* burning.
QUEIMAÇÃO *s.f.* firing, burning, impertinence, annoyance.
QUEIMADA *s.f.* burned-over land, forest fire, clearing land by burning.
QUEIMADO *adj.* burnt, carbonized, scorched, seared / *s.m.* burn.
QUEIMADURA *s.f.* burn.
QUEIMAR *v.* to burn, to flame; to burn out.
QUEIXA *s.f.* complaint.
QUEIXAR-SE *v.* to make a grievance, to complain, to grumble, to whine.
QUEIXO *s.m.* chin, lower jaw.
QUEM *pron.* who.
QUENGA *s.f.* prostitute.
QUÊNIA *s.f.* Kenya.
QUENIANO *adj.* Kenyan / *s.m.* Kenyan.
QUENTE *adj.2gên.* hot, warm.
QUENTURA *s.f.* warmth, heat.
QUEPE *s.m.* kepi, flat-topped hat.
QUERATINA *s.f.* keratin.
QUERELA *s.f.* complaint, indictment, lawsuit.
QUERELAR *v.* to sue, to make a formal accusation, to complain.
QUERER *v.* to want.
QUERIDO *adj.* dear, darling.
QUERMESSE *s.f.* kermess, outdoor fair or festival, bazaar.
QUEROSENE *s.m.* kerosene.
QUERUBIM *s.m.* cherub, cherubim, angel.
QUESITO *s.m.* enquiry, query, question, subject, issue, topic.
QUESTÃO *s.f.* question, case, issue, matter; controversy, debate, dispute.
QUESTIONAR *v.* to question.
QUESTIONÁRIO *s.m.* questionnaire.
QUIADO *s.m.* okra.
QUIÇÁ *adv.* perhaps, maybe.
QUICAR *v.* to jump, to leap; to be furious.

QUICHE *s.2gên.* quiche.
QUÍCHUA *adj.2gên.* Quechua / *s.m.* Quechua.
QUIETAR *v.* to quiet, to make quiet, to calm, to pacify; to remain silent.
QUIETO *adj.* quiet, still.
QUIETUDE *s.f.* quietude, quietness, tranquility; still, hush, calm.
QUILATE *s.m.* karat, carat; fineness.
QUILO *s.m.* kilo; chyle.
QUILOGRAMA *s.m.* kilogram.
QUILOHERTZ *s.m.* kilohertz.
QUILOLITRO *s.m.* kiloliter, kilolitre.
QUILOMETRAGEM *s.f.* mileage, milage, kilometre measuring.
QUILOMÉTRICO *adj.* kilometric.
QUILÔMETRO *s.m.* kilometre, kilometer.
QUILOWATT *s.m.* kilowatt.
QUIMERA *s.f.* chimera; phantasm, unreality.
QUÍMICA *s.f.* Chemistry.
QUÍMICO *s.m.* chemist / *adj.* chemical.
QUIMIOTERAPIA *s.f.* chemotherapy.
QUIMO *s.m.* chyme.
QUIMONO *s.m.* kimono.
QUINA *s.f.* set of five; corner or edge of a tableshop; quinine.
QUINHÃO *s.m.* portion, part, division, lot, destiny.
QUINHENTOS *num.* five hundred.
QUINQUAGÉSIMO *num.* five hundredth, fiftieth.
QUINQUÊNIO *s.m.* quinquennium.
QUINQUILHARIA *s.f.* gewgaws, fripperies; children's toys, trifles, bagatelles.

QUINTA-FEIRA *s.f.* Thursday.
QUINTAL *s.m.* back yard, back garden.
QUINTETO *s.m.* quintet.
QUINTO *num.* fifth, fifth part.
QUINTUPLICAR *v.* to quintuple.
QUÍNTUPLO *s.m.* quintuple.
QUINZE *num.* fifteen.
QUINZENA *s.f.* period of fifteen days, fortnight, two weeks.
QUINZENAL *adj.2gên.* fortnightly, biweekly, bimonthly.
QUIOSQUE *s.m.* kiosk; bookstall, newsstand.
QUIROMANCIA *s.f.* chiromancy, palmistry.
QUISTO *adj.* cyst, well-loved.
QUITAÇÃO *s.f.* quittance, discharge, release; quitter.
QUITANDA *s.f.* greengrocery, small shop.
QUITANDEIRO *s.m.* greengrocer.
QUITAR *v.* to quit, to cease, to desist, to release, to abandon, to leave.
QUITE *adj.2gên.* even, quit; square, quits.
QUITUTE *s.m.* titbit, canapé, light snack, dainty, delicacy.
QUIXOTE *s.m.* ingenious and idealistic individual.
QUIXOTESCO *adj.* quixotic, chivalrous.
QUIXOTISMO *s.m.* quixotism.
QUOCIENTE *s.m.* quotient.
QUÓRUM *s.m.* quorum.
QUOTA *s.f.* share.
QUOTIDIANO *s.m.* everyday, daily.
QUOTIZAR *v.* to distribute shares, to assess, to estimate.

Rr

R, r *s.m.* the eighteenth letter of the Portuguese alphabet.
RÃ *s.f.* frog.
RABANADA *s.f.* French toast.
RABANETE *s.m.* radish.
RÁBANO *s.m.* turnip, horseradish.
RABEAR *v.* to fidget, to be restless, to skid.
RABECA *s.f.* fiddle, violin.
RABIAR *v.* to rage, to become enraged.
RABICHO *s.m.* pigtail; love, passion.
RÁBICO(A) *adj.* rabic.
RABINO *s.m.* rabbi.
RABISCAR *v.* to scribble, to doodle.
RABISCO *s.m.* scribble, doodling, scribbling.
RABO *s.m.* tail.
RABO DE CAVALO *s.m.* ponytail.
RABUDO(A) *adj.* long-tailed, tailed; lucky.
RABUGENTO(A) *adj.* sullen, cross, grumpy.
RAÇA *s.f.* race (humana), breed (animal).
RAÇÃO *s.f.* animal food, fodder.
RACHA *s.m.* crack; illegal street race.
RACHADO *adj.* cracked, cleft.
RACHADURA *s.f.* crack, cleaving.
RACHAR *v.* to crack, to split, to chop.
RACIAL *adj.2gên.* racial.
RACIOCINAR *v.* to reason, to think.
RACIOCÍNIO *s.m.* thought, consideration.
RACIONAL *adj.2gên.* logical, reasonable.
RACIONALIZAR *v.* to rationalize.
RACIONAMENTO *s.m.* rationing.
RACIONAR *v.* to ration, to restrict supply of.
RACISMO *s.m.* racism.
RACISTA *adj.2gên.* racist / *s.2gên.* racist.
RADAR *s.m.* radar.
RADIAÇÃO *s.f.* radiation.
RADIADOR *s.m.* radiator.
RADIAL *adj.2gên.* radial.
RADIALISTA *s.2gên.* broadcaster.
RADIANO(A) *adj.* radian.
RADIANTE *adj.2gên.* radiante, brilliant, splendid.
RADIAR *v.* to radiate, to sparkle, to beam.
RADICADO(A) *adj.* rooted, inveterate.
RADICAL *adj.2gên.* radical.
RADICALISMO *s.m.* radicalism.
RADICALIZAÇÃO *s.f.* radicalization.
RADICALIZAR *v.* to radicalize.
RADICAR *v.* to take root, to root.

RADÍCULA *s.f.* radicule, rootlet.
RÁDIO *s.m.* radio (aparelho), radium (química), radius (osso).
RADIOATIVIDADE *s.f.* radioactivity.
RADIOATIVO(A) *adj.* radioactive.
RADIOCOMUNICAÇÃO *s.f.* radio communication.
RADIODIFUSÃO *s.f.* radio diffusion, radio broadcasting.
RADIOFONIA *s.f.* radiophony.
RADIOFREQUÊNCIA *s.f.* radio frequency.
RADIOGRAFIA *s.f.* radiography.
RADIOLOGIA *s.f.* radiology.
RADIOLOGISTA *s.2gên.* radiologist.
RADIOMETRIA *s.f.* radiometry.
RADIÔMETRO *s.m.* radiometer.
RADIOTERAPIA *s.f.* radiotherapy.
RADIOTRANSMISSÃO *s.f.* radio transmission.
RAIA *s.f.* line, stroke, racing lane.
RAIAR *v.* to dawn, to radiate, to shine, to sparkle.
RAINHA *s.f.* queen.
RAIO *s.m.* ray (de sol), spoke (de roda), lightning (relâmpago).
RAIVA *s.f.* rage, fury, rabies (animal).
RAIVECER *v.* to rage, to rave.
RAIVOSO(A) *adj.* enraged, angry, raving.
RAIZ *s.f.* root.
RAJADA *s.f.* wind gust, squall.
RAJADO(A) *adj.* striped, streaked.
RALADO(A) *adj.* grated; wounded.
RALADOR *s.m.* grater, rasper.
RALAR *v.* to grate, to rasp.
RALÉ *s.f.* lower class.
RALI *s.m.* rally, auto rally.
RALO *s.m.* grater, strainer; drain / *adj.* thin, rare.
RAMA *s.f.* foliage.
RAMAGEM *s.f. m.q.* rama.
RAMAL *s.m.* telephone extension, extension number.
RAMALHETE *s.m.* little branch, cluster, bouquet.
RAMEIRA *s.f.* prostitute.
RAMIFICAÇÃO *s.f.* ramification, propagation.
RAMIFICAR *v.* to subdivide, to furcate.
RAMO *s.m.* branch, bough, twig.
RAMOSO(A) *adj.* branchy, twiggy, ramose.
RAMPA *s.f.* ramp, incline, slope.

RANÇAR *v.* to grow rancid.
RANCHO *s.m.* ranch; shack, shanty; fare, ration, chow; hut, shelter.
RANCIDEZ *s.f.* rancidity, staleness.
RANÇO *s.m.* rancidity, rank smell, mustiness.
RANCOR *s.m.* resentment, grudge.
RANCOROSO(A) *adj.* rancorous, grudging, resentful.
RANÇOSO(A) *adj.* rancid, stale, musty.
RANGAR *v.* to eat, to chow down.
RANGENTE *adj.2gên.* creaking, grating.
RANGER *v.* to squeak, to cerak, to grate.
RANGIDO *s.m.* squeaking, creaking, grating.
RANGO *s.m.* food, meal.
RANHURA *s.f.* groove, slot, slit.
RANZINZA *s.2gên.* sullen, sulky, crabby.
RAPADO(A) *adj.* scraped, close-shaven.
RAPAR *v.* to scrape, to scratch, to cut short.
RAPARIGA *s.f.* girl, maiden.
RAPAZ *s.m.* boy, lad.
RAPAZIADA *s.f.* spree, folly.
RAPAZOLA *s.m.* lad, young man.
RAPÉ *s.m.* snuff.
RAPIDEZ *s.f.* speed, quickness.
RÁPIDO(A) *adj.* fast, quick.
RAPINA *s.f.* rapine, robbery, plunder.
RAPOSA *s.f.* fox.
RAPOSO *s.m.* male fox; cunning fellow.
RAPTADO(A) *adj.* kidnapped.
RAPTAR *v.* to kidnap, to abduct.
RAPTO *s.m.* abduction, kidnapping.
RAQUETA *s.f.* racket, snowshoe.
RAQUETE *s.f.* racket.
RAQUÍTICO(A) *adj.* rachitic, rickety.
RAQUITISMO *s.m.* rachitis, rickets.
RAREFEITO(A) *adj.* rarefied.
RARIDADE *s.f.* rarity, scarcity.
RARO(A) *adj.* rare, scarce, thin.
RASANTE *adj.2gên.* grazing, sweeping, skimming.
RASCUNHAR *v.* to sketch, to outline.
RASCUNHO *s.m.* sketch, draft, drawing.
RASGADO(A) *adj.* ripped, torn, rent.
RASGAR *v.* to tear, to rip, to rend.
RASGO *s.m.* rip, tear, scratch.
RASO(A) *adj.* plain, shallow, level.
RASPA *s.f.* shavings, filings.
RASPAGEM *s.f.* scrapings, shavings; abrasion.
RASPÃO *s.m.* scratch, slight injury.

RASPAR v. to scrape, to scratch; to scamper off, to run away.
RASTEAR. v. m.q. rastrear.
RASTEIRA s.f. treacherous act.
RASTEIRO(A) adj. creeping, crawling; humble, modest.
RASTEJADOR(A) s.m. searcher, tracker, tracer.
RASTEJANTE adj.2gên. searching, tracing.
RASTEJAR v. to search, to track, to trace.
RASTEJO s.m. tracing, tracking, investigation.
RASTELO s.m. rake, harrow.
RASTO s.m. m.q. rastro.
RASTREAR v. to track down, to trace, to look for.
RASTRO s.m. track, trace, spoor, clue.
RASURA s.f. erasure, obliteration.
RASURADO(A) adj. erased, blotted out.
RASURAR v. to erase, to obliterate, to blot out.
RATA s.f. female rat; blunder, failure, flop.
RATAZANA s.f. female rat; odd person.
RATEAR v. to prorate, to portion out, to divide.
RATEIO s.m. distribution, proration, division.
RATIFICAÇÃO s.f. ratification, confirmation.
RATIFICAR v. to ratify, to confirm.
RATO s.m. mouse, rat.
RATOEIRA s.f. mousetrap, trick, trap.
RAZÃO s.f. reason.
RAZOÁVEL adj.2gên. reasonable.
RÉ s.f. reverse gear; female defendant.
REABASTECER v. to resupply, to replenish.
REABERTURA s.f. reopening.
REABILITAÇÃO s.f. rehabilitation, rehab.
REABILITADO(A) adj. rehabilitated.
REABILITAR v. to rehabilitate.
REABRIR v. to reopen.
REABSORVER v. to reabsorb.
REAÇÃO s.f. reaction.
REACIONÁRIO(A) adj. reactionary.
READAPTAÇÃO s.f. readaptation.
READAPTAR v. to readapt.
READMISSÃO s.f. readmission.
READMITIR v. to readmit.
REAGENTE adj.2gên. reagent.
REAGIR v. to react, to respond, to resist.
REAJUSTAR v. to readjust.
REAJUSTE s.m. readjustment.
REAL adj.2gên. real, royal / s.m. real.
REALÇAR v. to enhance, to emphasize, to highlight, to intensify.
REALCE s.m. distinction, enhancement.
REALEJO s.m. hurdy-gurdy.
REALEZA s.f. royalty, regality, kingship.
REALIDADE s.f. reality.
REALISMO s.m. realism.
REALISTA adj.2gên. realist.
REALÍSTICO(A) adj. realistic, lifelike.
REALIZAÇÃO s.f. fulfilment, achievement.
REALIZADO(A) adj. realized, achieved.
REALIZADOR(A) adj. achiever, accomplisher / s.m. achiever, accomplisher.
REALIZAR v. to perform, to carry out; to accomplish, to achieve.
REALMENTE adv. really, indeed.
REATAR v. to rebind, to reattach.
REATIVIDADE s.f. reactivity.
REATIVO(A) adj. reactive.
REATOR s.m. reactor, converter.
REAVER v. to get back, to recover, to reobtain, to retrieve.
REBAIXA s.f. reduction, diminution.
REBAIXADO(A) adj. lowered, debased; relegated (futebol).
REBAIXAMENTO s.m. lowering; relegation (futebol).
REBAIXAR v. to lower, to decrease in value; to relegate (futebol).
REBANHO s.m. herd, troop, livestock.
REBATE s.m. alarm, surprise attack, discount.
REBATER v. to strike again, to repel, to return.
REBATIDO(A) adj. repelled, disproved.
REBELAR v. to revolt, to rebel; to rise against.
REBELDE adj.2gên. rebel, deserter, insurgent.
REBELDIA s.f. rebellion, revolt.
REBELIÃO s.f. rebellion, mutiny, insurrection.
REBENTO s.m. child, scion; shoot.
REBITE s.m. rivet, clinch.
REBOBINAR v. to rewind, to reel again.
REBOCAR v. to plaster, to tow.
REBOLAR v. to swing, to sway.
REBOQUE s.m. towage; tow truck, trailer.
REBOTE s.m. rebound.
REBU s.m. confusion, disorder.
REBULIÇO s.m. noise, uproar, confusion.
REBUSCADO(A) adj. refined.

REBUSCAR v. to search again; to refine, to rummage.
RECADO s.m. message.
RECAÍDA s.f. relapse, setback.
RECAIR v. to fall back, to relapse.
RECALCADO(A) adj. repressed, frustrated.
RECALCAR v. to step on, to tread, to repress.
RECALQUE s.m. repression, suppression.
RECAPITULAR v. to recapitulate, to summarize, to review.
RECARGA s.f. recharge, reload.
RECARREGAR v. to recharge, to reload.
RECATADO(A) adj. modest, prudent, proper.
RECAUCHUTADO(A) adj. retreaded; recapped.
RECAUCHUTAR v. to retread; to recap.
RECEAR v. to fear, to dread.
RECEBER v. to receive.
RECEBIMENTO s.m. receipt, reception.
RECEIO s.m. fear, apprehension.
RECEITA s.f. prescription; recipe; income, revenue.
RECEITAR v. to prescribe.
RECÉM adv. recently.
RECÉM-NASCIDO(A) s.m. newborn, newly born.
RECENTE adj. recent.
RECEOSO(A) adj. afraid, fearful.
RECEPÇÃO s.f. reception.
RECEPCIONISTA s.2gên. receptionist.
RECEPTÍVEL adj. receptible.
RECEPTIVO(A) adj. receptive / s.m. reception staff.
RECESSÃO s.f. recession.
RECESSIVO(A) adj. recessive.
RECESSO s.m. recess, break; timeout.
RECHAÇAR v. to repulse, to resist, to throw back.
RECHEAR v. to stuff, to fill, to cram.
RECHEIO s.m. stuffing; dressing.
RECIBO s.m. receipt.
RECICLAGEM s.f. recycling.
RECICLAR v. to recycle.
RECIFE s.m. reef.
RECINTO s.m. enclosure, precinct.
RECIPIENTE s.m. container.
RECÍPROCO(A) adj. reciprocal, mutual.
RECITAL s.m. recital, performance.
RECITAR v. to recite, to perform.
RECLAMAÇÃO s.f. complaint, demand.
RECLAMAR v. to complain, to nag.
RECLAME s.m. advertisement; claim, complaint.
RECLINAR v. to recline, to lean back, to lie down.
RECLINÁVEL adj.2gên. reclinable.
RECLUSÃO s.f. reclusion, confining.
RECOLHER v. to collect.
RECOMEÇAR v. to recommence, to begin again, to restart.
RECOMEÇO s.m. restart, recommencement.
RECOMENDAÇÃO s.f. recommendation.
RECOMENDAR v. to recommend, to praise.
RECOMPENSA s.f. reward.
RECOMPENSAR v. to reward, to compensate.
RECOMPOR v. to recompose, to renew.
RECONCILIAÇÃO s.f. reconciliation.
RECONCILIAR v. to reconcile, to appease.
RECONFORTANTE adj.2gên. restorative, restoring.
RECONFORTAR v. to restore, to comfort.
RECONFORTO s.m. reinvigoration, comfort.
RECONHECER v. to recognize, to admit.
RECONHECIMENTO s.m. recognition, gratitude; reward.
RECONSIDERAR v. to reconsider, to rethink.
RECONSTITUIR v. to reconstitute, to rebuild.
RECONSTRUÇÃO s.f. reconstruction, reestablishment.
RECONSTRUIR v. to rebuid, to reorganize, to reestablish.
RECORDAÇÃO s.f. souvenir; memory.
RECORDAR v. to recall, to recollect, to remember.
RECORDE s.m. record, feat.
RECORDISTA adj.2gên. record holder, record breaker.
RECORRER v. to search, to investigate; to appeal to.
RECORTADO(A) adj. indented, jagged.
RECORTAR v. to cut out.
RECORTE s.m. carving, pruning.
RECREAÇÃO s.f. fun, recreation, amusement.
RECREATIVO(A) adj. recreational, amusing.
RECREIO s.m. break, break time, recreation.
RECRIAR v. to recreate.
RECRIMINAR v. to recriminate.

RECRUTA *s.2gên.* recruit, new member.
RECUPERAÇÃO *s.f.* recovery, retrieval.
RECUPERAR *v.* to recover, to regain.
RECURSO *s.m.* resource; appeal.
RECURVAR *v.* to recurve; to twist.
RECUSA *s.f.* refusal, denial.
RECUSAR *v.* to refuse, to disclaim, to deny.
REDAÇÃO *s.f.* essay; editorial room.
REDATOR(A) *s.m.* editor, journalist.
REDE *s.f.* net, network.
REDEMOINHO *s.m.* whirl, eddy, vortex.
REDENÇÃO *s.f.* redemption, ransom.
REDENTOR(A) *s.m.* redeemer, saviour.
REDIGIR *v.* to write, to write down, to compose.
REDIMIR *v.* to redeem, to ransom.
REDOMA *s.f.* bell jar, glass shade.
REDONDEZA *s.f.* roundness; neighbourhood.
REDONDO(A) *adj.* round, circular, spherical.
REDOR *s.m.* circle, environs.
REDUÇÃO *s.f.* reduction.
REDUNDANTE *adj.2gên.* redundant.
REDUTÍVEL *adj.2gên.* reductible, divisible.
REDUTO *s.m.* redoubt, stronghold.
REDUTOR(A) *s.m.* reducer, reducing agent.
REDUZIR *v.* to reduce, to diminish.
REELEGER *v.* to reelect.
REELEIÇÃO *s.f.* reelection.
REEMBOLSAR *v.* to reimburse, to pay back.
REEMBOLSO *s.m.* reimbursement, repayment.
REENCARNAÇÃO *s.f.* reincarnation.
REENCARNAR *v.* to reincarnate.
REFAZER *v.* to make over, to repair.
REFEIÇÃO *s.f.* meal.
REFEITÓRIO *s.m.* refectory, dining hall.
REFÉM *s.2gên.* hostage.
REFERÊNCIA *s.f.* reference.
REFERENDO *s.m.* referendum.
REFERENTE *adj.2gên.* referring, regarding.
REFIL *s.m.* refill.
REFINAR *v.* to refine, to purify.
REFINARIA *s.f.* refinery.
REFLETIR *v.* to reflect, to deflect, to ponder.
REFLETOR *s.m.* reflector.
REFLEXÃO *s.f.* reflection.
REFLEXO *s.m.* reflection; reflex.
REFLORESCER *v.* to reflower.
REFLORESTAMENTO *s.m.* reforestation.
REFLORESTAR *v.* to reforest.

REFLUXO *s.m.* reflow, ebb, reflux.
REFOGAR *v.* to braise.
REFORÇADO(A) *adj.* reinforced; robust.
REFORÇAR *v.* to reinforce, to strengthen.
REFORÇO *s.m.* reinforcement, reinforcing.
REFORMA *s.f.* reform.
REFORMADO(A) *adj.* reformed person, retired officer.
REFORMAR *v.* to reform, to remodel.
REFORMATÓRIO *s.m.* reformatory.
REFRAÇÃO *s.f.* refraction.
REFRÃO *s.m.* refrain, chorus, saying.
REFRESCANTE *adj.2gên.* refreshing.
REFRESCAR *v.* to refresh.
REFRESCO *s.m.* refreshment, comfort.
REFRIGERADOR *s.m.* refrigerator, fridge.
REFRIGERANTE *s.m.* soda, pop, soft drink / *adj.2gên.* refrigerant.
REFÚGIO *s.m.* refuge, shelter, retreat.
REFUTAR *v.* to refute, to disprove.
REGADOR *s.m.* watering can, sprinkling.
REGALIA *s.f.* prerogative, liberty.
REGAR *v.* to water, to irrigate, to sprinkle.
REGATA *s.f.* regatta; halter.
REGÊNCIA *s.f.* regency, government.
REGENERAÇÃO *s.f.* regeneration.
REGENERAR *v.* to regenerate, to reproduce.
REGENERATIVO(A) *adj.* regenerative; reproducing.
REGENTE *s.2gên.* regent, governor, ruler.
REGIÃO *s.f.* region.
REGIME *s.m.* regime, administration; diet, regimen.
REGIONAL *adj.2gên.* regional.
REGISTRAR *v.* to register, to write down; to record.
REGISTRO *s.m.* register, record, registration.
REGO *s.m.* channel, duct, trench.
REGRA *s.f.* norm, standard, rule.
REGRAR *v.* to regulate, to guide, to direct.
REGRESSÃO *s.f.* regressin, returning.
REGRESSO *s.m.* return, regress.
RÉGUA *s.f.* ruler.
REGULAR *adj.2gên.* regular, constant / *v.* to regulate, to rule.
REI *s.m.* king.
REINO *s.m.* kingdom.
REJEIÇÃO *s.f.* rejection.
REJEITAR *v.* to reject.
RELAÇÃO *s.f.* relationship, connection.

RELÂMPAGO *s.m.* lightning.
RELATAR *v.* to tell, to report.
RELATIVO(A) *adj.* relative, concerning.
RELEVANTE *adj.2gên.* outstanding, relevant.
RELIGIÃO *s.f.* religion.
RELÓGIO *s.m.* clock (de parede), watch (de pulso).
REMAR *v.* to row.
REMENDAR *v.* to mend.
REMORSO *s.m.* remorse.
REMOTO(A) *adj.* remote, distant.
REMOVER *v.* to move, to remove.
RENDA *s.f.* lace; income, revenue.
REPARAR *v.* to repair, to fix, to mend.
REPARO *s.m.* repair, mending.
REPARTIR *v.* to separate, to slice, to divide.
REPETIÇÃO *s.f.* repetition.
REPLETO(A) *adj.* replete, filled up.
REPOLHO *s.m.* cabbage.
REPORTAGEM *s.f.* article, newspaper report.
REPRESA *s.f.* dam, dike.
RÉPTIL *s.2gên.* reptile.
REQUEIJÃO *s.m.* cottage cheese, cream cheese.
REQUISIÇÃO *s.f.* request, requisition.
REQUISITO *s.m.* requirement.
RESENHA *s.f.* review.
RESERVA *s.f.* reserve (natural), booking (hotel).
RESIDÊNCIA *s.f.* residence, dwelling.
RESOLVER *v.* to resolve, solve.
RESPEITAR *v.* to respect.
RESPEITO *s.m.* respect.
RESPIRAÇÃO *s.f.* breathing.
RESPONSABILIDADE *s.f.* responsibility.
RESPOSTA *s.f.* answer, response.
RESULTADO *s.m.* result.
RETORNO *s.m.* return.
RÉU *s.m.* criminal defendant, accused, respondent, criminal.

REUNIÃO *s.f.* meeting.
REVELAÇÃO *s.f.* revelation.
REVISTA *s.f.* magazine (publicação), review (inspeção).
REVÓLVER *s.m.* gun, revolver.
REZAR *v.* to pray.
RIACHO *s.m.* stream, brook.
RICO(A) *adj.* rich, wealthy.
RIGIDEZ *s.f.* rigidity, strictness.
RIM *s.m.* kidney.
RIO *s.m.* river.
RIR *v.* to laugh.
ROCHA *s.f.* rock.
ROLAR *v.* to roll.
ROLHA *s.f.* cork.
ROMÃ *s.f.* pomegranate.
ROMANCE *s.m.* novel, tale, fable.
ROMÂNTICO(A) *adj.* romantic.
RONCAR *v.* to snore.
RONCO *s.m.* snore.
ROSA *s.f.* rose (flor), pink (cor).
ROSBIFE *s.m.* roast beef.
ROSCA *s.f.* thread (parafuso); bagel (alimento).
ROSTO *s.m.* face.
ROTA *s.f.* route, direction, course.
ROTEIRO *s.m.* script; itinerary, route.
RÓTULO *s.m.* tag, label.
ROUBAR *v.* to rob, to steal.
ROUPA *s.f.* clothes.
ROXO(A) *adj.* purple, violet / *s.m.* purple, violet.
RUA *s.f.* street.
RUÍDO *s.m.* noise.
RUIM *adj.2gên.* awful, bad.
RUIVO(A) *adj.* red-haired, auburn.
RUMO *s.m.* bearing; route, course, direction.
RUPESTRE *adj.* growing on rocks, rupestrian.
RUPTURA *s.f.* rupture, breakage, rip, crack.
RURAL *adj.2gên.* rural.
RÚSTICO(A) *adj.* rustic.

S, s *s.m.* the nineteenth letter of the Portuguese alphabet.
SÁBADO *s.m.* Saturday.
SABÃO *s.m.* soap.
SABÁTICO(A) *adj.* sabbatical.
SABATINA *s.f.* weekly review; Saturday prayers.
SABATINAR *v.* to recapitulate.
SABEDORIA *s.f.* wisdom, learning.
SABER *v.* to know / *s.m.* knowledge.
SABIÁ *s.m.* red-bellied thrush.
SABICHÃO *s.m.* wiseacre, wise person.
SABIDO(A) *adj.* known.
SABINA *s.f.* savin.
SÁBIO(A) *adj.* wise.
SABÍVEL *adj.* knowable.
SABONETE *s.m.* toilet soap.
SABONETEIRA *s.f.* soap dish.
SABOR *s.m.* taste, flavour.
SABOREAR *v.* to relish, to savor, to taste.
SABOROSO(A) *adj.* tasty, delicious.
SABOTAGEM *s.f.* sabotage.
SABOTAR *v.* to sabotage.
SABRE *s.m.* saber, sword.
SABUGAR *v.* to flog.
SABUGO *s.m.* pith; slough.
SABUGUEIRO *s.m.* elder.
SABUJAR *v.* to fawn on, to flatter.
SABUJO *s.m.* bloodhound.
SACA *s.f.* sack, bag.
SACADA *s.f.* balcony, terrace.
SACADO(A) *s.m.* drawee.
SACADOR(A) *s.m.* drawer.
SACANA *adj.* lewd, libertine.
SACANAGEM *s.f.* lewdness, mockery.
SACANEAR *v.* to act scandalously.
SACÃO *s.m.* jolt, jump.
SACAR *v.* to draw; to pull out; to understand.
SACARÍDEO *s.m.* saccharide.
SACARINA *s.f.* saccharin.
SACA-ROLHAS *s.m.* corkscrew.
SACAROSE *s.f.* sucrose.
SACERDÓCIO *s.m.* priesthood.
SACERDOTAL *adj.2gên.* sacerdotal, priestly.
SACERDOTE *s.m.* clergyman, vicar, priest.
SACERDOTISA *s.f.* clergywoman, vicar, priestess.

SACHA *s.f.* hoe.
SACHAR *v.* to hoe.
SACHÊ *s.m.* sachet.
SACI *s.m.* saci.
SACIADO(A) *adj.* satiated.
SACIAR *v.* to sate, to satiate, to glut.
SACIÁVEL *adj.2gên.* satiable.
SACIEDADE *s.f.* satiation, satiety.
SACO *s.m.* bag, sack.
SACOLA *s.f.* bag, tote bag.
SACOLEJAR *v.* to shake.
SACOLEJO *s.m.* shaking.
SACRAMENTAR *v.* to transubstantiate.
SACRAMENTO *s.m.* sacrament.
SACRIFICADOR *s.m.* sacrificer / *adj.* sacrificing.
SACRIFICANTE *adj.2gên.* sacrificing / *s.2gên.* sacrificer.
SACRIFICAR *v.* to sacrifice, to offer to God.
SACRIFÍCIO *s.m.* sacrifice.
SACRILÉGIO *s.m.* profanation.
SACRISTÃO *s.m.* sacristan.
SACRISTIA *s.f.* sacristy.
SACRO *adj.* sacred, holy.
SACUDIDA *s.f.* shake.
SACUDIDELA *s.f.* light shock.
SACUDIR *v.* to shake, to quake, to jerk.
SÁDICO(A) *adj.* sadist, sadistic.
SADIO(A) *adj.* healthy, sound.
SAFADEZA *s.f.* shamelessness.
SAFADO(A) *adj.* lewd; naughty.
SAFANÃO *s.m.* flounce, push.
SAFAR *v.* to unload, to steal; to duck out.
SAFÁRI *s.m.* safari.
SAFENA *s.f.* saphena.
SAFIRA *s.f.* sapphire.
SAFRA *s.f.* anvil, crop, harvest.
SAGA *s.f.* saga.
SAGACIDADE *s.f.* sagacity, wisdom.
SAGAZ *adj.* sage, wise.
SAGRADO(A) *adj.* sacred, holy.
SAGU *s.m.* sago.
SAGUÃO *s.m.* lobby.
SAGUI *s.m.* tamarin, sagoin.
SAIA *s.f.* skirt.
SAIBRO *s.m.* gravel.
SAÍDA *s.f.* exit, way out.
SAÍDO(A) *adj.* gone out.
SAIMENTO *s.m.* funeral.
SAIOTE *s.m.* petticoat.
SAIR *v.* to go out, to leave, to quit.
SAL *s.m.* salt.
SALA *s.f.* room; living-room.
SALADA *s.f.* salad.
SALADEIRA *s.f.* salad dish, salad bowl.
SALAFRÁRIO(A) *adj.* libertine, rake.
SALAMANDRA *s.f.* salamander.
SALAME *s.m.* salami.
SALÃO *s.m.* salon, ballroom, great hall.
SALÁRIO *s.m.* wage, salary, paycheck.
SALAZ *adj.2gên.* libertine.
SALDAR *v.* to liquidate.
SALDO *s.m.* balance, rest, outcome.
SALEIRO *s.m.* salt shaker, salt cellar.
SALETA *s.f.* small hall, sitting room.
SALGADINHO *s.m.* snack crisps; appetizer.
SALGADO *s.m.* snack / *adj.* salty.
SALGAR *v.* to salt, to cure.
SALGUEIRO *s.m.* willow; food.
SALIÊNCIA *s.f.* salience, prominence.
SALIENTAR *v.* to point, to emphasize.
SALIENTE *adj.* noteworthy, outstanding.
SALINA *s.f.* salt mine, salt works.
SALINIDADE *s.f.* salinity.
SALINIZAÇÃO *s.f.* salinization.
SALINO(A) *adj.* saline.
SALITRE *s.m.* saltpetre.
SALIVA *s.f.* saliva.
SALIVAÇÃO *s.f.* salivation.
SALIVANTE *adj.2gên.* salivating.
SALIVAR *v.* to salivate / *adj.* salivary.
SALMÃO *s.m.* salmon.
SÁLMICO(A) *adj.* psalmodical.
SALMISTA *s.2gên.* psalmist.
SALMO *s.m.* psalm.
SALMONELA *s.f.* salmonella.
SALMOURA *s.f.* brine, pickle.
SALPICADO(A) *adj.* sprinkled.
SALPICAR *v.* to sprinkle, to splash.
SALSA *s.f.* parsley; salsa.
SALSÃO *s.m.* celery.
SALSEIRA *s.f.* sauce-boat, saucer.
SALSEIRO *s.m.* conflict, disorder.
SALSICHA *s.f.* sausage.
SALSINHA *s.f.* parsley.
SALTAR *v.* to leap, to jump.
SALTEADO(A) *adj.* attacked; alternated.
SALTIMBANCO *s.m.* juggler, acrobat.
SALTO *s.m.* leap, hop, jump; shoe heel.
SALUBRE *adj.2gên.* salubrious, healthy.

SALUDAR *v.* to quack; to conjure.
SALUTAR *adj.* salutary.
SALVAÇÃO *s.f.* salvation.
SALVADOR(A) *adj.* saviour.
SALVAMENTO *s.m.* salvation, rescue.
SALVAR *v.* to save.
SALVA-VIDAS *s.2gên.* lifeguard; lifesaver; lifebelt.
SALVO(A) *adj.* safe, sheltered.
SAMBA *s.m.* samba.
SAMBAR *v.* to dance the samba.
SAMBISTA *s.2gên.* samba composer, samba dancer.
SAMURAI *s.m.* samurai.
SANAR *v.* to cure, to heal.
SANATIVO(A) *adj.* sanative.
SANATÓRIO *s.m.* sanatorium, sanitarium.
SANÁVEL *adj.2gên.* curable.
SANÇÃO *s.f.* sanction, degree.
SANCIONAR *v.* to sanction, to confirm.
SANDÁLIA *s.f.* sandal.
SÂNDALO *s.m.* sandalwood.
SANDEU *s.m.* fool, madman.
SANDICE *s.f.* foolishness, nonsense.
SANDUÍCHE *s.m.* sandwich.
SANDUICHEIRA *s.f.* sandwich maker.
SANEAMENTO(A) *s.m.* sanitation.
SANEAR *v.* to improve, to sanitize.
SANFONA *s.f.* accordion.
SANFONADO(A) *adj.* pleated.
SANFONEIRO(A) *s.m.* accordionist.
SANGRAR *v.* to bleed.
SANGRENTO *adj.* bloody, bleeding.
SANGRIA *s.f.* bleeding, blood-letting; sangria.
SANGUE *s.m.* blood.
SANGUE-FRIO *s.m.* coldness.
SANGUINÁRIO(A) *adj.* cruel, bloodthirsty.
SANGUÍNEO(A) *adj.* sanguine.
SANGUINOLÊNCIA *s.f.* bloodshedding.
SANHA *s.f.* wrath, fury, rage.
SANIDADE *s.f.* sanity; hygiene.
SANITÁRIO *s.m.* water closet / *adj.* sanitary, healthful.
SANITARISTA *s.2gên.* sanitarian, hygienist.
SANTEIRO(A) *adj.* fanatic.
SANTIDADE *s.f.* holiness, sanctity.
SANTIFICAR *v.* to sanctify.
SANTINHO(A) *adj.* virtuous.
SANTO(A) *s.m.* saint / *adj.* holy, sacred.
SANTUÁRIO *s.m.* sanctuary.

SÃO *adj.* sound, healthy; saint.
SAPATA *s.f.* low shoe.
SAPATARIA *s.f.* shoe store.
SAPATEADO *s.m.* tapdance.
SAPATEAR *v.* to tapdance.
SAPATEIRO(A) *s.m.* shoemaker.
SAPATETA *s.f.* slipper.
SAPATILHA *s.f.* ballet shoe.
SAPATO *s.m.* shoe.
SAPECA *adj.2gên.* coquette; flirt.
SAPECAR *v.* to parch.
SAPEQUICE *s.f.* coquetry.
SAPIÊNCIA *s.f.* wisdom.
SAPIENTE *adj.2gên.* wise.
SAPO *s.m.* toad.
SAPOTI *s.m.* sapodilla.
SAQUE *s.m.* sack, pillage; serve; draft.
SAQUEADOR(A) *s.m.* plunderer, pillager.
SAQUEAR *v.* to plunder, to pillage.
SAQUEIO *s.m.* sack, pillage.
SARACOTEAR *v.* to sway, to ramble.
SARACOTEIO *s.m.* rambling.
SARADO(A) *adj.* healed, cured; ripped.
SARAIVA *s.f.* hail, hailstone.
SARAMPO *s.m.* measles.
SARAR *v.* to heal, to cure.
SARAU *s.m.* soiree.
SARÇA *s.f.* bramble; thorn.
SARCASMO *s.m.* sarcasm.
SARCÁSTICO(A) *adj.* sarcastic.
SARCÓFAGO *s.m.* sarcophagus, stone coffin.
SARCOMA *s.m.* sarcoma.
SARDA *s.f.* freckle.
SARDENTO(A) *adj.* freckled.
SARDINHA *s.f.* sardine.
SARDO(A) *adj.* Sardinian.
SARDOSO(A) *adj. m.q.* sardento.
SARGENTO *s.m.* sergeant.
SARGO *s.m.* sargus.
SARJA *s.f.* serge.
SARJETA *s.f.* gutter, drain.
SARNA *s.f.* itch, mange.
SARNENTO(A) *adj.* scabious, itchy.
SARRO *s.m.* tartar.
SATÃ *s.m.* Satan.
SATANÁS *s.m. m.q.* satã.
SATÂNICO *adj.* satanic, devilish.
SATANISMO *s.m.* satanism.
SATANISTA *adj.2gên.* satanist.
SATÉLITE *s.m.* satellite.

SÁTIRA *s.f.* satire, lampoon.
SATIRIÃO *s.m.* satyrium.
SATÍRICO *adj.* satiric / *s.m.* satirist.
SATIRIZAR *v.* to satirize.
SÁTIRO(A) *adj.* satyr, lecherous.
SATISFAÇÃO *s.f.* satisfaction.
SATISFATÓRIO(A) *adj.* satisfactory.
SATISFAZER *v.* to satisfy.
SATISFEITO(A) *adj.* pleased, happy.
SATURAÇÃO *s.f.* saturation.
SATURADO *adj.* saturated; sick, tired.
SATURAR *v.* to saturate.
SAUDAÇÃO *s.f.* greeting, salutation.
SAUDADE *s.f.* longing, yearning, missing.
SAUDAR *v.* to salute, to greet.
SAUDÁVEL *adj.2gên.* healthy.
SAÚDE *s.f.* health.
SAUDOSO(A) *adj.* nostalgic.
SAUNA *s.f.* sauna.
SAÚVA *s.f.* sauba ant.
SAVANA *s.f.* savanna.
SAX *s.m. m.q.* saxofone.
SAXOFONE *s.m.* sax, saxophone.
SAXOFONISTA *s.2gên.* saxophonist.
SAZÃO *s.m.* season; opportunity.
SAZONAL *adj.2gên.* seasonal.
SE *conj.* if, whether.
SÉ *s.f.* see, cathedral.
SEBE *s.f.* hedge, fence.
SEBO *s.m.* tallow, suet; antiquarian (de livros).
SEBORREIA *s.f.* seborrhea.
SEBOSO(A) *adj.* fatty, tallowy.
SECA *s.f.* drought.
SECADOR *s.m.* drier, dryer.
SECAGEM *s.f.* drying, airing.
SECANTE *adj.2gên.* drying / *s.m.* dryer.
SEÇÃO *s.f.* section; slice.
SECAR *v.* to dry; to dry up.
SECATIVO(A) *adj.* siccative.
SECO(A) *adj.* dry.
SECREÇÃO *s.f.* secretion.
SECRETARIA *s.f.* secretariat, office.
SECRETARIADO *s.m.* clerkship.
SECRETÁRIA ELETRÔNICA *s.f.* answering machine.
SECRETÁRIO(A) *adj.* secretary.
SECRETO(A) *adj.* secret, private.
SECULAR *adj.2gên.* secular.
SÉCULO *s.m.* century.

SECUNDAR *v.* to assist.
SECUNDÁRIO(A) *adj.* secondary.
SEDA *s.f.* silk.
SEDAÇÃO *s.f.* sedation.
SEDATIVO(A) *adj.* sedative.
SEDE *s.f.* thirst; headquarters.
SEDENTÁRIO(A) *adj.* sedentary.
SEDENTO *adj.* thirsty, desirous.
SEDIMENTAR *v.* to subside / *adj.2gên.* sedimentary.
SEDIMENTO *s.m.* sediment, deposit.
SEDOSO(A) *adj.* silky, smooth.
SEDUÇÃO *s.f.* seduction.
SEDUTOR(A) *adj.* seductive / *s.m.* seducer.
SEDUZIR *v.* to seduce.
SEDUZÍVEL *adj.2gên.* seducible.
SEGA *s.f.* harvest.
SEGAR *v.* to harvest, to reap.
SEGMENTO *s.m.* segment.
SEGREDO *s.m.* secret.
SEGREGAÇÃO *s.f.* segregation.
SEGREGAR *v.* to segregate.
SEGUIDA *s.f.* following, continuation.
SEGUIDO(A) *adj.* followed; continuous.
SEGUIDOR(A) *s.m.* follower.
SEGUINTE *adj. 2gên.* next, following.
SEGUIR *v.* to follow.
SEGUNDA-FEIRA *s.f.* Monday.
SEGUNDO(A) *adj.* second / *num.* second / *prep.* according to.
SEGURADO(A) *s.m.* insured, policyholder.
SEGURADOR(A) *s.m.* insurer, underwriter.
SEGURADORA *s.f.* insurance company.
SEGURANÇA *s.f.* safety; security.
SEGURAR *v.* to hold, to grasp; to insure.
SEGURO(A) *adj.* secure, safe / *s.m.* insurance.
SEIO *s.m.* breast.
SEIS *num.* six.
SEISCENTOS *num.* six hundred.
SEITA *s.f.* sect, faction.
SEIVA *s.f.* sap, vigor.
SELA *s.f.* saddle.
SELADO(A) *adj.* saddled.
SELAR *v.* to saddle, to stamp; to seal.
SELEÇÃO *s.f.* selection.
SELECIONAR *v.* to select, to choose.
SELÊNIO *s.m.* selenium.
SELETIVO(A) *adj.* selective.
SELETO(A) *adj.* select.

SELETOR(A) *adj.* selector.
SELIM *s.m.* saddle; seat.
SELO *s.m.* seal, signet, stamp, postage stamp, cachet.
SELVA *s.f.* forest, jungle.
SELVAGEM *adj.2gên.* wild; uncivilized.
SEM *prep.* without.
SEMÁFORO *s.m.* traffic light.
SEMANA *s.f.* week.
SEMANAL *adj.2gên.* weekly.
SEMBLANTE *s.m.* visage, look.
SEMEAR *v.* to sow, to seed, to plant.
SEMELHANÇA *s.f.* similarity.
SEMELHANTE *adj.2gên.* like, similar.
SEMELHAR *v.* to resemble, to look like.
SÊMEN *s.m.* semen.
SEMENTE *s.f.* seed.
SEMESTRAL *adj.2gên.* semi-annual.
SEMESTRE *s.m.* semester.
SEMINÁRIO *s.m.* seminar / *adj.* seminary.
SEMINARISTA *adj.2gên.* seminarist.
SEMITOM *s.m.* semitone, half tone.
SEMIVOGAL *s.f.* semivowel.
SÊMOLA *s.f.* semolina.
SEMPRE *adv.* always.
SENADO *s.m.* senate, upper house.
SENÃO *conj.* otherwise.
SENDA *s.f.* footpath.
SENHA *s.f.* password.
SENHOR *s.m.* sir, mister.
SENHORA *s.f.* madam, lady.
SENHORIO(A) *s.m.* landlord.
SENIL *adj.2gên.* senile.
SENSAÇÃO *s.f.* sensation, feeling.
SENSACIONAL *adj.2gên.* sensational.
SENSACIONALISMO *s.m.* sensationalism.
SENSATEZ *s.f.* wisdom.
SENSATO(A) *adj.* sensible, rational.
SENSIBILIDADE *s.f.* sensibility; sensitivity.
SENSITIVO(A) *adj.* sensory.
SENSÍVEL *adj.2gên.* sensible.
SENSO *s.m.* sense, course.
SENSORIAL *adj.2gên.* sensory.
SENSUAL *adj.2gên.* sexy.
SENTADO(A) *adj.* seated.
SENTAR *v.* to seat, to place.
SENTENÇA *s.f.* sentence.
SENTIDO(A) *adj.* grieved, touchy / *s.m.* sense, feeling, meaning.
SENTIMENTAL *adj.2gên.* emotional.

SENTIMENTO *s.m.* feeling.
SENTINELA *s.2gên.* watchman, guard.
SENTIR *v.* to feel.
SEPARAÇÃO *s.f.* separation, split.
SEPARADO(A) *adj.* separate; estranged.
SEPARAR *v.* to separate, to part.
SEPTO *s.m.* septum.
SEPULCRO *s.m.* grave, tomb.
SEPULTAR *v.* to bury.
SEPULTO(A) *adj.* buried.
SEQUELA *s.f.* sequel, result.
SEQUÊNCIA *s.f.* sequence.
SEQUENCIAL *adj.2gên.* sequential.
SEQUESTRADO(A) *adj.* kidnapped.
SEQUESTRADOR *s.m.* kidnapper.
SEQUESTRAR *v.* to kidnap, to abduct.
SEQUESTRO *s.m.* kidnapping.
SEQUILHO *s.m.* cracknel, dry biscuit.
SER *v.* to be / *s.m.* being, creature.
SERÃO *s.m.* evening work.
SEREIA *s.f.* mermaid.
SERELEPE *adj.2gên.* lively, excited.
SERENATA *s.f.* serenade.
SERENIDADE *s.f.* serenity.
SERENO(A) *adj.* serene, calm.
SERIADO *s.m.* series, TV series.
SERIAL *adj.2gên.* serial.
SÉRIE *s.f.* series; grade (escola).
SERIEDADE *s.f.* seriousness, gravity.
SERIGRAFIA *s.f.* serigraphy, silk screening.
SERINGA *s.f.* syringe.
SERINGUEIRO(A) *s.m.* tapper.
SÉRIO(A) *adj.* serious.
SERMÃO *s.m.* preach; reprimand.
SERPENTE *s.f.* serpent.
SERPENTEAR *v.* to wind, to meander.
SERPENTINA *s.f.* serpentine.
SERRA *s.f.* saw; mountain range.
SERRAÇÃO *s.f.* sawing.
SERRADO(A) *adj.* cut, sawn.
SERRADOR(A) *s.m.* sawyer.
SERRAGEM *s.f.* sawdust.
SERRALHARIA *s.f.* locksmith's workshop.
SERRALHEIRO(A) *s.m.* locksmith.
SERRANO(A) *adj.* mountaineer.
SERRAR *v.* to saw.
SERROTE *s.m.* handsaw.
SERTANEJO(A) *s.m.* inlander, backcountry dweller.
SERTÃO *s.m.* backcountry, outback.

SERVENTE s.2gên. servant, attendant.
SERVENTIA s.f. usefulness; slavery.
SERVIÇAL s.2gên. servant, menial.
SERVIÇO s.m. service.
SERVIDÃO s.f. servitude, slavery.
SERVIDOR(A) s.m. server, attendand.
SERVIL adj.2gên. servile; slavish.
SERVO(A) adj. s.m. servant, slave.
SESSÃO s.f. session.
SESSENTA num. sixty.
SESTA s.f. nap, siesta.
SETA s.f. arrow; dart.
SETE num. seven.
SETECENTOS num. seven hundred.
SETEMBRO s.m. September.
SETENTA num. seventy.
SETOR s.m. sector; section.
SEU pron. his / adj. his.
SEVERO(A) adj. severe, rigid.
SEXO s.f. sex.
SEXTA-FEIRA s.f. Friday.
SEXTETO s.m. sextet.
SEXTO num. sixth.
SEXUAL adj.2gên. sexual.
SEXUALIDADE s.f. sexuality.
SIBILANTE adj.2gên. sibilant.
SIBILAR v. to sibilate, to hiss.
SIDERAL adj.2gên. sidereal.
SIDRA s.f. cider.
SIFÃO s.m. siphon.
SÍFILIS s.f. syphilis.
SIGILO s.m. secret.
SIGILOSO(A) adj. secret.
SIGLA s.f. abbreviation; initials.
SIGNIFICADO s.m. meaning.
SIGNIFICAR v. to mean, to signify.
SIGNIFICATIVO(A) adj. significant.
SIGNO s.m. Zodiac sign (astrologia), sign.
SÍLABA s.f. syllable.
SILENCIAR v. to make silent.
SILÊNCIO s.m. silence, stillness.
SILENCIOSO(A) adj. quiet, silent.
SILHUETA s.f. silhouette.
SÍLICA s.f. silica.
SILICONE s.m. silicone.
SILO s.m. silo, granary.
SILVESTRE adj.2gên. sylvan, savage.
SILVO s.m. whistle, hiss.
SIM adv. yes.
SIMBÓLICO(A) adj. symbolic.

SIMBOLIZAR v. to symbolize.
SÍMBOLO s.m. symbol.
SIMETRIA s.f. symmetry.
SIMÉTRICO(A) adj. symmetric.
SIMILAR adj.2gên. similar.
SÍMIO s.m. simian, ape.
SIMPATIA s.f. affection, affinity.
SIMPÁTICO(A) adj. nice, friendly.
SIMPATIZANTE adj.2gên. supporter.
SIMPATIZAR v. to sympathise.
SIMPLES adj.2gên. simple.
SIMPLICIDADE s.f. simplicity.
SIMPLIFICAR v. to simplify.
SIMPÓSIO s.m. symposium.
SIMULAÇÃO s.f. simulation; sham.
SIMULADO s.m. simulate, false.
SIMULADOR(A) s.m. simulator / adj. faker, pretender.
SIMULAR v. to simulate; to fake, to pretend.
SIMULTÂNEO(A) adj. simultaneous.
SINA s.f. fate, fortune, destiny.
SINAGOGA s.f. synagogue.
SINAL s.m. sign; signal.
SINALIZAR v. to signalise.
SINCERIDADE s.f. sincerity.
SINCERO(A) adj. sincere, honest.
SÍNCOPE s.f. syncope, syncopation.
SINCRONIA s.f. synchronicity.
SINCRONIZAR v. to synchronise.
SINDICAL adj.2gên. syndical.
SINDICATO s.m. syndicate, trade union.
SÍNDICO(A) s.m. condominium manager.
SÍNDROME s.f. syndrome.
SINERGIA s.f. synergy.
SINETA s.f. hand bell.
SINFONIA s.f. symphony.
SINGELO(A) adj. plain, simple.
SINISTRO(A) adj. sinister, evil / s.m. accident, disaster.
SINO s.m. bell.
SINÔNIMO s.m. synonym.
SINOPSE s.f. synopsis, summary.
SINTAGMA s.m. syntagma.
SINTÁTICO(A) adj. syntactic.
SINTAXE s.f. syntax.
SÍNTESE s.f. synthesis.
SINTÉTICO(A) adj. synthetic.
SINTETIZADOR s.m. synthesiser.
SINTETIZAR v. to synthesise.

SINTOMA *s.m.* symptom.
SINTONIA *s.f.* syntony.
SINTONIZAR *v.* to syntonise.
SINUCA *s.f.* snooker; pool.
SINUOSIDADE *s.f.* sinuosity.
SINUOSO(A) *adj.* sinuous.
SINUSITE *s.f.* sinusitis.
SIRENE *s.f.* siren.
SIRI *s.m.* crab.
SIRIGAITA *adj.* flirt.
SÍSMICO(A) *adj.* seismic.
SISMÓGRAFO(A) *s.m.* seismograph.
SISTEMA *s.m.* system.
SISTEMATIZAR *v.* to systematise.
SÍTIO *s.m.* farm; place, local.
SITUAÇÃO *s.f.* situation, position.
SITUAR *v.* to place, to situate.
SÓ *adj.* alone / *adv.* only, just.
SOAR *v.* to sound, to toll.
SOB *prep.* under, below.
SOBERANIA *s.f.* sovereignty.
SOBERANO(A) *adj.* sovereign.
SOBERBA *s.f.* pride.
SOBERBO(A) *adj.* proud, arrogant.
SOBRA *s.f.* surplus, remainder.
SOBRADO *s.m.* two-story house.
SOBRANCELHA *s.f.* eyebrow.
SOBRAR *v.* to exceed, to remain.
SOBRE *prep.* on; about.
SOBREAVISO *s.m.* precaution.
SOBRECARGA *s.f.* overload.
SOBRECARREGAR *v.* to overload
SOBRELOJA *s.f.* mezzanine.
SOBREMESA *s.f.* dessert.
SOBRENATURAL *adj.2gên.* supernatural.
SOBRENOME *s.m.* last name, family name, surname.
SOBREPESO *s.m.* overweight.
SOBREPOR *v.* to superpose.
SOBRESSAIR *v.* to protrude, to jut out.
SOBRETUDO *s.m.* overcoat / *adv.* especially, over all.
SOBREVIVENTE *adj.2gên.* surviving / *s.2gên.* survivor.
SOBREVIVER *v.* to survive.
SOBREVOAR *v.* to fly over.
SOBRIEDADE *s.f.* sobriety.
SOBRINHA *s.f.* niece.
SOBRINHO *s.m.* nephew.
SÓBRIO(A) *adj.* sober.

SOCAR *v.* to hit, to punch.
SOCIAL *adj.2gên.* social
SOCIALISMO *s.m.* socialism.
SOCIÁVEL *adj.2gên.* sociable.
SOCIEDADE *s.f.* society.
SÓCIO(A) *s.m.* partner.
SOCIOLOGIA *s.f.* sociology.
SOCIÓLOGO(A) *s.m.* sociologist.
SOCO *s.m.* clog, punch.
SOCO-INGLÊS *s.m.* knuckleduster.
SOCORRER *v.* to help.
SOCORRISTA *s.2gên.* paramedic.
SOCORRO *s.m.* help, aid / *interj.* help!
SODA *s.f.* pop, soda.
SÓDIO *s.m.* sodium.
SODOMIZAR *v.* to sodomise.
SOFÁ *s.m.* sofa, couch.
SOFISTICADO *adj.* sophisticated.
SOFREDOR *adj.* suffering; sufferer.
SOFRER *v.* to bear; to suffer.
SOFRIDO(A) *adj.* tough, hard.
SOGRA *s.f.* mother-in-law.
SOGRO *s.m.* father-in-law.
SOL *s.m.* sun.
SOLAR *adj.2gên.* solar / *s.m.* solar.
SOLÁRIO *s.m.* solarium.
SOLAVANCO *s.m.* jolt. bump.
SOLDA *s.f.* solder; weld; welding.
SOLDADO *s.2gên.* soldier.
SOLDADOR(A) *s.m.* welder.
SOLDAR *v.* to solder.
SOLEIRA *s.f.* sill, threshold.
SOLENE *adj.2gên.* solemn.
SOLENIDADE *s.f.* solemnity.
SOLETRAR *v.* to spell.
SOLFEJO *s.m.* solfeggio.
SOLICITAÇÃO *s.f.* request.
SOLICITAR *v.* to ask, to request.
SOLÍCITO(A) *adj.* solicitous, thoughtful.
SOLIDÃO *s.f.* loneliness, solitude.
SOLIDARIEDADE *s.f.* solidarity.
SOLIDÁRIO(A) *adj.* solidary, supportive.
SOLIDEZ *s.f.* solidity; firmness.
SÓLIDO(A) *adj.* solid / *s.m.* solid.
SOLISTA *s.2gên.* soloist.
SOLITÁRIO(A) *adj.* lonely.
SOLO *s.m.* soil, ground; solo.
SOLSTÍCIO *s.m.* solstice.
SOLTAR *v.* to release; to discharge.
SOLTEIRO(A) *adj.* single, bachelor.

SOLTO(A) *adj.* free, unattached.
SOLUÇÃO *s.f.* solution.
SOLUÇAR *v.* to hiccup.
SOLUCIONAR *v.* to solve.
SOLUÇO *s.m.* hiccup.
SOLÚVEL *adj.2gên.* solvable; soluble.
SOLVENTE *adj.2gên.* solvent, solute / *s.m.* solvent.
SOM *s.m.* sound.
SOMA *s.f.* sum.
SOMAR *v.* to sum, to add.
SOMBRA *s.f.* shadow, shade.
SOMBREADO *s.m.* shading / *adj.* shaded.
SOMBRINHA *s.f.* umbrella, brolly.
SOMBRIO(A) *adj.* grim.
SOMENTE *adv.* only.
SONÂMBULO(A) *s.m.* sleepwalker.
SONAR *s.m.* sonar.
SONATA *s.f.* sonata.
SONDA *s.f.* dipstick, probe.
SONDAGEM *s.f.* probing.
SONDAR *v.* to sound.
SONECA *s.f.* snooze, nap, doze.
SONEGAÇÃO *s.f.* fraud.
SONEGAR *v.* to dodge, to steal.
SONETO *s.m.* sonnet.
SONHADOR(A) *s.m.* dreamer.
SONHAR *v.* to dream.
SONHO *s.m.* dream.
SONÍFERO *s.m.* opiate.
SONO *s.m.* sleep.
SONOLÊNCIA *s.f.* sleepiness.
SONOLENTO(A) *adj.* sleepy.
SONOPLASTA *s.2gên.* sound technician.
SONORIDADE *s.f.* sonority.
SONORO(A) *adj.* resonant.
SONSO(A) *adj.* sly.
SOPA *s.f.* soup.
SOPEIRA *s.f.* tureen.
SOPRANO *s.2gên.* soprano / *adj.* soprano.
SOPRAR *v.* to blow.
SOPRO *s.m.* blow.
SÓRDIDO(A) *adj.* sordid.
SORRATEIRO(A) *adj.* sneaky.
SORTE *s.f.* luck, destiny.
SORTEAR *v.* to sort, to raffle.
SORTEIO *s.m.* raffle.
SORTUDO(A) *adj.* lucky.
SORVETE *s.m.* ice cream.
SORVETERIA *s.f.* ice cream shop.

SÓSIA *s.2gên.* doppelganger.
SOSSEGADO(A) *adj.* quiet, calm.
SOSSEGAR *v.* to calm.
SOSSEGO *s.m.* peace, rest.
SÓTÃO *s.m.* loft, attic.
SOTAQUE *s.m.* accent.
SOVA *s.f.* beating.
SOVACO *s.m.* armpit.
SOVAR *v.* to knead, to thrash.
SOZINHO(A) *adj.* alone.
SUA *pron.* her / *adj.* her.
SUAR *v.* to sweat.
SUAVE *adj.2gên.* soft, smooth, gentle.
SUAVIDADE *s.f.* smoothness.
SUAVIZAR *v.* to sweeten; to understate.
SUBALTERNO(A) *s.m.* subaltern, subordinate.
SUBESTIMAR *v.* to underestimate.
SUBIDA *s.f.* ascension, rise; increase.
SUBIR *v.* to climb; to raise.
SÚBITO(A) *adj.* sudden, rapid.
SUBJETIVO(A) *adj.* subjective.
SUBJUNTIVO *s.m.* subjunctive.
SUBLIME *adj.2gên.* sublime, majestic.
SUBMARINO *s.m.* submarine.
SUBMETER *v.* to dominate, to subject.
SUBMISSÃO *s.f.* submission.
SUBMISSO(A) *adj.* submissive, obedient.
SUBORDINADO(A) *adj.* subordinated, minion.
SUBORDINAR *v.* to subordinate; to subsume.
SUBORNAR *v.* to bribe.
SUBORNO *s.m.* bribery.
SUBSOLO *s.m.* subsoil, underground.
SUBSTÂNCIA *s.f.* substance, matter.
SUBSTANTIVO *s.m.* noun.
SUBSTITUIR *v.* to substitute.
SUBSTITUTO(A) *s.m.* substitute / *adj.* supply.
SUBTÍTULO *s.m.* subtitle.
SUBTRAÇÃO *s.f.* subtraction.
SUBTRAIR *v.* to take away; to subtract.
SUBURBANO(A) *adj.* suburban.
SUBÚRBIO *s.m.* outskirts; suburb.
SUCATA *s.f.* scrap.
SUCÇÃO *s.f.* suction.
SUCESSÃO *s.f.* succession.
SUCESSIVO(A) *adj.* successive.
SUCESSO *s.m.* success.
SUCESSOR(A) *s.m.* successor.
SUCINTO(A) *adj.* succint.

SUCO *s.m.* juice.
SUCULENTO(A) *adj.* juicy.
SUCUMBIR *v.* to succumb.
SUDÁRIO *s.m.* sudarium.
SUDESTE *adj.* southeast / *s.m.* southeast.
SÚDITO(A) *s.m.* subject, vassal.
SUDOESTE *adj.* southwest / *s.m.* southwest.
SUDORESE *s.f.* profuse sweating.
SUÉTER *s.m.* sweater.
SUFICIENTE *adj.2gên.* sufficient / *s.m.* enough / *adv.* enough.
SUFIXO *s.m.* suffix.
SUFLÊ *s.m.* soufflé.
SUFOCANTE *adj.2gên.* suffocating.
SUFOCAR *v.* to suffocate.
SUFOCO *s.m.* suffocation.
SUFRÁGIO *s.m.* suffrage.
SUGAR *v.* to suck, to absorb.
SUGERIR *v.* to suggest.
SUGESTÃO *s.f.* suggestion.
SUGESTIVO(A) *adj.* suggestive.
SUICIDA *adj.2gên.* suicidal.
SUICÍDIO *s.m.* suicide.
SUÍNO(A) *s.m.* swine, pig, hog / *adj.* swinish.
SUÍTE *s.f.* suite.
SUJAR *v.* to soil.
SUJEIRA *s.f.* dirt.
SUJEITO(A) *adj.* subject / *s.m.* subject.
SUJO(A) *adj.* dirty; filthy.
SUL *adj.* south / *s.m.* south.
SULCO *s.m.* furrow, groove.
SULTÃO *s.m.* sultan.
SUMÁRIO *s.m.* summary, table of contents.
SUMIÇO *s.m.* disappearance.
SUMIDO(A) *adj.* disappeared, hidden, missing.
SUMIR *v.* to disappear, to vanish.
SUMO *s.m.* juice, sap.
SUNGA *s.f.* trunks.
SUOR *s.m.* sweat.
SUPERAÇÃO *s.f.* overcoming.
SUPERAR *v.* to overcome.
SUPERDOSE *s.f.* overdose.
SUPERDOTADO(A) *adj.* genius, talented.
SUPERFICIAL *adj.2gên.* superficial.
SUPERFÍCIE *s.f.* surface.
SUPÉRFLUO(A) *adj.* superfluous.
SUPERIOR *adj.2gên.* superior.
SUPERIORIDADE *s.f.* superiority.
SUPERLATIVO *s.m.* superlative.
SUPERMERCADO *s.m.* supermarket.
SUPERPOPULAÇÃO *s.f.* overpopulation.
SUPERSÔNICO(A) *adj.* supersonic.
SUPERSTIÇÃO *s.f.* superstition.
SUPERVISÃO *s.f.* supervision.
SUPERVISIONAR *v.* to supervise.
SUPERVISOR(A) *s.m.* supervisor.
SUPIMPA *adj.2gên.* fine, great.
SUPINO *s.m.* supine; bench press.
SUPLANTAR *v.* to supplant.
SUPLEMENTAR *v.* to supplement / *adj.2gên.* suplementary.
SUPLEMENTO *s.m.* supplement.
SUPLÊNCIA *s.f.* supplying.
SUPLENTE *adj.2gên.* substitute, proxy.
SUPLETIVO *s.m.* adult education.
SÚPLICA *s.f.* pleading, supplication.
SUPLICAR *v.* to supplicate, to beg.
SUPOR *v.* to suppose, to assume, to guess.
SUPORTAR *v.* to support; to bear, to stand.
SUPORTÁVEL *adj.2gên.* supportable; bearable.
SUPORTE *s.m.* support; pillar.
SUPOSIÇÃO *s.f.* supposition.
SUPOSITÓRIO *s.m.* suppository.
SUPOSTO(A) *adj.* putative.
SUPREMACIA *s.f.* supremacy.
SUPREMO(A) *adj.* supreme.
SUPRESSÃO *s.f.* suppression.
SUPRIMENTO *s.m.* supply; fill.
SUPRIMIR *v.* to suppress, to abolish.
SUPRIR *v.* to supply, to furnish.
SURDEZ *s.f.* deafness.
SURDINA *s.f.* sordine; mute.
SURDO(A) *adj.* deaf.
SURFAR *v.* to surf; to navigate the internet.
SURFISTA *s.2gên.* surfer.
SURGIMENTO *s.m.* outbreak.
SURGIR *v.* to appear, to arise.
SURPREENDENTE *adj.2gên.* surprising, amazing, remarkable.
SURPREENDER *v.* to surprise, to astonish.
SURPRESA *s.f.* surprise.
SURPRESO(A) *adj.* surprised, astonished.
SURRA *s.f.* thrashing, beating.
SURRADO(A) *adj.* worn out; beaten.
SURRAR *v.* to beat, to thrash.
SURREAL *adj.2gên.* surreal.
SURREALISMO *s.m.* surrealism.

SURREALISTA *adj.2gên.* surrealist, surrealistic.
SURTIR *v.* to result in, to work.
SURTO *s.m.* outbreak, boom.
SUSCETÍVEL *adj.2gên.* susceptible.
SUSCITAR *v.* to rouse, to excite.
SUSPEITA *s.f.* suspicion.
SUSPEITAR *v.* to suspect.
SUSPEITO(A) *adj.* suspect, suspicious.
SUSPENDER *v.* to suspend, to hang.
SUSPENSÃO *s.f.* suspension.
SUSPENSE *s.m.* suspense; thriller.
SUSPENSO(A) *adj.* suspended, hanging; interrupted.
SUSPENSÓRIO(A) *adj.* suspensory / *s.m.* suspenders.
SUSPIRAR *v.* to sigh.
SUSPIRO *s.m.* sigh; merengue (alimento).
SUSSURRAR *v.* to rustle, to whisper.
SUSSURRO *s.m.* rustle, whisper.
SUSTAR *v.* to stop; to cancel out.
SUSTENTAÇÃO *s.f.* sustenance; lift.
SUSTENTADOR(A) *adj.* supporting / *s.m.* supporter.
SUSTENTAR *v.* to support.
SUSTENTÁVEL *adj.2gên.* sustainable.
SUSTENTO *s.m.* maintenance, support.
SUSTO *s.m.* fright, scare.
SUTIÃ *s.m.* brassiere, bra.
SUTIL *adj.2gên.* subtle.
SUTILEZA *s.f.* subtlety.
SUTURA *s.f.* suture.
SUTURAR *v.* to suture.
SUVENIR *s.m.* souvenir.
SWING *s.m.* swing (música); swinging.

T t

T, t *s.m.* the twentieth letter of the Portuguese alphabet.
TABACAL *s.m.* tobacco field, tobacco plantation.
TABACARIA *s.f.* tobacco shop.
TABACO *s.m.* tobacco.
TABAGISTA *s.2gên.* tobacco smoker.
TABEFE *s.m.* slap, blow.
TABELA *s.f.* chart, list, table.
TABELIÃO *s.m.* notary public.
TABERNA *s.f.* tavern.
TABLADO *s.m.* platform, stage.
TABLETE *s.m.* tablet, bar.
TABLOIDE *s.m.* tabloid/ *adj.2gên.* tabloid.
TABU *s.m.* taboo.
TÁBUA *s.f.* board, plank.
TABUADA *s.f.* multiplication table.
TABULEIRO *s.m.* board.
TAÇA *s.f.* cup.
TACADA *s.f.* blow.
TACHO *s.m.* pan, bowl.
TÁCITO(A) *adj.* tacit.
TACITURNO(A) *adj.* taciturn, moody.
TACO *s.m.* stick.
TAGARELA *s.2gên.* babbler, chatterbox / *adj.2gên.* babbler, chatterbox.
TAGARELAR *v.* to chatter.
TAL *pron.* such, like.
TALA *s.f.* splint.
TALÃO *s.m.* book.
TALCO *s.m.* talc, talcum.
TALENTO *s.m.* talent, ability.
TALENTOSO(A) *adj.* talented, able.
TALHER *s.m.* flatware, tableware.
TALHO *s.m.* cut.
TALISMÃ *s.m.* talisman, amulet.
TALO *s.m.* bind, stalk.
TALVEZ *adv.* perhaps, maybe.
TAMANCO *s.m.* clog.
TAMANDUÁ *s.m.* tamandua.
TAMANHO *s.m.* size / *adj.* such.
TAMBÉM *adv.* also, too, as well.
TAMBOR *s.m.* drum.
TAMBORILAR *v.* to drum.
TAMBORIM *s.m.* tambourine.
TAMPA *s.f.* lid, cover(ing).
TAMPADO(A) *adj.* covered.
TAMPAR *v.* to cover.
TAMPOUCO *adv.* either, neither.
TANGA *s.f.* loincloth; thong bikini.

TANGENCIAL *adj.2gên.* tangential.
TANGENTE *s.f.* tangent / *adj.2gên.* tangent.
TANGERINA *s.f.* tangerine.
TANGÍVEL *adj.2gên.* tangible.
TANGO *s.m.* tango.
TANQUE *s.m.* tank.
TANTO(A) *adj.* so much, so many.
TÃO *adv.* so, such.
TAPA *s.m.* slap.
TAPADO(A) *adj.* stupid.
TAPAR *v.* to close, to cover.
TAPEAÇÃO *s.f.* swindle, bogus.
TAPEAR *v.* to deceive.
TAPEÇARIA *s.f.* tapestry.
TAPETE *s.m.* mat, carpet.
TAPIOCA *s.f.* tapioca.
TAPUME *s.m.* fence; enclosure.
TAQUIGRAFIA *s.f.* shorthand.
TAQUÍMETRO *s.m.* speedometer.
TARA *s.f.* tare.
TARADO(A) *adj.* perverted, degenerated.
TARANTELA *s.f.* tarantella.
TARÂNTULA *s.f.* tarantula.
TARDAR *v.* to delay, to tarry.
TARDE *s.f.* afternoon / *adv.* late.
TAREFA *s.f.* job, task.
TARIFA *s.f.* tariff, tax.
TARIFAR *v.* to tariff.
TÁRTARO *s.m.* tartar, Tartarus / *adj.* tartar.
TARTARUGA *s.f.* turtle.
TATEAR *v.* to grope; to fumble.
TÁTICA *s.f.* tactic.
TÁTIL *adj.2gên.* tactile.
TATO *s.m.* feel; tact.
TATU *s.m.* armadillo.
TATUAGEM *s.f.* tattoo.
TATUAR *v.* to tattoo.
TAUTOLOGIA *s.f.* tautology.
TAVERNA *s.f.* tavern, bar.
TAXA *s.f.* tax; rate.
TAXAÇÃO *s.f.* taxation.
TAXAR *v.* to tax.
TÁXI *s.m.* taxi; cab.
TAXIDERMIA *s.f.* taxidermy.
TAXÍMETRO *s.m.* taximeter.
TAXISTA *s.2gên.* taxi driver.
TCHAU *interj.* bye!
TE *pron.* you.
TEAR *s.m.* loom.
TEATRAL *adj.2gên.* dramatic.
TEATRALIZAR *v.* to theatricalize.
TEATRO *s.m.* theater.
TECELAGEM *s.f.* weaving.
TECELÃO *s.m.* weaver.
TECER *v.* to weave.
TECIDO *s.m.* cloth, fabric, tissue.
TECLA *s.f.* key.
TECLADO *s.m.* keyboard.
TECLAR *v.* to type.
TÉCNICA *s.f.* technique.
TÉCNICO(A) *adj.* technical / *s.m.* technician.
TECNOLOGIA *s.f.* technology.
TECNOLÓGICO(A) *adj.* technological.
TÉDIO *s.m.* boredom, tedium.
TEDIOSO(A) *adj.* boring.
TEGUMENTO *s.m.* tegument.
TEIA *s.f.* web.
TEIMAR *v.* to insist, to persist.
TEIMOSIA *s.f.* pertinacity.
TEIMOSO(A) *adj.* insistent.
TELA *s.f.* screen; canvas.
TELECINESIA *s.f.* telekinesis.
TELECOMUNICAÇÃO *s.f.* telecommunication.
TELEFÉRICO *s.m.* cablecar.
TELEFONAR *v.* to call, to telephone.
TELEFONE *s.m.* phone, telephone.
TELEFONEMA *s.m.* phone call.
TELEFONIA *s.f.* telephony.
TELEFÔNICO(A) *adj.* telephonic.
TELEFONISTA *s.2gên.* telephonist.
TELEGRAFAR *v.* to telegraph.
TELEGRAFIA *s.f.* telegraphy.
TELEGRÁFICO(A) *adj.* telegraphic.
TELÉGRAFO *s.m.* telegraph.
TELEGRAMA *s.m.* telegram.
TELEJORNAL *s.m.* tv newscast.
TELEPATIA *s.f.* telepathy.
TELEPÁTICO(A) *adj.* telephatic.
TELESCÓPICO(A) *adj.* telescopic.
TELESCÓPIO *s.m.* telescope.
TELESPECTADOR(A) *s.m.* televiewer.
TELEVISÃO *s.f.* television.
TELEVISIONAR *v.* to broadcast.
TELEVISOR *s.m.* television.
TELHA *s.f.* tile.
TELHADO *s.m.* roof.
TEMA *s.m.* subject, theme, topic.
TEMÁTICA *s.f.* theme.
TEMÁTICO(A) *adj.* thematic.
TEMER *v.* to fear, to dread.
TEMERÁRIO(A) *adj.* daring; risky; reckless.
TEMEROSO(A) *adj.* fearful.
TEMIDO(A) *adj.* fearsome, frightening.

TEMÍVEL *adj.2gên.* appalling, terrible.
TEMOR *s.m.* fear.
TÊMPERA *s.f.* temper.
TEMPERADO(A) *adj.* seasoned, spicy.
TEMPERAMENTAL *adj.2gên.* temperamental.
TEMPERAMENTO *s.m.* temper, character.
TEMPERANÇA *s.f.* temperance.
TEMPERAR *v.* to sauce, to spice.
TEMPERATURA *s.f.* temperature.
TEMPERO *s.m.* seasoning, condiment.
TEMPESTADE *s.f.* storm.
TEMPESTEAR *v.* to storm.
TEMPESTUOSO(A) *adj.* stormy.
TEMPLÁRIO *s.m.* templar.
TEMPLO *s.m.* temple.
TEMPO *s.m.* time; weather; duration.
TEMPO LIVRE *s.m.* leisure; free time.
TÊMPORA *s.f.* temple.
TEMPORADA *s.f.* season.
TEMPORAL *s.m.* tempest, storm / *adj.2gên.* temporal.
TEMPORALIDADE *s.f.* temporality.
TEMPORÁRIO(A) *adj.* temporary, transitory.
TENACIDADE *s.f.* tenacity.
TENAZ *adj.* tenacious.
TENDA *s.f.* tent.
TENDÃO *s.m.* tendon.
TENDÊNCIA *s.f.* tendency.
TENDENCIOSO(A) *adj.* tendencious.
TENEBROSIDADE *s.f.* gloom, darkness.
TENEBROSO(A) *adj.* tenebrous, gloomy.
TENENTE *s.2gên.* lieutenant.
TÊNIS *s.m.* tennis (esporte); sneakers.
TÊNIS DE MESA *s.m.* ping-pong, table tennis.
TENISTA *s.2gên.* tennis player.
TENOR *s.m.* tenor.
TENRO(A) *adj.* mild; tender.
TENSÃO *s.f.* tension.
TENSO(A) *adj.* tense.
TENTAÇÃO *s.f.* temptation.
TENTACULAR *adj.2gên.* tentacular.
TENTÁCULO *s.m.* tentacle.
TENTADOR(A) *adj.* tempter.
TENTAR *v.* to try.
TENTATIVA *s.f.* try.
TÊNUE *adj.* tenuous, thin.
TEOCRACIA *s.f.* Theocracy.
TEOLOGIA *s.f.* Theology.
TEOLÓGICO(A) *adj.* theological.
TEÓLOGO(A) *s.m.* theologian.
TEOR *s.m.* contents, tenor.

TEOREMA *s.f.* theorem.
TEORIA *s.f.* theory.
TEÓRICO(A) *adj.* theoretical / *s.m.* theoretician.
TEORIZAR *v.* to theorize.
TÉPIDO(A) *adj.* tepid.
TER *v.* to have, to own.
TERAPEUTA *s.2gên.* therapist.
TERAPÊUTICO(A) *adj.* therapeutic.
TERAPIA *s.f.* therapy.
TERÇA-FEIRA *s.f.* Tuesday.
TERCEIRIZAR *v.* to outsource.
TERCEIRO *num.* third.
TERCETO *s.m.* tercet.
TERÇO *s.m.* third; chaplet.
TERÇOL *s.m.* sty.
TERMAL *adj.2gên.* thermal.
TERMELÉTRICO(A) *adj.* thermoeletric.
TÉRMICO(A) *adj.* thermic.
TERMINAÇÃO *s.f.* termination, ending.
TERMINAL *s.m.* terminal / *adj.2gên.* terminal.
TERMINAR *v.* to finish, to end.
TÉRMINO *s.m.* terminal, end.
TERMINOLOGIA *s.f.* terminology.
TERMODINÂMICA *s.f.* thermodynamics.
TERMÓGRAFO *s.m.* thermograph.
TERMÓLISE *s.f.* thermolysis.
TERMÔMETRO *s.m.* thermometer.
TERMONUCLEAR *adj.2gên.* thermonuclear.
TERMOSTATO *s.m.* thermostat.
TERNO *s.m.* suit.
TERNO(A) *adj.* tender, delicate.
TERNURA *s.f.* terderness.
TERRA *s.f.* ground, land (terreno); world (mundo), Earth (planeta).
TERRAÇO *s.m.* balcony.
TERRÁQUEO(A) *s.m.* earthling.
TERREMOTO *s.m.* earthquake.
TERRENO *s.m.* ground, land.
TÉRREO *s.m.* downstairs.
TERRESTRE *adj.* earthly; earthy.
TERRIFICAR *v.* to terrify.
TERRÍFICO(A) *adj.2gên.* terryfying.
TERRITORIAL *adj.2gên.* territorial.
TERRITÓRIO *s.m.* territory, region.
TERRÍVEL *adj.2gên.* terrible, awful.
TERROR *s.m.* terror, horror.
TERRORISMO *s.m.* terrorism.
TERRORISTA *s.2gên.* terrorist.
TERRORIZAR *v.* to terrorize.
TESE *s.f.* thesis.

TESOURA *s.f.* scissors.
TESOURARIA *s.f.* treasury.
TESOUREIRO *s.m.* treasurer.
TESOURO *s.m.* treasure; treasury.
TESTA *s.f.* brow, forehead.
TESTAMENTO *s.m.* will, testament.
TESTAR *v.* to test.
TESTE *s.m.* test, examination, trial.
TESTEMUNHA *s.f.* witness.
TESTEMUNHAR *v.* to witness.
TESTÍCULO *s.m.* testicle.
TETO *s.m.* ceiling.
TEU *pron.* your, yours.
TÊXTIL *adj.2gên.* textile.
TEXTO *s.m.* text.
TEXUGO *s.m.* badger.
TIARA *s.f.* tiara.
TIGELA *s.f.* bowl.
TIGRE *s.m.* tiger.
TIJOLO *s.m.* brick.
TIL *s.m.* tilde.
TILINTAR *v.* to chink.
TIMBRE *s.m.* timber; frank.
TIME *s.m.* team.
TIMIDEZ *s.f.* shyness, timidity.
TÍMIDO(A) *adj.* shy.
TÍMPANO *s.m.* tympanum.
TINGIR *v.* to tinge, to colour.
TINTA *s.f.* ink; paint.
TINTEIRO *s.m.* ink bottle.
TINTURA *s.f.* dye.
TIA *s.f.* aunt.
TIO *s.m.* uncle.
TÍPICO(A) *adj.* typical.
TIPO *s.m.* kind, sort; type.
TIRANIA *s.f.* tyranny.
TIRANO(A) *s.m.* tyrant.
TIRAR *v.* to take away; to remove.
TÍTULO *s.m.* title.
TIRO *s.m.* shoot, shot; gunshot.
TOALETE *s.m.* toilet.
TOALHA *s.f.* towel.
TOCA *s.f.* den, burrow.
TOCAIA *s.f.* ambush.
TOCA-DISCOS *s.m.* record-player, CD player.
TOCAR *v.* to touch; to play.
TOCHA *s.f.* torch.
TODAVIA *conj.* yet, however.
TODO(A) *adj.* all / *s.m.* whole.
TOLERÂNCIA *s.f.* tolerance.
TOLERAR *v.* to tolerate.
TOLICE *s.f.* stupidity, silliness.

TOLO(A) *adj.* fool.
TOM *s.m.* tone (som); shade (cor).
TOMADA *s.f.* socket, plug.
TOMAR *v.* to take; to drink.
TOMATE *s.m.* tomato.
TOMBAR *v.* to fall down.
TONALIDADE *s.f.* shade; tonality.
TONELADA *s.f.* ton.
TONTEIRA *s.f.* dizziness.
TONTO(A) *adj.* dizzy; fool.
TONTURA *s.f.* dizziness.
TOPETE *s.m.* forelock.
TOPO *s.m.* top; peak.
TOQUE *s.m.* touch.
TORÇÃO *s.f.* twisting.
TORCICOLO *s.m.* torticollis.
TORCIDA *s.f.* wick.
TORMENTO *s.m.* torment; misery.
TORNADO *s.m.* tornado.
TORNAR *v.* to return, to turn; to become.
TORNOZELO *s.m.* ankle.
TORRADA *s.f.* toast.
TORRADEIRA *s.f.* toaster.
TORRAR *v.* to toast.
TORRE *s.f.* tower.
TORRENCIAL *adj.2gên.* torrential.
TORTA *s.f.* pie.
TORTO(A) *adj.* twisted, bent.
TORTURA *s.f.* torture.
TORTURAR *v.* to torture.
TOSSE *s.f.* cough.
TOSSIR *v.* to cough.
TOTAL *adj.2gên.* complete, full / *s.m.* total, sum.
TOUCA *s.f.* bonnet.
TOUPEIRA *s.f.* mole.
TOURO *s.m.* bull (animal); Taurus (astrologia).
TÓXICO(A) *adj.* toxic.
TRABALHADOR(A) *s.m.* worker / *adj.* hard-working, diligent.
TRABALHAR *v.* to labour, to work.
TRABALHO *s.m.* work, job.
TRABALHOSO(A) *adj.* hard, arduous.
TRABUCO *s.m.* trebuchet.
TRAÇA *s.f.* bookworm.
TRAÇAR *v.* to draw, to delineate.
TRACEJAR *v.* to draw, to outline.
TRAÇO *s.m.* trace; vestige.
TRADIÇÃO *s.f.* tradition.
TRADICIONAL *adj.2gên.* traditional.
TRADICIONALISMO *s.m.* traditionalism.

TRADICIONALISTA *adj.2gên.* traditionalist.
TRADUÇÃO *s.f.* translation.
TRADUTOR(A) *s.m.* translator.
TRADUZIR *v.* to translate.
TRÁFEGO *s.m.* traffic.
TRAFICANTE *s.2gên.* dealer; smuggler.
TRAFICAR *v.* to deal.
TRÁFICO *s.m.* traffic.
TRAGÉDIA *s.f.* tragedy.
TRÁGICO(A) *adj.* tragic.
TRAGICOMÉDIA *s.f.* tragicomedy.
TRAIÇÃO *s.f.* betrayal, treason.
TRAIÇOEIRO(A) *adj.* treacherous.
TRAIDOR(A) *s.m.* betrayer, traitor.
TRAIR *v.* to betray.
TRAJE *s.m.* vestment; costume; clothes.
TRAJETO *s.m.* way; route, passage.
TRAJETÓRIA *s.f.* trajectory.
TRAMA *s.f.* intrigue; plot.
TRAMBIQUE *s.m.* swindle, fraud.
TRAMBIQUEIRO(A) *s.m.* swindler.
TRAMPOLIM *s.m.* trampoline.
TRANÇA *s.f.* plait.
TRANCADO(A) *adj.* locked.
TRANCAFIADO(A) *adj.* arrested.
TRANCAFIAR *v.* to arrest, to lock.
TRANCAR *v.* to lock.
TRANCO *s.m.* jolt.
TRANQUILIDADE *s.f.* tranquility.
TRANQUILIZAR *v.* to tranquilize.
TRANQUILO(A) *adj.* tranquil; calm; quiet.
TRANSAÇÃO *s.f.* transaction, negotiation.
TRANSCENDENTE *adj.2gên.* transcendent.
TRANSCENDER *v.* to transcend.
TRANSCORRER *v.* to elapse.
TRANSFERÊNCIA *s.f.* transfer; transference.
TRANSFERIR *v.* to transfer.
TRANSFORMAÇÃO *s.f.* transformation.
TRANSFORMAR *v.* to transform.
TRANSFUSÃO *s.f.* transfusion.
TRANSGREDIR *v.* to transgress; to break.
TRANSGRESSÃO *s.f.* transgression.
TRANSITAR *v.* to transit.
TRÂNSITO *s.m.* traffic.
TRANSLÚCIDO(A) *adj.* translucent.
TRANSMISSÃO *s.f.* transmission.
TRANSMISSOR *s.m.* transmitter.
TRANSMITIR *v.* to transmit.
TRANSPARÊNCIA *s.f.* transparency.
TRANSPARENTE *adj.2gên.* transparent.
TRANSPIRAR *v.* to perspire, to sweat.
TRANSPLANTE *s.m.* transplant.

TRANSPORTAR *v.* to transport.
TRANSPORTE *s.m.* transport.
TRANSTORNAR *v.* to derange.
TRANSTORNO *s.m.* derangement.
TRANSVERSAL *adj.2gên.* transversal.
TRAPAÇA *s.f.* fraud.
TRAPACEAR *v.* to cheat.
TRAPACEIRO(A) *s.m.* cheater.
TRAPALHADA *s.f.* confusion; mess.
TRAPÉZIO *s.m.* trapezium.
TRAPO *s.m.* rag; shred.
TRAQUEIA *s.f.* trachea.
TRAQUINAGEM *s.f.* prank.
TRAQUINAS *adj.2gên.* mischievous.
TRASEIRO *s.m.* bottom, backside / *adj.* posterior, back; rear.
TRASTE *s.m.* rogue.
TRATADOR(A) *s.m.* caretaker.
TRATAMENTO *s.m.* treatment.
TRATAR *v.* to treat; to deal with.
TRATOR *s.m.* tractor.
TRAUMA *s.m.* trauma.
TRAUMÁTICO(A) *adj.* traumatic.
TRAUMATIZAR *v.* to traumatize.
TRAVAR *v.* to lock.
TRAVESSA *s.f.* bystreet, lane; dish.
TRAVESSÃO *s.m.* dash.
TRAVESSEIRO *s.m.* pillow.
TRAVESSO(A) *adj.* mischievous.
TRAVESSURA *s.f.* prank; trick.
TRAVESTI *s.m.* transvestite.
TRAZER *v.* to bring.
TRECHO *s.m.* passage.
TRECO *s.m.* stuff; indisposition.
TRÉGUA *s.f.* truce.
TREINADOR(A) *s.m.* trainer, coach.
TREINAMENTO *s.m.* training.
TREINAR *v.* to practice, to train.
TREM *s.m.* train.
TREMA *s.f.* dieresis, umlaut.
TREMENDO *adj.* terrific, tremendous.
TREMER *v.* to shiver, to tremble.
TREMOR *s.m.* quake; shiver.
TRENÓ *s.m.* sled; sleigh.
TREPADEIRA *s.f.* creeper.
TREPAR *v.* to climb.
TREPIDAÇÃO *s.f.* vibration; tremor.
TREPIDAR *v.* to jounce.
TRÊS *num.* three.
TREVA *s.f.* darkness.
TREVO *s.m.* clover.
TREZE *num.* thirteen.
TREZENTOS *num.* three hundred.

TRÍADE *s.f.* triad.
TRIAGEM *s.f.* seletion.
TRIANGULAR *adj.2gên.* triangular.
TRIÂNGULO *s.m.* triangle.
TRIBO *s.f.* tribe.
TRIBUFU *s.m.* ugly person.
TRIBUNAL *s.m.* tribunal, court.
TRIBUTAÇÃO *s.f.* taxation.
TRIBUTAR *v.* to tax.
TRIBUTO *s.m.* tribute.
TRICICLO *s.m.* tricycle.
TRICÔ *s.m.* tricot, knitting.
TRICOTAR *v.* to knit.
TRIDENTE *s.m.* trident.
TRIDIMENSIONAL *adj.2gên.* three-dimensional.
TRIGÊMEO *s.m.* triplet.
TRIGO *s.m.* wheat.
TRILHA *s.f.* trail.
TRILHAR *v.* to tread.
TRILHO *s.m.* rail.
TRILOGIA *s.f.* trilogy.
TRIMESTRE *s.m.* trimester.
TRINCAR *v.* to crush; to snap.
TRINCHEIRA *s.f.* trench.
TRINCO *s.m.* latch.
TRINTA *num.* thirty.
TRIO *s.m.* trio.
TRIPÉ *s.m.* tripod.
TRIPLICAR *v.* to triplicate.
TRIPULAÇÃO *s.f.* crew.
TRISTE *adj.2gên.* sad, unhappy.
TRISTEZA *s.f.* sorrow, sadness.
TRITURADOR *s.m.* crusher.
TRITURAR *v.* to crush; to mash.
TRIUNFAR *v.* to triumph.
TRIUNFO *s.m.* triumph.
TRIVIAL *adj.2gên.* trivial; common.
TROCA *s.f.* exchange.
TROCADILHO *s.m.* pun.
TROCAR *v.* to exchange.
TROCO *s.m.* change.
TROÇO *s.m.* thing.
TROFÉU *s.m.* trophy.
TROMBA *s.f.* trunk.
TROMBADA *s.f.* crash, collision.
TROMBAR *v.* to bump, to collide.
TRONCO *s.m.* trunk.
TRONO *s.m.* throne.
TROPA *s.f.* troop.
TROPEÇAR *v.* to stumble.
TROPICAL *adj.2gên.* tropical.
TRÓPICO *s.m.* tropic.
TROUXA *s.f.* bundle.
TROVÃO *s.m.* thunder.
TROVEJAR *v.* to thunder.
TUA *pron.* your, yours.
TUBA *s.f.* tuba.
TUBARÃO *s.m.* shark.
TUBÉRCULO *s.m.* tubercle.
TUBERCULOSE *s.f.* tuberculosis.
TUBO *s.m.* tube.
TUBULAÇÃO *s.f.* tubing, piping.
TUBULAR *adj.2gên.* tubular.
TUCANO *s.m.* toucan.
TUDO *pron.* all, everything.
TUFÃO *s.m.* typhoon, hurricane.
TUFO *s.m.* tuft.
TULE *s.m.* tulle.
TULIPA *s.f.* tulip.
TUMBA *s.f.* tomb, grave; tombstone.
TUMOR *s.m.* tumor.
TÚMULO *s.m.* tomb, grave.
TUMULTO *s.m.* tumult, disturbance.
TUMULTUAR *v.* to disorder.
TÚNEL *s.m.* tunnel.
TÚNICA *s.f.* tunic; vestment.
TURBANTE *s.m.* turban.
TURBILHÃO *s.m.* eddy.
TURBINA *s.f.* turbine.
TURBULÊNCIA *s.f.* turbulence.
TURBULENTO(A) *adj.* turbulent.
TURCO(A) *s.m.* Turkish / *adj.* Turkish.
TURISMO *s.m.* tourism.
TURISTA *s.2gên.* tourist.
TURMA *s.f.* gang, group.
TURNÊ *s.f.* touring, roadshow.
TURNO *s.m.* shift.
TURQUESA *s.f.* turquoise.
TURQUIA *s.f.* Turkey.
TURVAR *v.* to dim.
TUTELA *s.f.* custody.
TUTELAR *adj.2gên.* tutelary.
TUTOR(A) *s.m.* guardian; tutor.
TUTORIAL *s.m.* tutorial.
TUTU *s.m.* tutu; buck.

Uu

U, u *s.m.* the twenty-first letter of the Portuguese alphabet.
UAI *interj.* oh!
UAU *interj.* wow!
UBICAÇÃO *s.f.* ubiety.
UBÍQUO(A) *adj.* ubiquitous, omnipresent.
UFA *interj.* whew, wow, phew.
UFANAR *v.* to render proud; to flatter.
UFANISTA *adj.2gên.* vainglorious.
UFOLOGIA *s.f.* Ufology.
UFOLOGISTA *s.2gên.* ufologist.
UFÓLOGO(A) *m.q.* ufologista.
UI *interj.* ugh, ouch!
UÍSQUE *s.m.* whiskey.
UIVAR *v.* to howl, to yowl; to yell, to yelp.
UIVO *s.m.* howl, yowl, yelling, yelp, bawling.
ÚLCERA *s.f.* ulcer.
ULCERAÇÃO *s.f.* soreness, achiness.
ULCERAR *v.* to ulcerate, to suppurate, to fester; to canker.
ULTERIOR *adj.* ulterior, subsequent.
ULTIMAMENTE *adv.* recently, lately.
ULTIMAR *v.* to terminate, to finish; to complete; to close.
ULTIMATO *s.m.* ultimatum.
ÚLTIMO(A) *adj.* last, preceding.
ULTRAJANTE *adj.2gên.* offensive, outrageous.
ULTRAJAR *v.* to insult; to outrage.
ULTRAJE *s.m.* offense, outrage.
ULTRALEVE *s.m.* hang-glider, ultralight.
ULTRAMAR *s.m.* overseas, ultramarine.
ULTRAPASSADO(A) *adj.* overpast.
ULTRAPASSAGEM *s.f.* overtaking, surpassingness, passing, crossing.
ULTRAPASSAR *v.* to exceed, to surpass.
ULTRASSECRETO *adj.* top-secret.
ULTRASSOM *s.m.* ultrasound, supersound.
ULTRASSÔNICO *adj.* ultrasonic.
ULTRASSONOGRAFIA *s.f.* ultrasonography, ultrasound.
ULTRAVIOLETA *adj.* ultraviolet.
ULULAR *v.* to ululate, to howl.
UM(A) *art.* a, an / *num.* one.
UMBANDA *s.f.* hoodoo, white magic.
UMBELA *s.f.* umbel.
UMBIGO *s.m.* navel.
UMBILICAL *adj.2gên.* umbilical.

UMBRAL *s.m.* doorjamb, doorpost, threshold.
UMECTANTE *adj.2gên.* emollient, moisturizing.
UMECTAR *v.* to humect, to moisten.
UMEDECEDOR *s.m.* moistener, moisturizer.
UMEDECER *v.* to moisten, to humidify.
UMEDECIDO(A) *adj.* humid, wet.
UMIDADE *s.f.* humidity, moisture.
UMIDIFICADOR *s.m.* humidifier.
UMIDIFICAR *v.* to humidify, to moisturize.
ÚMIDO(A) *adj.* humid, wet, moist, damp.
UNÂNIME *adj.2gên.* unanimous.
UNANIMIDADE *s.f.* unanimity.
UNÇÃO *s.f.* unction, inunction, anointment, anointing.
UNDÉCIMO *num.* eleventh part, eleventh.
UNGIDO(A) *adj.* anointed, consecrated.
UNGIR *v.* to anoint, to oil.
UNGUENTO *s.m.* unguent, salve, ointment, unction.
UNHA *s.f.* nail.
UNHADA *s.f.* nail scratch; claw.
UNHAR *v.* to scratch, to claw, to tear; to layer.
UNHEIRO *s.m.* hangnail, agnail, whitlow.
UNIÃO *s.f.* union, alliance.
UNICELULAR *adj.* unicellular.
ÚNICO(A) *adj.* unique, only.
UNICOLOR *adj.2gên.* unicoloured.
UNICÓRNIO *s.m.* unicorn.
UNIDADE *s.f.* unit; unity.
UNIDIMENSIONAL *adj.2gên.* unidimensional.
UNIDIRECIONAL *adj.2gên.* unidirectional.
UNIDO(A) *adj.* united, joined, allied; linked.
UNIFICAÇÃO *s.f.* unification, unity.
UNIFICADO(A) *adj.* unified.
UNIFICAR *v.* to unify.
UNIFORME *adj.2gên.* uniform / *s.m.* uniform.
UNIFORMIDADE *s.f.* uniformity, uniformness.
UNIFORMIZADO(A) *adj.* uniformed.
UNIFORMIZAR *v.* to uniformize, to unify.
UNILATERAL *adj.2gên.* unilateral.
UNILÍNGUE *adj.2gên.* monolingual.
UNÍPARO(A) *adj.* uniparous.
UNIPESSOAL *adj.2gên.* unipersonal.
UNIPOLAR *adj.2gên.* unipolar.
UNIR *v.* to join, to unite, to connect.

UNISSEX *adj.2gên.* unisex.
UNISSEXUAL *adj.2gên.* unisexual.
UNISSONANTE *adj.2gên.* unison.
UNÍSSONO(A) *adj.* unison.
UNITÁRIO(A) *adj.* unitarist, unitarian.
UNIVALENTE *adj.2gên.* univalent, monovalent.
UNIVALVE *adj.2gên.* univalve.
UNIVALVULAR *adj.2gên.* univalvular.
UNIVERSAL *adj.2gên.* universal.
UNIVERSALIDADE *s.f.* universality.
UNIVERSALISMO *s.m.* universalism.
UNIVERSALISTA *adj.2gên.* universalist, universalistic.
UNIVERSALIZAÇÃO *s.f.* universalization.
UNIVERSALIZAR *v.* to universalize, to make universal, to generalize.
UNIVERSIDADE *s.f.* university.
UNIVERSITÁRIO(A) *adj.* academic, scholastic / *s.m.* collegian.
UNIVERSO *s.m.* universe.
UNIVITELINO(A) *adj.* univitelline.
UNÍVOCO(A) *adj.* univocal.
UNO(A) *adj.* one, sole, single.
UNTAR *v.* to anoint, to grease, to butter, to salve, to oil.
UNTUOSIDADE *s.f.* unctuousness, greasiness.
UNTUOSO(A) *adj.* unctuous, greasy, soapy.
UPA *interj.* hop, jump, go.
URÂNIO *s.m.* uranium.
URANO *s.m.* Uranus.
URBANISMO *s.m.* urbanism, city planning.
URBANISTA *adj.2gên.* urbanist.
URBANIZAÇÃO *s.f.* urbanization.
URBANIZADO(A) *adj.* built up, urbanized.
URBANIZAR *v.* to urbanize.
URBANO(A) *adj.* urban.
URBANÓLOGO *adj.* urbanologist.
URBE *s.f.* city, town.
URDIMENTO *s.m.* warp.
URDIR *v.* to warp, to weave, to machinate.
UREIA *s.f.* urea.
URETER *s.m.* ureter.
URETRA *s.f.* urethra.
URGÊNCIA *s.f.* urgency, haste.
URGENTE *adj.2gên.* urgent.
URGIR *v.* to urge, to press; to instigate; to claim.
ÚRICO *adj.* uric.

URINA *s.f.* urine.
URINAR *v.* to urinate.
URINÁRIO(A) *adj.* urinary.
URINOL *s.m.* potty, urinal.
URNA *s.f.* urn, casket; ballot-box.
UROLOGIA *s.f.* urology.
UROLOGISTA *adj.2gên.* urologist.
URRAR *v.* to roar.
URRO *s.m.* roar, roaring; bawl, howl.
URSO *s.m.* bear.
URSO-POLAR *s.m.* polar bear.
URTICANTE *adj.2gên.* urticant, stinging.
URTICÁRIA *s.f.* urticaria, hives.
URTIGA *s.f.* nettle, stinging nettle.
URTIGÃO *s.m.* scratchbush.
URUGUAIO(A) *adj.* Uruguayan.
URUBU *s.m.* vulture.
USADO(A) *adj.* used, usual; secondhand.
USAR *v.* to use, to wear.
USINA *s.f.* plant, factory.
USO *s.m.* use; application.
USUAL *adj.2gên.* usual.
USUÁRIO(A) *adj.* user / *s.m.* user.
USUFRUIR *v.* to enjoy, to usufruct.
USUFRUTO *s.m.* usufruct.
USURA *s.f.* usury, gombeen; avarice, ambition.
USURÁRIO(A) *s.m.* usurer, money jobber.
USURPADOR(A) *adj.* usurper, encroacher.
USURPAR *v.* to usurp, to encroach.
UTENSÍLIO *s.m.* utensil.
UTENTE *s.2gên.* user.
UTERINO *adj.* uterine.
ÚTERO *s.m.* uterus, womb.
ÚTIL *adj.2gên.* useful, practical.
UTILIDADE *s.f.* utility, usefulness.
UTILITÁRIO(A) *adj.* utilitarian.
UTILITARISMO *s.m.* utilitarism.
UTILITARISTA *adj.2gên.* utilitarian.
UTILIZAÇÃO *s.f.* utilization, application.
UTILIZAR *v.* to utilize, to use.
UTOPIA *s.f.* utopia, chimera.
UTÓPICO(A) *adj.* utopian, chimerical.
UVA *s.f.* grape.
UVA-PASSA *s.f.* raisin.
ÚVULA *s.f.* uvula.

V v

V, v *s.m.* the twenty-second letter of the Portuguese alphabet.
VACA *s.f.* cow (animal); beef (carne).
VACAÇÃO *s.f.* rest, repose.
VACÂNCIA *s.f.* holiday, vacation.
VACILAÇÃO *s.f.* vacillation.
VACILAR *v.* to vacillate, to hesitate.
VACILATÓRIO(A) *adj.* vacillatory.
VACINA *s.f.* vaccine, inoculation.
VACINAÇÃO *s.f.* inoculation, vaccination.
VACINAR *v.* to vaccinate, to inoculate with vaccine.
VACUIDADE *s.f.* vacuity, emptiness.
VÁCUO *s.m.* vacuum; gap, void.
VACÚOLO *s.m.* vacuole.
VADIAGEM *s.f.* vagrancy, idleness.
VADIAR *v.* to idle.
VADIO(A) *s.m.* loafer, idler.
VAGA *s.f.* vacancy.
VAGABUNDAGEM *s.f.* vagabondage.
VAGABUNDEAR *v.* to laze, to idle; to tramp.
VAGABUNDO(A) *s.m.* roamer, idler / *adj.* vagabond, erratic.
VAGA-LUME *s.m.* firefly.
VAGAMUNDO *s.m.* vagabond, tramp.
VAGÃO *s.m.* wagon.
VAGAR *v.* to wander, to roam.
VAGAREZA *s.f.* slowness, sluggishness.
VAGAROSO(A) *adj.* slow; leisurely.
VAGEM *s.f.* green bean.
VAGINA *s.f.* vagina.
VAGINAL *adj.2gên.* vaginal.
VAGO(A) *adj.* empty; vague.
VAGUEAR *v.* to rove, to perambulate.
VAIA *s.f.* hoot.
VAIAR *v.* to hoot.
VAIDADE *s.f* vanity.
VAIDOSO(A) *adj.* vain.
VAIVÉM *s.m.* swing.
VALA *s.f.* ditch.
VALE *s.m.* valley.
VALÊNCIA *s.f.* valence.
VALENTÃO(ONA) *s.m.* bully, daredevil.
VALENTE *adj.2gên.* brave.
VALENTIA *s.f.* bravery.
VALE-POSTAL *s.m.* money order.
VALER *v.* to value; to be valid.

VALETA *s.f.* channel, gutter.
VALETE *s.m.* knave, jack.
VALIA *s.f.* price, value.
VALIDAÇÃO *s.f.* validation.
VALIDADE *s.f.* validity.
VALIDAR *v.* to validate; to authenticate.
VALIDEZ *s.f.* validity.
VÁLIDO(A) *adj.* valid.
VALIOSO(A) *adj.* valuable.
VALISE *s.f.* small suitcase, valise.
VALOR *s.m.* value.
VALORIZAÇÃO *s.f.* valorization; esteem.
VALORIZAR *v.* to valorize, to value.
VALOROSO(A) *adj.* valorous; valiant.
VALSA *s.f.* waltz.
VALSISTA *s.2gên.* waltzer / *adj.* waltzing.
VALVA *s.f.* valve.
VÁLVULA *s.f.* valve.
VALVULAR *adj.* valvular.
VAMPIRO(A) *s.m.* vampire.
VANDALISMO *s.m.* vandalism.
VANDALIZAR *v.* to vandalize.
VÂNDALO *s.m.* vandal.
VANGLÓRIA *s.f.* vainglory, vanity.
VANGLORIAR *v.* to praise, to venerate.
VANGUARDA *s.f.* vanguard.
VANGUARDISMO *s.m.* vanguardism.
VANGUARDISTA *s.2gên.* vanguardist / *adj.* avant-garde.
VANIDADE *s.f.* vanity.
VANTAGEM *s.f.* advantage.
VANTAJOSO(A) *adj.* advantageous, beneficial.
VÃO(Ã) *s.m.* interspace, gap / *adj.* vain.
VAPOR *s.m.* vapour, steam.
VAPORAR *v.* to evaporate.
VAPORIZAÇÃO *s.f.* vaporization.
VAPORIZADOR *s.m.* evaporator; spray.
VAPORIZAR *v.* to vaporize; to pulverize.
VAPOROSIDADE *s.f.* vaporousness.
VAQUEIRO(A) *s.m.* cowboy.
VAQUEJADA *s.f.* rodeo.
VAQUINHA *s.f.* kitty, pool.
VARA *s.f.* stick, rod.
VARAL *s.m.* clothesline.
VARANDA *s.f.* terrace, porch.
VARÃO *s.m.* man.
VARAPAU *s.m.* stick; tall person.
VARAR *v.* to pierce, to trespass
VAREJISTA *s.2gên.* retailer / *adj.* retail.

VAREJO *s.m.* retail.
VARETA *s.f.* rod.
VARIABILIDADE *s.f.* variability.
VARIAÇÃO *s.f.* range, variation.
VARIADO(A) *adj.* different, diverse.
VARIANTE *s.f.* variation.
VARIAR *v.* to diversify.
VARIÁVEL *s.f.* variable / *adj.* variable.
VARICELA *s.f.* chickenpox, varicella.
VARIEDADE *s.f.* variety, diversity.
VARÍOLA *s.f.* smallpox.
VÁRIOS *adj.* several, various, many.
VARONIL *adj.* manly, virile.
VARREDOR *s.m.* dustman, garbage collector.
VARREDURA *s.f.* sweep.
VARRER *v.* to sweep.
VÁRZEA *s.f.* dale, lea.
VASCULAR *adj.2gên.* vascular.
VASCULHAR *v.* to search thoroughly.
VASECTOMIA *s.f.* vasectomy.
VASELINA *s.f.* vaseline.
VASILHA *s.f.* bowl, vessel.
VASILHAME *s.m.* holder.
VASO *s.m.* vase, flowerpot.
VASSALAGEM *s.f.* vassalage.
VASSALO *s.m.* vassal, liege.
VASSOURA *s.f.* brush, broom.
VASSOURADA *s.f.* sweep.
VASTIDÃO *s.f.* hugeness, expanse.
VASTO(A) *adj.* immense; colossal; vast.
VATICÍNIO *s.m.* prognostication.
VAZADO(A) *adj.* empty, hollow.
VAZAMENTO *s.m.* leak.
VAZÃO *s.f.* sewage; outflow.
VAZAR *v.* to leak.
VAZIO(A) *adj.* empty / *s.m.* emptiness.
VEADO *s.m.* deer (animal).
VEDAÇÃO *s.f.* gasket.
VEDAR *v.* to seal.
VEDETE *s.f.* vedette.
VEEMÊNCIA *s.f.* vehemence.
VEEMENTE *adj.2gên.* vehement.
VEGETAÇÃO *s.f.* vegetation.
VEGETAL *s.m.* vegetable.
VEGETAR *v.* to vegetate.
VEGETARIANO(A) *s.m.* vegetarian / *adj.* vegetarian.
VEIA *s.f.* vein.
VEICULAR *adj.2gên.* vehicular.

VEÍCULO *s.m.* vehicle.
VELA *s.f.* candle.
VELADO(A) *adj.* veiled.
VELAR *v.* to watch.
VELEIRO *s.m.* sailing ship.
VELEJAR *v.* to sail.
VELHARIA *s.f.* oldness; antiqueness.
VELHICE *s.f.* old age; senescence.
VELHO(A) *adj.* old; elderly.
VELHOTE *adj.* oldie.
VELOCIDADE *s.f.* speed.
VELOCÍMETRO *s.m.* speedometer.
VELOCÍPEDE *s.m.* velocipede.
VELOCISTA *s.2gên.* sprinter.
VELÓRIO *s.m.* deathwatch.
VELOZ *adj.2gên.* fast, speedy.
VELUDO *s.m.* velvet.
VENCEDOR(A) *s.m.* winner / *adj.* winning.
VENCER *v.* to win.
VENDA *s.f.* sale, selling.
VENDAR *v.* to blindfold.
VENDAVAL *s.m.* windstorm.
VENDEDOR(A) *s.m.* salesman / *s.f.* saleswoman.
VENDER *v.* to sell.
VENDINHA *s.f.* kiosk.
VENENO *s.m.* poison.
VENENOSO(A) *adj.* poisonous.
VENERABILIDADE *s.f.* venerability.
VENERAÇÃO *s.f.* veneration, reverence.
VENERAR *v.* to adore, to venerate.
VENERÁVEL *adj.2gên.* venerable.
VENÉREO(A) *adj.* venereal.
VENETA *s.f.* fancy, whim.
VENEZIANA *s.f.* Venetian blind, shutter.
VENOSO *adj.* veiny, venous.
VENTANIA *s.f.* blow, wind.
VENTAR *v.* to blow.
VENTILAÇÃO *s.f.* airing, ventilation.
VENTILADOR *s.m.* fan.
VENTILAR *v.* to fan, to ventilate.
VENTO *s.m.* wind.
VENTOINHA *s.f.* wheathercock; blower.
VENTOSA *s.f.* sucker.
VENTRE *s.m.* belly; womb.
VENTRÍCULO *s.m.* ventricle.
VENTRILOQUISMO *s.m.* ventriloquism.
VENTRÍLOQUO *s.m.* ventriloquist.
VENTURA *s.f.* venture; hap.
VÊNUS *s.f.* Venus.

VER *v.* to see.
VERACIDADE *s.f.* veracity, truth.
VERANEIO *adj.* summer.
VERÃO *s.m.* summer.
VERBA *s.f.* appropiation.
VERBAL *adj.* verbal, oral.
VERBALIZAR *v.* to verbalize.
VERBETE *s.m.* entry.
VERBO *s.m.* verb.
VERDADE *s.f.* truth.
VERDADEIRO(A) *adj.* true, truthful.
VERDE *s.m.* green / *adj.* green.
VERDURA *s.f.* vegetable.
VEREADOR(A) *s.m.* assemblyman / *s.f.* assemblywoman.
VEREDICTO *s.m.* verdict.
VERGÃO *s.m.* wheal, welt.
VERGAR *v.* to bend.
VERGONHA *s.f.* shame.
VERGONHOSO(A) *adj.* shameful, disgraceful.
VERÍDICO(A) *adj.* true.
VERIFICAR *v.* to verify.
VERME *s.m.* worm.
VERMELHO *s.m.* red / *adj.* red.
VERMICIDA *s.m.* vermicide, vermifuge.
VERNÁCULO *s.m.* vernacular / *adj.* vernacular.
VERNIZ *s.m.* varnish, polish.
VEROSSÍMIL *adj.2gên.* likely.
VEROSSIMILHANÇA *s.f.* likelihood.
VERRUGA *s.f.* wart.
VERSALETE *s.m.* small capital.
VERSÃO *s.f.* version.
VERSÁTIL *adj.2gên.* versatile.
VERSATILIDADE *s.f.* versatility.
VERSÍCULO *s.m.* verse.
VERSIFICAR *v.* to versify.
VERSO *s.m.* verse; back.
VÉRTEBRA *s.f.* vertebra.
VERTEBRADO(A) *adj.* vertebrate.
VERTEBRAL *adj.* vertebral, spinal.
VERTENTE *s.f.* hillside, watershed.
VERTER *v.* to pour.
VERTICAL *adj.2gên.* vertical, perpendicular.
VÉRTICE *s.m.* cloakroom.
VERTIGEM *s.f.* dizziness, vertigo.
VESGO(A) *adj.* squinter, lazy eye.
VESGUICE *s.f.* squint-eyedness.
VESÍCULA *s.f.* vesicle.

VESPA *s.f.* wasp.
VESPEIRO *s.m.* vespiary, wasps' nest.
VESPERTINO(A) *adj.* vespertine.
VESTIÁRIO *s.m.* cloakroom.
VESTIBULAR *s.m.* entrance exam, prelim.
VESTIDO *s.m.* dress.
VESTÍGIO *s.m.* sign, trace.
VESTIR *v.* to dress, to put on.
VESTUÁRIO *s.m.* garment.
VETAR *v.* to refuse, to reject.
VETERANO(A) *s.m.* veteran.
VETERINÁRIO(A) *s.m.* veterinary, vet.
VETO *s.m.* veto; interdiction.
VÉU *s.m.* veil.
VEXAME *s.m.* humiliation.
VEZ *s.f.* turn, time.
VIA *s.f.* way / *prep.* via, by.
VIA LÁCTEA *s.f.* Milky Way.
VIABILIDADE *s.f.* availability.
VIADUTO *s.m.* viaduct.
VIAGEM *s.f.* trip, journey.
VIAJAR *v.* to travel.
VIA-SACRA *s.f.* via crucis.
VIATURA *s.f.* car.
VIÁVEL *adj.* viable, workable.
VÍBORA *s.f.* viper.
VIBRAÇÃO *s.f.* vibration; tremor.
VIBRADOR *s.m.* vibrator.
VIBRANTE *adj.2gên.* vibrant, vibrating.
VIBRAR *v.* to vibrate.
VIBRATÓRIO(A) *adj.* vibratile, vibratory.
VICIADO(A) *adj.* addicted.
VICIAR *v.* to addict.
VÍCIO *s.m.* addiction.
VICIOSO *adj.* vicious.
VIDA *s.f.* life; existence.
VIDEIRA *s.f.* vine, grape.
VIDÊNCIA *s.f.* clairvoyance.
VIDENTE *s.2gên.* clairvoyant.
VÍDEO *s.m.* video.
VIDRAÇA *s.f.* window; glass.
VIDRAÇARIA *s.f.* glasshouse.
VIDRACEIRO(A) *s.m.* glazier.
VIDRO *s.m.* glass.
VIELA *s.f.* alley.
VIÉS *s.m.* obliquity, sloping.
VIGA *s.f.* beam.
VIGARICE *s.f.* swindle, fraud.
VIGÁRIO *s.m.* parson.
VIGARISTA *s.2gên.* hustler, con.
VIGENTE *adj.2gên.* actual, present.
VIGÉSIMO *num.* twentieth.
VIGIA *s.2gên.* guard, watchman.
VIGIAR *v.* to guard, to watch.
VIGILÂNCIA *s.f.* surveillance.
VIGILANTE *adj.2gên.* vigilant, watchful.
VIGÍLIA *s.f.* watch, vigil.
VIGOR *s.m.* energy, force.
VIGOROSO(A) *adj.* vigorous, vivid.
VIL *adj.2gên.* vile.
VILA *s.f.* villa.
VILANIA *s.f.* villainy.
VILÃO(Ã) *s.m.* villain.
VILAREJO *s.m.* village.
VILIPENDIAR *v.* to vilify.
VILIPÊNDIO *s.m.* slander, vilification.
VIME *s.m.* vime, wicker.
VINAGRE *s.m.* vinegar.
VINCAR *v.* to stress, to accentuate.
VINCO *s.m.* crease, plait.
VINCULAÇÃO *s.f.* linkage; joining.
VINCULAR *v.* to link, to attach.
VÍNCULO *s.m.* link, nexus.
VINDA *s.f.* coming, arrival.
VINDOURO(A) *adj.* coming.
VINGADOR(A) *s.m.* avenger.
VINGANÇA *s.f.* revenge.
VINGAR *v.* to revenge.
VINGATIVO(A) *adj.* vengeful, vindictive.
VINHA *s.f.* vine.
VINHEDO *s.m.* vineyard.
VINHETA *s.f.* vignette.
VINHO *s.m.* wine.
VINÍCOLA *s.f.* winery.
VINICULTURA *s.f.* winery.
VINTE *num.* twenty.
VIOLA *s.f.* viola.
VIOLAÇÃO *s.f.* violation.
VIOLÃO *s.m.* guitar.
VIOLAR *v.* to transgress.
VIOLÁVEL *adj.2gên.* violable.
VIOLÊNCIA *s.f.* violence.
VIOLENTAR *v.* to coerce, to constrain; to rape.
VIOLENTO(A) *adj.* violent.
VIOLETA *s.f.* violet.
VIOLINISTA *s.2gên.* violinist.
VIOLINO *s.m.* violin.
VIOLONCELO *s.m.* cello.
VIR *v.* to come.

VIRA-CASACA *s.2gên.* switcher, floater.
VIRADA *s.f.* turning.
VIRA-LATA *adj.2gên.* mongrel; pooch.
VIRAR *v.* to turn.
VIRGEM *s.2gên.* virgin.
VIRGEM *s.f.* Virgo (astrologia).
VIRGINDADE *s.f.* virginity.
VÍRGULA *s.f.* comma.
VIRIL *adj.2gên.* male.
VIRILHA *s.f.* groin.
VIRILIDADE *s.f.* virility.
VIROLOGIA *s.f.* virology.
VIROSE *s.f.* virosis.
VIRTUAL *adj.2gên.* virtual.
VIRTUDE *s.f.* virtue.
VIRTUOSO(A) *adj.* virtuous; virtuoso.
VÍRUS *s.m.* virus.
VISÃO *s.f.* vision; eyesight.
VISAR *v.* to aim, to drive; to spot.
VÍSCERA *s.f.* viscus.
VISCONDE *s.m.* viscount.
VISCOSO(A) *adj.* sticky, viscous.
VISEIRA *s.f.* visor, eyeshade.
VISIBILIDADE *s.f.* visibility.
VISIONÁRIO(A) *adj.* visionary.
VISITA *s.f.* visit.
VISITANTE *s.2gên.* visitor, guest.
VISITAR *v.* to visit.
VISÍVEL *adj.2gên.* visible.
VISLUMBRAR *v.* to glimpse.
VISOR *s.m.* viewer; sighthole, display.
VISTA *s.f.* sight, vision.
VISTO *s.m.* visa.
VISTORIAR *v.* to inspect.
VISUAL *adj.2gên.* visual.
VISUALIZAR *v.* to visualize, to see.
VITAL *adj.2gên.* vital.
VITALÍCIO *adj.* lifelong, tenured.
VITALIDADE *s.f.* vitality.
VITALIZAR *v.* to vitalize.
VITAMINA *s.f.* vitamin.
VITELA *s.f.* veal, heifer; calf.
VITELO *s.m.* vitellus, male calf.
VITICULTOR(A) *s.m.* viticulturist.
VITICULTURA *s.f.* viticulture, viniculture.
VÍTIMA *s.f.* victim.
VITÓRIA *s.f.* victory, win.
VITORIOSO(A) *adj.* victorious, triumphant.
VITRAL *s.m.* glass pane.
VITRINE *s.f.* showcase.

VITROLA *s.f.* phonograph.
VIÚVA *s.f.* widow.
VIÚVO *s.m.* widower.
VIVA *s.m.* cheer / *interj.* hooray!
VIVAZ *adj.2gên.* vivacious, lively.
VIVEIRO *s.m.* rookery, aviary.
VIVÊNCIA *s.f.* life, existance.
VIVENCIAR *v.* to live, to experience.
VIVENDA *s.f.* dwelling house.
VIVENTE *adj.2gên.* living.
VIVER *v.* to live.
VIVIDO(A) *adj.* experienced.
VÍVIDO(A) *adj.* lurid, vivid, colorful.
VIVÍPARO(A) *adj.* viviparous.
VIVO(A) *adj.* alive; lively.
VIZINHANÇA *s.f.* neighbourhood.
VIZINHO(A) *s.m.* neighbour.
VÔ *s.m.* grandfather, grandpa.
VOADOR(A) *s.m.* flier / *adj.* flying.
VOAR *v.* to fly.
VOCABULÁRIO *s.m.* vocabulary.
VOCÁBULO *s.m.* word, term.
VOCAÇÃO *s.f.* vocation.
VOCACIONAL *adj.2gên.* vocational.
VOCAL *adj.2gên.* vocal, oral.
VOCÁLICO(A) *adj.* vocalic.
VOCALISE *s.f.* vocalise.
VOCALISTA *s.2gên.* singer, vocalist.
VOCÊ *pron.* you.
VOCÊS *pron.* you.
VOCIFERAR *v.* to vociferate; to bawl.
VOGA *s.f.* vogue.
VOGAL *s.f.* vowel.
VOLANTE *adj.2gên.* movable, portable / *s.m.* steering wheel.
VOLÁTIL *adj.2gên.* volatile; mercurial.
VOLATILIDADE *s.f.* volatility.
VOLEIBOL *s.m.* volleyball.
VOLTA *s.f.* turn; return.
VOLTAGEM *s.f.* voltage.
VOLTAR *v.* to turn; to return.
VOLTÍMETRO *s.m.* voltmeter.
VOLUME *s.m.* volume.
VOLUMOSO(A) *adj.* voluminous, bulky; large.
VOLUNTÁRIO(A) *s.m.* volunteer / *adj.* voluntary.
VOLÚPIA *s.f.* ecstasy.
VOLUPTUOSO(A) *adj.* voluptuous.
VOLÚVEL *adj.2gên.* voluble, inconstant; fickle.
VOMITAR *v.* to throw up, to puke.

VÔMITO *s.m.* puke, vomit.
VONTADE *s.f.* will, wish.
VOO *s.m.* flight.
VORAZ *adj.2gên.* voracious.
VÓRTICE *s.m.* vortex.
VOTAÇÃO *s.f.* voting, election.
VOTANTE *s.2gên.* voter, elector.
VOTAR *v.* to vote.
VOTO *s.m.* vote; promise, vow.
VOZ *s.f.* voice.
VOZEIRÃO *s.m.* strong voice.
VOZERIO *s.m.* brawl.
VULCÂNICO *adj.* volcanic.
VULCÃO *s.m.* volcano.
VULGAR *adj.2gên.* vulgar.
VULNERÁVEL *adj.2gên.* vulnerable.
VULTO *s.m.* figure; form.
VULVA *s.f.* vulva.

W w

W, w *s.m.* the twenty-third letter of the Portuguese alphabet.
WAFFLE *s.m.* waffle.
WALKIE-TALKIE *s.m.* walkie-talkie.
WALKMAN *s.m.* walkman.
WATT *s.m.* watt.
WATT-HORA *s.m.* watt-hour.
WATTÍMETRO *s.m.* wattmeter.
W.C. *s.m. abrev.* water closet.
WINDSURFE *s.m.* windsurf.
WINDSURFISTA *s.2gên.* windsurfer.
W.O. *s.m. abrev.* walkover.
WORKSHOP *s.m.* workshop.
WWW *s.f.* world wide web.

Xx

X, x *s.m.* the twenty-fourth letter of the Portuguese alphabet.
XÁCARA *s.f.* ballad, ditty.
XADREZ *s.m.* chess (jogo); chessboard (tabuleiro); check (tecido).
XADREZISTA *s.2gên.* chess player.
XALE *s.m.* shawl.
XAMÃ *s.m.* shaman.
XAMPU *s.m.* shampoo.
XÂNTICO *adj.* xanthic.
XARÁ *s.2gên.* namesake.
XAROPE *s.m.* syrup.
XAVECO *s.m.* xebec, old boat.
XENOFILIA *s.f.* xenophilism
XENÓFILO *s.m.* xenophile / *adj.* xenophile.
XENÓFOBO *s.m.* xenophobe.
XENÔNIO *s.m.* xenon.
XEPA *s.f.* meal, food.
XEQUE *s.m.* check; political crisis.
XEQUE-MATE *s.m.* mate, checkmate.
XERETA *adj.* nosy / *s.2gên.* gossip, disturber.
XERETAR *v.* to snoop.
XERIFE *s.m.* sheriff.
XEROCAR *m.q.* xerocopiar.
XEROCÓPIA *s.f.* Xerox copy.
XEROCOPIAR *v.* to xerox.
XEROGRAFIA *s.f.* xerography.
XEROX *s.m.* Xerox copier.
XEXELENTO *s.m.* disagreeable.
XI *interj.* pish!.
XÍCARA *s.f.* cup.
XIITA *s.2gên.* Shiite.
XILINDRÓ *s.m.* jail, prison.
XINGAR *v.* to abuse; to chide, to scold.
XODÓ *s.m.* flirtation; sweetheart.

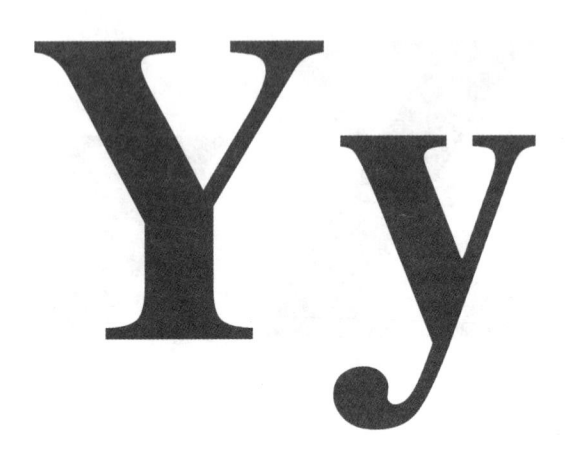

Y, y *s.m.* the twenty-fifth letter of the Portuguese alphabet.
YAKISOBA *s.m. yakisoba.*
YAKUZA *s.f. yakuza.*

YB *abrev.* ytterbium.
YD *abrev.* yard (jarda).
YIN-YANG *s.m. yin-yang.*
YOM KIPPUR *s.m. yom kippur.*

Z

Z, z *s.m.* the twenty-sixth letter of the Portuguese alphabet.
ZABUMBA *s.m.* bass drum.
ZAGA *s.f.* assagai.
ZAGUEIRO *s.m.* fullback.
ZAGUNCHAR *v.* to dart, to spear, to blame, to reprove.
ZAGUNCHO *s.m.* dart, javelin.
ZAMBEMBE *adj.2gên.* mediocre, inferior.
ZAMBIANO *adj.* Zambian.
ZAMPAR *v.* to eat greedily, to devour; to pack up.
ZANGA *s.f.* aversion, indignation, crossness.
ZANGADO *adj.* angry.
ZANGÃO *s.m.* drone.
ZANGAR *v.* to annoy.
ZANZAR *v.* to ramble, to rove, to wander, to roam.
ZANZIBAR *s.m.* Zanzibar.
ZANZIBARITA *s.2gên.* Zanzibari.
ZANZO *s.m.* queensland hemp.
ZAPEAR *v.* to zap.
ZARABATANA *s.f.* blow-pipe, blowtube, blowgun.
ZARANZAR *v.* to loiter, to walk awkwardly.
ZARCÃO *s.m.* minium, red lead.
ZARELHO *s.m.* mischievous child; scatterbrain.
ZAROLHO *adj.* one-eyed, squint-eyed.
ZARPAR. *v.* to weigh anchor, to sail away / to escape, to run away.
ZAVAR *v.* to bite furiously.
ZEBRA *s.f.* zebra.
ZÉFIRO *s.m.* zephyr.
ZELADOR *s.m.* janitor, watcher, keeper, caretaker.
ZELADORA *s.f.* janitress, watcher, keeper, caretaker.
ZELADORIA *s.f.* the janitor's office, the janitor's job.
ZELAR *v.* to ensure, to watch over, to take care.
ZELO *s.m.* zeal, warmth.
ZELOSO(A) *s.m.* zealous, earnest.
ZEN *adj.* zen.
ZENITAL *adj.* zenithal.
ZÊNITE *s.m.* zenith.
ZEPELIM *s.m.* zeppelin.

ZÉ-POVINHO *s.m.* people, populace, pleb.
ZERAR *v.* to reset.
ZERO *num.* zero.
ZEUGMA *s.m.* zeugma.
ZIGOMA *s.m.* zygoma.
ZIGOMÁTICO *adj.* zygomatic, jugal.
ZIGOTO *s.m.* zygote.
ZIGUE-ZAGUE *s.m.* zigzag, sinuosity.
ZIGUEZAGUEANTE *adj.2gên.* zigzagging, zigzaggy.
ZILHÃO *s.m.* zillion.
ZIMBRAR *v.* to lash, to flog, to switch.
ZINCO *s.m.* zinc.
ZINCOGRAVURA *s.f.* zincograph, zincography.
ZÍNGARO *s.m.* zingaro, zingano, gypsy.
ZIPAR *v.* to zip.
ZÍPER *s.m.* zip, zipper, zip-fastener.
ZIRCÔNIO *s.m.* zirconium.
ZIRCONITA *s.f.* zircon.
ZIZIAR *v.* to chirr, to chirp.
ZOADA *s.f.* whizzing, buzz, noise.
ZOAR *v.* to buzz.
ZODIACAL *adj.2gên.* zodiacal.
ZODÍACO *s.m.* zodiac.
ZOEIRA *s.f.* whizzing, disorder, noise.
ZOMBADOR(A) *s.m.* scoffer, jester, jeerer, mocker.
ZOMBAR *v.* to mock, to scoff, to jeer, to sneer.
ZOMBARIA *s.f.* mockery, sneer, jeer.
ZOMBETEIRO *adj.* taunting, mocking / *s.m.* mocker.
ZONA *s.f.* zone, mess.
ZONEAMENTO *s.m.* zoning.
ZONEAR *v.* to zone, to cause a brawl.
ZONZAR *v.* to stun, to make dizzy.
ZONZEAR *v. m.q.* zonzar.
ZONZEIRA *s.f.* dizziness, giddiness.
ZONZO *adj.* dizzy.
ZOOBIOLOGIA *s.f.* zoo biology.
ZOOFAGIA *s.f.* zoophagy.
ZOÓFAGO *s.m.* zoophagan / *adj.* zoophagous.
ZOOFILIA *s.f.* zoophilia, zoophily.

ZOÓFILO *s.m.* zoophilist, zoophilous / *adj.* zoophilic.
ZOOFOBIA *s.f.* zoophobia.
ZOÓLATRA *adj.* zootheist, zoolater.
ZOOLATRIA *s.f.* zootheism, zoolatry.
ZOOLOGIA *s.f.* zoology.
ZOOLÓGICO *s.m.* zoo, zoological garden / *adj.* zoologic, zoological.
ZOÓLOGO *s.m.* zoologist.
ZOOMAGNÉTICO *adj.* zoomagnetic.
ZOOMAGNETISMO *s.m.* zoomagnetism.
ZOOMANCIA *s.f.* zoomancy.
ZOOMANIA *s.f.* excessive love for animals.
ZOOMETRIA *s.f.* zoometry.
ZOOMORFISMO *s.m.* zoomorphism.
ZOONOSE *s.f.* zoonosis.
ZOOPATOLOGIA *s.f.* zoopathology.
ZOOQUÍMICA *s.f.* zoochemistry.
ZOOSPERMA *s.f.* zoosperm.
ZOÓSPORO *s.m.* zoospore.
ZOOTAXIA *s.f.* zootaxy, sistematic zoology.
ZOOTECNIA *s.f.* zootechny.
ZOOTÉCNICO *adj.* zootechnic.
ZOOTERAPIA *s.f.* zootherapy, veterinary therapeutics.
ZOOTOMIA *s.f.* zootomy.
ZOOTOMISTA *s.2gên.* zootomist.
ZOPEIRO *adj.* lame, crippled, timid.
ZOPO *s.m.* lame person, totterer, lazybones.
ZOROÁSTRICO *adj.* Zoroastrian.
ZOROASTRISMO *s.m.* Zoroastrianism.
ZORRA *s.f.* huge mess.
ZORRILHO *s.m.* skunk, zorril.
ZORRO *s.m.* zorro; lazybones, knave.
ZOTE *s.2gên.* simpleton, imbecile, idiot / *adj.2gên.* silly, idiotic.
ZUIR *v.* to whiz, to hum, to buzz.
ZUMBI *s.m.* zombie.
ZUMBIDO *s.m.* hum, buzz, whiz.
ZUMBIR *v.* to hum, to buzz, to drone, to murmur.
ZUNIR *v.* to whiz, to whir, to drone, to buzz.
ZURRO *s.m.* bray, braying, heehaw.

INGLÊS/PORTUGUÊS

Aa

A, a s. primeira letra do alfabeto inglês; lá (nota musical) /*art*. um(a).
ABACK *adv*. para trás, atrás; surpreso, perplexo(a).
ABAFT *adv*. à popa; a ré / *prep*. atrás; perante a ré de.
ABANDON *v*. abandonar, desamparar.
ABANDONED *adj*. abandonado(a); vicioso(a), perverso(a).
ABANDONMENT *s*. abandono, renúncia; desamparo.
ABASE *v*. rebaixar, humilhar.
ABASED *adj*. humilhado(a), degradado(a).
ABASEMENT *s*. degradação, humilhação.
ABASH *v*. embaraçar, envergonhar.
ABASHED *adj*. envergonhado(a).
ABATE *v*. diminuir, abater.
ABATTOIR *s*. matadouro.
ABBEY *s*. abadia, mosteiro.
ABBOT *s*. abade.
ABBREVIATE *v*. abreviar; resumir.
ABBREVIATION *s*. abreviação; resumo.
ABDICATE *v*. abdicar, renunciar.
ABDOMEN *s*. abdome.
ABDUCT *v*. raptar, abduzir.

ABDUCTEE *s*. sequestrado, raptado.
ABDUCTOR *s*. sequestrador; abdutor (anatomia).
ABERRANT *adj*. aberrante, anômalo(a); extravagante.
ABERRATION *s*. aberração; desvio; anomalia, irregularidade.
ABET *v*. instigar, incitar.
ABEYANCE *s*. suspensão, inatividade temporária.
ABEYANT *adj*. pendente, jacente.
ABHOR *v*. detestar, odiar.
ABHORRENCE *s*. aversão, repugnância.
ABHORRENT *adj*. detestável, repugnante.
ABIDE *v*. suportar; morar, residir.
ABILITY *s*. capacidade, habilidade, competência.
ABIOTIC *adj*. relativo a abiose; sem vida.
ABJECT *adj*. abjeto, miserável, vil, desprezível.
ABJURE *v*. abjurar, renunciar.
ABLAZE *adj*. em chamas; inflamado(a).
ABLE *adj*. capaz, hábil, apto(a).
ABLY *adv*. habilmente.
ABNEGATE *v*. abnegar.

ABNEGATION s. abnegação.
ABNORMAL adj. anormal; irregular.
ABNORMALITY s. anormalidade; irregularidade.
ABOARD adv. a bordo / prep. a bordo de, dentro de.
ABOLISH v. abolir.
ABOLITION s. abolição.
ABOLITIONIST s. abolicionista.
ABOMINABLE adj. abominável, odioso(a); desagradável, repugnante.
ABOMINATE v. abominar, detestar.
ABORT v. abortar; dar à luz prematuramente; interromper; frustrar.
ABORTION s. aborto; malogro, fracasso.
ABOUND v. abundar, fartar; ser rico em, estar cheio de.
ABOUT adv. aproximadamente; perto de, relativo a, a respeito de; junto a.
ABOVE prep. sobre; superior; além / adj. acima, referido / adv. acima, no alto.
ABRADE v. abradar, raspar, esfolar, friccionar.
ABRASION s. abrasão; erosão; desgaste; esfoladura, escoriação.
ABRASIVE adj. abrasivo(a).
ABRASIVE PAPER s. lixa.
ABRASIVE WHEEL s. rebolo.
ABREAST adv. lado a lado; em frente a; na mesma altura; manter o padrão.
ABRIDGE v. abreviar, resumir; diminuir, reduzir; privar.
ABRIDGEMENT s. abreviação, resumo; diminuição; sinopse.
ABROAD adv. no exterior, fora do país.
ABROGABLE adj. cancelável, anulável.
ABROGATE v. anular, abolir; liquidar.
ABROGATION s. anulação.
ABRUPT adj. abrupto(a); confuso(a); truncado(a).
ABRUPTION s. interrupção brusca; ruptura; desmembramento.
ABSCESS s. abcesso, apostema.
ABSCOND v. esconder-se, evadir-se, esquivar-se.
ABSCONDENCE s. evasão, fuga.
ABSCONDER s. fugitivo, foragido, desertor.
ABSENCE s. ausência, afastamento; falta, carência; distração.
ABSENT v. ausentar-se, afastar-se / adj. ausente; desaparecido; distraído.
ABSENTEEISM s. absenteísmo.

ABSINTHE s. absinto.
ABSOLUTE adj. absoluto(a), inteiro(a), total / s. absoluto(a).
ABSOLUTELY adv. absolutamente.
ABSOLUTION s. absolvição, remição; perdão, indulgência.
ABSOLUTISM s. absolutismo, despotismo.
ABSOLUTIST s. absolutista / adj. absolutista.
ABSOLVE v. absolver, isentar, perdoar.
ABSONANT adj. discordante, desarmonioso(a); insensato(a).
ABSORB v. absorver, assimilar.
ABSORBED adj. absorvido, absorto.
ABSORBENT adj. absorvente.
ABSORPTION s. absorção; interesse, dedicação; consumo; assimilação.
ABSTAIN v. abster-se, privar-se.
ABSTAINER s. abstinente, abstêmio.
ABSTEMIOUS adj. abstêmio.
ABSTINENCE s. abstinência.
ABSTRACT adj. abstrato(a) / s. abstrato, resumo, sumário.
ABSTRACTION s. abstração; furto, subtração; separação; distração.
ABSURD adj. absurdo(a), ridículo(a).
ABUNDANCE s. abundância, fartura.
ABUNDANT adj. abundante, opulento(a).
ABUSE v. abusar, maltratar / s. abuso; injúria.
ABUSIVE adj. ofensivo, insultante.
ABUT v. tocar, confinar, terminar; estar em contato.
ABYSMAL adj. péssimo(a).
ABYSS s. abismo.
ACADEMIC adj. acadêmico(a); teórico(a); universitário(a) / s. acadêmico.
ACADEMY s. academia; escola superior; conservatório.
ACCEDE v. aquiescer; aderir, associar-se; alcançar (cargo).
ACCELERATE v. acelerar, apressar; antecipar.
ACCELERATION s. aceleração.
ACCELERATOR s. acelerador.
ACCENT s. acento; sotaque.
ACCEPT v. aceitar; assumir.
ACCEPTABLE adj. aceitável, admissível; agradável.
ACCEPTANCE s. aceitação; aprovação, consentimento; acordo.
ACCESS s. acesso / v. acessar, entrar.
ACCESSIBLE adj. acessível.

ACCESSION s. acessão; aquiescência; adesão; aquisição.
ACCESSORIZE v. usar acessórios.
ACCESSORY s. acessório, suplemento / adj. acessório(a), suplementar.
ACCIDENT s. acidente, desastre.
ACCIDENTAL adj. acidental, inesperado(a).
ACCLAIM s. aclamação / v. aplaudir, aclamar.
ACCLAMATION s. aclamação, ovação, aplauso.
ACCLIMATE v. aclimatizar, adaptar.
ACCLIVITY s. ladeira, escarpa.
ACCOLADE s. louvor; honra; cerimonial.
ACCOMMODATE v. alojar, acomodar.
ACCOMMODATING adj. obsequioso(a), complacente.
ACCOMMODATION s. alojamento, acomodação.
ACCOMPANY v. acompanhar, escoltar.
ACCOMPLICE s. cúmplice.
ACCOMPLISH v. concluir; realizar.
ACCOMPLISHMENT s. realização; cumprimento.
ACCORD s. acordo / v. conceder; concordar.
ACCORDANCE s. acordo, conformidade, harmonia.
ACCORDINGLY adv. de acordo; portanto, consequentemente.
ACCORDION s. acordeão, sanfona.
ACCOST v. abordar.
ACCOUNT s. conta / v. calcular, acertar contas.
ACCOUNTABLE s. responsável.
ACCOUNTANCY s. contabilidade.
ACCOUNTANT s. contador(a).
ACCREDIT v. acreditar, abonar; confiar; autorizar; reconhecer, aprovar.
ACCREDITED adj. autorizado(a), aprovado(a).
ACCRUE v. acumular; advir, resultar.
ACCRUED INTEREST s. juros acumulados.
ACCULTURATE v. aculturar.
ACCUMULATE v. acumular.
ACCUMULATIVE adj. acumulativo.
ACCURACY s. exatidão, precisão.
ACCURATE adj. correto(a), preciso(a).
ACCURSED adj. amaldiçoado(a).
ACCUSATION s. acusação; incriminação.
ACCUSE v. acusar, denunciar.
ACCUSED s. acusado(a) / adj. acusado(a).

ACCUSTOM v. acostumar, habituar-se.
ACE s. ás (carta do baralho).
ACENTRIC adj. acêntrico, fora do centro.
ACEPHALOUS adj. acéfalo.
ACERBIC adj. amargo(a), azedo(a); áspero(a), severo(a).
ACETATE s. acetato / v. tratar com ácido acético.
ACETIC adj. acético.
ACETONE s. acetona.
ACHE s. dor / v. doer.
ACHIEVE v. alcançar, atingir, realizar.
ACHIEVEMENT s. realização, conquista.
ACHILLES HEEL s. calcanhar de aquiles.
ACID s. ácido / adj. azedo, acre.
ACKNOWLEDGE v. reconhecer; admitir; confirmar.
ACME s. auge, ápice.
ACNE s. acne.
ACORN s. bolota.
ACOUSTIC adj. acústico.
ACOUSTICS s. acústica.
ACQUAINT v. informar; familiarizar.
ACQUAINTANCE s. conhecido(a).
ACQUIESCE v. condescender, consentir.
ACQUIRE v. adquirir, obter.
ACQUISITION s. aquisição, obtenção.
ACQUISITIVE adj. aquisitivo; ganancioso, ávido.
ACQUIT v. absolver, inocentar.
ACQUITTAL s. absolvição, soltura.
ACRE s. acre (medida agrária).
ACRID adj. acre, azedo(a).
ACRIMONIOUS adj. mordaz, cáustico(a), amargo(a).
ACROBAT s. acrobata.
ACRONYM s. acrônimo.
ACROSS adj. cruzado(a) / adv. do outro lado / prep. através de.
ACROSTIC s. acróstico.
ACT s. ação, ato / v. atuar.
ACTING s. atuação, encenação / adj. ativo(a), em exercício.
ACTION s. ação, ato.
ACTIONER s. filme de ação.
ACTIVATE v. acionar, ativar.
ACTIVE adj. ativo(a), em atividade.
ACTIVELY adv. ativamente.
ACTIVIST s. ativista, militante.
ACTIVITY s. atividade.
ACTOR s. ator.

ACTRESS s. atriz.
ACTUAL adj. real, verdadeiro.
ACTUALITY s. realidade.
ACTUALIZE v. realizar, efetivar; contar, narrar de forma realística.
ACTUALLY adv. na verdade, de fato, realmente.
ACTUARY s. atuário, estatístico.
ACTUATE v. acionar, pôr em funcionamento (uma máquina); motivar.
ACTUATION s. acionamento; estímulo.
ACUITY s. acuidade.
ACUMEN s. perspicácia.
ACUTE adj. agudo(a); estridente, alto (som); assinalado com acento agudo.
AD abrev. d.C. (depois de Cristo).
ADAGE s. adágio, provérbio, ditado.
ADAGIO s. adágio / adj. vagaroso.
ADAMANT adj. inflexível, duro(a) / s. pedra, magnetita.
ADAMIC adj. adâmico.
ADAM'S APPLE s. pomo de adão.
ADAPT v. adaptar, ajustar.
ADAPTABLE adj. adaptável, ajustável.
ADAPTATION s. adaptação, acomodação.
ADD v. somar, adicionar, acrescentar.
ADDER s. víbora; máquina de somar.
ADDICT s. viciado(a).
ADDICTED adj. viciado(a) em; fanático(a) por; dependente de.
ADDICTION s. vício, dependência.
ADDICTIVE adj. viciante.
ADDITION s. adição, acréscimo.
ADDITIVE adj. aditivo.
ADDLE v. confundir, aturdir.
ADDRESS s. endereço / v. endereçar.
ADDRESS BAR s. barra de endereços.
ADDRESSEE s. destinatário.
ADDRESSER s. remetente; orador; suplicante.
ADEPT adj. hábil / s. perito.
ADEQUATE adj. adequado(a); suficiente, satisfatório(a).
ADHERE v. aderir, grudar.
ADHERENCE s. adesão.
ADHESIVE s. adesivo, cola / adj. adesivo, aderente.
ADHESIVE TAPE s. fita isolante; esparadrapo.
ADIABATIC adj. adiabático.
ADIPOSE s. adipose, gordura / adj. adiposo, gorduroso.

ADJACENCY s. adjacência, vizinhança; arredores.
ADJACENT adj. adjacente, vizinho(a).
ADJECTIVE s. adjetivo.
ADJOIN v. juntar, adicionar, unir.
ADJOINING adj. adjacente, contíguo(a).
ADJOURN v. suspender; adiar; transferir.
ADJUDGE v. julgar; condenar.
ADJUNCT s. adjunto; auxiliar, ajudante; adjunto adverbial.
ADJUNCTION s. adjunção.
ADJUNCTIVE adj. adjuntivo(a).
ADJURE v. adjurar.
ADJUST v. ajustar, adaptar; acostumar-se, adaptar-se.
ADJUSTABLE adj. ajustável.
ADJUSTMENT s. ajuste, regulagem.
ADJUTANT s. ajudante, auxiliar.
AD-LIB v. improvisar.
ADMAN s. publicitário(a).
ADMEASURE v. repartir, partilhar.
ADMIN s. administração.
ADMINICLE s. corroboração.
ADMINISTER v. administrar, ministrar, dirigir.
ADMINISTRATION s. administração, direção.
ADMIRABLE adj. admirável.
ADMIRAL s. almirante.
ADMIRATION s. admiração (por algo ou alguém).
ADMIRE v. admirar, apreciar.
ADMISSION s. entrada; ingresso; confissão.
ADMIT v. admitir, deixar entrar.
ADMITTANCE s. admissão, aceitação.
ADMIXTURE s. mistura.
ADMONISH v. admoestar, repreender, censurar.
ADMONITION s. admoestação, reprimenda.
AD NAUSEAM adv. sem parar.
ADO s. pressa; alvoroço.
ADOBE s. barro seco; tijolo cru.
ADOLESCENCE s. adolescência, juventude.
ADOLESCENT s. adolescente / adj. adolescente, juvenil.
ADOPT v. adotar, admitir.
ADOPTION s. adoção.
ADOPTIVE adj. adotivo(a).
ADORABLE adj. adorável, admirável.
ADORE v. adorar.
ADORN v. adornar, ornar.
ADORNMENT s. adorno, enfeite.

ADOWN adv. para baixo / prep. sobre ou ao longo de.
ADRENALINE s. adrenalina.
ADRIFT adv. à deriva / adj. desgovernado(a).
ADROIT adj. hábil, ágil.
ADROITNESS s. habilidade, destreza; talento.
ADRY adj. seco, sedento, sequioso.
ADSCITITIOUS adj. suplementar, adicional.
ADSCRIPT s. servo (feudal).
ADSORB v. adsorver.
ADSORPTION s. adsorção.
ADULATE v. adular, bajular.
ADULATION s. adulação, lisonja.
ADULT s. adulto(a) / adj. adulto(a).
ADULTERATE v. adulterar, falsificar.
ADULTERER s. adúltero.
ADULTERESS s. mulher infiel, adúltera.
ADULTEROUS adj. adúltero(a).
ADULTERY s. adultério.
ADULTHOOD s. maioridade.
ADUMBRATE v. adumbrar.
ADUST adj. queimado(a); triste, taciturno(a), melancólico(a).
ADVANCE s. avanço / adj. antecipado(a) / v. adiantar, avançar.
ADVANCED adj. avançado(a), adiantado(a), desenvolvido(a).
ADVANTAGE s. vantagem, supremacia / v. aproveitar-se, favorecer.
ADVANTAGEOUS adj. vantajoso(a), proveitoso(a).
ADVANTAGEOUSNESS s. vantagem.
ADVENT s. advento, chegada.
ADVENTISM s. adventismo.
ADVENTITIOUS adj. acidental, inesperado(a).
ADVENTURE s. aventura, façanha / v. aventurar-se.
ADVENTURER s. aventureiro(a).
ADVENTUROUS adj. aventureiro(a), audaz, intrépido(a).
ADVERB s. advérbio.
ADVERSARIAL adj. antagonista, adversário(a) (política).
ADVERSARY s. adversário(a), inimigo(a), oponente.
ADVERSE adj. adverso(a).
ADVERSITY s. adversidade, dificuldade.
ADVERT s. anúncio (coloquial) / v. advertir; chamar a atenção.
ADVERTENCE s. advertência.

ADVERTISE v. anunciar, publicar; fazer propaganda.
ADVERTISEMENT s. anúncio, propaganda.
ADVERTISER s. anunciante.
ADVERTISING s. publicidade, propaganda, anúncio.
ADVICE s. conselho, aviso, parecer.
ADVISABILITY s. prudência, conveniência.
ADVISABLE adj. aconselhável, recomendável; oportuno.
ADVISE v. aconselhar, recomendar.
ADVISEMENT s. conselho.
ADVISER s. conselheiro(a), consultor(a).
ADVISORY adj. consultivo; conselheiral.
ADVOCACY s. amparo, defesa (de uma ideia); advocacia.
ADVOCATE v. advogar / s. advogado(a).
ADVOCATORY adj. relativo a advocacia.
ADYTUM s. santuário de templos antigos.
AEGEAN adj. egeu.
AEGIS s. proteção; patrocínio; direção, controle.
AEOLIAN adj. eólico(a), eólio.
AEON s. era, eternidade.
AERATE v. ventilar, arejar; gaseificar (uma bebida).
AERIAL s. antena / adj. aéreo(a).
AEROBATICS s. acrobacia aérea, voo acrobático.
AEROBIC adj. aeróbico.
AEROBICS s. ginástica, aeróbica.
AERODROME s. aeroporto de pequeno porte.
AERODYNAMIC(AL) adj. aerodinâmico.
AERODYNAMICS s. aerodinâmica.
AEROGRAM s. aerograma, radiograma.
AEROGRAPH s. aerógrafo, meteorógrafo.
AEROLITE s. aerolito, meteorito.
AEROMECHANIC adj. aeromecânico.
AEROMECHANICS s. aeromecânica.
AERONAUT s. aeronauta, aviador.
AERONAUTICS s. aeronáutica.
AEROPLANE s. aeroplano, avião.
AEROSOL s. aerossol.
AERY adj. etéreo(a).
AESTHETE s. esteta.
AESTHETIC adj. estético(a).
AESTHETICISM s. esteticismo.
AETIOLOGY s. etiologia.
AFAR adv. de longe; a distância.

AFFABLE *adj.* afável, cortês, amável.
AFFABLENESS *s.* amabilidade, afabilidade.
AFFAIR *s.* assunto; negócio; romance, caso.
AFFECT *v.* afetar; comover.
AFFECTATION *s.* afetação, artificialidade.
AFFECTED *adj.* afetado(a).
AFFECTION *s.* afeto, afeição, simpatia.
AFFECTIONATE *adj.* afetuoso, carinhoso.
AFFECTIVE *adj.* afetivo(a).
AFFIDAVIT *s.* depoimento juramentado.
AFFILIATE *v.* afiliar, incorporar / *s.* filial, associado.
AFFINITY *s.* afinidade.
AFFIRM *v.* afirmar, assegurar; firmar, confirmar.
AFFIRMATIVE *adj.* afirmativo / *s.* afirmativa, confirmação.
AFFIX *v.* afixar, colar, juntar / *s.* afixo, anexo.
AFFLICT *v.* afligir.
AFFLUENCE *s.* afluência, abundância, riqueza.
AFFLUENT *adj.* abundante / *s.* afluente.
AFFLUX *s.* afluxo, grande quantidade (líquidos).
AFFORD *v.* poder gastar, ter dinheiro suficiente.
AFFORDABLE *adj.* disponível, acessível.
AFFOREST *v.* reflorestar.
AFFORESTATION *s.* reflorestamento.
AFFRANCHISE *v.* libertar, emancipar.
AFFRANCHISEMENT *s.* libertação, isenção, emancipação.
AFFRAY *v.* assustar / *s.* desordem.
AFFRICATE *s.* africada.
AFFRICATIVE *adj.* fricativo.
AFFRIGHT *adj.* susto, terror / *v.* assustar, aterrorizar.
AFFRONT *s.* afronta, ofensa / *v.* insultar, ofender.
AFFUSION *s.* infusão; asperção (batismo).
AFGHAN *s.* afegã, afegão / *adj.* afegão.
AFIELD *adv.* muito longe, afastado.
AFIRE *adj.* incendiado(a); entusiasmado(a) / *adv.* em chamas.
AFLAME *adj.* chamejante, flamejante; cintilante.
AFLOAT *adj.* flutuante; inundado.
AFLUTTER *adj.* esvoaçante, adejante; irrequieto(a), agitado(a).
AFOOT *adj.* sendo planejado; em andamento / *adv.* a pé.

AFOUL *adj.* confuso(a), emaranhado(a) / *adv.* confusamente, em colisão.
AFRAID *adj.* assustado(a), amedrontado(a).
AFRESH *adv.* de novo, mais uma vez.
AFRICAN *adj.* africano(a) / *s.* africano(a).
AFT *adv.* na popa, perto dela ou em direção a ela.
AFTER *adv.* depois, após / *prep.* atrás de, depois / *adj.* posterior.
AFTER ALL *adv.* apesar de tudo, afinal.
AFTERBIRTH *s.* placenta.
AFTERCARE *s.* pós-tratamento.
AFTEREFFECT *s.* efeito posterior; efeito colateral.
AFTERGLOW *s.* arrebol, resplendor, cor avermelhada do crepúsculo.
AFTERLIFE *s.* pós-morte, além-túmulo.
AFTERMATH *s.* consequências.
AFTERNOON *s.* tarde / *adj.* à tarde.
AFTERPAINS *s.* cólicas uterinas (após o parto).
AFTERS *s.* sobremesa (coloquial).
AFTER-SAILS *s.* vela de popa.
AFTERSHAVE *s.* loção pós-barba.
AFTERSHOCK *s.* pequeno terremoto.
AFTERTASTE *s.* gosto posterior (geralmente desagradável).
AFTERWARDS *adv.* posteriormente, mais tarde.
AFTERWORD *s.* posfácio.
AGAIN *adv.* de novo, outra vez, novamente.
AGAINST *prep.* contra, contrário.
AGAPE *adj.* boquiaberto(a).
AGATE *s.* ágata.
AGAZE *adv.* contemplativamente.
AGE *s.* idade; época.
AGED *adj.* idoso(a), velho(a).
AGEDNESS *s.* velhice; sazonação.
AGEISM *s.* etarismo, preconceito etário.
AGELESS *adj.* perene, eterno.
AGENCY *s.* agência.
AGENDA *s.* ordem do dia, pauta; agenda.
AGENT *s.* agente.
AGENTIAL *adj.* intermediário(a), representativo(a).
AGGLOMERATE *s.* aglomerado / *v.* aglomerar, acumular, amontoar / *adj.* aglomerado(a).
AGGLOMERATION *s.* aglomeração, ajuntamento, acumulação.

AGGLUTINATE *v.* aglutinar, unir, justapor / *adj.* aglutinado(a), justaposto(a), reunido(a).
AGGLUTINATION *s.* aglutinação.
AGGLUTINATIVE *adj.* aglutinativo, aglutinante.
AGGRANDIZE *v.* engrandecer, enaltecer, exaltar; exagerar.
AGGRANDIZEMENT *s.* engrandecimento, enaltecimento; ampliação.
AGGRANDIZER *s.* engrandecedor, enaltecedor.
AGGRAVATE *v.* agravar, piorar; irritar, provocar.
AGGRAVATING *adj.* agravante; desagradável, aborrecido(a).
AGGRAVATION *s.* agravação, piora; exagero; irritação.
AGGRAVATOR *s.* o que ou quem agrava, provoca.
AGGREGATE *s.* agregado / *v.* agregar, unir.
AGGREGATION *s.* acúmulo, coleção, agregação, combinação.
AGGREGATIVE *adj.* agregativo(a), acumulativo(a), coletivo(a); social.
AGGRESS *v.* agredir, atacar.
AGGRESSION *s.* agressão, ataque, injúria; agressividade.
AGGRESSIVE *adj.* agressivo(a); enérgico(a), ativo(a).
AGGRESSIVENESS *s.* agressividade.
AGGRESSOR *s.* agressor(a).
AGGRIEVE *v.* afligir, entristecer; lesar, prejudicar.
AGGRIEVED *adj.* aflito(a); magoado(a).
AGHAST *adj.* horrorizado(a); espantado(a).
AGILE *adj.* rápido, ágil, expedito, ativo, esperto.
AGILITY *s.* agilidade.
AGING *s.* envelhecimento.
AGIO *s.* ágio.
AGIOTAGE *s.* agiotagem.
AGITATE *v.* agitar.
AGITATELY *adv.* agitadamente.
AGITATION *s.* agitação; alvoroço; comoção, excitação.
AGITATOR *s.* agitador, sublevador, ativista.
AGLET *s.* agulheta.
AGLITTER *adj.* brilhante.
AGLOW *adj.* incandescente.
AGNATE *s.* agnado, agnato / *adj.* agnado(a), aparentado(a).
AGNATIC *adj.* agnato, agnado (antropologia).
AGNATION *s.* agnação, parentesco paterno.
AGNOMEN *s.* agnome, alcunha.
AGNOMINATE *v.* denominar, atribuir nome a.
AGNOSTIC *s.* agnóstico / *adj.* agnóstico.
AGNOSTICISM *s.* agnosticismo.
AGO *adv.* atrás, há tempo / *adj.* passado.
AGOG *adj.* ávido(a), entusiasmado(a), impaciente / *adv.* impacientemente.
AGOING *adv.* em movimento, em andamento.
AGONIC *adj.* ágono.
AGONISTIC(AL) *adj.* agonístico(a), combativo(a).
AGONIZE *v.* agonizar; agoniar; afligir-se.
AGONIZING *adj.* angustiante, agonizante.
AGONY *s.* agonia, aflição.
AGORAPHOBIA *s.* agorafobia.
AGRAFFE *s.* agrafo.
AGRAPHIA *s.* agrafia.
AGRARIAN *adj.* agrário(a), campestre.
AGRARIANISM *s.* agrarianismo.
AGREE *v.* concordar, combinar.
AGREEABILITY *s.* agradabilidade, amabilidade; concordância.
AGREEABLE *adj.* agradável, aprazível; disposto(a); de acordo.
AGREED *adj.* combinado, acordado; concordante.
AGREEMENT *s.* acordo, contrato, consentimento.
AGRESTIC *adj.* agreste, rural, rústico.
AGRICULTURAL *adj.* agrícola, agrário(a).
AGRICULTURE *s.* agricultura.
AGRICULTURIST *s.* agricultor, fazendeiro; agrônomo.
AGROBIOLOGY *s.* agrobiologia.
AGROCHEMICAL *s.* agente agroquímico.
AGRONOMIC(AL) *adj.* agronômico.
AGRONOMIST *s.* agrônomo.
AGRONOMY *s.* agronomia.
AGROUND *adv.* de modo encalhado / *adj.* encalhado(a).
AGUE *s.* malária, sezão, febre intermitente.
AGUED *adj.* febril.
AGUISH *adj.* malarífero (malária); intermitente; febril, com calafrios.
AH *interj.* ai!, ai-ai!
AHA *interj.* ah.

AHCHOO *interj.* atchim.
AHEAD *adv.* adiante, à frente.
AHEAP *adv.* em pilhas, amontoadamente.
AHEM *interj.* ahã, aham.
AHISTORICAL *adj.* não histórico.
AHOY *interj.* olá! (usada por marinheiros).
AID *s.* ajuda / *v.* ajudar, auxiliar.
AIDE *s.* ajudante.
AIDER *s.* quem presta socorro, ajuda.
AIDLESS *adj.* indefeso, desprotegido.
AIDS *abrev.* AIDS.
AIGRETTE *s.* penacho.
AIL *v.* sentir ou causar dor; estar doente, indisposto.
AILING *adj.* enfermo, doente.
AILMENT *s.* indisposição, doença.
AIM *v.* apontar, visar / *s.* pontaria, alvo, objetivo.
AIMER *s.* o que mira, visa.
AIMLESS *adj.* incerto, sem propósito.
AIMLESSNESS *s.* sem propósito, sem finalidade.
AIR *s.* ar, atmosfera / *v.* arejar, ventilar.
AIRBASE *s.* base aérea.
AIRBED *s.* colchão de ar.
AIR BLADDER *s.* bexiga, vesícula.
AIR-BOMB *s.* bomba aérea.
AIRBORNE *adj.* aerotransportado; aéreo.
AIR BRAKE *s.* freio pneumático.
AIR-BRICK *s.* tijolo furado.
AIRBRUSH *s.* aerógrafo.
AIR CONDITIONER *s.* ar-condicionado.
AIR CONDITIONING *s.* sistema de ar-condicionado.
AIR CORRIDOR *s.* corredor aéreo.
AIR COVER *s.* cobertura aérea.
AIRCRAFT *s.* aeronave.
AIRCRAFT CARRIER *s.* porta-aviões.
AIRCREW *s.* tripulação de avião.
AIRDRAIN *s.* respiradouro.
AIRFARE *s.* tarifa aérea.
AIRFIELD *s.* aeródromo, campo de aviação.
AIRFLOW *s.* corrente de ar.
AIRFOIL *s.* plano aerodinâmico.
AIR FORCE *s.* força aérea.
AIRFREIGHT *s.* carga aérea.
AIR FRESHENER *s.* ambientador.
AIRGUN *s.* espingarda de ar comprimido.
AIRHEAD *s.* cabeça de vento, tolo.
AIR HOSTESS *s.* aeromoça.
AIRILY *adv.* despreocupada; alegremente.

AIRING *s.* ventilação.
AIR-JACKET *s.* colete salva-vidas.
AIRLESS *adj.* sem ar corrente, mal ventilado.
AIRLINE *s.* linha aérea.
AIRLINER *s.* avião de passageiros.
AIRMAIL *s.* correio aéreo.
AIRMAN *s.* piloto, aviador.
AIR MATTRESS *s.* colchão de ar.
AIR PISTOL *s.* pistola de ar.
AIRPLANE *s.* avião, aeroplano.
AIRPLAY *s.* transmissão, radiodifusão.
AIR POCKET *s.* bolsa de ar.
AIRPORT *s.* aeroporto.
AIR PRESSION *s.* pressão atmosférica.
AIRPROOF *s.* selado(a), hermético(a), à prova de ar.
AIR PUMP *s.* bomba de ar.
AIR QUALITY *s.* qualidade do ar.
AIR RAID *s.* ataque aéreo em massa, incursão aérea.
AIRSCREW *s.* hélice.
AIR SHIP *s.* dirigível (balão).
AIRSPACE *s.* espaço aéreo.
AIRSTREAM *s.* corrente de ar (geralmente forte).
AIR STRIKE *s.* ataque aéreo.
AIR STRIP *s.* pista de pouso.
AIR TERMINAL *s.* terminal aéreo.
AIRTIGHT *adj.* hermético(a).
AIRTIME *s.* radiodifusão.
AIR TRAP *s.* sifão.
AIR VALVE *s.* válvula de escape (de ar).
AIRWAVES *s.* ondas sonoras.
AIRWAY *s.* rota ou linha aérea.
AIRWORTHINESS *s.* navegabilidade aérea.
AIRWORTHY *adj.* aeronavegável.
AIRY *adj.* arejado(a), vaporoso(a).
AIRY-FAIRY *adj.* impraticável; fantasioso(a).
AISLE *s.* nave de igreja; corredor, passagem.
AITCH *s.* a letra h.
AJAR *adj.* entreaberto(a).
AJUTAGE *s.* bica (de água).
AKIMBO *adj.* arqueado, curvado / *adv.* com as mãos na cintura.
AKIN *adj.* consanguíneo.
ALABASTER *s.* alabastro.
ALABASTRINE *adj.* alabastrino.
ALACRITY *s.* vivacidade.
ALAR *adj.* alado, que possui asas.
ALARM *s.* alarme / *v.* alarmar.
ALARM CLOCK *s.* despertador.

ALARMED *adj.* alarmado, sobressaltado, assustado.
ALARMING *adj.* alarmante.
ALARMIST *adj.* alarmista, pessimista.
ALAS *interj.* ai de mim!
ALASKA *s.* Alasca.
ALBANIA *s.* Albânia.
ALBATROSS *s.* albatroz.
ALBEIT *conj.* embora, apesar de.
ALBESCENT *adj.* albescente, albino.
ALBINISM *s.* albinismo.
ALBINO *s.* albino(a) / *adj.* albino(a).
ALBUM *s.* álbum.
ALCAIC *s.* verso alcaico / *adj.* alcaico.
ALCAZAR *s.* castelo, fortaleza.
ALCHEMIC(AL) *adj.* alquímico.
ALCHEMIST *s.* alquimista.
ALCHEMY *s.* alquimia.
ALCOHOL *s.* álcool.
ALCOHOLIC *s.* alcóolatra / *adj.* alcoólico.
ALCOHOLISM *s.* alcoolismo.
ALCOHOLIZATION *s.* alcoolização.
ALCOHOLIZE *v.* alcoolizar.
ALCOPOP *s.* refrigerante alcoólico.
ALCORAN *s.* Alcorão.
ALCOVE *s.* alcova.
ALDERMAN *s.* conselheiro municipal.
ALDERMANSHIP *s.* vereança, vereação.
ALE *s.* cerveja inglesa (coloquial).
ALEATORY *adj.* aleatório, casual; sujeito ao acaso.
ALEE *adj.* sota-ventado / *adv.* a sota-vento.
ALEHOUSE *s.* taverna, bar.
ALEMBIC *s.* alambique.
ALERT *adj.* atento(a), alerta / *v.* alertar.
ALERTNESS *s.* precaução, vigilância; agilidade, ligeireza.
ALEWIFE *s.* proprietária (taverna, bar).
ALEXANDRIAN *s.* verso alexandrino / *adj.* alexandrino.
ALEXIA *s.* alexia.
ALGA *s.* alga.
ALGEBRA *s.* álgebra.
ALGEBRAIC *adj.* algébrico.
ALGEBRAIST *s.* algebrista.
ALGERIA *s.* Argélia.
ALGID *adj.* álgido, glacial, algente, muito frio.
ALGIDITY *s.* algidez, frialdade.
ALGOID *adj.* algoide; alga.
ALGOPHOBIA *s.* algofobia.
ALGORITHM *s.* algoritmo.

ALGORITHMIC *adj.* algorítmico.
ALIAS *s.* alcunha, pseudônimo / *adv.* aliás.
ALIBI *s.* álibi; desculpa.
ALIBLE *adj.* nutritivo, alimentício.
ALIDADE *s.* alidade, alidada.
ALIEN *s.* estrangeiro(a); alienígena / *adj.* estranho(a).
ALIENABILITY *s.* alienabilidade.
ALIENATE *v.* alienar.
ALIENATION *s.* alienação; loucura, demência.
ALIENATOR *s.* alienador.
ALIENISM *s.* alienismo, loucura, insanidade mental.
ALIENIST *s.* alienista, médico psiquiatra.
ALIFORM *adj.* aliforme, em formato de asa.
ALIGHT *adj.* aceso, ardente / *v.* desmontar, descer / *adv.* em chamas.
ALIGN *v.* alinhar, enfileirar.
ALIGNER *s.* alinhador.
ALIGNMENT *s.* alinhamento.
ALIKE *adj.* semelhante / *adv.* igualmente.
ALIMENT *s.* alimento, mantimento, nutrição.
ALIMENTAL *adj.* nutritivo(a).
ALIMENTARY *adj.* alimentar; nutritivo(a).
ALIMENTATION *s.* alimentação, nutrição; sustento, substância.
ALIMENTATIVE *adj.* alimentício(a), nutritivo(a).
ALIMONY *s.* pensão alimentícia; manutenção.
ALIQUOT *s.* parte alíquota / *adj.* alíquota.
ALITERACY *s.* analfabetismo.
ALITERATE *s.* analfabeto, iletrado / *adj.* analfabeto(a), iletrado(a).
ALIVE *adj.* vivo(a), animado(a).
ALKALESCENT *adj.* alcalescente (estado alcalino).
ALKALI *s.* álcali; sal alcalino / *adj.* alcalino.
ALKALIFY *v.* alcalinizar.
ALKALINE *adj.* alcalino(a).
ALKALINE EARTHS *s.* terras alcalinas.
ALKALOID *s.* alcaloide / *adj.* alcaloide.
ALL *adj.* todo(s), toda(s); inteiro / *s.* totalidade, tudo.
ALLAH *s.* Alá.
ALLAY *v.* acalmar.
ALL CLEAR *s.* barra limpa (coloquial).
ALL-DAY *adj.* o dia inteiro.
ALLEGATION *s.* alegação, afirmação; asserção; desculpa, pretexto.

ALLEGE v. alegar.
ALLEGEABLE s. passível de ser alegado.
ALLEGEDLY adv. supostamente.
ALLEGIANCE s. lealdade, submissão.
ALLEGIANT adj. fiel, obediente.
ALLEGORIC(AL) adj. alegórico(a).
ALLEGORIST s. alegorista.
ALLEGORISTIC adj. alegórico(a).
ALLEGORIZE v. alegorizar.
ALLEGORY s. alegoria, parábola; emblema.
ALLEGRO s. alegro, rápida, alegre.
ALLELUIA s. aleluia / *interj.* aleluia!
ALLERGIC adj. alérgico(a).
ALLERGY s. alergia.
ALLEVIATE v. aliviar.
ALLEVIATION s. alívio.
ALLEVIATIVE adj. aliviador, paliativo.
ALLEY s. viela, ruela.
ALLEY CAT s. gato de rua; mulherengo.
ALLEYWAY s. beco, travessa, rua estreita.
ALLHALLOWS s. Dia de Todos os Santos.
ALLIANCE s. aliança.
ALLIED adj. aliado, unido; associado; parente.
ALLIGATOR s. jacaré.
ALLIGATOR PEAR s. abacate.
ALL-IMPORTANT adj. muito importante, importantíssimo(a).
ALL-IN adj. tudo incluído.
ALL-INCLUSIVE adj. com tudo incluso.
ALLITERATE adj. aliterar.
ALLITERATION s. aliteração (gramática).
ALLITERATIVE adj. aliterativo(a).
ALL-NIGHT adj. toda a noite.
ALLOCABLE adj. distribuível, atribuível.
ALLOCATE v. alocar, partilhar, repartir.
ALLOCATION s. divisão, partilha; designação, localização.
ALLOCATOR s. distribuidor, aquele que partilha.
ALLOCATUR s. confirmação de mandato.
ALLOCUTION s. alocução, discurso autoritário.
ALLOPHANE s. alofana (variedade de argila).
ALLOPHONE s. alofone.
ALLOT v. distribuir proporcionalmente; outorgar, conceder.
ALLOTABLE adj. distribuível.
ALLOTER s. distribuidor.
ALLOTMENT s. partilha, lote, cota.
ALLOTTEE s. sócio, parceiro; beneficiado.
ALL-OUT adj. total / adv. todo o possível.

ALL-OVER adj. por toda a parte.
ALLOW v. permitir, autorizar.
ALLOWABLE adj. permissível, admissível.
ALLOWANCE s. pensão, mesada, ajuda de custo.
ALLOWEDLY adv. reconhecidamente.
ALLOY s. liga, fusão.
ALLOYING s. fusão de metais.
ALLOY STEEL s. aço fundido.
ALL-POWERFUL adj. todo-poderoso, que tem total poder.
ALL-PURPOSE adj. para todos os fins.
ALL-PURPOSE FLOUR s. farinha de trigo.
ALL RIGHT adv. certo, correto; satisfatoriamente / adj. certo, correto; satisfatoriamente.
ALL-ROUND adj. em redor / adv. em todos os sentidos.
ALL SAINT'S DAY s. Dia de Todos os Santos (1º de novembro).
ALL SOULS' DAY s. dia de finados (2º de novembro).
ALL TOLD adv. ao final de tudo, ao todo.
ALLUDE v. aludir, insinuar.
ALLURE s. fascinação, sedução / v. fascinar, persuadir, convencer.
ALLURER s. tentador, sedutor.
ALLURING adj. tentador(a), atraente.
ALLURINGNESS s. fascinação, sedução.
ALLUSION s. alusão, menção, insinuação.
ALLUVIAL s. sedimento aluviano / adj. aluvial, aluviano.
ALLUVION s. aluvião, cheia, inundação.
ALLUVIUM s. aluvião.
ALLY s. aliado(a) / v. aliar-se.
ALMANAC s. almanaque; calendário anual.
ALMIGHTINESS s. onipotência.
ALMIGHTY adj. onipotente, todo-poderoso.
ALMIGHTY GOD s. Deus Todo-Poderoso.
ALMOND s. amêndoa.
ALMONER s. esmoler, caridoso, esmolador.
ALMONRY s. esmolaria.
ALMOST adv. quase, perto de.
ALMS s. esmola, dádiva.
ALMSGIVER s. esmolador, esmoler.
ALMSGIVING s. ato de caridade.
ALMSHOUSE s. albergue noturno, abrigo para indigentes.
ALMSMAN s. mendigo.
ALMSWOMAN s. mendiga.
ALOFT adv. em cima, no alto.

ALONE *adj.* sozinho(a) / *adv.* somente, apenas.
ALONG *prep.* ao longo de, por / *adv.* junto a.
ALONGSHORE *adv.* junto à costa, ao longo da costa.
ALONGSIDE *adv.* ao lado, ao longo, lado a lado / *prep.* ao lado de, ao longo de.
ALOOF *adj.* afastado(a), reservado(a), indiferente / *adv.* a distância, de longe.
ALOOFNESS *s.* indiferença, desinteresse.
ALOUD *adv.* em voz alta.
ALP *s.* montanha alta; cume, topo da montanha.
ALPENGLOW *s.* brilho das montanhas.
ALPENHORN *s.* corneta (Alpes).
ALPENSTOCK *s.* bordão de alpinista.
ALPHA *s.* alfa (alfabeto grego).
ALPHABET *s.* alfabeto, abecedário.
ALPHABETIC(AL) *adj.* alfabético.
ALPHABETIZE *v.* alfabetizar.
ALPINE *adj.* alpino.
ALPINISM *s.* alpinismo.
ALPINIST *s.* alpinista.
ALPS *s.* Alpes.
ALREADY *adv.* já.
ALSATIAN DOG *s.* cão pastor.
ALSO *adv.* também, além disso.
ALSO-RAN *s.* não classificado, perdedor.
ALTAR *s.* altar, mesa de sacrifício.
ALTAR BOY *s.* coroinha (igreja).
ALTARPIECE *s.* enfeite de altar (igreja).
ALTER *adv.* alterar, modificar.
ALTERABILITY *s.* alterabilidade, possibilidade de alteração.
ALTERABLE *adj.* alterável, modificável.
ALTERATION *s.* alteração.
ALTERATIVE *s.* alterante / *adj.* alterativo, alternante.
ALTERCATE *v.* altercar, discutir com calor.
ALTERCATION *s.* altercação, contenda, briga.
ALTERNANT *adj.* alternante.
ALTERNATE *adj.* alternado(a) / *v.* alternar, revezar.
ALTERNATIVE *s.* alternativa, opção / *adj.* alternativo(a).
ALTERNATIVENESS *s.* qualidade de ser ou estar alternado.
ALTERNATOR *s.* alternador, gerador.
ALTHORN *s.* saxotrompa.
ALTHOUGH *conj.* embora, apesar de, contudo.
ALTIMETER *s.* altímetro (instrumento).
ALTIMETRY *s.* altimetria.
ALTITUDE *s.* altitude.
ALTITUDINAL *adj.* altitudinal, altitúdico.
ALTO *s.* contralto; alto; viola, saxotrompa.
ALTO-CUMULUS *s.* alto-cúmulo.
ALTOGETHER *adv.* o todo, no total, inteiramente.
ALTO-RILIEVO *s.* alto-relevo.
ALTRUISM *s.* altruísmo.
ALTRUIST *s.* altruísta.
ALTRUISTIC *adj.* altruístico.
ALUMINIZE *v.* aluminar, revestir com alumínio.
ALUMINOUS *adj.* aluminoso(a), que contém alumínio.
ALUMINUM *s.* alumínio.
ALUMNA *s.* bacharelada, graduada.
ALUMNUS *s.* bacharel, graduado.
ALVEOLAR *adj.* alveolar.
ALVEOLATE *adj.* alveolado.
ALVEOLUS *s.* alvéolo; arco alveolar.
ALVINE *adj.* alvino, intestinal.
ALWAYS *adv.* sempre, continuamente.
AM *v.* sou, estou, 1ª pessoa do singular, presente do verbo *to be* / *abrev.* da manhã.
AMAIN *adv.* rapidamente, a toda velocidade; violentamente, com toda a força.
AMALGAM *s.* amálgama; mistura; fusão.
AMALGAMATE *v.* fazer amálgama; unir, misturar, amalgamar.
AMALGAMATION *s.* amalgamação.
AMANUENSIS *s.* amanuense, copista, secretário.
AMARANTH *s.* amaranto.
AMARYLLIS *s.* amarílis, açucena.
AMASS *v.* acumular, amontoar.
AMASSABLE *adj.* acumulável, amontoável.
AMASSER *s.* acumulador, amontoador, colecionador.
AMASSMENT *s.* aglomeração, amontoamento.
AMATEUR *adj.* amador(a) / *s.* amador(a).
AMATEURISH *adj.* superficial, amador, malfeito.
AMATEURISHNESS *s.* amadorismo.
AMATIVE *adj.* amativo, amoroso, sensual, erótico.
AMATORY *adj.* amativo, amoroso.
AMAUROTIC *adj.* amaurótico(a).

AMAZE v. pasmar, maravilhar / s. assombro, estupefação.
AMAZED adj. assombrado(a), maravilhado(a), pasmado(a).
AMAZEDNESS s. estupefação, complexidade, consternação.
AMAZEMENT s. espanto, perplexidade.
AMAZING adj. surpreendente, espantoso(a); fantástico(a).
AMAZON s. Amazonas.
AMAZONIAN adj. amazônio, amazônico, amazonense.
AMAZONITE s. amazonita.
AMBAGES s. ambiguidade; ambages, subterfúgios.
AMBAGIOUS adj. ambagioso(a), indireto(a), ambíguo(a).
AMBASSADOR s. embaixador; emissário.
AMBASSADORIAL adj. diplomático(a), representativo(a).
AMBASSADORSHIP s. embaixada.
AMBASSADRESS s. embaixatriz, embaixadora.
AMBER s. âmbar / adj. ambárico, ambarino.
AMBERGIS s. âmbar-gris, âmbar-cinzento, âmbar-pardo.
AMBIDEXTERITY s. ambidestria; ambidestrismo; destreza.
AMBIDEXTROUS adj. ambidestro(a); destro(a), extremamente ágil; ardiloso(a).
AMBIENCE s. ambiente.
AMBIGUITY s. ambiguidade.
AMBIGUOUS adj. ambíguo, vago, incerto.
AMBIT s. âmbito, perímetro; divisa, fronteira, raia, limite.
AMBITION s. ambição, aspiração.
AMBITIONLESS adj. sem ambição, sem interesse.
AMBITIOUS adj. ambicioso(a).
AMBITIOUSNESS s. caráter ambicioso.
AMBIVALENCE s. ambivalência.
AMBIVALENT adj. ambivalente.
AMBIVERSION s. ambiversão.
AMBLE s. esquipação; passo lento ou cômodo (de cavalo) / v. esquipar, andar lento.
AMBLER s. esquipador.
AMBO s. ambão, púlpito.
AMBROSIA s. ambrosia.
AMBROSIAL adj. ambrósio, ambrosíaco, muito saboroso.
AMBROSIAN adj. ambrosiano.

AMBRY s. depósito, despensa, recanto.
AMBULANCE s. ambulância.
AMBULANCE MAN s. paramédico.
AMBULATE v. andar, ambular.
AMBULATORY adj. ambulatório, ambulante; ambulativo; alterável.
AMBUSH s. emboscada, tocaia / v. emboscar.
AMBUSHMENT s. cilada.
AMEBA s. ameba.
AMELIORABLE adj. melhorável, aperfeiçoável.
AMELIORATE v. melhorar, aperfeiçoar.
AMELIORATION s. melhoria, melhoramento, aperfeiçoamento.
AMELIORATIVE adj. melhorativo(a).
AMELIORATOR s. benfeitor, beneficiador.
AMEN s. amém / interj. amém!
AMENABILITY s. responsabilidade; acessibilidade, afabilidade; subserviência.
AMENABLE adj. receptivo(a), afável; responsável.
AMEND v. emendar; aperfeiçoar.
AMENDABLE adj. emendável, melhorável, aperfeiçoável.
AMENDATORY adj. corretivo, com caráter de correção.
AMENDER s. emendador, benfeitor.
AMENDMENT s. correção; melhoramento; emenda.
AMENDS s. reparação, indenização.
AMENITIES s. comodidades.
AMENITY s. afabilidade, cortesia, gentileza.
AMENTIA s. demência, amência.
AMERCE v. multar, punir.
AMERCEABLE adj. sujeito a multa ou sanção.
AMERCEMENT s. multa, pena.
AMERICAN s. americano(a) / adj. americano(a).
AMERICANISM s. americanismo.
AMERICANIZE v. americanizar.
AMETHYST s. ametista.
AMETHYSTINE adj. ametístico.
AMETROPIA s. ametropia.
AMIABILITY s. amabilidade, afabilidade; bondade.
AMIABLE adj. amável, afável.
AMIANTUS s. amianto.

AMICABILITY s. amizade, cordialidade, benevolência, sinceridade.
AMICABLE adj. amigável, afável.
AMID prep. no meio de, entre.
AMIDE s. amida.
AMIDSHIP(S) s. a meia-nau.
AMIGO s. amigo, colega.
AMISS adj. defeituoso(a), errado(a) / adv. defeituosamente.
AMITY s. amizade.
AMMONIA s. amônia.
AMMONIAC s. amoníaco / adj. amoníaco, amoniacal.
AMMONIFICATION s. amonificação.
AMMUNITION s. munição.
AMMUNITION CHEST s. caixa de munição.
AMMUNITION CLIP s. pente carregador (de munição).
AMNESIA s. amnésia.
AMNESIAC adj. amnésico.
AMNESIC adj. amnéstico.
AMNESTY s. anistia / v. anistiar.
AMOEBA s. ameba.
AMOEBAN adj. amebiano.
AMOEBIC adj. amébico.
AMOEBIFORM adj. amebiforme, em forma de ameba.
AMONG prep. entre vários, no meio de.
AMORAL adj. amoral.
AMORALITY s. amoralidade.
AMORIST adj. namorador, galanteador.
AMOROUS adj. amoroso(a).
AMOROUSNESS s. amorosidade.
AMORPHISM s. amorfismo, amorfia.
AMORPHOUS adj. amorfo, não cristalino.
AMORPHOUSNESS s. amorfia, deformidade.
AMORT adj. desfalecido, sem vida.
AMORTIZABLE adj. amortizável.
AMORTIZATION s. amortização.
AMORTIZE v. amortizar.
AMOUNT s. soma, quantidade, quantia / v. equivaler, corresponder.
AMPERAGE s. amperagem.
AMPHIBIAN s. anfíbio.
AMPHITHEATER s. anfiteatro.
AMPHORA s. ânfora.
AMPHORIC adj. anfórico.
AMPICILLIN s. penicilina semissintética.
AMPLE adj. amplo, suficiente, vasto.
AMPLENESS s. amplitude.
AMPLIATION s. ampliação, aumento.
AMPLIFIABLE adj. ampliável.
AMPLIFICATION s. ampliação; extensão.
AMPLIFIER s. amplificador.
AMPLIFY v. ampliar, aumentar.
AMPLITUDE s. amplitude; tamanho; abrangência; abundância.
AMPLY adv. muito; amplamente; abundantemente.
AMPOULE s. ampola.
AMPULE s. ampulheta, relógio de areia.
AMPUTATE v. amputar; cortar.
AMPUTATION s. amputação; corte.
AMPUTATOR s. amputador.
AMPUTEE s. amputado; mutilado.
AMUCK adj. cheio de fúria / adv. furiosamente.
AMULET s. amuleto.
AMUSE v. divertir, distrair.
AMUSED adj. divertido, entretido.
AMUSEMENT s. divertimento, passatempo.
AMUSER s. aquele que alegra.
AMUSING adj. divertido.
AMYGDALA s. amígdala.
AMYGDALIC adj. amigdalar.
AMYGDALIN s. amigdalina.
AMYGDALOID s. amigdaloide / adj. amigdaloide.
AMYL s. amido.
AMYLACEOUS adj. amidoado.
AMYOTROPHY s. amiotrofia.
AN art. um(a).
ANABOLIC adj. anabólico(a).
ANABOLISM s. anabolismo, assimilação.
ANACHRONISM s. anacronismo.
ANACHRONISTIC adj. anacrônico(a); envelhecido(a), antiquado(a).
ANADEM s. grinalda.
ANAEMIA s. anemia.
ANAEMIC adj. anêmico(a).
ANAEROBE s. anaeróbio.
ANAEROBIC adj. anaeróbico.
ANAESTHESIA s. anestesia.
ANAESTHESIOLOGIST s. anestesiologista.
ANAESTHETIC adj. anestésico.
ANAESTHETIZE v. anestesiar.
ANAGRAM s. anagrama.
ANAL adj. anal, retal.
ANALGESIC s. analgésico / adj. analgésico(a).

ANALOG(UE) *adj.* analógico(a) / *s.* análogo(a), semelhante.
ANALOGIC *adj.* analógico(a).
ANALOGIZE *v.* fazer analogia, traçar um paralelo; comparar.
ANALOGOUS *adj.* análogo(a), semelhante.
ANALOGOUSNESS *s.* analogia.
ANALOGY *s.* analogia, semelhança; comparação.
ANALPHABETIC *adj.* não alfabético; fora da ordem alfabética; analfabeto / *s.* analfabeto.
ANALYSIS *s.* análise.
ANALYST *s.* analista; psicanalista.
ANALYTIC *adj.* analítico; operativo.
ANALYZABLE *adj.* analisável, inspecionável.
ANALYZE *v.* analisar.
ANALYZER *s.* analisador.
ANAPHASE *s.* anáfase.
ANARCH *s.* anarquista; revolucionário(a).
ANARCHIAL *adj.* anárquico.
ANARCHIC *adj.* anárquico(a), desgovernado(a).
ANARCHISM *s.* anarquismo.
ANARCHIST *s.* anarquista.
ANARCHY *s.* anarquia.
ANATHEMA *s.* horror; excomunhão; condenação.
ANATHEMATISATION *s.* anatematização, excomunhão; maldição; reprovação.
ANATHEMATIZE *v.* excomungar.
ANATOMIC *adj.* anatômico(a).
ANATOMISE *v.* anatomizar; analisar em detalhes.
ANATOMIST *s.* anatomista.
ANATOMIZE *v.* anatomizar; dissecar.
ANATOMY *s.* anatomia.
ANCESTOR *s.* antepassado.
ANCESTRAL *adj.* hereditário; ancestral.
ANCESTRESS *s.* ancestral (feminino), mãe primitiva.
ANCESTRY *s.* descendência, linhagem.
ANCHOR *s.* âncora / *v.* ancorar.
ANCHORAGE *s.* ancoradouro.
ANCHORESS *s.* ermitã.
ANCHORETTE *s.* apresentadora (programa de televisão).
ANCHORITE *s.* eremita.
ANCHORLESS *adj.* sem âncora.
ANCHORS *s.* freios de carro.
ANCHOVY *s.* anchova.

ANCIENT *s.* antigo, ancião / *adj.* antigo, velho, remoto.
ANCIENTNESS *s.* antiguidade.
ANCILLA *s.* ancila, serva, escrava.
ANCILLARY *adj.* auxiliar, assistente, subordinado.
ANCON *s.* cotovelo; suporte.
AND *conj.* e.
ANDEAN *adj.* dos Andes, andino(a).
ANDES *s.* Andes.
ANDIRON *s.* cano da chaminé.
ANDROCRACY *s.* governo dos homens, soberania do sexo masculino.
ANDROGEN *s.* andrógeno, hormônio masculino.
ANDROGENOUS *adj.* relativo a andrógeno.
ANDROGYNEITY *s.* androginia.
ANDROGYNOUS *adj.* andrógino, bissexual, hermafrodita.
ANDROGYNY *s.* androginia.
ANDROID *s.* androide.
ANDROPHOBIA *s.* androfobia.
ANECDOTAGE *s.* conjunto de anedotas.
ANECDOTE *s.* anedota, piada.
ANECDOTIC *adj.* anedótico(a).
ANEMIA *s.* anemia.
ANEMIC *adj.* anêmico, fraco.
ANEMOMETER *s.* anemômetro (aparelho).
ANEMOSCOPE *s.* anemoscópio, cata-vento.
ANENCEPHALIA *s.* anencefalia.
ANENCEPHALIC *adj.* anencefálico.
ANENCEPHALOUS *adj.* anencéfalo.
ANENT *prep.* com respeito a, concernente a.
ANESTHESIA *s.* anestesia.
ANESTHESIOLOGIST *s.* anestesista.
ANESTHESIOLOGY *s.* anestesiologia.
ANESTHETIC *s.* anestésico.
ANESTHETISE *v.* anestesiar, aplicar anestesia.
ANESTHETIST *s.* anestesista.
ANEURISM *s.* aneurisma.
ANEW *adv.* de novo; de uma forma diferente.
ANFRACTUOSITY *s.* sinuosidade.
ANFRACTUOUS *adj.* sinuoso.
ANGEL *s.* anjo.
ANGELFACE *s.* anjo, cara de anjo (coloquial).
ANGELIC(AL) *adj.* angelical; angélico.
ANGELOLATRY *s.* angelolatria, adoração de anjos.

ANGER s. raiva, fúria / v. zangar-se, irritar-se.
ANGLE s. ângulo; anzol.
ANGLED adj. angular.
ANGLER s. pescador amador.
ANGLERFISH s. peixe predatório grande.
ANGLES s. anglos (tribo germânica).
ANGLEWORM s. isca de vermes.
ANGLIAN s. anglo / adj. ânglico.
ANGLICAN s. anglicano(a) / adj. anglicano(a).
ANGLICANISM s. anglicanismo.
ANGLICE adv. em inglês.
ANGLICISE v. anglicizar.
ANGLICISM s. anglicismo.
ANGLICIST s. anglicista.
ANGLICIZATION s. anglicização.
ANGLING s. pesca à vara.
ANGLIST s. anglicista.
ANGLO s. anglo.
ANGLO-AMERICAN s. anglo-americano.
ANGLOCENTRIC adj. anglocentrismo.
ANGLOMANIA s. anglomania.
ANGLOMANIAC s. anglomaníaco.
ANGLOPHIL(E) s. anglófilo.
ANGLOPHILIA s. anglofilia.
ANGLOPHOBE s. anglófobo.
ANGLOPHOBIA s. anglofobia.
ANGLOPHONE s. anglófono / adj. anglófono.
ANGLO-SAXON s. anglo-saxão / adj. anglo-saxônico.
ANGOLA s. Angola.
ANGOLAN s. angolano / adj. angolano.
ANGRILY adv. com raiva, furiosamente.
ANGRINESS s. fúria, raiva.
ANGRY adj. zangado(a), furioso(a), irado(a), raivoso(a).
ANGST s. medo, temor, ansiedade / v. demonstrar medo, temor, ansiedade.
ANGUISH s. sofrimento, angústia, agonia.
ANGULAR adj. angular; anguloso(a); inflexível, rígido(a).
ANGULARITY s. angularidade; dureza; determinação.
ANGULARNESS s. rigidez, austeridade; transversalidade; próprio de ósseo.
ANGULATE v. tornar anguloso / adj. angulado(a), com ângulos.
ANGULATION s. angulação.
ANHEDONIA s. anedonia.
ANHEDRAL adj. xenomórfico.
ANHIDROSIS s. anidrose, ausência de suor.
ANHYDROUS adj. anidro, sem água.
ANILE adj. referente à pessoa idosa, senil.
ANILITY s. senilidade, velhice.
ANIMADVERT v. criticar severamente; censurar.
ANIMAL s. animal / adj. animal.
ANIMALISATION s. animalização; brutalização; processo de animalizar.
ANIMALISE v. animalizar; tornar-se brutal; tornar bruto.
ANIMALISM s. animalismo; sensualidade; bestialidade.
ANIMALISTIC adj. animalístico, animal.
ANIMALITY s. animalidade, bestialidade.
ANIMATE v. avivar; animar / adj. animado(a), vivo(a).
ANIMATED adj. animado, vivo, dinâmico, vigoroso.
ANIMATER s. animador, incentivador.
ANIMATION s. animação; alma, espírito.
ANIMISM s. animismo.
ANIMIST s. animista.
ANIMOSITY s. animosidade; hostilidade.
ANIMUS s. rancor; inimizade; ódio.
ANISE s. anis, erva-doce.
ANISEED s. semente de erva-doce.
ANKLE s. tornozelo.
ANKLEBONE s. o osso do calcanhar.
ANKLET s. tornozeleira.
ANKYLOSE v. ancilosar(-se), enrijecer(-se).
ANKYLOSIS s. ancilose, anquilose, acampsia.
ANLAGE s. princípio, origem, começo.
ANNALIST s. analista; cronista.
ANNALS s. anais; crônicas, história.
ANNEAL v. temperar; enrijecer.
ANNEALER s. recozedor, fortalecedor.
ANNEX s. anexo / v. anexar.
ANNEXABLE s. anexável.
ANNEXATION s. anexação, incorporação.
ANNIHILATE v. aniquilar, exterminar.
ANNIHILATION s. aniquilação, destruição.
ANNIHILATIVE adj. que aniquila, destrutivo; anulador; destrutor, exterminador.
ANNIHILATOR s. aniquilador.
ANNIVERSARY s. aniversário, festa de aniversário.
ANNOTATE v. explanar, explicar; adicionar notas ou comentários.
ANNOTATION s. anotação; observação.
ANNOTATOR s. comentarista, anotador.

ANNOUNCE v. anunciar, declarar.
ANNOUNCEMENT s. aviso, comunicado, publicação.
ANNOUNCER s. locutor(a); anunciante.
ANNOY v. aborrecer, irritar.
ANNOYANCE s. aborrecimento, amolação.
ANNOYING adj. irritante, aborrecido(a), chato(a).
ANNUAL adj. anual / s. anual, anuário.
ANNUALLY adv. anualmente.
ANNUITY s. anuidade.
ANNUL v. anular; exterminar.
ANNULARITY s. forma anular, forma de anel.
ANNULARY adj. circular, em forma de anel, redondo.
ANNULATE adj. anular, em forma de anel.
ANNULLABLE adj. anulável.
ANNULMENT s. anulação, cancelamento; exterminação, liquidação.
ANNUNCIATE v. anunciar, declarar, proclamar.
ANNUNCIATION s. anunciação, anúncio, aviso.
ANOINT v. untar.
ANOINTMENT s. unção.
ANOMALISM s. anomalismo.
ANOMALISTIC adj. anomalístico(a).
ANOMALOUS adj. anômalo(a).
ANOMALY s. anomalia.
ANOMIA s. anomia.
ANON adv. já; agora; imediatamente; depois, mais tarde.
ANONYM s. anônimo(a), desconhecido(a); pseudônimo(a).
ANONYMA adj. inominado, sem nome.
ANONYMITY s. anonímia, anonimato.
ANONYMIZE adj. anonimizar, tornar anônimo.
ANONYMOUS adj. anônimo(a), desconhecido(a).
ANONYMOUSNESS s. anonimidade, obscuridade.
ANORECTIC adj. anorético(a).
ANOREXIA s. anorexia.
ANOREXIC adj. anoréxico(a) / s. anoréxico(a).
ANORGANIC adj. não orgânico.
ANOTHER pron. outro, um outro / adj. outro(a), um(a) outro(a).
ANSWER v. responder / s. resposta.
ANSWERABLE adj. responsável; respondível.
ANSWERABLENESS s. responsabilidade.
ANSWERING MACHINE s. secretária eletrônica.
ANSWERPHONE s. m.q. answering machine.
ANT s. formiga.
ANTACID s. antiácido.
ANTAGONISM s. antagonismo.
ANTAGONIST s. antagonista, inimigo, opositor; adversário.
ANTAGONISTIC adj. antagônico(a), contrário(a), oposto(a).
ANTAGONIZE v. antagonizar, contrariar.
ANTARCTIC s. região antártica / adj. antártico(a).
ANTARCTICA s. Antártica, Antártida.
ANTARCTIC OCEAN s. Oceano Antártico.
ANTEATER s. tamanduá.
ANTEBELLUM adj. pré-guerra.
ANTECEDE v. anteceder, vir antes de.
ANTECEDENCE s. antecedência; preferência.
ANTECEDENT s. antecedente; suposição anterior / adj. antecedente, precedente.
ANTECESSOR s. antecessor, predecessor.
ANTECHAMBER s. antecâmara; sala de recepção; salão de entrada.
ANTEDATE v. antedatar.
ANTELOPE s. antílope.
ANTE MERIDIEM adv. antes do meio-dia.
ANTENATAL s. pré-natal / adj. pré-natal.
ANTENUPCIAL adj. antenupcial.
ANTERIOR adj. anterior; o que vem antes.
ANTERIORITY s. prioridade, precedência.
ANTERIORLY adv. antes disso.
ANTEROOM s. sala de entrada; sala de espera.
ANTHEM s. hino.
ANTHILL s. formigueiro.
ANTHOLOGIST s. antologista.
ANTHOLOGIZE v. praticar antologia.
ANTHOLOGY s. antologia.
ANTHOPHILOUS adj. antófilo.
ANTHROPO adj. antropoide.
ANTHROPOCENTRIC adj. antropocêntrico.
ANTHROPOCENTRISM s. antropocentrismo.
ANTHROPOCENTRIST s. antropocentrista.
ANTHROPOGENY s. antropogenia.
ANTHROPOLOGIC(AL) adj. antropológico.
ANTHROPOLOGIST s. antropólogo.

ANTHROPOLOGY s. antropologia.
ANTHROPOPHAGITE s. antropófago.
ANTHROPOPHAGY s. antropofagia.
ANTIACID adj. antiácido.
ANTIAIRCRAFT adj. antiaéreo.
ANTIALLERGENIC adj. antialérgico.
ANTIANXIETY adj. anxiolítico / s. antiansiedade.
ANTIBACTERIAL adj. antibacteriano, contra bactérias.
ANTIBIOTIC s. antibiótico / adj. antibiótico.
ANTIBODY s. anticorpo.
ANTIC s. farsa; travessura / adj. ridículo, grotesco / v. agir como palhaço.
ANTICARIOUS adj. anticárie.
ANTICHRIST s. anticristo, falso profeta.
ANTICIPATE v. prever; antecipar.
ANTICIPATION s. expectativa; antecipação.
ANTICLIMAX s. anticlímax.
ANTICLOCKWISE adv. sentido anti-horário.
ANTI-DAZZLE adj. que reduz o reflexo da luz.
ANTIDOTE s. antídoto.
ANTIFREEZE s. anticongelante / adj. anticongelante.
ANTI-INFLAMMATORY adj. anti-inflamatório / s. remédio anti-inflamatório.
ANTIQUARY s. antiquário.
ANTIQUATED adj. antiquado(a), fora de moda.
ANTIQUE s. antiguidade, objeto antigo.
ANTIQUITY s. antiguidade.
ANTI-SEMITE s. antissemita.
ANTI-SEMITISM s. antissemitismo.
ANTISEPTIC s. antisséptico / adj. antisséptico.
ANTI-SOCIAL adj. antissocial.
ANTLER s. chifre; armação.
ANVIL s. bigorna.
ANXIETY s. ansiedade, ânsia, inquietação.
ANXIOUS adj. preocupado(a), inquieto(a).
ANY pron. qualquer um(a), algum(a) / adj. qualquer, quaisquer.
ANYBODY pron. ninguém; alguém.
ANYHOW adv. de qualquer modo.
ANYONE pron. ninguém; alguém.
ANYTHING pron. alguma coisa; qualquer coisa.
ANYWAY adv. de qualquer modo.
ANYWHERE adv. onde quer que seja, em qualquer lugar.
APACE adv. rapidamente.
APANTHROPIA s. apantropia, misantropia.

APART adv. à parte, a distância, além de.
APARTHEID s. separação.
APARTMENT s. apartamento.
APATHETIC adj. apático(a), indiferente.
APATHY s. apatia, indiferença.
APE s. macaco / v. imitar, macaquear.
APERIENT adj. laxante, purgativo.
APERITIF s. aperitivo.
APERTURE s. abertura, orifício.
APEX s. ápice, cume.
APHONIA s. afonia, perda da voz.
APHONIC adj. afônico, sem voz.
APHORISM s. aforismo, provérbio, ditado.
APHRODISIAC s. afrodisíaco / adj. afrodisíaco.
APHTHA s. afta.
APIARY s. apiário.
APICULTURIST s. apicultor.
APIECE adv. cada um; por cabeça; por peça.
APLOMB s. serenidade, calma; desenvoltura.
APNEA s. apneia.
APOCALYPSE s. apocalipse.
APOCALYPTICAL adj. apocalíptico.
APOLITICAL adj. apolítico.
APOLOGETIC adj. cheio de desculpas, apologético.
APOLOGIZE v. pedir desculpas, desculpar-se.
APOLOGY s. desculpa; defesa.
APOSTLE s. apóstolo.
APOSTROPHE s. apóstrofe.
APOTHEGM s. apotegma, aforismo, máxima.
APOTHEOSIS s. apoteose.
APPALL v. horrorizar, intimidar, amedrontar.
APPALLING adj. terrível, horrível, apavorante.
APPARATUS s. aparelho, utensílio.
APPAREL s. vestuário, traje / v. vestir, trajar.
APPARENT adj. aparente; evidente, claro.
APPARENTLY adv. aparentemente, evidentemente; claramente; visivelmente.
APPARITION s. fantasma, espectro; aparição.
APPEAL s. apelação; simpatia; atração / v. apelar.
APPEAR v. aparecer, surgir.
APPEARANCE s. aparência.
APPEASE v. apaziguar; satisfazer.
APPELLANT adj. apelante, suplicante / s. apelante, recorrente.
APPELLATION s. apelação judicial.
APPENDICITIS s. apendicite.
APPENDIX s. apêndice; peça acessória de um órgão.
APPERCEIVE v. aperceber-se, perceber; ser.

APPERTAIN v. pertencer; referir-se a.
APPETENCE s. apetência, apetite.
APPETITE s. apetite.
APPETIZER s. aperitivo, tiragosto.
APPETIZING adj. apetitoso(a).
APPLAUD v. aplaudir, aclamar.
APPLAUSE s. aplauso, aclamação.
APPLE s. maçã.
APPLE PIE s. torta de maçã.
APPLE-POLISH v. adular, bajular.
APPLIANCE s. aplicação, utilização.
APPLICABILITY s. aplicabilidade, pertinência.
APPLICANT s. candidato(a), pretendente.
APPLICATION s. aplicação.
APPLICATIVE adj. aplicável, prático.
APPLIED adj. aplicado, empregado, usado.
APPLIER s. aplicador.
APPLY v. aplicar, usar, empregar.
APPOINT v. nomear, designar, apontar.
APPOINTED adj. marcado; designado, nomeado, apontado.
APPOINTER s. nomeador.
APPOINTMENT s. encontro marcado; compromisso; nomeação.
APPORTION s. dividir em partes iguais, repartir.
APPORTION v. partilhar, repartir; distribuir.
APPOSITE adj. adequado, apropriado.
APPOSITION s. justaposição; aposição.
APPRAISAL s. avaliação, cálculo.
APPRAISE v. avaliar, estimar.
APPRECIATE v. apreciar, estimar, prezar.
APPRECIATION s. avaliação, estimativa.
APPRECIATIVE adj. apreciativo, compreensivo.
APPREHEND v. prender, deter; sentir apreensão, recear.
APPREHENSIBLE adj. compreensível; concebível; apreensível.
APPREHENSION s. apreensão, preocupação.
APPREHENSIVE adj. apreensivo(a), preocupado(a), receoso(a).
APPRENTICE s. aprendiz, praticante.
APPRENTICESHIP s. aprendizado, aprendizagem.
APPRISE v. avisar, informar.
APPROACH s. aproximação / v. aproximar-se.
APPROACHABLE adj. acessível.

APPROACHABLENESS s. acessibilidade, facilidade.
APPROBATE v. aprovar formalmente.
APPROBATION s. aprovação; aceitação.
APPROBATORY adj. aprobatório, laudatório.
APPROPRIATE v. apropriar-se, apoderar-se / adj. apropriado, adequado.
APPROPRIATION s. apropriação.
APPROVAL s. aprovação, consentimento.
APPROVE v. autorizar, aprovar, apoiar.
APPROVEMENT s. aprovação, concordância.
APPROXIMATE adj. aproximado, quase correto / v. aproximar(-se).
APPROXIMATELY adv. aproximadamente.
APPROXIMATION s. aproximação.
APRICOT s. damasco.
APRIL s. abril.
APRIL FOOL'S DAY s. dia da mentira (1º de abril).
APRON s. avental.
APT adj. adequado(a); apto(a), competente.
APTITUDE s. aptidão, talento, habilidade.
AQUALUNG s. equipamento de mergulho.
AQUAMARINE s. água-marinha.
AQUANAUT s. mergulhador, aquanauta.
AQUAPLANE s. aquaplano / v. aquaplanar.
AQUARIAN adj. aquariano (astrologia).
AQUARIUM s. aquário.
AQUARIUS s. Aquário (astrologia).
AQUATIC adj. aquático, da água.
AQUEDUCT s. aqueduto.
AQUILINE adj. aquilino, próprio da águia.
AQUIVER adj. trêmulo.
AQUOSITY s. aquosidade.
ARAB adj. árabe / s. árabe.
ARABESQUE s. arabesco / adj. arabesco.
ARABIAN s. árabe / adj. árabe.
ARABIC adj. arábico, árabe.
ARABLE s. terra arável / adj. arável, cultivável.
ARACHNID s. aracnídeo.
ARACHNOID adj. aracnoide.
ARAMAIC s. aramaico / adj. aramaico.
ARBITER s. árbitro, juiz.
ARBITRARY adj. arbitrário.
ARBITRATION s. arbitragem.
ARBOR s. árvore.
ARBOREAL adj. arbóreo.
ARBORICULTURE s. arboricultura.
ARBORISATION s. arborização.
ARC s. arco.

ARCADE s. arcada; galeria.
ARCANE adj. secreto; misterioso.
ARCH s. arco / v. curvar.
ARCHAEOLOGIC(AL) adj. arqueológico.
ARCHAEOLOGIST s. arqueólogo(a).
ARCHAEOLOGY s. arqueologia.
ARCHAIC adj. arcaico, antigo.
ARCHAISE v. tornar arcaico.
ARCHAISM s. arcaísmo.
ARCHBISHOP s. arcebispo.
ARCHDIOCESAN adj. arquidiocesano.
ARCHDIOCESE s. arquidiocese, arcebispado.
ARCHENEMY s. arqui-inimigo(a).
ARCHEOLOGIC adj. arqueológico.
ARCHEOLOGIST s. arqueólogo.
ARCHEOLOGY s. arqueologia.
ARCHER s. arqueiro.
ARCHERY s. tiro de arco.
ARCHETYPE s. arquétipo.
ARCHETYPIC adj. arquetípico.
ARCHIMAGE s. grande mago; feiticeiro.
ARCHIMEDEAN adj. arquimediano.
ARCHIPELAGO s. arquipélago.
ARCHITECT s. arquiteto(a).
ARCHITECTONIC(AL) adj. arquitetônico.
ARCHITECTURAL adj. arquitetônico, arquitetural.
ARCHITECTURE s. arquitetura.
ARCHIVE s. arquivo.
ARCHIVIST s. arquivista.
ARCHLY adv. astuciosamente, engenhosamente.
ARCHNESS s. travessura.
ARCHRIVAL s. arquirrival.
ARCTIC adj. ártico (Polo Norte).
ARCTIC OCEAN s. Oceano Ártico.
ARCTICS s. galochas, botas de borracha.
ARDENCY s. ardência; calor.
ARDENT adj. ardente.
ARDUOUS adj. árduo.
ARE v. 2ª pessoa do singular, 1ª, 2ª e 3ª pessoa do plural, presente do verbo to be.
AREA s. área, zona, região.
AREAL adj. regional.
ARENA s. arena.
ARENACEOUS adj. arenoso.
ARGENTINA s. Argentina.
ARGENTINE adj. argênteo, de prata, prateado; argentino.
ARGH interj. eca.

ARGIL s. argila, barro.
ARGOT s. gíria, linguajar coloquial.
ARGUE v. discutir, argumentar, debater.
ARGUMENT s. briga, discussão, debate.
ARGUMENTATIVE adj. argumentativo, lógico.
ARHYTHMIA s. arritmia.
ARIA s. ária, melodia.
ARID adj. árido, seco.
ARIDITY s. aridez, seca.
ARIES s. Áries (astrologia).
ARIGHT adv. corretamente, certamente.
ARIOSE adj. melódico.
ARISE v. aparecer.
ARISTOCRACY s. aristocracia, nobreza.
ARISTOCRAT s. aristocrata, nobre.
ARITHMETIC s. aritmética.
ARITHMOMETER s. máquina calculadora.
ARK s. arca, barco grande.
ARM s. braço; arma.
ARMADILLO s. tatu.
ARMAMENT s. armamento, equipamento bélico.
ARMCHAIR s. poltrona, cadeira de braços.
ARMED adj. armado, munido de armas.
ARMFUL s. braçada.
ARMHOLE s. cava (de roupa, axila).
ARMLESS s. sem braço; sem armas.
ARMLET s. braço de mar, bracelete armila, manilha.
ARMOR s. armadura.
ARMORED adj. blindado.
ARMORY s. arsenal; armaria, depósito de armas.
ARMPIT s. axila.
ARMREST s. braço de poltrona.
ARMY s. exército.
AROMA s. aroma, fragrância.
AROMATIZE v. aromatizar, tornar aromático.
AROUND adv. em volta, cerca de / prep. em redor de, em torno de.
AROUSE v. despertar; provocar; estimular.
AROUSED adj. excitado, estimulado, agitado.
ARRAIGN v. processar; denunciar.
ARRANGE v. organizar, arrumar.
ARRANGEMENT s. acordo; disposição; combinação; arranjo.
ARRANT adj. completo, total, notório.
ARRAY s. banco de dados; ordem; coleção.
ARREARS s. atrasos; dívidas atrasadas.

ARREST v. prender, deter, aprisionar / s. apreensão, detenção, prisão.
ARRIVAL s. chegada.
ARRIVE v. chegar.
ARRIVISTE s. arrivista.
ARROGANCE s. arrogância.
ARROGANT adj. arrogante.
ARROGATE v. arrogar, usurpar.
ARROGATION s. pretensão; usurpação.
ARROW s. flecha, seta.
ARSENIC s. arsênico, veneno / adj. de arsênico, venenoso.
ARSON s. incêndio culposo.
ARSONIST s. incendiário.
ART s. arte.
ARTEFACT s. artefato.
ARTERIAL adj. arterial.
ARTERY s. artéria.
ARTESIAN adj. artesiano.
ARTFUL adj. ardiloso; esperto.
ARTFULNESS s. astúcia; artifício; habilidade.
ART GALLERY s. museu; galeria de arte.
ARTHRALGIA s. artralgia, dor articular.
ARTHRITIS s. artrite.
ARTHROLOGY s. artrologia.
ARTICHOKE s. alcachofra.
ARTICLE s. artigo.
ARTICULATE v. articular, expressar / adj. articulado, bem escrito.
ARTICULATENESS s. eloquência.
ARTIFACT s. instrumento, objeto, artefato; produto manufaturado.
ARTIFICE s. artifício, ardil, estratagema.
ARTIFICIAL adj. artificial.
ARTILLERY s. artilharia.
ARTISAN s. artesão(ã).
ARTIST s. artista.
ARTISTIC adj. artístico.
ARTLESS adj. natural; simples; sem arte.
ART SCHOOL s. escola de artes.
ARTWORK s. obra de arte.
ARTY adj. artístico.
ARUGULA s. rúcula.
ARVO s. tarde, noitinha (Austrália).
ARYAN s. ariano / adj. ariano.
AS prep. como, na qualidade de / adv. tão, tanto quanto.
ASCEND v. subir; ascender.
ASCENDANCE s. predomínio, domínio; ascendência.
ASCENT s. subida, ascensão.
ASCERTAIN v. averiguar, verificar, apurar.
ASCRIBABLE adj. atribuível, aplicável.
ASCRIBE v. atribuir, designar.
ASEPSIS s. assepsia.
ASEPTIC adj. asséptico, desinfetado.
ASEXUAL s. assexuado / adj. assexual, assexuado, sem sexo.
ASEXUALITY s. assexualidade.
ASEXUALIZATION s. assexualização.
ASEXUALIZE v. tornar assexuado; castrar (-se), esterilizar(-se).
ASH s. cinza.
ASHAMED adj. envergonhado(a).
ASHEN adj. cinzento.
ASHORE adv. em terra firme.
ASHPLANT s. bengala.
ASHTRAY s. cinzeiro.
ASH WEDNESDAY s. Quarta-feira de Cinzas.
ASIA s. Ásia.
ASIAN adj. asiático(a) / s. asiático(a).
ASIDE adv. de lado, ao lado; longe, a distância.
ASININE adj. asinino, asno; estúpido.
ASK v. perguntar; convidar; pedir.
ASKANCE adv. de soslaio, desconfiadamente.
ASKEW adj. torto, retorcido.
ASLANT adv. diagonalmente; obliquamente.
ASLEEP adj. adormecido; dormente.
ASLOPE adj. inclinado, oblíquo / adv. de maneira oblíqua, inclinada.
ASPARAGUS s. aspargo.
ASPECT s. aspecto, aparência.
ASPECTABLE adj. visível.
ASPERITY adj. aspereza, rudeza.
ASPERSE v. aspergir; caluniar, difamar.
ASPERSION s. calúnia, difamação; borrifo, respingo.
ASPERSORIUM s. aspersório (instrumento).
ASPHALT s. asfalto / v. asfaltar.
ASPHYXIAL adj. asfixiante, sufocante.
ASPHYXIANT s. asfixiante / adj. asfixioso, asfíxico.
ASPHYXIATION s. asfixia, sufocamento.
ASPIRATE v. aspirar (pronúncia).
ASPIRATION s. aspiração, desejos.
ASPIRATOR s. aspirador.
ASPIRE v. aspirar, ansiar, almejar.
ASPIRIN s. aspirina.
ASS s. jumento, asno; imbecil (coloquial).

ASSAIL v. assaltar, atacar.
ASSAILANT s. assaltante / adj. assaltante.
ASSAILMENT s. ataque, assalto.
ASSASSIN s. assassino.
ASSASSINATE v. assassinar.
ASSASSINATION s. assassinato.
ASSAULT v. assaltar, atacar, agredir / s. assalto, ataque, agressão.
ASSEMBLE v. reunir, ajuntar, agregar; montar, armar.
ASSEMBLY s. reunião, assembleia, junta.
ASSENT s. aprovação, consentimento / v. consentir, aprovar.
ASSERT v. afirmar, declarar.
ASSERTION s. afirmação, declaração.
ASSERTIVE adj. assertivo, afirmativo.
ASSERTIVENESS s. assertividade.
ASSESS v. avaliar, calcular, estimar.
ASSESSABLE adj. sujeito a impostos; que pode ser avaliado.
ASSESSMENT s. avaliação; taxação.
ASSESSOR s. assessor; avaliador; conselheiro.
ASSESSORSHIP s. assistência, perícia.
ASSET s. vantagem, trunfo.
ASSETS s. espólio.
ASSEVERATE v. asseverar, assegurar, afirmar, declarar.
ASSEVERATION s. asseveração, declaração, afirmação.
ASSHOLE s. idiota; imbecil.
ASSIDUITY s. assiduidade, perseverança, persistência; diligência.
ASSIDUOUS adj. assíduo; persistente, diligente, trabalhador.
ASSIGN v. designar, apontar.
ASSIGNMENT s. tarefa; designação.
ASSIMILATE v. assimilar; assemelhar.
ASSIMILATION s. assimilação; assemelhação.
ASSIST v. ajudar, auxiliar, assistir.
ASSISTANCE s. ajuda, auxílio, assistência.
ASSISTANT s. assistente, auxiliar.
ASSIZE s. sessão de um tribunal; veredito; julgamento.
ASS-KISSER s. puxa-saco, bajulador, adulador.
ASSOCIATE v. associar / s. associado(a).
ASSOCIATION s. associação; sociedade; companhia; união; junção.
ASSOCIATIVE adj. associativo.
ASSOIL v. absolver; perdoar.
ASSONANCE s. assonância.
ASSONANT adj. assonante.

ASSORT v. agrupar, classificar.
ASSORTED adj. sortido, variado, classificado.
ASSORTMENT s. variedade, sortimento.
ASSUAGE v. suavizar, aliviar; acalmar.
ASSUAGEMENT s. alívio; pacificação.
ASSUASIVE adj. calmante, aliviador.
ASSUMABLE adj. assuntível.
ASSUME v. supor, presumir; assumir.
ASSUMEDLY adv. supostamente, teoricamente.
ASSUMPTION s. suposição, hipótese.
ASSURANCE s. garantia; confiança.
ASSURE v. garantir, afirmar.
ASSURED adj. garantido, segurado.
ASTERISK s. asterisco.
ASTERN adv. à popa, a ré; atrás.
ASTEROID s. asteroide.
ASTHMA s. asma.
ASTHMATIC adj. asmático / s. asmático.
ASTIGMATISM s. astigmatismo.
ASTIR adj. ativo, agitado em movimento; fora da cama.
ASTONISH v. espantar, surpreender, pasmar.
ASTONISHMENT s. assombro, grande surpresa, pasmo.
ASTOUND v. pasmar, surpreender.
ASTRAL adj. astral, de estrelas.
ASTRAY adj. desviado, perdido.
ASTRICT v. restringir, limitar, confinar.
ASTRICTION s. restrição.
ASTRIDE adj. escarranchado / adv. escarranchadamente.
ASTRINGE v. comprimir, constringir.
ASTROLOGER s. astrólogo.
ASTROLOGICAL adj. astrológico.
ASTROLOGY s. astrologia.
ASTRONAUT s. astronauta.
ASTRONOMER s. astrônomo.
ASTRONOMIC(AL) adj. astronômico; extraordinário.
ASTRONOMY s. astronomia.
ASTROPHYSICIST s. astrofísico.
ASTROPHYSICS s. astrofísica.
ASTUTE adj. astuto, ardiloso.
ASUNDER adv. em partes; separadamente.
ASYLUM s. manicômio.
ASYMMETRIC adj. assimétrico.
ASYMMETRY s. assimetria.
ASYMPTOMATIC adj. assintomático.
ASYNCHRONISM s. assincronismo.

ASYSTEMATIC *adj.* assistemático, sem sistematização.
AT *prep.* em, a.
ATHEISM *s.* ateísmo.
ATHEIST *s.* ateísta, ateu, ateia.
ATHENS *s.* Atenas.
ATHLETE *s.* atleta.
ATHLETICS *s.* atletismo.
ATLANTIC OCEAN *s.* Oceano Atlântico.
ATLAS *s.* atlas.
ATMOSPHERE *s.* atmosfera.
ATOM *s.* átomo.
ATOMIZER *s.* pulverizador.
ATONE *v.* reparar; harmonizar.
ATROCIOUS *adj.* atroz, cruel.
ATTACH *v.* prender, fixar; anexar.
ATTACHÉ *s.* adido, diplomata.
ATTACHMENT *s.* acessório; anexo; ação de fixar.
ATTACK *v.* atacar, agredir / *s.* ataque, acesso súbito; agressão.
ATTAIN *v.* alcançar, chegar a, atingir.
ATTAINABLE *adj.* atingível, alcançável.
ATTEMPT *s.* tentativa, intento / *v.* tentar.
ATTEND *v.* cursar; assistir; prestar atenção.
ATTENDANCE *s.* frequência; atenção.
ATTENDANT *s.* encarregado(a), atendente.
ATTENTION *s.* atenção, cuidado.
ATTENTIVE *adj.* atento(a), atencioso(a), cuidadoso(a).
ATTIC *s.* sótão.
ATTIRE *s.* vestimenta, traje.
ATTITUDE *s.* atitude, postura.
ATTORNEY *s.* procurador, representante, advogado.
ATTRACT *v.* atrair; puxar para si.
ATTRACTION *s.* atração.
ATTRACTIVE *adj.* atraente, atrativo.
ATTRIBUTABLE *adj.* atribuível.
ATTRIBUTE *v.* atribuir / *s.* atributo, qualidade.
ATTRITION *s.* atrito, fricção.
ATTUNE *v.* afinar.
ATYPICAL *adj.* atípico.
AUBERGINE *s.* berinjela.
AUBURN *adj.* ruivo, castanho avermelhado.
AUCTION *v.* leiloar / *s.* leilão.
AUCTIONEER *s.* leiloeiro(a).
AUDIBLE *adj.* audível.
AUDIENCE *s.* público, audiência.
AUDIO *s.* áudio / *adj.* auditivo.
AUDIOVISUAL *adj.* audiovisual.

AUDIT *v.* fazer auditoria, examinar / *s.* auditoria, exame.
AUDITION *s.* audição.
AUDITOR *s.* auditor(a).
AUGMENT *v.* aumentar, acrescentar / *s.* aumento, acréscimo.
AUGUR *v.* augurar, prognosticar / *s.* profeta, adivinho.
AUGUST *s.* agosto.
AUGUSTNESS *s.* majestade; dignidade.
AULD *adj.* velho (regional).
AUNT *s.* tia.
AUNTIE *s.* titia.
AURA *s.* aura, essência.
AURICULAR *adj.* auricular.
AURORA *s.* aurora.
AUSPICE *s.* auspício.
AUSPICIOUS *adj.* favorável, auspicioso.
AUSTERE *adj.* austero.
AUSTERITY *s.* severidade, austeridade.
AUSTRALIA *s.* Austrália.
AUSTRALIAN *adj.* australiano(a) / *s.* australiano(a).
AUSTRIA *s.* Áustria.
AUSTRIAN *adj.* austríaco(a).
AUTEUR *s.* diretor (cinema).
AUTHENTIC *adj.* autêntico, genuíno.
AUTHENTICATE *v.* autenticar.
AUTHENTICATION *s.* autenticação.
AUTHENTICITY *s.* autenticidade.
AUTHOR *s.* autor(a).
AUTHORESS *s.* autora.
AUTHORITARIAN *adj.* autoritário(a) / *s.* autoritário(a).
AUTHORITARIANISM *s.* autoritarismo.
AUTHORITATIVE *adj.* autorizado.
AUTHORITY *s.* autoridade.
AUTHORIZE *v.* autorizar, permitir.
AUTISM *s.* autismo.
AUTISTIC *adj.* autista.
AUTO *s.* automóvel.
AUTOBAHN *s.* autoestrada, rodovia.
AUTOBIOGRAPHY *s.* autobiografia.
AUTOCRACY *s.* autocracia.
AUTOCRAT *s.* autocrata.
AUTOCRATIC *adj.* autocrático, despótico.
AUTOGRAPH *s.* autógrafo / *v.* autografar.
AUTOIMMUNE *adj.* autoimune.
AUTOIMMUNITY *s.* autoimunidade.
AUTOMATE *v.* automatizar.
AUTOMATIC *adj.* automático.

AUTOMATIVE *adj.* automotivo.
AUTOMATON *s.* autômato; robô.
AUTOMOBILE *s.* automóvel.
AUTONOMIC *adj.* autônomo.
AUTONOMY *s.* autonomia.
AUTOPILOT *s.* piloto automático.
AUTOPSY *s.* autópsia.
AUTUMN *s.* outono.
AUXILIARY *adj.* auxiliar, ajudante.
AVAIL *v.* aproveitar / *s.* proveito, lucro.
AVAILABILITY *s.* disponibilidade.
AVAILABLE *adj.* disponível, acessível.
AVALANCHE *s.* avalanche.
AVANT-GARDE *s.* vanguarda / *adj.* de vanguarda.
AVARICE *s.* cobiça, avareza.
AVAST *interj.* pare!, basta! (náutica).
AVATAR *s.* avatar.
AVE *abrev.* av.
AVENGE *v.* vingar(-se).
AVENGEMENT *s.* vingança, desforra.
AVENGER *s.* vingador.
AVENUE *s.* avenida.
AVER *v.* assegurar, asseverar.
AVERAGE *s.* média, proporção.
AVERSE *adj.* averso, adverso.
AVERSION *s.* aversion.
AVERT *v.* prevenir, evitar, desviar.
AVIARY *s.* viveiro de aves, aviário.
AVIATION *s.* aviação.
AVIATOR *s.* aviador.
AVID *adj.* ávido(a), ansioso(a).
AVIDITY *s.* avidez, cobiça.
AVOCADO *s.* abacate.
AVOCATION *s.* passatempo, hobby.
AVOID *v.* evitar; escapar, fugir.
AVOIDABLE *adj.* evitável.
AVOIDANCE *s.* fuga, evasão, desculpa.
AVOW *v.* declarar francamente, confessar.
AVOWAL *s.* confissão, declaração.
AVUNCULAR *adj.* avuncular.
AW *interj.* oh.
AWAIT *v.* esperar, aguardar.
AWAKE *v.* despertar / *adj.* acordado(a).
AWAKEN *v.* despertar, acordar.
AWARD *v.* conceder, premiar / *s.* prêmio, recompensa.
AWARE *adj.* informado(a), ciente; atento(a).
AWARENESS *s.* consciência, conhecimento.
AWASH *adj.* inundado; alagado.
AWAY *adv.* fora, à distância / *adj.* ausente, distante.
AWE *s.* terror, grande medo.
AWE-INSPIRING *adj.* impressionante, espantoso.
AWESOME *adj.* imponente, temeroso.
AWFUL *adj.* terrível, horrível.
AWHILE *adv.* por algum tempo, pouco tempo.
AWKWARD *adj.* desajeitado(a), inábil, embaraçoso.
AWKWARDNESS *s.* inabilidade, inaptidão, embaraço.
AWNING *s.* toldo, tenda.
AWOKE *adj.* desperto / *v.* despertar.
AWRY *adv.* de esguelha / *adj.* torto, oblíquo.
AXE *s.* machado / *v.* reduzir, cortar.
AXLE *s.* eixo.
AY *adv.* sim (coloquial) / *interj.* ah! oh! ai!
AYE *adv.* sempre, indefinidamente.
AZALEA *s.* azaleia.
AZTEC *s.* asteca / *adj.* asteca.
AZURE *adj.* azul-celeste.

Bb

B, B s. segunda letra do alfabeto inglês; si (nota musical).
B.A. s. sigla de Bachelor of Arts.
BAA v. balar, balir / s. balido (carneiro).
BABBLE v. balbuciar / s. balbucio, murmúrio.
BABBLER s. tagarela, falador.
BABE s. bebê; gata, garota.
BABEL s. Babel, Babilônia; algazarra.
BABOON s. babuíno.
BABY s. bebê, nenê; filhote.
BABYHOOD s. primeira infância.
BABYISH adj. infantil, pueril, de criança.
BABYSIT v. pajear, cuidar de criança.
BABYSITTER s. babá.
BABYSITTING s. cuidado de crianças, tomar conta de crianças.
BACCALAUREATE s. bacharelado.
BACHELOR s. bacharel; solteiro.
BACHELOR DEGREE s. bacharelado, graduação.
BACHELORHOOD s. bacharelado; celibato.
BACHELOR OF ARTS s. bacharelado em Artes.
BACHELOR OF SCIENCE s. bacharelado em Ciências Exatas.
BACHELOR PARTY s. despedida de solteiro.
BACILLUS s. bacilo; bactéria.
BACK s. costas, dorso, parte traseira / v. recuar, voltar atrás.
BACKACHE s. dor nas costas.
BACKBENCHER s. legislador, deputado.
BACKBITE s. calúnia / v. caluniar.
BACKBITING adj. traiçoeiro, desleal.
BACKBOARD s. tabela (basquete).
BACKBONE s. coluna vertebral; firmeza, determinação.
BACKCOUNTRY s. roça, interior, sertão.
BACKDATE v. pré-datar; antedatar.
BACKDOOR adj. ilícito, clandestino; às escondidas.
BACKDROP s. cenário, pano de fundo (teatro).
BACKED adj. apoiado, respaldado.
BACKED-UP adj. entupido, bloqueado.
BACKER s. financiador, patrocinador; apoiador.
BACKFIELD s. ataque (futebol americano).
BACKFIRE v. sair pela culatra; falhar, dar errado.
BACKGAMMON s. jogo de gamão.

BACKGROUND s. fundo, segundo plano; conhecimento; respaldo.
BACKGROUNDER s. informe à imprensa.
BACKHAND s. parte de trás da mão / adj. inesperado.
BACKHANDED adj. de duas caras, mentiroso.
BACKHOE s. escavadeira, escavadora.
BACKING adj. reforço, apoio, suporte.
BACKLASH s. retrocesso / v. retroceder.
BACKLIST s. catálogo / v. pôr na lista, reservar.
BACKLOG s. reserva, provisão / v. acumular, estocar.
BACKPACK s. mochila / v. viajar (mochilão).
BACKPACKER s. mochileiro, viajante.
BACKPACKING adj. viajante, mochileiro.
BACKREST s. descanso, encosto (cadeira).
BACKROOM s. fundos; área privativa/reservada.
BACKSEAT s. banco traseiro (carro) / adj. subalterno, subordinado.
BACKSIDE s. traseiro; bumbum.
BACKSLASH s. barra invertida (\).
BACKSLIDE v. apostar, desviar; recair.
BACKSPACE v. retroceder, voltar / s. retrocesso, volta.
BACKSTAGE adv. bastidores; nos bastidores.
BACKSTOP s. escora, escudo, barreira / v. sustentar, apoiar.
BACKSTREET s. rua secundária / adj. ilícito, clandestino.
BACKSTROKE s. nado de costas (natação).
BACKTALK v. dar patada / s. desaforo.
BACKTRACK v. retomar, regressar; voltar a fazer.
BACKUP s. cópia de segurança / adj. substituto.
BACKWARD adj. atrasado, retrógrado.
BACKWARD LOOKING s. pensamento conservador.
BACKWARDNESS s. retardamento, atraso; lentidão.
BACKWARD STEP s. passo para trás; retrocesso.
BACKWASH s. esteira; corrente (marítima).
BACKWATER s. lugar isolado; fim do mundo.
BACKWOODS s. mato; interior, sertão.
BACKYARD s. quintal; parte dos fundos.
BACON s. bacon, toucinho defumado.

BACTERIA s. bactéria (germes).
BACTERIAL adj. bacteriano.
BACTERICIDAL adj. bactericida.
BACTERIOLOGICAL adj. bacteriológico.
BACTERIOLOGY s. bacteriologia.
BACTERIUM s. bactéria (micro-organismo).
BAD adj. mau, vilão, ruim.
BADGE s. crachá, distintivo, emblema.
BADLY adv. mal, não bem; muito, demais.
BADNESS s. maldade, ruindade.
BAD-TEMPERED adj. mal-humorado.
BAFFLE v. desconcertar, confundir / s. confusão.
BAFFLED adj. perplexo, confuso.
BAFFLING adj. desconcertante.
BAG s. mala; bolsa; sacola.
BAGEL s. rosquinha (pão).
BAGGAGE s. bagagem.
BAGGIE s. sacolinha, saquinho.
BAGMAN s. caixeiro-viajante.
BAGGY adj. folgado, largo.
BAGPIPES s. gaita de foles.
BAGUETTE s. baguete.
BAIL s. fiança / v. libertar sob fiança, afiançar.
BAILER s. balde.
BAILEY s. muralha externa.
BAILIFF s. oficial de justiça.
BAIT s. isca / v. iscar; apoquentar.
BAKE v. assar, cozer.
BAKER s. padeiro.
BAKERY s. padaria.
BAKESHOP s. m.q. bakery.
BAKING s. fornada / adj. escaldante, quente.
BAKING PAN s. forma.
BAKING POWDER s. fermento em pó.
BAKING SODA s. bicarbonato de sódio.
BAKING TRAY s. assadeira.
BALANCE s. balança, equilíbrio; saldo / v. equilibrar, balancear.
BALANCED adj. equilibrado; balanceado.
BALCONY s. varanda; sacada, balcão.
BALD adj. careca, calvo / v. ficar careca.
BALDERDASH s. palavrório; conversa mole.
BALDING adj. diz-se de que está ficando calvo.
BALDNESS s. calvície; careca.
BALDY adj. carequinha, sem cabelo.
BALE s. fardo, desgraça / v. enfardar.
BALEFUL adj. maligno, fatal; doloroso.
BALER s. enfardadeira; embaladeira.
BALK v. recusar-se, negar-se; empacar.

BALL s. bola; novelo; baile.
BALLAD s. balada (composição musical e forma fixa de poema).
BALLAST s. lastro / v. lastrar, colocar lastro.
BALL BEARING s. rolimã; rolamento.
BALLERINA s. bailarina.
BALLET s. balé.
BALL GAME s. jogo de bola; situação complicada.
BALLISTIC adj. balístico / s. balística.
BALLOON s. balão; bexiga.
BALLOT s. votação; voto.
BALLOT BOX s. urna eleitoral; urna.
BALLOT PAPER s. cédula eleitoral.
BALLPARK s. estádio de baseball.
BALLPOINT adj. esferográfico.
BALLPOINT PEN s. caneta esferográfica.
BALLROOM s. salão de baile.
BALLYHOO s. sensacionalismo; clamor, tumulto.
BALM s. bálsamo.
BALMY adj. ameno, suave, brando.
BALSAM s. bálsamo.
BALSAMIC adj. balsâmico.
BALTIC adj. báltico.
BALUSTRADE s. balaustrada.
BAMBOO s. bambu.
BAMBOOZLE v. desnortear, desorientar.
BAN v. proibir, interditar / s. proibição.
BANAL adj. banal.
BANALITY s. banalidade.
BANANA s. banana.
BAND s. banda; faixa, fita; orquestra.
BANDAGE v. enfaixar, atar / s. atadura, bandagem.
BAND-AID s. curativo.
BANDANA s. bandana.
BANDIT s. bandido.
BANDITRY s. banditismo.
BANDLEADER s. líder; maestro.
BANDSTAND s. coreto.
BANDWAGON s. carro de propaganda política; condição de ficar na moda; popularidade.
BANE s. ruína, perdição; desgraça.
BANG v. bater / s. explosão, estrondo, pancada.
BANGER s. lata-velha, carro velho.
BANGLE s. bracelete, pulseira.
BANGS s. franja (de cabelo).
BANISH v. banir, expulsar.

BANISHMENT s. banimento, expulsão.
BANISTER s. corrimão; balaústre.
BANK s. banco; margem de rio / v. manter em banco, depositar.
BANKCARD s. cartão (banco).
BANKER s. banqueiro.
BANKING s. transações bancárias; bancário.
BANKING NOTE s. cédula, nota.
BANKRUPT adj. falido, sem dinheiro.
BANKRUPTCY s. falência.
BANK STATEMENT s. extrato bancário.
BANNER s. faixa, estandarte; bandeira.
BANNING s. proibição, banimento.
BANNS s. proclama de casamento.
BANQUET v. fazer banquete / s. banquete.
BAPTISE v. batizar.
BAPTISM s. batismo, iniciação.
BAPTISMAL adj. batismal.
BAPTIST s. batista.
BAR s. bar; barra / v. barrar; obstruir.
BARB s. farpa, lasca.
BARBARIAN s. bárbaro / adj. bárbaro.
BARBARIC adj. bárbaro, selvagem.
BARBARISM s. barbarismo.
BARBAROUS adj. bárbaro; incivilizado.
BARBECUE s. churrasco.
BARBED adj. farpado; cruel, mordaz.
BARBED WIRE s. arame farpado.
BARBER s. barbeiro, cabeleireiro.
BARBERSHOP s. barbearia.
BAR CODE s. código de barras.
BARD s. bardo; poeta.
BARE adj. despido, nu / v. descobrir, revelar.
BAREBONE s. esqueleto.
BAREFACED adj. descarado; insolente, cara de pau.
BAREFOOT adj. descalço.
BAREHEADED s. sem chapéu; descoberto.
BARELY adv. dificilmente, mal, apenas.
BARENESS s. nudez; pobreza.
BARGAIN v. barganhar, pechinchar / s. barganha, pechincha.
BARGAINING s. negociação; pechincha.
BARGE s. barcaça, chata / v. entrar abruptamente.
BARGEPOLE s. varejão.
BARITONE s. barítono.
BARK s. latido; casca de árvore / v. latir, ladrar.
BARKING s. latido / adj. doido, insano.
BARLEY s. cevada (grão e planta).

BARM s. lêvedo de cerveja; fermento.
BARMAID s. garçonete.
BARMAN s. garçom; *barman*.
BARN s. celeiro, estábulo.
BARNEY s. rolo, briga.
BARNYARD s. terreiro, quintal.
BAROMETER s. barômetro.
BAROMETRIC *adj.* barométrico.
BARON s. barão.
BARONAGE s. nobreza.
BARONESS s. baronesa.
BARONET s. baronete.
BARONY s. baronato.
BAROQUE *adj.* barroco; complexo.
BARQUE s. barca.
BARRACK s. barraca, barracão; quartel.
BARRAGE s. barragem.
BARRE s. barra.
BARREL s. barril, tonel; cano de arma.
BARREN *adj.* árido, estéril, improdutivo.
BARRICADE s. barricada / v. bloquear com uma barricada.
BARRIER s. barreira, obstáculo.
BARRING *prep.* exceto, salvo / s. impedimento.
BARRISTER s. advogado.
BARROW s. carrinho de mão, padiola.
BARTENDER s. garçom (de bar); *barman*.
BARTER v. trocar, permutar / s. comércio de troca.
BASAL *adj.* basal, fundamental.
BASE v. basear-se / s. base.
BASEBALL s. beisebol.
BASEBOARD s. rodapé.
BASEBORN *adj.* ilegítimo.
BASED *adj.* baseado; com base em.
BASELESS *adj.* infundado; inconsistente.
BASELINE v. estabelecer padrão / s. linha de base; padrão.
BASEMAN s. jogador de base (beisebol).
BASEMENT s. porão.
BASH v. socar, esmurrar, golpear.
BASHFUL *adj.* envergonhado, acanhado.
BASHFULLY *adv.* timidamente.
BASHING s. surra, ofensa, ultraje.
BASIC *adj.* básico; essencial, mínimo.
BASICALLY *adv.* basicamente.
BASICS s. essencial, elementos fundamentais.
BASIL s. manjericão.
BASIN s. bacia; pia de banheiro.

BASIS s. base.
BASK v. tomar sol, aquecer-se.
BASKET s. cesto, cesta.
BASKETBALL s. basquetebol.
BASKETRY s. cestaria.
BASS s. som ou tom baixo, grave / *adj.* grave (som)
BASSET s. bassê.
BASSIST s. baixista.
BASTARD s. filho ilegítimo; bastardo.
BASTARDISE v. declarar ilegítimo, bastardo; corromper.
BASTE v. regar.
BAT s. morcego; bastão / v. bater, golpear.
BATCH s. maço, lote / v. agrupar.
BATE v. reduzir, abater; moderar.
BATED *adj.* suspenso, retido.
BATH s. banheira, banho.
BATHE v. tomar banho; banhar-se.
BATHER s. banhista.
BATHHOUSE s. balneário.
BATHING s. banho, lavagem.
BATHROBE s. roupão de banho.
BATHROOM s. banheiro.
BATHTUBE s. banheira.
BATON s. cassetete; bastão.
BATTALION s. batalhão.
BATTEN v. fixar, prender.
BATTER v. espancar, bater / s. batedor.
BATTERED *adj.* maltratado, espancado.
BATTERER s. batedor; agressor.
BATTERING s. bateção; espancamento.
BATTERY s. agressão; bateria, pilha.
BATTING s. batedura.
BATTLE s. batalha, disputa, combate.
BATTLEFIELD s. campo de batalha.
BATTLEFRONT s. linha de frente.
BATTLEGROUND s. área de conflitos.
BATTLEMENT s. muralha, parapeito.
BATTLER s. combatente; soldado.
BATTLESHIP s. encouraçado, couraçado.
BAUBLE s. bugiganga, ninharia.
BAUD s. baud (informática).
BALK v. recusar-se, negar-se.
BAWDY *adj.* indecente, imoral.
BAWL v. gritar, berrar / s. grito, berro.
BAY s. baía, enseada; latido grave / v. ladrar; amarrar a caça.
BAYLEAF s. louro, loureiro.
BAYONETTE s. baioneta.
BAY WINDOW s. janela com sacada.

BAZAAR s. bazar.
BAZOOKA s. bazuca.
BC abrev. a.C. (antes de Cristo).
BE v. ser, estar.
BEACH s. praia / v. encalhar; naufragar.
BEACH BALL s. bola de praia.
BEACH CHAIR s. cadeira de praia.
BEACHFRONT s. beira-mar.
BEACH TOWEL s. toalha de praia.
BEACH UMBRELLA s. guarda-sol.
BEACHWEAR s. roupa de banho ou praia.
BEACON s. farol, sinalizador, baliza.
BEAD s. gota; conta de rosário.
BEADLE s. sacristão.
BEAGLE s. bigle, beagle (raça de cachorro).
BEAK s. bico.
BEAKER s. copo com bico, taça; proveta.
BEAM s. viga, suporte; raio, feixe de luz / v. sorrir.
BEAMING adj. brilhante, luminoso; radiante.
BEAN s. feijão, vagem; grão; fava.
BEANPOLE s. estaca; varapau.
BEANSPROUT s. broto de feijão.
BEANSTALK s. pé de feijão; ramo.
BEAR s. urso / v. suportar.
BEARABLE adj. suportável, tolerável.
BEARD s. barba.
BEARDED adj. barbado, barbudo.
BEARDLESS adj. sem barba, imberbe.
BEARER s. portador, carregador, titular.
BEARING s. comportamento, postura; posição, rumo.
BEAST s. animal, besta, fera.
BEASTLY adj. bestialmente, animalescamente.
BEAT v. bater em, tocar / s. batida, golpe; ritmo, compasso.
BEATER s. batedeira; batedor.
BEATING s. surra, derrota, açoitamento.
BEAT IT interj. fora!
BEATITUDE s. beatitude.
BEAUTICIAN s. esteticista.
BEAUTIFICATION s. embelezamento.
BEAUTIFUL adj. belo, bonito, lindo.
BEAUTIFULLY adv. lindamente, belamente.
BEAUTIFULNESS s. beleza, formosura.
BEAUTIFY v. embelezar; decorar.
BEAUTY s. beleza, beldade.
BEAUTY PARLOR s. salão de beleza.
BEAVER s. castor.

BECAUSE conj. porque, pela razão de.
BECAUSE OF prep. por causa de.
BECK s. sinal, aceno / v. acenar, fazer sinal.
BECKON v. acenar / s. gesto, aceno.
BECOME v. tornar-se, transformar-se em.
BECOMING adj. elegante, atrativo, vistoso.
BED s. cama.
BEDAZZLE v. deslumbrar.
BEDBUG s. percevejo; pulga.
BEDCLOTHES s. roupa de cama.
BEDEVIL v. atormentar, importunar.
BEDDING s. m.q. bedclothes.
BEDGOWN s. camisola.
BEDLAM s. confusão, tumulto.
BEDRAGGLED adj. molhado, lameado; sujo.
BEDRIDDEN adj. acamado; confinado.
BEDROCK s. fundamento, alicerce (construção).
BEDROOM s. quarto de dormir.
BEDSIDE s. cabeceira.
BEDSIDE LAMP s. lâmpada de cabeceira.
BEDSPREAD s. colcha.
BED-TABLE s. mesa de cabeceira, criado-mudo.
BEDTIME s. hora de dormir.
BEE s. abelha.
BEECH s. faia.
BEEF s. carne de boi.
BEEFBURGER s. hambúrguer bovino.
BEEFEATER s. guarda da torre de Londres.
BEEFSTEAK s. bife (carne bovina).
BEEFY adj. musculoso, carnudo; sarado.
BEEHIVE s. colmeia.
BEEKEEPER s. apicultor.
BEEKEEPING s. apicultura.
BEELINE s. caminho mais curto, linha reta.
BEEP s. bipe / v. bipar; buzinar.
BEER s. cerveja.
BEET s. beterraba.
BEETLE s. besouro; escaravelho.
BEETROOT s. beterraba.
BEFALL v. suceder, sobrevir; acontecer.
BEFIT v. convir, condizer.
BEFORE prep. antes de, diante de / conj. antes que / adv. antes, anteriormente, à frente.
BEFOREHAND adv. anteriormente, antecipadamente.
BEFORETIME adv. antigamente, anteriormente.
BEFRIEND v. fazer amizade.
BEFUDDLE v. estontear, confundir.

BEG v. implorar, suplicar.
BEGET v. gerar, procriar.
BEGGAR s. mendigo.
BEGGARY s. pobreza, miséria, penúria.
BEGIN v. começar, iniciar.
BEGINNER s. principiante, iniciante.
BEGINNING s. início, começo; origem.
BEGONE interj. fora! vá embora.
BEGRUDGE v. invejar, ressentir.
BEGUILE v. seduzir, encantar; iludir.
BEGUILING adj. atraente, encantador.
BEHALF s. interesse, favor; em nome de.
BEHAVE v. comportar-se, conduzir-se.
BEHAVIOUR s. comportamento, ação, conduta.
BEHAVIOURAL adj. comportamental.
BEHAVIOURISM s. comportamentalismo; behaviourismo.
BEHAVIOURIST s. behaviourista.
BEHEAD v. decapitar, degolar.
BEHEADING s. decapitação.
BEHEMOTH s. beemote; gigante.
BEHIND prep. atrás de / adv. atrás, detrás.
BEHOLD v. contemplar, observar, notar, ver.
BEHOLDEN adj. endividado; obrigado.
BEHOLDER s. observador; espectador.
BEIGE adj. bege / s. bege.
BEIJING s. Pequim.
BEING s. ser, existência.
BEIRUTE s. Beirute (Líbano).
BEJEWEL v. adornar com joias.
BELATED adj. atrasado, tardio.
BELCH v. arrotar; vomitar / s. arroto.
BELEAGUER v. importunar, assediar.
BELFRY s. campanário, torre dos sinos.
BELGIAN s. belga / adj. belga.
BELGIUM s. Bélgica.
BELIE v. desmentir; dar ideia falsa de; caluniar.
BELIEF s. opinião; crença, fé.
BELIEVABLE adj. acreditável; plausível.
BELIEVE v. acreditar, crer, confiar.
BELIEVER s. crente.
BELITTLE v. depreciar; desdenhar.
BELITTLING adj. desprezível, desdenhoso.
BELL s. sino, sineta; campainha.
BELLBIRD s. araponga.
BELLBOY s. mensageiro de hotel.
BELLIED adj. barrigudo.
BELLIGERENT adj. agressivo, hostil / s. beligerante.
BELLMAN s. porteiro.

BELLOW v. mugir, berrar / s. berro, urro, grito.
BELLOWS s. fole.
BELLY s. barriga, ventre.
BELLYACHE s. dor de barriga, cólica.
BELLY BUTTON s. umbigo.
BELLY DANCE s. dança do ventre.
BELONG v. pertencer a; ser membro de.
BELONGINGS s. pertences.
BELOVED s. amado, querido / adj. querido.
BELOW prep. abaixo, sob / adv. embaixo.
BELT s. cinto / v. surrar.
BELTWAY s. via circular; rodoanel.
BEMOAN v. reclamar; queixar-se.
BEMUSE v. confundir.
BEMUSED adj. preocupado, perturbado, confuso.
BENCH s. banco (assento); bancada.
BEND v. dobrar.
BENDABLE adj. flexível.
BENEATH prep. abaixo de, debaixo de, inferior a / adv. debaixo.
BENEFACTOR s. benfeitor.
BENEFACTRESS s. benfeitora.
BENEFICENCE s. beneficência.
BENEFICENT adj. beneficente.
BENEFICIAL adj. benéfico, proveitoso.
BENEFICIARY s. beneficiário.
BENEFIT s. benefício, auxílio / v. beneficiar.
BENEVOLENCE s. benevolência.
BENEVOLENT adj. benévolo, bondoso.
BENIGN adj. benigno, bondoso; gentil.
BENT s. inclinação / adj. inclinado.
BEQUEST s. legado.
BEREAVE v. privar de; roubar.
BEREAVED adj. de luto.
BERET s. boina.
BERGAMOT s. tangerina, bergamota.
BERLIN s. Berlim.
BERM s. acostamento; margem de um canal.
BERRY s. baga, fruto; semente, grão.
BERSERK adj. frenético, furioso / s. guerreiro nórdico.
BERTH v. atracar, ancorar / s. beliche (navio); cabine (trem); ancoradouro.
BESCREEN v. cobrir, ocultar, esconder.
BESEECH v. implorar, suplicar.
BESET v. atacar, assaltar.
BESIDE prep. junto de, ao lado de.
BESIDES prep. além de; exceto / adv. além disso.
BESIEGE v. sitiar; assediar.

BESPEAK v. indicar, testemunhar.
BEST adj. melhor / s. o melhor, o máximo.
BESTIAL adj. bestial, animal.
BESTIALITY s. bestialidade.
BESTIARY s. bestiário.
BEST MAN s. padrinho de casamento.
BESTOW v. outorgar, entregar; conceder.
BESTSELLER adj. best-seller.
BESTSELLING adj. grande sucesso.
BET v. apostar / s. aposta.
BETHINK v. refletir, considerar.
BETRAY v. trair.
BETRAYAL s. traição.
BETRAYER s. traidor.
BETTER adj. melhor / v. melhorar.
BETTERMENT s. benfeitoria, melhoria.
BETTING s. aposta.
BETTING SHOP s. casa de apostas.
BETTOR s. jogador, apostador.
BETWEEN prep. entre / adv. no meio de dois.
BEVERAGE s. bebida.
BEVY s. bando, rebanho.
BEWARE v. ter cuidado.
BEWILDER v. desnortear, confundir, desorientar.
BEWILDERED adj. atordoado, confuso.
BEWILDERING adj. desconcertante; desorientador.
BEWITCH v. encantar, enfeitiçar.
BEWITCHING adj. encantador, sedutor; fascinante.
BEWITCHMENT s. feitiço, encantamento.
BEWRAY v. trair, revelar (segredo).
BEYOND prep. além de / adv. além.
BEYONDNATURE s. sobrenatural.
BIANNUAL adj. bienal, bianual.
BIAS s. viés; parcialidade.
BIASED adj. preconceituoso, parcial, tendencioso.
BIB s. babador.
BIBLE s. Bíblia.
BIBLICAL adj. bíblico.
BIBLIOGRAPHIC adj. bibliográfico.
BIBLIOGRAPHY s. bibliografia.
BIBLIOPHILE s. bibliófilo.
BICARBONATE s. bicarbonato.
BICENTENARY s. bicentenário.
BICENTENNIAL adj. bicentenário.
BICEP s. bíceps.
BICKER v. brigar, disputar / s. briga, contenda.
BICKERING s. disputa, rixa.
BICYCLE s. bicicleta.
BICYCLIST s. ciclista.
BID s. lance; oferta; proposta / v. oferecer; propor.
BIDDABLE adj. dócil, obediente.
BIDDER s. licitante, arrematante.
BIDDING s. licitação; comando; ordem.
BIDE v. viver, residir; aguardar, esperar.
BIDET s. bidê.
BIFOCAL adj. bifocal.
BIFOCALS s. óculos bifocais.
BIFURCATE v. bifurcar.
BIFURCATION s. bifurcação.
BIG adj. grande; volumoso.
BIGAMIST s. bígamo.
BIGAMY s. bigamia.
BIG DIPPER s. montanha-russa.
BIGGEST adj. maior; superior.
BIG-HEADED adj. metido, convencido.
BIG-HEARTED adj. generoso, bondoso; gentil.
BIGMOUTH s. boca grande, bocudo; tagarela.
BIGOT s. fanático.
BIGOTED adj. intolerante, fanático.
BIGOTRY s. intolerância; fanatismo.
BIG TOE s. dedão (pé).
BIG TOP s. tenda de circo.
BIJOU s. bijuteria.
BIKE s. bicicleta.
BIKER s. ciclista.
BIKINI s. biquíni.
BILATERAL adj. bilateral.
BILE s. bílis; fel.
BILINGUAL adj. bilíngue.
BILINGUISM s. bilinguismo.
BILL s. conta, fatura; bico (trabalho informal).
BILLBOARD s. quadro para cartazes; outdoor.
BILLET s. alojamento, aquartelamento; boleto.
BILLIARDS s. bilhar / adj. de bilhar.
BILLION s. bilhão.
BILLIONAIRE s. bilionário.
BIMBO s. oportunista.
BIN s. caixa, lata; cesto de lixo.
BINARY s. binário / adj. binário.
BIND v. amarrar, ligar, atar / s. faixa, cinta, atadura.
BINDER s. amarrador; fichário; encadernador; fita, tira.
BINDING s. ligação; amarração / adj. que liga, amarra.
BINGE s. bebedeira; farra.

BINGO s. bingo / *interj.* é isso aí.
BINOCULARS s. binóculos.
BIOCHEMICAL *adj.* bioquímico.
BIOCHEMIST s. bioquímico.
BIOCHEMISTRY s. bioquímica.
BIODEGRADABLE *adj.* biodegradável.
BIODIVERSITY s. biodiversidade.
BIOENGINEERING s. bioengenharia.
BIOETHICS s. bioética.
BIOGRAPHER s. biógrafo, biografista.
BIOGRAPHICAL *adj.* biográfico.
BIOGRAPHY s. biografia.
BIOHAZARD *adj.* risco biológico.
BIOLOGIC *adj.* biológico.
BIOLOGIST s. biologista, biólogo.
BIOLOGY s. biologia.
BIOMASS s. biomassa.
BIONIC *adj.* biônico.
BIOPIC s. filme biográfico.
BIOPSY s. biópsia.
BIORHYTHM s. biorritmo.
BIOSPHERE s. biosfera.
BIOTECHNOLOGICAL *adj.* biotecnológico.
BIOTECHNOLOGY s. biotecnologia.
BIPED s. bípede.
BIPOLAR *adj.* bipolar.
BIRCH s. bétula (árvore).
BIRD s. pássaro, ave.
BIRDCAGE s. gaiola.
BIRDER s. observador de pássaros.
BIRDHOUSE s. casinha de pássaro.
BIRDSEED s. alpiste.
BIRDSONG s. canto de passarinho.
BIRDWATCHER s. ornitófilo; observador de pássaros.
BIRO s. esferográfica.
BIRTH s. nascimento; parto, nascença.
BIRTHCAKE s. bolo de aniversário.
BIRTHDAY s. aniversário (data do nascimento).
BIRTHMARK s. marca de nascença.
BIRTHPLACE s. local do nascimento; naturalidade.
BIRTHRATE s. taxa de natalidade.
BIRTHSTONE s. pedra da sorte.
BISCUIT s. biscoito, bolacha.
BISECT v. dividir ao meio; bifurcar.
BISECTION s. bifurcação.
BISEXUAL s. bissexual / *adj.* bissexual.
BISEXUALITY s. bissexualidade.
BISHOP s. bispo (igreja e xadrez).

BISON s. bisão, búfalo.
BISTRO s. bistrô.
BIT s. pedaço; pitada; partícula.
BITCH s. cadela; cachorra.
BITE s. mordida; picada / v. morder.
BITER s. mordedor.
BITING *adj.* cortante, mordaz.
BITTER *adj.* amargo.
BITTERLY *adv.* amargamente; veementemente.
BITTERNESS s. rancor, mágoa, amargura.
BITTERSWEET *adj.* agridoce.
BITTER-TASTING s. gosto amargo; amargura.
BITUMEN s. betume; asfalto.
BIWEEKLY *adv.* quinzenalmente / *adj.* quinzenal.
BIZ *abrev.* negócio.
BIZARRE *adj.* bizarro.
BLAB v. tagarelar, falar muito / s. tagarelice, tagarela.
BLABBER s. tagarela.
BLACK *adj.* preto, negro / s. preto, negro.
BLACKBERRY s. amora silvestre.
BLACKBOARD s. lousa.
BLACKEN v. denegrir, difamar; pretejar.
BLACKLIST v. pôr na lista negra / s. lista negra.
BLACKMAIL s. chantagem, extorsão / v. chantagear, extorquir.
BLACKNESS s. negridão, negrura; escuridão.
BLACKOUT s. apagão, escurecimento; blecaute.
BLACK PEPPER s. pimenta-do-reino.
BLACK SHEEP s. ovelha negra.
BLACKSMITH s. ferreiro.
BLACKTOP s. asfalto.
BLADDER s. bexiga (órgão).
BLADE s. lâmina.
BLAG s. lábia, manha / v. convencer.
BLAH s. blá-blá-blá.
BLAME s. culpa / v. culpar.
BLAMELESS *adj.* inocente, sem culpa.
BLAMEWORTHY *adj.* culpável; censurável.
BLAND *adj.* brando, suave; insosso.
BLANK s. espaço vazio, em branco / *adj.* em branco, vago.
BLANK CHEQUE s. cheque em branco.
BLANKET s. cobertor, manta de lã / v. cobrir por completo.

BLANKLY *adv.* inexpressivamente; vagamente.
BLANKNESS *s.* brancura, claridade.
BLASPHEME *v.* blasfemar.
BLASPHEMOUS *adj.* blasfemo; desrespeitoso.
BLASPHEMY *s.* blasfêmia.
BLAST *s.* rajada de vento; estrondo, explosão / *interj.* droga!
BLASTING *adj.* destruidor, destrutivo / *s.* explosão.
BLATANT *adj.* descarado, barulhento, ruidoso.
BLATANTLY *adv.* descaradamente.
BLAZE *s.* fogo; labareda; chama / *v.* arder; resplandecer.
BLAZER *s.* casaco esportivo, jaqueta.
BLAZING *adj.* rápido, acelerado; flamejante.
BLAZON *v.* ostentar, exibir / *s.* brasão.
BLEACH *s.* água sanitária / *v.* branquear, alvejar.
BLEACHED *adj.* oxigenado; branqueado.
BLEACHERS *s.* arquibancada descoberta.
BLEAK *adj.* sombrio, desolado, deserto.
BLEAKNESS *s.* desolação, solidão; desamparo.
BLEAT *v.* balir (carneiro, bode).
BLEED *v.* sangrar.
BLEEDING *adj.* sangrento.
BLEEDING HEART *s.* pessoa boa, humanitário.
BLEEP *s.* bipe / *v.* apitar, emitir som.
BLEMISH *s.* mancha; marca; defeito / *v.* manchar, sujar, desfigurar.
BLEND *s.* mistura / *v.* misturar.
BLENDER *s.* liquidificador.
BLENDING *s.* combinação; mistura.
BLESS *v.* abençoar; benzer; glorificar.
BLESSED *adj.* sagrado, santificado, abençoado.
BLESSING *s.* bênção, graça divina.
BLIGHT *v.* fazer secar (planta), arruinar / *s.* ferrugem; inseto ou pulgão.
BLIMEY *interj.* caramba! nossa!
BLIND *adj.* cego / *v.* cegar, encobrir / *s.* cortina, persiana.
BLINDED *adj.* cego.
BLINDFOLD *v.* vendar, tapar (os olhos) / *s.* venda / *adj.* vendado.
BLINDING *adj.* cegante, ofuscante / *s.* cegueira.
BLINDLY *adv.* às cegas, cegamente.
BLINDNESS *s.* cegueira; ignorância.

BLINDSIDE *s.* ponto cego / *v.* pegar de surpresa.
BLINK *v.* piscar / *s.* piscadela.
BLINKER *s.* pisca-pisca; farol.
BLINKING *adj.* piscante.
BLISS *s.* felicidade, alegria, êxtase.
BLISSFUL *adj.* feliz; bem-aventurado.
BLISSFULLY *adv.* alegremente; extasiadamente.
BLISTER *s.* bolha; vesícula / *v.* empolar, inchar.
BLISTERING *adj.* acelerado; muito quente.
BLITHE *adj.* alegre, jovial.
BLITHELY *adv.* contentemente, alegremente.
BLITZ *s.* bombardeio; ataque relâmpago, repentino.
BLITZKRIEG *s.* ataque relâmpago.
BLIZZARD *s.* nevasca; temporal com neve e frio.
BLOAT *v.* inchar / *s.* inchaço, inchação.
BLOATED *adj.* inchado.
BLOB *s.* gota, bolha.
BLOC *s.* coligação política; bloco.
BLOCK *s.* bloco; quadra, quarteirão / *v.* obstruir, bloquear.
BLOCKADE *s.* bloqueio / *v.* bloquear.
BLOCKAGE *s.* obstrução; bloqueio; impedimento.
BLOCKBUSTER *s.* sucesso de bilheteria.
BLOCKHEAD *s.* cabeça-dura; lerdo, tolo.
BLOCK LETTER *s.* letra de forma.
BLOG *s.* diário eletrônico; blogue.
BLOGGER *s.* blogueiro.
BLOKE *s.* cara, sujeito.
BLOND *adj.* claro, louro / *s.* claro, louro.
BLONDE *adj. m.q.* blond.
BLOOD *s.* sangue.
BLOODBANK *s.* banco de sangue.
BLOODBATH *s.* massacre; banho de sangue.
BLOODCURDLING *adj.* horripilante.
BLOODHOUND *s.* cão de caça; detetive, espião.
BLOODLINE *s.* linhagem, estirpe.
BLOOD RELATIVE *s.* parente consanguíneo.
BLOODSHED *s.* matança, carnificina.
BLOODSTAIN *s.* mancha de sangue.
BLOODSTREAM *s.* corrente sanguínea.
BLOODTHIRSTY *adj.* sanguinário, cruel.
BLOODY *adj.* sangrento / *v.* sangrar, fazer sangrar.
BLOOM *s.* flor / *v.* florescer.

BLOOMER s. gafe, mancada; vacilo.
BLOOMING adj. florido; viçoso, exuberante.
BLOSSOM s. florescência / v. florescer, florir.
BLOT s. borrão de tinta, mancha / v. borrar, rasurar.
BLOTCHY adj. manchado.
BLOTTER s. mata-borrão.
BLOTTING PAPER s. papel mata-borrão.
BLOUSE s. blusa.
BLOW v. soprar / s. golpe; soco; florescência.
BLOWER s. soprador (máquina para limpar folhas).
BLOWING s. sopro, assopro.
BLOW-UP s. explosão.
BLUE adj. azul; deprimido, triste / s. azul.
BLUE-BLOODED adj. sangue azul; rico, metido.
BLUE-COLLAR s. operário; peão.
BLUES s. blues (gênero musical).
BLUFF v. blefar, enganar / s. blefe; logro.
BLUNDER s. gafe, asneira / v. cometer uma gafe, errar.
BLUNT adj. cego, sem corte (faca); obtuso.
BLUNTNESS s. aspereza, rudeza.
BLUR s. borrão; nódoa; falta de clareza / v. embaçar.
BLURB s. sinopse; resumo; sumário.
BLURRED adj. confuso, embaçado.
BLURT OUT v. falar sem pensar.
BLUSH v. corar / s. rubor.
BLUSHER s. ruge.
BLUSHING adj. vermelho, corado.
BLUSTER s. tormenta / v. vangloriar-se.
BLUSTERING adj. fanfarrão; fanfarrona; estrondoso.
BLUSTERY adj. ventoso, tempestuoso.
BO abrev. body odor (cê-cê, sovaqueira).
BOAR s. javali; porco não castrado.
BOARD s. quadro de avisos; tábua; prancha.
BOARDING adj. de embarque.
BOARDROOM s. sala de reunião.
BOARDWALK s. passadiço, calçadão.
BOAST v. gabar-se / s. ostentação.
BOASTER s. convencido, aquele que se vangloria.
BOASTING adj. vanglorioso.
BOAT s. bote, barco.
BOATER s. chapéu de palha.
BOATHOUSE s. garagem de barcos.
BOATING TRIP s. viagem de barco.
BOATMAN s. barqueiro; remador.
BOBBING s. carretel, bobina.
BOBBY s. policial, tira (coloquial).
BOBSLEIGH s. trenó duplo / v. andar de trenó.
BOCCIE s. bocha.
BODILY adj. corporal / adv. à força.
BODY s. corpo; cadáver.
BODYBUILDER s. halterofilista.
BODYBUILDING s. musculação.
BODYGUARD s. guarda-costas.
BODYWORK s. lataria, carroceria de automóvel.
BOG s. pântano, brejo / v. atolar.
BOGEY s. meleca (de nariz).
BOGEYMAN s. bicho papão; cuca.
BOGUS adj. falso, adulterado / s. falsificação, adulteração.
BOHEMIAN adj. boêmio / s. boêmio.
BOIL v. ferver / s. ebulição, fervura; furúnculo, tumor.
BOILER s. caldeira.
BOILERMAKER s. caldeireiro.
BOILERPLATE s. chapa de caldeira.
BOILER SUIT s. macacão.
BOILING adj. fervente.
BOISTEROUS adj. tumultuoso, impetuoso; rude.
BOLD adj. corajoso, valente; atrevido; nítido; negrito (tipografia).
BOLDFACE s. negrito.
BOLDLY adv. ousadamente; audaciosamente.
BOLDNESS s. coragem, ousadia; atrevimento.
BOLIVIA s. Bolívia.
BOLL s. casulo, cápsula.
BOLT s. trinco; pino; parafuso; ferrolho.
BOLUS s. bolo alimentar.
BOMB s. bomba / v. bombardear.
BOMBARD v. bombardear.
BOMBARDIER s. artilheiro, bombardeiro.
BOMBARDMENT s. bombardeio; bombardeamento.
BOMBASTIC adj. bombástico.
BOMBER s. bombardeio; piloto de bombardeio.
BOMBING s. ataque com bombas.
BOMBSHELL s. bomba, granada explosiva; mulherão.
BONA FIDE adj. genuíno, legítimo / adv. de boa fé.
BONBON s. bombom.

BOND *s.* compromisso; vínculo; bônus; título / *v.* unir, ligar.
BONDAGE *s.* escravidão, servidão.
BONDHOLDER *s.* portador de um título.
BONDING *s.* laço.
BONE *s.* osso; chifre; espinha de peixe / *v.* desossar.
BONE-IDLE *adj.* extremamente preguiçoso.
BONFIRE *s.* fogueira.
BONNET *s.* capô; touca usada por mulheres.
BONNY *adj.* galante, sadio; formoso.
BONUS *s.* bônus, bonificação; bênção.
BONY *adj.* ossudo.
BOO *v.* vaiar / *s.* vaia / *interj.* uh!
BOOBY-TRAP *s.* armadilha; carga explosiva.
BOOK *s.* livro / *v.* reservar, registrar.
BOOKABLE *adj.* reservável.
BOOKCASE *s.* estante.
BOOKING *s.* reserva.
BOOKING AGENT *s.* agente de reservas.
BOOKING OFFICE *s.* bilheteria.
BOOKKEEPER *s.* guarda-livros.
BOOKKEEPING *s.* contabilidade.
BOOKLET *s.* folheto, livreto, apostila.
BOOKMAKER *s.* agenciador de apostas.
BOOKMAN *s.* livreiro; estudioso.
BOOKMARK *s.* marcador de páginas.
BOOK REVIEW *s.* crítica literária.
BOOKSELLER *s.* livreiro, vendedor de livros.
BOOKSHELF *s.* prateleira para livros.
BOOKSHOP *s.* m.q. bookstore.
BOOKSTALL *s.* banca de livros.
BOOKSTORE *s.* livraria.
BOOKWORM *s.* traça, cupim.
BOOM *s.* barulho; estrondo / *v.* retumbar.
BOON *s.* benefício; bênção.
BOOST *s.* estímulo, aumento, impulso / *v.* estimular, impulsionar, aumentar.
BOOSTER *s.* propugnador; dínamo.
BOOT *v.* carregar (coloquial) / *s.* bota; vantagem.
BOOTBLACK *s.* engraxate.
BOOTH *s.* barraca, tenda; cabine.
BOOTLEG *s.* contrabando, pirata / *adj.* contrabando, pirata / *v.* piratear, contrabandear.
BOOTLEGGER *s.* contrabandista, muambeiro.
BOOTLESS *adj.* descalço; inútil.
BOOTMAKER *s.* sapateiro.
BOOTY *s.* saque; pilhagem.

BOOZE *s.* bebida alcoólica; bebedeira.
BORDER *s.* margem, borda; fronteira, limite / *v.* limitar-se com.
BORDERLAND *s.* região fronteiriça.
BORDERLINE *adj.* fronteiriço / *s.* linha divisória.
BORE *v.* entediar; perfurar (buraco) / *s.* chato; buraco.
BORED *adj.* entediado, chateado.
BOREDOM *s.* tédio, enfado, aborrecimento.
BORESOME *adj.* cansativo, enfadonho.
BORING *adj.* chato, enfadonho / *s.* perfuração, sondagem.
BORN *adj.* nascido.
BORNE *adj.* transportado, carregado.
BOROUGH *s.* município; distrito, bairro.
BORROW *v.* pedir algo emprestado / *s.* empréstimo.
BORROWER *s.* mutuário; quem pede emprestado.
BORROWING *s.* empréstimo.
BOSOM *s.* peito.
BOSOM FRIEND *s.* amigo íntimo.
BOSS *s.* chefe, patrão / *v.* mandar, dirigir, controlar.
BOSSY *adj.* mandão, dominante.
BOSUN *s.* contramestre (barco ou navio).
BOTANIC *adj.* botânico.
BOTANIST *s.* botânico.
BOTANY *s.* botânica.
BOTCH *v.* estropiar, estragar / *s.* remendo malfeito.
BOTH *adj.* ambos / *pron.* ambos / *conj.* não só, tanto que.
BOTHER *v.* atrapalhar, incomodar; preocupar / *s.* preocupação; incômodo.
BOTHERSOME *adj.* aborrecido, amolante.
BOTTLE *s.* garrafa / *v.* engarrafar.
BOTTLENECK *s.* gargalo de garrafa; passagem estreita.
BOTTLE NOSE *s.* nariz vermelho.
BOTTLE OPENER *s.* abridor de garrafas.
BOTTOM *s.* fundo; parte mais baixa.
BOTTOMLESS *adj.* ilimitado; sem fundo.
BOTULISM *s.* botulismo.
BOUGH *s.* ramo; galho de árvore.
BOULDER *s.* pedra grande, rocha.
BOULEVARD *s.* bulevar; rua, avenida.
BOUNCE *v.* saltar, quicar; ser devolvido / *s.* salto, pulo.

BOUND s. pulo / v. pular / adj. com destino a.
BOUNDARY s. fronteira, limite.
BOUNDLESS adj. ilimitado, sem limites, infinito.
BOUQUET s. ramalhete, buquê; aroma de vinho, fragrância.
BOURGEOIS adj. burguês, da classe média / s. burguês.
BOURGEOISIE s. burguesia.
BOURSE s. bolsa de valores.
BOUT s. ataque, combate.
BOUTIQUE s. butique.
BOVINE s. bovino / adj. bovino.
BOW s. arco (flechas); reverência / v. fazer reverência, curvar-se.
BOWEL s. intestino.
BOWER s. caramanchão.
BOWL s. tigela, bacia; boliche / v. arremessar a bola.
BOWLEGGED adj. de pernas tortas.
BOWLER s. lançador, arremessador (críquete).
BOWLING s. jogo de boliche; críquete.
BOWLING ALLEY s. pista de boliche.
BOWLING BALL s. bola de boliche.
BOWLING-GREEN s. gramado (críquete).
BOWLS s. jogo de bolas; tigela, bacia.
BOWMAN s. arqueiro.
BOW-TIE s. gravata-borboleta.
BOX s. caixa; urna / v. encaixotar; boxear.
BOXCAR s. vagão fechado.
BOXED adj. encaixado.
BOXER s. boxeador; samba-canção; boxer (raça de cachorro).
BOXING s. pugilismo, boxe.
BOY s. menino, moço, rapaz.
BOYCOTT s. boicote / v. boicotar.
BOYFRIEND s. namorado.
BOYHOOD s. juventude, meninice.
BOYISH adj. jovial, pueril, infantil.
BOZO s. bobo, tolo; idiota.
BRA s. sutiã.
BRACE s. aparelho odontológico; braçadeira / v. suportar, apoiar; fixar.
BRACELET s. pulseira, bracelete.
BRACING adj. tonificante, fortificante / s. amarração, suporte, esteio.
BRACKEN s. samambaia.
BRACKET s. suporte; parêntese.
BRAG v. gabar-se.

BRAID s. trança de cabelo; cadarço / v. trançar, entrelaçar.
BRAILLE s. braile.
BRAIN s. cérebro, miolo; inteligência.
BRAINCHILD s. ideia, obra.
BRAIN-FAG s. cansaço cerebral.
BRAINLESS adj. sem cérebro, desmiolado.
BRAINPOWER s. inteligência; intelectualidade.
BRAINSTORM v. pensar, inspirar / s. inspiração, ideia.
BRAINWASHING s. lavagem cerebral.
BRAINWAVE s. inspiração; onda cerebral.
BRAINY adj. inteligente, esperto.
BRAISE v. refogar, guisar.
BRAKE v. frear, brecar / s. freio, breque.
BRAKING s. freada; frenagem.
BRAN s. farelo.
BRANCH s. galho; ramo de árvore; filial.
BRANCH BANK s. filial de banco; agência bancária.
BRAND s. marca de fábrica, marca registrada / v. marcar (gado).
BRANDED adj. marcado, rotulado.
BRANDER s. marcador; gerente de marca.
BRANDISH v. brandir, ostentar.
BRAND-NEW adj. novinho em folha.
BRANDY s. conhaque.
BRASH adj. frágil, quebradiço; grosseiro, impetuoso / s. indisposição, mal-estar.
BRASILIA s. Brasília.
BRASS s. latão, metal.
BRASSARD s. distintivo, emblema.
BRASSBAND s. banda de sopro.
BRAT s. pirralho, fedelho.
BRATTY adj. levado, danado; travesso.
BRAVADO s. bravata, desafio.
BRAVE adj. valente, corajoso / s. bravo (valente) / v. desafiar.
BRAVERY s. coragem, bravura.
BRAWL s. disputa, rixa, briga / v. brigar.
BRAWLER s. brigão.
BRAWN s. musculatura, vigor.
BRAWNY adj. musculoso, vigoroso.
BRAY v. zurrar / s. zurro, ornejo.
BRAZE v. soldar.
BRAZEN adj. descarado, atrevido; de latão / v. tornar atrevido.
BRAZIER s. caldeireiro; braseiro.
BRAZIL s. Brasil.
BRAZILIAN adj. brasileiro.
BRAZIL NUT s. castanha-do-pará.

BREACH s. brecha, abertura; ruptura, quebra, violação.
BREAD s. pão.
BREAD BIN s. caixa de pão.
BREADCRUMB s. migalha de pão.
BREADTH s. largura, amplitude.
BREADWINNER s. arrimo de família, ganha-pão.
BREAK s. quebra; brecha; fenda; interrupção, intervalo / v. quebrar, fraturar.
BREAKDOWN s. avaria; colapso, crise (de nervos); análise.
BREAKFAST s. café da manhã.
BREAKING s. fratura; ruptura; bancarrota.
BREAKTHROUGH s. avanço; descoberta.
BREAK-UP s. decaída, colapso; separação; fim; dissolução.
BREAKWATER s. quebra-mar.
BREAST s. peito.
BREAST-FEED v. amamentar.
BREATH s. fôlego; hálito; respiração.
BREATHE v. respirar, inspirar, inalar.
BREATHING s. respiração; aspiração.
BREATHLESS adj. sem fôlego, ofegante; esbaforido.
BREATHTAKING adj. emocionante; excitante; extraordinário.
BREED v. criar (gado); reproduzir-se / s. raça, casta, criação.
BREEDING s. procriação, geração, parição.
BREEZE s. brisa, vento leve; pó de cinza.
BREEZY adj. vivaz, alegre; com brisa.
BREW s. bebida fervida ou fermentada / v. fazer cerveja, fazer bebida para fervura.
BREWER s. cervejeiro.
BREWERY s. cervejaria.
BREWING s. preparação; fábrica de bebida fermentada.
BRIBE s. suborno / v. subornar.
BRIBELESS adj. insubornável.
BRIBER s. subornador.
BRICK s. tijolo; bloco para construção.
BRICKBUILT adj. construído de tijolos.
BRICKEN s. feito de tijolo.
BRICKLAYER s. pedreiro.
BRICKWALL s. muro de tijolos.
BRIDAL adj. nupcial, de noiva / s. casamento.
BRIDE s. noiva.
BRIDEGROOM s. noivo.
BRIDESMAID s. dama de honra.
BRIDGE s. ponte.
BRIDLE s. freio (de cavalo), rédea / v. colocar rédea ou freio.
BRIEF adj. breve, curto / s. sumário, síntese / v. instruir.
BRIEFCASE s. pasta executiva.
BRIEFING s. instruções resumidas.
BRIEFLY adv. rapidamente, resumidamente, brevemente.
BRIGHT adj. claro; brilhante; inteligente.
BRIGHTEN v. iluminar; clarear.
BRIGHTEN UP v. animar-se.
BRIGHTNESS s. brilho, luminosidade; inteligência.
BRILLIANCE s. brilho, luminosidade, claridade.
BRILLIANT adj. brilhante, luminoso; genial / s. diamante; brilho, resplendor.
BRIM s. borda, aba.
BRIMLESS s. sem borda, sem aba.
BRINE s. salmoura / v. salgar.
BRING v. trazer.
BRINK s. beira de precipício.
BRISK adj. vigoroso, enérgico; ativo / v. estimular, animar.
BRISTLE s. cerda / v. eriçar, arrepiar.
BRITAIN s. Grã-Bretanha.
BRITISH adj. britânico / s. britânico.
BRITON adj. m.q. British.
BRITTLE adj. frágil, quebradiço, inseguro.
BROACH v. abordar um assunto; perfurar, espetar / s. furador, alargador, espeto.
BROAD adj. amplo, vasto; largo.
BROADCAST v. transmitir, difundir / s. transmissão.
BROCCOLI s. brócolis.
BROCHURE s. folheto, panfleto; brochura.
BROIL v. grelhar.
BROKE adj. sem dinheiro, quebrado.
BROKEN adj. quebrado; partido.
BROKEN DOWN adj. desmoronado, decaído; deprimido.
BROKER s. corretor, agente, intermediário.
BROLLY s. guarda-chuva.
BRONCHITIS s. bronquite.
BRONZE s. bronze / v. bronzear-se.
BROOCH s. broche.
BROOD s. ninhada, filhotes; prole / v. chocar.
BROODING adj. taciturno, pensativo.
BROOK s. riacho, córrego / v. tolerar, sofrer, aguentar.
BROOM s. vassoura / v. varrer.

BROOMSTICK s. cabo da vassoura.
BROTH s. caldo, sopa.
BROTHEL s. bordel, prostíbulo.
BROTHER s. irmão; confrade; irmandade.
BROTHER-IN-LAW s. cunhado.
BROW s. fronte, testa; sobrancelha.
BROWN adj. castanho, marrom / s. castanho, marrom.
BROWNIE s. brownie; bandeirante (menina).
BROWN PAPER s. papel pardo, papel de embrulho.
BROWN SUGAR s. açúcar mascavo.
BROWSE v. pastar (gado); folhear / s. broto.
BRUISE s. hematoma, contusão, pisadura / v. contundir, machucar.
BRUNCH s. brunch (refeição que serve de café da manhã e almoço).
BRUNETTE adj. morena, de cabelo escuro / s. mulher de cabelo escuro.
BRUNT s. ímpeto; força.
BRUSH s. escova, escovão; pincel, brocha / v. escovar; varrer.
BRUSHWOOD s. lenha; mato; gravetos.
BRUSQUE adj. ríspido, brusco, rude.
BRUSSELS s. Bruxelas.
BRUSSELS SPROUTS s. couve-de-bruxelas.
BRUTAL adj. brutal, cruel.
BRUTE s. bruto; besta; animal irracional / adj. bruto, animalesco.
BRUTISHNESS s. brutalidade.
BUBBLE s. bolha, borbulha / v. borbulhar.
BUBBLE BATH s. banho de espuma.
BUBBLE GUM s. chiclete, goma de mascar.
BUCCOLIC adj. bucólico.
BUCK s. corça macho (animal); pulo; pinote; dólar (coloquial) / v. lutar contra, resistir.
BUCKET s. balde, tina / v. baldear.
BUCKLE s. fivela; curva, dobra / v. afivelar; dobrar, curvar.
BUD s. broto; botão de flor; origem / v. brotar, florescer.
BUDDHA s. Buda.
BUDDHISM s. budismo.
BUDDIHIST s. budista / adj. budista.
BUDDING adj. em ascensão, nascente, que está emergindo.
BUDDY s. companheiro, amigo; camarada.
BUDGE v. mover-se, mexer-se, sair do lugar.
BUDGET s. orçamento; receita; verba / v. orçar, planejar gastos.

BUFF adj. da cor do couro / s. couro de búfalo / v. polir com couro.
BUFFALO s. búfalo; bisão.
BUFFER s. para-choque; memória intermediária (informática).
BUFFET s. bufê; lanchonete; bofetada / v. esbofetear.
BUG s. inseto; bicho; erro, defeito, falha (informática); grampo, escuta.
BUGGY s. carrinho de bebê.
BUGLE s. corneta, clarim / v. tocar corneta ou clarim.
BUILD v. construir, edificar / s. estatura, constituição física.
BUILDING s. edifício, construção, estrutura.
BULB s. bulbo; lâmpada elétrica.
BULGARIA s. Bulgária.
BULGE s. bojo; protuberância / v. inchar; bojar.
BULK s. volume; tamanho.
BULK BUYING s. compra no atacado.
BULKY adj. volumoso; grande.
BULL s. touro.
BULL-CALF s. bezerro macho.
BULLDOG s. buldogue.
BULLDOZER s. escavadora; que intimida.
BULLET s. bala (revólver), projétil.
BULLETIN s. comunicado, boletim, publicação regular.
BULLET-PROOF adj. à prova de bala.
BULLFIGHT s. tourada.
BULLION s. barra de ouro ou prata; lingotes.
BULLOCK s. boi, bovino.
BULLRING s. arena.
BULL'S EYE s. no alvo, na mosca; tiro certeiro.
BULLY s. valentão / v. amedrontar, provocar, intimidar.
BUM s. nádegas / v. soar forte; zunir / adj. ordinário, vagabundo.
BUMP s. batida, baque, sacudida / v. bater contra.
BUMPER s. para-choque / adj. abundante.
BUMPER CAR s. carro de batida (parque de diversões).
BUMPTIOUS adj. presunçoso, arrogante, convencido.
BUMPY adj. acidentado, desigual; esburacado.
BUN s. pão doce; coque de cabelo, birote.
BUNCH s. grupo; cacho de fruta; ramalhete / v. agrupar-se.

BUNDLE s. embrulho, trouxa, maço / v. embrulhar, empacotar.
BUNGALOW s. chalé, bangalô.
BUNGLE v. estragar; fracassar, fazer malfeito.
BUNION s. joanete.
BUNK s. beliche; bobagem, besteira.
BUNKER s. abrigo subterrâneo, casamata.
BUNNY s. coelhinho.
BUOY s. boia.
BUOYANT adj. flutuante.
BURDEN s. carga, peso, encargo / v. sobrecarregar.
BUREAU s. escritório, repartição pública, agência; escrivaninha; cômoda.
BUREAUCRACY s. burocracia.
BURGLAR s. assaltante, arrombador.
BURGLARY s. assalto, arrombamento.
BURIAL s. enterro, sepultamento.
BURLY adj. robusto, corpulento.
BURMA s. Birmânia.
BURN v. queimar; acender; incinerar / s. queimadura; queimada.
BURNER s. bico de gás, maçarico, queimador.
BURNING adj. ardente / s. combustão, incêndio, queimadura.
BURROW s. toca / v. cavar, fazer uma toca.
BURSARY s. bolsa de estudos; tesouraria.
BURST v. arrebentar, estourar, explodir / s. rajada; estouro, rompimento.
BURST UP s. colapso.
BURY v. enterrar, sepultar.
BUS s. ônibus.
BUSH s. arbusto; mato, moita.
BUSHY adj. espesso, cerrado, frondoso.
BUSILY adv. atarefadamente.
BUSINESS s. negócio; trabalho; assunto, negócio.
BUSK v. fazer espetáculos de rua.
BUSKER s. artista de rua, músico ambulante.
BUS STOP s. ponto de ônibus.
BUST s. busto, peito (escultura) / adj. quebrado / v. estourar; quebrar.

BUSTER s. bebedeira; vento intenso.
BUSTLE s. animação, alvoroço / v. apressar-se, alvoroçar-se.
BUSTLING adj. movimentado.
BUSY adj. ocupado, atarefado, movimentado / v. ocupar-se com algo.
BUSYBODY adj. intrometido.
BUT conj. mas, porém / adv. apenas; exceto, além.
BUTCHER s. açougueiro; carniceiro / v. chacinar; abater.
BUTCHERY s. matadouro; carnificina.
BUTLER s. mordomo.
BUTT s. pancada, alvo; traseiro; ponta (cigarro).
BUTTER s. manteiga / v. untar; bajular.
BUTTERCUP s. botão-de-ouro.
BUTTERFLY s. borboleta.
BUTTERINE s. margarina.
BUTTOCK s. nádega, traseiro.
BUTTON s. botão / v. abotoar.
BUXOM adj. rechonchudo; robusta; curvilíneo.
BUY v. comprar / s. compra, aquisição.
BUYER s. comprador.
BUZZ s. zumbido, zunido; cochicho, rumor / v. zumbir; cochichar.
BUZZER s. cigarra (campainha), campainha elétrica.
BUZZWORD s. modismo, clichê, jargão.
BY prep. por; de; com; via; perto de, ao lado de; pelo.
BYE interj. até logo, tchau.
BY-ELECTION s. eleição suplementar.
BYGONE adj. passado, antigo.
BYPASS s. desvio, passagem secundária / v. contornar; evitar.
BYPRODUCT s. derivado.
BYSTANDER s. espectador, observador.
BYTE s. byte (informática).
BYWORD s. provérbio; lema; máxima.

Cc

C, c s. terceira letra do alfabeto inglês; dó (nota musical); representa o número 100 em algarismos romanos; centígrado (temperatura).
CAB s. táxi; cabine (de caminhão ou trem).
CABALLERO s. cavalheiro; montador de cavalo.
CABANA s. cabana, barraca.
CABARET s. cabaré.
CABBAGE s. repolho, couve / v. furtar, roubar.
CABIN s. cabana; camarote (náutica); cabine (aeronáutica).
CABINET s. gabinete; escritório.
CABINETMAKER s. marceneiro.
CABINETRY s. marcenaria.
CABLE s. cabo; amarra.
CABLE CAR s. bonde elétrico; teleférico.
CABLE TV s. tv a cabo.
CABRIOLET s. conversível; cabriolé (carruagem).
CACAO s. cacau.
CACHE s. esconderijo, estoque (alimentos) / v. esconder, ocultar; salvar.
CACKLE v. gargalhar; cacarejar; tagarelar / s. cacarejo; gargalhada; tagarelice.
CACOPHONY s. cacofonia; dissonância.
CACTUS s. cacto.
CADAVER s. cadáver.
CADDIE s. caddie, carregador (golfe).
CADDY s. carregador de tacos; caixa, lata ou cofre.
CADENCE s. cadência, ritmo (música).
CADET s. cadete; caçula; irmão mais novo.
CADGE v. mendigar, esmolar.
CAESAR s. César; imperador.
CAESAREAN s. cesariana.
CAFE s. café, restaurante.
CAFETERIA s. lanchonete, cantina.
CAFFEINE s. cafeína.
CAGE s. gaiola, jaula / v. engaiolar, enjaular.
CAGED adj. engaiolado.
CAGEY adj. cauteloso, cuidadoso.
CAGOULE s. casaco de náilon.
CAIRO s. Cairo (capital do Egito).
CAJOLE v. lisonjear, adular, bajular.
CAKE s. bolo; torta.

CALAMITY s. calamidade, catástrofe; desgraça.
CALCAREOUS adj. calcário.
CALCIFICATION s. calcificação.
CALCIFY v. calcificar.
CALCINE s. cinza mineral / v. calcinar.
CALCIUM s. cálcio.
CALCULATE v. calcular, fazer cálculos, avaliar.
CALCULATED adj. calculado.
CALCULATING adj. calculista, perspicaz.
CALCULATION s. cálculo, avaliação, cômputo.
CALCULATOR s. calculadora.
CALCULUS s. cálculo (matemática).
CALDERA s. caldeira, caldeirão.
CALENDAR s. calendário.
CALENDAR DAY s. data; dia útil.
CALENDARISE v. agendar, marcar no calendário.
CALF s. vitela; bezerro; barriga da perna, panturrilha.
CALFSKIN s. couro de bezerro.
CALIBER s. calibre.
CALIBRATE v. calibrar.
CALIBRATION s. calibração.
CALIBRATOR s. calibrador.
CALIBRE s. m.q. caliber.
CALIFORNIA s. Califórnia.
CALIPH s. califa.
CALL v. chamar, telefonar, convocar / s. chamada, visita, telefonema.
CALLBACK v. retorno; ligar de volta.
CALLBOX s. cabine telefônica, orelhão.
CALLER s. visitante; pessoa que chama ao telefone.
CALLIGRAPHER s. calígrafo.
CALLIGRAPHIC adj. caligráfico.
CALLIGRAPHY s. caligrafia.
CALLING s. tendência; ligação / adj. telefônico.
CALLING CARD s. cartão de visita.
CALLIOPE s. órgão a vapor.
CALLOUS adj. cruel, insensível; calejado; endurecido.
CALLOUSNESS s. calosidade; desumanidade, insensibilidade.
CALLOW adj. inexperiente, bisonho, imaturo.
CALLUS s. calo / v. calejar.

CALM s. calma, calmaria / adj. calmo / v. acalmar.
CALMING s. calma, calmaria / adj. calmante.
CALMLY adv. calmamente, sossegadamente.
CALMNESS s. calmaria, tranquilidade, sossego.
CALORIC adj. calórico.
CALORIE s. caloria.
CALORIFIC adj. calorífico.
CALVE v. parir, dar à luz (bezerro).
CALYPSO s. calipso (gênero musical).
CALYX s. cálice.
CAMARADERIE s. camaradagem.
CAMBODIA s. Camboja.
CAMCORDER s. filmadora; câmera digital.
CAMEL s. camelo.
CAMELOPARD s. girafa.
CAMERA s. máquina fotográfica.
CAMERAMAN s. cinegrafista.
CAMEROON s. Camarão (país africano).
CAMISOLE s. blusa, blusinha; corpete.
CAMOMILE s. camomila.
CAMOUFLAGE s. camuflagem / v. camuflar.
CAMP s. campo; acampamento / v. acampar.
CAMPAIGN s. campanha / v. fazer campanha.
CAMPAIGNER s. defensor; candidato.
CAMPANILE s. campanário.
CAMPER s. campista; indivíduo acampado.
CAMPFIRE s. fogueira.
CAMPGROUND s. local para acampar.
CAMPING s. acampamento.
CAMPSITE s. área de acampamento.
CAMPUS s. campus, cidade universitária.
CAMPY adj. ridículo, afetado.
CAN v. poder, ser capaz de; enlatar / s. lata.
CANADA s. Canadá.
CANADIAN s. canadense / adj. canadense.
CANAL s. canal.
CANARIES s. Ilhas Canárias.
CANARY s. canário (pássaro).
CANCEL v. cancelar, invalidar / s. cancelamento, revogação.
CANCELLATION s. cancelamento, anulação, supressão.
CANCER s. Câncer (signo); câncer, cancro.
CANCEROUS adj. cancinógeno; canceroso.
CANDELABRA s. candelabro, lustre.

CANDID *adj.* franco, sincero, ingênuo.
CANDIDA *s.* cândida.
CANDIDACY *s.* candidatura.
CANDIDATE *s.* candidato; aspirante.
CANDIDATURE *s.* candidatura.
CANDLE *s.* vela.
CANDLELIGHT *s.* luz de vela.
CANDLER *s.* fabricante de velas.
CANDLESTICK *s.* castiçal.
CANDLEWICK *s.* pavio, mecha; novelo.
CANDOUR *s.* franqueza, sinceridade.
CANDY *s.* doce, bala confeitada, bombom.
CANDYFLOSS *s.* algodão-doce.
CANE *s.* cana; bengala, vara; bambu.
CANINE *adj.* canino / *s.* cão.
CANISTER *s.* lata; vasilha.
CANKER *s.* úlcera, gangrena; cancro.
CANNABIS *s.* maconha.
CANNED *adj.* enlatado; em conserva.
CANNED-GOODS *s.* conservas, enlatados.
CANNERY *s.* fábrica de conservas.
CANNIBAL *s.* canibal.
CANNIBALISE *v.* canibalizar; praticar canibalismo.
CANNIBALISM *s.* canibalismo.
CANNIBALISTIC *adj.* canibal, canibalesco.
CANNING *s.* enlatado.
CANNING PROCESS *s.* processo de enlatar; enlatamento.
CANNON *s.* canhão.
CANNONBALL *s.* bala de canhão.
CANNON FOLDER *s.* bucha de canhão.
CANNY *adj.* astuto, engenhoso, sagaz.
CANOE *s.* canoa, piroga / *v.* navegar em canoa, remar em canoa.
CANOEING *s.* canoagem (esporte).
CANOEIST *s.* canoeiro, remador (canoa).
CANON *s.* cânone.
CANONICAL *adj.* canônico.
CANONISATION *s.* canonização.
CANONISE *v.* canonizar.
CANON LAW *s.* lei canônica, direito canônico.
CAN OPENER *s.* abridor de latas.
CANOPY *s.* cobertura, toldo.
CANTEEN *s.* cantina; cantil.
CANTICLE *s.* cântico.
CANVAS *s.* lona, tenda; quadro ou pintura a óleo.
CANVASS *v.* sondar; fazer campanha / *s.* exame minucioso.
CANVASSER *s.* angariador, cabo eleitoral.
CANVASSING *s.* angariação.
CANYON *s.* desfiladeiro, cânion.
CANYONING *s.* canyoning (esporte radical).
CAP *s.* gorro, boné, quepe; tampa / *v.* tampar; completar.
CAPABILITY *s.* capacidade; competência; aptidão.
CAPABLE *adj.* capaz; competente; apto.
CAPACITANCE *s.* capacitância.
CAPACITOR *s.* condensador; capacitor.
CAPACITY *s.* capacidade, aptidão.
CAPE *s.* capa; cabo, promontório.
CAPER *s.* alcaparra; cambalhota / *v.* saltar, brincar.
CAPILLARY *s.* capilar / *adj.* capilar.
CAPITAL *s.* capital; patrimônio, ganhos.
CAPITALISATION *s.* capitalização.
CAPITALISE *v.* capitalizar; iniciar com letra maiúscula.
CAPITALISM *s.* capitalismo.
CAPITALIST *s.* capitalista / *adj.* capitalista.
CAPITALISTIC *adj.* capitalista.
CAPITAL LETTER *s.* letra maiúscula, capitular.
CAPITATION *s.* capitação.
CAPITULATE *v.* capitular; render-se.
CAPITULATION *s.* capitulação.
CAPRICE *s.* capricho.
CAPRICIOUS *adj.* caprichoso, voluntarioso.
CAPRICORN *s.* Capricórnio (astrologia).
CAPSIZE *v.* virar, emborcar, capotar / *s.* capotagem.
CAPSULAR *adj.* capsular.
CAPSULE *s.* cápsula.
CAPTAIN *s.* capitão / *v.* capitanear, chefiar, comandar.
CAPTAINCY *s.* capitania.
CAPTION *s.* legenda (cinema, tv); captura, confisco.
CAPTIOUS *adj.* capcioso, ardiloso.
CAPTIVATE *v.* cativar, atrair.
CAPTIVATING *adj.* cativante.
CAPTIVE *s.* cativo, prisioneiro / *adj.* cativo, preso.
CAPTIVE AUDIENCE *s.* público cativo.
CAPTIVE MARKET *s.* monopólio.
CAPTIVE USE *s.* uso próprio.
CAPTIVITY *s.* cativeiro, prisão.
CAPTOR *s.* captor, apreensor.

CAPTURE v. prender, capturar / s. captura, aprisionamento.
CAR s. carro, automóvel.
CARAFE s. garrafa de mesa.
CARAMEL s. caramelo; bala de caramelo.
CARAMELISE v. caramelizar, caramelar.
CARAT s. quilate.
CARAVAN s. trailer (veículo); caravana.
CARBINE s. carabina, espingarda curta.
CARBOHYDRATE s. carboidrato.
CARBON s. carbono.
CARBONACEOUS adj. carbonífero, carbonoso.
CARBONATE v. carbonatar / s. carbonato.
CARBONATION s. carbonatação.
CARBONIFEROUS adj. carbonífero.
CARBONISE v. carbonizar; queimar.
CARBURETTOR s. carburador.
CARCASS s. carcaça; esqueleto.
CARCINOMA s. carcinoma, tumor maligno.
CARD s. cartão; carta de baralho; ficha.
CARDBOARD s. papelão; cartolina.
CARDHOLDER s. sócio; portador, titular.
CARDIAC adj. cardíaco.
CARDIGAN s. casaco de lã, cardigã.
CARDINAL adj. cardeal; cardinal / s. cardeal.
CARD INDEX s. fichário.
CARDIOLOGIST s. cardiologista.
CARDIOLOGY s. cardiologia.
CARDIOPULMONARY adj. cardiopulmonar.
CARDIOVASCULAR adj. cardiovascular.
CARE s. cuidado, cautela, precaução / v. importar-se com; cuidar de.
CAREER s. carreira, profissão / v. correr a toda velocidade.
CAREER FAIR s. feira de emprego.
CAREER FIELD s. campo profissional.
CAREER GOAL s. meta profissional.
CAREER PLAN s. plano de carreira.
CAREFREE adj. despreocupado, alegre, feliz.
CAREFUL adj. cuidadoso, cauteloso, meticuloso.
CAREFULLY adv. cuidadosamente.
CAREGIVER s. enfermeiro; cuidador.
CARELESS adj. descuidado, negligente, desleixado.
CARELESSNESS s. descuido, negligência, desatenção.
CARER s. cuidador; acompanhante.
CARESS v. acariciar / s. carícia, carinho.

CARETAKER s. zelador, vigia, porteiro.
CAREWORN adj. aflito(a), ansioso(a), preocupado(a)
CARGO s. carga, carregamento, frete.
CAR HIRE s. aluguel de carros.
CARIBBEAN s. Caribe; caraíba / adj. caribenho, caraíba.
CARICATURE s. caricatura.
CARIES s. cáries (dentária).
CARING adj. humanitário, afetuoso.
CARNAGE s. carnificina, massacre.
CARNAL adj. carnal, mundano, sexual.
CARNATION s. cravo / adj. vermelho, encarnado.
CARNAUBA s. carnaúba (cera).
CARNIVAL s. carnaval; folia, desfile.
CARNIVORE s. carnívoro.
CARNIVOROUS adj. carnívoro.
CAROUSEL s. carrossel; esteira rolante.
CARP s. carpa (peixe).
CAR PARK s. estacionamento.
CARPENTER s. carpinteiro.
CARPENTRY s. carpintaria.
CARPET s. tapete, carpete / v. atapetar.
CARPET SWEEPER s. limpador de tapetes.
CAR PHONE s. telefone de carro.
CARRIAGE s. carruagem; vagão ferroviário.
CARRIER s. transportadora; portador; mensageiro.
CARRIER BAG s. sacola.
CARRION s. carniça.
CARROT s. cenoura.
CARROT CAKE s. bolo de cenoura.
CARROT JUICE s. suco de cenoura.
CARRY v. levar, carregar, transportar.
CARRY ON v. seguir em frente; continuar.
CART s. carroça; carrinho de mão / v. transportar em carroça.
CARTEL s. cartel.
CARTER s. carreteiro, carroceiro.
CARTILAGE s. cartilagem.
CARTOGRAPHER s. cartógrafo.
CARTOGRAPHIC adj. cartográfico.
CARTOGRAPHY s. cartografia.
CARTON s. caixa; bandeja de ovos.
CARTOON s. desenho animado; história em quadrinhos; caricatura; papelão / v. fazer caricatura.
CARTOONIST s. cartunista.
CARTRIDGE s. cartucho; rolo de filme.

CARVE v. esculpir, entalhar.
CARVER s. escultor, entalhador.
CARVING s. entalhe; escultura.
CARVING KNIFE s. faca de trinchar.
CASCADE s. cascata, cachoeira.
CASE s. caso; causa judicial; estojo, caixa.
CASEBOOK s. livro de registro; folha clínica.
CASEIN s. caseína (proteína do leite).
CASH s. dinheiro (em espécie); pagamento à vista / v. descontar.
CASH CARD s. cartão de banco.
CASH DISPENSER s. caixa eletrônico.
CASHEW s. castanha de caju; cajueiro.
CASHIER s. caixa; operador de caixa.
CASHLESS adj. sem dinheiro.
CASHMERE s. caxemira (lã); caxemira (idioma).
CASH REGISTER s. caixa registradora.
CASING s. embalagem; cobertura; revestimento.
CASINO s. cassino.
CASK s. barril, tonel.
CASKET s. cofrezinho; porta-joias; caixinha.
CASSAVA s. mandioca.
CASSEROLE s. caçarola; panela.
CASSETTE s. fita cassete.
CASSETTE PLAYER s. toca-fitas.
CASSETTE RECORDER s. gravador.
CAST v. lançar, atirar / s. lance; elenco (teatro); molde.
CASTANET s. castanhola (instrumento musical).
CASTAWAY s. náufrago; pária / adj. rejeitado, inútil; náufrago.
CASTE s. casta; classe social.
CASTER s. roldana, rodízio.
CASTER SUGAR s. açúcar branco refinado, de confeiteiro.
CASTIGATE v. castigar, punir; repreender.
CASTING s. distribuição de papéis (teatro, cinema).
CASTING VOTE s. voto decisivo.
CAST IRON s. ferro fundido.
CASTLE s. castelo, fortaleza; torre.
CASTOR s. castor.
CASTOR OIL s. óleo de mamona.
CASTRATE v. castrar; capar.
CASTRATION s. castração.
CASTRATOR s. castrador.

CASUAL adj. informal, esportivo / s. trabalho temporário.
CASUALLY adv. casualmente, eventualmente.
CASUALTY s. vítima; acidente, desastre, infortúnio.
CAT s. gato.
CATACLYSM s. cataclismo; desastre social.
CATACLYSMIC adj. cataclísmico.
CATACOMB s. catacumba.
CATALOGUE s. catálogo / v. catalogar, classificar.
CATALOGUER s. catalogador.
CATALYSE v. catalisar.
CATALYSED adj. catalisado.
CATALYSIS s. catálise.
CATALYST s. catalisador.
CATALYTIC adj. catalítico.
CATAPULT s. catapulta; estilingue / v. catapultar.
CATARACT s. catarata, cachoeira.
CATARRH s. catarro
CATASTROPHE s. catástrofe.
CATASTROPHIC adj. catastrófico.
CATCH v. pegar, apanhar, prender; surpreender / s. captura, presa.
CATCHER s. receptor, apanhador.
CATCHING adj. contagioso, infeccioso; contagiante, cativante.
CATCHPHRASE s. bordão; slogan.
CATCHWORD s. chamada; deixa, frase feita.
CATCHY adj. sugestivo; atrativo.
CATECHISM s. catecismo.
CATECHIST s. catequista.
CATEGORICAL adj. categórico.
CATEGORISATION s. categorização.
CATEGORISE v. categorizar.
CATEGORY s. categoria, classe, série, grupo.
CATER v. abastecer, fornecer, suprir.
CATERER s. fornecedor (mantimentos); bufê.
CATERING s. abastecimento; bufê.
CATERING HALL s. refeitório; salão de festas.
CATERING TRUCK s. van de entrega (comida).
CATERPILLAR s. lagarta; esteira (de trator, tanque).
CATFISH s. peixe-gato; relacionamento virtual.
CATHARSIS s. catarse.

CATHEDRAL s. catedral.
CATHETER s. cateter.
CATHODE s. catódio, cátodo.
CATHODIC adj. catódico.
CATHOLIC adj. católico / s. católico.
CATHOLIC CHURCH s. Igreja Católica.
CATHOLICISM s. catolicismo.
CATHOLIC SCHOOL s. escola católica.
CATNAP s. soneca / v. tirar uma soneca.
CATTLE s. gado; rebanho.
CATTLE BREEDING s. pecuária; criação de gado.
CATTLEMAN s. vaqueiro.
CATTY adj. malévolo, maldoso; traiçoeiro.
CATWALK s. passarela.
CAUCASIAN s. caucasiano, caucásio / adj. caucasiano, caucásio.
CAUCUS s. comitê eleitoral, convenção de um partido político.
CAUDAL adj. caudal.
CAULDRON s. caldeirão.
CAULIFLOWER s. couve-flor.
CAUSAL adj. causal.
CAUSALITY s. causalidade.
CAUSATION s. causação.
CAUSATIVE adj. causativo, causador.
CAUSE s. causa, razão, origem / v. causar, originar.
CAUSTIC adj. cáustico.
CAUTION s. cautela; aviso / v. avisar, acautelar, advertir.
CAUTIOUS adj. cauteloso; prudente.
CAUTIOUSLY adv. cuidadosamente, cautelosamente.
CAVALCADE s. cavalgada.
CAVALIER s. cavaleiro / adj. espontâneo.
CAVALRY s. cavalaria.
CAVE s. caverna, gruta, toca / v. desabar; desistir.
CAVEMAN s. homem das cavernas, troglodita.
CAVERN s. caverna, gruta.
CAVERNOUS adj. cavernoso.
CAVIAR s. caviar.
CAVIL v. sofismar, cavilar / s. picuinha.
CAVITY s. cavidade; cárie.
CD abrev. CD.
CEASE v. cessar, terminar, parar; falecer.
CEASEFIRE s. cessar-fogo.
CEASELESS adj. incessante, contínuo.

CEDAR s. cedro.
CEDE v. ceder; renunciar.
CEILING s. teto, forro; ápice.
CELEBRANT s. celebrante, festejante.
CELEBRATE v. celebrar, festejar, comemorar.
CELEBRATED adj. célebre, famoso.
CELEBRATION s. celebração, comemoração.
CELEBRATORY adj. comemorativo, celebrativo.
CELEBRITY s. celebridade / adj. célebre.
CELERY s. aipo.
CELESTIAL adj. celestial.
CELIBACY s. celibato.
CELIBATE adj. celibatário.
CELL s. cela; célula; pilha.
CELLAR s. adega, celeiro, porão.
CELLIST s. violoncelista.
CELLO s. violoncelo.
CELLOPHANE s. celofane.
CELLOPHANE TAPE s. fita durex.
CELLPHONE s. telefone celular, celular.
CELLULAR adj. celular.
CELLULITE s. celulite.
CELLULOID s. celuloide / adj. celuloide.
CELSIUS s. Celsius (escala de temperatura).
CELT s. adj. celta.
CELTIC adj. m.q. celt.
CEMENT s. cimento, argamassa / v. cimentar, consolidar.
CEMENT MIXER s. betoneira, misturador (cimento).
CEMETERY s. cemitério.
CENSOR v. censurar / s. censor.
CENSORSHIP s. censura.
CENSURE v. criticar, repreender, censurar / s. crítica, repreensão.
CENSUS s. censo, recenseamento.
CENT s. cêntimo, centavo.
CENTAUR s. centauro (mitologia).
CENTENARY num. centenário / adj. centenário.
CENTENNIAL s. centenário / adj. centenário, secular.
CENTERFOLD s. página central (revista).
CENTERPIECE s. destaque, ponto central.
CENTIGRADE adj. centígrado.
CENTIMETER s. centímetro.
CENTIPEDE s. centopeia.

CENTRAL *adj.* central, principal.
CENTRAL HEATING *s.* aquecimento central.
CENTRALISATION *s.* centralização.
CENTRALISE *v.* centralizar.
CENTRALITY *s.* centralidade.
CENTRE *s.* centro, meio, núcleo / *v.* centrar, concentrar-se.
CENTRIFUGAL *adj.* centrífugo.
CENTRIFUGE *s.* centrífuga.
CENTRIST *s.* centrista.
CENTURION *s.* centurião.
CENTURY *s.* século.
CEPHALIC *adj.* cefálico.
CERAMIC *adj.* cerâmico / *s.* cerâmica.
CEREAL *s.* cereais / *adj.* cereal.
CEREAL BAR *s.* barra de cereais.
CEREAL BOWL *s.* tigela de cereal.
CEREBRAL *adj.* cerebral.
CEREBRUM *s.* cérebro.
CEREMONIAL *adj.* cerimonial.
CEREMONY *s.* cerimônia, solenidade.
CERISE *s.* cereja / *adj.* cereja.
CERTAIN *adj.* seguro, certo, evidente / *pron.* algum(ns).
CERTAINLY *adv.* certamente, seguramente; com certeza.
CERTAINTY *s.* certeza, segurança, convicção.
CERTIFICATE *s.* certidão, certificado, atestado, diploma.
CERTIFICATION *s.* certificação.
CERTIFIED *adj.* autorizado, certificado.
CERTIFIED MAIL *s.* encomenda registrada.
CERTIFY *v.* certificar, atestar, garantir.
CERVICAL *adj.* cervical.
CERVIX *s.* cerviz, nuca.
CESSATION *s.* cessação.
CESSION *s.* cessão.
CESSPOOL *s.* fossa, poço negro.
CHAFE *v.* roçar, atritar, friccionar / *s.* arranhão, esfoladura.
CHAGRIN *s.* desgosto, pesar, humilhação / *v.* afligir, vexar.
CHAIN *s.* corrente, cordilheira, cadeia / *v.* acorrentar; prender.
CHAINSAW *s.* motosserra.
CHAIN STORE *s.* sucursal, filial.
CHAIR *s.* cadeira; assento.
CHAIRMAN *s.* presidente (empresa, companhia).
CHAIRMANSHIP *s.* presidência.
CHAIRPERSON *s.* presidente, dirigente.
CHAIRWOMAN *s.* presidenta, dirigente.
CHALET *s.* chalé.
CHALICE *s.* cálice (religioso), taça.
CHALK *s.* giz, greda.
CHALKBOARD *s.* lousa; quadro.
CHALKY *adj.* calcário, esbranquiçado; de giz.
CHALLENGE *s.* desafio, provocação / *v.* desafiar, provocar.
CHALLENGER *s.* desafiador, provocador.
CHALLENGING *adj.* desafiante, desafiador, estimulante.
CHAMBER *s.* câmara, gabinete; compartimento.
CHAMELEON *s.* camaleão.
CHAMOIS *s.* camurça.
CHAMP *s.* campeão / *v.* mastigar, morder.
CHAMPAGNE *s.* champanhe.
CHAMPION *s.* campeão, vencedor / *v.* defender / *adj.* excelente, ótimo.
CHAMPIONSHIP *s.* campeonato, competição.
CHANCE *s.* oportunidade, possibilidade / *v.* arriscar a sorte.
CHANCEL *s.* capela-mor; presbitério.
CHANCELLOR *s.* chanceler; reitor.
CHANCERY *s.* chancelaria.
CHANDELIER *s.* lustre, candelabro.
CHANGE *v.* mudar, trocar / *s.* troca, mudança, troco (dinheiro).
CHANGEABLE *adj.* instável, mutável, inconstante.
CHANGE OVER *v.* permutar, trocar.
CHANGEOVER *s.* mudança; comutação.
CHANGING *adj.* variável, mutante / *s.* troca, mudança.
CHANNEL *s.* canal / *v.* canalizar.
CHANNELISATION *s.* canalização.
CHANNELISE *v.* canalizar, direcionar.
CHANT *s.* canto, cântico / *v.* cantar, entoar.
CHANTER *s.* cantor.
CHAOS *s.* caos; confusão.
CHAOTIC *adj.* caótico.
CHAP *s.* sujeito, cara; rachadura, fenda / *v.* rachar.
CHAPEL *s.* capela.
CHAPLAIN *s.* capelão.
CHAPLAINCE *s.* capelania.
CHAPPED *adj.* rachado.
CHAPTER *s.* capítulo.

CHAPTER HEADING s. título de capítulo.
CHAR v. tostar, queimar / s. carvão mineral.
CHARACTER s. caráter, personalidade; reputação; personagem.
CHARACTERISATION s. caracterização.
CHARACTERISE v. caracterizar, retratar.
CHARACTERISTIC adj. característico / s. traço, característica.
CHARACTERISTICALLY adv. caracteristicamente.
CHARADE s. charada.
CHARCOAL s. carvão vegetal.
CHARGE s. encargo; carga; acusação / v. carregar (bateria); acusar; cobrar.
CHARGEABLE adj. cobrável, carregável; acusável.
CHARGE ACCOUNT s. conta corrente.
CHARGE CARD s. cartão de débito.
CHARGED adj. carregado.
CHARGELESS adj. de graça, sem despesa.
CHARISMA s. carisma.
CHARISMATIC adj. carismático.
CHARITABLE adj. caridoso, bondoso, generoso.
CHARITY s. caridade; instituição de caridade.
CHARLADY s. diarista (mulher).
CHARLATAN s. charlatão; fraude.
CHARM s. charme, encanto / v. encantar, enfeitiçar.
CHARMED adj. encantado.
CHARMER s. sedutor, encantador.
CHARMING adj. encantador, gracioso, charmoso.
CHARRED adj. tostado, queimado.
CHART s. mapa, gráfico / v. traçar, mapear.
CHARTER s. alvará, licença; fretamento / v. fretar.
CHARTERED adj. fretado.
CHARTERED BUS s. ônibus fretado.
CHASE v. perseguir, caçar / s. perseguição, caçada.
CHASER s. perseguidor.
CHASM s. abismo, brecha, fenda na terra.
CHASSIS s. chassi.
CHASTE adj. casto, puro.
CHASTEN v. castigar, punir, açoitar.
CHASTENED adj. reprimido, castigado, punido.
CHASTISE v. castigar.
CHASTISEMENT s. reprimenda, correção.
CHASTITY s. castidade; modéstia.
CHAT v. conversar, tagarelar, bater papo / s. conversa, bate-papo.
CHATROOM s. sala de bate-papo (virtual).
CHAT SHOW s. programa de entrevistas.
CHATTER s. tagarelice, conversa fiada / v. tagarelar.
CHATTY adj. conversador, falador.
CHAUFFEUR s. chofer, motorista particular.
CHAUVINISM s. chauvinismo.
CHAUVINIST s. chauvinista; sexista.
CHAUVINISTIC adj. chauvinista, sexista.
CHEAP adj. barato, econômico; de má qualidade.
CHEAPEN v. degradar, rebaixar.
CHEAPLY adv. preço baixo; barato.
CHEAPNESS s. barateza; falta de qualidade.
CHEAPSKATE s. pão-duro, sovina.
CHEAT v. trapacear, enganar; colar (na prova) / s. trapaça.
CHEATER s. trapaceiro; enrolão.
CHECK v. verificar, conferir / s. inspeção, verificação; cheque.
CHECK BOOK s. talão de cheque.
CHECKED adj. marcado, checado.
CHECKERBOARD s. tabuleiro de damas.
CHECKING ACCOUNT s. conta corrente.
CHECKLIST s. lista; check-list.
CHECKMATE s. xeque-mate / v. derrotar.
CHECK UP v. verificar, conferir; exame médico rotineiro.
CHEEK s. bochecha, descaramento.
CHEEKILY adv. atrevidamente; insolentemente.
CHEEKY adj. insolente, atrevido.
CHEEP v. piar / s. pio, gorjeio.
CHEER v. aplaudir, alegrar-se / interj. saúde! / s. alegria, ânimo.
CHEERFUL adj. alegre, agradável, animado.
CHEERFULLY adv. alegremente, animadamente.
CHEERFULNESS s. alegria, satisfação, contentamento.
CHEERLEADER s. animador de torcida; líder de torcida.
CHEERLEADING s. animação de torcida.
CHEERLESS adj. triste, desanimado, melancólico.
CHEERS v. torcer; brindar / s. saúde! (brinde).

CHEESE s. queijo.
CHEESECAKE s. torta de queijo.
CHEESY adj. brega, cafona; de mau gosto.
CHEETAH s. chita, guepardo.
CHEF s. chefe de cozinha.
CHEMICAL adj. químico / s. produto químico.
CHEMISE s. camisola.
CHEMIST s. químico; farmacêutico.
CHEMISTRY s. química.
CHEMOTHERAPEUTIC adj. quimioterápico, quimioterapêutico.
CHEMOTHERAPY s. quimioterapia.
CHEQUE s. cheque.
CHEQUERED adj. acidentado.
CHERISH v. tratar com carinho, estimar.
CHERISHED adj. querido, estimado.
CHERRY s. cereja; cerejeira.
CHERRY-PICK v. manipular.
CHERUB s. querubim.
CHESS s. xadrez.
CHESSBOARD s. tabuleiro de xadrez.
CHEST s. peito, tórax; arca; baú.
CHESTNUT s. castanha; castanheira (árvore, madeira).
CHEST OF DRAWERS s. cômoda.
CHEW v. mastigar; remoer, ruminar.
CHEWER s. mastigador.
CHEWING GUM s. goma de mascar, chiclete.
CHEWY adj. alimento duro.
CHIC adj. elegante, chique.
CHICK s. pintinho; moça, menina.
CHICKEN s. galinha, frango.
CHICKENHEARTED adj. medroso, covarde.
CHICKENPOX s. catapora, varicela.
CHICKPEA s. grão-de-bico / adj. de grão-de-bico.
CHIDE v. ralhar / s. repreensão.
CHIEF s. chefe / adj. principal, superior.
CHIEF EXECUTIVE s. diretor geral.
CHIEFLY adv. principalmente, sobretudo.
CHIFFON s. fita.
CHILBLAIN s. frieira; micose.
CHILD s. criança; filho.
CHILD-FRIENDLY adj. próprio para crianças.
CHILDBIRTH s. parto; natal.
CHILDCARE s. assistência infantil.
CHILDHOOD s. infância, meninice.
CHILDISH adj. infantil, pueril; ingênuo, imaturo.
CHILDLESS adj. sem filho.

CHILDLIKE adj. pueril, infantil, inocente.
CHILDMINDER s. babá.
CHILDREN s. crianças, filhos.
CHILE s. Chile.
CHILEAN s. chileno.
CHILL s. friagem, frio; resfriado / v. congelar, esfriar, refrigerar.
CHILLI s. pimenta malagueta.
CHILLING adj. assustador.
CHILLY adj. frio.
CHIME s. carrilhão / v. soar, bater (sinos).
CHIMERA s. quimera (mitologia).
CHIMERIC adj. quimérico.
CHIMNEY s. chaminé.
CHIMPANZEE s. chimpanzé.
CHIN s. queixo.
CHINA s. louça, porcelana; China (país).
CHINATOWN s. distrito chinês.
CHINESE s. chinês / adj. chinês.
CHINK s. fresta, abertura.
CHIN UP v. erguer a cabeça; continuar.
CHIP s. chip; lasca, fragmento, pedaço.
CHIPBOARD s. papelão, compensado.
CHIPPER adj. esperto, animado; vivaz, ativo.
CHIPS s. batatas fritas.
CHIROPODIST s. pedicuro, quiropodista.
CHIROPODY s. quiropodia.
CHIRP v. piar, gorjear / s. gorjeio, cricri (grilo).
CHISEL s. formão, cinzel / v. cinzelar, talhar.
CHIT s. talão, bilhete; penhor.
CHITCHAT s. conversa fiada, mexerico.
CHIVALROUS adj. cavalheiresco; cavalheiro, galante.
CHIVALRY s. cavalheirismo, bravura.
CHIVE s. cebolinha, cebolinha verde.
CHLORIDE s. cloreto.
CHLORINATE v. clorar; tratar com cloro.
CHLORINATION s. cloração.
CHLORINE s. cloro, alvejante.
CHLORINE BLEACH s. água sanitária.
CHLOROFORM s. clorofórmio / v. cloroformizar.
CHLOROPHYLL s. clorofila.
CHOCK v. calçar, atravancar / s. calço, apoio, escora / adv. seguramente.
CHOCK-A-BLOCK adj. abarrotado, repleto.
CHOCOHOLIC s. chocólatra.
CHOCOLATE s. chocolate, bombom.
CHOICE s. escolha, opção / adj. de qualidade, seleto.

CHOIR s. coro, coral.
CHOIRBOY s. menino de coral, cantor.
CHOIR MASTER s. mestre de coro.
CHOKE v. engasgar; estrangular, asfixiar / s. sufocação, asfixia, estrangulação.
CHOKED adj. mudo; engasgado.
CHOKER s. gargantilha.
CHOKING s. sufocação, asfixia / adj. sufocante, asfixiante.
CHOLERA s. cólera.
CHOLESTEROL s. colesterol.
CHOMP v. mastigar fortemente.
CHOOSE v. escolher, preferir; decidir, resolver.
CHOOSER s. escolhedor; quem escolhe.
CHOOSY adj. exigente, difícil de contentar.
CHOP v. picar; cortar / s. golpe; mudança.
CHOPPER s. helicóptero; cutelo, machadinha.
CHOPPY adj. agitado, revolto.
CHOPSTICKS s. pauzinhos, palitos; hashi.
CHORAL adj. coral / s. coral.
CHORAL DIRECTOR s. maestro de coro.
CHORAL GROUP s. coro, coral.
CHORAL MUSIC s. música de coro.
CHORD s. acorde.
CHORE s. tarefa do cotidiano; tarefa, afazer.
CHOREOGRAPH v. coreografar.
CHOREOGRAPHER s. coreógrafo.
CHOREOGRAPHY s. coreografia.
CHORISTER s. corista.
CHORTLE v. casquinar, rir / s. riso, casquinada.
CHORUS s. coro; refrão.
CHOSEN adj. decidido, escolhido.
CHRISM s. crisma.
CHRIST s. Cristo, Jesus Cristo.
CHRISTEN v. batizar; dar nome.
CHRISTENDOM s. cristandade.
CHRISTENING s. batismo.
CHRISTIAN adj. cristão / s. cristão.
CHRISTIANITY s. Cristianismo, cristandade.
CHRISTIAN NAME s. nome de batismo, prenome.
CHRISTMAS s. Natal / adj. de Natal, natalino.
CHRISTMAS EVE s. véspera de Natal.
CHRISTMASTIME s. período natalino.
CHRISTMAS TREE s. árvore de Natal.
CHROMATIC adj. cromático.
CHROMATIC SCALE s. escala cromática.
CHROME s. cromo / adj. cromado.
CHROMOSOMAL adj. cromossômico.
CHROMOSOME s. cromossomo.
CHRONIC adj. crônico; persistente.
CHRONICLE s. crônica, relato / v. registrar; narrar, relatar.
CHRONICLER s. cronista.
CHRONOGRAPH s. cronógrafo.
CHRONOLOGICAL adj. cronológico.
CHRONOLOGY s. cronologia.
CHRONOMETRE s. cronômetro.
CHRYSALIS s. crisálida.
CHRYSANTHEMUM s. crisântemo.
CHUBBY adj. gordinho, fofinho; bochechudo.
CHUCK v. jogar, atirar, arremessar.
CHUCKLE s. riso contido / v. rir consigo mesmo.
CHUFFED adj. orgulhoso, satisfeito.
CHUG s. estampido / v. trepidar, estrepitar.
CHUM s. camarada, amigo íntimo.
CHUNK s. pedaço, naco / v. ordenar.
CHUNKY adj. corpulento, massudo.
CHURCH s. igreja / v. rezar, orar.
CHURCHGOER s. devoto, igrejeiro; praticante.
CHURCHMAN s. clérigo.
CHURCHYARD s. cemitério.
CHURL s. camponês; pessoa rude; avarento, sovina.
CHURLISH adj. rude, grosseiro; avarento, sovina.
CHURN s. batedeira / v. agitar, bater violentamente.
CHUTE s. rampa, ladeira íngreme; tobogã (em piscina); calha.
CHUTNEY s. molho picante.
CIA abrev. CIA.
CICADA s. cigarra (inseto).
CIDER s. sidra.
CIGAR s. charuto.
CIGAR BOX s. caixa de charutos.
CIGAR CUTTER s. corta-charutos.
CIGARETTE s. cigarro.
CIGAR SMOKER s. fumante.
CILANTRO s. coentro.
CINDER s. cinza; carvão em brasa.
CINE-CAMERA s. câmera cinematográfica.
CINE-FILM s. filme cinematográfico.
CINEMA s. cinema; filme.
CINEMATIC adj. cinematográfico.
CINEMATOGRAPHER s. cineasta, cinegrafista.
CINEMATOGRAPHY s. cinematografia.

CINNAMON s. canela; casca de caneleira.
CIPHER s. cifra; criptograma / v. calcular; cifrar.
CIRCA prep. cerca de; aproximadamente.
CIRCLE s. círculo / v. rodear, circular.
CIRCUIT s. circuito; volta.
CIRCUIT BREAKER s. interruptor, disjuntor.
CIRCUITOUS adj. circundante, tortuoso.
CIRCUITRY s. circuito eletrônico; conexão.
CIRCULAR adj. circular, redondo / s. circular.
CIRCULATE v. circular.
CIRCULATION s. circulação; tiragem (jornal), distribuição.
CIRCULATORY adj. circulatório.
CIRCULATORY DISEASE s. doença cardiovascular.
CIRCULATORY SYSTEM s. sistema circulatório.
CIRCUMCISE v. circuncidar.
CIRCUMCISION s. circuncisão.
CIRCUMFERENCE s. circunferência.
CIRCUMFERENTIAL adj. circunferencial.
CIRCUMFLEX s. circunflexo.
CIRCUMSPECT adj. prudente, circunspeto, cauteloso.
CIRCUMSTANCE s. circunstância, condição; situação econômica.
CIRCUMSTANTIAL adj. circunstancial.
CIRCUMVENT v. burlar, lograr; contornar.
CIRCUMVENTION s. circundamento, evasão.
CIRCUS s. circo.
CIRRHOSIS s. cirrose.
CISTERN s. caixa d'água, cisterna, tanque de água.
CITATION s. citação, menção.
CITE v. citar, mencionar, referir-se a.
CITIZEN s. cidadão, civil; habitante.
CITIZENRY s. povo, cidadãos (coletivo).
CITIZENSHIP s. cidadania.
CITRIC adj. cítrico.
CITRIC ACID s. ácido cítrico.
CITRON s. cidra / adj. amarelado.
CITRUS adj. cítrico / s. suco cítrico.
CITRUS FRUIT s. fruta cítrica.
CITY s. cidade.
CIVIC adj. cívico, citadino; municipal.
CIVIL adj. civil; gentil, cortês.
CIVILIAN s. civil / adj. civil.

CIVILISATION s. civilização.
CIVILISE v. civilizar.
CIVILISED adj. civilizado, educado, culto.
CIVILITY s. civilidade, polidez, cortesia.
CIVIL LAW s. direito civil.
CIVIL WAR s. guerra civil.
CLACK v. estalar, estripar / s. estalido.
CLAIM v. exigir, alegar, afirmar / s. reclamação, reivindicação; afirmação.
CLAIMANT s. requerente, pretendente, demandante.
CLAIRVOYANCE s. clarividência, vidência.
CLAIRVOYANT adj. vidente, clarividente.
CLAM s. molusco, marisco.
CLAMBER v. escalar (com dificuldade) / s. escalada, subida.
CLAMMY adj. úmido, pegajoso, grudento.
CLAMOUR v. clamar, protestar / s. clamor, rebuliço.
CLAMOUROUS adj. clamoroso.
CLAMP v. grampear, segurar / s. grampo, fixador.
CLAN s. clã.
CLANDESTINE adj. clandestino.
CLANG v. retinir, soar, ressoar / s. tinido, clangor.
CLAP v. aplaudir / s. palmada; aplauso.
CLAP HANDS v. bater palmas; aplaudir.
CLAPPING s. aplausos, palmas / adj. aplausível.
CLARIFICATION s. esclarecimento, elucidação.
CLARIFY v. esclarecer, clarificar, elucidar.
CLARINET s. clarinete, clarineta.
CLARION s. clarim, trombeta.
CLARITY s. clareza, lucidez, limpidez.
CLASH s. estrondo; conflito / v. confrontar; enfrentar; chocar-se.
CLASP s. gancho; fecho; abraço / v. afivelar, apertar, abraçar.
CLASS v. classificar / s. classe, categoria; aula / adj. de classe.
CLASSIC s. e adj. clássico, convencional, típico.
CLASSICAL adj. clássico.
CLASSICALLY adv. classicamente.
CLASSICISM s. Classicismo.
CLASSIFIABLE adj. classificável.
CLASSIFICATION s. classificação.
CLASSIFIED adj. secreto, confidencial, restrito.

CLASSIFIER s. classificador.
CLASSIFY v. classificar.
CLASSMATE s. colega de classe.
CLASSROOM s. sala de aula.
CLASSWORK s. exercícios em sala.
CLATTER s. ruído, tropel, algazarra.
CLAUSE s. cláusula; oração, frase (gramática).
CLAUSTROPHOBIA s. claustrofobia.
CLAUSTROPHOBIC adj. claustrofóbico.
CLAVICLE s. clavícula.
CLAW s. pata; garra / v. arranhar, agarrar.
CLAW BACK v. recuperar.
CLAY s. argila, barro.
CLAYEY adj. argiloso, barrento.
CLEAN v. limpar; fazer faxina / adj. limpo, honesto, puro.
CLEANER s. limpador, lavador; pessoa da limpeza.
CLEANING s. limpeza.
CLEANNESS s. limpeza; asseio.
CLEANSE v. purificar, limpar, purgar.
CLEANSER s. creme de limpeza; removedor.
CLEAN-SHAVEN adj. sem barba, de barba feita.
CLEANSING adj. purificante, purificador.
CLEAN-UP s. limpeza total; faxina.
CLEAR adj. claro / v. clarear; remover, retirar.
CLEARANCE s. remoção; desobstrução.
CLEARANCE SALES s. liquidação.
CLEARING s. clareira; roça; ajuste, acerto.
CLEARING HOUSE s. câmara de compensação.
CLEARLY adv. claramente.
CLEAVE v. rachar-se, fender-se.
CLEAVER s. cutelo; machadinha.
CLEF s. clave (notação musical).
CLEFT s. fissura, racha, fenda / adj. rachado, fendido.
CLEMENCY s. clemência.
CLEMENT adj. clemente.
CLEMENTINE s. tangerina, mandarina, clementina.
CLENCH v. agarrar, prender / s. aperto.
CLENCHED adj. apertado, cerrado.
CLERGY s. clero.
CLERGYMAN s. pastor, padre, ministro da igreja, clérigo.
CLERICAL adj. clerical, eclesiástico / s. clérigo, padre.

CLERK s. balconista; escrevente; auxiliar de escritório; funcionário.
CLEVER adj. inteligente, esperto, engenhoso.
CLEVERLY adv. sabiamente.
CLEVERNESS s. inteligência; habilidade.
CLEW s. indício; vestígio.
CLICK v. estalar, tinir; clicar / s. estalido, clique.
CLIENT s. cliente, freguês.
CLIENTELE s. clientela.
CLIFF s. penhasco, precipício.
CLIMACTIC adj. culminante; ápice.
CLIMATE s. clima; atmosfera; humor.
CLIMATE CHANGE s. mudanças climáticas.
CLIMATIC adj. climático.
CLIMATOLOGY s. climatologia.
CLIMAX s. clímax.
CLIMB v. subir, escalar, trepar / s. subida, escalada.
CLIMBER s. alpinista.
CLIMBING s. alpinismo, escalamento; ascensão.
CLIME s. clima.
CLINCH v. rebitar, segurar; fechar acordo; ganhar / s. rebitamento; agarramento.
CLING v. agarrar-se, grudar-se, prender-se.
CLINGING adj. grudento, apegado.
CLINIC s. clínica, consultório; clínico.
CLINICAL adj. clínico.
CLINK v. tinir, tilintar / s. tinido, som de vidro.
CLIP s. clipe, grampo / v. cortar; grampear, apertar.
CLIPPING s. recorte de jornal; clipagem.
CLIQUE s. panelinha, roda, grupo de pessoas.
CLITORAL adj. clitoriano.
CLITORIS s. clitóris.
CLOAK s. manto, capote; disfarce, pretexto / v. encobrir, mascarar.
CLOAKROOM s. vestiário, chapelaria (teatro, restaurante).
CLOCK s. relógio, medidor, taxímetro / v. cronometrar.
CLOCKWISE adv. em sentido horário / adj. sentido horário.
CLOCKWORK s. mecanismo / adj. regular, automático.
CLOD s. torrão de terra.
CLOG s. tamanco; obstáculo, obstrução / v. obstruir, entupir.

CLOISTER s. claustro; convento, mosteiro, retiro.
CLONE s. clone / v. clonar.
CLONING s. clonagem.
CLOSE adj. próximo, íntimo / v. fechar; terminar.
CLOSE-BY adj. perto, vizinho, adjacente.
CLOSELY adv. intimamente.
CLOSET s. armário, quartinho, cubículo.
CLOSE-UP s. primeiro plano, fotografia tirada de perto, vista.
CLOSURE s. fechamento, fim, encerramento.
CLOT s. coágulo / v. coagular.
CLOTH s. tecido, pano.
CLOTHE v. vestir-se, pôr roupa, revestir, cobrir.
CLOTHES s. roupa, traje, vestuário.
CLOTHESLINE s. varal, corda.
CLOTHING s. roupa, vestuário.
CLOUD s. nuvem.
CLOUDLESS adj. claro, sem nuvens; tempo limpo.
CLOUDY adj. nublado (tempo); confuso, turvo.
CLOUT v. esbofetear, murro / s. cascudo.
CLOVE s. cravo-da-índia; dente de alho.
CLOVER s. trevo, trifólio.
CLOWN s. palhaço / v. fazer palhaçadas.
CLOY v. fartar, saciar, saturar.
CLOYING adj. enjoativo.
CLUB s. clube; porrete, cacete / v. golpear.
CLUCK v. cacarejar / s. cacarejo.
CLUE s. pista, indício.
CLUELESS adj. desinformado, ignorante.
CLUMP s. moita; torrão, pedaço.
CLUMSY adj. desajeitado, desastrado.
CLUSTER v. agrupar-se, apinhar-se / s. grupo; cacho; enxame.
CLUTCH s. embreagem; ninhada; aperto / v. apertar; chocar.
CLUTTER v. entulhar, desarrumar / s. desordem, bagunça.
CLUTTERED adj. desarrumado, abarrotado.
CM s. cm, centímetro.
C/O abrev. a/c.
COACH s. treinador; carruagem; ônibus / v. treinar, ensinar.
COACHING s. treinamento.
COAGULATE v. coagular.

COAGULATION s. coagulação.
COAL s. carvão.
COALITION s. coligação, união, coalizão.
COALMINE s. mina de carvão.
COARSE adj. grosseiro, grosso, vulgar.
COARSEN v. engrossar, ficar grosseiro.
COARSENESS s. aspereza, grosseria, rudeza.
COAST s. costa, praia, beira-mar; litoral.
COASTAL adj. costeiro, litorâneo.
COAST GUARD s. guarda costeira.
COASTLINE s. litoral, contorno.
COAT s. casaco; plumagem / v. cobrir, revestir.
COBBLE s. remendo (de sapatos); pedra de calçamento / v. remendar.
COBBLER s. sapateiro.
COBRA s. naja (cobra).
COBWEB s. teia de aranha.
COCAINE s. cocaína.
COCK s. galo, frango; ave macho.
COCKPIT s. compartimento do piloto.
COCKROACH s. barata.
COCKSURE adj. absolutamente certo, convencido.
COCKTAIL s. coquetel.
COCKY adj. convencido, petulante, arrogante.
COCOA s. cacau; chocolate (bebida).
COCONUT s. coco.
COCONUT JUICE s. água de coco.
COCOON s. casulo / v. encasular, fazer casulo.
COD s. bacalhau.
CODE s. código / v. codificar, decodificar.
CODED adj. codificado.
CODED MESSAGE s. mensagem criptografada.
CODER s. codificador.
CODIFICATION s. codificação.
CODFISH m. q. cod.
CODIFY v. codificar, decodificar; sistematizar.
COEFFICIENT s. coeficiente.
COERCE v. coagir, compelir, forçar.
COERCION s. coerção, repressão.
COERCIVE adj. coercivo.
COEXIST v. coexistir.
COEXISTENCE s. coexistência.
COFFEE s. café (bebida).
COFFEE BREAK s. pausa para o café.
COFFER s. arca; cofre.
COFFIN s. caixão, ataúde.

COG s. dente de engrenagem.
COGENT adj. convincente, forçoso.
COGNAC s. conhaque, bebida alcoólica.
COGNATE s. cognato / adj. cognato.
COGNISABLE adj. cognoscível, conhecível.
COGNISANCE s. conhecimento, discernimento.
COGNISANT adj. ciente, competente.
COGNITION s. cognição.
COGNITIVE adj. cognitivo.
COHABIT v. coabitar; viver junto.
COHABITATION s. coabitação.
COHERENCE s. coerência.
COHERENT adj. coerente.
COHESION s. coesão.
COHESIVE adj. coeso, conexo, lógico.
COIL s. bobina, espiral, rolo / v. enrolar, bobinar.
COIN s. moeda.
COINAGE s. sistema monetário; cunhagem.
COINCIDE v. coincidir; acontecer ao mesmo tempo.
COINCIDENCE s. coincidência.
COINCIDENT adj. coincidente.
COLANDER s. coador, escorredor de macarrão.
COLD s. frio; resfriado / adj. frio; gélido; insensível.
COLD-BLOODED adj. cruel, de sangue-frio.
COLD-HEARTED adj. desalmado, cruel.
COLDLY adv. friamente.
COLDNESS s. frieza, friagem.
COLESLAW s. salada de repolho.
COLIC s. cólica.
COLISEUM s. coliseu.
COLLABORATE v. colaborar.
COLLABORATION s. colaboração.
COLLABORATIVE adj. cooperativo, participativo.
COLLABORATOR s. colaborador, cooperador.
COLLAGEN s. colágeno.
COLLAPSE s. colapso, desabamento / v. desabar, ruir.
COLLAPSIBLE adj. dobrável, desmontável, articulado.
COLLAR s. gola; colarinho; coleira (animal).
COLLARBONE s. clavícula.
COLLATERAL s. parente colateral; garantia / adj. paralelo, colateral.

COLLEAGUE s. colega.
COLLECT v. coletar, colecionar; juntar; cobrar.
COLLECTION s. coleção; arrecadação, cobrança.
COLLECTIVISM s. coletivismo.
COLLECTIVIST s. coletivista / adj. coletivista.
COLLECTOR s. coletor, cobrador; colecionador.
COLLEGE s. faculdade, centro de ensino superior.
COLLIDE v. colidir, chocar-se.
COLLISION s. colisão; conflito.
COLLOCATE v. colocar, encadear.
COLLOCATION s. colocação; disposição.
COLLOQUIAL adj. coloquial; informal.
COLLOQUIALISM s. coloquialismo.
COLLOQUIUM s. colóquio; seminário acadêmico.
COLON s. cólon (anatomia); dois pontos (:).
COLONEL s. coronel.
COLONIAL adj. colonial.
COLONISATION s. colonização.
COLONISE v. colonizar.
COLONISER s. colonizador.
COLONY s. colônia, povoação.
COLOUR s. cor / v. colorir, pintar.
COLOURANT s. corante.
COLOURATION s. coloração.
COLOURBLIND adj. daltônico.
COLOURFUL adj. colorido.
COLOURING s. coloração; colorido.
COLT s. potro; cavalo filhote.
COLUMN s. coluna.
COLUMNIST s. colunista.
COMA s. coma.
COMB s. pente; crista (de ave, de onda); favo (de mel) / v. pentear.
COMBAT v. combater / s. combate.
COMBATANT s. combatente / adj. combatente.
COMBINATION s. combinação; associação.
COMBINE v. combinar; unir-se, associar-se.
COMBINER s. combinador.
COMBUSTIBLE s. combustível / adj. combustível.
COMBUSTION s. combustão.
COME v. vir; chegar; aproximar-se.
COMEBACK s. volta, retorno / v. voltar, retornar.
COMEDIAN s. humorista, comediante.

COMEDIC *adj.* cômico.
COMEDY *s.* comédia.
COMER *s.* visitante, visita.
COMET *s.* cometa.
COMFORT *s.* bem-estar, conforto / *v.* consolar, confortar.
COMFORTABLE *adj.* confortável, cômodo.
COMFORTABLY *adv.* confortavelmente.
COMFORTING *adj.* reconfortante, confortante.
COMIC *s.* cômico; revista em quadrinhos, gibi.
COMIC STRIP *s.* história em quadrinhos, tirinhas.
COMING *s.* chegada, vinda; próximo.
COMMA *s.* vírgula.
COMMAND *s.* ordem, comando / *v.* mandar, comandar.
COMMANDER *s.* comandante, chefe.
COMMANDMENT *s.* mandamento, preceito.
COMMEMORATE *v.* comemorar, celebrar.
COMMENCE *v.* iniciar, começar.
COMMEND *v.* elogiar, recomendar.
COMMENSURATE *adj.* compatível; proporcional; igual.
COMMENT *s.* comentário, observação / *v.* comentar.
COMMENTARY *s.* comentário, explicação.
COMMENTATOR *s.* comentarista.
COMMERCE *s.* comércio.
COMMERCIAL *s.* anúncio / *adj.* comercial; mercantil.
COMMISSION *s.* comissão, encargo / *v.* encomendar; encarregar.
COMMISSIONER *s.* comissário.
COMMIT *v.* cometer; confinar, encerrar; comprometer-se.
COMMITMENT *s.* compromisso; promessa.
COMMITTEE *s.* comitê.
COMMODITY *s.* mercadoria; artigo de utilidade.
COMMON *adj.* comum, popular, usual.
COMMONLY *adv.* geralmente.
COMMON SENSE *s.* bom senso; juízo.
COMMOTION *s.* tumulto, distúrbio; agitação.
COMMUNAL *adj.* comum.
COMMUNICATE *v.* comunicar-se.
COMMUNICATION *s.* comunicação.
COMMUNION *s.* comunhão, participação.
COMMUNIQUÉ *s.* comunicado oficial.
COMMUNISM *s.* comunismo.
COMMUNIST *adj.* comunista / *s.* comunista.
COMMUNITY *s.* comunidade.
COMMUTE *v.* viajar diariamente; comutar, trocar.
COMPACT *adj.* compacto / *s.* caixa de pó de arroz / *v.* comprimir.
COMPACT DISC *s.* disco compacto, CD.
COMPANION *s.* companheiro.
COMPANIONSHIP *s.* companheirismo, camaradagem.
COMPANY *s.* companhia.
COMPARATIVE *adj.* comparativo; relativo.
COMPARATIVELY *adv.* relativamente, comparativamente.
COMPARE *v.* comparar.
COMPARISON *s.* comparação.
COMPARTMENT *s.* compartimento.
COMPASS *s.* bússola.
COMPASS CARD *s.* rosa dos ventos.
COMPASSES *s.* compasso.
COMPASSION *s.* compaixão, piedade.
COMPATIBILITY *s.* compatibilidade.
COMPATIBLE *adj.* compatível, conciliável.
COMPEL *v.* obrigar, compelir, forçar.
COMPELLING *adj.* convincente; persuasivo; irresistível.
COMPENSATE *v.* indenizar, compensar.
COMPENSATION *s.* indenização.
COMPETE *v.* competir.
COMPETENT *adj.* competente, capacitado.
COMPETITION *s.* competição, disputa.
COMPETITIVE *adj.* competitivo.
COMPETITOR *s.* competidor.
COMPLACENCY *s.* complacência; satisfação consigo.
COMPLAIN *v.* queixar-se; reclamar.
COMPLAINT *s.* queixa, denúncia, reclamação.
COMPLAISANT *adj.* complacente, afável, cortês.
COMPLEMENT *v.* complementar / *s.* complemento.
COMPLEMENTARY *adj.* complementar.
COMPLETE *adj.* completo, terminado / *v.* completar, terminar, concluir.
COMPLETELY *adv.* completamente, inteiramente, totalmente.

COMPLETENESS s. perfeição; inteireza, integralidade.
COMPLETION s. conclusão; acabamento.
COMPLEX s. complexo / adj. complexo, complicado.
COMPLEXION s. tez, cútis; caráter, natureza.
COMPLIANCE s. submissão; condescendência; conformidade.
COMPLICATE v. complicar; dificultar.
COMPLICATED adj. complicado, complexo.
COMPLICATION s. complicação.
COMPLIMENT s. elogio; cumprimento / v. elogiar; cumprimentar.
COMPLIMENTARY adj. lisonjeiro; grátis.
COMPLOT s. conspiração, trama.
COMPLY v. cumprir; estar de acordo com; condescender.
COMPONENT s. peça; componente / adj. componente.
COMPOSE v. compor.
COMPOSED adj. sereno, calmo, tranquilo.
COMPOSER s. compositor.
COMPOSITION s. composição; redação.
COMPOST s. compostagem, adubo.
COMPOSURE s. serenidade, compostura, calma.
COMPOUND adj. composto / s. composto, combinação / v. misturar, compor.
COMPREHEND v. compreender, entender.
COMPREHENSIVE adj. abrangente, completo; compreensivo.
COMPRESS s. compressa / v. comprimir, reduzir.
COMPROMISE v. comprometer, chegar a um acordo / s. acordo.
COMPULSION s. compulsão.
COMPULSIVE adj. compulsivo; inveterado (jogador).
COMPULSORY adj. obrigatório, compulsório.
COMPUTER s. computador.
COMPUTERIZE v. informatizar.
COMPUTING s. computação, informática.
COMRADE s. camarada, companheiro.
COMRADESHIP s. camaradagem.
CONCEAL v. omitir; esconder, ocultar.
CONCEDE v. reconhecer, admitir, ceder.
CONCEIT s. presunção, vaidade.
CONCEITED adj. vaidoso, convencido.

CONCEIVE v. conceber.
CONCENTRATE v. concentrar / s. concentrado.
CONCENTRATION s. concentração.
CONCEPT s. conceito.
CONCEPTION s. concepção.
CONCERN s. interesse; preocupação / v. dizer respeito a, interessar.
CONCERNING prep. a respeito de, acerca de, relativo a.
CONCERT s. concerto.
CONCERTED adj. conjunto, coordenado, de comum acordo.
CONCERTINA s. sanfona, harmônica.
CONCESSION s. concessão.
CONCISE adj. conciso, breve, resumido.
CONCLUDE v. concluir; deduzir, inferir.
CONCLUSIVE adj. conclusivo, decisivo.
CONCORD s. acordo; concórdia.
CONCOURSE s. saguão.
CONCRETE s. concreto / adj. concreto.
CONCUR v. concordar; coincidir.
CONDEMN v. condenar.
CONDENSATION s. condensação.
CONDENSE v. condensar; resumir.
CONDIMENT s. condimento, tempero.
CONDITION s. condição / v. condicionar.
CONDITIONER s. condicionador; amaciante (de roupas).
CONDOLENCES s. pêsames, condolências.
CONDOM s. camisinha, preservativo.
CONDOMINIUM s. condomínio.
CONDONE v. perdoar, desculpar; tolerar.
CONDUCE v. conduzir, levar, tender.
CONDUCT v. conduzir, dirigir, administrar / s. conduta, procedimento.
CONE s. cone; casquinha (sorvete); pinha.
CONFECTIONER s. confeiteiro.
CONFER v. conferir, outorgar, deliberar.
CONFERENCE s. congresso, conferência.
CONFESS v. confessar.
CONFESSION s. confissão.
CONFESSOR s. confessor.
CONFETTI s. confete.
CONFIDE v. confiar.
CONFIDENCE s. confiança.
CONFIDENT adj. confiante, certo, seguro.
CONFIDENTIAL adj. confidencial, secreto.
CONFINE v. confinar, limitar.
CONFINEMENT s. prisão, confinamento.

CONFINES s. confins.
CONFIRM v. confirmar; aprovar.
CONFIRMATION s. confirmação.
CONFISCATE v. confiscar / adj. confiscado.
CONFLICT v. divergir, discordar / s. conflito.
CONFLICTING adj. divergente, conflitante, contraditório.
CONFORM v. conformar-se, adaptar-se.
CONFOUND v. confundir, desconcertar.
CONFRONT v. enfrentar, confrontar.
CONFRONTATION s. confronto, acareação.
CONFUSE v. confundir, desorientar.
CONFUSED adj. confuso, desorientado.
CONFUSION s. confusão, desordem, balbúrdia.
CONGEAL v. congelar-se.
CONGENIAL adj. simpático; agradável; apropriado.
CONGESTION s. congestão; congestionamento.
CONGRATULATE v. parabenizar.
CONGRATULATION s. felicitação; parabéns.
CONGREGATE v. reunir-se.
CONGREGATION s. congregação.
CONGRESS s. congresso.
CONGRESSMAN s. deputado; congressista.
CONJUGATE v. conjugar; unir, ligar.
CONJURE v. fazer truques; invocar; evocar; conjurar, adjurar.
CONJURER s. mágico; conjurador.
CONK OUT v. pifar, falhar (coloquial); cair no sono.
CONMAN s. vigarista.
CONNECT v. conectar, unir, associar.
CONNECTION s. conexão, ligação, relação.
CONQUER v. conquistar, vencer.
CONQUEROR s. conquistador, vencedor.
CONQUEST s. conquista.
CONSCIENCE s. consciência.
CONSCIOUS adj. consciente, cônscio, ciente.
CONSCRIPT s. recruta / adj. conscrito, recrutado, alistado.
CONSCRIPTION s. conscrição (militar).
CONSENT s. consentimento / v. consentir.
CONSEQUENCE s. consequência.
CONSEQUENTLY adv. consequentemente.
CONSERVATION s. conservação.
CONSERVATIVE adj. conservador / s. conservador.
CONSERVATORY s. conservatório (música); estufa.
CONSERVE s. conserva / v. preservar, conservar.
CONSIDER v. considerar, refletir.
CONSIDERABLE adj. considerável.
CONSIDERATE adj. atencioso.
CONSIDERATION s. consideração; respeito, estima.
CONSIGNMENT s. consignação; remessa.
CONSIST v. consistir.
CONSISTENCY s. consistência.
CONSISTENT adj. estável, consistente, coerente.
CONSOLATION s. consolação, conforto, consolo.
CONSOLE s. consolo / v. confortar, consolar.
CONSONANT s. consoante / adj. consoante, harmonioso.
CONSORT s. cônjuge, consorte.
CONSORTIUM s. consórcio.
CONSPIRACY s. conspiração, trama.
CONSTABLE s. policial; condestável.
CONSTANT adj. constante.
CONSTIPATED adj. constipado.
CONSTIPATION s. constipação, prisão de ventre.
CONSTITUENCY s. distrito eleitoral.
CONSTITUENT s. eleitor, constituinte.
CONSTITUTE v. constituir.
CONSTITUTION s. constituição.
CONSTRAIN v. constranger, obrigar, compelir.
CONSTRAINT s. coação; restrição; confinamento.
CONSTRUCT v. construir.
CONSTRUCTION s. construção.
CONSTRUE v. interpretar; explicar.
CONSUL s. cônsul.
CONSULT v. consultar; prestar consultoria.
CONSULTANT s. consultor.
CONSUME v. consumir.
CONSUMER s. consumidor.
CONSUMER GOODS s. bens de consumo.
CONSUMPTION s. consumação.
CONTACT s. contato / v. contatar, comunicar.
CONTACT LENS s. lente de contato.
CONTAGIOUS adj. contagioso.
CONTAIN v. conter.
CONTAINER s. recipiente, contêiner.
CONTAMINATE v. contaminar.

CONTEMPLATE v. contemplar.
CONTEMPORARY adj. contemporâneo / s. contemporâneo.
CONTEMPT s. desprezo, desdém.
CONTEMPTIBLE adj. desprezível.
CONTENT v. contentar / s. contentamento; conteúdo.
CONTENTED adj. contente.
CONTENTMENT s. contentamento, satisfação.
CONTEST s. concurso, competição / v. disputar.
CONTESTANT s. adversário; concorrente.
CONTEXT s. contexto.
CONTINENT s. continente.
CONTINENTAL adj. continental.
CONTINGENCY s. contingência, eventualidade.
CONTINGENT s. contingente (de soldados).
CONTINUAL adj. contínuo.
CONTINUALLY adv. continuamente.
CONTINUATION s. prolongamento, continuação.
CONTINUE v. continuar, prosseguir.
CONTINUOUS adj. contínuo.
CONTINUOUS FORMS s. formulários contínuos.
CONTORT v. contorcer.
CONTOUR s. contorno; curva de nível.
CONTRABAND s. contrabando.
CONTRACT v. contrair; contratar / s. contrato.
CONTRACTION s. contração.
CONTRACTOR s. contratante, empreiteiro.
CONTRADICT v. contradizer, contestar.
CONTRAPTION s. geringonça, engenhoca (coloquial).
CONTRARY s. contrário, oposto / adj. teimoso; desfavorável, adverso.
CONTRAST s. contraste / v. contrastar; comparar.
CONTRAVENE v. infringir, transgredir, violar; contradizer.
CONTRIBUTE v. contribuir.
CONTRIBUTION s. contribuição; donativo; taxa, tributo.
CONTRIBUTOR s. contribuinte; colaborador.
CONTROL s. controle / v. controlar.
CONTROLLER s. controlador, fiscal, inspetor.
CONTROL ROOM s. sala de controle.
CONTROL TOWER s. torre de controle.
CONTROVERSIAL adj. polêmico, controverso.
CONTROVERSY s. controvérsia.
CONVALESCE v. convalescer.
CONVENE v. convocar; reunir-se.
CONVENIENCE s. utilidade; conveniência; comodidade.
CONVENIENT adj. conveniente, apropriado; prático.
CONVENT s. convento.
CONVENTION s. convenção.
CONVERSATION s. conversação, conversa.
CONVERSE v. conversar / adj. contrário, oposto.
CONVERSELY adv. inversamente.
CONVERSION s. conversão, troca.
CONVERT v. converter / s. convertido.
CONVERTIBLE s. conversível (carro) / adj. conversível.
CONVEY v. transportar; comunicar, expressar; enviar.
CONVICT v. condenar / s. presidiário, condenado.
CONVICTION s. convicção; condenação.
CONVINCE v. convencer.
CONVINCING adj. convincente.
CONVOY s. escolta, proteção / v. escoltar, comboiar.
COO v. arrulhar; namorar / s. arrulho.
COOK v. cozinhar / s. cozinheiro.
COOKBOOK s. livro de receitas culinárias.
COOKER s. fogão.
COOKERY s. culinária.
COOKING s. cozinha; arte culinária / adj. de cozinha.
COOL adj. fresco; frio; legal (coloquial) / v. resfriar.
COOLNESS s. frigidez, frieza.
COOP s. gaiola; viveiro / v. prender, confinar, cercar.
COOPERATE v. cooperar, colaborar.
COOPERATIVE s. cooperativa / adj. cooperativo.
COORDINATE v. coordenar / s. coordenadas.
CO-OWNERSHIP s. copropriedade, condomínio.
COP s. tira, policial (coloquial).
COPPER s. cobre; tira, policial (coloquial).
COPULATE v. ter relações sexuais, copular.

COPY v. copiar / s. cópia, reprodução / v. copiar, reproduzir.
COPYRIGHT s. direitos autorais / adj. protegido por direitos autorais.
CORAL s. coral / adj. coral, coralino.
CORD s. corda, cordão; fio.
CORDIAL adj. cordial / s. cordial.
CORDIALITY s. cordialidade.
CORDON s. cordão de isolamento.
CORDUROY s. veludo cotelê.
CORE s. caroço de frutas; centro, núcleo; essência.
CORIANDER s. coentro.
CORK s. cortiça, rolha de cortiça / adj. de cortiça.
CORKSCREW s. saca-rolhas.
CORN s. milho.
CORN BREAD s. pão de milho, broa de milho.
CORNED BEEF s. carne enlatada.
CORNER s. esquina; canto; ângulo; escanteio (futebol).
CORNET s. cornetim (instrumento).
CORNFIELD s. trigal; milharal.
CORNFLAKES s. flocos de milho.
CORNFLOUR s. amido de milho, maisena.
CORNY adj. granuloso, em grão.
CORONARY s. coronária / adj. coronário, coronal.
CORONATION s. coroação.
CORONET s. pequena coroa, diadema.
CORPORAL adj. corporal / s. cabo (militar).
CORPORATE adj. corporativo, coletivo.
CORPORATION s. corporação.
CORPS s. corpo (militar, do exército); corporação.
CORPSE s. cadáver, defunto.
CORRAL s. curral.
CORRECT v. corrigir; repreender / adj. correto, certo.
CORRECTNESS s. precisão; correção.
CORRESPOND v. corresponder.
CORRESPONDENCE s. correspondência.
CORRESPONDENT s. correspondente.
CORRIDOR s. corredor, passagem.
CORRODE v. corroer.
CORROSION s. corrosão.
CORRUPT adj. corrupto, desonesto / v. corromper.
CORRUPTION s. corrupção.
CORSAGE s. corpinho; corpete; buquê.

CORSET s. espartilho, cinta feminina.
CORSICA s. Córsega.
COSMETIC s. cosmético / adj. artificial; cosmético.
COSMOS s. cosmo, universo.
COSSET v. paparicar, mimar.
COST v. custar / s. preço, valor, custo.
CO-STAR s. coadjuvante.
COSTA RICA s. Costa Rica.
COST-EFFECTIVE adj. rentável.
COSTLY adj. caro.
COST OF LIVING s. custo de vida.
COSTUME s. traje, roupa nacional ou regional; fantasia.
COSTUME-JEWELLERY s. bijuteria.
COSY adj. aconchegante, confortável.
COT s. berço; cama estreita; choupana.
COTTAGE s. casa de campo ou de verão; chalé, cabana.
COTTAGE CHEESE s. requeijão.
COTTON s. algodão / adj. de algodão.
COTTON-CANDY s. algodão-doce.
COTTON WOOL s. algodão bruto ou em rama.
COUCH s. sofá.
COUCHETTE s. leito.
COUGAR s. puma (animal).
COUGH s. tosse, tossidela / v. tossir.
COUGH DROP s. pastilha para tosse.
COUNCIL s. conselho, assembleia.
COUNCIL ESTATE s. conjunto habitacional.
COUNCILOR s. conselheiro; vereador.
COUNSEL s. conselho / v. aconselhar, recomendar.
COUNT v. contar / s. conta, soma; conde.
COUNTENANCE v. tolerar, aprovar / s. apoio, auxílio.
COUNTER s. balcão; contador; oposto, contrário / v. contrariar / adj. oposto.
COUNTERACT v. contrapor-se, opor-se.
COUNTERBALANCE s. contrapeso / v. contrabalançar.
COUNTERFEIT v. falsificar / s. falsificação; imitação / adj. falsificado.
COUNTERFOIL s. canhoto (talão de cheque).
COUNTERMAND v. revogar / s. revogação.
COUNTERPART s. equivalente, contraparte, duplicata.
COUNTERSIGN v. autenticar, rubricar.
COUNTLESS adj. inumerável, incontável.

COUNTRY s. país; pátria; campo, interior; zona, região.
COUNTRY HOUSE s. casa de campo.
COUNTRYMAN s. camponês; compatriota, patrício.
COUNTRYSIDE s. campo, zona rural, interior.
COUNTY s. condado, município, comarca.
COUP s. golpe de estado.
COUPLE s. par, casal, dupla.
COUPLING s. ligação, junção.
COUPON s. cupom, bilhete, talão.
COURAGE s. coragem, bravura.
COURIER s. correio; mensageiro; guia.
COURSE s. curso; rumo; direção; prato (comida).
COURT s. corte (de justiça, real); quadra para jogos / v. cortejar.
COURTEOUS adj. cortês, amável.
COURTESAN s. cortesã, meretriz.
COURTESY s. cortesia, favor.
COURT-HOUSE s. palácio de justiça.
COURT-MARTIAL s. corte marcial; conselho de guerra.
COURTROOM s. sala de tribunal.
COUSIN s. primo.
COVE s. enseada.
COVENANT s. compromisso; convenção; pacto.
COVER s. cobertura, capa / v. cobrir, tampar.
COVERAGE s. cobertura.
COVERING s. camada, revestimento, cobertura.
COVERLET s. coberta, colcha.
COVERT adj. velado, secreto, encoberto / s. abrigo.
COVET v. cobiçar; desejar.
COW s. vaca / v. intimidar; amedrontar.
COWARD s. covarde / adj. covarde, medroso.
COWARDICE s. covardia.
COWARDLY adj. covarde / adv. covardemente.
COWBOY s. vaqueiro, boiadeiro; trambiqueiro, picareta.
COWPOX s. vacina; varíola bovina.
CRAB s. caranguejo, siri.
CRACK s. rachadura; estalo; droga; craque (esportista) / v. quebrar, estalar.
CRACKBRAINED adj. louco, doido.
CRACKER s. biscoito de água e sal; bombinha de São João.

CRADLE s. berço; terra natal / v. embalar.
CRAFT s. nave; artesanato; ofício, profissão; técnica / v. elaborar.
CRAFTSMAN s. artesão.
CRAFTY adj. astuto, ladino.
CRAG s. penhasco, rochedo.
CRAMP s. grampo; cãibra, cólica.
CRAMPED adj. apertado, espremido; espasmódico.
CRANE s. guindaste, grua.
CRANK s. manivela; pessoa excêntrica (coloquial).
CRASH s. batida; estampido; desastre; quebra / v. bater; quebrar.
CRASH COURSE s. curso intensivo.
CRASH HELMET s. capacete de proteção.
CRASH LANDING s. aterrissagem forçada.
CRATE s. caixote; engradado / v. encaixotar, engradar.
CRAVAT s. gravata larga.
CRAWL v. engatinhar, arrastar-se / s. rastejo; estilo de natação.
CRAYFISH s. lagostim.
CRAYON s. giz de cera, creiom.
CRAZE s. moda, febre, interesse passageiro.
CRAZY adj. louco, maluco, doido.
CREAK s. rangido / v. ranger, estalar.
CREAM s. creme; nata / adj. de creme.
CREAM CHEESE s. queijo cremoso.
CREAMERY s. fábrica de laticínios.
CREAMY adj. cremoso.
CREASE v. amassar; vincar; enrugar / s. vinco, prega, dobra; ruga.
CREATOR s. criador, autor.
CREATURE s. criatura, ser humano; animal.
CREDENCE s. crédito, crença.
CREDIBILITY s. credibilidade.
CREDIBLE adj. acreditável, crível.
CREDIT v. creditar / s. crédito, empréstimo.
CREDIT CARD s. cartão de crédito.
CREDITOR s. credor.
CREED s. credo, crença; doutrina.
CREEK s. riacho, córrego.
CREEP v. rastejar; engatinhar / s. arrepio, calafrio.
CREEPER s. trepadeira; rastreador; rastejador.
CREEPY adj. horripilante, arrepiador.
CREMATE v. cremar.
CREMATION s. cremação.
CREMATORIUM s. crematório.

CREPE s. crepe, panqueca.
CRESCENT s. meia-lua, crescente.
CRESS s. agrião.
CREST s. crista; topo.
CRETE s. Creta.
CREVICE s. fenda, fissura.
CREW s. tripulação.
CRIB s. berço com grades altas; manjedoura.
CRICK s. cãibra.
CRICKET s. grilo; críquete (esporte).
CRIME s. crime, delito.
CRIMINAL s. criminoso / adj. criminoso, criminal.
CRINGE v. encolher-se, recuar.
CRINKLE s. ruga; dobra; amassadura de papel.
CRIPPLE v. aleijar; mutilar / s. aleijado.
CRISIS s. (pl. crises) crise.
CRISP adj. torrado, crocante / v. encrespar; torrar.
CRISSCROSS adj. cruzado, riscado com linhas cruzadas / v. riscar, marcar.
CRITERION s. (pl. criteria) critério.
CRITIC s. crítico; detrator / adj. crítico.
CRITICAL adj. grave; decisivo, crucial.
CRITICISM s. crítica; censura; desaprovação.
CRITICIZE v. criticar, censurar.
CROAK v. coaxar / s. coaxo.
CROATIA s. Croácia.
CROCHET s. crochê / v. fazer crochê.
CROCKERY s. cerâmica (louça de barro).
CROCODILE s. crocodilo.
CROCUS s. açafrão.
CROFT s. pequena chácara, sítio.
CRONY s. comparsa; amigo íntimo.
CROOK s. vigarista, trapaceiro; curva, dobra / adj. torto, tortuoso; desonesto.
CROONER s. cantor de rádio.
CROP s. colheita, safra / v. cortar, tosar.
CROSS s. cruz; cruzamento / v. cruzar.
CROSSEYED s. vesgo; estrábico.
CROSSING s. travessia; cruzamento; faixa para pedestres.
CROSSWORD s. palavras cruzadas.
CROTCH s. virilha.
CROUCH s. agachamento / v. agachar-se, curvar-se.
CROW s. corvo, gralha; grito de alegria; canto de galo / v. cantar (galo).
CROWBAR s. pé de cabra, alavanca.

CROWD s. multidão, grupo / v. reunir-se, aglomerar-se.
CROWDED adj. lotado, abarrotado, cheio.
CROWN s. coroa; copa de árvore / v. coroar.
CRUCIAL adj. decisivo, crucial.
CRUCIFIX s. crucifixo.
CRUCIFIXION s. crucificação.
CRUDE adj. bruto, cru; rude, grosseiro.
CRUDENESS s. crueza, rudeza.
CRUEL adj. cruel.
CRUELTY s. crueldade.
CRUISE s. cruzeiro (marítimo), viagem / v. viajar, percorrer os mares.
CRUMB s. migalha; miolo do pão.
CRUMBLE v. esfarelar, desfazer-se, quebrar, desmoronar.
CRUMBLY adj. farelento, quebradiço.
CRUMPLE v. amarrotar, amassar, enrugar.
CRUNCH s. mastigação ruidosa / v. mastigar, morder algo (ruidosamente).
CRUNCHY adj. crocante.
CRUSADE s. cruzada.
CRUSH v. esmagar, espremer / s. aglomeração; paixão.
CRUST s. crosta de pão, casca; borra (de vinho).
CRUTCH s. muleta.
CRUX s. ponto crucial.
CRY v. chorar, gritar, exclamar / s. grito, choro.
CRYING s. choro, pranto, gritaria.
CRYPTIC adj. enigmático; escondido, oculto.
CRYSTAL s. cristal.
CUB s. filhote de urso ou raposa; lobinho (escoteiro).
CUBA s. Cuba.
CUBBYHOLE s. cubículo; lugar pequeno e fechado.
CUBE s. cubo; terceira potência / v. elevar ao cubo.
CUBE ROOT s. raiz cúbica.
CUBIC adj. cúbico.
CUBICLE s. cubículo; pequeno compartimento.
CUCUMBER s. pepino.
CUDDLE s. abraço / v. abraçar, afagar.
CUE s. taco de bilhar; sugestão, dica / v. dar sugestão, dica.
CUFF s. bainha de calça; punho de manga; tapa, soco; algema / v. esbofetear.

CUISINE s. cozinha.
CULL v. selecionar; abater animais.
CULMINATION s. auge, clímax.
CULOTTES s. saia-calça.
CULPRIT s. culpado, acusado.
CULT s. culto, veneração; moda.
CULTIVATE v. cultivar.
CULTIVATION s. cultivo.
CULTURE s. cultura.
CULTURED adj. culto; refinado.
CUMBERSOME adj. desajeitado; embaraçoso.
CUNNING s. astúcia / adj. engenhoso, astuto.
CUP s. xícara.
CUPBOARD s. armário, guarda-louça.
CUPPED s. em forma de xícara.
CUP TIE s. jogo eliminatório.
CURATOR s. curador.
CURB v. refrear, restringir / s. freio; restrição; meio-fio.
CURD s. coalho, coágulo / v. coagular, coalhar.
CURDLE v. coalhar; engrossar; solidificar.
CURE s. cura; remédio / v. curar, tratar; defumar.
CURELESS adj. sem cura, incurável.
CURFEW s. toque de recolher.
CURIOUS adj. curioso.
CURL s. cacho; espiral / v. cachear, enrolar.
CURLER s. bobe de cabelos.
CURLY adj. cacheado, enrolado, ondulado.
CURRANT s. groselha; uva-passa.
CURRENCY s. moeda.
CURRENT s. corrente / adj. atual.
CURRENT ACCOUNT s. conta corrente.
CURRENTLY adv. atualmente.
CURRICULUM s. programa de estudos; currículo.
CURRICULUM VITAE s. currículo, histórico profissional.

CURSE s. maldição, praga / v. xingar; amaldiçoar, rogar praga.
CURSED adj. maldito, amaldiçoado.
CURSOR s. cursor (informática).
CURSORY adj. superficial, apressado.
CURT adj. curto, áspero; breve.
CURTAIL v. restringir; reduzir.
CURTAIN s. cortina.
CURVE s. curva / v. fazer a curva.
CUSHION v. amortecer / s. almofada; amortecedor.
CUSTARD s. creme (baunilha); manjar ou pudim.
CUSTODIAN s. guardião; zelador.
CUSTODY s. custódia, tutela.
CUSTOM s. costume, hábito; clientela.
CUSTOMARY adj. costumeiro, habitual.
CUSTOMER s. cliente.
CUSTOMS s. alfândega.
CUSTOMS DUTY s. imposto alfandegário.
CUT v. cortar, reduzir / s. corte, redução.
CUTE adj. gracinha, atraente.
CUTICLE s. cutícula.
CUTLERY s. talheres.
CUTTER s. cortador.
CUTTING adj. cortante, afiado; mordaz / s. recorte de jornal.
CYANIDE s. cianeto, cianureto.
CYCLE s. ciclo; bicicleta / v. andar de bicicleta.
CYCLING s. ciclismo.
CYCLIST s. ciclista.
CYLINDER s. cilindro, tambor (gás).
CYNIC s. cínico, cético.
CYNICAL adj. cínico, cético.
CYNICISM s. cinismo, ceticismo.
CYPRESS s. cipreste.
CYST s. cisto, quisto.
CYSTITIS s. cistite.
CZECH adj. checo / s. checo, idioma checo.

Dd

D, d *s.* quarta letra do alfabeto inglês; ré (nota musical); representa o número 500 em algarismos romanos.
DAB *v.* tocar de leve / *s.* toque; perito(a), experto(a).
DABBLE *v.* interessar-se em (coloquial); salpicar, borrifar.
DAD *s.* papai.
DADDY *s. m.q.* dad.
DAFT *adj.* tolo, ridículo.
DAGGER *s.* punhal, adaga.
DAILY *s.* jornal diário / *adj.* diário / *adv.* diariamente.
DAINTY *adj.* delicado, delicioso / *s.* gulodice.
DAIRY *s.* leiteria; fábrica de laticínios.
DAIRY PRODUCTS *s.* laticínios.
DAIS *s.* estrado, plataforma (discurso).
DAISY *s.* margarida.
DALE *s.* vale.
DAM *s.* represa, dique / *v.* represar.
DAMAGE *v.* danificar / *s.* prejuízo; dano.
DAME *s.* dama, mulher.
DAMN *s.* maldição / *v.* condenar, amaldiçoar.
DAMNING *adj.* prejudicial, condenatório.
DAMP *s.* umidade / *adj.* úmido / *v.* umedecer.
DAMPEN *v.* umedecer.
DAMPNESS *s.* umidade.
DAMSEL *s.* rapariga; donzela.
DAMSON *s.* ameixa pequena e roxa.
DANCE *s.* dança / *v.* dançar; bailar.
DANCER *s.* dançarino(a).
DANCING *s.* dança / *adj.* dançante.
DANDELION *s.* dente-de-leão (botânica).
DANDRUFF *s.* caspa.
DANE *s.* dinamarquês(esa).
DANGER *s.* perigo, risco.
DANGEROUS *adj.* perigoso, arriscado.
DANGLE *v.* balançar.
DANISH *adj.* dinamarquês(esa) / *s.* dinamarquês(esa).
DAPPER *adj.* garboso; esperto.
DARE *v.* atrever-se, ousar / *s.* desafio, ousadia.
DAREDEVIL *s.* atrevido; valente / *adj.* valentão, atrevido.
DARING *s.* ousadia, audácia / *adj.* ousado, atrevido.

DARK *adj.* escuro.
DARKEN *v.* escurecer.
DARKNESS *s.* escuridão; trevas.
DARKROOM *s.* câmara escura.
DARLING *adj.* querido(a) / *s.* querido(a).
DARN *v.* cerzir, remendar / *s.* remendo, cerzidura.
DART *s.* dardo / *v.* precipitar-se, jogar dardos.
DARTBOARD *s.* jogo de dardos.
DASH *s.* hífen; colisão; movimento rápido / *v.* arremessar, colidir.
DASHBOARD *s.* painel de instrumentos.
DASHING *adj.* arrojado, enérgico, vivo; elegante.
DATA *s.* dados, informações, detalhes.
DATABASE *s.* banco de dados.
DATA-MINING *s.* mineração de dados.
DATA PROCESSING *s.* processamento de dados.
DATE *s.* data; encontro; tâmara / *v.* namorar.
DATED *adj.* antiquado, fora de moda; datado.
DAUB *s.* argamassa, barro / *v.* borrar; sujar.
DAUGHTER *s.* filha.
DAUGHTER-IN-LAW *s.* nora.
DAUNT *v.* amedrontar, intimidar.
DAUNTING *adj.* desanimador(a).
DAUNTLESS *adj.* destemido(a), corajoso(a).
DAWN *v.* amanhecer / *s.* alvorada, amanhecer, madrugada.
DAY *s.* dia.
DAYBREAK *s.* romper do dia, aurora, alvorada.
DAY-DREAM *s.* devaneio.
DAYLIGHT *s.* luz do dia.
DAYLIGHT-SAVING TIME *s.* horário de verão.
DAZE *s.* ofuscação / *v.* aturdir, ofuscar / *adj.* aturdido, confuso.
DAZZLE *s.* deslumbramento, fascinação / *v.* deslumbrar, encantar.
DAZZLING *s.* deslumbrante, fascinante, ofuscante.
DEAD *s.* defunto / *adj.* morto.
DEADEN *v.* amortecer, abafar (som), aliviar (dor).
DEAD END *s.* beco sem saída.
DEADLINE *s.* prazo final; data limite.
DEADLY *adj.* fatal, mortal.

DEAF *s.* surdo.
DEAFEN *v.* ensurdecer.
DEAFNESS *s.* surdez.
DEAL *s.* negócio; acordo, trato; quantidade / *v.* negociar; tratar; lidar.
DEALER *s.* negociante; vendedor; traficante (drogas, armas); carteador (cartas).
DEAN *s.* reitor(a); decano, deão.
DEARLY *adv.* ternamente; muito.
DEATH *s.* morte.
DEATH-BED *s.* leito de morte.
DEATH PENALTY *s.* pena de morte.
DEBACLE *s.* fracasso, derrota.
DEBASE *v.* degradar, humilhar.
DEBAUCH *s.* deboche; bacanal, devassidão.
DEBAUCHERY *s.* decadência, devassidão.
DEBIT *s.* débito; dívida / *v.* debitar.
DEBRIS *s.* escombros.
DEBT *s.* dívida.
DEBUNK *v.* desmascarar, desiludir.
DEBUT *s.* estreia, debute; primeira tentativa.
DECADE *s.* década.
DECANT *v.* decantar.
DECAY *s.* ruína; decadência; cárie / *v.* enfraquecer; decair; cariar.
DECEASE *s.* morte, óbito.
DECEIVE *v.* enganar, iludir.
DECEMBER *s.* dezembro.
DECENT *adj.* decente, honesto, apropriado.
DECEPTION *s.* engano, fraude, trapaça.
DECEPTIVE *adj.* enganoso, ilusório.
DECIDE *v.* decidir, resolver; julgar.
DECIDED *adj.* decidido, resolvido.
DECIDEDLY *adv.* decididamente, resolutamente.
DECIMAL *s.* decimal / *adj.* decimal.
DECISION *s.* decisão, resolução.
DECISIVE *adj.* decisivo.
DECK *s.* convés, deque.
DECKCHAIR *s.* espreguiçadeira.
DECLARATION *s.* declaração; depoimento.
DECLARE *v.* declarar.
DECLINE *s.* declínio, decadência / *v.* recusar, declinar.
DECODE *v.* decifrar.
DECOMPOSE *v.* decompor(-se); apodrecer.
DECOR *s.* decoração, cenário.
DECORATE *v.* decorar.
DECORATION *s.* decoração.
DECORATIVE *adj.* decorativo.

DECORATOR s. decorador(a).
DECORUM s. decoro, decência.
DECOY s. chamariz, isca, engodo.
DECREASE s. decréscimo; diminuição, redução / v. diminuir, reduzir.
DECREE s. decreto / v. decretar.
DEDICATE v. dedicar, consagrar.
DEDICATION s. dedicação, dedicatória.
DEDUCE v. deduzir, inferir.
DEDUCTION s. dedução.
DEED s. escritura; ação, obra.
DEEM v. estimar; considerar; julgar; crer.
DEEP adj. profundo, fundo / s. profundidade.
DEEPEN v. aprofundar.
DEEPLY adv. profundamente.
DEER s. veado, cervo.
DEER-SKIN s. camurça.
DEFACE v. desfigurar, deformar.
DEFAULT s. falta; revelia; descumprimento / v. faltar a alguma obrigação.
DEFEAT s. derrota, frustração / v. derrotar, frustrar.
DEFECT s. defeito / v. desertar.
DEFECTIVE adj. defeituoso.
DEFEND v. defender, proteger.
DEFENDER s. defensor(a); advogado de defesa.
DEFENSE s. defesa, proteção.
DEFENSELESS adj. indefeso, desprotegido.
DEFENSIVE adj. defensivo / s. defensiva.
DEFER v. adiar, protelar; submeter-se, condescender.
DEFIANCE s. desafio, rebeldia.
DEFIANT adj. desafiador(a).
DEFICIENCY s. deficiência.
DEFICIT s. déficit.
DEFILE s. desfiladeiro, passagem estreita / v. profanar; desonrar; corromper.
DEFINE v. definir, explicar.
DEFINITE adj. definitivo.
DEFINITELY adv. sem dúvida, definitivamente.
DEFINITIVE adj. conclusivo; definido.
DEFLATE v. esvaziar, desinflar; deflacionar.
DEFLATION s. esvaziamento; deflação.
DEFLECT v. desviar.
DEFOREST v. desflorestar, desmatar.
DEFORM v. deformar, desfigurar.
DEFORMITY s. deformidade, deformação.
DEFRAUD v. trapacear, defraudar.

DEFRAY v. custear.
DEFROST v. descongelar, degelar.
DEFT adj. destro; esperto, hábil.
DEFUNCT adj. extinto, morto.
DEFUSE v. neutralizar; desarmar, desativar.
DEFY v. desafiar, provocar.
DEGENERATE v. degenerar / adj. degenerado(a), corrompido(a).
DEGREE s. grau; estágio, classe; diploma.
DEHYDRATED adj. desidratado.
DEICE v. descongelar, remover o gelo.
DEITY s. divindade, deidade.
DEJECT v. abater, desanimar.
DEJECTED adj. deprimido, desanimado.
DELAY s. demora, atraso / v. atrasar, demorar, retardar.
DELECTABLE adj. gostoso, deleitável.
DELEGATE s. delegado(a), representante / v. delegar, encarregar.
DELEGATION s. delegação.
DELETE v. eliminar; deletar (informática); apagar, excluir.
DELIBERATE v. deliberar / adj. deliberado, intencional.
DELIBERATELY adv. propositalmente.
DELICACY s. delicadeza, iguaria.
DELICATE adj. delicado(a); frágil; diplomático.
DELICATESSEN s. guloseimas; casa de mercearias finas.
DELICIOUS adj. delicioso, gostoso.
DELIGHT s. prazer, deleite, encanto / v. encantar, deleitar.
DELIGHTED adj. encantado(a).
DELIGHTFUL adj. encantador(a).
DELINQUENT s. delinquente / adj. delinquente.
DELIRIOUS adj. delirante.
DELIVER v. entregar.
DELIVERANCE s. libertação, livramento.
DELIVERY s. entrega; parto.
DELUDE v. iludir.
DELUGE s. dilúvio / v. inundar.
DELUSION s. ilusão, desilusão.
DEMAND s. demanda / v. demandar, perguntar; exigir.
DEMANDING adj. exigente.
DEMEAN v. rebaixar, humilhar.
DEMEANOR s. conduta, comportamento.
DEMENTED adj. demente, louco.
DEMISE s. falecimento, morte.

DEMISTER s. desembaçador de para-brisa.
DEMO s. manifestação, passeata, demonstração (coloquial).
DEMOCRACY s. democracia.
DEMOCRAT s. democrata.
DEMOCRATIC adj. democrático(a).
DEMOLISH v. demolir.
DEMONSTRATE v. demonstrar.
DEMONSTRATION s. demonstração, manifestação.
DEMONSTRATOR s. manifestante, demonstrador(a).
DEMORAL v. desmoralizar.
DEMOTE v. degradar, rebaixar de graus.
DEMURE adj. recatado; acanhado.
DEN s. covil; espelunca.
DENIAL s. negação, recusa.
DENIM s. brim.
DENMARK s. Dinamarca.
DENOMINATION s. denominação.
DENOUNCE v. denunciar, delatar.
DENSE adj. denso; estúpido (coloquial).
DENSELY adv. densamente.
DENSITY s. densidade.
DENT s. entalhe; dente (de engrenagem, roda, pente) / v. dentear.
DENTAL adj. dentário, dental.
DENTIST s. dentista.
DENTISTRY s. odontologia.
DENTURES s. dentadura.
DENY v. recusar, negar.
DEODORANT s. desodorante.
DEPART v. partir, sair.
DEPARTMENT s. departamento, seção.
DEPARTMENT STORE s. magazine, loja de departamentos.
DEPARTURE s. partida, saída.
DEPEND v. depender.
DEPENDABLE adj. confiável.
DEPENDANT s. dependente.
DEPEND ON v. depender de.
DEPICT v. retratar; pintar.
DEPLETED adj. reduzido(a).
DEPLOY v. dispor; desenrolar-se, estender-se.
DEPOPULATION s. despovoamento.
DEPORT v. deportar, exilar.
DEPORTMENT s. comportamento, conduta.
DEPOSE v. depor, destituir.
DEPOSIT v. depositar / s. depósito, fiança.

DEPOT s. estação, terminal; armazém, depósito.
DEPRAVE v. depravar, perverter.
DEPRECIATE v. depreciar.
DEPRESS v. deprimir; humilhar.
DEPRESSED adj. deprimido(a).
DEPRESSING adj. deprimente, depressivo(a).
DEPRESSION s. depressão.
DEPRIVATION s. privação; pobreza.
DEPRIVE v. privar; destituir.
DEPRIVED adj. carente, necessitado(a).
DEPTH s. profundidade, profundeza; fundo.
DEPUTATION s. delegação.
DEPUTY s. deputado(a), representante.
DERAIL v. descarrilhar.
DERAILMENT s. descarrilhamento.
DERANGED adj. transtornado(a), desordenado(a), louco(a).
DERELICT adj. abandonado(a); infiel.
DERIVE v. derivar, originar.
DERRICK s. guindaste.
DESCENDANT s. descendente.
DESCRIBE v. descrever.
DESCRIPTION s. descrição.
DESCRIPTIVE adj. descritivo(a).
DESECRATE v. profanar, violar.
DESERT v. desertar / s. deserto.
DESERTER s. desertor.
DESERVE v. merecer.
DESERVING adj. digno(a).
DESIGN v. projetar; desenhar / s. desenho; projeto; esboço.
DESIGNATE v. nomear, designar / adj. designado(a), nomeado(a).
DESIGNER s. artista gráfico; estilista; projetista.
DESIRE s. desejo / v. desejar, cobiçar.
DESK s. mesa, escrivaninha, carteira escolar; balcão.
DESOLATE adj. deserto(a); desolado(a), triste / v. desolar.
DESPAIR s. desesperança; desespero / v. desesperar-se.
DESPERATE adj. desesperado, desesperador; sem esperança.
DESPERATELY adv. desesperadamente.
DESPERATION s. desespero.
DESPICABLE adj. vil, desprezível.
DESPISE v. desprezar.
DESPITE prep. apesar de.

DESPOND v. desesperar, desanimar.
DESPONDENT adj. desanimado(a), desesperado(a).
DESSERT s. sobremesa.
DESTINATION s. destino, destinação.
DESTINED adj. destinado.
DESTINY s. destino; sorte.
DESTITUTE adj. necessitado(a); destituído(a); indigente.
DESTROY v. destruir.
DESTRUCTION s. destruição.
DETACH v. separar.
DETACHED adj. imparcial; isolado, separado.
DETACHMENT s. distanciamento, afastamento; imparcialidade.
DETAIL s. detalhe / v. detalhar.
DETAIN v. deter.
DETECT v. perceber, detectar.
DETECTION s. descoberta, detecção.
DETECTIVE s. detetive, investigador.
DETENTION s. prisão, detenção, retenção.
DETER v. dissuadir; intimidar.
DETERGENT s. detergente.
DETERIORATE v. deteriorar-se, estragar.
DETERMINE v. demarcar; determinar; decidir.
DETERMINED adj. resoluto(a), determinado(a).
DETEST v. detestar, abominar.
DETONATE v. detonar, explodir.
DETONATOR s. detonador.
DETOUR s. desvio.
DETRIMENTAL adj. prejudicial, danoso(a).
DEVALUE v. desvalorizar.
DEVASTATE v. devastar, arruinar.
DEVELOP v. desenvolver, progredir; elaborar; revelar.
DEVELOPMENT s. desenvolvimento, evolução; revelação.
DEVICE s. aparelho, dispositivo, mecanismo.
DEVIL s. diabo, demônio.
DEVILISH adj. diabólico(a), maligno(a).
DEVIOUS adj. malandro(a), desonesto(a); tortuoso(a).
DEVISE v. inventar; imaginar.
DEVOLUTION s. devolução, restituição.
DEVOTE v. devotar-se, dedicar.
DEVOTEE s. adepto(a); devoto(a); fã.
DEVOTION s. devoção.
DEVOUR v. devorar.

DEVOUT adj. devoto; sincero, dedicado.
DEW s. orvalho; sereno.
DEWDROP s. gota de orvalho.
DEXTERITY s. destreza, aptidão, habilidade.
DIABETES s. diabetes, diabete.
DIABOLICAL adj. horrível, diabólico(a).
DIAGNOSIS s. diagnóstico.
DIAGONAL s. diagonal / adj. diagonal.
DIAGRAM s. diagrama.
DIAL s. mostrador, indicador; disco / v. discar.
DIALECT s. dialeto.
DIALLING CODE s. código de área.
DIALOGUE s. diálogo / v. dialogar.
DIAMETER s. diâmetro.
DIAMOND s. diamante; brilhante; losango.
DIAPHRAGM s. diafragma.
DIARRHEA s. diarreia.
DIARY s. diário; agenda.
DICE s. jogo de dados; dado / v. cortar em cubos.
DICTATE v. ditar; dar ordens.
DICTATION s. ditado; ordem.
DICTATOR s. ditador.
DICTATORSHIP s. ditadura.
DICTION s. dicção.
DICTIONARY s. dicionário.
DIDACTIC s. didático, instrutivo.
DIDDLE v. trapacear, enganar.
DIE v. morrer; dado.
DIEHARD adj. conservador.
DIESEL s. diesel.
DIET s. regime; dieta.
DIFFER v. discordar, divergir.
DIFFERENCE s. diferença.
DIFFERENT adj. diferente, distinto.
DIFFERENTIATION s. diferenciação.
DIFFERENTLY adv. diferentemente, diversamente.
DIFFICULT adj. difícil.
DIFFICULTY s. dificuldade.
DIFFUSE v. difundir.
DIFFUSION s. difusão, propagação; dispersão.
DIG v. cavar / s. escavação.
DIGEST s. digesto; resumo / v. digerir.
DIGESTIBLE adj. digestível.
DIGESTION s. digestão.
DIGESTIVE adj. digestivo.
DIGGING s. escavação.
DIGIT s. dígito.

DIGITAL *adj.* digital.
DIGNIFIED *adj.* digno, honrado, nobre.
DIGNIFY *v.* dignificar.
DIGNITY *s.* dignidade; decência.
DIGRESS *v.* divagar.
DIGS *s.* pensão, alojamento, aposento.
DIKE *s.* dique, barragem.
DILAPIDATED *adj.* arruinado.
DILATE *v.* dilatar(-se).
DILEMMA *s.* dilema.
DILIGENT *adj.* diligente.
DILUTE *v.* diluir.
DIM *v.* ofuscar / *adj.* escuro; ofuscado(a).
DIME *s.* moeda de dez centavos.
DIMENSION *s.* dimensão; tamanho; medida.
DIMINISH *v.* diminuir.
DIMINUTION *s.* diminuição, redução.
DIMINUTIVE *s.* diminutivo / *adj.* diminutivo, diminuto.
DIMMER *s.* regulador para iluminação.
DIMNESS *s.* obscuridade.
DIMPLE *s.* covinha no rosto.
DIN *s.* alarido (de gente); barulhada (de máquinas).
DINE *v.* jantar.
DINER *s.* aquele que janta; vagão restaurante.
DINETTE *s.* pequena sala de jantar.
DING *s.* tinido de sino / *v.* tinir, ressoar.
DINGY *adj.* sujo(a); desbotado(a).
DINING ROOM *s.* sala de jantar.
DINNER *s.* jantar; ceia.
DIP *s.* mergulho / *v.* mergulhar; molhar.
DIPHTONG *s.* ditongo.
DIPLOMA *s.* diploma.
DIPLOMAT *s.* diplomata.
DIPSWITCH *s.* interruptor.
DIRE *adj.* terrível, fatal.
DIRECT *adj.* direto; franco / *v.* dirigir; conduzir.
DIRECTION *s.* direção.
DIRECTLY *adv.* diretamente.
DIRECTOR *s.* diretor(a).
DIRECTORY *s.* catálogo, lista telefônica.
DIRIGIBLE *s.* dirigível / *adj.* dirigível.
DIRT *s.* sujeira.
DIRTINESS *s.* porcaria; sujidade.
DIRTY *adj.* sujo / *v.* sujar.
DISABILITY *s.* incapacidade; deficiência.
DISABLED *adj.* inválido, incapacitado.
DISADVANTAGE *s.* desvantagem.

DISAFFECTION *s.* desafeição, desamor, inimizade.
DISAGREE *v.* discordar.
DISAGREEABLE *adj.* desagradável.
DISAGREEMENT *s.* desacordo, discordância, divergência.
DISAPPEAR *v.* desaparecer.
DISAPPEARANCE *s.* desaparecimento.
DISAPPOINT *v.* decepcionar, desapontar.
DISAPPOINTMENT *s.* desapontamento, decepção.
DISAPPROVAL *s.* desaprovação.
DISAPPROVE *v.* desaprovar, reprovar.
DISARM *v.* desarmar(-se).
DISARMAMENT *s.* desarmamento.
DISARRAY *s.* desordem; confusão.
DISASTER *s.* desastre, calamidade.
DISBAND *v.* dispersar.
DISBELIEF *s.* descrença.
DISC *s.* disco.
DISCARD *v.* descartar.
DISCERN *v.* identificar; discernir.
DISCERNING *adj.* perspicaz, discernente.
DISCHARGE *v.* dispensar, descarregar / *s.* descarga; dispensa.
DISCIPLE *s.* discípulo(a).
DISCIPLINARY *adj.* disciplinar.
DISCIPLINE *s.* disciplina / *v.* disciplinar.
DISC JOCKEY *s.* radialista.
DISCLAIM *v.* negar.
DISCLAIMER *s.* renúncia, repúdio.
DISCLOSE *v.* revelar; descobrir.
DISCLOSURE *s.* revelação.
DISCO *s.* discoteca.
DISCOLORATION *s.* descoloração.
DISCOLORED *adj.* descolorado, desbotado.
DISCOMFIT *v.* desconcertar, embaraçar.
DISCOMFORT *s.* desconforto, incômodo.
DISCONCERT *v.* desconcertar.
DISCONNECT *v.* desligar, desconectar.
DISCONNECTION *s.* desconexão.
DISCONTENT *s.* descontentamento.
DISCONTENTED *adj.* descontente.
DISCONTINUE *v.* interromper.
DISCORD *s.* discórdia, desarmonia / *v.* discordar.
DISCORDANT *adj.* discordante.
DISCOUNT *s.* desconto / *v.* descontar.
DISCOURAGE *v.* desanimar, desencorajar.
DISCOURAGEMENT *s.* desencorajamento.

DISCOURAGING *adj.* desencorajador.
DISCOURSE *s.* conversa, diálogo, discurso.
DISCOURTEOUS *adj.* descortês; grosseiro, indelicado.
DISCOVER *v.* descobrir.
DISCOVERY *s.* descoberta, descobrimento.
DISCREDIT *v.* desacreditar; desabonar / *s.* descrédito.
DISCREET *adj.* discreto.
DISCREPANCY *s.* discrepância.
DISCRETE *adj.* discreto.
DISCRETION *s.* discrição.
DISCRIMINATE *v.* discriminar.
DISCRIMINATING *adj.* criterioso(a); perspicaz; discriminador(a).
DISCRIMINATION *s.* discriminação.
DISCURSIVE *adj.* discursivo.
DISCUSS *v.* discutir, tratar de um assunto.
DISCUSSION *s.* discussão, debate.
DISDAIN *s.* desdém / *v.* desdenhar.
DISDAINFUL *adj.* desdenhoso.
DISEASE *s.* doença, enfermidade.
DISEASED *adj.* doente, enfermo.
DISEMBARK *v.* desembarcar.
DISEMBODY *v.* desincorporar, desencarnar.
DISFAVOR *s.* desaprovação / *v.* desaprovar.
DISFIGURE *v.* desfigurar.
DISGRACE *s.* desgraça, vergonha, desonra / *v.* desonrar, desgraçar.
DISGRACEFUL *adj.* vergonhoso(a), infame.
DISGRUNTLED *adj.* descontente, desapontado(a).
DISGUISE *s.* disfarce; máscara / *v.* disfarçar, mascarar.
DISGUST *s.* repugnância / *v.* repugnar.
DISGUSTING *adj.* repugnante; desgostoso(a).
DISH *s.* prato, travessa; iguaria.
DISHEVELED *adj.* despenteado(a); desalinhado(a).
DISHONEST *adj.* desonesto(a).
DISHONOR *s.* desonra / *v.* desonrar.
DISHONORABLE *adj.* desonroso.
DISHTOWEL *s.* pano de prato.
DISHWASHER *s.* máquina de lavar louças.
DISILLUSION *v.* desiludir / *s.* desilusão.
DISINFECTANT *s.* desinfetante.
DISINTEGRATE *v.* desintegrar.
DISJOINTED *adj.* desconexo(a), deslocado(a).
DISK *s.* disco; disquete (coloquial).

DISK DRIVE *s.* unidade de disco (informática).
DISKETTE *s.* disquete (informática).
DISLIKE *s.* aversão, antipatia; desagrado / *v.* antipatizar.
DISLOCATE *v.* deslocar.
DISLODGE *v.* desalojar.
DISLOYAL *adj.* desleal, infiel.
DISMAL *adj.* deprimente, triste, sombrio.
DISMANTLE *v.* desmontar.
DISMAY *s.* desânimo / *v.* consternar.
DISMISS *v.* demitir; despedir.
DISMISSAL *s.* demissão.
DISMOUNT *v.* desmontar.
DISOBEDIENT *adj.* desobediente.
DISOBEY *v.* desobedecer.
DISORDER *s.* desordem.
DISORDERLY *adj.* desordenado, confuso / *adv.* desordenadamente.
DISORGANIZATION *s.* desorganização.
DISORIENT *v.* desorientar.
DISOWN *v.* repudiar; desconhecer; negar.
DISPARAGING *adj.* depreciativo.
DISPARATE *adj.* desigual, diferente / *s.* disparate.
DISPARITY *s.* desigualdade, disparidade.
DISPASSIONATE *adj.* imparcial, impassível, controlado.
DISPATCH *s.* despacho; remessa / *v.* enviar.
DISPEL *v.* dissipar; dispersar.
DISPENSE *v.* dispensar, atribuir, conceder.
DISPENSER *s.* distribuidor automático, dispensador.
DISPERSE *v.* dispersar, disseminar.
DISPIRITED *adj.* desanimado, deprimido.
DISPLACE *v.* deslocar, substituir.
DISPLAY *s.* exibição / *v.* mostrar; exibir.
DISPLEASE *v.* ofender; desagradar.
DISPLEASURE *s.* desgosto, desprazer; aborrecimento.
DISPOSABLE *adj.* descartável, disponível.
DISPOSAL *s.* venda, uso; disposição, disponibilidade.
DISPOSE *v.* dispor, arranjar, ordenar.
DISPOSED *adj.* disposto; preparado.
DISPOSITION *s.* disposição; temperamento.
DISPROVE *v.* refutar; contestar.
DISPUTE *v.* questionar / *s.* disputa.
DISQUALIFY *v.* desqualificar.

DISREGARD v. ignorar, desconsiderar / s. desconsideração, indiferença.
DISRESPECT s. desrespeito, desconsideração / v. desrespeitar.
DISRUPT v. perturbar, interromper.
DISRUPTION s. interrupção, rompimento.
DISSATISFACTION s. descontentamento.
DISSATISFY v. descontentar.
DISSECT v. dissecar.
DISSEMBLE v. dissimular.
DISSERTATION s. dissertação.
DISSIMILAR adj. diferente.
DISSIMULATE v. dissimular, fingir.
DISSIPATE v. dissipar.
DISSOLVE v. dissolver.
DISSUADE v. dissuadir.
DISTANCE s. distância.
DISTANT adj. distante.
DISTASTE s. desagrado; aversão.
DISTASTEFUL adj. repugnante, desagradável.
DISTEND v. estender-se, expandir, alargar.
DISTENDED adj. inchado, distendido.
DISTIL v. destilar.
DISTILLERY s. destilaria.
DISTINCT adj. distinto.
DISTINCTION s. distinção.
DISTINGUISH v. distinguir.
DISTINGUISHED adj. distinto(a); famoso(a).
DISTORT v. distorcer; torcer; corromper.
DISTRACT v. distrair.
DISTRACTED adj. distraído.
DISTRACTION s. distração.
DISTRESS s. aflição; angústia / v. afligir.
DISTRESSING adj. angustiante, penoso.
DISTRIBUTE v. distribuir.
DISTRIBUTION s. distribuição.
DISTRICT s. distrito, bairro.
DISTRUST s. desconfiança / v. desconfiar.
DISTURB v. perturbar, incomodar.
DISTURBANCE s. distúrbio, perturbação.
DISTURBED adj. perturbado.
DISTURBING adj. perturbador, inquietante.
DISUSED adj. abandonado(a), fora de uso.
DITCH v. abandonar, livrar-se de / s. fosso, vala.
DITHER v. vacilar (coloquial).
DITTO s. idem, o mesmo.
DIVAN s. divã.
DIVE s. mergulho / v. mergulhar.
DIVER s. mergulhador.

DIVERS adj. diversos, vários.
DIVERSE adj. diverso(a), diversificado(a).
DIVERSIFY v. diversificar.
DIVERSION s. diversão, distração; desvio.
DIVERSITY s. diversidade.
DIVERT v. desviar; distrair.
DIVIDE v. dividir, repartir.
DIVINE adj. divino(a).
DIVING s. salto ornamental, mergulho.
DIVING BOARD s. trampolim.
DIVINITY s. divindade.
DIVISION s. divisão; seção, departamento.
DIVORCE s. divórcio / v. divorciar-se de.
DIVORCED adj. divorciado.
DIVORCEE s. divorciada.
DIVULGE v. divulgar, revelar.
DIZZINESS s. tontura, vertigem.
DIZZY adj. tonto(a), atordoado(a) / v. causar desmaios; atordoar.
DJ abrev. DJ, discotecário, locutor.
DO v. fazer, executar.
DOCENT s. docente, guia.
DOCILE adj. dócil.
DOCK s. doca, embarcadouro / v. atracar (navios).
DOCKYARD s. estaleiro.
DOCTOR s. doutor(a), médico(a).
DOCTRINE s. doutrina.
DOCUMENT s. documento / v. documentar.
DOCUMENTARY adj. documentário / s. documentário (filme).
DOE s. coelha; corça.
DOG s. cachorro, cão / v. perseguir.
DOINGS s. atividades; ações.
DO-IT-YOURSELF s. faça você mesmo.
DOLEFUL adj. triste; doloroso.
DOLL s. boneca.
DOLLAR s. dólar.
DOLL UP v. embonecar-se (coloquial).
DOLPHIN s. golfinho.
DOMAIN s. domínio, propriedade.
DOME s. cúpula, abóbada.
DOMESTIC adj. doméstico, caseiro; nacional, interno.
DOMESTICATED adj. domesticado(a).
DOMINATE v. dominar.
DOMINATION s. dominação.
DOMINEERING adj. mandão(ona), dominador(a).
DOMINION s. domínio, poder absoluto.
DOMINOES s. jogo de dominó.

DON s. dom. fidalgo.
DONATE v. doar, contribuir.
DONE adj. completo, pronto.
DONKEY s. burro, asno.
DONOR s. doador(a).
DONUT s. sonho (doce).
DOOM s. julgamento; sentença; perdição / v. condenar.
DOOMSDAY s. dia do julgamento final.
DOOR s. porta; acesso.
DOORBELL s. campainha.
DOOR-HANDLE s. maçaneta.
DOOR-MAT s. capacho.
DOPE s. narcótico, droga / v. dopar, drogar.
DOPE FIEND s. drogado, viciado em narcóticos.
DORMANT adj. inativo, latente.
DORMITORY s. dormitório; alojamento estudantil.
DOSAGE s. dosagem, dose.
DOSE s. dose / v. dosar.
DOT s. ponto / v. pontilhar.
DOTE v. adorar.
DOTTED LINE s. linha pontilhada.
DOUBLE adj. duplo; dobro / v. dobrar / s. duplo, dobro; cópia; dublê.
DOUBLY adv. duplamente.
DOUBT s. dúvida / v. duvidar, hesitar.
DOUBTFUL adj. duvidoso, incerto.
DOUBTLESS adv. sem dúvida.
DOUSE v. encharcar, ensopar.
DOVE s. pomba.
DOWDY adj. deselegante, desleixado.
DOWN s. penugem, penas; buço / adv. para baixo.
DOWNSTAIRS adv. embaixo, para baixo / s. andar térreo / adj. de baixo.
DOWNSTREAM adj. rio abaixo.
DOWNTOWN s. centro da cidade.
DOWRY s. dote.
DOZE s. soneca / v. cochilar.
DOZEN s. dúzia.
DRAB adj. monótono, sem graça.
DRAFT s. rascunho, esboço; saque; corrente de ar / v. rascunhar, esboçar.
DRAG s. peso, chato (coloquial) / v. arrastar-se.
DRAGON s. dragão.
DRAGONFLY s. libélula.

DRAIN s. dreno; bueiro / v. drenar; escoar; enfraquecer, esvair.
DRAINAGE s. drenagem.
DRAINPIPE s. cano de esgoto.
DRAKE s. pato; marreco.
DRAMA s. drama; peça de teatro.
DRAPE s. cortina; cortinado / v. ornar; cobrir.
DRASTIC adj. drástico; grave.
DRAW v. desenhar, traçar; empatar / s. empate.
DRAWER s. gaveta.
DRAWING s. desenho; sorteio; saque.
DREAD s. terror / v. temer.
DREADFUL adj. terrível, horrível.
DREAM s. sonho / v. sonhar.
DREAMY adj. sonhador(a).
DREARY adj. monótono(a); lúgubre.
DREDGE v. dragar / s. draga.
DREGS s. escória, resíduos; ralé.
DRENCH s. remédio líquido / v. encharcar.
DRESS v. vestir; temperar / s. vestido.
DRESSING s. ação de vestir-se; tempero, condimento.
DRESSING-DOWN s. surra; correção.
DRESSING GOWN s. roupão.
DRESSMAKER s. costureira.
DRESSY adj. chique.
DRIBBLE v. driblar; babar / s. baba, saliva; drible (futebol).
DRIED adj. seco, desidratado.
DRIFT v. derivar, ir à deriva / s. vento; correnteza.
DRILL v. furar / s. furadeira; broca.
DRINK s. bebida / v. beber.
DRINKABLE adj. bebível.
DRINKING WATER s. água potável.
DRIP s. gota, gotejamento / v. pingar, gotejar.
DRIPPING s. gordura, banha; gotejamento / adj. gorduroso, encharcado.
DRIVE s. passeio de carro / v. dirigir.
DRIVEL s. bobagem, disparate; baba; saliva.
DRIVER s. motorista.
DRIVING s. direção.
DRIVING LICENCE s. carteira de motorista.
DRIVING MIRROR s. retrovisor.
DRIVING SCHOOL s. autoescola.
DRIZZLE s. chuvisco, garoa / v. garoar.
DROLL s. engraçado, divertido.
DRONE s. zangão; zumbido / v. zunir, zumbir.

DROOP s. inclinação, abatimento / v. inclinar-se, pender; desanimar.
DROOPING s. tristeza; gotejamento / adj. gotejante.
DROP s. gota, pingo / v. cair; deixar cair, derrubar.
DROPLET s. gotinha, gotícula.
DROP-OFF s. decadência.
DROPPER s. conta-gotas.
DROUGHT s. seca.
DROWN v. afogar-se.
DROWSE s. sonolência, soneca / v. cochilar, dormitar.
DROWSY adj. sonolento(a).
DRUG s. remédio; droga / v. drogar; ingerir drogas.
DRUG-ADDICT s. viciado(a) em drogas.
DRUGGIST s. farmacêutico(a).
DRUGSTORE s. drogaria; farmácia.
DRUM s. tambor, bateria; tímpano / v. rufar, tocar tambor.
DRUMMER s. baterista.
DRUNK adj. bêbado(a), embriagado(a).
DRUNKARD s. alcoólatra, bêbado.
DRUNKENNESS s. bebedeira; embriaguez.
DRY v. secar / adj. seco; árido.
DRY CLEANING s. lavagem a seco.
DRYER s. secador.
DRYNESS s. secura, aridez; ironia.
DRY-NURSE s. ama-seca, aia.
DUAL adj. duplo.
DUBBED adj. dublado.
DUBIOUS adj. duvidoso, incerto.
DUCHESS s. duquesa.
DUCK s. pato(a).
DUCKLING s. filhote de pato.
DUCT s. ducto, canal, tubo.
DUE s. dívida / adj. devido.
DUEL s. duelo.
DUET s. dueto, duo.
DUFFEL BAG s. mochila, saco de pano grosso.
DUKE s. duque.
DULL adj. enfadonho, monótono; nublado (tempo).
DULLY adv. desanimadamente.
DULY adv. devidamente; no tempo devido.
DUMB adj. estúpido, obtuso.
DUMMY s. manequim; imbecil (coloquial); testa de ferro.
DUMP s. espelunca; depósito de lixo / v. esvaziar, despejar.
DUMPY adj. gorducho(a), rechonchudo(a).
DUNCE s. estúpido, bronco.
DUNE s. duna.
DUNG s. estrume, esterco.
DUNGAREES s. macacão, jardineira.
DUPE s. incauto, ingênuo / v. enganar.
DUPLEX s. casa geminada / adj. duplex, duplo.
DUPLICATE s. duplicata, réplica / v. duplicar, copiar / adj. duplicado.
DUPLICITY s. duplicidade; fingimento, fraude.
DURABLE adj. durável, duradouro.
DURING prep. durante.
DUST s. poeira, pó / v. tirar o pó.
DUSTY adj. empoeirado.
DUTCH adj. holandês(esa) / s. língua holandesa.
DUTIFUL adj. respeitoso, obediente.
DUTY s. dever, obrigação; taxa, imposto; tarefa, função.
DWARF s. anão(ã).
DWELL v. morar, habitar, residir.
DWELLER s. morador, habitante.
DYE s. tintura / v. tingir.
DYER s. tintureiro.
DYING adj. moribundo, agonizante; último.
DYKE s. dique; represa.
DYNAMIC adj. dinâmico.
DYNAMICS s. dinâmica.
DYNAMITE s. dinamite / v. dinamitar.

E e

E, e s. quinta letra do alfabeto inglês; mi (nota musical).
EACH adj. cada / pron. cada qual / adv. para cada um, cada um.
EAGER adj. ávido, ansioso; impaciente.
EAGERLY adv. ansiosamente.
EAGERNESS s. ânsia; avidez; entusiasmo.
EAGLE s. águia.
EAGLE EYE s. olhos de águia; boa visão.
EAR s. orelha.
EARACHE s. dor de ouvido.
EARBUD s. fone de ouvido.
EAR CANAL s. canal auditivo.
EAR DEAFENING adj. ensurdecedor.
EARDRUM s. tímpano.
EAR FOR MUSIC s. ouvido para música; boa audição.
EARL s. conde.
EARLIER adj. adiantado, anterior, prévio / adv. mais cedo, anteriormente.
EARLIEST adj. mais antigo, anterior.
EARLY adv. cedo / adj. prematuro, precoce.
EARMARK v. reservar, destinar / s. marca de identificação.
EARN v. ganhar; receber.
EARN A LIVING v. ganhar a vida.
EARNEST adj. intenso; sério, grave.
EARNINGS s. salário, ordenado; ganhos.
EARPHONE s. fone de ouvido.
EAR PLUGS s. protetor auricular.
EARRING s. brinco.
EARTH s. Terra (planeta); terra (solo), terreno.
EARTHBOUND adj. terrestre, mundano.
EARTHEN adj. barroso, argiloso.
EARTHLING s. terráqueo.
EARTHLY adj. terrestre, terreno; mundano.
EARTHQUAKE s. terremoto; comoção.
EARTHWARE s. louça de barro, cerâmica / adj. de louça.
EARTHWORK s. aterro, terraplenagem.
EARTHWORM s. minhoca.
EARTHY adj. terrento, cheiro de terra.
EARWAX s. cerume, cerúmen; cera de ouvido.
EASE s. facilidade, conforto, alívio / v. facilitar, aliviar.
EASEL s. cavalete (de pintor).

EASEMENT *s.* mitigação, alívio.
EASIER *adj.* mais fácil.
EASILY *adv.* facilmente.
EASINESS *s.* facilidade, tranquilidade.
EAST *s.* leste, oriente / *adj.* oriental, do leste.
EASTER *s.* Páscoa.
EASTERLY *adv.* oriental, oriundo do ou em direção ao leste.
EASTERN *adj.* oriental; do oriente.
EASTERNER *s.* habitante do leste.
EASTWARD *adv.* ao leste.
EASY *adj.* fácil; tranquilo, simples.
EASY CHAIR *s.* poltrona; espreguiçadeira.
EASYGOING *adj.* descontraído; fácil de lidar.
EAT *v.* comer; corroer, destruir.
EATABLE *s.* comestível / *adj.* comestível, comível.
EATER *s.* comedor; devorador.
EATERY *s.* lanchonete, restaurante.
EATING *adj. m.q.* eatable.
EATING DISORDER *s.* distúrbio alimentar.
EAVE *s.* beiral do telhado; calha.
EAVESDROP *v.* escutar atrás da porta; espiar.
EAVESDROPPER *s.* bisbilhoteiro, intrometido; enxerido.
EBB *s.* decadência; maré baixa / *v.* baixar, diminuir, declinar.
EBONY *s.* ébano.
EBULLIENT *adj.* efervescente; vivaz.
ECCENTRIC *adj.* excêntrico, extravagante / *s.* excêntrico, extravagante.
ECCENTRICITY *s.* excentricidade.
ECCLESIASTICAL *adj.* eclesiástico.
ECHO *s.* eco, ressonância / *v.* ecoar.
ECHO CHAMBER *s.* câmara de ressonância.
ECLAIR *s.* bomba (doce), ecler.
ECLETIC *adj.* eclético.
ECLIPSE *s.* eclipse, escurecimento / *v.* ofuscar, eclipsar.
ECLIPTIC *adj.* eclíptico.
ECOLOGICAL *adj.* ecológico.
ECOLOGIST *s.* ecologista.
ECOLOGY *s.* ecologia.
ECONOMIC *adj.* econômico.
ECONOMICAL *adj.* rentável, econômico.
ECONOMICALLY *adv.* economicamente.
ECONOMICS *s.* economia (ciência).

ECONOMISE *v.* economizar.
ECONOMIST *s.* economista.
ECONOMY *s.* economia.
ECONOMY CLASS *s.* classe econômica.
ECOSYSTEM *s.* ecossistema.
ECOTOURISM *s.* ecoturismo.
ECOTOURIST *s.* ecoturista.
ECSTASY *s.* êxtase; euforia.
ECSTATIC *adj.* extático.
ECUADOR *s.* Equador.
ECUMENICAL *adj.* ecumênico.
ECUMENISM *s.* ecumenismo.
ECZEMA *s.* eczema; doença de pele.
EDEMA *s.* edema.
EDEN *s.* Éden; paraíso.
EDGE *s.* borda, beira, aba / *v.* afiar, mover.
EDGER *s.* afiador, amolador.
EDGING *s.* orla, borda; fita, barra.
EDGY *adj.* inquieto, impaciente; provocativo.
EDIBLE *adj. m.q.* eatable.
EDICT *s.* mandato, decreto.
EDIFICATION *s.* edificação.
EDIFICE *s.* edifício, construção.
EDIFY *v.* edificar; instruir, aperfeiçoar.
EDINBURGH *s.* Edimburgo (Escócia).
EDIT *v.* editar, revisar / *s.* edição, corte, modificação.
EDITING *s.* edição, revisão, correção / *adj.* editor.
EDITION *s.* edição, publicação.
EDITOR *s.* editor.
EDITORIAL *adj.* editorial / *s.* editorial.
EDITORIALISE *v.* editorar.
EDUCATE *v.* educar, ensinar, instruir.
EDUCATED *adj.* educado; instruído, culto.
EDUCATION *s.* educação, formação, instrução.
EDUCATIONAL *adj.* educativo, educacional.
EDUCATIVE *adj.* educativo.
EDUCATOR *s.* educador.
EEK *interj.* vixe! credo! nossa!
EEL *s.* enguia.
EERIE *adj.* estranho, assustador; horripilante.
EERILY *adv.* assustadoramente.
EFFACE *v.* apagar, obliterar, eclipsar.
EFFECT *s.* efeito, resultado / *v.* efetuar, executar.
EFFECTIVE *adj.* eficaz, efetivo; apto.

EFFECTIVELY *adv.* efetivamente.
EFFECTIVENESS *s.* eficácia, eficiência.
EFFECTS *s.* bens móveis; posse, objetos pessoais.
EFFECTUAL *adj.* eficaz, efetivo.
EFFECTUATE *v.* efetuar.
EFFEMINATE *adj.* afeminado; delicado.
EFFERVESCENCE *s.* efervescência.
EFFERVESCENT *adj.* efervescente.
EFFICACIOUS *adj.* eficaz.
EFFICACY *s.* eficácia.
EFFICIENCY *s.* eficiência.
EFFICIENT *adj.* eficiente, competente.
EFFICIENTLY *adv.* eficientemente.
EFFORT *s.* esforço; empenho; conquista.
EFFORTLESS *adj.* fácil, sem esforço; natural.
EFFORTLESSLY *adv.* facilmente.
EFFRONTERY *s.* descaramento, insolência.
EFFUSE *v.* efundir, derramar; espalhar.
EFFUSION *s.* efusão.
EFFUSIVE *adj.* efusivo, caloroso.
EGALITARIAN *s.* igualitário / *adj.* igualitário.
EGALITARIANISM *s.* igualitarismo.
EGALITARIST *s.* igualitarista.
EGG *s.* ovo; óvulo.
EGGPLANT *s.* berinjela.
EGGSHELL *s.* casca de ovo / *adj.* fino.
EGO *s.* ego.
EGOCENTRIC *adj.* egocêntrico.
EGOISM *s.* egoísmo; vaidade.
EGOIST *s.* egoísta.
EGOTISM *s. m.q.* egoism.
EGREGIOUS *adj.* egrégio; odioso, ofensivo.
EGRESS *s.* egressão, saída.
EGYPT *s.* Egito.
EGYPTIAN *adj.* egípcio / *s.* egípcio.
EIGHT *num.* oito.
EIGHTEEN *num.* dezoito.
EIGHTEENTH *num.* décimo oitavo.
EIGHTH *num.* oitavo.
EIGHTIES *s.* anos 80; década de 80.
EIGHTIETH *num.* octogésimo.
EIGHTY *num.* oitenta.
EIRE *s.* Irlanda.
EITHER *adj.* um ou outro; cada, qualquer / *adv.* tampouco / *conj.* ou.
EJACULATE *v.* ejacular / *s.* sêmen.
EJACULATION *s.* ejaculação; exclamação.
EJECT *v.* expulsar; lançar; expelir.
EJECTION *s.* ejeção.
EJECTOR *s.* ejetor.
EKE *v.* aumentar, alargar, acrescentar; ganhar a vida com dificuldade.
ELABORATE *v.* aperfeiçoar; elaborar; detalhar / *adj.* complicado; elaborado.
ELABORATELY *adv.* elaboradamente.
ELABORATION *s.* elaboração.
ELAPSE *v.* transcorrer; passar, decorrer.
ELASTIC *s.* elástico / *adj.* flexível, elástico.
ELASTIC BAND *s.* elástico, borrachinha (de juntar dinheiro).
ELASTICISE *v.* elastificar; esticar.
ELASTICITY *s.* elasticidade.
ELATE *v.* elevar, exaltar; alegrar.
ELATED *adj.* exultante.
ELATION *s.* exaltação, júbilo; elevação.
ELBOW *s.* cotovelo / *v.* cotovelar.
ELDER *adj.* mais velho; primogênito; ancião.
ELDERCARE *s.* atendimento a idosos.
ELDERLY *adj.* idoso / *s.* idoso.
ELDEST *adj.* mais velho; primogênito.
ELECT *s.* predestinado, escolhido / *v.* eleger, escolher.
ELECTED *adj.* eleito, escolhido.
ELECTION *s.* eleição, votação.
ELECTIONEERING *s.* campanha eleitoral, ser candidato.
ELECTIVE *adj.* eletivo.
ELECTOR *s.* eleitor.
ELECTORAL *adj.* eleitoral.
ELECTORATE *s.* eleitorado.
ELECTRIC *adj.* elétrico; vibrante.
ELECTRICAL *adj.* elétrico.
ELECTRICIAN *s.* eletricista.
ELECTRICITY *s.* eletricidade.
ELECTRIFICATION *s.* eletrificação.
ELECTRIFY *v.* eletrificar.
ELECTROCARDIOGRAM *s.* eletrocardiograma.
ELECTROCARDIOGRAPHY *s.* eletrocardiografia.
ELECTROCUTE *v.* eletrocutar.
ELECTROCUTION *s.* eletrocussão.
ELECTRODE *s.* eletrodo.
ELECTRON *s.* elétron.
ELECTRONIC *adj.* eletrônico.
ELECTRONIC DEVICE *s.* aparelho eletrônico.
ELECTRONIC MAIL *s.* correio eletrônico, e-mail.
ELECTRONIC MUSIC *s.* música eletrônica.

ELECTRONICS s. eletrônica (ciência).
ELEGANCE s. elegância.
ELEGANT adj. elegante, gracioso.
ELEGANTLY adv. elegantemente.
ELEGIAC adj. elegíaco (poema); chorão.
ELEGY s. elegia, lamento (poema e música).
ELEMENT s. elemento.
ELEMENTAL adj. elementar.
ELEMENTARY adj. elementar; rudimentar.
ELEMENTARY EDUCATION s. educação básica.
ELEMENTARY SCHOOL s. escola primária.
ELEPHANT s. elefante.
ELEVATE v. elevar; levantar, erguer.
ELEVATED adj. elevado; erguido.
ELEVATION s. elevação, altura.
ELEVATOR s. elevador.
ELEVEN num. onze.
ELEVENTH num. décimo primeiro; undécimo.
ELF s. (pl. elves) duente; gnomo.
ELFIN adj. élfico; delicado, pequeno.
ELIDE v. eliminar.
ELIGIBILITY s. elegibilidade.
ELIGIBLE adj. elegível, qualificado.
ELIMINATE v. eliminar, remover, excluir.
ELIMINATION s. eliminação.
ELIMINATOR s. eliminatória (esporte); eliminador.
ELITE s. elite / adj. elite.
ELITISM s. elitismo.
ELITIST s. elitista / adj. elitista.
ELK s. alce (animal).
ELLIPSE s. elipse, oval (forma).
ELOCUTION s. elocução.
ELONGATE v. alongar, prolongar.
ELONGATED adj. alongado, comprido.
ELONGATION s. prolongação, prolongamento.
ELOPE v. fugir, escapar, evadir-se.
ELOPEMENT s. fuga, evasão, escapada.
ELOQUENCE s. eloquência.
ELOQUENT adj. eloquente.
ELOQUENTLY adv. eloquentemente.
EL SALVADOR s. El Salvador (América Central).
ELSE adv. mais; em vez de / conj. ou, senão / adj. diverso.
ELSEWHERE adv. em outro lugar.
ELUCIDATE v. elucidar, esclarecer.

ELUCIDATION s. elucidação.
ELUDE v. esquivar; iludir; evitar.
ELUSIVE adj. ardiloso; evasivo, esquivo.
EMACIATE v. emaciar, definhar.
EMACIATED adj. definhado, emagrecido.
E-MAIL s. correio eletrônico / v. enviar mensagem.
EMANATE v. emanar, exalar, irradiar.
EMANATION s. emanação, exalação.
EMANCIPATE v. emancipar; libertar-se.
EMANCIPATION s. emancipação, libertação.
EMASCULATE v. emascular, castrar.
EMBALM v. embalsamar.
EMBANK v. deter, represar; aterrar.
EMBANKMENT s. aterro, talude; dique, barreira.
EMBARGO s. proibição, interdição; embargo.
EMBARK v. embarcar.
EMBARKATION s. embarque; embarcação.
EMBARRASS v. constranger; embaraçar.
EMBARRASSED adj. desconfortável, constrangido.
EMBARRASSING adj. embaraçoso, desagradável.
EMBARRASSMENT s. constrangimento; embaraço.
EMBASSADOR s. embaixador.
EMBASSY s. embaixada.
EMBATTLED adj. sitiado; pronto para combater.
EMBED v. embutir.
EMBEDDED adj. encaixado, embutido.
EMBELLISH v. embelezar, enfeitar, ornar.
EMBELLISHER s. decorador, embelezador.
EMBELLISHMENT s. ornamento, embelezamento; adorno.
EMBER s. brasa, tição.
EMBEZZLE v. desviar, fraudar.
EMBEZZLEMENT s. apropriação indevida.
EMBITTER v. amargar, amargurar; angustiar.
EMBITTERED adj. amargo; amargurado, sofrido.
EMBITTERMENT s. amargura; ressentimento.
EMBLEM s. emblema; símbolo.
EMBLEMATIC adj. emblemático; simbólico.
EMBODIMENT s. incorporação; encarnação.

EMBODY v. incorporar; encarnar.
EMBOLDEN v. encorajar, animar.
EMBOLISM s. embolia.
EMBOSOM v. abraçar, acariciar, afagar.
EMBOSS v. realçar, ornar com relevos.
EMBOSSED adj. realçado, ornado.
EMBRACE v. abraçar, envolver / s. abraço; aceitação.
EMBROIDER v. bordar; ornar, enfeitar.
EMBROIDERY s. bordado.
EMBRYO s. embrião; feto.
EMBRYOLOGY s. embriologia.
EMBRYONIC adj. embrionário.
EMEND v. emendar, corrigir.
EMENDATION s. emenda, correção.
EMERALD s. esmeralda.
EMERGE v. emergir, aparecer, surgir.
EMERGENCY s. emergência / adj. de emergência.
EMERGENCY EXIT s. saída de emergência.
EMERGENCY ROOM s. sala de emergência.
EMERGENT adj. emergente.
EMIGRANT s. emigrante / adj. emigrante.
EMIGRATE v. emigrar.
EMIGRATION s. emigração.
EMINENCE s. eminência.
EMINENT adj. eminente; notável, famoso.
EMIRATE s. emirado.
EMISSARY s. emissário.
EMISSION s. emissão.
EMIT v. emitir, liberar.
EMITTER s. emissor.
EMOTE v. emocionar-se, comover-se.
EMOTION s. emoção.
EMOTIONAL adj. emocional; emotivo.
EMOTIONAL HEALTH s. saúde emocional.
EMOTIONAL INTELLIGENCE s. inteligência emocional.
EMOTIONALLY adv. emocionalmente.
EMOTIVE adj. m.q. emotional.
EMPATHETIC adj. empático; compreensivo.
EMPATHIC adj. m.q. empathetic.
EMPATHISE v. sentir empatia; simpatizar.
EMPATHY s. empatia, compaixão.
EMPEROR s. imperador.
EMPHASIS s. ênfase; destaque.
EMPHASISE v. enfatizar; destacar, ressaltar.
EMPHATIC adj. enfático, categórico.
EMPHATICALLY adv. enfaticamente.
EMPIRE s. império.

EMPIRICAL adj. empírico.
EMPIRISM s. empirismo.
EMPLACEMENT s. posição; situação.
EMPLOY v. empregar; usar, aplicar.
EMPLOYABLE adj. empregável; aplicável.
EMPLOYEE s. empregado, colaborador.
EMPLOYER s. empregador, patrão.
EMPLOYMENT s. emprego, trabalho.
EMPOISON v. envenenar.
EMPOISONMENT s. envenenamento.
EMPORIUM s. empório.
EMPOWER v. autorizar; capacitar; habilitar.
EMPOWERMENT v. fortalecimento, autorização.
EMPRESS s. imperatriz.
EMPTINESS s. vácuo, vazio; frieza; futilidade.
EMPTY adj. vazio, vago; inútil / v. esvaziar; desocupar.
EMULATE v. emular, imitar, copiar.
EMULATION s. emulação, imitação.
EMULATOR s. emulador; imitador.
EMULSION s. emulsão.
ENABLE v. tornar possível; habilitar, permitir.
ENABLER s. facilitador, possibilitador.
ENACT v. decretar, legalizar.
ENACTMENT s. representação; decreto, lei.
ENAMEL s. esmalte / v. esmaltar.
ENAMOUR v. enamorar, encantar.
ENAMOURED adj. enamorado, encantado.
ENCAGE v. engaiolar, enjaular.
ENCAMP v. acampar.
ENCAMPMENT s. acampamento.
ENCAPSULATE v. encapsular; sintetizar, resumir.
ENCAPSULATION s. encapsulamento; resumo.
ENCASE v. encaixotar, encaixar; revestir.
ENCHAIN v. acorrentar; prender.
ENCHANT v. encantar, maravilhar.
ENCHANTED adj. encantado, enfeitiçado.
ENCHANTER s. feiticeiro; mágico.
ENCHANTING adj. encantador, cativante.
ENCHANTMENT s. encantamento.
ENCHANTRESS s. feiticeira, sedutora.
ENCIRCLE v. circundar; cercar, envolver.
ENCLASP v. abraçar, cingir.
ENCLAVE s. enclave.

ENCLOSE v. cercar; anexar, incluir.
ENCLOSED adj. incluso, anexado; fechado.
ENCLOSURE s. cerco, anexo, inclusão.
ENCODE v. codificar.
ENCODER s. codificador.
ENCOMPASS v. abranger, abarcar.
ENCORE s. bis / v. pedir bis.
ENCOUNTER s. encontro; conflito / v. encontrar, deparar.
ENCOURAGE v. encorajar, apoiar.
ENCOURAGEMENT s. encorajamento, estímulo; apoio.
ENCOURAGING adj. encorajador, animador.
ENCROACH v. invadir, usurpar; violar.
ENCROACHMENT s. invasão, intrusão.
ENCRUST v. cobrir, revestir; incrustar.
ENCRUSTED adj. incrustado, revestido.
ENCRYPT v. criptografar; cifrar.
ENCRYPTION s. criptografia, codificação.
ENCUMBER v. embaraçar, dificultar.
ENCUMBRANCE s. ônus, encargo; estorvo.
ENCYCLICAL adj. encíclico, circular.
ENCYCLOPAEDIA s. enciclopédia.
ENCYCLOPAEDIC adj. enciclopédico.
ENCYCLOPEDIA s. m.q. encyclopaedia.
ENCYCLOPEDIC s. m.q. encyclopaedic.
END s. fim, final / v. terminar; dar um fim.
ENDANGER v. arriscar, expor; pôr em risco.
ENDANGERED adj. ameaçado; em extinção.
ENDANGERMENT s. risco, perigo.
ENDEAR v. ser benquisto, tornar estimável.
ENDEARING adj. simpático, terno, afetuoso.
ENDEARMENT s. afeto, carinho, ternura.
ENDEAVOUR s. tentativa; empenho / v. esforçar-se.
ENDGAME s. final, fim de jogo.
ENDING s. conclusão, fim, término.
ENDIVE s. chicória; endívia.
ENDLESS adj. infinito; infindável.
ENDOCRINE s. endócrino (hormônio).
ENDOCRINOLOGIST s. endocrinologista.
ENDOCRINOLOGY s. endocrinologia.
ENDORPHIN s. endorfina.
ENDORSE v. endossar, aprovar; apoiar.
ENDORSEMENT s. aval, endosso, aprovação.
ENDORSER s. patrocinador; apoiador.
ENDOSCOPE s. endoscópio.

ENDOSCOPY s. endoscopia.
ENDOW v. dotar, prendar; doar.
ENDOWMENT s. doação, dote.
ENDPOINT s. ponto final.
ENDURABLE adj. sofrível, suportável, tolerável.
ENDURANCE s. tolerância, duração, resistência.
ENDURE v. aturar, suportar, resistir.
ENDURING adj. duradouro, persistente.
ENEMY adj. inimigo / s. inimigo.
ENERGETIC adj. energético; animado.
ENERGISE v. energizar.
ENERGISER s. energizador, tônico, estimulante.
ENERGY s. energia; força.
ENERVATING adj. enervante; debilitante.
ENFEEBLE v. enfraquecer, debilitar.
ENFOLD v. enrolar, encobrir.
ENFORCE v. fazer cumprir, obrigar, impor.
ENFORCEABLE adj. obrigatório, executável.
ENFORCED adj. imposto; executado.
ENFORCEMENT s. execução.
ENFORCER s. mandante.
ENFRAME v. emoldurar, enquadrar.
ENGAGE v. comprometer-se, noivar; empenhar.
ENGAGED adj. ocupado; noivo.
ENGAGEMENT s. noivado; compromisso.
ENGAGEMENT RING s. anel de noivado.
ENGAGING adj. atraente, sedutor, insinuante.
ENGENDER v. engendrar, gerar.
ENGINE s. motor; máquina, locomotiva.
ENGINEER s. engenheiro.
ENGINEER DRIVER s. maquinista (trem).
ENGINEERING s. engenharia.
ENGLAND s. Inglaterra.
ENGLISH adj. inglês / s. inglês (idioma).
ENGLISHMAN s. inglês.
ENGLISHWOMAN s. inglesa.
ENGORGE v. entupir, obstruir.
ENGRAVE v. gravar, esculpir, estampar.
ENGRAVING s. gravura, estampa.
ENGROSS v. absorver, prender.
ENGROSSED adj. absorto, abstraído.
ENGULF v. tragar, engolfar; subjugar.
ENHANCE v. ressaltar; aumentar, melhorar.
ENHANCEMENT s. realce; intensificação.
ENHANCER s. realçador, melhorador.

ENIGMA s. enigma; mistério.
ENIGMATIC adj. enigmático; misterioso.
ENJOIN v. impor, ordenar; proibir.
ENJOY v. desfrutar; divertir-se; deleitar-se.
ENJOYABLE adj. agradável, divertido.
ENJOYMENT s. prazer, satisfação, divertimento.
ENLACE v. envolver, enlaçar.
ENLARGE v. ampliar, alargar, aumentar.
ENLARGEMENT s. ampliação, aumento.
ENLIGHTEN v. iluminar, esclarecer.
ENLIGHTENED adj. esclarecido, informado, culto.
ENLIGHTENING adj. informativo, revelador.
ENLIGHTENMENT s. iluminação, esclarecimento.
ENLIST v. alistar-se, recrutar.
ENLISTMENT s. alistamento, recrutamento.
ENLIVEN v. avivar, alentar; animar.
ENMITY s. inimizade.
ENNOBLE v. enobrecer; nobilitar.
ENNUI s. enfado, tédio.
ENORMITY s. enormidade.
ENORMOUS adj. enorme.
ENORMOUSLY adv. enormemente.
ENOUGH adj. suficiente, bastante / interj. basta!
ENQUIRE v. inquirir, indagar.
ENQUIRING adj. investigador, inquiridor.
ENQUIRY s. investigação.
ENRAGE v. enfurecer, encolerizar.
ENRAGED adj. enraivecido, enfurecido.
ENRAPTURE v. encantar, enlevar.
ENRICH v. enriquecer.
ENRICHMENT s. enriquecimento.
ENROLL v. matricular-se, inscrever-se; alistar-se.
ENROLLMENT s. matrícula, inscrição.
ENSCONCE v. abrigar, agasalhar, acolher.
ENSEMBLE s. vestuário, conjunto; grupo; conjunto (música).
ENSHRINE v. preservar; santificar.
ENSIGN s. bandeira, insígnia; emblema.
ENSLAVE v. escravizar.
ENSLAVEMENT s. escravidão, escravização.
ENSLAVER s. escravocrata.
ENSNARE v. pegar, apanhar; ludibriar.
ENSUE v. resultar, suceder.
ENSUING adj. seguinte, subsequente.
ENSURE v. assegurar, proteger, garantir.

ENTAIL v. envolver, requerer.
ENTAILMENT s. vinculação, vínculo.
ENTANGLE v. emaranhar, enredar.
ENTANGLEMENT s. embaraço, estorvo.
ENTER v. entrar, passar para dentro.
ENTERPRISE s. empresa; empreendimento, iniciativa.
ENTERPRISING adj. empreendedor.
ENTERTAIN v. entreter, divertir.
ENTERTAINER s. humorista, animador.
ENTERTAINING adj. divertido, interessante.
ENTERTAINMENT s. diversão, entretenimento.
ENTHRALL v. cativar, fascinar, encantar.
ENTHRALLING adj. cativante, encantador.
ENTHRONE v. entronar; dar poder a.
ENTHUSE v. entusiasmar-se.
ENTHUSIASM s. entusiasmo, interesse.
ENTHUSIAST s. entusiasta, apaixonado.
ENTHUSIASTIC adj. entusiástico, entusiasta; entusiasmado, ardente.
ENTHUSIASTICALLY adv. entusiasticamente.
ENTICE v. atrair; incitar, instigar.
ENTICEMENT s. sedução, tentação; instigação.
ENTIRE adj. inteiro, todo, completo.
ENTIRELY adv. inteiramente, totalmente.
ENTIRETY s. totalidade.
ENTITLE v. intitular; autorizar.
ENTITLEMENT s. subvenção, direito.
ENTITY s. entidade, ente.
ENTOMB v. enterrar, sepultar.
ENTOURAGE s. séquito; cortejo, facção.
ENTRAILS s. estranhas; vísceras.
ENTRANCE s. entrada, portão.
ENTRANT s. estreante; aprendiz.
ENTRAP v. enganar, lograr; armar cilada.
ENTRAPMENT s. cilada, enredo, armadilha.
ENTREAT v. pedir, rogar, solicitar.
ENTREATY s. solicitação, pedido.
ENTREPRENEUR s. empresário.
ENTREPRENEURIAL adj. empresarial.
ENTREPRENEURSHIP s. empreendedorismo.
ENTRUST v. confiar; incumbir, encarregar.
ENTRY s. entrada, ingresso; verbete (dicionário).
ENTRY FORM s. ficha de registro; formulário.
ENTRYWAY s. entrada.

ENUMERATE v. enumerar; listar.
ENUMERATION s. enumeração; lista.
ENUMERATOR s. enumerador.
ENUNCIATE v. enunciar, articular, pronunciar.
ENUNCIATION s. enunciação, declaração.
ENVELOP v. envolver, envelopar, embrulhar.
ENVELOPE s. envelope.
ENVIABLE adj. invejável, cobiçável.
ENVIOUS adj. invejoso; cobiçoso.
ENVIRONMENT s. meio ambiente.
ENVIRONMENTAL adj. ambiental.
ENVIRONMENTALISM s. ambientalismo.
ENVIRONMENTALIST s. ambientalista.
ENVIRONMENTALLY adv. ambientalmente.
ENVIRONS s. arredores, imediações.
ENVISAGE v. prever, imaginar, considerar.
ENVISION v. antever, prever.
ENVOY s. enviado; representante.
ENVY s. inveja, cobiça / v. invejar, cobiçar.
ENWRAP v. envolver, embrulhar, empacotar.
ENZYMATIC adj. enzímico, enzimático.
ENZYME s. enzima.
EOLIAN adj. eólico.
EPHEMERAL adj. efêmero.
EPIC adj. épico, heroico / s. épico, epopeia.
EPICENTRE s. epicentro.
EPIDEMIC s. epidemia / adj. epidêmico, alastrante.
EPIDEMIOLOGICAL adj. epidemiológico.
EPIDEMIOLOGIST s. epidemiologista.
EPIDEMIOLOGY s. epidemiologia.
EPIDERMAL adj. epidérmico.
EPIDERMIS s. epiderme.
EPIGRAM s. epigrama.
EPILEPSY s. epilepsia.
EPILEPTIC s. epiléptico, epilético / adj. epiléptico, epilético.
EPILOGUE s. epílogo.
EPIPHANY s. epifania; aparição.
EPISODE s. episódio; capítulo.
EPISODIC adj. episódico; em partes.
EPISTLE s. epístola, carta, missiva.
EPISTOLARY adj. epistolar.
EPITAPH s. epitáfio.
EPITHET s. epíteto; apelido, codinome.
EPOCH s. época, era, período.
EQUABLE adj. uniforme, igual.

EQUAL s. semelhante, igual / adj. igual a, equivalente a.
EQUALISATION s. equalização.
EQUALISE v. igualar; empatar, equalizar.
EQUALISER s. equalizador, igualador.
EQUALITY s. igualdade; equidade.
EQUALLY adv. igualmente.
EQUATE v. equiparar; igualar.
EQUATION s. equação.
EQUATOR s. Equador (linha e país).
EQUATORIAL adj. equatorial.
EQUILIBRIUM s. equilíbrio.
EQUINE adj. equino, hípico (cavalo).
EQUINOX s. equinócio.
EQUIP v. equipar, prover, preparar.
EQUIPAGE s. equipagem, apetrechos.
EQUIPMENT s. equipamento.
EQUIPPED adj. equipado.
EQUITABLE adj. imparcial; equitativo.
EQUITATION s. equitação.
EQUITY s. patrimônio, participação.
EQUIVALENCE s. equivalência.
EQUIVALENT s. equivalente / adj. equivalente.
EQUIVOCAL adj. ambíguo, confuso; equívoco.
EQUIVOCALLY adv. equivocadamente.
EQUIVOCATE v. equivocar-se.
EQUIVOCATION s. equivocação.
ERA s. era, época; período.
ERADICATE v. erradicar, eliminar, exterminar.
ERADICATION s. erradicação.
ERASABLE adj. apagável.
ERASE v. apagar.
ERASER s. borracha; apagador.
ERASURE s. apagamento, desmancho.
ERE conj. antes de / prep. antes.
ERECT adj. ereto, reto / v. levantar, erguer, erigir.
ERECTILE adj. erétil.
ERECTION s. ereção.
ERECTOR s. eretor, elator; elevador.
ERGO adv. portanto, logo; por conseguinte.
ERGONOMIC adj. ergonômico.
ERGONOMICS s. ergonomia.
ERODE v. causar erosão, corroer, desgastar
ERODED adj. corroído, deteriorado.
EROSION s. erosão, desgaste.

EROSIVE *adj.* erosivo.
EROTIC *adj.* erótico.
EROTICA *s. m.q.* erotic art.
EROTIC ART *s.* arte erótica.
EROTICISM *s.* erotismo.
EROTIC LITERATURE *s.* literatura erótica.
ERR *v.* errar; falhar; enganar-se.
ERRAND *s.* recado, mensagem; missão, incumbência.
ERRANT *adj.* errante.
ERRATIC *adj.* errático; instável, inconstante.
ERRATUM *s.* errata.
ERRONEOUS *adj.* errôneo.
ERROR *s.* erro; falha.
ERST *adv.* outrora; antigamente.
ERSTWHILE *adj.* anterior, antigo.
ERUDITE *adj.* erudito.
ERUDITION *s.* erudição.
ERUPT *v.* entrar em erupção, estourar.
ERUPTION *s.* erupção, explosão.
ERUPTIVE *adj.* eruptivo.
ESCALADE *s.* escalada.
ESCALATE *v.* intensificar-se; aumentar.
ESCALATION *s.* agravamento, intensificação.
ESCALATOR *s.* escada rolante.
ESCAPADE *s.* peripécia, aventura; fuga, escapadela.
ESCAPE *s.* fuga, evasão / *v.* escapar, evadir-se.
ESCAPEE *s.* foragido, fugitivo.
ESCAPEMENT *s.* escapamento.
ESCAPISM *s.* escapismo.
ESCAPIST *adj.* escapista.
ESCARGOT *s.* caramujo; escargot (prato).
ESCHEW *v.* evitar; fugir de; afastar-se de.
ESCORT *s.* escolta; acompanhante / *v.* acompanhar, escoltar.
ESKIMO *s.* esquimó.
ESOPHAGUS *s.* esôfago.
ESOTERIC *adj.* esotérico.
ESPECIAL *adj.* especial.
ESPECIALLY *adv.* sobretudo, especialmente.
ESPIONAGE *s.* espionagem.
ESPIRIT *s.* espírito.
ESPLANADE *s.* esplanada.
ESPOUSAL *s.* casamento, núpcias.
ESPOUSE *v.* casar-se, desposar.
ESPRESSO *s.* expresso (café).
ESSAY *s.* ensaio, redação; dissertação.
ESSAYIST *s.* ensaísta.

ESSENCE *s.* essência.
ESSENTIAL *adj.* essencial; necessário.
ESSENTIALLY *adv.* basicamente.
ESTABLISH *v.* estabelecer, fundar, instituir.
ESTABLISHED *adj.* estabelecido, fundado.
ESTABLISHMENT *s.* estabelecimento, instituição, fundação.
ESTATE *s.* propriedade; conjunto de bens, patrimônio.
ESTEEM *s.* estima, consideração / *v.* estimar.
ESTHETIC *adj.* estético / *s.* estética.
ESTIMATE *s.* estimativa, avaliação / *v.* estimar, avaliar.
ESTIMATED *adj.* estimado; aproximado.
ESTIMATED INCOME *s.* renda estimada.
ESTIMATED LIFE *s.* expectativa de vida.
ESTIMATION *s.* cálculo, estimativa; opinião.
ESTIMATOR *s.* avaliador.
ESTRANGE *v.* afastar; tornar estranho.
ESTRANGED *adj.* separado, marginalizado.
ESTRANGEMENT *s.* distanciamento.
ESTROGEN *s.* estrógeno, estrogênio.
ESTRUS *s.* estro; cio.
ESTUARY *s.* estuário.
ETC. *abrev.* etc.
ETCH *v.* gravar, entalhar.
ETCHING *s.* água-forte, gravura, entalhe.
ETERNAL *adj.* eterno, perpétuo.
ETERNAL LIFE *s.* vida eterna.
ETERNALLY *adv.* eternamente.
ETERNAL YOUTH *s.* juventude eterna.
ETERNITY *s.* eternidade, perpetuidade.
ETHANE *s.* etano.
ETHANOL *s.* etanol.
ETHER *s.* éter.
ETHEREAL *adj.* etéreo; refinado.
ETHIC *s.* ética.
ETHICAL *adj.* ético, decente.
ETHICALLY *adv.* eticamente.
ETHICS *s.* ética (filosofia).
ETHIOPIA *s.* Etiópia.
ETHIOPIAN *s.* etíope / *adj.* etíope.
ETHNIC *adj.* étnico.
ETHNICALLY *adv.* etnicamente.
ETHNICITY *s.* etnia.
ETHNOGRAPHIC *adj.* etnográfico.
ETHNOGRAPHY *s.* etnografia.
ETHNOLOGY *s.* etnologia.

ETHOS s. etos, ethos.
ETHYL s. etílico; etilo.
ETIQUETTE s. etiqueta; boas maneiras.
ETYMOLOGICAL adj. etimológico.
ETYMOLOGY s. etimologia.
EUCALYPTUS s. eucalipto.
EUGENIC adj. eugênico (genética).
EULOGISE v. elogiar; louvar, enaltecer.
EULOGY s. elogio, louvor.
EUNUCH s. eunuco; homem castrado.
EUPHEMISM s. eufemismo.
EUPHORIA s. euforia.
EUPHORIC adj. eufórico.
EUREKA interj. eureca; heureca.
EUROPE s. Europa.
EUROPEAN s. europeu / adj. europeu.
EUROPEAN UNION s. União Europeia (UE).
EUROZONE s. zona do Euro.
EUTHANASIA s. eutanásia.
EUTHANISE v. praticar a eutanásia; sacrificar.
EVACUATE v. evacuar, abandonar, desocupar.
EVACUATION s. evacuação.
EVACUEE s. refugiado, evacuado, deslocado.
EVADE v. evadir, sonegar; escapar; evitar.
EVADER s. fugitivo, desertor.
EVALUATE v. avaliar; analisar.
EVALUATION s. avaliação; análise.
EVALUATIVE adj. avaliatório, avaliativo.
EVALUATOR s. avaliador.
EVANESCENCE s. evanescência, desvaneio.
EVANESCENT adj. evanescente.
EVANGELICAL adj. evangélico.
EVANGELICALISM s. evangelismo.
EVANGELISE v. evangelizar.
EVANGELISM s. m.q. evangelicalism.
EVANGELIST s. evangelista.
EVANGELISTIC adj. evangélico, evangelizador.
EVAPORATE v. evaporar; desaparecer.
EVAPORATION s. evaporação.
EVAPORATOR s. evaporador.
EVASION s. fuga; evasão.
EVASIVE adj. evasivo, ambíguo.
EVE s. véspera; Eva.
EVEN adj. plano, liso; par (número) / adv. mesmo, até; ainda que / v. nivelar; compensar.

EVENING s. noite, anoitecer / adj. noturno.
EVENING DRESS s. traje a rigor.
EVENLY adv. equilibradamente.
EVENNESS s. igualdade; imparcialidade; regularidade.
EVENT s. acontecimento, evento, ocorrência.
EVENTFUL adj. movimentado, agitado; acidentado.
EVENTUAL adj. final, consequente, eventual.
EVENTUALITY s. eventualidade, contingência.
EVENTUALLY adv. finalmente, por fim.
EVER adv. sempre; já, alguma vez; nunca, jamais.
EVERGREEN adj. duradouro.
EVERLASTING adj. perpétuo, eterno / s. eternidade.
EVERLASTINGLY adv. ininterruptamente; para sempre.
EVERMORE adv. eternamente.
EVERY adj. todo; cada um.
EVERYBODY pron. todo mundo, todos.
EVERYDAY adj. diário; todos os dias.
EVERYONE pron. todo mundo; todos.
EVERYTHING pron. tudo.
EVERYWHERE adv. em todo lugar; em toda parte.
EVICT v. despejar, desapossar, desapropriar.
EVICTION s. evicção, despejo.
EVIDENCE s. prova, evidência, indício.
EVIDENT adj. evidente, óbvio, visível.
EVIDENTLY adv. evidentemente, obviamente.
EVIL s. maldade, mal / adj. mau, ruim.
EVILDOER s. malfeitor.
EVILNESS s. maldade.
EVINCE v. evidenciar, provar.
EVITABLE adj. evitável.
EVOCATION s. evocação.
EVOCATIVE adj. evocativo.
EVOKE v. evocar, invocar.
EVOLUTION s. evolução.
EVOLUTIONARY adj. evolutivo, evolucionário.
EVOLUCIONIST s. evolucionista.
EVOLVE v. desenvolver; evoluir.
EWE s. ovelha.

EXACERBATE v. agravar; exacerbar.
EXACT adj. exato, preciso.
EXACTING adj. exigente; minucioso.
EXACTLY adv. exatamente.
EXAGGERATE v. exagerar.
EXAGGERATION s. exagero.
EXALT v. exaltar; louvar.
EXALTATION s. exaltação; elevação.
EXAM s. exame; prova.
EXAMINATION s. exame; investigação.
EXAMINE v. examinar; investigar.
EXAMINER s. examinador.
EXAMPLE s. exemplo.
EXASPERATE v. exasperar, irritar-se.
EXASPERATED adj. exasperado.
EXASPERATION s. exasperação.
EXCAVATE v. escavar, cavar.
EXCAVATION s. escavação.
EXCEED v. exceder, ultrapassar.
EXCEEDANCE s. excedente.
EXCEEDINGLY adv. extremamente.
EXCEL v. sobressair; distinguir-se.
EXCELLENCE s. excelência; primazia.
EXCELLENT adj. excelente, ótimo.
EXCEPT prep. exceto / v. excluir, isentar.
EXCEPTION s. exceção, exclusão.
EXCEPTIONAL adj. excepcional.
EXCERPT s. trecho, passagem.
EXCESS s. excesso, demasia.
EXCESSIVE adj. excessivo.
EXCHANGE s. troca; intercâmbio / v. trocar, cambiar.
EXCITE v. excitar; agitar.
EXCITEMENT s. excitação; agitação.
EXCITING adj. emocionante, excitante.
EXCLAIM v. exclamar.
EXCLAMATION s. exclamação.
EXCLAMATION MARK s. ponto de exclamação.
EXCLUDE v. excluir; eliminar.
EXCLUSIVE adj. exclusivo, único.
EXCURSION s. excursão.
EXCUSE s. desculpa / v. desculpar.
EXECUTE v. executar.
EXECUTION s. execução, realização.
EXECUTIVE s. executivo / adj. executivo.
EXECUTOR s. testamenteiro; executor testamentário.
EXEMPTION s. dispensa, isenção.

EXERCISE s. exercício / v. exercer; fazer exercício.
EXERT v. exercer; mostrar.
EXHIBIT s. obra exposta, exibição, exposição / v. exibir, expor.
EXHIBITION s. exposição, mostra.
EXILE s. exílio / v. exilar.
EXIST v. existir; viver.
EXISTENCE s. existência.
EXIT s. saída / v. sair.
EXODUS s. êxodo.
EXONERATE v. isentar; exonerar.
EXOTIC adj. exótico.
EXPAND v. expandir, dilatar; desenvolver.
EXPANSE s. extensão.
EXPANSION s. expansão, dilatação.
EXPECT v. esperar, aguardar, contar com.
EXPECTATION s. expectativa.
EXPEDIENCE s. conveniência, utilidade.
EXPEDIENT adj. conveniente, útil / s. expediente, meio.
EXPEDITION s. expedição.
EXPEL v. expelir, expulsar.
EXPEND v. gastar; despender.
EXPENDABLE adj. prescindível; descartável; dispensável.
EXPENDITURE s. gastos.
EXPENSE s. despesa, gastos, custo.
EXPENSIVE adj. caro, dispendioso, custoso.
EXPERIENCE s. experiência, prática / v. experimentar.
EXPERIENCED adj. experiente.
EXPERIMENT s. experimento, tentativa / v. fazer experiências, tentar.
EXPERT adj. perito / s. especialista, perito, experto.
EXPERTISE s. perícia.
EXPIRATION s. expiração; vencimento.
EXPIRE v. expirar, vencer, caducar.
EXPLAIN v. explicar, elucidar.
EXPLANATION s. explicação, esclarecimento.
EXPLICIT adj. explícito.
EXPLODE v. explodir, estourar.
EXPLOIT v. explorar recursos / s. façanha, proeza.
EXPLORE v. explorar um lugar, investigar, examinar.
EXPLORER s. explorador; desbravador.
EXPLOSION s. explosão, estouro.

EXPLOSIVE *adj.* explosivo / *s.* explosivo.
EXPORT *s.* exportação / *v.* exportar.
EXPORTER *s.* exportador.
EXPOSE *v.* expor, exibir.
EXPOSED *adj.* exposto; desprotegido.
EXPOSER *s.* expositor.
EXPOSURE *s.* exposição, exibição.
EXPOUND *v.* expor, esclarecer.
EXPRESS *adj.* expresso; urgente; rápido / *v.* expressar.
EXPRESSION *s.* expressão, manifestação; fórmula algébrica.
EXPRESSIVE *adj.* expressivo, significativo.
EXPRESSLY *adv.* expressamente.
EXPRESSWAY *s.* rodovia.
EXPULSION *s.* expulsão, exclusão.
EXPURGATE *v.* expurgar, limpar, purificar.
EXTANT *adj.* existente; sobrevivente.
EXTEND *v.* estender, prolongar; prorrogar.
EXTENSION *s.* extensão; ampliação.
EXTENSIVE *adj.* extenso, extensivo.
EXTENSIVELY *adv.* extensivamente.
EXTENT *s.* alcance, grau.
EXTERIOR *adj.* externo / *s.* exterior; aspecto.
EXTERNAL *adj.* externo, exterior.
EXTINCT *adj.* extinto.
EXTINGUISH *v.* extinguir, apagar.
EXTINGUISHER *s.* extintor.
EXTIRPATOR *s.* extirpador.
EXTORT *v.* extorquir.
EXTRA *s.* extraordinário; aumento / *adj.* adicional / *adv.* extra, super.
EXTRACT *v.* extrair; deduzir / *s.* extrato, resumo, passagem.
EXTRADITE *v.* extraditar.
EXTRAORDINARY *adj.* extraordinário, notável.
EXTRAVAGANCE *s.* extravagância.
EXTRAVAGANT *adj.* extravagante.
EXTREME *adj.* extremo / *s.* extremo.
EXTREMELY *adv.* extremamente.
EXTRICATE *v.* livrar, soltar.
EXTROVERT *s.* extrovertido.
EXUDE *v.* aparecer.
EYE *s.* olho / *v.* olhar.
EYEBALL *s.* globo ocular.
EYEBROW *s.* sobrancelha.
EYELASH *s.* cílio, pestana.
EYELESS *adj.* sem vista; cego.
EYELID *s.* pálpebra.
EYESHADOW *s.* sombra para os olhos.
EYESIGHT *s.* visão, vista.
EYESORE *s.* terçol.
EYEWITNESS *s.* testemunha ocular.

Ff

F, f s. sexta letra do alfabeto inglês; fá (nota musical).
FAB abrev. fabuloso (gíria).
FABLE s. fábula.
FABLED adj. famoso, lendário.
FABRIC s. tecido, pano; estrutura; construção.
FABRICATE v. fabricar; confeccionar.
FABRICATION s. fabricação, construção.
FABULOUS adj. fabuloso, incrível.
FACADE s. fachada.
FACE s. cara, rosto / v. encarar.
FACELESS adj. descarado; anônimo; sem rosto.
FACE-LIFT s. cirurgia plástica facial.
FACE-OFF s. enfrentamento.
FACET adj. faceta.
FACETIOUS adj. jocoso, brincalhão.
FACE-TO-FACE adv. face a face.
FACE VALUE s. valor nominal.
FACIAL adj. facial.
FACILE adj. fácil; simples.
FACILITATE v. facilitar.
FACILITATION s. facilitação.
FACILITATOR s. facilitador.
FACILITIES s. facilidades; instalações; recursos.
FACILITY s. facilidade.
FACING s. material de revestimento; cobertura.
FACSIMILE s. fac-símile, reprodução.
FACT s. fato, acontecimento.
FACTION s. facção.
FACTIONAL adj. faccionário, partidário.
FACTOR s. fator.
FACTORIZE v. fatorar.
FACTORY s. fábrica.
FACTUAL adj. real, efetivo, fatual.
FACULTY s. faculdade; capacidade; habilidade.
FAD s. mania; moda passageira.
FADE v. desbotar; murchar; enfraquecer.
FADED adj. desbotado, descolorido.
FADING s. desvanecimento, desaparecimento / adj. passageiro, transitório.
FAG s. trabalho enfadonho; homossexual (coloquial e pejorativo).

FAGGOT s. feixe, molho de paus ou varas; pacote de ferro para soldar; homossexual (pejorativo).
FAIL v. reprovar; falhar, fracassar / s. reprovação.
FAILED adj. falido.
FAILING s. defeito, falha.
FAIL-SAFE adj. relativo à prevenção contra falhas, à prova de falhas.
FAILURE s. falha, deficiência; fracasso; reprovação.
FAIN adj. contente, satisfeito, com prazer; obrigado, forçado.
FAINT s. desmaio / v. desmaiar / adj. fraco, leve.
FAINTHEARTED adj. medroso.
FAINTING s. desmaio, desfalecimento / adj. desfalecente, desmaiado, fraco.
FAINTLY adv. fracamente, vagamente.
FAINTNESS s. fraqueza, debilidade; tontura.
FAIR s. feira / adj. satisfatório; formoso; louro; justo, imparcial.
FAIR-CONDITIONED adj. de boa índole, benigno.
FAIRGROUND s. área descoberta, para feiras ou parques de diversões.
FAIR-HAIRED adj. louro, claro.
FAIRLY adv. com justiça, honestamente.
FAIRNESS s. justiça, integridade, imparcialidade; formosura.
FAIR PLAY s. jogo limpo, retidão.
FAIRWAY s. águas navegáveis; parte lisa do campo de golfe entre os buracos.
FAIRY s. fada.
FAIRYLAND s. reino das fadas.
FAIRYTALE s. conto de fadas.
FAITH s. fé, crença.
FAITHFUL adj. fiel, leal.
FAITHFULLY adv. fielmente, lealmente.
FAITHFULNESS s. fidelidade.
FAITHLESS adj. infiel, incrédulo, descrente; desleal, traiçoeiro; que falta aos seus compromissos.
FAKE s. falsificação; fraude; falso / v. fingir; falsificar; imitar.
FAKER s. falsificador, tapeador, embusteiro, simulador.
FALCON s. falcão.
FALL v. cair / s. queda; outono.
FALLACIOUS adj. falacioso, fraudulento.
FALLACY s. falácia.
FALLBACK s. retirada / v. bater em retirada.
FALLEN adj. caído(a), triste.
FALLIBLE adj. falível.
FALLING s. queda, caída, inclinação, caimento.
FALLING STAR s. estrela cadente.
FALLOUT s. partículas radioativas.
FALLOW adj. pousio, não cultivado.
FALSE adj. falso(a).
FALSELY adv. falsamente.
FALSENESS s. falsidade.
FALSE TEETH s. dentadura.
FALSETTO s. falsete.
FALSIFICATION s. falsificação.
FALTER s. vacilação / v. vacilar.
FALTERING adj. hesitante, vacilante / s. fraqueza, hesitação, vacilação.
FAME s. fama, reputação.
FAMED adj. afamado, famoso.
FAMILIAL adj. que diz respeito à família, familiar, da família.
FAMILIAR adj. familiar; íntimo; conhecido.
FAMILIARITY s. familiaridade.
FAMILIARIZATION s. familiarização.
FAMILIARIZE v. familiarizar-se, habituar-se.
FAMILY s. família; linhagem.
FAMILY NAME s. sobrenome.
FAMINE s. penúria, inanição.
FAMISHED adj. faminto, morto de fome.
FAMOUS adj. famoso, afamado, ilustre.
FAMOUSLY adv. famosamente.
FAN s. fã; leque, ventilador / v. abanar.
FANATIC s. fanático(a).
FANATICISM s. fanatismo.
FANCIED adj. imaginário.
FANCIFUL adj. extravagante, fantástico(a); fantasioso(a).
FANCY s. capricho; fantasia / adj. luxuoso(a) / v. imaginar, querer (coloquial).
FANCY BALL s. baile à fantasia.
FANCY DRESS s. fantasia (roupa).
FANDANGO s. fandango, dança de origem espanhola.
FANE s. templo, santuário.
FANFARE s. fanfarra; fanfarrice, ostentação.
FANG s. dente canino; raiz do dente.
FANTASTIC adj. fantástico(a).
FANTASY s. imaginação, fantasia.

FAQ *abrev.* FAQ (perguntas frequentes).
FAR *adj.* distante, remoto(a) / *adv.* muito longe.
FARAWAY *adj.* remoto(a), longínquo(a); distraído(a), pensativo(a).
FARCE *s.* farsa; pantomima.
FARCICAL *adj.* ridículo(a).
FARE *s.* tarifa, preço de passagem.
FAREWELL *s.* despedida, adeus / *adj.* de despedida.
FAR-FETCHED *adj.* forçado, trazido à força, afetado, não natural, artificial.
FAR-FLUNG *adj.* vasto, extenso, dilatado.
FARINA *s.* farinha (de cereais, batatas, nozes); amido, fécula.
FARM *s.* fazenda / *v.* cultivar.
FARMED *adj.* cultivado.
FARMER *s.* fazendeiro(a).
FARM HAND *s.* lavrador(a), trabalhador(a) agrícola.
FARMHOUSE *s.* casa de fazenda.
FARMING *s.* agricultura, lavoura, cultivo.
FARMLAND *s.* terra de cultivo.
FARMSTEAD *s.* fazenda, dependências da fazenda.
FARMYARD *s.* pátio de fazenda.
FARO *s.* faraó, jogo de azar.
FAR-OFF *adj.* distante, longínquo, remoto / *adv.* ao longe, a grande distância.
FAR-REACHING *adj.* de longo alcance.
FARRIER *s.* ferrador.
FARROW *s.* ninhada de leitões, leitãozinho.
FARSIGHTED *adj.* hipermetrope; perspicaz.
FARSIGHTEDNESS *adj.* hipermetropia; sagacidade.
FART *v.* peidar (coloquial) / *s.* peido (coloquial).
FARTHER *adj.* mais distante, mais afastado / *adv.* mais longe.
FASCIA *s.* fachada (placa com o nome da loja), painel de instrumentos de carros.
FASCINATE *v.* fascinar, cativar.
FASCINATING *adj.* fascinante, cativador, sedutor.
FASCINATION *s.* fascinação, encanto.
FASCISM *s.* fascismo.
FASCIST *s.* fascista / *adj.* fascista.
FASHION *s.* moda, uso, costume / *v.* modelar, amoldar.
FASHIONABLE *adj.* da moda, elegante.

FASHIONABLY *adv.* à moda, conforme a moda, elegantemente.
FASHION SHOW *s.* desfile de modas.
FAST *adv.* rapidamente / *adj.* rápido(a) / *s.* jejum / *v.* jejuar.
FAST-ACTING *adj.* de ação rápida.
FASTBACK *s.* carroçaria.
FASTBALL *s.* bola rápida (beisebol).
FASTEN *v.* fixar; prender; apertar.
FASTENER *s.* presilha; prendedor; zíper.
FASTENING *s.* fecho, gancho, ferrolho.
FAST FOOD *s.* comida pronta servida rapidamente.
FASTIDIOUS *adj.* fastidioso(a); difícil de contentar; enfadonho.
FASTIDIOUSNESS *adj.* meticuloso, perfeccionista.
FAT *adj.* gordo(a) / *s.* gordura.
FATAL *adj.* fatal.
FATALISM *s.* fatalismo.
FATALIST *s.* fatalista.
FATALITY *s.* fatalidade.
FATALLY *adv.* fatalmente.
FATE *s.* destino; sorte.
FATED *adj.* fadado, predestinado.
FATEFUL *adj.* fatídico, decisivo.
FAT-FREE *adj.* sem gordura.
FATHEAD *s.* cabeça-dura.
FATHER *s.* pai, genitor; padre.
FATHERHOOD *s.* paternidade.
FATHER-IN-LAW *s.* sogro.
FATHERLAND *s.* terra natal.
FATHERLESS *s.* órfão de pai.
FATHERLY *adj.* paternal / *adv.* paternalmente.
FATHOM *v.* sondar, penetrar.
FATIGUE *s.* fadiga, cansaço / *v.* fatigar, cansar.
FATNESS *s.* gordura.
FATTEN *v.* engordar.
FATTENING *adj.* engordativo, que engorda.
FATTY *s.* gorducho(a) / *adj.* gorduroso, oleoso.
FATUITY *s.* fatuidade; insensatez.
FATUOUS *adj.* fátuo, insensato, vaidoso, tolo; irreal, ilusório.
FAUCET *s.* torneira.
FAULT *s.* culpa; falta, defeito / *v.* criticar.
FAULTLESS *adj.* perfeito, sem falha.
FAULTY *adj.* defeituoso(a), imperfeito(a).

FAUN s. fauno.
FAUNA s. fauna.
FAUVISM s. fauvismo.
FAUX-MONNAYEUR s. pessoa que fabrica moeda falsa; falso devoto.
FAUX PAS s. gafe, mancada.
FAVE s. música, filme ou pessoa favorita.
FAVOR s. favor / v. favorecer.
FAVORABLE adj. favorável.
FAVORABLENESS s. benevolência.
FAVORABLY adv. favoravelmente.
FAVORED adj. favorecido.
FAVORING adj. favorecedor.
FAVORITE adj. predileto, preferido / s. favorito(a).
FAVORITISM s. favoritismo.
FAWN s. cervo / adj. bege / v. adular, bajular.
FAWNER s. adulador, bajulador.
FAWNING s. adulação, bajulação.
FAWNINGLY adv. servilmente.
FAX s. fax / v. enviar via fax (coloquial).
FAZE v. perturbar.
FBI abrev. FBI.
FEAL adj. leal, fiel / v. esconder.
FEALTY s. lealdade, fidelidade.
FEAR s. medo, temor / v. temer, recear.
FEARFUL adj. terrível, horrendo; medroso, receoso.
FEARFULLY adv. terrivelmente; medrosamente, receosamente.
FEARFULNESS s. terribilidade, horror; medo, receio.
FEARLESS adj. destemido(a), audaz.
FEARLESSLY adv. destemidamente, intrepidamente.
FEARLESSNESS s. destemor, audácia.
FEARSOME adj. espantoso, medonho, terrível.
FEARSOMELY adv. espantosamente, terrivelmente.
FEARSOMENESS s. espanto, timidez, terror.
FEASIBILITY s. viabilidade, possibilidade, praticabilidade.
FEASIBLE adj. viável, factível, exequível.
FEAST s. banquete, festa / v. festejar, banquetear.
FEASTER s. festejador, epicurista.
FEAT s. façanha, proeza.

FEATHER s. pena, pluma / v. empenar, emplumar-se.
FEATHERED adj. emplumado, empenado, coberto ou adornado de penas.
FEATHERING s. plumagem.
FEATHER-WEIGHT s. peso-pena.
FEATURE s. feição, traço, aspecto fisionômico / v. apresentar, caracterizar.
FEATURED adj. de destaque, tratado com especial destaque.
FEATURE-FILM s. longa-metragem.
FEATURE-LENGTH adj. de conteúdo ou teor integral (filme, reportagem).
FEATURELESS adj. sem traços característicos.
FEBRILE adj. febril.
FEBRUARY s. fevereiro.
FECES s. fezes.
FECKLESS adj. ineficaz.
FECUNDITY s. fecundidade.
FEDERAL adj. federal.
FEDERALISM s. federalismo.
FEDERALIST s. federalista / adj. federalista.
FEDERALLY adv. de modo federal.
FEDERATE v. federar (-se), reunir em federação, confederar(-se).
FEDERATION s. federação.
FED UP adj. de saco cheio, farto (coloquial).
FEE s. taxa; honorários.
FEEBLE adj. ineficaz; fraco, débil.
FEEBLE-MINDED adj. fraco de espírito.
FEEBLENESS s. debilidade, fraqueza.
FEED v. alimentar / s. ração, comida.
FEEDBACK s. retorno, resposta.
FEEDER s. alimentador, cevador; cabo alimentador.
FEEDING s. alimentação, pastagem.
FEEDING BOTTLE s. mamadeira.
FEEL s. tato; sensação / v. sentir; perceber.
FEELER s. antena de inseto; tentáculo.
FEEL-GOOD adj. que tem a intenção de fazer os outros felizes e/ou satisfeitos.
FEELING s. sentimento.
FEIGN v. fingir, simular, pretextar; aparentar, dissimular, disfarçar.
FEINT s. finta.
FEISTY adj. arrojado.
FELICITY s. felicidade.
FELINE adj. felino.
FELL v. lançar por terra, cortar / s. derrubada.
FELLOW s. camarada, companheiro.

FELLOW-MAN s. semelhante, membro da raça humana.
FELLOWSHIP s. amizade; comunidade; corporação.
FELON s. criminoso, bandido.
FELONY s. crime, delito grave.
FELT s. feltro.
FEMALE s. fêmea / adj. do sexo feminino, fêmea.
FEMININE adj. feminino(a) / s. feminino(a).
FEMININITY adj. feminilidade.
FEMINISM s. feminismo.
FEMINIST s. feminista.
FEMINIZE v. feminizar(-se), efeminar(-se).
FEMORAL adj. femoral.
FEMUR s. fêmur.
FEN s. pântano, brejo.
FENCE s. cerca, grade, muro / v. cercar; esgrimir.
FENCER s. esgrimidor, esgrimista, mestre de esgrima; construtor de cercas.
FENCING s. esgrima; cercas.
FEND v. defender-se; desviar.
FENDER s. para-lama; limpa trilhos; guarda, proteção.
FENNEL s. erva-doce.
FERAL adj. feroz, selvagem.
FERMENT v. fermentar / s. fermento, levedura.
FERMENTATION s. fermentação.
FERN s. samambaia.
FEROCIOUS adj. feroz, intenso.
FEROCITY s. ferocidade.
FERRET s. furão (animal); cadarço, fita; ferrão.
FERRIC adj. férrico, férreo.
FERROUS adj. ferroso.
FERRULE s. virola.
FERRY s. balsa / v. transportar em balsa.
FERRYBOAT s. barco de passagem, balsa.
FERTILE adj. fértil, fecundo.
FERTILIZATION s. fertilização.
FERTILIZE v. fertilizar, adubar.
FERTILIZER s. fertilizante, adubo.
FERVENT adj. ardente; abrasador; intenso.
FERVENTLY adv. fervorosamente.
FERVID adj. férvido, ardente.
FERVOR s. fervor, calor intenso, abrasamento, ardência.
FEST s. festa.

FESTER v. inflamar-se, supurar / s. chaga, pústula.
FESTIVAL s. festival, grande festa.
FESTIVE adj. festivo, alegre.
FESTIVITY s. festividade, solenidade.
FESTOON v. engrinaldar / s. festão, grinalda.
FETCH s. estratagema; busca / v. ir buscar.
FETCHING adj. atraente, encantador.
FETID adj. fétido, fedido.
FETISH s. fetiche.
FETISHISM s. fetichismo.
FETTER s. grilhão; cadeias, algemas.
FETTUCCINE s. fettuccine, massa italiana.
FEUD s. disputa; rixa / v. brigar, degladiar-se.
FEUDAL adj. feudal.
FEUDALISM s. feudalismo.
FEVER s. febre.
FEVERISH adj. febril.
FEVERISHNESS s. indisposição febril.
FEW pron. poucos(as) / adj. poucos(as).
FEWER adj. menos.
FEWEST adj. o menor.
FIANCÉ s. noivo.
FIANCÉE s. noiva.
FIASCO s. fiasco, malogro, fracasso.
FIAT s. sanção, decreto.
FIB s. lorota / v. contar lorotas.
FIBER s. filamento, fio, fibra.
FIBERGLASS s. fibra de vidro.
FICHE s. ficha.
FICKLE adj. volúvel, instável.
FICTION s. ficção.
FICTIONAL adj. de ficção, imaginário.
FICTIONALIZE v. romancear, adaptar.
FICTITIOUS adj. fictício, falso, artificial.
FIDDLE s. violino / v. tocar violino.
FIDDLER s. violinista.
FIDELITY s. fidelidade, lealdade, exatidão.
FIDGET v. inquietar-se, impacientar-se.
FIDGETY adj. irrequieto, inquieto, desassossegado, impaciente, agitado.
FIDUCIARY s. confidente / adj. fiduciário; firme, seguro.
FIE interj. fora! que vergonha!
FIELD s. campo.
FIELDER s. zagueiro, que intercepta a bola (beisebol, críquete).
FIELD-GLASS s. binóculo.
FIELD-WORK s. trabalho científico de campo.

FIEND s. demônio; espírito maligno.
FIENDISH adj. diabólico, cruel (coloquial).
FIERCE adj. feroz, selvagem; ardente, fogoso.
FIERCELY adv. ferozmente, furiosamente, encarniçadamente.
FIERCENESS s. ferocidade, fúria.
FIERY adj. fogoso; furioso.
FIFA abrev. FIFA (Federação Internacional de Futebol).
FIFTEEN num. quinze.
FIFTH num. quinto.
FIFTY num. cinquenta.
FIFTY-FIFTY adv. meio a meio.
FIG s. figo.
FIGHT s. briga, luta / v. lutar, brigar.
FIGHTER s. combatente, lutador; avião de caça.
FIGHTING s. batalha, luta / adj. combatente, lutador.
FIGMENT s. imaginário, imaginação; ficção.
FIGURATION s. figuração.
FIGURATIVE adj. figurado, figurativo, representativo.
FIGURATIVELY adv. figurativamente.
FIGURE s. figura; cifra, número / v. figurar; fazer sentido.
FIGURED adj. figurado, adornado, simbolizado, calculado; figurativo.
FIGURE OUT v. compreender; calcular, imaginar.
FIGURINE s. estatueta, manequim.
FIJI s. Fiji (ilhas do Pacífico).
FILAMENT s. filamento.
FILAMENTOUS adj. filamentoso, fibroso.
FILCH v. afanar, furtar.
FILE s. pasta; arquivo; fio, arame; lima (ferramenta) / v. arquivar; limar, lixar.
FILER s. assistente administrativo.
FILIAL s. filial, relativo aos filhos.
FILING s. arquivamento.
FILING-CABINET s. fichário, arquivo.
FILL v. preencher algo, encher, ocupar; obturar.
FILLET s. filé (lombo de vitela ou boi); filete, friso; faixa.
FILL-IN s. tapa-buraco, substituto.
FILLING s. recheio; obturação.
FILLING STATION s. posto de gasolina.
FILLY s. potranca; garota namoradeira; folgazona (coloquial).

FILM s. filme, película / v. filmar.
FILMING s. filmagem.
FILMMAKER s. cineasta.
FILMY adj. membranoso; fino, tênue; nevoento, turvo.
FILTER s. filtro / v. filtrar.
FILTER-TIPPED adj. filtrado.
FILTHY adj. indecente; corrupto; imundo.
FIN s. barbatana, nadadeira.
FINAL adj. final, último, decisivo.
FINALE s. final (música: parte final de uma sinfonia, ópera, peça).
FINALIST s. finalista.
FINALITY s. finalidade, fim.
FINALIZATION s. finalização.
FINALIZE v. concluir, finalizar.
FINALLY adv. finalmente.
FINANCE s. finanças / v. financiar, custear.
FINANCIAL adj. financeiro.
FINANCIALLY adv. financeiramente.
FINANCIER s. financiador(a); financista.
FINANCING s. financiamento.
FIND v. achar, encontrar; buscar.
FINDER s. achador, descobridor, inventor.
FINDING s. veredicto, decisão; achado, descoberta.
FIND OUT v. descobrir.
FINE adj. fino(a), excelente, refinado(a) / interj. ótimo! excelente! / s. multa / v. multar.
FINE ARTS s. belas-artes.
FINELY adv. finalmente.
FINER adj. melhor.
FINERY s. enfeites, ornatos.
FINESSE s. sutileza, finura.
FINGER s. dedo.
FINGERBOARD s. braço do violão, do violino, etc.
FINGERED adj. manuseado.
FINGERPRINT s. impressão digital.
FINGERPRINTING s. datiloscopia, processo de obtenção de impressões digitais.
FINGERTIP s. ponta do dedo.
FINICKY adj. enjoado(a); fresco(a) (diz-se coloquialmente de comida).
FINISH s. fim; chegada; acabamento / v. terminar; concluir.
FINISHED s. acabado, pronto.
FINISHER s. rematador, retocador, aperfeiçoador; golpe final, decisivo.

FINITE *adj.* finito, limitado.
FINK *s.* delator; fura-greve; espião (industrial; sindical), pelego.
FINLAND *s.* Finlândia.
FINN *s.* finlandês.
FINNISH *s.* finlandês(esa) / *adj.* finlandês(esa).
FIR *s.* pinheiro.
FIRE *s.* fogo; incêndio / *v.* atirar, disparar; demitir.
FIREARM *s.* arma de fogo.
FIREBALL *s.* bola de fogo; foguete.
FIREBOX *s.* fornalha.
FIREBRAND *s.* tição; ativista político, agitador.
FIRECRACKER *s.* fogo de artifício, bombinha.
FIRED *adj.* demitido.
FIRE ESCAPE *s.* escada de incêndio.
FIREFIGHT *s.* tiroteio.
FIREFIGHTING *s.* corpo de bombeiros.
FIREFLY *s.* pirilampo, vaga-lume.
FIREMAN *s.* bombeiro.
FIREPLACE *s.* lareira, fogueira.
FIREPROOF *adj.* à prova de fogo.
FIRESIDE *s.* lareira.
FIRE STORM *s.* incêndio.
FIRETRUCK *s.* caminhão de bombeiros.
FIREWOOD *s.* lenha.
FIREWORKS *s.* fogos de artifício.
FIRING *s.* demissão; descarga.
FIRING SQUAD *s.* pelotão de fuzilamento.
FIRM *s.* firma / *adj.* firme / *v.* fixar, firmar.
FIRMAMENT *s.* firmamento.
FIRMLY *adv.* firmemente.
FIRMNESS *s.* firmeza.
FIRST *adj.* primeiro(a) / *s.* primeiro(a) / *adv.* antes de tudo.
FIRST AID *s.* primeiros socorros.
FIRST-BORN *s.* primogênito.
FIRST-CLASS *adj.* de primeira classe.
FIRST-FLOOR *s.* andar térreo.
FIRST-HAND *adj.* de primeira mão.
FIRST LADY *s.* primeira dama.
FIRSTLY *adv.* em primeiro lugar, primeiramente.
FIRST NAME *s.* primeiro nome, prenome.
FISCAL *s.* fiscal (financeiro, imposto).
FISH *s.* peixe / *v.* pescar.
FISHBONE *s.* espinha.
FISH BOWL *s.* aquário.
FISHERMAN *s.* pescador.
FISHERY *s.* peixaria.

FISHHOOK *s.* anzol.
FISHING *s.* pesca, pescaria.
FISHMONGER *s.* peixeiro.
FISHNET *s.* rede de pesca.
FISHPOND *s.* viveiro, aquário.
FISSION *s.* fendimento, divisão em partes.
FISSURE *s.* fissura, fenda.
FIST *s.* punho; mão fechada.
FIST-FIGHT *s.* luta com os punhos livres (sem luvas).
FIT *adj.* em boa forma, em condições, apto(a), adequado(a) / *v.* caber, servir.
FITNESS *s.* aptidão; conveniência.
FITTED *adj.* instalado (carpete); fixo no lugar (armário); mobiliado (quarto).
FITTING *adj.* apropriado, ajustado, adequado / *s.* assentamento, ajuste, encaixe.
FITTINGLY *adv.* convenientemente, propriamente, adequadamente.
FITTING ROOM *s.* provador.
FITTINGS *s.* móveis; utensílios; acessórios.
FIVE *num.* cinco.
FIX *v.* fixar; consertar / *s.* dificuldade (coloquial).
FIXATE *v.* fixar, firmar, determinar a posição de, estabilizar.
FIXATION *s.* fixação, estabilidade.
FIXATIVE *s.* fixativo, fixador / *adj.* fixativo, fixador.
FIXED *adj.* fixo, estável.
FIXER *s.* fixador, reparador.
FIXITY *s.* fixidez, firmeza, estabilidade; caráter permanente.
FIXTURE *s.* fixação, fixidez.
FIZZLE *s.* crepitação, chiadeira; fiasco / *v.* sibilar, assobiar, chiar; crepitar.
FIZZY *adj.* efervescente, espumante.
FLAB *s.* flacidez.
FLABBERGAST *v.* espantar, pasmar.
FLABBY *adj.* frouxo, mole, balofo.
FLACCID *adj.* flácido.
FLAG *s.* bandeira; emblema / *v.* fraquejar, decair, esmorecer.
FLAGGED *adj.* pavimentado, coberto de pedras.
FLAGPOLE *s.* mastro.
FLAGSTONE *s.* laje.
FLAIL *v.* debulhar, malhar cereais; abanar os braços, agitar-se; açoitar, bater.
FLAIR *s.* olfato, faro, instinto.

FLAK s. críticas; artilharia antiaérea (militar).
FLAKE s. floco, lasca / v. lascar; escamar; cobrir de flocos.
FLAMBOYANT adj. espalhafatoso(a), extravagante.
FLAME s. chama, lume.
FLAMING adj. flamejante, ardente, brilhante; exagerado, extravagante.
FLAMINGO s. flamingo.
FLAMMABLE adj. inflamável.
FLAN s. torta doce.
FLANK s. flanco, ala / v. ladear, flanquear.
FLANNEL s. flanela.
FLAP s. borda, aba, ponta / v. ondular, bater, agitar.
FLARE s. sinal luminoso, chama.
FLARED adj. boca-de-sino, alargado.
FLASH s. clarão, lampejo / v. brilhar, lampejar.
FLASHBACK s. lembrança repentina de um fato do passado.
FLASH BULB s. clarão de lâmpada; *flash* (câmera).
FLASHING s. pisca-pisca.
FLASHLIGHT s. lanterna, lanterna de bolso; cintilação; clarão de luz; origem de luz artificial.
FLASHY adj. flamejante, cintilante.
FLASK s. frasco; cantil; garrafa térmica.
FLAT s. apartamento; a parte plana de algo / adj. plano, liso, sem relevo.
FLATBED s. plataforma.
FLATFOOT s. pé chato.
FLATIRON s. ferro de passar.
FLATLY adv. de modo chato ou plano.
FLATMATE s. companheiro de apartamento.
FLAT-OUT adj. direto, simples, positivo; irrestrito, total.
FLATTEN v. desanimar; achatar, nivelar, alisar.
FLATTER v. lisonjear; bajular.
FLATTERER s. lisonjeador; adulador.
FLATTERING adj. lisonjeiro.
FLATTERY s. bajulação; lisonja.
FLATULENCE s. flatulência.
FLATWARE s. louça.
FLAUNT s. ostentação, pompa / v. ostentar, alardear.
FLAVOUR s. sabor, gosto / v. aromatizar; temperar, condimentar.
FLAVOURED adj. saboroso; aromático, aromatizado.
FLAVOURING s. aromatizante, condimento, tempero.
FLAVOURLESS adj. sem gosto, sem sabor, insípido.
FLAW s. defeito, falha, fenda; furacão, tufão, ventania / adj. defeituoso.
FLAWED adj. com imperfeições, com falhas.
FLAWLESS adj. sem defeito, sem mancha, perfeito, impecável.
FLAWLESSLY adv. perfeitamente, isento de defeitos, impecavelmente.
FLAX s. linho (botânica).
FLAXEN adj. de linho, linhoso.
FLAY v. esfolar, tirar a pele de, descascar, pelar; criticar severamente.
FLEA s. pulga.
FLEABAG s. hotel ou pensão inferior; pessoa suja e malquista.
FLECK s. mancha na pele, pinta.
FLEDGELING s. avezinha; novato.
FLEE v. fugir, escapar.
FLEECE s. lã / v. tosquiar.
FLEET s. frota / adj. rápido(a), veloz / v. mover-se rapidamente.
FLEETING adj. passageiro; fugaz.
FLEMISH adj. flamengo, habitante da região de Flandres / s. flamengo, língua falada na Bélgica.
FLESH s. carne (do homem e dos animais).
FLESHY adj. carnudo, gordo, corpulento.
FLEUR-DE-LIS s. flor de lis.
FLEX s. cabo, condutor / v. dobrar-se, curvar-se.
FLEXIBILITY s. flexibilidade, elasticidade.
FLEXIBLE adj. flexível, adaptável.
FLICK s. peteleco / v. dar um peteleco.
FLICKER v. tremular / s. vislumbre.
FLICKERING adj. bruxuleante, tremeluzente; trêmulo, vacilante, vibrante.
FLIER s. aviador, voador.
FLIGHT s. voo; fuga; lance (de escadas).
FLIMSY s. papel fino, papel de cópia / adj. delgado(a), frágil.
FLINCH v. vacilar; retroceder-se; esquivar-se / s. recuo, desistência, hesitação.
FLING s. arremesso; farra amorosa / v. lançar, precipitar-se.
FLIP s. sacudidela; gemada / v. atirar para o ar; sacudir.
FLIP-FLOP s. chinelo de dedo.

FLIPPANCY s. petulância, leviandade, frivolidade, impertinência.
FLIPPANT adj. petulante, impertinente.
FLIPPER s. nadadeira; barbatana.
FLIRT v. flertar, namorar / s. paquerador(a), namorador(a).
FLIRTATIOUS adj. dado ao flerte, coquete, galanteador.
FLIT s. movimento leve / v. esvoaçar.
FLOAT s. boia; flutuação / v. flutuar.
FLOATATION s. flutuação, ato ou efeito de boiar.
FLOATER s. o que flutua; pessoa que troca frequentemente de residência, de emprego; vira-casaca.
FLOATING adj. flutuante.
FLOCK s. rebanho, manada, revoada; floco de lã / v. andar em bandos, reunir-se.
FLOG v. fustigar, açoitar.
FLOGGER s. açoitador, fustigador.
FLOOD s. inundação, enchente / v. inundar, transbordar.
FLOODGATE s. comporta.
FLOODING s. inundação.
FLOODLIGHT s. holofote.
FLOOR s. chão, solo, piso; andar / v. assoalhar.
FLOORING s. pavimento, soalho.
FLOOR LAMP s. abajur de pé.
FLOOZY s. mulher imoral e vulgar.
FLOP v. fracassar / s. fracasso, malogro.
FLOPPY adj. frouxo(a), mole, bambo(a) (coloquial).
FLORA s. flora.
FLORAL adj. floral.
FLORENCE s. Florença.
FLORESCENT s. florescente.
FLORET s. florzinha.
FLORID adj. florido(a).
FLORIDA s. Flórida.
FLORIST s. florista, floricultor(a).
FLORIST'S s. floricultura.
FLOSS s. fios de seda.
FLOTSAM s. fragmentos de naufrágio, restos de navio.
FLOUNCE s. babado; gesto de impaciência.
FLOUNDER s. linguado (peixe) / v. atrapalhar-se; debater-se.
FLOUR s. farinha.
FLOURISH s. floreio / v. florescer, prosperar.
FLOURISHING adj. próspero; notável.

FLOUT v. desrespeitar, insultar / s. escárnio, insulto.
FLOW s. fluxo; fluência / v. fluir; escorrer.
FLOW CHART s. fluxograma.
FLOWER s. flor / v. florir, desabrochar.
FLOWER BED s. canteiro de flores.
FLOWERPOT s. vaso de plantas.
FLOWERY adj. floreado(a), florido(a).
FLOWING adj. corrente, fluente.
FLU s. gripe, influenza.
FLUB. s. erro, estrago / v. errar, estragar.
FLUCTUATE v. flutuar, oscilar.
FLUCTUATION s. flutuação; variação, oscilação.
FLUE s. cano de chaminé, fumeiro; penugem; rede / v. afunilar.
FLUENCY s. fluência, abundância, espontaneidade de estilo.
FLUENT adj. fluente.
FLUENTLY adv. fluentemente, correntemente, com facilidade.
FLUFF s. penugem / v. afofar.
FLUFFY adj. macio(a); de pelúcia; fofo(a).
FLUID s. fluido, líquido.
FLUIDNESS s. fluidez.
FLUKE s. sorte, acaso.
FLUNK s. fracasso, reprovação / v. fracassar, reprovar.
FLUORESCENCE s. fluorescência.
FLUORESCENT adj. fluorescente.
FLUORIDE s. fluoreto.
FLUORINE s. flúor.
FLURRY s. lufada, refrega, rajada de vento; pancada de chuva, aguaceiro.
FLUSH s. rubor / v. corar; dar a descarga.
FLUSHED adj. corado(a); excitado(a); ansioso(a).
FLUSTER s. fervura, agitação nervosa, perturbação / v. agitar, aquecer; confundir, perturbar.
FLUSTERED adj. atrapalhado(a); agitado(a), excitado(a).
FLUTE s. flauta.
FLUTIST s. flautista.
FLUTTER s. agitação; palpitação / v. palpitar.
FLUVIAL adj. fluvial.
FLUX s. fluxo, curso, fluência, corrente.
FLY s. mosca / v. voar.
FLYAWAY s. fugitivo, fujão / adj. folgado, solto (vestido); leviano, volúvel.

FLYCATCHER s. papa-moscas; mosqueiro, armadilha para moscas.
FLYING s. aviação / adj. voador; flutuante.
FLYING SAUCER s. disco voador.
FLYOVER s. viaduto, passarela.
FLYWHEEL s. pêndulo; volante.
FM abrev. FM (frequência de rádio).
FOAL s. potro, poldro / v. parir, dar cria.
FOAM s. espuma / v. espumar.
FOAMY adj. espumante, espumoso.
FOB v. despachar alguém, livrar-se de; enganar.
FOCALIZE v. focar, focalizar.
FOCAL POINT s. foco, centro.
FOCUS s. foco / v. enfocar, focar.
FOCUSED adj. focado, centrado.
FODDER s. forragem / v. alimentar (o gado).
FOE s. inimigo, adversário.
FOETAL s. fetal.
FOETUS s. feto.
FOG s. nevoeiro, neblina.
FOGGY adj. nebuloso, nevoento, cerrado.
FOG LIGHT s. farol de neblina.
FOIBLE s. fraco, ponto fraco, fraqueza, defeito.
FOIL s. rastro de caça; folha metálica; lâmina delgada / v. frustrar.
FOIST v. impingir, empurrar; insinuar.
FOLD s. dobra; vinco / v. dobrar(-se); entrelaçar os dedos.
FOLDABLE adj. dobrável, flexível.
FOLDER s. pasta de papéis, envoltório.
FOLDING s. dobragem, dobradura / adj. dobradiço.
FOLDING CHAIR s. cadeira dobradiça.
FOLIAGE s. folhagem, ramagem.
FOLK s. povo; gente; nação / adj. folclórico, popular, comum.
FOLK DANCE s. dança folclórica.
FOLKLORE s. folclore.
FOLKLORIC adj. folclórico, popular.
FOLK SONG s. canção popular.
FOLKSY adj. simples, amável, sociável.
FOLKWAY s. costume, hábito.
FOLLOW v. seguir, suceder.
FOLLOWER s. seguidor(a).
FOLLOWING s. cortejo, séquito / adj. seguinte, próximo.
FOLLY s. loucura, doidice.

FOMENT v. fomentar, promover, excitar, estimular.
FOND adj. carinhoso, afetuoso; afeiçoado.
FONDLE v. acariciar, afagar.
FONT s. fonte (informática); pia de água benta.
FOOD s. comida, alimento.
FOOD POISONING s. intoxicação alimentar.
FOOD PROCESSOR s. multiprocessador de alimentos.
FOODSTUFF s. gêneros alimentícios.
FOOLISH adj. tolo; insensato.
FOOLISHNESS s. loucura, insensatez.
FOOLPROOF adj. infalível, perfeitamente seguro (coloquial).
FOOT s. (pl. feet) pé.
FOOTBALL s. futebol americano; bola de futebol americano.
FOOTBALL MATCH s. partida de futebol.
FOOTBRIDGE s. passarela, ponte para pedestres.
FOOTHOLD s. apoio para os pés, lugar onde pôr o pé.
FOOTLOCKER s. maleta com objetos pessoais.
FOOTLOOSE adj. livre, desembaraçado(a).
FOOTNOTE s. nota de rodapé.
FOOTPATH s. atalho; vereda.
FOOTPRINT s. pegada.
FOOTSTEP s. som de passo, pegada, passo.
FOOTWEAR s. calçados.
FOOTY adj. pobre, sem valor.
FOR prep. para; por.
FORAGE s. forragem.
FORBEAR v. conter, reprimir.
FORBEARANCE s. paciência, clemência, abstenção, omissão.
FORBEARING adj. paciente, indulgente.
FORBID v. proibir.
FORBIDDEN adj. proibido.
FORBIDDING adj. proibitivo, medonho, ameaçador.
FORCE s. força / v. forçar.
FORCED adj. forçado, obrigado, compelido, constrangido, compulsório.
FORCEFUL adj. vigoroso, forte.
FORCEFULLY adv. à força, vigorosamente, violentamente.
FORCEPS s. tórceps.
FORCIBLY adv. à força, forçosamente.

FORD s. parte rasa do rio.
FORE s. parte dianteira, frente; proa / adj. dianteiro, anterior.
FOREARM s. antebraço.
FOREBODE v. agourar.
FOREBODING s. agouro, presságio.
FORECAST s. previsão / v. prever, predizer.
FORECLOSE v. excluir, impedir, barrar, privar alguém.
FOREFATHER s. antepassado.
FOREFINGER s. dedo indicador.
FOREFOOT s. pata dianteira.
FOREFRONT s. em primeiro plano, vanguarda; testa.
FOREGO v. anteceder.
FOREGOING adj. precedente, antecedente.
FOREHEAD s. testa, fronte.
FOREIGN adj. estrangeiro.
FORELOCK s. topete, madeixa.
FOREMAN s. capataz, contramestre, feitor.
FOREMENTIONED adj. mencionado anteriormente, supracitado.
FOREMOST adj. dianteiro, primeiro (lugar, tempo, ordem), o principal.
FORERUNNER s. precursor, prognóstico, presságio.
FORESEE v. prever, antever, calcular, pressupor, pressagiar.
FOREST s. floresta, mata, selva.
FORESTER s. guarda-florestal.
FOREVER adv. para sempre, eternamente.
FOREWORD s. prefácio, introdução.
FORFEITURE s. confisco, perda, privação (de direitos).
FORGE s. fornalha / v. forjar; falsificar.
FORGER s. falsificador(a), falsário(a); forjador, ferreiro.
FORGERY s. falsificação.
FORGET v. esquecer.
FORGETFUL adj. esquecido(a).
FORGETFULNESS s. esquecimento.
FORGIVE v. perdoar, desculpar.
FORGIVENESS s. perdão.
FORGO v. renunciar a, abandonar, privar-se de.
FORK s. garfo; bifurcação / v. bifurcar.
FORKED adj. bifurcado(a).
FORKLIFT s. empilhadeira.
FORLORN adj. desolado(a); abandonado(a).
FORM s. formulário, forma.

FORMAL adj. formal; cerimônia.
FORMALISATION s. ato de formalizar, formalização.
FORMALISE v. formalizar.
FORMALISM s. formalismo.
FORMALITY s. formalidade.
FORMALLY adv. formalmente, cerimoniosamente.
FORMAT s. formato; formatar (informática).
FORMATION s. formação, disposição, ordem, estrutura, arranjo.
FORMATIVE adj. formativo.
FORMER adj. anterior.
FORMERLY adv. anteriormente, antigamente, outrora.
FORMIDABLE adj. formidável, tremendo.
FORMULA s. fórmula.
FORMULATE v. formular, expor com precisão ou sistematicamente.
FORMULATOR s. formulador.
FORNICATE v. fornicar / adj. arqueado.
FORNICATION s. fornicação, toda relação sexual ilícita; adultério; idolatria.
FORSAKE v. abandonar, renunciar a.
FORSOOTH adv. certamente, realmente, na verdade, pois não, deveras.
FORSWEAR v. abjurar, renegar, repudiar.
FORT s. forte, fortificação, castelo.
FORTIETH s. a quadragésima parte; quadragésimo.
FORTH adv. adiante; para frente.
FORTHCOMING s. aparecimento, chegada, vinda, aproximação / adj. prestes a aparecer, por vir, vindouro, próximo, futuro.
FORTHRIGHT s. caminho reto / adj. franco, direto, reto, sem rodeios / adv. direto à frente, em linha reta para a frente.
FORTHWITH adv. em seguida, sem demora, imediatamente.
FORTIFICATION s. fortificação, fortaleza, fortalecimento, forte, baluarte.
FORTIFIED adj. fortificado.
FORTIFY v. fortalecer, fortificar.
FORTITUDE s. fortaleza, coragem, resistência.
FORTNIGHT s. quinzena.
FORTNIGHTLY adj. quinzenal / adv. quinzenalmente.
FORTRESS s. fortaleza, castelo forte.
FORTUITOUS adj. fortuito, acidental, casual, improviso, eventual, imprevisto.

FORTUNATE *adj.* felizardo(a), afortunado(a), venturoso(a).
FORTUNATELY *adv.* felizmente, afortunadamente.
FORTUNE *s.* fortuna; sina, sorte.
FORTUNETELLER *s.* adivinho(a), cartomante.
FORTUNETELLING *s.* adivinhação, cartomancia.
FORTY *num.* quarenta.
FORUM *s.* foro, fórum.
FORWARD *adj.* para frente, dianteiro; avançado / *v.* enviar; avançar.
FORWARDNESS *s.* ardor, precipitação, prontidão, solicitude; adiantamento, progresso.
FOSSE *s.* fosso, canal, cova.
FOSSIL *s.* fóssil.
FOSSILISE *v.* fossilizar, tornar fóssil, petrificar, procurar ou colecionar fósseis.
FOSTER *v.* nutrir, alimentar, promover, patrocinar; acariciar, acalentar, encorajar.
FOUL *s.* infração, falta / *adj.* desonesto(a), ilícito(a).
FOUND *v.* fundar, construir.
FOUNDATION *s.* fundação; fundamento, alicerce.
FOUNDED *adj.* fundado.
FOUNDER *s.* fundador(a).
FOUNDING *s.* exposto(a); enjeitado(a).
FOUNDRY *s.* fundição.
FOUNT *s.* fonte; manancial, origem.
FOUNTAIN *s.* chafariz, fonte; bebedouro.
FOUNTAIN-PEN *s.* caneta-tinteiro.
FOUR *num.* quatro.
FOURSOME *s.* partida de golfe dupla; quarteto, grupo de quatro.
FOURSQUARE *s.* quadrado / *adj.* quadrado, quadrangular; franco.
FOURTEEN *num.* catorze.
FOURTH *num.* quarto(a).
FOWL *s.* ave ou pássaro; aves domésticas (galinha) / *v.* caçar.
FOX *s.* raposa.
FOXHOUND *s.* cão de caça (a raposas).
FOX-TROT *s.* fox-trote (dança); trote / *v.* dançar o foxtrote.
FOXY *adj.* semelhante à raposa, vulpino; astuto, manhoso, malicioso.
FOYER *s.* salão de teatro, vestíbulo.
FRACTION *s.* fração.

FRACTIONAL *adj.* fracionário, fracionado; parcial; insignificante.
FRACTURE *s.* fratura / *v.* fraturar.
FRAGILE *adj.* frágil, quebradiço, delicado.
FRAGILITY *s.* fragilidade, debilidade.
FRAGMENT *s.* fragmento / *v.* fragmentar.
FRAGMENTATION *s.* fragmentação.
FRAGMENTED *adj.* fragmentado.
FRAGRANCE *s.* fragrância, aroma, perfume.
FRAGRANT *adj.* perfumado(a), fragrante.
FRAIL *s.* seira (cesto de junco) / *adj.* frágil, delicado.
FRAILTY *s.* *m.q.* fragility.
FRAME *s.* estrutura; moldura; armação / *v.* emoldurar.
FRAME OF MIND *s.* estado de espírito, disposição.
FRAMER *s.* moldureiro, enquadrador.
FRAMEWORK *s.* armação; treliça; estrutura.
FRANCE *s.* França.
FRANCHISE *s.* concessão; franquia.
FRANK *adj.* franco, honesto / *v.* franquear.
FRANKLY *adv.* francamente.
FRANKNESS *s.* franqueza, sinceridade.
FRANTIC *adj.* frenético; furioso; desesperado.
FRANTICALLY *adv.* freneticamente.
FRATERNAL *adj.* fraternal, fraterno.
FRATERNITY *s.* fraternidade.
FRAUD *s.* fraude, embuste; impostor(a), embusteiro.
FRAUGHT *adj.* carregado, abastecido, provido, cheio.
FRAY *s.* rixa, briga / *v.* esfiapar, desfiar.
FRAZZLE *s.* farrapo, frangalho / *v.* desgastar(-se), esgotar(-se).
FRAZZLED *adj.* exausto, irritado, confuso.
FREAK *s.* anormal, excentricidade, aberração / *adj.* esquisito(a), grotesco(a).
FREAKISH *adj.* caprichoso, esquisito, excêntrico.
FRECKLE *s.* sarda (na pele).
FRECKLED *adj.* sardento(a).
FREE *adj.* livre; grátis / *v.* livrar; libertar.
FREEDMAN *s.* liberto.
FREEDOM *s.* liberdade.
FREE GIFT *s.* brinde.
FREEHAND *s.* carta branca, plenos poderes / *adj.* à mão livre.
FREELANCE *s.* colaborador, trabalhador independente.

FREE-LOADER s. penetra, bicão.
FREELY adv. livremente.
FREEMAN s. homem livre.
FREEMASON s. maçom, membro da maçonaria.
FREEMASONRY s. maçonaria.
FREEPOST s. postagem paga pelo destinatário.
FREESTYLE s. estilo livre (em competição).
FREE TRADE s. comércio livre.
FREEWAY s. autoestrada, rodovia.
FREE-WILL s. livre-arbítrio.
FREEZE s. congelamento / v. congelar.
FREEZER s. congelador.
FREEZING s. congelação / adj. glacial, frio.
FREIGHT s. frete, carga.
FRENCH s. francês(esa) / adj. francês(esa).
FRENCH FRIES s. batatas fritas.
FRENETIC adj. frenético.
FRENZY s. frenesi, furor.
FREQUENCY s. frequência.
FREQUENT adj. frequente / v. frequentar.
FREQUENTLY adv. frequentemente.
FRESH adj. fresco.
FRESHEN UP v. refrescar-se.
FRESHLY adv. com aspecto sadio, juvenil; recentemente.
FRESHMAN s. calouro; estudante novato.
FRESHNESS s. frescor, frescura.
FRESHWATER adj. de água doce.
FRET s. lamúria, choradeira, aborrecimento / v. amofinar-se, irritar-se.
FRIAR s. frade, monge.
FRICASSEE s. fricassê.
FRICATIVE adj. fricativo.
FRICTION s. fricção, atrito.
FRIDAY s. sexta-feira.
FRIDGE s. geladeira.
FRIED adj. frito; bêbado; confuso.
FRIEND s. amigo(a).
FRIENDLY adj. amigável / adv. amigavelmente.
FRIENDSHIP s. amizade; afeição.
FRIGHT s. medo, susto, pavor.
FRIGHTEN v. assustar, amedrontar.
FRIGHTENED adj. com medo, aterrorizado(a).
FRIGHTENING adj. assustador(a).
FRIGHTFUL adj. assustador(a), espantoso(a).
FRIGID adj. frígido, frio.
FRILL s. franja de tecido; franja de cabelo; enfeite.
FRINGE s. franja.
FRISK s. pulo, cambalhota / v. saltar, pular.
FRISKY adj. animado(a), brincalhão(ona), travesso(a).
FRITTER s. pedaço; bolinho frito / v. dissipar; fragmentar.
FRIVOLITY s. frivolidade, futilidade.
FRIVOLOUS adj. frívolo, fútil.
FRIZZY adj. crespo(a), encrespado(a).
FRO adv. de, atrás, para trás; cá, lá.
FROCK s. vestido ou saia; roupa solta (camisola, túnica, manto).
FROG s. rã.
FROLIC s. brincadeira, travessura / v. brincar, traquinar.
FROM prep. de; proveniente de.
FRONT s. frente; dianteira.
FRONTAGE s. fachada.
FRONTAL s. frontal.
FRONTIER s. fronteira.
FROSH s. calouro, novato (informal).
FROST s. geada / v. gear.
FROSTED adj. fosco; coberto de geada.
FROSTING s. glacê para cobertura de bolos.
FROSTY adj. coberto de geada; gelado(a).
FROTH s. espuma / v. espumar.
FROWN s. franzimento de sobrancelhas, carranca.
FROZEN adj. congelado(a).
FRUIT s. fruto, fruta; produto.
FRUITCAKE s. bolo de frutas; louco, maníaco (gíria).
FRUITERER s. fruteiro, vendedor de frutas.
FRUITFUL adj. proveitoso(a); frutífero(a); fecundo(a).
FRUITLESS adj. infrutífero, que não dá resultados.
FRUSTATE v. frustrar; malograr.
FRUSTRATED adj. frustrado.
FRUSTRATION s. frustração.
FRY s. fritada / v. fritar.
FRYING PAN s. frigideira.
FUDDLE s. bebedeira, embriaguez / v. embriagar(-se).
FUDDY-DUDDY s. careta.
FUDGE s. doce de açúcar / v. falsificar, camuflar.

FUEL s. combustível / v. abastecer com combustível.
FUG s. bafo, ar abafado.
FUGITIVE s. fugitivo(a), foragido(a) / adj. fugitivo(a), fugaz.
FULFIL v. cumprir a palavra, satisfazer um desejo.
FULFILLMENT s. satisfação; cumprimento; realização.
FULL adj. cheio(a), lotado(a).
FULL AGE s. maioridade.
FULL GROWN adj. maduro(a); adulto(a).
FULL MOON s. lua cheia.
FULLNAME s. nome completo.
FULLNESS s. plenitude, abundância.
FULL-TIME adj. por tempo integral / adv. por tempo integral.
FULLY adv. completamente, inteiramente.
FULSOME adj. enjoativo(a), grosseiro(a), repugnante.
FUME s. fumo / v. fumegar.
FUMES s. gases.
FUN s. diversão, brincadeira / adj. engraçado.
FUNCTION s. função / v. funcionar.
FUNCTIONAL adj. prático(a), funcional.
FUNCTIONARY s. funcionário, funcionário público.
FUND s. fundo, capital, valor disponível.
FUNDAMENTAL adj. fundamental.
FUNDAMENTALISM s. fundamentalismo.
FUNDAMENTALIST s. fundamentalista.
FUNDAMENTALLY adv. fundamentalmente.
FUNERAL s. funeral, enterro.
FUNERARY adj. funerário.
FUNFAIR s. parque de diversões.
FUNGUS s. fungo; cogumelo.
FUNK s. medo, pavor / v. atemorizar, intimidar.
FUNNEL s. funil.

FUNNY adj. divertido(a), engraçado(a); esquisito(a), estranho(a).
FUR s. pelo de animal; pele, peliça.
FURBISH v. lustrar, polir; restaurar.
FUR-COAT s. casaco de peles.
FURIOUS adj. furioso(a), irado(a).
FURL s. enrolamento / v. enrolar(-se).
FURLOUGH s. licença / v. licenciar, conceder licença a.
FURNACE s. forno, fornalha.
FURNISH v. mobiliar, suprir.
FURNISHED adj. mobiliado.
FURNISHINGS s. mobília; guarnições.
FURNITURE s. móveis, mobília.
FUROR s. furor, exaltação.
FURROW s. sulco; ranhura / v. sulcar, entalhar.
FURRY adj. peludo(a).
FURTHER adj. adicional, outro / adv. além disso, demais / v. promover.
FURTHERMORE adv. além disso, outrossim, demais.
FURY s. fúria.
FUSE s. fusível / v. fundir.
FUSE-BOX s. caixa de fusíveis.
FUSELAGE s. fuselagem.
FUSIBLE adj. fusível, fundível.
FUSILIERS s. fuzileiros.
FUSION s. fusão, união.
FUSS s. escândalo, espalhafato, alvoroço; preocupação exagerada.
FUSSY adj. espalhafatoso(a); exigente; meticuloso(a).
FUSTY adj. bolorento, mofento, abafado, sufocante.
FUTURE adj. futuro(a) / s. futuro.
FUTURISM s. futurismo.
FUTURIST adj. futurista.
FUZZ s. flocos, penugem, felpa.
FUZZY adj. flocoso(a), felpudo(a).

Gg

G, g s. sétima letra do alfabeto inglês; sol (nota musical).
GAB v. tagarelar / s. conversa, bate-papo.
GABBLE v. tagarelar / s. tagarelice.
GABBY adj. tagarela, conversador, falador.
GAD v. perambular.
GADFLY s. implicante.
GADGET s. invenção, engenhoca.
GADGETRY s. parafernália.
GAELIC s. gaélico (escocês ou irlandês) / adj. gaélico (escocês ou irlandês).
GAFF s. gafe, vacilo.
GAG s. mordaça, censura, piada / v. amordaçar, censurar.
GAGA adj. gagá, caduco; enamorado, apaixonado.
GAGGLE s. bando, revoada, amontoado.
GAIETY s. alegria.
GAILY adv. alegremente, felizmente.
GAIN s. ganho, lucro, conquista / v. ganhar, obter.
GAINER s. beneficiário; ganhador.
GAINFUL adj. vantajoso, lucrativo.
GAIT s. modo de andar, andadura.
GALA s. gala, pompa / adj. de gala, de festa.
GALACTIC adj. galáctico.
GALAXY s. galáxia.
GALE s. ventania, vento forte.
GALL s. vesícula; assadura, amargor / v. irritar, atormentar.
GALLANT s. galante, garboso, cortês / adj. galante, garboso, cortês.
GALLANTRY s. galanteio, cavalheirismo.
GALLEON s. galeão (navio).
GALLERY s. galeria.
GALLEY s. galera; galé; cozinha de navio.
GALLIC s. Gália / adj. gaulês, gálico (francês).
GALLING adj. irritante.
GALLON s. galão (medida).
GALLOP s. galope / v. galopar.
GALLOWS s. forca; enforcamento.
GALLOWS HUMOR s. humor negro.
GALLSTONE s. cálculo biliar; pedra nos rins.
GALORE adv. em abundância / adj. abundante.
GALVANISE v. galvanizar; reanimar, estimular.

GAMBIT s. gambito (xadrez); cambito.
GAMBLE s. risco, aposta / v. apostar (jogos); arriscar.
GAMBLER s. jogador, apostador.
GAMBLING s. jogo / adj. referente a jogo.
GAMBLING DEBT s. dívida de aposta.
GAMBOL s. cambalhota / v. pular, dar saltos.
GAME s. jogo, partida.
GAMEKEEPER s. guarda-caça.
GAMETE s. gameta.
GANDER s. ganso macho.
GANG s. grupo, bando, gangue, quadrilha.
GANGLY adj. grandalhão, desengonçado.
GANGRENE s. gangrena.
GANGSTER s. gângster, facínora, bandido.
GANGWAY s. passagem; ponte de embarque (navio).
GAOL v. prender / s. cadeia.
GAP s. brecha, vão, abertura, lacuna.
GAPE s. bocejo / v. ficar boquiaberto; bocejar.
GAPING adj. muito aberto, escancarado.
GARAGE s. garagem; oficina / v. guardar na garagem.
GARB s. traje, roupa, veste / v. vestir, usar.
GARBAGE s. lixo.
GARBAGE COLLECTOR s. gari.
GARBAGE DUMP s. aterro sanitário.
GARBLE v. deturpar, falsificar, adulterar.
GARDEN s. jardim, horta / v. cuidar de jardim.
GARDENER s. jardineiro.
GARDENING s. jardinagem; horticultura.
GARGLE v. gargarejar / s. gargarejo.
GARISH adj. berrante; extravagante.
GARLAND s. guirlanda, grinalda.
GARLIC s. alho.
GARMENT s. peça de roupa, vestuário.
GARNER v. acumular, armazenar.
GARNET s. granada; vermelho-escuro.
GARNISH v. enfeitar, ornar / s. guarnição, enfeite.
GARRISON s. guarnição (tropas) / v. guarnecer.
GAS s. gás; gasolina; acelerador (carro) / v. acelerar.
GAS COOKER s. fogão a gás.
GAS CYLINDER s. botijão de gás.
GASEOUS adj. gasoso.
GASH s. talho, corte, ferida profunda / v. talhar, cortar.
GASKET s. junta, vedação.
GAS MASK s. máscara de gás.
GAS METER s. medidor de gás.
GASOLINE s. gasolina.
GAS STATION s. posto de gasolina.
GASSY adj. gasoso, flatulento.
GASTRIC adj. gástrico.
GASTRIC JUICE s. suco gástrico.
GASTRIC ULCER s. úlcera gástrica.
GASTRITIS s. gastrite.
GASTROINTESTINAL adj. gastrointestinal.
GASTRONOMIC adj. gastronômico.
GASTRONOMY s. gastronomia.
GASWORKS s. fábrica de gás.
GATE s. portão, porta, cancela.
GATECRASHER s. penetra, bicão (de festa).
GATEHOUSE s. guarita, portaria.
GATEKEEPER s. porteiro, guardião.
GATEWAY s. porta, entrada; passagem, portal.
GATHER v. reunir, juntar, coletar.
GATHERER s. coletor, apanhador.
GATHERING s. reunião, encontro; ato de reunir.
GAUCHE adj. desajeitado, acanhado, desastroso.
GAUDY adj. afetado, exagerado; cafona, brega.
GAUGE s. escala; calibre (armas); medidor / v. padronizar, calibrar.
GAUNT adj. magro, descarnado, esquelético.
GAUZE s. gaze.
GAVEL s. martelo (juiz, leiloeiro).
GAWK v. ficar pasmo, boquiaberto.
GAWKY adj. atrapalhado, desajeitado.
GAY adj. homossexual; alegre / s. homossexual.
GAZE s. olhar fixo / v. olhar fixamente, fitar.
GAZEBO s. toldo, marquise.
GAZELLE s. gazela.
GAZER s. observador, espectador.
GAZETTE s. gazeta, jornal, noticiário.
GAZETTEER s. gazetista; dicionário geográfico.
GDP abrev. PIB (Produto Interno Bruto).
GEAR s. engrenagem; equipamento, marcha (carro) / v. engrenar.
GEARBOX s. caixa de câmbio.
GEARSTICK s. alavanca do câmbio; marcha.

GECKO s. lagartixa.
GEE interj. xii! puxa! oba!
GEEK s. estranho, esquisito; nerd.
GEEKY adj. nerd, inteligente.
GEISHA s. gueixa.
GEL s. gel.
GELATIN(E) s. gelatina / adj. gelatinoso.
GELD v. castrar, capar (animal).
GELDING s. castração.
GEM s. joia, gema, pedra preciosa.
GEMINI s. Gêmeos (astrologia).
GENDER s. gênero.
GENE s. gene.
GENEALOGICAL adj. genealógico.
GENEALOGICAL TREE adj. árvore genealógica.
GENEALOGIST s. genealogista.
GENEALOGY s. genealogia.
GENERAL s. general (militar) / adj. geral, generalizado.
GENERAL ELECTION s. eleição nacional.
GENERAL IDEA s. ideia geral.
GENERALISATION s. generalização.
GENERALISE v. generalizar.
GENERALIST s. generalista.
GENERALITY s. generalidade.
GENERALLY adv. geralmente.
GENERATE v. gerar, criar, causar.
GENERATION s. geração, criação.
GENERATIONAL adj. geracional.
GENERATIVE adj. generativo, gerativo.
GENERATOR s. gerador, genitor; produtor.
GENERIC adj. genérico.
GENEROSITY s. generosidade.
GENEROUS adj. generoso; abundante.
GENEROUSLY adv. generosamente.
GENESIS s. gênese, gênesis; origem.
GENETIC adj. genético.
GENETICALLY adv. geneticamente.
GENETIC ENGINEERING s. engenharia genética.
GENETICIST s. geneticista.
GENETICS s. genética.
GENEVA s. Genebra.
GENIAL adj. genial, cordial, amável.
GENIE s. gênio, espírito.
GENITAL adj. genital.
GENITALIA s. genitália; órgãos genitais.
GENIUS s. gênio, capacidade, destreza.
GENOCIDAL adj. genocida.
GENOCIDE s. genocídio.
GENOME s. genoma.
GENRE s. gênero (arte).
GENTEEL adj. distinto, refinado, elegante.
GENTILE s. gentio.
GENTLE adj. suave, brando, moderado.
GENTLEMAN s. cavalheiro; senhor.
GENTLEMAN'S AGREEMENT s. acordo de cavalheiros.
GENTLENESS s. meiguice; doçura, suavidade.
GENTLY adv. gentilmente, paulatinamente.
GENTRY s. pequena nobreza.
GENUINE adj. genuíno; autêntico.
GENUINELY adv. genuinamente.
GEOCENTRIC adj. geocêntrico.
GEOGRAPHER s. geógrafo.
GEOGRAPHIC adj. geográfico.
GEOGRAPHY s. geografia.
GEOLOGIST s. geólogo.
GEOLOGY s. geologia.
GEOMETRIC adj. geométrico.
GEOMETRY s. geometria.
GEOPOLITICAL adj. geopolítico.
GEOPOLITICS s. geopolítica.
GERANIUM s. gerânio.
GERIATRIC adj. geriátrico / s. geriátrico.
GERIATRICS s. geriatria.
GERM s. micróbio, germe.
GERMAN adj. alemão, germano / s. alemão, germano.
GERMANE adj. pertinente, apropriado.
GERMANY s. Alemanha.
GERMICIDAL adj. germicida, desinfetante.
GERMINAL adj. germinal.
GERMINATE v. germinar.
GERMINATION s. germinação.
GERUND s. gerúndio.
GESTATION s. gestação; gravidez.
GESTATIONAL adj. gestacional.
GESTICULATE v. gesticular.
GESTURE s. gesto, aceno, trejeito.
GET v. tornar, receber, obter, ganhar.
GET ABOUT v. espalhar-se; circular; viajar muito.
GET ALONG v. entender-se com, lidar com; progredir.
GET AROUND v. rodear, viajar de lugar em lugar.
GET AT v. alcançar, certificar-se.

GET AWAY v. partir, ir embora, escapar.
GET BACK v. voltar, receber de volta, regressar.
GET BY v. passar despercebido.
GET DOWN v. abaixar, descer; entristecer.
GET IN v. entrar.
GET OFF v. sair, decolar / s. decolagem.
GET ON v. subir.
GET OUT v. sair.
GET-TOGETHER v. reunir-se / s. reunião informal.
GET UP v. levantar-se; animar-se.
GET-UP s. enfeite, arranjo.
GHASTLY adj. horrível, medonho, pavoroso.
GHETTO s. gueto.
GHOST s. fantasma; espectro.
GHOSTLY adj. fantasmagórico.
GHOSTWRITER s. escritor-fantasma / v. escrever em nome de alguém.
GHOUL s. fantasma; homem detestável; ladrão de túmulos.
GHOULISH adj. macabro, mórbido.
GIANT s. gigante / adj. gigantesco, enorme.
GIBBON s. gibão (macaco).
GIDDINESS s. tontura, vertigem, distração.
GIDDY adj. tonto, zonzo; frívolo.
GIFT s. presente; dom, dádiva / v. presentear.
GIFTED adj. dotado, talentoso, prodígio.
GIG s. bico (trabalho informal); show, concerto.
GIGANTIC adj. gigantesco.
GIGGLE v. dar risadinhas / s. risadinha.
GIGGLY adj. riso amarelo.
GIGOLO s. gigolô, michê.
GILD v. dourar, laminar.
GILDED adj. dourado; superficial (bonito por fora).
GILT s. douradura, douração.
GIMMICK s. macete, truque.
GIN s. gim.
GINGER s. gengibre; pessoa ruiva.
GINGERBREAD s. biscoito de gengibre.
GINGERLY adv. cuidadosamente, cautelosamente.
GINGIVITIS s. gengivite.
GIRAFFE s. girafa.
GIRD v. cingir, prender.
GIRDER s. viga mestra, suporte principal.
GIRL s. menina, garota.
GIRLFRIEND s. namorada.
GIRL FRIEND s. amiga.
GIRLISH adj. de menininha; de mocinha.
GIRTH s. medida da cintura, corpulência.
GIST s. essência, ponto principal.
GIVE v. dar, doar, ceder, entregar.
GIVE AWAY v. trair, denunciar.
GIVEAWAY s. prêmio, brinde.
GIVE BACK v. devolver; dar de volta.
GIVE IN v. ceder.
GIVEN adj. dado, doado; especificado, determinado.
GIVER s. doador; presenteador.
GIVE UP v. desistir; renunciar.
GLACE adj. glacê.
GLACIAL adj. glacial, frio, apático.
GLACIER s. geleira.
GLAD adj. contente, alegre.
GLADDEN v. alegrar, contentar.
GLADE s. clareira.
GLADIATOR s. gladiador.
GLADLY adv. alegremente.
GLADNESS s. alegria.
GLAMORISE v. glorificar, exaltar, elogiar.
GLAMOROUS adj. glamoroso, deslumbrante.
GLAMOROUSLY adv. glamourosamente.
GLAMOUR s. fascínio, encanto, deslumbre.
GLANCE s. relance, olhada / v. dar uma olhadinha.
GLANCING adj. oblíquo, inclinado.
GLAND s. glândula.
GLANDULAR adj. glandular.
GLANS s. glande.
GLARE s. luminosidade, clarão; olhar penetrante / v. olhar com raiva.
GLARING adj. feroz, irritado; ofuscante.
GLASS s. vidro; copo; lupa.
GLASSES s. óculos.
GLASSHOUSE s. estufa; vidraçaria.
GLASSWARE s. vidraria; objetos de vidro.
GLASSY adj. vítreo, vidrado.
GLAUCOMA s. glaucoma.
GLAZE s. verniz; esmalte / v. envidraçar, vitrificar.
GLAZED adj. vitrificado.
GLAZIER s. vidraceiro.
GLAZING s. envidraçamento, vitrificação.

GLEAM v. brilhar, reluzir / s. lampejo, vislumbre.
GLEAMING adj. brilhante, reluzente.
GLEAN v. colher, compilar, obter.
GLEANER s. respigador.
GLEE s. regozijo, alegria, deleite.
GLEEFUL adj. alegre.
GLEN s. vale estreito e profundo.
GLIB adj. lisonjeiro, volúvel; superficial.
GLIDE s. deslizamento / v. planar, deslizar.
GLIDER s. planador (piloto ou avião).
GLIDING s. voo sem motor; asa-delta.
GLIMMER s. lampejo, luz trêmula / v. vislumbrar.
GLIMMERING s. vislumbre / adj. luzente.
GLIMPSE s. espiada, olhadinha / v. olhar de relance.
GLINT s. raio de luz, lampejos / v. cintilar; reluzir.
GLISTEN v. brilhar / s. brilho, resplendor.
GLITTER s. brilho; purpurina / v. reluzir, refletir a luz.
GLITTERING adj. brilhante, cintilante.
GLOATING s. soberba, arrogância / adj. soberbo, arrogante.
GLOB s. bolha, pingo, gota.
GLOBAL adj. mundial; global.
GLOBALISATION s. globalização.
GLOBALISE v. globalizar.
GLOBALLY adv. globalmente.
GLOBE s. globo, esfera.
GLOBULAR adj. globular; esférico.
GLOBULE s. glóbulo.
GLOOM s. escuridão; tristeza / v. ficar triste, melancólico.
GLOOMY adj. escuro; sombrio, triste, melancólico.
GLORIFICATION s. glorificação.
GLORIFY v. glorificar, honrar.
GLORIOUS adj. glorioso, ilustre.
GLORY s. glória; honra.
GLOSS s. brilho, lustro; brilho labial (cosmético) / v. polir, lustrar.
GLOSSARY s. glossário.
GLOSSY adj. lustroso, polido; reluzente.
GLOVE s. luva.
GLOVE COMPARTMENT s. porta-luvas.
GLOW v. irradiar, brilhar / s. brilho, fulgor.
GLOWER v. olhar furioso / s. encarada.
GLOWING adj. radiante, reluzente, brilhante.
GLUCOSE s. glicose.
GLUE s. cola, grude / v. colar, grudar.
GLUED adj. colado, grudado.
GLUM adj. carrancudo, de mau humor.
GLUT s. fartura, abundância / v. fartar, saturar.
GLUTTEN s. glúten.
GLUTTON s. glutão, comilão.
GLUTTONY s. gula, glutonaria.
GLYCERINE s. glicerina.
GLYCEROL s. glicerol.
GNARL s. nó / v. torcer, deformar.
GNARLED adj. retorcido; áspero.
GNARLY adj. nodoso, retorcido.
GNAT s. mosquito.
GNAW v. roer, mastigar; atormentar.
GNAWING s. mastigação / adj. implicante, perturbante.
GNOME s. gnomo; anãozinho.
GO v. ir, passar / s. tentativa, ida / interj. vai!
GO AHEAD v. ir em frente, avançar.
GOAL s. meta, objetivo; gol (futebol).
GOALKEEPER s. goleiro.
GOALPOST s. trave do gol.
GOALSCORER s. artilheiro, goleador.
GOAT s. cabra, bode; Capricórnio (astrologia).
GOATEE s. barbicha, cavanhaque.
GOATSKIN s. couro de cabra.
GO AWAY v. ir embora.
GO BACK v. voltar.
GOBBLE v. devorar, engolir.
GO-BETWEEN s. intermediário, negociador.
GOBLET s. cálice, taça.
GOBLIN s. duende, elfo.
GOD s. Deus.
GODCHILD s. afilhado.
GODDAUGHTER s. afilhada.
GODDESS s. deusa.
GODFATHER s. padrinho; chefão / v. apadrinhar.
GODHEAD s. divindade.
GODLESS adj. ateu, ímpio.
GODLIKE adj. divino, venerado.
GODLY adj. devoto, pio.
GODMOTHER s. madrinha / v. amadrinhar.
GODSEND s. dádiva do céu.
GODSON s. afilhado.
GOER s. frequentador.

GOING s. andamento; curso da vida / adj. andante, em movimento.
GOLD s. ouro.
GOLDEN adj. dourado, de ouro.
GOLDFINCH s. pintassilgo.
GOLDFISH s. peixe-dourado.
GOLDMINE s. mina de ouro.
GOLF s. golfe.
GOLFER s. jogador de golfe.
GONE adj. ido, partido.
GONG s. gongo.
GONORRHEA s. gonorreia.
GOO s. gosma, meleca.
GOOD adj. bom.
GOODBYE interj. até logo! adeus!
GOOD-FOR-NOTHING s. pessoa inútil.
GOOD FRIDAY s. Sexta-feira Santa.
GOOD-HUMOURED adj. bem-humorado.
GOOD-LOOKING adj. bonito, de boa aparência.
GOODLY adj. considerável.
GOOD-NATURED adj. de boa índole.
GOODNESS s. bondade / interj. céus!
GOOD NIGHT interj. boa noite.
GOODS s. mercadorias; bens, posses.
GOODWILL s. boa vontade, benevolência.
GOODY s. velhinha; beata; gulodice.
GOOEY adj. grudento.
GOOF s. bobo, pateta.
GOOGLE v. pesquisar na internet.
GOON s. pessoa estúpida (coloquial).
GOOSE s. (pl. geese) ganso.
GOOSEBERRY s. groselha, groselheira.
GORE v. ferir / s. sangue.
GORGE s. garganta, goela (anatomia); desfiladeiro, garganta (geografia).
GORGEOUS adj. magnífico, deslumbrante.
GORILLA s. gorila.
GORP s. granola.
GORSE s. tojo.
GORY adj. sangrento, ensanguentado.
GOSH interj. Deus!; caramba!
GOSPEL s. evangelho / adj. evangélico.
GOSSAMER s. teia de aranha, fio delgado; transparente.
GOSSIP s. fofoca, fofoqueiro / v. fofocar.
GOTH s. godo, gótico / adj. godo, gótico.
GOTHIC adj. gótico.
GOUACHE s. guache.
GOUGE v. arrancar, escavar.
GOVERN v. governar, administrar.
GOVERNESS s. governanta.
GOVERNMENT s. governo, administração.
GOVERNOR s. governador.
GOWN s. vestido longo; beca, toga.
GPS abrev. GPS (Sistema de Posicionamento Global).
GRAB v. agarrar.
GRACE s. graça, elegância / v. adornar, decorar.
GRACEFUL adj. gracioso, elegante.
GRACEFULLY adv. graciosamente.
GRACIOUS adj. afável; elegante, luxuoso.
GRADATION s. gradação.
GRADE s. classe; grau / v. classificar.
GRADE CROSSING s. passagem de nível.
GRADE SCHOOL s. escola primária.
GRADIENT s. declive, inclinação.
GRADUAL adj. gradual.
GRADUALLY adv. gradualmente, paulatinamente.
GRADUATE s. graduado, diplomado / v. formar-se, graduar-se.
GRADUATION s. formatura, graduação, colação de grau.
GRAFFITI s. pichação, grafite.
GRAFT s. enxerto / v. enxertar.
GRAIN s. grão.
GRAINED adj. granulado.
GRAM s. grama (unidade de massa).
GRAMMAR s. gramática.
GRAMMARIAN s. gramático.
GRAMMATICAL adj. gramatical.
GRAMMATICALLY adv. gramaticalmente.
GRAND adj. esplêndido, formidável.
GRANDCHILD s. neto (genérico).
GRANDDAUGHTER s. neta.
GRANDEUR s. grandeza.
GRANDFATHER s. avô.
GRANDIOSE adj. grandioso, imponente.
GRANDMOTHER s. avó.
GRANDNESS s. grandeza.
GRANDPARENTS s. avós.
GRANDSON s. neto.
GRANGER s. granjeiro.
GRANITE s. granito.
GRANNY s. vovó.
GRANT v. conceder / s. subsídio, subvenção.
GRANULATED adj. granulado.

GRAPE s. uva; videira.
GRAPH s. gráfico.
GRAPHIC adj. gráfico.
GRAPHIC ARTS s. artes gráficas.
GRAPPLE s. agarramento, luta / v. atracar-se com.
GRASP v. agarrar, pegar.
GRASPING adj. avaro, avarento; ganancioso.
GRASS s. grama, gramado.
GRASS ROOTS s. povo comum, zonas rurais.
GRASSHOPPER s. gafanhoto.
GRATE v. ralar; ranger.
GRATEFUL adj. agradecido, grato.
GRATER s. ralador.
GRATING adj. rangedor, rilhador / s. grade, barras de ferro.
GRATITUDE s. gratidão.
GRATUITY s. gratificação, gorjeta.
GRAVE s. cova, sepultura / adj. sério, grave / v. gravar, esculpir.
GRAVEL s. cascalho, pedregulho.
GRAVESTONE s. lápide, túmulo.
GRAVEYARD s. cemitério.
GRAVITY s. gravidade (física), seriedade (formal).
GRAVY s. molho ou caldo de carne.
GRAY adj. cinzento, cinza / s. cinza.
GREASE s. gordura, banha; graxa / v. engraxar; lubrificar.
GREASY adj. gorduroso, oleoso.
GREAT adj. genial; grande, vasto; formidável.
GREAT GRANDDAUGHTER s. bisneta.
GREAT GRANDFATHER s. bisavô.
GREAT GRANDMOTHER s. bisavó.
GREAT GRANDSON s. bisneto.
GREATLY adv. imensamente, muito.
GREATNESS s. grandeza.
GREECE s. Grécia.
GREED s. ganância; gula.
GREEK s. grego / adj. grego.
GREEN adj. verde; imaturo, inexperiente / s. verde.
GREEN CARD s. autorização de residência nos EUA.
GREENERY s. verdura, hortaliças.
GREENGROCER s. verdureiro, quitandeiro.
GREENHOUSE s. estufa.

GREENISH adj. esverdeado.
GREENLAND s. Groenlândia.
GREENS s. verduras.
GREET v. acolher; saudar, cumprimentar.
GREETING s. saudação, cumprimento.
GREETING CARD s. cartão comemorativo; saudação.
GRENADE s. granada.
GREY adj. m.q. gray.
GREY-HAIRED adj. grisalho.
GREYISH adj. cinzento, acinzentado.
GRID s. grade; grelha; linhas (de coordenadas).
GRIDDLE s. forma redonda para bolo.
GRIEF s. pesar, aflição.
GRIEVANCE s. queixa, mágoa.
GRIEVE v. afligir; chorar a perda de alguém.
GRILL s. grelha / v. grelhar.
GRILLE s. grade (de proteção).
GRIM adj. desagradável, carrancudo, severo.
GRIMY adj. encardido.
GRIND v. moer, triturar.
GRIP s. aderência, cabo, alça / v. agarrar.
GRIPE s. aperto, agarramento.
GRIPPING adj. fascinante.
GRISLY adj. medonho, terrível.
GRISTLE s. nervo; cartilagem.
GRIZZLY BEAR s. urso-pardo.
GROAN s. gemido / v. gemer.
GROCER s. dono de mercearia.
GROCERIES s. mantimentos.
GROCERY s. mercearia.
GROGGY adj. grogue, embriagado; tonto, zonzo.
GROIN s. virilha.
GROOM s. noivo.
GROOVE s. ranhura, entalhe, sulco / v. entalhar, sulcar.
GROSS s. grosa (medida) / adj. inteiro, total, bruto / v. totalizar.
GROSSLY adv. inteiramente, extremamente; grosseiramente.
GROTESQUE adj. grotesco.
GROTTO s. gruta, caverna.
GROTTY adj. repugnante.
GROUND s. terreno, terra, chão, solo; fundamento / v. fundamentar, basear.
GROUND-FLOOR s. andar térreo.
GROUNDING s. base, fundamentos; primeira demão (pintura).

GROUNDWORK s. preparação; base, princípio fundamental.
GROUSE s. galo silvestre / v. resmungar.
GROUT s. reboco / v. rebocar.
GROVE s. arvoredo, bosque.
GROVEL v. abaixar-se, humilhar-se, rastejar.
GROW v. crescer; cultivar; aumentar.
GROWING adj. crescente / s. crescimento.
GROWL v. rosnar, rugir / s. rosnado, rugido.
GROWN adj. crescido, adulto.
GROWTH s. crescimento, aumento.
GROW UP v. tornar-se adulto, desenvolver-se.
GRUB s. larva, lagarta; boia (comida).
GRUBBY adj. sujo, imundo.
GRUDGE v. ter rancor; invejar alguém / s. rancor, ressentimento.
GRUELING adj. árduo, cansativo, penoso.
GRUESOME adj. horrível, medonho.
GRUFF adj. rude, brusco; áspero.
GRUMBLE v. resmungar / s. queixa.
GRUMPY adj. rabugento, resmungão.
GRUNT s. grunhido / v. grunhir, resmungar.
GUARANTEE s. garantia / v. garantir.
GUARD s. guarda, vigia / v. vigiar, proteger.
GUARDED adj. cauteloso, precavido.
GUARDIAN s. tutor, guardião.
GUARDIANSHIP s. tutela.
GUATEMALA s. Guatemala.
GUAVA s. goiaba.
GUERRILLA s. guerrilheiro.
GUESS v. adivinhar, imaginar / s. suposição.
GUEST s. convidado; hóspede.
GUESTROOM s. quarto de hóspedes.
GUFFAW v. gargalhar / s. gargalhada.
GUIDANCE s. orientação; supervisão.
GUIDE s. guia / v. guiar, orientar.
GUIDE-BOOK s. guia de viagem.
GUIDED adj. guiado.
GUIDELINE s. orientação, diretriz.
GUIDEPOST s. sinalização, placa de trânsito.
GUIDER s. guia, condutor.
GUILE s. astúcia, malícia, fraude.
GUILELESS adj. sincero, sem malícia, ingênuo.
GUILT s. culpa.
GUILTLESS adj. inocente.
GUILTY adj. culpado.
GUITAR s. violão, guitarra.
GULF s. golfo.
GULL s. gaivota / v. enganar.
GULLET s. esôfago, garganta, goela.
GULLY s. rego, bueiro.
GULP v. engolir, tragar / s. trago, gole.
GUM s. goma, chiclete; gengiva.
GUMBALL s. bala de chiclete.
GUMBOOTS s. galochas.
GUMPTION s. juízo; bom senso.
GUN s. arma, pistola, espingarda / v. atirar.
GUNFIRE s. tiroteio.
GUNK s. porcaria, imundice.
GUNMAN s. pistoleiro.
GUNPOINT s. ponta ou mira de arma.
GUNPOWDER s. pólvora.
GURK s. arroto / v. arrotar.
GURU s. guru.
GUST s. rajada de vento; gosto, gozo, deleite.
GUSTO s. garra, entusiasmo.
GUT s. intestino, tripa; coragem.
GUTTER s. calha; sarjeta; rego.
GUY s. cara, sujeito, rapaz.
GUYANA s. Guiana.
GUZZLE s. bebedeira / v. empanturrar-se, encher a cara de.
GYMNASIUM s. ginástica; ginásio de esporte.
GYMNAST s. ginasta.
GYMNASTICS s. ginástica.
GYNECOLOGIST s. ginecologista.
GYP s. trapaceiro (coloquial) / v. lograr, enganar.
GYPSY s. cigano.
GYVE s. algema / algemar.

Hh

H, h *s.* oitava letra do alfabeto inglês.
HA *interj.* ai!, ah!
HABERDASHERY *s.* loja de armarinho; loja de roupas masculinas.
HABIT *s.* hábito, costume.
HABITUAL *adj.* habitual.
HACK *s.* corte / *v.* cortar; invadir um sistema de computador ilegalmente (coloquial).
HACKER *s.* pirata de computador (coloquial).
HACKNEYED *adj.* corriqueiro; vulgar.
HAIL *s.* granizo; saudação / *v.* chover granizo; saudar.
HAILSTONE *s.* pedra de granizo.
HAIR *s.* cabelo; pelo.
HAIRBRUSH *s.* escova de cabelo.
HAIRCUT *s.* corte de cabelo.
HAIRDO *s.* penteado de mulher (coloquial).
HAIRDRESSER *s.* cabeleireiro(a).
HAIRPIN *s.* grampo de cabelo.
HAIR-RAISING *adj.* horripilante, de arrepiar os cabelos.
HAIR SPRAY *s.* laquê.
HAIRY *adj.* peludo; cabeludo.
HALE *adj.* vigoroso, são / *v.* puxar, levantar.
HALF *s.* (*pl.* halves) metade, meio / *adj.* meio, metade de / *adv.* pela metade.
HALF-BAKED *adj.* meio assado (pão); inexperiente.
HALF-BRED *adj.* raça mista, bastardo.
HALFCASTE *s.* mestiço(a).
HALF-MAST *s.* meio-mastro; pôr a bandeira a meio-mastro.
HALFMOON *s.* meia-lua.
HALL *s.* saguão; entrada.
HALLMARK *s.* marca de qualidade (de metais preciosos).
HALLOWED *adj.* sagrado.
HALLOWEEN *s.* dia das bruxas.
HALLWAY *s.* corredor, entrada.
HALT *s.* parada, interrupção; descanso / *v.* deter-se, parar.
HALTER *s.* cabresto / *v.* amarrar com corda.
HALVE *v.* dividir ao meio.
HAM *s.* presunto.
HAMBURGER *s.* hambúrguer; almôndega.
HAMLET *s.* lugarejo; vilarejo.
HAMMER *s.* martelo / *v.* martelar.
HAMMOCK *s.* rede (de dormir).

HAMPER s. cesto grande; empecilho, estorvo / v. impedir, tolher.
HAMSTER s. hamster.
HAND s. mão / v. dar, entregar.
HANDBAG s. bolsa (de mulher); maleta.
HANDBILL s. folheto.
HANDBOOK s. manual.
HANDBRAKE s. freio de mão.
HANDCUFF s. algema / v. algemar.
HANDFUL s. punhado.
HANDICAP s. incapacidade, deficiência / v. prejudicar.
HANDICRAFT s. artesanato; habilidade manual.
HANDIWORK s. obra, trabalho manual.
HANDKERCHIEF s. lenço de bolso.
HANDLE s. maçaneta, asa, alça, cabo da xícara / v. manusear; lidar com.
HANDLE BARS s. guidão de bicicleta.
HANDLER s. tratador, treinador (animais); manejador (computador); encarregado.
HANDMADE adj. feito à mão.
HANDOUT s. doação, donativo; folheto.
HANDRAIL s. corrimão.
HANDSHAKE s. aperto de mão.
HANDSOME adj. atraente, bonito; generoso.
HANDWRITING s. caligrafia.
HANDY adj. habilidoso, prático; à mão.
HANDYMAN s. biscateiro.
HANG v. pendurar; enforcar.
HANGAR s. hangar, galpão.
HANGER s. cabide.
HANGING s. enforcamento.
HANGMAN s. carrasco; forca (jogo).
HANG ON v. esperar, aguardar.
HANGOVER s. ressaca.
HANG-UP s. problema, grilo (coloquial).
HAPHAZARD adj. por acaso / adv. casualmente.
HAPPEN v. acontecer, ocorrer.
HAPPENING s. acontecimento, ocorrência.
HAPPILY adv. felizmente, alegremente.
HAPPINESS s. felicidade, alegria.
HAPPY adj. feliz, alegre.
HARASS v. importunar, molestar, incomodar.
HARASSMENT s. perseguição, assédio, tormento.
HARBOR s. porto; abrigo, refúgio / v. abrigar, proteger.
HARD adj. duro; difícil.
HARD DISK s. disco rígido (informática).

HARDEN v. endurecer.
HARDLY adv. dificilmente.
HARDNESS s. dureza.
HARDSHIP s. privação, dificuldade.
HARD UP adj. sem dinheiro; em apuros.
HARDWARE s. ferragens; hardware (informática).
HARD-WEARING adj. resistente, durável.
HARD-WORKING adj. trabalhador(a), aplicado.
HARDY adj. resistente, robusto.
HARE s. lebre.
HARE-BRAINED adj. maluco.
HARLOT s. prostituta.
HARM s. dano / v. prejudicar.
HARMFUL adj. prejudicial.
HARMLESS adj. inofensivo.
HARMONICA s. gaita; harmônio.
HARMONIOUS adj. harmonioso.
HARMONY s. harmonia.
HARNESS s. correia, arreios / v. arrear (cavalo).
HARP s. harpa / v. tocar harpa.
HARPOON s. arpão.
HARROW s. rastelo, ancinho.
HARSH adj. desarmonioso; áspero; estridente; duro.
HARVEST s. colheita / v. colher.
HASH s. picadinho, guisado.
HASHISH s. haxixe.
HASSLE s. complicação, trabalhão (coloquial).
HASTE s. pressa / v. apressar.
HASTEN v. acelerar, apressar-se.
HASTILY adv. depressa, apressadamente.
HASTY adj. ligeiro, rápido, apressado; precipitado.
HAT s. chapéu.
HATCH s. ninhada; escotilha; abertura / v. sair do ovo; chocar, incubar.
HATCHET s. machadinha.
HATE s. ódio / v. odiar.
HATEFUL adj. odioso, detestável.
HATRED s. ódio, aversão.
HAUL v. puxar, arrastar.
HAUNT v. assombrar / s. abrigo, lugar preferido.
HAVE v. ter, possuir.
HAVEN s. porto, ancoradouro; refúgio / v. abrigar.
HAVERSACK s. mochila; farnel.

HAVOC s. destruição, devastação / v. destruir, devastar.
HAWAII s. Havaí.
HAWK s. falcão, gavião.
HAY s. feno.
HAY-LOFT s. palheiro.
HAYSTACK s. monte de feno.
HAZARD s. perigo, risco / v. aventurar, arriscar (jogos).
HAZARDOUS adj. perigoso, arriscado.
HAZE s. neblina, cerração / v. enevoar, obscurecer; judiar, maltratar.
HAZELNUT s. avelã.
HAZY adj. nebuloso; vago, confuso.
HE pron. ele.
HEAD s. cabeça / v. encabeçar.
HEADACHE s. dor de cabeça.
HEADING s. cabeçalho, título.
HEADLIGHT s. farol de automóvel.
HEADLINE s. título, manchete (de jornal).
HEAD-ON adv. de ponta-cabeça; de frente.
HEADPHONE s. fone de ouvido.
HEADQUARTERS s. quartel-general; sede.
HEADSTRONG adj. teimoso, obstinado.
HEADY adj. estonteante, inebriante; violento, irrefletido; forte.
HEAL v. curar, cicatrizar, sarar.
HEALTH s. saúde.
HEALTHY adj. saudável, sadio(a).
HEAP s. pilha / v. empilhar.
HEAR v. ouvir, escutar.
HEARING s. audição; interrogatório.
HEARING AID s. aparelho para surdez.
HEARSAY s. boato, rumor.
HEARSE s. carro funerário.
HEART s. coração.
HEARTACHE s. mágoa.
HEART ATTACK s. ataque cardíaco.
HEARTBEAT s. batida do coração.
HEARTBREAKING adj. angustiante, de partir o coração.
HEARTBROKEN adj. angustiado, de coração partido.
HEARTBURN s. azia; inveja.
HEARTEN v. animar.
HEART FAILURE s. parada cardíaca.
HEARTFELT adj. sincero, cordial.
HEARTLAND s. área central.
HEARTLESS adj. sem coração, insensível.
HEAT s. calor / v. aquecer.
HEATED adj. aquecido.

HEATER s. aquecedor.
HEATHEN s. pagão(ã).
HEATING s. aquecimento, calefação.
HEAT STROKE s. insolação.
HEAT WAVE s. onda de calor.
HEAVEN s. paraíso, céu.
HEAVENLY adj. divino, celestial.
HEAVILY adj. muito, em grande quantidade; pesadamente.
HEAVY adj. pesado; cansativo.
HEAVYWEIGHT s. peso-pesado.
HEBREW s. hebreu, hebraico / adj. hebraico.
HECTIC adj. frenético; febril; corado / s. tísica.
HEDGE s. cerca viva, cerca, sebe / v. cercar, restringir.
HEED s. cuidado, atenção / v. prestar atenção.
HEEL s. calcanhar; salto de sapato.
HEFTY adj. robusto, pesado, forte.
HEIFER s. novilha, bezerra.
HEIGHT s. altura, altitude.
HEIGHTEN v. elevar, intensificar, levantar.
HEIR s. herdeiro.
HEIRESS s. herdeira.
HEIRLOOM s. relíquia de família, peça de herança.
HELICOPTER s. helicóptero.
HELIPORT s. heliporto.
HELIUM s. hélio (química).
HELL s. inferno / interj. droga! (coloquial).
HELLISH adj. terrível, infernal.
HELLO interj. olá!, oi!, alô!
HELM s. leme, direção, timão (navio).
HELMET s. capacete.
HELP s. ajuda, auxílio, socorro / v. ajudar, auxiliar.
HELPER s. ajudante.
HELPFUL adj. prestativo, útil.
HELPING s. porção (de comida); ajuda.
HELPLESS adj. indefeso; desamparado.
HELPMATE s. ajudante.
HEM s. bainha / v. fazer a bainha.
HEMISPHERE s. hemisfério.
HEMORRHAGE s. hemorragia.
HEMORRHOIDS s. hemorroidas.
HEN s. galinha; fêmea de qualquer ave.
HENCE adv. portanto, por isso.
HENCEFORTH adv. de agora em diante.
HENCHMAN s. capanga.
HEPATITIS s. hepatite.
HER adj. dela / pron. lhe, a ela, sua, seu, a.

HERALD s. precursor(a); mensageiro / v. anunciar, trazer notícias.
HERB s. erva; forragem, capim.
HERD s. rebanho, manada.
HERE adv. aqui, cá.
HEREABOUT(S) adv. por aqui.
HEREAFTER adv. daqui por diante, depois / s. futuro.
HEREBY adv. por este meio, por isto.
HEREDITY s. hereditariedade.
HERESY s. heresia.
HERETIC s. herege / adj. herege.
HERITAGE s. patrimônio; herança.
HERMETICALLY adv. hermeticamente.
HERMIT s. eremita.
HERNIA s. hérnia.
HERO s. herói; protagonista.
HEROIN s. heroína (droga).
HEROINE s. heroína (pessoa); protagonista.
HERON s. garça.
HERRING s. arenque (peixe).
HERS pron. dela, seu, sua.
HERSELF pron. ela mesma, se, a si mesma.
HESITANT adj. indeciso, hesitante.
HESITATE v. hesitar, vacilar.
HESITATION s. indecisão, hesitação.
HETEROSEXUAL adj. heterossexual.
HEW v. cortar com machado, derrubar.
HEYDAY s. auge, apogeu.
HI interj. oi!
HIBERNATE v. hibernar.
HICCOUGH v. soluçar / s. soluço.
HICCUP v. m.q. hiccough.
HICK s. caipira (coloquial).
HIDE v. esconder, ocultar.
HIDE-AND-SEEK s. esconde-esconde.
HIDEAWAY s. esconderijo, refúgio.
HIERARCHY s. hierarquia.
HI-FI adj. alta-fidelidade / s. aparelho (de alta-fidelidade) (coloquial).
HIGH adj. alto, elevado, superior.
HIGHBORN adj. de alta linhagem; de nascimento ilustre.
HIGHBROW s. intelectual, erudito.
HIGH CHAIR s. cadeira alta, cadeira de bebê.
HIGHER EDUCATION s. ensino superior.
HIGH-HAT adj. grã-fino, arrogante.
HIGH-HEELED adj. de salto alto.
HIGHLIGHT v. realçar, ressaltar; iluminar / s. ponto alto, melhor momento.

HIGHLY adv. altamente, muito, extremamente.
HIGHNESS s. alteza.
HIGH SCHOOL s. escola secundária.
HIGH SEASON s. alta temporada.
HIGHWAY s. estrada, rodovia.
HIJACK v. sequestrar (avião).
HIJACKER s. sequestrador (de avião).
HIKE s. caminhada / v. caminhar.
HIKER s. andarilho(a), aquele(a) que caminha bastante.
HILARIOUS adj. hilário, hilariante, divertido.
HILL s. colina, ladeira, morro.
HILLSIDE s. encosta.
HILLY adj. montanhoso.
HILT s. cabo, punho (de faca ou de espada).
HIMSELF pron. ele mesmo, se, a si mesmo.
HIND s. corça (fêmea do veado) / adj. traseiro posterior.
HINDER v. retardar, atrapalhar.
HINDRANCE s. estorvo, obstáculo, impedimento.
HINDSIGHT s. retrospecto; compreensão tardia.
HINDU adj. hindu / s. hindu.
HINGE s. dobradiça / v. colocar em dobradiças.
HIP s. quadril; anca.
HIPPOPOTAMUS s. hipopótamo.
HIRE s. aluguel, arrendamento / v. alugar, arrendar, contratar.
HIS adj. dele / pron. dele, seu(s), sua(s).
HISS s. assobio, silvo / v. assobiar, sibilar.
HISTORIAN s. historiador(a).
HISTORIC(AL) adj. histórico(a).
HISTORY s. história, narração.
HIT v. bater, acertar, atingir / s. golpe, pancada.
HITCHHIKE v. pedir carona.
HI-TECH s. alta tecnologia.
HIVE s. colmeia.
HOARFROST s. geada.
HOARSE adj. rouco.
HOB s. placa de aquecimento (de fogão).
HOBBLE v. mancar; impedir.
HOBBY s. passatempo preferido.
HOCKEY s. hóquei.
HOE s. enxada.
HOG s. porco capado.
HOIST v. içar, levantar.
HOLD v. segurar, pegar.

HOLDER s. recipiente, vasilhame; portador(a); titular, proprietário.
HOLDING s. participação, sociedade, título.
HOLD ON v. esperar; firmar, segurar.
HOLD UP s. assalto à mão armada; atraso; engarrafamento.
HOLE s. buraco, orifício, toca / v. esburacar, furar.
HOLIDAY s. folga, feriado, dia santo; férias.
HOLINESS s. santidade.
HOLLAND s. Holanda.
HOLLOW adj. oco, vazio / s. cavidade, buraco.
HOLLY s. azevinho (botânica).
HOLOCAUST s. holocausto, destruição.
HOLY adj. sagrado, santo.
HOMAGE s. homenagem.
HOME s. casa, lar / adv. para casa.
HOME ADDRESS s. endereço residencial.
HOME COMPUTER s. computador doméstico.
HOMELESS adj. desabrigado, sem lar / s. mendigo.
HOMEMADE adj. caseiro, feito em casa.
HOMETOWN s. cidade natal.
HOMEWORK s. lição de casa.
HOMOGENEOUS adj. homogêneo.
HOMOSEXUAL adj. homossexual / s. homossexual.
HONDURAS s. Honduras.
HONEST adj. honesto, franco, sincero.
HONESTLY adv. honestamente, francamente.
HONESTY s. honestidade, honradez, franqueza.
HONEY s. mel; doçura, querido(a) (coloquial).
HONEYCOMB s. favo de mel.
HONEYMOON s. lua de mel.
HONK v. buzinar.
HONOR v. honrar / s. honra, dignidade.
HONORABLE adj. honrado, honesto, ilustre, decente.
HONORARY adj. honorário.
HOOD s. capuz; capô.
HOODWINK v. tapear, enganar, lograr; vendar os olhos.
HOOF s. casco, pata.
HOOK s. gancho; anzol (pesca) / v. prender, fisgar.
HOOLIGAN s. desordeiro(a), vândalo.
HOOP s. arco (de barril), aro, argola.
HOOT s. vaia; pio (coruja); barulho (de buzina) / v. piar; buzinar; vaiar.
HOOTER s. buzina, sirene.
HOOVER s. aspirador de pó / v. aspirar (com o aspirador).
HOP s. pulo / v. pular em um pé só.
HOPE v. esperar, ter esperança / s. esperança.
HOPEFUL adj. esperançoso, otimista.
HOPEFULLY adv. esperançosamente, com otimismo.
HOPELESS adj. desesperado; inútil; impossível.
HORDE s. multidão, horda.
HORIZON s. horizonte.
HORIZONTAL adj. horizontal.
HORMONE s. hormônio.
HORN s. chifre, corno; buzina (carro); trompa, corneta (música).
HORNET s. vespão.
HORNY adj. córneo, caloso; excitado sexualmente (coloquial).
HOROSCOPE s. horóscopo.
HORRIBLE adj. horrível.
HORRID adj. terrível, antipático.
HORRIFY v. horrorizar.
HORROR s. horror, pavor.
HORSE s. cavalo.
HORSEBACK s. garupa de cavalo / adv. a cavalo.
HORSEFLY s. mutuca.
HORSEHAIR s. crina de cavalo.
HORSESHOE s. ferradura.
HORTICULTURE s. horticultura.
HOSE s. mangueira (tubo flexível).
HOSPICE s. asilo; hospício.
HOSPITABLE adj. hospitaleiro.
HOSPITAL s. hospital.
HOSPITALITY s. hospitalidade.
HOST s. anfitrião; apresentador; hóstia (religião) / v. hospedar, receber.
HOSTAGE s. refém.
HOSTEL s. albergue, hospedaria.
HOSTESS s. anfitriã; recepcionista.
HOSTILE adj. hostil, inimigo.
HOSTILITY s. hostilidade.
HOT adj. quente; ardente, picante.
HOT-BLOODED adj. de sangue quente, fogoso.
HOT DOG s. cachorro-quente.
HOTEL s. hotel.
HOTELIER s. hoteleiro(a).
HOTHOUSE s. estufa de plantas.
HOT LINE s. linha direta.

HOTLY adv. ardentemente, calorosamente.
HOTPLATE s. chapa elétrica.
HOUND s. cão de caça / v. caçar, perseguir.
HOUR s. hora.
HOURLY adj. de hora em hora / adv. de hora em hora.
HOUSE s. casa, residência / v. alojar, acomodar.
HOUSE ARREST s. prisão domiciliar.
HOUSEBREAKING s. arrombamento, furto.
HOUSEKEEPER s. governanta.
HOUSEMAID s. doméstica, arrumadeira.
HOUSEWARMING s. festa de inauguração de uma casa nova.
HOUSEWIFE s. (pl. housewives) dona de casa.
HOUSEWORK s. trabalhos domésticos.
HOUSING s. alojamento, moradia.
HOVEL s. cabana, choupana.
HOW adv. como, de qual maneira.
HOWEVER adv. de qualquer modo / conj. contudo, porém, todavia.
HOWL s. uivo, urro, grito / v. uivar, berrar.
HUB s. cubo (da roda); centro.
HUBBUB s. algazarra, tumulto.
HUBCAP s. calota.
HUFF s. raiva; mau humor / v. gritar, xingar.
HUG s. abraço / v. abraçar; acariciar.
HUGE adj. enorme, imenso.
HUGENESS s. vastidão, imensidão.
HULL s. casco (de navio); casca (de ervilha, vagem) / v. descascar.
HUMAN s. humano / adj. humano.
HUMAN BEING s. ser humano.
HUMANITARIAN adj. humanitário.
HUMANITY s. humanidade.
HUMBLE v. humilhar / adj. humilde, modesto; submisso.
HUMBLENESS s. humildade, modéstia.
HUMID adj. úmido.
HUMIDITY s. umidade.
HUMILIATE v. humilhar.
HUMILITY s. humildade.
HUMMINGBIRD s. beija-flor.
HUMOR s. humor, graça.
HUMP s. corcunda, corcova, giba / v. corcovar, curvar.
HUNCH s. pressentimento, palpite; corcova, corcunda / v. corcovar.
HUNCHBACK s. corcunda.
HUNDRED num. cem, cento
HUNGARIAN s. húngaro / adj. húngaro.

HUNGER s. fome.
HUNGER STRIKE s. greve de fome.
HUNGRY adj. faminto, com fome.
HUNT s. caça, caçada / v. caçar, perseguir.
HUNTER s. caçador(a).
HUNTING s. caça.
HURDLE s. barreira (no esporte); obstáculo.
HURRICANE s. furacão, tufão.
HURRIED adj. apressado.
HURRY s. pressa / v. apressar.
HURT s. ferida, dor / v. ferir, machucar, ofender.
HURTFUL adj. ofensivo.
HUSBAND s. marido.
HUSH s. silêncio / v. silenciar / interj. quieto! silêncio!
HUSK s. casca; exterior.
HUSKY adj. rouco; forte, robusto / s. cão esquimó; idioma dos esquimós.
HUT s. cabana; barraca.
HYBRID s. híbrido.
HYDRANT s. hidrante.
HYDRAULIC adj. hidráulico.
HYDROELECTRIC adj. hidroelétrico.
HYDROGEN s. hidrogênio.
HYENA s. hiena.
HYGIENE s. higiene.
HYMEN s. hímen.
HYMN s. hino, cântico.
HYPE s. exageração (coloquial).
HYPERACTIVE adj. hiperativo.
HYPERACTIVITY s. hiperatividade.
HYPERINFLATION s. hiperinflação.
HYPERLINK s. hiperlink, link.
HYPERMARKET s. hipermercado.
HYPERSENSITIVE adj. hipersensível.
HYPERTENSION s. hipertensão.
HYPERTENSIVE adj. hipertensivo.
HYPERTEXT s. hipertexto.
HYPNOSIS s. hipnose.
HYPNOTIST s. hipnotizador(a).
HYPNOTIZE v. hipnotizar.
HYPOCRISY s. hipocrisia.
HYPOCRITE s. hipócrita.
HYPOTHERMIA s. hipotermia.
HYPOTHESIS s. hipótese.
HYPOTHESIZE v. conjurar, fazer uma hipótese.
HYPOTHETICAL adj. hipotético.
HYSTERICAL adj. histórico.
HYSTERICS s. histeria.

Ii

I, i s. nona letra do alfabeto inglês; representa o número um em algarismos romanos.
I *pron.* eu.
IAMBIC *adj.* iâmbico.
IBID *adv.* no mesmo lugar, na mesma obra.
IBIDEM *adv.* m.q. ibid.
ICE s. gelo / v. gelar.
ICEBERG s. iceberg.
ICEBOX s. geladeira.
ICEBREAKER s. quebra-gelo.
ICE CREAM s. sorvete.
ICE CUBE s. cubo de gelo.
ICED *adj.* gelado.
ICE HOCKEY s. hockey no gelo.
ICELAND s. Islândia.
ICELANDIC s. islandês / *adj.* islandês.
ICE LOLLY s. picolé.
ICEMAN s. vendedor de gelo.
ICE RINK s. rinque de patinação, pista de gelo.
ICE-SKATE v. patinar no gelo / s. patins de gelo.
ICE SKATER s. patinador.
ICING s. glacê.
ICKY *adj.* nojento, repulsivo.
ICON s. ícone.
ICONIC *adj.* icônico.
ICY *adj.* gelado; gélido.
IDEA s. ideia, plano.
IDEAL s. ideal / *adj.* ideal.
IDEALISM s. idealismo.
IDEALIST s. idealista, sonhador.
IDEALIZE v. idealizar.
IDEALLY *adv.* idealmente, perfeitamente.
IDEM *pron.* idem, a mesma coisa.
IDENTICAL *adj.* idêntico; igual, semelhante.
IDENTIFIABLE *adj.* identificável.
IDENTIFICATION s. identificação.
IDENTIFIER s. identificador.
IDENTIFY v. identificar, reconhecer.
IDENTIKIT s. retrato falado.
IDENTITY s. identidade.
IDEOLOGICAL *adj.* ideológico.
IDEOLOGUE s. ideólogo.
IDEOLOGY s. ideologia.
IDIOCY s. idiotice.

IDIOM s. idioma, dialeto; expressão idiomática.
IDIOMATIC adj. idiomático.
IDIOPATHIC adj. idiopático; doença.
IDIOSYNCRASY s. idiossincrasia.
IDIOSYNCRATIC adj. estranho, singular, peculiar.
IDIOT s. idiota.
IDIOTIC adj. idiota.
IDLE adj. ocioso, inútil, à toa / v. desocupar.
IDLENESS s. indolência, inatividade.
IDLER s. preguiçoso.
IDOL s. ídolo.
IDOLATRY s. idolatria; devoção.
IDOLISE v. idolatrar, adorar; venerar.
IDYLL s. idílio.
IDYLLIC adj. idílico; bucólico.
IF conj. se / s. suposição, objeção.
IFFY adj. duvidoso, incerto.
IF SO adv. neste caso, se assim for.
IF THAT adv. m.q. if so.
IGLOO s. iglu.
IGNITE v. acender, incendiar.
IGNITION s. ignição; combustão.
IGNITION KEY s. chave de ignição.
IGNOBLE adj. ignóbil, desonroso.
IGNORANCE s. ignorância.
IGNORANT adj. ignorante, desinformado.
IGNORE v. ignorar.
IGUANA s. iguana, réptil.
ILK s. laia, feitio.
ILL adj. doente, indisposto / s. mal, desgosto.
ILL-ADVISED adj. imprudente, mal-aconselhado.
ILL-AFFECTED adj. mal-intencionado, indisposto.
ILL-BRED adj. malcriado, mal-educado.
ILLEGAL adj. ilegal, ilegítimo.
ILLEGALITY s. ilegalidade.
ILLEGALLY adv. ilegalmente.
ILLEGIBLE adj. ilegível.
ILLEGITIMATE adj. ilegítimo, bastardo.
ILL FEELING s. má vontade; rancor, mal-estar.
ILLICIT adj. ilícito.
ILLITERACY s. analfabetismo.
ILLITERATE adj. analfabeto, iletrado, ignorante / s. analfabeto, iletrado, ignorante.
ILL LUCK s. desgraça, infortúnio.
ILL-MANNERED adj. mal-educado, rude, grosseiro.
ILLNESS s. doença, enfermidade.
ILLOGICAL adj. ilógico, incoerente.
ILL-TEMPERED s. mal-humorado, resmungão.
ILL-TREATMENT s. maus-tratos.
ILLUMINATE v. iluminar.
ILLUMINATED adj. iluminado; culto.
ILLUMINATING adj. iluminador, iluminante.
ILLUMINATION s. iluminação.
ILLUSION s. ilusão.
ILLUSIONIST s. ilusionista, mágico.
ILLUSIVE adj. ilusivo, enganoso.
ILLUSORY adj. ilusório, enganador.
ILLUSTRATE v. ilustrar, esclarecer, descrever.
ILLUSTRATED adj. ilustrado, esclarecido.
ILLUSTRATION s. ilustração; esclarecimento.
ILLUSTRATIVE adj. ilustrativo.
ILLUSTRATOR s. ilustrador; desenhista.
ILLUSTRIOUS adj. glorioso, renomado, ilustre.
IMAGE s. imagem.
IMAGERY s. imagens, estátuas, figuras; fantasias.
IMAGINABLE adj. imaginável.
IMAGINARY adj. imaginário.
IMAGINATION s. imaginação.
IMAGINATIVE adj. imaginativo, inventivo, criativo.
IMAGINE v. imaginar, supor, pensar.
IMBALANCE s. desequilíbrio.
IMBECILE s. imbecil.
IMBIBE v. absorver, embeber.
IMBUE v. embeber, saturar; tingir, imbuir.
IMF abrev. FMI (Fundo Monetário Internacional).
IMITATE v. imitar, copiar.
IMITATION s. imitação, cópia, falso.
IMITATIVE adj. imitativo.
IMITATOR s. imitador.
IMMACULATE adj. impecável, imaculado; limpo.
IMMANENT adj. imanente, inerente.
IMMATERIAL adj. imaterial, irrelevante; espiritual.

IMMATURE *adj.* imaturo.
IMMATURITY *s.* imaturidade.
IMMEASURABLE *adj.* imensurável, desmedido.
IMMEDIACY *s.* imediatismo, urgência.
IMMEDIATE *adj.* imediato, urgente, próximo.
IMMEDIATELY *adv.* imediatamente; diretamente.
IMMEMORIAL *adj.* imemorial.
IMMENSE *adj.* imenso, enorme.
IMMENSITY *s.* imensidade.
IMMERSE *v.* imergir, submergir; mergulhar.
IMMERSED *adj.* imerso, mergulhado, submerso.
IMMERSION *s.* imersão.
IMMIGRANT *s.* imigrante / *adj.* imigrante.
IMMIGRATE *v.* imigrar.
IMMIGRATION *s.* imigração.
IMMINENT *adj.* iminente.
IMMOBILE *adj.* imóvel, fixo.
IMMOBILISATION *s.* imobilização.
IMMOBILISE *v.* imobilizar.
IMMOBILISER *s.* imobilizador.
IMMOBILITY *s.* imobilidade.
IMMODERATE *adj.* imoderado, excessivo.
IMMOLATION *s.* imolação, sacrifício.
IMMORAL *adj.* imoral.
IMMORTAL *adj.* imortal, eterno.
IMMORTALITY *s.* imortalidade.
IMMORTALISE *v.* imortalizar.
IMMORTALITY *s.* imortalidade.
IMMOVABLE *adj.* imóvel.
IMMUNE *adj.* imune.
IMMUNISATION *s.* imunização.
IMMUNITY *s.* imunidade.
IMMUNIZE *v.* imunizar.
IMMUNOLOGIC *adj.* imunológico.
IMMUNOLOGY *s.* imunologia.
IMMUTABLE *adj.* imutável.
IMP *s.* pestinha, criança levada.
IMPACT *s.* impacto, colisão, choque.
IMPACTED *adj.* impactado, compactado.
IMPAIR *v.* prejudicar, deteriorar.
IMPAIRED *adj.* debilitado, danificado.
IMPAIRMENT *s.* enfraquecimento, dano.
IMPALE *v.* empalar, espetar.
IMPART *v.* dar, conceder, comunicar.
IMPARTIAL *adj.* imparcial, neutro; justo.
IMPARTIALITY *s.* imparcialidade.

IMPASSABLE *adj.* impraticável, intransponível.
IMPASSE *s.* impasse, situação difícil.
IMPASSIONED *adj.* ardoroso, fervoroso.
IMPASSIVE *adj.* impassível; insensível.
IMPATIENCE *s.* impaciência.
IMPATIENT *adj.* impaciente; apressado.
IMPAYABLE *adj.* impagável.
IMPEACH *v.* acusar, contestar; impedir, culpar.
IMPEACHMENT *s.* impedimento legal de exercer mandato; contestação.
IMPECCABLE *adj.* impecável.
IMPEDE *v.* impedir, obstruir; frustrar.
IMPEDMENT *s.* impedimento, obstáculo.
IMPEL *v.* impelir, incitar; estimular.
IMPELLER *s.* impulsor, impulsionador.
IMPEND *v.* impender, pairar (sobre); ameaçar.
IMPENDING *adj.* iminente, que está prestes a acontecer.
IMPENETRABLE *adj.* impenetrável.
IMPERATIVE *s.* imperativo / *adj.* autoritário.
IMPERCEPTIBLE *adj.* imperceptível.
IMPERFECT *adj.* imperfeito, defeituoso / *s.* imperfeito.
IMPERFECTION *s.* imperfeição.
IMPERIAL *adj.* imperial.
IMPERIALISM *s.* imperialismo.
IMPERIALIST *adj.* imperialista / *s.* imperialista.
IMPERIOUS *adj.* imperioso, arrogante, soberbo.
IMPERISHABLE *adj.* imperecível, perdurável.
IMPERMANENT *adj.* impermanente; transitório.
IMPERMEABLE *adj.* impermeável.
IMPERMISSIBLE *adj.* não permissível; proibitivo.
IMPERSONAL *adj.* impessoal.
IMPERSONALITY *s.* impessoalidade.
IMPERSONATE *v.* personificar, representar; imitar.
IMPERSONATION *s.* disfarce, imitação.
IMPERSONATOR *s.* impostor, imitador.
IMPERTINENT *adj.* impertinente; insolente.
IMPETUOUS *adj.* impetuoso.
IMPETUS *s.* incentivo, estímulo, ímpeto.

IMPIETY s. impiedade.
IMPIOUS adj. ímpio, irreverente, incrédulo.
IMPISH adj. travesso, danado; pestinha.
IMPLACABLE adj. implacável.
IMPLANT v. implantar / s. implante.
IMPLANTABLE adj. implantável.
IMPLANTATION s. implantação.
IMPLAUSIBLE adj. improvável, implausível.
IMPLEMENT v. executar, implementar / s. implemento, instrumento.
IMPLEMENTATION s. implementação.
IMPLICATE s. implicante / v. implicar, envolver / adj. implícito.
IMPLICATION s. implicação, envolvimento.
IMPLICIT adj. implícito.
IMPLIED adj. implicado; subentendido.
IMPLODE v. implodir.
IMPLODED adj. implodido.
IMPLORE v. implorar, suplicar.
IMPLORING s. súplica / adj. implorante.
IMPLOSION s. implosão.
IMPLY v. inferir, deduzir; sugerir.
IMPOLITE adj. indelicado, grosseiro, descortês.
IMPORT v. importar, relevar / s. importação, importância.
IMPORTANCE s. importância; valor, influência.
IMPORTANT adj. importante; considerável.
IMPORTATION s. importação.
IMPORTED adj. importado.
IMPORTER s. importador.
IMPORTUNE v. importunar.
IMPORTUNATE adj. importuno, incômodo.
IMPOSE v. impor, obrigar; coagir.
IMPOSING adj. imponente, majestoso.
IMPOSITION s. imposição.
IMPOSSIBILITY s. impossibilidade.
IMPOSSIBLE adj. impossível.
IMPOSTOR s. impostor, fraude.
IMPOTENCE s. impotência.
IMPOTENT adj. impotente, incapaz.
IMPOUND v. confiscar; encerrar, fechar.
IMPOVERISH v. empobrecer.
IMPOVERISHED adj. empobrecido.
IMPOVERISHMENT s. empobrecimento.
IMPRACTICABLE adj. impraticável, inexequível, impossível.
IMPRACTICAL adj. impraticável; pouco prático.

IMPRECISE adj. impreciso.
IMPRECISION s. imprecisão.
IMPREGNABLE adj. impregnável.
IMPREGNATE v. impregnar; emprenhar / adj. impregnado; prenhe.
IMPREGNATION s. impregnação; fecundação.
IMPRESS v. impressionar; imprimir; incutir.
IMPRESSION s. impressão.
IMPRESSIONABLE adj. impressionável.
IMPRESSIONISM s. impressionismo.
IMPRESSIONIST s. impressionista.
IMPRESSIVE adj. impressionante.
IMPRINT s. impressão; marca; carimbo / v. imprimir, carimbar.
IMPRISON v. encarcerar, prender; aprisionar.
IMPRISONMENT s. aprisionamento; confinamento.
IMPROBABLE adj. improvável.
IMPROMPTU adj. improvisado; improviso.
IMPROPER adj. impróprio, inconveniente.
IMPROPRIETY s. impropriedade; indecência, ato impróprio.
IMPROVE v. melhorar, progredir, aperfeiçoar.
IMPROVEMENT s. melhora, melhoria; progresso.
IMPROVIDENT adj. improvidente, negligente.
IMPROVISATION s. improvisação.
IMPROVISATIONAL adj. improvisado.
IMPROVISATOR s. improvisador; repentista.
IMPROVISE v. improvisar.
IMPRUDENT adj. imprudente.
IMPUGN v. impugnar.
IMPULSE s. impulso.
IMPULSIVE adj. impulsivo.
IMPUNITY s. impunidade.
IMPURE adj. impuro.
IMPURITY s. impureza.
IMPUTATION s. imputação; inculpação.
IMPUTE v. imputar.
IN prep. em, dentro de.
INABILITY s. inaptidão, incapacidade.
INACCESSIBLE adj. inacessível.
INACCURACY s. inexatidão, incorreção, imprecisão.

INACCURATE *adj.* impreciso, inexato, incorreto.
INACTION *s.* inação, inércia.
INACTIVATE *v.* desativar, inativar.
INACTIVATION *s.* inativação.
INACTIVE *adj.* inativo.
INACTIVITY *s.* inatividade.
INADEQUACY *s.* inadequação.
INADEQUATE *adj.* inadequado.
INADMISSIBLE *adj.* inadmissível.
INADVERTENT *adj.* inadvertido.
INADVISABLE *adj.* desaconselhável, sem conselho.
INALIENABLE *adj.* inalienável.
INANE *adj.* inane; vão, oco, fútil.
INANIMATE *adj.* inanimado.
INANITY *s.* bobagem, inanidade.
INAPLICABLE *adj.* inaplicável, irrelevante.
INAPPROPRIATE *adj.* inadequado, impróprio; inapropriado.
INAPT *adj.* inapto, incapaz.
INAPTITUDE *s.* inaptidão, incapacidade.
INARTICULATE *adj.* inarticulado, indistinto.
INASMUCH AS *adv.* na medida em que, visto que.
INATTENTION *s.* negligência, desatenção.
INATTENTIVE *adj.* desatento.
INAUDIBLE *adj.* inaudível.
INAUGURAL *adj.* inicial, inaugural.
INAUGURATE *v.* inaugurar.
INAUGURATION *s.* inauguração.
INAUSPICIOUS *adj.* desfavorável, nefasto.
IN-BETWEEN *adj.* intermediário / *prep.* entre, no meio.
INBOARD *adj.* interno.
INBORN *adj.* inato, inerente.
INBOX *s.* caixa de entrada.
INBRED *adj.* congênito; inato.
INBUILT *adj.* inerente, embutido; incorporado.
INCALCULABLE *adj.* incalculável.
INCANDESCENT *adj.* incandescente.
INCANTATION *s.* encantamento, magia.
INCAPABILITY *s.* incapacidade.
INCAPABLE *adj.* incapaz; incapacitado.
INCAPACITATE *v.* incapacitar, desqualificar.
INCAPACITY *s.* deficiência; incapacidade.
INCARCERATE *v.* encarcerar; aprisionar.
INCARCERATION *s.* encarceramento; prisão.

INCARNATE *v.* encarnar, personificar / *adj.* encarnado.
INCARNATION *s.* encarnação; personificação.
INCENDIARY *adj.* incendiário; provocativo.
INCENSE *s.* incenso / *v.* enraivecer; perfumar.
INCENTIVE *s.* incentivo, estímulo.
INCEPTION *s.* início, começo.
INCERTITUDE *s.* incerteza.
INCESSANT *adj.* incessante.
INCESSANTLY *adv.* incessantemente, sem parar.
INCEST *s.* incesto.
INCESTUOUS *adj.* incestuoso.
INCH *s.* polegada (equivalente a 2,54 cm).
INCIDENCE *s.* incidência, ocorrência.
INCIDENT *s.* incidente, acontecimento, ocorrência.
INCIDENTAL *adj.* incidental.
INCIDENTALLY *adv.* a propósito; incidentalmente.
INCINERATE *v.* incinerar, cremar.
INCINERATION *s.* incineração, cremação.
INCINERATOR *s.* incinerador.
INCIPIENT *adj.* incipiente.
INCISE *v.* incisar, entalhar; cortar.
INCISION *s.* incisão, corte.
INCISIVE *adj.* incisivo; eficaz, cortante.
INCISOR *s.* incisivo (dente);
INCITE *v.* provocar, incitar; estimular, instigar.
INCITEMENT *s.* incitação, provocação.
INCLEMENT *adj.* inclemente; severo, rigoroso.
INCLINATION *s.* tendência, inclinação; aptidão.
INCLINE *s.* inclinação, declive; rampa / *v.* inclinar; influenciar.
INCLUDE *v.* incluir.
INCLUDING *prep.* inclusive.
INCLUSION *s.* inclusão.
INCLUSIVE *adj.* incluído; incluso.
INCOGNITO *adj.* incógnito / *adv.* incognitamente.
INCOHERENCE *s.* incoerência.
INCOHERENT *adj.* incoerente.
INCOME *s.* renda, rendimento, lucro.
INCOME TAX *s.* imposto de renda.

INCOMING *adj.* de chegada; de entrada, entrante.
INCOMMUNICADO *adj.* incomunicável.
INCOMPARABLE *adj.* incomparável; único.
INCOMPATIBLE *adj.* incompatível.
INCOMPETENCE *s.* incompetência.
INCOMPETENT *adj.* incompetente.
INCOMPLETE *adj.* incompleto.
INCOMPLETENESS *s.* incompletude.
INCOMPREHENSIBLE *adj.* incompreensível.
INCOMPREHENSION *s.* incompreensão.
INCONCEIVABLE *adj.* inconcebível; inimaginável.
INCONCLUSIVE *adj.* inconclusivo.
INCONSEQUENTIAL *adj.* irrelevante, sem importância.
INCONSIDERATE *adj.* sem consideração; descortês.
INCONSISTENCE *s.* inconsistência; contradição.
INCONSISTENT *adj.* inconsistente.
INCONTESTABLE *adj.* incontestável.
INCONTINENCE *s.* incontinência.
INCONTINENT *adj.* incontinente, que não se controla.
INCONVENIENCE *s.* inconveniência, incômodo / *v.* incomodar, molestar.
INCONVENIENT *adj.* inconveniente, inoportuno.
INCORPORATE *v.* incorporar, unir / *adj.* incorporado, unido.
INCORPORATED COMPANY *s.* sociedade anônima.
INCORPORATION *s.* incorporação, corporação.
INCORRECT *adj.* incorreto, errado.
INCORRIGIBLE *adj.* incorrigível.
INCORRUPTIBLE *adj.* incorruptível.
INCREASE *s.* aumento, acréscimo / *v.* aumentar, acrescentar.
INCREASING *adj.* crescente.
INCREASINGLY *adv.* progressivamente, de modo crescente.
INCREDIBLE *adj.* incrível, inacreditável.
INCREDULOUS *adj.* incrédulo.
INCREMENT *s.* aumento, incremento.
INCREMENTAL *adj.* incremental.
INCRIMINATE *v.* incriminar.
INCRIMINATING *adj.* incriminador.

INCRIMINATION *s.* condenação, incriminação.
INCUBATE *v.* incubar.
INCUBATION *s.* incubação.
INCUBATOR *s.* incubadora, chocadeira (elétrica), estufa.
INCUBUS *s.* pesadelo / *adj.* íncubo.
INCUMBENCE *s.* incumbência.
INCUMBENT *s.* titular; beneficiado, incumbente.
INCUR *v.* incorrer; atrair sobre si.
INCURABLE *adj.* incurável.
INCURSION *s.* incursão; investida; invasão.
INDEBTED *adj.* em dívida com, endividado.
INDECENCY *s.* indecência, obscenidade.
INDECENT *adj.* indecente; obsceno.
INDECISION *s.* indecisão.
INDECISIVE *adj.* indeciso, hesitante.
INDEED *adv.* certamente, de fato, realmente.
INDEFATIGABLE *adj.* infatigável.
INDEFENSIBLE *adj.* indefensável.
INDEFINITE *adj.* indefinido, vago.
INDEFINITELY *adv.* indefinidamente.
INDEMNIFICATION *s.* indenização.
INDEMNIFY *v.* assegurar; indenizar, ressarcir.
INDEMNITY *s.* indenização.
INDENTURE *s.* contrato; escritura / *v.* contratar.
INDEPENDENCE *s.* independência.
INDEPENDENT *adj.* independente.
INDEPENDENTLY *adv.* independentemente.
INDESCRIBABLE *adj.* indescritível.
INDESTRUCTIBLE *adj.* indestrutível.
INDETERMINACY *s.* indeterminação.
INDETERMINATE *adj.* indeterminado.
INDEX *s.* *(pl. indexes)* índice / *v.* indexar.
INDEXATION *s.* indexação.
INDEXER *s.* indexador.
INDIA *s.* Índia.
INDIAN *s.* indiano; indígena, índio / *adj.* indiano; indígena, índio.
INDIAN OCEAN *s.* Oceano Índico.
INDICATE *v.* indicar, sinalizar, mostrar.
INDICATION *s.* indício, indicação.
INDICATIVE *s.* indicativo / *adj.* indicativo.
INDICATOR *s.* indicador; seta, pisca-pisca.

INDICES s. índices.
INDICT v. acusar, indicar, culpar.
INDICTABLE adj. acusável.
INDICTMENT s. acusação, indiciamento; incriminação.
INDIE adj. gravadora independente / s. gravadora independente.
INDIFFERENCE s. indiferença.
INDIFFERENT adj. indiferente.
INDIGENOUS adj. indígena; nativo.
INDIGENT adj. indigente; carente.
INDIGESTION s. indigestão.
INDIGNANT adj. indignado.
INDIGNANTLY adv. indignamente.
INDIGNATION s. indignação.
INDIGNITY s. indignidade, humilhação.
INDIGO s. anil; índigo / adj. azul-escuro.
INDIRECT adj. indireto.
INDIRECTION s. dissimulação, rodeio.
INDIRECTLY adv. indiretamente.
INDISCREET adj. indiscreto.
INDISCRETION s. indiscrição.
INDISCRIMINATE adj. indiscriminado.
INDISPENSABLE adj. indispensável, essencial.
INDISPUTABLE adj. incontestável, indisputável.
INDISTINCT adj. indistinto, confuso.
INDISTINGUISHABLE adj. indistinguível.
INDIUM s. índio (elemento químico).
INDIVIDUAL s. indivíduo / adj. individual.
INDIVIDUALISATION s. individualização.
INDIVIDUALISE v. individualizar.
INDIVIDUALISM s. individualismo.
INDIVIDUALIST s. individualista.
INDIVIDUALISTIC adj. individualista.
INDIVIDUALITY s. individualidade.
INDIVIDUALLY adv. individualmente.
INDIVISIBLE adj. indivisível.
INDOCTRINATE v. doutrinar.
INDOCTRINATION s. doutrinação.
INDOLENCE s. indolência.
INDOLENT adj. preguiçoso, indolente.
INDOMITABLE adj. indomável.
INDONESIA s. Indonésia.
INDONESIAN s. indonésio / adj. indonésio.
INDOOR adj. interno; de dentro.
INDOORS adv. no interior, dentro de.
INDUBITABLE adj. indubitável.
INDUCE v. induzir, persuadir; provocar.

INDUCEMENT s. incentivo, persuasão; estímulo.
INDUCER s. induzidor.
INDUCT v. introduzir; iniciar; recrutar.
INDUCTANCE s. indutância; coeficiente.
INDUCTEE s. alistado; conscrito.
INDUCTION s. introdução; indução.
INDUCTIVE adj. indutivo.
INDULGE v. condescender; ceder, satisfazer.
INDULGENCE s. deleite, satisfação; indulgência.
INDULGENT adj. indulgente; tolerante, complacente.
INDULGENTLY adv. indulgentemente.
INDUSTRIAL s. industrial / adj. industrial.
INDUSTRIALISATION s. industrialização.
INDUSTRIALISE v. industrializar.
INDUSTRIALIST s. industrialista.
INDUSTRIALIZED adj. industrializado.
INDUSTRIOUS adj. trabalhador, laborioso.
INDUSTRIOUSNESS s. diligência, destreza.
INDUSTRY s. indústria.
INDWELL v. habitar, residir, morar.
INEBRIATE v. inebriar, intoxicar.
INEDIBLE adj. incomível, intragável.
INEFFABLE adj. inefável, indizível.
INEFFECTIVE adj. ineficaz, ineficiente; inútil.
INEFFECTUAL adj. inútil, ineficaz.
INEFFICIENCY s. ineficiência, inutilidade.
INEFFICIENT adj. ineficiente.
INELIGIBLE adj. inelegível.
INEPT adj. inepto; desajeitado.
INEPTITUDE s. inépcia, inaptidão.
INEQUALITY s. desigualdade; discrepância.
INEQUITABLE adj. injusto, iníquo.
INEQUITY s. injustiça; iniquidade.
INERT adj. inerte.
INERTIA s. inércia.
INERTIAL adj. inerte, inercial.
INESCAPABLE adj. inevitável, fatal.
INESSENTIAL adj. desnecessário; não essencial.
INESTIMABLE adj. inestimável; precioso, raro.
INEVITABILITY s. inevitabilidade.
INEVITABLE adj. inevitável.
INEVITABLY adv. inevitavelmente.
INEXACT adj. inexato, dúbio.

INEXCUSABLE *adj.* imperdoável, indesculpável.
INEXHAUSTIBLE *adj.* inexaurível, inesgotável.
INEXISTENCE *s.* inexistência.
INEXISTENT *adj.* inexistente.
INEXORABLE *adj.* inexorável.
INEXORABLY *adv.* inexoravelmente.
INEXPEDIENT *adj.* inconveniente, inadequado.
INEXPENSIVE *adj.* barato, econômico.
INEXPENSIVELY *adv.* economicamente.
INEXPERIENCE *s.* inexperiência.
INEXPERIENCED *adj.* inexperiente
INEXPERT *adj.* desajeitado; pouco hábil.
INEXPERTISE *s.* imperícia.
INEXPLICABLE *adj.* inexplicável.
INEXPLICABLY *adv.* inexplicavelmente.
INEXPLICIT *adj.* obscuro, pouco claro.
INEXPRESSIBLE *adj.* inexprimível, indizível.
INEXPRESSIVE *adj.* inexpressivo.
INEXTENSIBLE *adj.* inextensível.
INEXTINGUISHABLE *adj.* inextinguível.
INEXTRICABLE *adj.* insolúvel.
INEXTRICABLY *adv.* intricadamente, insoluvelmente.
INFALLIBLE *adj.* infalível.
INFAMOUS *adj.* infame.
INFAMY *s.* infâmia.
INFANCY *s.* infância.
INFANT *s.* criança pequena; infante.
INFANTILE *adj.* infantil.
INFANTRY *s.* infantaria (exército).
INFANTRY MAN *s.* soldado da infantaria.
INFANT SCHOOL *s.* pré-escola.
INFARCT *s.* enfarte, enfarto.
INFATUATE *v.* apaixonar.
INFATUATION *s.* paixão.
INFECT *v.* contagiar, infectar.
INFECTED *adj.* infectado.
INFECTION *s.* infecção.
INFECTIOUS *adj.* contagioso, infeccioso.
INFECTIVE *adj.* infectante.
INFECUND *adj.* que não fecunda.
INFELICITOUS *adj.* infeliz, lamentável, inapropriado.
INFELICITY *s.* infelicidade, infortúnio, tolice.
INFER *v.* deduzir, inferir.

INFERENCE *s.* dedução, conclusão, inferência.
INFERIOR *adj.* inferior / *s.* subalterno.
INFERIORITY *s.* inferioridade.
INFERIORITY COMPLEX *s.* complexo de inferioridade.
INFERNAL *adj.* infernal.
INFERNO *s.* inferno.
INFERTILE *adj.* infértil.
INFERTILITY *s.* infertilidade.
INFERTILITY CLINIC *s.* clínica de infertilidade.
INFERTILITY TREATMENT *s.* tratamento de infertilidade.
INFEST *v.* infestar.
INFESTATION *s.* infestação.
INFIDEL *s.* infiel, pagão.
INFIDELITY *s.* infidelidade.
INFIELD *s.* campo interno (beisebol).
INFIELDER *s.* defensor do campo interno (beisebol).
INFIGHTING *s.* rivalidade, conflito interno.
INFILTRATE *v.* infiltrar, penetrar.
INFILTRATION *s.* infiltração.
INFILTRATOR *s.* infiltrado; intruso, espião.
INFIMUM *adj.* ínfimo.
INFINITE *adj.* infinito.
INFINITELY *adv.* infinitamente.
INFINITIVE *s.* infinitivo.
INFINITUDE *s.* infinitude.
INFINITY *s.* infinito, infinidade.
INFIRM *adj.* enfermo, débil, fraco.
INFIRMARER *s.* enfermeiro.
INFIRMARY *s.* enfermaria.
INFIRMITY *s.* fraqueza, enfermidade.
INFLAME *v.* inflamar.
INFLAMED *adj.* inflamado.
INFLAMMABLE *adj.* inflamável.
INFLAMMATION *s.* inflamação.
INFLAMMATORY *adj.* inflamatório.
INFLATABLE *adj.* inflável.
INFLATE *v.* inflar, encher de ar.
INFLATION *s.* inflação.
INFLATIONARY *adj.* inflacionário.
INFLECT *v.* modular, flexionar; inflectir (gramática).
INFLECTED *adj.* flexionado, modulado (gramática).
INFLECTION *s.* inflexão, modulação.

INFLECTIVE *adj.* flexivo, modulado (gramático).
INFLEXIBILITY *s.* inflexibilidade.
INFLEXIBLE *adj.* inflexível.
INFLEXION *s. m.q.* inflection.
INFLICT *v.* infligir.
INFLICTION *s.* inflição, inflicção.
INFLORESCENCE *s.* inflorescência, florescimento.
INFLORESCENT *adj.* florescente.
INFLOW *s.* influxo, afluxo; entrada.
INFLUENCE *s.* influência, prestígio / *v.* influenciar.
INFLUENCE PEDDLING *s.* tráfico de influência.
INFLUENTIAL *adj.* influente.
INFLUENZA *s.* gripe, influenza.
INFLUX *s.* afluxo; influxo.
INFOGRAPH *s.* infografia (gênero jornalístico).
INFOGRAPHIC *adj.* infográfico.
INFORM *v.* informar.
INFORMAL *adj.* informal.
INFORMALITY *s.* informalidade.
INFORMALLY *adv.* informalmente.
INFORMANT *s.* informante.
INFORMATICS *s.* informática; computação.
INFORMATION *s.* informação, conhecimento.
INFORMATION DESK *s.* balcão de informações; recepção.
INFORMATION SCIENCE *s.* ciência da informação.
INFORMATIVE *adj.* informativo.
INFORMER *s.* informante, delator.
INFRACTION *s.* infração, violação.
INFRARED *s.* infravermelho / *adj.* infravermelho.
INFRASTRUCTURAL *adj.* infraestrutural.
INFRASTRUCTURE *s.* infraestrutura.
INFREQUENT *adj.* infrequente.
INFRINGE *v.* infringir, transgredir.
INFRINGEMENT *s.* infração, violação; transgressão.
INFURIATE *v.* enraivecer; enfurecer.
INFURIATING *adj.* enfurecedor, exasperador.
INFUSE *v.* infundir.
INFUSIBLE *adj.* infusível.
INFUSION *s.* infusão.

INGEMINATE *v.* reiterar, repetir.
INGENIOUS *adj.* engenhoso; inventivo.
INGÉNUE *s.* inocente, ingênuo.
INGENUITY *s.* engenho, talento, habilidade.
INGENUOUS *adj.* ingênuo, simples.
INGEST *v.* ingerir.
INGESTION *s.* ingestão.
INGLORIOUS *adj.* inglório, vergonhoso.
INGRATE *s.* ingrato / *adj.* ingrato.
INGRATIATE *v.* ser agraciado com; agradar.
INGRATIATING *adj.* insinuante, atraente.
INGRATITUDE *s.* ingratidão.
INGREDIENT *s.* ingrediente.
INGRESS *s.* ingresso, admissão; entrada.
INGRESSIVE *adj.* ingressante.
INGROWN *adj.* encravado; inato.
INGURGITATE *v.* ingurgitar, encher até transbordar; engolir.
INHABIT *v.* habitar, morar, residir.
INHABITABLE *adj.* habitável.
INHABITANCE *s.* moradia, habitação.
INHABITANT *s.* habitante, morador.
INHALANT *s.* inalante, inalador.
INHALATION *s.* inalação; inspiração.
INHALE *v.* inalar, inspirar; tragar.
INHALER *s.* inalador.
INHARMONIC *adj.* inarmônico.
INHARMONIOUS *adj.* desarmonioso, desafinado.
INHERENT *adj.* inerente, inato.
INHERIT *v.* herdar.
INHERITABLE *adj.* hereditário, herdável.
INHERITANCE *s.* herança.
INHERITOR *s.* herdeiro.
INHESION *s.* inerência.
INHIBIT *v.* inibir.
INHIBITING *adj.* inibitivo.
INHIBITION *s.* inibição.
INHIBITOR *s.* inibidor.
INHIBITORY *adj.* inibitório.
INHOSPITABLE *adj.* inóspito, inospitaleiro.
INHUMAN *adj.* desumano, cruel.
INHUMANE *adj.* bárbaro, desumano.
INHUMANITY *s.* desumanidade.
INHUMATION *s.* enterro, sepultamento.
INHUME *v.* enterrar, sepultar.
INIMICAL *adj.* inimigo, hostil; nocivo, prejudicial.
INIMITABLE *adj.* inimitável.

INIQUITOUS *adj.* iníquo; injusto.
INIQUITY *s.* injustiça, maldade.
INITIAL *adj.* inicial / *s.* inicial.
INITIALISE *v.* iniciar, começar.
INITIALLY *adv.* inicialmente; a princípio.
INITIAND *s.* iniciante / *adj.* iniciante.
INITIATE *v.* iniciar, começar / *adj.* iniciado, começado.
INITIATION *s.* iniciação, começo.
INITIATIVE *s.* iniciativa.
INJECT *v.* injetar.
INJECTION *s.* injeção.
INJECTOR *s.* injetor (mecânica).
INJUNCTION *s.* injunção, determinação.
INJURE *v.* ferir, lesar, machucar.
INJURED *s.* ferido, machucado.
INJURIOUS *adj.* injurioso, pernicioso.
INJURY *s.* ferimento, lesão.
INJUSTICE *s.* injustiça.
INK *s.* tinta de escrever.
INKLING *s.* suspeita; alusão, indireta.
INKPOT *s.* tinteiro.
INKWELL *s. m.q.* inkpot.
INKY *adj.* sujo de tinta.
INLAID *adj.* incrustado.
INLAND *adv.* em terra firme.
IN-LAW *s.* parentes de casamento.
INLAY *s.* embutido / *v.* incrustar.
INLET *s.* enseada, baía.
INMATE *s.* interno, presidiário
INMOST *adj.* íntimo, interno.
INN *s.* pousada: hospedaria, estalagem.
INNARDS *s.* vísceras; entranhas.
INNATE *adj.* inato.
INNATELY *adv.* inerentemente; de modo inato.
INNER *adj.* íntimo, interior.
INNER CITY *s.* região metropolitana.
INNERMOST *adj.* íntimo, secreto, profundo.
INNER TUBE *s.* câmara de ar (pneu).
INNERVATE *v.* inervar.
INNERVATION *s.* inervação.
INNINGS *s.* turno, a vez de jogar (beisebol).
INNOCENCE *s.* inocência.
INNOCENT *adj.* inocente.
INNOCENTLY *adv.* inocentemente.
INNOCUOUS *adj.* inócuo; sem ofensa.
INNOVATE *v.* inovar.
INNOVATION *s.* inovação, novidade; descoberta.

INNOVATIVE *adj.* inventivo; original.
INNOVATOR *s.* inovador.
INNOVATORY *adj.* inovador; que inova.
INNUENDO *s.* sugestão; insinuação, alusão.
INNUMERABLE *adj.* inumerável.
INOCULATE *v.* inocular, vacinar.
INOCULATION *s.* inoculação, vacinação.
INODOROUS *adj.* inodoro; sem cheiro.
INOFFENSIVE *adj.* inofensivo.
INOPERABLE *adj.* inoperável.
INOPERATIVE *adj.* inoperante.
INORDINATE *adj.* imoderado; excessivo.
INORGANIC *adj.* inorgânico.
INPATIENT *s.* paciente, internado / *adj.* paciente, internado.
INPUT *s.* entrada; contribuição.
INQUEST *s.* inquérito, sindicância.
INQUIETUDE *s.* inquietude; ansiedade.
INQUIRE *v.* perguntar, investigar.
INQUIRER *s.* inquiridor, investigador.
INQUIRING *adj.* investigador; que pergunta.
INQUIRY *s.* inquérito, investigação, inquirição.
INQUISITION *s.* inquisição.
INQUISITIVE *adj.* inquiridor, investigante.
INQUISITOR *s.* interrogador, inquiridor.
INROAD *s.* invasão.
INSANE *adj.* insano.
INSANITARY *adj.* insalubre; anti-higiênico.
INSANITY *s.* insanidade, loucura.
INSATIABLE *adj.* insaciável.
INSCRIBE *v.* inscrever, endereçar.
INSCRIPTION *s.* inscrição; dedicatória.
INSCRUTABLE *adj.* impenetrável, inescrutável.
INSECT *s.* inseto / *adj.* inseto.
INSECTICIDAL *adj.* inseticida.
INSECTICIDE *s.* inseticida.
INSECURE *adj.* inseguro.
INSECURITY *s.* insegurança.
INSEMINATION *s.* inseminação; fecundação.
INSENSIBLE *adj.* inconsciente, insensato.
INSENSITIVE *adj.* insensível.
INSENSITIVITY *s.* insensibilidade.
INSEPARABLE *adj.* inseparável.
INSERT *v.* inserir, introduzir / *s.* inserção.
INSERTION *s.* inserção; enxerto.

IN-SERVICE *adj.* contínuo; relativo a cursos de treinamento na empresa.
INSHORE *adv.* em direção a costa, para a costa.
INSIDE *s.* interior / *adj.* interior / *adv.* dentro / *prep.* dentro de.
INSIDER *s.* membro, pessoa de dentro; espião.
INSIDIOUS *adj.* insidioso, traiçoeiro.
INSIGHT *s.* discernimento; perspicácia, argúcia; percepção.
INSIGHTFUL *adj.* perspicaz.
INSIGNIA *s.* insígnia, emblema.
INSIGNIFICANCE *s.* insignificância.
INSIGNIFICANT *adj.* insignificante.
INSINCERE *adj.* falso; desonesto.
INSINUATE *v.* insinuar; dar a entender.
INSINUATION *s.* insinuação.
INSIPID *adj.* insípido, sem graça.
INSIST *v.* insistir, persistir.
INSISTENCE *s.* insistência.
INSISTENT *adj.* insistente.
INSOFAR *conj.* à medida que.
INSOLE *s.* palmilha (sapato).
INSOLENCE *s.* insolência.
INSOLENT *adj.* insolente.
INSOLUBLE *adj.* insolúvel.
INSOLVENCY *s.* insolvência; falência.
INSOLVENT *adj.* insolvente; falido.
INSOMNIA *s.* insônia.
INSOMNIAC *s.* insone / *adj.* insone.
INSOUCIANCE *s.* despreocupação, indiferença.
INSPECT *v.* inspecionar, examinar.
INSPECTION *s.* inspeção, fiscalização, vistoria.
INSPECTOR *s.* inspetor, fiscal.
INSPECTORATE *s.* inspetoria, fiscalização; superintendência.
INSPIRATION *s.* inspiração.
INSPIRATIONAL *adj.* inspirativo, inspirador.
INSPIRE *v.* inspirar.
INSPIRED *adj.* inspirado.
INSPIRER *s.* inspirador; que inspira.
INSPIRING *adj.* estimulante; inspirador.
INSTABILITY *s.* instabilidade.
INSTALL *v.* instalar, estabelecer; empossar.
INSTALLATION *s.* instalação; emposse.
INSTALLER *s.* instalador.
INSTALLMENT *s.* prestação, parte; fascículo, capítulo.
INSTANCE *s.* exemplo, caso, ocasião.
INSTANT *s.* instante, momento / *adj.* imediato, instantâneo.
INSTANTANEOUS *adj.* instantâneo.
INSTANTANEOUSLY *adv.* instantaneamente.
INSTANTIATE *v.* provar, exemplificar.
INSTANTLY *adv.* instantaneamente, imediatamente.
INSTATE *v.* admitir, instalar; introduzir.
INSTEAD *adv.* em vez, em lugar de.
INSTEP *s.* dorso do pé.
INSTIGATE *v.* instigar, induzir, incitar.
INSTIGATION *s.* instigação.
INSTIGATOR *s.* instigador, agitador.
INSTINCT *s.* instinto; impulso.
INSTINCTIVE *adj.* instintivo.
INSTINCTIVELY *adv.* instintivamente.
INSTINCTUAL *adj.* inato, instintivo.
INSTITUTE *s.* instituto, associação / *v.* instituir, iniciar.
INSTITUTION *s.* instituição, instituto.
INSTITUTIONAL *adj.* institucional.
INSTITUTIONALISATION *s.* institucionalização.
INSTITUTIONALISE *v.* institucionalizar.
INSTRUCT *v.* instruir, ensinar.
INSTRUCTION *s.* instrução; ensino.
INSTRUCTIONAL *adj.* instrutivo, instrucional; educativo.
INSTRUCTIVE *adj.* instrutivo.
INSTRUCTOR *s.* instrutor.
INSTRUMENT *s.* instrumento.
INSTRUMENTAL *adj.* instrumental.
INSTRUMENTALIST *s.* instrumentista.
INSTRUMENTATION *s.* instrumentação.
INSUBORDINATE *adj.* insubordinado, indisciplinado.
INSUBORDINATION *s.* insubordinação; desobediência.
INSUBSTANTIAL *adj.* insubstancial; irreal, imaterial.
INSUFFERABLE *adj.* insuportável.
INSUFFICIENCY *s.* insuficiência; deficiência.
INSUFFICIENT *adj.* insuficiente.
INSUFFLATE *v.* insuflar, encher de ar.
INSUFFLATOR *s.* insuflação.
INSULA *s.* ínsula; parte do cérebro.
INSULAR *adj.* estreito, bitolado.

INSULATE v. isolar; separar.
INSULATING adj. isolante.
INSULATION s. isolamento.
INSULATOR s. isolador.
INSULIN s. insulina.
INSULT s. ofensa, insulto / v. insultar, ofender.
INSULTING adj. ofensivo, insultante, insultuoso.
INSUPERABLE adj. insuperável.
INSURABLE adj. segurável.
INSURANCE s. seguro.
INSURANCE POLICY s. apólice de seguro.
INSURE v. segurar; assegurar.
INSURED adj. assegurado; que tem seguro.
INSURER s. corretor de seguros; seguradora.
INSURGENCE s. insurreição, insurgência; revolta.
INSURGENT s. insurgente / adj. insurgente.
INSURMOUNTABLE adj. insuperável, intransponível.
INSURRECTION s. insurreição.
INTACT adj. intato, ileso.
INTAGLIO s. entalhe, gravura.
INTAKE s. entrada, admissão; consumo.
INTANGIBLE adj. intangível.
INTEGER s. inteireza, todo; número inteiro.
INTEGRAL adj. integral, essencial / s. integral, total.
INTEGRANT adj. integrante.
INTEGRATE v. integrar, incorporar.
INTEGRATION s. integração; combinação.
INTEGRATIVE adj. integrador.
INTEGRITY s. integridade, honestidade, totalidade.
INTELLECT s. intelecto, inteligência.
INTELLECTUAL adj. intelectual, culto / s. intelectual.
INTELLECTUALLY adv. intelectualmente.
INTELLIGENCE s. inteligência.
INTELLIGENT adj. inteligente.
INTELLIGIBLE adj. inteligível, compreensível.
INTEND v. pretender, planejar, ter a intenção de.
INTENDED adj. pretendido / s. pretendente.
INTENSE adj. intenso.

INTENSELY adv. extremamente, intensamente.
INTENSIFICATION s. intensificação.
INTENSIFIER s. intensificador.
INTENSIFY v. intensificar.
INTENSITY s. intensidade; força.
INTENSIVE adj. intensivo.
INTENT s. intenção, intento / adj. intencionado, atento.
INTENTION s. intenção.
INTENTIONAL adj. intencional; deliberado.
INTENTIONALLY adv. de propósito, intencionalmente.
INTENTLY adv. atentamente.
INTER v. enterrar, sepultar.
INTERACT v. interagir.
INTERACTION s. interação, relacionamento.
INTERACTIVE adj. interativo.
INTERATIVITY s. interatividade.
INTERBREED v. mestiçar, miscigenar.
INTERCEDE v. interceder.
INTERCEPT v. interceptar, interromper.
INTERCEPTION s. interrupção, intercepção.
INTERCEPTOR s. interceptor, interceptador.
INTERCESSION s. intercessão.
INTERCHANGE s. intercâmbio, troca / v. intercambiar.
INTERCHANGEABLE adj. permutável, intercambiável.
INTERCITY s. Interurbano.
INTERCOLLEGIATE adj. intercolegial.
INTERCOM s. interfone (coloquial).
INTERCONNECT v. interconectar.
INTERCONNECTION s. interconexão.
INTERCONTINENTAL adj. intercontinental.
INTERCOURSE s. intercurso, intercâmbio; relações sexuais.
INTERCULTURAL adj. intercultural.
INTERDEPARTMENTAL adj. interdepartamental, que acontece entre departamentos.
INTERDEPENDENCE s. interdependência, dependência mútua.
INTERDEPENDENT adj. mutuamente dependente, interdependente.
INTERDICT v. interditar, interdizer / s. interdição, proibição.

INTERDICTION s. interdição; proibição.
INTERDISCIPLINARY adj. interdisciplinar.
INTEREST s. interesse; vantagem / v. interessar-se.
INTERESTED adj. interessado.
INTERESTING adj. interessante.
INTERESTINGLY adv. de maneira interessante.
INTERFACE s. interface / v. interagir.
INTERFACING s. interface; interconexão.
INTERFERE v. interferir, intervir.
INTERFERENCE s. intromissão, interferência.
INTERFERING adj. interferente / s. interferência.
INTERGALACTIC adj. intergaláctico.
INTERGOVERNAMENTAL adj. intergovernamental.
INTERIM adj. interino, provisório / s. ínterim.
INTERIOR s. interno, interior / adj. interno, interior.
INTERJECT v. interromper; interpor.
INTERJECTION s. interjeição.
INTERLACE v. entrelaçar-se.
INTERLINE adj. integrado / v. entrelinhar.
INTERLINK s. interligação.
INTERLOCK v. engrenar; ligar-se, integrar-se.
INTERLOCUTOR s. interlocutor.
INTERLOCUTORY adj. interlocutório.
INTERLOPER s. intruso.
INTERLUDE s. interlúdio (música), intervalo.
INTERMARRIAGE s. casamento dentro da família, incesto.
INTERMARRY v. ficar parente por casamento; casar dentro da família.
INTERMEDIARY s. intermediário / adj. intermediário.
INTERMEDIATE adj. intermediário / v. intermediar.
INTERMENT s. enterro, sepultamento.
INTERMINABLE adj. interminável.
INTERMISSION s. intervalo, intermissão.
INTERMITTENT adj. intermitente.
INTERMIX v. misturar.
INTERN v. internar / s. médico-residente.
INTERNAL adj. interno.
INTERNALISATION s. interiorização.
INTERNALISE v. internalizar.
INTERNALLY adv. internamente.

INTERNATIONAL adj. internacional.
INTERNATIONALISATION s. internacionalização.
INTERNATIONALISE v. internacionalizar.
INTERNATIONALISM s. internacionalismo.
INTERNATIONALIST s. internacionalista.
INTERNATIONALLY adv. internacionalmente.
INTERNEE s. interno; detento, prisioneiro.
INTERNET s. internet.
INTERNMENT s. internação, internamento; confinamento.
INTERNSHIP s. estágio; residência (médico).
INTEROFFICE s. entre escritórios.
INTEROFFICE MEMO s. memorando interno.
INTERPERSONAL adj. interpessoal.
INTERPLANETARY adj. interplanetário.
INTERPLAY s. interação / v. interagir.
INTERPOSE v. interpor, intervir; vetar.
INTERPRET v. interpretar, traduzir.
INTERPRETATION s. interpretação.
INTERPRETATIVE adj. interpretativo.
INTERPRETER s. intérprete, tradutor.
INTERPRETING s. interpretação.
INTERRACIAL adj. inter-racial.
INTERRELATE v. correlacionar; inter--relacionar.
INTERRELATED adj. inter-relacionado; correlacionado.
INTERRELATION s. inter-relação, correlação.
INTERRELATIONSHIP s. inter--relacionamento, relação mútua.
INTERROGATE v. interrogar.
INTERROGATION s. interrogatório.
INTERROGATIVE adj. interrogativo.
INTERROGATOR s. interrogador.
INTERROGATORY adj. interrogatório.
INTERRUPT v. interromper, suspender.
INTERRUPTER s. interruptor; disjuntor.
INTERRUPTION s. interrupção.
INTERSCHOLASTIC adj. interescolar, que diz respeito a várias escolas.
INTERSECT v. cruzar, dividir.
INTERSECTION s. cruzamento, intersecção.
INTERSESSION s. férias escolares.
INTERSPERSE v. interpor, intercalar.
INTERSTATE adj. interestadual.
INTERSTELLAR adj. interestelar.

INTERTWINE v. entrelaçar.
INTERURBAN adj. interurbano.
INTERVAL s. intervalo.
INTERVENE v. intervir, interpor; mediar.
INTERVENING adj. intermediário, interferente.
INTERVENTION s. intervenção.
INTERVENTIONIST s. intervencionista / adj. intervencionista.
INTERVIEW s. entrevista / v. entrevistar.
INTERVIEWEE s. entrevistado.
INTERVIEWER s. entrevistador.
INTESTINAL adj. intestinal.
INTESTINE s. intestino.
INTIMACY s. intimidade.
INTIMATE v. intimar, insinuar / adj. íntimo, familiar.
INTIMATELY adv. intimamente.
INTIMATION s. intimação; sugestão.
INTIMIDATE v. intimidar.
INTIMIDATING adj. intimidador.
INTIMIDATION s. intimidação.
INTO prep. em; dentro; para dentro.
INTOLERABLE adj. intolerável.
INTOLERANCE s. intolerância.
INTOLERANT adj. intolerante.
INTONATION s. entonação.
INTONE v. entoar; entonar.
INTOXICANT s. intoxicante; bebida alcoólica.
INTOXICATE v. embriagar, inebriar; extasiar.
INTOXICATED adj. embriagado.
INTOXICATING adj. intoxicante.
INTOXICATION s. intoxicação, embriaguez.
INTRACTABLE adj. intratável.
INTRAMUSCULAR adj. intramuscular.
INTRANET s. intranet.
INTRANSIGENCE s. intransigência, intolerância.
INTRANSIGENT adj. intransigente.
INTRANSITIVE adj. intransitivo.
INTRANSITIVITY s. intransitividade.
INTRASTATE adj. estadual.
INTRAUTERINE adj. intrauterino, relativo ao interior do útero.
INTRAVENOUS adj. intravenoso.
INTREPID adj. intrépido.
INTRICACY s. complexidade; dificuldade.
INTRICATE adj. complicado, complexo.
INTRIGUE s. intriga / v. intrigar.
INTRIGUING adj. intrigante.
INTRINSIC adj. intrínseco; inerente.
INTRINSICALLY adv. intrinsecamente.
INTRO abrev. introdução.
INTRODUCE v. introduzir, mostrar; apresentar alguém.
INTRODUCTION s. introdução, apresentação.
INTRODUCTORY adj. introdutório.
INTROSPECTION s. introspecção.
INTROSPECTIVE adj. introspectivo.
INTROVERT s. introvertido / v. introverter.
INTROVERTED adj. introvertido.
INTRUDE v. irromper, penetrar; intervir.
INTRUDER s. intruso, intrometido; bicão (de festa).
INTRUSION s. intrusão.
INTRUSIVE adj. intrometido; invasivo.
INTUIT v. intuir.
INTUITION s. intuição, percepção.
INTUITIVE adj. intuitivo.
INTUITIVELY adv. instintivamente.
INUNDATE v. inundar.
INUNDATION s. inundação.
INURE v. habituar; endurecer.
INVADE v. invadir.
INVADER s. invasor.
INVADING adj. invasor, invasivo.
INVALID v. invalidar / adj. nulo, inválido.
INVALIDATE v. invalidar; tornar inválido.
INVALIDATION s. invalidação; anulação.
INVALIDITY s. invalidade, invalidez.
INVALUABLE adj. inestimável.
INVARIABLE adj. invariável.
INVARIABLY adv. invariavelmente.
INVASION s. invasão.
INVASIVE adj. invasivo, agressivo.
INVEIGH v. injuriar, censurar.
INVENT v. inventar.
INVENTION s. invenção, invento.
INVENTIVE adj. inventivo; criativo.
INVENTIVENESS adj. inovação, criatividade.
INVENTOR s. inventor.
INVENTORY s. inventário; estoque.
INVERSE s. inverso / adj. inverso.
INVERSION s. inversão.
INVERT v. inverter; reverter.

INVERTEBRATE s. invertebrado / adj. invertebrado.
INVERTED adj. invertido, inverso.
INVERTED COMMA s. aspas.
INVEST v. investir; aplicar.
INVESTIGATE v. investigar.
INVESTIGATION s. investigação; pesquisa.
INVESTIGATIVE adj. investigativo.
INVESTIGATOR s. investigador.
INVESTIGATORY adj. investigante, investigador.
INVESTMENT s. investimento.
INVESTOR s. investidor; aplicador.
INVIDIOUS adj. invejoso; hostil.
INVIGILATE v. fiscalizar; vigiar.
INVIGILATOR s. fiscal (de exame), vigilante.
INVIGORATE s. avigorar, revigorar, fortificar, avivar, animar.
INVIGORATING adj. revigorante; reanimador.
INVINCIBLE adj. invencível; invicto.
INVIOLABLE adj. inviolável.
INVISIBLE adj. invisível.
INVITATION s. convite.
INVITATIONAL s. restrito, somente para convidados.
INVITE v. convidar; chamar.
INVITEE s. convidado.
INVITING adj. convidativo, tentador; atraente.
INVOCATION s. invocação.
INVOICE s. fatura / v. faturar, cobrar.
INVOICING s. fatura; faturação.
INVOKE v. invocar, apelar; evocar.
INVOLUNTARY adj. involuntário.
INVOLVE v. envolver, incluir.
INVOLVED adj. envolvido, incluso; comprometido.
INVOLVEMENT s. envolvimento, comprometimento.
INVULNERABLE adj. invulnerável.
INWARD adj. íntimo, interior / adv. para dentro / s. interior.
INWARDLY adv. secretamente, por dentro.
IODINE s. iodo.
ION s. íon.
IONIC adj. iônico.
IONISE v. ionizar.
IOU abrev. vale, nota promissória (coloquial).
IQ abrev. QI (quociente de inteligência).
IRAN s. Irã.
IRANIAN s. iraniano / adj. iraniano.
IRAQ s. Iraque.
IRAQI s. iraquiano / adj. iraquiano.
IRASCIBLE adj. irascível, irritável.
IRATE adj. irado, colérico.
IRE s. ira, raiva.
IRELAND s. Irlanda.
IRIS s. íris.
IRISH s. irlandês / adj. irlandês.
IRK v. aborrecer, irritar.
IRKSOME adj. cansativo; aborrecido.
IRON s. ferro / v. passar roupa / adj. de ferro.
IRONIC adj. irônico, sarcástico.
IRONICALLY adv. ironicamente.
IRONING s. roupa passada / v. passar (a ferro).
IRONING BOARD s. tábua de passar roupa.
IRONMONGER s. ferreiro, ferrageiro.
IRONY s. ironia; sarcasmo.
IRONWARE s. ferragens.
IRRADIATE v. irradiar.
IRRADIATION s. irradiação.
IRRATIONAL adj. irracional.
IRRATIONALITY s. irracionalidade.
IRRECONCILABLE adj. irreconciliável.
IRREDUCIBLE adj. irreduzível, irredutível.
IRREFUTABLE adj. irrefutável.
IRREGULAR adj. irregular.
IRREGULARITY s. irregularidade.
IRRELEVANCE s. irrelevância.
IRRELEVANT adj. irrelevante.
IRREPARABLE adj. irreparável.
IRREPLACEABLE adj. insubstituível.
IRREPRESSIBLE adj. irreprimível; incontrolável.
IRRESISTIBLE adj. irresistível.
IRRESPECTIVE adj. sem consideração, sem restrição.
IRRESPONSIBLE adj. irresponsável.
IRRETRIEVABLE adj. irrecuperável.
IRRETRIEVABLY adv. irreparavelmente.
IRREVERENCE s. irreverência.
IRREVERENT adj. irreverente.
IRREVERSIBLE adj. irreversível.
IRREVOCABLE adj. irrevogável; inalterável.
IRRIGATE v. irrigar.
IRRIGATION s. irrigação.

IRRITABLE *adj.* irritável.
IRRITANT *s.* irritante.
IRRITATE *v.* irritar, provocar.
IRRITATING *adj.* m.q. irritable.
IRRITATION *s.* irritação.
IS *v.* 3ª pessoa do singular, presente do verbo *to be*.
ISLAM *s.* Islã, Islamismo.
ISLAMIC *adj.* islâmico.
ISLAMISM *s.* Islamismo.
ISLAMIST *s.* islamita.
ISLAND *s.* ilha; Islândia.
ISLANDER *s.* ilhéu.
ISLE *s.* ilhota, ilha.
ISLET *s.* ilhota.
ISOLATE *v.* isolar.
ISOLATED *adj.* isolado; solitário.
ISOLATION *s.* isolamento.
ISRAEL *s.* Israel.
ISRAELI *s.* israelense / *adj.* israelense.
ISSUANCE *s.* emissão.
ISSUE *s.* questão; edição; tema / *v.* distribuir; emitir.
ISSUER *s.* emissor.
IT *pron.* o, a, lhe, ele, ela.
ITALIAN *s.* italiano / *adj.* italiano.
ITALIC *s.* itálico (tipografia).
ITALICISE *v.* italicizar; por em itálico.
ITALY *s.* Itália.
ITCH *s.* comichão, coceira / *v.* coçar, desejar.
ITCHY *adj.* que coça.
ITEM *s.* item; assunto, número (edição).
ITEMISE *v.* especificar, relacionar.
ITERATE *v.* iterar.
ITERATION *s.* iteração.
ITERATIVE *adj.* iterativo.
ITINERANT *adj.* itinerante.
ITINERARY *s.* itinerário.
ITS *pron.* dele, dela.
ITSELF *pron.* ele mesmo, a si mesmo.
IVORY *s.* marfim / *adj.* de marfim.
IVY *s.* hera (planta).

J j

J, j *s.* décima letra do alfabeto inglês.
JAB *s.* golpe, estocada, espetada /
v. cutucar, espetar, ferir com a ponta de algo.
JACK *s.* macaco (mecânica); valete (baralho).
JACKAL *s.* chacal.
JACKASS *s.* asno, burro.
JACKET *s.* jaqueta, casaco curto.
JACK-IN-THE-BOX *s.* caixa de surpresa.
JACKPOT *s.* bolada, sorte grande.
JACK-STRAW *s.* boneco de palha, espantalho.
JAIL *s.* cadeia, prisão / *v.* encarcerar.
JAM *s.* geleia; congestionamento, engarrafamento / *v.* amontoar, apinhar-se.
JAMAICA *s.* Jamaica.
JAMB *s.* ombreira, jamba, batente.
JANITOR *s.* zelador.
JANUARY *s.* janeiro.
JAPAN *s.* Japão.
JAPANESE *s.* japonês(esa) /
adj. japonês(esa).
JAR *s.* jarro, pote, frasco / *v.* destoar; irritar.
JARGON *s.* jargão.
JASMIN(E) *s.* jasmim.
JAUNT *s.* excursão, caminhada /
v. perambular, vaguear.
JAUNTY *adj.* animado, vivo.
JAVELIN *s.* dardo de arremesso, lança.
JAW *s.* maxilar, mandíbula.
JAYWALKER *s.* pedestre imprudente.
JAZZ *s.* jazz.
JAZZ UP *v.* animar.
JEALOUS *adj.* ciumento(a).
JEALOUSY *s.* ciúme.
JEAN *s.* fustão de algodão.
JEANS *s.* calças de brim.
JEEP *s.* jipe.
JEER *s.* zombaria, vaia / *v.* zombar, vaiar.
JELLY *s.* gelatina, geleia.
JELLYFISH *s.* água-viva.
JERK *s.* empurrão; sacudida; idiota (coloquial) / *v.* sacudir.
JERKIN *s.* jaqueta.
JERKY *adj.* aos trancos; idiota (coloquial).
JERSEY *s.* suéter de lã; jérsei (tecido).
JEST *s.* gracejo / *v.* gracejar.
JESUS *s.* Jesus.

JET s. jato, jorro, esguicho.
JETTY s. molhe, quebra-mar.
JEW s. judeu / adj. judaico.
JEWEL s. joia, pedra preciosa, gema.
JEWELER s. joalheiro.
JEWELRY s. joias, joalheria.
JEWESS s. judia / adj. judia.
JEWISH adj. judaico, hebreu.
JIFFY s. instante, momento (coloquial).
JIGSAW s. quebra-cabeça.
JILT v. namorar, flertar.
JIMMY s. pé de cabra, alavanca.
JINGLE s. música de propaganda / v. tilintar, soar.
JOB s. emprego; tarefa.
JOBBERY s. agiotagem, especulação.
JOBCENTER s. agência de emprego.
JOBLESS adj. desempregado.
JOCKEY s. jóquei; impostor.
JOCUND adj. alegre, divertido.
JOG s. sacudida / v. cutucar, empurrar; correr.
JOGGING s. corrida.
JOIN s. ligação, junção / v. juntar, ligar.
JOINER s. marceneiro.
JOINT s. junta, articulação, união / adj. articulado; conjunto.
JOINT ACCOUNT s. conta conjunta.
JOKE s. piada, gracejo, brincadeira / v. brincar.
JOKER s. curinga (cartas); brincalhão.
JOLLY adj. alegre, divertido / adv. muito, bastante (coloquial).
JORDAN s. Jordânia.
JOSTLE s. colisão, choque / v. acotovelar, empurrar.
JOURNAL s. jornal especializado, revista, diário.
JOURNALISM s. jornalismo.
JOURNALIST s. jornalista.
JOURNEY s. viagem, jornada.
JOWL s. mandíbula.
JOY s. alegria, felicidade.
JOYFUL adj. alegre, jovial.
JOY-RIDE s. passeio temerário (de automóvel).
JOYSTICK s. alavanca de controle.

JUBILEE s. jubileu.
JUDGE s. juiz, árbitro / v. julgar, avaliar, criticar.
JUDGEMENT s. julgamento, crítica.
JUDICIAL adj. judicial, forense.
JUDICIARY s. poder judiciário; comarca; jurisdição.
JUDO s. judô.
JUG s. jarro, jarra; moringa; canto do rouxinol.
JUGGLER s. malabarista.
JUICE s. suco, sumo.
JUICY adj. suculento; picante; interessante.
JUKEBOX s. jukebox.
JULY s. julho.
JUMBLE s. desordem, confusão / v. remexer, confundir.
JUMBLE SALE s. bazar, venda de artigos em saldos.
JUMBO s. colosso (coloquial) / adj. colossal, gigantesco.
JUMP s. salto, pulo / v. saltar, pular.
JUMPER s. saltador; avental; suéter.
JUMPING-BOARD s. trampolim.
JUNCTION s. cruzamento, entroncamento.
JUNCTURE s. conjuntura, momento.
JUNE s. junho.
JUNGLE s. selva; bagunça.
JUNIOR s. jovem / adj. mais novo; subalterno.
JUNIOR SCHOOL s. escola primária.
JUNK s. sucata, refugo.
JUNK FOOD s. comida sem valor nutritivo.
JUNKIE adj. drogado(a), viciado(a).
JUPITER s. Júpiter.
JUROR s. jurado.
JURY s. júri.
JUST adj. justo, correto / adv. justamente, exatamente, quase, apenas.
JUSTICE s. justiça.
JUSTIFICATION s. justificativa, causa.
JUSTIFY v. justificar.
JUT v. sobressair.
JUTE s. juta.
JUVENILE s. jovem, menor / adj. juvenil, imaturo.

K k

K, k *s.* décima primeira letra do alfabeto inglês.
KABUKI *s.* cabúqui (gênero dramático japonês).
KAISER *s.* kaiser; imperador, líder.
KALEIDOSCOPE *s.* caleidoscópio.
KAMIKAZE *s.* camicase; ataque suicida.
KAMPUCHEA *s.* Camboja.
KAMPUCHEAN *s.* cambojano / *adj.* cambojano.
KANGAROO *s.* canguru.
KAPPA *s.* capa (décima letra do alfabeto grego, K).
KAPUT *adj.* destruído, inválido, arruinado.
KARAOKE *s.* karaokê.
KARAT *s.* quilate (de ouro).
KARATE *s.* caratê.
KARMA *s.* carma.
KARMIC *adj.* cármico; de carma.
KART *s.* kart.
KASHMIR *s.* Caxemira (região no sudoeste da Ásia).
KAYAK *s.* caiaque (esporte).
KAZAKHSTAN *s.* Cazaquistão.
KEBAB *s.* espetinho, churrasquinho.

KEEK *s.* olhadela, espreitadela / *v.* olhar, mirar.
KEEL *v.* embocar, tombar.
KEEL OVER *v.* capotar, cair; desfalecer.
KEEN *adj.* entusiasmado, muito interessado; intenso.
KEENLY *adv.* entusiasticamente, intensamente.
KEEP *v.* guardar; manter, conservar; ficar, permanecer.
KEEPER *s.* guardião, zelador; goleiro (futebol).
KEEPING *s.* cuidado, custódia; manutenção, sustento.
KEEPSAKE *s.* lembrança, dádiva, presente.
KEG *s.* barril.
KELVIN *s.* kelvin (medida de temperatura).
KEN *s.* compreensão / *v.* saber, conhecer.
KENNEL *s.* canil; casinha de cachorro / *v.* levar para o canil.
KENYA *s.* Quênia.
KENYAN *s.* queniano / *adj.* queniano.
KERATIN *s.* queratina, ceratina.
KERB *s.* meio-fio.

KERCHIEF s. lenço; mantilha.
KERNEL s. núcleo, cerne, miolo; parte central.
KEROSENE s. querosene.
KETCHUP s. ketchup; molho de tomate.
KETTLE s. chaleira; caldeira.
KETTLEDRUM s. timbale, tímpano (instrumento musical).
KEY s. chave; tecla, código / adj. essencial, fundamental.
KEYBOARD s. teclado.
KEYBOARDIST s. tecladista (músico).
KEYHOLE s. buraco da fechadura.
KEYNOTE s. ideia central; tema; nota chave (música).
KEYPAD s. teclado numérico.
KEYRING s. chaveiro (porta-chaves).
KEYWORD s. palavra-chave; termo importante.
KHAKI s. brim cáqui; caqui (fruto) / adj. cáqui (cor).
KHAN s. cã.
KIBBLE s. comida de cachorro / v. moer, esmagar.
KIBBUTZ s. kibutz (colônia agrícola em Israel).
KICK v. chutar, dar pontapé, espernear / s. pontapé, chute.
KICKBACK s. comissão; suborno, propina.
KICKER s. jogador; batedor de faltas (futebol).
KICKOFF s. chute inicial, tiro de meta (futebol).
KID s. criança; cabrito / v. brincar.
KID BROTHER s. irmão caçula.
KIDDER s. brincalhão, piadista.
KIDDY s. criança pequena.
KIDNAP v. sequestrar, raptar.
KIDNAPPER s. sequestrador.
KIDNAPPING s. sequestro, rapto.
KIDNEY s. rim.
KID SISTER s. irmã caçula.
KILL v. matar, abater / s. matança, extermínio.
KILLER s. assassino, matador / adj. difícil de lidar.
KILLING s. assassinato; matança / adj. cansativo.
KILLJOY s. estraga-prazeres; desmancha-prazeres.
KILN s. fornalha, forno.
KILOGRAM s. quilograma (Kg).
KILOMETER s. quilômetro (Km).
KILOWATT s. quilowatt (Kw).
KILT s. kilt; saiote escocês.
KIMONO s. quimono.
KIN s. parente, família.
KINAESTHETIC adj. cinestético.
KIND adj. generoso, amável / s. espécie, classe, tipo.
KINDERGARTEN s. jardim de infância.
KIND-HEARTED adj. bom coração, bondoso.
KINDLE v. acender, iluminar; dar cria (ninhada).
KINDLY adv. amavelmente, gentilmente.
KINDNESS s. bondade, gentileza.
KINDRED s. família, parentes / adj. aparentado, afim.
KINETIC adj. cinético.
KING s. rei / adj. enorme, grande.
KINGDOM s. reino, monarquia; domínio.
KINGLY adj. real, majestoso / adv. majestosamente, regiamente.
KINGSHIP s. monarquia; realeza.
KING-SIZE adj. tamanho grande, maior que o comum.
KINK s. torcicolo; nó, enrosco.
KINKY adj. excêntrico, pervertido.
KINLESS adj. sem parentes.
KIOSK s. quiosque.
KIPPER s. arenque defumado.
KIRMESS s. quermesse.
KISMET s. destino, sina.
KISS s. beijo / v. beijar.
KIT s. estojo; equipamento.
KITCHEN s. cozinha.
KITCHEN SINK s. pia de cozinha.
KITCHENWARE s. utensílios de cozinha.
KITE s. papagaio de papel, pipa.
KITSCH s. cafona, brega; deselegante / adj. cafona, brega; deselegante.
KITTEN s. gatinho (filhote).
KITTY s. gatinho; vaquinha (contribuição).
KLEPTOMANIAC s. cleptomaníaco.
KNACK s. habilidade, jeito.
KNAVE s. patife, cafajeste.
KNEAD v. amassar.
KNEE v. dar joelhada / s. joelho.
KNEECAP s. rótula (anatomia).

KNEEL v. ajoelhar-se; ficar de joelhos.
KNELL s. badalada; toque de campainha.
KNICKERS s. calcinha; calçolas.
KNICK-KNACK s. bagatela; bugiganga.
KNIFE s. faca / v. esfaquear.
KNIFE-GRINDER s. amolador de faca.
KNIGHT s. cavaleiro; cavalo (xadrez).
KNIGHTHOOD s. fidalguia, nobreza; cavalheirismo.
KNIT v. tricotar; entrelaçar / s. tricô.
KNITTING s. tricô; malha, união.
KNITTING MACHINE s. máquina de tricotar.
KNITTING NEEDLE s. agulha de tricô.
KNITWEAR s. roupa de malha.
KNOB s. maçaneta, puxador.
KNOCK s. pancada, batida / v. bater; colidir.
KNOCKING s. pancadas, barulho, ruído anormal de motor.
KNOCKOUT s. nocaute / v. nocautear.
KNOCK OVER v. atropelar.
KNOT s. nó, laço; câimbra / v. atar, amarrar.
KNOTTY adj. cheio de nós, nodoso.
KNOW v. saber, conhecer, entender.
KNOW-ALL s. sabichão; sabe tudo.
KNOW-HOW s. experiência, prática, conhecimento.
KNOWING s. conhecimento, sabedoria / adj. intencional; sagaz, astuto.
KNOWINGLY adv. sabiamente, intencionalmente.
KNOWLEDGE s. conhecimento, instrução; dados (informática).
KNOWLEDGEABLE adj. versado, instruído, entendido.
KNOWN adj. conhecido, reconhecido.
KNUCKLE s. nó dos dedos, junta, articulação.
KNUCKLEHEAD s. pessoa tola, estúpida.
KNURL s. nó, saliência, bossa.
KOALA s. coala.
KOOK s. maluco, excêntrico.
KORAN s. Alcorão, Corão.
KORANIC adj. relativo ao Alcorão.
KOREA s. Coreia.
KOREAN adj. coreano / s. coreano.
KOSHER adj. apropriado, permitido; legítimo.
KRYPTON s. criptônio (elemento químico).
KUDOS s. glória, fama, elogio, enaltecimento.
KWAIT s. Kwait.

Ll

L, l *s.* décima segunda letra do alfabeto inglês / *abrev.* de *liter*; representa o número 50 em algarismos romanos.
LAB *abrev.* laboratório.
LABEL *s.* etiqueta, rótulo / *v.* rotular, etiquetar.
LABIAL *adj.* labial.
LABILE *adj.* lábil, variável.
LABORATORY *s.* laboratório.
LABORIOUS *adj.* laborioso, custoso.
LABOUR *s.* trabalho, faina; parto / *v.* trabalhar, labutar.
LABOURED *adj.* forçado; elaborado, trabalhoso.
LABOURER *s.* operário, trabalhador.
LABYRINTH *s.* labirinto.
LABYRINTHINE *adj.* labiríntico, intrincado, confuso.
LACE *s.* renda; cadarço / *v.* amarrar (sapatos).
LACERATE *v.* dilacerar, lacerar.
LACERATION *s.* laceração.
LACK *s.* falta, carência / *v.* faltar, carecer.
LACKADAISICAL *adj.* apático; lânguido.
LACKEY *s.* lacaio.
LACKING *adj.* carente, deficiente, desprovido de.
LACKLUSTER *adj.* embaçado, apagado; sem brilho.
LACONIC *adj.* lacônico.
LACQUER *s.* fixador; laquê.
LACRIMAL *adj.* lacrimal.
LACTATE *v.* lactar; aleitar, secretar leite.
LACTATION *s.* lactação.
LACTIC *adj.* lácteo, láctico, relativo ao leite.
LACTOSE *s.* lactose.
LACTOSE INTOLERANCE *s.* intolerância à lactose.
LACY *adj.* rendado.
LAD *s.* rapaz, moço.
LADDER *s.* escada de mão.
LADDIE *s.* rapazinho; garoto.
LADE *v.* carregar.
LADEN *adj.* carregado, onerado.
LADING *s.* carregamento.
LADLE *s.* concha de sopa / *v.* servir com a concha.
LADY *s.* senhora; dama.
LADYBUG *s.* joaninha.

LADYLIKE *adj.* refinado, elegante.
LADYLOVE *s.* amada, namorada, amante.
LADYSHIP *s.* senhoria; dignidade de senhora.
LAG *s.* atraso, defasagem / *v.* ficar para trás, retardar-se.
LAGGARD *s.* retardatário / *adj.* vagaroso.
LAGOON *s.* lagoa, laguna.
LAID-BACK *adj.* descontraído; tranquilo.
LAIR *s.* covil, toca.
LAKE *s.* lago.
LAM *v.* fugir; bater, golpear, socar.
LAMB *s.* cordeiro.
LAMBSWOOL *s.* merino; lã de cordeiro / *adj.* merino; lã de cordeiro.
LAME *adj.* manco, coxo / *v.* mancar, coxear.
LAME EXCUSE *s.* desculpa esfarrapada.
LAMELY *adv.* indevidamente; com defeito.
LAMENT *s.* lamento, queixa, choro / *v.* lamentar-se.
LAMENTABLE *adj.* lamentável.
LAMENTATION *s.* lamento, lamentação.
LAMINATE *s.* laminado / *v.* laminar / *adj.* laminado.
LAMINATION *s.* laminação, laminagem.
LAMP *s.* lâmpada, lanterna.
LAMPPOST *s.* poste de iluminação.
LAMPSHADE *s.* abajur; quebra-luz.
LANCE *s.* lança / *v.* lancetar, perfurar.
LANCER *s.* lanceiro.
LANCET *s.* bisturi; lanceta.
LAND *s.* terra; região; solo / *v.* pousar, desembarcar.
LANDFALL *s.* deslizamento de terra.
LANDFILL *s.* aterro sanitário.
LANDHOLDER *s.* proprietário (de terras).
LANDHOLDING *s.* posse de terras.
LANDING *s.* aterrissagem, pouso; desembarque.
LANDLADY *s.* proprietária (de estalagem), senhoria.
LANDLORD *s.* proprietário (de estalagem), senhorio.
LANDMARK *s.* lugar conhecido, ponto de referência.
LANDOWNER *s.* latifundiário(a).
LANDSCAPE *s.* paisagem, cenário.
LANDSCAPER *s.* paisagista.
LANDSCAPING *s.* paisagismo.
LANDSLIDE *s.* desmoronamento, deslizamento de terra.
LANDSMAN *s.* lavrador, camponês.
LANE *s.* caminho, raia; pista, faixa.
LANGUAGE *s.* língua, linguagem, idioma.
LANGUID *adj.* lânguido, abatido.
LANGUIDLY *adv.* lentamente.
LANGUISH *v.* debilitar, adoecer, definhar.
LANK *adj.* liso; magro, delgado / *v.* decair.
LANKY *adj.* magrelo, esbelto.
LANTERN *s.* lanterna.
LAP *s.* volta; colo; regaço; lambida.
LAPEL *s.* lapela.
LAPIDARY *adj.* lapidário.
LAPLAND *s.* Lapônia.
LAPSE *s.* lapso de tempo; erro, deslize / *v.* escoar, decorrer.
LAPTOP *s.* computador portátil.
LAPWING *s.* quero-quero (pássaro).
LARCENY *s.* apropriação indébita; furto, roubo.
LARD *s.* banha de porco, toucinho / *v.* engordar.
LARDER *s.* despensa.
LARGE *adj.* grande, abundante, amplo.
LARGELY *adv.* em grande parte, amplamente.
LARGE-SCALE *adj.* em grande escala.
LARGESS *s.* presente, dádiva.
LARIAT *s.* laço.
LARK *s.* brincadeira, travessura; cotovia.
LARVA *s.* larva (inseto).
LARYNGEAL *adj.* laríngeo, laringiano, que se refere à laringe.
LARYNGITIS *s.* laringite.
LARYNX *s.* laringe.
LASAGNA *s.* lasanha.
LASCIVIOUS *adj.* lascivo.
LASER *s.* raio *laser* / *adj.* raio *laser*.
LASER PRINTER *s.* impressora a *laser*.
LASH *s.* chicotada; cílio / *v.* chicotear, açoitar.
LASHING *s.* açoitamento, ataque ou censura severa.
LASS *s.* moça.
LASSO *s.* laço / *v.* laçar.
LAST *adj.* último / *adv.* em último lugar / *v.* durar.
LASTING *adj.* duradouro, durável.
LASTLY *adv.* finalmente, por fim.
LAST MINUTE *adj.* última hora.
LATCH *s.* trinco / *v.* trancar; fechar com trinco.
LATE *adj.* atrasado / *adv.* tarde, tardio.

LATECOMER s. retardatário.
LATELY adv. ultimamente, recentemente.
LATENCY s. latência.
LATENESS s. atraso, demora.
LATENT adj. latente.
LATER adj. posterior / adv. mais tarde.
LATERAL adj. oblíquo, inclinado, lateral.
LATEST adj. último; últimas (notícias).
LATEX s. látex / adj. de látex.
LATH s. ripa, sarrafo.
LATHE s. torno mecânico.
LATHER s. espuma (de sabão) / v. ensaboar.
LATIN s. latim / adj. latino.
LATIN AMERICA s. América Latina.
LATIN AMERICAN adj. latino-americano.
LATITUDE s. latitude; largura.
LATITUDINAL adj. latitudinal.
LATRINE s. latrina, privada, cloaca.
LATTER adj. posterior, último; moderno, mais recente.
LATTICE s. treliça.
LAUD s. louvor, elogio / v. louvar, elogiar.
LAUDABLE adj. louvável.
LAUGH s. riso, risada / v. rir, gargalhar.
LAUGHABLE adj. ridículo, risível.
LAUGHING s. riso, risada / adj. risonho; cômico.
LAUGHINGSTOCK s. alvo de riso.
LAUGHTER s. gargalhada; rir muito.
LAUNCH s. lancha; lançamento, inauguração / v. lançar.
LAUNCHER s. lançador.
LAUNCH PAD s. plataforma de lançamento.
LAUNDER v. lavar e passar; higienizar.
LAUNDERING s. lavagem; lavagem de dinheiro.
LAUNDRESS s. lavadeira.
LAUNDRY s. lavanderia.
LAVATORY s. lavatório, toalete, vaso sanitário.
LAVENDER s. lavanda.
LAVISH adj. generoso, abundante / v. esbanjar.
LAVISHLY adv. abundantemente.
LAVISHNESS s. opulência; grandiosidade.
LAW s. lei, norma, regra.
LAW COURT s. tribunal de justiça.
LAWFUL adj. lícito, legal, legítimo.
LAWFULLY adv. legalmente.
LAWLESS adj. ilegal, ilegítimo; sem lei.

LAWLESSNESS s. ilegalidade.
LAWMAKER s. legislador.
LAWMAN s. homem da lei; policial.
LAWN s. gramado, relvado.
LAWN MOWER s. cortador de grama.
LAW SCHOOL s. faculdade de Direito.
LAWSUIT s. ação judicial, processo.
LAWYER s. advogado.
LAX s. diarreia / adj. relaxado, frouxo.
LAXATIVE s. laxante / adj. laxativo.
LAXITY s. negligência; lassidão, frouxidão.
LAY adj. leigo; laico / v. colocar, pôr, derrubar / s. postura.
LAYABOUT s. vadio, preguiçoso.
LAYAWAY s. consórcio, prestação.
LAY-BY s. acostamento (estrada).
LAYER s. camada; estrato (geologia).
LAYETTE s. enxoval de bebê.
LAYING s. postura; assentamento.
LAYMAN s. leigo.
LAYOFF s. dispensa, demissão.
LAYOUT s. desenho, plano, esquema.
LAYPERSON s. m.q. layman.
LAZE v. vadiar, folgar / s. ócio.
LAZILY adv. preguiçosamente.
LAZINESS s. indolência, preguiça.
LAZY adj. preguiçoso; relaxado, negligente.
LAZYBONES s. folgado, vida mansa.
LB abrev. libra.
LEAD s. chumbo; dianteira; conduta / v. liderar; conduzir.
LEADEN adj. cinzento; feito de chumbo.
LEADER s. líder; guia.
LEADERSHIP s. liderança, comando.
LEAD-FREE adj. sem chumbo.
LEADING adj. principal.
LEADING LADY s. protagonista.
LEADING LIGHT s. luz guia; destaque.
LEAD SINGER s. vocalista.
LEAF s. (pl. leaves) folha (de planta).
LEAFLESS adj. desfolhado.
LEAFLET s. folheto.
LEAF THROUGH v. folhear rapidamente.
LEAFY adj. frondoso; com muitas folhas.
LEAGUE s. liga, aliança; légua.
LEAK s. vazamento, goteira, escape / v. vazar, gotejar, escapar.
LEAKY adj. avariado; furado, esburacado.
LEAN adj. magro, delgado / s. inclinação / v. inclinar, encostar; depender.

LEANING s. inclinação, propensão / adj. inclinado, propenso.
LEAP s. salto, pulo / v. pular, saltar.
LEAPFROG s. jogo de pular sela; pular carniça.
LEAP YEAR s. ano bissexto.
LEARN v. aprender; ficar sabendo.
LEARNED adj. instruído, culto.
LEARNER s. principiante, discípulo, aprendiz.
LEARNING s. saber, erudição; aprendizagem.
LEASE s. aluguel, arrendamento / v. arrendar, alugar.
LEASEHOLDER s. arrendatário.
LEASH s. correia, trela / v. amarrar, prender.
LEASING s. aluguel.
LEAST adj. menor, mínimo / adv. pelo menos, menos / s. menor, mínimo.
LEATHER s. couro / adj. de couro / v. cobrir com couro.
LEAVE v. deixar, partir, abandonar / s. licença, permissão.
LEAVE BEHIND v. deixar para trás, abandonar.
LEAVEN s. levedura, fermento / v. fermentar, levedar.
LEAVE OUT v. omitir, extraviar.
LEAVER s. desistente.
LEAVING s. partida, ida.
LEBANESE s. libanês / adj. libanês.
LEBANON s. Líbano.
LECHER s. libertino, devasso.
LECHEROUS adj. lascivo, luxurioso.
LECTERN s. púlpito, atril, leitoril.
LECTURE s. palestra, discurso / v. dar uma palestra, discursar.
LECTURE HALL s. salão de conferências.
LECTURER s. palestrante, conferencista, professor.
LECTURE ROOM s. sala de palestras.
LEDGE s. peitoril, saliência, orla.
LEDGER s. lápide; livro de registro (contabilidade).
LEECH s. sanguessuga.
LEEK s. alho-poró.
LEEWAY s. liberdade de ação, à deriva.
LEFT s. esquerda / adj. canhoto / adv. à esquerda.
LEFT-HANDED adj. canhoto.
LEFTISM s. esquerdismo.
LEFTIST s. esquerdista / adj. esquerdista.
LEFTOVER s. sobra, resto.
LEFTWARDS adv. à esquerda.
LEFT-WING s. ala esquerdista / adj. esquerdista.
LEG s. perna.
LEGACY s. legado, herança.
LEGAL adj. legal, legítimo.
LEGALISATION s. legalização.
LEGALISE v. legalizar.
LEGALISM s. legalismo.
LEGALITY s. legalidade.
LEGALLY adv. legalmente.
LEGEND s. lenda; legenda.
LEGENDARY adj. legendário; lendário.
LEGIBILITY s. legibilidade.
LEGIBLE adj. legível, nítido.
LEGIBLY adv. legivelmente.
LEGION s. legião; multidão.
LEGIONARY adj. legionário.
LEGISLATE v. legislar.
LEGISLATION s. legislação.
LEGISLATIVE adj. legislativo.
LEGISLATIVE ASSEMBLY s. Assembleia Legislativa.
LEGISLATOR s. legislador.
LEGISLATURE s. legislatura.
LEGITIMACY s. legitimidade.
LEGITIMATE adj. legítimo, autêntico / v. legitimar, legalizar, validar.
LEGITIMISE v. legitimar, justificar, autenticar.
LEGROOM s. espaço para as pernas.
LEISURE s. lazer.
LEISURELY adj. calmo, vagaroso / adv. vagarosamente.
LEISUREWEAR s. roupa casual.
LEMON s. limão.
LEMONADE s. limonada.
LEMON DROP s. bala de limão (doce).
LEMON SQUEEZER s. espremedor de limão.
LEMON TREE s. limoeiro; pé de limão.
LEND v. emprestar.
LENDER s. credor, emprestador.
LENDING s. empréstimo.
LENGTH s. comprimento; duração, tamanho.
LENGTHEN v. alongar, estender.
LENGTHWISE adj. longitudinal / adv. longitudinalmente.
LENIENCE s. leniência, indulgência, calma, suavidade.

LENIENT *adj.* indulgente, brando.
LENS *s.* lente.
LENT *s.* quaresma (religião).
LENTEN *adj.* quaresmal; parcimonioso, escasso.
LENTIL *s.* lentilha.
LEO *s.* Leão (astrologia).
LEOPARD *s.* leopardo.
LEPER *s.* leproso, hanseniano.
LEPROSY *s.* lepra, mal de Hansen.
LESBIAN *s.* lésbica / *adj.* lésbico.
LESBIANISM *s.* lesbianismo.
LESION *s.* lesão, ferida, machucado.
LESS *s.* inferior, menor, menos / *adj.* inferior, menor, menos / *adv.* menos / *prep.* sem, menos.
LESSEN *v.* diminuir, reduzir.
LESSENING *s.* redução, diminuição / *adj.* diminuidor.
LESSER *adj.* menor, inferior.
LESSON *s.* aula, lição.
LET *v.* deixar, permitir; alugar / *s.* dificuldade.
LET DOWN *v.* baixar, humilhar, decepcionar.
LETDOWN *s.* desapontamento, humilhação.
LET IN *v.* deixar entrar; permitir.
LETHAL *adj.* letal, mortal.
LETHARGIC *adj.* letárgico.
LETHARGY *s.* letargia.
LETTER *s.* letra; carta.
LETTER BOMB *s.* carta-bomba.
LETTERBOX *s.* caixa de correio; caixa postal.
LETTERED *adj.* letrado, erudito.
LETTERHEAD *s.* timbre, cabeçalho.
LETTERING *s.* letras; inscrição.
LETTUCE *s.* alface.
LET-UP *s.* diminuição, pausa, intervalo.
LEUKAEMIA *s.* leucemia.
LEUKAEMIC *adj.* leucêmico.
LEVEL *s.* nível; superfície plana / *adj.* plano, nivelado / *v.* nivelar.
LEVELER *s.* nivelador; igualitário.
LEVER *s.* alavanca.
LEVERAGE *s.* influência.
LEVITATE *v.* levitar.
LEVITATION *s.* levitação.
LEVITY *s.* leviandade, leveza.
LEVY *s.* coleta, taxação / *v.* arrecadar.
LEXICAL *adj.* lexical.
LEXICON *s.* léxico; vocabulário.
LIABILITY *s.* responsabilidade; obrigação.
LIABLE *adj.* responsável.
LIAISE *v.* estabelecer contato, ligação.
LIAR *s.* mentiroso.
LIBEL *s.* difamação, calúnia / *v.* difamar.
LIBELOUS *adj.* difamatório, acusatório.
LIBERAL *s.* liberal / *adj.* liberal.
LIBERALISATION *s.* liberalização.
LIBERALISE *v.* liberalizar.
LIBERALISM *s.* liberalismo.
LIBERATE *v.* libertar, liberar.
LIBERATING *adj.* liberalizante, libertador.
LIBERATION *s.* liberação, libertação.
LIBERATOR *s.* libertador.
LIBERTARIAN *s.* libertário / *adj.* libertário.
LIBERTINE *s.* libertino.
LIBERTY *s.* liberdade.
LIBIDINOUS *adj.* libidinoso, lascivo.
LIBIDO *s.* libido.
LIBRA *s.* Libra (astrologia).
LIBRARIAN *s.* bibliotecário.
LIBRARIANSHIP *s.* biblioteconomia.
LIBRARY *s.* biblioteca.
LIBYA *s.* Líbia.
LICENSE *s.* licença, autorização.
LICENSED *adj.* licenciado, autorizado.
LICENSE PLATE *s.* placa (de carro).
LICENTIATE *s.* licenciado; licenciatura.
LICK *s.* lambida / *v.* lamber.
LICKING *s.* lambida; surra, sova.
LID *s.* tampa.
LIE *s.* mentira, falsidade / *v.* jazer, deitar-se; mentir.
LIEGE *s.* senhor feudal, soberano.
LIEUTENANT *s.* tenente.
LIFE *s.* vida; validade (produtos).
LIFEBELT *s.* cinto de segurança.
LIFEBLOOD *s.* força vital.
LIFEBOAT *s.* barco salva-vidas.
LIFEGUARD *s.* salva-vidas.
LIFE INSURANCE *s.* seguro de vida.
LIFEJACKET *s.* colete salva-vidas.
LIFELESS *adj.* sem vida, morto; inanimado.
LIFELIKE *adj.* natural; tal como a vida.
LIFELONG *adj.* que dura a vida toda, vitalício.
LIFESAVING *s.* salvamento; primeiros socorros.
LIFE SENTENCE *s.* pena de prisão perpétua.

LIFESPAN s. duração de vida; vida útil (produtos).
LIFESTYLE s. estilo de vida.
LIFETIME s. tempo de vida, existência.
LIFT v. levantar, suspender / s. elevador; carona.
LIFTER s. elevador; levantador.
LIFTING s. levantamento.
LIGAMENT s. ligamentos (anatomia).
LIGATE v. ligar, conectar.
LIGATION s. ligação.
LIGATURE s. ligadura.
LIGHT s. luz / v. acender, iluminar / adj. claro, leve, delicado.
LIGHTS s. semáforo.
LIGHTEN v. iluminar, acender; clarear; aliviar.
LIGHTER s. isqueiro; barcaça, chata.
LIGHT-HEARTED adj. alegre, despreocupado.
LIGHTHOUSE s. farol.
LIGHTING s. iluminação, ignição.
LIGHTLY adv. ligeiramente, levemente.
LIGHTNESS s. leveza, claridade; brandura.
LIGHTNING s. relâmpago; raio.
LIGHTNING BUG s. vaga-lume.
LIGHTNING ROD s. para-raios.
LIGHT-YEAR s. ano-luz.
LIKE v. gostar / prep. como / adj. parecido, semelhante / s. igual, semelhante.
LIKEABLE adj. agradável, simpático.
LIKELIHOOD s. probabilidade; semelhança.
LIKELY adj. provável, plausível / adv. provavelmente.
LIKEN v. comparar.
LIKENESS s. semelhança, aparência.
LIKEWISE adv. igualmente, do mesmo modo.
LIKING s. simpatia; preferência.
LILAC s. lilás / adj. lilás.
LILT s. cadência, ritmo (música).
LILY s. lírio; flor-de-lis.
LILY PAD s. vitória-régia; nenúfar (flor).
LIMB s. membro, limbo.
LIMBER UP v. fazer aquecimento.
LIME s. limeira, limão, lima; cal.
LIME JUICE s. suco de limão.
LIMELIGHT s. centro das atenções; publicidade.
LIMESTONE s. pedra calcária.
LIMIT s. limite / v. limitar.
LIMITATION s. limitação.

LIMITED s. trem ou ônibus expresso / adj. limitado.
LIMITED COMPANY s. sociedade anônima.
LIMITED EDITION s. edição limitada.
LIMITER s. limitador.
LIMITING adj. limitante, limitativo.
LIMOUSINE s. limusine.
LIMP v. mancar / adj. frouxo; manco.
LIMPID adj. límpido, claro.
LINE s. linha, corda; fila, reta; linho / v. enfileirar-se; riscar.
LINEAGE s. linhagem, estirpe.
LINEAL adj. linear.
LINEARITY s. linearidade.
LINED adj. pautado; enrugado.
LINEN s. linho; roupa de cama.
LINER s. transatlântico; delineador.
LINESMAN s. juiz de linha; bandeirinha.
LINE-UP v. enfileirar, alinhar / s. alinhamento; formação.
LINGER v. demorar, perdurar-se; persistir.
LINGERIE s. *lingerie,* roupa íntima feminina.
LINGERING adj. prolongado, vagaroso.
LINGUAL adj. lingual.
LINGUIST s. linguista.
LINGUISTIC adj. linguístico.
LINGUISTICS s. linguística (ciência).
LINK s. elo, conexão, ligação / v. unir, conectar, ligar.
LINKUP s. conexão, acoplamento; fusão.
LINSEED s. linhaça.
LINT s. fiapo.
LION s. leão.
LIONESS s. leoa.
LIP s. lábio, beiço; borda.
LIPSTICK s. batom.
LIQUEFIER s. liquidificador.
LIQUEFY v. liquidificar, liquefazer.
LIQUEUR s. licor.
LIQUID s. líquido, fluido / adj. líquido, fluido.
LIQUIDATE v. liquidar, saldar.
LIQUIDATION s. liquidação.
LIQUIDITY s. liquidez.
LIQUID SOAP s. sabão líquido.
LIQUOR s. licor, bebida alcoólica.
LIQUOR STORE s. loja de bebidas.
LISBON s. Lisboa.
LISP s. pronúncia defeituosa / v. balbuciar.
LIST v. listar, enumerar / s. lista; tabela.
LISTED adj. registrado.

LISTEN v. escutar, ouvir.
LISTENER s. ouvinte.
LISTENING s. escuta.
LISTING s. alistamento; relação.
LISTLESS adj. indiferente, desatento, apático.
LIT adj. iluminado, acendido.
LITANY s. ladainha, litania.
LITER s. litro.
LITERACY s. alfabetização.
LITERAL adj. literal, factual.
LITERALLY adv. literalmente.
LITERARY adj. literário.
LITERATE adj. alfabetizado.
LITERATURE s. literatura.
LITIGANT s. litigante.
LITIGATE v. litigar.
LITIGATION s. litígio; processo.
LITRE s. m.q. liter.
LITTER s. lixo; ninhada / v. jogar o lixo.
LITTERBIN s. lata de lixo.
LITTLE adj. pequeno, pouco / adv. pouco, escassamente.
LITTLE FINGER s. dedo mindinho.
LITTORAL s. litoral / adj. litorâneo.
LITURGICAL adj. litúrgico.
LITURGY s. liturgia; ritual religioso.
LIVE v. viver, morar / adj. vivo; ao vivo.
LIVEABLE adj. suportável; habitável.
LIVELIHOOD s. meios de vida, sustento.
LIVELONG adj. durável; por muito tempo.
LIVELY adj. vivo, vigoroso, animado.
LIVEN UP v. animar.
LIVER s. fígado.
LIVESTOCK s. criação de gado.
LIVID adj. lívido.
LIVING adj. vivo, vivente / s. sustento, modo de vida.
LIVING BEING s. ser vivo.
LIVING CONDITION s. condição de vida.
LIVING LANGUAGE s. língua viva.
LIVING MATTER s. matéria viva; matéria orgânica.
LIVING ROOM s. sala de estar.
LIVING STANDARD s. padrão de vida.
LIVING WAGE s. salário mínimo.
LIZARD s. lagarto.
LOAD s. peso, carga / v. carregar.
LOADED adj. carregado.
LOADING s. carregamento; carga.

LOAF s. filão de pão, pão (de forma); vadiagem, ociosidade / v. vadiar.
LOAFER s. vadio.
LOAN s. empréstimo / v. emprestar.
LOAN SHARK s. agiota.
LOBBY s. saguão, vestíbulo; pressão / v. pressionar.
LOBSTER s. lagosta.
LOCAL adj. local.
LOCALITY s. localidade.
LOCALLY adv. nos arredores, localmente.
LOCATE v. localizar, situar; fixar residência.
LOCATION s. local, localização, posição, locação.
LOCH s. lago.
LOCK s. fechadura, cadeado / v. trancar.
LOCKER s. armário; depósito.
LOCKET s. medalhão.
LOCKSMITH s. serralheiro.
LOCKUP s. local que serve como prisão / v. trancafiar.
LOCOMOTIVE s. locomotiva / adj. locomotivo.
LOCUST s. gafanhoto.
LODGE s. guarita; residência temporária; alojamento / v. alojar.
LOFT s. sótão; apartamento pequeno e de luxo.
LOG s. tora, lenha; diário de bordo ou de voo / v. registrar.
LOGBOOK v. registrar / s. livro de registro, diário.
LOGE s. camarote de teatro.
LOGIC s. lógica.
LOGICAL adj. lógico.
LOGO s. logotipo.
LOIN s. lombo.
LOITER v. perder tempo, tardar.
LOLL v. refestelar-se; pôr a língua para fora.
LOLLIPOP s. pirulito.
LONDON s. Londres.
LONDONER s. londrino.
LONE adj. solitário.
LONELINESS s. solidão, isolamento.
LONELY adj. só, solitário.
LONG adj. longo, comprido / adv. muito tempo / v. ansiar por algo, desejar.
LONG-DISTANCE adj. longa distância / adv. de longa distância.
LONG-HAIRED adj. peludo, cabeludo.
LONGHAND s. escrita manual.
LONGISH adj. um tanto longo.

LONGITUDE s. longitude.
LONG-LIFE adj. vida longa.
LONG-RANGE adj. de longo alcance.
LONG-TERM adj. a longo prazo.
LOO s. banheiro.
LOOK v. olhar; parecer / s. olhar; aparência.
LOOK FOR v. procurar.
LOOK OUT v. tomar cuidado.
LOOK OVER v. examinar.
LOOM s. tear / v. assomar, surgir.
LOONY s. débil mental / adj. maluco.
LOOP s. laço, laçada / v. enlaçar.
LOOSE s. liberdade / adj. solto, folgado, vago / v. soltar, desamarrar.
LOOSELY adv. folgadamente, livremente.
LOOSEN v. afrouxar, desatar, soltar.
LOOT v. saquear, pilhar / s. saque, pilhagem.
LOP OFF v. podar, cortar.
LOP-SIDED adj. torto, distorcido.
LORD s. Deus; o senhor, lorde.
LORDLIKE adj. nobre, senhoril; arrogante.
LORRY s. caminhão.
LOSE v. perder.
LOSER s. perdedor.
LOSS s. perda, dano prejuízo.
LOST adj. perdido, desorientado.
LOT s. porção; lote; destino / v. lotear, dividir.
LOTION s. loção.
LOTTERY s. loteria.
LOUD adj. alto; barulhento / adv. alto, em voz alta.
LOUD-HAILER s. megafone.
LOUDLY adv. ruidosamente, em voz alta.
LOUDSPEAKER s. alto-falante.
LOUNGE s. saguão; bar social / v. espreguiçar-se, vadiar.
LOUSE s. (pl. lice) piolho.
LOUSY adj. piolhento; vil, torpe.
LOVEBLE adj. adorável, amável.
LOVE s. amor / v. amar.
LOVE AFFAIR s. caso de amor.
LOVELESS adj. sem amor.
LOVE LIFE s. vida sentimental.
LOVELY adj. encantador, gracioso.
LOVER s. amante.
LOVING adj. carinhoso.
LOW adj. baixo / adv. baixo.
LOW-CUT adj. decotado.
LOWER adj. inferior; mais baixo / v. reduzir, baixar.
LOW-FAT adj. magro, de baixa caloria.
LOWING s. mugido.
LOWLAND s. planície.
LOWLY adj. humilde, modesto; vil, inferior.
LOW-SPIRITED adj. deprimido.
LOW TIDE s. maré baixa.
LOYAL adj. leal, fiel.
LOYALTY s. lealdade, fidelidade.
LUBRICATE v. lubrificar.
LUCK s. sorte; acaso.
LUCKILY adv. felizmente, afortunadamente.
LUCKY adj. sortudo, afortunado.
LUG s. puxão, arranco / v. puxar pelas orelhas.
LUGGAGE s. bagagem.
LUGGAGE RACK s. porta-bagagem.
LULL s. calmaria, bonança / v. acalmar, acalentar.
LULLABY s. canção de ninar / v. ninar.
LUMBER s. restos de madeira / v. mover-se com dificuldade.
LUMBERING adj. pesado.
LUMBERJACK s. lenhador.
LUMINOUS adj. luminoso.
LUMP s. torrão; inchação, inchaço.
LUNATIC s. louco, lunático / adj. louco, lunático.
LUNCH s. almoço / v. almoçar.
LUNCH TIME s. hora do almoço.
LUNG s. pulmão.
LURCH s. desamparo; balanço brusco / v. dar uma guinada, cambalear.
LURK v. espreitar; emboscar.
LUSH adj. viçoso, exuberante.
LUST s. luxúria / v. cobiçar.
LUSTER s. lustre, brilho.
LUSTY adj. robusto, vigoroso.
LUXEMBOURG s. Luxemburgo.
LUXURY s. luxo / adj. de luxo.
LYING s. mentira / adj. mentiroso.
LYING-IN s. resguardo, situação de estar deitado.
LYNCH v. linchar.
LYRICAL adj. lírico.
LYRICS s. letra de música.

Mm

M, m *s.* décima terceira letra do alfabeto inglês; representa o número 1.000 em algarismos romanos.
MA *abrev.* mestrado, título de mestre.
MA'AM *abrev.* madame, senhora.
MACABRE *adj.* lúgubre, funesto, macabro.
MACAW *s.* arara.
MACHIAVELLIAN *adj.* maquiavélico, astuto.
MACHINATE *v.* maquinar.
MACHINATION *s.* maquinação.
MACHINE *s.* máquina.
MACHINE-GUN *s.* metralhadora / *v.* metralhar.
MACHINERY *s.* maquinaria; maquinismo.
MACHINIST *s.* operador de máquina.
MACHISMO *s.* machismo.
MACHO *adj.* macho, valentão.
MACKINTOSH *s.* capa impermeável.
MACROSCOPIC *adj.* macroscópico.
MAD *adj.* louco, demente, insensato; furioso.
MADAM *s.* senhora, madame.
MADDEN *v.* enlouquecer, enfurecer.
MADDENING *adj.* irritante, exasperador.
MADE *adj.* feito, fabricado.
MADE-TO-ORDER *adj.* feito sob medida.
MADE-UP *adj.* inventado, mentiroso.
MADHOUSE *s.* hospício.
MADLY *adv.* loucamente.
MADMAN *s.* louco, alienado.
MADNESS *s.* loucura; raiva.
MAGAZINE *s.* revista, periódico.
MAGENTA *s.* magenta, carmim.
MAGGOT *s.* larva, verme.
MAGIC *s.* magia / *adj.* mágico.
MAGICAL *adj.* mágico, encantado.
MAGICALLY *adv.* magicamente.
MAGICIAN *s.* mago, ilusionista.
MAGISTERIAL *adj.* magistral; autoritário.
MAGISTRATE *s.* magistrado, juiz.
MAGMA *s.* magma.
MAGNANIMITY *s.* magnanimidade.
MAGNANIMOUS *adj.* magnânimo, clemente.
MAGNATE *s.* magnata.
MAGNESIUM *s.* magnésio.
MAGNET *s.* ímã, magneto.
MAGNETIC *adj.* magnético; atrativo.

MAGNETISATION s. magnetização.
MAGNETISE v. magnetizar.
MAGNETISM s. magnetismo; atração.
MAGNIFICATION s. ampliação; aumento.
MAGNIFICENCE s. magnificência.
MAGNIFICENT adj. magnífico, grandioso.
MAGNIFY v. magnificar, ampliar.
MAGNITUDE s. magnitude, grandeza.
MAHARAJAH s. marajá.
MAID s. criada, empregada.
MAIDEN s. solteirona, donzela.
MAIDENHEAD s. virgindade; hímen.
MAIDENHOOD s. virgindade.
MAIDEN NAME s. nome de solteira.
MAIDSERVANT s. criada.
MAIL s. correio; correspondência / v. expedir, enviar pelo correio.
MAILBAG s. sacola de cartas.
MAILBOX s. caixa de correio.
MAILING s. mala direta, envelope.
MAILLOT s. maiô; malha.
MAILMAN s. carteiro.
MAIM s. lesão, mutilação / v. mutilar, desfigurar.
MAIN s. encanamento / adj. principal, essencial.
MAINLAND s. continente.
MAINLY adv. principalmente.
MAINSTREAM s. corrente principal / adj. que está na moda.
MAINTAIN v. manter, cuidar; persistir.
MAINTAINABLE adj. sustentável.
MAINTENANCE s. sustento; manutenção.
MAIZE s. milho.
MAJESTIC adj. majestoso, grandioso.
MAJESTY s. majestade, grandeza.
MAJOR s. major; maior de idade / adj. muito importante.
MAJORDOMO s. mordomo, camareiro.
MAJORITY s. maioria; maioridade.
MAKE v. fazer, fabricar, produzir / s. marca, fabricação.
MAKE-BELIEVE s. imaginação, fingimento / adj. imaginação, fingimento / v. fingir, simular.
MAKE DO v. contentar-se.
MAKEOVER s. transformação.
MAKE OVER v. refazer, renovar.
MAKER s. fabricante, fazedor.
MAKESHIFT s. provisório, temporário / adj. provisório, temporário.
MAKE-UP s. maquiagem, composição; constituição.
MAKING s. fabricação; ato de fazer.
MALADJUSTED adj. malfeito, desajustado.
MALADY s. doença, aflição, problema.
MALAISE s. mal-estar, indisposição.
MALARIA s. malária.
MALARIAL adj. malárico.
MALCONTENT s. descontente / adj. descontente.
MALE s. macho, varão / adj. masculino, macho.
MALEFICENT adj. maléfico.
MALEVOLENCE s. malevolência, maldade.
MALEVOLENT adj. malevolente, malévolo.
MALFORMATION s. malformação.
MALFORMED adj. malformado.
MALFUNCTION s. mau funcionamento.
MALICE s. malícia.
MALICIOUS adj. malicioso.
MALIGN v. caluniar, difamar / adj. maligno, maléfico.
MALIGNANCY s. malignidade, virulência.
MALIGNANT adj. maligno.
MALL s. centro de compras; *shopping center*.
MALLEABLE adj. maleável, flexível.
MALLET s. maço, malho; marreta.
MALNOURISHED adj. subnutrido, mal alimentado.
MALNUTRITION s. desnutrição.
MALPRACTICE s. negligência, imperícia.
MALT s. malte, maltado / v. maltar.
MALTREAT v. maltratar.
MALTREATMENT s. maus-tratos.
MAMMAL s. mamífero.
MAMMALIAN s. mamífero / adj. mamífero.
MAMMOGRAM s. mamografia.
MAMMOGRAPHY s. mamografia.
MAMMOTH s. mamute / adj. gigantesco.
MAN s. (*pl. men*) homem.
MANACLE s. algema; constrangimento / v. algemar; restringir.
MANAGE v. administrar, gerenciar, dirigir.
MANAGEABLE adj. maleável; controlável; dócil.
MANAGEMENT s. administração, gerência; gestão, conduta.
MANAGER s. gerente, diretor, administrador.
MANDATE v. ordenar, exigir / s. mandato, ordem.

MANDATORY s. mandatário / adj. obrigatório.
MANDIBLE s. mandíbula, queixada.
MANDIBULAR adj. mandibular.
MANDOLIN s. bandolim (instrumento).
MANE s. crina, juba.
MANEUVER v. manobrar / s. manobra.
MANEUVRABLE adj. móvel, manobrável.
MANGA s. mangá (quadrinho japonês).
MANGE s. sarna.
MANGER s. manjedoura.
MANGO s. manga (fruta).
MANGO TREE s. mangueira; pé de manga.
MANGROVE s. mangue.
MANGY adj. sarnento, sórdido, sujo.
MANHANDLE v. maltratar.
MANHOLE s. bueiro.
MANHOOD s. masculinidade; virilidade.
MANHUNT s. perseguição, caça.
MANIA s. mania.
MANIAC s. maníaco, fanático.
MANIACAL adj. maníaco.
MANICURE v. cortar, aparar / s. manicure.
MANICURIST s. manicuro, manicure.
MANIFEST v. manifestar, revelar / s. manifesto, evidente / adj. manifesto, evidente.
MANIFESTATION s. manifestação.
MANIFESTO s. manifesto; declaração.
MANIFOLD s. coletor / adj. múltiplo, variado.
MANIKIN s. manequim.
MANIPULATE v. manipular, manejar, influenciar.
MANIPULATION s. manipulação.
MANIPULATOR adj. manipulador, controlador.
MANKIND s. humanidade; ser humano.
MANLINESS s. brio, dignidade; virilidade.
MANLY adj. másculo, viril.
MANNEQUIN s. modelo, manequim.
MANNER s. modo, maneira, conduta.
MANNERISM s. maneirismo (arte).
MANNERLESS adj. sem modos, indelicado.
MANPOWER s. potencial humano, mão de obra.
MANSE s. residência paroquial; presbítero.
MANSION s. mansão.
MANSLAUGHTER s. homicídio culposo.
MANTLE s. manto, capote; bastão.

MANUAL adj. manual, feito com as mãos / s. manual.
MANUALLY adv. manualmente.
MANUFACTURE v. manufaturar, fabricar / s. manufatura, fabricação.
MANUFACTURER s. fabricante.
MANUFACTURING s. manufatura, fabricação.
MANURE s. esterco, estrume.
MANUSCRIPT s. manuscrito.
MANY pron. muito(s), muita(s) / adj. muito(s), muita(s).
MAP s. mapa / v. mapear; planejar.
MAR v. frustrar, arruinar.
MARATHON s. maratona.
MARATHON RUNNER s. maratonista.
MARBLE s. mármore; bolinha de gude.
MARBLED adj. marmorizado, marmoreado.
MARCH s. março; marcha / v. marchar, protestar.
MARCHER s. marchante.
MARCHING adj. operante; em marcha.
MARE s. égua.
MARGARINE s. margarina.
MARGIN s. margem, beira.
MARGINAL s. marginal / adj. marginal.
MARGINALISATION s. marginalização.
MARGINALISE v. marginalizar.
MARIJUANA s. maconha.
MARINATE v. temperar, marinar.
MARINE s. Marinha (forças armadas) / adj. marinho, do mar.
MARINE BIOLOGY s. biologia marinha.
MARINER s. marinheiro.
MARIONETTE s. fantoche, marionete.
MARISH s. pântano / adj. pantanoso.
MARITAL adj. marital, do casamento.
MARITAL STATUS s. estado civil.
MARITIME adj. marítimo.
MARK s. marca, sinal; nota escolar / v. marcar, assinalar, corrigir.
MARKDOWN s. remarcação, redução (preço).
MARKED adj. marcado.
MARKER s. marcador, indicador.
MARKET s. mercado / v. anunciar, apresentar (produto).
MARKETABLE adj. vendável, comercializável.
MARKETER s. negociante, marqueteiro.
MARKETING s. publicitário, mercadológio; *marketing*.

MARKETPLACE s. mercado; lugar para compras.
MARKUP s. remarcação, aumento (preços).
MARMALADE s. marmelada; geleia.
MARMOT s. marmota.
MARQUEE s. tenda, marquise.
MARQUIS s. marquês.
MARQUISE s. marquesa.
MARRIAGE s. casamento, matrimônio.
MARRIED adj. casado; unido.
MARROW s. medula, tutano.
MARRY v. casar-se; ajustar, acomodar.
MARS s. Marte.
MARSH s. pântano, brejo.
MARSHAL s. marechal (militar) / v. ordenar, guiar.
MARSHLAND s. pântano.
MARSHY adj. pantanoso.
MARTIAL v. dispor, ordenar / adj. marcial.
MARTIAL ART s. arte marcial.
MARTIAN s. marciano / adj. marciano.
MARTYR s. mártir / v. martirizar.
MARTYRDOM s. martírio, tormento.
MARVEL s. maravilha / v. maravilhar-se.
MARVELOUS adj. maravilhoso, magnífico.
MARVELOUSLY adv. maravilhosamente.
MARVELOUSNESS s. maravilha.
MARXISM s. marxismo.
MARXIST s. marxista / adj. marxista.
MASCARA s. rímel (cosmético).
MASCOT s. mascote.
MASCULINE adj. masculino.
MASCULINITY s. masculinidade.
MASH s. purê, mistura, papa / v. amassar, espremer.
MASHED adj. amassado, espremido.
MASK s. máscara; disfarce / v. mascarar, ocultar.
MASKED BALL s. baile de máscaras.
MASOCHISM s. masoquismo.
MASOCHIST s. masoquista.
MASON s. pedreiro; maçom.
MASONRY s. pedreiro (profissão); alvenaria; maçonaria.
MASQUERADE v. mascarar / s. mascarada.
MASS s. multidão, massa; missa / v. juntar-se, amontoar-se.
MASSACRE v. massacrar / s. massacre.
MASSAGE s. massagem / v. massagear.
MASSEUR s. massagista (homem).
MASSEUSE s. massagista (mulher).
MASSIVE adj. maciço, sólido.
MASSIVELY adv. massivamente.
MASS MEDIA s. meios de comunicação de massa.
MASTER s. mestre, dono, senhor / v. dominar, controlar.
MASTERFUL adj. perito, erudito, hábil.
MASTERLY adv. magistralmente.
MASTERPIECE s. obra-prima.
MASTERY s. domínio, controle.
MASTURBATE v. masturbar-se.
MASTURBATION s. masturbação.
MAT s. esteira, capacho, tapete.
MATCH s. fósforo; jogo, partida; igual; companheiro / v. combinar, unir.
MATCHBOX s. caixa de fósforo.
MATCHING adj. correspondente, apropriado.
MATCHMAKER s. casamenteiro.
MATCHSTICK s. palito de fósforo.
MATE s. companheiro, colega / v. dar xeque-mate no xadrez; acasalar-se.
MATERIAL s. matéria; material, substância; tecido / adj. material, essencial.
MATERIALISE v. materializar
MATERIALISM s. materialismo.
MATERIALIST s. materialista.
MATERIALLY adv. materialmente.
MATERNAL adj. maternal.
MATERNITY s. maternidade.
MATERNITY HOSPITAL s. maternidade.
MATHEMATICAL adj. matemático; rigoroso, exato.
MATHEMATICIAN s. matemático (estudante, especialista).
MATHEMATICS s. matemática.
MATINEE s. matinê.
MATING s. acasalamento, cruzamento.
MATRIARCH s. matriarca.
MATRICULATE v. matricular.
MATRICULATION s. matrícula.
MATRIMONIAL adj. matrimonial.
MATRIMONY s. matrimônio.
MATRIX s. matriz.
MATRON s. matrona.
MATT adj. fosco, sem brilho.

MATTER s. questão, assunto, matéria / v. importar, significar.
MATTING s. capacho.
MATTRESS s. colchão.
MATURATION s. maturação.
MATURE adj. maduro / v. amadurecer.
MATURITY s. maturidade.
MAUDLIN adj. sentimental, piegas, choroso.
MAUL v. maltratar, estropiar.
MAUSOLEUM s. mausoléu.
MAVERICK s. dissidente, rebelde, independente / adj. dissidente, rebelde, independente.
MAWKISH adj. enjoativo, repugnante.
MAXILLARY adj. maxilar.
MAXIM s. máxima; aforismo.
MAXIMAL adj. máximo.
MAXIMISATION s. maximização.
MAXIMISE v. maximizar; aumentar.
MAXIMUM adj. máximo.
MAY s. maio (mês) / v. poder, ter permissão.
MAYBE adv. talvez, possivelmente.
MAYDAY s. SOS, mayday / interj. SOS, mayday.
MAY DAY s. Dia do Trabalho.
MAYHEM s. desordem, caos.
MAYONNAISE s. maionese.
MAYOR s. prefeito.
MAYORAL adj. referente a prefeito.
MAZE s. labirinto.
MBA abrev. Mestre em Administração de Empresas.
MC abrev. mestre de cerimônias, membro do congresso.
MD abrev. doutor em Medicina.
ME pron. me, mim, comigo.
MEADOW s. prado, campina.
MEAGER adj. escasso, insuficiente.
MEAL s. refeição.
MEALTIME s. hora da refeição.
MEALY adj. farinhento, farináceo.
MEAN adj. avarento; maldoso / s. meio, média / v. significar, querer dizer.
MEANDER v. vaguear, vagar.
MEANDERING s. passeio / adj. sinuoso.
MEANIE s. malvado.
MEANING s. sentido, significado / adj. expressivo, significativo.
MEANINGFUL adj. significativo.

MEANINGFULLY adv. significativamente.
MEANINGLESS adj. sem sentido.
MEANLY adv. maldosamente, vilmente.
MEANNESS s. maldade, mesquinhez.
MEANS s. meio, forma, modo, recurso.
MEANTIME adv. entretanto, enquanto isso.
MEANWHILE adv. enquanto isso, ao passo que.
MEASLES s. sarampo.
MEASURABLE adj. mensurável, medível.
MEASURE v. medir; comparar; tirar as medidas / s. medida.
MEAT s. carne (alimento).
MEATBALL s. almôndega.
MEATY adj. carnudo, carnoso.
MECHANIC s. mecânico / adj. mecânico.
MECHANISATION s. mecanização.
MECHANISE v. mecanizar.
MECHANISM s. mecanismo.
MEDAL s. medalha.
MEDALLION s. medalhão.
MEDALLIST s. medalhista.
MEDDLE v. intrometer-se, intervir.
MEDDLING s. intromissão / adj. intrometido.
MEDIA s. meios de comunicação, mídia.
MEDIAL adj. mediano, medial.
MEDIATE v. mediar, arbitrar.
MEDIATION s. mediação.
MEDIATOR s. mediador.
MEDICAL adj. médico.
MEDICAL CARE s. tratamento médico.
MEDICAMENT s. medicamento.
MEDICATE v. medicar; curar, tratar.
MEDICATION s. medicação.
MEDICINAL adj. medicinal, curativo.
MEDICINE s. medicina, remédio.
MEDIOCRE adj. medíocre.
MEDIOCRITY s. mediocridade.
MEDITATE v. meditar, ponderar.
MEDITATION s. meditação.
MEDIUM adj. médio, moderado / s. meio.
MEDLEY s. mistura, miscelânea, confusão / adj. misturado.
MEEK adj. manso, submisso, meigo.
MEET v. encontrar; reunir-se; conhecer.
MEETING s. reunião; encontro.

MEGALOMANIAC s. megalomaníaco / adj. megalomaníaco.
MEGAPHONE s. megafone.
MELANCHOLIC s. melancólico, deprimido / adj. melancólico, deprimido.
MELANCHOLY s. melancolia.
MELANIN s. melanina.
MELODIC adj. melódico.
MELODRAMA s. melodrama.
MELODY s. melodia.
MELON s. melão.
MELT v. derreter, desfazer.
MELTING adj. derretido.
MEMBER s. membro; sócio, associado.
MEMBERSHIP s. filiação, associação.
MEMBRANE s. membrana.
MEMO s. memorando, circular.
MEMOIRIST s. memorialista.
MEMORABLE adj. memorável, notável.
MEMORIAL s. memorial / adj. memorial.
MEMORIALISE v. comemorar, recordar.
MEMORISATION s. memorização.
MEMORISE v. memorizar, decorar; guardar.
MEMORISER s. memorizador.
MEMORY s. memória, lembrança, recordação.
MEN s. homens.
MENACE s. ameaça / v. ameaçar.
MENACING adj. ameaçador.
MEND v. remendar, recuperar, reparar / s. remendo, reparo.
MENDACIOUS adj. mentiroso, desonesto.
MENDACITY s. desonestidade.
MENINGITIS s. meningite.
MENOPAUSE s. menopausa.
MENSES s. fluxo menstrual; menstruação.
MENSTRUATE v. menstruar; ficar menstruada.
MENSTRUATION s. menstruação.
MENSWEAR s. roupas masculinas.
MENTAL adj. mental; louco (coloquial).
MENTALIST s. mentalista.
MENTALITY s. mentalidade.
MENTALLY adv. mentalmente.
MENTALLY ILL adj. deficiente mental.
MENTHOL s. mentol / adj. mentolada.
MENTHOLATED adj. mentolado.
MENTION v. mencionar, citar, referir-se / s. menção.
MENTOR s. mentor, mestre / v. guiar, orientar.
MENU s. cardápio, menu.

MEOW v. miar / s. miau, miado.
MERCANTILE adj. mercantil.
MERCENARY s. mercenário; interesseiro / adj. mercenário; interesseiro.
MERCHANDISE v. promover, divulgar / s. mercadoria.
MERCHANDISING s. propaganda, divulgação.
MERCIFUL adj. misericordioso, piedoso, clemente.
MERCIFULLY adv. misericordiosamente.
MERCILESS adj. impiedoso, desumano, cruel.
MERCURY s. Mercúrio.
MERCY s. piedade, misericórdia.
MERE s. lago, lagoa, charco / adj. mero, simples.
MERELY adv. meramente; somente.
MERGE v. fundir; misturar, juntar.
MERGER s. fusão, aliança, junção.
MERIDIAN s. meridiano / adj. meridiano.
MERINGUE s. merengue, suspiro.
MERIT s. mérito / v. merecer.
MERITOCRACY s. meritocracia.
MERITORIOUS adj. meritório.
MERMAID s. sereia.
MERRILY adv. animadamente.
MERRIMENT s. alegria, animação.
MERRY adj. animado, feliz, divertido.
MERRY-GO-ROUND s. carrossel.
MESCALINE s. mescalina.
MESMERISM s. mesmerismo; hipnotismo.
MESMERIZATION s. fascinação; hipnose.
MESMERIZE v. hipnotizar; cativar.
MESMERIZER s. hipnotizador; que fascina.
MESS s. confusão, desordem, bagunça / v. bagunçar, sujar, desarrumar.
MESSAGE s. mensagem, recado.
MESSENGER s. mensageiro.
MESSIAH s. Messias; salvador, redentor.
MESSY adj. sujo, desarrumado, bagunçado.
MESTIZO adj. mestiço.
MET abrev. meteorológico, meteorologia.
METABOLIC adj. metabólico.
METABOLISE v. metabolizar.
METABOLISM s. metabolismo.
METAL s. metal.
METALLIC adj. metálico.
METALLURGICAL adj. metalúrgico.
METALLURGY s. metalurgia.

METAMORPHIC *adj.* metamórfico.
METAMORPHISM *s.* metamorfismo.
METAMORPHOSE *v.* metamorfosear.
METAMORPHOSIS *s.* metamorfose.
METAPHOR *s.* metáfora.
METAPHORIC *adj.* metafórico.
METAPHORICALLY *adv.* metaforicamente.
METAPHYSICAL *adj.* metafísico, transcendente.
METAPHYSICS *s.* metafísica (ciência).
METASTASIS *s.* metástase.
METE *v.* distribuir, repartir.
METEOR *s.* meteoro.
METEORITE *s.* meteorito.
METEOROLOGICAL *adj.* meteorológico.
METEOROLOGIST *s.* meteorologista.
METEOROLOGY *s.* meteorologia.
METHANE *s.* metano (gás).
METHANOL *s.* metanol.
METHOD *s.* método, procedimento.
METHODICAL *adj.* metódico, sistemático.
METHODICALLY *adv.* metodicamente.
METHODIST *s.* metodista.
METHODOLOGICAL *adj.* metodológico.
METHODOLOGY *s.* metodologia.
METICULOUS *adj.* meticuloso.
METICULOUSLY *adv.* meticulosamente.
METICULOUSNESS *s.* meticulosidade.
METRE *s.* metro, medidor / *v.* medir.
METRIC *adj.* métrico.
METRIC SYSTEM *s.* sistema métrico.
METROPOLIS *s.* metrópole.
METROPOLITAN *s.* metropolitano / *adj.* metropolitano.
METTLE *s.* ânimo, vigor; caráter, índole.
MEW *s.* gaivota; miado / *v.* miar.
MEXICAN *s.* mexicano / *adj.* mexicano.
MEXICO *s.* México.
MICRO *abrev.* microcomputador.
MICROBE *s.* micróbio.
MICROORGANISM *s.* micro-organismo.
MICROPHONE *s.* microfone.
MICROSCOPE *s.* microscópio.
MICROWAVE OVEN *s.* forno de micro-ondas
MID *adj.* meio, meados; semi.
MIDDAY *s.* meio-dia.
MIDDLE *s.* meio, centro, metade / *adj.* médio, central.
MIDDLE AGE *s.* meia-idade / *adj.* de meia-idade.
MIDGE *s.* mosquito.
MIDGET *s.* anão; pigmeu / *adj.* muito pequeno.
MIDNIGHT *s.* meia-noite.
MIDRIFF *s.* diafragma.
MIDTERM *s.* meio período / *adj.* de meio período.
MIDWIFE *s.* parteira.
MIDWIFERY *s.* obstetrícia; trabalho de parteira.
MIGHT *s.* força, potência.
MIGHTILY *adv.* extremamente.
MIGHTY *adj.* poderoso, potente.
MIGRAINE *s.* enxaqueca.
MIGRANT *s.* migrante / *adj.* migrante.
MIGRATE *v.* migrar, emigrar.
MIGRATION *s.* migração.
MIGRATORY *adj.* migratório; nômade.
MILD *adj.* brando, meigo; ameno, suave.
MILDEW *s.* mofo, bolor.
MILDLY *adv.* moderadamente.
MILDNESS *s.* suavidade, brandura.
MILE *s.* milha (1.600 metros).
MILEAGE *s.* quilometragem.
MILITANCE *s.* militância.
MILITANT *s.* militante, combativo / *adj.* militante, combativo.
MILITARISM *s.* militarismo.
MILITARISTIC *adj.* militarista; militar.
MILITARY *adj.* militar.
MILITATE *v.* militar, lutar; fazer militância.
MILITIA *s.* milícia.
MILITIAMAN *s.* miliciano.
MILK *s.* leite / *v.* ordenhar, extrair.
MILKING *s.* ordenha.
MILKMAN *s.* leiteiro.
MILKY *adj.* leitoso, lácteo.
MILKY WAY *s.* Via Láctea.
MILL *s.* moinho, engenho, fábrica / *v.* moer, triturar.
MILLENNIUM *s.* milênio.
MILLER *s.* moleiro, dono de moinho.
MILLING *s.* moagem, moedura.
MILLION *s.* milhão / *adj.* milhão.
MILLIONAIRE *s.* milionário.
MILLSTONE *s.* mó, pedra de moinho; carga pesada.
MIME *s.* mímica / *v.* imitar, fazer mímicas.

MIMETIC *adj.* mimético, talento para imitar.
MIMIC *s.* mímico, imitador / *adj.* mímico, imitativo / *v.* imitar.
MIMICRY *s.* mimetismo; imitação.
MINCE *s.* picadinho de carne / *v.* moer, picar.
MIND *s.* mente, intelecto / *v.* concentrar-se, dedicar-se.
MINDFUL *adj.* consciente, diligente.
MINDSET *s.* mentalidade.
MINE *s.* mina / *pron.* meu, minha / *v.* minerar, extrair.
MINEFIELD *s.* campo minado.
MINER *s.* mineiro.
MINIATURE *s.* miniatura / *adj.* miniatura.
MINIM *s.* mínima.
MINISTER *s.* ministro; sacerdote, pastor.
MINISTRY *s.* ministério; clero.
MINOR *adj.* menor, secundário, de pouca importância / *s.* menor (de idade).
MINT *s.* hortelã, menta; casa da moeda.
MINUS *s.* sinal de menos (-) / *adj.* menos, negativo.
MINUTE *s.* minuto.
MINX *s.* rapariga, mulher à toa.
MIRACLE *s.* milagre.
MIRAGE *s.* miragem.
MIRE *s.* lodo, lama / *v.* atolar; envolver-se em dificuldades.
MIRROR *s.* espelho / *v.* espelhar, refletir.
MISADVENTURE *s.* desgraça, infelicidade, infortúnio.
MISAPPLY *v.* empregar mal, desviar.
MISCELLANEOUS *adj.* variado, misto.
MISER *s.* avarento, sovina / *adj.* avarento, sovina.
MISERABLE *adj.* triste, infeliz, desgraçado, miserável.
MISERY *s.* miséria, penúria; tristeza, aflição.
MISFORTUNE *s.* infortúnio, desgraça, infelicidade.
MISGIVING *s.* apreensão; pressentimento.
MISGUIDE *v.* desencaminhar.
MISHANDLE *v.* maltratar, manejar mal.
MISS *s.* falha, erro; saudade; senhorita, moça / *v.* perder, errar; sentir falta.
MISSILE *s.* míssil, projétil.
MISSING *adj.* ausente, extraviado, que falta, desaparecido.
MISSION *s.* missão.
MISSIVE *s.* missiva, carta.

MISTAKE *s.* erro / *v.* errar.
MISTER *s.* senhor.
MISTREAT *v.* maltratar.
MISTRESS *s.* senhora, título dado a mulher casada.
MISTRUST *s.* desconfiança / *v.* desconfiar.
MISTY *adj.* nebuloso.
MISUNDERSTAND *v.* entender mal, interpretar mal.
MISUNDERSTANDING *s.* equívoco, mal-entendido, desavença.
MIX *v.* misturar, mesclar / *s.* mistura, mescla.
MIXED-UP *s.* confusão / *adj.* confuso.
MIXER *s.* batedeira, misturador.
MOBILE *adj.* móvel.
MOBILITY *s.* mobilidade.
MODE *s.* modo, maneira, meio.
MODEL *s.* modelo, maquete / *v.* modelar, moldar.
MODERATE *adj.* moderado, módico / *v.* moderar.
MODERN *adj.* moderno.
MODEST *adj.* modesto.
MOIST *s.* umidade.
MOISTEN *v.* umedecer.
MOLE *s.* verruga, pinta; porto, dique; toupeira / *v.* cavar, escavar.
MOLECULE *s.* molécula.
MOLEST *v.* molestar, importunar; agredir.
MOLTEN *adj.* fundido.
MOMENT *s.* momento, instante.
MONARCH *s.* monarca.
MONDAY *s.* segunda-feira.
MONETARY *adj.* monetário.
MONEY *s.* dinheiro.
MONEYED *adj.* endinheirado, ostentoso.
MONK *s.* monge, frade.
MONKEY *s.* macaco.
MONKEY BUSINESS *s.* macaquice; trapaça.
MONSTER *s.* monstro.
MONTAGE *s.* montagem.
MONTH *s.* mês.
MONUMENT *s.* monumento.
MOOD *s.* humor, disposição.
MOON *s.* lua.
MOONLIGHT *s.* luar / *adj.* iluminado pela lua, enluarado.
MOOT *s.* debate, disputa / *v.* debater.
MOPPET *s.* boneca de pano.

MORAL s. moral.
MORALITY s. moralidade.
MORALIZE v. moralizar.
MORBID adj. doentio, mórbido.
MORE adj. mais / adv. além do mais; ainda.
MOREOVER adv. além disso, além do mais.
MORGUE s. necrotério.
MORNING s. manhã / adj. matinal, da manhã.
MORTAR s. argamassa; morteiro (militar); pilão.
MORTGAGE s. hipoteca / v. hipotecar.
MOSAIC s. mosaico.
MOSLEM adj. muçulmano, islamita.
MOSS s. musgo.
MOST s. maior parte de, maioria de / adv. o(a) mais, muito / adj. mais.
MOTE s. partícula (de pó), molécula.
MOTH s. traça; mariposa.
MOTHER s. mãe; madre, freira.
MOTHERHOOD s. maternidade.
MOTHER-IN-LAW s. sogra.
MOTHERLAND s. pátria.
MOTIVE s. motivo, razão.
MOTLEY adj. variado, multicolor / s. roupa colorida usada pelos bufões.
MOTOR s. motor.
MOULD s. mofo, bolor, fungo; molde, modelo, forma / v. mofar; moldar.
MOULDY adj. mofado, bolorento.
MOUNTAIN s. montanha
MOUNTAIN RANGE s. cordilheira, cadeia de montanhas.
MOUSE s. (pl. mice) camundongo.
MOUSETRAP s. ratoeira.
MOUTH s. boca; foz.
MOUTHFUL s. bocado.
MOVE s. movimento / v. mover.
MOVIE s. filme.
MOVIES s. cinema.
MOVING adj. comovente, tocante.
MOW s. celeiro / v. aparar, cortar, ceifar.
MR abrev. Sr.
MRS abrev. Sra.
MS abrev. Srta.
MUCH adv. muito / s. grande quantidade.
MUCK s. sujeira, porcaria; esterco.

MUCKY adj. imundo, sujo; vil.
MUD s. lama, barro, lodo.
MUDDLE s. confusão, desordem / v. confundir, desorganizar.
MUDDY s. barrento, enlameado / v. enlamear.
MUDGUARD s. para-lama.
MUFF s. pessoa desajeitada.
MUFFLE s. focinho.
MUFFLER s. luva de boxe; amortecedor.
MUG s. caneca; otário (coloquial).
MUGGY adj. abafado.
MULBERRY s. amora; amoreira.
MULCT v. multar / s. multa, penalidade.
MULE s. mula; chinelo de quarto.
MULTIPLE s. múltiplo / adj. múltiplo.
MULTIPLY v. multiplicar.
MUM s. mamãe (coloquial) / adj. silencioso, calado.
MUMBLE s. resmungo / v. resmungar.
MUMMY s. múmia; mamãe (coloquial).
MUMPS s. caxumba.
MUNICIPAL s. municipal.
MURDER s. assassinato, homicídio / v. assassinar, matar.
MURKY adj. escuro, obscuro.
MURMUR s. murmúrio / v. murmurar, sussurrar.
MUSCLE s. músculo.
MUSEUM s. museu.
MUSHROOM s. cogumelo.
MUSIC s. música.
MUST s. obrigação, dever, necessidade / v. dever, ter de, ser obrigado a.
MUSTARD s. mostarda.
MUTE adj. mudo, calado / v. silenciar.
MUTINY s. motim, rebelião / v. amotinar-se, revoltar-se.
MUTUAL s. mútuo, recíproco; comum.
MY pron. meu, minha.
MYSELF pron. me, eu mesmo, mim mesmo, a mim.
MYSTERIOUS adj. misterioso.
MYSTERY s. mistério, enigma, segredo.
MYSTIC s. místico / adj. místico.
MYTH s. mito; fábula.

Nn

N, n *s.* décima quarta letra do alfabeto inglês / *abrev.* Norte.
NAB *v.* surrupiar, furtar.
NAH *interj.* não!
NAIL *s.* unha; prego / *v.* pregar, cravar.
NAILBRUSH *s.* escova de unhas.
NAIVE *adj.* ingênuo.
NAIVETE *s.* ingenuidade, inocência.
NAIVETY *s.* ingenuidade.
NAKED *adj.* nu, exposto, despido.
NAKEDNESS *s.* nudez.
NAME *s.* nome / *v.* nomear, dar nome a.
NAMELESS *adj.* desconhecido; anônimo.
NAMELY *adv.* nomeadamente.
NAMEPLATE *s.* placa de identificação.
NAMESAKE *s.* xará.
NANNY *s.* babá.
NANOSECOND *s.* nanossegundo.
NANOTECHNOLOGY *s.* nanotecnologia.
NAP *s.* soneca, sesta / *v.* cochilar, dormir.
NAPALM *s.* napalm.
NAPE *s.* nuca.
NAPHTHA *s.* nafta.
NAPHTHALENE *s.* naftalina.
NAPKIN *s.* guardanapo.
NAPPY *s.* fralda.
NARCISSISM *s.* narcisismo.
NARCISSIST *s.* narcisista.
NARCISSUS *s.* narciso.
NARCOLEPSY *s.* narcolepsia.
NARCOTIC *s.* narcótico / *adj.* narcótico.
NARRATE *v.* narrar, contar.
NARRATION *s.* narração.
NARRATIVE *s.* narrativa / *adj.* descritivo.
NARRATOR *s.* narrador.
NARROW *adj.* estreito; limitado / *v.* estreitar, apertar; limitar.
NARROWLY *adv.* estritamente.
NARROWNESS *s.* estreiteza.
NASAL *adj.* nasal, nasalado.
NASALISATION *s.* nasalização.
NASALISE *v.* nasalar, nasalizar.
NASALITY *s.* nasalidade.
NASALLY *adv.* nasalmente.
NASCENT *adj.* nascente.
NASTINESS *s.* sordidez, maldade.
NASTILY *adv.* maldosamente.
NASTY *adj.* vil, sórdido, repugnante.

NATAL *adj.* terra natal; local de nascimento.
NATION *s.* nação.
NATIONAL *s.* nacional / *adj.* nacional.
NATIONALISATION *s.* nacionalização.
NATIONALISE *v.* nacionalizar.
NATIONALISM *s.* nacionalismo.
NATIONALIST *s.* nacionalista / *adj.* nacionalista.
NATIONALITY *s.* nacionalidade.
NATIONWIDE *adv.* em todo o país.
NATIVE *s.* nativo / *adj.* natural, nativo.
NATIVITY *s.* natividade.
NATO *abrev.* OTAN (Organização do Tratado do Atlântico Norte).
NATURAL *adj.* natural; nato, inato.
NATURALISATION *s.* naturalização.
NATURALISE *v.* naturalizar.
NATURALISM *s.* naturalismo.
NATURALIST *s.* naturalista.
NATURALISTIC *adj.* naturalístico.
NATURALLY *adv.* naturalmente.
NATURE *s.* natureza, universo; caráter, índole.
NATURISM *s.* naturismo, nudismo.
NATURIST *s.* naturista, nudista.
NAUGHTY *adj.* malcriado; travesso; malicioso.
NAUSEA *s.* náusea; nojo, ânsia.
NAUSEATE *v.* nausear, enjoar.
NAUSEATING *adj.* nauseante, nojento, asqueroso.
NAUSEOUS *adj.* nauseado, enjoado.
NAUTICAL *adj.* náutico.
NAUTICALLY *adv.* nauticamente.
NAUTICAL MILE *s.* milha náutica.
NAVAL *adj.* naval.
NAVAL ACADEMY *s.* Academia Naval.
NAVAL COLLEGE *s.* colégio naval.
NAVAL SCHOOL *s.* escola da marinha.
NAVEL *s.* umbigo.
NAVIGABLE *adj.* navegável.
NAVIGATE *v.* navegar; abrir caminho.
NAVIGATION *s.* navegação.
NAVIGATIONAL *adj.* náutico, marítimo.
NAVIGATOR *s.* navegador.
NAVY *s.* marinha; frota / *adj.* azul-marinho.
NAYSAYER *s.* contraditor; pessoa do contra.
NAZI *s.* nazista.
NAZIFY *v.* transformar em nazi.
NAZISM *s.* nazismo.

NBA *abrev.* de National Basketball Association.
NEANDERTHAL *s.* neandertal / *adj.* neandertal.
NEAR *adj.* próximo; vizinho / *adv.* perto, a pouca distância / *prep.* junto a.
NEARBY *adj.* próximo / *adv.* perto.
NEARLY *adv.* quase.
NEARNESS *s.* proximidade.
NEARSIGHTED *adj.* míope.
NEAT *adj.* arrumado, organizado.
NEATLY *adv.* organizadamente.
NEATNESS *s.* asseio, limpeza, esmero.
NEBULA *s.* nebulosa.
NEBULOUS *adj.* nebuloso, nublado.
NECESSARILY *adv.* necessariamente.
NECESSARY *adj.* necessário, essencial.
NECESSITATE *v.* necessitar, precisar.
NECESSITY *s.* necessidade; pobreza.
NECK *s.* pescoço; gola (roupa).
NECKING *s.* amassos, apertão.
NECKLACE *s.* colar.
NECKLINE *s.* decote.
NECKTIE *s.* gravata.
NECROMANCER *s.* necromante.
NECROPOLIS *s.* necrópole; cemitério.
NECROSIS *s.* necrose.
NECROTIC *adj.* necrótico.
NECTAR *s.* néctar.
NECTARINE *s.* nectarina.
NEED *s.* necessidade, precisão / *v.* precisar, necessitar.
NEEDFUL *adj.* necessário, indispensável.
NEEDINESS *s.* pobreza, carência.
NEEDLE *s.* agulha, alfinete / *v.* alfinetar.
NEEDLEPOINT *s.* ponto cheio.
NEEDLESS *adj.* desnecessário.
NEEDLESSLY *adv.* desnecessariamente.
NEEDLEWORK *s.* bordado.
NEEDY *adj.* necessitado, carente.
NEFARIOUS *adj.* abominável, nefário.
NEGATE *v.* negar.
NEGATION *s.* negação.
NEGATIVE *s.* negativo / *adj.* negativo.
NEGATIVE ANSWER *s.* resposta negativa.
NEGATIVE ATTITUDE *s.* atitude negativa.
NEGATIVE POLE *s.* polo negativo (pilha).
NEGATIVE SIGN *s.* mau agouro; sinal negativo.

NEGATIVELY *adv.* negativamente.
NEGATIVENESS *s.* negatividade.
NEGATIVISM *s.* negativismo.
NEGATIVIST *s.* negativista.
NEGATIVITY *s.* negatividade.
NEGATOR *s.* que nega; negador.
NEGLECT *s.* negligência, desleixo / *v.* negligenciar.
NEGLECTED *adj.* abandonado, negligenciado.
NEGLECTFUL *adj.* negligente.
NEGLIGENCE *s.* negligência, descuido.
NEGLIGENT *adj.* negligente.
NEGLIGIBLE *adj.* insignificante.
NEGOTIABLE *adj.* negociável.
NEGOTIATE *v.* negociar.
NEGOTIATED *adj.* negociado, combinado.
NEGOTIATING *s.* negociação.
NEGOTIATION *s.* negociação.
NEGOTIATOR *s.* negociador.
NEGRITUDE *s.* negritude.
NEIGH *v.* rinchar, relinchar / *s.* rincho, relincho.
NEIGHBOUR *s.* vizinho.
NEIGHBOURHOOD *s.* vizinhança.
NEITHER *pron.* nenhum / *conj.* nem / *adv.* tampouco.
NEMESIS *s.* nêmesis, ruína, castigo.
NEO *adj.* neo, novo.
NEOCLASSICAL *adj.* neoclássico.
NEOCLASSICISM *s.* neoclassicismo.
NEOCOLONIAL *adj.* neocolonial; neocolono.
NEOCOLONIALISM *s.* neocolonialismo.
NEOCOLONIALIST *s.* neocolonialista.
NEOCONSERVATISM *s.* neoconservadorismo.
NEOCONSERVATIVE *s.* neoconservador / *adj.* cauteloso, moderado.
NEO-LIBERAL *s.* neoliberal.
NEO-LIBERALISM *s.* neoliberalismo.
NEOLITHIC *adj.* neolítico.
NEOLOGISE *v.* neologizar, neologismar.
NEOLOGISM *s.* neologismo.
NEOLOGIST *s.* neologista.
NEON *s.* néon / *adj.* de néon.
NEONATAL *adj.* neonatal.
NEONATE *s.* neonato, recém-nascido.
NEONATOLOGY *s.* neonatologia.
NEOPHYTE *s.* neófito, noviço.
NEOPLASM *s.* neoplasma.
NEOPLASTIC *adj.* neoplástico.
NEOPRENE *s.* neoprene; borracha sintética.
NEPAL *s.* Nepal.
NEPHEW *s.* sobrinho.
NEPHRITIS *s.* nefrite.
NEPOTISM *s.* nepotismo.
NEPTUNE *s.* Netuno.
NERD *s.* nerd; esquisito, antissocial.
NERVE *s.* nervo; ousadia.
NERVOUS *adj.* nervoso.
NERVOUSLY *adv.* ansiosamente.
NEST *s.* ninho / *v.* aninhar, criar ninho.
NESTED *adj.* encaixado, aninhado.
NESTING *s.* aninhamento, aninhador.
NESTLE *v.* aninhar-se, acomodar-se.
NET *s.* rede; armadilha / *adj.* líquido / *v.* obter lucro líquido; apanhar.
NETBALL *s.* netball (esporte).
NETHER *adj.* inferior, mais baixo.
NETHERLANDS *s.* Países Baixos.
NETIQUETTE *s.* netiqueta (etiqueta na internet).
NETSPEAK *s.* internetês.
NETTING *s.* tela, tecido de rede.
NETTLE *v.* exasperar / *s.* urtiga.
NETWORK *s.* rede, cadeia.
NETWORKED *adj.* computadores interligados.
NETWORKING *s.* rede de comunicação.
NEURAL *adj.* neural, nerval; nervoso.
NEURALGIA *s.* neuralgia, nevralgia.
NEURITIS *s.* neurite.
NEUROLOGICAL *adj.* neurológico.
NEUROLOGIST *s.* neurologista.
NEUROLOGY *s.* neurologia.
NEURON *s.* neurônio.
NEURONAL *adj.* neuronal.
NEUROSIS *s.* neurose.
NEUROSURGEON *s.* neurocirurgião.
NEUROSURGERY *s.* neurocirurgia.
NEUROTIC *s.* neurótico / *adj.* neurótico.
NEUROTRANSMITTER *s.* neurotransmissor.
NEUTER *v.* capar / *adj.* gênero neutro.
NEUTRAL *adj.* neutro; imparcial.
NEUTRAL GROUND *s.* área neutra.
NEUTRALISATION *s.* neutralização.
NEUTRALISE *v.* neutralizar.
NEUTRALISER *s.* neutralizador.
NEUTRALITY *s.* neutralidade, imparcialidade.

NEUTRAL TERRITORY s. território neutro.
NEUTRAL ZONE s. zona neutra.
NEUTRINO s. neutrino.
NEUTRON s. nêutron.
NEUTRON BOMB s. bomba de nêutron.
NEVER adv. nunca, jamais.
NEVER-ENDING adj. interminável, infinito; sem fim.
NEVERLAND s. Terra do Nunca.
NEVER MIND interj. deixa para lá! esquece!
NEVERMORE adv. nunca mais.
NEVER SO adv. nunca antes.
NEVERTHELESS adv. no entanto; contudo.
NEVUS s. sinal, marca de nascença.
NEW adj. novo; recente; outro.
NEWBIE s. novato, iniciante.
NEWBORN s. recém-nascido.
NEWCOMER s. recém-chegado.
NEW EDITION s. nova edição.
NEWFOUND adj. recém-descoberto.
NEW GENERATION s. nova geração.
NEWLY adv. recentemente; recém.
NEWLYWED adj. recém-casados.
NEWS s. notícia, novidade; informação.
NEWSAGENT s. jornaleiro.
NEWSCAST s. noticiário; telejornal.
NEWSFLASH s. plantão de notícias.
NEWSLETTER s. informativo.
NEWSMAN s. repórter.
NEWSPAPER s. jornal.
NEWSROOM s. sala de redação.
NEWSSTAND s. banca de jornal.
NEWSWORTHY adj. notável.
NEW-YEAR s. Ano-Novo; Réveillon.
NEWT s. salamandra.
NEXT s. próximo; seguinte / adj. próximo, ao lado de, a seguir.
NEXUS s. conexão, ligação.
NGO abrev. de Non-Governmental Organisation; ONG.
NIBBLE v. beliscar, mordiscar.
NIBBLER s. roedor.
NICE adj. simpático, agradável, bonito.
NICELY adv. gentilmente.
NICETY s. delicadeza; cortesia.
NICHE s. nicho; lugar.
NICK s. pequeno corte, entalhe; prisão / v. cortar, entalhar.
NICKLE v. niquelar / s. níquel; moeda de cinco centavos.

NICKNAME s. apelido, alcunha / v. apelidar.
NICOTINE s. nicotina.
NICOTINE ADDICTION s. tabagismo.
NIECE s. sobrinha.
NIFTY adj. elegante, atraente.
NIGGLE v. reclamar, implicar / s. implicância.
NIGGLING adj. reclamão.
NIGHT s. noite.
NIGHTCAP s. touca antes de dormir.
NIGHTCLUB s. clube noturno; balada.
NIGHTCLUBBING s. vida noturna / adj. baladeiro.
NIGHTDRESS s. camisola.
NIGHTFALL s. anoitecer; crepúsculo.
NIGHTGOWN s. robe.
NIGHTINGALE s. rouxinol.
NIGHTLIFE s. vida noturna.
NIGHTLIGHT s. lâmpada noturna.
NIGHTLY adv. durante a noite; toda noite / adj. noturno.
NIGHTMARE s. pesadelo.
NIGHTMARISH adj. atemorizante, aterrorizador.
NIGHTSHADE s. beladona.
NIGHTSPOT s. balada, boate.
NIGHTSTAND s. criado-mudo; cabeceira.
NIGHTTIME s. noite / adj. noturno.
NIGHT-WALKER s. sonâmbulo.
NIGHTWEAR s. roupa de dormir.
NIHILISM s. niilismo.
NIHILIST s. niilista.
NIHILISTIC adj. niilista.
NIL s. nada; inexistência; zero.
NILE s. Nilo (rio).
NIMBLE adj. ágil, ligeiro, esperto.
NIMBLY adv. agilmente.
NIMBUS s. nimbo, halo.
NIMROD s. bobo, bocó.
NINE num. nove.
NINETEEN num. dezenove.
NINETEENTH num. décimo nono.
NINETIES s. anos 90; década de 90.
NINETIETH num. nonagésimo.
NINETY num. noventa.
NINJA s. ninja.
NINTH num. nono.
NIP v. dar um gole; dar uma mordida / s. gole.
NIPPER s. garra; pinça; alicate; aquele que belisca.

NIPPLE s. mamilo; bico de mamadeira.
NIPPON s. Japão.
NIPPY adj. cortante, penetrante.
NIRVANA s. nirvana.
NITRATE s. nitrato.
NITRIFICATION s. nitrificação.
NITRITE s. nitrito.
NITROCELLULOSE s. nitrocelulose.
NITROGEN s. nitrogênio.
NITROGEN OXIDE s. óxido de nitrogênio.
NITROGLYCERINE s. nitroglicerina.
NIX v. vetar, proibir / s. nada.
NO adv. não, nenhum / adj. nenhum / s. não, recusa / pron. nenhum, nenhuma.
NOB s. grã-fino.
NOBILITY s. nobreza.
NOBLE adj. nobre, honroso.
NOBLE BIRTH s. berço de ouro.
NOBLE GAS s. gás nobre.
NOBLEMAN s. nobre; aristocrático.
NOBLY adv. nobremente.
NOBODY pron. ninguém.
NOCTURNAL adj. noturno.
NOCTURNE s. noturno.
NOD v. acenar / s. aceno, sinal.
NODAL adj. nodal.
NODE s. nodo.
NODULAR adj. nodular.
NODULE s. nódulo.
NOEL s. natal.
NOHOW adv. de modo algum.
NOISE s. ruído, barulho.
NOISELESS adj. silencioso, calado.
NOISEMAKER s. chocalho, matraca.
NOISILY adv. ruidosamente.
NOISY adj. barulhento, ruidoso.
NOMAD s. nômade.
NOMADIC adj. nômade.
NOMADISM s. nomadismo.
NOMENCLATURE s. nomenclatura.
NOMINAL adj. nominal.
NOMINATE v. nomear; designar.
NOMINATION s. nomeação; indicação.
NOMINATIVE adj. nominativo.
NOMINATOR s. nomeador, nomeante; indicador.
NOMINEE s. nomeado; candidato.
NONALCOHOLIC adj. sem álcool.
NONBELIEVER s. incrédulo, descrente.
NONCHALANT adj. calmo, sereno.
NONCOMMITTAL adj. hesitante, evasivo.
NONCOMPLIANCE s. descumprimento; inadimplência.
NONCONFORMING adj. inconformista.
NONCONFORMIST s. rebelde, dissidente.
NONCONFORMITY s. inconformismo.
NONCOOPERATION s. falta de cooperação.
NONCUSTODIAL adj. não tutelar.
NONDESCRIPT adj. desinteressante.
NONDESTRUCTIVE adj. indestrutível.
NONDISCLOSURE s. sigilo.
NONDISCRIMINATION s. indiscriminação.
NONDISCRIMINATORY adj. indiscriminatório.
NONE adv. de modo algum / pron. ninguém, nenhum, nada / adj. nenhum.
NONENTITY s. insignificância.
NONESSENTIAL adj. desnecessário.
NONESUCH adj. inigualável, ímpar.
NONETHELESS adv. todavia, contudo.
NONEXCLUSIVE adj. inclusivo.
NONEXEMPT adj. sem isenção.
NONEXISTENT adj. inexistente.
NONFAT adj. sem gordura.
NONFATAL adj. não fatal.
NONFICTION s. não ficção / adj. não ficcional.
NONGOVERNMENTAL adj. não governamental.
NONLINEAR adj. não linear.
NONNATIVE adj. estrangeiro; não nativo.
NONPARTISAN adj. não partidário.
NONPAYMENT s. dívida, falta de pagamento.
NONPRESCRIPTION s. sem receita.
NONPROFIT adj. beneficente; sem fins lucrativos.
NONPROLIFERATION s. não proliferação.
NONPUBLIC adj. particular, privado.
NONRECURRING adj. não recorrente.
NONREFUNDABLE adj. não reembolsável.
NONRESIDENTIAL adj. não residencial.
NONSENSE s. absurdo, besteira.
NONSENSICAL adj. ridículo, tolo.
NONSMOKER s. não fumante.
NONSMOKING adj. não fumante.
NONSPECIFIC adj. inespecífico.
NONSTANDARD adj. não padronizado.
NONSTARTER s. inviável.

NONSTICK *adj.* antiaderente.
NONSTOP *adj.* contínuo, direto, sem parada / *adv.* continuamente.
NONSTRUCTURAL *adj.* não estrutural.
NONSIRURGICAL *adj.* não cirúrgico.
NONTOXIC *adj.* atóxico; sem veneno.
NONTRADITIONAL *adj.* não tradicional.
NONUNIFORM *adj.* desigual.
NONVERBAL *adj.* não verbal.
NONVERBAL COMMUNICATION *s.* comunicação não verbal.
NONVIOLENT *adj.* pacífico, não violento.
NOODLE *v.* improvisar / *s.* bobo, inocente; macarrão.
NOOK *s.* recanto, refúgio.
NOON *s.* meio-dia.
NOONDAY *s. m.q.* noon.
NOOSE *s.* forca; nó, laço.
NOPE *adv.* não.
NOR *conj.* nem, tampouco / *adv.* nem, também não.
NORDIC *adj.* nórdico, escandinavo.
NORM *s.* norma, regra, padrão.
NORMAL *s.* normal; padrão / *adj.* normal.
NORMALCY *s. m.q.* normality.
NORMALITY *s.* normalidade.
NORMALISATION *s.* normalização.
NORMALISE *v.* normalizar.
NORMALLY *adv.* normalmente.
NORMADY *s.* Normandia (Europa).
NORMATIVE *adj.* normativo.
NORSE *s.* nórdico / *adj.* nórdico.
NORTH *s.* norte / *adj.* do norte.
NORTHBOUND *adv.* para o norte.
NORTHEAST *adj.* nordestino / *adv.* ao nordeste / *s.* nordeste.
NORTHEASTERN *adj.* nordestino; do nordeste.
NORTHERN *adj.* nortista; do norte.
NORTHERNER *s.* nortista.
NORTHERN HEMISPHERE *s.* Hemisfério Norte.
NORTHERN LIGHTS *s.* aurora boreal.
NORTHWARD *adv.* para o norte.
NORTHWEST *s.* noroeste.
NORTHWESTERN *adj.* do noroeste.
NORWAY *s.* Noruega.
NORWEGIAN *s.* norueguês / *adj.* norueguês.
NOSE *s.* nariz; focinho; faro.
NOSEBLEED *s.* sangramento nasal.

NOSEDIVE *v.* mergulhar; despencar / *s.* mergulho; queda.
NOSTALGIA *s.* nostalgia.
NOSTALGIC *adj.* nostálgico.
NOSTRIL *s.* narina.
NOSTRUM *s.* panaceia.
NOSY *adj.* intrometido, abelhudo.
NOT *adv.* não.
NOTABLE *adj.* notável / *s.* celebridade, pessoa notável.
NOTABLY *adv.* notavelmente.
NOTARIAL *adj.* notarial.
NOTARISE *v.* autenticar, validar.
NOTARY *s.* tabelião, notário; escrivão.
NOTATE *v.* anotar.
NOTATION *s.* notação.
NOTCH *v.* entalhar, chanfrar / *s.* entalhe, encaixe.
NOTE *s.* nota (bilhete, música, dinheiro); tom / *v.* notar, observar.
NOTEBOOK *s.* caderno; computador portátil.
NOTED *adj.* notório, célebre.
NOTEPAD *s.* bloco de anotações.
NOTEPAPER *s.* papel de rascunho.
NOTEWORTHY *adj.* digno de nota.
NOTHING *s.* nada, ninharia, nulidade / *adv.* em vão, nada.
NOTHINGNESS *s.* nada; insignificância.
NOTICE *s.* anúncio, notificação, aviso / *v.* notar, perceber; avisar, notificar.
NOTICEABLE *adj.* evidente, notável.
NOTICEABLY *adv.* notavelmente, visivelmente.
NOTICEBOARD *s.* quadro de aviso.
NOTIFIABLE *adj.* notificável.
NOTIFICATION *s.* notificação.
NOTIFIER *s.* informante.
NOTIFY *v.* notificar; avisar, alertar.
NOTION *s.* noção; ideia.
NOTIONAL *adj.* nocional; teórico, hipotético.
NOTORIETY *s.* notoriedade, renome, fama.
NOTORIOUS *adj.* notório; renomado.
NOTORIOUSLY *adv.* notoriamente.
NOTWITHSTANDING *adv.* não obstante; no entanto.
NOUGHT *s.* nada, zero.
NOUN *s.* substantivo.
NOURISH *v.* nutrir, alimentar; acalentar.
NOURISHING *adj.* nutritivo.

NOURISHMENT s. alimento, sustento; nutrição.
NOUS s. intelecto, inteligência.
NOVEL s. romance, novela.
NOVELIST s. escritor, romancista.
NOVELLA s. conto.
NOVELTY s. novidade, inovação.
NOVEMBER s. novembro.
NOVENA s. novena.
NOVICE s. novato, noviço / *adj.* novato.
NOW *adv.* agora, já, presentemente / *conj.* assim sendo.
NOWADAYS *adv.* hoje em dia, atualmente.
NOWAY *adv.* de modo algum.
NOWHERE *adv.* lugar nenhum.
NOW OR NEVER *interj.* agora ou nunca!
NOXIOUS *adj.* nocivo.
NOXIOUSLY *adv.* nocivamente.
NOXIOUS WEED s. erva daninha.
NOZZLE s. bocal.
NTH *adj.* enésimo; inespecífico.
NU s. ni, letra N do alfabeto grego.
NUANCE s. nuance.
NUB s. nó.
NUBILE *adj.* núbil, atraente.
NUCLEAR *adj.* nuclear.
NUCLEAR BOMB s. bomba nuclear.
NUCLEAR ENERGY s. energia nuclear.
NUCLEUS s. núcleo.
NUDE *adj.* nu artístico.
NUDISM s. nudismo.
NUDIST s. nudista / *adj.* nudista.
NUDITY s. nudez.
NUGGET s. pepita.
NUISANCE s. chateação; incômodo.
NULL *adj.* nulo.
NULLIFICATION s. cancelamento.
NULLIFY *v.* anular, cancelar.
NUMB *v.* entorpecer / *adj.* dormente, paralisado;

NUMBER s. número; algarismo / *v.* numerar.
NUMBERING s. numeração / *adj.* enumerador.
NUMERAL s. numeral.
NUMERATE *v.* computar, calcular.
NUMERIC *adj.* numérico.
NUMEROLOGY s. numerologia.
NUMEROUS *adj.* numeroso, abundante.
NUN s. freira.
NUNNERY s. convento.
NUPTIAL *adj.* nupcial.
NURSE s. enfermeiro / *v.* cuidar de.
NURSEMAID s. babá; ama de leite.
NURSERY s. berçário, creche, escola maternal.
NURSING s. enfermagem; cuidado.
NUT s. noz; porca (de parafuso); maluco, doido.
NUTCRACKER s. quebra-nozes.
NUTMEG s. noz-moscada.
NUTRIENT s. nutriente / *adj.* nutritivo, nutriente.
NUTRITION s. nutrição.
NUTRITIONAL *adj.* nutricional.
NUTRITIONIST s. nutricionista.
NUTRITIVE *adj.* nutritivo.
NUTS s. maluco, doido.
NUTSHELL s. casca.
NUTTY *adj.* de nozes.
NUZZLE *v.* fuçar, xeretar.
NY *abrev.* de New York; Nova Iorque.
NYLON s. náilon / *adj.* de náilon.
NYMPH s. ninfa.
NYMPHET s. ninfeta.
NYMPHOMANIA s. ninfomania.
NYMPHOMANIAC *adj.* ninfomaníaca.
NYP *abrev.* de Not Yet Published; no prelo.
NYSTAGMUS s. nistagmo.
NZ *abrev.* de New Zealand; Nova Zelândia.

Oo

O, o s. décima quinta letra do alfabeto inglês.
OAF s. tolo, parvo.
OAK s. carvalho.
OAR s. remo / v. remar.
OARSMAN s. remador.
OASIS s. oásis.
OAT s. aveia / adj. de aveia.
OATH s. juramento, promessa; praga, blasfêmia.
OATMEAL s. farinha ou mingau de aveia.
OATMEAL COOKIE s. biscoito de aveia.
OBDURATE adj. obstinado; teimoso.
OBEDIENCE s. obediência.
OBEDIENT adj. obediente.
OBEDIENTLY adv. obedientemente.
OBEISANCE s. reverência.
OBELISK s. obelisco.
OBESE adj. obeso.
OBESITY s. obesidade.
OBEY v. obedecer.
OBFUSCATE v. obscurecer.
OBFUSCATION s. ofuscação.
OBITUARY s. obituário.
OBJECT s. objeto (gramática), objetivo; objeção / v. objetar, ser contra.
OBJECTIFICATION s. objetivação; coisificação.
OBJECTIFY v. objetivar, materializar.
OBJECTION s. objeção.
OBJECTIONABLE adj. censurável; objetável.
OBJECTIVE s. objetivo / adj. objetivo.
OBJECTIVELY adv. objetivamente.
OBJECTIVITY s. objetividade; imparcialidade.
OBLIGATE v. obrigar, forçar, compelir.
OBLIGATION s. obrigação, compromisso.
OBLIGATORY adj. obrigatório.
OBLIQUE adj. oblíquo (gramática), evasivo; inclinado.
OBLITERATE v. obliterar, destruir, suprimir.
OBSCENE adj. obsceno.
OBSCENITY s. obscenidade, indecência.
OBSCURE adj. obscuro / v. obscurecer.
OBSCURITY s. obscuridade.
OBSERVABLE adj. observável.
OBSERVANT adj. observador.
OBSERVATION s. observação.

OBSERVATORY s. observatório.
OBSERVE v. observar, notar, reparar.
OBSERVER s. observador.
OBSESS v. obcecar-se; atormentar.
OBSESSION s. obsessão.
OBSESSIVE adj. obsessivo.
OBSOLETE adj. obsoleto.
OBSTACLE s. obstáculo, empecilho.
OBSTETRIC adj. obstétrico.
OBSTETRICIAN s. obstetra.
OBSTINATE adj. teimoso, obstinado.
OBSTINATELY adv. obstinadamente.
OBSTRUCT v. obstruir, impedir; bloquear.
OBSTRUCTION s. obstrução, impedimento.
OBSTRUCTIVE adj. obstrutivo.
OBTAIN v. obter, conseguir, adquirir.
OBTAINABLE adj. adquirível, atingível.
OBTRUSIVE adj. indiscreto, inoportuno.
OBTUSE adj. obtuso, tolo.
OBVIATE v. tornar óbvio; obviar.
OBVIOUS adj. óbvio, evidente.
OBVIOUSLY adv. obviamente, evidentemente.
OCCASION s. ocasião.
OCCASIONAL adj. ocasional.
OCCASIONALLY adv. ocasionalmente.
OCCIDENTAL adj. ocidental.
OCCLUSION s. oclusão.
OCCLUSIVE adj. oclusivo / s. consoante oclusiva (gramática).
OCCULT adj. oculto, secreto / v. ocultar, esconder.
OCCULTISM s. ocultismo.
OCCUPANCY s. posse, ocupação.
OCCUPANT s. ocupante; inquilino, residente.
OCCUPATION s. ocupação, profissão.
OCCUPATIONAL adj. ocupacional.
OCCUPY v. ocupar; residir, habitar.
OCCUR v. ocorrer, acontecer.
OCCURRENCE s. ocorrência; caso.
OCEAN s. oceano; vastidão (figurativo).
OCEANFRONT s. beira-mar / adj. costeiro, litoral.
OCEANIC adj. oceânico.
OCH interj. oh, ah!
OCTOGONAL adj. octogonal, formado por oito ângulos e oito lados.
OCTAVE s. oitava (escala musical).
OCTOBER s. outubro.
OCTOPUS s. polvo.

ODD adj. estranho, esquisito; ocasional; ímpar (número).
ODDNESS s. extravagância, esquisitice.
ODDITY s. peculiaridade, extravagância.
ODDLY adv. estranhamente.
ODE s. ode, poema.
ODIOUS adj. odioso.
ODOUR s. fedor; cheiro, fragrância.
ODOURLESS adj. inodoro, sem cheiro.
ODYSSEY s. odisseia (poema épico); longa viagem.
OF prep. de.
OFF adj. desligado, apagado, livre / adv. embora / prep. fora, fora de, distante.
OFFENCE s. ofensa, insulto, afronta; delito, crime.
OFFEND v. ofender, irritar; cometer delito, crime.
OFFENDER s. ofensor, infrator, criminoso.
OFFENDING adj. ofensivo.
OFFENSIVE adj. ofensivo, agressivo, insultante / s. ofensiva, ataque.
OFFER s. oferta, oferecimento / v. ofertar, oferecer.
OFFERING s. oferecimento, oferenda.
OFFICE s. escritório; agência, posto.
OFFICEHOLDER s. funcionário público.
OFFICER s. oficial, policial (militar); funcionário.
OFFICIAL adj. autorizado, oficial / s. funcionário público.
OFFICIAL LANGUAGE s. idioma, língua oficial.
OFFICIALLY adv. oficialmente, formalmente.
OFFICIAL SPOKESMAN s. porta-voz oficial.
OFFICIATE v. oficializar, formalizar.
OFFSET s. compensação, equivalência / v. compensar, equiparar.
OFFSIDE s. impedimento / adj. impedido (futebol).
OFFSPRING s. filho prole; filhotinho (animal).
OFFSTAGE s. bastidor / adv. nos bastidores.
OFTEN adv. frequentemente, geralmente.
OGRE s. ogro; mal-educado, grosso.
OH interj. oh!
OIL s. óleo; petróleo / v. lubrificar.
OILFIELD s. campo petrolífero.
OILY adj. oleoso, gorduroso; bajulador.

OINK v. grunhir / s. grunhido (de porco).
OINTMENT s. pomada.
O.K. adj. certo, correto / adv. bem / interj. tudo certo!
OKAY adj. m.q. o.k.
OKRA s. quiabo.
OLD adj. velho, antigo, idoso.
OLD AGE s. velhice.
OLDER adj. mais velho, idoso; veterano.
OLD-FASHIONED adj. antiquado, fora de moda.
OLE interj. olé!
OLFACTORY adj. olfativo, olfatório, sentido do olfato.
OLIGARCH s. oligarca.
OLIGARCHY s. oligarquia.
OLIVE s. azeitona; oliveira.
OLYMPIC adj. olímpico / s. olimpíadas.
OLYMPIC GAMES s. olimpíadas, jogos olímpicos.
OMELET s. omelete.
OMEN s. presságio, agouro.
OMISSION s. omissão.
OMIT v. omitir; deixar de fora.
OMNIPOTENCE s. onipotência.
OMNIPOTENT adj. onipotente; todo-poderoso.
OMNIPRESENT adj. onipresente.
OMNISCIENCE s. onisciência.
OMNISCIENT adj. onisciente.
OMNIVORE s. onívoro.
ON prep. sobre, em cima de; no, na, nos, nas / adv. sobre, em cima de; a partir de / adj. ligado, funcionando.
ONCE conj. uma vez que, desde que / adv. outrora, uma vez.
ONCE AGAIN adv. mais uma vez.
ONCOLOGIST s. oncologista.
ONCOLOGY s. oncologia, estudo dos tumores.
ONCOMING adj. aproximado, perto.
ONE num. um / adj. único, um todo / pron. alguém.
ONEROUS adj. oneroso, pesado, apreensivo, árduo.
ONESELF pron. mesmo, si próprio.
ONGOING adj. em andamento.
ONION s. cebola.
ONLOOKER s. espectador, assistente; curioso.
ONLY adv. somente, apenas / adj. único, só / conj. só que, exceto.
ONOMATOPEIA s. onomatopeia.
ONSET s. ataque, assalto; início, começo.
ONSHORE adj. litoral / adv. próximo ao litoral.
ONSIDE adv. em posição legal (futebol).
ONSLAUGHT s. ataque violento; investida.
ONSTAGE adj. no palco / adv. no palco.
ONTO prep. em, sobre, a.
ONUS s. ônus; responsabilidade, carga, peso.
ONYX s. ônix / adj. de ônix.
OOPS interj. opa! epa!
OPACITY s. opacidade.
OPAL s. opala.
OPAQUE adj. opaco.
OPEN adj. aberto; livre, desimpedido / v. abrir.
OPENER s. abridor; saca-rolhas.
OPENING s. abertura; início; estreia; inauguração.
OPENLY adv. abertamente.
OPENNESS s. franqueza; abertura.
OPERA s. ópera.
OPERABLE adj. operável.
OPERATE v. fazer funcionar, operar.
OPERATING adj. operante; em andamento.
OPERATION s. operação, funcionamento.
OPERATIONAL adj. operacional.
OPERATOR s. operador; telefonista.
OPHTHALMOLOGIST s. oftalmologista.
OPHTHALMOLOGY s. oftalmologia.
OPINE v. opinar; manifestar opinião.
OPINION s. opinião, parecer.
OPPONENT s. oponente, rival, adversário.
OPPORTUNE adj. oportuno, conveniente.
OPPORTUNITY s. oportunidade.
OPPORTUNISM s. oportunismo.
OPPORTUNIST s. oportunista.
OPPORTUNITY s. oportunidade.
OPPOSE v. opor-se, resistir, discordar.
OPPOSING adj. oponente, inimigo; oposto.
OPPOSING PARTY s. oposição (política).
OPPOSITE adj. oposto, contrário / s. oposto, oponente / adv. defronte a, em frente a.
OPPOSITION s. oposição, rivalidade.

OPPRESS v. oprimir, tiranizar; sobrecarregar.
OPPRESSION s. opressão.
OPPRESSIVE adj. opressor; opressivo.
OPPRESSOR s. tirano, opressor.
OPT v. optar, escolher.
OPTIC adj. óptico.
OPTIC NERVE s. nervo óptico.
OPTICAL adj. óptico.
OPTICAL ILLUSION s. ilusão de óptica.
OPTICIAN s. oculista.
OPTIMAL adj. ótimo.
OPTIMISATION s. otimização.
OPTIMISE v. otimizar.
OPTIMISM s. otimismo.
OPTIMIST s. otimista.
OPTIMISTIC adj. otimista.
OPTION s. opção, alternativa; adicional.
OPTIONAL adj. opcional.
OPTIONALLY adv. opcionalmente.
OPULENCE s. opulência, abundância.
OPULENT adj. opulento, farto, abundante.
OPUS s. (pl. opera) obra; composição (musical ou literária).
OR conj. ou, senão.
ORACLE s. oráculo.
ORAL adj. oral.
ORALLY adv. oralmente.
ORANGE s. laranja / adj. alaranjado.
ORANGEADE s. laranjada; suco de laranja.
ORANGUTAN s. orangotango.
ORATION s. oração, oratória; discurso.
ORATOR s. orador.
ORATORIO s. oratório (religião).
ORATORY s. oratória, eloquência.
ORBIT v. orbitar / s. órbita / adj. órbita.
ORBITAL adj. orbital.
ORC s. orca (baleia).
ORCHARD s. pomar.
ORCHESTRA s. orquestra.
ORCHESTRAL adj. orquestral.
ORCHESTRATE v. orquestrar.
ORCHESTRATION s. orquestração.
ORCHID s. orquídea.
ORDAIN v. ordenar, mandar.
ORDER s. ordem, comando; pedido / v. encomendar, pedir, ordenar.
ORDERED adj. ordenado, em ordem; pedido, solicitado.

ORDERLY adj. organizado, arrumado / s. atendente.
ORDINAL adj. ordinal (número).
ORDINANCE s. ordenação, regulamentação.
ORDINARY s. ordinário, comum / adj. ordinário, comum.
ORDINATE v. ordenar, dar ordens / s. ordenado / adj. ordenado.
ORDINATION s. ordenação.
OREGANO s. orégano.
ORGAN s. órgão.
ORGANIC adj. orgânico.
ORGANISM s. organismo.
ORGANIST s. organista (músico).
ORGANISATION s. organização.
ORGANISATIONAL adj. organizacional; empresarial.
ORGANISE v. organizar.
ORGANISER s. organizador; agenda (coloquial).
ORGASM s. orgasmo; clímax.
ORGASMIC adj. orgástico; prazeroso.
ORGY s. orgia.
ORIENT s. Oriente / v. orientar(-se).
ORIENTAL adj. oriental, do oriente.
ORIENTATION s. orientação.
ORIFICE s. orifício.
ORIGAMI s. origami (arte).
ORIGIN s. origem.
ORIGINAL adj. original, único / s. original, único.
ORIGINALITY s. originalidade; inventividade.
ORIGINALLY adv. originalmente.
ORIGINATE v. originar, causar.
ORIGINATION s. criação, geração.
ORIGINATOR s. inventor, criador.
ORNAMENT v. ornamentar, ornar / s. ornamento, decoração.
ORNAMENTAL adj. ornamental, decorativo.
ORNAMENTATION s. ornamentação.
ORNATE adj. ornamentado, embelezado.
ORPHAN s. órfão / adj. órfão / v. ficar órfão.
ORPHANAGE s. orfanato.
ORTHODOX adj. ortodoxo.
ORTHODOXY s. ortodoxia, conformidade com uma doutrina.
ORTHOGRAPHIC adj. ortográfico.
ORTHOGRAPHY s. ortografia.

ORTHOPAEDIC adj. ortopédico.
ORTHOPAEDIST s. ortopedista.
OSCILLATE v. oscilar, balançar; vibrar, vacilar.
OSCILLATION s. oscilação.
OSCILLATOR s. oscilador.
OSCILLATORY adj. oscilante; oscilatório.
OSSIFY v. ossificar.
OSTENSIBLE adj. ostensivo.
OSTENSIBLY adv. ostensivamente.
OSTENTATION s. ostentação.
OSTENTATIOUS adj. ostentoso.
OSTEOPOROSIS s. osteoporose.
OSTRACISM s. ostracismo; esquecimento.
OSTRACISE v. condenar; banir, excluir.
OSTRICH s. avestruz.
OTHER pron. outro(s) / adj. outro, diferente.
OTHERWISE adv. de outra maneira, por outro lado / conj. senão; do contrário.
OTTER s. lontra.
OUCH interj. ai!
OUGHT TO v. dever, ter que.
OUNCE s. onça (animal); onça (medida de peso).
OUR pron. nosso(s), nossa(s).
OURSELVES pron. nos; nós mesmos.
OUST v. expulsar, remover, ejetar.
OUT adv. fora, para fora / interj. fora! saia! / adj. publicado (obra); ausente.
OUTAGE s. interrupção, parada.
OUTBACK s. interior, área distante, cafundó.
OUTBOX s. caixa de saída.
OUTBREAK s. eclosão, surto (doença); deflagração; revolta.
OUTCAST s. excomungado, pária.
OUTCLASS v. exceder, ultrapassar.
OUTCOME s. resultado; efeito.
OUTCRY s. clamor; protesto, tumulto.
OUTDATED adj. antiquado, fora de moda.
OUTDISTANCE v. ultrapassar; ir além.
OUTDO v. exceder, superar.
OUTDOOR adj. exterior, ao ar livre.
OUTFIT v. equipar, aparelhar / s. equipamento, roupas.
OUTFITTER s. abastecedor, fornecedor.
OUTFLOW s. derramamento, escoamento; gasto (dinheiro).
OUTGOING adj. extrovertido / s. despesas, gastos.
OUTGROWTH s. rebento, broto.

OUTLAW v. proscrever; banir, proibir / s. foragido, banido.
OUTLET s. tomada, soquete (eletricidade); ponta de estoque (loja).
OUTLINE s. contorno, esboço / v. delinear, esboçar, resumir.
OUTLOOK s. previsão, percepção, prognóstico.
OUTLYING adj. remoto, afastado.
OUTMODED adj. obsoleto, antiquado; démodé.
OUTPUT v. gerar, produzir / s. emissão; saída; produção.
OUTRAGE v. ultrajar / s. ultraje, atrocidade.
OUTRAGED adj. indignado, ultrajado, ofendido.
OUTRAGEOUS adj. ultrajante, extravagante.
OUTREACH v. expandir-se, estender-se / s. alcance.
OUTRUN v. ultrapassar; correr mais rápido.
OUTSIDE s. exterior / adj. externo / adv. lá fora, para fora / prep. fora de.
OUTSIDER s. estranho; forasteiro.
OUTSIZE adj. de tamanho extra grande.
OUTSKIRT s. arredores; periferia.
OUTSORCE v. terceirizar a mão de obra.
OUTSOURCING s. terceirização; subcontratação.
OUTSPOKEN adj. franco, sincero.
OUTSTANDING adj. excepcional, extraordinário.
OUTSTRETCH v. estender, esticar, estirar.
OUTSTRIP v. ultrapassar, exceder.
OUTWARD adj. externo, exterior; para fora.
OUTWARDLY adv. externamente.
OUTWEIGH v. sobrepesar; prevalecer; ser mais importante.
OVAL s. oval, ovalado / adj. oval, ovalado.
OVARY s. ovário.
OVATION s. ovação, aclamação; aplausos.
OVEN s. forno.
OVER prep. por cima de, sobre / adj. excedente; acabado / adv. de novo.
OVERACT v. extrapolar, exagerar; exceder.
OVERACTIVE adj. hiperativo.
OVERAGE s. excesso, abundância / adj. idade avançada.
OVERALL adj. geral, todo / adv. no geral, totalmente / s. macacão (roupa); bata.

OVERBALANCE v. desequilibrar, exceder.
OVERBEAR v. dominar, forçar, oprimir.
OVERBEARING adj. dominador, autoritário.
OVERBOOK v. reservar além da capacidade.
OVERBURDEN v. sobrecarregar / s. sobrecarga.
OVERCAST adj. nublado, encoberto.
OVERCHARGE v. cobrar muito caro.
OVERCOAT s. sobretudo (vestimenta), capote.
OVERCOME v. superar, triunfar; vencer, derrotar.
OVERCOOK v. cozinhar demais; cozinhar por muito tempo.
OVERCROWD v. superlotar; exceder a capacidade.
OVERCROWDED adj. superlotado, abarrotado, repleto.
OVERCROWDING s. superlotação.
OVERDO v. abusar, exagerar.
OVERDONE adj. exagerado, excessivo.
OVERDOSE s. dose excessiva; superdose / v. ter *overdose*.
OVERDRAFT s. saque a descoberto; débito (bancário).
OVERDRAW v. sacar a descoberto; debitar.
OVERDRAWN adj. endividado; no vermelho.
OVERDRESSED adj. formal demais, vestir em excesso.
OVERDRIVE s. sobremarcha.
OVERDUB v. sobrepor sons / s. superposição de sons.
OVERDUE adj. atrasado, vencido (prazo).
OVEREAGER adj. extremamente ansioso.
OVEREAGERLY adv. demasiadamente ansioso.
OVEREAGERNESS s. ansiedade excessiva.
OVEREAT v. comer demais; empanturrar-se.
OVEREATER s. comilão, fominha, glutão.
OVEREATING s. gula, gulodice, glutonaria.
OVEREMPHASISE v. dar muita ênfase.
OVEREMPHASISED adj. superenfatizado; destacado.
OVERESTIMATE v. sobrevalorizar, superestimar.
OVEREXCITED adj. superexcitado.
OVEREXPOSE v. expor demais.
OVEREXPOSURE s. superexposição.
OVEREXTEND v. estender demais.
OVERFILL v. encher demais; fazer transbordar.
OVERFLIGHT s. sobrevoo.
OVERFLY v. sobrevoar.
OVERFLOW s. inundação, transbordamento / v. transbordar, inundar.
OVERFLOWING adj. cheio, transbordante.
OVERFULL adj. satisfeito, empanturrado, lotado.
OVERGROW v. crescer demais.
OVERGROWN adj. muito alto; que cresceu demais.
OVERGROWTH s. crescimento excessivo.
OVERHANGING adj. suspenso, pendurado.
OVERHAUL v. revisar; fazer revisão (carro).
OVERHEAD s. gastos gerais / adj. elevado, suspenso / adv. em cima.
OVERHEAR v. ouvir por acaso; escutar casualmente.
OVERHEAT v. superaquecer; sobreaquecer.
OVERHEATED adj. superaquecido; agitado.
OVERHEATING s. superaquecimento.
OVERJOY v. arrebatar, enlevar, regozijar / s. arrebatamento, arroubo.
OVERJOYED adj. radiante, enlevado; cheio de alegria.
OVERKILL s. exagero; uso excessivo de.
OVERLAID adj. coberto, tapado, revestido.
OVERLAND adj. terrestre / adv. por terra, sobre a terra.
OVERLAP v. sobrepor / s. sobreposição.
OVERLAY s. revestimento, cobertura / v. revestir, cobrir.
OVERLEAF adv. no verso; do outro lado.
OVERLIE v. cobrir, tapar.
OVERLOAD v. sobrecarregar / s. sobrecarga.
OVERLOOK v. ignorar, deixar passar / s. terraço, mirante.
OVERLORD s. soberano, senhor supremo.
OVERLY adv. excessivamente; demais.
OVERNIGHT adv. durante a noite / adj. noturno / v. pernoitar / s. pernoite.
OVERPAID adj. pago excessivamente.
OVERPASS v. atravessar; ultrapassar / s. passagem elevada (ponte, viaduto).
OVERPAY v. pagar demais.
OVERPOPULATE v. superpovoar.
OVERPOPULATED adj. superpovoado, populoso.
OVERPOPULATION s. superpopulação.
OVERPOWER v. dominar, subjugar, derrotar.
OVERPOWERING adj. opressor, esmagador.
OVERPRICE v. cobrar muito caro.
OVERPRICED adj. caríssimo, preço elevado.
OVERPRINT v. imprimir por cima.

OVERPRODUCTION s. superprodução.
OVERPROTECTION s. superproteção.
OVERPROTECTIVE adj. superprotetor.
OVERQUALIFIED adj. superqualificado.
OVERRATE v. superestimar.
OVERRATED adj. superestimado.
OVERREACH v. sobrepujar; fracassar.
OVERREACT v. reagir exageradamente.
OVERREACTION s. reação exagerada.
OVERSEA adv. além-mar / adj. exterior, estrangeiro.
OVERSEE v. supervisionar, inspecionar.
OVERSEER s. supervisor; gerente.
OVERSHADOW v. eclipsar, ofuscar, ensombrecer, obscurecer.
OVERSHOOT v. passar dos limites.
OVERSIZED adj. enorme, desproporcional.
OVERSLEEP v. perder a hora; dormir demais.
OVERTIME s. hora extra (trabalho); serão.
OVERTURE s. abertura, proposta.
OVERVIEW s. panorama; resumo, síntese.
OVERWEIGHT s. sobrepeso / adj. gordo, pesado.
OVERWORK v. trabalhar demais / s. trabalho extra.
OVERWRITE v. sobrescrever, reescrever; escrever bastante.
OVERZEALOUS adj. superzeloso; fanático.
OVULATE v. ovular.
OVULATION s. ovulação.
OVUM s. óvulo.
OWE v. dever, ter dívidas.
OWING s. devido, que não foi pago.
OWL s. coruja.
OWN v. possuir, ter / adj. próprio.
OWNER s. dono, proprietário.
OWNERSHIP s. propriedade; posse.
OX s. (pl. oxen) boi.
OXIDE s. óxido, combinação de oxigênio com outro elemento.
OXYGEN s. oxigênio / adj. oxigenado.
OXYGENATE v. oxigenar.
OXYGENATION s. oxigenação.
OXYMORON s. paradoxo, oximoro.
OYSTER s. ostra.
OZONE s. ozônio.

Pp

P, p s. décima sexta letra do alfabeto inglês / abrev. página, fósforo (química).
PACE s. passo, compasso; ritmo, marcha.
PACEMAKER s. marca-passo (aparelho).
PACER s. marchador, galopador (cavalo).
PACIFIC adj. pacífico, sossegado.
PACIFIC OCEAN s. Oceano Pacífico.
PACIFIER s. pacificador; chupeta (figurativo).
PACIFISM s. pacifismo.
PACIFIST s. pacifista / adj. pacifista.
PACIFY v. acalmar, pacificar, aliviar.
PACK v. empacotar; fazer as malas / s. pacote, embrulho; bando, quadrilha; matilha.
PACKAGE s. pacote, embrulho.
PACKAGER s. empacotador, embalador.
PACKAGING s. embalagem, acondicionamento.
PACKED s. abarrotado, acumulado.
PACKING CASE s. caixa de embalagem.
PACT s. pacto, trato, acordo.
PAD s. bloco de papel; almofada (de carimbo).
PADDED adj. acolchoado, recheado.
PADDING s. enchimento.
PADDLE s. remo curto; raquete / v. remar.
PADDLER s. remador.
PADDOCK s. cercado para cavalos; pastagem, picadeiro.
PADLOCK v. trancar com cadeado / s. cadeado.
PAGAN s. pagão / adj. pagão.
PAGANISM s. paganismo.
PAGANIZE v. tornar-se pagão.
PAGE s. página; mensageiro; pajem.
PAGEANT s. cortejo, espetáculo; desfile alegórico.
PAGEANTRY s. pompa, ostentação.
PAGEBOY s. mensageiro; serviçal.
PAGINATE v. paginar.
PAGINATION s. paginação.
PAGING s. m.q. pagination.
PAGODA s. pagode (templo pagão).
PAID adj. pago.
PAIL s. balde.
PAIN s. dor, sofrimento, mágoa.
PAINFUL adj. doloroso, penoso.

PAINFULLY *adv.* penosamente; dolorosamente.
PAINKILLER *s.* analgésico.
PAINLESS *adj.* indolor; sem dor.
PAINSTAKING *adj.* detalhista, minucioso, meticuloso.
PAINSTAKINGLY *adv.* meticulosamente.
PAINT *s.* pintura, tinta / *v.* pintar.
PAINTBALL *s.* paintball (jogo).
PAINTBRUSH *s.* pincel, brocha.
PAINTER *s.* pintor.
PAINTING *s.* pintura, quadro (arte).
PAINTWORK *s.* pintura (objetos, residência).
PAIR *s.* par, dupla / *v.* juntar, unir.
PAKISTAN *s.* Paquistão.
PAKISTANI *s.* paquistanês / *adj.* paquistanês.
PAL *s.* camarada, companheiro.
PALACE *s.* palácio.
PALADIN *s.* paladino.
PALATABLE *adj.* palatável, degustável.
PALATAL *s.* fonema palatal (linguística) / *adj.* palatal.
PALATE *s.* paladar; palato (céu da boca).
PALATIAL *adj.* palaciano, suntuoso.
PALAVER *s.* rebuliço, confusão.
PALE *adj.* pálido, claro / *v.* empalidecer.
PALEFACE *s.* cara pálida.
PALELY *adv.* palidamente.
PALENESS *s.* palidez.
PALEONTOLOGIST *s.* paleontólogo.
PALEONTOLOGY *s.* paleontologia.
PALESTINE *s.* Palestina.
PALESTINIAN *s.* palestino / *adj.* palestino.
PALETTE *s.* palheta, paleta.
PALING *s.* estaca; cerca.
PALLADIUM *s.* paládio (química).
PALLIATIVE *s.* paliativo, que acalma / *adj.* paliativo, que acalma.
PALLID *adj.* pálido, descorado.
PALM *s.* palma da mão; palmeira; palmo (medida).
PALMISTRY *s.* quiromancia.
PALPABLE *adj.* palpável.
PALPATION *s.* palpação, apalpação.
PALPITATE *v.* palpitar; pulsar.
PALPITATION *s.* palpitação; pulsação, tremor.
PALSIED *adj.* paralítico, paralisado.

PALSY *s.* paralisia muscular.
PALTRY *adj.* desprezível, irrisório; reles.
PAMPER *v.* mimar, deleitar.
PAMPHLET *s.* panfleto.
PAN *s.* panela, caçarola; Pã (mitologia).
PANACHE *s.* petulância, insolência.
PANAMA *s.* Panamá.
PANCAKE *s.* panqueca.
PANCREAS *s.* pâncreas.
PANDEMIC *s.* pandemia / *adj.* pandêmico.
PANDEMONIUM *s.* pandemônio, confusão, caos.
PANE *s.* vidraça, vidro de janela.
PANEL *s.* painel; comitê, júri.
PANELLIST *s.* palestrante, orador, conferencista.
PANHANDLE *s.* cabo de frigideira.
PANHANDLER *s.* pedinte, mendigo (figurativo).
PANIC *v.* ficar em pânico / *s.* pânico.
PANICKY *adj.* assustado.
PANORAMA *s.* panorama.
PANORAMIC *adj.* panorâmico.
PANTHER *s.* pantera.
PANTIES *s.* calcinha.
PANTRY *s.* despensa, copa.
PANTS *s.* calças.
PAPACY *s.* papado, pontificado; governo papal.
PAPAYA *s.* mamão papaia.
PAPER *s.* papel; jornal; redação, trabalho (escolar); documentos.
PAPERBACK *s.* brochura.
PAPERBOARD *s.* papelão.
PAPERBOY *s.* jornaleiro.
PAPER-MILL *s.* fábrica de papel.
PAPERWORK *s.* papelada; tarefas administrativas.
PAPRIKA *s.* páprica (condimento), pimentão.
PARABLE *s.* parábola.
PARABOLIC *adj.* parabólico.
PARACHUTE *s.* paraquedas / *v.* saltar de paraquedas.
PARACHUTING *s.* paraquedismo.
PARADE *s.* desfile, parada / *v.* desfilar.
PARADIGM *s.* paradigma.

PARADIGMATIC adj. paradigmático.
PARADISE s. paraíso.
PARADISIAC adj. paradisíaco.
PARADOX s. paradoxo; disparate.
PARADOXICAL adj. paradoxal.
PARADOXICALLY adv. paradoxalmente.
PARAFFIN s. parafina.
PARAGRAPH s. parágrafo.
PARAKEET s. periquito.
PARALLEL s. paralelo; linha paralela; semelhança / adj. paralelo.
PARALLELISM s. paralelismo.
PARALYMPICS s. paraolimpíadas.
PARALYSE v. paralisar; imobilizar, neutralizar.
PARALYSIS s. paralisia.
PARALYTIC adj. paralítico.
PARAMEDIC s. paramédico / adj. paramédico.
PARAMETER s. parâmetro.
PARAMETRIC adj. paramétrico.
PARAMILITARY s. paramilitar, grupo que exerce funções militares / adj. paramilitar.
PARAMOUNT adj. primordial; preeminente.
PARANOIA s. paranoia.
PARANOID adj. paranoico.
PARANORMAL s. paranormal / adj. paranormal.
PARAPET s. parapeito.
PARAPHERNALIA s. parafernália.
PARAPHRASE v. parafrasear / s. paráfrase.
PARAPLEGIA s. paraplegia; paralisia das pernas.
PARAPLEGIC s. paraplégico.
PARAPSYCHOLOGY s. parapsicologia, premonição.
PARASITE s. parasita.
PARASITISM s. parasitismo.
PARASOL s. guarda-sol; sombrinha.
PARATROOPER s. paraquedista.
PARCEL s. pacote, embrulho / v. embrulhar.
PARCH v. secar, ressecar; tostar.
PARCHED adj. sedento, ressecado; com sede.
PARCHMENT s. pergaminho.
PARDON s. perdão, indulto / v. perdoar; desculpar.
PARENT s. pai ou mãe, pais.
PARENTAGE s. ascendência, parentesco.

PARENTAL adj. parental.
PARENTHESIS s. parêntese.
PARENTHOOD s. paternidade ou maternidade.
PARENTING s. criação.
PARIS s. Paris.
PARISH s. paróquia; igreja.
PARISHIONER s. paroquiano.
PARISIAN s. parisiense / adj. parisiense.
PARITY s. paridade, igualdade, equivalência.
PARK s. parque; estádio (esportes) / v. estacionar.
PARKING LOT s. estacionamento.
PARKLAND s. parque.
PARKWAY s. autoestrada; via expressa.
PARLANCE s. fala, linguajar.
PARLEY v. discutir, conversar / s. discussão, conversa.
PARLIAMENT s. parlamento.
PARLIAMENTARIAN s. parlamentar, parlamentarista.
PARLIAMENTARY adj. parlamentar.
PARLOUR s. sala de visitas, salão.
PARMESAN s. parmesão (queijo).
PAROCHIAL adj. paroquial, paroquiano.
PARODY s. paródia, zombaria / v. parodiar, imitar.
PARROT s. papagaio.
PARRY v. desviar (de golpes), evitar, evadir.
PARSIMONIOUS adj. parcimonioso.
PARSIMONY s. parcimônia.
PARSLEY s. salsa, salsinha.
PARSON s. pároco, vigário.
PART s. parte, pedaço / v. partir, repartir.
PARTAKE v. partilhar, participar.
PARTIAL adj. parcial.
PARTIALITY s. predileção; parcialidade.
PARTIALLY adv. parcialmente.
PARTICIPANT s. participante.
PARTICIPATE v. participar.
PARTICIPATION s. participação.
PARTICIPATORY s. participativo.
PARTICIPLE s. particípio (gramática).
PARTICLE s. partícula, pequena parte.
PARTICULAR adj. particular, específico, próprio.
PARTICULARISE v. particularizar.
PARTICULARITY s. particularidade.
PARTICULARLY adv. particularmente.

PARTING s. divisão, separação / adj. de despedida.
PARTISAN adj. partidário, sectário.
PARTISANSHIP s. partidarismo.
PARTITION s. divisão; partição.
PARTLY adv. em parte, parcialmente.
PARTNER s. sócio, parceiro.
PARTNERSHIP s. parceria, associação; sociedade.
PART-TIME adv. de meio expediente, de meio período / adj. de meio expediente, de meio período.
PARTY s. festa; partido político, grupo.
PARTYING s. festejo, festa.
PASCHAL adj. pascal, pascoal.
PASS s. passagem / v. passar, entregar; ser aprovado.
PASSABLE adj. transitável, passável, razoável.
PASSAGE s. passagem, corredor; citação.
PASSAGEWAY s. passagem, corredor.
PASSENGER s. passageiro, viajante.
PASSER-BY s. transeunte.
PASSING adj. passageiro, fugaz.
PASSION s. paixão.
PASSIONATE adj. apaixonado.
PASSIONATELY adv. apaixonadamente.
PASSIVE adj. passivo; inerte, indiferente.
PASSIVELY adv. passivamente.
PASSIVE VOICE s. voz passiva (gramática).
PASSIVITY s. passividade.
PASSPORT s. passaporte.
PASSWORD s. senha.
PAST s. passado, antigo / adj. passado, antigo / prep. depois, após.
PASTA s. macarrão, massa.
PASTE v. colar / s. pasta, cola, massa.
PASTEL s. pastel (cor, arte) / adj. pastel (cor, arte).
PASTEURISATION s. pasteurização.
PASTEURISE v. pasteurizar.
PASTIME s. passatempo.
PASTORAL adj. pastoril, pastoral.
PASTRY s. pastelaria.
PASTURE s. pasto.
PASTY adj. pastoso, pálido.
PAT v. dar tapinha, acariciar / s. palmada, tapinha.
PATCH s. retalho; remendo / v. remendar.

PATENT s. patente; direito, licença / adj. patente; óbvio / v. patentear.
PATERNAL adj. paternal, paterno.
PATERNALISM s. paternalismo.
PATERNALISTIC adj. paternalista.
PATERNITY s. paternidade.
PATH s. caminho, trajetória, trilha.
PATHETIC adj. patético, deplorável.
PATHFINDER s. desbravador, pioneiro.
PATHOLOGICAL adj. patológico.
PATHOLOGIST s. patologista.
PATHOLOGY s. patologia.
PATHOS s. pena, compaixão.
PATHWAY s. caminho, atalho, trilha.
PATIENCE s. paciência.
PATIENT s. paciente / adj. paciente.
PATIENTLY adv. pacientemente.
PATIO s. pátio, terraço.
PATISSERIE s. confeitaria.
PATRIARCH s. patriarca.
PATRIARCHAL adj. patriarcal.
PATRIARCHATE s. patriarcado.
PATRIMONY s. patrimônio.
PATRIOT s. patriota / adj. patriota.
PATRIOTIC adj. patriótico; cívico.
PATRIOTISM s. patriotismo.
PATROL s. patrulha, ronda / v. patrulhar, rondar.
PATROLMAN s. patrulheiro.
PATRON s. patrono.
PATRONAGE s. clientela; apoio, suporte.
PATRONISE v. apadrinhar, amparar, patrocinar.
PATTER s. lábia, conversa fiada.
PATTERN s. padrão, modelo; estampado / v. modelar, moldar.
PATTERNED adj. padronizado, estampado.
PAUSE v. pausar, parar / s. pausa, intervalo.
PAVEMENT s. calçada; pavimentação.
PAW s. pata (pé de animal) / v. dar patadas.
PAWN v. penhorar / s. peão (xadrez).
PAY v. pagar, remunerar.
PAYABLE adj. pagável.
PAYBACK s. reembolso, retribuição.
PAYDAY s. dia de pagamento.
PAYER s. pagador.
PAYMENT s. pagamento.
PAYOFF s. suborno; recompensa.
PAYOUT s. indenização; dividendo, lucro.
PAYROLL s. folha de pagamento.

PC *abrev.* computador pessoal.
PEA *s.* ervilha.
PEACE *s.* paz; sossego.
PEACEABLE *adj.* pacífico.
PEACEFUL *adj.* calmo, tranquilo.
PEACEFULLY *adv.* pacificamente.
PEACEFULNESS *s.* quietude, tranquilidade.
PEACEMAKER *s.* pacificador, reconciliador.
PEACETIME *s.* tempo de paz.
PEACH *s.* pêssego.
PEACHY *adj.* ótimo, formidável.
PEACOCK *s.* pavão.
PEAK *s.* pico; cume.
PEAL *v.* repicar, ressoar.
PEANUT *s.* amendoim.
PEAR *s.* pera.
PEARL *s.* pérola.
PEASANT *s.* camponês; caipira (pejorativo).
PEASANTRY *s.* campesinato.
PECK *v.* bicar; dar beijinhos.
PECKER *s.* picareta, picador; pica-pau, bico (de aves).
PECTORAL *s.* peitoral / *adj.* peitoral.
PECULIAR *adj.* peculiar.
PECULIARITY *s.* peculiaridade.
PEDAGOGICAL *adj.* pedagógico.
PEDAGOGUE *s.* pedagogo.
PEDAGOGY *s.* pedagogia.
PEDESTRIAN *s.* pedestre.
PEDIATRIC *adj.* pediátrico.
PEDIATRICIAN *s.* pediatra.
PEDIATRICS *s.* pediatria.
PEDOPHILIA *s.* pedofilia.
PEDOPHILIAC *s.* pedófilo / *adj.* pedófilo.
PEE *v.* fazer xixi.
PEEK *v.* piar, dar pios / *v.* espreitar.
PEEL *s.* casca (de fruta) / *v.* descascar.
PEELER *s.* descascador.
PEELING *s.* descascamento, casca / *adj.* descamante.
PEEP *v.* espiar, dar uma olhadinha.
PEEPHOLE *s.* olho mágico (da porta).
PEEV *v.* irritar, provocar / *s.* irritação, tormento.
PEEVED *adj.* irritado, atormentado.
PEEVISH *adj.* rabugento, irritadiço, teimoso.
PEG *s.* pregador (de roupa) / *v.* fixar, vincular.
PEJORATIVE *adj.* pejorativo, depreciativo.
PELICAN *s.* pelicano.

PELVIC *adj.* pélvico.
PELVIS *s.* pélvis.
PEN *v.* escrever, compor / *s.* caneta.
PENAL *adj.* penal, punível.
PENALISE *v.* penalizar; punir.
PENALTY *s.* penalidade (esporte); pênalti (futebol); multa, pena.
PENANCE *s.* penitência / *v.* penitenciar, punir.
PENCIL *v.* escrever a lápis / *s.* lápis.
PEND *v.* pender; ter inclinação a.
PENDING *adj.* pendente.
PENDULUM *s.* pêndulo.
PENETRATE *v.* penetrar, infiltrar, permear.
PENETRATING *adj.* penetrante; sagaz, perspicaz.
PENETRATION *s.* penetração.
PENGUIN *s.* pinguim.
PENICILLIN *s.* penicilina.
PENINSULA *s.* península.
PENIS *s.* pênis.
PENITENCE *s.* penitência, arrependimento.
PENITENCIARY *s.* penitenciária; prisão.
PENITENT *adj.* penitente.
PENKNIFE *s.* canivete.
PENNANT *s.* flâmula.
PENNILESS *adj.* sem dinheiro; duro, quebrado.
PENNY *s.* (*pl. pence*) moeda inglesa (1/100 da libra); centavo.
PENSION *s.* pensão, aposentadoria.
PENSIONABLE *adj.* aposentável.
PENSIONER *s.* pensionista, pensionário.
PENSIVE *adj.* pensativo.
PENTAGON *s.* pentágono (geometria).
PENTHOUSE *s.* cobertura (apartamento).
PENT-UP *adj.* reprimido, contido.
PENULTIMATE *adj.* penúltimo.
PENUMBRA *s.* penumbra.
PEOPLE *s.* povo; gente; multidão.
PEPPER *s.* pimenta.
PEPPERY *adj.* apimentado; picante.
PER *prep.* por (por dia, por cento); conforme.
PERCEIVE *v.* perceber, compreender, notar.
PERCENTAGE *s.* porcentagem.
PERCEPTIBLE *adj.* perceptível, discernível.
PERCEPTION *s.* percepção, ideia, noção.
PERCEPTIVE *adj.* perceptivo.

PERCH v. empoleirar-se / s. poleiro.
PERCUSSION s. percussão.
PERCUSSIONIST s. percussionista.
PERDITION s. perdição (religião).
PEREGRINE adj. peregrino.
PERENNIAL adj. perene.
PERFECT adj. perfeito / v. aperfeiçoar.
PERFECTION s. perfeição; excelência.
PERFECTIONISM s. perfeccionismo.
PERFECTIONIST s. perfeccionista / adj. perfeccionista.
PERFECTLY adv. perfeitamente.
PERFORATE v. perfurar.
PERFORATION s. perfuração.
PERFORM v. realizar, fazer, desempenhar; interpretar.
PERFORMANCE s. desempenho, execução, atuação.
PERFORMER s. artista, ator, intérprete.
PERFORMING s. realização, atuação, execução.
PERFUME s. perfume.
PERFUMERY s. perfumaria.
PERHAPS adv. talvez, quiçá, porventura.
PERIMETER s. perímetro.
PERIOD s. período, época; menstruação (coloquial); ponto final (gramática).
PERIODIC adj. periódico, intermitente.
PERIODICAL adj. periódico (jornal, revista, artigos).
PERIODICALLY adv. periodicamente, regularmente.
PERIODICITY s. periodicidade.
PERIPHERAL adj. periférico.
PERIPHERY s. periferia; arredores.
PERISCOPE s. periscópio.
PERISH v. perecer, falecer; sucumbir.
PERISHABLE adj. perecível.
PERJURE v. prestar falso testemunho, perjurar.
PERJURY s. perjúrio.
PERK s. benefício, vantagem / v. animar-se.
PERKY adj. animado, alegre; ousado, altivo.
PERMANENCE s. permanência.
PERMANENT adj. permanente, duradouro.
PERMANENTLY adv. permanentemente.
PERMEABLE adj. permeável.
PERMEATE v. penetrar, permear.
PERMEATION s. infiltração, impregnação.
PERMISSIBLE adj. permissível, admissível.
PERMISSION s. permissão, autorização.
PERMISSIVE adj. permissivo.
PERMIT v. permitir, autorizar / s. permissão, licença.
PERMUTATION s. permutação, troca.
PERMUTE v. permutar.
PERNICIOUS adj. pernicioso, nocivo, maligno.
PERPENDICULAR adj. perpendicular.
PERPETRATE v. perpetrar; praticar.
PERPETRATION s. perpetração, execução.
PERPETUAL adj. perpétuo, eterno.
PERPETUATE v. perpetuar.
PERPETUATION s. perpetuação, perpetuamento.
PERPETUITY s. perpetuidade, eternidade.
PERPLEX v. confundir, atrapalhar; ficar perplexo.
PERPLEXING adj. desconcertante, confuso, perplexo.
PERPLEXITY s. perplexidade, atordoamento.
PERSECUTE v. perseguir, importunar.
PERSECUTION s. perseguição.
PERSEVERANCE s. perseverança.
PERSEVERE v. perseverar, persistir.
PERSEVERING adj. perseverante, persistente.
PERSIMMON s. caqui (fruta).
PERSIST v. persistir.
PERSISTENCE s. persistência, permanência.
PERSISTENT adj. persistente, duradouro.
PERSISTENTLY adv. persistentemente.
PERSON s. pessoa, indivíduo.
PERSONA s. personalidade; personagem (artes).
PERSONABLE adj. formoso, elegante.
PERSONAL adj. privado, individual, pessoal.
PERSONAL COMPUTER s. computador pessoal.
PERSONALISE v. personalizar, individualizar.
PERSONALITY s. personalidade.
PERSONALLY adv. pessoalmente; particularmente.
PERSONIFICATION s. personificação.
PERSONIFY v. personificar
PERSPECTIVE s. perspectiva.
PERSPICACIOUS adj. perspicaz.
PERSPICACITY s. perspicácia.

PERSPIRATION s. transpiração, suor.
PERSPIRE v. suar; transpirar.
PERSUADE v. persuadir, convencer.
PERSUASION s. persuasão.
PERSUASIVE adj. persuasivo, convincente.
PERT adj. atrevido, ousado.
PERTAIN v. pertencer a; referir-se a, ser próprio de.
PERTINENCE s. pertinência, relevância.
PERTINENT adj. pertinente, adequado.
PERTNESS s. atrevimento, ousadia.
PERTURB v. perturbar.
PERTURBATION s. perturbação, transtorno.
PERTURBING adj. perturbador.
PERU s. Peru (país).
PERUSE v. ler atentamente, examinar.
PERUVIAN s. peruano / adj. peruano.
PERVERSE adj. perverso, maldoso.
PERVERSION s. perversão, depravação.
PERVERSITY s. perversidade.
PERVERT s. pervertido, depravado / v. perverter, corromper.
PESSIMISM s. pessimismo.
PESSIMIST s. pessimista.
PEST s. peste, praga.
PESTER v. incomodar, importunar / s. importuno.
PESTICIDE s. pesticida.
PESTILENCE s. pestilência, peste; má influência.
PET s. animal de estimação.
PETAL s. pétala.
PETITION s. petição.
PETRIFIED adj. petrificado, paralisado.
PETRIFY v. petrificar.
PETROCHEMICAL adj. petroquímico.
PETROL s. gasolina.
PETROLEUM s. petróleo.
PETTING s. carícias, carinho.
PETTY adj. mesquinho, sem importância.
PETULANT adj. mal-humorado, petulante.
PHALANX s. falange.
PHANTASM s. fantasma.
PHANTASMAGORIC adj. fantasmagórico.
PHANTOM s. fantasma.
PHARAOH s. faraó.
PHARISEE s. fariseu.
PHARMACEUTIC adj. farmacêutico.
PHARMACIST s. farmacêutico.

PHARMACY s. farmácia.
PHARYNGITIS s. faringite.
PHARYNX s. faringe.
PHASE s. fase, etapa.
PHEASANT s. faisão.
PHENOMENAL adj. fenomenal, admirável.
PHENOMENON s. (pl. phenomena) fenômeno.
PHEROMONE s. feromônio.
PHEW interj. ufa!
PHILANTHROPIST s. filantropo.
PHILANTHROPY s. filantropia.
PHILHARMONIC s. filarmônica / adj. filarmônico.
PHILIPPINE s. filipino / adj. filipino.
PHILIPPINES s. Filipinas.
PHILOLOGICAL adj. filológico.
PHILOLOGY s. filologia.
PHILOSOPHER s. filósofo.
PHILOSOPHIC s. filosófico.
PHILOSOPHISE v. filosofar.
PHILOSOPHY s. filosofia.
PHOBIA s. fobia.
PHOBIC adj. fóbico.
PHOENIX s. fênix (mitologia).
PHONEME s. fonema (gramática).
PHONEMIC adj. fonêmico, fonemático (gramática).
PHONETICS s. fonética.
PHONIC adj. fônico.
PHONOLOGY s. fonologia.
PHOSPHATE s. fosfato (química).
PHOSPHOR s. fósforo.
PHOTOCOPY v. fotocopiar / s. fotocópia.
PHOTOGRAPH s. fotografia.
PHRASAL adj. frasal.
PHRASE s. frase.
PHYSICAL adj. físico.
PHYSICALLY adv. fisicamente.
PHYSICS s. física.
PHYSIOLOGY s. fisiologia.
PIANIST s. pianista.
PIANO s. piano.
PICK v. apanhar, pegar.
PICKER s. colhedor, apanhador.
PICKET s. piquete, estaca.
PICKLE s. picles.
PICKUP TRUCK s. caminhonete.
PICNIC s. piquenique.
PICTURE s. quadro, pintura, tela; retrato.

PIE s. torta, pastelão, empadão.
PIECE s. pedaço, fatia; peça.
PIER s. cais, embarcadouro.
PIERCE v. penetrar, furar; romper.
PIERCING adj. penetrante; perfurante, cortante.
PIETY s. piedade; abnegação.
PIG s. porco, leitão.
PIGEON s. pombo.
PIGMENT s. pigmento.
PIGSTY s. chiqueiro, pocilga.
PIKE s. posto de pedágio; pico (de montanha).
PILE s. pilha, montão.
PILFER v. furtar; afanar.
PILGRIM s. peregrino, romeiro.
PILL s. pílula.
PILLAR s. pilar, coluna.
PILLOW s. travesseiro.
PILOT s. piloto / v. pilotar, conduzir.
PIMPLE s. espinha (acne).
PIN s. alfinete; broche; pino.
PINAFORE s. avental para crianças.
PINBALL s. fliperama.
PINCERS s. pinça; alicate.
PINCH s. beliscão.
PINCUSHION s. alfineteira, pregadeira.
PINE s. pinheiro.
PINEAPPLE s. abacaxi.
PINK adj. cor-de-rosa; rosado / v. enrubescer.
PINNACLE s. cume, pináculo, auge.
PIONEER s. pioneiro, precursor / adj. pioneiro, precursor.
PIP s. caroço, semente.
PIPE s. cano, tubo; encanamento; cachimbo.
PIQUANT adj. picante; pungente.
PIRATE s. pirata.
PISCES s. Peixes (astrologia).
PISTOL s. pistola.
PISTON s. pistão.
PIT s. cova; fossa; mina de carvão.
PITCH s. arremesso; tom (música).
PITCHER s. jarro, cântaro; arremessador.
PITEOUS adj. lastimável, comovente.
PITFALL s. perigo; armadilha, cilada.
PITIFUL adj. comovente, lamentável; deplorável.
PITILESS adj. impiedoso, cruel.
PITTANCE s. ninharia; miséria.
PITY s. compaixão, pena, piedade.

PIVOT s. eixo; pino; pivô.
PIXIE s. duende, elfo.
PLACARD s. placar.
PLACATE v. apaziguar.
PLACE s. lugar; posto; assento / v. pôr, colocar; encomendar.
PLACID adj. plácido, sereno.
PLAGUE s. praga, peste.
PLAIN s. planície / adj. claro, evidente; simples; liso, plano.
PLAIT s. dobra; trança / v. trançar.
PLAN s. plano, projeto, esquema / v. planejar, projetar.
PLANE s. avião; plano (geometria) / adj. plano, raso.
PLANET s. planeta.
PLANNER s. projetista, planejador.
PLANNING s. planejamento.
PLANT s. planta; fábrica, usina / v. plantar, semear.
PLANTATION s. plantação.
PLASMA s. plasma.
PLASTIC s. plástico / adj. plástico.
PLASTIC SURGERY s. cirurgia plástica.
PLATINUM s. platina / adj. de platina.
PLATOON s. pelotão.
PLATTER s. travessa (de louça).
PLAY s. jogo, partida; peça teatral / v. jogar, brincar, divertir-se; representar.
PLAYBOY s. farrista, boêmio (coloquial).
PLEA s. apelo; petição; argumento.
PLEAD v. defender, advogar; apelar, suplicar.
PLEASANT adj. agradável.
PLEASE adv. por favor / v. agradar, dar prazer a.
PLEASING adj. agradável, gentil.
PLEASURE s. prazer, satisfação.
PLENTY s. abundância, fartura / adj. abundante.
PLIABLE adj. flexível, maleável.
PLIGHT s. apuro, situação difícil; compromisso.
PLOT s. trama, conspiração; lote; enredo de uma história / v. tramar; traçar.
PLUG s. pino; tomada.
PLUM s. ameixa.
PLUMAGE s. plumagem.
PLUMBER s. encanador.
PLUME s. pluma, pena.

PLUMP *adj.* roliço, rechonchudo.
PLUNGE *s.* salto; mergulho.
PLURAL *s.* plural / *adj.* plural.
PLUS *s.* sinal de adição (+) / *prep.* mais / *adj.* positivo.
PLUSH *adj.* de pelúcia.
PM *abrev.* p.m.
PNEUMATIC *adj.* pneumático.
PNEUMONIA *s.* pneumonia.
POCKET *s.* bolso / *adj.* de bolso / *v.* embolsar.
POD *s.* vagem (de feijão); bando, cardume.
PODCAST *s.* podcast, arquivo de áudio digital.
PODGY *adj.* atarracado.
PODIUM *s.* pódio.
POEM *s.* poema.
POET *s.* poeta.
POETIC *adj.* poético.
POETRY *s.* poesia.
POIGNANT *adj.* comovente, pungente.
POINT *s.* ponto; objetivo; relevância / *v.* indicar, evidenciar.
POINTLESS *adj.* inútil, fora de propósito.
POISE *s.* equilíbrio, estabilidade.
POISON *s.* veneno / *v.* envenenar.
POISONING *s.* envenenamento.
POKE *v.* atiçar; cutucar.
POKER *s.* pôquer, atiçador.
POLAND *s.* Polônia.
POLAR *adj.* polar.
POLARIZE *v.* polarizar.
POLICE *s.* polícia / *v.* policiar.
POLIO *s.* poliomielite, pólio.
POLISH *s.* polonês / *adj.* polonês.
POLITE *adj.* gentil, cortês, educado.
POLITIC *adj.* político, astuto.
POLL *s.* votação; pesquisa, sondagem.
POLLEN *s.* pólen.
POLLUTE *v.* poluir, contaminar.
POLLUTION *s.* poluição.
POLYESTER *s.* poliéster.
POLYGAMY *s.* poligamia.
POLYTECHNIC *s.* politécnica / *adj.* politécnico.
POMEGRANATE *s.* romã.
POMP *s.* pompa, ostentação.
POMPOUS *adj.* pomposo, empolado.
PONDER *v.* ponderar, refletir, considerar.
PONTIFF *s.* pontífice.
PONTIFICATE *v.* pontificar / *s.* pontificado, papado.

PONY *s.* pônei.
POOL *s.* poça, charco; tanque, reservatório; piscina.
POOR *adj.* pobre.
POORNESS *s.* pobreza.
POP *s.* ruído seco; estouro (som), estalo / *v.* estalar, saltar.
POPCORN *s.* pipoca.
POPE *s.* papa.
POPEYED *adj.* com os olhos arregalados.
POPPY *s.* papoula.
POPULAR *adj.* popular; familiar; na moda.
POPULATE *v.* povoar.
POPULOUS *adj.* populoso.
PORCELAIN *s.* porcelana / *adj.* de porcelana.
PORCH *s.* pórtico; varanda, sacada.
PORCUPINE *s.* porco-espinho.
PORKCHOP *s.* costeleta de porco.
PORNOGRAPHIC *adj.* pornográfico.
POROUS *adj.* poroso.
PORPOISE *s.* toninha, boto.
PORT *s.* porto, ancoradouro.
PORTABLE *adj.* portátil.
PORTER *s.* porteiro; carregador, bagageiro.
PORTION *s.* porção, parcela.
PORTLY *adj.* corpulento; imponente.
PORTRAIT *s.* retrato.
PORTUGAL *s.* Portugal.
PORTUGUESE *s.* português / *adj.* português.
POSE *s.* postura; pose / *v.* posar; propor; fazer posar.
POSH *adj.* requintado, de luxo, chique.
POSITION *s.* posição; situação / *v.* posicionar.
POSITIVE *adj.* positivo; certo; definitivo.
POSSIBILITY *s.* possibilidade.
POST *v.* pôr no correio, postar / *s.* poste, pilar.
POSTER *s.* cartaz, pôster.
POSTERITY *s.* posteridade.
POSTGRADUATE *s.* pós-graduado / *adj.* pós-graduado.
POST MERIDIEM *adj.* entre o meio-dia e a meia-noite.
POST OFFICE *s.* agência do correio.
POT *s.* panela, caçarola, pote.
POTATO *s.* batata.
POTENT *adj.* potente, poderoso, forte.
POTENTIAL *s.* potencial / *adj.* potencial.

POTION s. poção.
POUND s. libra (0,454 quilograma); libra (£) / v. golpear, socar.
POVERTY s. pobreza; escassez.
POWDER s. pó / v. polvilhar.
POWDERED MILK s. leite em pó.
POWER s. poder; força.
POWERFUL adj. poderoso; influente.
PRACTICAL adj. prático.
PRAGMATIC adj. pragmático.
PRAISE s. louvor, elogio / v. elogiar, louvar.
PRAM s. carrinho de bebê (coloquial).
PRANK s. travessura, brincadeira / v. brincar, traquinar.
PRAY v. rezar, orar.
PREACH v. pregar, fazer sermão.
PRECARIOUS adj. precário.
PRECAUTION s. precaução, prevenção.
PRECIOUS adj. precioso, valioso.
PRECIPICE s. precipício.
PRECIPITATE adj. precipitado, apressado / v. precipitar; apressar.
PRECISE adj. exato, preciso.
PREFACE s. prefácio; introdução / v. prefaciar.
PREFECT s. monitor escolar.
PREFER v. preferir.
PREFIX s. prefixo.
PREGNANCY s. gravidez.
PRELUDE s. prelúdio (música); introdução.
PREMATURE adj. prematuro.
PREMIER s. primeiro-ministro / adj. principal.
PREMISE s. premissa.
PREMIUM s. prêmio; recompensa.
PREOCCUPATION s. preocupação.
PREPARATION s. preparação.
PREPARATORY adj. preparatório.
PREPARE v. preparar.
PREPOSITION s. preposição.
PREROGATIVE s. prerrogativa; privilégio.
PRESCRIBE v. prescrever, receitar.
PRESENCE s. presença, comparecimento.
PRESENT s. presente, atualidade; oferta / v. apresentar; presentear.
PRESERVATION s. preservação, conservação.
PRESERVATIVE s. preservativo / adj. preservativo, conservante.
PRESERVE v. preservar, proteger, conservar.

PRESIDE v. presidir.
PRESIDENCY s. presidência.
PRESS s. imprensa, jornalismo (meio de comunicação) / v. apertar, pressionar.
PRESSURE s. pressão.
PRESTIGE s. prestígio, influência.
PRESUME v. presumir, supor; inferir, deduzir.
PRESUPPOSE v. pressupor, conjeturar.
PRETEND v. fingir, simular.
PRETENDER s. pretendente; embusteiro, simulador.
PRETENSION s. pretensão; ostentação.
PRETEXT s. pretexto.
PRETTY adj. bonito, atraente / adv. bastante.
PREVAIL v. prevalecer, imperar.
PREVENT v. prevenir, evitar, impedir.
PREVIEW s. antecipação, pré-estreia.
PREVIOUS adj. prévio, anterior; apressado, prematuro.
PRICE s. preço / v. fixar o preço.
PRICK s. picada, ferroada / v. picar, furar.
PRICKLE s. espinho, ferrão.
PRIDE s. orgulho, soberba; brio.
PRIEST s. padre, sacerdote.
PRIMARY s. primário; principal; fundamental / adj. primário; principal; fundamental.
PRIMATE s. primaz; primata.
PRIMITIVE s. primitivo, aborígene / adj. primitivo, rudimentar.
PRINCE s. príncipe.
PRINCESS s. princesa.
PRINCIPAL s. dirigente; diretor de colégio.
PRINCIPLE s. princípio; caráter.
PRINT s. impressão; cópia; letra / v. imprimir; publicar.
PRIORITY s. prioridade.
PRISON s. prisão, cárcere, cadeia.
PRIVACY s. privacidade; isolamento, retiro.
PRIVATE adj. particular, privado / s. soldado raso.
PRIVILEGE s. privilégio.
PRIZE s. prêmio, recompensa / adj. premiado.
PROBABILITY s. probabilidade.
PROBLEM s. problema.
PROCEDURE s. procedimento, método; norma.
PROCEED v. proceder; prosseguir, avançar.
PROCESS s. processo / v. tratar, processar.
PROCURE v. obter, conseguir.

PRODIGY s. prodígio.
PRODUCT s. produto.
PROFILE s. perfil; contorno.
PROFOUND adj. profundo.
PROFOUNDLY adv. profundamente.
PROGRAM s. programa / v. programar.
PROGRESS s. progresso, avanço, desenvolvimento / v. progredir, evoluir.
PROJECT s. projeto, plano / v. projetar.
PROJECTOR s. projetor.
PROLONG v. prolongar, estender.
PROMENADE s. passeio / v. passear.
PROMISE s. promessa / v. prometer.
PROMOTE v. promover.
PROMPT adj. pronto, rápido, pontual / v. induzir, incitar.
PRONOUN s. pronome.
PRONOUNCE v. pronunciar, declarar.
PRONUNCIATION s. pronúncia.
PROOF s. prova; evidência.
PROPERTY s. propriedade; posses, bens.
PROPHECY s. profecia, predição.
PROPOSE v. propor; pedir em casamento.
PROSAIC adj. prosaico, trivial.
PROSE s. prosa.
PROSPER v. prosperar, progredir.
PROSTITUTE s. prostituta, meretriz.
PROTECT v. proteger, amparar.
PROTEIN s. proteína.
PROTEST s. protesto / v. protestar.
PROTOCOL s. protocolo / v. protocolizar.
PROUD adj. orgulhoso; imponente; soberbo.
PROVE v. testar; provar.
PROVERB s. provérbio.
PROVIDE v. prover, munir, suprir.
PROVINCE s. província; o interior.
PROVOCATION s. provocação; estímulo; incitamento.
PROVOKE v. provocar, desafiar, afrontar.
PROW s. proa.
PSYCHIATRIC adj. psiquiátrico.
PSYCHIATRIST s. psiquiatra.
PSYCHOLOGICAL adj. psicológico.
PSYCHOLOGIST s. psicólogo.
PUB abrev. bar, botequim.

PUBLIC s. público, notório / adj. público, notório.
PUBLICATION s. publicação.
PUBLICITY s. publicidade.
PUBLISH v. publicar, divulgar, difundir.
PUFF s. sopro; baforada / v. soprar, bufar.
PUFFY adj. inchado; balofo.
PULL v. puxar / s. puxão.
PULLOVER s. pulôver.
PULP s. polpa (de fruta).
PULSATE v. palpitar, pulsar.
PULVERIZE v. pulverizar, vaporizar.
PUMMEL v. esmurrar, socar.
PUMPKIN s. abóbora.
PUNCH s. soco, murro; ponche (bebida alcoólica) / v. socar, esmurrar.
PUNISH v. punir, castigar.
PUNY adj. débil, fraco.
PUPPET s. marionete, fantoche; boneca.
PUPPET SHOW s. teatro de marionetes.
PUPPY s. filhote de cachorro.
PURCHASE s. compra, aquisição / v. comprar.
PURE adj. puro, imaculado.
PURIFICATION s. purificação.
PURIST s. purista.
PURITAN s. puritano / adj. puritano.
PURITANISM s. puritanismo.
PURITY s. pureza.
PURPLE adj. roxo, purpúreo / s. roxo, púrpura.
PURPOSE s. propósito, finalidade.
PURSE s. carteira de mulher; porta-moedas.
PURSER s. comissário de bordo.
PUSH v. empurrar / s. empurrão.
PUSSY s. bichano, gatinha.
PUT v. pôr, colocar.
PUTRID adj. podre, putrefato.
PUZZLE s. charada, enigma; quebra-cabeça / v. confundir.
PYJAMAS s. pijama.
PYRAMID s. pirâmide.
PYROTECHNIC adj. pirotécnico.
PYTHON s. píton, pitão (cobra).

Q q

Q, q s. décima sétima letra do alfabeto inglês.
QATAR s. Catar (país árabe).
QC abrev. controle de qualidade.
QUACK v. grasnar / s. grasnido (pato).
QUACKERY s. charlatanismo, charlatanice (coloquial).
QUADRANGLE s. quadrilátero.
QUADRANT s. quadrante.
QUADRATIC adj. quadrático.
QUADRICEPS s. quadríceps.
QUADRILLE s. quadrilha (dança).
QUADRIPLEGIA s. tetraplegia, quadriplegia.
QUADRIPLEGIC s. quadriplégico, tetraplégico / adj. quadriplégico, tetraplégico.
QUADRUPLE adj. quádruplo.
QUADRUPLET s. quádruplo, quadrigêmeo.
QUAFF v. engolir; tragar.
QUAIL s. codorna.
QUAINT adj. curioso; esquisito, estranho.
QUAKE v. tremer, estremecer / s. tremor; abalo sísmico.
QUALIFIABLE adj. qualificável.
QUALIFICATION s. qualificação; habilitação.
QUALIFIED adj. qualificado, habilitado.
QUALIFIER s. qualificador (gramática).
QUALIFY v. qualificar; capacitar, habilitar.
QUALITATIVE adj. qualitativo.
QUALITATIVELY adv. qualitativamente.
QUALITY s. qualidade, propriedade.
QUALITY CONTROL s. controle de qualidade.
QUALITY OF LIFE s. qualidade de vida.
QUALM s. apreensão, receio.
QUANTIFIABLE adj. quantificável.
QUANTIFICATION s. quantificação.
QUANTIFIER s. quantificador.
QUANTIFY v. quantificar, avaliar.
QUANTITATIVE adj. quantitativo.
QUANTITY s. quantidade; porção, soma.
QUANTUM s. quantum, quantidade, importância, fração, porção.
QUARANTINE v. ficar em quarentena / s. quarentena.
QUARREL s. disputa, rixa, briga / v. discutir, brigar.
QUARRELLING s. discussão, bate-boca / adj. briguento.
QUARRELSOME s. briguento, brigão.

QUARRY s. pedreira.
QUART s. quarto (medida de líquido).
QUARTER s. quarto, quarta parte; trimestre; quarteirão; moeda norte-americana e canadense de 25 centavos.
QUARTERFINAL s. quarta de final (esporte).
QUARTET s. quarteto.
QUARTZ s. quartzo.
QUASAR s. quasar (astronomia).
QUASH v. anular, revogar (sentença).
QUASI adv. quase.
QUATRAIN s. quarteto, quadra; verso com quatro linhas.
QUAVERING adj. trêmulo.
QUAY s. cais; desembarcadouro.
QUAYSIDE s. cais / adj. situado à beira do cais.
QUEASINESS s. náusea, enjoo; mal-estar.
QUEASY adj. enjoado, nauseado.
QUEBEC s. Québec; província canadense.
QUEEN s. rainha; dama (baralho e xadrez).
QUEENLY adj. majestoso, real.
QUEER adj. esquisito, estranho; indisposto; homossexual (pejorativo).
QUEERLY adv. de modo singular, esquisitamente.
QUELL v. domar, sufocar, reprimir.
QUENCH v. extinguir, saciar.
QUENCHER s. refresco, algo que mata a sede.
QUERY v. pesquisar, consultar / s. pesquisa, consulta (informática).
QUEST s. busca, procura, pesquisa.
QUESTION s. pergunta, dúvida, questão / v. indagar, questionar.
QUESTION MARK s. ponto de interrogação (?).
QUESTIONABLE adj. questionável.
QUESTIONER s. questionador; interrogador.
QUESTIONING adj. interrogativo; duvidoso.
QUESTIONNAIRE s. questionário.
QUEUE v. formar fila / s. fila.
QUIBBLE s. ninharia, picuinha.
QUIBBLING adj. de pirraça.
QUICHE s. quiche (culinária).
QUICK adj. rápido, ágil, ligeiro.
QUICKEN v. apressar-se.
QUICKLY adv. rapidamente, depressa.
QUICKNESS s. rapidez.
QUICKSAND s. areia movediça.
QUICKSILVER s. mercúrio / adj. explosivo, impulsivo.
QUID s. libra esterlina (coloquial).
QUIESCENT adj. quieto, calmo, sossegado.
QUIET adj. calmo, tranquilo / s. tranquilidade.
QUIETEN v. sossegar, acalmar, aquietar.
QUIETLY adv. calmamente, pacientemente.
QUIETNESS s. calma, quietude; sossego.
QUIETUDE s. quietude, tranquilidade.
QUIFF s. topete.
QUILL s. pena, pluma.
QUILT s. colcha de retalhos / v. forrar, acolchoar.
QUILTED adj. acolchoado.
QUILTER s. acolchoador.
QUINCE s. marmelo (fruta).
QUINTET s. quinteto.
QUINTUPLET s. quíntuplo.
QUIRK s. peculiaridade, esquisitice.
QUIRKY adj. bizarro, excêntrico, extravagante.
QUIT v. renunciar, desistir; parar, abandonar.
QUITE adv. totalmente, completamente; muito, um bocado.
QUITTER adj. derrotista, que desiste com facilidade (pejorativo).
QUIVER v. tremer, tremular / s. tremor.
QUIXOTIC adj. quixotesco; idealista, romântico.
QUIZ s. teste, competição (de conhecimento) / v. examinar oralmente.
QUORUM s. quórum.
QUOTA s. cota, parcela; limite.
QUOTABLE adj. citável, digno de citação; conciso.
QUOTATION s. cotação; citação.
QUOTATION MARK s. marca de citação; aspas (" ").
QUOTE v. citar, mencionar; cotar, estimar.
QUOTIENT s. quociente; resultado.

Rr

R, r *s.* décima oitava letra do alfabeto inglês.
RABBI *s.* rabino.
RABBIT *s.* coelho.
RACE *s.* corrida; competição; raça humana / *v.* competir.
RACIAL *adj.* racial.
RACIST *adj.* racista / *s.* racista.
RACK *s.* estante; prateleira; suporte.
RACY *adj.* espirituoso(a); vivo(a), esperto(a), animado(a).
RADAR *s.* radar.
RADIATE *v.* irradiar; emitir / *adj.* radiado.
RADIATION *s.* radiação.
RADICAL *adj.* radical, extremo.
RADIO *s.* rádio.
RADISH *s.* rabanete.
RAFFLE *s.* rifa; sorteio / *v.* rifar, sortear.
RAFT *s.* balsa / *v.* viajar (em balsa ou jangada).
RAG *s.* trapo, farrapo.
RAGE *s.* raiva, furor, ira / *v.* enfurecer-se.
RAGGED *adj.* esfarrapado, maltrapilho.
RAID *s.* ataque repentino; batida policial.
RAIDER *s.* invasor, atacante.
RAIL *s.* grade; corrimão; trilho.
RAILROAD *s.* ferrovia, estrada de ferro.
RAIN *s.* chuva / *v.* chover.
RAINBOW *s.* arco-íris.
RAINCOAT *s.* capa de chuva.
RAINDROP *s.* pingo de chuva.
RAISE *s.* elevação, aumento, subida / *v.* subir, levantar, erguer; criar, educar.
RAISER *s.* produtor, criador, cultivador; fundador, causador, inspirador.
RAISIN *s.* passa, uva-passa.
RAM *s.* carneiro / *v.* bater, golpear.
RAMBLE *s.* excursão a pé; caminhada / *v.* vaguear, perambular.
RAMP *s.* rampa, ladeira.
RANCH *s.* rancho, fazenda.
RANDOM *adj.* casual, ao acaso, aleatório / *s.* acaso; impetuosidade.
RANDY *adj.* excitado, sensual.
RANGE *s.* extensão; alcance; cordilheira / *v.* agrupar, ordenar, estender-se.
RANK *s.* linha, ordem, grau, fila, fileira / *v.* enfileirar, classificar, ordenar.
RANSOM *s.* resgate.
RAP *s.* batida breve e seca; estilo musical.
RAPE *s.* estupro; violação; rapto / *v.* estuprar, violar.

RAPID *adj.* rápido, ligeiro / *s.* rápido, correnteza.
RAPPORT *s.* harmonia, conformidade.
RARE *adj.* raro; malpassado (carne).
RARELY *adv.* raramente.
RARITY *s.* raridade.
RASH *adj.* impetuoso, precipitado / *s.* urticária, irritação na pele.
RASPBERRY *s.* framboesa.
RAT *s.* rato / *adj.* pessoa de má índole, vil.
RATE *s.* taxa; razão, proporção / *v.* avaliar, estimar.
RATHER *adv.* preferivelmente; bastante, muito.
RATIFY *v.* ratificar, endossar.
RATIONAL *adj.* racional.
RAT TRAP *s.* ratoeira; casa velha e descuidada.
RAVAGE *v.* devastar; saquear / *s.* devastação.
RAVE *s.* delírio, desvario; fúria; festa animada / *v.* delirar, enfurecer.
RAVEL *s.* confusão.
RAVEN *v.* devorar / *s.* corvo.
RAVENOUS *adj.* faminto; voraz; ávido.
RAVISH *v.* arrebatar, cativar; raptar, violar.
RAY *s.* raio (de luz, calor).
RAZE *v.* arrasar; aniquilar; demolir; riscar; apagar.
RAZOR *s.* navalha, lâmina de barbear / *v.* cortar com navalha.
REACH *v.* alcançar, atingir, chegar / *s.* alcance.
REACT *v.* reagir.
READ *v.* ler.
READER *s.* leitor(a); livro (de leitura escolar).
READILY *adv.* facilmente; prontamente.
READING *s.* leitura / *adj.* de leitura.
READJUST *v.* reajustar.
READY *adj.* pronto, preparado, terminado, acabado.
REAFFIRM *v.* reafirmar, reiterar.
REAFFIRMATION *s.* reafirmação.
REAL *adj.* real, autêntico, verdadeiro.
REALITY *s.* realidade, verdade.
REALIZATION *s.* realização, percepção.
REALIZE *v.* realizar; dar-se conta de, imaginar, perceber.
REALLY *adv.* realmente, de fato; sem dúvida.
REASON *s.* razão, motivo / *v.* raciocinar, pensar.

REASONABLE *adj.* razoável, sensato.
REBEL *s.* rebelde / *adj.* revoltoso, rebelde / *v.* rebelar-se.
REBUFF *s.* repulsa, recusa; esnobada / *v.* repelir; esnobar.
RECALL *v.* recordar; convocar; chamar de volta / *s.* chamada de volta; recolhimento de produtos com defeitos.
RECAP *v.* recapitular / *s.* pneu recauchutado.
RECEDE *v.* retroceder.
RECEIVE *v.* receber; acolher.
RECENT *adj.* recente.
RECEPTION *s.* recepção; audiência.
RECEPTIVE *adj.* receptivo.
RECIPE *s.* receita.
RECIPIENT *s.* recipiente, recebedor, destinatário.
RECITE *v.* recitar, declamar; relatar, contar.
RECKLESS *adj.* despreocupado, descuidado; imprudente.
RECLINE *v.* reclinar-se, recostar-se.
RECOGNIZE *v.* reconhecer; aceitar, admitir.
RECOIL *v.* retroceder; recuar.
RECOMMEND *v.* recomendar.
RECOMPENSE *s.* recompensa / *v.* recompensar.
RECONCILE *v.* reconciliar.
RECONSIDER *v.* reconsiderar, reavaliar.
RECORD *s.* registro, anotação / *v.* gravar; registrar; gravar em disco.
RECREATE *v.* recriar.
RECREATION *s.* recreação, passatempo, divertimento.
RED *adj.* vermelho / *s.* vermelho.
REDEEMER *s.* Redentor.
RED-HAIRED *adj.* ruivo.
RED PEPPER *s.* malagueta; pimentão.
REDUCE *v.* reduzir; rebaixar.
REDWOOD *s.* pau-brasil, sequoia.
REEL *s.* molinete; carretel, bobina / *v.* bobinar, enrolar.
REFER *v.* referir-se, reportar; recorrer.
REFERENCE *s.* referência, respeito, menção.
REFILL *s.* carga sobressalente para suprir outra, refil / *v.* reabastecer.
REFLEX *s.* reflexo; reflexão / *adj.* reflexivo / *v.* recurvar.
REFORM *s.* reforma, melhoria / *v.* reformar.
REFRESH *v.* refrescar, revigorar.
REFRESHMENT *s.* refresco; refeição ligeira; descanso, repouso.

REFRIGERATION s. refrigeração.
REFRIGERATOR s. geladeira.
REFUGE s. refúgio, asilo.
REFUSE v. recusar, rejeitar, negar / s. refugo.
REFUTE v. refutar, contradizer.
REGARD s. consideração, atenção; estima / v. considerar, julgar, dizer respeito a.
REGARDING prep. relativo a, a respeito de, com referência a.
REGARDS s. cumprimentos, saudações.
REGENT s. regente, reinante / adj. regente, reinante.
REGION s. região, área, território.
REGISTER s. registro, arquivo, lista / v. registrar, inscrever.
REGRET s. arrependimento, remorso / v. arrepender, lastimar, lamentar.
REIGN s. reinado; domínio / v. reinar.
REIN s. rédea.
REINDEER s. rena.
RELATE v. contar; relacionar.
RELATION s. relação, relacionamento.
RELATIVE s. parente / adj. relativo.
RELAX v. relaxar, descontrair, descansar.
RELEASE v. liberar, soltar (nota, publicação) / s. soltura, exibição, lançamento.
RELIABLE adj. confiável, de confiança, seguro.
RELIEF s. alívio; relevo, saliência.
RELIGION s. religião.
REMAIN s. sobra, resto / v. permanecer, ficar, restar.
REMARK s. observação, comentário / v. comentar, observar.
REMEDY s. remédio / v. remediar.
REMEMBER v. lembrar, recordar.
REMINDER s. lembrança, lembrete.
REMISS adj. remisso, preguiçoso, indolente, lento.
REMNANT s. resto; retalho.
REMOTE adj. remoto, distante.
REMOVE v. tirar; remover.
RENEW v. renovar, refazer, repetir; recomeçar.
RENEWAL s. renovação, recomeço.
RENT s. aluguel / v. alugar.
REPAIR s. conserto / v. consertar.
REPEAT s. repetição / v. repetir.
REPLACE v. repor, substituir.
REPLACEMENT s. reposição, substituição.
REPLY s. resposta / v. responder, replicar.
REPORT s. relatório; reportagem; boletim de escola / v. informar, comunicar.
REPROACH s. repreensão, censura / v. repreender.
REPROVE v. reprovar, criticar.
REPUBLIC s. república.
REPULSE v. rejeitar, repelir, recusar / s. repulsa, recusa, rejeição.
REPUTE s. reputação, fama, renome / v. reputar, julgar.
REQUEST s. pedido, requerimento, solicitação / v. solicitar, requerer, pedir.
REQUIRE v. requerer, exigir, necessitar.
REQUISITE s. requisito / adj. requerido.
RESALE s. revenda.
RESCUE s. salvamento, resgate / v. resgatar, salvar, socorrer.
RESEARCH s. pesquisa, busca / v. pesquisar, examinar, investigar.
RESEMBLE v. assemelhar-se, parecer-se com.
RESERVE s. reserva, restrição / v. reservar, guardar.
RESIDE v. residir.
RESIST v. resistir, opor-se.
RESOLVE s. resolução / v. resolver, decidir, solucionar.
RESORT s. local turístico; refúgio.
RESOURCE s. recurso, meio, expediente.
RESPECT s. respeito, consideração / v. respeitar.
RESPOND v. responder, reagir.
REST s. descanso, repouso; resto, restante, sobra / v. descansar; sobrar.
RESTART v. reiniciar, recomeçar / s. reinício, recomeço.
RESTLESS adj. impaciente.
RESULT s. resultado, consequência / v. resultar.
RESUME v. reatar, retomar, recuperar.
RESUMÉ s. currículo profissional; resumo, sumário.
RETAIL v. vender a varejo / s. varejo.
RETAIN v. reter, manter.
RETARD s. demora, atraso / v. demorar-se, atrasar-se.
RETICENT adj. reticente, reservado.
RETIRE v. aposentar-se, reformar-se.
RETORT s. réplica / v. replicar.
RETURN v. retornar, regressar, voltar / s. retorno, regresso, volta.
REVENGE s. vingança, desforra / v. vingar-se.

REVERSE s. contrário, reverso, oposto / adj. contrário, reverso, oposto / v. revogar, inverter, anular.
REVIEW v. rever, revisar, examinar / s. resenha, revisão, exame, inspeção.
REWARD s. recompensa, gratificação / v. recompensar, retribuir.
REWRITE v. reescrever.
RHINOCEROS s. rinoceronte.
RHYME s. rima; verso; poesia / v. rimar, fazer versos.
RHYTHM s. ritmo, cadência.
RIB s. costela.
RIBALD adj. irreverente, devasso, dissoluto.
RIBBON s. fita, faixa.
RICE s. arroz.
RICH adj. rico.
RICHES s. riquezas, bens.
RID v. libertar, livrar-se.
RIDE s. carona / v. passear; cavalgar.
RIDICULE s. ridículo.
RIGHT s. direito, correto, justo / adj. certo, correto, direito / adv. à direita; corretamente, justamente.
RIGID adj. rígido, firme, duro, inflexível.
RIGOROUS adj. rigoroso, severo.
RILE v. aborrecer, irritar.
RIM s. borda, beira; aro, aba.
RING s. anel; círculo; toque de campainha ou telefone / v. tocar, soar, telefonar.
RINK s. pista de patinação, rinque.
RIOT s. desordem, distúrbio / v. provocar distúrbios.
RIPE adj. maduro (fruta) / v. amadurecer.
RISE s. levantamento, ascensão / v. ascender, subir, erguer-se.
RITUAL adj. ritual, cerimonial.
RIVER s. rio.
ROAD s. estrada.
ROAR v. rugir, urrar / s. rugido, urro.
ROAST BEEF s. rosbife.
ROB v. roubar.
ROBBER s. ladrão.
ROBBERY s. furto, roubo.
ROBE s. roupão, robe; manto.
ROBOT s. robô.
ROBUST adj. robusto, vigoroso, forte.
ROCK s. rocha, pedra / v. balançar-se; embalar (criança).

ROCKET s. foguete / v. disparar.
ROD s. vara, haste.
RODEO s. rodeio.
ROLLER COASTER s. montanha-russa.
ROMAN adj. romano / s. romano.
ROMANCE s. romance; caso amoroso; história de amor.
ROMANTIC adj. romântico.
ROOF s. telhado.
ROOM s. quarto, aposento, sala.
ROOSTER s. galo.
ROOT s. raiz.
ROPE s. corda, cabo, cordame.
ROSE s. rosa (flor).
ROSEBUD s. botão de rosa.
ROSEBUSH s. roseira.
ROSEMARY s. alecrim.
ROTARY adj. rotativo, giratório.
ROUGH adj. áspero, tosco; bruto, violento.
ROUGHNESS s. aspereza, rudeza.
ROUND adj. redondo / s. rodada / prep. em volta de, ao redor de / v. rodear.
ROUTINE s. rotina, hábito / adj. rotineiro, de rotina.
ROW s. fileira, fila; briga, motim / v. enfileirar; remar; brigar.
ROWER s. remador.
ROYAL adj. real; monárquico.
RUB v. esfregar, friccionar; polir; apagar (com a borracha).
RUBBER s. borracha; camisinha.
RUBY s. rubi.
RUDDER s. leme.
RUDE adj. grosso, grosseiro, rude.
RUMMAGE SALE s. bazar (de caridade).
RUN s. corrida / v. correr; administrar, dirigir.
RUNNER s. corredor; aquele que corre.
RUNT s. nanico, anão, pigmeu.
RURAL adj. rural, campestre.
RUSH s. ímpeto, pressa, agitação / v. apressar-se, acelerar.
RUSH HOUR s. horário de pico.
RUSSIA s. Rússia.
RUST s. ferrugem / v. enferrujar.
RUSTY adj. enferrujado.
RUTHLESS adj. cruel, implacável, desumano.

S

S, s *s.* décima nona letra do alfabeto inglês.
SABBATH *s.* sabá, sábado dos judeus, dia de descanso.
SABBATIC *adj.* sabático.
SABER *v.* golpear com sabre / *s.* sabre (espada).
SABOT *s.* tipo de tamanco.
SABOTAGE *s.* sabotagem / *v.* sabotar.
SABOTEUR *s.* sabotador, terrorista.
SABULOUS *adj.* sabuloso, areento, arenoso.
SAC *s.* bolsa, cavidade, receptáculo.
SACERDOTAL *adj.* sacerdotal.
SACERDOTALISM *s.* sacerdotalismo, clericalismo.
SACHEM *s.* chefe de tribo; chefe, líder, dirigente.
SACHET *s.* sachê.
SACK *s.* saco; bolsa; demissão / *v.* demitir; saquear; ensacar.
SACKCLOTH *s.* pano de saco, aniagem.
SACKER *s.* saqueador, espoliador; o responsável por demitir.
SACRAL *adj.* sacro, relativo ao osso sacro; sagrado.
SACRAMENT *s.* sacramento.
SACRAMENTAL *s.* cerimônia, sacramento / *adj.* sacramental.
SACRED *adj.* sagrado; consagrado; religioso.
SACREDNESS *s.* santidade; sacralidade.
SACRIFICE *s.* sacrifício / *v.* sacrificar.
SACRIFICIAL *adj.* sacrificial, sacrificatório.
SACRILEGE *s.* sacrilégio.
SACRILEGIOUS *adj.* sacrilégio, injurioso, insultante.
SACRISTAN *s.* sacristão.
SACRISTY *s.* sacristia.
SACROSANCT *adj.* consagrado, sacrossanto, sagrado, inviolável.
SAD *adj.* triste; deplorável.
SADDEN *v.* entristecer; entristecer-se.
SADDLE *s.* sela / *v.* selar; impor; dominar.
SADDLEBAG *s.* alforje; sacola, bolsa.
SADDLER *s.* seleiro.
SADDLERY *s.* selaria.
SADISM *s.* sadismo.
SADIST *s.* sadista.
SADISTIC *adj.* sadista, sádico.
SADLY *adv.* tristemente; lamentavelmente.
SADNESS *s.* tristeza.
SADOMASOCHISM *s.* sadomasoquismo.

SAFARI s. safári.
SAFE adj. seguro / s. cofre.
SAFEBREAKER s. arrombador de cofres.
SAFEGUARD s. salvaguarda / v. proteger, salvaguardar.
SAFEKEEPING s. guarda, custódia.
SAFE LIGHT s. lanterna de câmara escura.
SAFELY adv. seguramente, sem perigo, sem dano.
SAFETY s. segurança, trava.
SAFETY BELT s. cinto de segurança.
SAFETY GLASS s. vidro de segurança.
SAFFRON s. açafrão / adj. amarelo alaranjado.
SAG s. caída, queda, inclinação / v. afundar, cair, decair.
SAGA s. saga, conto lendário, lenda.
SAGACIOUS adj. perspicaz, sagaz, esperto.
SAGACIOUSNESS s. sagacidade, perspicácia, inteligência.
SAGACITY s. m.q. sagaciousness.
SAGE s. sábio, inteligente / adj. sábio, prudente.
SAGENESS s. sabedoria, inteligência; sagacidade.
SAGGY adj. propenso a ceder, inclinado, caído.
SAGITTARIAN s. sagitariano.
SAGITTARIUS s. Sagitário (astrologia).
SAHARA s. Saara.
SAHIB s. senhor (tratamento dado aos europeus na Índia).
SAID adj. citado, mencionado.
SAIL s. vela de navio / v. navegar, velejar; deslizar.
SAILBOAT s. veleiro.
SAILCLOTH s. lona.
SAILER s. navio a vela.
SAILING s. navegação / adj. de vela.
SAILMAKER s. pessoa que faz ou conserta veleiros.
SAILOR s. marinheiro, marujo.
SAILORLY adj. relativo a marinheiro.
SAINT adj. santo / s. santo.
SAINTED adj. santificado.
SAINTHOOD s. santidade.
SAKE s. objetivo, propósito, razão; saquê.
SALACIOUS adj. lascivo, obsceno, indecente.
SALACIOUSNESS s. lascívia, luxúria.
SALAD s. salada.

SALAMANDER s. salamandra.
SALAMI s. salame.
SALARIED adj. assalariado.
SALARY s. salário, remuneração.
SALE s. venda, liquidação.
SALEABILITY s. qualidade do que é vendável, passível de ser vendido.
SALEABLE adj. passível de venda, vendível.
SALEROOM s. sala de exposição ou de vendas; sala para leilão.
SALESCLERK s. balconista.
SALESMAN s. vendedor.
SALESWOMAN s. vendedora.
SALIENCE s. saliência; importância, destaque.
SALIENT s. ângulo protuberante / adj. saliente, importante, considerável.
SALIFY v. salificar, converter em sal.
SALINA s. salina, local onde se produz sal por evaporação.
SALINE s. salino; remédio salino / adj. salina; salgado.
SALIVA s. saliva.
SALIVARY adj. salivar, de saliva.
SALIVATE v. salivar.
SALIVATION s. salivação.
SALLOW v. ficar pálido / adj. amarelo, amarelado, pálido.
SALLOWISH adj. de cor amarelada.
SALLOWNESS s. abatimento, palidez.
SALLY s. ataque repentino / v. irromper, investir; atacar.
SALMON s. salmão.
SALMONELLA s. salmonela.
SALON s. sala, salão.
SALOON s. bar, botequim, salão (de navio).
SALT s. sal / v. salgar.
SALTCELLAR s. saleiro.
SALTISH adj. salgado.
SALTSHAKER s. saleiro.
SALTWATER s. água salgada.
SALTY adj. salgado.
SALUBRIOUS adj. salubre.
SALUTARY adj. benéfico; saudável, salubre.
SALUTATION s. cumprimento, saudação.
SALUTE s. continência; saudação / v. bater continência; saudar.
SALVAGE s. salvamento / v. salvar.
SALVATION s. salvação, redenção.
SALVE s. pomada, remédio / v. aliviar, mitigar.

SAMARITAN s. samaritano; bondoso, solidário / adj. samaritano; bondoso, solidário.
SAME adj. mesmo, igual / adv. igualmente / pron. o mesmo.
SAMENESS s. similaridade, mesmice.
SAMP s. farinha de milho cozido.
SAMPLE s. amostra / v. testar, provar.
SAMPLER s. o que tira amostras, classificador.
SANATORIUM s. sanatório.
SANATORY adj. sanativo.
SANCTIFICATION s. santificação.
SANCTIFY v. santificar.
SANCTION s. sanção / v. sancionar, penalizar.
SANCTITY s. santidade.
SANCTUARY s. santuário.
SAND s. areia / v. jogar areia; encher de areia.
SANDAL s. sandália.
SANDBAG s. saco de areia.
SANDBAR s. banco de areia.
SANDBOX s. caixa de areia.
SANDCASTLE s. castelo de areia.
SANDGLASS s. ampulheta.
SANDPAPER s. lixa / v. lixar.
SANDPIPER s. maçarico.
SANDPIT s. poço de areia, areeiro.
SANDSTONE s. arenito (rocha).
SANDSTORM s. tempestade de areia.
SANDWICH s. sanduíche.
SANDY adj. arenoso.
SANE adj. são, sadio, sensato.
SANGUINARY adj. sanguinário.
SANGUINE adj. sanguíneo.
SANITARY adj. sanitário.
SANITATION s. saneamento.
SANITISE v. sanear, desinfetar.
SANITY s. sanidade.
SANSKRIT s. sânscrito.
SAPHEAD s. bobo.
SAPIENCE s. sapiência, sabedoria.
SAPPHIRE s. safira.
SAPPY adj. cheio de vida, sucoso, vigoroso, forte; bobo.
SARACEN s. sarraceno, mouro, árabe.
SARCASM s. sarcasmo, ironia.
SARCASTIC adj. sarcástico.
SARCASTICALLY adv. sarcasticamente.
SARCOMA s. sarcoma (tumor maligno).
SARCOPHAGUS s. sarcófago.
SARDINE s. sardinha.
SARDINIA s. Sardenha (Itália).
SARDONIC adj. sardônico; sarcástico.
SARS abrev. SRAG (Síndrome Respiratória Aguda Grave).
SARTOR s. alfaiate.
SARTORIAL adj. sartorial; bem-vestido.
SAS abrev. SAS (Serviço Aéreo Especial).
SASH s. cinto, cinturão, faixa.
SASSY adj. ousado, presumido, corajoso.
SATAN s. diabo, satã.
SATANIC adj. satânico.
SATANISM s. satanismo.
SATANIST s. satanista.
SATE v. saciar-se.
SATELLITE s. satélite.
SATIATE v. saciar, fartar / adj. saciado, satisfeito.
SATIN s. cetim / adj. acetinado.
SATIRE s. sátira.
SATIRICAL adj. satírico.
SATIRISE v. satirizar.
SATIRIST s. satirista.
SATISFACTION s. satisfação.
SATISFACTORY adj. satisfatório.
SATISFIED adj. satisfeito.
SATISFY v. satisfazer; saciar; corresponder.
SATISFYING adj. gratificante, agradável.
SATURATE v. saturar.
SATURATION s. saturação; satisfação.
SATURDAY s. sábado.
SATURN s. Saturno.
SATYR s. sátiro (mitologia).
SATYRIC adj. m.q. satirical.
SAUCE s. molho, tempero.
SAUCEPAN s. caçarola, panela grande.
SAUCER s. pires.
SAUCINESS s. atrevimento; travessura.
SAUCY adj. atrevido; provocante, malicioso.
SAUDI s. saudita, árabe-saudita / adj. saudita, árabe-saudita.
SAUERKRAUT s. chucrute.
SAUNA s. sauna.
SAUSAGE s. salsicha; linguiça.
SAUTÉ s. sauté / v. saltear / adj. salteado.
SAVAGE adj. selvagem; cruel; feroz.
SAVAGERY s. selvageria.
SAVANNA s. savana.
SAVANT s. sábio, culto.
SAVE v. salvar, guardar, economizar.
SAVER s. poupador, que economiza.

SAVING s. salvação; economia, poupança / adj. econômico, salvador / prep. fora, exceto.
SAVIOUR s. salvador, resgatador.
SAVOR s. sabor, gosto / v. saborear, provar.
SAVORY adj. saboroso, cheiroso.
SAW s. serra, serrote / v. serrar, cortar com serra.
SAWDUST s. serragem, serradura.
SAWMILL s. serraria.
SAWYER s. serrador.
SAXON s. inglês; anglo-saxão; saxônio / adj. inglês; anglo-saxão; saxônio.
SAXOPHONE s. saxofone.
SAXOPHONIST s. saxofonista.
SAY v. dizer; mandar, dar ordens.
SAYING s. provérbio, ditado.
SCAB s. casca (machucado) / v. cicatrizar.
SCABBARD s. bainha.
SCABBY adj. desprezível, nojento; sarnento.
SCABIES s. sarna, escabiose.
SCABROUS adj. rude; repulsivo; complicado.
SCAFFOLD s. andaime.
SCALABLE adj. escalável.
SCALD s. queimadura (com água fervente) / v. escaldar.
SCALDING adj. escaldante.
SCALE s. escala, régua, metro; escama; balança / v. escalar; pesar.
SCALENE s. triângulo escaleno / adj. escaleno.
SCALLION s. cebolinha.
SCALP s. escalpo / v. escalpar.
SCALPEL s. escapelo, bisturi.
SCALPER s. esfolador; cambista (teatro).
SCALY adj. escamoso.
SCAM s. fraude, logro / v. fraudar.
SCAMMER s. fraudador.
SCAMP s. patife, malandro, velhaco.
SCAN s. exame, varredura / v. escanear, examinar.
SCANDAL s. escândalo, vexame, calúnia.
SCANDALISE v. escandalizar.
SCANDALOUS adj. escandaloso.
SCANDINAVIA s. Escandinávia.
SCANDINAVIAN s. escandinavo / adj. escandinavo.
SCANNER s. escâner; tomógrafo, leitor.
SCANT adj. escasso; insuficiente / v. limitar, escassear, reduzir.
SCANTILY adv. escassamente.

SCANTY adj. escasso, raro.
SCAPEGOAT s. bode expiatório.
SCAPULA s. escápula, omoplata (anatomia).
SCAR v. cicatrizar, deixar marca / s. cicatriz.
SCARAB s. escaravelho (besouro).
SCARCE adj. escasso, raro.
SCARCELY adv. raramente.
SCARCENESS s. escassez, raridade, parcimônia, falta.
SCARCITY s. escassez, carência, falta.
SCARE s. susto, espanto / v. assustar, espantar.
SCARECROW s. espantalho; maltrapilho.
SCARED adj. assustado.
SCAREMONGER s. alarmista.
SCARF s. cachecol; lenço de pescoço.
SCARLET s. escarlate / adj. escarlate.
SCARP s. escarpa, declive / v. escarpar.
SCARY adj. assustador; repulsivo.
SCATHE s. dano, trauma / v. ferir, machucar; criticar.
SCATHING adj. nocivo, mordaz, corrosivo.
SCATHINGLY adv. mordazmente, de forma fulminante.
SCATOLOGIC adj. escatológico.
SCATOLOGY s. escatologia.
SCATTER s. dispersão, dissipação / v. espalhar, difundir; dispersar-se.
SCATTERBRAIN s. cabeça de vento, pessoa distraída.
SCATTERBRAINED adj. distraído, descuidado.
SCATTERED adj. espalhado, disperso.
SCAVENGE v. vascular, revirar; cavucar.
SCENARIO s. cenário.
SCENE s. vista, panorama; cena.
SCENERY s. vista, cenário.
SCENIC adj. pictórico, pitoresco; cênico.
SCENT s. perfume; aroma, odor / v. farejar.
SCENTED adj. perfumado, cheiroso.
SCEPTICAL adj. céptico, descrente.
SCEPTICISM s. ceticismo.
SCEPTRE s. cetro.
SCHEDULE s. horário; lista; programa / v. programar.
SCHEDULED adj. programado, planejado.
SCHEDULER s. organizador, planejador.
SCHEDULING s. programação; agendamento.
SCHEMA s. esquema, programa, esboço.

SCHEMATIC s. esquema, diagrama / adj. esquemático.
SCHEMATIZE v. esquematizar.
SCHEME s. plano, método; esquema / v. planejar; tramar, maquinar.
SCHEMER s. conspirador, maquinador.
SCHISM s. cisma.
SCHIZOID adj. esquizoide, antissocial.
SCHIZOPHRENIA s. esquizofrenia.
SCHIZOPHRENIC s. esquizofrênico / adj. esquizofrênico.
SCHOLAR s. culto, erudito; acadêmico; bolsista.
SCHOLARLY adj. erudito, sábio, douto.
SCHOLARSHIP s. bolsa de estudos.
SCHOOL s. escola.
SCHOOLBOOK s. livro escolar, livro didático.
SCHOOLDAYS s. dias letivos.
SCHOOLING s. escolaridade, educação.
SCHOOLMATE s. colega de escola.
SCHOOLWORK s. trabalho escolar.
SCHOOLYARD s. pátio.
SCIATIC adj. ciático.
SCIATICA s. ciática (anatomia).
SCIENCE s. ciência.
SCIENTIFIC adj. científico.
SCIENTIFICALLY adv. cientificamente.
SCIENTIST s. cientista.
SCILICET adv. a saber; ou seja.
SCINTILLA s. centelha, partícula.
SCINTILLANT adj. cintilante.
SCINTILLATE v. cintilar.
SCISSION s. corte, divisão, separação.
SCISSOR v. tesourar, cortar com tesoura.
SCISSORS s. tesoura.
SCLEROSIS s. esclerose.
SCLEROTIC adj. esclerótico.
SCOFF s. zombaria, escárnio / v. zombar, ridicularizar.
SCOLD s. mulher ranzinza; megera / v. repreender, censurar.
SCOLDING s. repreensão, bronca.
SCOLIOSIS s. escoliose, curvatura lateral da coluna vertebral.
SCONCE s. candeeiro; cachola, cabeça / v. fortificar.
SCONE s. bolinho, broinha.
SCOOP s. concha, colher / v. cavar, cavoucar.
SCOOT v. apressar-se, correr.
SCOOTER s. patinete; lambreta.
SCOPE s. escopo; âmbito, alcance.
SCORCH v. queimar, chamuscar / s. queimadura leve.
SCORE s. contagem (de pontos) / v. marcar (pontos).
SCOREBOARD s. placar.
SCOREBOOK s. livro em que se registra a pontuação em uma competição.
SCORECARD s. cartão de pontuação; boletim.
SCORER s. marcador; artilheiro.
SCORING s. marcação, pontuação.
SCORN s. desprezo, desdém / v. desprezar, desdenhar.
SCORNFUL adj. desdenhoso; que despreza.
SCORNFULLY adv. desdenhosamente.
SCORPIO s. Escorpião (astrologia).
SCORPION s. escorpião.
SCOT s. escocês.
SCOTCH s. escocês (dialeto e uísque) / adj. escocês (dialeto e uísque) / v. ferir; praticar incisões.
SCOTLAND s. Escócia.
SCOTTISH s. escocês / adj. escocês; da Escócia.
SCOUNDREL s. patife, canalha.
SCOUNTMASTER s. chefe de um grupo de escoteiros.
SCOURGE s. flagelo.
SCOUT s. escoteiro, patrulheiro / v. explorar, conhecer.
SCOUT CAR s. carro militar blindado, sem capota.
SCOUTCRAFT s. escoteirismo, bandeirantismo.
SCOUTER s. escoteiro acima de 18 anos.
SCOUTING s. vigia, observação; escotismo.
SCOW s. barcaça para transportar areia.
SCOWL s. carranca, mau humor / v. falar com raiva.
SCRABBLE s. rabisco; arranhão; raspagem / v. rabiscar; arranhar; raspar.
SCRAG s. pessoa magra, animal magro.
SCRAGGEDNESS s. magreza, aspereza.
SCRAGGLY adj. esparso, irregular.
SCRAGGY adj. alto e magro; áspero, rugoso, eriçado.
SCRAM v. sair rapidamente, dar de pinote, sumir.

SCRAMBLE s. passeio, escalada ou subida sobre terreno áspero; luta / v. misturar, mexer; lutar; embaralhar.
SCRAMBLINGLY adv. desordenadamente, a esmo, apressadamente.
SCRAP s. pedaço, parte; sucata, ferro-velho / v. descartar.
SCRAPBOOK s. álbum de recortes / v. colecionar recortes.
SCRAPE v. lixar, limpar; raspar; coçar / s. arranhão; complicação.
SCRAPER s. avarento, pão-duro; raspadeira, raspador.
SCRAP HEAP s. monte de sucata; atitude de desprezo.
SCRAPINGS s. economias; restos.
SCRAPIRON s. ferro-velho, sucata.
SCRAPPY adj. desconexo, fragmentário.
SCRATCH s. arranhão; unhada / v. arranhar, coçar.
SCRATCH-AND-WIN s. raspadinha (tipo de loteria).
SCRATCH LINE s. linha de largada (esporte).
SCRATCH PAD s. bloco de anotações, de rascunho.
SCRATCH PAPER s. papel para rascunho.
SCRAWL s. rabisco, garrancho / v. rabiscar, garatujar.
SCRAWLY adj. rabiscado, ilegível (letra).
SCREAK s. rangido, chiado / v. ranger, chiar.
SCREAM s. grito, berro / v. gritar, berrar.
SCREAMER s. gritador, berrador.
SCREAMING s. gritaria / adj. gritante.
SCREECH s. berro, grito / v. gritar, chiar, berrar.
SCREECHY adj. estridente, agudo.
SCREED s. longo discurso; lenga-lenga.
SCREEN s. tela (TV, cinema, etc.).
SCREENING s. classificação; projeção; teste.
SCREENPLAY s. roteiro.
SCREENSAVER s. protetor de tela.
SCREEN STAR s. astro de cinema.
SCREENWRITER s. roteirista.
SCREENWRITING s. escrita de roteiros.
SCREW s. parafuso, tarraxa / v. aparafusar, atarraxar.
SCREWBALL s. pessoa excêntrica.
SCREWDRIVER s. chave de fenda.
SCREWED adj. parafusado, atarraxado.
SCREW WRENCH s. chave de parafuso.
SCREWY adj. caótico, confuso.

SCRIBBLE s. rabiscos, garranchos / v. rabiscar, escrevinhar.
SCRIBE s. escriba, escrevente, copiador / v. gravar, registrar, marcar.
SCRIMMAGE s. conflito, choque, luta, briga / v. brigar, lutar.
SCRIMP v. apertar, estreitar; economizar.
SCRIMPY adj. escasso, apertado.
SCRIP s. recibo, certificado de posse, documento.
SCRIPT s. escrita; roteiro; manuscrito / v. escrever roteiro.
SCRIPTED adj. roteirizado, programado.
SCRIPTURAL adj. escritural; bíblico.
SCRIPTURE s. Escritura, Bíblia.
SCRIPTWRITER s. roteirista.
SCRIVENER s. escrivão, escrevente.
SCROLL s. pergaminho; rolo de papel / v. paginar, rolar.
SCROLLING s. rolagem / adj. rotante, de rolagem.
SCROOGE v. economizar / s. avarento, sovina.
SCROOP s. farfalho (som) / v. farfalhar.
SCROTAL adj. escrotal.
SCROTUM s. testículos, escroto.
SCROUNGE v. filar, pedir, explorar.
SCRUB s. moita, arbustos; esfregação / v. esfregar, friccionar.
SCRUBBER s. esfregador, esfregão; purificador.
SCRUBBY adj. inferior, miserável.
SCRUFF s. nuca.
SCRUFFY adj. desleixado, imundo, sujo.
SCRUM s. alinhamento; tumulto, motim.
SCRUNCH s. rangido, estalido / v. ranger; mastigar, esmagar.
SCRUNCHIE s. elástico de cabelo.
SCRUPLE s. escrúpulo; receio, hesitação / v. recear, ter escrúpulos, hesitar.
SCRUPULOUS adj. escrupuloso, cauteloso; exigente, meticuloso.
SCRUPULOUSLY adv. escrupulosamente, de forma meticulosa.
SCRUTABLE adj. escrutável, que pode ser examinado ou investigado.
SCRUTINEER s. escrutinador.
SCRUTINISE v. escrutar, perscrutar cuidadosa e minuciosamente; inquirir.

SCRUTINISER s. escrutador; investigador.
SCRUTINY s. escrutínio, exame minucioso.
SCUBA s. cilindro de mergulho.
SCUBA DIVER s. mergulhador; esportista que mergulha.
SCUD s. movimento rápido, deslize / v. movimentar-se, deslizar.
SCUFF s. chinelo; ato de arrastar os pés / v. esfolar; arrastar os pés.
SCUFFLE s. briga, rixa, disputa / v. disputar, brigar.
SCUFF s. tipo de pantufa.
SCULPT v. esculpir; gravar, entalhar.
SCULPTOR s. escultor.
SCULPTRESS s. escultora.
SCULPTURAL adj. escultural.
SCULPTURE s. escultura; gravura / v. esculpir; gravar.
SCUM s. escuma, espuma; escória, lixo / v. escumar; tirar a sujeira.
SCUMBAG s. pessoa desprezível, asquerosa (gíria).
SCUMMY adj. espumoso, espumento.
SCUNNER s. aversão, desgosto / v. desgostar, sentir-se mal.
SCURF s. caspa.
SCURFY adj. escamoso; esfoliado.
SCURRILE adj. baixo, grosseiro, indecente.
SCURRILELY adv. vilmente, grosseiramente.
SCURRILOUSNESS s. baixeza, indecência.
SCURRY v. correr, apressar / s. pressa.
SCUT s. rabinho, cauda curta.
SCUTTLE v. correr, escapulir / s. correria, corrida; escotilha, portinhola (navio).
SCUTTLER s. fugitivo.
SEA s. mar / adj. marinho, do mar.
SEA-BATHING s. banho de mar.
SEABED s. solo oceânico, fundo do mar.
SEA-BIRD s. ave marinha.
SEABOARD s. litoral, costa.
SEABORN adj. nascido no mar, oriundo do mar.
SEA-BREEZE s. brisa do mar.
SEA-COAST s. orla, encosta.
SEA-FIGHT s. batalha naval.
SEAFLOOR s. fundo do mar.
SEAFOOD s. fruto do mar.
SEA GULL s. gaivota.
SEA HORSE s. cavalo-marinho.
SEAL s. foca; vedação, lacre / v. selar, lacrar.
SEAMAN s. marinheiro.
SEA PIKE s. peixe-agulha.

SEAPORT s. porto.
SEAQUAKE s. maremoto.
SEAR v. queimar, tostar; arder.
SEARCH s. busca; pesquisa, exame / v. procurar; investigar.
SEARCHER s. pesquisador, investigador.
SEARCHING adj. rigoroso, minucioso.
SEARCHLESS adj. impenetrável, sem acesso.
SEARCHLIGHT s. holofote.
SEARING adj. abrasador; causticante.
SEASCAPE s. paisagem marinha.
SEASHELL s. concha.
SEASHORE s. litoral, costa.
SEASICK adj. enjoado, mareado.
SEASICKNESS s. enjoo, náusea.
SEASIDE s. beira-mar.
SEASON s. época, temporada, estação / v. temperar, condimentar.
SEASONAL adj. sazonal.
SEASONALITY s. sazonalidade.
SEASONED adj. maduro, sazonado; temperado.
SEASONING s. tempero, condimento.
SEAT s. assento, banco, lugar / v. acomodar, assentar.
SEATBELT s. cinto de segurança.
SEATED adj. sentado, assentado.
SEATING s. assento.
SEAWARD adj. na direção do mar, voltado para o mar.
SEAWAY s. rota marítima; canal.
SEAWEED s. alga marinha.
SEAWORTHY adj. navegável.
SEC adj. seco; momento, segundo (coloquial) / abrev. segundo.
SECEDE v. separar-se, cindir-se, afastar-se.
SECEDER s. separatista, dissidente.
SECERN v. distinguir, segregar.
SECESSION s. secessão, separação.
SECLUDE v. afastar, isolar.
SECLUDED adj. isolado, retirado.
SECLUSION s. exclusão, isolamento.
SECOND adj. segundo, suplementar / s. segundo / adv. em segundo lugar.
SECONDARY adj. secundário.
SECONDARY SCHOOL s. escola secundária; ensino médio.

SECOND-HAND s. ajuda / adj. usado, de segunda mão / adv. indiretamente.
SECONDLY adv. em segundo lugar.
SECRECY s. sigilo, reserva.
SECRET s. segredo, enigma / adj. secreto, oculto.
SECRETARIAL adj. secretarial.
SECRETARIAT s. secretariado, secretaria.
SECRETARY s. secretário.
SECRETE v. secretar, expelir.
SECRETION s. secreção.
SECRETIVE s. segredista.
SECRETIVELY adv. discretamente.
SECRETLY adv. secretamente.
SECRETORY adj. secretório, secretor.
SECT s. seita; facção.
SECTION s. seção, parte; artigo; gomo.
SECTIONAL adj. seccional, secional.
SECTOR s. setor, ala.
SECULAR adj. secular; muito antigo.
SECURE adj. seguro, preso / v. prender; assegurar.
SECURELY adv. seguramente; firmemente.
SECURITIES s. títulos (finanças).
SECURITY s. segurança; garantia, fiança.
SECURITY COUNCIL s. Conselho de Segurança (ONU).
SECURITY GUARD s. segurança, geralmente de grandes valores ou quantias de dinheiro.
SECURITY SERVICE s. Serviço de Segurança.
SEDAN s. sedã.
SEDATE adj. sossegado, sedado / v. sedar.
SEDATION s. sedação.
SEDATIVE s. sedativo / adj. sedativo.
SEDENTARY adj. sedentário, inativo.
SEDIMENT s. sedimento.
SEDIMENTARY adj. sedimentário.
SEDIMENTATION s. sedimentação.
SEDUCE v. seduzir, persuadir.
SEDUCER s. sedutor.
SEDUCTION s. sedução, atração; fascínio.
SEE v. ver, enxergar, olhar.
SEED s. semente, caroço / v. semear.
SEEDLESS adj. sem semente (fruta).
SEEDLING s. muda (de planta).
SEEING s. vista, visão / conj. visto que, desde que, haja vista.
SEEK v. procurar, buscar, esforçar-se por.
SEEM v. parecer, dar a impressão de.
SEEMINGLY adv. aparentemente.
SEEP v. penetrar, infiltrar-se.

SEEPAGE s. vazamento, infiltração.
SEESAW s. gangorra; balanço / v. balançar.
SEGMENT s. segmento / v. segmentar.
SEGMENTATION s. segmentação.
SEGREGATE v. segregar / adj. segregado.
SEGREGATION s. segregação, separação.
SEISMIC adj. sísmico.
SEISMOLOGY s. sismologia.
SEIZE v. agarrar, pegar; tomar, confiscar.
SEIZED adj. amarrado, agarrado.
SEIZURE s. confisco.
SELDOM adv. raramente.
SELECT v. selecionar, escolher / adj. selecionado.
SELECTION s. seleção.
SELECTIVE adj. seletivo.
SELECTIVELY adv. seletivamente, de modo seleto.
SELECTIVITY s. seletividade.
SELECTNESS s. excelência, exclusividade.
SELECTOR s. selecionador; eleitor.
SELF s. eu, ego, a própria pessoa / pron. si, mesmo.
SELF-ADMIRATION s. autoadmiração, vaidade.
SELF-AFFIRMATION s. autoafirmação.
SELF-CONFIDENCE s. confiança em si mesmo, autoconfiança.
SELF-CONTROL s. autocontrole.
SELF-EDUCATED s. autodidata.
SELF-ESTEEM s. autoestima, amor-próprio.
SELF-INTEREST s. interesse próprio.
SELFISH adj. egoísta.
SELFISHNESS s. egoísmo.
SELF-LEARNING s. autoaprendizagem.
SELFLESS adj. altruísta.
SELL v. vender, negociar.
SELLER s. vendedor.
SELLING s. venda.
SELL-OFF s. liquidação.
SELL-OUT s. esgotado, lotado (espetáculo); vendido, traidor.
SEMANTIC adj. semântico, significativo.
SEMANTICS s. semântica (ciência).
SEMBLANCE s. semelhança, aparência.
SEMEN s. sêmen, esperma.
SEMESTER s. semestre.
SEMINAL adj. seminal.
SEMINAR s. seminário.
SEMINARIAN s. seminarista.

SEMIOLOGY s. semiologia.
SEMIOTIC adj. semiótico.
SENATE s. senado.
SENATOR s. senador.
SEND v. mandar, enviar, despachar.
SENDER s. remetente.
SENESCENCE s. senescência, velhice.
SENILE adj. senil, velho.
SENIOR s. mais velho, sênior / adj. superior, sênior.
SENIORITY s. precedência, primazia, superioridade.
SENSATION s. sensação.
SENSATIONAL s. sensacional, fabuloso.
SENSATIONALISE v. exagerar; escandalizar.
SENSATIONALISM s. sensacionalismo.
SENSATIONALIST s. sensacionalista / adj. sensacionalista.
SENSE s. senso, sentido, percepção / v. sentir, perceber.
SENSELESS adj. sem sentido; absurdo.
SENSIBILITY s. sensibilidade.
SENSIBLE adj. sensato, sábio, cauteloso.
SENSIBLY adv. sensatamente.
SENSITISE v. sensibilizar.
SENSITIVE adj. sensível, sensitivo, delicado.
SENSITIVITY s. sensibilidade.
SENSOR s. sensor.
SENSORY adj. sensorial, sensitivo.
SENSUAL adj. sensual.
SENSUALITY s. sensualidade.
SENT adj. enviado.
SENTENCE s. sentença, frase, oração.
SENTIMENT s. sentimento.
SENTIMENTAL adj. sentimental.
SENTIMENTALISM s. sentimentalismo.
SENTIMENTALITY s. sentimentalidade.
SENTINEL s. sentinela.
SENTRY s. guarda, vigia; sentinela.
SEPARABLE adj. separável.
SEPARATE adj. separado, diferente / v. separar, apartar.
SEPARATELY adv. separadamente.
SEPARATION s. separação, divisão.
SEPARATISM s. separatismo.
SEPARATIST s. separatista / adj. separatista.
SEPARATOR s. separador, centrífuga.
SEPIA s. sépia / adj. sépia.
SEPTEMBER s. setembro.
SEPTIC adj. séptico.
SEPTUM s. septo.
SEPULCHRE s. sepulcro.
SEQUENCE s. sequência, série.
SEQUENTIAL adj. sequencial; consecutivo.
SEQUENTIALLY adv. sequencialmente.
SEQUESTER v. isolar, afastar, separar.
SEQUESTRATION s. sequestro.
SEQUIN s. lantejoula.
SERAPH s. serafim, anjo.
SERENADE s. serenata, seresta / v. fazer serenata.
SERENDIPITOUS adj. afortunado.
SERENE adj. sereno, tranquilo.
SERENITY s. serenidade.
SERGEANT s. sargento.
SERIAL s. seriado, novela / adj. serial, em série.
SERIES s. série; sucessão.
SERIGRAPH s. serigrafia, impressão sobre seda.
SERIOUS adj. sério; grave, crítico.
SERIOUSLY adv. seriamente / interj. sério!
SERIOUSNESS s. seriedade.
SERMON s. sermão.
SEROTONIN s. serotonina.
SERPENT s. serpente, cobra.
SERVANT s. criado, empregado, servo.
SERVE v. atender, servir.
SERVER s. servidor (internet).
SERVICE s. serviço; manutenção.
SERVICEABLE adj. útil, prestável, prestativo.
SERVILE adj. servil.
SERVING s. porção (comida).
SERVITUDE s. servidão, serventia.
SESSION s. sessão.
SET s. jogo, grupo, conjunto; aparelho / v. ajustar; pôr; estabelecer.
SETTING s. colocação, assentamento; moldura, armação, engaste; cenário.
SETTLE v. assentar; estabelecer-se; liquidar, pagar (dívida).
SETTLEMENT s. colonização, assentamento; decisão, acordo.
SETUP s. instalação, configuração, arranjo.
SEVEN num. sete.
SEVENTEEN num. dezessete.
SEVENTY num. setenta.
SEVERAL adj. vários, diversos.
SEVERE adj. severo; austero.
SEVERELY adv. severamente.

SEVERITY s. severidade.
SEW v. coser, costurar.
SEWAGE s. esgoto.
SEWER s. encanamento.
SEWING s. costura.
SEX s. sexo / adj. sexual.
SEXINESS s. sexualidade.
SEXOLOGY s. sexologia.
SEXTON s. sacristão.
SEXUAL adj. sexual.
SEXUALITY s. m.q. sexiness.
SEXUALLY adv. sexualmente.
SEXY adj. erótico, excitante.
SHABBY adj. nojento, desprezível.
SHACK s. barracão, choça.
SHACKLE s. algema; obstáculo / v. algemar, acorrentar.
SHADE s. penumbra, sombra, tom / v. escurecer, sombrear.
SHADING s. sombreado, nuança.
SHADOW s. sombra.
SHADY adj. sombreado; sombrio.
SHAGGY adj. felpudo; peludo.
SHAKE v. sacudir, tremer, agitar.
SHAKEN adj. abalado, chocado.
SHAKINESS s. instabilidade.
SHAKY adj. duvidoso, instável, abalado.
SHALLOWNESS s. superficialidade; frivolidade.
SHAM s. imitação, farsa.
SHAMAN adj. pajé; xamã.
SHAMANISM s. xamanismo.
SHAME s. vergonha; pena, lástima / v. envergonhar.
SHAMEFUL adj. vergonhoso, desonroso, indecente.
SHAMEFULLY adv. vergonhosamente.
SHAMELESS adj. descarado, sem-vergonha.
SHAMELESSLY adv. descaradamente.
SHAMING s. vergonha, humilhação.
SHAMPOO s. xampu / v. lavar os cabelos.
SHANTY s. cabana, palhoça, barraco.
SHANTYTOWN s. favela.
SHAPE s. forma, figura, contorno / v. formar, dar forma.
SHAPED adj. modelado, moldado.
SHAPELESS adj. amorfo, disforme.
SHAPELY adj. formoso, bem-feito.
SHARE s. parte, porção; cota / v. dividir, compartilhar.
SHARK s. tubarão.

SHARP adj. esperto, perspicaz; afiado, pontudo.
SHARPEN v. afiar, amolar, apontar.
SHARPENER s. apontador, amolador, afiador.
SHARPLY adv. bruscamente.
SHAVE v. barbear, depilar.
SHAVER s. barbeador.
SHE pron. ela.
SHEAR v. tosquiar, tosar.
SHEARER s. tosquiador, aparador.
SHEEN s. brilho, resplendor.
SHEEP s. ovelha, carneiro.
SHEER v. guinar, desviar / adj. absoluto, completo.
SHEET s. lençol; folha (de papel); chapa, placa.
SHEIK s. xeique, xeque.
SHELF s. estante, prateleira.
SHELL s. concha, casca, casco.
SHELLFISH s. molusco, crustáceo.
SHELTER s. abrigo, refúgio / v. abrigar, proteger.
SHEPHERD v. pastorear / s. pastor.
SHERIFF s. xerife.
SHIELD s. escudo / v. proteger, defender.
SHIFT v. mover, mudar, trocar / s. mudança, troca.
SHIFTY adj. esperto, safado, astuto; negligente, inconstante, volúvel, desonesto.
SHIN s. canela (da perna).
SHINBONE s. tíbia.
SHINE s. brilho / v. brilhar.
SHINY adj. brilhante, lustroso.
SHIP s. navio, barco / v. embarcar, enviar.
SHIP-BOARD s. bordo de navio / adj. que ocorre(u) no navio.
SHIRK s. vagabundo / v. esquivar-se, faltar ao dever.
SHIRT s. camisa.
SHOCK s. choque, impacto / v. chocar, colidir; escandalizar.
SHOE s. sapato.
SHOEMAKER s. sapateiro.
SHOP s. loja / v. fazer compras.
SHORE s. margem, costa.
SHORT adj. curto; breve; baixo.
SHOT s. tiro, disparo; tentativa; injeção.

SHOULDER s. ombro.
SHOW v. mostrar, exibir / s. mostra, exibição.
SHRIMP s. camarão.
SHRUB s. arbusto.
SHUFFLE v. embaralhar / s. truque, embuste.
SHUN v. afastar-se de, evitar.
SHUNT v. manobrar, desviar / s. desvio, manobra.
SHUT v. fechar, tapar / adj. fechado, tapado.
SHUT-DOWN s. paralisação, parada temporária.
SHY adj. tímido, reservado, acanhado.
SHYLY adv. timidamente.
SHYNESS s. timidez, acanhamento.
SIAMESE s. siamês, siamesa, língua da Tailândia / adj. siamês.
SIBERIA s. Sibéria.
SIBERIAN s. siberiano / adj. siberiano.
SICILIAN s. siciliano / adj. siciliano.
SICILY s. Sicília.
SICK s. doente; vômito / adj. enjoado, farto.
SICKEN v. ficar doente, ficar enjoado.
SICKENING adj. repugnante, enjoativo.
SICKLE s. foice.
SICKLY adj. doentio.
SIDE s. lado; margem.
SIDEBURNS s. costeletas.
SIDE-LINE s. ocupação secundária, bico.
SIDEREAL adj. sideral.
SIDEWALK s. calçada.
SIDEWAYS adj. de lado, lateral / adv. para um lado, lateralmente.
SIFT v. peneirar.
SIGHT s. vista; visão.
SIGN s. indício; sinal; signo (astrologia) / v. assinar, inscrever.
SIGNATURE s. assinatura.
SIGNIFICANCE s. importância, consequência, significação, significado.
SIGNIFICANT adj. significante.
SIGNIFICATIVE s. significativo.
SIGNIFY v. significar.
SILENCE s. silêncio / v. silenciar.
SILENCER s. silenciador.
SILENT adj. silencioso, calado.
SILENTLY adv. silenciosamente.
SILHOUETTE s. silhueta.
SILICONE s. silicone / adj. de silicone.
SILK s. seda / adj. de seda.
SILKEN adj. sedoso, macio, suave.
SILKWORM s. bicho-da-seda.
SILLY adj. bobo, idiota, ridículo.
SILVER s. prata / adj. de prata, prateado.
SILVERWARE s. prataria, utensílios de prata.
SIMILAR adj. parecido, semelhante.
SIMILARITY s. semelhança.
SIMPLE adj. simples, fácil.
SIMPLICITY s. simplicidade.
SIMPLIFICATION s. simplificação.
SIMPLIFY v. simplificar.
SIMPLISTIC adj. simplista.
SIMPLY adv. simplesmente.
SIMULATE v. simular.
SIMULATED adj. simulado.
SIMULATION s. simulação.
SIMULATOR s. simulador.
SIMULTANEITY s. simultaneidade.
SIMULTANEOUS adj. simultâneo.
SIMULTANEOUSLY adv. simultaneamente.
SIN s. pecado / v. pecar.
SINCE adv. desde, desde então / conj. desde que, visto que / prep. desde.
SINCERE adj. sincero.
SINCERELY adv. sinceramente, atenciosamente.
SINCERITY s. sinceridade.
SINFUL adj. pecaminoso, pecador.
SING v. cantar.
SINGER s. cantor.
SINGING s. canto.
SINGLE adj. único, só; solteiro.
SINGLY adv. individualmente; isoladamente.
SINGULAR s. singular.
SINGULARITY s. singularidade.
SINISTER adj. sinistro; ameaçador.
SINK s. pia / v. afundar.
SINNER s. pecador.
SINUSITIS s. sinusite.
SIP s. gole, trago / v. tragar, bebericar.
SIR s. senhor.
SISTER s. irmã.
SISTER-IN-LAW s. cunhada.
SIT v. sentar-se, sentar, acomodar.
SITE s. local, lugar.
SITUATION s. situação.
SIX num. seis.
SIXTEEN num. dezesseis.
SIXTY num. sessenta.
SIZE s. tamanho, área, dimensão.

SKATE s. patim / v. patinar.
SKELETON s. esqueleto.
SKID s. derrapagem, escorregão / v. derrapar, escorregar.
SKILFUL adj. habilidoso.
SKILL s. habilidade, destreza.
SKIN s. pele.
SKIT s. paródia, sátira.
SKULL s. crânio; caveira.
SKUNK s. gambá.
SKY s. céu.
SLANDER s. calúnia / v. difamar, caluniar.
SLANG s. gíria; jargão.
SLAP s. palmada, tapa / v. esbofetear, dar tapas.
SLAVE s. escravo.
SLEAZY adj. sórdido.
SLEEP s. sono / v. dormir.
SLEIGH s. trenó.
SLICE s. fatia, pedaço, porção / v. fatiar, cortar em fatias.
SLICK adj. jeitoso, liso.
SLIDE s. escorregador / v. deslizar, escorregar.
SLIGHT adj. fraco, franzino; mínimo, leve.
SLIM adj. magro / v. emagrecer.
SLIP s. tropeção, escorregão, erro, lapso / v. escapar, fugir, escapulir.
SLIPPER s. chinelo.
SLOGAN s. frase; lema, moto.
SLOP v. transbordar, derramar / s. lavagem (comida que se dá aos porcos).
SLOPE s. ladeira, rampa.
SLOT s. fenda, abertura.
SLOW adj. lento, vagaroso / v. reduzir, diminuir.
SLUMBER s. sono leve, soneca / v. dormir, tirar uma soneca.
SLUR s. calúnia, insulto / v. desprezar, passar por cima.
SLY adj. astuto, malicioso.
SMACK s. estalo feito com os lábios, beijoca; pancada, palmada.
SMALL adj. pequeno.
SMALLPOX s. varíola.
SMART adj. inteligente, esperto; elegante.
SMASH s. quebra, choque / v. despedaçar.
SMELL s. cheiro / v. cheirar.
SMILE s. sorriso / v. sorrir.
SMOKE s. fumaça / v. fumar.

SMOOTH adj. macio, suave, liso / v. alisar, suavizar.
SMOTHER v. sufocar, asfixiar, abafar / s. nuvem de fumaça, de poeira.
SMUDGE s. mancha / v. manchar, sujar.
SMUG adj. metido, convencido.
SMUTTY adj. obsceno, indecente; sujo.
SNACK s. petisco, lanche.
SNAG s. obstáculo, dificuldade.
SNAIL s. lesma, caracol.
SNAKE s. cobra, serpente.
SNAP s. estalo / v. estalar.
SNARE s. armadilha, cilada / v. apanhar em armadilha, trair, enganar.
SNEEZE s. espirro / v. espirrar.
SNIFF s. farejada, fungada / v. fungar, cheirar, farejar.
SNOOKER s. sinuca, bilhar.
SNOOZE s. soneca / v. cochilar.
SNORE s. ronco / v. roncar.
SNOW s. neve / v. nevar.
SO adv. tão; desse modo, assim; de maneira que, logo.
SOAK v. encharcar, deixar de molho.
SOAP s. sabão.
SOB s. soluço / v. soluçar.
SOBER adj. sóbrio; sério.
SOCCER s. futebol.
SOCIABLE adj. sociável.
SOCIAL adj. social.
SOCIAL SECURITY s. Previdência Social.
SOCIETY s. sociedade.
SOCIOLOGIST s. sociólogo.
SOCIOLOGY s. sociologia.
SOCKET s. tomada, soquete.
SODA s. refrigerante.
SODDEN adj. encharcado.
SOFA s. sofá.
SOFT adj. macio, suave.
SOLAR adj. solar.
SOLDIER s. soldado.
SOLID adj. sólido.
SOLIDARITY s. solidariedade.
SOLITARY adj. solitário.
SOLUBLE adj. solúvel.
SOLUTION s. solução.
SOME pron. alguns, algumas, uns, umas.
SOMETHING pron. algo, alguma coisa.
SOMETIME adv. algum dia.
SOMETIMES adv. às vezes, de vez em quando.

SON s. filho.
SONG s. canção.
SONNET s. soneto.
SOON adv. logo, brevemente, cedo.
SOPHISTICATE adj. sofisticado / v. sofisticar.
SOPHISTICATION s. sofisticação.
SORE adj. doloroso, dolorido, machucado / s. machucado, mágoa.
SORRY adj. arrependido / interj. perdão! como? sinto muito!
SOS abrev. SOS (pedido de socorro).
SOUP s. sopa.
SOUR adj. azedo; ácido.
SOUTH s. sul / adj. do sul / adv. para o sul.
SOUTHERN CROSS s. Cruzeiro do Sul.
SOUVENIR s. lembrança, recordação.
SPA s. fonte de água; estância hidromineral.
SPACE s. espaço, lugar; intervalo.
SPAGHETTI s. espaguete.
SPAIN s. Espanha.
SPANIARD s. espanhol.
SPANISH adj. espanhol / s. espanhol.
SPANK v. dar palmadas; bater, espancar.
SPARE adj. desocupado; de sobra, extra, disponível / v. poupar, economizar.
SPARROW s. pardal.
SPARSE adj. escasso, esparso.
SPASM s. espasmo.
SPAWN v. desovar, criar, gerar / s. desova (de peixes), cria, prole.
SPEAK v. falar.
SPECIAL adj. especial.
SPECIES s. espécie.
SPECIFIC adj. específico, preciso.
SPEED s. velocidade, rapidez / v. acelerar.
SPELL v. soletrar, escrever / s. feitiço, encanto; período.
SPEND v. gastar, consumir.
SPERM s. esperma.
SPEW v. vomitar, lançar / s. vômito.
SPHERE s. esfera.
SPICE s. tempero, condimento / v. temperar, condimentar.
SPIDER s. aranha.
SPIKE s. ponta; espiga.
SPILL v. derramar, transbordar.
SPINACH s. espinafre.
SPINE s. espinha dorsal; espinho; lombada (de livro).
SPIRE s. agulha; pináculo.
SPIRIT s. espírito, alma; atitude.
SPIRITS s. bebida alcoólica; humor.
SPIRITUAL adj. espiritual.
SPIT v. cuspir / s. cuspe, saliva.
SPITE s. rancor, ressentimento.
SPITTLE s. saliva, cuspe.
SPLEEN s. baço.
SPLIT s. fenda; brecha.
SPLURGE s. ostentação / v. ostentar.
SPLUTTER v. gaguejar, balbuciar.
SPONGE s. parasita; esponja / v. esfregar (com esponja); parasitar.
SPONSOR s. patrocinador.
SPONSORSHIP s. patrocínio.
SPONTANEITY s. espontaneidade.
SPONTANEOUS adj. espontâneo.
SPONTANEOUSLY adv. espontaneamente.
SPOON s. colher.
SPORADIC adj. esporádico.
SPORT s. esporte.
SPOT s. lugar, local; pinta, espinha / v. localizar, descobrir (coloquial).
SPRAIN s. distensão, deslocamento, entorse / v. torcer, deslocar.
SPRAY s. spray, borrifador, pulverizador / v. borrifar, pulverizar.
SPRING s. primavera; mola; nascente; salto.
SPRITE s. duende.
SPY s. espião / v. espionar.
SQUAD s. pelotão, esquadra.
SQUARE s. quadrado; praça / adj. quadrado.
SQUID s. lula.
STAB s. punhalada, facada / v. apunhalar, cravar.
STABILITY s. estabilidade.
STADIUM s. estádio.
STAFF s. pessoal, empregados.
STAG s. veado adulto.
STAGNANT adj. estagnado.
STAID adj. sério; sossegado; calmo.
STAIR s. degrau; escada.
STAKE s. estaca; aposta / v. apostar; fixar em estaca ou poste.
STALWART adj. robusto, forte; fiel, leal.
STAMINA s. resistência, força.
STAMP s. selo, carimbo, marca / v. bater o pé, carimbar, selar.
STAND s. posição, postura; barraca, estande, banca / v. tolerar, aguentar.
STANDARD s. padrão / adj. padrão, modelo.

STAND BY s. alerta, reserva, lista de espera.
STAPLE s. grampo (de papel) / *adj.* principal / v. grampear.
STAR s. estrela, astro; celebridade / v. estrelar.
STARFISH s. estrela-do-mar.
STARK *adj.* severo, rigoroso, inflexível.
STARRY *adj.* estrelado.
START s. princípio, começo, início / v. começar, iniciar, dar partida.
STATE s. estado / v. declarar, afirmar.
STATIC *adj.* estático, parado, imóvel / s. estática, interferência (rádio).
STATION s. estação (de ônibus, trem); emissora de rádio.
STATISTIC s. estatística.
STATUE s. estátua.
STATUTE s. estatuto; lei.
STAY s. estada, permanência / v. ficar, permanecer.
STEAK s. filé, bife.
STEAM s. vapor; fumaça / v. cozinhar a vapor, emitir vapor.
STEEL s. aço / *adj.* de aço.
STEP s. passo, degrau; medida / v. andar, dar um passo, pisar.
STEREO s. estéreo.
STERN *adj.* severo, austero, duro.
STICK s. galho; vara; bastão; bengala / v. perfurar, espetar; colar, grudar.
STILL *adv.* ainda, ainda assim, contudo / *adj.* quieto, calmo, parado.
STIMULATE v. estimular.
STING s. picada, ferroada / v. picar.
STINK s. catinga, fedor / v. feder.
STOCK s. estoque, reserva / v. estocar, armazenar.
STOMACH s. estômago.
STONE s. pedra, rocha; caroço, semente; pedra preciosa, joia, gema.
STOP s. parada / v. parar.
STOPPAGE s. paralisação, parada, interrupção.
STORAGE s. armazenagem.
STORE s. loja, depósito, armazém / v. armazenar, pôr em estoque.
STORM s. tempestade, temporal.
STORY s. história, conto, narrativa.
STOVE s. fogão.
STRAIGHT *adj.* correto; honrado; direto, reto; liso.

STRAIN s. tensão, esforço; deslocamento / v. esforçar-se; deslocar, luxar.
STRAIT s. estreito / *adj.* estreito.
STRANGE *adj.* desconhecido, estranho.
STRANGLE v. estrangular, sufocar.
STRATEGIC *adj.* estratégico.
STRATEGY s. estratégia.
STRAWBERRY s. morango.
STREAK s. traço, listra, risca / v. riscar.
STREAM s. riacho; córrego.
STREET s. rua.
STRENGTH s. força, resistência.
STRESS s. pressão, tensão, cansaço, esforço / v. estressar.
STRIFE s. luta, conflito.
STRIKE v. bater, atingir, atacar / s. greve; ataque; golpe.
STRING s. fio, barbante.
STROKE s. pancada, golpe; derrame, apoplexia.
STRONG *adj.* forte, firme.
STRUCTURAL *adj.* estrutural.
STRUCTURALISM s. estruturalismo.
STRUCTURALIST s. estruturalista.
STUDENT s. estudante.
STUDY s. estudo; escritório (em uma casa) / v. estudar.
STUPID s. estúpido, idiota / *adj.* estúpido, idiota.
STY s. chiqueiro; terçol.
STYLE s. estilo, maneira.
SUBJECT s. assunto; matéria; sujeito (gramática) / v. sujeitar, submeter.
SUBMARINE s. submarino.
SUBMIT v. submeter, apresentar.
SUBSCRIBE v. fazer a assinatura de, assinar; consentir, concordar.
SUBSTANCE s. substância, essência.
SUBSTITUTE s. substituto, reserva / *adj.* substituto, reserva / v. substituir.
SUBURB s. subúrbio.
SUBWAY s. passagem subterrânea; metrô.
SUCCESS s. sucesso, êxito.
SUCH *adj.* desta maneira / *adv.* como tal, assim mesmo / *pron.* semelhante, tal, tão, tanto.
SUE v. processar, acionar.
SUEDE s. camurça / *adj.* de camurça.
SUET s. sebo.
SUFFICIENT *adj.* suficiente.
SUGAR s. açúcar.

SUIT s. terno (roupa); petição / v. processar; cair bem, ficar bem (roupas).
SUITCASE s. mala.
SULLEN adj. rabugento, teimoso, carrancudo.
SUMMARY s. resumo; sumário.
SUMMER s. verão.
SUN s. sol.
SUNDAY s. domingo.
SUNGLASSES s. óculos de sol.
SUPERMARKET s. supermercado.
SUPPLIER s. fornecedor(a).
SUPPLY v. fornecer, abastecer / s. fornecimento, abastecimento.
SUPPORT s. apoio, suporte, sustento / v. apoiar, sustentar.
SUPPOSE v. supor, presumir, imaginar.
SURE adj. claro, certo, seguro; com certeza.
SURF s. surfe.
SURGERY s. cirurgia.
SURNAME s. sobrenome.
SURPRISE s. surpresa / v. surpreender.
SURVEY s. inspeção, vistoria; pesquisa, levantamento / v. pesquisar.
SURVIVAL s. sobrevivência.
SUSPECT adj. suspeito / s. suspeito / v. suspeitar, desconfiar.
SUSPENSE s. suspense, tensão.
SUSTAIN v. sustentar, manter.
SWALLOW s. andorinha; gole, trago / v. engolir.
SWAMP s. pântano, brejo.
SWAN s. cisne.
SWAP s. permuta, troca / v. trocar, permutar.
SWARM s. aglomeração, multidão; enxame (abelhas).
SWEAT s. suor, transpiração / v. suar, transpirar.
SWEATY adj. suado.
SWEET s. doce / adj. doce; amável, gentil.
SWELL v. inchar, dilatar.
SWIM v. nadar.
SWING s. balanço, oscilação / v. balançar, oscilar.
SYLLABLE s. sílaba.
SYLLABUS s. programa de estudo; resumo.
SYMBIOSIS s. simbiose.
SYMBIOTIC adj. simbiótico.
SYMBOL s. símbolo.
SYMBOLIC adj. simbólico.
SYMBOLICALLY adv. simbolicamente.
SYMBOLISE v. simbolizar, representar.
SYMBOLISM s. simbolismo.
SYMMETRICAL adj. simétrico.
SYMMETRY s. simetria.
SYMPATHETIC adj. solidário, compreensivo.
SYMPATHY s. solidariedade, compreensão, empatia.
SYMPHONIC adj. sinfônico.
SYMPHONY s. sinfonia.
SYMPTOM s. sintoma.
SYMPTOMATIC adj. sintomático.
SYNC v. sincronizar / s. sincronização.
SYNCOPE s. síncope.
SYNDROME s. síndrome.
SYNONYM s. sinônimo.
SYNONYMOUS adj. sinônimo.
SYNONYMY s. sinonímia.
SYNTACTIC adj. sintático.
SYNTAX s. sintaxe.
SYNTHESIS s. síntese.
SYNTHESISE v. sintetizar.
SYNTHETIC adj. sintético, artificial.
SYPHILIS s. sífilis.
SYRUP s. xarope.
SYSTEM s. sistema; organização.
SYSTEMATIC adj. sistemático.
SYSTEMATICALLY adv. sistematicamente.
SYSTEMATISE v. sistematizar.
SYSTEMIC adj. sistêmico.

T

T, t s. vigésima letra do alfabeto inglês.
TAB s. tabulador; tabulação / v. tabular (informática).
TABBY s. gato malhado.
TABERNACLE s. tabernáculo.
TABLE s. mesa; tabela, lista; tabuada.
TABLE CLOTH s. toalha de mesa.
TABLESPOON s. colher de sopa.
TABLET s. tablete, comprimido; placa comemorativa.
TABLEWARE s. utensílios de mesa.
TABLOID s. tabloide; sensacionalista / adj. tabloide; sensacionalista.
TABOO s. tabu / adj. tabu.
TABULAR adj. tabular.
TABULATE v. tabular; fazer tabulações.
TABULATION s. tabulação.
TACHYCARDIA s. taquicardia.
TACIT adj. tácito.
TACITLY adv. tacitamente.
TACITURN adj. taciturno; silencioso.
TACK v. fixar, prender.
TACKLE v. derrubar; atacar, abordar.
TACKY adj. pegajoso, grudento.

TACT s. tato.
TACTFUL adj. tático, delicado, diplomata.
TACTFULLY adv. diplomaticamente.
TACTIC s. tática, estratégia.
TACTICAL adj. tático, estratégico.
TACTICIAN s. tático, estrategista.
TACTILE adj. tátil, palpável.
TACTLESS adj. insensível.
TADPOLE s. girino.
TAG s. etiqueta, identificação, rótulo.
TAGGING s. etiquetagem, marcação.
TAIL s. rabo, cauda.
TAILGATE v. colar na traseira do carro da frente / s. porta traseira.
TAILLIGHT s. lanterna, luz traseira.
TAILOR v. costurar sob medida / s. alfaiate.
TAILORED adj. ajustado, sob medida.
TAINT v. estragar, macular / s. mancha, nódoa.
TAINTED adj. contaminado, envenenado.
TAKE v. tomar; pegar; levar; embarcar (ônibus, trem, etc.).
TAKEN adj. tomado, entendido.
TAKE-OFF s. decolar; decolagem, partida.

TAKE OUT v. tirar, extrair.
TAKEOVER v. assumir o controle / s. aquisição, conquista.
TAKER s. comprador, receptor; tomador.
TAKING s. captura, tomada (filmagens) / adj. cativante, encantador.
TALC s. talco / v. passar talco.
TALE s. conto, história; fofoca, fuxico.
TALENT s. talento, aptidão.
TALENTED adj. talentoso, habilidoso.
TALISMAN s. talismã.
TALK s. conversa, papo / v. conversar, falar, dizer.
TALKATIVE adj. falador, tagarela.
TALKATIVENESS s. tagarelice, falação.
TALKING s. fala, discurso.
TALL adj. alto, grande.
TALLOW s. sebo (gordura animal).
TAMARIND s. tamarindo (fruto).
TAMBOURINE s. tamborim.
TAME v. domesticar, dominar, subjugar / adj. domesticado, dócil, manso.
TAMEABLE adj. domável, domesticável.
TAMER s. dominador, domador.
TAMPON s. tampão.
TAN v. bronzear / s. bronzeado, cor morena / abrev. tangente.
TANG s. sabor forte, gosto.
TANGENT s. tangente.
TANGENTIAL adj. tangencial.
TANGERINE s. tangerina, mexerica.
TANGIBLE adj. tangível.
TANGO v. dançar tango / s. tango.
TANGY adj. picante, ácido.
TANK s. reservatório, tanque, cisterna; tanque de guerra.
TANKARD s. caneca de cerveja.
TANKER s. carro-tanque; petroleiro.
TANNED adj. curtido, bronzeado, moreno.
TANNERY s. curtume.
TANTALISE v. atormentar, provocar.
TANTALISING adj. tentador, irresistível.
TANTALISINGLY adv. tentadoramente.
TAP v. dar um tapinha; abrir a torneira / s. torneira, bica.
TAPE s. fita adesiva; fita magnética / v. gravar, colar.
TAPE RECORDER s. gravador.
TAPESTRY s. tapeçaria.
TAPEWORM s. solitária, tênia.

TAPPER s. grampo, extrator, batedor.
TAPPING s. batida, pancadinha.
TAR s. alcatrão.
TARANTELLA s. tarantela (dança italiana).
TARANTULA s. tarântula.
TARDY adj. tardio, vagaroso.
TARE s. tara.
TARGET s. alvo, objetivo, meta.
TARGETING s. mira, pontaria.
TARIFF s. tarifa; lista de preços; taxa de importação / v. taxar, tarifar.
TAROT s. tarô.
TARSUS s. tarso.
TARTAR s. tártaro (molho); sarro, tártaro.
TASK s. tarefa, trabalho / v. encarregar, incumbir.
TASKMASTER s. capataz; chefe de serviço.
TASTE s. sabor, gosto, paladar / v. experimentar, provar, saborear.
TASTEFUL adj. gostoso, saboroso.
TASTEFULLY adv. saborosamente.
TASTELESS adj. insípido, insosso.
TASTER s. provador, degustador.
TASTING s. degustação / adj. saboroso.
TASTY adj. gostoso, saboroso.
TATTER v. rasgar, esfarrapar / s. farrapo, trapo.
TATTOO s. tatuagem / v. tatuar, fazer uma tatuagem.
TAUNT v. provocar, insultar, zombar / s. insulto, troça.
TAURUS s. Touro (astrologia).
TAUTOLOGY s. tautologia; redundância.
TAVERN s. taberna; bar.
TAX s. imposto, tributo, encargo, taxa / v. tributar, taxar.
TAXABLE adj. taxável.
TAXATION s. taxação.
TAXI s. táxi.
TAXIDERMIST s. taxidermista.
TAXIDERMY s. taxidermia.
TAXMAN s. coletor de impostos.
TAXONOMIC adj. taxonômico.
TAXONOMY s. taxonomia.
TAXPAYER s. contribuinte.
TEA s. chá.
TEABAG s. saquinho de chá.
TEACH v. ensinar, educar, lecionar.

TEACHABLE *adj.* educável; que pode ser ensinado.
TEACHER *s.* professor, educador.
TEACHING *s.* ensino, instrução.
TEACUP *s.* xícara de chá.
TEAM *s.* time, equipe.
TEAMMATE *s.* colega de time.
TEAM UP *v.* juntar, reunir.
TEAMWORK *s.* trabalho de equipe.
TEAPOT *s.* bule.
TEAR *s.* rasgão; lágrima / *v.* rasgar, arrancar; chorar.
TEARDROP *s.* lágrima.
TEARFUL *adj.* choroso, lacrimoso.
TEARFULLY *adv.* lastimosamente.
TEAROOM *s.* salão de chá.
TEASE *v.* caçoar; provocar, atiçar / *s.* provocação.
TEASER *s.* provocador, atiçador, implicante.
TEASING *s.* provocação (maliciosa).
TEASPOON *s.* colher de chá.
TEAT *s.* teta (animais).
TEATIME *s.* hora do chá; chá da tarde.
TECHNICAL *adj.* técnico.
TECHNICALITY *s.* tecnicidade.
TECHNICALLY *adv.* tecnicamente.
TECHNICIAN *s.* técnico.
TECHNIQUE *s.* técnica; modo de fazer.
TECHNOLOGICAL *adj.* tecnológico.
TECHNOLOGICALLY *adv.* tecnologicamente.
TECHNOLOGY *s.* tecnologia.
TECTONIC *adj.* tectônico (geologia).
TEDDY *s.* urso de pelúcia.
TEDIOUS *adj.* chato, maçante, tedioso.
TEDIUM *s.* tédio.
TEENAGE *adj.* adolescente; jovem.
TEENAGER *s.* adolescente, jovem.
TEETHE *v.* endentecer; nascer os dentes.
TEETHING *s.* dentição / *adj.* dentição.
TELECOMMUNICATION *s.* telecomunicação.
TELEGRAM *s.* telegrama.
TELEGRAPH *v.* telegrafar / *s.* telégrafo.
TELEPATHIC *adj.* telepático.
TELEPATHY *s.* telepatia.
TELEPHONE *s.* telefone / *v.* telefonar, ligar.
TELEPHONIC *adj.* telefônico.
TELEPHONY *s.* telefonia.
TELESCOPE *s.* telescópio.
TELESCOPIC *adj.* telescópico.

TELEVISE *v.* televisionar.
TELEVISION *s.* televisão; TV.
TELL *v.* dizer; contar, relatar.
TELLER *s.* operador de caixa; contador de história.
TELLTALE *s.* informante, fofoqueiro / *adj.* revelador.
TEMERITY *s.* temeridade; ousadia, audácia.
TEMP *s.* temporário, interino.
TEMPER *s.* temperamento, humor / *v.* moderar, suavizar.
TEMPERA *s.* têmpera.
TEMPERAMENT *s.* temperamento.
TEMPERAMENTAL *adj.* temperamental.
TEMPERATURE *s.* temperatura; febre.
TEMPEST *s.* temporal, tempestade.
TEMPESTUOUS *adj.* tempestuoso.
TEMPLATE *s.* molde, padrão.
TEMPLE *s.* templo.
TEMPO *s.* tempo, ritmo (música).
TEMPORAL *adj.* temporal.
TEMPORARILY *adv.* temporariamente.
TEMPORARY *adj.* temporário, provisório.
TEMPT *v.* tentar, seduzir, instigar.
TEMPTATION *s.* tentação.
TEMPTING *adj.* tentador, atraente, sedutor.
TEN *num.* dez.
TENABLE *adj.* sustentável, defensável.
TENACIOUS *adj.* tenaz, obstinado.
TENACITY *s.* tenacidade.
TENANCY *s.* inquilinato.
TENANT *s.* ocupante, inquilino.
TEND *v.* tender, inclinar-se.
TENDENCIOUS *adj.* tendencioso.
TENDENCY *s.* tendência, propensão, hábito.
TENDENTIOUSLY *adv.* tendenciosamente.
TENDER *adj.* frágil, afetuoso, meigo.
TENDERNESS *s.* ternura, suavidade, amabilidade.
TENDINITIS *s.* tendinite.
TENDON *s.* tendão.
TENET *s.* princípio, pressuposto.
TENNIS *s.* tênis (esporte).
TENOR *s.* tenor (música) / *adj.* tenor (música).
TENSE *s.* tempo verbal (gramática) / *adj.* tenso, nervoso.
TENSION *s.* tensão, pressão.
TENT *s.* tenda, barraca.
TENTACLE *s.* tentáculo.

TENTATIVE s. tentativa; experiência; experimental.
TENTATIVELY adv. provisoriamente.
TENTH num. décimo.
TENUOUS adj. tênue, delgado.
TENURE s. estabilidade.
TENURED adj. vitalício.
TERCENTENARY s. tricentenário / adj. tricentenário.
TERM s. termo, condição; trimestre, semestre.
TERMINAL s. terminal / adj. terminal.
TERMINATE v. terminar, acabar, concluir.
TERMINATION s. término, terminação; conclusão.
TERMINOLOGICAL adj. terminológico.
TERMINOLOGY s. terminologia.
TERMINUS s. terminal, ponto final.
TERMITE s. cupim.
TERRACE v. dispor em terraço / s. terraço.
TERRAIN s. terreno.
TERRESTRIAL adj. terrestre.
TERRIBLE adj. terrível, horrível, péssimo.
TERRIBLY adv. terrivelmente.
TERRIFIC adj. formidável, espetacular.
TERRIFICALLY adv. maravilhosamente.
TERRIFY v. aterrorizar, apavorar.
TERRIFYING adj. aterrorizante.
TERRITORIAL adj. territorial.
TERRITORY s. território.
TERROR s. terror.
TERRORISE v. aterrorizar, amedrontar.
TERRORISM s. terrorismo.
TERRORIST s. terrorista.
TERSE adj. conciso, sucinto; curto e grosso.
TEST s. prova, ensaio; teste, exame / v. testar, examinar.
TESTAMENT s. testamento.
TESTAMENTARY adj. testamentário.
TESTER s. provador, examinador.
TESTICLE s. testículo.
TESTICULAR adj. testicular.
TESTIFY v. testemunhar.
TESTIMONIAL s. testemunho.
TESTIMONY s. declaração, testemunho.
TESTOSTERONE s. testosterona.
TETANUS s. tétano.
TEXT s. texto.
TEXTURE s. textura.
THAN conj. que, do que.

THANK s. agradecimento; muito obrigado / v. agradecer.
THANKFUL adj. agradecido, reconhecido.
THANKFULLY adv. felizmente.
THANKLESS adj. mal-agradecido; ingrato.
THAT pron. (pl. those) aquele; que / conj. que, para que, a fim de que.
THE art. o, a, os, as.
THEATRE s. teatro.
THEFT s. roubo.
THEIR pron. seu(s), dele(s).
THEM pron. os, a eles, lhes.
THEMATIC adj. temático.
THEME s. tema, tópico.
THEMSELVES pron. eles mesmos, elas mesmas.
THEN adv. então, em seguida, logo.
THERE adv. aí, ali, lá.
THERMOMETER s. termômetro.
THESAURUS s. enciclopédia, coleção de palavras ou frases.
THEY pron. eles, elas.
THIGH s. coxa.
THIN adj. magro / v. afinar.
THING s. coisa.
THINK v. pensar, achar; julgar.
THIRD num. terceiro.
THIRST s. sede, vontade, ânsia.
THIRSTY adj. sedento.
THIRTEEN num. treze.
THIRTY num. trinta.
THIS pron. (pl. these) este, esta.
THOUSAND num. mil.
THREAT s. ameaça, perigo.
THREATEN v. ameaçar.
THREE num. três.
THROAT s. garganta.
THROUGH prep. por, através de, durante.
THROW s. arremesso, lance / v. arremessar, lançar.
THUMB s. polegar.
THUMP s. murro, pancada / v. golpear, bater.
THUNDER s. trovão / v. trovejar.
THURSDAY s. quinta-feira.
TICKET s. passagem, bilhete; multa.
TIE s. gravata; empate / v. amarrar, atar, empatar.

TIGER s. tigre.
TIGHT adj. esticado; apertado.
TIME s. tempo, hora, momento; espaço de tempo, época, ocasião.
TIRE v. cansar, esgotar / s. pneu.
TITLE s. título.
TO prep. a, para, ao / adv. em direção a; partícula utilizada antes do verbo para designar o infinitivo.
TODAY s. hoje / adv. hoje.
TOE s. dedo do pé.
TOGETHER adv. juntos.
TOILET s. banheiro; vaso sanitário, privada.
TOLERANCE s. tolerância.
TOMATO s. tomate.
TOMB s. tumba, túmulo.
TOMORROW s. amanhã / adv. amanhã.
TONE s. tom, tonalidade.
TONIC s. tônico.
TONIGHT adv. esta noite, hoje à noite, à noite / s. esta noite.
TOO adv. também, igualmente; demais; muito.
TOOL s. ferramenta, instrumento.
TOOTH s. (pl. teeth) dente.
TOP adj. mais alto, máximo, principal / s. cume, pico, ponto mais alto.
TOPIC s. tópico, assunto.
TORMENT s. tormento / v. torturar.
TORTOISE s. tartaruga (da terra).
TORTURE s. tortura / v. torturar, atormentar.
TOSS v. atirar, lançar, chacoalhar, agitar / s. agitação, arremesso, sacudida.
TOTAL adj. total / s. total, soma.
TOTALLY adv. totalmente.
TOUCH s. toque, tato / v. tocar.
TOUGH adj. duro, forte, valentão.
TOUPEE s. peruca, topete postiço.
TOUR s. viagem, excursão / v. excursionar.
TOURIST s. turista.
TOWEL s. toalha.
TOWER s. torre, fortaleza.
TOWN s. cidade.
TOXIC adj. tóxico.
TOY s. brinquedo.
TRACE s. traço; indício; rastro, pista / v. rastrear, descobrir.
TRACK s. rastro, pista; trilha; faixa de um CD / v. rastrear, localizar.
TRACTOR s. trator.

TRADE s. comércio; negócio.
TRADEMARK s. marca registrada.
TRAFFIC s. trânsito, tráfego; tráfico.
TRAGEDY s. tragédia.
TRAGIC adj. trágico.
TRAIN s. trem.
TRANSFER s. transferência / v. transferir.
TRANSFORM v. transformar.
TRANSLATE v. traduzir.
TRANSPORT s. transporte / v. transportar.
TRAP s. armadilha, cilada / v. prender, aprisionar.
TRAPEZE s. trapézio.
TRAPPINGS s. decoração, ornamento.
TRASH s. lixo, refugo; besteira (coloquial); ralé.
TRAVEL s. viagem / v. viajar.
TRAY s. bandeja.
TREASON s. traição.
TREATY s. tratado, acordo, pacto.
TREE s. árvore.
TREMBLE s. tremor / v. tremer, estremecer.
TRIBE s. tribo.
TRICK s. truque, ardil / v. enganar, pregar uma peça.
TRIP s. viagem, passeio; tropeço / v. tropeçar.
TRIPOD s. tripé.
TRIUMPH s. triunfo / v. triunfar.
TROOP s. grupo, bando, tropa.
TROPHY s. troféu.
TROPIC s. trópico / adj. trópico.
TROUBLE s. problema, dificuldade, encrenca / v. importunar, incomodar.
TROUBLESOME adj. importuno, problemático, desagradável.
TROUSERS s. calças compridas.
TROUT s. truta.
TRUCE s. trégua, folga.
TRUCK s. caminhão.
TRUE adj. verdadeiro; legítimo; real.
TRULY adv. exatamente, verdadeiramente, sinceramente.
TRUSS v. atar, amarrar, fixar / s. armação, suporte, andaime.
TRUST s. confiança, responsabilidade, crédito / v. confiar.
TRUTH s. verdade.
TRY s. tentativa / v. tentar.
T-SHIRT s. camiseta.
TUESDAY s. terça-feira.

TUMULT s. tumulto.
TUNIC s. túnica.
TUNING s. sintonização, afinação.
TUNNEL s. túnel.
TUNNY s. atum.
TURBAN s. turbante.
TURBINE s. turbina.
TURN s. volta, giro; vez, ocasião / v. girar.
TURNIP s. nabo.
TURNOVER s. faturamento; circulação, rotatividade.
TWELVE num. doze.
TWENTY num. vinte.
TWICE adv. duas vezes.
TWIST s. torção, giro, guinada / v. retorcer, retorcer.
TWO num. dois.
TYPE s. tipo, espécie, classe.
TYPEWRITER s. máquina de escrever.
TYPICAL adj. típico, característico.
TYPICALLY adv. tipicamente.
TYPOGRAPHY s. tipografia.
TYPOLOGY s. tipologia.
TYRANNICAL adj. tirânico.
TYRANNISE v. tiranizar; tornar-se tirano.
TYRANNY s. tirania.
TYRANT s. tirano.
TYRO s. novato, calouro.

Uu

U, u s. vigésima primeira letra do alfabeto inglês; representa o Urânio na tabela periódica.
UBIQUITY s. onipresença.
UFO abrev. OVNI (objeto voador não identificado).
UFOLOGIST s. ufólogo, ufologista.
UFOLOGY s. ufologia; ovniologia.
UGH interj. eca! argh!
UGLIFY v. tornar feio; enfear.
UGLINESS s. feiura; fealdade.
UGLY adj. feio; repulsivo, perigoso.
UH interj. hein, hã, o quê!
UK abrev. Reino Unido.
UKRAINE s. Ucrânia.
UKRANIAN s. ucraniano / adj. ucraniano.
ULCER s. úlcera; lesão.
ULCERATION s. formação de úlceras; ulceração.
ULTIMATE adj. último.
ULTIMATELY adv. finalmente, por fim; enfim.
ULTIMATUM s. ultimato, intimação.
ULTRA s. radical (política) / adj. radical (política).
ULTRALIGHT adj. ultraleve.
ULTRASONIC adj. ultrassônico.
ULTRASOUND s. ultrassom, ultrassonografia.
ULTRAVIOLET s. ultravioleta.
UMBILICAL adj. umbilical.
UMBILICAL CORD s. cordão umbilical.
UMBRAGE s. ressentimento.
UMBRELLA s. guarda-chuva.
UMLAUT s. trema (¨).
UN abrev. ONU (Organização das Nações Unidas).
UNABASHED adj. desavergonhado, descarado.
UNABLE adj. ser incapaz, impossibilitado.
UNABRIDGED adj. inteiro, integral.
UNACCEPTABLE adj. inaceitável.
UNACCOMPANIED adj. desacompanhado; solista.
UNACCOUNTABLE adj. inexplicável; incontável.
UNACCUSTOMED adj. desacostumado, desabituado.
UNADORNED adj. simples, sem enfeite.

UNADULTERATED adj. autêntico, natural; íntegro.
UNAFRAID adj. destemido.
UNAIDED adj. desamparado, sem ajuda.
UNAIDED EYE adv. a olho nu.
UNALIGNED adj. desalinhado, desordenado.
UNALTERED adj. inalterado.
UNAMBIGUOUS adj. claro, inequívoco; sem ambiguidade.
UNAMBIGUOUSLY adv. inequivocamente.
UNANIMITY s. unanimidade.
UNANIMOUS adj. unânime.
UNANIMOUSLY adv. unanimemente.
UNANNOUNCED adj. improvisado; inesperado.
UNANSWERABLE adj. irrespondível, incontestável.
UNANSWERED adj. sem resposta.
UNAPPEALING adj. sem apelo, desagradável.
UNAPPETISING adj. insosso, sem gosto.
UNAPPROACHABLE adj. inacessível, inabordável.
UNAPPROVED adj. desaprovado.
UNARMED adj. desarmado.
UNASHAMED adj. sem-vergonha; cara de pau.
UNASHAMEDLY adv. descaradamente, despudoradamente.
UNASSUMING adj. modesto, despretensioso.
UNATTACHED adj. descomprometido.
UNATTAINABLE adj. inatingível, inacessível.
UNATTENDED adj. abandonado, desacompanhado.
UNATTRACTIVE adj. sem atrativos, desinteressante; feio.
UNAUTHORISED adj. proibido, desautorizado.
UNAVAILABLE adj. indisponível.
UNAVOIDABLE adj. inevitável.
UNAVOIDABLY adv. inevitavelmente.
UNAWARE adj. inconsciente, sem saber, sem notar.
UNAWARENESS s. desconhecimento, inconsciência.
UNBALANCE v. desequilibrar, desestabilizar.
UNBALANCED adj. desequilibrado, desajustado.
UNBEARABLE adj. insuportável, intolerável.
UNBEARABLY adv. insuportavelmente.
UNBEATABLE adj. invencível, imbatível.
UNBEATEN adj. invicto.
UNBECOMING adj. impróprio, inapropriado.
UNBELIEF s. incredulidade; desconfiança.
UNBELIEVABLE adj. inacreditável; incrível.
UNBELIEVABLY adv. inacreditavelmente.
UNBELIEVER s. incrédulo, cético, descrente.
UNBIASED adj. imparcial.
UNBIND v. desatar, desamarrar.
UNBLEACHED adj. encardido.
UNBLOCK v. desbloquear, desimpedir.
UNBLOCKED adj. desimpedido, desbloqueado.
UNBOTTON v. desabotoar.
UNBREAKABLE adj. inquebrável.
UNBROKEN adj. inteiro, intato.
UNCANNILY adv. estranhamente, assombrosamente.
UNCANNINESS s. estranheza.
UNCANNY adj. incomum, misterioso, estranho.
UNCAP v. destampar; retirar a tampa.
UNCARING adj. indiferente, apático.
UNCEASING adj. incessante, ininterrupto.
UNCEASINGLY adv. incessantemente.
UNCENSORED adj. livre, sem censura.
UNCERTAIN adj. incerto, indeciso, inseguro, duvidoso.
UNCERTAINTY s. incerteza, indecisão.
UNCHAIN v. desacorrentar; libertar-se.
UNCHALLENGEABLE adj. incontestável, indiscutível.
UNCHALLENGEABLY adv. incontestavelmente, indiscutivelmente.
UNCHANGEABLE adj. imutável, invariável, inalterável.
UNCHANGEABLENESS s. imutabilidade, inalterabilidade.
UNCHANGEABLY adv. imutavelmente, invariavelmente.
UNCHANGED adj. inalterado, sem modificação.
UNCHARACTERISTIC adj. incomum, atípico.
UNCLASSIFIABLE adj. inclassificável.
UNCLASSIFIED adj. não classificado.
UNCLE s. tio, titio.

UNCLEAN *adj.* impuro, imoral, sujo.
UNCLEANLINESS *s.* sujeira, impureza, imoralidade.
UNCLEAR *adj.* confuso, obscuro.
UNCOMFORTABLE *adj.* incômodo; desconfortável.
UNCOMFORTABLY *adv.* desconfortavelmente.
UNCOMMITTED *adj.* descomprometido.
UNCOMMON *adj.* raro, incomum.
UNCOMMUNICATIVE *adj.* retraído, reservado, taciturno.
UNCOMPLETED *adj.* incompleto.
UNCOMPLICATE *v.* descomplicar.
UNCOMPLICATED *adj.* descomplicado.
UNCOMPROMISING *adj.* inflexível, teimoso.
UNCONCERNED *adj.* indiferente, despreocupado.
UNCONDITIONAL *adj.* incondicional.
UNCONDITIONALLY *adv.* incondicionalmente.
UNCONFIDENT *adj.* sem autoconfiança.
UNCONFINED *adj.* desimpedido.
UNCONFIRMED *adj.* não confirmado.
UNCONNECTED *adj.* desconectado.
UNCONSCIONABLE *adj.* irracional.
UNCONSCIOUS *adj.* inconsciente, desacordado.
UNCONSCIOUSLY *adv.* inconscientemente.
UNCONSTITUTIONAL *adj.* inconstitucional.
UNCONSTITUTIONALLY *adv.* inconstitucionalmente.
UNCONTROLLABLE *adj.* incontrolável.
UNCONTROLLABLY *adv.* incontrolavelmente.
UNCONTROLLED *adj.* descontrolado, incontrolado.
UNCONVENTIONAL *adj.* incomum, não convencional.
UNCOOKED *adj.* cru, não cozido.
UNCOORDINATED *adj.* descoordenado, desajeitado.
UNCORRECTED *adj.* incorreto.
UNCOUNTABLE *adj.* incontável.
UNCOVER *v.* descobrir, revelar, destapar.
UNDECIDED *adj.* indeciso, hesitante.
UNDEFINED *adj.* indefinido.
UNDENIABLE *adj.* inegável.

UNDENIABLY *adv.* inegavelmente.
UNDER *prep.* debaixo de, embaixo, por baixo, sob.
UNDERAGE *adj.* menor de idade.
UNDERARM *s.* axila.
UNDERBELLY *s.* baixo-ventre; parte inferior.
UNDERCLASS *s.* classe baixa; classes D e E.
UNDERCLOTHES *s.* roupa íntima.
UNDERCOVER *adj.* secreto, disfarçado.
UNDERCUT *v.* reduzir, baratear.
UNDERDEVELOPED *adj.* subdesenvolvido; imaturo, prematuro.
UNDERDEVELOPMENT *s.* subdesenvolvimento
UNDERESTIMATE *v.* subestimar.
UNDERESTIMATION *s.* subestimação, menosprezo.
UNDERFLOOR *adj.* subsolo.
UNDERFOOT *adv.* embaixo, debaixo do pé.
UNDERGO *v.* submeter-se a; passar por.
UNDERGRADUATE *s.* estudante universitário.
UNDERGROUND *s.* metrô /
adv. subterrâneo / *adj.* subterrâneo.
UNDERGROWTH *s.* subdesenvolvimento; definhamento.
UNDERLAY *v.* escorar, forrar / *s.* camada, base
UNDERLINE *v.* sublinhar, enfatizar /
s. sublinhado.
UNDERLING *s.* subalterno.
UNDERMOST *adj.* ínfimo, inferior.
UNDERNEATH *adj.* debaixo, embaixo, abaixo
adv. debaixo, embaixo, abaixo.
UNDERNOURISHED *adj.* subnutrido.
UNDERPAID *adj.* mal pago.
UNDERPANTS *s.* roupa íntima (calcinha ou cueca).
UNDERPASS *s.* passagem subterrânea.
UNDERPAY *v.* pagar mal; pagar pouco.
UNDERPIN *v.* sustentar, basear, escorar.
UNDERPRIVILEGED *adj.* desprovido, carente.
UNDERRATE *v.* subestimar.
UNDERRATED *adj.* desprezado, subestimado.
UNDERSCORE *v.* ressaltar, enfatizar.
UNDERSEA *adj.* submarino.
UNDERSELL *v.* desvalorizar, desmerecer (alguém); vender por um preço menor que o real ou o da concorrência.
UNDERSTAND *v.* entender, compreender, reconhecer.
UNDERSTANDABLE *adj.* compreensível.

UNDERSTANDABLY adv. compreensivelmente.
UNDERSTANDING s. compreensão, entendimento / adj. compreensivo.
UNDERSTATE v. atenuar, suavizar, abrandar.
UNDERTAKE v. empreender; aceitar, afirmar.
UNDERTAKER s. agente funerário.
UNDERTAKING s. empreendimento.
UNDERTONE s. meio-tom (música); insinuação.
UNDERVALUE v. subestimar, depreciar.
UNDERWATER adj. subaquático, submerso.
UNDERWEAR adj. roupa de baixo.
UNDERWEIGHT adj. abaixo do peso.
UNDERWHELM v. desapontar, ser inexpressivo.
UNDERWORLD s. submundo; mundo subterrâneo.
UNDERWRITE v. subscrever.
UNDESERVED adj. desmerecido, injusto.
UNDESERVEDLY adv. injustamente, de forma não merecida.
UNDESERVING adj. desmerecedor, indigno.
UNDESIRABLE s. indesejável / adj. indesejável.
UNDESIRED adj. indesejado.
UNDETECTABLE adj. imperceptível.
UNDETECTED adj. despercebido.
UNDETERMINED adj. indeterminado.
UNDEVELOPED adj. não desenvolvido, embrionário.
UNDIGESTED adj. indigesto, mal digerido.
UNDIGNIFIED adj. indigno; sem dignidade.
UNDISCIPLINED adj. indisciplinado.
UNDISCLOSED adj. secreto, oculto.
UNDISCOVERABLE adj. indetectável, oculto.
UNDISCOVERED adj. desconhecido.
UNDISCRIMINATING adj. indiscriminado.
UNDISGUISED adj. manifesto, sem disfarces.
UNDIVISED adj. inteiro, íntegro.
UNDO v. desfazer; cancelar.
UNDONE adj. desfeito; desatado.
UNDOUBTED adj. incontestável.
UNDOUBTEDLY adv. indubitavelmente, incontestavelmente, certamente.
UNDRESS v. despir-se; tirar a roupa.
UNDRESSED adj. nu, pelado, desnudo.
UNDRINKABLE adj. não potável.
UNDUE adj. indevido, exagerado.
UNDULATE v. ondular.

UNDULATING adj. ondulante.
UNDULATION s. ondulação.
UNDULY adv. indevidamente, injustamente.
UNDYING adj. imortal, imperecível.
UNEARTH v. desenterrar, desencavar.
UNEARTHLY adj. sobrenatural, não terrestre.
UNEASE s. desconforto, inquietação.
UNEASILY adv. desconfortavelmente.
UNEASINESS s. ansiedade, inquietação.
UNEASY adj. inquieto, desconfortável.
UNECONOMIC adj. gastador, esbanjador.
UNEDITED adj. não editado; inédito.
UNEDUCATED adj. inculto, ignorante.
UNEMOTIONAL adj. impassível, sem emoção.
UNEMPLOYABLE adj. imprestável, inútil.
UNEMPLOYED adj. desempregado; em desuso.
UNEMPLOYMENT s. desemprego.
UNENDING adj. eterno, interminável.
UNENTHUSIASTIC adj. sem entusiasmo.
UNENVIABLE adj. indesejado, não invejável.
UNEQUAL adj. desigual, irregular.
UNEQUALLED adj. inigualável, sem igual.
UNEQUIVOCAL adj. inequívoco.
UNERRING adj. infalível, seguro.
UNETHICAL adj. antiético; imoral.
UNEVEN adj. desigual, desnivelado.
UNEVENLY adv. irregularmente.
UNEVENTFUL adj. rotineiro, monótono.
UNEXCITING adj. desinteressante.
UNEXPECTED adj. inesperado.
UNEXPECTEDLY adv. inesperadamente.
UNEXPLAINABLE adj. inexplicável.
UNEXPLAINED adj. inexplicado, que não se pode explicar.
UNEXPLORED adj. inexplorado.
UNEXPOSED adj. protegido, abrigado.
UNFAILING adj. infalível, confiável.
UNFAIR adj. injusto.
UNFAIRLY adv. injustamente.
UNFAIRNESS s. injustiça; parcialidade.
UNFAITHFUL adj. infiel.
UNFAMILIAR adj. desconhecido, estranho.
UNFASHIONABLE adj. antiquado, obsoleto.
UNFASTEN v. desatar, soltar, desafivelar.
UNFAVOURABLE adj. desfavorável.
UNFEELING adj. insensível, impiedoso.
UNFETTER v. libertar, liberar, livrar.
UNFILLED adj. vazio, vago.

UNFILTERED *adj.* sem filtro.
UNFINISHED *adj.* inacabado, incompleto.
UNFIT *adj.* incapaz, inadequado.
UNFLAGGING *adj.* incansável, resistente.
UNFOCUSED *adj.* desfocado, desconcentrado.
UNFOLD *v.* desenrolar, desdobrar.
UNFORCED *adj.* espontâneo, voluntário.
UNFORGETTABLE *adj.* inesquecível.
UNFORGIVABLE *adj.* imperdoável.
UNFORGIVING *adj.* rancoroso, implacável.
UNFORSEEABLE *adj.* imprevisível.
UNFORSEEN *adj.* imprevisto.
UNFORTUNATE *adj.* infeliz, lamentável, desventurado.
UNFORTUNATELY *adv.* lamentavelmente, infelizmente.
UNFOUNDED *adj.* infundado.
UNFREEZE *v.* descongelar, degelar.
UNFRIENDLINESS *s.* hostilidade, antipatia.
UNFRIENDLY *adj.* hostil, antipático.
UNFUNNY *adj.* sem graça, chato.
UNGODLY *adj.* ímpio, herege, incrédulo.
UNGRACIOUS *adj.* indelicado, descortês.
UNGRAMMATICAL *adj.* gramaticalmente incorreto.
UNGREATFUL *adj.* ingrato.
UNGUARDED *adj.* desprotegido, imprudente.
UNHAPPILY *adv.* infelizmente.
UNHAPPINESS *s.* infelicidade, infortúnio.
UNHAPPY *adj.* infeliz, triste.
UNHARMED *adj.* ileso, sem ferimento.
UNHEALTHY *adj.* insalubre, prejudicial; enfermo, doentio.
UNHEARD *adj.* desconhecido.
UNHEATED *adj.* frio, gelado.
UNHELPFUL *adj.* inútil, de pouca serventia.
UNHOLY *adj.* profano, pecaminoso.
UNHOOK *v.* desenganchar, desprender.
UNHURRIED *adj.* devagar, sem pressa.
UNHYGIENIC *adj.* anti-higiênico.
UNI *abrev.* universidade.
UNICORN *s.* unicórnio.
UNICYCLE *s.* monociclo.
UNIDENTIFIED *adj.* não identificado, irreconhecível.
UNIFICATION *s.* unificação.
UNIFORM *adj.* uniforme / *s.* uniforme / *v.* uniformizar.

UNIFORMITY *s.* uniformidade.
UNIFORMLY *adv.* uniformemente.
UNIFY *v.* unificar; unir.
UNILATERAL *adj.* unilateral.
UNILATERALISM *s.* unilateralismo.
UNIMAGINABLE *adj.* inimaginável.
UNIMAGINATIVE *adj.* sem imaginação.
UNIMPAIRED *adj.* inalterado, intato.
UNIMPEDED *adj.* desimpedido, livre.
UNIMPORTANT *adj.* insignificante, reles.
UNIMPRESSED *adj.* indiferente, insensível.
UNIMPRESSIVE *adj.* inexpressivo, insignificante.
UNINFORMED *adj.* desinformado, ignorante.
UNINHABITABLE *adj.* inabitável.
UNINHABITED *adj.* inabitado, desabitado.
UNINHIBITED *adj.* desinibido.
UNINITIATED *adj.* inexperiente.
UNINJURED *adj. m.q.* unharmed.
UNINSPIRED *adj.* sem inspiração.
UNINSPIRING *adj.* tedioso, pouco inspirador.
UNINSTALL *v.* desinstalar; remover.
UNINTELLIGENT *adj.* iletrado, ignorante; estúpido.
UNINTELLIGIBLE *adj.* ininteligível, incompreensível.
UNINTENDED *adj.* involuntário, sem querer.
UNINTENTIONAL *adj.* involuntário, não intencional.
UNINTENTIONALLY *adv.* involuntariamente.
UNINTERESTING *adj.* chato, enfadonho.
UNINTERRUPTED *adj.* incessante, contínuo, constante.
UNINVITED *adj.* intruso, intrometido.
UNINVITING *adj.* nada convidativo.
UNION *s.* união; sindicato trabalhista.
UNIQUE *adj.* único; só; ímpar.
UNIQUELY *adv.* exclusivamente; unicamente.
UNISEX *adj.* unissex.
UNISON *s.* acordo, concordância / *adj.* uníssono.
UNIT *s.* unidade.
UNITARY *adj.* unitário, individual.
UNITE *v.* unir, aderir; unir-se.
UNITED *adj.* unido.
UNITISE *v.* unificar, juntar.
UNITY *s. m.q.* unit.
UNIVERSAL *adj.* universal.
UNIVERSALITY *s.* universalidade.
UNIVERSALLY *adv.* universalmente.

UNIVERSE s. universo.
UNIVERSITY s. universidade, academia.
UNJUST adj. injusto.
UNJUSTIFIABLE adj. injustificável.
UNJUSTIFIED adj. injustificado.
UNKIND adj. indelicado.
UNKNOWN adj. desconhecido, ignorado.
UNLACE v. desatar, desfazer.
UNLAWFUL adj. ilegal, ilícito.
UNLAWFULLY adv. ilicitamente.
UNLEARN v. desaprender.
UNLEASH v. desencadear; livrar.
UNLESS conj. a menos que, a não ser que.
UNLIKE prep. ao contrário de / adj. distinto / v. ser hostil.
UNLIKELY adv. improvável.
UNLIMITED adj. ilimitado.
UNLOAD v. descarregar, despejar.
UNLOADING adj. descarga.
UNLOCK v. destrancar, abrir.
UNLUCKY adj. azarado; sem sorte.
UNMADE adj. desfeito, desarrumado.
UNMAKE v. desfazer, desmanchar.
UNMARRIED adj. solteiro.
UNMASK v. revelar, expor; desmascarar.
UNMERCIFUL adj. impiedoso.
UNMISTAKABLE adj. inequívoco, inconfundível.
UNNATURAL adj. artificial; afetado; anormal.
UNNECESSARILY adv. desnecessariamente.
UNNECESSARY adj. desnecessário, inútil.
UNPLEASANT adj. desagradável, antipático.
UNPLUG v. desligar.
UNPOPULAR adj. impopular.
UNREAL adj. irreal, ilusório.
UNSAFE adj. perigoso, inseguro.
UNSUITABLE adj. inadequado, impróprio.
UNSURE adj. inseguro, incerto.
UNTIL prep. até / conj. até que.
UNUSUAL adj. incomum, inusitado.
UNWRAP v. desembrulhar.
UP adj. avançado, adiantado / adv. em cima; para cima, acima / prep. em cima, para cima, acima.
UPCOMING adj. iminente, vindouro.
UPDATE v. atualizar.
UPGRADE v. elevar o nível, melhorar / s. elevação, melhoria, subida.
UPKEEP s. manutenção.
UPSTAIRS adv. em cima / s. andar de cima / adj. do andar superior.
UPSTREAM adv. rio acima.
UP-TO-DATE adj. moderno; atualizado, em dia.
URANUS s. Urano.
URBAN adj. urbano, da cidade.
URGENCY s. urgência, premência.
URINATE v. urinar.
US pron. nos, nós.
USAGE s. uso, costume.
USE s. uso (utilidade) / v. usar.
USEFUL adj. útil, proveitoso, aproveitável.
USUAL adj. usual, habitual, normal.
USUALLY adv. usualmente.
UTENSIL s. utensílio.
UTILISE v. utilizar.
UTILITY s. utilidade.
UTTER adj. completo, total, absoluto / v. proferir, expressar, dizer.
UTTERLY adv. completamente, totalmente.

V v

V, v s. vigésima segunda letra do alfabeto inglês; representa o número cinco em algarismos romanos.
VACANCY s. vaga, vacância.
VACANT adj. vago, vazio.
VACANTLY adv. vagamente; ociosamente.
VACATE v. vagar, desocupar; abrir vaga.
VACATION s. férias / v. tirar férias.
VACATIONER s. veranista; que está de férias.
VACCINATE v. vacinar; dar vacina.
VACCINATION s. vacinação.
VACCINE s. vacina.
VACILLATE v. vacilar, hesitar.
VACUUM s. vácuo; aspirador de pó / v. aspirar com aspirador de pó.
VACUUM CLEANER s. aspirador de pó.
VAGABOND s. vagabundo, andarilho.
VAGINA s. vagina (anatomia).
VAGINAL adj. vaginal.
VAGRANCY s. vagabundagem, vadiagem.
VAGRANT s. errante, nômade / adj. errante, nômade.
VAGUE adj. vago.
VAGUELY adv. vagamente.
VAIN adj. vaidoso; vão, fútil.
VAINLY adv. inutilmente; em vão.
VALENTINE s. namorado; cartão remetido no Dia dos Namorados.
VALET v. servir / s. manobrista.
VALID adj. válido, vigente.
VALIDATE v. validar, autenticar.
VALIDATION s. validação, comprovação.
VALITY s. validade.
VALLEY s. vale.
VALUABLE adj. valioso, precioso.
VALUATE v. valorar, valorizar.
VALUATION s. avaliação.
VALUE s. valor, apreço / v. avaliar, calcular o preço de.
VALUER s. avaliador, perito.
VALVE s. válvula; pistão.
VALVULAR adj. valvular.
VAMPIRE s. vampiro.
VAN s. caminhonete, furgão / v. transportar em van.
VANDAL s. vândalo, bárbaro.
VANDALISE v. vandalizar.

VANDALISM s. vandalismo.
VANE s. cata-vento; ventoinha.
VANGUARD s. vanguarda.
VANILLA s. baunilha.
VANISH v. desaparecer, sumir.
VANITY s. vaidade.
VANTAGE s. vantagem; perspectiva.
VAPID adj. insípido, enfadonho; monótono.
VAPORISATION s. vaporização.
VAPORISE v. vaporizar; converter em vapor.
VAPORISER s. vaporizador.
VAPOUR v. vaporizar / s. vapor; névoa, bruma.
VARIABILITY s. variabilidade.
VARIABLE adj. variável / s. variável.
VARIANCE s. divergência, disparidade.
VARIANT s. variante / adj. variante.
VARIATION s. variação, alteração.
VARIETY s. variedade, diversidade.
VARIOUS adj. vários, diversos.
VARNISH s. verniz, esmalte / v. envernizar.
VARY v. variar.
VARYING adj. variado, cambiante, inconsistente.
VASCULAR adj. vascular.
VASE s. vaso, jarra.
VASECTOMY s. vasectomia.
VASELINE s. vaselina.
VAST adj. vasto, enorme, imenso.
VASTLY adv. vastamente, imensamente.
VAULT s. abóbada, galeria arqueada; salto, pulo / v. pular.
VEAL s. carne de vitela (culinária).
VEAL CHOP s. costela de vitela (culinária).
VECTOR s. vetor.
VEGETABLE s. vegetal, verdura, hortaliça / adj. vegetal.
VEGETARIAN s. vegetariano / adj. vegetariano.
VEGETARIANISM s. vegetarianismo.
VEGETATE v. vegetar.
VEGETATION s. vegetação.
VEGETATIVE adj. vegetativo.
VEHEMENCE s. veemência; ardor, amor.
VEHEMENT adj. veemente.
VEHEMENTLY adv. veementemente.
VEHICLE s. veículo.
VEHICULAR adj. veicular.
VEIL v. vendar, cobrir / s. véu.

VEILED adj. velado, disfarçado.
VEIN s. veia (anatomia).
VELOCITY s. velocidade.
VELODROME s. velódromo.
VELVET s. veludo.
VELVETY adj. aveludado; macio.
VEND v. vender, comercializar.
VENDETTA s. vendeta; vingança.
VENDING s. vendas / adj. de venda.
VENDOR s. vendedor.
VENERABLE adj. venerável.
VENERATE v. venerar.
VENERATION s. veneração.
VENEREAL adj. venéreo.
VENGEANCE s. vingança.
VENGEFUL adj. vingativo.
VENOM s. veneno, peçonha; ódio.
VENOMOUS adj. venenoso, peçonhento.
VENOUS adj. venoso (veia).
VENT s. abertura, orifício, respiradouro.
VENTILATE v. ventilar, arejar.
VENTILATION s. ventilação.
VENTILATOR s. ventilador.
VENTRICLE s. ventrículo (anatomia).
VENTRICULAR adj. ventricular (coração).
VENTRILOQUIST s. ventríloquo.
VENTRILOQUY s. ventriloquia.
VENTURE s. empreendimento, projeto / v. aventurar-se, arriscar-se.
VENUS s. Vênus.
VERACITY s. veracidade, verdade.
VERB s. verbo.
VERBAL adj. verbal, oral.
VERBALISE v. verbalizar, oralizar.
VERBALLY adv. verbalmente, oralmente.
VERBATIM adj. literal / adv. palavra por palavra, literalmente.
VERDICT s. veredicto.
VERGE s. limite, margem, beira.
VERIFIABLE adj. verificável.
VERIFICATION s. verificação.
VERIFY v. verificar, conferir.
VERITY s. verdade.
VERNACULAR s. vernáculo / adj. vernacular.
VERNAL adj. vernal, primaveril.
VERSATILE adj. versátil, volúvel.
VERSATILITY s. versatilidade.
VERSE s. verso, versículo (Bíblia), poesia; estrofe.

VERSED *adj.* versado, entendido.
VERSION *s.* versão; tradução.
VERSO *s.* verso; parte de trás.
VERSUS *prep.* versus, contra.
VERTEBRA *s.* vértebra.
VERTEBRAL *adj.* vertebral.
VERTEBRATE *s.* vertebrado.
VERTEX *s.* vértice, ápice.
VERTICAL *adj.* vertical.
VERTICALLY *adv.* verticalmente.
VERTIGO *s.* vertigem, tontura.
VERVE *s.* entusiasmo.
VERY *adv.* muito.
VESICLE *s.* vesícula.
VESICULAR *adj.* vesicular.
VESSEL *s.* vaso sanguíneo; vasilhame; navio, barco.
VEST *v.* vestir-se; investir / *s.* colete, túnica.
VESTIBULE *s.* vestíbulo.
VESTIGE *s.* vestígio.
VESTMENT *s.* vestimenta.
VESTRY *s.* sacristia (igreja).
VET *v.* examinar, investigar / *s.* veterano de guerra.
VETERAN *s.* veterano, experiente / *adj.* veterano, experiente.
VETERINARIAN *s.* veterinário (médico).
VETERINARY *s.* veterinário (local); veterinária (medicina).
VETO *v.* vetar, proibir, barrar / *s.* veto.
VEX *v.* aborrecer, importunar, vexar.
VEXATION *s.* vexação, amolação.
VEXATIOUS *adj.* vexatório, vexante, vexativo.
VEXATIOUSLY *adv.* de modo vexante, aborrecidamente, penosamente.
VIA *prep.* via, por meio de, através.
VIABILITY *s.* viabilidade.
VIABLE *adj.* viável.
VIADUCT *s.* viaduto.
VIBE *abrev.* vibração.
VIBRANCY *s.* brilho, esplendor; vitalidade.
VIBRANT *adj.* vibrante.
VIBRATE *v.* vibrar, oscilar, tremer.
VIBRATION *s.* vibração.
VIBRATORY *adj.* vibratório.
VICAR *s.* vigário, pároco.
VICARAGE *s.* casa paroquial.
VICARIOUSLY *adv.* indiretamente.

VICE *s.* vício, deficiência / *prep.* em vez de, em lugar de.
VICINITY *s.* vizinhança, cercania.
VICIOUS *adj.* viciado; mau, depravado.
VICIOUS CIRCLE *s.* círculo vicioso.
VICISSITUDE *s.* vicissitude.
VICTIM *s.* vítima.
VICTIMHOOD *s.* vitimização.
VICTIMISATION *s.* vitimação.
VICTIMISE *v.* vitimar.
VICTIMLESS *adj.* sem vítima.
VICTORIOUS *adj.* vitorioso, triunfante.
VICTORY *s.* vitória.
VIE *v.* competir, concorrer.
VIEW *s.* vista; cenário / *v.* ver, observar, enxergar.
VIEWER *s.* visor, espectador.
VIEWING *s.* inspeção, exame.
VIEWPOINT *s.* ponto de vista.
VIGIL *s.* vigília.
VIGILANCE *s.* vigilância.
VIGILANT *adj.* vigilante; atento.
VIGILANTE *s.* justiceiro.
VIGOROUS *adj.* vigoroso; vivaz.
VIGOROUSLY *adv.* vigorosamente; com vigor.
VIGOUR *s.* energia, vitalidade; vigor.
VILE *adj.* vil, repugnante.
VILIFY *v.* caluniar, difamar; vilipendiar.
VILLAGE *s.* aldeia, povoado, vilarejo.
VILLAGER *s.* aldeão.
VILLAIN *s.* vilão, bandido.
VINAIGRETTE *s.* vinagrete.
VINDICATE *v.* vindicar.
VINDICATION *s.* vindicação.
VINE *s.* vinha, videira.
VINEGAR *s.* vinagre.
VINEYARD *s.* vinhedo.
VINTAGE *s.* vindima (safra de vinho) / *adj.* vintage; antigo.
VINYL *s.* vinil.
VIOLATE *v.* violar, violentar; profanar.
VIOLATION *s.* violação.
VIOLATOR *s.* violador.
VIOLENCE *s.* violência, força.
VIOLENT *adj.* violento, agressivo.
VIOLENTLY *adv.* violentamente.
VIOLET *s.* violeta; roxo / *adj.* violeta; roxo.
VIOLIN *s.* violino.
VIOLINIST *s.* violinista.
VIOLIST *s.* violista.

VIOLONCELIST s. violoncelista.
VIOLONCELLO s. violoncelo.
VIP abrev. VIP (pessoa muito importante).
VIPER s. víbora; traiçoeiro, maldoso.
VIRAL adj. viral; que se espalha rapidamente.
VIRGIN s. virgem, donzela / adj. virgem, donzela.
VIRGINAL adj. virginal.
VIRGINITY s. virgindade.
VIRGO s. Virgem (astrologia).
VIRILE adj. viril, másculo, varonil.
VIRILITY s. virilidade.
VIROLOGY s. virologia.
VIRTUAL adj. virtual.
VIRTUALLY adv. virtualmente.
VIRTUE s. virtude; mérito.
VIRTUOSITY s. virtuosidade, virtuosismo.
VIRTUOSO s. músico virtuoso; habilidoso.
VIRTUOUS adj. virtuoso; de virtude.
VIRULENCE s. virulência.
VIRULENT adj. virulento.
VIRUS s. vírus; virose.
VISA s. visto.
VISAGE s. semblante, rosto, aspecto.
VISCERAL adj. visceral.
VISCOSE s. viscose.
VISCOSITY s. viscosidade.
VISCOUNT s. visconde.
VISCOUS adj. viscoso.
VISCUS s. víscera.
VISE v. tornear / s. torno, torninho.
VISIBILITY s. visibilidade.
VISIBLE adj. visível, perceptível.
VISIBLY adv. visivelmente, evidentemente.
VISION s. vista; visão.
VISIONARY s. visionário / adj. visionário.
VISIT s. visita / v. visitar.
VISITATION s. visitação.
VISITING s. visitante, convidado / adj. visitante, convidado.
VISITOR s. visitador, visitante.
VISOR s. viseira.
VISTA s. vista, imagem, panorama.
VISUAL adj. visual.
VISUALISATION s. visualização.
VISUALISE v. visualizar.
VISUALLY adv. visualmente.
VITAL adj. essencial, vital.
VITALISATION s. vitalização.
VITALISE v. vitalizar.
VITALISM s. vitalismo.
VITALIST adj. vitalista.
VITALITY s. vitalidade.
VITALLY adv. vitalmente, essencialmente.
VITAMIN s. vitamina.
VITAMINISE v. vitaminar; adicionar vitamina.
VITIATE v. viciar, adulterar, corromper.
VITREOUS adj. vítreo; de vidro.
VIVACIOUS adj. vivaz, animado.
VIVACITY s. vivacidade.
VIVID adj. vívido.
VIVIDLY adv. vividamente.
VIVISECTION s. vivissecção.
VOCABULARY s. vocabulário.
VOCAL adj. vocal; da voz.
VOCAL CORDS s. cordas vocais.
VOCALIC s. vogal vocálica / adj. vocálico.
VOCALISATION s. vocalização.
VOCALISE v. vocalizar.
VOCALISM s. vocalismo.
VOCALIST s. vocalista.
VOCALLY adv. vocalmente.
VOCATION s. vocação; tendência, inclinação.
VOCATIONAL adj. vocacional, profissional.
VOCATIVE adj. vocativo (gramática).
VOCIFERATE v. vociferar.
VOCIFEROUS adj. vociferante.
VODKA s. vodca.
VOGUE s. voga, moda.
VOICE s. voz.
VOICED adj. sonoro (gramática); vocal.
VOICELESS adj. áfono; não sonoro (gramática); mudo.
VOID v. invalidar / s. vazio, lacuna / adj. vazio, livre, isento.
VOIDABLE adj. anulável.
VOILE s. voile; tecido transparente.
VOL abrev. volume.
VOLATILE adj. volátil, inconstante.
VOLATILITY s. volatilidade.
VOLCANIC adj. vulcânico.
VOLCANISM s. vulcanismo.
VOLCANO s. vulcão.
VOLCANOLOGY s. vulcanologia.
VOLITION s. volição, vontade.
VOLITIONAL adj. volitivo, voluntário
VOLITIONALLY adv. voluntariamente.

VOLLEY v. rebater / s. voleio.
VOLLEYBALL s. voleibol.
VOLT s. volt.
VOLTAGE s. voltagem.
VOLTMETER s. voltímetro.
VOLUBILITY s. volubilidade, fluência.
VOLUBLE adj. volúvel, loquaz.
VOLUBLY adv. voluvelmente.
VOLUME s. volume.
VOLUMETRIC adj. volumétrico.
VOLUMETRICALLY adv. volumetricamente.
VOLUMINOUS adj. volumoso.
VOLUMINOUSLY adv. volumosamente.
VOLUMISE v. adicionar volume; aumentar.
VOLUNTARILY adv. voluntariamente.
VOLUNTARY adj. voluntário, espontâneo.
VOLUNTEER v. ser voluntário / s. voluntário.
VOLUNTEERISM s. voluntarismo.
VOLUPTUOUS adj. voluptuoso, libidinoso.
VOLUPTUOUSLY adv. voluptuosamente.
VOMIT v. vomitar / s. vômito.
VOMITING s. vômito.
VOODOO s. vodu / adj. vodu.
VORACIOUS adj. voraz.
VORACIOUSLY adv. vorazmente.
VORTEX s. vórtice.
VOTE s. voto; votação / v. votar.
VOTER s. eleitor.
VOTING s. votação.
VOUCH v. garantir, atestar, assegurar / s. garantia, fiança.
VOUCHER s. documento; recibo.
VOW v. fazer os votos, jurar / s. voto (promessa).
VOWEL s. vogal.
VOYAGE s. viagem (espacial ou marítima).
VOYAGER s. viajante.
VULGAR adj. vulgar.
VULGARITY s. vulgaridade.
VULNERABILITY s. vulnerabilidade.
VULNERABLE adj. vulnerável.
VULTURE s. abutre, urubu.
VULVA s. vulva (anatomia).

W w

W, w s. vigésima terceira letra do alfabeto inglês / *abrev.* oeste.
WACKY *adj.* doido, estranho, excêntrico.
WAD *v.* estofar, acolchoar / *s.* maço, pilha.
WADDLE *v.* bambolear, gingar / *s.* ginga.
WADE *v.* caminhar, vadear.
WAFER *s.* bolacha, biscoito; hóstia (religião).
WAFFLE *v.* falar sem parar / *s.* conversa-fiada.
WAFT *v.* flutuar, soprar (vento) / *s.* rajada, lufada (vento).
WAG *v.* sacudir, abanar / *s.* abano, sacudida.
WAGE *v.* promover, empreender / *s.* salário, ordenado, soldo.
WAGER *s.* aposta / *v.* apostar, arriscar.
WAGGLE *v.* sacudir, agitar / *s.* balanço, sacolejo.
WAGGON *s.* carroça, vagão; caminhão.
WAGGONER *s.* condutor; motorista.
WAIL *s.* lamento, gemido / *v.* lamentar-se, gemer.
WAIN *s.* carroça.
WAIST *s.* cintura.
WAISTBAND *s.* cinta, cós.
WAIT *s.* espera / *v.* esperar, aguardar.
WAITER *s.* garçom.
WAITING *adj.* de espera.
WAITING LIST *s.* lista de espera.
WAITRESS *s.* garçonete.
WAIVE *v.* renunciar a, abrir mão de, ceder.
WAIVER *s.* renúncia, desistência, abandono.
WAKE *v.* acordar, despertar.
WAKEN *v.* despertar, acordar; ficar atento.
WALES *s.* País de Gales.
WALK *s.* passeio, caminhada / *v.* andar a pé, passear.
WALKABLE *adj.* andável; próprio para caminhar; possível para ir a pé.
WALKER *s.* andador; pedestre; andarilho.
WALKING *s.* andamento, caminhada.
WALKWAY *s.* caminho, passagem; passarela.
WALL *s.* parede, muro / *v.* cercar, murar.
WALLED *adj.* murado, cercado.
WALLET *s.* carteira (de dinheiro).

WALLFLOWER s. goivo-amarelo (botânica); pessoa tímida, inibida (figurativo).
WALLOP v. surrar, espancar / s. pancada, bofetada.
WALLPAPER s. papel de parede / v. revestir a parede com papel.
WALLY s. bobo, tolo.
WALNUT s. noz; imbuia (madeira).
WALRUS s. morsa (animal).
WALTZ v. dançar valsa / s. valsa.
WAN adj. pálido, descorado; débil, fraco.
WAND s. varinha mágica; varinha de condão.
WANDER v. vagar, perambular; divagar.
WANDERER s. errante, perambulante, viajante.
WANDERING adj. divagante, divagador.
WANE v. decrescer, diminuir / s. recaída, declínio.
WANK v. masturbar-se.
WANNABE s. pessoa que finge ser o que não é.
WANT v. querer, desejar / s. necessidade, vontade.
WANT AD s. anúncio, classificado.
WANTED adj. procurado (foragido); desejado, almejado.
WANTING adj. carente, desprovido.
WANTON adj. injustificado, gratuito; impudico.
WAR v. guerrear, fazer guerra / s. guerra, conflito.
WARD s. ala; tutela, custódia.
WARDEN s. diretor, administrador; guarda.
WARDER s. carcereiro, guarda, sentinela.
WARDROBE s. armário, guarda-roupa.
WAREHOUSE s. armazém, depósito / v. armazenar.
WARFARE s. conflito, guerra.
WARHEAD s. ogiva.
WARILY adv. cautelosamente.
WARINESS s. cuidado, prudência, cautela.
WARLIKE adj. bélico, militar.
WARLOCK s. bruxo, feiticeiro.
WARLORD s. déspota, chefe militar; senhor da guerra.
WARM adj. quente, aquecido; cordial / v. aquecer, esquentar.
WARMER s. aquecedor / adj. caloroso; mais quente.
WARMLY adv. calorosamente.

WARMONGER s. quem instiga, provoca uma guerra.
WARMTH s. calor, quentura; amabilidade, cordialidade.
WARM UP s. aquecimento; preparação.
WARN v. prevenir, avisar, advertir.
WARNING s. aviso, prevenção, advertência / adj. preventivo.
WARP v. entortar, empenar / s. empenamento.
WARPED adj. torto, empenado.
WARPLANE s. avião de guerra.
WARRANT v. justificar, garantir, afiançar / s. mandado (de prisão); garantia.
WARRANTEE s. afiançado, garantido.
WARRANTY s. garantia.
WARREN s. toca, viveiro de coelhos.
WARRIOR s. guerreiro.
WARSAW s. Varsóvia (Polônia).
WARSHIP s. navio de guerra.
WART s. verruga.
WARTHOG s. javali.
WARTIME s. tempo de guerra / adj. tempo de guerra.
WARTY adj. verruguento, verrugoso.
WARY adj. cauteloso, cuidadoso.
WASH s. lavagem, banho / v. lavar, limpar.
WASHABLE adj. lavável.
WASHBASIN s. lavatório, pia.
WASHBOARD s. tábua de bater roupa, tanque / adj. tanquinho.
WASHBOWL s. bacia.
WASHCLOTH s. toalha de rosto.
WASHER s. máquina de lavar roupa; lavador.
WASHING s. lavagem, limpeza / adj. de lavar.
WASHOUT s. fracasso.
WASHROOM s. banheiro.
WASHY adj. aguado, ralo, fraco.
WASP s. vespa.
WASTAGE s. desperdício.
WASTE s. perda, sobras; desperdício; lixo / v. perder, desperdiçar.
WASTEBASKET s. lixeira, cesto de lixo.
WASTEBIN s. lata de lixo.
WASTED adj. gasto, desperdício; bêbado (figurativo).
WASTEFUL adj. gastador, esbanjador; ineficaz.

WATCH s. relógio de pulso; cuidado / v. olhar, vigiar; observar, assistir a.
WATCHABLE adj. possível de assistir a.
WATCHER s. espectador, observador.
WATCHFUL adj. vigilante.
WATCHMAN s. guarda, vigia.
WATER v. regar, molhar, irrigar / s. água.
WATERCOLOUR s. aquarela.
WATERCOURSE s. curso d'água, curso fluvial.
WATERCRESS s. agrião.
WATERFALL s. cachoeira; queda-d'água.
WATERING s. regador / adj. regador.
WATERLILY s. nenúfar; vitória-régia.
WATERLOGGED adj. alagado, ensopado.
WATERMARK s. marca-d'água.
WATERMELON s. melancia.
WATERMILL s. moinho d'água; azenha.
WATERPROOF v. impermeabilizar / s. capa de chuva / adj. à prova d'água.
WATERY adj. aguado, aquoso; ralo.
WAVE s. onda, ondulação; sinal, aceno / v. acenar; ondular.
WAVER v. vacilar, fraquejar, hesitar / s. oscilação, indecisão.
WAVY adj. ondulado, ondulante, flutuante.
WAX s. cera / v. encerar.
WAXY adj. ceroso, cheio de cera.
WAY s. caminho; modo, jeito; forma; maneira.
WC abrev. banheiro.
WE pron. nós.
WEAK adj. fraco, frágil; mole, molenga.
WEAKEN v. enfraquecer, debilitar.
WEAKLING s. franzino, débil; fracote, fraquinho.
WEAKLY adv. debilitadamente.
WEAKNESS s. fraqueza.
WEALTH s. riqueza, fortuna, abundância.
WEALTHY adj. rico, opulento.
WEAPON s. arma.
WEAPONRY s. armamento.
WEAR v. usar (roupa, sapatos); vestir, trajar.
WEARABLE adj. usável, possível de vestir.
WEARILY adv. exaustivamente.
WEARING adj. desgastante.
WEARY adj. cansado, fatigado; desgastante.
WEASEL v. evitar, escapar / s. fuinha (animal).
WEATHER s. tempo (meteorológico) / v. deteriorar, estragar.
WEATHERCOCK s. cata-vento.
WEATHERED adj. desgastado.
WEATHERMAN s. meteorologista.
WEAVER s. tecelão.
WEAVING s. tecelagem.
WEB s. teia; rede; trama.
WEBSITE s. site, página na internet.
WED v. casar-se, unir, ligar.
WEDDING s. casamento.
WEDLOCK s. matrimônio, casamento, união.
WEDNESDAY s. quarta-feira.
WEED v. excluir, cortar, eliminar / s. erva daninha, alga.
WEEDKILLER s. herbicida.
WEEK s. semana.
WEEKDAY s. dia útil, dia da semana.
WEEKEND s. fim de semana.
WEEKLY adv. semanalmente.
WEEP v. chorar, choramingar.
WEEPING s. choradinha / adj. chorão, choramingador.
WEEPY adj. chorão, choroso.
WEIGH v. pesar, ponderar; avaliar.
WEIGHT s. peso, fadiga.
WEIGHTING s. peso, relevância, importância.
WEIGHTLESS adj. leve, sem peso; irrelevante.
WEIGHTLIFTER s. halterofilista; levantador de pesos.
WEIGHTLIFTING s. levantamento de pesos (esporte).
WEIR s. represa, açude.
WEIRD adj. estranho, esquisito.
WELCOME s. acolhimento, recepção / adj. bem-vindo / v. dar boas-vindas.
WELCOMING adj. acessível, receptivo.
WELD s. solda / v. soldar, fundir, unir.
WELDER s. soldador.
WELFARE s. saúde, bem-estar.
WELL adv. bem, estar bem / s. cisterna, fonte, poço / interj. bem.
WELLHEAD s. nascente, manancial; fonte.
WELLINGTON s. galocha.
WELLSPRING s. nascente, fonte.
WELSH s. galês / adj. galês.
WEREWOLF s. lobisomem.
WEST s. oeste / adj. ocidental / adv. para o oeste.
WESTERN s. faroeste (cinema) / adj. ocidental, do oeste.

WESTERNISE v. ocidentalizar.
WESTERNIZATION s. ocidentalização.
WET adj. úmido, molhado / v. molhar, umedecer.
WHALE s. baleia.
WHALER s. baleeiro (barco), caçador de baleia.
WHALING s. pesca de baleia.
WHARF s. cais, pier, porto.
WHAT pron. que, qual, quais / interj. o quê?!
WHATEVER pron. qualquer coisa / interj. tanto faz.
WHATSOEVER adv. qualquer que seja, que quer seja.
WHEAL s. vergão.
WHEAT s. trigo.
WHEE interj. oba!
WHEEL s. roda / v. rolar.
WHEELCHAIR s. cadeira de rodas.
WHEEZE v. ofegar.
WHEEZY adj. ofegante, arfante.
WHEN adv. quando.
WHENCE adv. de onde, daí / conj. por isso; por que motivo.
WHENEVER adv. quando for, a qualquer hora.
WHERE pron. onde / adv. aonde / conj. onde.
WHEREAS conj. ao passo que, enquanto que.
WHEREBY adv. pelo qual, no qual; por meio de.
WHEREVER adv. onde quer que seja; aonde for.
WHETHER conj. se, quer, ou.
WHETSTONE s. pedra de amolar.
WHEW interj. ufa!
WHEY s. soro.
WHICH pron. que, qual, quais.
WHICHEVER pron. qualquer que seja.
WHILE s. um tempo / conj. durante, enquanto / adv. embora, porém.
WHIM s. capricho, extravagância.
WHINE s. gemido, lamento, choro / v. gemer, choramingar.
WHINER s. resmungão, chorão.
WHINING s. lamento / adj. lamentoso.
WHINNY v. rinchar, relinchar / s. relincho.
WHINY adj. irritante, perturbador.
WHIP v. chicotear, açoitar / s. chicote.
WHIPLASH s. chicotada.
WHIPPING s. flagelação, açoitamento.

WHIR v. zunir, zumbir, zoar / s. zunido, zumbido.
WHISK v. bater; mover rápido / s. batedor (culinária).
WHISKER s. bigode, fio de cabelo.
WHISKEY s. uísque.
WHISPER v. sussurrar, cochichar / s. sussurro; boato.
WHISTLE v. apitar, assobiar / s. apito.
WHISTLEBLOWER s. delator, informante; dedo-duro.
WHITE s. branco / adj. branco.
WHITEN v. branquear, clarear.
WHITENER s. alvejante; branqueador.
WHITENESS s. brancura, palidez; alvura.
WHITEWASH v. caiar, passar cal / s. cal.
WHIZZ v. fazer zumbido; zumbir.
WHO abrev. OMS (Organização Mundial da Saúde).
WHO pron. que, o qual, quem.
WHOA interj. ôa! pera lá.
WHOEVER pron. quem quer que seja, quem for.
WHOLE adj. todo, inteiro, completo / s. todo, conjunto, totalidade.
WHOLESALE v. vender por atacado / adj. de atacado / adv. por atacado.
WHOLESALER s. atacadista.
WHOLESOME adj. sadio, saudável; benéfico.
WHOLLY adv. completamente.
WHOM pron. de quem, para quem.
WHOOP v. gritar, bradar / s. grito, berro.
WHOOPEE interj. oba! viva!
WHOOSH s. som sibilante; som do sopro do ar.
WHOPPER s. lorota, grande mentira.
WHOSE pron. cujo(s), cuja(s).
WHOSOEVER pron. quem quer que seja.
WHY s. motivo, razão / adv. por que, por que razão / pron. por que, pelo qual / conj. por que.
WICK s. pavio, mecha.
WICKED adj. malvado, perverso.
WICKEDLY adv. perversamente.
WIDE adj. largo, extenso, amplo.
WIDELY adv. amplamente.
WIDEN v. alargar, ampliar.
WIDENING adj. largo, amplo, expandido.
WIDOW s. viúva / adj. viúva.
WIDOWED adj. enviuvado.

WIDOWER s. viúvo / adj. viúvo.
WIDOWHOOD s. viuvez.
WIDTH s. largura.
WIFE s. esposa.
WIG s. peruca.
WILD adj. selvagem, agreste; violento, louco.
WILDLIFE s. animais selvagens; vida selvagem.
WILDLY adv. descontroladamente.
WILDNESS s. selvageria.
WILL s. vontade, desejo, determinação; testamento.
WILLFUL adj. teimoso, obstinado.
WILLFULLY adv. teimosamente.
WILLPOWER s. força de vontade.
WILY adj. esperto, astuto.
WIN v. ganhar, vencer.
WIND s. vento.
WINDOW s. janela, vitrine.
WINDY adj. com vento, ventoso.
WINE s. vinho.
WING s. asa; ala.
WINNER s. vencedor, vitorioso.
WINTER s. inverno.
WIRE s. arame.
WIRELESS s. rádio / adj. sem fios, por meio do rádio.
WIRY adj. resistente, rijo; de arame.
WISDOM s. sabedoria; ciência; bom senso.
WISE adj. sábio; sensato, prudente.
WISH s. desejo / v. desejar.
WISTFUL adj. pensativo, saudoso, melancólico.
WITCH s. bruxa, feiticeira.
WITH prep. com.
WITHOUT prep. sem.
WITHSTAND v. resistir a.
WITNESS s. testemunha / v. testemunhar, presenciar.
WITTY adj. espirituoso; engenhoso.
WIZARD s. feiticeiro, mago.
WOLF s. lobo.
WOMAN s. (pl. women) mulher.
WONDERFUL adj. maravilhoso, espetacular.
WOOD s. madeira, lenha; floresta, bosque.
WORD s. palavra.
WORK s. trabalho, emprego, profissão / v. trabalhar.
WORLD s. mundo.
WORM s. verme, lombriga.
WORRIED adj. preocupado; aflito.
WORRY s. preocupação / v. preocupar, afligir.
WORSE adv. pior / adj. pior.
WORST s. o pior / adv. pior / adj. pior.
WRING s. torção; aperto / v. torcer, espremer.
WRITE v. escrever.
WRONG s. injustiça; erro / adj. errado, incorreto / adv. erradamente, erroneamente.

Xx

X, x *s.* vigésima quarta letra do alfabeto inglês; representa o número dez em algarismos romanos; representa um valor indeterminado.
X-CHROMOSOME *s.* cromossomo X.
XENON *s.* xenônio (química).
XENOPHOBIA *s.* xenofobia.
XENOPHOBIC *adj.* xenofóbico.
XEROX *v.* fotocopiar, xerocar / *s.* fotocópia.
X FACTOR *s.* fator X.
XI *s.* letra do alfabeto grego, csi.
X-IRRADIATION *s.* irradiação.
XMAS *abrev.* Natal.
X-RATED *adj.* imoral, indecente.
X-RAY *s.* radiografia, raio X / *v.* tirar chapa, radiografar.
XYLEM *s.* xilema, lenho.
XYLOGRAPH *s.* xilogravura.
XYLOGRAPHIC *adj.* xilográfico.
XYLOPHONE *s.* xilofone (música).
XYLOPHONIST *s.* xilofonista.

Y y

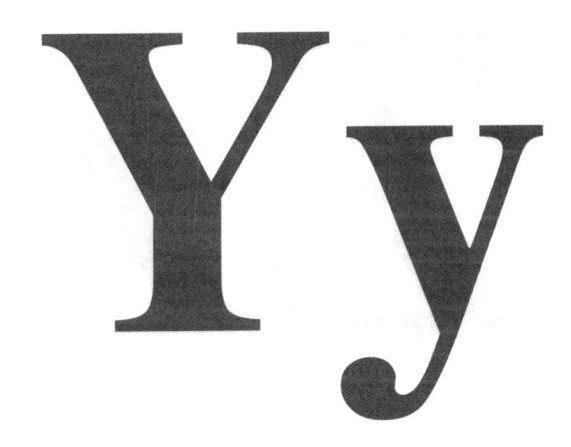

Y, y s. vigésima quinta letra do alfabeto inglês.
YARD s. quintal, pátio; jardim frontal; jarda (unidade de medida equivalente a 91,4 cm).
YAWN s. bocejo / v. bocejar.
YEAR s. ano.
YEARNING s. anseio, aspiração, desejo / adj. ansioso, desejoso.
YEAST s. levedura, levedo; fermento.
YELL s. grito, berro / v. gritar, berrar.
YELLOW s. amarelo / adj. amarelo / v. amarelar.
YELP s. latido, ganido / v. latir, ganir.
YES s. sim / adv. sim, é mesmo.
YESTERDAY s. ontem / adv. ontem.
YET adv. ainda / conj. porém, contudo, no entanto.
YIELD s. rendimento, lucro, produto / v. render, produzir.
YOGA s. ioga.
YOLK s. gema de ovo.
YONDER adv. além, acolá, mais longe / adj. longínquo.
YOU pron. você, tu, vós, vocês.
YOUNG adj. jovem, moço.
YOUR adj. teu(s), tua(s); seu(s), sua(s).
YOURSELF pron. teu mesmo, a você mesmo(a), próprio(a).
YOUTH s. juventude, mocidade.

Zz

Z, z *s.* vigésima sexta letra do alfabeto inglês.
ZANY *adj.* tolo(a), bobo(a).
ZEAL *s.* zelo, fervor.
ZEBRA *s.* zebra.
ZERO *num.* zero.
ZEST *s.* vivacidade, entusiasmo; gosto, sabor; prazer.

ZINC *s.* zinco / *v.* zincar, galvanizar.
ZIP CODE *s.* código de endereçamento postal (CEP).
ZODIAC *s.* zodíaco.
ZONE *s.* zona, região.
ZOO *s.* zoológico.
ZOOLOGIST *s.* zoólogo(a).